EC SHIPPING LAW

LLOYD'S SHIPPING LAW LIBRARY

Time Charters, third edition
by Michael Wilford, Terence Coghlin
and John D. Kimball
(1989)

The Ratification of Maritime Conventions
edited by The Institute of Maritime
Law, University of Southampton
(1990)

Laytime and Demurrage, second edition
by John Schofield
(1990)

The Law of Shipbuilding Contracts
by Simon Curtis
(1991)

EC Shipping Law
by Vincent Power
(1992)

EC SHIPPING LAW

BY

VINCENT POWER
B.C.L.(N.U.I.), LL.M.(Cantab.), B.L. (King's Inns)
Director of EEC and Competition Law,
A. & L. Goodbody,
Dublin, New York, London
and Brussels

LLP

LONDON NEW YORK HAMBURG HONG KONG
LLOYD'S OF LONDON PRESS LTD
1992

Lloyd's of London Press Ltd
Legal Publishing and Conferences Division
One Singer Street, London EC2A 4LQ

USA AND CANADA
Lloyd's of London Press Inc
Suite 308, 611 Broadway
New York, NY 10012 USA

GERMANY
Lloyd's of London Press GmbH
59 Ehrenbergstrasse
2000 Hamburg 50, Germany

SOUTH EAST ASIA
Lloyd's of London Press (Far East) Ltd
Room 1101, Hollywood Centre
233 Hollywood Road
Hong Kong

British Library Cataloguing-in-Publication Data
A catalogue record for
this book is available from the
British Library

ISBN 1–85044–312–2

Text set 10 on 12 Linotron 202 Times by
Megaron, Cardiff, Wales
Printed in Great Britain by
Bookcraft Ltd, Midsomer Norton, Avon

Preface

The boundaries of the European Community (EC) are not the boundaries of shipping. There is no way that the EC will ever control all aspects of shipping as if the industry were in an EC-controlled incubator. Nonetheless, the EC is concerned with shipping and the legal regulation of this international industry. The purpose of this book is to describe and discuss the EC law relating to shipping.

There are extensive extracts from various documents, reports, communications, opinions and cases. These verbatim extracts are designed to assist those readers who do not have ready access to these publications and no excuse is made for facilitating such readers.

The advice and assistance of many people have been sought and gratefully received. I must mention Caroline Boyle of the Chamber of Shipping (formerly the General Council of British Shipping); Martin Garside, Research Assistant of NUMAST; Andrew Keates of Stephenson Harwood, Solicitors, London; Bill Packard; and Tom Walsh, Senior Consultant, Price Waterhouse in Cork, Ireland. There are others, too numerous to mention or too shy (such as EC Commission officials), so that they did not want to be mentioned. I thank them all. The errors in this book are mine and not theirs. Special mention must also be made of the courteous and helpful staff at Lloyd's of London Press Ltd.

The love, guidance and support of my parents, grandmother and of Edwina (who transformed from girlfriend to fiancée to wife during this book!) are appreciated more than they will ever know. The book is dedicated to each of them.

The law is stated as at 1 January 1992, although references have been made to subsequent developments where they have been known to me.

Dublin
October 1992

VINCENT J. G. POWER

Contents

Preface	v
Table of Cases	li
Table of Legislation, Etc.	lxv
Table of EC Decisions	lxxv
Table of Reports and Publications	lxxvii
Table of Abbreviations	lxxix
Bibliography	lxxxii

CHAPTER 1 INTRODUCTION

1.1 The European Community			1
1.1.1	The Three European Communities		1
1.1.2	The evolution of the EC		1
1.1.3	The EC is the world's largest trading bloc		2
1.1.4	Population		2
1.1.5	The 1992 Programme		2
1.1.6	Transport in the EC		3
1.1.7	Future of the EC		3
1.2 Shipping in the EC			3
1.2.1	EC Shipping policy		3
	1.2.1.1	Strategic significance of shipping for the EC	3
	1.2.1.2	Shipping has an important role in the EC's internal market	4
	1.2.1.3	Shipping is an important employer in the EC	5
	1.2.1.4	Shipping is an important earner of foreign currency	5
	1.2.1.5	Open/non-protectionist policy	6
	1.2.1.6	Internal balances	7
	1.2.1.7	Social dimension to EC shipping policy	7
	1.2.1.8	Environmental dimension to EC shipping policy	8
	1.2.1.9	Competition dimension to EC shipping policy	8
	1.2.1.10	EC shipping policy and its relationship to the international obligations of the EC Member States	8
	1.2.1.11	Staggered or strategic development of EC shipping policy?	8
	1.2.1.12	There is no comprehensive Community shipping policy	8
1.2.2	EC shipping law		10
1.3 International Organisations and Shipping			10
1.3.1	Introduction		10

1.3.2 United Nations (UN) 11
1.3.3 The Intergovernmental Maritime Consultative Organisation (IMCO) and the International Maritime Organisation (IMO) 12
1.3.3.1 Introduction 12
1.3.3.2 The Intergovernmental Maritime Consultative Organisation 12
1.3.3.4 The International Maritime Organisation 13
1.3.4 International Labour Organisation (ILO) 14
1.3.4.1 Introduction 14
1.3.4.2 Organic and organisational structure 14
1.3.4.3 Activities 15
1.3.4.4 Relations with the EC 15
1.3.5–1.3.7 United Nations Conference on Trade and Development (UNCTAD) 15
1.3.8 United Nations Commission on International Trade Law (UNCITRAL) 16
1.3.9 Economic Commission for Europe (ECE) 16
1.3.10 United Nations Environment Programme (UNEP) 17
1.3.10.1 Introduction 17
1.3.10.2 Organisation 17
1.3.10.3 Activities 17
1.3.11 International Maritime Satellite Organisation (INMARSAT) 18
1.3.11.1 Membership 18
1.3.11.2 Organic structure and operation 19
1.3.11.3 Assessment 19
1.3.12 United Nations Educational, Scientific and Cultural Organisation (UNESCO) 19
1.3.13 World Health Organisation (WHO) 19
1.3.14 International Atomic Energy Agency (IAEA) 19
1.3.15 Organisation for Economic Co-operation and Development (OECD) 20
1.3.16 Customs Co-operation Council 20
1.3.17 Consultative Shipping Group 20
1.3.18 General Agreement on Tariffs and Trade (GATT) 21
1.3.19 Ministerial Conference of West and Central African States (MINCONMAR) 21
1.3.20 European Free Trade Association 21
1.3.21 Comecon 21
1.3.22 International Non-Governmental Organisations 22
1.3.23 Assessment 22

1.4 Outline of this book 23

CHAPTER 2 A COMMERCIAL OVERVIEW OF SHIPPING IN THE EC

2.1 Introduction 25

2.2 State of Shipping in the EC 25

2.2.1 Introduction 25
2.2.2 Tonnage 26
2.2.2.1 Tonnage owned and registered in the EC 27
2.2.2.2 Tonnage beneficially owned in the EC but registered outside the EC 27
2.2.2.3 Distribution of gross tonnage registered in EC Member States 27

2.2.3 Age profile 28
2.2.4 Market sectors 28
2.2.4.1 Cargo 28
2.2.4.2 Passengers 29
2.2.4.3 Oil tankers 30
2.2.4.4 Ore and bulk carriers 30
2.2.4.5 Containers 30
2.2.4.6 Liquid gas carriers 31
2.2.4.7 Combination carriers 31
2.2.4.8 Assessment 31
2.2.5 Employment 31
2.2.5.1 Merchant marine 31
2.2.5.2 Shipbuilding 32
2.2.6 Technology 32
2.2.7 Taxation 33
2.2.8 Protectionism 33
2.2.9 Flagging-out 33
2.2.10 The future 33

2.3 An Overview of Shipping in Each Member State 34

2.3.1 Introduction 34
2.3.1.1 Attitudes and policies of Member States 34
2.3.2 Belgium 35
2.3.2.1 Introduction 35
2.3.2.2 Number of ships 35
2.3.2.3 Tonnage 36
2.3.2.4 Age Profile 36
2.3.2.5 Employment 36
2.3.2.6 General comments 36
2.3.3 Denmark 36
2.3.3.1 Number of ships 36
2.3.3.2 Tonnage 37
2.3.3.3 Age profile 37
2.3.3.4 Employment 37
2.3.3.5 General comments 37
2.3.4 France 38
2.3.4.1 Number of ships 38
2.3.4.2 Tonnage 38
2.3.4.3 Age profile 38
2.3.4.4 Employment 38
2.3.4.5 General comments 38
2.3.5 Germany 39
2.3.5.1 Number of ships 39
2.3.5.2 Tonnage 39
2.3.5.3 Age profile 39
2.3.5.4 Employment 39
2.3.5.5 General comments 39
2.3.6 Greece 40
2.3.6.1 Introduction 40
2.3.6.2 Number of ships 40
2.3.6.3 Tonnage 41

2.3.6.4 Age Profile 41
2.3.6.5 Employment 41
2.3.6.6 General comments 41
2.3.7 Ireland 42
2.3.7.1 Introduction 42
2.3.7.2 Number of ships 42
2.3.7.3 Tonnage 43
2.3.7.4 Age profile 43
2.3.7.5–2.3.7.6 General comments 43
2.3.8 Italy 43
2.3.8.1 Introduction 43
2.3.8.2 Number of ships 43
2.3.8.3 Tonnage 44
2.3.8.4 Age profile 44
2.3.8.5–2.3.8.6 General comments 44
2.3.9 Luxembourg 44
2.3.10 The Netherlands 45
2.3.10.1 Introduction 45
2.3.10.2 Number of ships 45
2.3.10.3 Tonnage 45
2.3.10.4 Age profile 45
2.3.10.5 Employment 45
2.3.10.6 General comments 45
2.3.11 Portugal 46
2.3.11.1 Introduction 46
2.3.11.2 Number of ships 46
2.3.11.3 Tonnage 46
2.3.11.4 Age profile 46
2.3.11.5 Employment 46
2.3.11.6 General comments 46
2.3.12 Spain 47
2.3.12.1 Introduction 47
2.3.12.2 Number of ships 47
2.3.12.3 Tonnage 47
2.3.12.4 Age profile 47
2.3.12.5 Employment 48
2.3.12.6 General comments 48
2.3.13 United Kingdom 48
2.3.13.1 Introduction 48
2.3.13.2 Number of ships 48
2.3.13.3 Tonnage 48
2.3.13.4 Age profile 49
2.3.13.5 Employment 49
2.3.13.6 General comments 49

2.4 EC in the Shipping World 50

2.4.1 Introduction 51
2.4.2 United States of America 51
2.4.3 The former USSR 51
2.4.4 China 51

2.4.5 Hong Kong 51
2.4.6 Norway 52
2.4.7 Developing countries 52
2.4.8 Open registries 52
2.4.9 Offshore registries 52
2.4.10 Bahamas 52
2.4.11 Cyprus 52
2.4.12 Comecon 53

2.5 Conclusion 53

CHAPTER 3 THE EUROPEAN COMMUNITY

3.1 Introduction 55

3.2 The Community 56

3.2.1 Introduction 56
3.2.2 European Coal and Steel Community (ECSC) 56
3.2.3 European Atomic Energy Community (EURATOM) 57
3.2.4 European Economic Community (EEC) 57

3.3 History of the Community 59

3.3.1 European Integration 59
3.3.2 Marshall Aid, the OEEC and the UN Economic Commission for Europe 59
3.3.3 Congress of Europe 60
3.3.4 Benelux Union 60
3.3.5 Council of Europe 60
3.3.6 NATO 60
3.3.7 Schumann Declaration 61
3.3.8 The European Coal and Steel Community (ECSC) 61
3.3.9 The EEC and Euratom 61
3.3.10 European Defence Treaty 62
3.3.11 European Free Trade Association 62
3.3.12 Britain's position 62
3.3.13 Merger Treaty 63
3.3.14 Customs Union 63
3.3.15 Accessions 63
3.3.16 Tindemans Report 64
3.3.17 European Monetary System 64
3.3.18 Direct elections to the European Parliament 64
3.3.19 Internal Market White Paper 64
3.3.20 Single European Act 65
3.3.21 Eastern Europe 65

3.4 Organic Structure of the European Community 65

3.4.1 Introduction 65
3.4.2 Commission 66
3.4.2.1 Introduction 66
3.4.2.2 Composition 66

3.4.2.3 Functions 66
3.4.2.4 Operation 66
3.4.2.5 DG IV: Competition 68
3.4.2.6 DG VII: Transport 68
3.4.3 Council of Ministers 69
3.4.3.1 Introduction 69
3.4.3.2 Composition 69
3.4.3.3 Functions 69
3.4.3.4 Operation and voting 70
3.4.3.5 Coreper 71
3.4.3.6 General Secretariat of the Council of Ministers 71
3.4.4 European Council 71
3.4.4.1 Introduction 71
3.4.4.2 Origin 71
3.4.4.3 Role 71
3.4.5 European Parliament 71
3.4.5.1 Introduction 71
3.4.5.2 Seat 72
3.4.5.3 Members 73
3.4.5.4 Tenure 73
3.4.5.5 Election 73
3.4.5.6 President and Officers of the Parliament 73
3.4.5.7 Bureau of the Parliament 73
3.4.5.8 Secretariat of the Parliament 73
3.4.5.9 Committees 73
3.4.5.10 Functions and operation 73
3.4.5.11 Future 74
3.4.6 Court of Justice of the European Communities 74
3.4.6.1 Introduction 74
3.4.6.2 Functions 74
3.4.6.3 Personnel 74
3.4.6.3.1 Judges 74
3.4.6.3.2 President of the Court 75
3.4.6.3.3 Registrar 75
3.4.6.3.4 Advocates-General 75
3.4.6.3.5 Legal Secretaries 75
3.4.6.3.6 Appointment process of Judges and Advocates-General 75
3.4.6.4 Operation of the Court 76
3.4.6.4.1 Seat 76
3.4.6.4.2 Plenary and chamber sessions 76
3.4.6.4.3 Court of First Instance 76
3.4.6.4.4 Lawyers 76
3.4.6.4.5 Languages 76
3.4.6.5 Procedure 77
3.4.6.5.1 Locus standi 77
3.4.6.5.2 Effect of judgments 77
3.4.6.5.3 Enforcement of judgments 77
3.4.6.6 Jurisdiction 77
3.4.6.6.1 Introduction 77

3.4.6.6.2 Article 169: Commission contending that a Member State has failed to fulfil a Treaty obligation 78
3.4.6.6.3 Article 170: A Member State contends that another Member State has failed to fulfil a Treaty obligation 78
3.4.6.6.4 Article 172: Unlimited jurisdiction with respect to penalties 79
3.4.6.6.5 Article 173: Actions to annul EC measures 79
3.4.6.6.6 Article 175: Actions for inactivity 80
3.4.6.6.7 Article 184: Plea of illegality 80
3.4.6.6.8 Article 179: Staff disputes 80
3.4.6.6.9 Article 177: Preliminary references 81
3.4.6.6.10 Opinions on external relations 81
3.4.7 Bodies 82
3.4.7.1 Economic and Social Committee 82
3.4.7.2 European Investment Bank 82
3.4.7.3 Court of Auditors 82

3.5 Community Law 82

3.5.1 Introduction 82
3.5.2 Sources of community law 83
3.5.2.1 Primary law 83
3.5.2.1.1 Foundation Treaties (including Annexes and Protocols) 83
3.5.2.1.2 Accession treaties 84
3.5.2.1.3 Institutional treaties 84
3.5.2.1.4 Financial treaties 84
3.5.2.1.5 Single European Act 85
3.5.2.1.6 Maastricht Treaty 85
3.5.2.2 Secondary law 85
3.5.2.2.1 Regulations 86
3.5.2.2.2 Directives 86
3.5.2.2.3 Decisions 87
3.5.2.2.4 Recommendations 87
3.5.2.2.5 Resolutions 87
3.5.2.2.7 Agreements 87
3.5.2.2.8 General principles of Community law 87
3.5.2.2.9 Case law of the Court of Justice 88
3.5.2.2.10 Opinions of the Advocates-General 88
3.5.3 Direct effect and direct applicability 88
3.5.4 Publication of community law 89
3.5.5 Relationship between community law and national laws 89
3.5.6 Interpretation of community law 90
3.5.7 Fundamental principles of EC law 91
3.5.7.1 Non-discrimination between EC nationals on the basis of nationality 91
3.5.7.2 Proportionality 91
3.5.7.3 Legitimate expectation 91
3.5.8 Enforcement of EC law in the courts of Member States 91
3.5.9 Challenging the legality of Community measures 91
3.5.9.1 Passing on 91
3.5.9.2 Prospective overruling 92

CHAPTER 4 EC TRANSPORT LAW

4.1 Introduction 93

4.1.1 Importance of transport in the EC 93
4.1.2 Need to achieve a common transport policy 94
4.1.3 Failure to achieve a common transport policy 94
4.1.4 Legal bases of EC transport law 95
4.1.5 Adoption and administration of EC transport law 95

4.2 Position of Transport in the EC Treaties 95

4.2.1 ECSC Treaty 95
4.2.1.1 Introduction 95
4.2.1.2 Article 4 of the ECSC Treaty 96
4.2.1.2.1 Text 96
4.2.1.2.2 Commentary 97
4.2.1.3 Article 70 of the ECSC Treaty 97
4.2.1.3.1 Text 97
4.2.1.3.2 Commentary 97
4.2.2 EEC Treaty 98
4.2.2.1 Introduction 98
4.2.2.2 Article 3 of the EEC Treaty 100
4.2.2.2.1 Text 100
4.2.2.2.2 Commentary 100
4.2.2.3 Article 61 101
4.2.2.3.1 Text 101
4.2.2.3.2 Commentary 101
4.2.2.4 Article 74 101
4.2.2.4.1 Text 101
4.2.2.4.2 Commentary 101
4.2.2.5 Article 75 102
4.2.2.5.1 Text 102
4.2.2.5.2 Commentary 102
4.2.2.6 Article 76 104
4.2.2.6.1 Text 104
4.2.2.6.2 Commentary 104
4.2.2.7 Article 77 105
4.2.2.7.1 Text 105
4.2.2.7.2 Commentary 105
4.2.2.8 Article 78 106
4.2.2.8.1 Text 106
4.2.2.8.2 Commentary 106
4.2.2.9 Article 79 106
4.2.2.9.1 Text 106
4.2.2.9.2 Commentary 106
4.2.2.10 Article 80 107
4.2.2.10.1 Text 107
4.2.2.10.2 Commentary 107
4.2.2.11 Article 81 108
4.2.2.11.1 Text 108
4.2.2.11.2 Commentary 108

4.2.2.12 Article 82 108
4.2.2.12.1 Text 108
4.2.2.12.2 Commentary 109
4.2.2.13 Article 83 109
4.2.2.13.1 Text 109
4.2.2.13.2 Commentary 109
4.2.2.14 Article 84 110
4.2.2.14.1 Text 110
4.2.2.14.2 Commentary 110
4.2.2.15 Relationship between the ECSC Treaty and the EEC Treaty 112

4.3 Transport Sectors 113

4.3.1 Road transport 113
4.3.1.1 Introduction 113
4.3.1.2 1962 Directive 113
4.3.1.3 Directive 65/269 113
4.3.1.3a Regulation 117/66 114
4.3.1.4 Regulation 1018/68 114
4.3.1.5 Regulation 543/69 114
4.3.1.6 Regulation 516/72 114
4.3.1.7 Regulation 517/72 114
4.3.1.8 1972 ASOR 114
4.3.1.9 Directive 74/561 114
4.3.1.10 Directive 74/562 115
4.3.1.11 Directive 76/914 115
4.3.1.12 Regulation 3237/76 115
4.3.1.13 1978 Customs Convention 115
4.3.1.15 Decision of 25 June 1979 115
4.3.1.16 1981 TIR Convention 115
4.3.1.17 ASOR Agreement 116
4.3.1.18 Directive 83/463 116
4.3.1.19 Directive 84/647 116
4.3.1.20 Regulation 3690/86 116
4.3.1.21 Regulation 1841/88 116
4.3.1.22 Regulation 4059/89 116
4.3.1.23 Regulation 3916/90 116
4.3.2 Rail transport 117
4.3.2.1 Introduction 117
4.3.2.2 Regulation 1192/69 117
4.3.2.3 1970 Resolution 117
4.3.2.4 Decision 75/327 117
4.3.2.5 Regulation 2830/77 117
4.3.2.6 Regulation 2183/78 117
4.3.2.7 Directive 80/1177 118
4.3.2.8 1981 Resolution 118
4.3.2.9 Decision 82/529 118
4.3.2.10 Decision 83/418 118
4.3.2.11 1984 Recommendation 118
4.3.2.12 1991 Package of Measures 118

4.3.3 Air transport 118
4.3.3.1 Introduction 118
4.3.3.2 A review of the measures adopted in the field of air transport 120
4.3.3.2.1 Council Decision 80/50 120
4.3.3.2.2 Council Direction 80/51 120
4.3.3.2.3 Council Directive 80/1266 120
4.3.3.2.4 Council Recommendation 81/560 120
4.3.3.2.5 Council Directive 83/416 121
4.3.3.2.6 Council Directive 86/216 121
4.3.3.2.7 Council Directive 87/601 121
4.3.3.2.8 Council Decision 87/602 121
4.3.3.2.9 Decision 87/359/EEC 121
4.3.3.2.10 Council Regulation 3975/87/EEC 121
4.3.3.2.11 Council Directive 80/51 122
4.3.3.2.12 Council Regulation 3976/87/EEC 122
4.3.3.2.13 Commission Regulation 2671/88 122
4.3.3.2.14 Commission Regulation 2672/88 122
4.3.3.2.15 Commission Regulation 2673/88 122
4.3.3.2.16 Commission Regulation 4261/88 122
4.3.3.2.17 Council Regulation 2299/89 122
4.3.3.2.18 Council Directive 89/629 123
4.3.3.2.19 Council Directive 90/449 123
4.3.3.2.20 Council Regulation 2342/90/EEC 123
4.3.3.2.21 Council Regulation 2343/90/EEC 123
4.3.3.2.22 Regulation 82/91 123
4.3.3.2.23 Regulation 83/91 123
4.3.3.2.24 Regulation 84/91 123
4.3.3.2.25 Regulation 294/91 124
4.3.3.2.26 Regulation 295/91 124
4.3.3.2.27 Regulation 3922/91 124
4.3.3.2.28 Directive 91/670 124
4.3.3.3 Conclusion 124
4.3.4 Inland waterway 124
4.3.4.1 Recommendation 335/68 124
4.3.4.2 Regulation 281/71 124
4.3.4.3 Directive 80/1119 125
4.3.4.4 Regulation 1101/89 125
4.3.4.5 Regulation 4060/89 125

4.4 General Matters 125

4.4.1 Transport committees 125
4.4.2 Competition 126
4.4.2.1 Regulation No. 11 of 1960 126
4.4.2.2 Regulation 141/62 126
4.4.2.3 Decision 65/271 126
4.4.2.4 Regulation 1017/68 126
4.4.2.5 Regulation 1629/69 126
4.4.2.6 Regulation 1630/69 127
4.4.2.7 Regulation 1107/70 127
4.4.2.8 Regulation 2988/74 127

4.4.3 Infrastructure 127
4.4.3.1 1964 Decision 127
4.4.3.2 Regulation 1108/70 127
4.4.3.3 Decision 78/174 128
4.4.3.4 Regulation 3600/82 128
4.4.3.5 Decision 84/519 128
4.4.3.6 Decision 84/520 128
4.4.3.7 Regulation 4059/86 128
4.4.3.8 Regulation 4070/87 128
4.4.3.9 Regulation 3359/90 129
4.4.4 Inspection of goods 129
4.4.5 Summertime arrangements 129
4.4.6 Public service 129
4.4.6.1 Regulation 1191/69 129
4.4.7 Passenger and luggage traffic 129
4.4.8 Prior examination and consultation in transport matters 129
4.4.9 External relations 130
4.4.10 General measures 130
4.4.11 Temporary Importation 130
4.4.11.1 Regulation 2249/91 130
4.4.12 Statistics 130
4.4.12.1 Directive 78/546 130

4.5 Conclusion 130

CHAPTER 5 HISTORICAL OVERVIEW OF EC SHIPPING LAW

5.1 Introduction 133

5.2 The Foundation Treaties 133

5.3 The 1960s 134

5.3.1 1960 Memorandum from the Commission to the Council 134
5.3.2 1961 Memorandum on the Basic Approach to be Adopted in the Common Transport Policy 134
5.3.3 1962 Action Programme for a Common Transport Policy 134
5.3.4 1962 Regulations on Competition and Shipping 134

5.4 The 1970s 135

5.4.1 Introduction 135
5.4.2 Bodson's proposals 135
5.4.3 The 1973 enlargement of the EC 136
5.4.4 Commission's Communication to Council on 25 October 1973 136
5.4.5 ECSC Rail Tariff 137
5.4.6 1973 Enlargement of the EC 137
5.4.7 1973 Oil crisis 137
5.4.8 1973 French Seaman's Case 137
5.4.9 1974 Ports 139
5.4.10 1975 French initiative 139

5.4.11 Non-Member States 139
5.4.12 Code of Conduct for Liner Conferences 139
5.4.13 1976 Interim Report drawn up on behalf of the European Parliament's Committee on Economic and Monetary Affairs on the Community Shipping Industry 140
5.4.14 1977 Interim Report drawn up on behalf of the Committee on Regional Policy, Regional Planning and Transport of the Sea Transport Problems in the Community 140
5.4.15 1977 Consultation procedure: Decision 77/587 141
5.4.16 1978 Decision on Relations with State Trading Countries: Decision 78/774 141
5.4.17 Tanker disasters 142
5.4.18 1978 Ship's inspection proposals 143
5.4.19 1978 Collection of Information Decision 143
5.4.20 1978 Decision in respect of liner trades between the EC and East Africa/Central America 143
5.4.21 1979 Ratification of the UN Code of Conduct for Liner Conferences 143
5.4.22 1979 Parliamentary Resolution on Shipping Accidents 143
5.4.23 1979 Parliamentary Resolution on the Community's Relations with the Comecon States in Maritime Shipping 144
5.4.24 1979 Economic and Social Committee Opinion on Flags of Convenience 144
5.4.25 Shipping crisis 144

5.5 The 1980s 144

5.5.1 Shipping crisis as well as port distortions 144
5.5.2 1980 Draft for a Council Resolution Concerning Priorities and the Timetable for Decisions to be taken by the Council in the Transport Sector during the Period up to the End of 1983 144
5.5.3 1980 Extension of the 1978 Collection of Information Decision 145
5.5.4 1980 Recommendation on the Torremolinos International Convention for the Safety of Fishing Vessels 145
5.5.5 1980 Proposal on Port Control of Pollution 145
5.5.6 1980 Parliamentary resolutions on oil pollution 145
5.5.7 1981 Accession to the EC of Greece 145
5.5.8 1981 Council Resolution on its Priorities in the Transport Sector up to 1983 145
5.5.9 1981 Decision extending the Collection of Information Regime in respect of the Far East 145
5.5.10 1981 Proposal on Competition Rules and Shipping 146
5.5.11 1981 Proposals on Concerted Research on Shore-Based Maritime Navigation Aid Systems 146
5.5.12 1982 Extension of the Collection of Information systems 146
5.5.13 1982 Memorandum of Understanding on Port-State Control 146
5.5.14 1983 Economic and Social Committee Opinion on the Commission's proposal on the application of Articles 85 and 86 to shipping 146
5.5.15 1983 Recommendation on SAR 147
5.5.16 1983 Countermeasures Decision 147
5.5.17 1983 Paraliament's case against the Commission for failure to elaborate proposals in the area of transport 147
5.5.18 1984 Commission Memorandum on Maritime Transport 147
5.5.19 1985 Progress Towards a Common Maritime Policy: Commission Communication 148

5.5.19.1 Introduction 148
5.5.19.2 Analysis of the Market 149
5.5.19.3 Proposals 149
5.5.19.4 Economic and Social Committee's Opinion 151
5.5.20 The 1986 Package 152
5.5.20.1 Regulation 4055/86 153
5.5.20.2 Regulation 4056/86 153
5.5.20.3 Statements 153
5.5.20.4 Assessment of the 1986 Package 154
5.5.21 The Single European Act 155
5.5.22 1987 Antwerp Meeting 155
5.5.23 1988 Shipbuilding Talks with Japan 155
5.5.24 1988 Commission Proposal on the Minimum Health and Safety Requirements for Improved Medical Treatment on Board Vessels 155
5.5.25 1988 Commission Programme 155
5.5.26 August 1989: Positive Measures 156
5.5.26.1 Proposal for a Council Regulation establishing a Community Ship Register and Providing for the Flying of the Community Flag by Sea-Going Vessels 156
5.5.26.2 Proposal for a Commission Recommendation on Improving the Effectiveness of Port State Control in the Community 156
5.5.26.3 Proposal for a Council of Ministers Regulation providing for a Common Definition of a Community Shipowner 156
5.5.26.4 Proposal for a Council of Ministers Regulation applying the Principle of Freedom to Provide Services to Maritime Transport within Member States 156
5.5.26.5 1990: Proposal for a Council Regulation regarding the Transfer of Ships from one Register to another within the Community 157
5.5.27 Financial and fiscal measures 157
5.5.28 June 1990 Resolution on Passenger Ferry Safety 157
5.5.29 1990 Proposal for a Council of Ministers Regulation to grant a Block Exemption for Consortia 157
5.5.29.1 1991: Permanent Dialogue on the Maritime Industry 158

5.6 The Future 158

CHAPTER 6 ESTABLISHMENT AND REGISTRATION

6.1 Right of Establishment 159

6.1.1 Concept of right of establishment 160
6.1.2 General rule on freedom of establishment 160
6.1.3 Prohibition of new restrictions 161
6.1.4 Implementation of the Treaty provisions on establishment 161
6.1.5 Mutual recognition of diplomas, certificates and qualifications 162
6.1.6 Exceptions to the freedom of establishment 163
6.1.6.1 Exception 1: Exercise of official authority 163
6.1.6.2 Exception 2: Public policy 163
6.1.6.3 Exception 3: Public security 164
6.1.6.4 Exception 4: Public health 164

6.2 Registration 164

6.2.1 Introduction 164
6.2.1.1 Traditional home registries 165
6.2.1.2 Traditional open registries 165
6.2.1.3 Offshore registries 166
6.2.1.4 International registries 166
6.2.2 International law on registration 167
6.2.2.1 Geneva Convention on the High Seas 1958 167
6.2.2.2 United Nations Convention of the Law of the Sea 1982 167
6.2.2.3 United Nations Convention on the Registration of Ships 1986 169

6.3 EC Perspective on Registration 170

6.3.1 Introduction 170
6.3.2 EC reaction to the UN Convention on the Registration of Ships 1986 171
6.3.2.1 Commission's Communication 171
6.3.2.2 Commission's proposal 173
6.3.2.3 European Parliament's Report 175
6.3.4 An EC register: EUROS 176
6.3.4.1 Proposal 176
6.3.4.2 Objective of the proposal 178
6.3.4.3 Legal bases 178
6.3.4.4 Market reaction 178
6.3.4.5 Establishment of the Register 179
6.3.4.6 Eligibility to be registered 179
6.3.4.7 Safety on EUROS-registered ships 181
6.3.4.12 Advantages of being registered on EUROS 184
6.3.4.13 Assessment of the proposal 184
6.3.5 Council regulation on the transfer of ships from one register to another within the Community 184
6.3.5.1 Introduction 184
6.3.5.2 Background to the proposal 185
6.3.5.3 Legislative history 186
6.3.5.3 Relationship between the Regulation and other rules 188
6.3.5.5 Legal bases 188
6.3.5.6 Interpretation 188
6.3.5.7 Application of the proposed Regulation 189
6.3.5.8 Obligation on Member State to register 190
6.3.5.9 No additional requirements for certificates 191
6.3.5.10 Divergences of interpretation 191
6.3.5.12 Committee of maritime experts 191
6.3.5.12.1 The Committee's procedure 192
6.3.5.12.2 Entry into force 192
6.3.5.13 "National Shipping Line" 192

6.4 Definition of a Community Shipowner 193

6.4.1 Introduction 193
6.4.2 Rationale for the Proposal 193
6.4.3 Legal bases 193
6.4.4 Purpose of the proposed Regulation 193
6.4.5 The concept of a Community shipowner 193

6.5 Parallel Registries 194

CHAPTER 7 FREEDOM TO SUPPLY MARITIME SERVICES

7.1–7.2 Introduction 197

7.3 UN Liner Code 197

7.4 Freedom to Provide Services in EC Law 197

7.5 Regulation 4055/86 198

7.5.1 Introduction 198
7.5.2 Purpose 198
7.5.3 Commercial background 199
7.5.4 Effect 199
7.5.5 Entry into force 199
7.5.6 Implementation 199
7.5.7 Basic provision: Article 1 199
7.5.7.1 Timetable: Article 2 200
7.5.8 Cargo-sharing arrangements in bilateral agreements: Articles 3 and 4 201
7.5.9 Cargo-sharing arrangements in future agreements: Article 5 201
7.5.10 Non-discrimination between EC nationals on the basis of nationality 202
7.5.11 Non-EC nationals 202
7.5.12 Temporary establishment 203
7.5.13 Review 203
7.5.14 Assessment 203
7.5.15 French-Corsican Case 203
7.5.16 Italy-Algeria Case 205

7.6 Cabotage 210

7.6.1 Introduction 210
7.6.2 Concept of cabotage 210
7.6.2.1 Definition 210
7.6.2.2 State cabotage 210
7.6.2.3 EC cabotage 210
7.6.3 Commercial overview of cabotage 211
7.6.4 Merits of cabotage 212
7.6.4.1 Arguments for cabotage 212
7.6.4.2 Arguments against cabotage 212
7.6.5 Cabotage in each of the member states 213
7.6.5.1 States which have cabotage restrictions 213
7.6.5.1.1 France 213
7.6.5.1.2 Greece 213
7.6.5.1.3 Italy 213
7.6.5.1.4 Portugal 214
7.6.5.1.5 Spain 214
7.6.5.2 States which do not have cabotage restrictions 214
7.6.5.2.1 Belgium 214
7.6.5.2.2 Germany 214

		7.6.5.2.3 Ireland	214
		7.6.5.2.4 United Kingdom	214
	7.6.5.3	States which have limited cabotage restrictions	215
		7.6.5.3.1 Denmark	215
	7.6.5.4	States for which the issue does not arise	215
		7.6.5.4.1 Luxembourg	215
7.6.6	Development of the concept of cabotage in EC Law		215
	7.6.6.1	Commission v. France	215
	7.6.6.2	1985 Communication from the Commission to the Council	215
	7.6.6.3	1986 December Package	216
	7.6.6.4	1988 Commission Programme	217
	7.6.6.5	1989 Positive Measures Programme	217
		7.6.6.5.1 A brief analysis of the Commission proposal	218
7.6.7	Outlook		220

CHAPTER 8 EMPLOYMENT AND SOCIAL SECURITY LAW

8.1 Introduction			221
8.2 EC Law and Employment Generally			222
8.2.1	Introduction		222
8.2.2	Free Movement of Workers		222
	8.2.2.1	Concept of "worker"	222
	8.2.2.2	Article 48 of the EEC Treaty	223
	8.2.2.3	Discrimination on the basis of nationality	224
		8.2.2.3.1 Exceptions to the right	224
		8.2.2.3.2 Public service	224
	8.2.2.4	Article 49 of the EEC Treaty	225
	8.2.2.5	Assessment	225
8.2.3	Working conditions		225
8.2.4	Equal pay		226
8.2.5	Non-discrimination on the basis of nationality between EC countries		226
8.2.6	Employment in shipping in the EC		227
	8.2.6.1	Introduction	227
		8.2.6.1.1 Merchant Marine	227
		8.2.6.1.2 Shipbuilding	227
	8.2.6.2	Hollesen Study	228
8.3 EC Law and the Employment of Seafarers			228
8.3.1	Training		228
	8.3.1.1	Hours of working	229
	8.3.1.2	Mutual recognition of qualifications	229
		8.3.1.2.1 Directive 87/540	229
		8.3.1.2.2 Belgium, Greece and Ireland	230
8.3.2	Taxation		230
8.4 EC Social Security Law			230
8.4.1	Introduction		230
8.4.2	Joint Committee on Maritime Transport		230

CHAPTER 9 INTRODUCTION TO EC COMPETITION LAW AND SHIPPING

9.1 Introduction 233

9.2 EEC Competition Law Generally 234

9.3 EC Competition Law and Shipping: The History of the Application of Articles 85 and 86 of the EEC Treaty 234

9.3.1 1962: Regulation 17/62 implementing EC competition law 234
9.3.2 1962: Regulation 141/62 disapplying EC competition law in the case of transport 235
9.3.3 1988: Regulation 1017/68 applying EC competition law to certain transport modes 235
9.3.4 1973: Accession of Denmark, Ireland and the UK to the EC 236
9.3.5 1974: Commission v. France 236
9.3.6 1978: Commission v. Belgium 236
9.3.7 1979: UNCTAD Code 236
9.3.8 Pre-regulation 4056/86 position 237
9.3.9 Regulation 4056/86 238

9.4 Overlap Between Competition Measures Relating to Transport and General Measures 238

9.5 Conclusion 238

CHAPTER 10 ARTICLES 85 AND 86 OF THE EEC TREATY

10.1 Article 85 241

10.1.1 Introduction 241
10.1.2 Text of Article 85 241
10.1.3 Basic concepts in Article 85 242
10.1.3.1 Undertaking 242
10.1.3.1.1 Introduction 242
10.1.3.1.2 Definition 242
10.1.3.1.3 Particular entities 243
10.1.3.2 Agreements, decisions and concerted practices 246
10.1.3.2.1 Introduction 246
10.1.3.2.2 Agreements between undertakings 247
10.1.3.2.3 Decisions by associations of undertakings 248
10.1.3.2.4 Concerted practices 249
10.1.3.2.5 Agreements, decisions and concerted practices entered into outside the EC 250
10.1.4 Objective or effect of preventing, restricting or distorting competition 250
10.1.4.1 Introduction 250
10.1.4.2 Object 250
10.1.4.3 Effect 251
10.1.4.4 Preventing, restricting and distorting competition 251
10.1.5 Effect on inter-State trade 251
10.1.5.1 Introduction 251

10.1.5.2 Examples 251
10.1.6 De minimis doctrine 252
10.1.6.1 Introduction 252
10.1.7 Agreements falling outside Article 85(1) 252
10.1.7.1 Commission notice agreements 253
10.1.7.2 Agreements within a single economic unit 253
10.1.7.3 Objective necessity 253
10.1.7.4 Commercial risk 254
10.1.7.5 Selective distribution system 254
10.1.7.6 Mergers 254
10.1.7.7 Transfer of assets 254
10.1.7.8 Exemption 254
10.1.8 Article 85(2): Voidness 255
10.1.8.1 Introduction 255
10.1.8.2 Text of Article 85(2) EEC 255
10.1.8.3 Penal aspect 255
10.1.8.4 Is this really a penalty at all? 255
10.1.9 Article 85(3): Exemptions 255
10.1.9.1 Introduction 255
10.1.9.2 Text of Article 85(3) EEC 255
10.1.9.3 Conditions for granting exemptions 256
10.1.9.3.1 Introduction 256
10.1.9.3.2 Benefit 256
10.1.9.3.3 Fair share to the consumers 256
10.1.9.3.4 No indispensable restrictions 256
10.1.9.3.5 No substantial elimination of competition 256
10.1.9.4 Individual exemptions 257
10.1.9.5 Block exemptions 257
10.1.9.5.1 Introduction 257
10.1.9.5.2 Examples 257
10.1.9.5.3 Opposition procedure 257
10.1.9.5.4 Comfort letters 257

10.2 Article 86 258

10.2.1 Introduction 258
10.2.2 Text of Article 86 EEC 258
10.2.3 Importance of economic evidence 259
10.2.4 Interpretation of Article 86 EEC 259
10.2.5 Economic rationale for Article 86 EEC 259
10.2.6 Check-list for the successful application of Article 86 EEC 260
10.2.7 Undertakings 260
10.2.8 Concept of a dominant position or dominance 260
10.2.8.1 Introduction 260
10.2.8.2 There is no definition in the EEC Treaty 261
10.2.8.3 The definition used by the EEC institutions 261
10.2.8.3.1 Introduction 261
10.2.8.3.2 The product or services market 262
10.2.8.3.3 Supply-side substitutability 264
10.2.8.4 Relevant geographical market 264
10.2.8.5 Relevant temporal market 265

10.2.11 Market power 265
10.2.11.1 Introduction 265
10.2.11.2 Measuring market power 265
10.2.11.3 Market shares 265
10.2.11.4 Barriers to entry 266
10.2.11.4.1 Economies of scale 266
10.2.11.4.2 Evidence of the undertakings 266
10.2.11.4.3 Price movements 266
10.2.11.4.4 Conduct 266
10.2.11.4.5 Overall strength and size of the undertaking(s) 266
10.2.11.4.6 Legal provisions 267
10.2.11.4.7 Deep pocket 267
10.2.12 Within the Common Market or a substantial part of it 267
10.2.13 Concept of "Abuse of a dominant Position" 267
10.2.13.1 Introduction 267
10.2.13.2 Definition of abuse 268
10.2.13.3 Exploitation 268
10.2.13.4 Anti-competitive abuses 268
10.2.14 Effect on inter-State trade 268

10.3 Competition Procedure 269

10.3.1 Role of the Commission 269
10.3.2 Role of the national authorities and courts 269
10.3.3 Initiation of proceedings 269
10.3.4 Notification 270
10.3.5 Complaints 270
10.3.6 Own-initiative investigations 270
10.3.7 Sector investigations 270
10.3.8 Conduct of proceedings 270
10.3.8.1 Fact-finding 270
10.3.8.2 Requests for information 270
10.3.8.3 Investigations 271
10.3.8.4 Legal professional privilege 271
10.3.9 Conclusion of proceedings 271
10.3.9.1 Introduction 271
10.3.9.2 Negative clearance 271
10.3.9.3 Exemption 271
10.3.9.4 Termination of proceedings 271
10.3.10 Internal compliance

CHAPTER 11 LINER CONFERENCES GENERALLY

11.1 Introduction 273

11.2 United Nations Code of Conduct for Liner Conferences 274

11.2.1 Introduction 274
11.2.2 UNCTAD negotiations 275
11.2.3 Objectives and principles of the Code 275

11.2.4	Signature and entry into force	276
11.2.5	Perspectives on the Code of Conduct	276
11.2.6	Application of the Code	277
11.2.7	Provisions of the Code relating to relations between conference members	278
	11.2.7.1 Introduction	278
	11.2.7.2 Membership	278
	11.2.7.3 Participation	278
	11.2.7.4 Decision-making	279
	11.2.7.5 Sanctions	279
	11.2.7.6 Self-policing	279
	11.2.7.7 Conference agreements	280
11.2.8	Provisions of the Code relating to relations with shippers	280
	11.2.8.1 Introduction	280
	11.2.8.2 Loyalty arrangements	280
	11.2.8.3 Dispensation	281
	11.2.8.4 Availability of tariffs	281
	11.2.8.5 Annual reports	281
	11.2.8.6 Consultation machinery	282
11.2.9	Provisions of the Code relating to freight rates	283
	11.2.9.1 Introduction	283
	11.2.9.2 Criteria for freight rate determination	283
	11.2.9.3 Conference tariffs and classification of tariff rates	283
	11.2.9.4 General freight-rate increases	283
	11.2.9.5 Promotional freight rates	284
	11.2.9.6 Surcharges	285
	11.2.9.7 Currency changes	286
11.2.10	Other substantive aspects of the Code	286

11.3 The UN Liner Code and EC Law 286

11.3.1	Introduction	286
11.3.2	Compatibility of the Code with EC Law	287
11.3.3	Regulation 954/79	287
11.3.4	Legislative history of Regulation 954/79	287
	11.3.4.1 1974: Commission Proposal	287
	11.3.4.2 1975: Commission Proposal	287
	11.3.4.2.1 Code of Conduct: EEC Treaty	288
	11.3.4.3 Council of Ministers Decision	288
11.3.5	Contents of Regulation 954/79	289
	11.3.5.1 Existing conference	289
	11.3.5.2 Cargo allocation	289
	11.3.5.3 OECD Member States	290
	11.3.5.4 Decision-making procedures	290
	11.3.5.5 Reservations and interpretative reservations	291
11.3.6	Implementation of the UN Code in EC Member States	291

CHAPTER 12 COMPETITION: REGULATION 4056/86

12.1 Introduction 293

12.2 Legislative History 293

12.2.1 Introduction 293
12.2.2 1981 Commission Proposal 294
12.2.3 1983 ECOSOC Opinion 295
12.2.4 1984 European Parliament's Report 295
12.2.5 1985 Amended Commission Proposal 296
12.2.6 1986: Commission Amendment 297

12.3 Entry into Force of the Regulation 297

12.4 Legal Bases of the Regulation 298

12.5 Legal Effects 299

12.6 Application of the Regulation 299

12.6.1 Text of Article 1 299
12.6.2 Effect of Article 1 300
12.6.3 Transport services 300
12.6.4 International transport services 300
12.6.5 Maritime services 300
12.6.6 Services other than tramp services 301
12.6.7 Transport users 301
12.6.8 Agreements between providers of ancillary services 302
12.6.9 Passenger traffic 302
12.6.10 Scope 302

12.7 Technical Agreements 302

12.7.1 Introduction 302
12.7.2 Text of Article 2 303
12.7.2.1 The introduction of uniform application of standards or types in respect of vessels and other means of transport, equipment, supplies or fixed installation 304
12.7.2.2 The exchange or pooling for the purpose of operating transport services, of vessels, space on vessels or slots or other means of transport, staff, equipment or fixed installations 304
12.7.2.3 The organisation and execution of successive or supplementary maritime transport operations and the establishment or application of inclusive rates and conditions for such operations 304
12.7.2.4 The co-ordination of transport timetables for connecting routes 305
12.7.2.5 The consolidation of individual assignments 305
12.7.2.6 The establishment or application of uniform rules concerning the stucture and the conditions governing the application of transport tariffs 305
12.7.3 Amendment 305

12.8 Block Exemption for Liner Conferences 305

12.8.1 Introduction 305
12.8.2 Liner conferences 305

12.8.3 Block exemption 306
12.8.4 Text of Article 3 of the Regulation 306
12.8.5 Condition attaching to the block exemption for liner conferences 308
12.8.5.1–12.8.5.3 Text of Article 4 308
12.8.5.4 Commission's Commentary on Article 4 308
12.8.5.5 Importance of Article 4: Commentary 308
12.8.6 Obligations attaching to the exemption 309
12.8.6.1 Introduction 309
12.8.6.2 Text of Article 5 309
12.8.6.3 Details of the obligations 310
12.8.6.4 Consultations 310
12.8.6.5 Loyalty arrrangements 310
12.8.6.6 Services not covered by the freight charges 311
12.8.6.7 Availability of tariffs 311
12.8.6.8 Notification to the Commission of awards at arbitration and recommendations 311

12.9 Block Exemption for Agreements Between Transport Users and Conferences Concerning the Use of Scheduled Maritime Transport Services 312

12.9.1 Introduction 312
12.9.2 Text of Article 6 of the Regulation 312
12.9.3 Definition of liner conferences 312
12.9.4 Definition of transport user 312

12.10 Monitoring of exempted Agreements 313

12.10.1 Introduction 313
12.10.2 Text of Article 7 of the Regulation 313
12.10.3 Commentary 314

12.11 Abuse of a dominant Position 315

12.11.1 Introduction 315
12.11.2 Text of Article 8 315
12.11.3 Commentary 316
12.11.4 Example 316

12.12 Conflicts of National Laws 316

12.12.1 Text of Article 9 of the Regulation 316
12.12.2 Commentary 317

12.13 Rules of Procedure 317

12.13.1 Complaints 318
12.13.1.1 Text of Article 10 318
12.13.1.2 Procedures on complaint or on the Commission's own initiative 318
12.13.1.3 Locus standi to submit a complaint 318
12.13.2 Result of procedures on complaint or on the Commission's own initiative 318
12.13.2.1 Introduction 318
12.13.2.2 Text of Article 11 318
12.13.2.3 Commentary on Article 319

12.13.3 Opposition procedure 320
12.13.3.1 Introduction 320
12.13.3.2 Text of Article 12 320
12.13.3.3 Commentary 320
12.13.4 Duration and revocation of individual exemption 322
12.13.4.1 Introduction 322
12.13.4.2 Text of Article 13 323
12.13.4.3 Renewal of the exemption 323
12.13.4.4 Revocation of the exemption 323
12.13.4.5 Amendment of the exemption 323
12.13.4.6 Prohibition of specified acts by the parties 323
12.13.4.7 Publication of the decision 324
12.13.5 Powers of the commission 324
12.13.5.1 Text of Article 14
12.13.5.2 Commentary 324
12.13.6 Liaison with the authorities of the member states: Article 15 324
12.13.6.1 Introduction 324
12.13.6.2 Text of Article 15 324
12.13.6.3 Commentary 325
12.13.7 Commission requests for information 326
12.13.7.1 Introduction 326
12.13.7.2 Text of Article 16 326
12.13.7.3 Commentary 326
12.13.8 Investigations 327
12.13.8.1 Introduction 327
12.13.8.2.1 Text of Article 18 327
12.13.8.2.2 Commentary 328
12.13.8.3 Investigations by authorities of the Members States 329
12.13.8.3.1 Introduction 329
12.13.8.3.2 Text of Article 17 329
12.13.8.4 Secrecy of information gathered 329
12.13.9 Fines and periodic penalty payments 330
12.13.9.1 Fines 330
12.13.9.1.1 Text of Article 19 330
12.13.9.1.2 Commentary 330
12.13.9.2 Periodic penalty payments 331
12.13.9.2.1 Text of Article 20 331
13.13.9.2.2 Commentary 332
12.13.10 Hearings of the parties and others 332
12.13.10.1 Introduction 332
12.13.10.2 Text of Article 23 332
12.13.10.3 Commentary 333
12.13.11 Review by the Court of Justice of the fines and periodical penalty payments 333
12.13.11.1 Introduction 333
12.13.11.2 Text of Article 21 333
12.13.11.3 Commentary 333
12.13.12 Publication of decisions 333
12.13.13 Implementing provisions 334

12.14 Procedure: Commission Regulation 4260/88 334

12.14.1 Introduction 334

12.14.2 Legal basis and background 334
12.14.3 Notification 334
12.14.3.1 Text of Article 1 of Regulation 4260/86 334
12.14.4 Complaints 335
12.14.4.1 Introduction 335
12.14.4.2 Text of Article 2 of Regulation 4260/86 335
12.14.5 Applications for exemptions 335
12.14.5.1 Introduction 335
12.14.5.2 Text of Article 4 of Regulation 4260/86
12.14.6 Hearings 336
12.14.6.1 Preliminary hearing 336
12.14.6.1.1 Text of Article 5 336
12.14.6.1.2 Text of Article 6 336
12.14.7 Communicating awards and recommendations 336

12.15 Practice to Date 336

12.15.1 Brazilian and Colombian coffee trades 336
12.15.2 Eurocorde 337
12.15.3 Gulfway 337
12.15.4 Israeli trades 337
12.15.5 RTM/P&O 338
12.15.6 Sealink/B&I (operating agreement) 338
12.15.7 Sealink/B&I (port dispute) 338
12.15.8 Sealink/SMZ 339
12.15.9 Sealink/SNCF 339
12.15.10 West and Central Africa cases 339
12.15.11 The 1237 Agreement 339
12.15.12 Irish Club rules 340

12.16 Assessment 340

CHAPTER 13 DUMPING: REGULATION 4057/86

13.1 Introduction 341

13.2 Council Regulation 4057/86 341

13.2.1 Introduction 341
13.2.2 Legal basis 344
13.2.3 Commercial background 344
13.2.4 Legal history 344
13.2.5 Entry into force 345
13.2.6 Purpose 345
13.2.7 Application 345
13.2.8 Concepts 345
13.2.8.1 Concept of dumping 345
13.2.8.2 Concept of an unfair pricing practice 346
13.2.8.3 Concept of non-commercial advantage 346
13.2.8.4 Concept of normal freight rates 347
13.2.8.5 Concept of "serious disruption of a freight pattern" 348

13.2.8.6 Concept of "injury to Community ship operators" 348
13.2.8.7 Concept of "Community interest" 349
13.2.8.8 Concept of third country shipowner 349
13.2.9 Role of EC institutions under the Regulation 350
13.2.9.1 The Commission 350
13.2.9.2 The Council of Ministers 350
13.2.9.3 The European Court of Justice 350
13.2.10 Complaints 350
13.2.10.1 Complaint procedure 350
13.2.10.2 Who may lodge a complaint? 351
13.2.10.3 Form of a complaint 351
13.2.10.4 Contents of the complaint 351
13.2.10.5 To whom is the complaint made? 352
13.2.10.6 Confidentiality of the complaint 352
13.2.10.7 Withdrawal of the complaint 352
13.2.11 Consultation 352
13.2.12 Initiation and investigation 353
13.2.12.1 Initiation 353
13.2.12.2 Contents of the investigation 353
13.2.12.3 Invitation to the allegedly guilty party to make their case 354
13.2.12.4 Co-operation 354
13.2.12.5 Confidentiality of information supplied 354
13.2.12.6 Conclusion of the first stages of investigation 354
13.2.12.7 Formal rights of the parties 355
13.2.13 Outcome of the Commission's investigations 355
13.2.13.1 Introduction 355
13.2.13.2 No action 355
13.2.13.3 Undertakings 355
13.2.13.3.1 Introduction 355
13.2.13.3.2 Duration of undertakings 356
13.2.13.3.3 Review of undertakings 356
13.2.13.4 Redressive duties 356
13.2.13.5 Power to impose redressive duties 356
13.2.13.6 Calculation of the redressive duties 356
13.2.13.7 Imposition of redressive duties 357
13.2.13.7.1 Collection of redressive duties 357
13.2.13.7.2 Duration of the redressive duties 357
13.2.13.7.3 Retroactivity of redressive duties 357
13.2.13.7.4 Review of redressive duties 357
13.2.13.7.5 Refunds of redressive duties 357
13.2.14 Appeals 358
13.2.15 Practice to date 358

CHAPTER 14 COMPETITION: REGULATION 4058/86

14.1 Introduction 361

14.2 Application 361

14.3 Legal cases 361

14.4 Legal history 361

14.5 Entry into force 362

14.6 Background 362

14.7 Concepts 362

14.8 Triggering event 363

14.9 Requests by a Member State for co-ordinated action 363

14.9.1 Introduction 363
14.9.2 Text of Article 3 363

14.10 Co-ordinated action 364

14.10.2 Text of Article 4 364
14.10.3 Diplomatic representations 364

14.11 Procedure 364

14.12 Action by Member States in default of Council action 365

14.12.1 Individual or group action 365
14.12.2 Urgent action 365
14.12.3 Report to the Commission 365

14.13 Consultation 365

14.14 OECD Member States 365

14.14.1 Introduction 365
14.14.2 Article 8 of the Regulation 365

14.15 History 366

CHAPTER 15 STATE AIDS

15.1 Introduction 367

15.2 Purposes of State Aids 367

15.3 Economics of State Aids 368

15.4 State Aids and EC Law Generally 369

15.4.1 Introduction 369
15.4.2 Introduction to the EEC Treaty rules 370
15.4.3 State aids in shipping and EC law 370
15.4.3.1 Compatibility of shipping State aids with EC LAW: the general principles 371

15.4.4 Article 92(1) of the EEC Treaty: the prohibition of certain types of aid 372
15.4.4.1 Article 92(1) 372
15.4.4.2 Purpose of Article 92 372
15.4.4.3 Concept of aid 373
15.4.4.3.1 Advantage 374
15.4.4.3.2 Aid is provided by a Member State or an emanation of such a State 375
15.4.4.3.3 Aid favours certain undertaking or the production of certain goods or services 376
15.4.4.3.4 Aid distorts competition 376
15.4.4.3.5 Effect on inter-state trade 377
15.4.4.3.6 Purpose of the aid 377
15.4.4.3.7 Juridical nature of Article 92 377
15.4.5 Article 92(2) of the EEC Treaty: the automatic authorisation of certain types of aid 377
15.4.5.1 Introduction 377
15.4.5.2 Text of Article 92(2) 378
15.4.5.3 Effect of compatibility 378
15.4.5.4 Aid having a social character 378
15.4.5.5 Natural disasters 378
15.4.5.6 Germany 378
15.4.6 Article 92(3) of the EEC Treaty: the authorisation of certain types of aid in certain circumstances 379
15.4.6.1 Introduction 379
15.4.6.2 Text of Article 92(3) 379
15.4.6.3 Criteria used by the Commission in deciding to authorise an aid 379
15.4.6.4 Economic development aids 380
15.4.6.5 Important European project 380
15.4.6.6 Serious disturbance in the economy 380
15.4.6.7 Development of certain economic activities 380
15.4.6.8 Sectoral aids 381
15.4.6.9 Aid to build a ship 381
15.4.6.10 Aid to reduce manning costs 381
15.4.6.11 Aid for crew relief/employment grants 382
15.4.6.12 Aid to training 382
15.4.6.13 Aid in the form of special taxation of certain shipping activities 382
15.4.6.14 Operating aid 382
15.4.6.15 Aid to investment 383
15.4.6.16 Restructuring aid 383
15.4.6.17 Environmental aid 383
15.4.6.18 Aid in the form of public authority holdings in company capital 384
15.4.6.19 Rescue aid 385
15.4.6.20 Regional policy aid 385
15.4.6.21 Research and development aid 386
15.4.6.22 Small and medium-sized enterprises 386
15.4.6.23 Other aids which are specified by the Council of Ministers 386
15.4.7 Article 93 of the Treaty: supervision 386
15.4.7.1 Text of Article 93 386
15.4.7.2 Existing aids 387
15.4.7.3 Contentious proceedings 387
15.4.7.4 New aids 388

15.4.7.5 Article 93 and the doctrine of direct effect 388
15.4.8 Article 94 of the EEC Treaty: the legislative powers 388
15.4.8.1 Introduction 388
15.4.8.2 Text of Article 94 388
15.4.9 Challenging State aids 388
15.4.10 Conclusions 389

15.5 State Aids and Shipbuilding 389

CHAPTER 16 CONSORTIA

16.1 Introduction 391

16.2 Juridical Nature of Consortia 392

16.3 Commercial View on Consortia 394

16.4 1990 Communication on Consortia 395

16.4.1 Introduction 395
16.4.2 Background to the communication on consortia 395

16.5 The Need for the Block Exemption 396

16.6 Contents of the Council of Ministers Regulation 397

16.6.1 Purpose 397
16.6.2 Form of the proposed block exemption 398
16.6.3 Scope of the block exemption 399
16.6.4 Provision for an exemption regulation 399
16.6.5 Duration and effect of the exemption 399
16.6.6 Consultation 399
16.6.7 Breaches 400
16.6.8 Entry into force 400

CHAPTER 17 EUROPEAN COMMUNITY MARINE ENVIRONMENTAL LAW

17.1 Introduction 401

17.2 The 1950s 402

17.2.1 1957: The EEC Treaty 402

17.3 The 1960s 402

17.3.1 Introduction 402
17.3.2 1967: Torrey Canyon 402

17.4 The 1970s 403

17.4.1 1972: UN Conference in Stockholm 403
17.4.2 1972 and 1973: EC responses to the UN Conference 404

17.4.3 1973: the first Action Programme 404
17.4.3.1 The Action Programmes 404
17.4.3.2 1973: The 1973 Action Programme 405
17.4.4 1973: establishment of an Environmental and Consumer Protection Service 405
17.4.5 1975: Paris Convention for the Prevention of Marine Pollution from Land-Based Sources 405
17.4.6 1975: Council Recommendation on the "Polluter Pays" principle 405
17.4.7 1976: discharge of effluent from land: Directive 76/464 405
17.4.8 1976: deliberate dumping of waste at sea 406
17.4.9 Bravo drilling rig in the Ekofisk field 406
17.4.10 1977: exploitation of marine and sub-marine resources, especially exploitation of the seabed 406
17.4.11 The Second Action Programme 407
17.4.12 Commission Communication to the Council of Ministers on the Reorganisation of the Community Shipbuilding Industry 407
17.4.13 Amoco Cadiz 408
17.4.14 1978: Copenhagen Summit 408
17.4.15 Council Resolution of 26 June 1978 408
17.4.15.1 Introduction 408
17.4.15.2 Background 408
17.4.15.3 Resolution in the context of the Action Programmes 408
17.4.15.4 Rationale of the Resolution 409
17.4.15.5 Essence of the Resolution 409
17.4.16 1978 Council Recommendation on Ratification of Safety Conventions 410
17.4.16.1 Introduction 410
17.4.16.2 Background to the Recommendation 411
17.4.16.3 Conventions referred to in the Recommendation 411
17.4.17 1978: measures relating to titanium oxide 411
17.4.18 Recommendation 79/114 on the ratification of the 1978 international Convention on Standards of Training, Certification and Watchkeeping for Seafarers 412

17.5 The 1980s 412

17.5.1 1980–1982: port state control 412
17.5.2 Commission Decision 80/686 setting up an advisory committee on the control and reduction of pollution caused by hydrocarbons discharged at sea 413
17.5.3 1982: United Nations Convention on the Law of the Sea (UNCLOS III) 413
17.5.4 1983: Communication 413
17.5.5 1983: Council Recommendation on SAR 413
17.5.6 1985: Single European Act amended the EEC Treaty 413
17.5.7 1986: Community information system 414
17.5.8 1987–1988: European Environmental Year 415
17.5.9 1987: The Fourth Action Programme 415
17.5.10 1987: European parliamentary question on the seaworthiness of vessels operating in Community waters 415
17.5.11 Mediterranean 416
17.5.12 Marine Science and Technology Programme (MAST) 1989–1992 416

17.6 The 1990s 416

17.6.1 Introduction 416
17.6.2 1990: European Environment Agency Regulation 417

17.6.3 1990 Resolution on the Prevention of Accidents causing Marine Pollution 417
17.6.3.1 Introduction 417
17.6.3.2 Background 417
17.6.3.3 Ensuring that EC ships are safe 418
17.6.3.4 Inspections on foreign ships docking in EC ports 418
17.6.3.5 Requests for the Commission to act 418
17.6.4 Environmental Information Directive 419
17.6.5 Shipment of radioactive wastes 419
17.6.6 North Sea 419

17.7 Conclusion 419

CHAPTER 18 SHIPBUILDING

18.1 Introduction 421

18.2 Commercial Overview 421

18.2.1 Protectionist practices 424

18.3 1977 Communication on Shipbuilding 424

18.3.1 Problems of EC shipbuilding 424
18.3.2 Objectives of EC intervention 425
18.3.4 EC action 426
18.3.4.1 Committee 427

18.4 1978 Council of Ministers Resolution 428

18.5 Commission Proposal 428

18.6 First Report on Shipbuilding 428

18.7 1986 Parliamentary Resolution 428

18.8 1987 Commission Communication on Shipbuilding 429

18.8.1 Key proposals 429
18.8.2 Reaction to the communication 429

18.9 Reneval Programme 429

18.9.1 Introduction 429
18.9.2 Establishment of the Reneval Programme 430
18.9.3 Purpose of the Reneval Programme 430
18.9.4 Criteria and areas of application: Article 3(1) 430
18.9.5 Decision-making process: Article 3(2) 431
18.9.6 Permitted activities for the Reneval Programme 431
18.9.7 Financing of the Reneval Programme 431
18.9.8 Form of the aid 432
18.9.9 Entities eligible for funding 432
18.9.10 Procedure 432
18.9.11 Duration of the programme 433
18.9.12 The Reneval Areas: the practice to date 433

18.9.12.1 France 433
18.9.12.1.1 Decision 90/205: Certain Coastal Zone of Le Havre, Dieppe and Fecamp 433
18.9.12.2 Germany 433
18.9.12.2.1 Decision 89/539/EEC: Kreisfreie Stadt in Lubeck 433
18.9.12.2.2 Decision 89/448/EEC: City Region of Hamburg-Zentrum 433
18.9.12.3 Netherlands 433
18.9.12.3.1 Decision 89/484: Rijn Delta and certain other areas 433
18.9.12.4 Spain 434
18.9.12.4.1 Decision 91/91: La Coruna, Pontevedra and Vizcaya 434
18.9.12.5 United Kingdom 434
18.9.12.5.1 Decision 89/541: Plymouth travel-to-work area 434
18.9.12.5.2 Decision 90/602: Wirral and Sefton 434

18.10 Shipbuilding Aids 434

18.10.1 First shipbuilding directive 436
18.10.2 Second shipbuilding directive 437
18.10.2.1 Study 438
18.10.2.1.1 Direct aids and intervention 439
18.10.2.1.2 Aids for the sale of ships 440
18.10.2.1.3 Investment aids 440
18.10.2.1.4 Emergency measures 440
18.10.3 Third shipbuilding directive 441
18.10.3.1 Background to the Directive 441
18.10.3.2 Essence of the Directive 441
18.10.3.3 Reporting mechanism 442
18.10.3.4 Emergency aid 443
18.10.4 Fourth shipbuilding directive 443
18.10.4.1 Introduction 443
18.10.4.2 Legal bases 443
18.10.4.3 Commercial background 443
18.10.4.4 Duration 443
18.10.4.5 Concept of shipbuilding 444
18.10.4.6 Concept of ship-conversion 444
18.10.4.7 Concept of ship-repair 444
18.10.4.8 Concept of sale 444
18.10.4.9 Concept of state aid 444
18.10.4.10 Credit facilities 445
18.10.4.11 Relationship between the Directive and the EEC Treaty rules relating to state aids 445
18.10.4.12 Investment aid 445
18.10.4.13 Rescue aids 445
18.10.4.14 Crisis aids 446
18.10.4.15 Cost-escalation insurance 447
18.10.4.16 Non-discrimination 447
18.10.5 Fifth shipbuilding directive 447
18.10.5.1 Introduction 447
18.10.5.2 Duration 447

18.10.5.3 Legal basis 448
18.10.5.4 Entry into force 448
18.10.5.5 Commercial Background 448
18.10.5.6 Duration 448
18.10.5.7 Concept of shipbuilding 448
18.10.5.8 Concept of ship-conversion 449
18.10.5.9 Concept of ship-repair 449
18.10.5.10 Concept of sale 449
18.10.5.11 Concept of aid 449
18.10.5.12 Credit facilities 449
18.10.5.13 Relationship between the Directive and the EEC Treaty rules relating to state aids 450
18.10.5.14 Investment aid 450
18.10.5.15 Rescue aids 450
18.10.5.16 Crisis aid 450
18.10.5.17 Cost-escalation insurance 451
18.10.5.18 Non-discrimination 451

18.10.6 Sixth shipbuilding directive 452
18.10.6.1 Duration 452
18.10.6.1.1 Article 4(5) 452
18.10.6.2 Implementation 453
18.10.6.3 Spain and Portugal 453
18.10.6.4 Assessment 453

18.10.7 Seventh shipbuilding directive 454
18.10.7.1 Background 454
18.10.7.1.1 Commission proposal 454
18.10.7.1.2 Opinion of the European Parliament 454
18.10.7.1.3 Opinion of the Economic and Social Committee 455
18.10.7.1.4 Commercial background 455
18.10.7.2 International context 455
18.10.7.3 Legal basis 455
18.10.7.4 Entry into force 455
18.10.7.5 Approach 455
18.10.7.6 Concept of aid 456
18.10.7.7 Concept of shipbuilding 456
18.10.7.8 Concept of ship-conversion 457
18.10.7.9 Concept of ship-repair 457
18.10.7.10 Concept of contract value before aid 457
18.10.7.11 Specific areas of the EC 457
18.10.7.11.1 Spain and Portugal 457
18.10.7.11.2 Greece 458
18.10.7.11.3 "German Democratic Republic" 458
18.10.7.12 Discriminatory practices 458
18.10.7.13 Aid to shipowners 458
18.10.7.14 Operating aid 459
18.10.7.14.1 Ceilings 459
18.10.7.15 Restructuring aid 460
18.10.7.15.1 Investment aid 460
18.10.7.15.2 Aid for closures 461
18.10.7.15.3 Aid for research and development 462
18.10.7.16 Monitoring 462

18.10.7.17 Spain 463
18.10.7.18 Balance 463

CHAPTER 19 THE EC'S RELATIONS IN SHIPPING MATTERS WITH REST OF THE WORLD

19.1 Introduction 465

19.2 The Law Relating to the External Relations of the EC 466

19.2.1 Introduction 466
19.2.2 Provisions of the EC Treaties 466
19.2.2.1 ECSC Treaty 466
19.2.2.2 Euratom or EAEC Treaty 466
19.2.2.3 EEC Treaty 467
19.2.2.3.1 Treaty-making powers 467
19.2.2.3.2 Relations with the United Nations and GATT 467
19.2.2.3.3 Relations with the Council of Europe 467
19.2.2.3.4 Relations with the Organisation for Economic Co-operation and Development 467

19.3 Consultation Procedure in Shipping Matters 468

19.3.1 Introduction 468
19.3.2 Purpose 468
19.3.3 Background 469
19.3.4 Legal bases 473
19.3.5 Scope of the consultation 473
19.3.6 Purposes of consultation 474
19.3.7 Channels and confidentiality of consultation 474
19.3.8 Review 474

19.4 Market Monitoring 475

19.4.1 Decision 78/774/EEC 475
19.4.1.1 Introduction 475
19.4.1.2 Legal bases 475
19.4.1.3 Legislative history 475
19.4.1.4 Article 1: The essence of the Decision 475
19.4.1.5 Article 2: Application 475
19.4.1.5.1 Amendment to Article 2(1) 476
19.4.1.6 Legislative resolution 476
19.4.1.7 Observations of the Committee 477
19.4.1.8 Article 3: Evaluation 477
19.4.1.9 Article 4: National legislation 477
19.4.1.10 Article 5: National systems 477
19.4.1.11 Article 6: Implementation 477
19.4.2 Decision 79/4/EEC 477
19.4.2.1 Introduction 477
19.4.2.2 Legal bases 478
19.4.2.3 Legislative history 478

	19.4.2.4 Factual background	478
	19.4.2.5 Extension of the information collected	478
	19.4.2.6 Assessment	479
19.4.3	Decision 80/1181/EEC	479
	19.4.3.1 Introduction	479
19.4.4	Decision 81/189/EEC	479
	19.4.4.1 Introduction	479
	19.4.4.2 Annex I	479
	19.4.4.3 Annex II	480
19.4.5	Decision 82/870/EEC	480
19.4.7	Decision 84/656/EEC	480
19.4.8	Decision 86/646/EEC	480
19.4.9	Decision 89/242/EEC	480
19.4.10	Decision 89/243/EEC	481
19.4.11	Decision 90/545/EEC	
	19.4.11.1 Introduction	481
	19.4.11.2 Background	481
	19.4.11.3 Essence of the Decision	481
19.5	*International Safety Conventions*	481
19.5.1	Introduction	481
19.5.2	1978 Council of Ministers Recommendation on the ratification of safety conventions	482
	19.5.2.1 Introduction	482
	19.5.2.2 Background to the Recommendation	482
	19.5.2.3 Conventions referred to in the Recommendation	483
	19.5.2.4 Procedure for ratification or accession	483
19.5.3	1978 Council of Ministers Recommendation on the ratification of the 1978 International Convention on Standards of Training, Certification and Watchkeeping for Seafarers	483
19.5.4	1983 Council of Ministers Recommendation on SAR	483
19.6	*Counter-Measures*	484
19.6.1	1983 Council Decision concerning counter-measures in the field of international merchant shipping	484
	19.6.1.1 Introduction	484
	19.6.1.2 Legal bases	484
	19.6.1.3 Factual background	484
	19.6.1.4 Obligation to consult	484
	19.6.1.5 Desirability of co-ordination of measures	484
	19.6.1.6 Procedural matters	485
	19.6.1.7 Counter-measures	485
19.7	*Bilateral relations*	485
19.7.1	Council Decision 87/476 relating to maritime transport between Italy and Algeria	485
19.8	*International Organisations*	485
19.8.1	United Nations	485

19.8.1.1 Introduction 485
19.8.1.2 Liner Conference 486
19.8.2 UNCLOS III 486
19.8.2.1 United Nations Economic Commission for Europe 486
19.8.3 International Maritime Organisation and International Maritime Consultative Organisation 486
19.8.4 International Labour Organisation 486
19.8.5 General Agreement on Tariffs and Trade as well as General Agreement on Trade in Services 487
19.8.6 European Free Trade Association 487

CHAPTER 20 THE EC AND SAFETY AT SEA

20.1 Introduction 489

20.1.1 International legislation 490

20.2 EC Measures and Developments 490

20.2.1 1978 Council Recommendation on ratification of safety conventions 490
20.2.1.1 Introduction 490
20.2.1.2 Background to the Recommendation 490
20.2.1.3 Conventions referred to in the Recommendation 491
20.2.2 1979 Council Recommendation on the 1978 International Convention on Standards of Training, Certification and Watchkeeping for Seafarers 491
20.2.3 Deep-sea pilots Directive 491
20.2.4 Tankers 491
20.2.5 Fishing vessels 491
20.2.6 Greek Government 491
20.2.7 1983 Council Recommendation on SAR 491
20.2.8 1987 European parliamentary Question on the Seaworthiness of Vessels Operating in Community Waters 492
20.2.9 1989: Parliament's Resolution on Safety at Sea 493
20.2.10 1990: Council of Ministers Resolution on Passenger Ferry Safety 493
20.2.11 Council Directive on the Minimum Safety and Health Requirements for Improved Medical Treatment on Board Vessels 494
20.2.11.1 Introduction 494
20.2.11.2 Background 494
20.2.11.3 Legal bases 495
20.2.11.4 Basic concepts 495
20.2.11.4.1 Antidote 495
20.2.11.4.2 Medical supplies 495
20.2.11.4.3 Owner 495
20.2.11.4.4 Vessel 495
20.2.11.4.5 Worker 496
20.2.11.5 Obligation to have medical supplies on board 496
20.2.11.6 Obligation on ships to carry antidotes 496
20.2.11.7 Allocation of responsibilities 497
20.2.11.8 Information and training 497
20.2.11.9 Training 498
20.2.11.10 Data centres 498
20.2.11.11 Inspection 498

20.2.11.12 Adaptation of the annexes 498
20.2.11.13 Entry into force 499
20.2.11.14 Conclusion 499

CHAPTER 21 NAVIGATION

21.1 Introduction 501

21.2 Decision 82/887 501

21.3 Decision 92/143: Radionavigation systems 501

21.3.1 Introduction 501
21.3.2 Legal bases 501
21.3.3 Legislative history 502
21.3.4 Technical background 502
21.3.5 Role of the Member States 502
21.3.6 Role of the Commission 503
21.3.7 Role of the Commission and Member States jointly 503

CHAPTER 22 PILOTAGE

22.1 Introduction 505

22.2 The 1978 North Sea Pilotage Directive 505

22.2.1 Introduction 505
22.2.2 Legal bases 505
22.2.3 Purpose 505
22.2.4 Obligation on certain states to provide qualified pilots 505
22.2.5 Member States are obliged to encourage ships which fly their flags to use qualified pilots 506
22.2.6 Implementation 506

22.3 1985 Commission Memorandum on Shipping 506

CHAPTER 23 PORTS AND PORT STATE CONTROL

23.1 Ports 507

23.2 Port State Control 510

23.2.1 Introduction 510
23.2.2 Commission proposal for a directive on Port State Control 510
23.2.3 The Memorandum of Understanding on Port Control 510
23.2.4 Commission Recommendation on improving the effectiveness of Port State control in the Community 511
23.2.4.1 Rationale 511
23.2.4.2 Ratification of the International Conventions covered by the Memorandum of Understanding 512
23.2.4.3 Implementation of the International Conventions covered by the Memorandum of Understanding 512
23.2.4.4 Follow-up 512

23.2.5 1982 Commission Opinion 513
23.2.5.1 1986 progress towards a Common Transport Policy: Maritime Transport 513

CHAPTER 24 CARRIAGE OF GOODS AND PASSENGERS BY SEA

24.1 Passenger Baggage 515

24.1.1 The proposed elimination of controls on passenger baggage on intra-community sea crossings 515
24.1.2 Background 515
24.1.3 Legal basis 515
24.1.4 Basic regime 515
24.1.5 Basic concepts relating to sea transport 516
24.1.6 Limitations 516
24.1.7 Committee on Community Transit 516
24.1.8 Application 516

24.2 Fares 517

24.3 Travel Allowances 518

CHAPTER 25 LITIGIOUS ASPECTS OF EC SHIPPING LAW: THE CONVENTION ON JURISDICTION AND THE ENFORCEMENT OF JUDGMENTS IN CIVIL AND COMMERCIAL MATTERS

25.1 Introduction 519

25.2 Scope of the Convention 521

25.2.1 Subject-matter of the Convention 521
25.2.2 Geographical scope 521

25.3 Jurisdiction 523

25.3.1 Introduction 523
25.3.1.1 General rule 523
25.3.1.2 Exceptions to the general rule on jurisdiction 523
25.3.1.3 Domicile 524
25.3.1.3.1 Convention provisions relating to domicile 524
25.3.1.3.2 UK statutory rules relating to domicile 524
25.3.2 General provisions 526
25.3.2.1 Persons domiciled in a contracting state 526
25.3.2.2 Defendants not domiciled in a contracting state 527
25.3.3 Special jurisdiction 528
25.3.3.1 Article 5: Introduction 528
25.3.3.2 Article 5(1): Contract 528
25.3.3.3 Article 5(2): Maintenance 529
25.3.3.4 Article 5(3): Tort, delict and quasi-delict 530
25.3.3.5 Article 5(4): Civil claims in criminal proceedings 530
25.3.3.6 Article 5(5): Branches, agencies and other establishments 531
25.3.3.7 Article 5(6): Trusts 531

25.3.3.8 Articlc 5(7): Salvage 531
25.3.3.9 Article 6: Special jurisdiction 533
25.3.3.10 Article 6(1): Co-defendants 534
25.3.3.11 Article 6(2): Third parties 534
25.3.3.12 Article 6(3): Counterclaims 534
25.3.3.13 Article 6(4): Certain combined actions 534
25.3.3.14 Article 6A: Limitation of liability actions in respect of the operation of ships 534
25.3.4 Insurance 537
25.3.5 Consumer contracts 539
25.3.6 Exclusive jurisdiction 539
25.3.6.1 Proceedings have as their object rights in rem 540
25.3.6.2 Tenancies of immovable property 540
25.3.6.3 Certain proceedings involving a company 540
25.3.6.4 Validity of Acts on public registers 540
25.3.6.5 Intellectual property proceedings 540
25.3.6.6 Enforcement of judgments 541
25.3.7 Prorogation of jurisdiction 541
25.3.7.1 Article 17: Jurisdiction agreements 541
25.3.7.2 Article 18: Jurisdiction by submission 542
25.3.8 Examination as to jurisdiction and admissibility 542
25.3.9 Lis pendens—related actions 543
25.3.10 Provisional, including protective, measures 543

25.4 Recognition and enforcement 554

25.4.1 Introduction 554
25.4.1.1 Concept of judgment 544
25.4.2 Recognition 554
25.4.2.1 Principle of recognition 544
25.4.2.2 Instances of non-recognition of judgments 544
25.4.2.2.1 Article 27(1): Public policy 545
25.4.2.2.2 Article 27(2): Judgment in default of appearance 545
25.4.2.2.3 Article 27(3): Conflicting judgments 545
25.4.2.2.4 Article 27(4): Preliminary questions and private international law 545
25.4.2.2.5 Article 27(5): Conflicts between judgments from non-contracting states 545
25.4.2.2.6 Article 28: Exceptions 546
25.4.2.2.7 Article 29: Prohibition on review of the substance of the judgment 546
25.4.2.2.8 Article 30 546
25.4.3 Enforcement 546
25.4.3.1 A foreign judgment ordering a periodic payment 550
25.4.3.2 Legal aid 550
25.4.3.3 No security, bond or deposit 550
25.4.4 Common rules for recognition and enforcement 550
25.4.5 Authentic instruments and court settlements 551
25.4.5.1 Approved settlements 551

25.5 Miscellaneous Matters 551

CHAPTER 26 THE CHALLENGES OF THE INTERNAL MARKET FOR SHIPPING: THE 1992 PROGRAMME

26.1 Introduction 553

26.1.1 Need to be aware of the 1992 programme and "Maastricht" 553
26.1.2 Great changes 553
26.1.3 Prospect of "1992" 554
26.1.4 Objectives of the EC 554

26.2 The Concept of the Internal Market 554

26.3 The Rationale for the Internal Market 554

26.3.1 Revitalisation of EC industry 555
26.3.1.1 Problems 555
26.3.1.2 Cure 555
26.3.2 Revitalisation of the EC organisation 555
26.3.2.1 Problem 555
26.3.2.2 Cure 556

26.4 Background to the Internal Market Programme 556

26.4.1 Introduction 556
26.4.2 Progress 556

26.5 The Contents of the Internal Market Programme 558

26.5.1 Physical barriers 558
26.5.1.2 Introduction 558
26.5.1.3 Movement of goods 559
26.5.1.3.1 Introduction 559
26.5.1.3.2 Single administrative document 559
26.5.1.3.3 Quota system 559
26.5.1.3.4 Cabotage of goods 559
26.5.1.3.5 Customs presentation charges 560
26.5.1.3.6 Transit advice note 560
26.5.1.3.7 Veterinary checks 560
26.5.1.3.8 Size of trucks on EC roads 560
26.5.1.3.9 Banalisation 560
26.5.1.4 Movement of persons 560
26.5.1.4.1 Schengen Agreement 561
26.5.1.4.2 Asylum 561
26.5.1.4.3 Non-active persons 561
26.5.2 Technical barriers 561
26.5.2.1 Introduction 561
26.5.2.2 The Commission's White Paper 562
26.5.2.3 New standards 563
26.5.2.4 Mutual recognition of qualifications 563
26.5.2.5 Capital movements 563
26.5.2.6 Free movement of capital 563
26.5.2.7 Balance of payments 564
26.5.3 Public procurement 564
26.5.3.1 Introduction 564

26.5.3.2 Supplies 564
26.5.3.3 Public works 565
26.5.3.4 Water, energy, transport and communication 565
26.5.3.5 Procedural rules for the award of public procurement contracts 565
26.5.3.6 Company law 565
26.5.3.6.1 Introduction 565
26.5.3.6.2 Merger control regulation 565
26.5.3.6.3 European company statute 566
26.5.3.6.4 European economic interest groupings 566
26.5.3.6.5 Single-member limited liability companies 567
26.5.3.6.6 Disclosure of information by branch offices 567
26.5.3.6.7 Amendments to the directives on accounts 567
26.5.3.6.8 Structure of Public Limited Companies 567
26.5.3.6.9 Small and medium-sized enterprises 568
26.5.3.7 Banking 568
26.5.3.7.1 Introduction 568
26.5.3.7.2 Second Banking Directive 568
26.5.3.7.3 Own funds Directive 568
26.5.3.7.4 Solvency ratio Directive 568
26.5.3.7.5 Large exposures 569
26.5.3.10 Insurance 569
26.5.3.10.1 Introduction 569
26.5.3.10.2 Non-life insurance 569
26.5.3.10.3 Freedom of establishment 569
26.5.3.10.4 Freedom to provide services 569
26.5.3.10.5 Life insurance 570
26.5.3.10.6 Reinsurance 570
26.5.3.10.7 Insurance intermediaries 570
26.5.3.11 Securities 570
26.5.3.12 Competition 570
26.5.3.12.1 Introduction 570
26.5.3.12.2 State aids 571
26.5.3.12.3 Mergers 571
26.5.3.13 Environment 571
26.5.3.14 Miscellaneous areas 572
25.5.4 Fiscal barriers 572
26.5.4.1 Introduction 572

26.6 External Dimension to the 1992 Programme 573

26.6.1 Introduction 573
26.6.2 Fortress Europe 574
26.6.3 Relations with international organisations 574
26.6.3.1 European Free Trade Association 574

26.7 Economic and Monetary Union 574

26.8 1992 and Shipping 575

CHAPTER 27 CONCLUSIONS

27.1 Introduction 577

27.2 The EC is on a trajectory of growth 577
27.3 The place of the EC in world shipping 577
27.4 EC shipping law is of recent origin 577
27.5 There is hardly any limit to the possible application of EC law to shipping yet there is a limit to the possible development of EC shipping law 578
27.6 EC transport policy has been slow to develop 578
27.7 EC shipping policy has not been entirely successful 579
27.8 Is shipping a public service or merely another service in the market place? 579
27.9 EC shipping law is only a component of international shipping law 579
27.10 The formulation of EC shipping law requires the involvement of all partners 579
27.11 EC shipping law and policy must seek to protect EC shipowners, seafarers and all those involved in the EC shipping industry 580

APPENDIX 1 TREATY OF ROME 581

APPENDIX 2 COUNCIL DECISIONS, RECOMMENDATIONS AND RESOLUTIONS

1. Council Decision of 13 September 1977 Setting up a Consultation Procedure on Relations between Member States and Third Countries in Shipping Matters and on Action Relating to Such Matters in International Organizations (77/587/EEC) 643

2. Council Recommendation of 26 June 1978 on the Ratification of Conventions on Safety in Shipping (78/584/EEC) 645

3. Council Resolution of 26 June 1978 Setting up an Action Programme of the European Communities on the Control and Reduction of Pollution Caused by Hydrocarbons Discharged at Sea 647

4. Council Decision of 19 September 1978 Concerning the Activities of Certain Third Countries in the Field of Cargo Shipping (78/774/EEC) 649

5. Council Decision of 19 December 1978 on the Collection of Information Concerning the Activities of Carriers participating in Cargo Liner Traffic in Certain Areas of Operation (79/41/EEC) 651

6. Council Recommendation of 21 December 1978 on the Ratification of the 1978 International Convention on Standards of Training, Certification and Watchkeeping for Seafarers (79/114/EEC) 653

7. Council Directive of 21 December 1978 Concerning Pilotage of Vessels by Deep-Sea Pilots in the North Sea and English Channel (79/115/EEC) 654

8. Council Directive of 21 December 1978 Concerning Minimum Requirements for Certain Tankers Entering or Leaving Community Ports (79/116/EEC) 655

9. Council Regulation of 15 May 1979 Concerning the Ratification by Member States of, or their accession to, the United Nations Convention on a Code of Conduct for Liner Conferences (79/954/EEC) 658

10. Council Directive of 6 December 1979 Amending Directive 79/116/EEC Concerning Minimum Requirements for Certain Tankers Entering or Leaving Community Ports (79/1034/EEC) 662

11. Council Recommendation of 23 September 1980 on the Ratification of the Torremolinos International Convention for the Safety of Fishing Vessels (1977) (80/907/EEC) 663

12. Council Decision of 4 December 1980 Amending and Supplementing Decision 79/4/EEC on the Collection of Information Concerning the Activities of Carriers Participating in Cargo Liner Traffic in Certain Areas of Operation (80/1181/EEC) 664

13. Council Decision of 26 March 1981 Establishing Detailed Rules for the Collection of Information Concerning the Activities of Carriers Participating in Cargo Liner Traffic between the Member States and the Far East (81/189/EEC) 665

14. Council Decision of 13 December 1982 Adopting a Concerted Action Project for the European Economic Community in the Field of Shore-Based Marine Navigation Aid Systems (82/887/EEC) 667

15. Council Decision of 16 December 1982 Extending the Collection of Information Concerning the Activities of Carriers Participating in Cargo Liner Traffic in Certain Areas of Operation, Carried out Under Decisions 79/4/EEC, 80/1181/EEC and 81/189/EEC (82/870/EEC) 671

16. Council Decision of 28 March 1983 on the Conclusion of the Community-Cost Concertation Agreement on a Concerted Action Project in the Field of Shore-Based Marine Navigation Aid Systems (Cost Project 301) 83/124/EEC) 672

17. Council Recommendation of 25 July 1983 on the Ratification of or Accession to the 1979 International Convention on Maritime Search and Rescue (SAR) (83/419/EEC) 678

18. Council Decision of 26 October 1983 Concerning Counter-Measures in the Field of International Merchant Shipping (83/573/EEC) 679

19. Council Decision of 18 December 1984 Extending the Collection of Information Concerning the Activities of Carriers Participating in Cargo Liner Traffic in Certain Areas of Operation (84/656/EEC) 680

20. Council Decision of 16 December 1986 Extending the Collection of Information Concerning the Activities of Carriers Participating in Cargo Liner Traffic in Certain Areas of Operation (86/646/EEC) 681

21. Council Regulation (EEC) No 4055/86 of 22 December 1986 Applying the Principle of Freedom to Provide Services to Maritime Transport between Member States and between Member States and Third Countries 682

22. Council Regulation (EEC) No 4056/86 of 22 December 1986 Laying Down Detailed Rules for the Application of Articles 85 and 86 of the Treaty to Maritime Transport 686

23. Council Regulation (EEC) No 4057/86 of 22 December 1986 on Unfair Pricing Practices in Maritime Transport 698

24. Council Regulation (EEC) No 4058/86 of 22 December 1986 Concerning Coordinated Action to Safeguard Free Access to Cargoes in Ocean Trades 706

25. Regulation No 4260/88 of 16 December 1988 on the Communications, Complaints and Applications and the Hearings Provided for in Council Regulation No. 4056/86 Laying down Detailed Rules for the Application of Articles 85 and 86 of the Treaty to Maritime Transport 709

26. Proposal for a Council Regulation Establishing a Community Ship Register and Providing for the Flying of the Community Flag by Sea-Going Vessels (COM(89) 266 Final) (Submitted by the Commission to the Council on 2 August 1989) (89/C 263/02) 717

27. Commission Recommendation on Improving the Effectiveness of Port State Control in the Community (COM(89) 266 Final (Submitted by the Commission to the Council on 2 August 1989) (89/C 263/03) 722

28. Council Resolution of 19 June 1990 on the Prevention of Accidents Causing Marine Pollution (90/C 206/01) 724

29. Resolution of the Council and of the Representatives of the Governments of the Member States, Meeting within the Council, of 19 June 1990 on Improving Passenger Ferry Safety (90/C 206/02) 726

30. Council Regulation (EEC) No 613/91 of 4 March 1991 on the Transfer of Ships from One Register to Another within the Community 727

31. Council Regulation (EEC) No 479/92 of 25 February 1992 on the Application of Article 85(3) of the Treaty to Certain Categories of Agreements, Decisions and Concerted Practices between Liner Shipping Companies (Consortia) 731

32. Council Decision of 25 February 1992 on Radionavigation Systems for Europe (92/143/EEC) 734

31. United Nations Convention on a Code of Conduct for Liner Conferences 736

Index 759

Table of Cases

All references are to paragraph numbers

AB Volvo *v.* Erik Veng [1989] 4 CMLR 122 (Case 238/87) 10.2.8.3.2
ABG, OJ 1977 L117/1; [1977] 2 CMLR D1 .... 10.2.10
ACF Chemiefarma NV *v.* Commission [1970] ECR 661 (Case 41/69) 10.1.3.2.2
AEG Telefunken *v.* Commission [1983] ECR 3151; [1984] 3 CMLR 325 (Case 107/82) 10.1.3.1.2, 10.1.3.2.2, 10.1.7.2
A.M. & S. Europe Ltd. *v.* Commission [1982] ECR 1575 .... 3.5.6
AOIP/Beyrard, OJ L6/8, 13 January 1976; [1976] 1 CMLR D14; CCH 9,801 ..... 10.1.3.1, 10.1.3.1.2
ARG/Unipart, OJ L45/34, 18 February 1988; [1988] 4 CMLR 513; CCH 10,968 .... 10.1.3.1
AROW *v.* BNIC, OJ 1982 L379/1; [1983] 2 CMLR 240 .... 10.1.3.2.3
ASPA (*Re*), OJ 1970 L148/9; [1970] CMLR D25 .... 10.1.3.2.3
Adams *v.* Commission [1985] ECR 3539 (Case 145/83, 53/84) 3.4.6.1, 19.3.7
Administrazione delle Finanze dello Stato *v.* Essevi SpA [1981] ECR 1413 (Cases 142 and 143/80) 3.4.6.6.2
Agreements on the Protection and Indemnity Clubs (*Re*) [1989] CMLR 178 (Case IV/30.373) 9.4
Ahlstrom (A.) Osakeyhtiö *v.* Commission [1988] ECR 5193; (Cases 89/85, 104/85, 114/85, 116/85 and 125–9/85) (the Wood Pulp case) 10.1.3.2.2, 12.6.4
Ahmed Saeed Flugreisen and Silver Line Reisburo *v.* Zentrale zur Bekämpfung unläuteren Wettbewerbs [1990] 4 CMLR 102 (Case 66/84) 4.3.3.1, 10.2.8.3.2, 12.11.1
Allue Coonan *v.* Università degli studi di Venezia (Case 33/88) 8.2.2.3.2
Aluminium Imports from Eastern Europe, OJ 1985 L92/1; [1987] 3 CMLR 813 .. 10.1.3.1.2, 10.1.5.2
Amministrazione delle Finanze Dello Stato *v.* Denkavit Italiano Srl [1980] ECR 1205; [1981] 3 CMLR 694 (Case 61/79) 15.4.4.3, 15.4.4.3.1
Amsterdam Bulb [1977] ECR 137; [1977] 2 CMLR 218 (Case 50/76) 3.5.2.2.1, 3.5.3
Analog Devices [1981] ECR 2781 (Case 122/80) 3.5.6
Apple and Pear Development Council *v.* Customs and Excise [1988] 2 CMLR 394 (Case 102/86) 3.5.6
Apple and Pear Development Council *v.* Lewis [1983] ECR 4083 (Case 222/82) 15.4.4.3.2
Auditeur du Travail *v.* Cagnon et Taquet [1975] ECR 171 (Case 69/74) 4.3.1.5

BAT *v.* Commission [1985] ECR 363; [1985] 2 CMLR 470 (Case 35/83) 10.1.3.1.2
BBI/Boosey and Hawkes (Interim Measures), OJ 1987 L286/36; [1988] 4 CMLR 67 ...... 10.2.8.3.2, 10.2.11.4.2
BL *v.* Commission [1987] 1 CMLR 185 (Case 226/84) 10.2.7, 10.2.8.3.2
BNIC *v.* Clair [1985] ECR 391; [1985] 2 CMLR 430 (Case 123/83) 10.1.3.1.2
BP *v.* Commission [1978] ECR 1513; [1978] 3 CMLR 174 (Case 77/77) 3.4.6.6.5, 10.2.12
BPB Industries plc, OJ 1989 L10/50, on appeal British Plasterboard Industries plc and British Gypsum *v.* Commission 10.2.8.4, 10.2.11.4.1
BPICA, OJ 1977 L299/18; [1977] 2 CMLR D43 .... 10.1.3.2.3
Barbara Erzbergbau AG *v.* High Authority [1960] ECR 173 (Cases 3–18/58, 23–26/58, 25, 26/58) 4.2.1.2.2, 4.2.1.3, 4.2.1.3.2, 4.2.2.10.2
Beguelin Import *v.* GL Import–Export [1971] ECR 949; [1972] CMLR 81 (Case 22/71) ... 10.1.3.2.5, 10.1.7.2, 12.6.1
Bekaert *v.* Procureur de la Republique de Rennes (Case 204/87) 6.1.2
Bela-Muhle *v.* Grows Farm [1977] ECR 1211 (Case 114/76) 3.5.2.2.8
Belasco *v.* Commission, on appeal (Case 246/86) 10.1.3.2.2
Belgian Roofing Felt, OJ 1986 L232/15, on appeal Case 246/86 Belasco *v.* Commission 10.1.3.2.2
Belgium *v.* Commission [1986] ECR 2321; (Case 40/85) 15.4.4.3
Belgium *v.* Commission (Case 142/87) 15.4.4.3
Belgium *v.* Commission [1986] ECR 2263; (Case 234/84) 15.4.4.3
Belgium (*Re*) *v.* Commission (Case 142/87) 15.4.4.3

Berghoefer GmbH *v.* ASA [1985] ECR 1517; [1980] 1 CMLR 566 (Case 221/84) 25.3.7.1
Berkeley Administration *v.* McClelland [1990] 1 All ER 958 .... 25.5
Bertini [1986] ECR 1893; [1987] 1 CMLR 774 (Cases 98, 162 and 258/85) 3.4.6.6.9
Bettray *v.* Staatssecretaris van Justitie [1991] 1 CMLR 459 (Case 344/87) 8.2.2.1
Bianco *v.* Andreas Kufferath, Giust. Civ. 1980, I, p. 103 (Italian Court of Cassation) 25.2.1
Bier *v.* Mines de Potasse d'Alsace. *See* Handelswerkrij Bier.
Binder *v.* Hauptzollamt Bad Reichenall (Case 161/86) 3.5.7.3
Blaizot *v.* University of Liège [1989] 1 CMLR 57 .... 3.5.7.3, 3.5.9.2
Boch (*Re*): Belgium *v.* Commission [1986] ECR 2321; [1988] 2 CMLR 301 (Case 40/85) 15.4.4.3
Borowitz *v.* Bundesversicherungsanstalt für Angestellte [1988] ECR (Case 21/87) 3.5.5
Bosch *v.* De Geus [1962] ECR 45 (Case 13/61) 3.5.2.2.8
Bourgoin *v.* Ministry of Agriculture [1985] 3 WLR 1027 .... 3.5.8
Brasserie de Haecht *v.* Wilkin [1967] ECR 407; [1968] CMLR 26 (Case 23/67) 10.1.4.3
Breeders' Rights: Roses, OJ 1985 L369/9; [1988] 4 CMLR 193 .... 10.1.3.1.2
British American Tobacco *v.* EC Commission [1987] ECR 4487 (Cases 142 and 156/87) .. 26.5.3.12.3
British Telecommunications, OJ 1982 L360/36; [1983] 1 CMLR 457, upheld on appeal Case 41/83 Italy *v.* Commission [1985] ECR 873; [1985] 2 CMLR 368 .... 10.2.8.4, 10.2.13.3, 10.2.13.4
Buitoni *v.* FORMA [1979] ECR 677, 684 (Case 122/78) 3.5.2.2.8
Bulk Oil *v.* Sun International (Case 174/84) 3.5.5

Camera Care Ltd. *v.* Victor Hasselblad AB, OJ 1982 L161/18; [1982] 2 CMLR 233 .... 10.1.3.2.2
Capolongo *v.* Azienda Agricola Maya [1973] ECR 611; [1974] 1 CMLR 230 (Case 77/72) . 15.4.4.3.7, 15.4.5.1
Casaquande [1974] ECR 773 (Case 9/74) 8.2.2.1
Case IV/33.045 .... 3.4.2.3, 12.15.5
Centrafarm *v.* Sterling Drug [1974] ECR 1147; [1974] 2 CMLR 480 (Case 15/74) . 10.1.3.1.2, 10.1.7.2
Central Wine Buyers (South Leicester) Ltd. *v.* Moet et Chandon (London) Ltd., OJ 1982 L94/7; [1982] 2 CMLR 166 .... 10.1.3.1.2
Centre Belge d'Etudes de Marche Tele-Marketing *v.* CLT [1986] 2 CMLR 558 (Case 311/84) 10.2.7, 10.2.11.2.1
Choquet [1978] ECR 2293; [1979] 1 CMLR 535 (Case 16/78) 6.1
CILFIT *v.* Ministry of Health [1982] ECR 3415; [1983] 1 CMLR 472 (Case 283/81) 3.4.6.6.9
Colombian Coffee (*Re*), OJ 1982 L360/31; [1983] 1 CMLR 703 .... 10.1.3.1.2
Coman *v.* Italy (Case 63/86) 6.1.2
Commercial Solvents *v.* Commission [1974] ECR 223; [1974] 1 CMLR 309 (Cases 6 and 7/73) 10.1.5.2, 10.1.7.2, 10.2.3, 10.2.8.3.2, 10.2.13.4, 10.2.14, 12.6.1
Commission *v.* Belgium: Re Public Employees [1980] ECR 3881 (Case 149/79) 8.2.2.3.2
Commission *v.* Belgium [1978] ECR 1881 (Case 156/77) 4.2.1.1, 4.2.2.1, 4.2.2.7.2, 9.3.6
Commission *v.* Belgium [1987] ECR 719; [1988] 1 CMLR 620 (Case 221/85) 6.1.2
Commission *v.* Council [1971] ECR 263; [1971] CMLR 355 (Case 22/70) 4.2.2.1
Commission *v.* Council [1987] ECR 1493; [1988] 2 CMLR 131 (Case 45/86) 3.5.9
Commission *v.* Council [1973] ECR 575 (Case 81/72) 3.5.2.2.8
Commission *v.* Council (Case 355/87) 14.2
Commission *v.* Council of Ministers, para. 6 (*Re* the ERASMUS Legislation) [1991] 1 CMLR 478 3.5.9
Commission *v.* Denmark [1982] ECR 4547 (Case 211/81) 3.4.6.6.2
Commission *v.* Denmark [1989] 1 CMLR 619 (Case 302/86) 17.7
Commission *v.* France [1969] ECR 523 (Cases 6 and 11/69) 3.4.6.6.5, 15.4.4.3, 15.4.4.3.6
Commission *v.* France [1971] ECR 1003 (Case 7/71) 3.4.6.6.2, 3.5.1
Commission *v.* France (The French Seamen's Case) [1974] ECR 359; [1974] 2 CMLR 216 (Case 167/73) 3.1., 3.2.4, 3.3.15, 3.4.6.6.2, 3.5.2.2.2, 3.5.3, 3.5.5, 4.2.2.1, 4.2.2.2.2, 4.2.2.7.2, 4.2.2.14.2, 5.2, 5.3.2, 5.4.6, 5.4.8, 6.1, 8.1, 8.2.2.1, 8.2.2.4, 9.3.4, 9.3.5, 9.3.6, 11.3.4.1, 12.2.5, 27.4, 27.5
Commission *v.* France [1983] ECR 3707 (Case 52/83) 15.4.4.3.6
Commission *v.* France [1985] ECR 439 (Case 290/83) 15.4.4.3.1
Commission *v.* France [1986] ECR 273; [1986] YBEL 247 (Case 270/83) 6.1, 6.1.2
Commission *v.* France (Case 216/84) 3.5.7.2
Commission *v.* France [1986] ECR 1225 (Case 307/84) 8.2.2.3.2
Commission *v.* Germany [1973] ECR 813 (Case 70/72) 15.4.9
Commission *v.* Greece (Case 147/86) 6.1.2
Commission *v.* Ireland [1978] ECR 417; [1978] 2 CMLR 466 (Case 61/77) 3.1, 3.4.6.6.2
Commission *v.* Ireland [1991] 2 CMLR 876 (Case 39/88) 3.4.6.6.2
Commission *v.* Italian Republic [1987] ECR 2625; [1988] CMLR 635 (Case 225/85) 8.2.2.3.2

Commission *v.* Italy [1968] ECR 423; [1969] CMLR 1 (Case 7/68) 6.1.6.1
Commission *v.* Italy [1968] ECR 423 (Case 39/72) 3.4.6.6.2
Commission *v.* Italy [1970] ECR 25 (Case 31/69) 3.4.6.6.2
Commission *v.* Italy [1970] ECR 111 (Case 7/69) 3.4.6.6.2
Commission *v.* Italy [1970] ECR 47 (Case 38/69) 3.4.3.4
Commission *v.* Italy [1973] ECR 101; [1973] CMLR 439 (Case 39/72) 3.4.6.6.2
Commission *v.* Italy [1974] ECR 709 (Case 173/73) 15.4.4.2
Commission *v.* Italy [1979] ECR 3247; [1980] 3 CMLR 446 (Case 159/78) 6.1.2
Commission *v.* Italy [1983] ECR 2525 (Case 203/82) 15.4.4.3.6
Commission *v.* Italy [1984] ECR 2793 (Case 51/83) 3.4.6.6.2
Commission *v.* Italy [1984] ECR 3395 (Case 254/83) 3.4.6.6.2
Commission *v.* Italy [1985] ECR 1127 (Case 2/84) 4.2.2.10.2
Commission *v.* United Kingdom [1988] 3 CMLR 437 (Case 60/86) 3.5.5
Compagnie des Hauts Fourneaux et Fonderies de Givers *v.* High Authority [1960] ECR 241 (Joined Cases 27–29/85) 4.2.1.2.2, 4.2.1.3.2
Compagnie Royale Asturienne des Mines SA and Rheinzink GmbH *v.* Commission [1984] ECR 1679; [1985] 1 CMLR 688 (Cases 29, 30/83) 10.1.3.1.2, 10.1.3.2.4, 10.1.4.2, 10.1.5.2
Conradi *et al v.* Direction de la Concurrences et des Prix des Hauts de la Seine *et al* (Case 198/86) 6.1.2
Consten and Grundig *v.* Commission [1966] ECR 299; [1966] CMLR 418 (Cases 56, 58/84) 9.2, 10.1.9.3.2
Continental Can *v.* Commission [1973] ECR 215; [1973] CMLR 199 (Case 6/72) 10.2.8.3.1, 10.2.8.3.2, 10.2.8.3.3
Co-operative Stemsel-en Kleurselfabriek *v.* Commission [1981] ECR 851; [1982] 1 CMLR 240 (Case 61/80) 10.1.3.1.2
Corfu Channel Case, The. (Merits): UK *v.* Albania [1949] ICJ Rep. 4 .... 17.1
Corrine Bodson *v.* Pompes Funèbres des Regions Libérées SA [1988] ECR 2479; [1989] 4 CMLR 984 .... 10.1.3.1.2
Corsica Ferries France *v.* Direction Générale des Douanes Françaises [1991] 2 CMLR 227 (The French–Corsican case) (Case 48/89) 7.5.15
Costa *v.* ENEL [1964] ECR 585; [1964] CMLR 426 (Case 6/64) ... 3.5.1, 3.5.5, 6.1.3, 15.4.7.5, 15.4.9
Council *v.* Parliament [1986] ECR 2155; [1986] 3 CMLR 94 (Case 34/86) 3.4.5.10
Cullet *v.* Leclerc [1985] ECR 305 (Case 231/83) 3.2.4

D J Smit Transport BV *v.* Commissie Grensoverschrijdend Beroepsvervoer [1983] ECR 73; [1983] 3 CMLR 106 (Case 126/82) 4.2.2.1
Da Veiga *v.* Staatssecretaris van Justitie [1991] 1 CMLR 217 (Case 9/88) 4.2.2.1
De Bloos *v.* Bouyer [1976] ECR 1497; [1977] 1 CMLR 60 (Case 14/76) 25.3.3.6
de Cavel *v.* de Cavel (No. 1) [1979] ECR 1055; [1979] 2 CMLR 547 .... 25.2.1, 25.4.1.1
de Cavel *v.* de Cavel (No. 2) [1980] ECR 731 .... 25.2.1
De Gexamenlijke Steenkolenmijnen in Limburg *v.* ECSC High Authority [1961] ECR 1 (Case 30/59) 15.4.4.3, 15.4.4.3.1
De Wolf *v.* Cox BV [1976] ECR 1758 .... 25.3.3.4
Decca Navigator Systems, OJ 1989 L43/27 .... 10.2.8.3.2
Defrenne *v.* Sabena (Case 80/70) 8.2.2.1
Defrenne *v.* Sabena [1976] ECR 455 (Case 43/75) 3.5.5
Denilauler *v.* Couchet Freres [1980] ECR 1553 .... 25.4.1.1
Derycke [1977] ECR 29 (Case 65/76) 4.3.1.5
Deufil GmbH and Co. KG *v.* Commission [1987] ECR 901; [1988] 1 CMLR 553 (Case 310/85) 15.4.4.3, 15.4.6.14
Deutsche Grammophon *v.* Metro [1971] ECR 487 (Case 78/70) 3.2.4
Distillers Company *v.* Commission [1980] ECR 2229; [1980] 3 CMLR 121 (Case 30/78) 10.1.3.2.2
Dona *v.* Mantero [1976] ECR 1333; [1976] 2 CMLR 578 .... 6.1
Dresser UK Ltd *v.* Falcongate Freight Management Ltd [1991] 2 Lloyd's Rep. 557 .... 25.3.9
Dymond *v.* G.B. Britton (Holdings) Ltd. [1976] 1 CMLR 133 .... 3.5.5

EATE Levy, OJ 1985 L219/35; [1988] 4 CMLR 698 .... 10.1.3.1.2
EC Commission *v.* EC Council [1971] ECR 263; [1971] CMLR 335 (Case 22/70) 4.2.2.5.2
ECS/AKZO, OJ 1983 L252/13; [1983] 3 CMLR 694 .... 10.2.11.3
E.D. and F. Man *v.* Intervention Board (Case 181/84) 3.5.2.2.8
EEC *v.* Anseau-Navewa, OJ 1982 L167/39; [1982] 2 CMLR 193 .... 10.1.3.1.2
EEC *v.* Associated Lead Manufacturers Ltd. (White Lead), OJ 1979 L21/16; [1979] 1 CMLR 464 .... 10.1.3.2.2

EMI Records Ltd. *v.* CBS UK Ltd. [1976] ECR 811; [1976] 2 CMLR 235 (Case 51/75) 10.1.3.2.2
ENI/Montedison, OJ 1987 L354/28; [1988] 4 CMLR 444 .... 10.1.3.2.2, 10.1.7.10
Effer *v.* Kantner [1982] ECR 987 .... 25.3.3.2
ERASMUS Legislation (*Re*): Commission *v.* Council of Ministers, para. 6 [1991] 1 CMLR 478 .... 3.5.9
Erauw-Jacquery *v.* La Hesbignonne [1988] 4 CMLR 576 (Case 27/87) 10.1.7.3
Erzbergbau (Barbara) AG *v.* High Authority [1960] ECR 173 (Cases 3.18/58, 23–26/58, 25, 26/58) 4.2.1.2.2, 4.2.1.3, 4.2.1.3.2, 4.2.2.10.2
European Parliament *v.* Council of Ministers [1985] ECR 1513; [1986] 1 CMLR 138 (Case 13/83) 4.1.5, 4.2.2.1, 4.2.2.5.2, 4.2.2.14.2
European Sugar Cartel (*Re*) [1973] CMLR D65 .... 10.2.12
Europemballage Corpn. and Continental Can Co. Inc. *v.* Commission [1973] ECR 215; [1973] CMLR 199 (Case 6/72) 10.2.4, 10.2.8.3, 10.2.8.3.2, 10.2.13.4, 26.5.3.12.3
Executif Regional Wallon and Glaverbel SA *v.* Commission [1988] ECR 1573; [1989] 2 CMLR 771 (Cases 62/87 and 72/87) 15.4.6.17

Federal Republic of Germany *v.* EC Commission [1987] ECR 4013; [1988] 1 CMLR 591 (Case 248/84) 15.4.2, 15.4.4.3.4
Fedetab, OJ 1978 L224/29; 1978 3 CMLR 524 .... 10.1.3.2.1
Fides, OJ 1979 L57/33; [1979] 1 CMLR 650 .... 10.1.3.1.2
Fietje [1980] ECR 3389 (Case 27/80) 3.4.6.2
Film Purchases by German Television Stations, OJ 1989 L284/36 .... 10.1.3.1.2
Fire Insurance (D), OJ 1982 L80/36; [1982] 2 CMLR 159 .... 10.1.3.1.2
Firma Steinike und Weinlig *v.* Bundesamt für Ernährung und Forstwirtschaft [1977] ECR 595; [1977] 2 CMLR 688 (Case 78/76) 15.4.2, 15.4.4.3.1, 15.4.4.3.2, 15.4.9
Fishery Price Information (*Re*) [1991] 2 CMLR 876 (Case C–39/88) 3.4.6.6.2
Floral (*Re*), OJ 1980 L39/51; [1980] 2 CMLR 285 .... 10.1.3.2.2
Ford *v.* Commission (No. 1) [1984] ECR 1129 (Cases 228, 229/82) 10.1.3.1.3
France *v.* Commission [1970] ECR 487; [1970] CMLR 351 (Case 47/69) 15.4.4.3.4, 15.4.4.3.5
France *v.* Commission [1988] ECR 4067 (Case 102/87) 15.4.4.3.5
France *v.* Commission [1990] ECR 351 (Case 301/87) 15.4.4.3
Franco-Japanese Ballbearings Agreement (*Re*), OJ 1974 L343/19; [1975] 1 CMLR D8 ...... 10.1.5.2
Freccia del Nord, The [1989] 1 Lloyd's Rep. 388 .... 25.3.9
French and Taiwanese Mushroom Packers (*Re*), OJ 1975 L29/26; [1975] 1 CMLR D83 ...... 10.1.5.2
French Seamen's Case [1974] ECR 359; [1974] 2 CMLR 216 (Case 167/73) 3.1, 3.2.4, 3.3.15, 3.4.6.6.2, 3.5.5, 4.2.2.1, 4.2.2.2.2, 4.2.2.7.2, 4.2.2.14.2, 5.2, 5.3.2, 5.4.6, 5.4.8, 6.1, 8.1, 8.2.2.1, 8.2.2.4, 9.3.4, 9.3.5, 9.3.6, 11.3.4.1, 12.2.5
Frubo *v.* Commission [1975] ECR 563; [1975] 2 CMLR 123 (Case 71/74) 10.1.3.1.2

GEMA, JO 1971 L134/15; [1971] CMLR D35 .... 10.2.1
GVL, OJ 1981 L370/49; [1982] 1 CMLR 221 .... 10.2.11.3
GVL *v.* Commission [1983] ECR 483; [1983] 3 CMLR 645 (Case 7/82) 10.1.5.2
Garden Cottage Foods *v.* Milk Marketing Board [1984] AC 130 .... 3.5.7.2, 3.5.8
General Motors *v.* Commission [1975] ECR 1367; [1976] 1 CMLR 95 (Case 26/75) 10.2.7
Gerling Konzern AG *v.* Amministrazione del Tesoro dello Stato [1983] ECR 2503; [1984] 3 CMLR 638 .... 25.3.4, 25.3.7.1
Germany *v.* Commission [1984] ECR 1451 (Case 84/82) 15.4.4.3, 15.4.4.3.1
Germany *v.* Commission [1987] ECR 4013; [1987] 1 CMLR 591 (Case 248/84) 15.4.4.3, 15.4.6.4, 15.4.6.7
Germany *v.* High Authority [1960] ECR 225 (Case 19/58) 4.2.1.2.2, 4.2.1.3, 4.2.1.3.2
Gondrand Frères [1981] ECR 1219 (Case 169/80) 3.5.2.2.8
Grad *v.* Finanzamt Traunstein [1970] ECR 825; [1971] 1 CMLR 1 (Case 9/70) 3.5.3, 4.2.2.6.2, 4.2.2.10.2
Gravier *v.* City of Liege (Case 293/84) 8.2.5
Greece *v.* Commission [1988] ECR 2875 (Case 57/86) 15.4.4.3
Greens, The *v.* European Parliament 1986 ECR 1339; [1987] 2 CMLR 343 (Case 294/83) ... 3.4.6.6.5
Greenwich Film Production *v.* SACEM [1979] ECR 3275; [1980] 1 CMLR 629 (Case 22/79) . 10.1.5.2
Grimaldi-Cobelfret *v.* BEBFC (Case IV/33.509, filed on 2 April 1990) 12.15.1
Gullung *v.* Conseil de l'Ordre des Avocats au Barreau de Colmar *et al.* [1988] 2 CMLR 57 (Case 292/86) 6.1

Hagen *v.* Fratelli [1980] CMLR 253 .... 3.4.6.6.9

Hasselblad, OJ 1982 L16/9; [1979] 1 CMLR 448 .... 10.1.3.2.2
Heineken [1984] ECR 3424 (Cases 91 and 127/83) 15.4.7.4
Handelswekrij G.J. Bier BV *v.* Mines de Potasse d'Alsace SA [1976] ECR 1735 .... 25.3.3.4
Hilti AG *v.* Commission (Case 98/88) 10.2.8.4
Hoekstra (nee Unger) *v.* BBDA (Case 75/63) 8.2.2.1
Hoffmann *v.* La Roche, OJ 1976 L223/27; [1977] 2 CMLR D25 .... 10.2.8.3.1, 10.2.8.3.2
Hoffmann-La Roche and Co AG *v.* Commission [1979] ECR 461; [1979] 3 CMLR 211 (Case 85/76) 3.5.2.2.8, 10.2.4, 10.2.8.3, 10.2.11.3, 10.2.11.4.5, 10.2.13.4
Hugin Kassaregister AB *v.* Commission [1979] ECR 1869; [1979] 3 CMLR 345 (Case 22/82) 10.1.5.1, 10.2.8.3.2, 10.2.11.4.6
Hydrotherm *v.* Anderoil [1984] ECR 2999; [1985] 3 CMLR 224; CCH 14,112 (Case 173/83) . 10.1.3.1, 10.1.3.1.2
Hyundai Marine Co. Ltd. (Case 136/89) 13.2.15

IAZ International Belgium NV *v.* Commission [1983] ECR 3369; [1984] 3 CMLR 276 (Case 96/82) 10.1.3.1.2, 10.1.3.2.3
ICI *v.* Commission [1972] ECR 619; [1972] CMLR 557 (Case 48/69) 10.1.3.2.4, 10.2.8.3.2, 12.6.1
Industrie Tessili Italiana Como *v.* Dunlop AG [1976] ECR 1473 .... 25.1, 25.3.3.2
Instituto Chemioterapico Italiano SpA and Commercial Solvents Corpn *v.* Commission [1974] ECR 223; [1974] 1 CMLR 309 (Joined Cases 6, 7/73) 10.2.4, 10.2.8.4.1, 10.2.8.5.4, 10.2.8.5.5
Intermills SA *v.* Commission [1984] ECR 3809; [1986] 1 CMLR 614 (Case 323/84) 15.4.4.3, 15.4.4.3.1, 15.4.4.3.2, 15.4.6.19, 15.4.7.3
International Fruit Co. *v.* Produktschap [1972] ECR 1219; [1975] 2 CMLR 1 (Cases 21–4/72) .. 3.5.3
Interpar *v.* GVLmbH, OJ 1982 L370/49; [1982] 1 CMLR 221 .... 10.1.3.1.2
Ireland *v.* France, OJ 1977 C142/8 (Case 58/77) 3.4.6.6.3
Irish Club Rules (Case IV/33.677) 12.15.12
Italian Cast Glass, OJ 1980 L383/19; [1982] 2 CMLR 61 .... 10.1.9.5.1
Italian Cast Glass (*Re*), OJ 1985 L376/62; [1985] 4 CMLR 178 .... 10.1.3.1.2
Italian Flat Glass, OJ 1989 L33/44 .... 10.1.3.2.4
Italian State *v.* Sacchi [1974] ECR 409; [1974] 2 CMLR 177 (Case 155/73) 10.1.3.1.2
Italy–Algeria Case 7.5.16
Italy *v.* Commission [1985] ECR 873; [1985] 2 CMLR 368 (Case 41/83) 10.1.3.1.2, 10.2.7, 10.2.8.4, 10.2.11.2.1
Italy *v.* Commission [1969] ECR 277; [1970] CMLR 17 (Case 1/69) 4.2.2.10.2
Italy *v.* Commission [1974] ECR 709; [1974] 2 CMLR 593 (Case 173/73) 15.4.4.3
Italy *v.* High Authority [1960] ECR 325 (Case 20/59) 4.2.1.3.2

Johnson and Johnson, OJ 1980 L377/16; [1981] 2 CMLR 287 .... 10.1.3.1.2
Johnston *v.* Chief Constable of the RUC [1986] ECR 1651 (Case 222/84) 3.5.6

Kalfelis *v.* Schroder, Munchmeyer, Hengst & Co. (Case 189/87) 25.3.3.4, 25.3.3.10
Kempf *v.* Staatssecretaris van Justitie (Case 139/85) 8.2.2.1
Kolpinghuis Nijmegen [1989] 2 CMLR 18 (Case 80/86) 3.5.3

LdPE, OJ 74/21, 17 March 1989; CCH 1989 I CEC 2,193 .... 10.1.3.1, 10.1.3.2.2
LTU *v.* Eurocontrol [1976] ECR 1541; [1979] 1 CMLR 88 .... 25.2.1
Lachmuller *v.* Commission [1960] ECR 463 Joined Cases 43/59 etc. and Ruling 1/78 [1978] ECR 2151 .... 3.1
Lambregts Transportbedrijf *v.* Belgian State [1989] ECR 2583; [1991] 1 CMLR 351 .... 7.5.15
Lawrie-Blum *v.* Land Baden-Württemberg [1986] ECR 2121; [1987] 3 CMLR 389 (Case 66/85) 8.2.2.1, 8.2.2.3.2
Levin *v.* Staatssecretaris van Justitie [1982] ECR 1035; [1982] 2 CMLR 454 (Case 53/81) 8.2.2.1
London European Airways *v.* Sabena, OJ 1988 L317/47; [1989] 4 CMLR 662 (Case IV/32.328) . 9.3.2, 9.4, 10.2.14, 12.6.3
Lord Bethell *v.* EC Commission [1982] ECR 2277; [1982] 3 CMLR 300 (Case 246/81) 4.3.3.1
L'Oreal NV *v.* De Nieuwe AMCK PVBA [1980] ECR 3775; [1981] 2 CMLR 235 (Case 31/80) 10.2.8.3.1
Lorenz *v.* Germany [1973] ECR 1471 (Case 120/73) 15.4.7.3, 15.4.7.5, 15.4.9
Luisi and Carbone *v.* Ministero del Tesoro [1984] ECR 377; [1985] 3 CMLR 52 (Cases 286/82 and 26/83) 3.5.6, 3.5.7.1
Lutticke *v.* Commission [1966] ECR 19 (Case 48/65) 3.4.6.6.2
Luxembourg *v.* Eruopean Parliament [1983] ECR 255 (Case 230/81) 3.5.2.1.1

Mackprang *v.* Commission [1971] ECR 797 (Case 15/71) 3.4.6.6.6
Magill TV Guide/ITP, BBC and RTE, OJ 1989 L78/43, on appeal Cases 76/89 etc. RTE *v.* Commission 10.2.8.4
Marc Rich & Co. AG *v.* Società Italiana Impianti S.p.A. [1992] 1 Lloyd's Rep. 342 .... 25.2.1
Marshall *v.* Southampton Area Health Authority [1986] ECR 723; [1986] 1 CMLR 688 (Case 152/84) 3.5.3
Marson *v.* Netherlands (Cases 35, 36/82) 8.2.2.1
Martin Peters Bauunternehmung GmbH *v.* Zuid Nederlandse Aannemers Vereniging [1983] ECR 987 .... 25.3.3.2, 25.3.3.4
Mecaniver-PPG, OJ 1985 L35/54; [1985] 3 CMLR 359 .... 10.1.7.10
Meeth *v.* Glacetal [1978] ECR 2133; [1979] 1 CMLR 520 (Case 23/78) 25.3.7.1
MELDOC, OJ 1986 L348/50 .... 10.1.3.1.2
Merck *v.* Hauptzollamt Hamburg-Jonas [1983] ECR 3781 (Case 292/82) 3.5.6
Meura (*Re*): Belgium *v.* Commission [1986] ECR 2263; [1988] 2 CMLR 331 (Case 234/84) ... 15.4.4.3
Michelin *v.* Commission [1983] ECR 3461; [1985] 1 CMLR 282 (Case 322/81) ... 10.2.8.3.1, 10.2.13.1
Miller *v.* Commission [1978] ECR 131 (Case 19/77) 3.5.2.2.3
Ministère Public *v.* Gauchard (Case 20/87) 6.1.2, 8.2.2.1
Ministère Public *v.* Ledoux [1988] ECR 3741 .... 7.5.15
Ministère Public *v.* Lucas Asjes [1986] ECR 1425; [1986] 3 CMLR 173 (Cases 209–213/84) ... 4.2.2.1, 4.3.3.1
Ministère Public *et al v.* Van Wesemael and Follachio [1979] ECR 35; [1979] 3 CMLR 87 (Case 110–111/78) 6.1
Molkerei-Zentrale Westfalen *v.* Hauptzollamt Paderborn [1968] ECR 143 (Case 28/67) 3.5.5
Moser *v.* Land Baden-Württemberg (Case 180/83) 8.2.2.1
Mulder *v.* Minister von Landbouw [1989] 2 CMLR 1 (Case 120/86) 3.5.7.3
Musique Diffusion Française *v.* Commission [1983] ECR 1825; [1983] 3 CMLR 221 (Cases 100–103/80) 10.1.3.1.2

Napier Brown-British Sugar, OJ 1988 L284/41 .... 10.2.11.4.3, 10.2.14
National Panasonic, OJ 1982 L354/28; [1983] 1 CMLR 497 .... 10.1.3.2.1, 10.1.3.2.2
National Panasonic (UK) Ltd. *v.* Commission [1979] ECR 2033 (Case 136/79) 3.5.2.2.8, 3.5.6
Nederlandsche Banden-Industrie Michelin NV *v.* Commission [1983] ECR 3461; [1985] 1 CMLR 282 (Case 322/81) 10.2.4, 10.2.8.3.1, 10.2.8.3.2, 10.2.8.5.5
Nehlsen *v.* Bremen [1979] ECR 3639 (Case 47/79) 4.3.1.5
Netherlands *v.* Commission [1968] ECR 1 (Case 28/66) 4.2.1.3.2
Netherlands *v.* High Authority [1962] ECR 213 (Case 9/61) 4.2.1.3.2
Netherlands *v.* High Authority [1960] ECR 355 (Case 25/59) 4.2.1.3.2
Netherlands and Leeuwarder Papierwarenfabriek BV *v.* Commission [1985] ECR 809; [1985] 3 CMLR 380 (Cases 296 and 318/82) 15.4.4.3, 15.4.4.3.2, 15.4.4.3.4, 15.4.4.3.6, 15.4.6.18
Netherlands State *v.* Ruffer [1980] ECR 3807; [1981] 3 CMLR 293 (Case 814/79) 25.2.1, 25.3.3.4
New Hampshire Insurance Co. *v.* Strabag Bau [1992] 1 Lloyd's Rep. 361 .... 25.3.4
Niederrheinshe Bergwerks-AG *et al v.* High Authority [1961] ECR 133 (Cases 2 and 3/60) ... 3.4.3.1
Nold *v.* Commission [1974] ECR 491 (Case 4/73) 3.5.2.2.8
Norddeutsches Vieh-und Fleischkontor *v.* BALM [1982] ECR 3583 (Cases 213/81 etc.) 15.4.4.3.2
Nordglimt, The [1987] 2 Lloyd's Rep. 470 .... 25.3.3.8
Nordsee *v.* Reederei Mond [1982] ECR 1095 (Case 102/81) 3.4.6.6.9
Nouvelles Frontières [1986] ECR 1425 (Cases 209 to 213/84) 4.2.2.1, 4.3.3.1, 9.3.5
Nungesser KG *v.* Commission [1982] ECR 2015; [1983] 1 CMLR 278, CJEC (Case 258/78) 10.1.3.1.2, 10.1.7.4
Nuovo CEGAM (*Re*), OJ 1984 L99/29; [1984] 2 CMLR 484 .... 10.1.3.2.2

Olympic Airways, OJ 1985 L46/51 .... 12.6.3
Olympic Airways (*Re*) [1985] 1 CMLR 730 .... 9.3.2, 9.4
Openbaar Ministerie *v.* van Tiggele [1978] ECR 25 (Case 82/77) 15.4.4.3.2
Ordre des Avocats au Barreau de Paris *v.* Klopp [1984] ECR 2971; [1985] 1 CMLR 99 (Case 107/83) 6.1

PVC, OJ L74/1, 17 March 1989; CCH 1989 1 CEC 2,167 .... 10.1.3.1, 10.1.3.1.2, 10.1.3.2.2
P and I Clubs, OJ 1985 L376/2; [1985] 4 CMLR 178 .... 10.1.3.1.2
Parliament *v.* Council, OJ 1983 C49/9 (Case 13/83) 3.4.6.6.6
Patrick *v.* Ministre des Affaires Culturelles [1977] ECR 1199; [1977] 2 CMLR 523 (Case 11/77) .. 6.1, 6.1.2

Penney's Trade Mark (*Re*), OJ 1978 L60/19; [1978] 2 CMLR 100 .... 10.1.3.2.2
Peters *v*. ZNAV. *See* Martin Peters.
Philip Morris Holland BV *v*. Commission [1980] ECR 2671; [1981] 2 CMLR 321 (Case 730/79) 15.4.4.3, 15.4.4.3.4, 15.4.4.3.5, 15.4.5.3, 15.4.6.3, 15.4.6.4, 15.4.9
Pigs Marketing Board *v*. Redmond [1978] ECR 2347; [1979] 1 CMLR 177 (Case 83/78) 3.5.6
Plaumann *v*. Commission [1963] ECR 95; [1964] CMLR 29 (Case 25/62) 3.4.6.6.5
Polypropylene, OJ 1986 L230/1, 18 August 1986; [1988] 4 CMLR 347; CCH 10,782, on appeal Cases 179/86 etc. Rhones-Poulenc SA *v*. Commission 10.1.3.1, 10.1.3.1.2, 10.1.3.2.2, 10.1.3.2.4, 10.1.5.2
Procureur du Roi *v*. Dassonville [1974] ECR 837; [1974] 2 CMLR 436 (Case 8/74) 3.5.5
Produits Bertrand *v*. Commission [1976] ECR 1; [1976] 1 CMLR 220 (Case 40/75) 15.4.4.3.5
Pronuptia *v*. Schillgalis [1986] 1 CMLR 414 (Case 161/84) 10.1.7.3
Putz *v*. Kawasaki Motors (UK) Ltd., OJ 1979 L16/9; [1979] 1 CMLR 448 .... 10.1.3.2.2

R. *v*. Commissioners for Customs and Excise, *ex p*. Tattersall Ltd. [1988] 3 CMLR 113 (Case 10/87) 3.4.6.6.9
R. *v*. HM Treasury *et al*., *ex p*. Daily Mail and General Trust Plc [1988] 3 CMLR 713 (Case 81/87) 6.1.2, 6.1.4
R. *v*. Royal Pharmaceutical Society of Great Britain, *ex p*. Secretary of State for Social Services [1989] 2 CMLR 751 (Cases 266 and 267/87) 3.5.5
R. *v*. Saunders [1979] ECR 1129; [1979] 2 CMLR 216 (Case 175/78) 8.2.2.1
R. *v*. Secretary of State for Transport, *ex p*. Factortame (No. 2) [1991] AC 603; [1990] 3 WLR 818; [1991] 1 All ER 70 (Case C213/89) 27.5
RAI/UNITEL, OJ L157/39, 15 June 1978; [1978] 3 CMLR 306; CCH 10,009 ..... 10.1.3.1, 10.1.3.1.2
RTEV *v*. Commission (Case 76/89) 10.2.8.4
RTM/P & O (Case 33.045) 12.15.5
Remia BV and Verenigde Bedrijven Nutricia NV *v*. Commission [1987] 1 CMLR 1 (Case 42/84) 10.1.3.1.2, 10.1.7.3
Reuter/BASF, OJ 1976 L254/40 [1976] 2 CMLR D44; CCH 9862 ...... 10.1.3.1, 10.1.3.1.2, 10.1.7.3
Rewe *v*. Hauptzollamt Kiel [1981] ECR 1805; [1982] 1 CMLR 449 (Case 158/80) 3.5.5, 3.5.8
Rewe-Zentral AG *v*. Bundesmonopolverwaltung für Branntwein [1979] ECR 649 (Case 120/78) (The Cassis de Dijon case) 26.5.2.2
Reyner *v*. Kingdom of Belgium [1974] ECR 631; [1974] 2 CMLR 305 (Case 2/74) 6.1.2
Rhones-Poulenc SA *v*. Commission (Case 179/86) 10.1.3.2.2, 10.1.3.2.4
Rosler *v*. Rottwinkel [1986] ECR 99; [1985] 1 CMLR 806 (Case 241/83) 25.3.6.2
Royal Scholten Honig *v*. Intervention Board [1978] ECR 2037 (Cases 103 and 145/77) 3.5.2.2.8
Royer [1976] ECR 497; [1976] 2 CMLR 619 (Case 48/75) 6.1.2
Rutili *v*. Commission [1974] ECR 491 (Case 36/75) 3.5.2.2.8
Rutili *v*. Ministre de l'Interieur [1975] ECR 1219; [1976] 1 CMLR 140 (Case 36/75) 8.2.2.1

STM *v*. Maschinenbau [1966] ECR 235; [1966] CMLR 357 (Case 56/65) 10.1.7.4
Saarland and Others *v*. Ministry of Commerce and Others [1989] 1 CMLR 529 (Case 187/87) .. 17.7
Saeed (Ahmed) Flugreisen and Silver Line Reisebüro *v*. Zentrale zur Bekämpfung unläuteren Wettbewerbs [1990] 4 CMLR 102 (Case 66/84) 4.3.3.1
San Giorgio [1983] ECR 3595; [1985] 2 CMLR 658 (Case 199/82) 3.5.9.1
Sanders *v*. Van der Patte [1977] ECR 2383; [1978] 1 CMLR 331 (Case 73/77) 25.3.6.2
Sanicentral GmbH *v*. Collin [1979] ECR 3423; [1979] 2 CMLR 164 .... 25.1, 25.2.1, 25.3.7.1
Schottle and Söhne OHG *v*. Finanzamt Traunstein [1977] ECR 247; [1977] 2 CMLR 98 (Case 20/76) 4.2.2.6.2
Sealink/B & I (Case IV/32.385) 12.15.6
Sealink/SMZ (Case IV/32.383, OJ No. C17/12, 89) 12.15.8
Sealink/SNCF (Case IV/32.385, OJ No. C17/8, 21 August 1989) 12.15.9
Siemens/Fanuc, OJ 1985 L376/29; [1988] 4 CMLR 948 .... 10.1.5.2
Simmenthal *v*. Commission [1979] ECR 777 (Case 92/78) 3.4.6.6.5
Simmenthal [1978] ECR 629; [1978] 3 CMLR 263 (Case 106/77) 3.5.8
Smit (D J) Transport BV *v*. Commissie Grensoverschrijdend Beroepsvervoer [1983] ECR 73; [1983] 3 CMLR 106 (Case 126/82) 4.2.2.1
Société Technique Minière *v*. Maschinenbau Ulm [1966] ECR 235; [1966] CMLR 357, CJEC (Case 56/65) 10.1.4.1, 10.1.5.2
Somafer *v*. Saar-Ferngas [1978] ECR 2183 .... 25.3.3.6
Sotgiu *v*. Deutsche Bundespost (Case 152/73) 8.2.2.3.2, 8.2.5
Steinhausser *v*. City of Biarritz [1985] ECR 1819; [1986] 1 CMLR 53 (Case 197/84) 6.1

Steymann v. Staatssecretaris van Justitie (Case 196/87) 6.1.1, 8.2.2.1
Stichting Sigarettenindustrie Agreements (*Re*), OJ 1982 L232/1; 3 CMLR 702 .... 10.1.3.2.2
Sugar Cartel, OJ 1973 L140/17 .... 10.1.5.1
Suiker Unie v. Commission [1975] ECR 1663; [1976] 1 CMLR 295 (Cases 40/73 etc.) 10.1.3.1.2, 10.1.3.2.4, 10.2.12, 10.2.13.4
Swansea Cork Ferries 15.4.4.3.2

Tepea v. Commission [1978] ECR 1391; [1978] 3 CMLR 392 (Case 28/77) 10.1.3.2.1, 10.1.3.2.2
Tetra Pak Rausing SDA v. Commission (Case 327/88) 10.2.14
Thieffry v. Conseil de l'Ordre des Avocats à la Cour de Paris [1977] ECR 765; [1977] 2 CMLR 373 (Case 71/76) 6.1, 6.1.5
Tokyo Electric Co. Ltd. v. Council of Ministers [1989] 1 CMLR 169 (Case 260/85) 3.4.6.4.5
Trail Smelter Arbitration, The: U.S. v. Canada (1941) 3 RIAA 1905 .... 17.1
Transports Lesage & Cie v. Hauptzollamt Freiburg [1970] ECR 861; [1971] CMLR 1 (Case 20/70) 4.2.2.10.2

Ugliola [1969] ECR 363 (Case 15/69) 8.2.2.1
Uniform Eurocheques, OJ 1989 L36/16 .... 10.1.3.1.2, 10.1.3.2.2
Union Transport v. Continental Lines [1992] 1 Lloyd's Rep. 229 .... 25.3.3.2
United Brands Co. v. Commission [1978] ECR 207; [1978] 1 CMLR 429; [1979] ECR 461; [1979] 3 CMLR 211 (Case 27/76) 10.2.4, 10.2.8.3, 10.2.8.3.2, 10.2.11.1, 10.2.11.4.1, 10.2.11.4.4, 10.2.11.4.7, 10.2.14
United Kingdom v. Commission [1988] 2 CMLR 169 (Case 305/85) 3.5.6, 3.5.7.1

Vacuum Interrupters Ltd. (*Re*) OJ 1977 L48/32; [1977] 1 CMLR D67 .... 10.1.5.2
Vaessen BV v. Morris, OJ 1979 L19/32; [1979] 1 CMLR 511 D14 .... 10.1.3.1.2
Van Ameyde v. UCI [1977] ECR 1091 (Case 90/76) 10.1.3.1.2
Van Der Koon v. Commission [1988] ECR 219 (Cases 67/85 etc.) 15.4.4.3.1, 15.4.4.3.2
Van Duyn v. Home Office [1974] ECR 1337; [1975] 1 CMLR 1 (Case 41/74) 3.5.5, 8.2.2.1, 8.2.2.3.1, 8.2.2.4
Van Gend en Loos v. Nederlandse Administratie der Belastingen [1963] ECR 1 (Case 26/62) 3.1, 3.5.5
Van Landewyck v. Commission [1980] ECR 3125; [1981] 3 CMLR 193 (Cases 209/78 etc.) 3.5.2.2.8, 10.1.3.1, 10.1.3.2.1, 10.1.3.2.2
Variola [1973] ECR 981 (Case 24/73) 3.5.2.2.1, 3.5.3
Vereeniging van Cementhandelaren v. Commission [1972] ECR 977; [1973] CMLR 7 (Case 8/72) 10.1.3.2.3
Volk v. Vervaecke [1969] ECR 295; [1969] CMLR 273 (Case 5/69) 10.1.6.1
Von Colson v. Land Nordheim-Westfalen [1984] ECR 1891; [1986] 2 CMLR 430 (Case 14/83) . 3.5.6

W. v. H. [1982] ECR 731; [1983] 2 CMLR 125 (Case 25/81) 25.2.1
WANO Schwarzpulver GmbH (*Re*), OJ 1978 L322/26; [1979] 1 CMLR 403 .... 10.1.9.3.5
Wagner v. Fohrmann [1964] ECR 195 (Case 101/63) 3.5.2.1.1
Walrave and Koch v. Association Union Cycliste Internationale *et al* [1974] ECR 1405; [1975] 1 CMLR 320 (Case 36/74) 6.1.2, 8.2.5, 12.6.1
Watson and Belmann [1976] ECR 1185; [1976] 2 CMLR 552 (Case 118/75) 6.1.1
Welded Steel Mesh, OJ L260/1, 6 September 1989; [1989] 2 CEC 2051 .... 10.1.3.1
West and Central Africa cases (Cases IV/32.447, 32.448 and 32.450) 12.15.10
Wood Pulp, OJ 1985 L85/1, [1985] 3 CMLR 474 .... 10.1.3.2.2
X/Open Group, OJ 1987 L35/36; [1988] 4 CMLR 542 .... 10.1.4.4

Zeiger v. Salinitri [1984] ECR 2397 .... 25.3.9
Zinc Producers' Group (*Re*), OJ 1984 L220/27; [1958] 2 CMLR 108 .... 10.1.3.1, 10.1.3.1.2
Zuchner v. Bayerische Vereinsbank AG [1981] ECR 2021; [1982] 1 CMLR 313 (Case 172/80) 10.1.3.2.4

EEC CASES

Case 19/58 Germany v. High Authority [1960] ECR 225 .... 4.2.1.2.2, 4.2.1.3, 4.2.1.3.2
Case 20/59 Italy v. High Authority [1960] ECR 325 .... 4.2.1.3.2

Cases 3–18/58, 23–26/58, 25/58, 26/58 Barbara Erzbergbau AG *v.* High Authority [1960] ECR 173 .... 4.2.1.2.2, 4.2.1.3, 4.2.1.3.2, 4.2.2.10.2
Case 25/59 Netherlands *v.* High Authority [1960] ECR 355 .... 4.2.1.3.2
Case 30/59 De Gexamenlijke Steenkolenmijnen in Limburg *v.* ECSC High Authority [1961] ECR 1 .... 15.4.4.3, 15.4.4.3.1
Case 43/59 Lachmuller *v.* Commission [1960] ECR 463 .... 3.1
Cases 2/60, 3/60, Niederrheinshe Bergwerks-AG *et al.* *v.* High Authority [1961] ECR 133 .... 3.4.3.1
Case 9/61 Netherlands *v.* High Authority [1962] ECR 213 .... 4.2.1.3.2
Case 13/61 Bosch *v.* De Geus [1962] ECR 45 .... 3.5.2.2.8
Case 25/62 Plaumann *v.* Commission [1963] ECR 95; [1964] CMLR 29 .... 3.4.6.6.5
Case 26/62 Van Gend en Loos *v.* Nederlandse Administratie der Belastingen [1963] ECR 1 .... 3.1, 3.5.5
Case 75/63 Hoekstra (nee Unger) *v.* BBDA 8.2.2.1
Case 101/63 Wagner *v.* Fohrmann [1964] ECR 195 .... 3.5.2.1.1
Case 6/64 Costa *v.* ENEL [1964] ECR 585; [1964] CMLR 426 .... 3.5.1, 3.5.5, 6.1.3, 15.4.7.5, 15.4.9
Case 48/65 Lütticke *v.* Commission [1966] ECR 19 .... 3.4.6.6.2
Case 56/65 Société Technique Minière (STM) *v.* Maschinenbau Ulm [1966] ECR 235; [1966] CMLR 357, CJEC 10.1.4.1, 10.1.5.2, 10.1.7.4
Case 28/66 Netherlands *v.* Commission [1968] ECR 1 .... 4.2.1.3.2
Case 23/67 Brasserie de Haecht *v.* Wilkin [1967] ECR 407; [1968] CMLR 26 .... 10.1.4.3
Case 28/67 Molkerei-Zentrale Westfalen *v.* Hauptzollamt Paderborn [1968] ECR 143 [1968] CMLR 187 .... 3.5.5
Case 7/68 Commission *v.* Italy [1968] ECR 423; [1969] CMLR 1 .... 6.1.6.1
Case 1/69 Italy *v.* Commission [1969] ECR 277; [1970] CMLR 17 .... 4.2.2.10.2
Case 5/69 Völk *v.* Vervaecke [1969] ECR 295; [1969] CMLR 273 .... 10.1.6.1
Case 6/69 Commission *v.* France [1969] ECR 523 .... 3.4.6.6.5, 15.4.4.3, 15.4.4.3.6
Case 7/69 Commission *v.* Italy [1970] ECR 111 .... 3.4.6.6.2
Case 11/69 *See* Case 6/69
Case 15/69 Ugliola [1969] ECR 363 [1970] CMLR 194 .... 8.2.2.1
Case 31/69 Commission *v.* Italy [1970] ECR 25 .... 3.4.6.6.2
Case 38/69 Commission *v.* Italy [1970] ECR 47 .... 3.4.3.4
Case 41/69 ACF Chemiefarma NV *v.* Commission [1970] ECR 661 .... 10.1.3.2.2
Case 47/69 France *v.* Commission [1970] ECR 487; [1970] CMLR 351 .... 15.4.4.3.4, 15.4.4.3.5
Case 48/69 ICI *v.* Commission [1972] ECR 619; [1972] CMLR 557 .... 10.1.3.2.4, 12.6.1
Case 9/70 Grad *v.* Finanzamt Traunstein [1970] ECR 825; [1971] 1 CMLR 1 .... 3.5.3, 4.2.2.6.2, 4.2.2.10.2
Case 20/70 Transports Lesage & Cie *v.* Hauptzollamt Freiburg [1970] ECR 861; [1971] CMLR 1 .... 4.2.2.10.2
Case 22/70 EC Commission *v.* EC Council [1971] ECR 263; [1971] CMLR 335 ..... 4.2.2.1, 4.2.2.5.2
Case 78/70 Deutsche Grammophon *v.* Metro [1971] ECR 487 .... 3.2.4
Case 80/70 Defrenne *v.* Sabena 8.2.2.1
Case 7/71 Commission *v.* France [1971] ECR 1003 .... 3.4.6.6.2, 3.5.1
Case 15/71 Mackprang *v.* Commission [1971] ECR 797 .... 3.4.6.6.6
Case 22/71 Béguelin Import *v.* GL Import–Export SA [1971] ECR 949; [1972] CMLR 81 . 10.1.3.2.5, 10.1.7.2, 12.6.1
Case 6/72 Europemballage Corpn. and Continental Can Co. Inc. *v.* Commission [1973] ECR 215; [1973] CMLR 199 .... 10.2.4, 10.2.8.3, 10.2.8.4.1, 10.2.8.4.2, 10.2.8.5.4, 10.2.8.8, 10.2.13.4, 26.5.3.12.3
Case 8/72 Vereeniging van Cementhandelaren *v.* Commission [1972] ECR 977; [1973] CMLR 7 .... 10.1.3.2.3
Cases 21–24/72 International Fruit Co. *v.* Produktschap [1972] ECR 1219; [1975] 2 CMLR 1 ... 3.5.3
Case 39/72 Commission *v.* Italy [1968] ECR 423 [1973] ECR 101; [1973] CMLR 439 .... 3.4.6.6.2
Case 70/72 Commission *v.* Germany [1973] ECR 813 .... 15.4.9
Case 77/72 Capolongo *v.* Azienda Agricola Maya [1973] ECR 611; [1974] 1 CMLR 230 ... 15.4.4.3.7, 15.4.5.1
Case 81/72 Commission *v.* Council [1973] ECR 575 .... 3.5.2.2.8
Case 4/73 Nold *v.* Commission [1974] ECR 491 .... 3.5.2.2.8
Cases 6–7/73 Instituto Chemioterapico Italiano SpA and Commercial Solvents Corpn. *v.* Commission [1974] ECR 223; [1974] 1 CMLR 309 .... 10.2.4, 10.2.8.4.1, 10.2.8.5.4, 10.2.8.5.5
Cases 6/73, 7/73 Commercial Solvents *v.* Commission [1974] ECR 223; [1974] 1 CMLR 309 . 10.1.5.2, 10.1.7.2, 10.2.3, 10.2.13.4, 10.2.14, 12.6.1
Case 24/73 Variola [1973] ECR 981 .... 3.5.2.2.1, 3.5.3

Case 40/73 Suiker Unie *v*. Commission [1975] ECR 1663; [1976] 1 CMLR 295 .... 10.1.3.1.2, 10.1.3.2.4, 10.2.12, 10.2.13.4
Case 120/73 Lorenz *v*. Germany [1973] ECR 1471 .... 15.4.7.3, 15.4.7.5, 15.4.9
Case 152/73 Sotgiu *v*. Deutsche Bundespost 8.2.2.3.2, 8.2.5
Case 155/73 Italian State *v*. Sacchi [1974] ECR 409; [1974] 2 CMLR 177 .... 10.1.3.1.2
Case 167/73 Commission *v*. France (The French Seamen's Case) [1974] ECR 359; [1974] 2 CMLR 216 .... 3.1, 3.2.4, 3.3.15, 3.4.6.6.2, 3.5.2.2.2, 3.5.3, 3.5.5, 4.2.2.1, 4.2.2.2.2, 4.2.2.7.2, 4.2.2.14.2, 5.2, 5.3.2, 5.4.6, 5.4.8, 6.1, 8.1, 8.2.2.1, 8.2.2.4, 9.3.4, 9.3.5, 9.3.6, 11.3.4.1, 12.2.5, 27.4, 27.5
Case 173/73 Italy *v*. Commission [1974] ECR 709; [1974] 2 CMLR 593 .... 15.4.4.2, 15.4.4.3
Case 2/74 Reyner *v*. Kingdom of Belgium [1974] ECR 631; [1974] 2 CMLR 305 .... 6.1.2
Case 9/74 Casagrande [1974] ECR 773 .... 8.2.2.1
Case 15/74 Centrafarm *v*. Sterling Drug [1974] ECR 1147; [1974] 2 CMLR 480 .... 10.1.3.1.2, 10.1.7.21
Case 36/74 Walrave and Koch *v*. Association Union Cycliste Internationale *et al*. [1974] ECR 1405; [1975] 1 CMLR 320 .... 6.1.2, 8.2.5, 12.6.1
Case 41/74 Van Duyn *v*. Home Office [1974] ECR 1337; [1975] 1 CMLR 1 .... 3.5.5, 8.2.2.1, 8.2.2.3.1, 8.2.2.4
Case 69/74 Auditeur du Travail *v*. Cagnon et Taquet [1975] ECR 171 .... 4.3.1.5
Case 71/74 Frubo *v*. Commission [1975] ECR 563; [1975] 2 CMLR 123 .... 10.1.3.1.2
Case 26/75 General Motors *v*. Commission [1975] ECR 1367; [1976] 1 CMLR 95 .... 10.2.7
Case 36/75 Rutili *v*. Commission [1974] ECR 491 .... 3.5.2.2.8
Rutili *v*. Ministre de l'Interieur [1975] ECR 1219; [1976] 1 CMLR 140 .... 8.2.2.1
Case 43/75 Defrenne *v*. Sabena [1976] ECR 455 .... 3.5.5
Case 48/75 Royer [1976] ECR 497; [1976] 2 CMLR 619 .... 6.1.2
Case 51/75 EMI Records Ltd. *v*. CBS UK Ltd. [1976] ECR 811; [1976] 2 CMLR 10.1.3.2.2
Case 14/76 De Bloos *v*. Bouyer [1976] ECR 1497; [1977] 1 CMLR 60 .... 25.3.3.6
Case 20/76 Schottle and Söhne OHG *v*. Finanzamt Traunstein [1977] ECR 247; [1977] 2 CMLR 98 .... 4.2.2.6.2
Case 27/76 United Brands Co. *v*. Commission [1978] ECR 207; [1978] 1 CMLR 429; [1979] ECR 461; [1979] 3 CMLR 211 .... 10.2.4, 10.2.8.3, 10.2.8.4, 10.2.11.1, 10.2.11.4.1, 10.2.11.4.7, 10.2.14
Case 50/76 Amsterdam Bulb [1977] ECR 137; [1977] 2 CMLR 218 .... 3.5.2.2.1, 3.5.3
Case 65/76 Derycke [1977] ECR 29 .... 4.3.1.5
Case 71/76 Thieffry *v*. Conseil de l'Ordre des Avocats à la Cour de Paris [1977] ECR 765; [1977] 2 CMLR 373 .... 6.1, 6.1.5
Case 78/76 Firma Steinike und Weinlig *v*. Bundesamt für Ernährung und Forstwirtschaft [1977] ECR 595; [1977] 2 CMLR 688 .... 15.4.2, 15.4.4.3.1, 15.4.4.3.2, 15.4.9
Case 85/76 Hoffmann-La Roche and Co. AG *v*. Commission [1979] ECR 461; [1979] 3 CMLR 211 .... 3.5.2.2.8, 10.2.4, 10.2.8.3, 10.2.11.3, 10.2.11.4.5, 10.2.13.4
Case 90/76 Van Ameyde *v*. UCI [1977] 1091 .... 10.1.3.1.2
Case 114/76 Bela-Muhle *v*. Grows Farm [1977] ECR 1211 .... 3.5.2.2.8
Case 11/77 Patrick *v*. Ministre des Affaires Culturelles [1977] ECR 1199; [1977] 2 CMLR 523 .... 6.1, 6.1.2
Case 19/77 Miller *v*. Commission [1978] ECR 131 .... 3.5.2.2.3
Case 28/77 Tepea *v*. Commission [1978] ECR 1391; [1978] 3 CMLR 392 .... 10.1.3.2.1, 10.1.3.2.2
Case 58/77 Ireland *v*. France, OJ 1977 C142/8 .... 3.4.6.6.3
Case 61/77 Commission *v*. Ireland [1978] ECR 417; [1978] 2 CMLR 466 .... 3.1, 3.4.6.6.2
Case 73/77 Sanders *v*. Van der Patter [1977] ECR 2383; [1978] 1 CMLR 331 .... 25.3.6.2
Case 77/77 BP *v*. Commission [1978] ECR 1513; [1978] 3 CMLR 174 .... 3.4.6.6.5, 10.2.12
Case 82/77 Openbaar Ministerie *v*. Van Tiggele [1978] ECR 25 .... 15.4.4.3.2
Case 103/77 Royal Scholten Honig *v*. Intervention Board [1978] ECR 2037 .... 3.5.2.2.8
Case 106/77 Simmenthal [1978] ECR 629; [1978] 3 CMLR 263 .... 3.5.8
Case 145/77 Royal Scholten Honig *v*. Intervention Board [1978] ECR 2037 .... 3.5.2.2.8
Case 156/77 Commission *v*. Belgium [1978] ECR 1881 .... 4.2.1.1, 4.2.2.1, 4.2.2.7.2, 9.3.6
Case 16/78 Choquet [1978] ECR 2293; [1979] 1 CMLR 535 .... 6.1
Case 23/78 Meeth *v*. Glacetal [1978] ECR 2133; [1979] 1 CMLR 520 .... 25.3.7.1
Case 30/78 Distillers Company *v*. Commission [1980] ECR 2229; [1980] 3 CMLR 121 ..... 10.1.3.2.2
Case 83/78 Pigs Marketing Board *v*. Redmond [1978] ECR 2347; [1979] 1 CMLR 177 .... 3.5.6
Case 92/78 Simmenthal *v*. Commission [1979] ECR 777 .... 3.4.6.6.5
Cases 110–111/78 Ministère Public *et al*. *v*. Van Wesemael and Follachio [1979] ECR 35; [1979] 3 CMLR 87 .... 6.1

Case 120/78 Rewe-Zentral AG *v.* Bundesmonopolverwaltung für Branntwein (The Cassis de Dijon case) [1979] ECR 649 .... 26.5.2.2
Case 122/78 Buitoni *v.* FORMA [1979] ECR 677, 684 .... 3.5.2.2.8
Case 159/78 Commission *v.* Italy [1979] ECR 3247; [1980] 3 CMLR 446 .... 6.1.2
Case 175/78 R. *v.* Saunders [1979] ECR 1129; [1979] 2 CMLR 216 .... 8.2.2.1
Case 209/78 Van Landewyck *v.* Commission [1980] ECR 3125; [1981] 3 CMLR 193 .... 3.5.2.2.8, 10.1.3.1, 10.1.3.2.1, 10.1.3.2.2
Case 258/78 Nungesser KG *v.* Commission [1982] ECR 2015; [1983] 1 CMLR 278, CJEC . 10.1.3.1.2, 10.1.7.4
Case 22/79 Greenwich Film Production *v.* SACEM [1979] ECR 3275; [1980] 1 CMLR 629 ... 10.1.5.2
Case 47/79 Nehlsen *v.* Bremen [1979] ECR 3639 .... 4.3.1.5
Case 61/79 Amministrazione delle Finanze Dello Stato *v.* Denkavit Italiano Srl [1980] ECR 1205; [1981] 3 CMLR 694 .... 15.4.4.3, 15.4.4.3.1
Cases 91/79, 92/79 Commission *v.* Italian Republic [1980] ECR 1099 .... 17.3.2.1
Case 136/79 National Panasonic (UK) Ltd. *v.* Commission [1979] ECR 2033 .... 3.5.2.2.8, 3.5.6
Case 149/79 Commission *v.* Belgium: Re Public Employees [1980] ECR 3881 .... 8.2.2.3.2
Case 730/79 Philip Morris Holland BV *v.* Commission [1980] ECR 2671; [1981] 2 CMLR 321 .... 15.4.4.3, 15.4.4.3.4, 15.4.4.3.5, 15.4.5.3, 15.4.6.3, 15.4.6.4, 15.4.9
Case 814/79 Netherlands State *v.* Ruffer [1980] ECR 3807; [1981] 3 CMLR 293 .... 25.2.1, 25.3.3.4
Case 27/80 Fietje [1980] ECR 3389 .... 3.4.6.2
Case 31/80 L'Oreal NV *v.* De Nieuwe AMCK PVBA [1980] ECR 3775; [1981] 2 CMLR 235 .... 10.2.8.3
Case 61/80 Co-operative Stemsel-en Kleurselfabriek *v.* Commission [1981] ECR 851; [1982] 1 CMLR 240 .... 10.1.3.1.2
Cases 100–103/80 Musique Diffusion Française *v.* Commission [1983] 3 CMLR 221 .... 10.1.3.1.2
Case 122/80 Analog Devices [1981] ECR 2781 .... 3.5.6
Cases 142/80 and 143/80 Administrazione delle Finanze dello Stato *v.* Essevi SpA [1981] ECR 1413 .... 3.4.6.6.2
Case 158/80 Rewe *v.* Hauptzollamt Kiel [1981] ECR 1805; [1982] 1 CMLR 449 .... 3.5.5, 3.5.8
Case 169/80 Gondrand Freres [1981] ECR 1219 .... 3.5.2.2.8
Case 172/80 Zuchner *v.* Bayerische Vereinsbank AG [1981] ECR 2021; [1982] 1 CMLR 313 .... 10.1.3.2.4
Case 25/81 W. *v.* H. [1982] ECR 731; [1983] 2 CMLR 125 .... 25.2.1
Case 53/81 Levin *v.* Staatssecretaris van Justitie [1982] ECR 1035; [1982] 2 CMLR 454 .... 8.2.2.1
Case 102/81 Nordsee *v.* Reederei Mond [1982] ECR 1095 .... 3.4.6.6.9
Case 211/81 Commission *v.* Denmark [1982] ECR 4547 .... 3.4.6.6.2
Case 213/81 Norddeutsches Vieh-und Fleischkontor *v.* BALM [1982] ECR 3583 .... 15.4.4.3.2
Case 230/81 Luxembourg *v.* European Parliament [1983] ECR 225 .... 3.5.2.1.1
Case 246/81 Lord Bethell *v.* EC Commission [1982] ECR 2277; [1982] 3 CMLR 300 .... 4.3.3.1
Case 283/81 CILFIT *v.* Ministry of Health [1982] ECR 3415; [1983] 1 CMLR 472 .... 3.4.6.6.9
Case 322/81 Nederlandsche Banden-Industrie Michelin NV *v.* Commission [1983] ECR 3461; [1985] 1 CMLR 282 .... 10.2.4, 10.2.8.3, 10.2.8.4.1, 10.2.8.5.5, 10.2.11.8, 10.2.13.1
Case 7/82 GVL *v.* Commission [1983] ECR 483; [1983] 3 CMLR 645 .... 10.1.5.2
Case 22/82 Hugin Kassaregister AB *v.* Commission [1979] ECR 1869; [1979] 3 CMLR 345 .. 10.1.5.1, 10.2.8.5.4, 10.2.11.4.6
Cases 35/82, 36/82 Marson *v.* Netherlands 8.2.2.1
Case 84/82 Germany *v.* Commission [1984] ECR 1451 .... 15.4.4.3, 15.4.4.3.1
Case 96/82 IAZ International Belgium *v.* Commission [1983] ECR 3369; [1984] 3 CMLR 276 .... 10.1.3.1.2, 10.1.3.2.3
Case 107/82 AEG Telefunken *v.* Commission [1983] ECR 3151; [1984] 3 CMLR 325 .... 10.1.3.1.2, 10.1.3.2.2, 10.1.7.2
Case 126/82 DJ Smit Transport BV *v.* Commissie Grensoverschrijdend Beroepsvervoer [1983] ECR 73; [1983] 3 CMLR 106 .... 4.2.2.1
Case 199/82 San Giorgio [1983] ECR 3595; [1985] 2 CMLR 658 .... 3.5.9.1
Case 203/82 Commission *v.* Italy [1983] ECR 2525 .... 15.4.4.3.6
Case 222/82 Apple and Pear Development Council *v.* Lewis [1983] ECR 4083 .... 15.4.4.3.2
Cases 228/82, 229/82 Ford *v.* Commission (No. 1) [1984] ECR 1129 .... 10.1.3.1.3
Case 286/82 Luisi and Carbone *v.* Ministero del Tesoro [1984] ECR 377; [1985] 3 CMLR 52 ... 3.5.6, 3.5.7.1
Case 292/82 Merck *v.* Hauptzollamt Hamburg-Jonas [1983] ECR 3781 .... 3.5.6
Case 296/82, 318/82 Netherlands and Leeuwarder Papierwarenfabriek BV *v.* Commission [1985] ECR 809; [1985] 3 CMLR 380 .... 15.4.4.3, 15.4.4.3.2, 15.4.4.3.4, 15.4.4.3.6, 15.4.6.18

Case 13/83 European Parliament *v.* Council of Ministers [1985] ECR 1513; [1986] 1 CMLR 138; OJ 1983 C49/9 .... 3.4.6.6.6, 4.2.2.1, 4.2.2.5.2, 4.2.2.14.2
Case 14/83 Von Colson *v.* Land Nordheim-Westfalen [1984] ECR 1891; [1986] 2 CMLR 430 ... 3.5.6
Case 26/83 Luisi and Carbone *v.* Ministero del Tesoro [1984] ECR 377; [1985] 3 CMLR 52 .... 3.5.6, 3.5.7.1
Cases 29/83, 30/83 Compagnie Royale Asturienne des Mines SA and Rheinzink GmbH *v.* Commission [1984] ECR 1679; [1985] 1 CMLR 688 .... 10.1.3.1.2, 10.1.3.2.4, 10.1.4.2, 10.1.5.2
Case 35/83 BAT *v.* Commission [1985] ECR 363; [1985] 2 CMLR 470 .... 10.1.3.1.2
Case 41/83 Italy *v.* Commission [1985] ECR 873; [1985] 2 CMLR 368 .... 10.1.3.1.2, 10.2.7, 10.2.8.4, 10.2.11.2.1
Case 51/83 Commission *v.* Italy [1984] ECR 2793 .... 3.4.6.62
Case 52/83 Commission *v.* France [1983] ECR 3707 .... 15.4.4.3.6
Case 91/83 Heineken [1984] ECR 3424 .... 15.4.7.4
Case 107/83 Ordre des Avocats au Barreau de Paris *v.* Klopp [1984] ECR 2971; [1985] 1 CMLR 99 .... 6.1
Case 123/83 BNIC *v.* Clair [1985] ECR 391; [1985] 2 CMLR 430 .... 10.1.3.1.2
Case 127/83 Heineken [1984] ECR 3424 .... 15.4.7.4
Case 145/83 Adams *v.* Commission [1985] ECR 3539 .... 3.4.6.1, 19.3.7
Case 173/83 Hydrotherm *v.* Anderoil [1984] ECR 2999; [1985] 3 CMLR 224; CCH 14, 112 .. 10.1.3.1, 10.1.3.1.2
Case 180/83 Moser *v.* Land Baden-Württemberg 8.2.2.1
Case 231/83 Cullet *v.* Leclerc [1985] ECR 305 .... 3.2.4
Case 241/83 Rosler *v.* Rottwinkel [1986] ECR 99; [1985] 1 CMLR 806 .... 25.3.6.2
Case 254/83 Commission *v.* Italy [1984] ECR 3395 .... 3.4.6.6.2
Case 270/83 Commission *v.* France [1986] ECR 273; [1986] YBEL 247 .... 6.1, 6.1.2
Case 290/83 Commission *v.* France [1985] ECR 439 .... 15.4.4.3.1
Case 294/83 Greens, The *v.* European Parliament [1986] ECR 1339; [1987] 2 CMLR 343 ... 3.4.6.6.5
Case 2/84 Commission *v.* Italy [1985] ECR 1127 .... 4.2.2.10.2
Case 42/84 Remia BV and Verenigde Bedrijven Nutricia NV *v.* Commission [1987] 1 CMLR 1 .... 10.1.3.1.2, 10.1.7.3
Cases 56/84, 58/84 Consten and Grundig *v.* Commission [1966] CMLR 418 .... 9.2, 10.1.9.3.2
Case 66/84 Ahmed Saeed Flugreisen and Silver Line Reisburo *v.* Zentrale zur Bekämpfung unläuteren Wettbewerbs [1990] 4 CMLR 102 .... 4.3.3.1, 12.11.1
Case 152/84 Marshall *v.* Southampton Area Health Authority [1986] ECR 723; [1986] 1 CMLR 688 .... 3.5.3
Case 174/84 Bulk Oil *v.* Sun International 3.5.5
Case 181/84 E.D. and F. Man *v.* Intervention Board 3.5.2.2.8
Case 197/84 Steinhauser *v.* City of Biarritz [1985] 1819; [1986] 1 CMLR 53 .... 6.1
Cases 209–213/84 Ministère Public *v.* Lucas Asjes (The Nouvelles Frontières case) [1986] ECR 1425; [1986] 3 CMLR 173 .... 4.2.2.1, 4.3.3.1, 9.3.5
Case 216/84 Commission *v.* France 3.5.7.2
Case 221/84 Berghoefer GmbH *v.* ASA [1985] ECR 1517; [1980] 1 CMLR 566 .... 25.3.7.1
Case 222/84 Johnston *v.* Chief Constable of the RUC [1986] ECR 1651 .... 3.5.6
Case 226/84 BL *v.* Commission [1987] 1 CMLR 185 .... 10.2.7, 10.2.8.5.6
Case 234/84 Meura (*Re*): Belgium *v.* Commission [1986] ECR 2263; [1988] 2 CMLR 331 .... 15.4.4.3
Case 248/84 Federal Republic of Germany *v.* EC Commission [1987] ECR 4013; [1988] 1 CMLR 591 .... 15.4.2, 15.4.4.3, 15.4.4.3.4, 15.4.6.4, 15.4.6.7
Case 293/84 Gravier *v.* City of Liege 8.2.5
Case 307/84 Commission *v.* France [1986] ECR 1225 .... 8.2.2.3.2
Case 311/84 Centre Belge d'Etudes de Marche Tele-Marketing *v.* CLT [1986] 2 CMLR 558 ... 10.2.7, 10.2.11.2.1
Case 323/84 Intermills SA *v.* Commission [1984] ECR 3809; [1986] 1 CMLR 614 .... 15.4.4.3, 15.4.4.3.1, 15.4.4.3.2, 15.4.6.19, 15.4.7.3
Cases 27–29/85 Compagnie des Hauts Fourneaux et Fonderies de Givers *v.* High Authority [1960] ECR 241 .... 4.2.1.2.2, 4.2.1.3.2
Case 40/85 Boch (*Re*): Belgium *v.* Commission [1986] ECR 2321; [1988] 2 CMLR 301 ...... 15.4.4.3
Case 66/85 Lawrie-Blum *v.* Land Baden-Württemberg [1986] ECR 2121; [1987] 3 CMLR 389 .... 8.2.2.1, 8.2.2.3.2
Case 67/85 Van Der Kooi *v.* Commission [1988] ECR 219 .... 15.4.4.3.1, 15.4.4.3.2
Case 89/85 *See* Cases 104/85 *etc.*
Case 98/55 Bertini [1986] ECR 1893; [1987] 1 CMLR 774 .... 3.4.6.6.9

Cases 104/85, 114/85, 116/85, 125–129/85 Ahlstrom (A.) Osakeyhtiö *v.* Commission (the Wood Pulp Case) [1988] ECR 5193 ... 10.1.3.2.2, 12.6.4
Case 139/85 Kempf *v.* Staatssecretaris van Justitie ... 8.2.2.1
Case 162/85 Bertini [1986] ECR 1893; [1987] 1 CMLR 774 ... 3.4.6.6.9
Case 221/85 Commission *v.* Belgium [1987] ECR 719; [1988] 1 CMLR 620 ... 6.1.2
Case 225/85 Commission *v.* Italian Republic [1987] ECR 2626; [1988] CMLR 635 ... 8.2.2.3.2
Case 258/85 Bertini [1986] ECR 1893; [1987] 1 CMLR 774 ... 3.4.6.6.9
Case 260/85 Tokyo Electric Co. Ltd. *v.* Council of Ministers [1989] 1 CMLR 169 ... 3.4.6.4.5
Case 305/85 United Kingdom *v.* Commission [1988] 2 CMLR 169 ... 3.5.6, 3.5.7.1
Case 310/85 Deufil GmbH and Co. KG *v.* Commission [1987] ECR 901; [1988] 1 CMLR 553 ... 15.4.4.3, 15.4.6.14
Case 34/86 Council *v.* Parliament [1986] ECR 2155; [1986] 3 CMLR 94 ... 3.4.5.10
Case 45/86 Commission *v.* Council [1987] ECR 1493; [1988] 2 CMLR 131 ... 3.5.9
Case 57/86 Greece *v.* Commission [1988] ECR 2875 ... 15.4.4.3
Case 60/86 Commission *v.* United Kingdom [1988] 3 CMLR 437 ... 3.5.5
Case 63/86 Coman *v.* Italy ... 6.1.2
Case 80/86 Kolpinghuis Nijmegen [1989] 2 CMLR 18 ... 3.5.3
Case 102/86 Apple and Pear Development Council *v.* Customs and Excise [1988] 2 CMLR 394 ... 3.5.6
Case 120/86 Mulder *v.* Minister von Landbouw [1989] 2 CMLR 1 ... 3.5.7.3
Case 147/86 Commission *v.* Greece ... 6.1.2
Case 161/86 Binder *v.* Hauptzollamt Bad Reichenall ... 3.5.7.3
Case 179/86 Rhones-Poulenc SA *v.* Commission (Polypropylene, OJ 1986 L230/1, 18 August 1986; [1988] 4 CMLR 347; CCH 10, 782 ... 10.1.3.1, 10.1.3.1.2, 10.1.3.2.2, 10.1.3.2.4, 10.1.5.2
Case 198/86 Conradi *et al.* *v.* Direction de la Concurrences et des Prix des Hauts da la Seine *et al.* ... 6.1.2
Case 246/86 Belasco *v.* Commission, on appeal ... 10.1.3.2.2
Case 292/86 Gullung *v.* Conseil de l'Ordre des Avocats au Barreau de Colmar *et al.* [1988] 2 CMLR 57 ... 6.1
Case 302/86 Commission *v.* Denmark [1989] 1 CMLR 619 ... 17.7
Case 10/87 R. *v.* Commissioners for Customs and Excise, *ex p.* Tattersall Ltd. [1988] 3 CMLR 113 ... 3.4.6.6.9
Case 20/87 Ministère Public *v.* Gauchard ... 6.1.2, 8.2.2.1
Case 21/87 Borowitz *v.* Bundesversicherungsanstalt für Angestellte ... 3.5.5
Case 27/87 Erauw-Jacquery *v.* La Hesbignonne [1988] 4 CMLR 576 ... 10.1.7.3
Case 62/87 Executif Regional Wallon and Glaverbel SA *v.* Commission [1988] ECR 1573; [1989] 2 CMLR 771 ... 15.4.6.17
Case 72/87 *See* Case 62/87
Case 81/87 R. *v.* HM Treasury *et al.*, *ex p.* Daily Mail and General Trust Plc [1988] 3 CMLR 713 ... 6.1.2, 6.1.4
Case 102/87 France *v.* Commission [1988] ECR 4067 ... 15.4.4.3.5
Cases 142/87, 156/87 British American Tobacco *v.* EC Commission [1987] ECR 4487 ... 26.5.3.12.3
Case 187/87 Saarland and Others *v.* Ministry of Commerce and Others [1989] 1 CMLR 529 ... 17.7
Case 189/87 Kalfelis *v.* Schroder, Munchmeyer, Hengst & Co. ... 25.3.3.4, 25.3.3.10
Case 196/87 Steymann *v.* Staatssecretaris van Justitie ... 6.1.1, 8.2.2.1
Case 204/87 Bekaert *v.* Procureur de la Republique de Rennes ... 6.1.2
Case 238/87 AB Volvo *v.* Erik Veng [1989] 4 CMLR 122 ... 10.2.8.5.4
Cases 266/87, 267/87 R. *v.* Royal Pharmaceutical Society of Great Britain, *ex p.* Secretary of State for Social Services [1989] 2 CMLR 751 ... 3.5.5
Case 301/87 France *v.* Commission [1990] ECR 351 ... 15.4.4.3
Case 344/87 Bettray *v.* Staatsscretaris van Justitie [1991] 1 CMLR 459 ... 8.2.2.1
Case 355/87 Commission *v.* Council ... 14.2
Case 9/88 Da Veiga *v.* Staatssecretaris van Justitie [1991] 1 CMLR 217 ... 4.2.2.1
Case 33/88 Allue Coonan *v.* Università degli studi di Venezia ... 8.2.2.3.2
Case 39/88 Fishery Price Information (*Re*): Commission *v.* Ireland [1991] 2 CMLR 876 ... 3.4.6.6.2
Case 98/88 Hilti AG *v.* Commission ... 10.2.8.4
Case 327/88 Tetra Pak Rausing SDA *v.* Commission ... 10.2.14
Case 76/89 RTE *v.* Commission (Magill TV Guide/ITP, BBC and RTE, OJ 1989 L78/43 ... 10.2.8.4
Case 136/89 Hyundai Marine Co. Ltd ... 13.2.15
Case 48/89 Corsica Ferries France *v.* Direction Générale des Douanes Françaises [1991] 2 CMLR 227 (The French–Corsican case) ... 7.5.15

Case 213/89 R. *v*. Secretary of State for Transport, *ex p*. Factortame (No. 2) [1991] AC 6; [1990] 3 WLR 818; [1991] 1 All ER 70 .... 27.5
Case IV/30.373 Agreements on the Protection and Indemnity Clubs (*Re*) [1989] CMLR 178 ... 9.4
Case IV/32.328 London European Airways *v*. Sabena, OJ 1988 L317/47; [1989] 4 CMLR 662 .. 9.3.2, 9.4, 10.2.14, 12.6.3
Case IV/32.383 Sealink/SMZ, OJ No. C17/12, 89 .... 12.15.8
Case IV/32.385 Sealink B & I 12.15.6
Sealink/SCNF, OJ No. C17/8, 21 August 1989 .... 12.15.9
Cases IV/32.447, 32.448, 32.450 West and Central Africa cases 12.15.10
Case IV/33.045 RTM/P & O 3.4.2.3, 12.15.5
Case IV/33.509 (filed on 2 April 1990) Grimaldi–Cobelfret *v*. BEBFC 12.15.1
Case IV/33.677 Irish Club Rules 12.15.12

Table of Legislation, Etc.

All references are to paragraph number

ACP (Lomé Convention) 8.3.1
Accession Convention 1978 .... 25.1
  art. 3 .... 25.2.1
    5(4) 25.3.3.7, 25.3.3.8
    6 .... 25.3.3.14
  arts. 7, 8 .... 25.3.4
  art. 11 .... 25.3.7.1
    13(2) 25.4.2.2.5
    14 .... 25.4.2.2.8
Accession Convention 1982 .... 25.1
Accession Convention 1989
  art. 7 .... 25.3.7.1
    8 .... 25.3.9
    15 .... 25.3.1.3.1
    17 .... 25.5
  Annex 1(a)(2) 1st sub-para. 25.4.2.2.4
    1(d)(2) 2nd sub-para. 25.4.2.2.5
    (4) 25.4.2.2.8
Act of Accession 1972 .... 4.3.1.3, 4.3.4.2, 4.4.2.1, 4.4.2.4, 4.4.2.5, 4.4.3.1, 4.4.6.1
  Protocol No. 3, art. 2 .... 6.5
Act of Accession 1979 .... 4.4.2.5, 4.4.6.1
Act of Accession of Greece 1981 ..... 4.3.3.2.5, 4.3.4.2, 4.4.6.1, 4.4.7, 5.5.7
Act of Accession of Spain and Portugal 1986
  arts. 25, 155 and Protocol 2 .... 3.5.2.1.1
Act of the Council concerning direct elections to the European Parliament 3.5.2.1.3
Arrest Convention 1952 .... 25.1, 25.3.3.8, 25.3.3.14
Athens Convention on the Carriage of Passengers and their Luggage by Sea 1974 .... 25.3.3.14
Barcelona Convention for the Protection of the Mediterranean Sea 1976 ...... 1.3.10.3
Belgium—
  Civil Code, art. 15 .... 25.3.2.1
  Judicial Code, art. 638 .... 25.3.2.1
Benelux Union Treaty 1958 .... 26.5.1.4.1
British Navigation Acts 1651 .... 15.1
Bulk Chemical Code (A.212 (VIII)) 6.3.5.6
Bulk Gas Code (A.328 (IX)) 6.3.5.6
Chicago Convention 1944, arts. 1, 16 ... 4.3.3.1
Civil Jurisdiction and Judgments Act 1982 .... 25.1 *et seq.*
  s. 2 .... 25.1
  s. 26 .... 25.3.3.8
  ss. 41–46 .... 25.3.1.3.2
Commission of the European Communities (EC Commission)
  Commission Regulations—
    335/68 .... 4.3.4.1
    1016/68 .... 4.3.1.3
    2598/70 .... 4.4.3.2
    281/71 .... 4.3.4.2
    2116/78 .... 4.4.3.2
    4260/86 .... 9.5, 12.13.13, 12.14.1, 12.14.2
      art. 1 .... 12.14.3.1
        2 .... 12.13.1.4, 12.14.4.1, 12.14.4.2
        4 .... 12.14.5.1, 12.14.5.2
      Annex I 12.14.5.2
    2671/88 .... 4.3.3.2.12
    2672/88 .... 4.3.3.2.13
    2673/88 .... 4.3.3.2.14
    1855/89 .... 4.4.10
    82/91 .... 4.3.3.2.20
    83/91 .... 4.3.3.2.21
    84/91 .... 4.3.3.2.22
    2249/91 .... 4.4.10
Conventions—
  Convention Establishing a Common Customs Co-operation Council 1.3.16
  Convention for Safe Containers 1972 .... 1.3.3
  Convention for the Prevention of Marine Pollution by Dumping from Ships and Aircraft, etc. 1972 (Oslo) 17.4.8
  Convention for the Prevention of Marine Pollution from Land-based Sources 1975 (Paris) 17.4.5
  Convention for the Prevention of Pollution of the Sea by Oil 1954 .... 1.3.3, 1.3.3.2
  Convention for the Prevention of Pollution from Ships 1973. See under MARPOL.
  Convention for the Safety of Fishing Vessels 20.2.5
  Convention for the Safety of Life at Sea. See under SOLAS.
  Convention on Certain Institutions Common to the Three Communities 1957 .... 3.5.2.1.3
  Convention on Civil Liability for Oil Pollution Damage 1969 .... 17.3.2

Conventions—*cont.*
Convention on Jurisdiction and the Enforcement of Judgments in Civil and Commercial Matters 1968 ...... 1.4, 25.1 *et seq.*
art. 1 .... 25.2.1
(4) 25.2.1
2 .... 25.3.2.1
arts. 2–6 .... 25.3.3.14
art. 3 .... 25.3.2.1, 25.3.2.2
4 .... 25.3.5
5 .... 25.3.3.1, 25.3.3.2, 25.3.3.9
(1) 25.3.3.2, 25.3.7.1
(2) 25.3.3.3
(3) 25.3.3.4
(4) 25.3.3.5
(5) 25.3.3.6, 25.3.5
(6) 25.3.3.7
(7) 25.3.3.8
arts. 5–6A 25.3.3
5–18 .... 25.3.2.1
art. 5A 25.3.1.3.2
6 .... 25.3.3.1, 25.3.3.9
(1) 25.3.3.10
(2) 25.3.3.11
(3) 25.3.3.12
(4) 25.3.3.13
6A 25.3.3.14
7 .... 25.3.4
arts. 7–12A 25.3.4
art. 8 .... 25.3.1.3.2, 25.3.4
arts. 9, 10,11 .... 25.3.4
art. 12 .... 25.3.4, 25.3.7.1
(5) 25.3.4
12A 25.3.4
13 .... 25.3.1.3.2, 25.3.5, 25.3.7
14 .... 25.3.5, 25.3.7
15 .... 25.3.5, 25.3.7, 25.3.7.1
16 ... 25.3.1.2, 25.3.2.2, 25.3.6, 25.3.7, 25.3.7.1, 25.3.8
(2) 25.3.1.3.2, 25.3.6.3, 25.3.6.5
arts. 16–18 .... 25.3.3.14
art. 17 .... 25.3.1.2, 25.3.3.2, 25.3.3.14, 25.3.4, 25.3.6, 25.3.7, 25.3.7.1
18 .... 25.3.3.14, 25.3.7, 25.3.7.1, 25.3.7.2
arts. 19, 20 .... 25.3.8
art. 21 .... 25.3.3.4, 25.3.9
22 .... 25.3.3.4, 25.3.3.14, 25.3.9
23 .... 25.3.3.4, 25.3.9
24 .... 25.3.10
25 ...... 25.4.1.1, 25.4.2.2, 25.4.2.2.1, 25.4.2.2.2, 25.4.2.2.3, 25.4.2.2.4, 25.4.2.2.5
26 .... 25.4.2.1
arts. 26–30 .... 25.4.1
art. 27 .... 25.4.2.2, 25.4.3
28 ...... 25.3.2.2, 25.4.2.2, 25.4.2.2.6, 25.4.3
29 .... 25.4.2.2, 25.4.2.2.7
30 .... 25.4.2.2.8
31 .... 25.4.3

Conventions—*cont.*
Convention on Jurisdiction and the Enforcement of Judgments in Civil and Commercial Matters 1968—*cont.*
arts. 31–45 .... 25.4.1
art. 32(2) 25.4.3
arts. 32–35 .... 25.4.3.2
33–36 .... 25.4.3
art. 37(1) 25.4.3
arts. 38, 39 .... 25.4.3
40(2), 42 .... 25.4.3
art. 41 .... 25.4.3
43 .... 25.4.3.1
44 .... 25.4.3.2
45 .... 25.4.3.3
46 .... 25.4.3, 25.4.4
arts. 46–49 .... 25.4.1, 25.4.4
art. 47 .... 25.4.3, 25.4.4
arts. 48, 49 .... 25.4.4
art. 50 .... 25.4.5
51 .... 25.4.5.1
arts. 52, 53 .... 25.3.1.3.1, 25.3.1.3.2
art. 54A 25.5
55 .... 25.1
57 .... 25.3.3.14
60 .... 25.2.2
63 .... 25.1
Protocol 1968,
art. V 25.3.3.11
Vb 25.3.3.2
Protocol on Interpretation 1971 ...... 25.1, 25.2.1
Convention on Load Lines 1966 .... 1.3.3, 6.3.5.6, 17.5.1, 23.2.3, 23.2.4.2
Convention on Nomenclature for the Classification of Goods in Customs Tariffs 1.3.16
Convention on Standards of Training, Certification and Watchkeeping for Seafarers 1978 ..... 1.3.3, 8.3.1, 17.4.18, 17.5.1, 19.5.1, 19.5.3, 20.2.2, 23.2.3, 23.2.4.2
Convention on the Dumping of Wastes at Sea, etc. 1975 (London) 17.4.8
Convention on the International Maritime Satellite Organisation 1976
arts. 1(d), 3(1), 6 .... 1.3.11
art. 3(3) 1.3.11.1
Convention on the International Regulations for Preventing Collisions at Sea 1972 .... 1.3.3, 17.5.1, 23.2.3, 23.2.4.2
Convention on the Protection of the Marine Environment of the Baltic Sea area 6.3.5.8
Convention on the Valuation of Goods for Customs Purposes 1.3.16
Convention relating to Intervention on the High Seas in Cases of Oil Pollution Casualties 1969 .... 17.3.2
art. 1 .... 17.3.2

Conventions—*cont.*
Convention relating to the Limitation of Liability for Maritime Claims 1976 . . . . . 25.3.3.14
Convention relating to the Limitation of Liability of Owners of Sea-going Ships 1957 . . . . . 25.3.3.14
Council of Ministers of the European Communities—
Council Directives—
64/220 . . . . . 6.1.4
64/225 . . . . . 26.5.3.10.6
69/262 (1st Shipbuilding Directive) . 18.10.1
71/304, 71/305, 71/306 . . . . . 26.5.3.1
72/273 (2nd Shipbuilding Directive) 18.10.2, 18.10.2.1, 18.10.3.1
73/148 . . . . . 6.1.4
73/240 . . . . . 26.5.3.10.3
74/49 . . . . . 4.3.1.2
74/59 . . . . . 18.10.3.1
74/562 . . . . . 6.1.4
74/643 . . . . . 18.10.2
75/432 (3rd Shipbuilding Directive) . . . 18.1, 18.10, 18.10.3, 18.10.3.1, 18.10.3.2, 18.10.3.3, 18.10.3.4
76/464 . . . . . 17.2.1, 17.4.7, 17.5.9
77/62 . . . . . 26.5.3.1
77/158 . . . . . 4.3.1.2
77/388 (VAT Directive) 3.5.2.2.2
78/175 . . . . . 4.3.1.2
78/176 . . . . . 17.4.17
78/338 (4th Shipbuilding Directive) . . . 18.10.4.1, 18.10.4.4, 18.10.4.5, 18.10.4.6, 18.10.4.7, 18.10.4.8, 18.10.4.9, 18.10.4.10, 18.10.4.11, 18.10.4.12, 18.10.4.13, 18.10.4.14, 18.10.4.15, 18.10.4.16, 18.10.5.5
78/546 . . . . . 4.3.1.11
78/660 . . . . . 26.5.3.6.7
79/115 . . . . . 5.5.20, 22.2.1 *et seq.*, 20.2.3, App. 2.7
79/116 . . . . . 5.5.20, 20.2.4, 20.2.6, App. 2.8
79/279 . . . . . 26.5.3.11
79/1034 . . . . . App. 2.10
80/49 . . . . . 4.3.1.2
80/51 . . . . . 4.3.3.2.2
80/390 . . . . . 26.5.3.11
80/737 . . . . . 4.4.5
80/767 . . . . . 26.5.3.1
80/1266 . . . . . 4.3.3.2.3
81/363 (5th Shipbuilding Directive) 18.4, 18.10.5.1, 18.10.5.2, 18.10.5.3, 18.10.5.4, 18.10.5.5, 18.10.5.6, 18.10.5.7, 18.10.5.8, 18.10.5.9, 18.10.5.10, 18.10.5.11, 18.10.5.12, 18.10.5.13, 18.10.5.14, 18.10.5.15, 18.10.5.16, 18.10.5.17, 18.10.5.18
82/50 . . . . . 4.3.1.2
82/121 . . . . . 26.5.3.11

Council of Ministers of the European Communities—*cont.*
Council Directives—*cont.*
82/880 . . . . . 18.10.5.2
83/206 . . . . . 4.3.3.2.2
83/349 . . . . . 26.5.3.6.7
83/416 . . . . . 4.3.3.1, 4.3.3.2.5, 4.3.3.2.6
83/418 . . . . . 4.3.2.8
83/463 . . . . . 4.3.1.14
83/572 . . . . . 4.3.1.2
83/643 . . . . . 4.4.4
84/647 . . . . . 4.3.1.2, 4.3.1.15
85/2 . . . . . 18.10.5.2
85/384 . . . . . 6.1.4
85/611 . . . . . 26.5.3.11
86/216 . . . . . 4.3.3.2.5, 4.3.3.2.6
87/53 . . . . . 4.3.1.14, 4.4.4
87/167 (6th Shipbuilding Directive) . . . 18.10.6, 18.10.6.1, 18.10.6.1.1, 18.10.6.2, 18.10.6.3, 18.10.7.1, 18.10.7.5
87/467 . . . . . 8.4.2
87/540 . . . . . 6.1.4, 8.3.1.2.1
87/601 . . . . . 4.3.3.1, 4.3.3.2.7, 4.3.3.2.17
87/602 . . . . . 4.3.3.1, 4.3.3.2.8
87/1544 . . . . . 4.3.1.16
88/295 . . . . . 26.5.3.1, 26.5.3.2
88/357 . . . . . 7.6.1, 26.5.3.10.4
88/361 . . . . . 26.5.2.6
88/627 . . . . . 26.5.3.11
89/48 . . . . . 6.1.5, 26.5.2.4
89/298 . . . . . 26.5.3.11
89/299 . . . . . 26.5.3.7.3
89/440 . . . . . 26.5.3.13
89/458 . . . . . 26.5.3.13
89/463 . . . . . 4.3.3.2.5
89/592 . . . . . 26.5.3.11
89/646 . . . . . 7.6.1, 26.5.3.7.2
89/647 . . . . . 26.5.3.8
89/665 . . . . . 26.5.3.1, 26.5.3.5
89/666 . . . . . 26.5.3.6.6
90/684 (7th Shipbuilding Directive) . . . 18.1, 18.10, 18.10.6.4, 18.10.7, 18.10.7.1, 18.10.7.1.1, 18.10.7.1.4, 18.10.7.2, 18.10.7.3, 18.10.7.4, 18.10.7.5, 18.10.7.6, 18.10.7.7, 18.10.7.8, 18.10.7.9, 18.10.7.10, 18.10.7.11.1, 18.10.7.11.2, 18.10.7.11.3, 18.10.7.12, 18.10.7.13, 18.10.7.14, 18.10.7.14.1, 18.10.7.15, 18.10.7.15.1, 18.10.7.15.2, 18.10.7.15.3, 18.10.7.16, 18.10.7.17
92/29 . . . . . 20.2.11 *et seq.*
12th Company Law Directive 26.5.3.6.5
Council Directive on the Minimum Safety and Health Requirements for Improved Medical Treatment on board Vessels (92/29) . . . . . 20.2.11 *et seq.*

Council of Ministers of the European Communities—*cont.*
Council Regulation applying the Principle of Freedom to Provide Services to Maritime Transport within Member States (Proposed) .... 5.5.26.4, 7.6.6.5 *et seq.*
Council Regulation concerning the Elimination of Controls and Formalities applicable to the Cabin and Checked Baggage of Passengers taking an intra-Community flight and the Baggage of Passengers making an intra-Community Sea Crossing (Proposed) .... 24.1 *et seq.*
Council Regulation establishing a Community Ship Register and Providing for the Flying of the Community Flag by Sea-going Vessels (Proposed) . 5.5.26.1, 6.3.4 *et seq.*, App. 2.26
Council Regulation laying down detailed Rules for the Application of Arts. 85 and 86 of the Treaty to Maritime Transport (Proposed) 9.3.8
Council Regulation on the Transfer of Ships from one Register to another within the Community ... 5.5.26.5, 6.3.5 *et seq.*, App. 2.30
Council Regulation Providing for a Common Definition of a Community Shipowner (Proposed) 5.5.26.3, 6.4
Council Regulation to Grant a Block Exemption for Consortia (Proposed) .... 5.5.29, 16.4 *et seq.*
Council Regulations—
11/60 .... 4.2.2.9.2, 4.4.2.1
17/62 ... 4.3.3.1, 4.4.2.2, 5.3.4, 9.3.1, 9.3.2, 9.4, 10.3.1, 10.3.10.2, 12.2.1, 12.2.5, 12.13, 16.5, 16.6.1, 16.6.2, 16.6.3, 16.6.4
art. 6 .... 10.3.9.3, 16.6.1, 16.6.7
8 .... 16.6.7
9(1) 10.1.9.4
10(3) 16.6.6
11 .... 10.3.8.2
15(6) 10.3.4
27/62 .... 10.3.10.2
141/62 .... 4.3.3.1, 4.4.2.2, 5.3.4, 5.4.8, 9.3.2., 10.3.10.2, 12.2.1, 12.2.5
art. 1 .... 9.3.2
165/65 .... 4.4.2.2
117/66 .... 4.3.1.3a
67/67 .... 10.1.9.5.2
1002/67 .... 4.4.2.2
1017/68 ..... 4.4.2.5, 4.4.2.6, 4.4.2.7, 5.3.4, 9.3.3, 9.4, 12.2.5, 12.8.5.4, 12.13, 16.5, 16.6.1, 16.6.2, 16.6.3, 16.6.4
art. 3 .... 12.7.2
11(4) 16.6.1, 16.6.7
13 .... 16.6.7
16(3) 16.6.6

Council of Ministers of the European Communities—*cont.*
Council Regulations—*cont.*
1018/68 .... 4.3.1.4
1612/68 .... 4.2.2.14.2, 5.4.8
543/69 .... 4.3.1.5
1191/69 .... 4.2.2.7.2, 4.4.6.1
1192/69 .... 4.3.2.2
1629/69 .... 4.4.2.5, 4.4.2.6, 9.3.3
1630/69 .... 4.4.2.5, 4.4.2.7, 9.3.3
1107/70 .... 4.2.2.7.2, 4.4.2.4, 15.4.8.1
1108/70 .... 4.3.4.2, 4.4.3.2
2598/70, 281/71 .... 4.4.3.2
1408/71 .... 8.2.2.1
516/72 .... 4.3.1.6
517/72 .... 4.3.1.7
2442/72 .... 4.3.1.6, 4.3.1.7
2988/74 .... 4.4.2.8
724/75 .... 18.9.8
1473/75 .... 4.2.2.7.2, 4.4.2.4
3237/76 .... 4.3.1.9, 4.3.1.13
2830/77 .... 4.3.2.5
1301/78 .... 4.3.1.7
2116/78 .... 4.4.3.2
2183/78 .... 4.3.2.6
2778/78 .... 4.3.1.6
954/79 ...... 5.4.20, 5.5.19.3, 5.5.20, 7.5.8, 11.3.1, 11.3.2.1, 11.3.3.1, 11.3.4, 11.3.4.3, 11.3.5, 12.2.1, 12.2.5, 19.8.1.2, App. 2.9
art. 1 .... 11.3.5
2 .... 11.3.5.1
3 .... 11.3.5.2
4 .... 11.3.5.3
5 .... 11.3.5.4
Annex I 11.3.5.5
1384/79 .... 4.4.3.2
2617/80 ...... 18.9.1, 18.9.6, 18.9.7, 18.9.8
3020/81 .... 4.3.1.9, 4.3.1.13
3021/81 .... 4.4.3.2
1658/82 .... 4.2.2.7.2, 4.4.2.4
3600/82 .... 4.4.3.4
1787/84 .... 18.9.1, 18.9.2, 18.9.7
2176/84 .... 13.2.2
3626/84 .... 4.2.2.9.2, 4.4.2.1
7 May 1985 .... 6.3.5.2
418/85 .... 10.1.9.5.1
2137/85 .... 26.5.3.6.4
3634/85 .... 18.9.8
3690/86 .... 4.3.1.13, 4.3.1.16
4055/86 . 3.5.2.2.1, 5.5.20, 5.5.20.1, 6.2.1.3, 7.5 *et seq.*, 7.6.1, 7.6.6.3, 9.3.8, 14.15, 19.1, 24.3.1, App. 2.21
art. 1 .... 7.5.7, 7.5.7.1, 7.5.9, 7.5.10, 7.6.6.3
2 .... 7.5.7.1
arts. 3, 4 .... 7.5.8
5, 6 .... 7.5.9
art. 7 .... 7.5.7, 7.5.11
8 .... 7.5.12
9 .... 7.5.10
10 .... 7.5.6

Council of Ministers of the European Communities—*cont.*
Council Regulations—*cont.*
4055/86—*cont.*
art. 11 .... 7.5.13
12 .... 7.5.4, 7.5.5,
4056/86 ..... 3.2.4, 3.5.2.2.1, 5.3.4, 5.5.20, 5.5.20.2, 5.5.20.3, 7.5.9, 7.6.6.3, 9.3.8, 9.4, 9.5, 10.3, 11.2.8.4, 11.2.8.6, 11.3.1, 12.1 *et seq.*, 13.2.7, 14.15, 16.2, 16.3, 16.4.2, 16.5, 16.6.1, 16.6.2, 16.6.3, 16.6.4, App. 2.22
art. 1 .... 12.6.1, 12.6.10
(2) 12.6.3, 12.6.4, 12.6.6
(3)(a) 12.6.6
(b) 12.6.9, 12.8.2, 12.8.3, 12.9.3
(c) 12.6.7
arts. 1–9 .... 12.1
art. 2 .... 12.6.8, 12.7.1, 12.7.2.4, 12.7.2.5, 12.7.2.6, 16.2, 16.3, 16.4.2
(1) 12.7.2
(c) 12.7.2.3
(2) 12.7.2
3 ..... 12.8.1, 12.8.3, 12.8.4, 12.8.5, 12.8.6.1, 12.8.6.2, 12.8.6.3, 12.8.6.8, 12.10.2, 12.10.3, 12.11.1, 12.11.3, 12.13.3.1, 12.13.3.3, 16.2, 16.3
4 ..... 12.8.1, 12.8.3, 12.8.4, 12.8.5, 12.8.5.1, 12.8.5.4, 12.8.5.5, 12.14.3.1, 12.15.1
5 .... 12.8.1, 12.8.5.3, 12.8.6.1, 12.8.6.2, 12.8.6.3, 12.8.6.5, 12.8.6.7, 12.8.6.8, 12.10.1, 12.10.2, 12.10.3, 12.13.9.1.1, 12.13.9.1.2
(1) 12.8.6.4, 12.9.1, 12.9.2
(2) 12.8.6.5, 12.9.1, 12.9.2, 12.14.3.1
(3) 12.8.6.6, 12.14.3.1
(5) 12.13.9.1.1, 12.13.9.1.2, 12.13.13, 12.14.2
6 .... 12.8.5, 12.8.5.1, 12.9.1, 12.9.2, 12.10.2, 12.10.3
7 .... 12.10.1, 12.10.2, 12.10.3, 12.13.1.1, 12.13.1.2, 12.13.2.2, 12.13.2.3, 12.13.5.1, 12.13.5.2, 12.13.9.1.1, 12.13.9.1.2, 12.13.9.2.1, 12.13.9.2.2, 12.15.1
(1) 12.10.1, 12.10.3
(2) 12.10.1, 12.10.3
(c) 12.10.3
8 .... 12.11.1, 12.11.2, 12.15.1
(1) 12.11.3
(2) 12.11.1, 12.11.3
(3) 12.11.3
9 .... 12.4, 12.12.1, 12.12.2
(1)(2)(3) 12.12.2

Council of Ministers of the European Communities—*cont.*
Council Regulations—*cont.*
4056/86—*cont.*
art. 10 .... 12.11.1, 12.11.2, 12.11.3, 12.13.1, 12.13.1.1, 12.13.1.2, 12.13.1.3, 12.13.3.2, 12.13.3.3, 12.13.6.2, 12.13.6.3, 12.13.13, 12.14.2, 12.14.4.2, 12.15.1, 12.15.4, 12.15.10
11 ... 12.13.2.1, 12.13.2.2, 12.13.2.3, 12.13,9.2.1, 12.13.9.2.2, 12.13.10.2, 12.13.10.3, 12.13.12
(1)(2)(3) 12.13.2.3
(4) 12.10.2, 12.10.3, 12.13.2.3, 12.13.3.3, 12.13.4.1, 12.13.4.2, 12.15.2, 12.15.3, 12.15.11, 16.6.1
12 ... 12.13.3.1, 12.13.3.2, 12.13.3.3, 12.13.9.1.1, 12.13.9.1.2, 12.13.13, 12.14.2, 12.14.5.2, 12.15.2, 12.15.3, 12.15.6, 12.15.8, 12.15.9, 12.15.11
(1)–(4) 12.13.3.3
(3) 12.13.3.3, 12.13.5.1, 12.13.5.2, 12.13.6.2, 12.13.6.3, 12.13.10.2, 12.13.10.3, 12.13.12
(4) 12.13.3.3, 12.13.4.1, 12.13.4.2, 12.13.6.2, 12.13.6.3, 12.13.10.2, 12.13.10.3, 12.13.12
13 ...... 12.13.4.1, 12.13.4.2, 16.6.7
(1) 12.13.9.1.1, 12.13.9.1.2
(1)–(3) 12.13.3.3
(2) 12.13.4.3
(3) 12.13.4.5, 12.13.4.6, 12.13.4.7, 12.13.9.2.1, 12.13.9.2.2, 12.13.10.2, 12.13.10.3, 12.13.12
14 .... 12.13.5.1, 12.13.5.2
15 .... 12.12.1, 12.12.2, 12.13.6, 12.13.6.1, 12.13.6.2, 12.13.6.3
(1) 12.13.6.3
(2) 12.13.3.2, 12.13.3.3, 12.13.6.3
(3) 16.6.6
(3)(4) 12.13.9.1.1, 12.13.9.1.2, 12.13.9.2.2
(3)–(6) 12.13.6.3
16 ... 12.13.7.1, 12.13.7.2, 12.13.7.3, 12.13.8.1
(2)–(6) 12.13.7.3
(3) 12.15.4, 12.15.10
(3)(5) 12.13.9.1.1, 12.13.9.1.2
(5) 12.13.9.1.2, 12.13.9.2.1, 12.13.9.2.2
17 .... 12.13.8.3.2, 12.13.8.4, 12.13.9.1.1, 12.13.9.1.2
(1)(2) 12.13.8.3.1
18 .... 12.13.8.2.1, 12.13.8.4, 12.13.9.1.1, 12.13.9.1.2
(1) 12.13.8.2.2, 12.13.8.3.1, 12.13.8.3.2
(2) .... 12.13.8.2.2.

Council of Ministers of the European Communities—*cont.*
Council Regulations—*cont.*
4056/86—*cont.*
art. 18(3) 12.13.8.3.1, 12.13.8.2.2, 12.13.8.3.2, 12.13.9.1.1, 12.13.9.1.2, 12.13.9.2.1, 12.13.9.2.2, 12.15.10
(4)(6) 12.13.8.2.2
19 .... 12.13.9.1.1, 12.13.9.1.2, 12.13.10.2, 12.13.10.3
(1) 12.13.9.1.2
(a) 12.13.9.1.2
(b) 12.13.7.2, 12.13.7.3
(c) 12.13.8.2.1, 12.13.8.2.2
(2)(3)(4) 12.13.9.1.2
20 .... 12.13.9.2.1, 12.13.9.2.2, 12.13.10.2, 12.13.10.3
(1) 12.13.9.2.2
(a) 12.13.9.2.2
(c) 12.13.7.2, 12.13.7.3, 12.13.9.2.2
(d) 12.13.8.2.1, 12.13.8.2.2, 12.13.9.2.2
(2)(3) 12.13.9.2.2
21 .... 12.13.11.1, 12.13.11.2, 12.13.11.3
22 .... 12.13.9.1.2, 12.13.9.2.2
23 .... 12.13.8.4, 12.13.10.2
(1) 12.14.6.1.1
(1)(2) 12.13.10.3, 12.13.13, 12.14.2
(3) 12.13.10.3
24(1)–(3) 12.13.8.4
25 .... 12.13.8.4
(1)(2) 12.13.2.3, 12.13.3.3, 12.13.4.7, 12.13.12
26 .... 12.13.6.2, 12.13.6.3, 12.13.13, 12.14.2
27 .... 12.3, 12.5
Section I, art 7 .... 12.13
II 12.10.2, 12.10.3, 12.13
4057/86 .... 3.5.2.2.1, 5.5.20, 5.5.20.2, 7.6.6.3, 13.1 *et seq.*, App. 2.23
Preamble 13.2.2
Recital 13.2.10.1
1, 3, 4 .... 13.2.3
3, 12 .... 13.2.7
5 .... 13.2.6, 13.2.8.4
6 .... 13.2.8.2
art. 1 .... 13.1, 13.2.6
2(2) 13.2.13.4.1
3(a)(d) 13.2.8.7
(b) 13.2.8.2
4(2) 13.2.8.5
5 .... 13.2.12.2
(1) 13.2.10.2, 13.2.10.3
(c) 13.2.12.2
(2) 13.2.11
(a)(b) 13.2.12.2
(2)(5) 13.2.10.4
(3) 13.2.10.5
(a) 13.2.12.2

Council of Ministers of the European Communities—*cont.*
Council Regulations—*cont.*
4057/86—*cont.*
art. 5(4) 13.2.10.7
(6) 13.2.10.2
6(1)–(4) 13.2.11
7(1) 13.2.11
(a) 13.2.12.1
9(1) 13.2.13.2
art. 10(1) 13.2.13.3.1
12 .... 13.2.8.6, 13.2.13.4.1
15(2) 13.2.13.7.2
16 .... 13.2.13.7.5
4058/86 .... 3.5.2.2.1, 5.5.20, 5.5.20.2, 5.5.20.3, 7.5.2, 7.6.6.3, 14.1 *et seq.*, App. 2.24
Recitals 14.6
art. 1 .... 14.8
2 .... 14.7
3 .... 14.9.1, 14.9.2, 14.11
4 .... 14.9.2, 14.10.2
(1)(b) 14.11
5 .... 14.11
6(1) 14.12.1, 14.12.2
(2) 14.12.2
(3) 14.12.3
7 .... 14.13
8 .... 14.14.2
9 .... 14.5
4059/86 .... 4.4.3.5
1544/87 .... 4.3.1.13
3975/87 .... 4.3.3.2.10, 4.3.3.2.15, 9.4, 12.13
3976/87 .... 4.3.3.2.11
4070/87 .... 4.4.3.4
1841/88 .... 4.3.1.16, 26.5.1.3.3
1969/88 .... 26.5.2.7
2423/88 .... 13.2.4
2506/88 .... 18.9.1
art. 1 .... 18.9.2
2 .... 18.9.3
3 .... 18.9.4
(1) 18.9.4, 18.9.12.4.1, 18.9.12.5.1, 18.9.12.5.2
(a) 18.9.4
(2)(3) 18.9.4, 18.9.5, 18.9.10
4 .... 18.9.6, 18.9.7, 18.9.9
5 .... 18.9.7
6 .... 18.9.8
(2) 18.9.9
7 .... 18.9.10
(2) 18.9.11
8 .... 18.9.7
9 .... 18.9.2
4260/88 .... 12.14.1, 12.14.4.1, 12.14.5.1, App. 2.25
5 .... 12.14.6.1.1
6 .... 12.14.6.1.2
Section I 12.14.1
II 12.14.6
4261/88 .... 4.3.3.2.10, 4.3.3.2.15

Council of Ministers of the European Communities—*cont.*
Council Regulations—*cont.*
4283/88 . . . . . 26.5.1.3.9
15/89
paras. 10, 12 . . . . . 13.2.15
1101/89 . . . . . 4.3.4.3
1102/89 . . . . . 4.3.4.3
1106/89 . . . . . 4.2.2.7.2, 4.4.2.4
2299/89 . . . . . 4.3.3.2.16
4059/89 . . . . . 26.5.1.3.4
4060/89 . . . . . 4.3.1.17
4064/89 . . . . . 10.1.5.1, 10.1.7.6, 16.2, 26.5.3.6.2, 26.5.3.12.3
art. 22(2) 16.2
1210/90 . . . . . 17.6.2
2342/90 . . . . . 4.3.3.1, 4.3.3.2.17
2343/90 . . . . . 4.3.3.1, 4.3.3.2.18, 4.3.3.2.19
2367/90 . . . . . 3.4.2.3
3359/90 . . . . . 4.4.3.6
259/91 . . . . . 4.3.3.2.23
479/92 . . . . . App. 2.31
Council Resolutions—
7 December 1970 . . . . . 4.3.2.3
26 June 1978 . . . . 17.4.14, 17.4.15, App. 2.3
17 May 1977 . . . . . 17.4.11
27 September 1978 . . . . . 18.4, 18.5
26 March 1981 . . . . . 5.5.8
15 December 1981 . . . . . 5.5.5
19 June 1990 (Ferry Safety) . . . . . 5.5.28, 20.2.10, App. 2.29
19 June 1990 (Marine Pollution) . . . . 17.4.6, 17.4.6.1, App. 2.28
Denmark—
Law on Civil Procedure
art. 246(2)(3) 25.3.2.1
arts. 653–656 . . . . . 25.5
Seamen's Law No. 420 of 18 June 1973 . . . . . 25.3.3.2
EAEC (European Atomic Energy Community) (Euratom) Treaty
art. 1 . . . . . 3.2.3
3 . . . . . 3.4.3.1
101 . . . . . 19.2.2.2
109 . . . . . 3.4.5.10
111 . . . . . 3.4.5.3, 3.4.5.6
arts. 118, 120 . . . . . 3.4.3.4
art. 136 . . . . . 3.4.6.2
arts. 161–163 . . . . . 3.5.2.2.1, 3.5.2.2.2
art. 208 . . . . . 3.3.9, 3.5.2.1.1
ECSC (European Coal and Steel Community) Treaty 1951
arts. 2, 3, 18, 24 . . . . . 3.2.2
art. 4 . . . . . 4.2.1.2
6 . . . . . 19.2.2.1
7 . . . . . 3.4.3.1
22 . . . . . 3.4.5.10
23 . . . . . 3.4.5.3, 3.4.5.6
28 . . . . . 3.4.3.4
31 . . . . . 3.4.6.2
arts. 58, 59, 64 . . . . . 10.2.8.2
art. 66(7) 10.2.8.2

ECSC (European Coal and Steel Community) Treaty 1951—*cont.*
art. 70 . . . . . 4.2.1.1, 4.2.1.2.2, 4.2.1.3
97 . . . . . 3.3.9, 3.5.2.1.1
EEC Treaty (Treaty of Rome) 1957 . . . . App. 1
art. 1 . . . . . 3.2.4
2 . . . . . 3.2.4, 4.2.2.2.1, 4.2.2.14.2, 10.2.4, 17.2.1, 26.1.4
3 . . . 4.2.2.1, 4.2.2.2, 4.2.2.2.1, 4.2.2.14.2
(c) 4.1.2, 8.2.1
(f) 10.2.4, 10.2.7
4 . . . . . 3.4.1, 3.4.3.1
(2) 3.4.7.1
(3) 3.4.1
5 . . . . . 4.2.2.9.2, 10.2.7
arts. 5(2), 6(1) 3.2.4
art. 7 . . . 1.2.2, 2.3.5.5, 3.5.6, 3.5.7.1, 4.2.2.1, 6.3.1, 6.3.2.1, 7.5.10, 7.6.4.2, 8.2.2.3, 8.2.5, 11.3.2, 11.3.2.1, 11.3.4.2.1, 12.13.9.2.1, 24.6, 26.5.1.4.1
(1) 3.1
8 . . . . . 3.3.14, 12.2.5
8a (as inserted by art. 13 of the Single European Act 1986) 11.1.5, 24.5.2, 26.2, 26.4.2
arts. 9(1), 10, 12–29 . . . . . 3.3.14
art. 12 . . . . . 4.2.2.6.2
26 . . . . . 3.4.6.6.10
arts. 30–34 . . . . . 3.5.5
art. 38(2) 4.2.2.14.2
39(2) 6.1.4
48 . . . . . 4.2.2.1, 4.2.2.14.2, 5.4.8, 8.2.2.1, 8.2.2.2
(2) 8.2.2.3
(4) 3.5.7.1, 8.2.2.3.1, 8.2.2.3.2
arts. 48–51 . 4.2.2.14.2, 6.3.2.1, 6.3.2.2, 8.2.1, 8.2.2
art. 49 . . . . . 8.2.2.4
52 . . . . . 6.1.2, 11.3.2.1
arts. 52–58 . . 6.1, 6.1.2, 6.3.2.1, 6.3.2.2, 8.2.1
art. 53 . . . . . 4.2.2.6.2, 6.1.3, 11.3.2.1
54 . . . . . 6.1.4
arts. 55–62 . . . . . 7.6.6.5.1
art. 56 . . . . . 6.1.6.1, 6.1.6.2, 6.1.6.3, 6.1.6.4
57 . . . . . 6.1.5
58 . . . . . 6.1.2, 6.1.4
59 . . . . . 4.2.2.4.2
arts. 59–66 . . . . . 8.2.1
art. 61 . . 4.2.2.1, 4.2.2.3, 4.2.2.3.1, 4.2.2.4.2, 7.6.6.5.1
(1) 4.2.2.1, 4.2.2.3.2, 4.2.2.14.2
arts. 67–73 . . . . . 6.3.2.1, 6.3.2.2
art. 74 . . . . . 4.2.2.4, 4.2.2.4.1, 4.2.2.4.2, 4.2.2.6.2, 4.2.2.14.2
arts. 74–83 . . . . . 5.3.2
74–84 . . . . . 1.2.2, 4.2.1.3.2, 4.2.2.1
art. 75 . . . . . 4.2.2.5, 4.2.2.5.1, 4.2.2.5.2
(1)(a)–(c) 4.2.2.5.2
(1)(3) 4.2.2.14.2
76 . . . . . 4.2.2.4.2, 4.2.2.6, 4.2.2.6.1, 4.2.2.6.2
77 . . . 4.2.2.7, 4.2.2.7.1, 4.2.2.7.2, 4.4.6.1

EEC Treaty (Treaty of Rome) 1957—*cont.*
art. 78 .... 4.2.2.8, 4.2.2.8.1, 4.2.2.8.2
79 .... 4.2.2.9, 4.2.2.9.1, 4.2.2.9.2
(1) 12.8.5.4
(3) 4.2.2.9.2, 4.4.2.1
80 .... 4.2.2.10, 4.2.2.10.1, 4.2.2.10.2
(2) 4.2.2.10.2
81 .... 4.2.2.11, 4.2.2.11.1, 4.2.2.11.2
82 .... 4.2.2.12, 4.2.2.12.1, 4.2.2.12.2
83 .. 4.2.2.13, 4.2.2.13.1, 4.2.2.13.2, 4.4.1
84 .... 4.2.2.1, 4.2.2.14, 4.2.2.14.1, 4.2.2.14.2, 5.2
(1)(2) 4.2.2.4.2, 4.2.2.14.2
(2) 4.2.2.14.2, 5.4.2, 5.4.6, 5.4.8, 5.5.21, 6.3.4.3, 6.3.5.5, 7.6.6.2, 9.3.5, 12.2.3, 12.4, 12.12.1, 12.12.2, 13.2.2, 14.3, 14.9.2, 19.3.4, 19.4.1.2, 19.4.1.5.1, 19.4.1.6, 19.4.1.7, 19.4.2.2, 19.4.11.2, 19.6.1.2, 21.3.2, 22.2.2
85 ... 1.2.2, 5.3.4, 5.4.8, 5.5.14, 5.5.19.4, 5.5.20.2, 7.6.6.3, 9.3, 9.3.1, 9.3.5, 9.3.8, 9.4, 9.5, 10.1 *et seq.*, 11.3.2.1, 12.1 *et seq.*
(1) 5.5.20.3, 10.1.7, 10.1.7.1, 10.1.7.2, 10.1.7.8, 12.7.2, 12.8.3, 12.9.1, 12.9.2, 12.13.1.1, 12.13.1.2, 12.13.2.2, 12.13.2.3, 12.13.3.2, 12.13.3.3, 12.13.5.1, 12.13.5.2, 12.13.9.1.1, 12.13.9.1.2, 12.13.9.2.1, 12.13.9.2.2, 16.4.2, 16.6.1, 16.6.4
(2) 12.8.4, 12.8.5.1, 12.13.4.2, 12.13.4.4, 12.13.4.5, 12.13.4.6, 16.2
(3) .. 4.3.3.2.11, 4.3.3.2.12, 4.3.3.2.13, 4.3.3.2.14, 5.5.19.3, 10.1.7.8, 12.2.5, 12.6.6, 12.7.1, 12.10.1, 12.10.2, 12.10.3, 12.13.2.2, 12.13.2.3, 12.13.3.2, 12.13.3.3, 12.13.4.2, 12.13.4.3, 12.13.5.1, 12.13.5.2, 12.13.9.1.1, 12.13.9.1.2, 12.13.10.2, 12.13.10.3, 12.15.2, 12.15.6, 12.15.8, 12.15.9, 12.15.12, 16.4.1, 16.5, 16.6.1, 16.6.4, 16.6.7
(b) 12.10.2, 12.10.3
arts. 85, 86 ... 1.4, 3.5.5, 5.3.4, 5.4.8, 5.5.14, 5.5.19.4, 5.5.20.2, 7.6.6.3, 9.3, 9.3.1, 9.3.8, 9.4, 9.5, 11.3.2.1, 12.1 *et seq.*
85–92 .... 11.3.2, 11.3.4.2.1
85–94 .... 5.3.4, 9.3.5, 24.6
art. 86 .... 5.3.4, 5.4.8, 5.5.14, 5.5.19.4, 5.5.20.2, 7.6.6.3, 9.3, 9.3.1, 9.3.2, 9.3.5, 9.3.8, 9.4, 9.5, 10.1.3.1.1, 10.2 *et seq.*, 12.1 *et seq.*, 16.6.1, 16.6.7
87 ...... 3.4.3.3, 9.3.1, 10.3.10.2, 12.2.3, 12.2.4, 12.4

EEC Treaty (Treaty of Rome) 1957—*cont.*
art. 88 .... 9.3.1, 9.3.8
89 .... 3.4.2.3, 9.3.1, 9.3.8, 12.13.1.3
90(1) 24.6
(2) 10.2.7, 10.2.11.2.1
(3) 24.6
92 .... 4.2.2.7.2, 5.5.19.3, 15.4.2, 15.4.3, 15.4.4.2, 15.4.4.3, 15.4.4.3.2, 15.4.4.3.3, 15.4.4.3.5, 15.4.4.3.6, 15.4.4.3.7, 15.4.7.1, 15.4.7.3, 15.4.7.4, 15.4.8.2, 15.4.9, 18.7, 18.10.3.2, 18.10.4.9, 18.10.4.11, 18.10.5.11, 18.10.5.13, 23.1
92(1) . 15.4.2, 15.4.4, 15.4.4.1, 15.4.4.3.1, 15.4.4.3.7
(2) .. 15.4.2, 15.4.5, 15.4.5.1, 15.4.5.2, 15.4.5.3, 15.4.9
(a) 15.4.5.4
(b) 15.4.5.5
(c) 15.4.5.6
(3) .. 15.4.2, 15.4.6, 15.4.6.1, 15.4.6.2, 15.4.6.3
(a) 15.4.6.4
(b) 15.4.6.5, 15.4.6.6, 15.4.6.17
(c) 15.4.3.1, 15.4.6.7, 15.4.6.16
(d) .. 15.4.6.23, 18.10.4.2, 18.10.5.3, 18.10.7.3
art. 93 ..... 5.5.19.3, 15.4.2, 15.4.3, 15.4.4.3, 15.4.7, 15.4.7.1, 15.4.8.2, 18.7, 18.10.3.2, 18.10.4.9, 18.10.4.11, 18.10.5.11, 18.10.5.13, 23.1
(1) 15.4.7.3
(3) 15.4.7.4, 15.4.7.5, 15.4.8.2, 15.4.9
94 .... 4.2.2.7.2, 15.4.2, 15.4.4.3, 15.4.4.3.7, 15.4.7.3, 15.4.8, 15.4.8.1, 15.4.8.2, 18.7
100 .... 17.2.1, 24.5.3
100A (as inserted by the Single European Act 1986) 3.4.3.4
100(3) 6.3.5.12.1
101 .... 19.2.2.3
110 .... 19.2.2.3
113 .... 5.4.2, 5.4.8, 18.10.4.2, 18.10.5.3, 18.10.7.3, 19.2.1, 19.2.2.3
114 .... 19.2.1
116 .... 5.4.2, 5.4.8
117 .... 8.2.3
118A 20.2.8.2
119 .... 8.2.4
arts. 129, 130 .... 3.4.7.2
art. 130R 6.3.5.12.1, 17.5.6
130T 17.5.6
arts. 137–144 (as amended) 3.4.5.3
art. 139 .... 3.4.5.10
140 .... 3.4.5.3, 3.4.5.6, 3.4.5.10
arts. 141, 142, 144, 145–154 (as amended) 3.4.3.1, 3.4.3.3
art. 146 .... 3.4.2.3, 3.4.3.4
148 .... 3.4.3.4
(2) 6.3.5.12.1, 20.2.11.12

EEC Treaty (Treaty of Rome) 1957—*cont.*
art. 149A 3.4.5.4, 3.4.5.10
150 .... 3.4.3.4
155 .... 3.4.2.3
164 .... 3.4.6.2, 3.4.6.3.4
arts. 164–188 .... 3.4.6.1
art. 165 (as amended) 3.4.6.3.1, 3.4.6.4.1
166 .... 3.4.6.3.4
167 .... 3.4.6.3.1, 3.4.6.3.6
168 .... 3.4.6.3.3
168A 3.4.6.4.3
169 ...... 3.4.6.6.2, 3.4.6.6.3, 4.2.2.14.2, 5.4.8, 6.3.2.2, 11.3.4.2.1, 15.4.7.3
170 .... 3.4.6.6.3, 15.4.7.3
171 .... 3.4.6.6.2, 3.4.6.6.3
172 .... 3.4.6.6.4, 12.13.9.1.2, 12.13.11.2, 12.13.11.3
173 .... 3.4.6.5.1, 3.4.6.6.5, 3.4.6.6.7, 15.4.5.3, 15.4.9
174 .... 3.5.7.3, 3.5.9.2
175 .... 3.4.6.6.6
177 ..... 3.4.6.6.9, 3.5.6, 3.5.7.3, 3.5.9.2, 25.1
179 .... 3.4.6.6.8
184 .... 3.4.6.6.7
186 .... 6.3.2.2
arts. 187–192 .... 3.4.6.5.3
art. 189 .... 3.5.6
(2) 3.5.2.2.1
(3) 3.5.2.2.2
(4) 3.5.2.2.3
arts. 189–190 .... 3.5.2.2.2
189–191 .... 3.5.2.2.1
art. 190 .... 3.5.2.2.2, 3.5.2.2.3
191(2) 3.5.2.2.3
arts. 193–198 .... 3.4.7.1
art. 198(1) 5.5.19.4
202 .... 3.4.5.10
arts. 207, 209 .... 12.13.9.1.2, 12.13.9.2.2
210, 211 .... 3.1
art. 220 .... 25.1, 25.2.1
224 .... 19.2.1
228 .... 3.4.6.6.10, 19.2.2.3.1
229 .... 19.2.2.3.2, 19.8.1.1
230 .... 19.2.2.3.3
231 .... 19.2.2.3.4
232 .... 4.2.1.1, 4.2.2.15
(1)(2) 3.5.2.1.1, 4.2.1.1
235 .... 3.5.9, 17.2.1
236 .... 19.2.2.3.1
240 .... 3.3.9, 5.2.1.1
European Defence Treaty 3.3.10
Federal Republic of Germany 4.2.2.12.1
Code of Civil Procedure,
art. 23 .... 25.3.2.1
Financial Treaties
Decision Creating the Communities' Own Resources 3.5.2.1.4
Treaty Amending Certain Budgetary Provisions 3.5.2.1.4
Financial Treaties—*cont.*
Treaty Amending Certain Financial Provisions 3.5.2.1.4
France—
Civil Code, arts. 14, 15 .... 25.3.2.1
French Merchant Seamen Code (13 December 1926) (as amended by Order No. 58–1358 of 27 December 1958)
s. 3(2) 4.2.2.14.2, 5.4.8
GATT (General Agreement on Tariffs and Trade) 1.3.18, 15.4.1, 19.8.5, 26.6.4.2
art. VI 13.1
Geneva Convention on the High Seas 1958—
art. 5(1) 6.2.2.1, 6.2.2.2, 6.2.2.3
Greece—
Code of Civil Procedure, art. 40 .... 25.3.2.1
Gulfway Agreement 12.15.3
Hague Convention 1965, art. 15 .... 25.3.8
ILO Constitution, arts. 2, 3(1), 7, 7(1), 10(1) 1.3.4.2
ILO Convention No. 147 Concerning Minimum Standards in Merchant Ships 1.3.4.4, 5.4.16, 19.5.2.3, 17.4.16.3, 17.5.1, 20.2.1.1, 20.2.1.3, 23.2.3, 23.2.4.2, 23.2.5.1
ILO Wages, Hours of Work and Manning (Sea) Recommendation (No. 109) 1958 .... 6.3.4.6
IMCO Convention 1948 ....1.3.3.2
art. 28(a) 1.3.3.4
IMO Convention
arts. 13–16, 17–27 ....1.3.3.4
IMO Convention on Standards of Seafarers' Training 6.3.1
International Conventions. *See* Convention
Italy—
Code of Civil Procedure, arts. 2, 4 Nos. 1 and 2 .... 25.3.2.1
Italian National Law No. 423/81 of 1 August 1981 .... 15.4.6.14
Korean Maritime Transportation Fostering Act, art. 16 .... 13.2.15
Lomé Convention (ACP) 8.3.1
Lugano Convention 1988 .... 25.2.2
Luxembourg Civil Code, arts. 14, 15 ... 25.3.2.1
Luxembourg Ship Registry 6.5
MARPOL (International Convention for the Prevention of Pollution by Ships 1973) 5.4.16, 14.16.3, 17.4.16.1, 17.5.1, 19.5.2.3, 20.2.1.1, 20.2.1.3, 23.2.3, 23.2.4.2, 23.2.5.1
Protocol 1978 .... 5.4.16, 6.3.5.6, 6.3.5.7, 17.4.16.1, 17.4.16.3, 19.5.2.3, 20.2.1.1, 20.2.1.3, 23.2.3, 23.2.4.2
Memorandum of Understanding on Port State Control 1982 .. 5.5.28, 17.5.1, 20.2.7, 23.2.3, 23.2.4.3
Merchant Shipping Act 1979, Scheds. 3, 4 .... 25.3.3.14

Merchant Shipping Act 1988 .... 6.3.1
Merchant Shipping (Liability of Shipowners and Others) Act 1958 .... 25.3.3.14
Merchant Shipping (Liner Conferences) Act 1982 .... 11.3.6
Merchant Shipping (Liner Conferences) (Mandatory Provisions) Regulations 1985 (SI 1985/406) 11.2.7.3
Navigation Acts 1651 .... 7.6.1
Netherlands—
Code of Civil Procedure, arts. 126(3), 127 .... 25.3.2.1
Portugal—
Code of Civil Procedure, arts. 65(1)(c), 65(2), 65A(c) 25.3.2.1
Code of Labour Procedure, art. 11 .. 25.3.2.1
SEA (Single European Act 1986) .. 1.1.2, 3.2.4, 3.3.24, 4.2.2.1, 5.5.21, 17.5.6, 26.2, 26.4.2, 26.5.3.13, 26.5.4.1
art. 1 .... 3.5.2.1.5
2 .... 3.4.4.1, 3.4.4.2
6(4) 6.1.4
13 .... 1.1.5
16 .... 4.2.2.14.2
(5) 6.3.5.5
art. 25 .... 17.5.6
30(5) 19.2.1
SOLAS (International Convention for the Safety of Life at Sea) 1974 .. 1.3.3, 1.3.3.2, 5.4.16, 6.3.5.6, 6.3.5.7, 17.5.1, 19.5.2.3, 20.2.1.1, 23.2.1, 23.2.3, 23.2.4.2
Protocol 1978 . 1.3.3, 5.4.16, 17.5.1, 19.5.2.3, 20.2.1.1, 20.2.1.3, 23.2.3, 23.2.4.2
San Sebastian Convention 25.1
Shipping Investment Grants Act 1987 (Ireland) 2.3.7.6, 15.4.1
Solemn Declaration on European Union 1983 .... 26.4.2
Spain—
Decree Law 22/62 (14 June 1962) and Decree Law 46/81 (29 December 1981) 24.6
Reg. No. 1382 (18 January 1985) 7.5.7.1, 24.3.1
Royal Decree No. 3269/82 (12 November 1982) 24.6
Spinelli Treaty 1984 .... 3.3.22, 26.4.2
Supreme Court Act 1981
ss. 20–22, 21(3) 25.3.3.8
TIR Convention 1975 .... 4.3.1.12, 4.3.1.13
Treaty amending, with regard to Greenland, the Treaties establishing the European Communities 3.5.2.1.2
Treaty establishing a Single Council and a Single Commission (The Merger Treaty) 1965 .... 3.2.2, 3.3.13, 3.5.2.1.3
art. 1 .... 3.4.2.5, 3.4.3.1, 3.4.3.3
2 .... 3.4.3.2, 3.4.3.4
4 .... 3.4.3.5
5 .... 3.4.3.4
9 .... 3.4.2.1
arts. 10, 11 .... 3.4.2.2
Treaty of Accession 1972 .... 4.2.2.7.2, 4.3.2.2, 4.4.2.2, 4.4.3.2
Treaty of Accession 1979 .... 4.2.2.7.2, 4.3.2.2, 4.3.2.4, 4.3.2.5, 4.3.2.6
Treaty of Accession 1985 .... 4.2.2.7.2, 4.3.2.2, 4.3.2.4, 4.3.2.5, 4.3.2.6, 4.3.2.8, 4.4.3.2
Treaty of Accession 1986 .... 4.4.3.2
Treaty of Accession of Denmark, Ireland and the UK (Cmnd. 7462) 3.5.2.1.2
Treaty of Accession of Greece (Cmnd. 7650) 3.5.2.1.2
Treaty of Accession of Spain and Portugal (Cmnd. 9634) 3.5.2.1.2
Treaty of Brussels 1972 .... 3.3.15
Treaty of Paris 1952 .... 3.2.2
UNCLOS III (Third United Nations Convention on the Law of the Sea) 1982 .... 1.3.2, 6.2.2.2, 17.5.3, 19.8.2
arts. 90, 91, 94 .... 6.2.2.2
arts. 192, 193 .... 17.5.3
UNCTAD Code (UN Convention on a Code of Conduct for Liner Conferences 1983) .... 1.3.7, 5.4.11, 5.4.20, 5.5.19.3, 7.5.8, 7.6.2.3, 9.3.7, 11.2 *et seq.*, 12.2.4, 12.2.5, 12.4, 12.8.4, 12.8.5, 12.8.5.3, 12.8.6.1, 12.16, 19.8.1.2, App. 2.33
UN Charter, arts. 57, 63 .... 1.3.4.1
UN Convention on Conditions for the Registration of Ships 1986 .... 6.3.2.3
art. 1 .... 6.2.2.3, 6.3.2
arts. 7, 8, 9, 10 .... 6.3.2.1
8, 9, 10 .... 6.3.2.2
US Shipping Act 1916 .... 11.1
US Shipping Act 1984 .... 11.1
Value Added Tax Act 1983 .... 3.5.2.2.2
Versailles Treaty Part XIII (ILO Constitution) 1.3.4.1
Vienna Convention on the Law of Treaties, arts. 19, 20, 21 .... 6.3.2.2

Table of EC Decisions

All references are to paragraph numbers

Commission of the European Communities (EC Commission)
Commission Decisions—
64/390 ... 4.2.2.13.2, 4.4.1
71/293 ... 4.2.1.3.2
72/261 ... 15.4.4.3.3
73/152 ... 4.2.1.3.2
77/260 ... 15.4.6.17
78/975 ... 4.2.1.3.2
79/496 ... 15.4.6.8
80/991 ... 4.2.2.13.2, 4.4.1
81/626 ... 15.4.6.8
81/2320 ... 15.4.6.16
82/73 ... 15.4.6.18
82/744 ... 15.4.6.14
83/472 ... 4.4.3.4
83/474 ... 4.4.3.4
85/13 ... 4.2.2.13.2, 4.4.1
85/67 ... 4.3.1.1, 4.4.3.4
85/383 ... 4.4.2.5, 4.4.2.7
85/516 ... 4.2.2.13.2, 4.4.1
87/15 ... 15.4.6.20
87/359 ... 4.3.3.2.9, 24.2
87/418 ... 15.4.4.3
87/423 ... 15.4.6.16
87/447 ... 4.2.2.13.2, 4.4.1
87/467 ... 4.2.2.13.2, 4.4.1
87/585 ... 15.4.6.19
88/167 ... 15.4.6.19
88/318 ... 15.4.6.4, 15.4.6.22
88/346 ... 17.4.5
89/296 ... 15.4.4.3
89/448 ... 18.9.12.2.2
89/484 ... 18.9.12.3.1
89/539 ... 18.9.12.2.1
89/541 ... 18.9.12.5.1
90/205 ... 18.9.12.1.1
90/449 ... 4.3.3.1.
90/602 ... 18.9.12.5.2

Commission of the European Communities (EC Commission)—*cont.*
Commission Decisions—*cont.*
91/91 ... 18.9.12.4.1
Council of Ministers of the European Communities
Council Decisions—
21 March 1962 ... 4.2.2.6.2, 4.4.8
22 June 1964 ... 4.4.3.1
13 May 1965 ... 4.4.3.1
65/271 ... 4.4.2.3
70/108 ... 4.4.3.1
72/426 ... 4.3.1.2
73/101 ... 4.2.2.7.2, 4.4.3.2, 4.4.6.1
73/402 ... 4.2.2.4.2, 4.2.2.6.2, 4.4.8
75/327 ... 4.2.2.8.2, 4.3.2.4
75/437 ... 17.3.4
77/587 ... 5.4.14, 5.5.19.3, 5.5.20, 5.5.20.3, 7.5.8, 7.5.9, 14.6, 14.13, 19.3.1 *et seq.*, App. 2
77/774 ... 13.2.3
78/174 ... 4.2.2.13.2, 4.4.1, 4.4.3.3
78/774 ... 5.4.15, 5.4.18, 5.5.20, 13.2.3, 19.4.1 *et seq.*, 19.4.11.2, 19.6.1.3, App. 2
21 December 1978 ... 5.4.19
25 June 1979 ... 4.3.1.12
79/4 ... 5.5.3, 19.4.2 *et seq.*,

Council of Ministers of the European Communities—*cont.*
Council Decisions—*cont.*
79/4—*cont.* 19.4.11.2, 19.6.1.3, App. 2
80/50 .... 4.3.3.2.1
80/1181 .... 19.4.3, 19.4.11.2, 19.6.1.3, App. 2
81/189 .... 5.5.9, 19.4.4, 19.6.1.3, App. 2
82/505 .... 4.3.1.8
82/870 .... 19.4.5, 19.6.1.3, App. 2
82/887 .... 5.5.11, 21.2, App. 2
83/124 .... App. 2
83/418 .... 4.3.2.8, 4.4.7
83/573 .... 5.5.16, 14.6, 19.4.1.10,

Council of Ministers of the European Communities—*cont.*
Council Decisions—*cont.*
83/573—*cont.* 19.4.6, 19.6.1.1 *et seq.* App. 2
84/656 .... 19.4.7, App. 2
86/646 .... 19.4.8, App. 2
87/373 .... 6.3.5.12.1
87/475 .... 14.2, 19.7.1
87/602 .... 4.3.3.2.8
89/242 .... 19.4.1.5.1, 19.4.8, 19.4.9, 19.4.10, 19.4.11.2
89/243 .... 19.4.2.6, 19.4.3.1, 19.4.5, 19.4.7.1, 19.4.8, 19.4.11.2
90/545 .... 19.4.2.5, 19.4.11, 19.4.11.2, 19.4.11.3

Table of Reports and Publications

All references are to paragraph numbers

Action Programmes for the Environment .... 17.4.3.1 *et seq.*
Adonnino Report 1985 .... 26.4.2
Annual Report (1974) on the General Activities of the Communities 5.4.8
Carossino Report on the Role of ports in the Common Transport Policy 23.1
Commission of the European Communities (EC Commission)—
Report from the Commission to the Council on the Implementation of the Four Regulations in the Field of Maritime Transport adopted by the Council on 22 December 1986, SEC (90) 1594, final, 1 August 1990 .... 14.15
para. 19 .... 13.2.15
64 .... 12.15.2, 12.15.7, 12.15.11
65 .... 12.15.6, 12.15.8, 12.15.9
66 .... 12.15.6
67 .... 12.15.5
paras. 68–69 .... 12.15.10
para. 75 .... 12.15.4
Report to Parliament on Community Port Policy (Doc. EP73.762) 23.1
Reports on Competition Policy—
1st (1971) .. 15.3, 15.4.4.3.2, 18.10, 18.10.1
2nd (1972) ... 15.4.4.3, 15.4.4.3.6, 15.4.6.6
3rd (1973) 18.10.2, 18.10.2.1
4th (1974) 15.4.6.17
5th (1975) 12.2.1
6th (1976) . 15.4.4.3.3, 15.4.6.17, 15.4.6.20, 15.4.6.22
8th (1978) 15.4.6.14, 15.4.6.18
9th (1980) 9.2
10th (1980) 15.4.4.3, 15.4.6.1, 15.4.6.3
11th (1981) 15.4.4.3.3, 15.4.4.3.4
12th (1983) 9.2, 15.4.1, 15.4.6.3
14th (1985) 9.2, 10.1.3.1.2
16th (1987) 9.2, 10.1.3.1.2, 15.4.6.11, 15.4.6.17
17th (1988) 12.15.2, 15.4.6.6, 15.4.6.22
18th (1989) 15.4.6.4
19th (1989) 12.6.9, 16.5
Seventh Annual Report to the European Parliament on Commission Monitoring of the Application of Community Law, COM (90) 288 final, 22 May 1990 .... 7.5.14
Dooge Report 1985 .... 26.4.2
Eighth General Report on the Activities of the European Communities (1974)
point 355 .... 5.4.8
Eleventh General Report on the Activities of the European Communities (1977)
point 379 .... 5.4.12
380 .... 5.4.15
382 .... 5.4.9
European Parliament
Interim Report on the Community Shipping Industry in 1976 (Doc. 479/76) 8.4.2
paras. 1, 2 .... 5.4.13
para. 14 .... 5.4.7, 7.6.4.1, 11.1, 11.2.5, 13.2.1, 18.2, 18.3.1, 18.10
Interim Report on the proposal for a Regulation laying down detailed rules for the application of Arts. 85 and 86 of the EEC Treaty to maritime transport (Doc. 1–249/84/A) 12.2.4
Interim Report on the sea transport problems in the Community (Doc. 5/77, 23 March 1977) 5.4.13, 19.8
paras. 1, 3 .... 4.2.2.14.2
para. 3 .... 5.2
4 .... 1.1.3, 19.1
22 .... 19.8.4
Report on the problems of maritime transport in the Community, 23 March 1977, PE 47.110/final 23.1
Report on the role of ports in the Common Transport Policy, 15 November 1982, PE 80/050 final 23.1
Report on Transport and Tourism (Doc. A3–0345/90) 6.3.5.3, 6.3.5.12.3
Report on UN Convention on Conditions for the Registration of Ships (COM (86) 523) final (Doc. A2–53/88) 6.3.2.3
Fifteenth General Report on the Activities of the European Communities (1981)
points 206, 487 .... 5.5.10

Fourteenth General Report on the Activities of the European Communities (1980)
point 426 .... 5.4.18, 5.5.3
Fourth General Report on the Activities of the European Communities (1970)
point 302 .... 5.4.2
Hollesen Study (published by EC Commission, June 1980) 8.2.6.2
Rochdale, Report of the Committee into Shipping (Cmnd. 4337) ... 2.3.13.6, 6.2.1.2
Sarlis Report (COM (89)) 266 final 6.3.5.3
Seefeld Reports—
Doc. 5/77, 23 March 1977, PE 47.110/def. 2.1, 5.4.2
Doc. EP No. 512/78, 5 January 1979, p. 54 .... 5.4.14
Seventh General Report on the Activities of the European Communities (1973)
point 403 .... 5.4.5
Spaak Report 4.1.2
Spierenburg Report 1979 .... 26.4.2
Tenth General Report on the Activities of the European Communities (1976)
point 439 .... 5.4.11
451 .... 5.4.10
Thirteenth General Report on the Activities of the European Communities (1979)
point 378 .... 5.4.11
382 .... 5.4.9
Tindemans Report 3.3.16, 26.4.2
Twelfth General Report on the Activities of the European Communities (1978)
point 370 .... 5.4.16
373 .... 5.4.9

Table of Abbreviations

ACP	African, Caribbean and Pacific Countries
AEA	Association of European Airlines
AJIL	American Journal of International Law
ANEC	US Atlantic-North Europe Conference
ASOR	Agreement on the International Carriage of Passengers by Road by means of occasional Coach and Bus Services
BES	Business Expansion Scheme
BIMCO	Baltic and International Maritime Council
BSC	British Shippers' Council
CAACE	Comité des Associations d'Armateurs des Communautés Européennes
CAP	Common Agricultural Policy
CCC	Customs Co-operation Council
CCT	Common Customs Tariff
CDE	Cahiers de Droit Européen
CEN	European Committee for Standardisation
CENLEC	European Committee for Electrotechnical Standardisation
CENSA	Council of European and Japanese National Shipowners' Associations
CFI	Court of First Instance
CJEC	Court of Justice of the European Communities
CMEA	Council for Mutual Economic Co-operation
CMLR	Common Market Law Reports
CML Rev.	Common Market Law Review
COMECON	Council for Mutual Economic Co-operation
COREPER	Committee of Permanent Representatives
COST	Co-operation Européenne dans la domaine de la recherche Scientifique et Technique
CSG	Consultative Shipping Group
CTP	Common Transport Policy
Dec.	Decision
DG	Directorate-General
Dir.	Directive
dwt	Deadweight tons
EAEC	European Atomic Energy Community ((Euratom) Treaty)
EC	European Community or European Communities
ECA	Economic Commission for Africa (UN)
ECE	Economic Commission for Europe (UN)
ECJ	Court of Justice of the European Communities
ECLA	Economic Commission for Latin America (UN)
ECLR	European Competition Law Review
ECMT	European Conference of Ministers of Transport
ECOSOC	Economic and Social Committee
ECSC	European Coal and Steel Community
ECU	European Currency Unit
EEC	European Economic Community
EEIG	European Economic Interest Grouping
EFTA	European Free Trade Association
EIB	European Investment Bank
ELR	European Law Review
EMS	European Monetary System

EP	European Parliament
ERDF	European Regional Development Fund
ESC	European Shippers' Council Economic and Social Committee
ESCAP	Economic Commission for Asia and the Pacific (UN)
ETSI	European Telecommunications Standardisation Institute
EUA	European Unit of Account
Euratom	European Atomic Energy Community
EUROS	Community Ship Register
FAO	Food and Agriculture Organisation
FASA	Federation of Asean Shipowners' Associations
GATS	General Agreement on Trade in Services
GATT	General Agreement on Tariffs and Trade
GCBS	General Council of British Shipping
GDP	Gross Domestic Product
GEMS	Global Environmental Monitoring System
grt	Gross Registered Tonnage
HMSO	Her Majesty's Stationery Office
IAEA	International Atomic Energy Agency
ICAO	International Civil Aviation Organisation (UN)
ICES	International Council for the Exploration of the Sea
ICHCA	International Cargo Handling Coordination Association
ILO	International Labour Organisation
IMCO	Intergovernmental Maritime Consultative Organisation
IMO	International Maritime Organisation
IMP	Integrated Mediterranean Programme
INMARSAT	International Maritime Satellite Organisation
INTERCARGO	International Association of Dry Cargo Shipowners
INTERTANKO	International Association of Independent Tanker Owners
IOC	International Oceanographic Commission
ITF	International Transport Federation
JBL	Journal of Business Law
J.Com.M.S.	Journal of Common Market Studies
JO	Journal Officiel
KSR	Kombinat Schiffbau Rostock
LIEI	Legal Issues of European Integration
LMCLQ	Lloyd's Maritime and Commercial Law Quarterly
LQR	Law Quarterly Review
MARPOL	International Convention for the Prevention of Pollution by Ships
MINCONMAR	Ministerial Conference of West and Central African States
MLR	Modern Law Review
NATO	North Atlantic Treaty Organisation
NEAC	North Europe-US Atlantic Conference
NIS	Norwegian International Ships Register
NUMAST	UK Seafaring Officers' Union
OECD	Organisation for Economic Cooperation and Development
OEEC	Organisation for European Economic Cooperation
OJ	Official Journal of the European Communities
Reg.	Regulation
SAD	Single Administrative Document
SAR	International Convention on Maritime Search and Rescue
SCOR	Scientific Commission on Oceanic Research
SE	Societas Europaea (European Company based on EC Law)
SEA	Single European Act
SIRP	Shipping Industry Rationalisation Plan (Korea)
SMEs	Small and Medium-sized Enterprises
SOLAS	International Convention for the Safety of Life at Sea
TEU	Twenty Foot Equivalent Unit
TIEP	Transport Infrastructural Experimental Programme
TOAS	Tolerated Outsider Agreements
u.a.	Units of Account
UK	United Kingdom
UN	United Nations

UNCITRAL	United Nations Commission on International Trade Law
UNCLOS III	Third United Nations Convention on the Law of the Sea
UNCTAD	United Nations Conference on Trade and Development
UNCTAD Code	UN Convention on a Code of Conduct for Liner Conferences
UNEP	United Nations Environment Programme
UNESCO	United Nations Educational Scientific and Cultural Organisation
US	United States of America
USSR	Union of Soviet Socialist Republics
VSM	Association of the West German Shipbuilding Industry and Marine Technology
VTS	Vessel Traffic Management Services
WHO	World Health Organisation
YEL	Yearbook of European Law

Terms

"Commission": The Commission of the European Communities
"Council of Ministers": The Council of Ministers of the European Communities
"Economic and Social Committee": The Economic and Social Committee of the European Communities

Bibliography

A. BOOKS AND ENCYCLOPEDIAS

Abbati, *Transport and European Integration* (1986)
Abecassis and Jarashow, *Oil Pollution from Ships* (2nd ed., 1985)
Ademuni-Odeke, *Shipping in International Trade Relations* (1988)
Alderton, *Sea Transport: Operation and Economics*
Arbuthnott and Edwards, *A Common Man's Guide to the Common Market* (2nd ed., 1989)
Armstrong, *The Rise of the International Organisation: A Short History* (1982)
Arnould, *Arnould on Marine Insurance* (16th ed., 1981)
Astle, *Legal Developments in Maritime Commerce* (1983)
Astle, *Shipping and the Law*
Baldwin, *Regulating the Airlines: Administrative Justice and Agency Discretion* (1985)
Barrington and Cooney, *Inside the EEC* (1984)
Barston and Birnie, *The Maritime Dimension* (1980)
Bates, *UK Marine Pollution Law* (1985)
Bates, *UK Marine Pollution Legislation* (1987)
Bayliss, *European Transport* (1965)
Bebr, *Development of Judicial Control of the European Communities* (1981)
Bekiashev and Serebriakov, *International Marine Organisations* (1981)
Bellamy & Child, *Common Market Law of Competition* (3rd ed., 1987)
Bernhardt, *Encyclopedia of Public International Law* (1983)
Berridge, *Politics of the South Africa Run: European Shipping and Pretoria* (1987)
Bes, *Bulk Carriers* (2nd ed., 1972)
Bessler & Williams, *Anti-Dumping and Anti-Subsidy Law: The European Communities* (1986)
Beth, Hader & Kappel, *25 Years of World Shipping*
Bieber, Pinder, Dehousie, Weiler (Eds.), *1992: One European Market* (1988)
Boczek, *Flags of Convenience* (1962)
Booker, *Containers: Conditions, Law & Practice of Carriage & Use* (1987, 2 vols.)
Bos, Stuyck and Wytinck, *Concentration Control in the European Economic Community* (1991)
Bourgoignie & Trubek, *Consumer Law, Common Market and Federalism* (1987)
Branch, *Economics of Shipping Practice & Management* (2nd ed., 1988)
Branch, *Elements of Shipping* (6th ed., 1989)
Breatey, *European Community Law on Financial Services* (1992)
Breatey & Quigley, *Completing the Internal Market of the European Community* (Looseleaf)
Breatey & Quigley, *Completing the Internal Market of the European Community: 1992 Handbook* (2nd ed., 1991)
Bredima, *Methods of Interpretation and Community Law* (1978)
Bredima-Savopoulou and Tzoannos, *The Common Shipping Policy of the EEC* (1990)
Brown & Wormell, *An Introduction to Working in the Lloyd's Market* (1987)
Burrows, *Free Movement in European Community Law* (1987)
Butler (Ed.), *The Law of the Sea and International Shipping: Anglo-Soviet Post-UNCLOS Perspectives* (1985)
Cheng, *The Law of International Air Transport* (1962)
Chrzanowski, *Introduction to Shipping Economics* (1985)
Churchill, *EEC Fisheries Law* (1987)
Clifford Chance, *Insurance in the EEC—The European Community's Programme for a New Regime* (1990)
Close, in Hailsham (Ed.), 52 *Halsbury's Laws of England* (4th ed.)
Clough and Randolph, *Shipping and EC Competition Law* (1991)

Clout, *Regional Variations in the European Community* (1986)
Coffey, *Economic Policies of the Common Market* (1979)
Colinvaux, *Carver on Carriage by Sea* (13th ed., 1982)
Dassesse and Isaacs, *EEC Banking Law*
Despicht, *Policies for Transport in the Common Market* (1964)
Dolmans, *Problems of Mixed Agreements* (1985)
Edwards and Wallace, *A Wider European Community?*
Edwards and Wallace, *The Council of Ministers of the European Community and the President in Office*
El-Agraa (Ed.), *The Economics of the European Community* (1985)
Ellen and Campbell, *International Maritime Fraud* (1981)
Emerson, *The Economics of 1992* (1988)
Erdmenger, *The European Community Transport Policy* (1983)
Ewart, *Bulk Carriers* (1983)
Fairplay, *World Shipping Statistics* (Annual Volumes)
Farthing, *International Shipping: An introduction to the policies, politics and institutions of the maritime world* (1987)
Fine, *Mergers and Joint Ventures in Europe* (1988)
Frankel, *World Shipping Industry* (1987)
Freeman and Whish (Eds.), *Butterworths Competition Law* (1991)
Freestone, *The Institutional Framework of the European Communities* (1988)
Furmston, Kerridge and Sufrin (Eds.), *The Effect on English Domestic Law of Membership of the European Communities and of Ratification of the European Convention on Human Rights* (1983)
Gaskell *et al.*, *Chorley & Giles' Shipping Law* (8th ed., 1987)
Gilman, *Competitive Dynamics of Container Shipping*
Gleed *et al.*, *Deloitte's 1992 Guide* (1989)
Goss, *Studies in Maritime Economics* (1968)
Graham & Hughes, *Containerisation in the Eighties* (1985)
Grammenos, *Bank Finance for Ship Purchase* (1979)
Gray, *Financial Risk Management in the Shipping Industry* (1986)
Gripaios, *Tramp Shipping* (1959)
Groux and Manin, *The European Communities in the International Order* (1984)
Gunner and Edwards, *Carriage of Crude Oil by Sea* (1986)
Hartley, *The Foundations of European Community Law* (2nd ed., 1988)
Hawkins, *Shipping Subsidies and the Balance of Payments* (1989)
Henry, *Carriage of Dangerous Goods by Sea: Role of the IMO in International Legislation* (1985)
Herman, *Shipping Conferences* (1983)
Hine, *The Political Economy of European Trade: An Introduction to the Trade Policies of the EEC* (1985)
Hoggart and Johnson, *An Idea of Europe* (1987)
Hopkins, *Business & Law for the Shipmaster* (6th ed., 1982)
Institute of Maritime Law, *Ratification of Maritime Conventions*
International Shipping Federation, *ISF Guide to International Maritime Labour Supply* (1990)
Ivamy, *Payne and Ivamy's Carriage of Goods by Sea* (13th ed., 1989)
Ivamy, *Encyclopedia of Shipping Law Sources (UK)* (1985)
Ivamy, *Casebook on Shipping* (4th ed., 1987)
Ivamy, *Chalmers' Marine Insurance Act 1906* (9th ed., 1983)
Ivamy, *Marine Insurance* (4th ed., 1985)
Ivamy, *Merchant Shipping (Liner Conferences) Act 1982* (1987)
Jackson, *Civil Jurisdiction and Judgments—Maritime Claims* (1987)
Jackson, *Enforcement of Maritime Claims* (1985)
Johnson, *Pollution Control Policy of the European Communities* (2nd ed., 1983)
Joll (Ed.), *Britain and Europe: Pitt to Churchill 1793–1940* (1961)
Jones, van der Woude & Lewis, *EEC Competition Law Handbook* (1990)
Kapteyn and Van Themaat, *Introduction to the Law of the European Communities* (2nd ed., edited by Gormley, 1989)
Katsipis, *European Integration and its Impact on Greek Cabotage*
Kelley and Onkelinx, *EEC Customs Law* (Updated work)
Kendall, *Business of Shipping* (5th ed., 1986)
Kennedy, *The Rise and Fall of the Great Powers* (1988)
Kerr, *The Common Market and How it Works* (3rd ed., 1987)
Kerse, *EEC Antitrust Procedure* (2nd ed., 1987)
Kramer, *EEC Consumer Law* (1986)
Lambeth, *Templeman on Marine Insurance* (6th ed., 1986)

Lasok and Bridge, *Law and Institutions of the European Communities* (4th ed., 1987)
Louis, *The Community Legal Order* (2nd ed., 1990)
Lowe, *The Transport and Distribution Managers' Guide to 1992* (1989)
Maitland-Walker, *Towards 1992: The Development of International Anti-Trust* (1990)
Mankabady, *International Maritime Organization* (vol. 1: 1986 and vol. 2: 1987)
Mankabady, *International Shipping Law* (1991)
Mathijsen, *A Guide to European Community Law* (4th ed., 1985)
McAlees and Drudy (Eds.), *Ireland and the European Community*
McGonigle & Zacher, Pollution Politics and International Law (1979)
McGovern, *International Trade Regulation* (2nd ed., 1986)
Meeson, *Practice and Procedure of the Admiralty Court* (1986)
Merkin, *Encyclopedia of Competition Law* (Looseleaf)
Metaxas, *The Economics of Tramp Shipping* (1971)
Metaxas, *Flags of Convenience* (1985)
Moreby and Springett, *The UK Shipping Industry: Critical Levels Study* (1990)
Newns & Parrington, *Double Taxation Relief for Shipping* (1988)
Nicoll and Salmon, *Understanding the European Communities* (1990)
Nordguist, *UN Convention on the Law of the Sea 1982* (1985)
O'Connell, *International Law of the Sea* (Vol. 1: 1983 and Vol. 2: 1984)
Oliver, *Free Movement of Goods* (2nd ed., 1988)
Olmi *et al.*, *Thirty Years of Community Law* (1983)
O'Keefe and Schermers (Eds.), *Essays in European Law and Integration* (1982)
O'Loughlin, *The Economics of Sea Transport* (1967)
Ovrebo, *Short Sea and Coastal Tramp Shipping in Europe* (1969)
Packard, *Ship and Sales* (2nd ed., 1988)
Parry and Hardy, *EEC Law* (2nd ed., 1981)
Pearson, *Container Ships & Shipping* (1988)
Pijpers, *European Political Co-operation in the 1980's* (1988)
Plummer, *Super Ferries of Britain, Europe, and Scandinavia* (1988)
Rasmussen, *On Law and Policy in the European Court of Justice* (1986)
Reukema, *Discriminatory Refusal of Carriage in North America* (1982)
Ridley, *Law of Carriage of Goods by Land, Sea and Air* (7th ed., 1989)
Ritter *et al.*, *EEC Competition Law: A Practitioner's Guide* (1991)
Rosenstein and Goldstein (Eds.), *Organisational Changes in Shipping in Europe and Israel* (1983)
Ruttley, *EEC Maritime Competition Law* (Forthcoming)
Schina, *State Aids under the EEC Treaty: Articles 92 to 94* (1987)
Singh, *Maritime Flag and International Law* (1978)
Singh, *International Maritime Law Conventions* (4 vols., 1983)
Sloggett, *Shipping Finance* (1984)
Smit and Herzog, *The Laws of the European Community* (Looseleaf, 1976)
Snyder, *New Directions in European Community Law* (1990)
Soni, *Control of Marine Pollution in International Law*
Spicer, *New Directions in Maritime Law* (1985)
Spyrou, *Energy & Ships* (1988)
Stopford, *Maritime Economics* (1988)
Sturmey, *The Code of Conduct and the Review Conference British Shipping and World Competition* (1962)
Sullivan, *The Marine Encyclopaedic Dictionary* (1988)
Swann, *The Economics of the Common Market* (6th ed., 1988)
Tinsley, *Short-Sea Bulk Trades: Dry Cargo Shipping in European Waters* (1984)
Tzoannos, *The Fiscal Regime for Shipowning Firms in the EEC* (1980)
Urwin, *Western Europe Since 1945*, (4th Edn., 1989)
Ussher, *European Community Law and National Law: The Irreversible Transfer?* (1981)
Vaughan, *Post-War Integration in Europe* (1976)
Volker and Steenbergen, *Leading Cases and Materials on the External Relations Law of the European Communities* (1985)
Wardley-Smith (Ed.), *Prevention of Oil Pollution* (1979)
Whitelegg, *Transport Policy in the EEC* (1988)
Wilson, *Carriage of Goods by Sea* (1988)

B. LAW REPORTS

Common Market Law Reports
Common Market Law Reports: Antitrust Supplements
European Court of Justice Reporter
European Court Reports
Lloyd's Law Reports
Reports of Cases before the Court

C. JOURNALS GENERALLY CONSULTED

Anglo-American Law Review
Cambridge Law Journal
Common Market Law Review
European Competition Law Review
European Court of Justice Reporter
European Economy
European Intellectual Property Review
European Law Review
European Transport Law
Fairplay
Freighting World
IMO News
International Business Lawyer
International and Comparative Law Quarterly
International Company and Commercial Law Review
Journal of Business Law
Journal of Common Market Studies
Journal of International Banking Law
Lloyd's Environmental Law International
Lloyd's Law Reports
Lloyd's List
Lloyd's Loading List
Lloyd's Maritime and Commercial Law Quarterly
Lloyd's Maritime Law Newsletter
Lloyd's Passenger Shipping International
Lloyd's Shipping Economist
Lloyd's Shipping Index
Lloyd's Ship Manager
Lloyd's Voyage Record
Modern Law Review
Netherlands Yearbook of International Law
P&I International
Product Liability International
Yearbook of European Law

D. OFFICIAL PUBLICATIONS

1. Council of Ministers

Doc. No. 11584/86 MAR 84 of 19 December 1986, Annex III.

2. Commission of the European Communities

A Future for the Community Shipping Industry: Measures to Improve the Operating Conditions of Community Shipping, 3 August 1989, COM(89) 266 final.

A Social Survey in Maritime Transport: Preparatory Study on the Employment and Social Impact of International and National Provisions regarding working conditions in Maritime Transport; and Distortions affecting both Employment and Competitivity of Community Nationals (Author: van Poelgeest, 1987).

Communication from the Commission on a Community Regime for Procurement in the Excluded Sectors: Water, Energy, Transport and Telecommunications (COM(88) 376 final).

Communication from the Commission to the Council on the Community's Relations with non-member countries in shipping matters, COM(76) 341 final, 30 June 1976.

Communication from the Commission to the Council on the United Nations Convention on Conditions for Registration of Ships, COM(86) 523 final, 25 September 1986.

Communication from the Commission to the Council, the European Parliament and the Economic and Social Committee, New Challenges for Maritime Industries (COM(91) 335 final), 20 September 1991.

Completing the Internal Market: White Paper from the Commission to the European Council, 1985.

Co-ordination of Investments in Transport Infrastructures, 1973 (Studies, Transport Series No. 3, Brussels, 1973).

Doc. No. 4130/MAR 3, 11.1.1988.

Doc. No. 10048/88 MAR 38 of 13.12.1988.

Guidelines for the Examination of State Aids to Community Shipping Companies, Annex I to Financial and Fiscal Measures Concerning Shipping Operations with Ships Registered in the Community, SEC(89) 921 final, 3 August 1989, COM(85) 90 final.

Progress Towards a Common Transport Policy: Maritime Transport, COM(85) 90 final, 14 March 1985. Reprinted in Bull. EC, Supp. 5/85 and reprinted in part in OJ C212 of 23.8.85, pp.2–21.

Proposal for a Council Decision on the common position to be adopted by Member States when signing and ratifying the United Nations Convention on conditions for registration of ships, COM(86) 523 final, 25 September 1986.

Proposal for a Council Decision on the LORAN-C radionavigation System, 21 January 1991, COM(91) 1 final.

Proposal for a Council Regulation (EEC) on the transfer of ships from one register to another within the Community, 1 June 1990, COM(90) 219 final.

Report from the Commission to the Council: Implementation of the Four Regulations in the Field of Maritime Transport adopted by the Council of Ministers on 22 December 1986, SEC(90) 1594 final, 1 August 1990.

The Community and Transport Policy, European File 10/85.

The European Community's Transport Policy, Periodical 3/1984.

The Community and Transport Policy, European File 16/83 (October 1983).

3. European Parliament

First Report of the Committee on Transport and Tourism on the Proposal from the Commission to the Council for: I. a Council Regulation establishing a Community Ship Register and providing for the flying of the Community flag by sea-going vessels; II. a Council Regulation on a Common Definition of a Community Shipowner; and III. a Council Regulation applying the Principle of Freedom to Provide Services to Maritime Transport within Member States, A3-0199/90, 25 July 1990, Rapporteur: Sarlis.

Interim Report drawn up on behalf of the Committee on Regional Policy, Regional Planning and Transport on the Sea Transport Problems in the Community, Working Documents; Doc. 5/77; 23 March 1977; Rapporteur: Mr. H. Seefeld.

Report drawn up on behalf of the Committee on Transport on the proposal for a Council decision on the common position to be adopted by Member States when signing and ratifying the United Nations Convention on Conditions for the Registration of Ships (COM(86) 523 final); Rapporteur: Mr. D. Romera I Alcazar, Doc. A 2–53/88, 18 May 1988.

Report of the Committee on Transport and Tourism on the Commission Proposal for a Council Regulation on the Transfer of Ships from one Register to Another within the Community, A3–0345/90, 3 December 1990, Rapporteur: Braun-Mosler.

Second Report of the Committee on Transport and Tourism on the Proposal from the Commission to the Council for: I. a Council Regulation establishing a Community Ship Register and providing for the flying of the Community flag by sea-going vessels; II. a Council Regulation on a Common Definition of a Community Shipowner; and III. a Council Regulation applying the Principle of Freedom to Provide Services to Maritime Transport within Member States, A3–0259/90, 22 October 1990, Rapporteur: Sarlis.

4. Economic and Social Committee

European Communities, *The European Community's Transport Policy* (2nd ed., 1984) (CB–NC–80–003–EN–C).

Opinion on Positive Measures for Maritime Transport, OJ No. C 56, 7 March 1990 (Rapporteur: Mr. Whitworth).

Opinion on the Progress Towards a Common Transport Policy: Maritime Transport, CES 1023/85 (27.11.85).

Opinion on the Progress Towards a Common Transport Policy: Maritime Transport, Second Part, CES (21.5.86).

Opinion on the Progress Towards a Common Transport Policy: Maritime Transport, COM(85) 90 final (TRA/116).
Opinion on the Proposal for a Council Regulation (EEC) on the transfer of a ship from one registry to another within the EC, COM(90) 219 final.

5. House of Lords

European Communities Committee 3rd Report 1983–1984: *Competition Policy: Shipping* (HL Paper 23).
European Communities Committee 9th Report 1985–1986: *European Maritime Transport Policy* (HL Paper 106).
European Communities Committee 28th Report 1989–1990: *Community Shipping Measures* (HL Paper 90).

6. UK Authorities and Inquiries

Committee of Inquiry into Shipping (1970, Cmnd. 4337).

E. ARTICLES, REPORTS AND SPEECHES

Abrahamson, "The Law of the Sea Convention and Shipping" (1986) 5 *Political Geography Quarterly* 13.
Allen, "Conferences Operating Out of the EC", at The Future of Shipping in Europe—Key Legal and Commercial Issues, London, 28–29 June 1990.
Anon, "Open for business or fortress Europe?", *Lloyd's Shipping Economist*, February 1990, p.12.
Anon, "Perestroika heralds a period of invigorating change for Soviet Shipping", *Lloyd's Shipping Economist*, September 1989, p.26.
Bayer, "Antitrust comes to Maritime Transport in the European Economic Community", (1987) 34 *Federal Bar News & Journal*, 299.
Bayliss, "Transport in the European Communities", (1979) 13 *Jo. of Transport Economics and Policy* 28.
Bellis, Vermulst and Musquar, "The New EEC Regulation on Unfair Pricing Practices in Maritime Transport: A Forerunner of the Extension of Unfair Trade Concepts to Services?", (1988) 22 JWTL 47.
Blank, "Creating a Level Playingfield for Shipping", *Liner Shipping in the 90's*, Amsterdam (Conference Proceedings), 12.11.91.
Bott, "What is the Future of Liner Conferences?", *Liner Shipping in the 90's*, Amsterdam (Conference Proceedings) 12.11.91.
Braure, "Perspectives nouvelles pour les lignes aeriennes europeennes", (1989) XXIV *European Transport Law* 441.
Bredima, "The Common Shipping Policy of the EEC", (1981) CML Rev
Bredima Savopoulout & Tzoannos, "In Search of a Common Shipping Policy for the EC", (1982) *Jo. Common Market Studies* 95.
Burke, "Towards a Shipping Policy for the EEC," Seatrade Conference, Brussels, 11.9.78.
Burke, "Shipping Policy: A View of Western Europe," Stockholm School of Economics, 22.6.1979.
Burns, "Registration of Vessels, Offshore, International and Euroregistry", at The Future of Shipping in Europe—Key Legal and Commercial Issues, London, 28–29 June 1990.
Close, "Article 84 EEC: The Development of Transport Policy in the Sea and Air Sectors", (1980) 5 ELR 188.
Close, "Inland Transport Services: Recent Developments in Community Policy", (1985) 22 CML Rev 587.
Collinson, "Economic Regulation of Transport under the Common Transport Policy of the European Communities", (1971–72) 24 *Stanford Law Review* 221.
Croxford *et al.*, "The Reform of the European Regional Development Fund: A Preliminary Assessment", (1987) XXVI *JCMS*.
Dassesse, "EEC Insurance Market and 1992: Significance of Fiscal and Tariff Issues", (1990) LMCLQ 176.
Dawbarn, "Intermodalism: How Distribution Systems are Developing", *Liner Shipping in the 90's*, Amsterdam (Conference Proceedings) 12.11.91.
De Clerq, "The United States and the European Community: Brothers Yet Foes?", [1987] 2 *European Affairs* 16.
De Croo, Inaugural address to the Antwerp Shipping symposium, "A Future for the Country Fleet", 6.5.87, reprinted in (1987) XXII *European Transport Law* in May 1987, p.194.
Edmondson, "Ship Finance in the EC Market", at *The Future of Shipping in Europe—Key Legal and Commercial Issues*, London, 28–29 June 1990.

Ehlers, "The History of the International North Sea Conferences", (1990) 5 *International Journal of Estuarine and Coastal Law* 1.
Erdmenger, "World Shipping in the 90's: An EEC Perspective of the Industry", Amsterdam, 14 November 1989.
Fante, "The Challenges for European Shipbuilding in the 90's", *Prospects for Bulk Shipping*, Amsterdam (Conference Proceedings), 13.11.91.
Feig, "Transport in the European Community", *EIU European Trends*, 1990, No. 2, p.42.
Fennel, "The Transport Policy Case", (1985) 10 *European Law Review* 264.
Gardner and Marlow, "An International Comparison of the Fiscal Treatment of Shipping", (1983) 31 *Journal of Industrial Economics* 397.
General Council of British Shipping, *Decline in the UK Registered Fleet*, (1986).
Giannopoulos, "The Economics of Flagging of Flagging Out", (1988) *Journal of Transport Economics and Policy*.
Giari, "European Community Seaport Policy: Competition or Cooperation?", (1982) 8 *Marine Affairs Journal* 1.
Goss, "Sense and Shipping Policies", [1987] 14 *Maritime Policy and Management* 83.
Goss, "Some Economic Aspects of Flag Discrimination", (1986) 13 *Maritime Policy and Management* 245.
Greaves, "Introduction to the EEC and the Shipping Market", London, 11 November 1988.
Greenwood, "Nationality and the Limits of the Free Movement of Persons in Community Law", (1987) Yb.E.Law 185.
Gwilliam, *Co-ordination of Investments in Transport Infrastructures*, Studies, Transport Series, No. 3 (1973).
Hammer, "The Outlook for Bulk Shipping in the 90's", *Prospects for Bulk Shipping*, Amsterdam (Conference Proceedings), 13.11.91.
Hayward, "The Oslo and Paris Commissions" (1990) 5 *International Journal of Estuarine and Coastal Law* 1.
Hickey, "The Application of the Competition Rules to Shipping", at The Future of Shipping in Europe—Key Legal and Commercial Issues, London, 28–29 June 1990.
Jones, "The North Sea Environment: Features and Problems" (1990) 5 *International Journal of Estuarine and Coastal Law* 66.
Juda, "The UNCTAD Liner Code: A Preliminary Examination of the Implementation of the Code of Conduct for Liner Conferences", (1985) JMLC 181.
Juglart, "Droit Commun et droit maritime" (1986) 38 *Droit Maritime Francais* 259.
Keates, "Shipping Law—European Aspects", at The Future of Shipping in Europe—Key Legal and Commercial Issues, London, 28–29 June 1990.
Kean, "Overbooking and Denied-Boarding" [1991] JBL 598.
Kippenberger, "Some Comments on the Development of the German Ship Financing Market", (1985) 3 *Maritime Industry* 19.
Kreis, "European Community Competition Policy and International Shipping", (1989–1990) 13 *Fordham International Law Journal* 411.
Lake, "The Lome III Convention—Europe's New Model for Dialogue and Development" (1985) 5 Yb.E.Law 21.
Lay, "Euro-American Relations", (1987?) Yb.E.Law 171.
MacAllister, "City Consequences of UK Fleet Decline Highlighted", Lloyd's List, 23 April 1990, p.3.
MacMillan, "Marine Insurance in the EC Market—Commercial Aspects", at The Future of Shipping in Europe—Key Legal and Commercial Issues, London, 28–29 June 1990.
McGee and Weatherill, "The Evolution of the Single Market: Harmonisation or Liberalisation" (1990) 53 MLR 578.
Micklitz, "Perspectives on a European Directive on the Safety of Technical Consumer Goods" (1986) 23 CML Rev 617.
Mikelis and Dean, *The Fleet Controlled by the European Community* (5th International Congress of the International Maritime Association of the East Mediterranean, Athens, 1990 and published by Lloyd's Register).
Moreby, "Labour—Regulations Affecting European Seafarers/Safety" at The Future of Shipping in Europe—Key Legal and Commercial Issues, London, 28–29 June 1990.
O'Donovan, "EC Policy on Marine Environment and Pollution", at The Future of Shipping in Europe—Key Legal and Commercial Issues, London, 28–29 June 1990.
Oliver, "Non-Community Nationals and the Treaty of Rome" (1985) Yb.E.Law 57.
Oliver and Yataganas, "The Harmonised System of Customs Classification", (1987?) Yb.E.Law 113.
Pelkmans, "The New Approach to Technical Harmonisation and Standardisation" (1987) 25 JCMS 249.

Penfold, "Bulk and Container Trade—A European Perspective", at The Future of Shipping in Europe—Key Legal and Commercial Issues, London, 28–29 June 1990.

Petropolous, "The European Community Transport Policy—An Overview", at The Future of Shipping in Europe—Key Legal and Commercial Issues, London, 28–29 June 1990.

Power, "International Market Opportunities: Cabotage, Shipbuilding and New Services", at The Future of Shipping in Europe—Key Legal and Commercial Issues, London, 28–29 June 1990.

Rabe, "Report on Recent Developments in EEC Legislation Pertaining to Maritime Transport" delivered to the International Bar Association Section on Business Law, 2–6 October 1989 (SG3281).

Riphagen, "The Transport Legislation of the European Communities, its Relationship to International Treaties and its Effect in Member States", (1965–1966) 3 CML Rev 291, p.291.

Roberts, "Doubts on a Common Transport Policy", (1967–1968) 5 CML Rev 193.

Robinson, "Clear of Tunnel Vision", *Financial Times Survey* "Transport Rules with the Continent", 5 April 1990, p.IV.

Sager, "Prospects for Liner Shipping in the 90's", Liner Shipping in the 90's, Amsterdam (Conference Proceedings), 12.11.91.

Schermers, "The Internal Effect of Community Treaty-making" in O'Keefe and Schermers (Eds.), *Essays in European Law and Integration* (1982).

Shah, "The UN Lines Code of Conduct: Some Key Issues regarding its Interpretation", (1981) 16 ETL 491.

Simmonds, "The Community's Participation in the UN Law of the Sea Convention", in O'Keefe and Schermers (Eds.), *Essays in European Law and Integration* (1982).

Simmonds, "International Maritime Organization" in Bernhardt (Ed.), *Encyclopedia of Public International Law*, vol. 5, page 104 (1983).

Sorensen, "The Air Transport Policy of the EEC", (1989) XXIV *European Transport Law* 411.

Stokes, "Significance of Directive on Ship Purchase Bank Finance", *Lloyd's List*, 26 March 1990, p.2.

Sturmey, "Pragmatic Competition and Liner Shipping", (1990) 14 *Marine Policy* 36.

Sweeney, "From Columbus to Co-operation—Trade and Shipping Policies from 1492 to 1992", (1989–1990) 13 *Fordham International Law Journal* 481.

Vandersanden, "L'application des règles de concurrence aux transports aeriens", (1989) XXIV *European Transport Law* 419.

Vigarie, "State Aids for Seaports: A Cartesian Position in the French Case", (1986) 13 *Marine Policy and Management* 127.

Volckaert, "Formulation of National Marine Policy: The Case of Belgium", (1988) 10 *Marine Policy* 90.

Von Brevern, "State Aid to Shipbuilding Industries and Shipping", at The Future of Shipping in Europe—Key Legal and Commercial Issues, London, 28–29 June 1990.

Voorst and Van Dam, "Europe 1992: Free Movement of Goods in the Wider Context of a Changing Europe", (1988) 25 CML Rev 683.

Weber, "Effect on EEC Air Transport Policy on International Cooperation", (1989) XXIV *European Transport Law* 448.

Weiss, "The Law of Public Procurement in EFTA and the EEC: the Legal Framework and its Implications", (1987) Yb.E.Law 59.

Wellans and Borchardt, "Soft Law in European Community Law", (1989) 14 ELRev 267.

Whish and Sufrin, "Article 85 and the Rule of Reason", (1987) Yb.E.Law 1.

Whittaker, "The EEC Directive on Product Liability", (1985) Yb.E.Law 233.

Yeutter, "We are Not Close to a Trade War", [1987] 3 European Affairs 25.

CHAPTER 1

Introduction

This book is an introduction to the law of the European Community[1] (EC) as it relates to shipping.[2]

1.1 THE EUROPEAN COMMUNITY

1.1.1 The Three European Communities

The EC consists of three interconnected international organisations: the European Coal and Steel Community (ECSC); the European Atomic Energy Community (Euratom)[3] and the European Economic Community (EEC). Of these, the last is the most significant for present purposes. Collectively, they constitute the EC.[4]

1.1.2 The evolution of the EC

The EC is growing: it began in 1952 with six Member States[5]; in 1973, it grew to nine States;[6] it then grew to ten States in 1981[7]; and since 1986, when Portugal and Spain joined, there have been twelve Member States: Belgium; Denmark; France; Germany; Greece; Ireland; Italy; Luxembourg; the Netherlands; Portugal; Spain; and the United Kingdom of Great Britain and Northern Ireland. Austria has applied to accede.[8] Sweden, Finland, Poland, Hungary, Czechoslovakia, Malta and Turkey[9] have also expressed interest in acceding. In time, other European States may accede to or associate themselves with the EC.

The EC is evolving. It has experienced dynamic development over the past few years.

1. The terms "European Community" and "European Communities" are often used interchangeably in legal literature. The former term will be used in this book.

2. In this context, "shipping" is taken to mean the "business of transporting goods and persons in ships from a dockside point across the sea for commercial purposes" (*Committee of Inquiry into Shipping*, Viscount Rochdale, London 1970, HMSO, Cmnd. 4337). On the definition of shipping, see also Bredima-Savopoulou and Tzoannos, *The Common Shipping Policy of the EEC* (1990), p. 12 *et seq.*.

This book does not involve a discussion of EC fishing law (on which see Churchill, *EEC Fishing Law* (1987)), inland waterways or shipbuilding *per se*, although shipbuilding is examined in Chapter 18, below.

3. This organisation is commonly abbreviated as either the EAEC or Euratom but the latter is used in this book.

4. On the EC generally, see Chapter 3, below.

5. *I.e.*, Belgium, France, the then Federal Republic of Germany, Italy, Luxembourg and the Netherlands. The Treaty of Paris was signed on 18 April 1951.

6. Denmark, Ireland and the UK acceded on 1 January 1973.

7. Greece acceded on 1 January 1981.

8. See "Austria to Remain Neutral within EEC", *Lloyd's List*, 18 July 1989.

9. Other States may seek to join over the course of time.

It began life in the 1950s as a group of three intergovernmental organisations and may end up by the late 1990s as an economic, monetary and political union. The EC is already playing a significant role in world affairs as a collective unit having diplomatic relations around the world. The EC, as a separate entity from its Member States, has the power to conclude certain types of international agreements within its sphere of competence and has concluded many such agreements to date. The EC has reached common positions on such issues as South Africa, Yugoslavia, Palestine and so on. It has concluded agreements with States as diverse as the People's Republic of China and Austria. Its foreign policy role has been strengthened since the adoption of the Single European Act (SEA).[10]

1.1.3 The EC is the world's largest trading bloc

The EC is the world's largest trading bloc. It has about 19% of the world's trade while the US and Japan have about 17% and 10% respectively. Its foreign trade with the rest of the world amounted to around ECU 680 billion[11] —this is more than double the Japanese total and some ECU 100 billion greater than the US figure. The gross domestic product (GDP) of the combined EC Member States is ECU3,669 billion which is smaller than the USA (ECU3,869 billion) but larger than Japan (which has a GDP of ECU 2,058 billion). The EC has a special relationship with the European Free Trade Association (EFTA) with about half of EFTA's exports going to the EC and about a quarter of the EC's exports going to EFTA.[12] There is no doubt that the EC is now being forced to "speak with one voice and to adopt a common position".[13]

1.1.4 Population

The EC has a population of 350 million—more than the former USSR (with 279 million), the USA (with 239 million) or Japan (with 121 million).

1.1.5 The 1992 Programme

The Internal Market Programme of the EC (known colloquially as the "1992 Programme")[14] has rejuvenated the EC in recent years. In June 1985, a plan was outlined by way of a Commission White Paper to integrate the twelve national markets of the EC into one single or internal market. If the twelve markets of the EC are integrated so as to become one internal market then it will be the largest single market in the world. The process of integration or internalisation is well under way and the timetable set down in Article 8a of the EEC Treaty[15] requires this process to be completed by 31 December 1992. In practical terms, this deadline is optimistic for two reasons: first, if all of the measures set out in the June 1985 White Paper were adopted by the EC, some would still require implementation in Member States and this will

10. On the SEA, see para.3.21 below. On the external relations of the EC generally, see Chapter 19, below.
11. The ECU is the European Currency Unit and is approximately equivalent to one US dollar in value.
12. The EC and EFTA collectively constitute the European Economic Area. On this Area, see Chapter 26, below.
13. The European Parliament's Committee on Regional Policy, Regional Planning and Transport, *Interim Report on the Sea Transport Problems in the Community* (1977), para. 4.
14. On this programme, see Chapter 26 below.
15. As inserted by Art.13 SEA.

probably not take place before the end of 1992 and secondly, despite the fact that there were almost 300 measures set out in the White Paper, more measures will be needed to achieve a true internal market.

1.1.6 Transport in the EC

Transport plays a significant role in the EC.[16] Expenditure in the EC on transport is very high as a proportion of expenditure generally in the Community—it amounts to some 14.3% (in 1985) and is second only to the two main categories of expenditure, namely sustenance (*i.e.* food and drink) as well as energy (*i.e.* fuel and light). Transport in the EC has traditionally been highly regulated by the governments of the EC Member States. There has been a large number of restrictive practices as well as technical and administrative regulations governing the sector. For a more detailed discussion of transport in the EC, see Chapter 4 below.

1.1.7 Future of the EC

The EC is currently on a path of spectacular growth and development. It may grow to replace the Member States in many spheres. It may well be the case that there are "a number of problems . . . the Community could tackle more effectively than individual Member States"[17] — the whole may be greater than the sum of the parts. Thus, on the level of world shipping, the EC (as an entity) should be more important and influential than the twelve separate Member States.

1.2 SHIPPING IN THE EC

Chapter 2 is a detailed commercial overview of shipping in the EC. It would however be useful at this stage to preview some basic facts about shipping and the EC.

1.2.1 EC Shipping policy

1.2.1.1 Strategic significance of shipping for the EC

There is no doubt about the strategic significance of shipping for the EC. About 90% of the EC's foreign trade is carried by sea. About one-third of the 750 million tonnes of goods carried each year between the Member States is carried by sea. Ships registered in EC Member States carry about 70% of the trade between Member States as well as 40% of the Community's external trade and there would be other ships used for this latter trade which are owned by nationals from EC Member States but registered outside the EC. The Commission has written that it:

16. See Chapter 4 below.
17. The Commission's Communication to the Council of Ministers entitled "*A Future for the Community Shipping Industry: Measures to Improve the Operating Conditions of Community Shipping*", COM(89)266 final, 3 August 1989, p. 9. In this context, note the concept of subsidiarity.

"considers that a strong Community fleet is essential to the Community both for economic and strategic reasons. As the leading world trading entity,[18] the Community should not be excessively dependent on third country fleets for its imports and exports, so losing control and influence on the price and quality of transport to and from its territory."[19]

The strategic significance of shipping to the EC means that the EC must have a shipping policy. As the Economic and Social Committee has commented:

"the Community needs a maritime transport policy concerned with the promotion of all maritime activities such as the carriage of goods and passengers by companies in Member States, the use of vessels registered in Member States and the employment of seafarers from Member States."[20]

The same Committee has also written that:

"there is no disputing the fact that if Member States do not want to lose their economic independence, and if they desire to keep control over their own means of transport and maintaining jobs, they must under all circumstances have a merchant fleet at their disposal . . . ."[21]

The Commission has commented:

"[a] cheap and efficient sea transport system is a basic prerequisite for expansion of [EC] trade, especially with non-member countries."[22]

1.2.1.2 Shipping has an important role in the EC's internal market

Shipping is an indispensable element in trade between the Member States as well as between Member States and third countries.[23] The EC is the world's largest trading bloc. Some 90% of the EC's foreign trade is carried by sea. Transport is vital for internal and external trade. The EC needs good transport, and preferably, its own transport fleet: as the Economic and Social Committee[24] has commented:

"[a] viable Community fleet, registered in Member States is essential if services to exporters and importers in the European Community are not to be dominated by third party shipping interests."[25]

Georgios Anastassopoulos, the then chairman of the Transport Committee of the European Parliament,[26] commented in 1987 that his Committee:

"strongly believe[d] that one could not in fact envisage a major trading and economic power, such as the Community, the largest in the world, with 90% of its external trade and 40%

18. *Ed.*, see para.1.1.3, above.

19. Commission of the European Communities, *Guidelines for the Examination of State Aids to Community Shipping Companies*, 1990, p. 3.

20. *Opinion of the Economic and Social Committee on the Communication and Proposals (II.3, II.4) by the Commission to the Council on Progress towards a Common Transport Policy—Maritime Transport*, (COM(85)90 final (TRA/116), para. 1.2

21. *EEC Shipping Policy—Flags of Convenience*, OJ C171 35, 9.7.79.

22. *Communication from the Commission to the Council on The Community's Relations with Non-Member Countries in Shipping Matters*, COM(76)341 final, para. 2.

23. See proposal for a Council Regulation establishing a Community ship register and providing for the flying of the Community flag by sea-going vessels, contained in the Commission's Communication to the Council entitled *A Future for the Community Shipping Industry: Measures to Improve the Operating Conditions of Community Shipping*, COM(89)266 final, 3 August 1989.

24. On this Committee, see para 3.4.7.1 below.

25. *Opinion of the Economic and Social Committee on the Communication and Proposals (II.3, II.4) by the Commission to the Council on Progress towards a Common Transport Policy—Maritime Transport*, COM(85)90 final (TRA/116), para. 1.1.

26. On the European Parliament, see para. 3.4.5 below.

of the Intra-Community [trade] carried by sea, without a Community fleet. That would leave the Community open at any time to all sorts of pressures by the other world trading and economic powers. It would deprive a wide-range of other industries from a basic element of support. It would have meant the loss of a major source of foreign currency and of a major client of European banking and insurance institutions and perhaps the last client of the remnants of the European shipbuilding industry. It would have signified a major loss of employment. The European ports, that happen to be among the largest in the world...would have also tremendously suffered."[27]

He went on to say that there were also defensive[28] and competition reasons supporting the existence of a strong EC shipping fleet.

Shipping is of strategic significance not only for the EC in terms of its relations with the rest of the world, but also in terms of its internal activities. About 40% of the internal trade in goods within the EC is carried by sea, with about half of the trade of the EC Member States being carried by EC carriers. Huge numbers of passengers are transported around the EC both on short and long-haul services. Shipping is the "dominant mode" for many trades.[29]

1.2.1.3 Shipping is an important employer in the EC

Shipping and Shipbuilding are substantial employment industries in the EC. It is almost impossible to calculate all those who benefit from a shipping industry in the EC — these people would include dockers, hauliers, ships' agents, ships' providers, shipbuilders, steel makers, shipping bankers, maritime lawyers as well as those people who work in factories which have been built near ports because of the availability of shipping services.

1.2.1.4. Shipping is an important earner of foreign currency

Shipping has traditionally been an important earner of foreign currency for some of ethe Member States of the EC. Foreign currency is earned not just in terms of charter and carriage fees, but also in terms of insurance premiums, interest on bank loans, shipbuilding contracts, ship-repair contracts, wages, bunkers, fuel, pilotage, harbour dues, legal fees and so on. This was reckoned to be about ECU 13,000 million in 1974.[30] Greece and the UK both earn vast amounts of foreign currency as a result of their involvement in shipping. The UK has, for example, also earned considerable amounts through the marine insurance as well as the financial and legal services it offers in the City of London.

27. See his address at the Antwerp Shipping Symposium, "A Future for the Community Fleet", 6 May 1987; reprinted in (1987) XXII *European Transport Law* at pp. 197–198.

28. The absence of a fleet during wartime can cause enormous difficulties for a State or Community: note, for example, the difficulties experienced by the UK during the Falklands (Malvinas) crisis.

29. The term used by the Economic and Social Committee in *Opinion of the Economic and Social Committee on the Communication and Proposals (II.3, II.4) by the Commission to the Council on Progress towards a Common Transport Policy—Maritime Transport* (COM(85)90 final (TRA/116), para. 1.2 for freight and passenger traffic between some Member States.

30. *Communication from the Commission to the Council on the Community's Relations with Non-Members Countries in Shipping Matters*, COM(76)341 final, 30 June 1976, para. 3.

1.2.1.5 Open/non-protectionist policy

The thrust of EC shipping policy as a whole[31] is towards encouraging and maintaining an open and free shipping market.[32] According to Dimitri Petropolous, the Head of the Maritime Transport Division in the Transport Directorate-General of the EC Commission,[33] because of, *inter alia*,

"the direction provided by the Treaty of Rome[34] towards a policy based on market economy principles . . ., the first objective for Community maritime transport policy must be to *safeguard free access to a free world shipping market*. Indeed there is nothing to be gained by a protectionist Community shipping policy. Although the Community is a big cargo generating area you can normally not reserve more than half of the cargo to your own ships—your trading partners can make their claims.[35] As the Community fleet is already carrying around 40% of the Community's foreign trade on vessels registered in the Community, the possible gain, if any, would be small and could place in jeopardy the revenue which the Community shipping industry gets from cross-trading between third countries. Moreover, the Community's shipping policy cannot simply look at the position of shipowners. An essential consideration of shipping policy must be that the Community's foreign trade should have the advantages of freight rates arrived at in fair and free competition. Therefore the Community has to defend itself against protectionist measures of other countries whilst at the same time bringing its own house in order in this respect."[36]

This openness is not surprising: first, the EC is generally in support of an open as well as free economy and secondly, most shipping companies in the EC are private profit-making organisations and not State-operated concerns. The openness of EC shipping policy does not mean that the EC will never protect the interests of its Member States. The European Parliament has said that: "the Community is not faced with a stark choice between a free market and protectionism, rather there can be a balanced and pragmatic approach applying selective defensive actions where the basic viability of the shipping industry is being undermined."[37] Much of the package of measures adopted by the Council of Ministers in December 1986[38] was based on the free market philosophy. On the other hand, the EC has protected the interests of its shipping. The dumping measures adopted by the Council of Ministers in 1986[39] were designed to protect EC shipping interests. It is true to say however that the EC has not been as vigilant as it might have been in protecting the interests of its shipping industry. Sometimes the EC does not achieve the balance between protection and openness—it was written in 1981:

"so far, the EC in the context of its economic and political relations with third countries has concentrated on promoting economic development and trade by providing through Conventions

31. The shipping policies of each EC Member State is examined in Chapter 2 below.

32. On shipping policies generally, see Bredima-Savopoulou and Tzoannos, *op. cit. cf.* footnote 2 above (1990), pp. 36–37.

33. On the EC Commission and its organisation generally, see para. 3.4.2 below.

34. *Ed.*, this Treaty (which is also known as the EEC Treaty) established the EEC and still governs its operation. On the Treaty, see para 3.2.4 below.

35. *Ed.*, see Chapter 11 below.

36. In a speech "The European Community Transport Policy—An Overview", in *The Future of Shipping in Europe—Key Legal and Commercial Issues*, London, 28–29 June 1990, pp. 4–5.

37. "The European Parliament's *Opinion on the Communication and Proposals by the Commission to the Council of Ministers on Progress towards a Common Transport Policy—Maritime Transport*", reprinted in OJ 1986 C207/31 at 32.

38. On these measures, see, *inter alia*, Chapter 5 below.

39. On these measures, see Chapter 5 below.

significant concessions concerning the free entry to its markets of industrial products and most agricultural products originating from those countries. These concessions have not, on the other hand, been reciprocated by the guarantees that the countries concerned will refrain from flag discrimination practices at the expense of the Community fleets.

It appears that whenever the Community has been confronted with a conflict between trade and development interests on one hand, and shipping interests on the other, it has opted in favour of the former."[40]

Conversely, the EC may not want to engage in protectionism and instead an open policy may well be the desired course of action. It is however interesting to note that the apparent openness of EC shipping policy is out of step with the twentieth century growth in the level of protectionism afforded by many States around the world to their fleets.[41] Cabotage[42] and cargo reservation are two instruments of such protectionism.

1.2.1.6 Internal balances

There is an interesting and delicate balance to be struck in the formulation of EC shipping policy. The interests of shipowners, seafarers, shippers, governments, as well as others involved in the transport industry, are sometimes not capable of harmonisation.[43] Shipowners may seek a protective market in which freight rates are fixed by means of an agreement between the shipowners but such a policy could be contrary to the interests of shippers. Some governments may wish to protect their national fleets and are therefore willing to offer State Aids[44] and this may be contrary to the wishes of other governments, shipowners from other States, the policy of the EC, and the well-being of the industry in general.

There is also a balance to be struck in terms of dividing competence between the Member States and the EC itself. The EC institutions are certainly very anxious to have power resting with them: in a 1984 press release, the Commission stated: "[t]he Commission believes that the best way of serving the interests of the Community fleet and its users and of achieving the Treaty objectives is to maintain *a trade-orientated, multilateral Community shipping policy*."[45]

1.2.1.7 Social dimension to EC shipping policy

EC shipping policy has a social dimension. The policy to be adopted by the Member States must have an employment protection dimension. A bi-partite committee was established in 1987 to advise the Commission on how best to promote social measures for the protection of seafarers in the EC. The "*Positive Measures*" Communication of 3 August 1989[46] contained a number of specific measures designed to improve the social conditions of seafarers. This may well be an aspect of EC shipping policy which will become more important as the EC develops its social policy after "1992".

40. Bredima-Savopoulou and Tzoannos, "In Search of a Common Shipping Policy for the EC" (1981) XX JCMS 95 at p. 97.

41. See Ademuni-Odeke, *Protectionism and the Future of International Shipping* (1984), *passim* and Hayman in Barston and Birnie, *The Maritime Dimension* (1980), p.130 *et seq*.

42. On cabotage see Chapter 7 below.

43. Lord Stanley Clinton Davies, former Commissioner for Transport, is reported to have said that each of these interest groups "has to comprehend the problems of the other; each has to be mutually supportive": see IP(85)60.

44. On State Aids, see Chapter 15 below.

45. P-95, December 1984, emphasis added.

46. On this Communication, see para. 5.5.26 below.

1.2.1.8 Environmental dimension to EC shipping policy

EC shipping policy is also concerned with the environment.[47] Some of the earliest legal measures adopted by the EC in the area of shipping were in relation to the protection of the marine environment. Indeed, EC environmental law developed more in the maritime sector than in many other sectors during the early years.

1.2.1.9 Competition dimension to EC shipping policy

In line with the EC's general policy in favour of an open and competitive market generally as well as its open and competitive policy towards shipping[48] in particular, a great deal of EC shipping law relates to competition. Chapters 10–16, below, deal specifically with this issue.

1.2.1.10 EC shipping policy and its relationship to the international obligations of the EC Member States

The shipping policy of the EC must take into account the international obligations of the EC Member States as well as the role of the EC in the world. It is not possible for the EC to take unilateral positions. The EC's shipping policy must be in compliance with the economic and commercial policies of the EC and its Member States. The external relations of the EC in shipping matters are examined in chapter 19 below.

1.2.1.11 Staggered or strategic development of EC shipping policy?

There is a choice between the development of EC shipping policy on a co-ordinated basis or in a piecemeal way. While there is some merit in providing for individual items, there is need for a co-ordinated approach. France has traditionally favoured the comprehensive framework approach. The piecemeal approach has been favoured by the UK, Greece, the EC institutions (to some extent) and the CAACE.[49] While the latter approach allows considerable flexibility and freedom in respect of those areas which are not regulated by the EC, there is surely considerable merit in having a comprehensive skeletal overview within which individual issues can be tackled as and when it is appropriate. There is need for a comprehensive and not just a modal approach to shipping and other transport areas.

1.2.1.12 There is no comprehensive Community shipping policy

It is sad to record that the EC does not as yet appear to have a uniform and comprehensive policy on shipping.[50] It is vital that such an important industry, which has suffered so badly in recent years, has an effective and well-designed policy for both the shorter and longer terms. While one cannot blame the decline in the fortunes of shipping on the EC, one must however consider whether the decline might not have been so great had the Member States of the EC been able to combine together

47. On the environment and shipping, see Chapter 17 below.
48. See para 1.2.1.5, above.
49. See the CAACE, "Annual Report 1978", Brussels, May 1979.
50. It is, of course, acknowledged that the adoption of such a policy is difficult given the diversity of interests and the absence of specific Treaty provisions.

and produce an effective policy. How protectionist should the EC have been? All is not lost, however, and one hopes that the Member States might formulate a common open and competitive policy on shipping so as to meet the challenge of the internal market and the twenty-first century.

The need for an EC shipping policy was skilfully and convincingly argued in an interim report published in 1977 by the European Parliament's Committee on Regional Policy, Regional Planning and Transport on Sea Transport Problems in the Community.[51] The Committee stated:

"7. In this introduction your Committee wishes to state its strong and unequivocal opposition to a number of arguments frequently advanced by those who are against the inclusion of sea transport in the European Community's terms of reference.

8. Sea transport, it is argued, should not be included in the Common Transport Policy because it is governed by 'special conditions' and cannot be made subject to the same rules as other means of transport.

Needless to say, this report does not call for the same conditions. The principles governing land transport quite clearly cannot be applied to sea transport as they stand. No one is suggesting that locomotives should be used to pull sea-going vessels. What is needed is a dynamic concept for a common sea transport policy which allows for world-wide contingencies and developments and the specific conditions governing sea transport. But it is equally clear that certain basic principles of the common economic policy of the European Community must also be applied to sea transport. The generally free-market basic structure of the Community, the principle of non-discrimination and a number of other fundamental principles must surely also be applied to sea transport. There can be no progress in the discussion on this subject if some demand that different and others that the same principles be applied as to the other means of transport without saying what these principles are: basic principles such as market economy, competition, equal treatment, and non-discrimination or "second-line principles" like those laid down in Articles 74 to 82 of the EEC Treaty.

9. Another frequently heard argument is that since sea transport is subject to world-wide ramifications and world-wide rules, it should not be forced into the "narrow confines" of Community regulations, which would only represent a step backwards compared with world-wide arrangements.

There is no logic to this argument, popular though it may be. What European industry is *not* subject to world-wide ramifications? Is it not simply true to say of the European economy, with its dependence on imports of raw materials and its vital need to export, that everything we do has world-wide ramifications? Even the cereals which grow in our fields are subject to world-wide rules, which in some respects go further than world arrangements for sea transport.

The reason why the "world-wide ramifications' argument has found so many adherents in transport policy is perhaps that at least one major mode of transport—rail transport—does not have such ramifications. However, the railways, with their regional monopolies, are the major exception among all other sectors of the economy. The ramifications of the other modes of transport (road transport, inland waterways, pipelines) are also continental rather than world-wide; however, it is only in relation to these and not to industry and agriculture that the world-wide ramifications of sea transport are unusual.

In addition, it is perfectly clear that any Community policy (whether on cereals or sea transport) must take account of existing international agreements and either conform to them or, if they are seen to be inadequate, attempt to supplement or correct them.

The world-wide ramifications of sea transport cannot be used as an argument against the application of Article 84(2) [of the EEC Treaty]. The Community is no longer a free trade area which is not developing a common external economic policy. In view of the world-wide ramifications of the Community's economy as a whole it is essential for sea transport to be included in the Community's external economic policy.

10. A further argument, usually muted, is that sea transport policy is better left in the hands of

51. Doc.5/77, 23 March 1977.

the maritime nations and city-ports, of economic circles close to shipping and possessing the necessary expertise, than in the hands of bureaucrats in Brussels."

1.2.2 EC shipping law

EC shipping law is in the early stages of development and, in-so-far as it has developed at all, it has been of recent origin. The law of the EC relating to shipping is primarily the law of the EEC rather than the law of either the ECSC or Euratom. There is not a great deal of *pure* EC shipping law: shipping (more accurately, sea transport) is mentioned only once in the EEC Treaty![52] Many aspects of shipping law and practice, such as the classification and technical standards of ships are essentially matters of national policy and scrutiny. The EC does, however, influence and control many areas of shipping. Indeed, it is quite surprising that there should be EC law on shipping at all. Maritime politics have traditionally been very nationalistic: traditionally, States have rarely conceded and only occasionally co-operated on such matters. Yet the EC Member States have co-operated in a remarkable (but limited) way.

In essence, there are two sources of EEC shipping law, namely, the EEC Treaty and the secondary legislation adopted under that Treaty (based in particular, on Article 84 of that Treaty).

It should be remembered that EC shipping law must be seen in the context of EC law generally. Thus the provisions of the EEC Treaty directly relating to transport, namely, Articles 74 to 84, must be seen in the context of the EEC Treaty as a whole, including such provisions as Articles 7[53] and 85.[54] This inter-relationship will be discussed in greater length later.[55] The remaining chapters of this book are devoted to examining some of the various aspects of EC shipping law.

1.3 INTERNATIONAL ORGANISATIONS AND SHIPPING

1.3.1 Introduction

Before examining the work of the EC in relation to shipping, it would be instructive to review the work of other international organisations in the area of shipping. Such a brief review will highlight the special nature of the EC in general, for example, in terms of organisation, as well as its role in shipping in particular.

Traditionally, shipping has been a matter for individual nation States.[56] States jealously guarded their sovereignty in shipping and maritime matters.[57] Many of the States founded since the Second World War have been particularly anxious to guard their newly found sovereignty in matters relating to the sea and trade. States are interested in shipping for legitimate (as well as not so legitimate) reasons. They are interested in matters such as ship finance, registration, deployment, crewing, competition, safety, design and operation. The mechanisms used by States include

52. EEC Treaty, Art. 84.
53. *I.e.* prohibition of discrimination on the basis of nationality.
54. On anti-competitive agreements, decisions and concerted practices.
55. See Chapter 4 below.
56. See Farthing, *International Shipping: An Introduction to the Policies, Politics and Institutions of the Maritime World*, (Lloyd's of London Press Ltd., 1987), Chapter 3.
57. See O' Connell, *International Law of the Sea* (1982), *passim*.

regulations, subsidies and various arrangements or agreements.

A small but significant change, however, took place over the last one hundred years. Shipping is not now a matter left entirely to the States themselves but is also a matter of legitimate concern for intergovernmental organisations as well.[58] It is only natural that there should be an international interest in shipping because it is, after all, one of the most international of all industries. It is contended that the *international* regulation of shipping will grow in the coming years at the expense of *national* regulation.[59] Such international regulation will be particularly evident in areas like the environment, cargo reservation, government subsidies, shipbuilding, taxes, safety and navigation. The signs are already there.

There is a large number of international organisations involved in shipping. Over time, some of the most significant, have included the Baltic and International Maritime Council (formerly Conference) (BIMCO), the Danube Commission, the Intergovernmental Maritime Consultative Organisation (IMCO) (now the International Maritime Organisation (IMO)),[60] the International Association of Independent Tanker Owners, the International Association of Lighthouse Authorities,[61] the International Chamber of Shipping, the International Maritime Pilots' Association, the International Maritime Satellite Organisation[62] and, the International Shipowners' Association. There are also organisations and institutions whose main concern lies elsewhere but which have an impact on shipping and such organisations and institutions include, for example, the International Atomic Energy Agency[63] and the United Nations Institute for Training and Research.[64] With such a large number of international organisations involved, it is important that there is no unproductive overlap in the work of these organisations[65] but sadly, there is some overlap. There are also international arrangements such as the North Sea Conferences[66] as well as the Oslo and Paris Commissions which have specific roles to play.

1.3.2 United Nations (UN)

The United Nations (UN) is the primary international organisation being the supreme universal organisation.[67] It was formed by fifty states at the San Francisco Conference in 1945 and on 2 March 1992, it had 175 Member States.

The UN has a large number of specialised agencies and only some of the ones more relevant to shipping are mentioned here. Others include the Food and Agriculture

58. This was in line with the trend towards the development of international organisations throughout the twentieth century: see Armstrong, *The Rise of the International Organisation: A Short History* (1982) and Bowett, *The Law of International Institutions* (4th ed., 1982).

59. On the increasing regulation of shipping activities, see Farthing, *op. cit.* at footnote 56, Chapter 1.

60. On this organisation, see para 1.3.3 below.

61. See Dolzer in Bernhardt (ed.), *Encyclopedia of Public International Law*, vol. 5, 1983, p. 52.

62. On this organisation, see para 1.3.11 below.

63. Szasz in Bernhardt (ed.), *op. cit.* at footnote 61, vol. 5, 1983, p. 52. See also Bischof, "Nuclear Ships" in Bernhardt (ed.), *op. cit.* at footnote 61, vol. 11, 1989, p. 240.

64. Diallo in Bernhardt (ed.), *op. cit.* at footnote 61, 1983, p. 336.

65. See the comments of Georgios Anastassopoulos to the Antwerp Shipping Symposium, "A Future for the Community Fleet" on 6 May 1987, reprinted in (1987) XXII *European Transport Law* at p. 201.

66. See Part 1 of (1990) *International Journal of Estuarine and Coastal Law*, Numbers 1–3.

67. On the UN see Bowett, *op. cit.* at footnote 58, Chapter 3; Goodrich, *The United Nations in Changing World* (1974); Gutteridge, *The United Nations in a Changing World* (1969); Hill, *The Law of the United Nations* (1964); Luard, *The United Nations: How it Works and What it Does* (1979). See also Frowein in Bernhardt (ed.), *op. cit.* at footnote 61, vol. 5, 1983, p. 272.

Organisation (FAO) and the UN Institute for Training and Research. The UN itself has been responsible for such conventions as the Third United Nations Convention on the Law of the Sea (UNCLOS III).[68]

In 1977, the European Parliament's Committee on Regional Policy, Regional Planning and Transport published an Interim Report on the Sea Transport Problems in the Community and stated: "[t]he most important negotiations on questions of world sea transport are at present being held within the framework of the United Nations."[69]

1.3.3 The Intergovernmental Maritime Consultative Organisation (IMCO) and the International Maritime Organisation (IMO)

1.3.3.1 Introduction

The International Maritime Organisation (IMO) is the primary international maritime organisation.[70] It has been described by the EC's Economic and Social Committee[71] as "the body 'par excellence' for dealing with shipping safety and protection of the marine environment."[72] The IMO is really the successor to the Intergovernmental Maritime Consultative Organisation (IMCO).

The IMCO and the IMO have been responsible for the adoption of a large number of Conventions and Recommendations over time. In terms of Conventions, they have been involved in the formulation of, among others, the International Convention for the Prevention of Pollution of the Sea by Oil 1954, the Safety of Life at Sea Convention 1960, the International Convention on Load Lines 1966, the Convention on the International Regulations for Preventing Collisions at Sea 1972, the Convention for Safe Containers 1972, the Safety of Life at Sea Convention (SOLAS) 1974, the International Convention on the International Maritime Satellite Organisation 1976, the Torremolinos Convention for the Safety of Fishing Vessels 1978, the Convention on Standards of Training, Certification and Watchkeeping 1978, the Safety of Life at Sea Protocol 1978, and the International Convention on Maritime Search and Rescue (SAR).

It is useful to divide the present analysis of the IMO into two parts: the IMCO and the IMO.

1.3.3.2 The Intergovernmental Maritime Consultative Organisation

The Intergovernmental Maritime Consultative Organisation (IMCO)[73] was a Specialised Agency of the UN.[74] It was one of the later Specialised Agencies to be formed, having been created only in 1958. However, it owed its origins to the United

68. See Simmonds, "The Status of the UN Convention on the Law of the Sea" (1985) 34 ICLQ 359 and "EEC Urged to Agree Law of the Sea Convention," *Lloyd's List*, 16 December 1982, p. 3.

69. Working Documents; Doc. 5/77; 23 March 1977; Rapporteur: Mr. H. Seefeld, para. 20.

70. On the IMO see Mankabady (ed.), *The International Maritime Organisation* (1984); and Simmonds in Bernhardt (ed.), *op. cit.* at footnote 61, vol. 11, p.104.

71. On this Committee, see para.3.4.7 below.

72. *Opinion of the Economic and Social Committee on the Proposal for a Council Regulation (EEC) on the transfer of ships from one register to another within the Community* (COM(90) 219 final), para. 2.2.

73. See Johnson, "IMCO: The First Four Years, 1959–1962" (1963) 12 ICLQ 31; Simmonds, "The Constitution of the Maritime Safety Committee of IMCO", (1963) 12 ICLQ 56; and Simmonds, "International Maritime Organisation" in Bernhardt (ed.), *op. cit.* at footnote 61 above, vol. 5, 1983, p. 104.

74. On UN Specialised Agencies, see Bowett, *op. cit.* at footnote 58, *passim*.

Maritime Authority (which was formed by the Allied Powers during the Second World War), the temporary United Maritime Consultative Council (which met in 1946), as well as the Provisional Maritime Consultative Council which was formed in 1947. The birth of IMCO was due to a Convention drawn up at the UN Maritime Conference held in Geneva in 1948 which was attended by thirty-five States (but not by the then USSR). This Convention, the IMCO Convention, provided for an Assembly which met for the first time in London in 1959 and confirmed the status of IMCO as a UN Specialised Agency. This Assembly later accepted responsibility for the administration and implementation of a number of international maritime agreements, including the International Convention for the Safety of Life at Sea, the International Code of Signals and the International Convention for the Prevention of Pollution of the Sea by Oil.

1.3.3.4 The International Maritime Organisation

The IMCO became the IMO in 1982 for reasons which are not relevant to the present work. Like the IMCO, the IMO has an Assembly[75] which meets every two years. The Assembly's membership is drawn from all the Member States of IMCO and acts as the IMO's policy-making organ. It also has a Council[76] which consists of twenty-four members which are elected for two-year terms. Six of the members represent those States having the largest interest in providing international shipping services; another six members represent States with the largest interest in international sea-borne trade; and the balance (i.e. twelve) represent those States which have special interests in maritime transport or navigation.[77] The IMO generally has 135 member states.

There are also a number of committees, including the Maritime Safety Committee which considers any matter within the scope of the Organisation and is concerned with aids to navigation, construction and equipment of vessels, manning from a safety standpoint, rules for the prevention of collisions, handling of dangerous cargoes, as well as maritime safety and procedures. This Committee operates through a number of sub-committees which deal with such issues as radio communications, navigation, training, containers, dangerous cargoes and bulk chemicals. Originally, the Maritime Safety Committee consisted of fourteen members:

> "elected by the Assembly from the Members, governments of those nations having an important interest in maritime safety, of which not less than eight shall be elected so as to ensure adequate representation of Members, governments of other nations with an important interest in maritime safety, such as nations interested in maritime safety, such as nations interested in the supply of large numbers of crews or in the carriage of large numbers of berthed and unberthed passengers, and of major geographical areas."[78]

This provision caused considerable controversy in the Organisation and led to an Advisory Opinion being sought from the International Court of Justice.[79] The details of that controversy and Opinion are dealt with extensively in other books but the only point which need concern present readers is that the possibility of becoming a member of this Committee is now open to all members of the IMO.

75. IMO Convention, Arts. 13–16.
76. IMO Convention, Arts. 17–27.
77. These twelve are elected in such a manner as to ensure the representation of the major geographical areas of the world.
78. IMCO Convention, Art.28(a).
79. *Constitution of IMCO Safety Committee (Advisory Opinion)*, ICJ Rep. 1960, p. 150.

The IMO has a successful Marine Environment Protection Programme which was established in 1973 and has been active since. Indeed, the EEC Council of Ministers has recognised the IMO as representing the focal point for preventing and combating marine pollution at international level.[80] Most importantly for present purposes, the EC has observer status at the IMO.

1.3.4 International Labour Organisation (ILO)

1.3.4.1 Introduction

The International Labour Organisation (ILO) has had a long and prestigious history.[81] It was founded in 1919 as part of the post-First World War reconstruction programme.[82] The ILO was formed in order to improve working conditions worldwide by means of international co-operation. The ILO now has the responsibility of promoting conditions in which all human beings, irrespective of race, creed or sex, are able to pursue their material well-being and their spiritual development in freedom and dignity, economic security and equal opportunity. Since 1946, the ILO has been one of the specialised agencies of the UN.[83] Today, it has around 150 Member States.

1.3.4.2 Organic and organisational structure

The permanent organisation of the ILO is divided into three parts: (a) a General Conference of Members' representatives; (b) a Governing Body composed of twenty-four government representatives, twelve employers' representatives and twelve employees' representatives;[84] and (c) the International Labour Office controlled by the Governing Body.[85]

The General Conference normally meets at least once a year.[86] It is composed of four representatives of each Member State, of whom two are government delegates and the other two delegates respectively represent the employers and the employees in the Member State.[87] These delegates may be accompanied by advisers. The General Conference discusses a broad range of issues as they relate to employment. The work of the General Conference leads to either Recommendations (which are never legally binding) or Conventions (i.e. treaties) (which become legally binding on a State when they entered into force, have been signed and ratified by the State).

The Governing Body consists of forty-eight persons: twenty-four representing governments; twelve representing employers and twelve representing workers.[88] It meets three times a year. The Governing Body is responsible for the ILO's programme generally.

80. Council of Ministers Resolution of 19 June 1990 on the Prevention of Accidents causing Marine Pollution, OJ C206/1, 18.8.1990.

81. On the ILO, see Galenson, *The International Labour Organisation: an American View* (1981); Jenks, *Social Justice in the Law of the Nations: the ILO Impact after Fifty Years* (1970); Shotell, *The Origins of the International Labour Organisation* (1934); and Vaticos, *International Labour Law* (1979).

82. The ILO Constitution was Part XIII of the Versailles Treaty.

83. On the relationship between the ILO and the UN, see the UN Charter, Arts. 57 and 63.

84. ILO Constitution, Art. 7.

85. ILO Constitution, Art. 2.

86. ILO Constitution, Art. 3(1).

87. ILO Constitution, Art. 3(1).

88. ILO Constitution, Art. 7(1).

The International Labour Office is the ILO's secretariat and its functions include:

> "the collection and distribution of information on all subjects relating to the international adjustment of conditions of industrial life and labour, and particularly the examination of subjects which it is proposed to bring before the Conference with a view to the conclusion of international Conventions, and the conduct of such special investigations as may be ordered by the Conference or by the Governing Body."[89]

There are other bodies as well, such as regional conferences, regional advisory committees and industrial committees. Most importantly, for present purposes, is the Joint Maritime Commission which is composed of shipowners' and seafarers' representatives. It deals with issues of employment at sea and prepares for the work of the maritime sessions of the International Labour Conference.

1.3.4.3 Activities

The ILO has been successful in improving the conditions of workers in many economic sectors (it was awarded the Nobel Peace Prize in 1969) but particularly in the area of shipping. Some of the general work of the ILO relates (incidentally) to shipping. The ILO has adopted over 150 Conventions and over 160 Recommendations on labour issues. Many of these would benefit seafarers.

The ILO has also taken a specific interest in shipping matters. It has adopted specific Conventions and Recommendations on the employment of seafarers.[90] The General Conference has held a number of sessions devoted exclusively to shipping matters. The ILO's Joint Maritime Commission (JMC), which meets more regularly than the General Conference, is a bipartite conference involving representatives of both employers and employees. Both the General Conference and the JMC have been quite successful in the area of seafarers, and over two dozen Conventions and almost two dozen Recommendations have been adopted in the area of shipping.

1.3.4.4 Relations with the EC

On 26 June 1978, the EEC Council of Ministers recommended, in Recommendation 78/584/EEC,[91] that Member States should (where appropriate and where they had not already done so) ratify or accede to the ILO's Convention No. 147 concerning minimum standards in merchant ships[92] as a matter of priority.

1.3.5–1.3.7 United Nations Conference on Trade and Development (UNCTAD)

The United Nations Conference on Trade and Development (UNCTAD) represents another substantial area of involvement by the UN in the area of shipping.[93] Many developing countries have found UNCTAD to be an useful forum for the expression of their views on, among other things, shipping.

89. ILO Constitution, Art. 10(1).
90. E.g. the 29 October 1976 Agreement on the Supervision of Working Conditions on Sea-Going Ships. See also Agritto, "Flags of Convenience and Sub-Standard Vessels: A Review of ILO's Approach to the Problem" (1974) *International Labour Review*, vol. 110.
91. OJ L194/17, 19.7.78.
92. Adopted in 1976.
93. On UNCTAD and shipping, see Corea, in Bernhardt (ed.), *op. cit.*, at footnote 54 above, vol. 5, 1983, p. 301 and Farthing, *op. cit.* at footnote 56 above, Chapter 8. See also Juda, "World Shipping, UNCTAD and the New International Economic Order" (1981) 35 *International Organization* 49.

The first meeting of UNCTAD took place in Geneva in 1964. Shipping was a small item on the long agenda of this first meeting. It was resolved that shipping would be dealt with by the Third Committee of the Conference which was the Committee dealing with Invisible Trade. It was later decided that shipping merited a Permanent Committee of its own and as a result, the Shipping Committee of the UNCTAD was formed. This Shipping Committee (now abolished), which consisted of some forty-five members, discussed shipping in the broad commercial and economic contexts. It has examined such issues as liner conferences,[94] multi-modal transport, ports, bulk trades and conditions for registration of ships.[95]

Discussions within UNCTAD on shipping have been heated at times. The Developed Countries were against public regulation of what they viewed as a private profit-making industry. Conversely, the developing States held diametrically opposed views favouring public regulation of what they viewed as a public service. The EC States have generally gathered in Group B within UNCTAD along with the developed States so as to fight against protectionist shipping policies.

UNCTAD has been closely involved in the issue of liner conferences.[96] The developing States were particularly hard-hitting in their criticism of the liner conference system. Eventually, an "agreement" was reached on the basis of consensus.[97] This agreement recognised the necessity of the liner conference system so as to secure stable rates and regular services but stated that, for the system to function properly, it is necessary that there should be close co-operation between shippers and the conferences. UNCTAD's Code of Conduct for Liner Conferences is the only multilateral cargo sharing agreement in which the EC Member States are involved. Some Member States have yet to ratify it, namely, Greece, Ireland, Italy, Luxembourg, Portugal and Spain.

UNCTAD is also deeply involved in the UN's Development Programme (UNDP) for Third World states and runs both the TRAINMAR (the training of managers from developing countries) and JOBMAR (assisting seafarers from developing countries to obtain "on the job" experience) programmes.

1.3.8 *United Nations Commission on International Trade Law* (UNCITRAL)

The United Nations Commission on International Trade Law (UNCITRAL) was created in 1966 to examine legal issues relating to international trade.[98] UNCITRAL has only occasionally concerned itself with shipping matters.

1.3.9 Economic Commission for Europe (ECE)

The Economic Commission for Europe (ECE) is part of the UN. It is the European counterpart of the UN Economic Commissions in Africa (ECA), Latin America (ECLA) as well as in Asia and the Pacific (ESCAP). ECE has little significance for

93. On UNCTAD and shipping, see Corea, in Bernhardt (ed.), *op. cit.*, at footnote 61 above, vol. 5, 1983, p. 301 and Farthing, *op. cit.*, at footnote 56, Chapter 8. See also Guest, *Lloyd's List*, 21 April 1992, p. 4.

94. On liner conferences, see Chapter 11 below.

95. Farthing, *op. cit* at footnote 56 above, p. 88.

96. On the liner conference system generally, see paras 11.1–11.3 below. See also Farthing, *op. cit.* at footnote 56 above, Chapter 7.

97. The agreement, is known as the Common Measures of Understanding on Shipping Questions.

98. Herrmann in Bernhardt (ed.), *op. cit.* at footnote 61 above, vol. 5, 1983, p. 297.

shipping generally but it has conducted some work in the area of cargo documentation (including customs clearance) and shipping procedures.

1.3.10 United Nations Environment Programme (UNEP)

1.3.10.1 Introduction

The United Nations Environment Programme (UNEP) has obvious relevance for shipping in terms of marine environmental protection.[99] UNEP was set up by UN General Assembly Resolution 2997 (XXVII) after the June 1972 UN Conference on the Human Environment held in Stockholm. That Conference produced an "Action Plan" of 109 Recommendations and declared twenty-six "Common Principles" on humanity's rights and duties in relation to the environment.[100] The Conference recommended that the UN give greater attention to the environment and as a result of this Recommendation as well as a report from the UN Secretary-General, Resolution 2997 (XXVII) was adopted so as to establish the UNEP. Interestingly, the UNEP is not a UN Specialised Agency but rather acts as a catalyst within the UN system.[101]

1.3.10.2 Organisation

Resolution 2997(XXVII) established three main organs: the Governing Council; the Environment Secretariat; and the Environment Fund. First, the Governing Council consists of a large number of States selected on a geographical basis (as is common with the UN family of organisations) and elected by the UN General Assembly. The purpose of the General Council is to promote international co-operation on the environment, recommend policies on the environment, review the programme of the Environment Fund (*infra*) and make regular reports to the UN General Assembly. Secondly, the Environment Secretariat serves as a focal point for environmental action and co-ordination within the UN system in such a way as to ensure a high degree of effective management. Acting on its own initiative, it submits proposals on environmental issues to the Governing Council. The Environment Secretariat is headed by a Secretary-General who is elected by the UN General Assembly. Thirdly, the Environment Fund is a fund composed of voluntary contributions from States. The purpose of the Fund is to contribute to environmental initiatives undertaken within the UN system. It should not be forgotten that the UN General Assembly is still the main authority for the UNEP. UNEP is based in Nairobi but has regional offices around the world.

1.3.10.3 Activities

The UNEP is more a catalyst than an actor in world environmental matters. Its Global

99. On UNEP see Bacon, "The Role of the United Nations Environmental Program in the Development of International Environmental Law" (1974) 12 CanYBIL 255; Dupuy, "United Nations Environment Programme" in Bernhardt (ed.), *op. cit.* at footnote 61 above, vol. 5, p. 319; and Hardy, "The United Nations Environmental Programme" in Teclaff and Ulton (eds), *International Environmental Law* (1974), p. 57.

100. One of the six areas of the action plan was the "oceans".

101. See Dupuy in Bernhardt (ed.), *op. cit.* at footnote 61 above, vol. 5, p. 319.

Environmental Monitoring System (GEMS) monitors environmental developments worldwide by analysing data from ships, aircraft, satellites and terrestrial observation stations worldwide. UNEP has been more specifically involved in shipping matters through its co-operation with the Food and Agriculture Organisation (FAO) and which was influential in regard to the adoption of the Barcelona Convention for the Protection of the Mediterranean Sea in 1976.[102] It facilitated a similar agreement in relation to Kuwait in 1978.[103] It has developed its Regional Seas Programme elsewhere as well, including thc Gulf of Guinea.

1.3.11 International Maritime Satellite Organisation (INMARSAT)

One organisation which is not strictly part of the UN family (despite its creation having been sponsored by one of the UN family) is the International Maritime Satellite Organisation (INMARSAT).[104] The purpose of this organisation is "to make provision for the space segment[105] necessary for improving maritime communications, thereby assisting in improving maritime communications, thereby assisting in improving distress and safety of life at sea communications, efficiency and management of ships, maritime public correspondence services and radio determination capabilities".[106] The organisation was established by the Convention on the International Maritime Satellite Organisation of 3 September 1976.[107] This Convention entered into force on 16 July 1979 and had been sponsored by the Intergovernmental Maritime Consultative Organisation (IMCO) (now the International Maritime Organisation (IMO)).

1.3.11.1 Membership

INMARSAT has a small but selective list of members. The US, the former USSR, UK and Norway are among its members. The organisation must act exclusively for peaceful purposes.[108]

Participation in INMARSAT is not however limited to States. The operators of equipment in the "space segment" will normally be State agencies, government departments and private organisations or companies rather than States themselves. Thus, the Convention allows for participation in the organisation by these operators—such operators are known as "Designated Entities" because they are designated by the States parties. Designated Entities sign an Operating Agreement (rather than the Convention) and come under the jurisdiction of the State party which designated them.

102. (1976) 15 ILM 290.

103. (1978) 17 ILM 511.

104. On INMARSAT generally, see Doyle, "The International Maritime Satelite Organisation: Origins and Structures" (1977) 5 *Journal of Space Law* 45; Fawcett, "INMARSAT", in Bernhardt (ed.), *op. cit.* at footnote 61 above, vol. 5, p. 35; Menon, "The International Maritime Satellite Organisation: An Important Milestone in Maritime Communications," (1977) 24 NILR 489; and Sondaal, "Current Situation in the Field of Maritime Communications Satellites: INMARSAT" (1980) 8 *Journal of Space Law* 9.

105. In this context, "space segment" means (according to Article 1(d) of the INMARSAT Convention) "the satellites, and the tracking, telemetry, command, control, monitoring and related facilities and equipment required to support the operation of these satellites". INMARSAT may own or lease the space segment: see INMARSAT Convention, Art. 6.

106. See Convention on the International Maritime Satellite Organisation of 3 September 1976, Art. 3(1).

107. Reprinted in (1976) 15 ILM 1051.

108. Convention on the International Maritime Satellite Organisation of 3 September 1976, Art. 3(3).

1.3.11.2 Organic structure and operation

INMARSAT is similar in many ways to INTELSAT. INMARSAT has an Assembly, a Council and a Director-General.

The Assembly consists of one representative from each State party to the INMARSAT Convention and each representative has one vote.

The Council administers INMARSAT while having "due regard for the views and recommendations of the Assembly".[109] It consists of a number of representatives of the "Designated Entities" which have the largest investment shares in the organisation and a smaller number of representatives of the "Designated Entities" which have been elected by the Assembly. The Council operates a system of weighted voting.

The Director-General is the "chief executive and legal representative of the Organisation".[110] He or she is responsible to and acts under the supervision of the Council.[111]

1.3.11.3 Assessment

It has been written that "INMARSAT is an outstanding example of modern international co-operation overcoming the saturation of frequencies, which caused long delays for shipping. It provides a telecommunications service which increases the efficiency of navigation and the safety of life at sea. As part of this service, it is contributing to the important development of transfrontier ground stations. It is also a means of collaboration between governments, industry and commerce".[112]

1.3.12 United Nations Educational, Scientific and Cultural Organisation (UNESCO)

The sometimes controversial United Nations Educational, Scientific and Cultural Organisation (UNESCO)[113] has some involvement in shipping matters. Its sub-organs include the International Oceanographic Commission (IOC), the International Council for the Exploration of the Sea (ICES) and the Scientific Commission on Oceanic Research (SCOR). These are all highly specialist organisations.

1.3.13 World Health Organisation (WHO)

The World Health Organisation (WHO) has involved itself with discussions on the health of seafarers. The work of this organisation touches on the shipping industry in terms of the health of seafarers and passengers alike.

1.3.14 International Atomic Energy Agency (IAEA)

The International Atomic Energy Agency has examined the issue of the liability of owners and operators of nuclear-powered ships as well as general issues relating to the carriage of nuclear materials by sea.

109. *Ibid.*
110. *Ibid.*
111. *Ibid.*
112. Fawcett, *op. cit.* at footnote 104 above, at p. 37.
113. See Partan in Bernhardt (ed.), *op. cit.* at footnote 61 above, vol. 5, 1983, p. 314.

1.3.15 Organisation for Economic Co-operation and Development (OECD)

The Organisation for Economic Co-operation and Development (OECD) is an international organisation which is closely involved in the economic development of its Member States.[114] It is based in Paris and has a permanent secretariat.

The OECD is deeply involved in shipping matters. Its annual reports on maritime transport are useful sources of information. Nonetheless the OECD has not been very successful in this area; in one of its Working Documents,[115] the European Parliament stated that the OECD was devoting attention to shipping but "without any striking success". It has close links with the Maritime Transport Ministers Committee (the so-called Conference Européenne des Ministres des Transports (CEMT)).

1.3.16 Customs Co-operation Council

The Customs Co-operation Council (CCC) is an inter-governmental organisation with a worldwide membership devoted to co-operation in customs matters.[116] It is based in Brussels. The origins of the CCC lay in the work of the Committee for European Economic Co-operation which led to the adoption of the Convention on Nomenclature for the Classification of Goods in Customs Tariffs,[117] the Convention on the Valuation of Goods for Customs Purposes[118] and the Convention Establishing a Common Customs Co-operation Council[119] being signed in Brussels on 15 December 1950.

The CCC has a Council composed of representatives of the Member States and these representatives are normally the heads of national customs authorities. This Council is assisted by technical committees and a General Secretariat.

According to the preamble of its constitutive instrument, the CCC has the task of securing the highest degree of harmony and uniformity in its Member States' customs systems.

The CCC has some impact on shipping in that the organisation is involved in harmonising customs law and procedures. Thus, its involvement is more related to shipping activities rather than the technical operation of ships.

1.3.17 Consultative Shipping Group

The Consultative Shipping Group (CSG), which originated in the 1960s, is an informal intergovernmental group involving some European States and Japan.[120] The UK Department of Transport has normally provided the Group's secretariat. The CSG

114. Art. 1 of the 1948 Convention founding the OECD provides that there is a need for policies designed "(a) to achieve the highest sustainable economic growth and employment and a rising standard of living in Member countries, while maintaining financial stability, and thus to contribute to the development of the world economy; (b) to contribute to sound economic expansion in Member as well as non-member countries in the process of development; and (c) to contribute to the expansion of world trade on a multilateral, non-discriminatory basis in accordance with international obligations." It is based in Paris and has a permanent secretariat.

115. Doc.5/77; 23 March 1977; Rapporteur: Mr H. Seefeld, para. 26.

116. On the CCC see Wolf in Bernhardt (ed.), *op. cit.* at footnote 61 above, vol. 5, p. 8.

117. UNTS, vol. 347, p. 127.

118. UNTS, vol. 171, p. 305.

119. UNTS, vol. 157, p. 129.

120. It is composed of Belgium, Denmark, Finland, France, Germany, Greece, Italy, Japan, the Netherlands, Norway, Spain, Sweden and the UK. The Group originated in the 1960s.

has had discussions with the US on the issue of adopting common measures in relation to third States pursuing flag discrimination practices. It also proved very important in the late 1960s when it drafted (after the 1968 UNCTAD II meeting)[121] guidelines for the behaviour of liner conferences and these guidelines became known as the CENSA Code when adopted by the shipowners' association, CENSA.

1.3.18 General Agreement on Tariffs and Trade (GATT)

The General Agreement on Tariffs and Trade (GATT) is an international arrangement relating to trade in goods.[122] The GATT originally concerned itself only with goods. Nowadays, however, the GATT has become involved in the area of services as well through the medium of the General Agreement on Trade in Services (GATS). GATS aims at, *inter alia*, the liberalisation of the world market in shipping. The current talks have not been easy. The EC would formally like shipping to be included in any GATS arrangements but has also sought certain derogations.[123]

1.3.19 Ministerial Conference of West and Central African States (MINCONMAR)

The Ministerial Conference of West and Central African States (MINCONMAR) is a interministerial group consisting of the shipping or maritime ministers from West and Central Africa.

1.3.20 European Free Trade Association (EFTA)

The EC has close links with the European Free Trade Association (EFTA).[124] EFTA has a minor involvement in shipping but because of that association's links with the EC, it is important to note that link in this section. EFTA has, for example, adopted a Scheme for the Reciprocal Recognition of Tests and Inspections carried out on Ships' Equipment in 1971. Apart from this, however, EFTA's involvement in shipping is more incidental than mainline, despite the significance of shipping for some of its Member States.

1.3.21 Comecon

The EC had talks with COMECON on shipping matters over many years.[125] Ultimately, official relations were established between the two organisations.[126] The

121. At UNCTAD II in 1968, it was resolved that the "governments of Member States of UNCTAD should urge liner conferences and equivalent organisations, directly or through the shipowner members of them, to make provisions in their constitution of working arrangements to the effect that they would discuss with shippers' councils or equivalent bodies questions pertaining to freight rates, conference practices, adequacy of shipping services and other matters of common interest within the consultation machinery of the country or group of countries concerned".

122. Jaenucke in Bernhardt (ed.), *op. cit.* at footnote 61 above, vol. 5, 1983, p. 20.

123. This is an evolving situation and negotiations are continuing at the time of writing.

124. See Krugman, "EFTA and 1992," EFTA Occasional Paper No. 23 (1988); Wallace and Wessels, "Towards a New Partnership: the EC and EFTA in the Wider Western Europe", EFTA Occasional Paper No. 28 (1989) and Weiss, "The European Free Trade Association after Twenty-Five Years" (1985) 5 Ybk. E. L. 287.

125. For example, see, "EEC-Comecon Talks", *Lloyd's List*, 19 March 1987, p. 1.

126. Council of Ministers Decision 88/345 approving the text of a Joint Declaration on the establishment of official relations between the EC and the Council for the Mutual Economic Assistance.

importance of COMECON declined in recent times because of the great changes in Eastern Europe in 1989–1991 and has now been dissolved.[127]

1.3.22 International Non-Governmental Organisations

As well as the *intergovernmental organisations* (IGOs), there are also *international non-governmental organisations* (NGOs) which are interested in shipping affairs. Examples include the Federation of ASEAN Shipowners' Associations (FASA); the International Committee of Passenger Lines (ICPL); the International Cargo-Handling Coordination Association (ICHCA); the International Association of Dry Cargo Shipowners (Intercargo); and, the International Association of Independent Tanker Owners (Intertanko).

The Comité des Associations d'Armateurs de Communautés Européenes (CAACE) was set up by European shipowners. After the enlargement of the EC in 1973, it transferred its headquarters to Brussels. The influence of the CAACE has been significant: it has been written: "CAACE makes its presence felt in the drafting of Community acts on shipping."[128]

1.3.23 Assessment

A number of points emerge from this brief survey of some of the international organisations (other than the EC) which are involved in shipping.

Shipping is only one of the EC's activities. It is thus quite different from the IMO, Intercargo or any of the other specialist shipping organisations. This means that the EC cannot adopt measures in the isolated context of shipping alone but must see shipping as an integral part of transport generally and the overall economy. This is both a blessing and a burden.

The European Parliament has stated in one of its Working Documents that "there is very little coordination of maritime policy at world level".[129] This is very true. The EC could well play a role in the international co-ordination of shipping policy.

While many of the organisations other than the EC are involved in the formulation of rules and laws on shipping, these organisations do not have the capacity to impose rules on their Member States. For example, the IMO may facilitate the conclusion of a Convention but such a Convention must be signed and ratified by the Member States before it becomes binding. Conversely, the EC, acting through its institutions,[130] has the capacity to impose binding rules on its Member States.

The EC is small and narrow in its membership when compared with many of the other international organisations involved in shipping. The EC has twelve Member States and all of them are Western democracies with highly developed economies sharing broadly similar values.

The EC's institutions[131] meet frequently and some are in almost permanent session. This is in contrast to the organs and institutions of some organisations which meet only annually or bi-annually.

127. See Robinson, "Winding-up of Comecon Delayed," *Financial Times*, 16 March 1991.

128. Bredima and Tzoannos, "In Search of a Common Shipping Policy for the EEC" (1981) XX *Journal of Common Market Studies* 95, at p. 98.

129. Doc.5/77; 23 March 1977; Rapporteur: Mr H. Seefeld, para. 26.

130. On the EC's institutions, see para. 3.4 below

131. *Ibid.*

Organically, the EC does not have a Secretary-General in the nature of such organisations as INMARSAT or the UN. While the President of the EC Commission[132] plays an important role in promoting the EC as a whole, he or she is not cast in the role of Secretary-General.

Politically, the EC must act with one voice in international negotiations relating to shipping. In 1977, the European Parliament's Committee on Regional Policy, Regional Planning and Transport published an Interim Report on the Sea Transport Problems in the Community and stated (after reviewing the work of international organisations in the area of shipping): "[the] Committee . . . feels that the Community should henceforth adopt a common position and speak with one voice in all these organizations."[133]

In conclusion, the EC is a unique institution in terms of international shipping: its scope is broader; its powers stronger and its aims more ambitious than any of the organisations typically involved in shipping.

1.4 OUTLINE OF THIS BOOK

This book deals with the shipping law of the EC. It does not deal with EC law relating to internal water transport, that is to say, either waterway or canal transport. Nor does it deal with fisheries law[134] or offshore installations.

Chapter 2 is a brief commercial overview of transport and shipping in the EC. It is imperative to understand the commercial perspective before dealing with the legal dimension to transport generally and shipping in particular.

Chapter 3 is an overview of EC law. It is designed for those readers who do not have an understanding or knowledge of EC law and for those readers this chapter is a necessary inclusion. Readers who are familiar with EC law may not need to read it.

Chapter 4 gives an overview of EC transport law generally. It is useful to be able to put the particular body of EC law relating to shipping into the overall context of EC transport law. Given the nature of the chapter, it is, of necessity, brief and somewhat elementary.

Chapter 5 traces the historical development of EC shipping law over the last thirty years and describes in detail the developments over the last fifteen years. This chapter encapsulates the history of EC shipping law.

The next chapter, Chapter 6, describes and discusses the law on freedom of establishment as it relates to shipping and the registration of ships in the light of the provisions of EC law. This chapter deals with EUROS — the EC's registry of shipping.

Chapter 7 deals with the complex but commercially vital area of freedom to provide shipping services. This chapter examines Regulation 4055/86[135] and the controversial issue of cabotage.[136]

Chapter 8 outlines the EC law relating to the employment of seafarers and their social conditions.

132. On the EC Commission, see para 3.4.2 below.
133. Working Documents; Doc. 5/77; 23 March 1977; Rapporteur: Mr H. Seefeld, para 20.
134. On EC fisheries law, see the excellent book, Churchill, *EEC Fisheries Law* (1987).
135. On Regulation 4055/86, see para. 7.4 below.
136. On Cabotage, see para. 7.5 below.

Chapter 9 discusses, in broad terms, the application of the competition law of the EC to shipping.

The next chapter examines Articles 85 and 86 of the EEC Treaty so as to provide a foundation for Chapter 12.

Chapter 11 looks at liner conferences generally and their relationship with competition law in the light of the United Nations Liner Code.

Chapter 12 examines Regulation 4056/86 which applied Articles 85 and 86 of the EEC Trcaty to maritime transport.

Chapter 13 examines Regulation 4057/86. This Regulation, which is loosely described as the "Dumping Regulation", attempts to deal with the "dumping" of low shipping rates on the EC market by non-EC companies benefiting from unfair non-commercial advantages.

Chapter 14 deals with Regulation 4058/86 which concerns co-ordinated action to safeguard free access to cargoes in ocean trade.

Chapter 15 relates to State aids in relation to shipping.

Chapter 16 describes and discusses the competition law relating to consortia.

Chapter 17 deals with the emerging law of the EC relating to the marine environment. This area is in a state of flux and development.

Shipbuilding is the subject-matter of Chapter 18.

The external relations of the EC in shipping matters is the subject of Chapter 19. The external relations of the EC in this matter have often been controversial and complex.

The EC law relating to maritime safety is dealt with in Chapter 20.

Chapter 21 examines the EC law relating to navigation.

A short chapter, Chapter 22, describes the EC law on pilotage.

Chapter 23 examines the EC law relating to ports and port state control.

The nascent EC law on the carriage of goods and passengers forms the basis of chapter 24.

The EC law relating to shipping litigation is examined in Chapter 25. This chapter focuses on the 1968 Convention on Jurisdiction and the Enforcement of Judgments in Civil and Commercial Matters.

The penultimate chapter examines the challenges of the internal market for shipping. The 1992 Programme has implications for most industries, including shipping.

The final chapter involves an appraisal of EC shipping law by drawing a number of conclusions on the present state and future development of this fascinating branch of EC law.

CHAPTER 2

A Commercial Overview of Shipping in the EC

2.1 INTRODUCTION

The purpose of this chapter is to provide a commercial overview of shipping[1] in the EC[2] and thereby outline the commercial background to EC shipping law. It is hoped that the chapter will be of particular interest to lawyers who may not be fully conversant with the commercial background to EC shipping law.

This overview relates to shipping activities (in the narrow sense) but it is important to remember that shipping is not a single industry but is related to many other economic activities such as shipbuilding and ship repair; tourism; pilotage; shipbroking; marine insurance; stevedoring; shipping finance; maritime law and so on.[3]

2.2 STATE OF SHIPPING IN THE EC

2.2.1 Introduction

The size of the EC's economy and its shipping fleet makes the EC a major player in the world shipping market. There was a steady and significant growth in the world shipping industry for many years until the end of the 1970s—from 1957 to the present day, the number of ships worldwide has doubled and the gross tonnage has quadrupled.[4] Growth within the EC was not however as dramatic as it was elsewhere in the world[5]; the Far East, the former USSR, the Chinas[6] and the Open Registry States[7] grew much more significantly. During the 1980s, however, the world experienced a shipping

1. For a commercial overview of shipping generally, see, *inter alia*, Kendall, *The Business of Shipping* (5th edn., 1988).

2. On transport generally in the EC, see, *inter alia*, Lowe, *The Transport and Distribution Manager's Guide to 1992* (1989), Chapter 2. On shipping in the EC generally, see Bredima-Savopoulou and Tzoannos, *The Common Shipping Policy of the EC* (1989), Chapters 1 and 2 as well as the excellent report prepared by Mikelis and Dean on "The Fleet Controlled by the European Community—Present Status and Some Historic Trends", a paper for the 5th International Congress of the International Maritime Association of the East Mediterranean, Athens, 28 May–1 June 1990 (referred to herein as Mikelis and Dean). Acknowledgement is given that extensive use of that report has been made in this chapter. See also the Seefeld Report Doc.5/77, 23 March 1977, PE47.110/def. See also Clinton Davis, 'The Future of the Community's Fleet' (1987) ETL 203.

3. See the comments of Hayman in Barston and Birnie, *The Maritime Dimension* (1980), at pp. 128–129.

4. Mikelis and Dean, *op. cit.* at footnote 2, Section 2.

5. Bredima-Savopoulou and Tzoannos comment (*op. cit.* at footnote 2, p. 8) that prior to 1980 the "total size of the combined EC fleets grew by a much smaller percentage than the corresponding size of the world total would or the other principal fleets, indicating that the decline in the relative position of the EC fleet had started long before the recent crisis". See also Mikelis and Dean, *op. cit.* at footnote 2, Section 2.

6. I.e. both the People's Republic of China and Taiwan.

7. Such as the Bahamas, Bermuda, Cyprus, Liberia and Panama.

crisis of "unprecedented gravity and duration".[8] Commenting on the 1957–1990 period, Mikelis and Dean observed: "[w]hereas a few [EC] flags appear to be maintaining the levels of their fleet, the majority are seen to have been in decline, especially during the 1980s."[9] The EC suffered more deeply and earlier[10] than the rest of the world during this crisis. In the 1975–1983 period, the absolute size of the merchant fleet under the flags of the EC Member States decreased only slightly. None the less its share of world tonnage fell from 29% to 23.3% during the same period. Conversely, the former socialist states', the open registry states' and developing countries' fleets grew during the same period. Whereas world shipping capacity fell by some 8% between 1981 and 1987, total EC-owned capacity (including ships registered outside the EC) fell by some 28%.[11] In 1989, the Member States of the EC had only 50% of the gross tonnage and 73% of the number of ships they had in 1980. EC-flagged tonnage represented some 32.7% of the world total in 1967 but this had fallen to 14.7% by 1989.[12] The decline in the EC's fortunes has been dramatic. For example, in the five-year period between 1984 and 1989, the EC-flagged fleet fell by one-third in terms of tonnage and in the 1981-1989 period, the EC registered fleet fell (in terms of world tonnage) from 29% to 15%.

So why did the EC suffer more than other regions? Writing in 1989, the Commission stated that the:

"prolonged recession in world trade with the accompanying excess shipping capacity, the erosion of comparative advantage of Community shipping and the growth of protectionist practices adopted by third countries have been the major causes of the decline of the Community fleet relative to world tonnage over the last decade. During the same period, open registry and other third country fleets, including those of developing countries, have continued to expand. *The expansion of non-Community merchant fleets has, inter alia, been based on the comparative advantage deriving from specific fiscal treatment and low manning, including social costs.* This loss of the EEC share of the world fleet shows that the competitive disadvantages of operating under Community flags have proved too great for many Community shipowners."[13] (Author's italics)

In essence, there are two reasons: the EC is a relatively high-cost and regulatory base from which to operate; and secondly, some other blocs and countries are more protectionist in their shipping policies. Undoubtedly, greater aid was given by some non-EC governments towards the acquisition and operation of ships than their EC counterparts. It is equally clear that many jurisdictions worldwide have lower taxes for shipping operations than EC jurisdictions. Indeed, the toleration by some non-EC States of sub-standard ships flying their flags[14] has meant that some non-EC operators have had an unfair and unsafe advantage over their EC counterparts. The depression in

8. Petropolous, "The European Community Transport Policy – An Overview", at *The Future of Shipping in Europe—Key Legal and Commercial Issues*, London, 28–29 June 1990, p. 1 (Personal Comments).

9. *Op. cit.* at footnote 2, para 2.

10. See Bredima-Savopoulou and Tzaonnos, *op. cit.* at footnote 2, p. 8. See also "Call for Action to Halt Fleet Decline", *Lloyd's List*, 7 May 1987, p. 1.

11. See Petropolous, "The European Community Transport Policy—An Overview", at *The Future of Shipping in Europe—Key Legal and Commercial Issues*, London, 28–29 June 1990, p. 4.

12. Mikelis and Dean, *op. cit.* at footnote 2, Section 2.

13. "Guidelines for the Examination of State Aids to Community Shipping Companies", Annex I to Commission of the European Communities, *Financial and Fiscal Measures Concerning Shipping Operations with Ships Registered in the Community*, SEC (89)921 final, 3 August 1989, emphasis added.

14. See Opinion of the Economic and Social Committee on the Communication and Proposals (II.3, II.4) by the Commission to the Council on *Progress towards a Common Transport Policy Maritime Transport* (COM (85)90 final) (TRA/116), para. 1.8.

the EC has stimulated joint action by the Member States of the EC—as Bredima-Savopoulou and Tzoannos have written:

"... joint Community action in the maritime field in the form of the package of the December 1986 regulations would not have materialised but for the prolonged crisis in international shipping and the relative decline in the total capacity of the fleet under Community flags."[15]

It is true to say that the package of positive measures published by the Commission in August 1989[16] would not have emerged either. Shipping in the EC is now in a depressed state relative to its boom days earlier this century. Both shore and onboard employment are at a low ebb. Shipbuilding is more unhealthy than ever.

2.2.2 Tonnage[17]

2.2.2.1 Tonnage owned and registered in the EC

Shipping tonnage registered in the twelve EC Member States was virtually halved between 1980 and 1988.[18] The share held by EC-registered ships of the world fleet fell to about 15.4% (59 million tonnes) in 1988 from a share of 29.7% (117 million tonnes) in 1980. During the 1984–1989 period, every Member State in the EC lost tonnage (apart from Luxembourg which is a special case[19]).[20]

2.2.2.2 Tonnage beneficially owned in the EC but registered outside the EC

There is a considerable amount of tonnage owned by entities within the EC but registered outside, particularly under flags of convenience.[21] UK, German, Greek and Belgian shipowners are very much prone to flagging out. Interestingly, Italian and Spanish owners shy away from flagging out. It will be recalled that tonnage owned by EC companies and registered anywhere in the world fell by 28.3% between 1981 and 1987.[22]

2.2.2.3 Distribution of gross tonnage registered in EC Member States

In 1989, the distribution of the gross tonnage registered in EC Member States was as follows:

15. *Op. cit.* at footnote 2, p. 7. On the December 1986 regulations, see para. 5.5 below.
16. On this package, see para. 5.5.26, below.
17. Tonnage is a more reliable indicator of the state of shipping than the number of ships because, in general, ships are becoming larger.
18. Commission of the European Communities, *A Future for the Community Shipping Industry: Measures to Improve the Operating Conditions of Community Shipping*, Statistical Table, Annex I.
19. See para. 2.3.9, below.
20. Mikelis and Dean, *op. cit.*, Section 2.
21. On flags of convenience generally, see Metaxas, *Flags of Convenience* (1985); and Commission of the European Communities, "Progress Towards a Common Transport Policy: Maritime Transport", COM (85)90 final.
22. Commission of the European Communities, *A Future for the Community Shipping Industry: Measures to Improve the Operating Conditions of Community Shipping*, p. 1.

State	*Tonnage*	*Percentage of the EC Total Tonnage*
Greece	21,324,340	35.3%
UK	7,645,750	12.6%
Italy	7,602,032	12.6%
Denmark	4,962,706	8.2%
France	4,413,464	7.3%
FRG	3,966,571	6.6%
Spain	3,961,941	6.6%
Netherlands	3,654,973	6.0%
Belgium	2,043,594	3.4%
Portugal	726,102	1.2%
Ireland	167,125	0.3%
Luxembourg	3,542	0.1%

Source: Mikelis and Dean, *op.cit.* at footnote 2.

Thus, the three leading shipping States controlled 60.5% of the combined EC fleet.

2.2.3. Age profile

The age profile of the EC fleet is most unfavourable to having a healthy shipping industry.[23] Older ships may be less safe, less sophisticated in terms of technology, more likely to pollute and more costly to operate. The EC fleet is now much older than many of the fleets of its competitors worldwide. Bredima-Savopoulou and Tzoannos have commented: "[t]he prolonged shipping crisis and the resulting negative pressures on the cash flow position of shipping companies . . . have discouraged investment activity in new ships."[24]

While increasing "ship age" is a worldwide phenomenon,[25] the EC has been particularly badly affected. Denmark and Germany are the two exceptions: 45% of Danish fleet is less than ten years old and over 70% of the German fleet is less than ten years old. However, the proportion of ships under ten years old is only 17% in the case of Italy; 27% in the cases of France and Greece; and 34% in the cases of Spain and the UK. Turning outside the EC, to take one example, half of the Hong Kong fleet is less than ten years old.

2.2.4 Market sectors

2.2.4.1 Cargo

Of the total EC fleet of 7,621 ships[26] of over 1,000 grt on 19 March 1990, there were some 2,705 cargo vessels amounting to 14,271,962 grt. More than 65% of them built were ten or more years old. The EC fleet represents 22.9% of the world's total of cargo ships.

23. See Bredima-Savopoulou and Tzoannos, *op. cit.* at footnote 2, p. 16 *et seq.*
24. *Op. cit.*, p. 16.
25. Bredima-Savopoulou and Tzoannos, *op. cit.*, comment (at p. 16) that "whilst the total number of ships on order worldwide, stood in September 1982 at 2428 representing approximately 60 million dwt".
26. Incidentally, there were 164 more on order amounting to only 750,532 grt.

2.2.4.2 Passengers

Of the total EC fleet of 7,621 ships of over 1,000 grt on 19 March 1990, there were some 504 passenger ships amounting to 3,725,351 grt.[27] There were 29 more amounting to 501,006 grt on order. Over a quarter of the 504 ships were over twenty-five years old and more than 77% were ten or more years old. The EC fleet represents 33.4% of the world's total of passenger ships. Many of these vessels were involved in the ferry business. Ferries constitute a strong sector of the shipping business in Europe.[28] There was a considerable expansion in car ferry traffic during the 1960s following on from the prosperity of the late 1950s and 1960s which resulted in increased car ownership, tourism, trade in goods and mobility of persons. The 1980s saw the introduction of the jumbo ferries. These ferries became *feasible* because of the number of passengers and vehicles being carried as well as *essential* because of the cost structure involved in the ferry business. Regularity of services is a key to success in this highly specialised business.[29] Ferries in Europe are, for the most part, liners rather than tramps. They are not generally part of conferences. There is a need for a strong combination of freight and passengers. Specialised cargo vessels frequently travel alongside car ferries.

In the late 1980s, two points did not augur well for ferries, namely, concerns over ferry safety[30] and the possible abolition of duty-free sales on board ferries within the EC. The *Herald of Free Enterprise* disaster in March 1987 highlighted the need for the highest standards of safety on board.[31] Tax-free or duty-free sales on board ferries constitute an important part of the revenue of many ferry companies within the EC. Dan Olsson of Stena Line has said:

> "[t]he question as to how the realisation of the internal European market will affect ferry traffic has long been discussed. In the Nordic countries, the discussion has primarily centred on the future of tax-free sales. In Sweden, Denmark, England and West Germany, tax-free sales on board play an important role. If tax-free sales were to be discontinued without the ferry companies being able to find some form of compensation for the loss of revenue, the effect would be profound, not only on the ferry traffic but also on society as a whole in the longer run. Were the revenues from tax-free to disappear, the ferries' freight rates and ticket prices would go up, for a start. It is difficult to say by exactly how much, but a rise in prices there would certainly be. As a consequence, travel for recreational purposes would be bound to gradually decline, the total number of ships would fall and the timetable would become more widely spaced. For the ferry traffic's freight haulage customers the scrapping of tax-free would similarly entail increased transport prices as well as reduced regularity of services. Accordingly, the buyer of transportation services would incur greater costs and the industry's competitiveness would be reduced. In the long run, the tax-free dependent tonnage may reach a considerably higher average age, given that profitability would not allow for replacements at the desired rate. To fend off this scenario, the tax-free-dependent operators must develop new travel and transportation products."[32]

None the less the future of ferries seems bright on some fronts. The 1990s are expected to bring more leisure time due mainly to shorter working hours, thus there may be an increase in short ferry holidays. The threat to the abolition of duty-free privileges has now receded.

27. On ferries in Europe, see, *inter alia*, Plummer, *Super Ferries of Britain, Europe and Scandinavia* (1988).
28. See Robinson, "Clear of Tunnel Vision" in *Financial Times Survey*, "Transport Links with the Continent", April 1990, p. IV.
29. Olsson, p. 2.
30. On ferry safety, see Chapter 20, below.
31. See Chapter 20, below.
32. *Op. cit.*, p. 7–8.

In respect of passengers liners, Europe is now relatively weak in the passenger liner/cruise ship sector. Europe was dominant for many decades but now it is the US and the former USSR that are the strongest in this sub-sector but with the UK, Italy and Greece still having some presence, albeit with some of their ships being flagged-out.

2.2.4.3 Oil tankers

Of the total EC fleet of 7,621 ships of over 1,000 grt on 19 March 1990, there were some 547 oil tankers amounting to 27,955,824 grt. There were only nine more on order (amounting to 572,824 grt). Over 83% of the existing fleet were ten or more years old. The EC's fleet represents 20.8% (in number) of the world's fleet of oil tankers. The EC's oil tanker fleet has fallen steadily in recent years — much more so than the world pattern.[33] There was, of course, a drop in the volume of crude oil carried by sea following the oil crises of 1973 and 1978 and a consequential drop in tanker rates. The EC-owned tanker fleet fell by about 40% and the EC-registered fleet by about 54% between 1981 and 1987. Mikelis and Dean comment:

"the EC-controlled oil tanker fleet represents 24.6% of the world tanker fleet, whilst the share of the Japanese and the Norwegian-controlled fleets are 12.1% and 10.1% respectively. While the total deadweight tonnage on the World Order Book represents 8.3% of the total existing tanker fleet, the corresponding EC figure is only 1.8%. This low measure of fleet renewal is in contrast to figures of 16.3% for Japanese and 11.5% for Norwegian oil tanker replacement tonnage. With the current tanker fleet being of a high age, with increasing newbuilding prices and limited berth availability, and finally with impending US legislation on double bottoms/double hulls for oil tankers, the figures should be of concern to the EC tanker-owning industry, almost half of whose current tonnage is over fifteen years old."[34]

2.2.4.4 Ore and bulk carriers[35]

The EEC fleet on 19 March 1990 included 1,314 ore and bulk carriers which made up 17% of the total EC fleet (in terms of number). The total gross tonnage was 29,969,102. This means that the EC fleet has about a quarter in number (in specific terms, 26.6%) of the world's ore and bulk carriers. The EC-owned capacity of the dry bulk market fell by about 13% and the EC-registered capacity, in the same sector, fell by about 40% between 1981 and 1987. The EC's bulk carrier fleet declined faster than the world total. In this sector Greece is particularly strong and has achieved dominance in this sector within the EC.

2.2.4.5 Containers

The number of container ships worldwide grew significantly between 1970 and 1987. During that period, container ships grew to represent 9.5% of the total EC fleet and 5.6% of the world fleet. The EC's share of the world container market has however fallen in recent times — in 1983, the EC held about 36% of the world market but by 1987 the share had fallen to 28%. Interestingly, Greece has not proved to be a significant player in the container market. The EC fleet on 19 March 1990 included 442 pure container ships (5.7%) amounting to 9,351,100 grt. This means that the EC fleet

33. See the comments of De Croo in his inaugural address to the Antwerp Shipping Symposium, "A Future for the Community Fleet", May 1987; reprinted in (1987) XXII *European Transport Law* at p. 194.
34. *Op. cit.* at footnote 2, Section 3.
35. On bulk carriers generally, see Bes, *Bulk Carriers* (2nd edn. 1972) and Ewart, *Bulk Carriers* (1983).

constituted by 1989 about 33.9% of the total number of container vessels worldwide. This may well be an area for EC shipping to prosper and develop—bearing in mind that about 55% of the world's general cargo is now shipped by container. Earnings are not necessarily linked to the tonnage of individual ship-types and some ro-ro ferries produce disproportionately high earnings to their tonnage.

2.2.4.6 Liquid gas carriers

There were 231 liquid gas carriers in the EC fleet as at 19 March 1990. These carriers amounted to 3,064,804 grt. The EC has a strong world presence in this sector with some 37.3% of the world total of liquid gas carriers. This is in line with the world's consumption of liquid gas and the technological strength of the EC merchant fleet.

2.2.4.7 Combination carriers

There were 106 combination carriers in the EC fleet on 19 March 1990. They represented 28.6% of the total number of combination carriers worldwide. The 106 combination ships represented 6,561,931 grt.

2.2.4.8 Assessment

Thus, it may be seen that the EC has proved to be particularly strong in certain sectors. It is submitted that these sectors are essentially those involving the highest level of technology.

2.2.5 Employment

The number of seafarers employed in the EC fell dramatically during the 1980s. Between 1980 and 1986, the total number of seafarers employed in the EC fell by about 138,000 (i.e. some 45%) to 169,000.[36] The number of non-EC nationals employed in EC ships fell to about 18,000.

The reason for the decline is said by the Commission to be due to two reasons, namely, the contraction of the EC fleet and the development of more technologically advanced ships with lower manning requirements. Both of these reasons are valid but it is submitted that the former is probably the stronger and more significant of the two. Furthermore, the relative cost[37] of using EC seafarers as opposed to certain non-EC nationals (such as Far Eastern nationals) is not to be underestimated under any circumstances.

2.2.5.1 Merchant marine

A table of persons employed in the merchant marine in some Member States for the year 1986 shows that Greece had the largest number of persons employed in this sector with the UK and Germany not too far behind. The full table is as follows:

36. See Commission of the European Communities, *A Future for the Community Shipping Industry: Measures to Improve the Operating Conditions of Community Shipping*, COM (89)266 final, 3 August 1989, para. 28 and Table 9.
37. Including, wages, social security contributions and taxes.

State	*No. of employees*	*% of State's total workers*
Belgium	2,928	0.08%
Denmark	9,779	0.40%
France	6,807	0.30%
Germany (FRG)	20,470	0.08%
Greece	31,934	0.90%
Netherlands	14,218	0.30%
Portugal	2,913[38]	0.07%
Spain	19,873	0.20%
UK	29,781	0.10%

2.2.5.2 Shipbuilding

A table of persons employed in the shipbuilding sector in each Member State for the year 1986 shows that the (then) Federal Republic of Germany had the largest number of persons employed in this sector with Spain and the Netherlands not too far behind. The full table is as follows:

Member State	*No.*	*% of State's total work*
Belgium	3,871	0.01%
Denmark	12,260	0.05%
France	13,498	0.06%
FRG	38,118	0.02%
Greece	6,328	0.02%
Ireland	1,000	0.1%
Italy	13,809	0.07%
Netherlands	15,300	0.03%
Portugal	14,150	0.04%
Spain	22,996	0.02%
UK	11,694	0.05%

Source: Bredima-Savopoulou and Tzoannos[39] as well as the author's own research

2.2.6 Technology

In many ways, the secret of European success in shipping in the past was due to its technological superiority. This technology gap has now been narrowed to the point where non-EC ships are now as technologically advanced (or more so, in some cases) than their EC counterparts. It is submitted that the EC could do a great deal for

38. 1985 figure.
39. *Op. cit.* At footnote 2 above.

shipping in the EC by promoting technological development in shipping so as to ensure that the non-human "cost base" improves as much as possible. A programme of technical grants and loans would be conducive to the improvement of the fortunes of EC shipping.

2.2.7 Taxation

The taxation of shipping activities is a critical concern. A company established in an open registry does not pay much or any income tax. The availability of low or no taxes in other jurisdictions has resulted in some EC shipping companies re-registering their fleets in other registries around the world. The EC needs a positive policy on taxation within the shipping industry.

2.2.8 Protectionism

Many non-EC States have protected their shipping fleets by protectionist measures.[40] This has materially affected EC fleets. Unfair pricing practices have been particularly harmful. The EC has responded in part.[41] Unfortunately, some EC States have also been unfairly protective of their own fleets and have forced national companies (especially the State-owned ones) to build and repair their ships in the shipyards of those States and these requirements have forced up these companies' costs. This matter is dealt with more fully in Chapters 15 (on State Aids) and 13 (on Dumping), below.

2.2.9 Flagging-out

A number of EC-based shipping companies have either "flagged out" to open registries outside the EC or even gone into other industries. This process is discussed in Chapter 6 below.

2.2.10 The future

In an effort to improve the situation, the Commission has considered a number of measures. In August 1989, the European Commission[42] communicated to the Council of Ministers[43] a set of draft regulations[44] which the Commission believes could improve matters somewhat. These measures include proposals for a Council Regulation establishing a Community ship register and providing for the flying of the Community flag by sea-going vessels,[45] a Commission Recommendation on improving the effectiveness of Port State control in the Community,[46] a Council of Minister's Regulation on a Common Definition of a Community Shipowner,[47] a Council Regulation applying the principle of freedom to provide services to maritime transport within Member States[48]—all of which will be discussed below. Suffice it to say at present,

40. See Chapters 11 and 13 below.
41. See Chapters 12 and 13 below.
42. On the Commission, see para. 3.4.2, below.
43. On the Council of Ministers, see para. 3.4.3, below.
44. On Regulations, see para. 5, above.
45. See Chapter 5, below.
46. See Chapter 5, below.
47. See Chapter 5, below.
48. See Chapter 5, below.

that these measures are (even if they were to be adopted) unlikely to be sufficient in themselves radically to alter the situation of EC shipping.

2.3 AN OVERVIEW OF SHIPPING IN EACH MEMBER STATE

2.3.1 Introduction

Traditionally, EC Member States have carried a large proportion of their own trade in nationally flagged ships. In recent years, however, Member States have experienced a decline in the share of national trade carried in national-flag ships. Most EC shipping companies are fully private in terms of ownership.[49] Those companies which are not privately-owned often operate in specialist sectors.[50] The importance of shipping for EC Member States is demonstrated by the fact that EC shipowners earn about one-half of their income as cross-traders between third states.

2.3.1.1 Attitudes and policies of Member States

As a general rule, the stance taken by each Member State in regard to shipping matters at the EC level is nearly always a direct correlation of the level of importance attached to shipping in that particular Member State and the relationship of shipping to other sectors such as shipbuilding, steel manufacture, ports, ship finance operations and industry generally. Bredima-Savopolou and Tzoannos make some incisive comments:

"There are many factors that influence government maritime policy in each country. First of all, the orientation of maritime policy depends on whether government philosophy is for liberalism in economic activity especially in trade relations with third countries or for interventionism. In practice this distinction is not clear. Another key element is the weight given to shipping relative to other industries. Sometimes, shipping is viewed as a trunk industry subservient to other sectors of the economy. In other instances it is treated as a key industry on its own merits.

The relative weight attached to shipping depends on the economic magnitude of the sector in the context of the national economy, the strategic importance attached to it for defence purposes and the political pressure that interested parties (e.g. maritime trade unions) can exercise.

It should also be pointed out that in some countries maritime policy is extricably linked to policies pursued for shipbuilding whilst in others the shipping industry is treated in isolation from other sectors of the national economy."[51]

It is clear that despite shipping being an important industry for the EC as a whole, it is not a major industry in each of the Member States of the EC, with the obvious exceptions of Denmark, Greece and the UK. It is of lesser significance in France and Germany. It is interesting to observe that shipbuilding is in some ways more important than shipping in Belgium, France and Germany.

All EC maritime Member States are protectionist of their shipping industries to some extent. Such protectionism takes such forms as building aids,[52] purchase aids, employment restrictions, rules on cabotage,[53] taxation,[54] international registries[55]

49. Commission, *Communication from the Commission on a Community Regime for Procurement in the Excluded Sectors: Water, Energy, Transport and Telecommunications* (COM(88) 376 final), para.223
50. *Ibid.*
51. *Op. cit.*, p. 33.
52. See Chapter 15, below.
53. See Chapter 7, below.
54. The positive effects of a favourable tax regime for shipping, must not be underestimated.
55. On international registries see Chapter 6, below.

as well as cargo reservation policies.[56] On balance, however, the EC Member States are in favour of an open shipping policy and have committed themselves to safeguarding and promoting open trade within the confines of free competition on a fair and commercial basis in international shipping.[57] The Member States have adopted such openess both in their own right[58] and within the EC[59] as well as in international fora such as the OECD[60] and UNCTAD.[61] Even when the EC Member States are protectionist, it has been concluded by Bredima-Savopolou and Tzoannos that "there is no clear-cut connection between the degree of protectionism afforded to national shipping and flag shares in the external trade of EC countries"[62] and "in those countries where some forms of protectionism exist, that these have not been sufficient to counterbalance the loss by national flag carriers of competitive advantage so as to preserve their market shares".[63]

It is to be noted that the figures (set out below) referring to "the EC total" mean the total of the twelve States which are *now* members of the EC even if they were not Member States at the date of the statistic.

2.3.2 Belgium[64]

2.3.2.1 Introduction

Belgium has fared well during the past decade relative to some of its fellow EC Member States. The Belgian fleet continued to grow (both in tonnage and ship numbers) from 1957 until 1986 — indeed, the tonnage quadrupled during that period. However, by 1989, the increases made in the 1957–1986 period in both numbers and tonnage had been virtually eliminated. Between 1984 and 1989 the gross tonnage registered had fallen from 2,406,714 to 2,043,594.

2.3.2.2 Number of ships

In 1970, the Belgian fleet had 230 ships (representing 0.4% of the world total and almost 3% of the then EC [65] total). In 1975, this figure had risen to 252 (representing 0.4% of the world total and 2.1% of the then EC [66] total). In 1987, this figure had risen to 350 ships (representing 0.5% of the world total and 2.5% of the then EC [67] total).

56. See Chapter 14, below.
57. See Council of Ministers Recommendation concerning Common Principles of Shipping Policy for Member Countries, 13 February 1987.
58. Note the stance of the UK in respect of cabotage.
59. Note the measures adopted in the area of competition: see Chapter 12, below.
60. On the OECD, see para. 1.3.15, above.
61. On UNCTAD, see para. 1.3.7, above.
62. *Op. cit.*, p. 45.
63. *Op. cit.*, p. 48.
64. See Volckaert, "Formulation of National Marine Policy: The Case of Belgium" (1988) 10 *Marine Policy* 90.
65. I.e. the total tonnage of what are now the twelve Member States of the EC.
66. *Ibid.*
67. *Ibid.*

2.3.2.3 Tonnage

In 1970, the Belgian fleet was almost 1,100,000 tons. By 1975, the fleet was almost 1,300,000 tons. By 1980, the tonnage reached 1,800,000 tons and by 1987, the tonnage reached 2,250,000.[70]

2.3.2.4 Age Profile

On 19 March 1990, of 195 ships owned by Belgian parent companies, 28 were less than four years or less, 48 were between five and nine years old, 51 were between ten and 14 years, 32 were between 15 and 19 years, 15 were between 20 and 24 years with 5 being 25 years or more.[71]

2.3.2.5 Employment

In 1986, there were 2,928 persons employed in the merchant marine (representing 0.09% of the total civilian labour force in 1986) and 3,871 persons employed in shipbuilding (representing 0.1% of the total civilian labour force in 1986).

2.3.2.6 General comments

Six points are worth noting. First, shipbuilding is more important (in terms of the number of jobs) than the merchant marine. Secondly, of the 195 ships (of over 1,000 grt) owned by Belgian parent companies, 102 (i.e. 52%) were registered in Belgium with the majority of the others being registered in Cyprus, Liberia and Singapore. Thirdly, under Belgian tax laws, there are accelerated depreciation allowances in respect of shipping activities. Fourthly, it appears that a number of Belgian ships may transfer registry to Luxembourg because of the changes in the latter's registry. Fifthly, the Règle Maritime des Transports (RMT) is the only State-owned shipping company and is an autonomous body under government supervision and providing ferry transport to and from the United Kingdom, in competition with other lines.[72] And, finally, of the 195 ships owned by Belgian parent companies, some 37 are ore and bulk carriers (just under 19%).

2.3.3 Denmark

2.3.3.1 Number of ships

The number of ships in the Danish fleet (about 1,250) is less than its high point of about 1,400 which was enjoyed in the mid-1970s but is still higher than the number which it had at any time during the 1960s or 1970s. In 1970, it had 1,210 ships (representing 2.3% of the world total). In 1975, this figure had risen to 1,371 (representing 2.15% of the world total and 11.6% of the then EC total). In 1987, this figure had fallen back to 1,256 ships (representing 1.6% of the world total and 10.7% of the then EC total).

70. Lloyd's Register of Shipping: *Statistical Tables.*
71. *Ibid.*
72. Commission, *Communication from the Commission on a Community Regime for Procurement in the Excluded Sectors: Water, Energy, Transport and Telecommunications* (COM(88) 376 final), para. 224.

2.3.3.2 Tonnage

In 1970, the Danish fleet was almost 3,400,000 tons. By 1975, the fleet was almost 4,500,000 tons. By 1980, the tonnage reached 5,500,000 tons and by 1989, the tonnage had fallen to 5,000,000.

2.3.3.3 Age Profile

On 19 March 1990, of 591 ships owned by Danish parent companies, 123 were less than four years or less, 171 were between five and nine years old, 106 were between ten and 14 years, 59 were between 15 and 19 years, 27 were between 20 and 24 years with 20 being 25 years or more.[73]

2.3.3.4 Employment

In 1986, there were 9,779 persons employed in the merchant marine (representing 0.4% of the total civilian Danish labour force in 1986) and 12,260 persons employed in shipbuilding (representing 0.5% of the total civilian labour force in 1986).

2.3.3.5 General comments

Denmark has not only its own registry but also an international registry as well. The Faroe Islands are also available as a registry. Of the 591 ships owned by Danish parent companies on 19 March 1990, 118 (i.e. 20%) were registered on the Danish registry and 235 (i.e. 40%) were registered on the Danish International Registry with the rest being registered around the world (in particular, in the Bahamas, Liberia and Singapore).

The K/S partnership scheme encourages investment in shipping by providing tax savings for the investor.

In Denmark, the DSB is the State-owned railway company and it operates a fleet of vehicle and train ferries. It is one of the few State-owned shipping companies in the EC but since 1984 it has worked in a way which is largely independent of government control.[75]

Under Danish tax law, it is possible to create tax-free reserves from operating profits or from book profits resulting from the sale of a ship and these reserves may then be used for the purchase of new ships.

The Danish company Maersk is the second largest container company in the world.

2.3.4 France

2.3.4.1 Number of ships

In 1970, the French fleet had over 1,400 ships. By 1975, the fleet had almost 1,400 ships.

73. Lloyd's Register of Shipping: *Statistical Tables.*

75. Commission, *Communication from the Commission on a Community Regime for Procurement in the Excluded Sectors: Water, Energy, Transport and Telecommunications* (COM(88)376 final), para. 225. On shipping in Denmark generally, see *Fairplay*, 19 July 1990 *passim.*

By 1980, the number had fallen to around 1,230 and by 1989, the number had fallen to around 950.

2.3.4.2 Tonnage

In 1970, the French fleet was almost 6,500,000 tons but by 1978, this rose dramatically to over 12,000,000 tons but had fallen even more dramatically to just over 4,500,000 by 1989 having been in "free-fall" since 1980.[76]

2.3.4.3 Age Profile

On 19 March 1990, of 298 ships owned by French parent companies, 22 were less than four years or less, 60 were between five and nine years old, 104 were between ten and 14 years, 64 were between 15 and 19 years, 14 were between 20 and 24 years with 16 being 25 years or more.[77]

2.3.4.4 Employment

In 1986, there were 6,807 persons employed in the merchant marine (representing 0.03% of the total French civilian labour force in 1986) and 20,916 persons employed in shipbuilding (representing 0.06% of the total civilian labour force in 1986).

2.3.4.5 General comments

A number of points are worth mentioning in regard to France and shipping. First, shipbuilding is more important than the merchant marine in terms of jobs. The French Government has consistently sought to encourage its shipping companies to build in France and thereby bolster French shipbuilding. Secondly, the government offers grants towards the acquisition of ships and operating subsidies. Thirdly, there are accelerated depreciation allowances in respect of shipping activities. Fourthly, France operates an unilateral cargo reservation system. Two-thirds of hydrocarbon imports and two-fifths of coal imports must be carried in French ships. All cargoes shipped on account of France must be carried onboard French ships. Fifthly, it is possible to create tax-free reserves from operating profits or from book profits resulting from the sale of a ship and these reserves may then be used for the purchase of new ships. Sixthly, a significant portion of France's external trade is carried on board French ships. Seventhly, some 16% of the French merchant fleet is owned by the Compagnie Generale Maritime (CGM) which is 99% State-owned and is thus one of the relatively few shipping companies in the EC which is State-owned.[80] And, finally, there is a very strong tendency among French parent companies to flag their ships either in France (62.7%) or in the French Antarctic Territory (10.4%).

76. Lloyd's Register of Shipping: *Statistical Tables*. See *Fairplay*, 12 July 1990, *passim*.
77. *Ibid*.
80. Commission, *Communication from the Commission on a Community Regime for Procurement in the Excluded Sectors: Water, Energy, Transport and Telecommunication* (COM(88) 376 final), para 227.

2.3.5 Germany

Germany has been going through great changes in recent years since reunification. This section examines in particular the fortunes of the then Federal Republic of Germany (as it was a Member State of the EC since the foundation of the EC).

2.3.5.1 Number of ships

In the late 1950s, the Federal Republic of Germany had about 2,200 ships under its flag; by the late 1960s this had risen to over 2,800; but by the late 1970s, it had fallen to about 1,850 and by the late 1980s, it had fallen to around 1,200.

2.3.5.2 Tonnage

At the start of 1990, the tonnage registered under the Federal Republic of Germany's flag was only marginally better than it was in 1957. It had about four million gross tons of ships flying its flag but this is less than half the tonnage flying the flag during the mid-1970s.

2.3.5.3 Age Profile

On 19 March 1990,[85] of 1,025 ships owned by German parent companies 157 were less than four years or less, 382 were between five and nine years old, 186 were between ten and 14 years, 130 were between 15 and 19 years, 58 were between 20 and 24 years with 58 being 25 years or more.[86]

2.3.5.4 Employment

In 1986, there were 20,470 persons employed in the merchant marine (representing 0.08% of the total civilian labour force in 1986) and 38,118 persons employed in shipbuilding (representing 0.02% of the total civilian labour force in 1985).

2.3.5.5 General comments

The German government offers grants towards the acquisition of ships.

Shipbuilding is more important (in terms of the number of jobs) than the merchant marine. The Federal Republic of Germany had a large shipbuilding industry with over 33,000 people employed at 80 yards. On 1 March 1990, an agreement entered into force between the Association of the West German Shipbuilding Industry and Marine Technology (VSM) and its East German equivalent, the Kombinat Schiffbau Rostock (KSR).[87] The agreement provides that the KSR became an associate member of the VSM with the two sides forming a co-ordination committee. The agreement also provided for an exchange of information and know-how, and jointly to work out schemes to improve competitiveness of the industry in Germany generally (both East and West). Under the terms of the Agreement, the VSM will represent the interests of the KSR in West Germany, the OECD, the Association of European Shipbuilders

85. Lloyd's Register of Shipping: *Statistical Tables.*
86. *Ibid.*
87. See *Lloyd's List*, March 1990.

(AWES) and the Committee of EEC Shipbuilders' Associations.

Of the 1,025 ships of over 1,000 grt owned by West German parent companies on 19 March 1990, 53.7% were registered in the FRG with the bulk of the others registered in Cyprus (15.4%), Antigua, Liberia and Panama.

It is possible to create tax-free reserves from operating profits or from book profits resulting from the sale of a ship and these reserves may then be used for the purchase of new ships.

The Federal Republic of Germany established a second register in April 1989, the so-called German International Register.[88] It is not open to foreign owners *per se*.[89] German seafaring unions oppose it. None the less shipping companies there regard it as a success because it has halted the flight of ships from the traditional German register to offshore registries around the world. In March 1990, it was reckoned that about 40% of the ships of the (then) Federal Republic of Germany were on the German International Register.[90]

Part of the traffic from what was East Germany will probably flow through Hamburg which is, after all, the fourth largest port in Europe. It has been estimated that about 5 million tons of "East Germany's" 25 million will flow through Hamburg.[91] This may even rise to 12 million tons by 1995.[92]

2.3.6 Greece

2.3.6.1 Introduction

Greece acceded to the EC in 1981. In general terms, Greece is the most important shipping nation within the EC at present—it represents one-third of the entire EC fleet. It earns about $1.3 billion per annum from shipping.

2.3.6.2 Number of ships

The growth in the number of ships under the Greek flag has been spectacular. In 1957, there were less than 400 ships under the Greek flag but by 1980 this figure had reached almost 4000. Unfortunately, this figure has fallen back to just under 1900 but the growth was still significant.

2.3.6.3 Tonnage

Just as the growth in the number of ships was spectacular, so too was the growth in the tonnage under the Greek flag. In 1957, there were less than two million gross tons registered under the Greek flag but by 1980, this had risen over 20-fold to over 41 million gross tons.

88. See Simon in *Lloyd's List*, 21 March 1990, p. 4 for a review of the first year. See also *Lloyd's List*, 22 December 1988, p. 2.

89. *Quaere* the legality of this in the light of Art. 7 of the EEC Treaty.

90. Simon in *Lloyd's List*, 21 March 1990, p. 4.

91. Kern, *Fairplay*, 24 May 1990, p. 20.

92. *Ibid.*

2.3.6.4 Age Profile

On 19 March 1990,[93] of 2,423 ships owned by Greek parent companies, 53 were less than four years or less, 243 were between five and nine years old, 544 were between ten and 14 years, 794 were between 15 and 19 years, 475 were between 20 and 24 years with 269 being 25 years or more.[94]

2.3.6.5 Employment

In 1986, there were 31,934 persons employed in the merchant marine (representing 0.9% of the total civilian labour force in 1986) and 6,328 persons employed in shipbuilding (representing 0.2% of the total civilian labour force in 1986).

2.3.6.6 General comments

Greece has specialised in the tramp or bulk markets and now has one of the largest bulk carrier fleets in the world.

The Greek Government offers grants towards the purchase of ships.

Of the 2,423 ships owned by Greek parent companies on 19 March 1990, only about 40% were registered on the Greek registry with large numbers registered in Cyprus (24%), Panama (12%), Liberia (6.6%) and Malta (6.6%).

A significant portion of Greece's external trade is carried on board Greek ships.

The Greek tax regime is particularly attractive for shipping. The Commission in its August 1989 publication, "Financial and Fiscal Measures Concerning Shipping Operations with Ships Registered in the Community"[95], analysed the tax regimes of each of the Member States as they relate to shipping and concluded that the Greek system, whereby shipping companies are subject only to a tonnage tax, is advantageous at times of medium and high profit.[96]

Greek tonnage rose steadily until 1981. Greece has fared badly in the shipping market over the last decade. In general terms, its fleet has expanded in terms of ship numbers although there has been a drop in tonnage.

Free movement of EC seafarers has applied to Greece since 1 January 1988.

The accession of Greece to the EC had a huge impact on shipping in the EC. Beyer de Ryke, a Member of the European Parliament, asked the Commission: "can the Commission provide a full report on the economic effects in [the maritime chartering] sector of Greece's entry into the common market and its consequences for chartering in other Member States?"[97] Commissioner Contogeorgis answered:

"As at April 1st 1981, the Greek merchant fleet, at 38.4 million grt represented about 10% of the world fleet and about 36.5% of the Community fleet. The accession of Greece increased the Community fleet by some 57%. The Community fleet now represents rather over 27% of the world fleet.[98] It is difficult to evaluate the consequences of this addition to the Community's

93. Lloyd's Register of Shipping: *Statistical Tables*.
94. *Ibid.*
95. SEC (89)921 final, 3 August 1989.
96. *Ibid.*, para. 7.
97. Written Question No. 531/81.
98. These figures represent the vessels under Greek registry only (approximately 3.900 of 40 million grt.). If we take the whole of the Greek-owned fleet into consideration these numbers would come up to about 4,400 ships of 50 million grt.

merchant fleet, as the Greek merchant fleet, unlike those of many of the other Member States, is mainly engaged in transport of bulk cargoes. This is a world wide transport market in which shipowners may generally participate freely, without regard to nationality, and in which there is little flag discrimination. As far as the method of chartering vessels is concerned, membership of the Community is not likely to lead to any major changes in this particular sector of the shipping market. This is especially true as far as the allocation of cargoes and freight rates are concerned.

On the other hand, it is clear that the importance of the Greek merchant fleet lends added weight to the Community in all international negotiations concerning shipping matters, especially those on the open registry and bulk shipping questions within the framework of UNCTAD and the OECD, in the work on shipping safety in IMCO and in the current discussions connected with the establishment of a second Hague Memorandum on Port State Control."

Bredima and Tzoannos recorded:

"The accession of Greece [to the EC] changed the structure of the Community fleet in terms of the types of ships and the trades these serve. The composition of the fleet of the [pre-existing] Nine [Member States represented] a heavier emphasis towards the transport of finished industrial goods and oil, than of dry commodities transported in bulk which consist of raw materials, such as iron ore, coal, grain etc. In contrast the Greek fleet has a big percentage of its capacity geared towards the transport of dry bulk commodities. Also, the percentage of tonnage in the Greek fleet which is in containers is insignificant compared to the fleet of the Nine.

Thus, the activities of the Greek fleet are to a large extent complementary to those of the other EC fleets and consequently the accession of Greece has resulted in a more balanced fleet in terms of the trades it can serve. That fleet is now capable of serving the needs of the Community in the transport by sea of both its exports and imports."[99]

2.3.7 Ireland

2.3.7.1 Introduction

Ireland acceded to the EC in 1973 along with Denmark and the UK and is by far one of the smaller shipping States in the EC. Shipping is however of considerable strategic significance for Ireland—after the completion of the Channel Tunnel between the UK and France, Ireland will be the only EC Member State which does not have a land link with the Continent of Europe.

2.3.7.2 Number of ships

Ireland has more ships now than it did in 1957 when the EEC was founded or in 1973 when it joined the EC. Indeed, Ireland has seen a consistent growth in the ship numbers since the mid-1970s, after a period of remarkable consistency in numbers during the period 1957 to 1977.

2.3.7.3 Tonnage

While Ireland has had good fortune in terms of ship numbers over the 1957–1989 period, it has not been so fortunate in terms of tonnage during that same period. While it has almost doubled the tonnage under its flag during that period, it has lost the gains made during the 1970s.

At mid-1989 the gross tonnage of ships registered in Ireland was 167,000.

99. (1981) XX JCMS 95, pp. 95–6.

2.3.7.4 Age Profile

On 19 March 1990,[100] of 51 ships owned by Irish parent companies, 8 were less than four years or less, 12 were between five and nine years old, 11 were between ten and 14 years, 7 were between 15 and 19 years, 6 were between 20 and 24 years with 4 being 25 years or more.[101]

2.3.7.5–2.3.7.6 General comments

The Irish Government offers grants towards the purchase of ships. The Shipping Investment Grants Act 1987[102] provides some funding towards the acquisition of certain types of ships less than seven years old. This Act is a successor to an earlier Act of 1969.

Of the fifty-one ships owned on 19 March 1990 by Irish parent companies, forty-two (i.e. 82%) were registered on the Irish flag with only a few almost evenly divided between the Bahamas, the UK and Panama.

The Irish taxation regime is particularly favourable towards the shipping industry. The Business Expansion Scheme (BES) — a tax scheme whereby the purchase of shares in certain types of, *inter alia*, shipping companies attracts tax relief — has helped foster some shipping companies. There is also a reduced corporation tax rate of 10% for shipping and shipping related services.

There are accelerated depreciation allowances in respect of shipping activities.

2.3.8 Italy

2.3.8.1 Introduction

Italy, one of the founder members of the EC, has always been a strong maritime nation. It has fared well during its membership of the EC since 1957 but the gross registered tonnage registered under its flag fell from 9,157,867 in 1984 to 7,602,032 in 1989. The ports of Amalfi, Genoa, Pisa and Venice were bustling ports.

2.3.8.2 Number of ships

The number of ships under the Italian flag has been quite consistent during the 1957–1989 period with only marginal variation over the time period. In the late 1950s, it had around 1,250 ships and in 1989, it had around 1,500 ships. Indeed, unlike France, the Federal Republic of Germany, the Netherlands and the UK, Italy now has more ships than it did in 1957.

2.3.8.3 Tonnage

In 1957, the gross tonnage was around 4,500,000, by 1970 this had risen to 7,000,000 grt, by 1979 this had risen to the high of over 11,500,000 tons but by 1989, it had fallen back to 7,500,000 grt.

100. Lloyd's Register of Shipping: *Statistical Tables.*
101. *Ibid.*
102. See Power in *Irish Current Law Statutes Annotated* 1987.

2.3.8.4 Age Profile

On 19 March 1990,[103] of 722 ships owned by Italian parent companies, 52 were less than four years or less, 88 were between five and nine years old, 136 were between ten and 14 years, 182 were between 15 and 19 years, 123 were between 20 and 24 years with 96 being 25 years or more.[104]

2.3.8.5–2.3.8.6 General comments

Italian shipowners are hesitant to flag out their vessels. Of the 722 vessels over 1,000grt owned by Italian parent companies on 19 March 1990, 679 (i.e. 94%) were on the Italian register.

The Italian Government offers grants towards the purchase of ships. There are accelerated depreciation allowances in respect of shipping activities.

2.3.9 Luxembourg

It may appear strange in a book about shipping in the EC to include a section on Luxembourg, the only landlocked Member State, but this State is important in a number of respects for present purposes. First, Luxembourg registered its first ship in 1988 and its second in 1989. No other ships had been registered there at any time during the State's membership of the EC. Thus, at the end of 1989, there were two ships registered in Luxembourg with a gross tonnage of around 35,000. Yet the creation of the register is an important development[105] which may prove significant in future years. Some companies may decide to register there because of the generous fiscal regime, low administration costs and an efficient mortgage registration system.

2.3.10 The Netherlands

2.3.10.1 Introduction

The Netherlands has been a strong maritime nation since at least the sixteenth century. The Dutch have traditionally been very strong in the liner (as opposed to tramp) sector.

2.3.10.2 Number of ships

The Dutch fleet has fallen almost consistently in the period between 1957 and 1989: it has fallen from a level of about 1900 ships in the late 1950s to about 1250 in the late 1980s.

Of the 656 ships (greater than 1,000 gross registered tons) registered on 19 March 1990, 6 were oil tankers, 48 were chemical and product carriers, 19 were liquid gas carriers, 25 were ore and bulk carriers, 29 were pure container ships, 350 were cargo ships, 17 were passenger ships and the remaining 162 were of various types.

2.3.10.3 Tonnage

The tonnage under the Dutch flag has remained quite consistent since 1957 despite the

103. Lloyd's Register of Shipping: *Statistical Tables*.
104. *Ibid.*
105. See Loesch, "New Ship Register", *International Financial Law Review*, February 1991, p. 54.

gyrations of the shipping market during that period. There were about 4.5 million gross tons under the Dutch flag in the late 1950s and just under 4 million gross tons by the end of the 1980s – although there were more than 5 million gross tons registered under the Dutch flag throughout the 1960s and 1970s.

2.3.10.4 Age profile

On 19 March 1990,[106] of 656 ships owned by Dutch parent companies 85 were less than four years or less, 194 were between five and nine years old, 166 were between ten and 14 years, 84 were between 15 and 19 years, 47 were between 20 and 24 years with 22 being 25 years or more.[107]

2.3.10.5 Employment

In 1986, there were 14,218 persons employed in the merchant marine (representing 0.3% of the total civilian labour force in 1986) and 15,300 persons employed in shipbuilding (representing 0.3% of the total civilian labour force in 1985).

2.3.10.6 General comments

The Netherlands is particularly strong in terms of cargo ships but is weak in terms of oil tankers and passenger ships. Of the 656 ships owned by Dutch parent companies on 19 March 1990, some 442 (i.e. 67%) were registered in the Netherlands and 37 (i.e. 5.6%) were registered in the Netherlands Antilles.

It is possible to create tax-free reserves from operating profits or from book profits resulting from the sale of a ship and these reserves may then be used for the purchase of new ships.

The Netherlands has introduced measures to reduce the cost of employing Dutch seafarers by granting relief on personal taxation and social security.

2.3.11 Portugal

2.3.11.1 Introduction

In 1988, the EC Commission estimated that between 85-90% of the capacity of the Portuguese fleet belonged to companies under State control.[108]

2.3.11.2 Number of ships

The number of ships under the Portuguese flag in 1989 was virtually identical to the number under that flag in 1957. Apart from a dramatic increase in numbers during the mid-1970s, the number of ships under the Portuguese flag has remained consistent at around 350 from the mid-1950s to the mid-1980s.

106. Lloyd's Register of Shipping: *Statistical Tables.*
107. *Ibid.*
108. Commission, *Communication from the Commission on a Community Regime for Procurement in the Excluded Sectors: Water, Energy, Transport and Telecommunications* (COM(88) 376 final), para. 230.

2.3.11.3 Tonnage

The tonnage registered under the Portuguese flag rose dramatically between the late 1950s (when it was just over 0.5 million gross tons) and the mid-1980s (when it reached over 1.5 million gross tons). It suffered a considerable decline in the late 1980s during which time the tonnage was more than halved.

2.3.11.4 Age profile

On 19 March 1990,[114] of 125 ships owned by Portuguese parent companies 6, were less than four years or less, 10 were between five and nine years old, 22 were between ten and 14 years, 25 were between 15 and 19 years, 16 were between 20 and 24 years with 42 being 25 years or more.[115] It is most significant that almost 40% of Portuguese ships are 25 years or more.

2.3.11.5 Employment

In 1985, there were 2,913 persons employed in the merchant marine (representing 0.07% of the total civilian labour force in 1986) and 14,150 persons employed in shipbuilding (representing 0.4% of the total civilian labour force in 1985).

2.3.11.6 General comments

Portugal is often underestimated as a maritime nation.[116] In recent times, Portugal is undergoing an extensive privatisation programme[117] and shipping companies such as Portline and Transinsular were prepared for sale. Portugal established an offshore registry in Madeira[118] in 1989 but it has not been very successful in attracting tonnage.

Of the 125 ships over 1,000grt owned by Portuguese parent companies on 19 March 1990, 90 (i.e. 72%) were registered in Portugal with the balance registered mainly in Panama.

The Portuguese Government provides operating subsidies. There are also accelerated depreciation allowances in respect of shipping activities.

2.3.12 Spain

2.3.12.1 Introduction

In 1988, it was estimated by the EC Commission that some 25% of the tonnage of the Spanish fleet was in the hands of the State.[119]

2.3.12.2 Number of ships

The Spanish fleet almost doubled in terms of ship numbers during the 1957–1989 period. In

114. Lloyd's Register of Shipping: *Statistical Tables*.
115. *Ibid.*
116. On Shipping in Portugal, see the "Special Report" in *Lloyd's List*, 20 March 1990, p. 6.
117. See *Lloyd's List*, 20 March 1990, p. 6.
118. *I.e.* the Atlantic Ocean.
119. Commission, *Communication from the Commission on a Community Regime for Procurement in the Excluded Sectors: Water, Energy, Transport and Telecommunications* (COM(88) 376 final), para. 228. For a survey of ports in Spain, see *Fairplay*, 27 September 1990.

the late 1950s, there were just over 1,200 ships on the Spanish registry but by the late 1980s this reached just under 2,400. Spain, in common with a number of States, reached a high point (in terms of ship numbers) during the mid-1970s but then went into some decline.

2.3.12.3 Tonnage

In spite of a large number of ships, the tonnage registered under the Spanish flag is relatively low. At present, about four million gross tons are registered under the Spanish flag. This is more than twice the figure in the late 1950s but less than half of the amount registered in the late 1970s when Spanish tonnage was at its highest.

2.3.12.4 Age profile

On 19 March 1990,[123] of 535 ships owned by Spanish parent companies, 64 were less than four years or less, 101 were between five and nine years old, 160 were between ten and 14 years, 85 were between 15 and 19 years, 62 were between 20 and 24 years with 38 being 25 years or more.[124]

2.3.12.5 Employment

In 1986, there were 19,873 persons employed in the merchant marine (representing 0.2% of the total civilian labour force in 1986) and 22,996 persons employed in shipbuilding (representing 0.2% of the total civilian labour force in 1986).

2.3.12.6 General comments

Of the 535 ships of over 1,000 grt owned by Spanish parent companies on 19 March 1990, 445 (i.e. 83%) were registered in Spain with the bulk of the remainder registered in the Canary Islands or Panama.

Spanish ships are used quite significantly in respect of the import of goods into Spain but not so much in respect of exports from Spain.

The Spanish Government offers grants towards the acquisition of ships. The Government provides operating subsidies. There are accelerated depreciation allowances in respect of shipping activities.

It is possible to create tax-free reserves from operating profits or from book profits resulting from the sale of a ship and these reserves may then be used for the purchase of new ships.

2.3.13 United Kingdom

2.3.13.1 Introduction

The shipping fortunes of the UK have waned in recent years.

120. *I.e.* the total tonnage of what are now the twelve Member States of the EC.
121. *Ibid.*
122. *Ibid.*
123. Lloyd's Register of Shipping: *Statistical Tables.*
124. *Ibid.*

2.3.13.2 Number of ships

On 19 March 1990, of 998 ships owned by UK parent companies, 48 were less than four years or less, 67 were between five and nine years old, 271 were between ten and 14 years, 215 were between 15 and 19 years, 137 were between 20 and 24 years with 90 being 25 years or more.

Of the 998 ships (greater than 1,000 gross registered tons) registered on 19 March 1990, 99 were oil tankers, 87 were chemical and product carriers, 36 were liquid gas carriers, 5 were combination carriers, 85 were ore and bulk carriers, 78 were pure container ships, 240 were cargo ships, 81 were passenger ships and the remaining 287 were of various types.

The size of the UK-registered fleet is not a true indicator of the real involvement of the UK in shipping. About half of the UK-owned tonnage is registered on other British flag registries (e.g. Isle of Man and Hong Kong) and one-fifth is registered in non-British registries.

2.3.13.3 Tonnage

In 1975, the gross tonnage was around 32,200,000 grt; this was the highest tonnage in the entire 1957–1989 period. In 1984, the tonnage was 15,874, 062 grt. By 1989, this had fallen to 7,200,000 grt.

2.3.13.4 Age profile

On 19 March 1990,[125] of 998 ships owned by UK parent companies, 67 were less than four years or less, 170 were between five and nine years old, 271 were between ten and 14 years, 215 were between 15 and 19 years, 137 were between 20 and 24 years with 90 being 25 years or more.[126]

2.3.13.5 Employment

In 1976, there were 58, 333 UK nationals employed as seafarers. In 1986, there were 29,781 persons employed in the merchant marine (representing 0.1% of the total civilian labour force in 1986) and 11,694 persons employed in shipbuilding (representing 0.5% of the total civilian labour force in 1986). By 1989, 17,838 UK nationals were employed as seafarers with 7,892 being officers and 9,946 being ratings.

2.3.13.6 General comments

As is well known, the UK was *the* shipping nation. However, since the late 1950s, the UK has seen a steady decline in the number of ships registered under its flag[127] – there are now less than half the number of ships registered under the UK flag than there were

125. Lloyd's Register of Shipping: *Statistical Tables*.
126. *Ibid.*
127. See Goss, "Sense and Shipping Policies" [1987] 14 *Maritime Policy Management*, No. 12, p. 83; Sturmey, *British Shipping and World Competition* (1962); and *Rochdale, Report of the Committee into Shipping*.

in the late 1950s. More worryingly, the amount of tonnage is less than one-third of the amount registered in the late 1950s and about one-fifth of the amount registered in the mid-1970s. The situation in the UK is now critical.[128] The decline is probably due to two factors: (a) the structural changes in shipping worldwide; and (b) the lack of government subsidies but presence of high labour costs and standards in the UK.[129] The City of London earns a considerable amount from shipping activities. The decline of the UK fleet is threatening this revenue stream.[130] It has been reckoned that owners, operators and managers in the UK would lose 52% of their business if the UK-owned and UK-flagged (UK or Crown Dependency) vessels of over 500 grt fell to zero from its 1988 level of 437 vessels of 8.6 million grt.[131] The City of London has £1.22 billion worth of marine-related earnings. And the City of London would lose 36% of its maritime business if there was a complete end to UK-owned and flagged operations, and a 16% loss if the current fleet level was halved.[132] It has also been calculated that the total loss of earnings would be over £226m — one-third of the current £852m level, if the UK fleet disappeared altogether.[133] Revenue from marine insurance would be down by some 33% or £148.5m[134]; shipbroking revenue would be down by some 38% or £38.4m[135]; revenue from maritime banking activity would be down by some 35% or £42m.[136] Indeed, earnings in the City of London from maritime law activities would fall by some 29% or about £21.8m were the UK merchant fleet to disappear. More generally, it has been reckoned that the gross foreign earnings of the industry in 1989 were £3 billion and net earnings were over £1.1 billion with more than £1 billion of import savings made in the form of freight on imports and passenger revenues from UK residents.

It is submitted that the UK merchant fleet will not disappear. The Business Expansion Scheme (BES) allows for tax-efficient investment in shipping. There are accelerated depreciation allowances in respect of shipping activities.

The UK has traditionally specialised in the liner market.

The Isle of Man is in a curious position *vis-à-vis* the EC.

The tunnel being built at present between Britain and France ("the Channel Tunnel") will have a small but significant effect on British shipping. However, a port such as Felixstowe currently handles more than twice the freight which the Channel Tunnel could handle at full capacity.[137]

There has been a steady decline in UK tonnage over the recent past.

The Business Expansion Scheme (BES)—a tax scheme whereby the purchase of shares in certain types of, *inter alia*, shipping companies attracts tax relief— has helped foster some shipping companies.

128. See the study prepared by Moreby and Springett, *The UK Shipping Industry: Critical Levels Study*, 1990. See also MacAllister, "City Consequences of UK Fleet Decline Highlighted", *Lloyd's List*, 23 April 1990, p. 3. Department of Transport, *British Shipping: Challenges and Opportunities* (1990), *passim*.

129. See General Council of British Shipping, *Decline in the UK Registered Fleet*, November 1986, *passim*.

130. MacAllister, "City Consequences of UK Fleet Decline Highlighted," *Lloyd's List*, 23 April 1990, p. 3.

131. See MacAllister, "City Consequences of UK Fleet Decline Highlighted," *Lloyd's List*, 23 April 1990, p. 3. reporting the Moreby and Springett study.

132. *Ibid.*

133. *Ibid.*

134. *Ibid.*

135. *Ibid.*

136. *Ibid.*

137. See the comments of the British Transport Secretary, Cecil Parkinson, MP, in *Lloyd's List*, 1 March 1990, p. 2.

Of the 998 ships of over 1,000 grt owned by UK parent companies on 19 March 1990, less than half, 422 (i.e. 42.2%) were registered in the UK. The bulk of the rest were registered in various flags of convenience around the world such as the Bahamas (82 ships or 8.2% of the total), Hong Kong (63 ships or 6.3% of the total), Isle of Man (57 ships or 5.7% of the total), Liberia (84 ships or 8.4% of the total) and Panama (50 ships or 5% of the total).

A significant portion of the UK's external trade is carried on board UK ships.

The UK is particularly strong in the tanker sector but is well represented in the others as well, in particular the cargo and passenger ship sectors. The 1990 study *British Shipping: Challenges and Opportunities* records that in terms of international revenue earned by the UK shipping industry, 32% is earned by the tanker sector, 26% in the container sector, 13% in the cruise sector, 10% in ro-ro, 8% in dry bulk and 11% in other dry. The report also noted that of the "UK shipping industry direct owned tonnage" some 61.2% was comprised of tankers with 20.6% being comprised of dry bulk cargo.

2.4 EC IN THE SHIPPING WORLD

2.4.1 Introduction

It would be useful at this juncture to review the position of the EC in the wider shipping world.

In 1957, about 44% of the world's fleet flew the flag of one of the (now) twelve States of the EC — today, only about 17.4% of the world's fleet flies the flag of an EC Member State — almost one-third less. In 1957, about 38% of the world's gross tonnage was registered in one of the States which is now a member of the EC but today the figure is only about 14.7% — again almost one-third less. The EC-controlled fleet has fallen to about 24.8% and 25.1% of world totals in terms of numbers and tonnage.

The decline in the EC fortunes has been quite dramatic in recent years. Over a six-year period from 1981 to 1987, the decline of the EC fleet was four times greater than that of the world fleet: the world shipping capacity (measured in deadweight tonnage) fell by 8% between 1981 and 1987 but the EC fleet fell by 28% during the same period.

As a general rule, the EC-controlled fleet is older than its counterparts around the world. Indeed, whatever modernisation is taking place in the EC is concentrated in the smaller ships sector.[138]

2.4.2 United States of America[139]

The US fleet grew by one-third during the 1980–1987 period. This progress has been due in part to the Jones Act. The contrast between the fortunes of shipping in the US and the EC is obvious. While the US suffered a decline both in terms of tonnage and ship numbers during the 1960s and early 1970s, the position has been entirely reversed in terms of US-registered ships and almost remedied in the case of US-registered

138. Mikelis and Dean, *op. cit.*, Section 3.

139. On relations between the US and the EC see, *inter alia*, De Clerq, "The United States and the European Communities: Brothers Yet Foes?" [1987] *European Affairs* 16 and Yeutter, "We are Not Close to a Trade War", [1987] 3 *European Affairs* 25. See a survey on US Maritime Industries in *Lloyd's List*, 30 December 1991, page 5.

tonnage. When the US and the EC are contrasted, one sees a decline in the EC's fortunes but an improvement in the fortunes of the US.

2.4.3 The former USSR

The former USSR was a major maritime nation and had been so since the late 1960s. It is possible that recent developments in relation to the privatisation of shipping companies in the former USSR may lead to further growth and development. The position of shipping in the CIS is now very serious: ships are ageing, there are bad debt problems and general economic chaos.

2.4.4 China

The Chinese flags have done well over the last decade. Both the Taiwanese and the People's Republic flags have risen steadily (indeed almost unstintingly) both in numbers and tonnage between 1961 and 1989.

2.4.5 Hong Kong

Hong Kong's fleet doubled from 4 million tons to 8.2 million tons between 1983 and 1986.[140]

2.4.6 Norway

Norway applied for EC membership and even signed a Treaty of Accession in 1972 but because of eventual opposition in Norway to membership, it has not joined the EC. If it had joined then the EC's shipping fortunes today might be better. There is speculation that it may yet join the EC.

Norway has traditionally been a strong maritime nation and it is interesting to note that while the Norwegian fleet's gross tonnage fell four-fold from a high of about 25 million grt in the mid-1970s to a low of about 6 million grt in 1987, there has only been a marginal decline in ship numbers. Indeed, since the low of 1987 there has been a doubling of tonnage in the Norwegian fleet due mainly to domestic legal changes, including the Norwegian International Ship Registry. An examination of the Norwegian-owned fleet shows an increase from 24 million grt in November 1988 to over 32 million in March 1990.[141] As a general principle, the Norwegian fleet has not suffered anything like the decline in ship numbers suffered by the EC and while it has suffered a severe drop in tonnage (like the EC), this is being remedied.

2.4.7 Developing countries

The shipping fleet of the developing countries grew by almost 60% during the 1980–1987 period. Four States contributed much to this increase, namely, the People's Republic of China, Hong Kong, Singapore and South Korea.

140. See the comments of De Croo in his inaugural address to the Antwerp Shipping symposium, "A Future for the Community Fleet", 6 May 1987; reprinted in (1987) XXII *European Transport Law* in May 1987, p. 194.

141. Mikelis and Dean, *op. cit.*, Section 3.

2.4.8 Open registries

The so-called "open registries" which have been created in recent years have grown rapidly to the detriment of the more traditional EC registries. These registries in such locations as Antigua, Saint Vincent and Vanuatu have attracted considerable interest.

2.4.9 Offshore registries

The so-called "offshore registries" such as Bermuda, Denmark, the Isle of Man and Norway have also proved attractive in that they allow a ship still to fly the flag of its own country while having many of the benefits of an open registry. These registries have proved a major threat to the future of shipping registered in EC Member States.[142]

2.4.10 Bahamas

The Bahamas has become a registry of considerable significance since 1982. Prior to the changes in 1982, the Bahamas fleet had a minute amount of tonnage — about a quarter of a million tons — but since then it has grown to almost 12 million tons.

2.4.11 Cyprus

Cypriot shipping has enjoyed a period of prosperity over the last quarter century. While suffering a decline in the late 1970s and early 1980s, Cyprus has enjoyed a period of considerable prosperity during the 1980s with a doubling in ship numbers and a nine-fold increase in gross tonnage. Again, the EC has not fared so well.

2.4.12 Comecon

The Council for Mutual Economic Co-operation (CMEA or Comecon) consists of eleven States, namely, Albania, Bulgaria, Czechoslovakia, Hungary, Poland, Romania and the USSR. During the 1975–1983 period, Comecon's container fleet grew seven-fold from 61,000 grt to 414,000 grt.[143]

There was an increase in the early 1970s in the threat posed to EC shippers by State-trading countries.

2.5 CONCLUSION

One of the challenges facing the EC in the years ahead is to strike a balance between a desire to have its own fleet (despite strong world competition) and a desire to have an effective competition policy.

The Economic and Social Committee commented in 1986 that ships:

> "registered in Community Member States are important cross-traders between other Member States and third countries and between third countries only. They face strong competition from flag of convenience shipping under other flags, and are threatened by the increasing trend towards cargo reservation and the desire of many non-Community States to build up their fleets."[144]

142. See "Clinton Davies Warns of Possible Dangers posed by Development of Offshore Registries", *Lloyd's List*, 1 April 1987, p. 1.
143. See Progress, Table 4.
144. TRA/116, para. 1.14.

It is interesting to note the trend in new orders placed by EC companies in contrast to the rest of the world: in 1986, it amounted to 11.42% of the total; in 1987, it rose to 14.63%; it 1988, this climbed to 16.96%; and fell in 1989 to 14.27%.[145] In each of those years, South Korea had placed a higher order than the EC and in 1989 Japan had placed an order three times as great.[146] It should not be forgotten that vessels registered under the flags of the Member States carry 70% of the EC's internal trade and 40% of external trade.

145. Source:Lloyd's Maritime Information Service, reprinted in *Lloyd's List*, 22 March 1990, p. 3.
146. *Ibid.*

CHAPTER 3

The European Community

3.1 INTRODUCTION

This chapter provides a general overview of the law, legal system, policies and institutions of the European Community (EC) in general.[1] Such an understanding of the EC is vital to comprehend subsequent chapters. The inclusion of such a long chapter is necessitated by the fact that many readers may be maritime or non-EC lawyers who are unfamiliar with the workings of the EC.

The legal consequences for each Member State of its involvement in the EC are enormous.[2] The EC is, in the words of the European Court of Justice (ECJ), "a new legal order of international law" (see Case 26/62 *van Gend en Loos*[2a]). Every citizen of an EC Member State has acquired new rights and duties.[3] A new legal order has been created.[4] There is hardly a sector of the economy which is not affected:

1. On community law generally, see Hartley, *The Foundations of European Community Law* (2nd edn., 1988); Kapteyn and Van Themaat, *Introduction to the Law of the European Communities* (2nd edn., 1988); Lasok and Bridge, *An Introduction to the Law of the European Communities* (4th edn., 1988); Mathijsen, *A Guide to European Community Law* (4th edn., 1985); Myles, *EEC Brief* (Belfast, 1979 and updates); Nugent, *The Government and Politics of the European Community* (1989); Olmi *et al.*, *Thirty Years of Community Law* (1983); Parry and Hardy, *EEC Law* (2nd edn., 1981); Smit and Herzog, *The Law of the European Community* (6th edn.); Stein, Hay and Waelbroeck, *European Community Law and Institutions in Perspective* (1976); Toth, *The Oxford Encyclopedia of European Community Law*; Vaughan (Ed.), *Law of the European Communities* (1986) (reprinted in Hailsham (Ed.), *Halsbury's Laws of England* (4th edn.), vols 51 and 52); as well as Wyatt and Dashwood, *The Substantive Law of the EEC* (2nd edn., 1987). See also Collins, *European Community Law in the UK* (3rd edn., 1984); Hartley, "Federalism, Courts and Legal Systems: The Emerging Constitution of the European Community" (1986) 34 AJCL 229; Mackenzie Stuart, *The European Communities and the Rule of Law* (1977); Schermers, *Judicial Protection in the European Communities* (3rd edn., 1983); Stein, "Lawyers, Judges and the Making of a Transnational Constitution" (1981) 75 *American Journal of International Law* 1. For cases on European Community law see, among other publications, the *European Court Reports* and the *Common Market Law Reports*. For collections of EC laws, see Simmonds (Ed.), *Encyclopedia of European Community Law* (updated). On the economics of the Communities see Coffey (Ed.), *Economic Policies of the Common Market* (1979); El-Agraa (Ed.), *The Economics of the European Community* (1985) and Swann, *The Economics of the Common Market* (6th edn., 1988). On the Communities generally see Arbuthnott and Edwards, *A Common Man's Guide to the Common Market* (2nd edn., 1989); Bieber (Ed.), *An Ever Closer Union* (1985); Budd and Jones, *The European Community: A Guide to the Maze* (3rd edn., 1989); Lodge, *The European Community and the Challenge of the Future* (1989); as well as Nicoll and Salmon, *Understanding the European Communities* (1990)

2. On the influence of the membership of the EC on English law see Collins, *European Community Law in the UK* (3rd edn., 1984) and Furmston, Kerridge and Sufrin (Eds), *The Effect on English Domestic Law of Membership of the European Communities and of Ratification of the European Convention on Human Rights* (1983).

2a. [1963] ECR 1; [1963] CMLR 105.

3. E.g. there can be no discrimination in matters covered by the EEC Treaty between citizens of Member States (EEC, Article 7, para.1). *Cf.* Case 167/73 *Commission v. France* [1974] ECR 359 and Case 61/77 *Commission v. Ireland* [1978] ECR 417. On the rights of individuals in European Community law see Toth, *Legal Protection of Individuals in the European Communities* (1978). See also Greenwood, "Nationality and the Limits of the Free Movement of Persons in Community Law" (1987) 7 Ybk. Eur. Law 185.

4. See Case 26/62 *Van Gend en Loos v. Nederlandse Administratie der Belastingen* [1963] ECR 1 at p. 29.

be it agriculture,[5] banking,[6] energy[7] or transport.[8] The social consequences are equally significant through environmental[9] and regional development policies.[10] And, politically, the EC represents a transfer of some aspects of sovereignty by the Member States to the Communities.[11]

3.2 THE COMMUNITY

3.2.1 Introduction

The EC consists of three international organisations[12] which are juristically separate but are, in practical terms, interlinked by shared organs and resources. The three Communities operate principally in the political, economic, social and financial spheres.

3.2.2 European Coal and Steel Community (ECSC)

The first of the three Communities is the European Coal and Steel Community (ECSC).[13] It was founded on 18 April 1951 under the Treaty of Paris which was signed by Belgium, the (then) Federal Republic of Germany, France, Italy, Luxembourg and the Netherlands.[14] Ireland, Denmark and the UK joined in 1973. Greece joined in 1981.

5. On agriculture, see *inter alios*, Buckwell, Harvey, Thompson and Parbou, *The Cost of the Common Agricultural Policy* (1982); Duchene, Szczepanik and Legg, *New Limits on European Agriculture: Politics and the Common Agricultural Policy* (1985); Hill, *The Common Agricultural Policy: Past, Present and Future* (1984); Marsh and Ritson, *Agricultural Policy and the Common Market* (1971); and Tracy, *Agriculture in Western Europe* (1982).

6. On banking see, *inter alios*, Crossick and Lindsay, *European Banking Law* (1983) and Lunt, *Legal Aspects of the ECU* (1989). See also Baltensperger and Dermine, "Banking Deregulation" (1987) *Economic Policy* 63.

7. See Gasteyger (Ed.), *The Future for European Energy Security* (1985) and Lucas, *Energy and the European Communities* (1977).

8. See Chapter 4, below, for the effects generally on transport.

9. See Johnson and Courcelle, *L'autre Europe "verte": La politique communautaire de l'environment* (1987).

10. See Clout, *Regional Variations in the European Community* (1986) as well as Yuill, Allen and Hull, *Regional Policy in the European Community* (1980).

11. See Case 26/62 *Van Gend en Loos v. Nederlandse Administratie der Belastingen* [1963] ECR 1, at p. 12. The EC has legal personality and legal capacity: see EEC Treaty, Articles 210, 211 and Joined Cases 43/59 etc. *Lachmuller v. Commission* [1960] ECR 463, at p. 472 and Ruling 1/78 [1978] ECR 2151.

12. On the law relating to international organisations generally, see, *inter alia*, Bebr, "Regional Organisations: a United Nations Problem" (1955) 49 AJIL 166; Bowett, *Law of International Institutions* (4th edn., 1984); Eagleton, *International Government* (1957); *op. cit.*, "International Personality of Intergovernmental Organisations" (1964) 4 IJIL 1, at p. 233; Jenks, "Some Constitutional Problems of International Organisations" (1945) 22 BYIL 12; Lauterpacht, "The Development of the Law of International Organization by the Decisions of International Tribunals" (1976) 4 RdC 388; Mangone, *A Short History of International Organisation* (1954); Njaya, "The Relevance of the Study of Common Problems of International Organisations to Developing Countries", UNESCO Doc.5HC-76/CONF.623/7; Potter, "Contemporary Problems of International Organisations" (1965) 59 AJIL 291; Schermers, *International Institutional Law* (2nd edn., 1980); Seyersted, "Objective International Personality of Intergovernmental Organisations" (1964) 34 Nor TIR 46; Sohn, "The Growth of the Science of International Organizations", in *The Relevance of International Law: Essays in Honour of Leo Gross*, (1968), pp. 251–269.

13. On the ECSC, see, in particular, Reuter, *La CECA* (1953).

14. Cmnd 7460; 261 UNTS 141. The Treaty entered into force on 25 July 1952. An annotated text is published in Simmonds (Ed.), *Encyclopedia of Community Law*, vol. BI.

Spain as well as Portugal joined in 1986. The operation of the ECSC is confined to the coal and steel sectors[15]—two sectors which were critical in the European economy of the early 1950s. The ECSC has as its task "to contribute, in harmony with the general economy of the Member States and through the establishment of a common market [in coal and steel], to economic expansion, growth of employment and a rising standard of living in the Member States."[16] It must "progressively bring about conditions which will of themselves ensure the most rational distribution of production at the highest possible level of productivity, while safeguarding continuity of employment and taking care not to provoke fundamental and persistent disturbances in the economies of Member States."[17] When first drafted, the ECSC Treaty contemplated a High Authority (a permanent executive supra-national body)[18], a Special Council of Ministers (to harmonise the actions of the High Authority and Member States), a Common Assembly (or Parliament, with no legislative powers but with some supervisory functions[19] and a Court of Justice (to solve legal disputes). It is not too surprising that the ECSC has little significance for shipping and relates only to shipping in so far as the ECSC is interested in shipping rates for the transport of coal and steel.[20]

3.2.3 European Atomic Energy Community (Euratom)

The European Atomic Energy Community (Euratom) was founded by the Treaty of Rome (a separate treaty from the one which established the European Economic Community (EEC)), signed on 25 March 1957 which became effective on 1 January 1958. Initially, EURATOM was composed of "the Six" (Belgium, France, the (then) Federal Republic of Germany, Italy, Luxembourg and the Netherlands), but has since been joined by Denmark, Ireland and the UK (in 1973), Greece (in 1981) as well as Portugal and Spain (in 1986). The task of Euratom is to contribute to the raising of the standard of living in the Member States and to the development of relations with each other countries by creating the conditions necessary for the speedy establishment and growth of nuclear industries.[21] Its sphere of operation is limited to the nuclear energy sector and is not of any great significance to shipping companies.[22]

3.2.4 European Economic Community (EEC)

The European Economic Community (EEC) was established by Article 1 of the Treaty of Rome which was signed on 25 March 1957 which became effective on 1 January 1958 and was amended by, *inter alia*, the Single European Act (SEA) of 1986.[23] Initially, it was composed of "the Six" (Belgium, France, the (then) Federal Republic of Germany, Italy, Luxembourg and the Netherlands), but has since been joined by Denmark, Ireland, and the UK (in 1973), Greece (in 1981) as well as Portugal and Spain (in 1986).

15. This is in contrast to the EEC which applies to virtually all sectors of the economy.
16. ECSC Treaty, Article 2.
17. ECSC Treaty, Article 2. Cf. ECSC, Article 3, for the objectives of the ECSC institutions.
18. ECSC, Article 18 (in its original form). The High Authority was abolished in 1967 by the Merger Treaty, see para. 3.3.13 below.
19. ECSC, Article 24 (as originally drafted).
20. See para.4.2.1, below.
21. Euratom, Article 1.
22. Except nuclear-powered ships in an indirect way.
23. On the SEA, see para. 3.3.20 below. It will also be amended by the Maastricht Treaty.

The task of the EEC is "by establishing a common market and progressively approximating the economic policies of Member States, to promote throughout the Community, a harmonious development of economic activities, a continuous and balanced expansion, an increase in stability, an accelerated raising of the standard of living and closer relations between the States belonging to it".[24] The activities[25] of the EEC include:

"(a) the elimination, as between Member States, of customs duties and of quantitative restrictions on the import and export of goods, and of all other measures having equivalent effect;
(b) the establishment of a common customs tariff and of a common commercial policy towards third countries;
(c) the abolition, as between Member States, of obstacles to freedom of movement for persons, services and capital[26];
(d) the adoption of a common policy in the sphere of agriculture;
(e) the adoption of a common policy in the sphere of transport;
(f) the institution of a system ensuring that competition in the common market is not distorted[27];
(g) the application of procedures by which the economic policies of Member States can be coordinated and disequilibria in their balances of payments remedied;
(h) the approximation of the laws of Member States to the extent required for the proper functioning of the common market;
(i) the creation of a European Social Fund in order to improve employment opportunities for workers and to contribute to the raising of their standard of living;
(j) the establishment of a European Investment Bank to facilitate the economic expansion of the Community by opening up fresh resources; [and]
(k) the association of the overseas countries and territories in order to increase trade and to promote jointly economic and social progress."[28]

Member States are obliged to "take all appropriate measures, whether general or particular, to ensure fulfilment of the obligations arising out of [the EEC] Treaty or resulting from action taken by the institutions of the Community. They shall facilitate the achievement of the Community's task".[29] States must "abstain from any measure which could jeopardise the attainment of the objectives" of the EEC Treaty.[30] They must co-ordinate their respective economic policies to the extent necessary to attain the objectives of the Treaties.[31]

Unlike the other two Communities (the ECSC and Euratom), the EEC's competence is not limited to a particular economic sector but covers virtually all economic activities.

24. EEC Treaty, Article 2.

25. I.e. the means by which the objectives will be achieved.

26. The removal of restrictions on the free movement of workers, services and capital has direct significance for shipping. Note for example, the free movement of seafarers as discussed by the European Court of Justice in Case 167/73 *Commission v. France* [1974] ECR 359; [1974] 2 CMLR 216 (in the case of workers (see Chapter 8, below)), the abolition of cabotage (in the case of services (see Chapter 7, below)) and, the availability of finance for ship acquisition from any bank in the EC.

27. The institution of a system of competition has proved significant in the case of shipping as in most other business sectors but only in the recent past because it was only with the entry into force of Regulation 4056/86 (OJ 1986 L378/4) that the competition rules applied to shipping. On EC competition law and shipping see, *inter alia*, Chapter 9 *et seq.* below and the references cited in it.

28. EEC Treaty, Article 5(2).

29. *Cf.* Case 78/70 *Deutsche Grammophon v. Metro* [1971] ECR 487; Case 231/83 *Cullet v. Leclerc* [1985] ECR 305.

30. EEC Treaty, Article 5(2).

31. EEC Treaty, Article 6(1).

3.3 HISTORY OF THE COMMUNITY

3.3.1 European Integration

The story of how the EC developed is fascinating.[32] The EC is the product of the spirit of European integration. The notion of European integration is not new but it has gathered momentum since the end of the Second World War. Thinkers and talkers such as Henry IV of France 400 years ago (with his "Great Republic of Europe" concept); William Penn 300 years ago (with his "European Parliament' concept); as well as Kant, Saint-Simon and Cattaneo 200 years ago each advanced notions of European integration. The first half of this century saw thinkers such as Coudenhove-Kalergi and Briand advocate the doctrine. Progress was however slow and difficult. The Second World War impressed on many people the dire need for European unity. Two eminent EC lawyers, Lasok and Bridge have written: "[t]he Second World War demonstrated the futility of conquests and the vulnerability of the sovereign state concept. The sovereign state could no longer guarantee the protection of the citizen and so the traditional concept of allegiance based on a *sui generis* contract broke down. Interdependence of states rather than independence became the key to post-war international relations . . . ."[33] In 1946, Winston Churchill spoke at Zurich University of the need to "recreate the European family, or as much of it as we can, and provide it with a structure under which it can dwell in peace, in safety and in freedom. We must build a kind of United States of Europe . . . The first step in the recreation of the European family must be a partnership between France and Germany". Integration, in this context, was undertaken so as to achieve both economic growth and political stability while avoiding war and domination by Stalinist Russia.

3.3.2 Marshall Aid, the OEEC and the UN Economic Commission for Europe

In June 1947 at Harvard University, General George Marshall, the then US Secretary of State, announced a plan for European relief (the Marshall Plan) under which the USA would offer cash aid on condition that Europe worked out a common programme for the relief of poverty and for economic reconstruction. Sixteen Western European States participated in a conference on the plan. Thirteen milliard dollars was given by the US to Europe in so-called Marshall Aid. The Marshall Plan led to the establishment of the Organisation of European Economic Co-operation (OEEC) in 1948.[34] This was an intergovernmental organisation consisting of a Council of Ministers, an Executive Committee and a Secretariat. Its Members were States and it operated along the classic lines of an international organisation: unanimity of Member States was required before action could be taken.[35] Its function was to administer Marshall Aid efficiently. The organisation constituted the first major attempt to achieve *economic* co-operation in Europe. The name of this organisation was changed in 1961[36] to the Organisation for Economic Co-operation and Development (OECD)

32. See Hoggart and Johnson, *An Idea of Europe* (1987); Kennedy, *The Rise and Fall of the Great Powers* (1988); Urwin, *Western Europe Since 1945* (4th edn., 1989); and Vaughan, *Post-War Integration in Europe* (1976). See also Nicoll and Salmon, *Understanding the European Communities* (1990), Chapter 1.
33. *Op. cit.* at footnote 1 above, p. 4.
34. Convention of 16 April 1948. TS59 (1949) (UK), p. 13.
35. See Nicoll and Salmon, *op. cit.* at footnote 1 above, p. 8.
36. Convention of 14 December 1960, TS21 (1962); Cmnd.1646.

when the USA and Canada joined. The European Community (in its corporate capacity) is now a member of OECD. The work of the OECD in the context of shipping is discussed in Chapter 1 above.[37]

The United Nations established an Economic Commission for Europe in 1947 with the purpose of exchanging information on coal, electricity and transport in Western Europe.[38]

3.3.3 Congress of Europe

A Congress of Europe was held in The Hague in May 1948. This was a gathering of many people who were influential either then or later in European politics, including such figures as Churchill, Eden, Macmillan and Mitterand. The Congress called for a European Parliament to be established. This did not happen. Instead, less representative institutions were established which lay within the control of the European States and these institutions formed part of the Council of Europe.

3.3.4 Benelux Union

Also in 1948, the Benelux Union was established between Belgium, the Netherlands and Luxembourg whereby customs barriers were removed and closer co-operation was established between those three States. This was to prove instrumental in the establishment in the Common Market of the EEC.

3.3.5 Council of Europe

Along with the OEEC,[39] another organisation, the Council of Europe was created at this time. It still survives today. It is an intergovernmental organisation consisting of over twenty-five States.[40] It has been largely unsuccessful in achieving its remit in the area of political co-operation, but it has succeeded well in the areas of human rights and culture. Its failure to achieve all of its goals is due in no small way to the limits placed on it by the Statute establishing it and the breadth of its membership. It is interesting to note that the opening up of Eastern Europe in recent years may well prove to be a blessing for the Council of Europe because many of the Eastern European States may join the Council. It has little significance for shipping but its Convention may well provide comfort for some companies which suffer loss.[41]

3.3.6 NATO

The North Atlantic Treaty Organisation (NATO) was established in 1949.[42] It is a collective security pact: armed aggression against one member constitutes armed aggression against all of the members. It consists of the non-neutral Western European

37. See para. 1.3.15, above.
38. See para. 1.3.9, above.
39. See para. 3.3.2, above.
40. The constitutive instrument is the Statute of the Council of Europe TS51 (1949); Cmnd. 7779.
41. A shipping company may well apply to the European Commission on Human Rights to vindicate, for example, property rights.
42. North Atlantic Treaty was signed in Washington DC on 4 April 1949, TS56 (1949 (U.K.)); Cmnd. 7789.

states along with the USA and Canada. France has withdrawn from NATO but remains a party to the Treaty. Ireland is the only EC Member State which is not a full member of NATO. The existence of NATO has probably meant that the EC has not had a military dimension up to this time. There are however indications that the EC is developing a security (if not, a military) dimension.

3.3.7 Schumann Declaration

All of this organisation and reorganisation of Europe led many to believe that further integration was possible, if not a prerequisite. On 9 May 1950, Robert Schumann, the French Foreign Minister, stated in the Salle de l'Horloge in Paris that a united Europe was essential for world peace. He went on to say that such a united Europe would not come about until there was a coming together of France and Germany. He proposed that the coal and steel production of those two former adversaries would be pooled under a common High Authority. The purpose was two-fold: first, to avoid the possibility that either State could build up a war industry (coal and steel being the significant raw materials for war, at least at that time) and secondly, to create economic growth through an enlarged market, albeit in limited economic sectors initially. France needed access to the German market so as to sell agricultural products. Conversely, Germany needed the French market as an outlet for manufactured goods. The Schumann Proposal led to the foundation of the European Coal and Steel Community (ECSC). Schumann's proposal was described at the time by President Truman of the US as "an act of constructive statesmanship".

3.3.8 The European Coal and Steel Community (ECSC)

The ECSC was founded in 1951 by means of a Treaty signed in Paris (known since as the Treaty of Paris) which entered into force in 1952. The ECSC proved to be an immediate success. This was the stimulus for the later birth of the European Economic Community (the EEC). The new organisation had a High Authority (later called the Commission),[43] a Council of Ministers,[44] an Assembly (later known as the Parliament)[45] and a Court of Justice.[46,47] The ECSC was a success—had it been a failure then in all probability neither the EEC nor the Euratom would ever have been created. The work of Schumann should always be seen in the context of the great work of Jean Monnet, the French businessman who also championed the cause of European Integration.

3.3.9 The EEC and Euratom

The Benelux countries[48] proposed the establishment of a common market in products other than coal and steel as well as services generally.[49] A conference was held in

43. On the Commission, see para. 3.4.2, below.
44. On the Council of Ministers, see para. 3.4.3, below.
45. On the Parliament, see para. 3.4.5, below.
46. On the Court of Justice, see para. 3.4.6, below.
47. On the institutions generally, see para. 3.4, below.
48. See para. 3.3.4, above. The Benelux countries consist of Belgium, The Netherlands and Luxembourg. Belgium and Luxembourg had formed an economic union in 1921.
49. Although invited, Britain did not take part in the new Communities because of (among other things) its Commonwealth responsibilities and its special link with the US.

Messina in June 1955 to discuss the proposals. Spaak (the Belgian Foreign Minister) was asked to report on the feasibility of a general economic union and the joint development and peaceful use of atomic energy. The Spaak Report was discussed in Venice in May 1956. The Foreign Ministers of the Six decided at that meeting to establish two new Communities (the EEC and Euratom).

The Foundation Treaties for both the EEC and Euratom were speedily drafted and later signed on 25 March 1957. Unlike the ECSC Treaty which was designed to last for fifty years,[50] the EEC and Euratom Treaties are of unlimited duration.[51] The EEC and Euratom were both established on 1 January 1958.

A Convention on certain institutions common to the EC entered into force on the same day as the EEC and Euratom Treaties.[52] The Convention provided for a single parliamentary assembly (i.e. the European Parliament) and a single Court of Justice for the three Communities as well as a single Economic and Social Committee for the EEC and the Euratom.

3.3.10 European Defence Treaty

In 1952, it was proposed that a European Defence Community would be established under a European Defence Treaty. This Community was still-born because of opposition on the part of some States, notably France.

3.3.11 European Free Trade Association

In 1959, the European Free Trade Association (EFTA) was founded by Austria, Denmark, Norway, Portugal, Sweden, Switzerland and the UK. This was an organisation of some non-EC European States designed to create a free trade area (but not a customs union) between them. Both Denmark and the UK left EFTA when they joined the EC in 1973. Austria has since announced its intention to join the EC and has formally applied for membership. The economic relationship between EC and EFTA is deepening and this new relationship will be discussed below.[53]

3.3.12 Britain's position

The position of the UK during the formation of the EC is interesting. The UK had opposed even the earliest plans for European federation put forward in 1929 by Astrid Briand at the General Assembly of the League of Nations.[54] Britain believed that its relationship with the Commonwealth of Nations prevented it from joining such a European alliance.[55] Nonetheless, it should not be forgotten that Lord Salisbury, the British Prime Minister, said in 1897: "[t]he federated action of Europe, if we can maintain it, is our sole hope of escaping from the constant terror and calamity of war, the constant pressure of the burdens of an armed peace, which weigh down the spirits

50. ECSC Treaty, Article 97.
51. EEC Treaty, Article 240 and Euratom Treaty, Article 208.
52. The Merger Treaty was signed on 8 April 1965 and entered into force on 29 June 1967.
53. This is the so-called European Economic Area.
54. See Nicoll and Salmon, *op. cit.* at footnote 1 above, p. 4.
55. See Joll (Ed.), *Britain and Europe: Pitt to Churchill 1793–1940* (1961).

and darken the prospect of every Nation in this part of the world. The Federation of Europe is the only hope we have."[56]

The UK applied to join the EC in 1961 but did not join. Nevertheless it renewed its applications in 1967 and 1970. The UK signed a Treaty of Accession to the EC on 22 January 1972 and joined on 1 January 1973. In 1975, the UK held a referendum on its continued membership of the EC and the people voted to remain in the EC.

3.3.13 Merger Treaty

In spite of the Convention on certain institutions common to the European Communities,[57] the three Communities had a number of overlapping institutions. This was inefficient. The Merger Treaty of 8 April 1965[58] established a Single Council of Ministers[59] and a Single Commission.[60] Thus, from mid-1967 (when the Merger Treaty entered into force) there was one Council of Ministers and one Commission for all three Communities (as well as one Parliament and one Court of Justice).

3.3.14 Customs Union[61]

Unlike the ECSC, the EEC "shall be based upon a customs union which shall cover *all* trade in goods and which shall involve the prohibition between Member States of customs duties on imports and exports and of all charges having their equivalent effect, and the adoption of a common customs tariff in their relations with third countries".[62,63] The Customs Union became fully operative on 1 July 1968 (eighteen months ahead of the timetable laid down in the Treaty).[64] A common external tariff was put in place.

3.3.15 Accessions

The Treaty of Brussels was signed on 22 January 1972 by Denmark, Ireland, Norway and the United Kingdom. The first three States ratified the Treaty but Norway did not—in a referendum the Norwegian people voted against joining the EC, largely because of the EC's fishing polices. Thus Ireland, the UK and Denmark joined the three Communities on 1 January 1973. The accession of Denmark and the UK (as well as Ireland to a lesser extent) brought shipping to the forefront in the EC and led to the Commission instituting proceedings against France over its Maritime Code.[65]

On 12 June 1975, Greece applied for membership of the Communities.[66] Greece joined on 1 January 1981 by means of the Accession Treaty of 28 May 1979. Its accession dramatically altered the shipping profile of the EC and its fleet accounts for

56. Cited by Harold Macmillan in *Tides of Fortune 1945–1955* (London, 1969), p. 151.
57. On the Convention, see para. 3.3.9, above.
58. JO 152/2 (1967).
59. On the Council of Ministers, see para. 4.3, below.
60. On the Commission, see para. 4.2, below.
61. A customs union involves the abolition of internal trade barriers and the creation of a common customs tariff towards the rest of the world. This latter element, the common customs tariff, is missing from a free trade area.
62. See EEC Treaty, Article 10.
63. EEC Treaty, Article 9(1), emphasis added. See EEC Treaty Articles 12–29, *passim*.
64. See EEC Treaty, Article 8.
65. See Case 167/73 *Commission v. France*, [1974] ECR 359.
66. On Greece, see para. 2.3.6 above.

almost half of the EC total.[67] The accession of the three States in 1973 and Greece in 1981 had an enormous impact on the development of a shipping policy in the EC: until 1973, 90 per cent. of transportation between the then six Member States in the EC was by means of inland transport but after the EC was enlarged to ten States, 90 per cent. of the trade between the old six and the new four was carried by sea.

Expansion also took place in the West. Spain and Portugal applied for membership in 1977[68] and became members on 1 January 1986.

3.3.16 Tindemans Report

The Tindemans Report was published in the mid-1970s. This report discussed the gradual development towards European Union through the media of greater co-operation among Member States on foreign policy issues, more frequent meetings of the heads of government, the strengthening of the role of the Council of Ministers and the creation of a two-speed plan for economic integration.

3.3.17 European Monetary System

The Council of Ministers decided to establish a European Monetary System (the so-called EMS). It was designed to create closer monetary co-operation leading to European monetary stability. It was introduced on 13 March 1979. This was a significant step on the road towards a monetary union programme which is currently being pursued and advanced in the EC and may lead to full monetary union by the end of the decade.

3.3.18 Direct elections to the European Parliament

While there had been a European Assembly (or Parliament) since the inception of the Communities, the members were nominated by their respective governments or parliaments and were not elected by the people until 1979. It was widely believed that the European Parliament would gain prestige and power by being directly elected by the people. Following the 1976 Act concerning the Election of the Representatives of the Assembly by Direct Universal Suffrage,[69] the first direct elections took place in June 1979 and now take place every five years.[70]

3.3.19 Internal Market White Paper

In June 1985, the Commission published its White Paper on the Completion of the Internal Market. This is one of the most important documents in the entire catalogue of EC documents. It set the objective that the Internal Market would be achieved by 31 December 1992.

67. See para. 2.3.6, above.
68. See Bull. 7/8–1977, 6 and Suppl. 9/78 in respect of Spain, and Bull. 3–1977, 8 and Suppl. 5/78 in respect of Portugal.
69. OJ 1976 L278/1
70. On the European Parliament generally, see Ritter *et al.*, *op. cit.* at footnote 1 above, pp. 131–145.

3.3.20 Single European Act

The Single European Act (SEA)[71] which was signed in Luxembourg on 17 February 1986 and in The Hague on 28 February 1986 constitutes one of the most significant documents in EC law and special attention must be paid to it here. The SEA was agreed upon by a meeting of the European Council in December 1985. The SEA amends the EEC Treaty quite extensively, particularly in the area of foreign policy. Traditionally, the Council of Ministers had to adopt legislation by way of a unanimous vote but the SEA allows for the adoption of many matters, including some quite controversial ones, by way of a majority vote. The SEA also reformed the powers of the Parliament.[72]

3.3.21 Eastern Europe[73]

The opening up of Eastern Europe is an event of huge significance for the EC as a whole. The unification of Germany has expanded the EC. The conclusion of numerous joint ventures with Eastern European companies creates both promise and problems for the EC. As Eastern Europe is currently in a state of flux, it would be inappropriate to draw any conclusions at this time.

3.4 ORGANIC STRUCTURE OF THE EUROPEAN COMMUNITY

3.4.1 Introduction

Community organs[74] are classified under EC law as either "institutions" (which are capable of taking decisions binding on Member States) or "bodies" (which are not capable of taking such binding decisions). The four institutions are the Commission of the European Communities,[75] the Council of Ministers of the European Communities,[76] the European Parliament[77] and the Court of Justice of the European Communities[78,79]. The bodies are too numerous to enumerate here but include the Economic and Social Committee[80] and most of them are essentially advisory in nature. All organs must act within the powers conferred on them under Community law[81] and are audited by the Court of Auditors.[82] Some of the organs are remote from the citizens of the EC.[83] A "comprehensive policy-making and regulatory task has . . . been allotted to the Institutions" in the EEC.[84]

The Council of Ministers is politically the most significant of the institutions. In

71. See Campbell, "The Single European Act and the Implications" (1985) 34 ICLQ 359 and Murphy, "The Single European Act" (1985) 30 Ir.Jur.(n.s.) 17, at p. 239.
72. See para. 3.4.5, below.
73. See *The Times Guide to Eastern Europe* (1991).
74. On the organic structure of the EC, see Kapteyn and Van Themaat, *op. cit.* at footnote 1 above, Chapter IV.
75. See para. 3.4.2, below.
76. See para. 3.4.3, below.
77. See para. 3.4.4, below.
78. See para. 3.4.5, below.
79. See EEC Treaty, Article 4.
80. See para. 3.4.7.1, below.
81. *Cf.* EEC Treaty, Article 4.
82. EEC Treaty, Article 4(3).
83. See Mackenzie Stuart (1979) 39 NILQ 95, at p. 98.
84. Kapteyn and Van Themaat, *op. cit.* at footnote 1 above, p. 31.

recent years, the Commission has an increased high public profile, particularly in connection with the 1992 Programme. The Parliament has a limited role. The Court has a monitoring function.

3.4.2 Commission

3.4.2.1 Introduction

The Commission is the central cog in the EC wheel. It is not just the permanent civil service of the EC but has a wider role. It is the EC's executive organ. One Commission serves the three Communities.[85] It is responsible for executing the decisions of the Council of Ministers.[86] It sends to the Council of Ministers various proposals which may ultimately find their way into Regulations, Directives and so on.[87]

3.4.2.2 Composition

It has seventeen members[88] who are appointed by agreement between the governments of the Member States on the basis of their general competence.[89] The number may be altered by a unanimous decision of the Council of Ministers.[90] The Commission must have at least one national from each Member State while France, Germany, Italy, Spain and the UK may have two nationals.[91] The Commission may not have non-EC nationals among its membership.[92] All Commissioners are appointed by the common accord of the governments of Member States on the basis of general competence and independence from national interests.[93] Commissioners are appointed for four-year renewable periods.[94] The Commission has a President with six Vice-Presidents.

3.4.2.3 Functions

The functions of the Commission fall into three broad categories: first, the guardian of the Treaties; secondly, the initiator and guardian of the EC policy; and thirdly, the EC's executive organ. The Commission ensures that the Foundation Treaties and measures taken pursuant to them are complied with by all Member States, Community institutions and the general public; it formulates recommendations or delivers opinions on matters dealt with in the Treaties, if they expressly so provide or if the Commission considers it necessary; the Commission has its own power of decision and participation in the shaping of measures taken by the Council of Ministers and by the European Parliament in the manner provided for in the Foundation Treaties; and exercises the powers conferred on it by the Council of Ministers for the implementation of the rules

85. See Merger Treaty, Article 9, see also Article 155 EEC.
86. On the Council of Ministers, see para. 3.4.3, below.
87. On EC law, see para. 3.5, below.
88. Merger Treaty, Article 10(1), as modified by the Treaties of Accession.
89. Merger Treaty, Article 10.
90. Merger Treaty, Article 10.
91. Merger Treaty, Article 10.
92. Merger Treaty, Article 10.
93. Merger Treaty, Article 10.
94. Merger Treaty, Article 11.

laid down by the latter.[95] Thus, for example, Commission Regulation 2367/90[96] implements Council of Ministers Regulation 4064/89[97] (the so-called Merger Control Regulation).[98] The Commission has the power to initiate legislation by proposing opinions or recommendations to the Council of Ministers for adoption. It does so either because the Foundation Treaties require it or because the Commission considers it necessary. It is worth noting that the Commission has the power to take its own decisions in some areas but they are limited.[99]

The Foundation Treaties specifically charge the Commission with the task of enforcing EC competition law.[100] This has provided the Commission with an opportunity to heighten public awareness of its existence and powers.

The Commission is independent of the Member States and thus it is independent in the exercise of its functions. This independence gives the Commission independence and authority.

The Commission can sometimes irritate or annoy Member States. It engages in "preaching, exhorting, cajoling, exposing uncomfortable truths, and [takes] the flak when things go wrong, as an honest broker often does"[101] so as to prompt those States into action. An example of the "honest broker" is to be found in Case No. IV/33.045 where it intervened to solve a dispute between an Irish shipping company and a UK harbour company.[102]

3.4.2.4 Operation

The Commission is based in Brussels but with offices in Luxembourg as well as information offices in the Member States. The Commission maintains delegations in a number of cities throughout the world. The seventeen-member collegiate Commission normally meets weekly. The Commission has a Secretary-General and some 10,000 employees.[103] It operates through Directorates-General—a concept like Government Departments or Ministries. Director-Generals preside over each Directorate-General. Some of these Directorates-General are sub-divided into Directorates.[104] A full list of the Directorates-General reads as follows:

DG I	External Relations
DG II	Economic and Financial Affairs
DG III	Internal Market and Industrial Affairs
DG IV	Competition
DG V	Employment, Social Affairs and Education
DG VI	Agriculture
DG VII	Transport

95. EEC, Article 155.
96. OJ 1990, L219/5.
97. OJ 1989 L395/1, 30 December 1989.
98. This Regulation deals with the merger or acquisition of undertakings and is not to be confused with the Merger Treaty which relates to the merging of certain EC institutions.
99. *Cf.* EEC, Articles 146 and 155.
100. EEC, Article 89.
101. Budd and Jones, *op. cit.* at footnote 1 above, p. 22.
102. For further details, see Chapter 12 below.
103. Many of these employees are engaged in language translation activities.
104. *E.g.* DG IV has five Directorates.

DG VIII	Development
DG IX	Personnel and Administration
DG X	Information, Spokesman's Group
DG XI	Environment, Consumer Protection and Nuclear Safety
DG XII	Science, Research and Development, Joint Research Centre
DG XIII	Information Market and Innovation
DG XIV	Fisheries
DG XV	Financial institutions and taxation
DG XVI	Regional Policy
DG XVII	Energy
DG XVIII	Credit and Investments
DG XIX	Budget
DG XX	Financial Control
DG XXI	Customs Union and Indirect Taxation
DG XXII	Coordination of Structural Instruments
DG XXIII	SME (Small and Medium-Sized Enterprises) Task Force

These Directorates are assisted by a Legal Service which advises the Commission on legal matters, determines the legality of all its decisions and represents it in proceedings before the Court of Justice. The Commission also has a Joint Maritime Committee.

3.4.2.5 DG IV: Competition

Directorate-General Four (DG IV) deals with competition. Its official address is the Berlaymont, rue de la Loi 200, B-1049 Brussels (telephone number: (32) 235-11-11 and telex number: (32) 21877 COMEU). The current Commissioner is Sir Leon Brittan, QC. Directorate A of DG IV deals with general competition and co-ordination. Directorate B of DG IV is entitled: "restrictive practices, abuses of dominant positions and other distortions of competition I: electrical and mechanical products; banking and insurance; media." Directorate C of DG IV is entitled: "restrictive practices, abuses of dominant positions and other distortions of competition II: minerals; energy; chemicals." It does not deal with coal and steel matters. Directorate D of DG IV is entitled: "restrictive practices, abuses of dominant positions and other distortions of competition III: steel and coal; transport; cars." Directorate E of DG IV is entitled: "State Aids". DG IV also has a Special Merger Task Force dealing with concentrations under the Regulation 4064/89.[105]

3.4.2.6 DG VII: Transport

Directorate-General VII (DG VII) deals with transport. Its official address is the Berlaymont, rue de la Loi 200, B-1049 Brussels (telephone number: (32) 235-11-11 and telex number: (32) 21877 COMEU). The current Commissioner is Karel van Miert. Its Director-General is Robert Coleman.

Directorate A of DG VII deals with maritime transport, legislation and transport economics.

Directorate B of DG VII deals with inland transport, market analysis, transport safety, as well as research and technology.

105. See footnote 97 above.

Directorate C of DG VII deals with air transport, transport infrastructure as well as social and ecological aspects of air transport.

3.4.3 Council of Ministers

3.4.3.1 Introduction

The Council of Ministers[106] is the institution through which the Member States act and decide.[107] It is a Community institution and not just an intergovernmental organ.[108] One Council of Ministers serves the three Communities.[109] Given the regime established by Article 84 of the EEC Treaty, the Council of Ministers has been given an extensive role to play in shipping matters.

3.4.3.2 Composition

It is composed of one representative from each Member State,[110] that is to say, the members of the Council of Ministers act, not on their own initiative, but on the instructions of their States.[111] Each government delegates one of its members. These representatives are the Foreign Ministers of the Member States but States may send other Ministers (e.g. agriculture, finance or transport) instead of the Foreign Minister because of the subject-matter under discussion.

3.4.3.3 Functions

The Council of Ministers exercises the powers and functions conferred on it by the Treaties.[112] It has the duty of ensuring that the objectives of the Foundation Treaties are attained. It also has the task of ensuring co-ordination of the general economic objectives of the Member States.[113] It must ensure co-ordination of the general economic policies of the Member States, have power to take decisions and confer on the Commission, in the acts which the Council of Ministers adopts, powers for the implementation of the rules which the Council of Ministers lays down.[114] The Council of Ministers has a representative role in international affairs. The Council of Ministers is the EC's legislature in that *it* adopts legislation and not the European Parliament. This legislation is usually embodied in Regulations and Directives.[115] The Council of Ministers can only act on a proposal from the Commission and does not have the power to initiate legislation but it can invite the Commission to bring forward

106. EEC, Articles 145–154 (as amended). See also Article 10 SEA.

107. On the balance between the Member States upholding their own nationalistic interests and the interests of the EC as a whole, see Cases 2 and 3/60 *Niederrheinische Bergwerks-AG et al. v. High Authority* [1961] ECR 133, at pp. 146–147.

108. See ECSC, Article 7; EEC, Article 4; and EAEC, Article 3.

109. Merger Treaty, Article 1.

110. Merger Treaty, Article 2. Deputies can be sent to Council of Ministers meetings. Where the deputies are not members of Government, they may not vote and the vote is cast by another member of the Council of Ministers.

111. This is in contradistinction to the Commission whose members are independent.

112. Merger Treaty, Article 1 and Article 145 EEC.

113. EEC, Article 145.

114. EEC, Article 145.

115. On community law, see para. 3.5 below.

proposals. The Treaties oblige the Council of Ministers to adopt appropriate Regulations and Directives to deal with particular matters in a number of special situations.[116]

3.4.3.4 Operation and voting

The Council of Ministers is bound by the Foundation Treaties. It operates in accordance with its own rules of procedure.[117] It meets in private. A general Council of Ministers meeting is normally held on the first Tuesday of every month. The Council of Ministers is presided over by a member acting as President. The Presidency rotates among the Member States in alphabetical order of the name of the State on a six-monthly basis.[118] The President has the principal functions of notifying the members of meetings of the Council of Ministers, putting issues to a vote as well as signing measures adopted by the Council of Ministers. The meetings are convened at the request of the President of the Council of Ministers, a member of the Council of Ministers or the Commission.[119] Instead of one State-one vote, there is a weighted voting system in operation.[120]

Member State	*Votes*
France	10
Germany	10
Italy	10
UK	10
Spain	8
Belgium	5
Greece	5
Netherlands	5
Portugal	5
Denmark	3
Ireland	3
Luxembourg	2

The Council of Ministers acts either unanimously, by a simple majority or by a qualified majority,[121] depending on the issue involved.[122] The simple majority is the general rule.[123] The absence of a Minister from a meeting is not fatal: any ministerial member of the Council of Ministers may cast a vote on behalf of another Member State.[124]

The Council of Ministers may adopt Regulations, Directives, Decisions, Recommendations and Opinions. Its acts are not international agreements.[125]

116. *E.g.* competition (EEC Article 87).

117. Merger Treaty, Article 5.

118. See EEC, Article 146 and the Merger Treaty, Article 2. See also Vaughan (Ed.), *Halsbury's Laws of England*, 4th edn., vol. 51, para. 1.81.

119. See Merger Treaty, Article 5.

120. See EEC, Article 148, The weights are: Belgium (5); Denmark (3); Germany (10); Greece (5); Spain (8); France (10); Ireland (3); Italy (10); Luxembourg (2); Netherlands (5); Portugal (5); and the UK (10).

121. A qualified majority requires fifty-four votes on a proposal from the Commission or fifty-four votes and eight Member States in favour in all other cases. Majority voting is of increased importance: see Article 100A as inserted by the SEA.

122. See EEC, Article 148.

123. EEC Treaty, Article 148 and Euratom Treaty, Article 118.

124. EEC Treaty, Article 150; Euratom Treaty, Article 120; and ECSC Treaty, Article 28.

125. See Case 38/69 *Commission* v. *Italy* [1970] ECR 47, at p. 56.

3.4.3.5 COREPER

A discussion of the Council of Ministers would be incomplete without mention of COREPER. Its legal basis is Article 4 of the Merger Treaty which provides that a "committee consisting of the Permanent Representatives[126] of the Member States shall be responsible for preparing the work of the Council and for carrying out the tasks assigned to it by the Council". It prepares and trims the agenda for the Council of Ministers. It is a medium for the interchange of information between the Member States and helps prepare the way for agreement at Council of Ministers meetings. It is important to stress that COREPER has no powers of decision.

3.4.3.6 General Secretariat of the Council of Ministers

The General Secretariat of the Council of Ministers, under a Secretary-General, is a permanent service to the Council of Ministers acting as a liaison between the Council of Ministers and COREPER.

3.4.4 European Council

3.4.4.1 Introduction

The European Council consists of the Heads of State or of Government of the Member States with the President of the Commission of the European Communities. They are assisted by the Ministers for Foreign Affairs of each Member State and a Member of the Commission.[127]

3.4.4.2 Origin

The European Council was not established by the Foundation Treaties.[128] In the past, summit meetings were arranged as the occasion demanded but since the early 1970s they are held at least twice yearly. Article 2 of the SEA provides that they shall meet at least twice a year.

3.4.4.3 Role

The European Council is politically very important. It is the final court of political appeal. Matters which have not been resolved at the Council of Ministers or Commission levels are often resolved at the European Council meetings.[129]

3.4.5 European Parliament

3.4.5.1 Introduction

The European Parliament[130] has traditionally had a modest and limited role. Its profile

126. These Permanent Representatives are in the nature of Ambassadors from the Member States to the EC.

127. SEA, Article 2.

128. See now the SEA, Article 2.

129. Sometimes this is done for effect—the political clout of a European Council meeting outweighs that of an "ordinary" Council of Ministers meeting.

130. Although originally called the "Assembly" in the Treaties, that body resolved that it be called the "European Parliament": Resolution of 30 March 1962 (JO 1962, 1045). See also Article 137 EEC.

has increased since the first direct elections in 1979 but it has not yet reached its full potential and it is not entirely analogous to parliaments in the Member States.

3.4.5.2 Seat

The Parliament has its plenary sessions principally in Strasbourg. It holds many of its committee meetings in Brussels. It has offices in Brussels, Luxembourg and Strasbourg. There is some support for centralising all of the Parliament's activities in Brussels.

3.4.5.3 Members

The Parliament consists of 518 members elected in elections held throughout the EC every five years.[132] The members are representatives of the *peoples* of the Member

Member State	*Members*
France	81
Germany	81
Italy	81
UK	81
Spain	60
Netherlands	25
Belgium	24
Greece	24
Portugal	24
Denmark	16
Ireland	15
Luxembourg	6[133]

States.[134] These members are arranged not in national delegations but are instead gathered in groups according to political outlook. Some MEPs are members of both national parliaments and the EC Parliament—those who are not members of national parliaments can often devote more time to their European Parliamentary duties. The members elect a President and officers from among themselves.[135]

3.4.5.4 Tenure

Members of the European Parliament are elected for a period of five years.[136]

3.4.5.5 Election

The fact that a person is a member of a national parliament does not mean that the person is ineligible for membership of the European Parliament. Prior to 1979, the members of the Parliament were nominated by the parliaments in the Member States. Since 1979, members of the Parliament have been directly elected by voters throughout the EC on the basis of universal suffrage. The direct elections in 1979 (at which 110

132. See EEC Treaty, Articles 137–144 (as amended) and D76/787 OJ 1976 L278/1 (as amended).
133. EEC Treaty, Article 140; ECSC Treaty, Article 23; and Euratom Treaty, Article 111.
134. EEC, Article 137.
135. EEC, Article 140.
136. EEC, Article 149A.

million people voted throughout the EC), 1984 and 1989 heightened public awareness in many EC Member States of the workings of the Parliament.

3.4.5.6 President and Officers of the Parliament

The Parliament elects its own president and officers from among its own members.[137]

3.4.5.7 Bureau of the Parliament

The Parliament has a Bureau composed of the President of the Parliament, twelve Vice-Presidents and five Questors. These Questors are officials who have special responsibility for financial and administrative matters relating to the Parliament.

3.4.5.8 Secretariat of the Parliament

The Parliament's Secretariat is in charge of the organisational and administrative aspects of the Parliament.

3.4.5.9 Committees

The Parliament has fifteen standing committees. Each of these Committees specialise in particular areas of EC policy. These standing committees prepare reports which form the bases of debates in the Parliament. Reference will be made throughout the book to the Transport Committee as well as the Economic and Monetary Affairs Committee.

3.4.5.10 Functions and operation

The functions of the Parliament are mainly advisory and supervisory. It has no legislative powers. It can question the Commission and ultimately dismiss it by motion of censure.[138] The Parliament has some control over the Community's budget; it can reject the Community budget[139] and it did so in 1979. It can reject harmonisation proposals[140] and it can institute proceedings in the European Court of Justice and it did so in respect of, among other matters, transport.[141]

The Parliament normally acts by an absolute majority of the votes cast[142] and in accordance with its own rules of procedure.[143]

The Parliament has some control over the Commission and the Council of Ministers. Both institutions must answer questions put to them by MEPs.[144]

The Parliament adopts resolutions on issues which it feels to be important. Its resolutions on competition policy,[145] agriculture and budgetary matters carry considerable weight within the Community.

137. EEC Treaty, Article 140; ECSC Treaty, Article 23; and Euratom Treaty, Article 111.
138. EEC, Article 144.
139. EEC, Article 202. *Cf.* Case 34/86 *Council v. Parliament* [1986] ECR 2155; [1986] 3 CMLR 94.
140. See EEC Article 149A.
141. See para. 5.5.17 below.
142. EEC, Article 141.
143. EEC, Article 142.
144. EEC, Article 140.
145. See Bellamy and Child, *Common Market Law of Competition* (3rd edn.), para. 1–033.

The Parliament must hold at least one annual session on the second Tuesday in March.[146] It may meet in extraordinary sessions at the request of a majority of its members, the Council of Ministers or the Commission.

3.4.5.11 Future

Many commentators believe that the Parliament will become more important as a political forum in the future, but this is a matter of great debate.

3.4.6 The European Court of Justice and the Court of First Instance

3.4.6.1 Introduction

The European Court of Justice of the European Communities[147] (the "ECJ") and the Court of First Instance (CFI) are the judicial institutions of the Communities. They provide a system of "checks and balances" in the institutional system of the EC by monitoring the conduct of the other institutions and ensure that they act in accordance with law.[148] The ECJ has existed since the foundation of the EC. The Court of First Instance, which was established to cope with the huge backlog of work, commenced operations in 1989.[149]

3.4.6.2 Functions

The principal function of the ECJ is to ensure that in the interpretation and application of the Treaties, "the law is observed".[150] Unlike some English courts (such as the High Court) which have an inherent jurisdiction, the ECJ must act within the limits of the powers conferred upon it by the Treaties. The court is, in part, a law-maker[151] because the nature of Community law constantly requires refinement and adaptation.[152]

3.4.6.3 Personnel

3.4.6.3.1 Judges

The ECJ and the CFI are each composed of thirteen judges.[153] Each Member State appoints one judge with the thirteenth judge coming from one of the Member States. The judges are appointed by the common accord of the governments of the Member States for a renewable period of six years. The judges are guaranteed

146. See EEC Treaty, Article 139; ECSC Treaty, Art. 22; and Euratom Treaty, Article 109.

147. EEC, Articles 164–188. See Brown and Jacobs, *The Court of Justice of the European Communities* (2nd edn., 1983); K. Lasok, *The European Court of Justice, Practice and Procedure* (1984). See also Slynn, "The Court of Justice of the European Communities" (1984) 33 ICLQ 409; Warner, "Some Aspects of the European Court" (1976) 14 JSPTL (n.s.) 15.

148. See, for example, *Adams v. Commission*.

149. On the Court of First Instance, see Millett, *The Court of First Instance* (1990). See also Kennedy, "The Essential Minimum: The Establishment of the Court of First Instance," (1989) 14 EL Rev. 7. The rules of procedure are published in OJ L136/1, 91.

150. EEC, Article 164; ECSC Treaty, Article 31; and Euratom Treaty, Article 136.

151. See Brown and Jacobs, *op. cit.* at footnote 147, Part Four.

152. *Cf.* Case 27/80 *Fietje* [1980] ECR 3389, at p. 3853.

153. EEC, Article 165 (as amended)

independence in the exercise of their functions and are in no way representatives of their States.[154]

3.4.6.3.2 President of the Court

The President of the ECJ holds office for a renewable period of three years and is appointed by the judges from among their own number by a majority vote by way of a secret ballot. Each of the chambers of the ECJ has a President who holds office for a renewable term of one year.

3.4.6.3.3 Registrar

The ECJ appoints, by secret ballot, its own registrar[155] who is in charge of the Court's administration[156] and is responsible for the conduct of cases. The registrar's duties are enumerated in the Protocol on the Statute of the Court and the Rules of Procedure. He or she is appointed for a renewable six-year period.

3.4.6.3.4 Advocates-General

The ECJ is assisted by six Advocates-General[157] who are similar in nature to the Commissaire du Gouvernement at the French Conseil d'Etat. These advocates are equal to judges in order of precedence, but they are *not* judges. It is the duty of the Advocates-General "acting with complete impartiality and independence, to make, in open court, reasoned submissions on cases brought before the Court of Justice, in order to assist the Court in the performance"[158] of its task of ensuring that in the interpretation and application of the Treaties the law is observed.[159] Normally one Advocate-General acts in each case. The Advocate-General summarises the arguments of the parties and makes reasoned arguments to the Court on the merits of the case and the options facing the Court, much in the manner of an *amicus curiae*. These opinions are highly influential and are usually followed by the Court.

3.4.6.3.5 Legal Secretaries

Each judge and Advocate-General is assisted by three legal secretaries. These legal secretaries assist in the drafting of opinions and judgments.

3.4.6.3.6 Appointment process of Judges and Advocates-General

Both judges and Advocates-General are chosen from "persons whose independence is beyond doubt and who possess the qualifications required for appointment to the highest judicial offices in their respective countries or who are jurisconsults of

154. EEC Treaty, Article 167.
155. EEC, Article 168.
156. On the Registry generally, see Brown and Jacobs, *op. cit.* at footnote 147 above, pp. 17–19.
157. On the Advocates-General see Brown and Jacobs, *op. cit.* at footnote 147 above, Chapter 4.
158. EEC, Article 166.
159. EEC, Article 164.

recognised competence; they shall be appointed by common accord of the Governments of the Member States for a term of six years".[160] Instead of all the judges and advocates being replaced at one time there is instead a partial replacement every three years.[161] As only some of the judges leave office, this ensures continuity. Judges and Advocates may be re-elected.[162] Judges can also be dismissed or resign.

3.4.6.4 Operation of the Court

3.4.6.4.1 Seat

The Court has its seat at Luxembourg. Despite the view of some commentators that this detachment from Brussels is advantageous to the Court, it is submitted that it would be more convenient (like Washington D.C.) if the Court were situated in Brussels where most of the other institutions are located.

3.4.6.4.2 Plenary and chamber sessions[163]

As a general rule, the Court sits in plenary session (i.e. all judges would sit on each case).[164] In some specific circumstances, namely, in cases brought by a Member State or a Community institution, or in a preliminary reference, the Court must sit in plenary session.[165] But, the Court may, and mostly does, sit in chambers of judges "either to undertake certain preparatory inquiries or to adjudicate on particular categories of cases in accordance with rules laid down for these purposes".[166] The chamber system means that more cases can be dealt with by the Court as a whole and specialisation is possible. Chambers have either three or six judges. At present, there are six chambers.

3.4.6.4.3 Court of First Instance

The Single European Act amended the Treaties[167] so as to provide for a Court of First Instance to hear some classes of cases (competition, coal and steel regulation as well as staff cases), subject to an appeal to the Court itself but only on points of law.

3.4.6.4.4 Lawyers[168]

Any lawyer who is a member of the Bar of a Member State is entitled to appear before the Court.

3.4.6.4.5 Languages

French is the working language of the Court but it also functions in the other official

160. EEC, Article 167.
161. EEC, Article 167.
162. EEC, Article 167.
163. See Brown and Jacobs, *op. cit.* at footnote 147, pp. 25–27.
164. EEC, Article 165.
165. EEC, Article 165.
166. EEC, Article 165.
167. See the new EEC, Article 168A.
168. Brown and Jacobs, *op. cit.* at footnote 147, Chapter 12.

languages of the EC, namely, Danish, Dutch, English, German, Greek, Italian, Portuguese and Spanish.[169] It may also function in Irish.

3.4.6.5 Procedure

The rules on practice and procedure generally of the ECJ are laid down in the Statute of the Court of Justice annexed, which is annexed as a Protocol to the Treaties and by its Rules of Procedure.[170] The ECJ relies heavily on the written and inquisitorial procedures. The parties to the case initially submit written arguments to the Court. The Court appoints a judge to investigate the case more fully. This judge collects evidence by examining both documents and witnesses. The Court then hears short oral arguments from the parties' lawyers. These arguments are not presented in an accusatorial way because there is, for example, no cross-examination of witnesses. After the oral stage, the Advocate-General delivers an opinion. The Advocate-General proposes a solution to the problem at issue and sets out the legal position. This opinion (which is much longer than the judgment of the Court) is very important in predicting the future of Community law. The Court delivers its judgment which is normally short and consists of two parts: the *motifs* (the reasons for the decision) and the *dispositif* (the ruling). The Court often adopts a teleological approach in its interpretation.

3.4.6.5.1 Locus standi

As a general rule, only Member States, the Commission, the Council of Ministers or the Parliament may bring actions in the Court.[171] Others may always bring cases on EC law before the courts in each of the Member States. Parties other than Member States and EC Institutions have limited rights before the ECJ. They may institute proceedings under Article 173 of the EEC Treaty[172] where the decision is of direct concern to them.[173]

3.4.6.5.2 Effect of judgments

A judgment has binding force from the date of its delivery.

3.4.6.5.3 Enforcement of judgments

If the ECJ gives judgments against a body or an individual in the form of a fine then the fine is enforceable as a judgment debt.[174]

3.4.6.6 Jurisdiction

3.4.6.6.1 Introduction

The jurisdiction of the ECJ may be classified under the following principal headings.

169. See Case 260/85 *Tokyo Electric Company Ltd v. Council of Ministers* [1989] 1 CMLR 169.
170. See OJ 1982 C39/1.
171. *Cf.* Case 206/84 *Re Co. Insurance Services: EC Commission v. Ireland* [1978] 2 CMLR 150.
172. On Article 173 of the EEC Treaty, see para. 3.4.6.6.5, below.
173. The action must be brought within two months.
174. EEC Treaty, Articles 187/192.

(a) the Commission contending that a Member State has failed to fulfil a Treaty obligation;[175] (b) a Member State contends that another Member State has failed to fulfil a Treaty obligation; (c) unlimited jurisdiction with respect to penalties; (d) actions to annul EC measures; (e) actions for inactivity; (f) pleas of illegality; (g) staff disputes; (h) preliminary references; and (i) opinions on external relations.

3.4.6.6.2 Article 169: Commission contending that a Member State has failed to fulfil a Treaty obligation

Article 169 of the EEC Treaty provides:

"if the Commission considers[176] that a Member State has failed to fulfil an obligation under this Treaty, it shall deliver a reasoned opinion on the matter after giving the State concerned the opportunity to submit its observations. If the State concerned does not comply with the opinion within the period laid down by the Commission, the latter may bring the matter before the Court of Justice."

This provision[177] allows the Commission to fulfil more easily its function as watchdog of the Treaty. It is a necessary function: the Commission issued 960 warnings to Member States during 1990.[178]

The Commission initiates the process by sending a letter[179] to the Member State concerned which must fully[180] set out the case against that State. If the Commission is not satisfied with the response (if any) to its letter then it may issue a non-legally binding Opinion on the matter.[181] The Commission may then decide, if there has been no response to the Opinion which is satisfactory to the Commission, to pursue the matter in the ECJ. If the Court "finds" that the Member State has failed to comply with the Treaty[182] then that State "shall be required to take the necessary measures to comply with the judgment of the Court".[183] An individual may not force the Commission to bring such proceedings.[184] Nor may the Member State defend the action by pleading internal circumstances (e.g. costs or lack of personnel).[185]

3.4.6.6.3 Article 170: A Member State contends that another Member State has failed to fulfil a Treaty obligation

Under Article 170 of the EEC Treaty "a Member State which considers that another

175. See para. 3.4.6.6.2, below.

176. *Ed.*, the Commission does not have to demonstrate a legal interest: Case 167/73 *Commission v. France* [1974] ECR 359 at pp. 368–369.

177. On Article 169 see Case 7/71 *Commission* v. *France* [1971] ECR 1003; Case 61/77 *Commission v. Ireland* [1978] ECR 417; [1978] 2 CMLR 466. See also Audretsch, *Supervision in European Community Law* (2nd edn.), *passim*; as well as Brown and Jacobs, *op. cit.* at footnote 147, pp. 75–82.

178. See Gardnér, "Flouting of EC Law by Member States Increases", *Financial Times*, 1 August 1991.

179. See Case 211/81 *Commission v. Denmark* [1982] ECR 4547, at p. 4557.

180. See Case 31/69 *Commission v. Italy* [1970] ECR 25, at p. 33; Case 7/69 *Commission v. Italy* [1970] ECR 111, at p. 117; and Case 51/83 *Commission v. Italy* [1984] ECR 2793, at p. 2804.

181. See Cases 142 and 143/80 *Administrazione delle Finanze dello Stato v. Essevi* SpA *et al.* [1981] ECR 1413, at pp. 1432–1433.

182. I.e. any provision of the EEC Treaty.

183. EEC, Article 171.

184. Case 48/65 *Lütticke v. Commission* [1966] ECR 19, at p. 27; Case 39/72 *Commission v. Italy* [1968] ECR 423, at p. 428, Case 7/71 *Commission v. France* [1971] ECR 1003, at p. 1016. See also Evans, (1979) 4 *European Law Review* 442.

185. See Case 254/83 *Commission v. Italy* [1984] ECR 3395; Case 39/72 *Commission v. Italy* [1973] ECR 101; [1973] CMLR 439; Case C-39/88 *Re Fishery Price Information: Commission v. Ireland* [1991] 2 CMLR 876.

Member State has failed to fulfil an obligation under this Treaty may bring the matter before the Court of Justice. Before a Member State brings an action against another Member State for an alleged infringement of an obligation under this Treaty, it shall bring the matter before the Commission. The Commission shall deliver a reasoned opinion after each of the States concerned has been given the opportunity to submit its own case and its observations on the other party's case both orally and in writing. If the Commission has not delivered an opinion within three months of the date on which the matter was brought before it, the absence of such opinion shall not prevent the matter from being brought before the Court of Justice." Article 170[186] is an alternative to the Article 169 procedure.[187] Ireland was the first State to invoke the procedure though the case was later withdrawn.[188] If the Court "finds" that the Member State has failed to comply with the Treaty then that State "shall be required to take the necessary measures to comply with the judgment of the Court".[189]

3.4.6.6.4 Article 172: Unlimited jurisdiction with respect to penalties

Article 172 of the EEC Treaty provides: "regulations made by the Council [of Ministers] pursuant to the provisions of this Treaty may give the Court of Justice unlimited jurisdiction in regard to the penalties provided for in such regulations".

3.4.6.6.5 Article 173: Actions to annul EC Measures

Under Article 173 of the EEC Treaty[190] "the Court of Justice shall review the legality of acts of the Council [of Ministers] and the Commission other than recommendations or opinions. It shall for this purpose have jurisdiction in actions brought by a Member State, the Council [of Ministers] or the Commission on grounds of lack of competence, infringement of an essential procedural requirement, infringement of this Treaty or of any rule of law relating to its application, or misuse of powers. Any natural or legal person may, under the same conditions, institute proceedings against a decision addressed to that person or against a decision which, although in the form of a regulation or a decision addressed to another person, is of direct and individual concern to the former". The proceedings provided for in this Article shall be instituted within two months of the publication of the measure, or of its notification to the plaintiff, or, in the absence thereof, of the day on which it came to the knowledge of the latter, as the case may be.

Who may seek annulment? Subject to the two-month time limit, Member States, the Council of Ministers and the Commission have an unlimited right to initiate proceedings under Article 173. Natural and legal persons must prove that they have a specific interest, that is to say, the measure is of "direct and individual concern" to them.[191]

186. See Brown and Jacobs, *op. cit.* at footnote 147, pp. 82–83.
187. On the Article 169 procedure see para. 3.4.6.6.2, above.
188. Case 58/77 *Ireland v. France* (OJ 1977 C142/8).
189. EEC, Article 171.
190. On Article 173 see Brown and Jacobs, *op. cit.* at footnote 147, pp. 93–110.
191. Case 25/62 *Plaumann v. Commission* [1963] ECR 95; [1964] CMLR 29; Case 77/77 *BP v. Commission* [1978] ECR 1513, at p. 1525.

On what grounds is annulment granted? Article 173 enumerates four grounds. First, if the institution lacked competence then the measure would be annulled.[192] Secondly, if there is an infringement of an essential procedural requirement then the measure would be annulled. Thirdly, any measures which are the result of an infringement of the Treaty or any rule of law relating to its application would be annulled. Fourthly, if a power is misused (i.e. used for an objective for which it was not granted) then any resultant measure would be annulled.[193]

The ECJ has held in Case 294/83 *The Greens v. European Parliament* that an action under Article 173 may be brought to annul an act of the Parliament even though such acts are not mentioned in Article 173 itself.[194]

3.4.6.6.6 Article 175: Actions for inactivity

A remedy must be available not only where an institution acts unlawfully but also where it fails to act. Under Article 175 of the EEC Treaty[195]: "should the Council [of Ministers] or the Commission, in infringement of this Treaty, fail to act, the Member States and the other institutions of the Community may bring an action before the Court of Justice to have the infringement established. The action shall be admissible only if the institution concerned has first been called to act. If, within two months of being so called upon, the institution concerned has not defined its position, the action may be brought within a further period of two months. Any natural or legal person may, under the conditions laid down in the preceding paragraphs, complain to the Court of Justice that an institution of the Community has failed to address to that person any act other than a recommendation or an opinion." Thus, the ECJ can be asked to declare that the failure of a Community institution to act, where it was legally obliged to do so, constitutes a breach of Community law. Unlike an action for annulment, an action for failure to act may be brought by the European Parliament.[196] A natural or legal person may bring proceedings under this procedure against an institution which fails to issue a binding act only when that person would have been the addressee.[197]

3.4.6.6.7 Article 184: Plea of illegality

Article 184 of the EEC Treaty states that notwithstanding the expiry of the period laid down in the third paragraph of Article 173,[198] any party may, in proceedings in which a regulation of the Council of Ministers or the Commission is in issue, plead the grounds specified in the first paragraph of Article 173, in order to invoke before the ECJ the inapplicability of that regulation.

3.4.6.6.8 Article 179: Staff disputes

The judicial tribunals of many international organisations have jurisdiction over

192. *Cf.* Cases 6 and 11/69 *Commission v. France* [1969] ECR 523, at p. 539.
193. Case 92/78 *Simmenthal v. Commission* [1979] ECR 777, at p. 804.
194. [1986] ECR 1339; [1987] 2 CMLR 343.
195. On Article 175 of the EEC Treaty, see Brown and Jacobs, *op. cit.*, pp. 110 112.
196. E.g. Case 13/83 *Parliament v. Council* OJ 1983 C49/9.
197. Case 15/71 *Mackprang v. Commission* [1971] ECR 797, at p. 804.
198. On Article 173, see para. 3.4.6.6.5 above.

disputes relating to staff within the organisations. Under Article 179 of the EEC Treaty[199] the ECJ has jurisdiction in any dispute between the Community and its servants within the limits and under the conditions laid down in the staff regulations or the conditions of employment. These matters are now heard by the Court of First Instance.

3.4.6.6.9 Article 177: Preliminary references

Article 177 of the EEC Treaty provides the ECJ with the competence to give preliminary rulings concerning, *inter alia*, the interpretation of the Treaty.[200] The Article states:

"The Court of Justice shall have jurisdiction to give preliminary rulings concerning:
(a) the interpretation of this Treaty;
(b) the validity and interpretation of acts of the institutions of the Community;
(c) the interpretation of the statutes of bodies established by an act of the Council, where those statutes so provide.

Where such a question is raised before any court or tribunal of a Member State, that court or tribunal may, if it considers that a decision on the question is necessary to enable it to give judgment, request the Court of Justice to give a ruling thereon.

Where any such question is raised in a case pending before a court or tribunal of a Member State, against whose decisions there is no judicial remedy under national law, that court or tribunal shall bring the matter before the Court of Justice."

Thus, where an issue arises in the course of litigation in a national court or tribunal[201] involving an interpretation of the Treaties then the national court or tribunal *may*[202] request the ECJ to give a preliminary ruling on the point at issue. A reference *must* be made by any court or tribunal against whose decisions there is no judicial remedy.[203]

Article 177 has been used by the courts in EC Member States on numerous occasions. The UK courts have used the procedure in such cases as Case 10/87 *R v Commissioners for Customs and Excise, ex p. Tattersall Ltd.*[204] The EC procedure deals, as a general rule, in "abstract questions" with the final judgment being left for the national court.

3.4.6.6.10 Opinions on external relations

Article 228 of the EEC Treaty[205] provides:

"1. Where this Treaty provides for the conclusion of agreements between the Community and one or more States or an international organisation, such agreements shall be negotiated by the Commission. Subject to the powers vested in the Commission in this field, such agreements shall be concluded by the Council, after consulting the Assembly where required by this Treaty.

199. See Brown and Jacobs, *op. cit.* at footnote 147 above, Chapter 8.

200. On the preliminary reference see Brown and Jacobs, *op. cit.* at footnote 147 above, Chapter 9; Gray, "Advisory opinions and the European Court of Justice" (1983) 8 EL Rev 24; Arnull, "Article 177 and the retreat from Van Duyn" (1983) 8 EL Rev. 365.

201. "Tribunal" in this context does not include "arbitral tribunal": see Case 102/81 *Nordsee v. Reederei Mond* [1982] ECR 1095.

202. The decision to refer is a critical one (given the cost, delay and other implications of a referral) and is for the national court but this court (see Cases 98, 162 and 258/85 *Bertini* [1986] ECR 1893; [1987] 1 CMLR 774) will normally hear the arguments of the parties to the case. Ultimately, it is a matter for the ECJ to decide on whether or not a reference should be made: Case 283/81 *CILFIT v. Ministry of Health* [1982] ECR 3415; [1983] 1 CMLR 472.

203. See *Hagen v. Fratelli* [1980] CMLR 253.

204. [1988] 3 CMLR 113.

205. See Brown and Jacobs, *op. cit.* at footnote 147 above, Chapter 10.

The Council, the Commission or a Member State may obtain beforehand the opinion of the Court of Justice as to whether an agreement envisaged is compatible with the provisions of this Treaty. Where the opinion of the Court of Justice is adverse, the agreement may enter into force only in accordance with Article 26.

2. Agreements concluded under these conditions shall be binding on the institutions of the Community and on Member States."

3.4.7 Bodies

3.4.7.1 Economic and Social Committee

The Economic and Social Committee (ECOSOC)[207] is an advisory body which delivers advisory reports on proposed regulations and draws up reports on matters such as competition. It assists the Council of Ministers and the Commission acting in an advisory capacity.[208] The Committee has played a significant role in shipping matters.

3.4.7.2 European Investment Bank

The non-profit making[209] European Investment Bank (EIB) is established under Article 129 of the EEC Treaty with the task of contributing "by having recourse to the capital market and utilising its own resources, to the balanced and steady development of the common market in the interest of the Community".[210] Its members are the Member States.[211] It grants loans and gives guarantees which facilitate the financing of: "(a) projects for developing less-developed regions; (b) projects for modernizing or converting undertakings or for developing fresh activities called for by the progressive establishment of the common market, where these projects are of such a size or nature that they cannot be entirely financed by the various means available in the individual Member States; (c) projects of common interest to several Member States which are of such a size or nature that they cannot be entirely financed by the various means available in the individual Member States."[212] The EIB is now to be seen in the light of the European Bank for Reconstruction and Development (EBRO) which will help to reconstruct and develop Eastern Europe.

3.4.7.3 Court of Auditors

A single Court of Auditors has served all three Communities since 1 June 1977. Its function is to ensure that the EC's financial resources are properly spent.

3.5 COMMUNITY LAW

3.5.1 Introduction

The laws enacted by the EC have a unique character and quality.[213] Unlike many other

207. EEC, Articles 193–198.
208. EEC, Articles 4(2).
209. EEC, Article 130.
210. EEC, Article 130.
211. EEC, Article 129.
212. EEC, Article 130.
213. On Community law generally, see Kapteyn and Van Themaat, *op. cit.* at footnote 1 above, pp. 36–51; Rawlinson and Cornwell-Kelly, *op. cit.* at footnote 1, Chapter 2.

international organisations, the EC has the power to make law which is binding on Member States and even persons in those States.[214] EC law is supreme and overrides any national laws of the Member States which may be in conflict.[215] In essence, there has been a transfer of some of the powers of the Member States to the EC.[216]

3.5.2 Sources of Community Law

3.5.2.1 Primary law

3.5.2.1.1 Foundation Treaties (including Annexes and Protocols)

The primary sources of community law are the Foundation Treaties—the treaties which established the three communities. These treaties are the Treaty of Paris establishing the ECSC; the Treaty of Rome establishing the EEC; and the second Treaty of Rome establishing Euratom. A number of other treaties and agreements have been concluded between the Member States which amend the Foundation Treaties. The Foundation Treaties set out the objectives of the EC.

Duration Unlike the ECSC Treaty which was designed to last for fifty years,[217] the EEC and Euratom Treaties are of unlimited duration.[218]

Territorial application The Foundation Treaties apply to both the land mass and the territorial sea of the Member States. They may have extra-territorial effect in certain cases.

Germany The Foundation Treaties gave special status to the then German Democratic Republic. The Treaties now apply to what was the German Democratic Republic (or East Germany).[219]

British Sovereign base on Cyprus The Foundation Treaties do not apply.

Faroe Islands The Foundation Treaties do not apply.

French Overseas Departments The Foundation Treaties are limited in their application to this territory.

Canary Islands The Foundation Treaties are limited in their application to this territory.[220] The Commission has however proposed that EC law would apply to the Canary Islands and EC law now applies for some purposes.[221]

Ceuta The Foundation Treaties are limited in their application to this territory.

Channel Islands The Foundation Treaties are limited in their application to these islands.

Isle of Man The Foundation Treaties are limited in their application to this territory.

214. See para. 1.3.23, above.
215. Case 6/64 *Costa v. ENEL* [1964] ECR 585.
216. See Case 7/71 *Commission v. France* [1971] ECR 1003, at p. 1018. See also Ussher, *European Community Law and National Law: the Irreversible Transfer?* (1981).
217. ECSC, Treaty, Article 97.
218. EEC, Article 240 and Euratom, Article 208.
219. Transitional arrangements were adopted to deal with the integration of the former GDR into the EC.
220. See Articles 25, 155 and Protocol 2 of the Act of Accession of Spain and Portugal.
221. COM(90)686 final.

Melilla The Foundation Treaties are limited in their application to this territory.

Mount Athos The Foundation Treaties are limited in their application to this territory.

Inter-relationship between the Foundation Treaties[222] Article 232(1) of the EEC Treaty (which was concluded in 1957) provides that the provisions of that Treaty do not affect the provisions of the ECSC Treaty (which was concluded in 1952). Article 232(2) of the EEC Treaty goes on to provide that the provisions of the EEC Treaty do not derogate from those of the Euratom Treaty which was concluded simultaneously. It is generally accepted that the EEC Treaty, which relates to all economic sectors *per se*, also applies to economic activities in the coal, nuclear energy and steel sectors, in so far as the ECSC and Euratom Treaties do not deal with the matter.[223] It is also generally accepted that the provisions of the Treaties relating to the Institutions which are common to the three Communities are to be interpreted by the Court, in so far as possible, in a uniform and harmonious manner.[224]

3.5.2.1.2 Accession treaties

Six new States have joined the EC since the foundation of the EC and each State has acceded to the Foundation Treaties. Thus, there have been three Accessions Treaties: the Treaty of Accession of Denmark, Ireland and the UK[225]; the Treaty of Accession of Greece[226]; and the Treaty of Accession of Spain and Portugal.[227] Each made significant changes to the Foundation Treaties. One area, namely Greenland, has left the EC. Thus there is one secession treaty, called the "Treaty amending, with regard to Greenland, the Treaties establishing the European Communities". The implications of this treaty are understandably marginal.

3.5.2.1.3 Institutional treaties

The institutional treaties include the Convention on Certain Institutions Common to the Three Communities[228]; the Treaty Establishing a Single Council and a Single Commission (the so-called Merger Treaty)[229] as well as the Act of the Council concerning Direct elections to the European Parliament.[230]

3.5.2.1.4 Financial treaties

There are treaties and other measures relating to financial and budgetary matters.

222. See Kapteyn and Van Themaat, *op. cit.* at footnote 1, Chapter II.

223. See *Deuxieme Rapport General sur l'Activité des Communautes Europeenes*, 1968, para. 655.

224. See Case 101/63 *Wagner v. Fohrmann* [1964] ECR 195 and Case 230/81 *Luxembourg v. European Parliament* [1983] ECR 255.

225. Cmnd. 7462. An annotated text is reprinted in *Encyclopedia of Community Law*, vol. BI. Norway was a party to this Treaty as well but did not ratify it.

226. Signed in Athens on 28 May 1979; Cmnd. 7650. An annotated text is contained in *Encyclopedia of Community Law*, vol. BII.

227. Signed in Madrid and Lisbon on 12 June 1985; Cmnd. 9634. An annotated text is reprinted in *Encyclopedia of Community Law*, vol. BII.

228. 1957.

229. 1965.

230. 1976.

These include the Decision Creating the Communities' Own Resources; the Treaty Amending Certain Budgetary Provisions; and, the Treaty Amending Certain Financial Provisions.

3.5.2.1.5 Single European Act

The Single European Act (SEA) was adopted by the Member States as part of their desire "to continue the work undertaken on the basis of the Treaties establishing the European Communities and to transform relations as a whole among their States into a European Union".[231] Title I, Article 1 of the SEA provides that the "European Communities and European Political Co-operation shall have as their objective to contribute together to making concrete progress towards European Unity".

3.5.2.1.6 Maastricht Treaty

A Treaty on European Union was signed in Maastricht on 7 February 1992. The Treaty provides for the establishment of a European Union involving an Economic and Monetary Union. There are many changes planned for the EC but at the time of writing, no date has been finalised for its entry into force.

3.5.2.2 Secondary Law

Two leading commentators on EC law have written:

"[t]he acts of general application–regulations and directives—are sometimes referred to as 'secondary legislation', the implication presumably being that the Treaties are in some sense 'primary legislation'. This classification is misleading since, although the implementing regulations of the Commission are often akin to subordinate or delegated legislation, there is nothing secondary, in character or in scope, about the basic regulations of the Council in such fields as agriculture, the free movement of workers, social security, and competition. This legislation is both as fundamental in character and as broad in scope as any national legislation, and its relationship to the founding Treaties is comparable to that which national legislation has to a national constitution, with the Court of Justice fulfilling the role of a constitutional court."[232]

Secondary legislation is published in the *Official Journal of the European Communities.*[233] There is a confusion of terminology between the three Treaties but this confusion is not of huge significance to shipping because shipping is almost exclusively concerned with the EEC and not the other two organisations. In simple terms, the differing terminology may be explained by the following table[234]:

231. Preamble to the SEA.

232. Brown and Jacobs, *op. cit.* at footnote 147, pp. 4–5.

233. The *Official Journal* (referred to as the OJ) is published almost daily in two forms: the first referred to as the "L" version contains legislation and other matters whose publication is compulsory as well as the "C" version which contains notices and matters whose publication is not compulsory (such as certain Commission proposals).

234. This table appeared in the Butterworths *Guide to the European Communities* (1989) at p. 11.

EEC Treaty	Euratom Treaty	ECSC Treaty
regulations directives decisions opinions recommendations	regulations directives decisions opinions recommendations	decisions recommendations opinions

The terminology used in this book relates to the EEC Treaty unless the context demonstrates otherwise.

3.5.2.2.1 *Regulations*

A Regulation[235] is adopted by either the Council of Ministers[236] or the Commission.[237] The Council of Ministers acts on the basis of a provision or provisions in a Foundation Treaty while the Commission normally acts on the basis of powers delegated to it from the Council of Ministers. A Regulation is general in application. It binds all the Member States from the date of its adoption or entry into force (whichever is specified in the Regulation). It must be published in the *Official Journal of the European Communities*.[238] A Regulation is binding in its entirety and is directly applicable in all Member States.[239] It has the same effect as if it were a national law. Regulations do not require implementing legislation[240] but they may have supplementary legislation in such matters as criminal enforcement. A Regulation has the purpose of achieving uniformity between the Member States. It must be reasoned and based on a provision in the relevant Foundation Treaty, normally the EEC Treaty. A Regulation is presumed to be valid until struck down by the ECJ. Any national legislation which conflicts with a Regulation is invalid and of no effect.

Regulations have been used on a number of occasions in regard to shipping matters, most notably, in the cases of Regulations 4055/86,[241] 4056/86,[242] 4057/86[243] and 4058/86.[244]

3.5.2.2.2 *Directives*

Not everything is capable of or suitable for uniform treatment throughout the EC by way of a Regulation. Directives require Member States to achieve a particular *result* but leave the *form and method* to the individual State.[245] Thus, Member States are obliged to amend their laws so as to bring them into line with Directives. The Member States must implement the Directive *in full* within the specified time limits—failure to

235. On regulations see EEC, Articles 189–91 and Euratom, Articles 161–163.
236. On the Council of Ministers, see para. 3.4.3, above.
237. On the Commission, see para 3.4.2, above.
238. In the "L" series of the OJ.
239. EEC Treaty, Article 189(2).
240. See Case 24/73 *Variola* [1973] ECR 981 and Case 50/76 *Amsterdam Bulb* [1977] ECR 137; [1977] 2 CMLR 218.
241. OJ 1986 L378/1.
242. OJ 1986 L378/3.
243. OJ 1986 L378/14.
244. OJ 1986 L378/21.
245. EEC, Article 189(3). On directives in EC law, see EEC Treaty, Articles 189–90 and Euratom Treaty, Articles 161–63. e.g. the EEC's VAT Directive (Dir. 77/388) was implemented in the UK by virtue of the Value Added Tax Act 1983. On national implementation, see Case 169/87 *Commission v. France* [1974] ECR 359; [1974] 2 CMLR 216.

do so exposes the Member State to possible enforcement proceedings being instituted by the Commission in the ECJ.[246] Directives must be based on a provision of the Foundation Treaties, most normally, the EEC Treaty.[247] The purpose of directives is to achieve approximation and harmonisation of the laws between the Member States but not uniformity.[248] Directives are addressed to Member States but may still create rights for individuals. Directives have been used in shipping matters.

3.5.2.2.3 Decisions

A decision is binding in its entirety on the State or the person to whom it is addressed.[249] Decisions must be reasoned and based on a provision of the Foundation Treaties (most normally, for present purposes, on a provision of the EEC Treaty).[250] While publication is not obligatory,[251] they are usually published in the *Official Journal of the European Communities*. Decisions are important in regard to the application of competition law to shipping in that a decision may be taken against an undertaking breaching EC competition law.

3.5.2.2.4 Recommendations

Occasionally, EC institutions merely *recommend* a course of action rather than order it. For example, the Council of Ministers has made a recommendation in respect of passenger ferry safety and the Commission has proposed a recommendation on improving the effectiveness of Port State Control.[252] Recommendations are not legally binding in themselves.

3.5.2.2.5 Resolutions

Bodies such as the European Parliament occasionally adopt resolutions on particular topics. These resolutions are not legally binding in themselves.

3.5.2.2.7 Agreements

The EC, in its international corporate capacity, frequently adopts agreements with other international organisations (which have the legal capacity to conclude such agreements) and States. Sometimes these agreements can form part of EC law.

3.5.2.2.8 General principles of Community law

Some principles of law common to all or many of the legal systems in Member States have been used by the European Court of Justice in reaching its decisions. It has used,

246. Note, in particular, the possibility of Article 169 proceedings.
247. See the EEC Treaty, Article 190 in the case of EEC Directives.
248. See Bebr, *Development of Judical Control of the European Communities* (Nijhoff, 1981), 584–588, 596–602.
249. EEC, Article 189(4). Advocate-General Warner said in Case 19/77 *Miller v. Commission* [1978] ECR 131, at p. 161 that decisions were not "law creating".
250. E.g. in the case of the EEC Treaty, Article 190.
251. EEC, Article 191(2).
252. On the Commission proposal, see OJ 1989 C263/15.

inter alia, the principles of legitimate expectation,[253] proportionality,[254] legal certainty,[255] the principles of human rights,[256] as well as equality and non-discrimination.[257]

3.5.2.2.9 *Case law of the Court of Justice*

Unlike the system of *stare decisis* operated by the British, American, Commonwealth and Irish courts, the ECJ does not feel obliged to follow its previous decisions and can freely depart from them without having to provide an explanation.

3.5.2.2.10 *Opinions of the Advocates-General*

The opinions of the Advocates-General[258] are not binding in themselves but they can be persuasive in future cases.

3.5.3 Direct effect and direct applicability

In accordance with the doctrine of direct applicability as set out in Article 189 of the EEC Treaty, Regulations[259] have direct applicability in Member States. Directives or Decisions do not have direct applicability under the EEC Treaty. This means that Regulations do not need to be re-enacted in the legislation of the Member States.[260]

Directives, decisions and certain articles of the Foundation Treaties are not given directly applicability under the EEC Treaty and require national legislation so as to implement them.[261] The ECJ has held, in a series of judgments,[262] that these measures may have direct effect. Direct effect means that a measure creates rights which may be relied upon by persons in litigation before the courts of the Member States and those courts must give effect to these measures. Directly effective measures may only be invoked *against* a Member State[263] (or an emanation of the State) but not *by* a Member State[264] (i.e. it only has "vertical effect" (State-Person) but not horizontal effect (e.g. person-person) which Regulations have). The ECJ adopted this reasoning because

253. I.e. the Community will not in any way contrary to the expectations legitimately held by those affected by the proposed action: see Case 81/72 *Commission v. Council* [1973] ECR 575.

254. I.e. Community action should not exceed what is actually necessary so as to achieve the objectives sought. *Cf.* Case 114/76 *Bela-Muhle v. Grows Farm* [1977] ECR 1211; Case 122/78 *Buitoni v. FORMA* [1979] ECR 677, 684; and Case 181/84 *ED and F Man v. Intervention Board.*

255. See Case 13/61 *Bosch v. De Geus* [1962] ECR 45; Case 85/76 *Hoffmann-La Roche v. Commission* [1979] ECR 461, at p. 510; Case 169/80 *Gondrand Freres* [1981] ECR 1219, at p. 1232; Case 4/73 *Nold v. Commission* [1974] ECR 491; and Cases 209/78 etc., *Van Landewyck v. Commission* [1980] ECR 3125, at p. 3248.

256. *Cf.* Case 36/75 *Rutili v. Commission* [1974] ECR 491 and Case 136/79 *National Panasonic v. Commission* [1979] ECR 2033.

257. Cases 103 and 145/77 *Royal Scholten Honig v. Intervention Board* [1978] ECR 2037, at p. 2072.

258. On Advocates-General, see para. 3.4.6.3.4, above.

259. On Regulations, see para. 3.5.2.2.1, above.

260. See Case 24/73 *Variola* [1973] ECR 981 and Case 50/76 *Amsterdam Bulb* [1977] ECR 137; [1977] 2 CMLR 218. See Arnull, "The Direct Effect of Directives: Grasping the Nettle" [1986] 35 ICLQ 932.

261. See Case 169/87 *Commission v. France* [1974] ECR 359; [1974] 2 CMLR 216.

262. See Case 9/70 *Grad v. Finanzant Traunstein* [1970] ECR 825; [1971] CMLR 1.

263. See Cases 21–4/72 *International Fruit Co v. Produktschap* [1972] ECR 1219; [1975] 2 CMLR 1; Case 152/84 *Marshall v. Southampton Area Health Authority* [1986] ECR 723; [1986] 1 CMLR 688.

264. See Case 80/86 *Kolpinghuis Nijimegen* [1989] 2 CMLR 18.

Member States or EC institutions have often failed to adopt laws to implement those measures. The Court is of the view that it would be illogical and inconsistent with the binding nature of the EC legal system not to allow persons to rely on these measures in so far as they establish clear, precise and legally complete obligations just because the Member States or the Institutions have failed to implement the measure.

3.5.4 Publication of community law

The secondary legislation, as well as many other instruments, are published in the EC's *Official Journal of the European Communities* (abbreviated as the OJ).[265] Since 1 January 1968, the *Official Journal* has been divided into two separate series, the "L" series which contains legislation and the "C" series which contains notices, proposals, information, as well as various communications.

3.5.5 Relationship between community law and national laws

The Community is an independent legal order which is capable of creating rights and duties affecting not only the Member States but individuals and other undertakings. Community law is part of the national law of each of the Member States.[266] Community law is superior to national law. Provisions of Community law which confer rights and duties[267] on individuals and so on are said to have direct effect.[268] Any measure which has direct effect is superior to any Member State law.[269] EC law takes precedence over the national law of the EC Member States irrespective of when the laws were adopted.[270] This rule applies to civil and criminal[271] law as well as, in certain case, the rules of professional organisations.[272] Incompatible national legislation is of no effect and should be "repealed"—if only for good legal order.[273] If an area of law has been made the subject of EC legislation then the Member States may no longer legislate in respect of that area.[274] Member States may continue to legislate where the EC has done no more than co-ordinate national legislation on a topic.[275] The courts of the Member States are obliged to ensure the effectiveness of EC law.[276]

265. On the OJ, see Kapteyn and Van Themaat, *op. cit.*, (2nd edn.), p. xxv.
266. See the comments of Oliver J. in *Dymond v. G. B. Britton (Holdings) Ltd* [1976] 1 CMLR 133, at p. 135.
267. E.g. EEC, Articles 30–4; 85–6.
268. See Hartley, *op. cit., passim*; Winter, "Direct Applicability and Direct Effect: Two Distinct and Different Concepts in Community Law", 9 CML Rev 425; Pescatore, "The Doctrine of 'Direct Effect': An Infant Disease of Community Law", 8 EL Rev 155. *Cf.* Case 26/62 *Van Gend en Loos* [1963] ECR 1; Case 6/64 *Costa v. ENEL* [1964] ECR 585; Case 28/67 *Molkerei-Zentrale Westfalen v. Hauptzollamt Paderborn* [1968] ECR 143; Case 41/74 *Van Duyn v. Home Office* [1974] ECR 1337; Case 43/75 *Defrenne v. Sabena* [1976] ECR 455, 474; Case 174/84 *Bulk Oil v. Sun International.*
269. On direct effect, see para. 3.5.3, above.
270. See Case 6/64 *Costa v. ENEL* [1964] ECR 585; [1964] CMLR 425.
271. See Case 8/74 *Procureur du Roi v. Dassonville* [1974] ECR 837; [1974] 2 CMLR 436.
272. See Cases 266 and 267/87 *R. v. Royal Pharmaceutical Society of Great Britain ex p. Secretary of State for Social Services* [1989] 2 CMLR 751.
273. See Case 167/73 *Commission v. France (the French Seafarers' case)* [1974] ECR 359; [1974] 2 CMLR 216.
274. Case 60/86 *Commission v. United Kingdom* [1988] 3 CMLR 437.
275. See Case 21/87 *Borowitz v. Bundesversicherungsanstalt für Angestellte* [1988] ECR.
276. See Case 158/80 *Rewe v. Hauptzollamt Kiel* [1981] ECR 1805; [1982] 1 CMLR 449.

3.5.6 Interpretation of community law[277]

The interpretation of EC law is a fascinating study. Judge Kutscher of the ECJ has (extra-judicially) identified four interpretative techniques or methods used by the ECJ: the literal; the historical; the comparative and the teleological. The literal method involves examining the obvious meaning in the literary context of the document. The historical method involves an analysis of the legislative history of the provision at issue. This is rarely used in practice.[278] The comparative approach involves a comparison of the laws of the various legal systems of the Member States[279]—while using this approach, the Court does not look for the lowest common denominator between the laws.

The teleological approach involves looking at the broad aims and goals of the legislators in enacting the provision. It avoids a literal approach. It is flexible but must not be too flexible.[280] The context of the legislation must be examined.[281] This approach is assisted by the use of recitals as preambular statements in the measures.[282] Juristic writings are far more important in the Court of Justice of the European Communities than in the British or Irish courts.[283] EC laws are multilingual,[284] being published in nine official languages.[285] Each text is equally authentic. If there is a divergence between the texts then each text must be interpreted in the light of the other texts.[286] Both the Advocates-General and the judges have examined words and expressions used in several languages. The interesting problem of how to interpret national legislation which has been enacted because of or on the basis of Community legislation was discussed by the ECJ said in *Johnston v. Chief Constable of the RUC* when the Court said: "in applying national law, and in particular the provisions of national legislation specifically introduced in order to implement [d]irective[s] . . . national courts are required to interpret their national law in the light of the wording and the purpose of the directive in order to achieve the result referred to in the third paragraph of Article 189 of the EEC Treaty".[287] Article 177 of the EEC Treaty[288] facilitates a uniform interpretation by allowing the ECJ to adopt a common approach to the interpretation of a particular provision in a measure.[289]

277. See Kutscher, "Methods of Interpretation as seen by a Judge at the Court of Justice", Judicial and Academic Conference 1976.

278. *Cf. National Panasonic (UK) Ltd v. EC Commission* [1980] ECR 2033.

279. See *A.M. & S. Europe Ltd v. Commission* [1982] ECR 1575.

280. See Case 122/80 *Analog Devices* [1981] ECR 2781.

281. See Case 292/82 *Merck v. Hauptzollamt Hamburg-Jonas* [1983] ECR 3781.

282. E.g. Case 83/78 *Pigs Marketing Board v. Redmond* [1978] ECR 2347; [1979] 1 CMLR 177.

283. See, for example, *A.M. & S. Europe Ltd v. Commission.*

284. EEC Treaty, Article 7. See, for example, Cases 286/82 and 26/83 *Luisi and Carbone v. Ministero del Tesoro* [1984] ECR 377; [1985] 3 CMLR 52; Case 305/85 *United Kingdom v. Commission* [1988] 2 CMLR 169.

285. Some measures are also published in the Irish language, but this is not an official language.

286. This is a frequent problem in international law.

287. Case 222/84 [1986] ECR 1651 at para. 53. See also Case 14/83 *von Colson v. Land Nordheim-Westfalen* [1984] ECR 1891; [1986] 2 CMLR 430.

288. On Article 177 of the EEC Treaty, see para.3.4.6.6.9, above.

289. See, for example, Case 102/86 *Apple and Pear Development Council v. Customs and Excise* [1988] 2 CMLR 394.

3.5.7 Fundamental principles of EC law

3.5.7.1 Non-discrimination between EC nationals on the basis of nationality

It is a fundamental general[290] principle of EC law that there may be no discrimination between nationals of EC Member States in any area of EC law.[291]

3.5.7.2 Proportionality

The doctrine of proportionality[292] provides that an action or course of conduct must be proportionate or appropriate to the objective to be achieved.[293]

3.5.7.3 Legitimate expectation

The doctrine of legitimate expectation[294] is recognised in EC law.[295] This means that EC law will protect the interests of someone who acted to his or her detriment on the basis of a "legitimate expectation".

3.5.8 Enforcement of EC law in the courts of Member States

All the courts in the EC Member States are obliged to apply EC law.[296] EC law may be raised as an issue in any court in the EC.[297] In the English courts, tort actions might be brought in relation to the breach of EC law on grounds such as breach of statutory duty or perhaps misfeasance in a public office.[298] Injunctions may be granted in those courts to restrain breaches of EC law.[299]

3.5.9 Challenging the legality of Community measures

It is possible to challenge the legality of EC legal measures in the ECJ. Article 235 of the EEC Treaty is sometimes used as the basis of EC measures. The ECJ has stated that this Article may be used "as the legal basis for a measure . . . only where no other provision of the [EEC] Treaty gives the Community institutions the necessary power to adopt the measure in question".[300]

3.5.9.1 Passing on

It is worth recalling that in the sphere of taxation (which is widely defined) the doctrine

290. Exceptions are permitted, see, for example, Article 48(4) of the EEC Treaty.
291. EEC Treaty, Article 7. See, for example, Cases 286/82 and 26/83 *Luisi and Carbone v. Ministero del Tesoro* [1984] ECR 377; [1985] 3 CMLR 52; Case 305/85 *United Kingdom v. Commission* [1988] 2 CMLR 169.
292. See *Garden Cottage Foods v. Milk Marketing Board* [1984] AC 130.
293. See, for example, Case 216/84 *Commission v. France*.
294. See Article 174 of the EEC Treaty. In respect of this principle and Article 177 of the EEC Treaty, see Case 24/86 *Blaizot v. University of Liège* [1989] CMLR 57.
295. See Case 120/86 *Mulder v. Minister von Landbouw* [1989] 2 CMLR 1. For the limits of the doctrine, see Case 161/86 *Binder v. Hauptzollamt Bad Reichenall*.
296. *Cf.* Case 106/77 *Simmenthal* [1978] ECR 629; [1978] 3 CMLR 263.
297. *Cf.* Case 158/80 *Rewe v. Hauptzollamt Kiel* [1981] ECR 1805; [1982] 1 CMLR 449.
298. See Rawlinson and Cornwell Kelly, *op. cit.*, at footnote 1 above, para.2.45. See *Bourgoin v. Ministry of Agriculture* [1985] 3 WLR 1027.
299. See *Garden Cottage Foods v. Milk Marketing Board* [1984] AC 130.
300. *Re the ERASMUS Legislation: Commission v. Council of Ministers*, para.6, [1991] 1 CMLR 478 at p. 495. See also Case 45/86 *Commission v. Council*, at para.13, [1987] ECR 1493; [1988] 2 CMLR 131.

of "passing on" means that where the burden of an illegally imposed tax has been passed on by a taxpayer to its customers, then Member States may deny the taxpayer the right to a repayment of the tax, notwithstanding that it has been struck down as illegal.[301] This prevents taxpayers obtaining windfalls when they successfully challenge tax-imposing measures.

3.5.9.2 Prospective overruling

The ECJ may declare that its decision that a measure is invalid would have effect only in respect of future transactions or in respect of transactions currently disputed.[302]

301. See Case 199/82 *San Giorgio* [1983] ECR 3595; [1985] 2 CMLR 658.
302. See Article 174 of the EEC Treaty. In respect of this principle and Article 177 of the EEC Treaty, see Case 24/86 *Blaizot v. University of Liège* [1989] 1 CMLR 57.

CHAPTER 4

EC Transport Law

4.1 INTRODUCTION

This chapter examines the law of the EC as it relates to transport[1] generally.[2] An understanding of the EC law relating to transport in general is useful in trying to understand the EC law relating to shipping in particular.

4.1.1 Importance of transport in the EC

Transport is an inherent part of any economic community—it is however particularly important in the EC's economy. First, it accounts for about 7% of the combined GDP of the EC Member States and this is more than agriculture—indeed, agriculture and transport are the only economic sectors which have Titles devoted to them in the original EEC Treaty. Only agriculture, commerce and transport have common policies under Article 3 of the EEC Treaty. Secondly, it is almost inevitable that even more money will be spent on transport in the coming years because of the opening up of the Middle and Eastern European markets as well as the anticipated completion of the EC's Internal Market.[3] Thirdly, it is worth remembering that transport is a huge employer around the EC.[4] Fourthly, the development of such freedoms as free movement of goods, services and persons presupposes a transport system. The integration of the EC demands the development of a transport system: there is a pressing need to have a low-cost, highly efficient, competitive transport system,

1. In the context of this chapter, "transport" is taken to mean the carriage of persons or goods from one place to another.

2. On EC transport law and policy generally see, Abbati, *Transport and European Integration* (1986); Commission of the European Communities, *The European Community's Transport Policy*, Periodical 3/1984; *op. cit.*, *The Community and Transport Policy*, European File 10/85; Greaves, *Transport Law of the European Community* (1991); Kapteyn and Van Themaat, *Introduction to the Law of the European Communities* (2nd edn., 1989, edited by Gormley), p. 705 *et seq.*; Kuyper, (1985/2) LIEI 69; Simons, *Recht en Onrecht in het Europees Vervoerbeleid* (Zwolle, 1986); Lasok and Bridge, *Law and Institutions of the European Communities* (4th edn., 1987), pp. 423–6; Mathijsen, *A Guide to European Community Law* (4th edn., 1985), pp. 162–6; Parry and Hardy, *EEC Law* (2nd edn., 1981), Chapter 19. See also Close, "Article 84 EEC: The Development of Transport Policy in the Sea and Air Sectors" (1980) 5 EL Rev. 188; *op. cit.*, "Inland Transport Services: Recent Developments in Community Policy" (1985) 22 *Common Market Law Review* 587; and Xureb (1989) 38 ICLQ 697. See also the Report of a Conference held on 4 and 5 March 1963 on "The Legal Provisions Relating to Transport in the Common Market" (British Institute of International and Comparative Law, Special Publication No. 2 (1963)).

On EC transport generally, see Despicht, *Policies for Transport in the Common Market* (1964); Feige, "Transport in the European Community", *EIU European Trends*, 1990, No. 2, p. 42; Gwilliam, *Co-ordination of Investments in Transport Infrastructures*, Studies, Transport Series, No. 3 (1973); and Swann, *The Economics of the Common Market*, 6th edn., 1988, p. 232 *et seq.*

3. On the Internal Market programme, see Chapter 24, below.

4. See EC Commission, *The Community and Transport Policy* (1985) (European File 10/85), p. 3.

allowing transport users a reasonable choice and transport operators a fair return on investment.

4.1.2 Need to achieve a common transport policy

Transport is one of the foundations of the EEC Treaty: the Treaty states that a common transport policy (CTP) is a necessary pre-requisite if the Common Market is ever to be achieved. A common policy envisages national policies being recast into one single EC policy: the national becomes supranational. The need to adopt such a policy was identified as early as the Spaak Report.[5] Article 3(c) of the EEC Treaty calls for the adoption of such a policy. The CTP is vital for the EC given its size and population. The EC has a population density of around 142 persons per square kilometre but it is unevenly spread (for example, The Netherlands has a population density of around 430 persons per square kilometre but Spain has a population density of around 75 persons per square kilometre). An effective CTP is essential.

There is a need to integrate all areas of transport policy: for example, there is a need to co-ordinate road and rail networks with the building and operation of ferryports. The CTP needs not only to be coherent in itself, but also integrated with many of the EC's other policies such as agriculture (e.g. the carriage of food aid), the environment (e.g. pollution), competition (e.g. prohibition of unfair pricing practices) and social policy (e.g. the Reneval Programme). The CTP must also take into account what is happening in European organisations (such as the Central Commission for the Navigation of the Rhine, the Moselle Commission, the European Conference of Ministers for Transport, the Council of Europe and the Economic Commission for Europe) as well as international bodies (such as the International Maritime Organisation and the United Nations Conference on Trade and Development). Sadly, neither internal nor external integration has yet taken place. The CTP needs to be not only a common policy but also a coherent one.

4.1.3 Failure to achieve a common transport policy

Despite the need for a CTP, such a policy remains elusive. The elements of the policy which have been adopted so far are unconnected and incomplete: it has been a "policy of little steps". The lack of achievement in achieving an EC transport policy is due, for the most part, to the lack of a common will on the part of the Member States because of their differing interests and attitudes. The Common Agricultural Policy (CAP) has been, despite its many critics, a remarkable achievement—the diversity of interests; the plethora of products; and the complexity of the politics involved have all been overcome to produce a common policy. There has been no such luck with the CTP: no clear-cut policy has been developed.

Various commentators have discussed the reasons for the failure of the EC to adopt an effective CTP. Lowe has argued that the:

> "reason that no great progress in this area has been made is that Member States have their own divergent views as to the priorities of transport as well as their own quite individual geographic, economic and cultural considerations. Certain states have adopted strict interventionist policies while others have adopted a much more liberal approach to government participation in transport. In particular, for example, we have seen the desire of some individual Member States to adopt and maintain protectionist policies towards their railway systems, waterways and ports.

5. See Abbati, *op. cit.* at footnote 2 above, para.2.3.1.

In other cases protection of road systems is important because of the inherent dependence of the smaller countries of Europe on their road networks. To date there has been no definable incentive for these considerations to be pushed aside in the common good but the implementation of the Single European Act now changes this position and the new vision of a single market provides the incentive."[6]

Other commentators have written that the reason for the non-achievement of this policy is that "the transport system developed in each Member State was designed to serve *national* needs (often military ones) rather than a wider territorial unit . . . [h]ence the problem of integration".[7] Member States take differing views on the degree to which States should intervene in transport affairs. It is anticipated that the future development of EC transport law on a global rather than modal basis will hopefully stimulate development.

4.1.4 Legal bases of EC transport law

The legal bases of EC transport law are: first, the general rules of the EC Treaties (in particular, Articles 74 to 84 of the EEC Treaty); secondly, the legislation adopted under those Treaties; and, thirdly, the case-law of the European Court of Justice.

4.1.5 Adoption and administration of EC transport law

The adoption of measures relating to EC transport lies mainly in the hands of the Council of Ministers and the Commission. The former institution is by far the more politically significant and is principally involved in the adoption rather than the *administration* of EC transport law and policy. The Council was stimulated into action in the 1980s after the ECJ condemned it for its inactivity in the area.[8] The administration of EC transport law and policy lies in the hands of the Commission. The work of these institutions in the area of transport has been discussed earlier.[9]

4.2 POSITION OF TRANSPORT IN THE EC TREATIES

Transport is dealt with in the ECSC Treaty and the EEC Treaty. It does not appear in the Euratom Treaty. This section analyses the provisions in the ECSC and the EEC Treaties.

4.2.1 ECSC Treaty

4.2.1.1 Introduction

The ECSC Treaty does not deal with transport at any great length. Indeed, for "the purposes of the partial integration aimed at by the Treaty establishing the European Coal and Steel Community – that is, integration of the sectors of coal and steel only—it may not be immediately apparent why intervention in regard to transport should be necessary"[10] at all. However,

"one of the main requirements of a Common Market is that all consumers in comparable positions should have equal access to the sources of production – in other words, that an end

6. *The Transport and Distribution Manager's Guide to 1992* (1989), pp. 19–20.
7. Lasok and Bridge, *op. cit.* at footnote 2 above, p. 423 (emphasis added).
8. Case 13/83 *European Parliament v. Council of Ministers* [1985] ECR 1513; [1986] 1 CMLR 138.
9. See para. 3.4, above.
10. Debois and Baeyens, "Transport in the European Coal and Steel Community" (1966) 1 *European Transport Law* 29, at p. 29.

should be made to all arrangements or practices making for discrimination between one producer, purchaser or consumer and another, notably in the matter of prices and conditions of sale, and to all import and export duties, all equivalent dues and charges, and all subsidies or impediments to the free movement of goods. By themselves, however, such measures would be largely ineffective if the prohibition on discriminatory practices did not extend to transport."[11]

It is true to say that the control of transport is vital in a common market where the products are as bulky and costly to transport as coal and steel.

The provisions of the ECSC Treaty relating to transport are purely sectoral and modal in outlook: they relate solely to coal as well as steel, and to the normal modes of transport for such commodities, namely road, rail and inland waterway. The emphasis in terms of mode is on rail transport: it was reckoned in 1966 that the carriage of coal and steel amounted to around half of the EC's total rail traffic and around one-fifth of the total inland-waterway traffic.[12]

The provisions of the ECSC Treaty are also limited in their ambition: they do not purport to demand the adoption of a common transport policy (unlike the later EEC Treaty), but are simply limited to the removal of distortions of competition. As Close has commented: "[g]enerally speaking, whilst envisaging the future harmonisation of national rates and conditions, the provisions of the ECSC Treaty devoted to transport leave tariff policy uncontrolled and are confined to the requirement that within any national system any discrimination must be abolished".[13] He went on to say that the "provisions of the ECSC Treaty devoted to transport leave tariff policy uncontrolled and are confined to the requirement that within any national system any must be abolished".[14]

In the light of Article 232 of the EEC Treaty, it is to be remembered that the EEC Treaty applies to the transport of coal and steel in so far as Article 70 of the ECSC Treaty (and any implementing measures) contain no special provisions to the contrary.

On the relationship between transport under the EEC Treaty and the ECSC Treaty regard must be had to Case 156/77 *Commission v. Belgium.*[15] It is also to be recalled that Article 232(1) of the EEC Treaty provides that the provisions of the EEC Treaty are not to affect the provisions of the ECSC Treaty and Article 232(2) of the EEC Treaty provides that its provisions do not derogate from the Euratom Treaty.

It has been suggested that while the provisions on transport in the EEC Treaty are wider, they are not as deep or as effective as those to be found in the ECSC Treaty.[16]

4.2.1.2 Article 4 of the ECSC Treaty

4.2.1.2.1 Text

"The following are recognized as incompatible with the common market for coal and steel and shall accordingly be abolished and prohibited within the Community, as provided in this Treaty:

. . . (b) measures or practices which discriminate between producers, between purchasers or between consumers, especially in prices and delivery terms or transport rates and conditions, and measures or practices which interfere with the purchaser's free choice of supplier . . . ."

11. *Op. cit.*, pp. 29–31.
12. *Op. cit.*, p. 35.
13. Close in Hailsham (ed.), *Halsbury's Laws of England* (4th edn.), vol. 52, para. 18.02 (footnote omitted).
14. Close, *op. cit.*, para. 18.02, footnote omitted.
15. [1978] ECR 1881.
16. See the comments of Debois and Baeyens, *op. cit.* at footnote 10 above, at p. 39.

4.2.1.2.2 Commentary

Article 4 prohibits, among other things, discrimination in the area of transport rates and conditions.[17] This is echoed in Article 70 of the ECSC Treaty.[18]

4.2.1.3 Article 70 of the ECSC Treaty[19]

4.2.1.3.1 Text

"It is recognized that the establishment of the common market necessitates the application of such rates and conditions for the carriage of coal and steel as will afford comparable price conditions to comparably placed consumers.

Any discrimination in rates and conditions of carriage of every kind which is based on the country of origin or destination of products shall be prohibited in traffic between Member States. For the purpose of eliminating such discrimination it shall in particular be obligatory to apply to the carriage of coal and steel to or from another country of the Community the scales, rates and all other tariff rules of every kind which are applicable to the internal carriage of the same goods on the same route.

The scales, rates and all other tariff rules of every kind applied to the carriage of coal and steel within each Member State and between Member States shall be published or brought to the knowledge of the High Authority.

The application of special internal rates and conditions in the interest of one or more coal- or steel-producing undertakings shall require the prior agreement of the High Authority, which shall verify that they are in accordance with the principles of this Treaty; it may make its agreement temporary or conditional.

Subject to the provisions of this Article, and to the other provisions of this Treaty, transport policy, including the fixing and altering of rates and conditions of carriage of every kind and the making of rates on a basis calculated to secure for the transport undertakings concerned a properly balanced financial position, shall continue to be governed by the laws or regulations of the individual Member States, as shall measures relating to coordination or competition between different modes of transport or different routes."

4.2.1.3.2 Commentary

The first paragraph of Article 70 represents the kernel of the ECSC law relating to transport: the establishment of the common market necessitates the application of such rates and conditions for the carriage of coal and steel as will afford comparable price conditions to comparably placed consumers. Close wrote:

"[t]he discrimination which the first paragraph of Article 70 envisages is that special internal rates and conditions afford different price conditions to comparably placed consumers. The comparability envisaged is to be evaluated from the point of view of transport. It would not be correct therefore for the comparison to take account of all the circumstances of the undertakings, such as the profitability of the deposits worked and the fact of being located in a less favoured region."[20,21]

17. See Joined Cases 3-18/58 *Barbara Erzberghau AG v. High Authority* [1960] ECR 173; Case 19/58 *Germany v. High Authority* [1960] ECR 225; and Joined Cases 27-29/58 *Compagnie des Hauts Fourneaux et Fonderies de Givers v. High Authority* [1960] ECR 241.

18. On ECSC Treaty, Article 70, see para.4.2.1.3, below.

19. On Article 70 ECSC, see Joined Cases 23-26/58 *Barbara Erzbergau v. High Authority* [1960] ECR 173; Case 19/58 *Germany v. High Authority* [1960] ECR 225, ECJ.

20. Joined Cases 3-18, 25, 26/58 *Barbara Erzberghau AG v. High Authority* [1960] ECR 173; Case 19/58 *Germany v. High Authority* [1960] ECR 225, ECJ; Joined Cases 27-29/58 *Compagnie des Hauts Fourneaux et Fonderies de Givers v. High Authority* [1960] ECR 241, ECJ. See also Commission Decision 73/152 (OJ L172/20, 28.6.73).

21. In Hailsham (ed.), *Halsbury's Laws of England* (4th edn), vol. 52, para. 18.03.

The second paragraph[22] provides that any discrimination in rates and conditions of carriage of every kind which is based on the country of origin or destination of products is prohibited in relation to traffic between Member States. The paragraph goes on to say that for the purpose of eliminating such discrimination it shall in particular be obligatory to apply to the carriage of coal and steel to or from another country of the Community the scales, rates and all other tariff rules of every kind which are applicable to the internal carriage of the same goods on the same route.

The third paragraph[23] provides that the scales, rates and all other tariff rules of every kind applied to the carriage of coal and steel within each Member State and between Member States must be published or brought to the knowledge of the Commission.[24] Commission Decision 73/152[25] obliges undertakings in the steel industry to publish lists or schedules of transport charges for sea routes between EC Member States.

The fourth paragraph provides that the application of special internal rates and conditions in the interest of one or more coal- or steel-producing undertakings requires the prior agreement of the Commission.[26] The Commission shall then verify that the rates and conditions are in accordance with the principles of the ECSC Treaty. The Commission may make its agreement temporary or conditional.[27]

The reservation of transport matters to Member States by means of the fifth paragraph has been whittled away by Articles 74 to 84 of the EEC Treaty.

It is essential to recall that by reason of Article 232 of the EEC Treaty, the EEC regime applies to coal and steel transport insofar as the ECSC Treaty does not apply.

Article 70 contemplates the elimination of discrimination on the basis of nationality in transport rates and conditions in the carriage of coal and steel.

The provisions of Article 79 of the EEC Treaty do not apply to the transportation of coal and steel.

4.2.2 EEC Treaty

4.2.2.1 Introduction

The EEC Treaty contains special[28] but limited[29] provisions. These provisions are principally contained in Articles 74–84[30] which constitute Title IV of Part Two[31] of the EEC Treaty. Article 3 states that one of the activities of the EEC is the adoption of a common transport policy. Article 61 also explicitly mentions transport (but in the context of freedom to provide services).[32] Transport is also to be seen in the wider

22. On this paragraph, see Joined Cases 3-18, 25, 26/58 *Barbara Erzbergbau AG v. High Authority* [1960] ECR 173.

23. On the third paragraph, see Case 20/59 *Italy v. High Authority* [1960] ECR 325; Case 25/59 *Netherlands v. High Authority* [1960] ECR 355; and Case 9/61 *Netherlands v. High Authority* [1962] ECR 213.

24. See also ECSC High Authority Recommendation 1/61.

25. OJ 1973 L172/20.

26. See Case 19/58 *Germany v. High Authority* [1960] ECR 225 and Case 28/66 *Netherlands v. Commission* [1968] ECR 1.

27. *E.g.* Commission Decision 71/293 and Decision 78/975 [1979] 2 CMLR 210.

28. The provisions are special in that agriculture and transport are the only two industries which have Titles in the EEC Treaty devoted to them.

29. The provisions in the EEC Treaty relating to transport are quite limited in terms of specifics and leave a great deal to be adopted by the Council of Ministers. This degree of discretion is at its greatest in the case of air and sea transport provisions. See Fennel (1980) 10 E.L. Rev. 264.

30. See Appendix I.

31. Part Two of the EEC Treaty is entitled "Foundations of the Community".

32. See para.4.2.2.3 and Chapter 7 below.

context of the other provisions of the EEC Treaty itself[33] in so far as they are not expressly disapplied.[34,35]

Apart from agriculture, transport is the only economic sector which has a special Title in the EEC Treaty. Yet the terms of the Transport Title are vague by contrast.

The provisions of the EEC Treaty are much broader in scope and ambition than the ECSC Treaty.[36] The modes of transport contemplated by the transport provisions of the EEC Treaty are rail, road, inland waterway, sea transport and air transport.[37] The EEC Treaty relates to the carriage of all persons as well as all goods not regulated by the ECSC Treaty. In essence, the EEC Treaty envisages the adoption of a comprehensive and ambitious common transport policy covering all modes,[38] and all cargoes[39] and persons.[40]

The EEC Treaty (as originally drafted) did not in itself oblige the speedy and thorough adoption of a common transport policy: there was ambiguity in the text, a lack of an agreed approach to transport issues generally in the EC and there was a requirement for unanimity in the Council of Ministers which was (and still is) always difficult to obtain. This situation has now changed (at least in part): the environment has been improved by the amendment of Article 84 EEC by the Single European Act[41] as well as the decisions and rulings of the European Court of Justice[42] in such cases as Case 22/70 *Commission v. Council*,[43] Case 167/73 *Commission v. France*,[44] Case 156/77 *Commission v. Belgium*,[45] Case 13/83 *European Parliament v. Council*[46] and Cases 209–213/84 *Ministere Public v. Asjes*.[47]

In reviewing the specific provisions on transport in the EEC Treaty, it is worth bearing in mind that the general provisions of the EEC Treaty also apply to transport. This principle has been confirmed[48] by the ECJ in Case 167/73 *Commission v. France*[49] when the court said:

"When Article 74 refers to the objectives of the Treaty, it means the provisions of Articles 2 and 3, the attainment of which the fundamental provisions applicable to the whole complex of

33. For example, the provisions relating to nationality (Article 7) (see, for example, Case 167/73 *Commission v. France* [1974] ECR 359; [1974] 2 CMLR 216) and free movement of workers (Article 48) (see, for example, Case 9/88 *Da Veiga v. Staatssecretaris van Justitie* [1991] 1 CMLR 217.

34. *E.g.* Article 61(1) of the EEC Treaty provides that freedom to provide services in the field of transport shall be governed by the provisions of the Title relating to transport.

35. Case 167/73 *Commission v. France* [1974] ECR 359; [1974] 2 CMLR 216.

36. On transport in the ECSC Treaty, see para. 4.2.1, above.

37. NB it does not specifically mention pipelines.

38. Apparently, other than pipelines and vacuum tubes — but there is no clear indication in the Treaty of this viewpoint.

39. Other than coal and steel.

40. None the less the articles and aims of the provisions in the EEC Treaty relating to transport are more limited in scope than the provisions in the ECSC Treaty relating to transport.

41. See para. 4.2.2.1.4 below.

42. On the European Court of Justice, see Chapter 3, above.

43. [1971] ECR 263; [1971] CMLR 355; see paras 00–00, below.

44. [1974] ECR 359; [1974] 2 CMLR 216; see paras 00–00, below.

45. [1978] ECR 1811.

46. [1985] ECR 1513; [1986] 1 CMLR 138. See Fennel (1985) 10 European Law Review 264.

47. [1986] ECR 1425.

48. The historical background to this debate is interesting but need not detain the present discussion. For the historical debate, see Abbati, *op. cit.* at footnote 2, at para. 2.3.6.

49. [1974] ECR 359; [1974] 2 CMLR 216 (known as the *French Merchant Seamen* or the *Code du Travail Maritime* case). See also Case 22/70 *Commission v. Council* [1971] ECR 263; [1971] CMLR 335; Case 156/77 *Commission v. Belgium* [1978] ECR 1811; Case 13/83 *European Parliament v. Council* [1985] ECR 1513, [1986] 1 CMLR 138; Cases 209–213/84 *Ministère public v. Asjes (the "Nouvelles Frontières")* [1986] ECR 1425; Case 66/86 *Ahmed Saeed Flugreisen v. Zentrale zur Bekämpfung Unlauteren Wettbewerbs e V* [1990] 4 CMLR 102.

economic activities seek to ensure. Far from involving a departure from these fundamental rules, the object of the rules relating to the common transport policy is to implement and complement them by means of common action. Consequently the said general rules must be applied in so far as they can achieve these objectives."

This principle was confirmed in Case 13/83 *European Parliament v. Council of Ministers.*[50] Thus, such sections of the EEC Treaty as competition,[51] non-discrimination on the basis of nationality,[52] freedom of establishment,[53] the common commercial policy, free movement of goods and so on apply to transport. It is worth noting however that the free movement of services in the field of transport is dealt with by the Title in the Treaty relating to transport and not by the ordinary provisions on freedom to provide services.[54]

In Case 13/83 *European Parliament v. Council*[55] the ECJ held, in an action brought by the Parliament against the Council of Ministers, that the Council of Ministers had failed in its duty under the EEC Treaty to ensure freedom to provide services in the sphere of international transport and to lay down conditions under which carriers not resident in one Member State could provide services in another EC Member State. This was the first Article 175 EEC Case brought to the ECJ by one EC institution against another. The ambiguity of the EEC Treaty provisions caused considerable (and unnecessary) doubt before the ECJ resolved some of the difficulties in Case 167/73 *Commission v. France*.

4.2.2.2 Article 3 of the EEC Treaty

4.2.2.2.1 Text

"For the purposes set out in Article 2,[56] the activities of the Community shall include, as provided in this Treaty, and in accordance with the timetable set out therein . . .

(e) the adoption of a common policy in the sphere of transport . . . ."

4.2.2.2.2 Commentary

This is a general[57] provision which sets the basis for the adoption of a common transport policy. Unfortunately, as will be seen, this policy has not yet been achieved. It is possible that a comprehensive CTP may never be achieved due to the differences

50. [1985] ECR 1513; [1986] 1 CMLR 138.

51. See the incisive analysis of Kapteyn and Van Themaat, *op. cit.*, p.713. See also Cases 209–213/84 *Ministere Public v. Asjes* [1986] ECR 1425; and Case 66/86 *Ahmed Saeed Flugreisen and Silver Line Reisebüro GmbH v. Zentrale zur Bekämpfung Unlauteren* [1990] 4 CMLR 102. In regard to state aids: see Case 156/77 *Commission v. Belgiun* [1978] ECR 1811.

52. See Article 7 EEC and see also Case 126/82 *DJ Smit Transport BV v. Commissie Grensoverschrijdend Beroepsvervoer* [1983] ECR 73; [1983] 3 CMLR 106.

53. See the General Programme for the Abolition of Restrictions on Freedom of Establishment, OJ English Special Edition (2nd Series), IX, p. 7. In the case of free movement of workers, see Case 167/73 *Commission v. France* [1974] ECR 359; [1974] 2 CMLR 216.

54. EEC Treaty, Article 61.

55. [1985] ECR 1513; [1986] 1 CMLR 138.

56. Article 2 of the EEC Treaty reads: "The Community shall have as its task, by establishing a common market and progressively approximating the economic policies of Member States, to promote throughout the Community a harmonious development of economic activities, a continuous and balanced expansion, an increase in stability, an accelerated raising of the standard of living and closer relations between the States belonging to it."

57. For a specific use of the provision, see Case 167/73 *Commission v. France* [1974] ECR 359; [1974] 2 CMLR 216.

between Member States and the fact that the borders of the EC are not the borders of transport, and thus the EC, despite its very best intentions, may be unable to legislate comprehensively for this most international of business sectors. It is important to note that while Article 3(e) calls for a CTP, the Treaty itself only prescribes a timetable and procedures but nothing more.

4.2.2.3 Article 61

4.2.2.3.1 Text

"1. Freedom to provide services in the field of transport shall be governed by the provisions of the Title relating to transport.

2. The liberalisation of banking and insurance services connected with movements of capital shall be effected in step with the progressive liberalisation of movement of capital."

4.2.2.3.2 Commentary

Article 61(1) is the only part of Article 61 which is relevant for present purposes. In essence, it removes transport from the ambit of the general provisions in the Chapter[58] on Services in Title III of the EEC Treaty[59] This area will be examined more thoroughly in Chapter 7, below.[60]

4.2.2.4 Article 74

4.2.2.4.1 Text

"The objectives of this Treaty shall, in matters governed by this Title, be pursued by Member States within the framework of a common transport policy."

4.2.2.4.2 Commentary

It is worth noting while reviewing Article 74 of the EEC Treaty that Article 84(1) of the same Treaty specifically provides that the provisions of the Transport Title are to apply only to rail, road and inland waterway while Article 84(2) provides that the Council of Ministers "may, acting by a qualified majority, decide whether, to what extent and by what procedure appropriate provisions may be laid down for sea and air transport". In effect, Articles 74 to 84 do not automatically apply to sea transport.

Kapteyn and Van Themaat contend that on the basis of Article 74 EEC as well as Articles 59 and 61 that a common transport policy *must* be established.[61] It is useful to compare Article 38 of the EEC Treaty (on agriculture) and Article 74 (on transport).

In accordance with Articles 74 and 76,[62] the Council of Ministers[63] adopted a Decision on 21 March 1962 (which has since been amended[64]) to institute a procedure for the prior examination and consultation on certain laws, regulations and administrative provisions proposed by Member States relating to rail, road and inland

58. *I.e.* Chapter 3.
59. *I.e.* the Title on free movement of persons, services and capital..
60. Chapter 7 deals with freedom to provides services.
61. *Op. cit.*, p. 714.
62. On Article 76 of the EEC Treaty, see para. 4.2.2.6, below.
63. On the Council of Ministers, see para. 3.4, above.
64. Dec.73/402/EEC, OJ 1973 L347/48.

waterway transport which are liable to substantially interfere with the implementation of the common transport policy. The procedure is two-fold: first, a Member State must notify the Commission and inform the other Member States of the proposed measure; and secondly, the Commission must address an Opinion or Recommendation to the relevant Member State and inform the other Member States of this Opinion or Recommendation.

4.2.2.5 Article 75

4.2.2.5.1 Text

"1. For the purpose of implementing Article 74, and taking into account the distinctive features of transport, the Council[65] above shall, acting unanimously until the end of the second stage[66] and by a qualified majority thereafter, lay down, on a proposal from the Commission[67] and after consulting the Economic and Social Committee[68] and the European Parliament[69]:

(a) common rules applicable to international transport to or from the territory of a Member State or passing across the territory of one or more Member States;
(b) the conditions under which non-resident carriers may operate transport services within a Member State;
(c) any other appropriate provisions.

2. The provisions referred to in (a) and (b) of paragraph 1 shall be laid down during the transitional period.[70]

3. By way of derogation from the procedure provided for in paragraph 1, where the application of provisions concerning the principles of the regulatory system for transport would be liable to have a serious effect on the standard of living and on employment in certain areas and on the operation of transport facilities, they shall be laid down by the Council acting unanimously. In so doing, the Council shall take into account the need for adaptation to the economic development which will result from establishing the common market."

4.2.2.5.2 Commentary

Article 75[71] is the legal basis for most of the secondary legislation in the area of transport. It is the means for the implementation of the common transport policy in relation to rail, road and inland waterway. It gives the Council of Ministers the power to elaborate and implement the Common Transport Policy. The Article "contains indisputably the most important provisions on transport in the whole of Title IV".[72]

Article 75 mentions the "distinctive features of transport". What is meant by this phrase? One author has commented that:

"[m]ost kinds of transport require heavy investments which, due to widely varying demand, often remain idle and unproductive for long periods. There is an enormous discrepancy between the infrastructure needed for various means of transport: some, like railways and inland shipping, need a specially designed infrastructure, while others, like road transport, use the road network jointly with millions of other users; another characteristic is that some means of transportation are in the hands of the State and are forced to offer services which are not economically justifiable. But whether nationalised or not, all forms of transport are subject to

65. *I.e.* the Council of Ministers. On the Council of Ministers, see para. 3.4.3, above.
66. *I.e.*. the second stage of the completion of the common market.
67. On the Commission, see Chapter 3, above.
68. On the Economic and Social Committee, see Chapter 3, above.
69. On the European Parliament, see Chapter 3, above.
70. The transitional period ended on 31 December 1969.
71. See Bellieni, "Comments on Article 75", *Jupiter*, No. 1, 1973.
72. Abbati, *op. cit.* at footnote 2 above, para.2.3.5.

severe requirements with regard to public safety. Finally, air and sea transport, extending far beyond the limits of the Community, are the object of many international agreements and regulations."[73]

Other distinctive characteristics include the division of ownership in the infrastructure and the means of transport; competition between modes; international dimension; dependence on infrastructure; the demand-led nature of the sector; high fixed costs; the large-scale nature of the industry; high employment levels; the role of transport in servicing other industries; the social function of the industry; and impossibility of storing up supply.

In Case 22/70 *Commission v. Council*[74] the European Court of Justice ruled that in those areas where the EC had developed a common transport policy it was the EC which was competent to negotiate international agreements as opposed to the Member States. Article 75 represents an element of this legal authority to negotiate international agreements. Article 75(1) of the EEC Treaty refers to the measures which may be enacted as being:

> "(a) common rules applicable to international transport to or from the territory of a Member State or passing across the territory of one or more Member States;
> (b) the conditions under which non-resident carriers may operate transport services within a Member State;
> (c) any other appropriate provisions."

Article 75(1)(*a*) relates to "international transport operations applying both in the case of carriage between Member States and in the case of carriage from a Member State to a third country".[75,76] Article 75(1)(*b*) is simple: it relates to the situation of where transport services are provided by a non-resident carriers entirely within a Member State (i.e. cabotage). The measures contemplated by Article 75(1)(*a*) and Article 75(1)(*b*) were both to have been adopted during the transitional period[77] but not all the measures were adopted.[78] It has been through Article 75(1)(*c*), the residual clause,the Council of Ministers has been able to "develop the notion of transport policy".[79] This is a very broad residual power.

Article 75(3) of the EEC Treaty is an unusual and important derogation because it permits a state to invoke its particular circumstances so as to prevent the adoption of a common transport policy.

Close has succinctly analysed Article 75 in the context of international agreements in the following terms:

"The legislative power[80] of the EC Council [of Ministers] for the purposes of the common transport policy extends to the conclusion of agreements with one or more third countries or an international organisation where the agreements form the subject of transport policy.[81] The power to enter into international commitments exists not only where internal measures have been adopted to attain the common transport policy, but also where the Community's

73. Mathijsen, *op. cit.* at footnote 2 above, p.163. See also Joined Cases 23–26/58 *Barbara Erzbergau AG v. High Authority* [1960] ECR 173.
74. [1971] ECR 263; [1971] CMLR 335. See also Opinion 1/76 *Laying-Up Fund* [1977] ECR 741.
75. Case 22/70 *EC Commission v. EC Council* [1971] ECR 263; [1971] CMLR 335.
76. Close, *op. cit.* at footnote 2 above, para.18.21.
77. EEC Treaty, Article 75(2).
78. See Case 13/83 *European Parliament v. EC Council of Ministers* [1985] ECR 1513; [1986] 1 CMLR 138.
79. Parry and Hardy, *op. cit.*, 19–05 citing Case 97/78 *Schumalla* [1978] ECR 2311.
80. *I.e.* under the EEC Treaty, Article 75.
81. Case 22/70 *EC Commission v. EC Council* [1971] ECR 263; [1971] CMLR 335, ECJ.

participation in an international agreement is necessary for the attainment of one of the Community's objectives. The Community may also co-operate in the setting up of an international organism in order to attain the common transport policy, and for this purpose to give it appropriate powers of decision and to define, in a manner appropriate to the objectives pursued, the nature, elaboration, implementation and effects of the provisions to be adopted within the organism. In so doing, however, the Community must respect its internal constitution."[82]

The international dimension of transport is to be seen in the context of Article 234 of the EEC Treaty.

Measures adopted under Article 75 of the EEC Treaty must not conflict with Article 70 of the EEC Treaty.

4.2.2.6 Article 76

4.2.2.6.1 Text

"Until the provisions referred to in Article 75(1) have been laid down, no Member State may, without the unanimous approval of the Council,[83] make the various provisions governing the subject when this Treaty enters into force less favourable in their direct or indirect effect on carriers of other Member States as compared with carriers who are nationals of that State."

4.2.2.6.2 Commentary

The essence of Article 76 of the EEC Treaty is that until the common transport policy has become a reality, no Member State may, as a general rule,[84] make the various national provisions[85] governing transport when the EEC Treaty entered into force, less favourable on carriers of other EC Member States than on its own nationals. In many ways, it is similar to Article 12 of the EEC Treaty which deals in much the same way with customs duties and charges having an equivalent effect. It is a standstill provision.

Article 76 attempted to crystallise the position[86] in respect of the original Member States as of 1 January 1958 for the original six Member States and the date of entry into the EC in respect of the newer States. It is a standstill clause.

Parry and Hardy record:

"To assist with the implementation of the standstill clause, the Council [of Ministers] instituted a procedure for prior examination and consultation in respect of legislative changes proposed by Member States in the transport sector.[87] Under this decision, Member States proposing legislation which may interfere substantially with the implementation of the common transport policy must notify the Commission and at the same time inform the other Member States. Other, peripheral matters, need not be notified, although the Commission may be kept abreast of events informally. The Commission is then required to address an opinion or recommendation to the Member State concerned, indicating whether it considers the measure proposed compatible with the common transport policy. Other Member States have an opportunity to comment. As both

82. Opinion 1/76 (draft agreement establishing a European laying-up fund for inland waterway vessels) [1977] ECR 741; [1977] 2 CMLR 279, ECJ.

83. *I.e.* the Council of Ministers. On the Council of Ministers, see para. 3.4.3, above.

84. The exception was where the Council of Ministers unanimously allowed otherwise.

85. Other than the right of establishment: EEC Treaty, Article 53.

86. See Case 9/70 *Grad v. Finanzamt Traunstein* [1970] ECR 825; [1971] 1 CMLR 1 and Case 20/76 *Schottle and Söhne OHG v. Finanzamt Traunstein* [1977] ECR 247; [1977] 2 CMLR 98.

87. Decision of 21 March 1962, JO 1962 720; OJ 1959-62, 96, amended by Decision 73/402, OJ 1973, L347/48.

Article 76 EEC and this decision are operative in the context of the progressive implementation of a common transport policy, the need for both will be reduced as the policy is implemented."[88]

The better view is that Article 76 is directly applicable.

Thus, in accordance with Articles 74[89] and 76, the Council of Ministers[90] adopted a Decision on 21 March 1962 (which has since been amended) to institute a procedure for the prior examination and consultation on certain laws, regulations and administrative provisions proposed by Member States relating to rail, road and inland waterway transport which are liable to interfere substantially with the implementation of the common transport policy. The procedure is two-fold: first, a Member State must notify the Commission and inform the other Member States of the proposed measure; and secondly, the Commission must address an Opinion or Recommendation to the relevant Member State and inform the other Member States of this Opinion or Recommendation.

4.2.2.7 Article 77

4.2.2.7.1 Text

"Aids shall be compatible with this Treaty if they meet the needs of co-ordination of transport or if they represent re-imbursement for the discharge of certain obligations inherent in the concept of a public service."

4.2.2.7.2 Commentary

Aids by States to transport are common[91] and need to be tightly controlled.[92]

Article 77 of the EEC Treaty provides that "aids shall be compatible with this Treaty if they meet the needs of co-ordination of transport or if they represent reimbursement for the discharge of certain obligations inherent in the concept of a public service".

Article 77 of the EEC Treaty is not an exception to the provisions contained in Articles 92 to 94 of that same Treaty on state aids[93]—instead it sets out two further forms of State aid which are permissible under Art. 92 of the EEC Treaty[94] namely, (a) aid which meet the needs of co-ordination of transport and (b) aid which represents reimbursement for the discharge of certain obligations inherent in the concept of a public service. Thus, Article 77 of the EEC Treaty should be read in conjunction with the other provisions of the EEC Treaty relating to State Aids.[95]

Kapteyn and Van Themaat make an interesting observation on Article 77:

"[t]he applicability to transport of Articles 92–94 EEC relating to aids was always assumed in the practice of the Commission and follows moreover from Article 77 EEC according to which state aids are deemed to be compatible with the Treaty if they meet the needs of co-ordination of transport or if they represent reimbursement for the discharge of certain obligations inherent in the concept of a 'public service'. It would of course be unnecessary to deem such aids compatible

88. *Op. cit.*, para. 19–06.
89. On Article 76 of the EEC Treaty, see para. 4.2.2.6, above.
90. On the Council of Ministers, see Chapter 3, above.
91. See para. 15.1, below.
92. See Chapter 15, below.
93. Case 156/77 *Commission v. Belgium* [1978] ECR 1881.
94. On Article 92 of the EEC Treaty, see Chapter 15, below.
95. Case 167/73 *Commission v. France* [1974] ECR 359; [1974] CMLR 216; Case 156/77 *Commission v. Belgium* [1978] ECR 1881.

if Article 92, according to which aids are in principle deemed incompatible with the common market, were not applicable. Article 77, therefore, is to be considered as a supplement to the exceptions to incompatibility mentioned in Article 92(2) and (3)."[96]

Article 77 is extended by means of secondary legislation. Regulation 1191/69[97] is a limitation on the public service obligations dimension to Article 77.[98] Articles 92 to 94 were applied by Regulation 1107/70[99] to road, rail and inland waterway transport.[100] It helped to clarify, in part, Regulation 1191/69.

4.2.2.8 Article 78

4.2.2.8.1 Text

"Any measures taken within the framework of this Treaty in respect of transport rates and conditions shall take account of the economic circumstances of carriers."

4.2.2.8.2 Commentary

Kapteyn and Van Themaat contend that Article 78 EEC implies "some sort of indication that the transport policy must be based on sound principles of economic rationality of transport, and that the concept of public service must not gain priority over principles of good economic management".[101,102] It is widely acknowledged that, to date, provision has been of little practical significance.[103]

4.2.2.9 Article 79

4.2.2.9.1 Text

"1. In the case of transport within the Community, discrimination which takes the form of carriers charging different rates and imposing different conditions for the carriage of the same goods over the same transport links on grounds of the country of origin or of destination of the goods in question, shall be abolished, at the latest, before the end of the second stage.

2. Paragraph 1 shall not prevent the Council[104] from adopting other measures in pursuance of Article 75(1)."

4.2.2.9.2 Commentary

Article 79 EEC sets out the general principle that in intra-EC trade, all discrimination taking the form of carriers charging different rates and imposing different conditions for the carriage of the same goods over the same transport links on the bases of the

96. *Op. cit.*, pp 713–14, footnote omitted.

97. JO 1969, L156/1; OJ 1969, 276.

98. This has been amended by the 1972, 1979 and 1985 Treaties of Accession as well as by Dec.73/101 (OJ L2/1, 1 January 1973).

99. JO 1970, L130, 15 June 1970, p.1; OJ 1970, 360.

100. This was both derogated from and extended by the 1972 Treaty of Accession; supplemented by Regulation 1658/82 (OJ L184/1, 29 June 1982); as well as amended by Regulation 1473/75 (OJ 1975, L152/1, 12 June 1975) and Regulation 1100/89 (OJ L116, 28 April 1989, p.24).

101. Article 78 EEC played a part in the elaboration of various measures, such as Dec.75/327 (OJ 1975 L152/3), relating to the improvement of the position of the railways.

102. *Op. cit.*, p. 717 (footnote reprinted in part).

103. See Parry and Hardy, *op. cit.*, para. 19–10.

104. *I.e.* the Council of Ministers. On the Council of Ministers, see para. 3.4.3, above.

country of origin or the country of destination must be abolished. Such discrimination was to be abolished by the end of the second stage of the transitional period. In essence, it required the abolition of discrimination in freight rates and conditions of EC transport.

In order to ensure the implementation of Article 79 EEC, the Council of Ministers adopted Regulation 11 of 27 June 1960[105] so as to oblige undertakings to notify their governments of any discriminatory practices (within the meaning of Article 79 EEC)[106] and to further oblige the governments to notify the Commission. Smit and Herzog were of the opinion that Regulation 11 enabled the Commission to impose upon carriers the burden of showing that their actions do not violate Article 79.[107]

It is to be presumed that this prohibition is directly applicable.[108,109]

4.2.2.10 Article 80

4.2.2.10.1 Text

"1. The imposition by a Member State, in respect of transport operations carried out within the Community, of rates and conditions involving any element of support or protection in the interest of one or more particular undertakings or industries shall be prohibited as from the beginning of the second stage,[110] unless authorised by the Commission.

2. The Commission shall, acting on its own initiative or on application by a Member State, examine the rates and conditions referred to in paragraph 1, taking account in particular of the requirements of an appropriate regional economic policy, the needs of underdeveloped areas and the problems of areas seriously affected by political circumstances on the one hand, and of the effects of such rates and conditions on competition between the different modes of transport on the other.

After consulting each Member State concerned, the Commission shall take the necessary decisions.

3. The prohibition provided for in paragraph 1 shall not apply to tariffs fixed to meet competition."

4.2.2.10.2 Commentary

Article 80 of the EEC Treaty[111] prohibits Member States imposing, in regard to transport operations carried out in the EC, rates and conditions[112] involving any element of support or protection in the interest of one or more particular undertakings or industries as and from the beginning of the second stage of the transitional period.

105. OJ English Special Edition, 1959–62, p.60. OJ No.52, 16 August 1960, p.1121. This Regulation was extended by the 1972 Treaty of Accession and amended by Regulation 3626/84 (OJ L335/4, 22 December 1984). See also the Commission Recommendation to the Member States on the application of Regulation 11 concerning the abolition of discrimination in transport rates and conditions, in implementation of Article 79(3) of the EEC Treaty (OJ No.50, 22 July 1961, p.975).

106. EEC Treaty, Article 5.

107. In *The Law of the European Community – A Commentary on the EEC Treaty* (1976), vol.2, para.74.04. On Article 79, see also Article 70 ELSC.

108. On the concept of direct applicability, see para. 3.5.3, above.

109. See Gaudet and Bayens (1969) *European Transport Law* 42; and Kapteyn and Van Themaat, *op. cit.*, p. 715, fn.169.

110. *I.e.*, the second stage of the development of the common market.

111. On Article 80 of the EEC Treaty, see, in particular, Case 1/69 *Italy v. Commission* [1969] ECR 277; [1970] CMLR 17.

112. See Joined Cases 3–18, 25, 26/58 *Barbara Erzberghau AG v. High Authority* [1960] ECR 173; Case 9/70 *Grad v. Finanzamt Traunstein* [1970] ECR 825; Case 20/70 *Transports Lesage & CIE v. Hauptzollamt Freiburg* [1970] ECR 861; [1971] CMLR 1.

This support or protection differs from a State Aid in that the benefit is a reduced transport bill rather than the direct payment of money. In essence, a Member State may not impose rates and conditions involving support or protection of undertakings.

Article 80(2) EEC provides that the Commission may however authorise the imposition of such support tariffs in exceptional cases. The exercise of this power is a matter of considerable significance.[113] In examining the rates and conditions, the Commission must take into account, on the one hand, the requirements of an appropriate regional policy and the needs of underdeveloped areas as well as, on the other hand, the problems of areas seriously affected by political circumstances.

It is to be presumed that Article 80 of the EEC Treaty is directly applicable.[114,115]

4.2.2.11 Article 81

4.2.2.11.1 Text

"Charges or dues in respect of the crossing of frontiers which are charged by a carrier in addition to the transport rates shall not exceed a reasonable level after taking the costs annually incurred thereby into account.

Member States shall endeavour to reduce these costs progressively.

The Commission may make recommendations to Member States for the application of this Article."

4.2.2.11.2 Commentary

Charges or dues in respect of crossing frontiers which are charged by a carrier in addition to the transport rates must not exceed a reasonable level and must be reduced progressively. It is important to note that the application of Art. 81 is left to the Member States and thus the Commission only has the power to make recommendations.

Commenting on Article 81 Parry and Hardy comment:

"Article 81 requires Member States to endeavour to reduce costs of charges or dues in respect of frontier crossings on a progressive basis. Although the article refers only to a reduction of these dues, the ultimate aim is complete elimination of such charges, for with the elimination of internal customs duties these charges can become substantial barriers to trade, and yet have no economic value to the transporter. The transporters in turn are required to pass on no more than a reasonable charge, having regard to the cost actually incurred. The Commission is given a power to make recommendations for the application of these provisions. The provision is probably now of marginal importance in view of the wide interpretation given to the provisions on elimination of measures having equivalent effect to quantitative restrictions."[116]

4.2.2.12 Article 82

4.2.2.12.1 Text

"The provisions of this Title shall not form an obstacle to the application of measures taken in the Federal Republic of Germany to the extent that such measures are required in order to

113. Case 1/69 *Italy v. Commission* [1969] ECR 277; [1970] CMLR 17 and Case 2/84 *Commission v. Italy* [1985] ECR 1127.

114. On the concept of direct applicability, see para. 3.5.3, above.

115. See Gaudet and Bayens (1969) *European Transport Law* 42; and Kapteyn and Van Themaat, *op. cit.*, p.715, fn 169.

116. *Op. cit.*, para.19-13.

compensate for the economic disadvantages caused by the division of Germany to the economy of certain areas of the Federal Republic affected by that division."

4.2.2.12.2 Commentary

Article 82 was a special provision in relation to Germany because of the divided nature of that country before unification in 1990.

4.2.2.13 Article 83

4.2.2.13.1 Text

"An Advisory Committee consisting of experts designated by the Governments of Member States, shall be attached to the Commission. The Commission, whenever it considers it desirable, shall consult the Committee on transport matters without prejudice to the powers of the transport section of the Economic and Social Committee."

4.2.2.13.2 Commentary

Article 83 allows for the establishment of a Transport Advisory Committee consisting of experts designated by the governments of the Member States. It would be attached to the Commission. This specific Treaty reference to the formation of an Advisory Committee (of which there are very few established under the Treaty) is indicative of the significance attached to transport by the framers of the Treaty. It would be independent of the Economic and Social Committee (ECOSOC).[117] The function of the Transport Committee would be more in the preparation of proposals rather than in the consideration of published proposals.

The rules of the Transport Committee were adopted in 1958[118] and amended in 1964.[119] It gives advice to the Commission.[120]

Council Decision 78/174 instituted a consultation procedure and set up a committee in the field of transport infrastructure.[121]

Commission Decision 80/991/EEC set up a Joint Committee on Inland Navigation.[122]

Commission Decision 85/13/EEC related to the setting up of a Joint Committee on Railways.[123]

Commission Decision 85/516/EEC set up a Joint Committee on Road Transport.[124] This Decision was later amended.[125]

Commission Decision 87/467/EEC set up a Joint Committee on Maritime Transport.[126]

Commission Decision 90/449/EEC set up a Joint Committee on Civil Aviation. [127]

117. On the ECOSOC, see para. 3.4.7.1, above.
118. OJ No.25, 27 November 1958, p. 509; OJ 1957–8, p. 72 (as amended).
119. See Dec.64/390/EEC, OJ P102, 29 June 1964, p. 1602. See also *Halsbury's Laws of England*, vol. 52, para. 18.32.
120. On the Commission, see para. 3.4.2, above.
121. OJ L54/16, 25 February 1978.
122. OJ L297/28, 6 November 1980.
123. OJ L8/26, 10 January 1985.
124. OJ L317/33, 28 November 1985.
125. See Decision 87/447/EEC (OJ L240/37, 22 August 1987).
126. OL 253/20, 4 September 1987.
127. OJ L 230/22, 24 August 1990.

4.2.2.14 Article 84

4.2.2.14.1 Text

"1. The provisions of this Title shall apply to transport by rail, road and inland waterway.

2. The Council may, acting by a qualified majority, decide whether, to what extent and by what procedure appropriate provisions may be laid down for sea and air transport.

The procedural provisions of Article 75(1) and (3) shall apply."

4.2.2.14.2 Commentary

It has been written that the specific mention of air, inland waterway, rail, road and sea in Article 84[128] excludes other forms of transport (such as pipelines) from the application of the Title on Transport.[129]

Article 84(2) (which is contained in Title IV (Part Two) of the EEC Treaty) is an empowering provision. It *prima facie* excludes sea and air transport from the CTP. It *allows* for provisions to be laid down for sea and air transport by the Council acting unanimously. The paragraph was inserted due to the wishes of The Netherlands who sought to have very little (if any) involvement by the EC in shipping matters. If the UK had been part of the original members of the EC then it would have been interesting to have seen its reaction to the inclusion of the second paragraph.

The second paragraph (as originally drafted) was a curiously drafted and novel provision in the EEC Treaty. It did not follow the pattern of similar provisions – they provide for the adoption[130] of measures by the Council of Ministers after a proposal by the Commission and the giving of opinions by the Parliament as well as the Economic and Social Committee – but this paragraph spoke simply of the Council acting unanimously to decide whether, to what extent and by what procedure appropriate provisions may be laid down for sea and air transport.

The European Parliament's Committee on Regional Policy, Regional Planning and Transport published an Interim Report on the Sea Transport Problems in the Community in 1977 in which it said:

"The [EEC] Treaty . . . excludes sea and air transport from the common transport policy. . . . There is no point in asking why the authors of the Treaty left sea transport out of the Common Transport policy during the negotiations at Val Duchesse in 1957. . . . It may be that they simply could not agree on rules for sea transport or that they intended to draw up special rules for sea transport but did not have the time before the Treaty was pronounced ready for signature by the Heads of Government, or they had specific reasons for excluding sea transport which are unknown to us."[131]

Article 84(2) EEC, before its amendment by Article 16 of the Single European Act, was described as a "notorious paragraph" which gave rise "to diametrically opposed interpretations".[132] After its amendment by the SEA, it reads: "The Council may, acting by a qualified majority, decide whether, to what extent and by what procedure

128. See Close, "Article 84 EEC: The Development of Transport Policy in the Sea and Air Sectors" (1980) 5 *European Law Review* 188.

129. See Close, "The Development of Transport Policy in the Sea and Air Sectors" (1980) 5 EL Rev. 189. See also Case 97/78 *Schumalla* [1978] ECR 2311.

130. Initially by unanimous vote and later by a qualified majority.

131. Working Documents; Doc.5/77; 23 March 1977; Rapporteur: Mr. H. Seefeld, paras 1 and 3.

132. Bird, "Further Debate on the Treaty of Rome, Article 84, Paragraph 2 as it may affect Maritime Transport" (1966) 2 *European Transport Law* 24, at p. 24.

appropriate provisions may be laid down for sea and air transport. The procedural provisions of Article 75(1) and (3) shall apply."

Prior to 1974, it was believed by many commentators that air and sea transport fell outside the scope of the Treaty because of Article 84(2) of the EEC Treaty. This restrictive view was adopted by many of the Member States. Not surprisingly, the Commission adopted a broader perspective. Article 84 EEC fell to be considered by the ECJ in Case 167/73 *Commission v. France*.[133] The case came about because of the accession to the EC of Ireland and the UK—two islands—which prompted the Commission to bring a test case to test the point. The net point was whether the rest of the EEC Treaty applied to sea transport. In that case, the Commission brought an action on the basis of Article 169 EEC[134] for a declaration that by not repealing, in so far as it affects the nationals of other EC Member States, the provisions of s. 3(2) of the French Merchant Seamen Code of 13 December 1926 (as amended by Order No. 58-1358 of 27 December 1958), the French Republic had not complied with its obligations under the provisions of the EEC Treaty relating to freedom of movement for workers generally and Articles 1, 4 and 7 of Council Regulation 1612/68 of 15 October 1968 on the freedom of movement of workers within the EC.[135] Section 3(2) of the French Act had provided that such proportion (as may be laid down by the French Minister of the Merchant Marine) of the crew of a French ship must be of French nationality.

The French Minister of the Merchant Marine had made an Order on 21 November 1960 (as amended on 12 June 1969) that, apart from special exemptions granted by particular competent local administrative authorities, the employment of seafarers on the bridge and in the engine rooms of merchant ships, fishing vessels or pleasure cruisers was reserved for French nationals and the employment generally was limited in the ratio of three-to-one. The Commission argued that such restrictions were incompatible with EC law. France argued, *inter alia*, that the rules of the EEC Treaty regarding freedom of movement for workers did not apply to transport and, in any event, not to maritime transport so long as the Council of Ministers had not so decided under Article 84(2) of the EEC Treaty. It is interesting to read the ECJ's judgment on the point:

"17. To determine whether, in the sphere of transport, Member-States are bound by the obligations provided in Articles 48 to 51 of the Treaty, it is proper to consider the place of Title IV of Part Two of the [EEC] Treaty, relating to transport, in the general system of the Treaty, and the place of Article 84(2) within Title IV.

18. Under Article 2 of the Treaty,[136] which is placed at the head of the general principles which govern it, the Community has as its task to promote throughout the Community a harmonious development of economic activities by establishing a Common Market and progressively approximating the economic policies of member-States.

19. The establishment of the Common Market thus refers to the whole of the economic activities in the Community.

20. The basic object of Part Two of the Treaty, devoted to the foundations of the Community, is to establish the basis of the Common Market, i.e. free movement of goods (Title I) and free movement of persons, services and capital (Title III).

21. Conceived as being applicable to the whole complex of economic activities, these basic rules can be rendered inapplicable only as a result of express provision in the Treaty.

133. [1974] ECR 359; [1974] 2 CMLR 216.
134. On Article 169 of the EEC Treaty, see para. 3.4.6.6.2, above.
135. On Regulation 1612/68, see Chapter 4, below.
136. On Article 2 of the EEC Treaty, see Chapter 3, above.

22. Such exemption is provided, in particular, by Article 38(2) under which the rules laid down for the establishment of the Common Market shall apply to agricultural products save as provided in Title II of this part of the Treaty.
23. As regards transport, which is the subject of Title IV of this part, it is proper to enquire, viewing Article 84(2) in the framework of this Title, whether the provisions of the Title contain a similar exemption.
24. When Article 74[137] refers to the objectives of the Treaty, it means the provisions of Articles 2 and 3, for the attainment of which the fundamental provisions applicable to the whole complex of economic activity are of prime importance.
25. Far from involving a departure from these fundamental rules, therefore, the object of the rules relating to the common transport policy is to implement and complement them by means of common action.
26. Consequently the said general rules must be applied in so far as they can achieve these objectives.
27. Since transport is basically a service, it has been found necessary to provide a special system for it, taking into account the special aspects of this branch of activity.
28. With this object, a special exemption has been provided by Article 61(1),[138] under which freedom to provide services in the field of transport 'shall be governed by the provisions of the Title relating to transport', thus confirming that the general rules of the Treaty must be applied insofar as they are not excluded.
29. Article 84(1) provides that the provisions of the Title relating to transport shall apply to transport by rail, road and inland waterway.
30. Article 84(2) provides that as regards maritime transport, the Council may decide whether, to what extent and by what procedure appropriate provisions may be laid down.
31. Far from excluding the application of the Treaty to these matters, it provides only that the special provisions of the Title relating to transport shall not automatically apply to them.
32. Whilst under Article 84(2), therefore, sea and air transport, so long as the Council has not decided otherwise, is excluded from the rules of Title IV of Part Two of the Treaty relating to the common transport policy, it remains, on the same basis as the other modes of transport, subject to the general rules of the Treaty.
33. It thus follows that the application of Articles 48 to 51 to the sphere of maritime transport is not optional but obligatory for member-States."

The European Court of Justice went on to state that in maintaining unamended the provisions of section 3(2) of the Merchant Seamen Code as regards the nationals of other Member States, France had failed to fulfil its obligations under Article 48 EEC and Article 4 of Regulation 1612/68.[139]

The regulation of maritime and air transport is provided for by Article 84(2) of the EEC Treaty (as amended by Article 16 of the Single European Act).

The EEC has been slow to act in terms of adopting a common transport policy (CTP). The Parliament instituted proceedings in the European Court of Justice against the Council of Ministers for failure to act.[140]

4.2.2.15 Relationship between the ECSC Treaty and the EEC Treaty

Article 232 of the EEC Treaty provides that that Treaty shall apply in relation to matters not already covered by the ECSC Treaty. Thus, the EEC Treaty can have application to the transport of coal and steel.

137. On Article 74 of the EEC Treaty, see para.4.2.2.4, above.
138. On Article 61(1) EEC, see para.4.2.2.3, above.
139. See Case 167/73 *Commission v. France* [1974] ECR 359; [1974] 2 CMLR 216 in the context of Article 48 EEC.
140. Case 13/83 *European Parliament v. EC Council* [1985] ECR 1513; [1986] 1 CMLR 138.

4.3 TRANSPORT SECTORS

This section examines the principal EC measures relating to each transport mode or sector. Some measures which are limited in scope to particular states are not examined. Some measures of limited interest have been excluded.

4.3.1 Road transport

4.3.1.1 Introduction

Road transport is of critical concern to the EC.[141] Some 80% of all the passenger inland transport market is met by the private motor car sector with the coach and bus service on the one hand and the railways on the other accounting for 10% each.[142] In terms of coach and bus passenger transport,[143] there are a large number of small operators who work in local or national markets and only a small number of transnational operators.

There has been significant progress in the area of road transport in recent years—for example, quantitative controls or restrictions on market entry are being phased out and are to be abolished by 1 January 1993.

For present purposes, it is worth noting that there is need for a connection to be drawn between a Member State's Ports Policy and its road transport policy.[144]

4.3.1.2 1962 Directive

The First Council Directive of 23 July 1962[145] (as amended[146]) established the common rules for the international carriage of certain goods between Member States. The Directive exempts the carriage of certain types of carriage of goods from any transport quota or authorisation system. The Directive goes on to provide that the carriage of certain other types of carriage of goods are subject to authorisation but there may be no quantitative restrictions involved.

4.3.1.3 Directive 65/269

On 13 May 1965 the Council of Ministers adopted Directive 65/269 concerning the standardisation of certain rules relating to authorisations for the carriage of goods by road between Member States.[147]

141. On EC road law and policy, see Turvey, *The Analysis of Economic Costs and Expenses in Road and Rail Transport*, Studies Transport Series No. 4, Brussels, April 1975.

142. *Panorama of EC Industry 1990*, 25–11.

143. *Panorama of EC Industry 1990*, 25–11.

144. See, for example, Commission Decision 85/67 (OJ L30/22, 2 February 1985).

145. OJ No. 70, 6 August 1962, p.2005.

146. As amended by Act of Accession 1972; Council Decision 72/426 (OJ L291/155, 28 December 1972); Council Directive 74/149/EEC (OJ L84/8, 29 March 1974); Council Directive 77/158/EEC (OJ L48/30, 19 February 1977); Council Directive 78/175/EEC (OJ L54/18, 25 February 1978); Council Directive 80/49/EEC (OJ L18, 24 January 1980, p.23); Council Directive 82/50/EEC (OJ L27/22, 4 February 1982); Council Directive 83/572/EEC (OJ L332/33, 28 November 1983) and Council Directive 84/647/EEC (OJ L335/72, 22 December 1984).

147. OJ 88/1469, 24 May 1965 (as amended). See also Commission Recommendation 741/67 (OJ 296/9, 6 December 1967) and Regulation 1016/68 prescribing the model control documents referred to in Articles 6 and 9 of Council Regulation 117/66/EEC.

4.3.1.3a Regulation 117/66

Regulation 117/66/EEC[148] (as amended[149]) introduced common rules for the international carriage of passengers by coach and bus.

4.3.1.4 Regulation 1018/68

One of the most serious issues in EC road transport law is that relating to the capacity of carriers from each Member State to operate throughout the EC without authorisation by Member States. Regulation 1018/68[150] allocated to EC Member States various quotas of EC-wide permits.

4.3.1.5 Regulation 543/69

Regulation 543/69[151] provided for compulsory minimum rest periods for truck-drivers.

4.3.1.6 Regulation 516/72

Regulation 516/72[152] (as amended[153]) introduced common rules for shuttle services by coach and bus between Member States.

4.3.1.7 Regulation 517/72

Regulation 517/72[154] (as amended[155]) introduced common rules for regular and special regular services.

4.3.1.8 1972 ASOR

In 1972, the Agreement on the International Carriage of Passengers by Road by means of Occasional Coach and Bus Services (ASOR) was signed by representatives of the EC Member States and some other European States (including Norway, Sweden and Finland).[156]

4.3.1.9 Directive 74/561

Council Directive 74/561 of 12 November 1974, sets out the rules on admission to the occupation of road haulage operator in national and international transport operations.[157]

148. OJ 147, 9 August 1966, p. 2688.
149. See Act of Accession 1972; Commission Regulation 1016/68/EEC (OJ L173, 22 July 1968, p. 8).
150. OJ 1968 L175/13.
151. JO 1969, L77/49; OJ 1969(1), 170. See Case 69/74 *Auditeur du Travail v. Cagnon et Taquet* [1975] ECR 171; Case 65/76 *Derycke* [1977] ECR 29; Case 47/79 *Nehlsen v. Bremen* [1979] ECR 3639.
152. OJ L67, 20 March 1972, p. 13.
153. Council Regulation (EEC) No.2442/72 (OJ L265, 24 November 1972, p. 7) and Council Regulation No.2778/78 (OJ L333, 30 November 1978, p. 4).
154. OJ L67, 20 March 1972, p. 19.
155. Council Regulation (EEC) No. 2442/72 (OJ L265, 24 November 1972, p. 7), Council Regulation (EEC) No. 1301/78 (OJ L158, 16 June 1978, p. 1). See also Regulation 1172/72 prescribing the form of the documents referred to in Council Regulation 517/72 and Council Regulation 516/72 (OJ L 134/1, 12 June 1972).
156. Signed in Dublin on 26 May 1982. The Agreement was approved on behalf of the EC by Council Decision 82/505/EEC (OJ L230, 5 August 1982, p. 38).
157. OJ L308/18, 19 November 1974 (as amended).

4.3.1.10 Directive 74/562

Council Directive 74/562 of 12 November 1974 sets out the rules on admission to the occupation of road transport operator in national and international transport operations.[158]

4.3.1.11 Directive 76/914

On 16 December 1976 the Council of Ministers adopted Directive 76/914 on the minimum level of training for some road transport drivers.[159]

4.3.1.12 Regulation 3237/76

On 21 December 1976, the Council of Ministers adopted Regulation 3237/76 on the advance implementation of the Technical Annexes and the advance use of the specimen TIR carnet of the Customs Convention on the international transport of goods under cover of TIR carnets (TIR Convention) of 14 November 1975.[160] This was later amended by Regulation 3020/81.[161]

4.3.1.13 1978 Customs Convention

The Customs Convention on the international transport of goods under cover of TIR carnets (the TIR Convention).[162]

4.3.1.15 Decision of 25 June 1979

The Council of Ministers adopted a Decision on 25 June 1979 on the acceptance of Resolution No.119 of the United Nations Commission for Europe which was intended to standardize the forms used for authorisations for international goods transported by road so as to facilitate road transport.

4.3.1.16 1981 TIR Convention

The Customs Convention on the international transport of goods under cover of TIR carnets of 14 November 1981 (the so-called TIR Convention) is of obvious significance in road transport.[163] In 1976, the Council of Ministers adopted a regulation, Regulation 3237/76[164] on the advance implementation of the Technical Annexes and the advance use of the specimen TIR carnet of the Customs Convention on the international transport of goods under cover of TIR carnets. Later, on 1 December 1986, the Council of Ministers adopted Regulation 3690/86[165] which concerned the abolition within the framework of the TIR Convention of customs facilities on exit from a Member State at a frontier between two Member States.[166]

158. OJ L308/23, 19 November 1974 (as amended).
159. OJ L357/36, 29 December 1976.
160. OJ L368/1, 31 December 1976.
161. OJ L302/6, 23 October 1981.
162. OJ L252/2, 14 September 1978. Implemented by Regulation 2112/78 OJ L 252/1, 14 September 1978.
163. OJ L252/2, 14 September 1978.
164. OJ L368/1, 31 December 1976 (as amended by Regulation 3020/81, OJ L302/6, 23 October 1981).
165. OJ L341/1, 4 December 1986. On the legal effect of a regulation, see para.3.5.2.2.1, above.
166. This was implemented by Regulation 1544/87 (OJ L144/7, 4 June 1987). On the legal effect of a Regulation, see Chapter 3, above.

4.3.1.17 ASOR Agreement

The Agreement on the International Carriage of Passengers by Road by means of occasional coach and bus service (ASOR) is worth noting.[167] This was agreed by the EC States as well as some other European States.

4.3.1.18 Directive 83/463

On 1 December 1983, the Council of Ministers adopted a Directive on the facilitation of physical inspections and administrative formalities in respect of the carriage of goods between Member States.[168]

4.3.1.19 Directive 84/647

In 1984, the Council of Ministers adopted Directive 84/647/EEC so as to make provision for the use of vehicles hired without drivers for the carriage of goods by road.[169]

4.3.1.20 Regulation 3690/86

The Council of Ministers adopted Regulation 3690/86 on 1 December 1986.[170] The regulation concerned the abolition within the framework of the TIR Convention of customs formalities on exit from a Member State at a frontier between two Member States. The regulation was implemented by Directive 87/1544.[171]

4.3.1.21 Regulation 1841/88

Regulation No.1841/88 quotas.[172]

4.3.1.22 Regulation 4059/89

Regulation 4059/89 laid down the conditions under which non-resident carriers may operate national road haulage services within a Member State. It was an important milestone on the road towards freedom to provide road services in the EC.

4.3.1.23 Regulation 3916/90

On 21 December 1990 the Council of Ministers adopted Regulation 3916/90 on measures to be taken in the event of a crisis in the market concerning the carriage of goods by road.[173]

167. OJ L230/39, 5 August 1982.
168. OJ L359/8, 22 December 1983. This Directive has been amended by Dir.87/53 (OJ L24/33, 27 January 1987).
169. OJ L335/72, 22 December 1984 (as amended by Dir. 90/398 OJ L202/46, 31 July 1990).
170. OJ L341/1, 4 December 1986.
171. OJ L144/7, 4 June 1987.
172. OJ L163, 30 June 1988.
173. OJ L375/10, 31 December 1990.

4.3.2 Rail transport

4.3.2.1 Introduction

Railways play an important role in the social life of the EC: they link many rural areas with urban centres.[174] None the less they have suffered a decline, in both passengers and freight carried, over the past few years relative to other modes of transport. Their share of the merchandise transported within the EC fell from 18% to 14% during the 1984–1989 period.

EC railway policy has tended to focus in on freight as opposed to passenger traffic. Its purpose has been to harmonise the financial aids given to railways and to generally improve the situation of railways.

Railways have always proved difficult to regulate. They are heavily subsidised[175] and they often serve a social function[176] An important issue relating to railways in the EC is their public service obligations.

4.3.2.2 Regulation 1192/69

On 26 June 1969, the Council of Ministers adopted Regulation 1192/69 on common rules for the normalisation of the accounts of railway undertakings.[177]

4.3.2.3 1970 Resolution

On 7 December 1970, the Council of Ministers adopted a Resolution on co-operation between railway undertakings.[178]

4.3.2.4 Decision 75/327

The Council of Ministers decided on 20 May 1975 to adopt Decision 75/327/EEC on the improvement of the situation of railway undertakings and the harmonisation of rules governing financial relations between such undertakings and States.[179]

4.3.2.5 Regulation 2830/77

On 12 December 1977, the Council of Ministers adopted Regulation 2830/77 on the measures necessary to achieve compatibility between the accounting systems and annual accounts of railway undertakings.[180]

174. See *Bulletin of the EC, No. 12, 1980, point 1.6.2.* See also Van Miert, "Railways with a European Dimension . . . and Fit for the Single Market", *Target 92*, August-September 1991, p. 1. On EC railway law and policy, see Turvey, *The Analysis of Economic Costs and Expenses in Road and Rail Transport*, Studies Transport Series No. 4, Brussels, April 1975.

175. It has been estimated that the level of this subsidy in the early 1980s was in the order of 20 billion ECU. see Nicoll and Salmon, *op. cit.*, p. 186.

176. An important issue relating to railways in the EC is their public service obligations.

177. OJ L156/8, 28 June 1969. This was amended by the 1972, 1979 and 1985 Treaties of Accession as well as Decision 101/73 (OJ L2/1, 1 January 1973).

178. OJ C5/1, 19 January 1971.

179. OJ L152/3, 12 June 1975. This was amended by the 1979 Treaty of Accession and supplemented by the 1985 Treaty of Accession. See also Regulation 3572/90 (OJ L353/12, 17 December 1990) and Dir. 91/440 (OJ L237/25, 24 August 1991).

180. OJ L334/13, 24 December 1977. This was amended by the 1979 Treaty of Accession and supplemented by the 1985 Treaty of Accession.

4.3.2.6 Regulation 2183/78

On 19 September 1978, the Council of Ministers adopted Regulation 2183/78 so as to lay down uniform costing principles for railway undertakings.[181]

4.3.2.7 Directive 80/1177

On 4 December 1980 the Council of Ministers adopted Directive 80/1177/EEC on statistical returns in respect of carriage of goods by rail, as part of regional statistics.[182]

4.3.2.8 1981 Resolution

The Council of Ministers adopted a Resolution on Community railway policy on 15 December 1981.[183]

4.3.2.9 Decision 82/529

Decision 82/529/EEC of 19 July 1982 set out rules on the fixing of rates for the international carriage of goods by rail.[184]

4.3.2.10 Decision 83/418

Council of Ministers Decision 83/418 of 25 July 1983 related to the commercial independence of the railways in the management of their international passenger and luggage traffic.[185]

4.3.2.11 1984 Recommendation

In 1984, the Council of Ministers adopted a recommendation[186] on the strengthening of co-operation of the national railway companies of the EC Member States in international passenger and goods transport.

4.3.2.12 1991 Package of Measures

On 29 July 1991, the Council of Ministers adopted Directive 91/440 on the development of the Community's railways.[187]

4.3.3 Air transport

4.3.3.1 Introduction

It would be quite beyond the scope of the present book to provide a detailed account of EC air transport law: a simple overview will suffice for present purposes.[188]

181. OJ L334/13, 24 December 1977. This was amended by the 1979 Treaty of Accession and supplemented by the 1985 Treaty of Accession.

182. OJ L350/23, 23 December 1980 (as amended).

183. OJ C157/1, 22 June 1982.

184. OJ L234/5, 9 August 1982 (as amended).

185. OJ L237/32, 26 August 1983. This was amended by the 1985 Treaty of Accession. See also Regulation 3572/90 (OJ L353/12, 17 December 1990).

186. Recommendation 646/84, OJ L333/63, 21 December 1984. On the legal effect of *a recommendation*, see Chapter 3, above.

187. OJ L237/25, 24 August 1991.

188. For a more detailed examination of this vast topic, see Baldwin, *Regulating the Airlines: Administrative Justice and Agency Discretion* (1985); Shawcross and Beaumont, *Air Law*, Division IX; Frere

For many years, air transport in the EC was more State-regulated,[189] expensive and State-supported than in most other parts of the world. Traditionally, air transport has been regulated by the Member States themselves and not the EC. The development of an EC-centred air transport policy has been hampered by the fact that the traditional approach to airline regulation is a State-sovereignty centred approach. Articles 1 and 6 of the Chicago Convention 1944 provide that each State has complete and exclusive sovereignty over its airspace. Thus, bilateral and multilateral agreements were the only ways of providing regulation.

EC air transport law owes its real origin to the Commission's first proposals in this area in 1979. In that year, the Commission published a memorandum outlining a number of proposals for legislation.[190] This led to Council Directive 83/416/EEC[191] on scheduled inter-regional air services which has since been revoked.

The 1979 memorandum was followed by another from the Commission in 1984 which was entitled "Progress Towards the Development of a Community Air Transport Policy".[192] The Council of Ministers did not immediately act on it.

The development of EC air transport law has been stimulated by such cases in the ECJ as Cases 209-213/84 *Ministere Public v. Lucas Asjes* (the so-called *Nouvelles Frontières* case).

In December 1987, the Council of Ministers finally agreed on a number of proposals in the "Progress Towards the Development of a Community Air Transport Policy"[193] memorandum. In specific terms, the Council of Ministers adopted measures on fares, capacity and access.[194] These measures are now referred to as the "first package". The significance of these measures is that they represent a diminution of the sovereignty of states in respect of air transport. The package applies to international air transport between Member State airports.

The Council of Ministers has adopted the so-called "second package'[195] in July 1990 which took effect from 1 November 1990. This package revoked the "first package" and introduced a more liberal regime but not as liberal a regime as originally proposed by the Commission.[196]

For many years, there was no secondary legislation allowing for EC competition law[197] to apply to air transport. This was due to Regulation 141/62/EEC[198] being specifically disapplied by Regulation 17/62/EEC.[199] This was similar to shipping. It is important to remember that despite the absence of such secondary rules, competition

Chormeley, *Air Law and the European Community* (1990) (this book was written by John Balfour); Close, "Article 84 EEC: The Development of Transport Policy in the Sea and Air Sections" (1980) 5 EL Rev. 188; Dagtoolou, "Air Transport and the European Communities" (1981) 6 EL Rev. 335, at p. 356.

189. States are heavily involved in this sector by their ownership and regulation.

190. "Contribution of the European Communities to the Development of Air Transport Services", EC Bull.Supp. 5/79.

191. OJ L237/19, 26 August 1983.

192. COM(84)72.

193. COM(84)72.

194. Council Directive 87/601/EEC (OJ L374/12, 31 December 1987) and Council Directive 87/602/EEC (OJ L374/19, 31 December 1987).

195. Council Regulation (EEC) 2342/90 (OJ L217/1, 11 August 1990) and Council Regulation 2343/90 (OJ L217/8, 11 August 1990).

196. See OJ C258/3, 11 October 1989. There is nothing preventing Member States from concluding or maintaining more liberal agreements.

197. On EC competition law generally, and EC competition law in relation to shipping, see Chapters 9 and 10, below.

198. OJ 1962, 29 November 1962, p. 2751.

199. OJ L13, 21 February 1961, p. 204.

law still applied to air transport.[200] Secondary legislation was however adopted in December 1987. This was modified in part in July 1990.

From 1 August 1990, the Commission has been assisted by a Joint Committee on Civil Aviation. This body, which was created by the Commission,[201] is composed of 50 people drawn from airlines, airports and employees' associations. Its purpose is to issue opinions and submit reports to the Commission on matters relating to the airline industry.

Thc 1992 Programme[202] has also stimulated activity. It is highly unlikely that a single market in air transport services will be created by the end of 1992 (the date scheduled for the completion of the Internal Market), but considerable progress will have been recorded by then.

4.3.3.2 A review of the measures adopted in the field of air transport

4.3.3.2.1 Council Decision 80/50

On 20 December 1979, the Council of Ministers adopted Decision 80/50 setting up a consultation procedure on relations between Member States and third countries in the field of air transport and on action relating to such matters within international organisations (such as ICAO).[203]

4.3.3.2.2. Council Directive 80/51

The Council of Ministers adopted Directive 80/51 on 20 December 1979 on the limitation of noise emissions from subsonic aircraft.[204] This was later amended by Directive 83/206.[205]

4.3.3.2.3 Council Directive 80/1266

On 16 December 1980, the Council of Ministers adopted Directive 80/1266 on future co-operation and mutual assistance between the Member States in the field of air accident investigation.[206]

4.3.3.2.4 Council Recommendation 81/560

On 13 July 1981, the Council of Ministers adopted Recommendation 81/560 on the carriage of express low weight cargo by air.[207]

200. See Cases 209-213/84 *Ministère Public v. Lucas Asjses* [1986] ECR 1425; [1986] 3 CMLR 173 and Case 66/86 *Ahmed Saeed Flugreisen and Silver Line Reisburo v. Zentrale zur Bekämpfung Unlauteren Wettbewerbs* [1990] 4 CMLR 102. See also Case 246/81 *Lord Bethell v. EC Commission* [1982] ECR 2277; [1982] 3 CMLR 300.

201. Commission Decision (EEC) 90/449 (OJ L230/22, 24 August 1990).

202. On the 1992 Programme generally, see Chapter 26, below.

203. OJ L18/24, 24 January 1980.

204. OJ L18/26, 24 January 1980.

205. OJ L363/27, 13 December 1989.

206. OJ L375/32, 31 December 1980.

207. OJ L203/51, 23 July 1981.

4.3.3.2.5 Council Directive 83/416

The Council of Ministers adopted Directive 83/416 on 25 July 1983 on the authorisation of scheduled inter-regional air services for the transport of passengers, mail and cargo between Member States.[208] This was supplemented by 1985 Act of Accession for Greece. It was also amended by two subsequent directives, Directive 86/216[209] and Directive 89/463.[210]

4.3.3.2.6 Council Directive 86/216

On 26 May 1986, the Council of Ministers adopted Directive 86/216 amending, on account of the accession of Portugal, Directive 83/416/EEC[211] concerning the authorisation of scheduled inter-regional air services for the transport of passengers, mail and cargo between Member States.[212]

4.3.3.2.7 Council Directive 87/601

The Council of Ministers adopted Directive 87/601 on 14 December 1987 on fares for scheduled air services between Member States.[213]

4.3.3.2.8 Council Decision 87/602

The Council of Ministers adopted Decision 87/602 on 14 December 1987 on the sharing of passenger capacity between air carriers on scheduled air services between Member States and on access for air carriers to scheduled air-service routes between Member States.[214]

4.3.3.2.9 Decision 87/359/EEC

The Commission adopted Decision 87/359/EEC on 22 June 1987 on reductions in air and sea transport fares available only to Spanish nationals resident in the Canary Islands and the Balearic Islands.[215]

4.3.3.2.10 Council Regulation 3975/87/EEC

Council Regulation 3975/87/EEC of 14 December 1987 lays down the procedure for the application of the rules on competition to undertakings in the transport sector.[216] This was implemented by Regulation 4261/88.[217] The application of competition law to air transport has had dramatic implications for the industry: there has been a dramatic reduction in air fares; an increase in routes; and a greater challenge for the airlines leading many to improve the quality of their services.[218]

208. OJ L237/19, 26 August 1983.
209. OJ L152/47, 6 June 1986.
210. OJ L226/14, 3 August 1989.
211. On which, see Chapter 4, above.
212. OJ L152/47, 6 June 1986.
213. OJ L374/12, 31 December 1987.
214. OJ L374/19, 31 December 1987.
215. OJ L194, 15 July 1987, p. 28.
216. OJ L374/1, 31 December 1987.
217. OJ L376/10, 31 December 1988. It was amended by Regulation 1284/91 (OJ L122/2, 17 May 1991).
218. On competition and air transport generally. See also various articles in *Lloyd's List*, including, 31 March 1987 (p. 1) on airline cartels.

4.3.3.2.11 Council Directive 80/51

On 20 December 1979 the Council of Ministers adopted Directive 80/51 on the limitation of noise emissions from subsonic aircraft.[219]

4.3.3.2.12 Council Regulation 3976/87/EEC

Council Regulation 3976/87/EEC of 14 December 1987 applied Article 85(3) of the EEC Treaty to certain categories of agreements and concerted practices in the air transport sector.[220] This has been amended by Regulation 2344/90.[221]

4.3.3.2.13 Commission Regulation 2671/88

On 26 July 1988, the Commission adopted Regulation 2671/88 on the application of Article 85(3) of the EEC Treaty to certain categories of agreements between undertakings, decisions of associations of undertakings and concerted practices concerning joint planning and co-ordination of capacity, sharing of revenue and consultation on tariffs on scheduled air services and slot allocation at airports.[222]

4.3.3.2.14 Commission Regulation 2672/88

On 26 July 1988, the Commission adopted Regulation No.2672/88 on the application of Article 85(3) of the EEC Treaty to certain categories of agreements between undertakings relating to computer reservation systems for air transport services.[223]

4.3.3.2.15 Commission Regulation 2673/88

Again on 26 July 1988, the Commission adopted Regulation 2673/88 on the application of Article 85(3) of the EEC Treaty to certain categories of agreements between undertakings, decisions of associations of undertakings and concerted practices concerning ground handling services.[224]

4.3.3.2.16 Commission Regulation 4261/88

On 16 December 1988, the Commission adopted Regulation 4261/88 on the complaints, applications and hearings provided for in Council Regulation No.3975/87 (EEC) laying down the procedure for the application of the rules on competition to undertakings in the air transport sector.[225]

4.3.3.2.17 Council Regulation 2299/89

The Council of Ministers adopted Regulation 2299/89 on 24 July 1989 on a code of conduct for computerised reservation systems.[226]

219. OJ L18/26, 24 January 1980 (as amended) by Directive 83/206 (OJ L117/15, 4 May 1983).
220. OJ L374/9, 31 December 1987.
221. OJ L217/15, 11 August 1990.
222. OJ L239/9, 30 August 1988.
223. OJ L239/13, 30 August 1988.
224. OJ L239.17, 30 August 1988.
225. OJ L376/10, 31 December 1988.
226. OJ L220/1, 29 July 1989.

4.3.3.2.18 Council Directive 89/629

On 4 December 1989 the Council of Ministers adopted Directive 89/629/EEC on the limitation of noise emissions from civil subsonic jet aeroplanes.[227]

4.3.3.2.19 Council Directive 90/449

On 30 July 1990 the Commission adopted Decision 90/449 setting up a Joint Committee on Civil Aviation.[228]

4.3.3.2.20 Council Regulation 2342/90/EEC

Council Regulation 2342/90/EEC[229] deals with fares on scheduled air services between EC Member States. It is a successor to the earlier Council Directive on fares, namely, Council Directive 87/601 of 14 December 1987.[230]

4.3.3.2.21 Council Regulation 2343/90/EEC

Regulation 2343/90 concerns access for air carriers to scheduled intra-Community air service routes and on the sharing of passenger capacity between air carriers on scheduled air services between the vast majority[231] of airports in the Member States of the EC.[232]

4.3.3.2.22 Regulation 82/91

The Commission adopted Regulation 82/91 on agreements, decisions and concerted practices concerning ground handling services.[233]

4.3.3.2.23 Regulation 83/91

The Commission adopted Regulation 83/91 on agreements between undertakings related to computer reservation systems for air transport services.[234]

4.3.3.2.24 Regulation 84/91

The Commission adopted Regulation 84/91 on the agreements, decisions and concerted practices concerning joint planning and co-ordination of capacity, consultations on passenger and cargo tariff rates on scheduled air services and slot allocations at airports.[235]

227. OJ L363/27, 13 December 1989.
228. OJ L230/22, 24 August 1990.
229. OJ L217/1, 11 August 1990. For the Commission's proposal, see OJ C258/3, 11 October 1989 and OJ C164/7, 5 July 1990. The opinion of the European Parliament as well as the Economic and Social Committee are reprinted in OJ C96/59, 17 April 1990 and OJ C112/17, 7 May 1990 respectively.
230. OJ L374/12, 31 December 1987.
231. i.e. other than Gibraltar, Porto as well as certain island airports in Greece and the Azores.
232. OJ L217/8, 11 August 1990.
233. OJ L10/7, 15 January 1991.
234. OJ L10/9, 15 January 1991.
235. OJ L10/14, 15 January 1991.

4.3.3.2.25 Regulation 294/91

The Council of Ministers has adopted Regulation 294/91 on the operation of air cargo services between Member States.[236]

4.3.3.2.26 Regulation 295/91

The Council of Ministers has adopted Regulation 295/91 on the common rules for compensation of those passengers denied boarding due to a scheduled flight being overbooked.[237]

4.3.3.2.27 Regulation 3922/91

The Council of Ministers adopted Regulation 3922/91 on 16 December 1991 on the harmonisation of technical requirements and administrative procedures in the field of civil aviation.[238]

4.3.3.2.28 Directive 91/670

The Council of Ministers adopted Directive 91/670 on 16 December 1991 on mutual acceptance of personnel licences for the exercise of functions in civil aviation.[239]

4.3.3.3 Conclusion

There are a great number of proposals in the area of air transport law embracing a review of the second package and measures on air traffic control, infrastructure, personnel licensing, cargo services, denied boarding compensation, airport consultation and charging, baggage formalities as well as new measures in the area of competition.[240]

4.3.4 Inland waterway

There has been a great deal of overcapacity in inland waterway transport. EC measures are designed to cope with this problem.

4.3.4.1 Recommendation 335/68

On 31 July 1968, the Commission adopted Recommendation 335/68 on the structural improvement of the market in the carriage of goods by inland waterway.[241]

4.3.4.2 Regulation 281/71

On 9 February 1971, the Commission adopted Regulation 281/71 determining the composition of the list of waterways of a maritime character provided for in Article 3(*e*) of Council Regulation (EEC) 1108/70 of 4 June 1970.[242]

236. OJ L36/1, 8 February 1991.
237. OJ L36/15, 8 February 1991.
238. OJ 1991 L374/4.
239. OJ 1991 L374/21.
240. See Frere Chormeley, *op. cit.* at footnote 188 above, Chapter 5.
241. OJ L218/10, 4 September 1968.
242. OJ L33/11, 10 February 1971. This was supplemented by both the 1972 and 1985 Acts of Accession It was also extended in scope by the 1972 Act of Accession.

4.3.4.3 Directive 80/1119

Directive 80/1119 deals with statistical returns in respect of carriage of goods by inland waterways.[243]

4.3.4.4 Regulation 1101/89

The Council of Ministers adopted Regulation 1101/89 on the subject of structural improvements in inland waterway transport.[244]

4.3.4.5 Regulation 4060/89

On 21 December 1989, the Council of Ministers adopted Reg. 4060/89 on the elimination of controls performed at the frontiers of Member States in the field of road and inland waterway transport.[245]

4.4 GENERAL MATTERS

4.4.1 Transport committees

Article 83 of the EEC Treaty provides for the establishment and operation of a transport committee. The rules of the Transport Committee were adopted in 1958[246] and amended in 1964.[247] Today, it advises the Commission[248] on matters relating to transport. Its role is more in the preparation of proposals rather than in the consideration of published proposals.

On 20 February 1978, the Council of Ministers instituted a consultation procedure and set up a committee in the field of transport infrastructure by way of Council Decision 78/174.[249]

A Joint Committee on Inland Navigation was set up by means of Commission Decision 80/991/EEC.[250]

A Joint Committee on Railways was established by virtue of Commission Decision 85/13/EEC.[251]

Commission Decision 85/516/EEC set up a Joint Committee on Road Transport.[252] This Decision was later amended.[253]

Commission Decision 87/467/EEC set up a Joint Committee on Maritime Transport.[254]

244. OJ L339/30, 15 December 1980 as amended.
245. OJ L116/25, 28 April 1989. This was implemented by Regulation 1102/89 (OJ L116/30, 28 April 1989) and amended by Regulation 3572/90 (OJ L353/12, 17 December 1990).
245. OJ L390/18, 30 December 1989.
246. OJ 25, 27 November 1958, p. 509; OJ 1957–58, p.72.
247. See Dec.64/390/EEC, OJ P102, 29 June 1964, p. 1602.
248. On the Commission, see para. 3.4.2, above.
249. OJ L54/16, 25 February 1978.
250. OJ L297/28, 6 November 1980.
251. OJ L8/26, 10 January 1985.
252. OJ L317/33, 28 November 1985.
253. See Decision 87/447/EEC (OJ L240/37, 22 August 1987).
254. OJ L253/20, 4 September 1987. See para.3.4.

4.4.2 Competition

Special rules operate in relation to competition and transport. These rules will be examined in detail in later chapters, below, and only a brief mention of the principal secondary legislative measures is contained in this chapter.[255]

4.4.2.1 Regulation No. 11 of 1960

The EEC Council adopted Regulation No. 11 of 1960 concerning the abolition of discrimination in transport rates and conditions, in implementation of Article 79(3) of the EEC Treaty.[256,257] A year later, the Commission issued Recommendation 722/61 to the Member States on the application of Regulation No. 11.[258]

4.4.2.2 Regulation 141/62

The Council adopted Regulation 141/62 so as to exempt transport from the application of Council Regulation 17/62.[259]

4.4.2.3 Decision 65/271

In respect of road, rail and inland waterways, Council Decision 65/271/EEC sought to harmonise certain provisions affecting competition in transport by rail, road and inland waterway.[260]

4.4.2.4 Regulation 1017/68

It was not until 19 July 1968 that the Council of Ministers adopted Regulation 1017/68 so as to apply the rules of competition to transport by rail, road and inland waterway.[261] This was the first real application of EEC competition law to transport, albeit only three modes of transport. The application of the Regulation is apparent from such Commission Decisions as Decision 85/383 of 10 July 1985 (relating to a proceeding under Article 2 of Regulation 1017/68) in relation to the French inland waterway charter traffic.[262]

4.4.2.5 Regulation 1629/69

Regulation 1017/68 was supplemented by Commission Regulation 1629/69 of 8 August 1969 on the form, content and other details of complaints pursuant to Article

255. See Chapter 10, below.

256. On Article 79(3) of the EEC Treaty, see para. 4.2.2.9.

257. OJ 52/1121, 16 August 1960. This was extended by means of the 1972 Act of Accession and amended by Regulation 3626/84 (OJ L335/4, 22 December 1984).

258. OJ 50/975, 22 July 1961.

259. OJ 124/2751, 28 November 1962. This was extended by the 1972 Treaty of Accession and amended by both Regulation 165/65 (OJ P210, 11 December 1965, p.3141) and Regulation 1002/67 (OJ P306, 16 December 1967, p. 1).

260. OJ 88, 24 May 1965, p.1500.

261. OJ L175/1, 23 July 1968. This Regulation was supplemented by and derogated from the 1972 Act of Accession as well as amended by the 1979 Act of Accession. It had been implemented by means of Regulation 1629/69 (OJ L209/1, 21 August 1969) and Regulation 1630/69 (OJ L209/11, 21 August 1969).

262. OJ L219/35, 17 August 1985.

10, applications pursuant to Article 12 and notifications pursuant to Article 14(1) of Regulation 1017/68.[263]

4.4.2.6 Regulation 1630/69

Regulation 1017/68 was also supplemented by Regulation 1630/69 of 8 August 1969 on the hearings provided for in Article 26(1) and (2) of Council Regulation (EEC) 1017/68 of 19 July 1968.[264] Examples of its enforcement include Commission Decision 85/383 of 10 July 1985 relating to a proceeding under Article 2 of the regulation in respect of French inland waterway charter traffic (the so-called EATE levy).[265]

4.4.2.7 Regulation 1107/70

Regulation 1107/70 adopted by the Council of Ministers on 4 June 1970 dealt with the granting of aids for transport by rail, road and inland waterway.[266]

4.4.2.8 Regulation 2988/74

The Council of Ministers adopted Regulation 2988/74 on 26 November 1974 concerning limitation periods in proceedings and the enforcement of sanctions under the rules of the EEC relating to transport and competition.[267]

4.4.3 Infrastructure

4.4.3.1 1964 Decision

On 22 June 1964 the Council of Ministers adopted a Decision on the organisation of a survey of infrastructure costs in respect of transport by rail, road and inland waterway.[268] Article 4 of the Decision was implemented by a Council Decision of 13 May 1965. This 1965 Decision was further amended by Council Decision 70/108 of 27 January 1970.[269]

4.4.3.2 Regulation 1108/70

The Council of Ministers adopted Regulation 1108/70 on 4 June 1970, to introduce an accounting system for expenditure on infrastructure in respect of transport by rail,road and inland waterway.[270] There have been other measures supplementing this

263. OJ L209/181, 21 August 1969.
264. OJ L209/11, 21 August 1969.
265. OJ L219/35, 17 August 1985.
266. OJ L130/1, 15 June 1970. This was amended by Regulation 1473/75 (OJ L152/1, 12 June 1975) and Regulation 1100/89 (OJ L116/24, 28 April 1989). It was derogated from by the 1972 Act of Accession. It was extended by the 1972 Act of Accession. Finally, it was supplemented by Regulation 1658/82 (OJ L184/1, 29 June 1982).
267. OJ L 319/1, 29 November 1974.
268. OJ 102, 29 June 1964, p.1598.
269. OJ L23/24, 30 January 1970. This was derogated from by the 1972 Act of Accession.
270. OJ L130/4, 15 June 1970. This has been implemented by Regulation 2598/70 (OJ L278/1, 23 December 1970) and Regulation 281/71 (OJ L33/11, 10 February 1971); amended by the 1972 and 1985 Treaties of Accession, Decision 73/101 (OJ L2/1, 1 January 1973) Regulation 1384/79 (OJ L167/1, 5 July 1979) as well as Regulation 3021/81 (OJ L302/8, 23 October 1981); and supplemented by the 1986 Treaty of Accession.

regulation, including Commission Regulation 2598/70 specifying the items to be included under the various headings in the forms of accounts shown in Annex I to the Regulation.[271]

4.4.3.3 Decision 78/174

On 20 February 1978, the Council of Ministers decided, by way of Decision 78/174,[272] to institute a consultation procedure and set up a committee in the field of transport infrastructure.

4.4.3.4 Regulation 3600/82

On 30 December 1982, the Council of Ministers adopted a Regulation on the granting of limited financial support in the field of transport infrastructure.[273] Examples of this limited financial support are the granting of limited financial support to such projects as the implementation of the Evzoni–Volos road section,[274] the implementation of the marshalling yard and customs station at Domodossola project,[275] and the implementation of the Wexford by-pass project.[276]

On 22 December 1987, the Council of Ministers adopted Regulation 4070/87 on the grant of support to transport infrastructure projects.[277]

4.4.3.5 Decision 84/519

Commission Decision 84/519/EEC of 26 June 1984 granting financial assistance for special measures of Community interest relating to transport infrastructure.[278]

4.4.3.6 Decision 84/520

Commission Decision 84/520 of 17 October 1984 granting financial assistance for special measures of Community interest relating to transport infrastructure.[279]

4.4.3.7 Regulation 4059/86

The Council of Ministers adopted Regulation 4059/86 on 22 December 1986 on the granting of financial support to transport infrastructure projects.[280]

4.4.3.8 Regulation 4070/87

On 22 December 1987, the Council of Ministers adopted Regulation 4070/87 on the grant of support to transport infrastructure projects.[281]

271. Regulation 2598/70, OJ L278/1, 23 December 1970. The scope of this Regulation was extended under the 1972 Accession Treaty but amended by Regulation 2116/78 (OJ L246/7, 8 September 1978).
272. OJ L54/16, 25 February 1978.
273. OJ L376/10, 31 December 1982.
274. Commission Decision 83/472; OJ L259/32, 20 September 1983.
275. Commission Decision 83/474; OJ L260/23, 21 September 1983.
276. Commission Decision 85/67; OJ L30/22, 2 February 1985.
277. OJ L380/33, 31 December 1987.
278. OJ L290/22, 7 November 1984.
279. OJ L290/25, 7 November 1984. This was amended by Decision 85/636, OJ L379/52, 31 December 1985.
280. OJ L378/24, 31 December 1986.
281. OJ L380/33, 31 December 1987.

4.4.3.9 Regulation 3359/90

The Council of Ministers adopted Regulation 3359/90 on 20 November 1990 in regard to an action programme in the field of transport infrastructure with a view to the completion of an integrated transport market in 1992.[282]

4.4.4 Inspection of goods

On 1 December 1983, the Council of Ministers adopted Directive 83/643 on the facilitation of physical inspections and administrative formalities in respect of the carriage of goods between Member States.[283] This Directive was amended in 1987 and 1991.[284]

4.4.5 Summertime arrangements

The adoption of measures relating to "summertime" lighting; that is to say, the changing of time so as to minimise travel in the dark, has been a part of EC transport law for more than a decade. On 22 July 1980, the Council of Ministers adopted Directive 80/737[285] on summertime arrangements. On 21 December 1988, the Council of Ministers adopted its fifth Directive[286] on summertime arrangements.[287]

4.4.6 Public service

4.4.6.1 Regulation 1191/69

Article 77 of the EEC Treaty[288] deals with (among other things) the concept of a public service. Council Regulation 1191/69 of 26 June 1969 on action by Member States concerning the obligations inherent in the concept of a public service in transport by rail, road and inland waterway.[289]

4.4.7 Passenger and luggage traffic

The Council of Ministers adopted Decision 83/418 on the commercial independence of the railways in the management of their international passenger and luggage traffic.[290]

4.4.8 Prior examination and consultation in transport matters

The EEC Council of Ministers adopted a Decision on 21 March 1962,[291] to institute a procedure on prior examination and consultation in respect of certain laws, regulations and administrative provisions concerning transport proposed in the Member States.

282. OJ L326/1, 24 November 1990.
283. OJ L359/8, 22 December 1981.
284. See Directive 87/53 (OJ L24/33, 27 January 1987) and Directive 91/342 (OJ L187/47, 13 July 1991).
285. OJ L205/17, 7 August 1980.
286. On the legal effect of a Directive, see para. 3.5.2.2.2, above.
287. OJ L17/57, 21 January 1989.
288. On Article 77 of the EEC Treaty, see para. 4.2.2.7, above.
289. OJ L156/1, 28 June 1969. This has been amended by the 1972, 1979 and 1985 Acts of Accession as well as Dec.73/101 (OJ L2/1, 1 January 1973).
290. OJ L237/32, 26 August 1983. This was amended by the 1985 Act of Accession.
291. OJ No.23, 3 April 1962, p.720.

This Decision has since been amended.[292] The current regime requires a Member State to notify the Commission and inform other Member States of measures relating to rail, road and inland waterway transport which are liable to interfere substantially with the implementation of the common transport policy. The Commission must, within two months of this notification, deliver an Opinion or a Recommendation to the relevant Member State and inform the other Member States of this Opinion or Recommendation.

4.4.9 External relations

The EC's capacity to conclude international agreements is of paramount importance in transport—one of the most international of all industries. This is a matter which is discussed in greater depth and length in Chapter 17, below.

4.4.10 General measures

On 14 December 1967, the Council of Ministers adopted Decision 67/790 on certain measures of common transport policy.[293]

4.4.11 Temporary Importation

4.4.11.1 Regulation 2249/91

Commission Regulation 2249/91/EEC[294] lays down provisions for the implementation of Regulation 1855/89/EEC for the temporary importation of means of transport.

4.4.12 Statistics

4.4.12.1 Directive 78/546

On 12 June 1978 the Council of Ministers adopted Directive 78/546 on statistical returns in respect of goods by road, as part of regional statistics.[295]

4.5 CONCLUSION

There is no harmonious approach to transport in the EC. The failure to adopt a common transport policy is regrettable. A document published by the Commission has described the costs of non-adoption in the following terms:

"1. it is in the interest of Member States to make the most of the substantial private and public investment in transport. Divergences in national policies damage effectiveness, profitability and productivity. The Community could monitor the compatibility of national programmes, harmonise them where desirable and create economies of scale. It could also give technical and financial aid to projects involving more than one Member State;
2. the success of other Community policies (agriculture, industry, regional development, energy, environment and tourism) relies heavily on the quality of Community transport services;

292. See Council Decision 73/402/EEC (OJ L347, 17 December 1973, p.48).
293. OJ 322/4, 30 December 1967.
294. OJ L204/31, 27 July 1991.
295. OJ L168/29, 26 June 1978 as amended.

3. the elimination of distortions of competition and discriminations affecting transport undertakings is an indispensable pre-condition to the genuine achievement of one of the basic principles of the common market: the free movement of people and goods."[296]

The internalisation of the EC market as well as the integration of Western and Eastern Europe will inevitably lead to transport having an even higher profile and importance in the EC. This greater profile and importance increases more than ever the need for accelerated progress on the adoption of a common transport policy.

The establishment by the Commission in 1990 of a group of independent experts for a project entitled "Transport in the Year 2000" provides some hope for the development of an effective CTP. It will be fascinating to see how EC transport law develops in the future.

296. EC Commission, *The Community and Transport Policy*, European File 16/83 (October 1983).

CHAPTER 5

Historical Overview of EC Shipping Law

5.1 INTRODUCTION

The purpose of this chapter is to provide an historical overview of the development of EC shipping law. While there is an obvious overlap with other chapters, a separate chapter providing an historical overview will also be of value. It is proposed to analyse the development of EC shipping law using four time-periods: (a) the Foundation Treaties[1]; (b) the 1960s[2]; (c) the 1970s[3]; and, finally, (d) the 1980s and early 1990s.[4]

A number of general trends emerge from an historical review of shipping in the EC. First, the EC has declined in its proportionate significance in world shipping: for example, in 1959 the fleets of the first nine Member States represented 40% of the world tonnage but by 1975 this had fallen to 25%.[5] Secondly, the size of the EC fleet (in terms of tonnage) has grown substantially: in 1959, the first nine Member States had a total of 40.1 million grt but this had grown to 71.3 million grt in 1975.[6] Thirdly, despite the aspiration to have a comprehensive system of EC shipping law, it will be impossible to achieve this aim because the world of shipping is wider than the world of the EC.[7]

5.2 THE FOUNDATION TREATIES

It will be recalled from Chapter 4, above, that shipping was mentioned only once in the EEC Treaty and was not expressly mentioned at all in the ECSC Treaty. The net effect of Article 84 of the EEC Treaty (the only treaty provision expressly referring to shipping) was that sea transport (like air transport) was excluded from the normal rules for formulating the common transport policy. None the less, the general rules of the EEC Treaty have always applied to sea and air transport.[8]

Why was sea transport excluded? The European Parliament's Committee on Regional Policy, Regional Planning and Transport published in 1977 an Interim Report on the Sea Transport Problems in the Community and stated:

> "There is no point in asking why the authors of the [EEC] Treaty left sea transport out of the Common Transport Policy during the negotiations at Val Duchesse in 1957 . . . It may be that they simply could not agree on rules for sea transport or that they intended to draw up special

1. See para. 5.2 below.
2. See para. 5.3 below.
3. See para. 5.4 below.
4. See para. 5.5 below.
5. COM(76)341 final.
6. COM(76)341 final.
7. This is a point which is discussed at greater length below.
8. This was confirmed in the case of sea transport by Case 167/73 *Commission v. France* [1974] ECR 359. There is greater discussion of this point later at paragraph 5.4.8, below.

rules for sea transport but did not have the time before the Treaty was pronounced ready for signature by the Heads of Government, or they had specific reasons for excluding sea transport which are unknown to us. In any case the situation is now completely different . . ."[9]

5.3 THE 1960s

The 1960s were a barren period for the development of EC shipping law.

5.3.1 1960 Memorandum from the Commission to the Council

In November 1960, the Commission sent a Memorandum to the Council of Ministers on the applicability of the competition rules of the EEC Treaty and the interpretation of the Treaty's application to sea and air transport.[10] At point 29 of the Memorandum, the Commission contended that maritime transport should be included in the measures adopted in the field of transport in furtherance of the EEC Treaty's objectives.

5.3.2 1961 Memorandum on the Basic Approach to be Adopted in the Common Transport Policy

This Memorandum is an important document because it sets out the Commission's position at the beginning of the 1960s on shipping. The Commission was of the view that the general rules of the EEC Treaty (but not the specific provisions of Articles 74 to 83 of the EEC Treaty, i.e. Title IV on Transport) applied to maritime transport. The Commission's view was ultimately vindicated in the ECJ's decision in Case 167/73 *Commission v. France*.[11]

5.3.3 1962 Action Programme for a Common Transport Policy

This grandly titled document was a Communication from the Commission to the Council of Ministers. It did not however contain any specific proposals. It merely confirmed the approach of the Commission in its 1960 Memorandum from the Commission to the Council of Ministers and 1961 Memorandum on the Basic Approach to be Adopted in the Common Transport Policy.

5.3.4 1962 Regulations on Competition and Shipping

Articles 85 to 94 of the EEC Treaty which relate to competition[12] were implemented by Regulation 17/62.

Some Member States opposed the application of Regulation 17/62 to shipping and on 14 June 1962, the Council requested the Commission to submit a proposal on the exemption of sea transport from the scope of Regulation 17/62. These States argued, *inter alia,* that the state of the development of the EC's transport policy was such that the full application of EC competition law would not be appropriate. The Commission then submitted a Proposal for a Council Regulation regarding the Temporary Non-

9. Working Documents, Doc. 5/77, 23 March 1977, Rapporteur: Mr H. Seefeld, para. 3.
10. Doc.VII/S/05230. Final of 12 November 1960.
11. [1974] ECR 359.
12. See Chapter 9 *et seq.*

Application of Articles 85 to 94 of the EEC Treaty to Sea and Air Transport. This proposal was adopted by the Council of Ministers on 26 November 1962 in the form of Regulation 141/62.

Regulation 141/62 exempted all modes of transport from the scope of Regulation 17/62. Article 1 of Regulation 141/62 provided:

"Regulation 17 shall not apply to agreements, decisions or concerted practices in the transport sector which have as their object or effect the fixing of transport rates and conditions, the limitation or control of the supply of transport or the sharing of transport markets; nor shall it apply to the abuse of a dominant position, within the meaning of Article 86 of the Treaty, within the transport market."

Regulation 141/62 was eventually rescinded in respect of road, rail and inland waterway transport by means of Regulation 1017/68 adopted on 19 July 1968.[13] These were the easier cases—the Preamble to Regulation 141/62 stated that "it is impossible to foresee whether and at what stage the Council will adopt appropriate provisions [for air and sea transport]; whereas . . . a limit to the period during which Regulation 17 shall apply can be set only for transport by rail, road and inland waterway". Indeed, it was not until the adoption of Regulation 4056/86, which was adopted in December 1986, (which repealed Regulation 141/62 in respect of shipping), that Articles 85 and 86 applied to shipping.

5.4 THE 1970s

5.4.1 Introduction

The 1970s saw the beginning of action on an EC shipping policy.[14] Work which began in the 1970s bore fruit throughout the 1970s but blossomed most spectacularly in the mid-1980s. Why the change from the 1960s? Bredima-Savopoulou and Tzoannos have observed seven factors:

"— the first enlargement of the EC in 1973 brought sea transport more to the fore, in that not only were the United Kingdom and Denmark both important shipping nations but also that the United Kingdom and Ireland were both islands,
— the world-wide shipping crisis and the concomitant tonnage surpluses getting worse since 1973,
— the expansion of flag discrimination and protectionist practices,
— the expansion of state trading country shipping, particularly in the liner trades,
— several tanker disasters which led to extensive oil spillages such as the accident of the *Amoco Cadiz* in March 1978 and to sensitizing of public opinion on marine pollution matters,
— the increasing number of questions, covering a wide range of shipping matters, submitted for the European Parliament and reflecting the revival of interest in shipping,
— the second enlargement of the Community in 1981 with the accession of Greece, a leading international maritime power."[15]

5.4.2 Bodson's proposals

Victor Bodson attended his last Council of Ministers meeting as Commissioner for Transport on 4 June 1970. At that meeting, he presented a report on the action to be taken at Community level on both sea and air transport.[16] Abbati has written:

13. OJ L175/1 of 23 July 1968.
14. See Editorial, "Towards a Shipping Code" in *The Economist*, 26 March 1977, p. 89.
15. *The Common Shipping Policy of the EEC* (1990), pp. 74–75.
16. See Bodson, "Le prospettive della politica commune di transporti" in *Automolisimo e Automobilismo industriale*, Nos 5–6, 1970.

"[i]n the Bodson report the Commission was not proposing that the Council adopt a full and proper policy on shipping. In view of the unanimity provision of Article 84(2) of the [EEC] Treaty[17] it instead listed a number of problems on which a swift Commmunity decision would be desirable. These can be summarized as:

(i) the need to establish proper links between the Community's commercial policy and action on shipping when it comes to negotiations on agreements with non-member countries based on Article 113 of the Treaty,[18] a particularly important point in respect of those non-Community countries which reserve cargo for ships of their own flag;
(ii) the adoption of a common approach towards international economic organizations like UNCTAD and the OECD, in accordance with the provisions of Article 116;[19]
(iii) the establishment of a procedure for co-operation between Member States in order better to protect their interests against flag discrimination by non-Community countries against the fleets of Member States;
(iv) the adoption of a common policy (harmonized at Community level) to policy on State aid for shipping aimed at improving the competitiveness of the fleets of the Member States and maintaining services felt to be essential;
(v) the standardisation of working conditions of crews."[20]

The European Parliament adopted a resolution on 12 April 1972 based on the Seefeld Report[21] accepting the Commission's objectives. This Report pointed out the need for the Community to develop a common shipping policy given the impending enlargement of the Community on 1 January 1973 by the accession of Denmark, Ireland and the UK.

5.4.3 The 1973 enlargement of the EC

On 1 January 1973, three new States, namely Denmark, Ireland and the UK—all of which are maritime nations (to varying degrees)—ensured that shipping would be an issue of growing significance. Norway had intended joining but, following a referendum, that State did not join. Even without Norway, the UK and Denmark were still important shipping States. The UK and Denmark accounted for half of the EC's fleet at that time.[22] It has been estimated that prior to the accession of Denmark, Ireland and the UK, some 90% of EC transport was by road, rail and inland waterway and after their accession, some 90% of the exports and imports between the three new and pre-existing six Member States were carried by sea.[23]

5.4.4 Commission's Communication to Council on 25 October 1973

The Commission Communication of 25 October 1973 to the Council on the Development of the Common Transport Policy explained the functions of transport

17. Now removed by the SEA.
18. For the current text of Article 113 of the Treaty see Appendix 1 below
19. For the current text of Article 116 of the Treaty see Appendix 1 below.
20. *Transport and European Integration* (1986) at para. 7.1. See also Fourth General Report on the Activities of the EEC (1970), point 302.
21. EP Working Document No. 10/1972.
22. See "Communication from the Commission to the Council on the Community's Relations with Non-Member Countries in Shipping Matters", COM(76)341 final, 30 June 1976, para. 2.3.
23. The Commission stated in its 1976 "Communication to the Council of Ministers on the Community's Relations with Non-Member Countries in Shipping Matters" (COM(76)314 final, para. 2.3) that the "importance of sea transport to the Community has increased following the accession of the three new Member States, since two of these States (the United Kingdom and Denmark) have very large merchant marine fleets (more than half the Community total) which make an important contribution to their balance of payments. Furthermore, the bulk of trade between these countries and the rest of the Community is carried by sea, so that 25% of trade within the Community now goes by sea, compared with 8% in the six nation Community."

within the EC framework and reiterated the importance of maritime transport within the framework of the new approach to the common transport policy.

5.4.5 ECSC Rail Tariff

In 1973, the Commission and the UK Government agreed that the ECSC Rail Tariff No. 1001 be extended to cover rail transport by ferry.[24]

5.4.6 1973 Enlargement of the EC

On 1 January 1973, Denmark, Ireland and the UK joined the EC. Ireland and the UK were the first ever island states to be members of the EC. This made shipping a more important issue than before. The Commission took the opportunity to take a test case against France to determine whether or not the general provisions of the EEC Treaty applied to shipping notwithstanding Article 84(2). This was the so-called *French Seamen's Case*.[25]

5.4.7 1973 Oil crisis

The oil crisis of 1973 (as well as the later oil crisis in 1978) caused considerable difficulties for the economies of the EC Member States. This particularly affected the oil tanker sector. The European Parliament's Committee on Economic and Monetary Affairs in its Interim Report on the Community Shipping Industry in 1976 recorded that by then:

> "[a] vast number of tankers [had] been laid up, which cuts the shipowner's costs considerably but by no means entirely. At the beginning of 1975, 45 tankers with a total deadweight of 1.6 million tons were laid up. By October [1986] these were 426 tankers of 34.9 million deadweight tons, representing almost 15% of the world tanker fleet. And 54% of this laid-up tonnage is composed of ships less than five years old."[26]

5.4.8 1973 French Seaman's Case

On 4 April 1974, the Court of Justice delivered its judgment in Case 167/73 *Commission v. France* (the *French Seamen's Case*).[27] This is the most important EC case on shipping. The ECJ was of the opinion that Article 48 EEC was directly applicable and, thus, France was in breach of its EEC Treaty obligations. More importantly perhaps, the judgment confirmed that sea transport was subject to the general rules of the EEC Treaty even if in the absence of a decision taken pursuant to Article 84(2) of the pre-SEA EEC, they are excluded from the rules of Title IV (Transport) of Part Two of the EEC Treaty. This judgment implied, according to the 1974 Annual Report on the General Activities of the Communities, "the applicability to sea and air transport of the rules of competition, of aids, of social policy, of taxation and of freedom of movement". The ECJ did not at that stage specifically identify those rules.

24. Seventh General Report on the Activities of the Communities (1973), point 403.
25. On this case, see para. 5.4.8 below.
26. Doc.479/76, Rapporteur: Mr J. L. Prescott, para. 14, citing *Finanstidende*, Copenhagen, 31 December 1975. On the report generally, see Chapter 5 below.
27. [1974] ECR 359.

The Commission brought the case against France as a test case so as to determine whether or not Article 48 of the EEC Treaty (which related to free movement of workers[28]) applied to the employment of seafarers.

The Commission instituted the proceedings on the basis of Article 169 of the EEC Treaty.[29] It sought a declaration that by not repealing, in so far as it affected the nationals of other EC Member States, the provisions of Section 3(2) of the French Merchant Seamen Code of 13 December 1926 (as amended by Order No. 58–1358 of 27 December 1958), France had not complied with its obligations under the provisions of the EEC Treaty relating to free movement of workers and, in particular, Articles 1, 4 and 7 of Regulation 1612/68 of 15 October 1968 on the free movement of workers within the EC. Section 3(2) of the 1926 Code (as amended) required that a proportion of the crew of a French ship be French nationals, with the exact proportion being laid down by way of a Ministerial Order. The Ministerial Order adopted (on 21 November 1960 and later amended on 12 June 1969) required that, apart from special exemptions, employment on the bridge and in the engine and wireless rooms on board merchant ships, fishing vessels and pleasure cruisers was to be reserved for French nationals.

Bredima-Savopoulou and Tzoannos have commented that the judgment:

> "was important not only for its legal implications but also for its political implications because it incorporated maritime transport in the process of European integration. Although a Court's judgment cannot be a substitute for a common policy—it cannot be an 'ersatz' of a common policy in the absence of acts of secondary law or of provisions of the Treaties—nevertheless the . . . judgment triggered actions; it had practical implications within 48 hours.[30] The judgment was delivered on 4 April 1978 and two days later the final act of the UN Conference on Trade and Development (UNCTAD IV Session) was initialled in Geneva. During the course of the Conference, the Commission had not appeared as representing the Community and had not negotiated on behalf of the Member States. The European Court's judgment, however, was such that the Community had no alternative but to seek a common position two days before signature of the final act of the Code. That was the effect of the judgment upon Articles 113 and 116 of the EEC Treaty, which were considered to be enlisted among the general rules of the Treaty that applied to shipping. Instead of that, and in spite of the Commission's efforts to establish a common view 'a la recherche du temps perdu', three Member States (France, Germany and Belgium) signed the Code. With regard to voting: France, Germany and Belgium voted in favour; the United Kingdom and Denmark voted against; Italy, the Netherlands and Greece abstained; Ireland and Luxembourg did not participate in the Conference . . . "

The judgment had another effect as well. The Eighth General Report on the Activities of the European Communities (1974) records that:

> "in view of the special characteristics of sea and air transport, which operate chiefly on the world market, the Commission has begun a series of informal consultations with shipowners and airlines in the Community in order to examine the possible practical implications of the application of the general rules of the [EEC] Treaty. The Commission intends to hold appropriate consultations with national experts."[31]

In some respects the judgment was not surprising. Had not the Council of Ministers already conceded the point many years before in adopting Regulation 141 of 1962 disapplying Articles 85 and 86 to maritime transport? Had Articles 85 and 86 (i.e. part

28. See Chapter 8 below.
29. On Article 169 EEC, see para. 3.4.6.6.2 above.
30. As the Eighth General Report on the Activities of the European Communities states at point 355: ". . . [t]he adoption by UNCTAD . . . of [the] Convention . . . necessitated rapid intervention by the Commission in order to safeguard the Community's interests."
31. Point 355.

of the general provisions of the EEC Treaty) not applied to sea transport then why did the Council of Ministers bother to adopt Regulation 141/62?

5.4.9 1974 Ports

The second exchange of views with the representatives of the chief EC ports took place on 19 February 1974. It was agreed that before deciding what EC action to take on ports, it was necessary to obtain a clearer picture of the management of the various EC ports from the institutional, structural and administrative angles, and also to define certain concepts relating to ports. The Commission chaired a working party composed of representatives of the ports which investigated these issues and which planned to report in 1975.

In June 1977, the representatives of the major ports approved the Report on the Current Situation of the Major Ports of the EC. The representatives also examined a Commission staff report on the then current situation on traffic links between the ports and their hinterlands.[32]

The Ports Working Group met six times during 1978 in pursuance of the instructions it received at the third plenary meeting of port authorities in June 1977.[33]

During 1979, the Ports Working Group met a total of five times in pursuance of the instructions it received at the third plenary meeting of port authorities in June 1977.[34,35]

5.4.10 1975 French initiative

On 8 December 1975, the French Government presented to the Council of Ministers a memorandum on the development of EC action on shipping.[36] The memorandum suggested "several lines of action both for harmonisation within the Commuity and for the protection of the Member States' economic interests against discrimination from outside the Community".[37] It proposed the "harmonisation of intra-Community sea transport from the point of view of intra-Community trade".

The Memorandum also stated that the French Government:

"feels that a common policy on sea transport cannot be achieved through scattered efforts, which might weaken the competitiveness of Member States' merchant fleets in the world. It considers it essential that a coherent whole be shaped starting from a clear-cut definition of the content of this common policy."

5.4.11 Non-Member States

In June 1976, the Commission sent a report to the Council of Ministers a communication on the EC's relations with non-EC states in shipping matters.

5.4.12 Code of Conduct for Liner Conferences

In November 1976, the Council of Ministers "turned its attention for the first time to the general problems of shipping and agreed that a common stance should be adopted

32. Eleventh General Report on the Activities of the European Communities, point 382.
33. Twelfth General Report on the Activities of the European Communities, point 373.
34. Bull. EC 6-1977, point 2.1.117.
35. Thirteenth General Report on the Activities of the European Communities, point 382.
36. Tenth General Report on the Activities of the European Communities, point 451.
37. *Ibid.*

on the Code of Conduct for Liner Conferences and on possible action at Community level".[38]

France, Germany and Belgium voted in favour of the Convention. In July 1976, the Commission decided not to initiate legal proceedings in the ECJ against the three States who had signed the Convention because they had undertaken not to ratify the Code for the moment and to seek a common Community approach.[39]

In December 1986, the Commission sent to the Council of Ministers a proposal for a Regulation in respect of accession to the UN Convention on a Code of Conduct for Liner Conferences.[40] The aim of this proposal was said to be "to avoid discrimination for reasons of nationality between the shipping lines of the Member States and, within the OECD, to maintain the principle of sharing cargoes among members of the liner conferences".[41]

It was not until 15 May 1979 that the Council of Ministers adopted the regulation concerning the accession of the Member States to the UN Convention on a Code of Conduct for Liner Conferences.[42] The Thirteenth General Report on the Activities of the European Communities recorded that the adoption of this Regulation "marked the achievement of a common approach which not only complied with the wishes of developing countries for access to liner conferences and cargo sharing but also maintained commercial arrangements for cargo sharing between OECD shipping lines and in liner trades between OECD countries".[43]

5.4.13 1976 Interim Report drawn up on behalf of the European Parliament's Committee on Economic and Monetary Affairs on the Community Shipping Industry

On 23 December 1976, the European Parliament's Committee on Economic and Monetary Affairs published its Interim Report on the Community Shipping Industry.[44] The report emphasised the need for further co-ordination in the shipping and shipbuilding fields among the EC Member States.[45] It also recognised the need for new ideas and policies in shipping and shipbuilding[46]—two industries which it saw as being interdependent.[47] The report canvassed the traditional reasons why shipping is important for the EC: the carriage of exports of EC goods; the carriage of basic raw materials and energy into the EC; the employment of persons on board ships as well as in ports and shipyards.

5.4.14 1977 Interim Report drawn up on behalf of the Committee on Regional Policy, Regional Planning and Transport on the Sea Transport Problems in the Community

The European Parliament's Committee on Regional Policy, Regional Planning and Transport published an Interim Report on the Sea Transport Problems in the Community.[48]

38. Tenth General Report on the Activities of the European Communities, point 439.
39. Tenth General Report on the Activities of the European Communities, point 451.
40. Bull. EC 12-1977, point 2.1.160.
41. Eleventh General Report on the Activities of the European Communities, point 379.
42. OJ L121 of 17 May 1979; Bull. EC 5-1979, point 2.1.120. See para. 5.4.20 below.
43. Point 378.
44. Doc.479/76, Rapporteur: Mr J. L. Prescott.
45. *Ibid.*, para. 1.
46. *Ibid.*
47. *Ibid.*, para. 2.
48. Working documents; Doc.5/77; 23 March 1977; Rapporteur: Mr H. Seefeld.

5.4.15 1977 Consultation procedure: Decision 77/587

In June 1976, a Communication was issued by the Commission to the Council of Ministers on the Community's relations with third countries in shipping matters.[49] The principal purpose of the paper was, according to the Commission itself, to stimulate debate in the Community on the possible scope and content of a Community shipping policy.[50] This Communication outlined the principal problems in the EC's relations with non-member countries in shipping.

On 13 September 1977 the Council of Ministers adopted, by way of Decision 77/587/EEC, a consultation procedure on relations between Member States and third countries and to facilitate action within international organisations.[51] This measure was designed to facilitate exchanges of information, where appropriate, on shipping matters of common interest. Such a common approach would, it was believed, allow the EC to combine the strengths of each of its Member States into one single bloc. Abbati has commented:

> "[e]ven though this Decision reflected only part of the Commission's proposal—the Commission wanted prior consultation in respect both of bilateral shipping agreements concluded between Member States and non-Community countries and of shipping matters discussed in international organisations, whereas the Council authorized consultation only in respect of the former, and after the event at that[52]—it nevertheless constituted the legal instrument which would serve as a basis, at Community level, for discussion of the most urgent problems facing sea transport without raising the thorny matter of the unanimous decisions required under Article 84(2). There is no denying that from 1978 onwards the fact that the Community had this institutionalised instrument for consultation between Member States went some way towards speeding up Community action on the major shipping problems facing the Member States."[53]

The Consultation Procedure has worked well—especially in the context of ongoing negotiations with the US and Japan.[54]

5.4.16 1978 Decision on Relations with State Trading Countries: Decision 78/774

A number of Comecon States, in particular, the USSR, the GDR and Poland were, during the late 1970s, posing a considerable threat to EC Member State fleets because they were able to offer very competitive rates. The Commission's analysis, contained in *Les transports maritimes des pays a commerce d'Etat et la Communaute*[55] clearly showed the penetration of the Eastern Bloc fleets into the EC liner market. The study showed that The Netherlands' share of bilateral trade with the Comecon countries was about 5% in 1976. The study also showed that of the bilateral liner trade between the USSR and the EC Member States, the USSR accounted for 64% of the trade with the UK in 1976, 75% with Germany in the same year and 83% with Belgium in the

49. Bull. EC 6-1976, point 2274.
50. *Progress*, p. 9.
51. See Council Decision 77/587/EEC of 13 September 1977 setting up a consultation procedure on relations between Member States and third countries in shipping matters and on action relating to such matters in international organisations (OJ L239/23, 17 September 1977). See also Bull. EC 9-1977, point 2.1.64.
52. And in fact came in for criticism from the European Parliament: see the Seefeld Report on the present state and progress of the common transport policy, Doc. EP No. 512/78 of 5 January 1979, p. 54.
53. *Op. cit.*, para. 7.1.
54. See Bredima-Savopoulou and Tzoannos, *op. cit.* at footnote 15 above, p. 78. See also Eleventh General Report on the Activities of the European Communities, point 380.
55. Brussels, 1978.

previous year. State-planned economies could offer long-term freight rates at a very competitive level.

The Commission's solution was a proposal that channels of communication be established which would provide regular information on market penetration by Comecon fleets and such communication would allow an effective response by the EC. This solution was embodied in a proposal for a Decision forwarded by the Commission to the Council in April 1978. This proposal envisaged the Council requesting each Member State to monitor the liner trade of the State-trading counties and allowing each Member State to adopt national retaliatory legislation.

The Commission's proposal was adopted, for the most part by the Council of Ministers in a Decision adopted on 19 September 1978. This was Decision 78/774/EEC of 19 September 1978 concerning the activities of certain third countries in the field of cargo shipping.[56] The Decision referred, in general terms, to collecting information on the activities of third countries whose practices are harmful to the shipping interests of the Member States and did not refer specifically to the State-trading countries—this was so as to placate the French representative on the Council of Ministers who did not want to strain Soviet-French relations.[57] This provided a system of data collection in regard to such routes as East Africa, Central America and the Far East.

5.4.17 Tanker disasters

There were many disasters involving oil tankers during the 1970s. These disasters, many of which occurred on the coasts of EC Member States (including the *Amoco Cadiz*) concentrated the minds of the EC on the need for action. The European Council discussed the matter in 1978.[58] On 26 June 1978, the Council of Ministers adopted a Recommendation on the ratification by the Member States of the International Convention on the Safety of Life at Sea (SOLAS 1974) and the International Convention on the Prevention of Pollution by Ships (MARPOL 1973), together with their 1978 Protocols as well as the International Labour Organisation's (ILO's) Convention No. 147 concerning minimum standards in merchant ships. The Council of Ministers also adopted a Declaration on the need for better enforcement of international measures for the prevention of marine pollution by ships and to ensure the safety of ships and the competence of crews.[59]

On 23 November 1978, the Council of Ministers adopted a statement on the subject of the Memorandum of Understanding of 2 March 1978 between certain North Sea maritime authorities on the maintenance of standards on board merchant vessels.[60]

On 21 December 1978, the Council of Ministers adopted a number of other measures, namely, a Recommendation that the Member States sign the 1978 IMCO Convention on standards for the training and certification of seafarers and watchkeeping by 1 April 1979 and ratify it by 31 December 1980 at the latest; a Directive aimed at raising qualification standards for North Sea and Channel pilots and encouraging vessels to make use of such pilots; and a Directive setting out minimum rules for certain tankers entering or leaving EC ports.

56. OJ L258, 21 September 1978.
57. See Abbati, *ibid.*
58. Bull. EC 4-1978, point 1.4.3.
59. See Twelfth General Report on the Activities of the European Communities, point 370.
60. Bull. EC 11-1978, point 2.1.91.

5.4.18 1978 Ship's inspection proposals

On 13 November 1978, the Commission sent a proposal to the Council of Ministers for a Decision rendering mandatory the procedures for ship inspection forming the subject of resolutions by the Intergovernmental Maritime Consultative Organisation.[61] The Parliament delivered its opinion.[62] The Economic and Social Committee also delivered its opinion.[63]

5.4.19 1978 Collection of Information Decision

On 19 September 1978, the Council of Ministers adopted a Decision on the shipping activities of certain non-EC Member States.[64] The Decision required all EC Member States to set up a system for gathering information on the activities of fleets of countries whose practices were seen as detrimental to the maritime interests of the EC Member States.

The application of the Decision was extended for a further two years on 4 December 1980.[65] It was also extended to include transport services between the EC and the Far East.[66]

5.4.20 1978 Decision in respect of liner trades between the EC and East Africa/Central America

On 21 December 1978, the Council of Ministers adopted a Decision on the application of the monitoring system established under the Decision described above to the activities of carriers operating in liner trades between the EC and East Africa as well as the EC and Central America.

5.4.21 1979 Ratification of the UN Code of Conduct for Liner Conferences

The adoption of the UN Code of Conduct for Liner Conferences forced the EC to think further about shipping law than it had previously done so. The Council of Ministers adopted Regulation 954/79 on 15 May 1979 on the ratification of the UN Code of Conduct for Liner Conferences. This measure has been described by Bredima-Savopoulou and Tzoannos as being the "most important Community act in shipping, until 1985".[67]

5.4.22 1979 Parliamentary Resolution on Shipping Accidents

In February 1979, the European Parliament adopted a Resolution on the best means of preventing accidents to shipping.[68]

61. OJ C284 of 28 November 1978.
62. OJ C39 of 12 December 1979.
63. OJ C128 of 21 May 1979.
64. See OJ L258, 21 September 1978; Bull. EC 9-1978, point 2 January 1967. For the Parliament's as well as the Economic and Social Committee's opinions on the proposal, see OJ C131 of 5 June 1978 and OJ C269 of 13 November 1978.
65. OJ L5, 9 January 1979.
66. See Fourteenth General Report on the Activities of the European Communities, point 426.
67. *Op. cit.*, at footnote 15 above p. 79.
68. OJ C67, 12 March 1979; Bull. EC 2-1979, point 2.3.10.

5.4.23 1979 Parliamentary Resolution on the Community's Relations with the Comecon States in Maritime Shipping

In May 1979, the Parliament adopted a Resolution on the Community's relations with the Comecon countries in maritime shipping matters.[69]

5.4.24 1979 Economic and Social Committee Opinion on Flags of Convenience

The Economic and Social Committee adopted an Opinion on Flags of Convenience.[70]

5.4.25 Shipping crisis

The shipping crisis which commenced in the 1970s continued on through the early and mid 1980s.

5.5 THE 1980s

5.5.1 Shipping crisis as well as port distortions

The shipping crisis which commenced in the 1970s continued on through the early and mid 1980s.

On 13 December 1984 the Commission presented a proposal designed to eliminate distortions of competition between ports arising from the variations in the national regulation of hinterland traffic.[71]

5.5.2 1980 Draft for a Council Resolution Concerning Priorities and the Timetable for Decisions to be taken by the Council in the Transport Sector during the Period up to the End of 1983

On 24 October 1980, the Commission submitted to the Council of Ministers a Draft for a Council of Ministers Resolution Concerning Priorities and the Timetable for Decisions to be taken by the Council in the Transport Sector during the Period up to the End of 1983.[72]

The Annex outlined the proposed priorities of the Council of Ministers in the area of shipping. Those priorities were:

- a system for monitoring the activities of certain third countries in sea transport;
- verifying the fulfilment of international safety standards by ships in EC ports, bringing EC interests to bear in relations between the Member States and third countries;
- state aids for shipping;
- rules on maritime transport; and
- social regulation in maritime transport.

69. OJ C140, 5 June 1979; Bull. EC 5-1979, point 2.3.20.
70. OJ C171, 9 July 1979; Bull. EC 4-1979, point 2.3.67.
71. OJ C14, 16 January 1985; Bull. EC 12-1984, point 2.1.203.
72. COM(80)582 final. Reprinted in OJ C294 of 13 November 1980, p. 6.

5.5.3 1980 Extension of the 1978 Collection of Information Decision

The application of the Decision of 19 December 1978 on the Collection of Information concerning the activities of carriers participating in cargo liner traffic in certain areas of operation[73] was extended for a further two years on 4 December 1980.[74] It was also extended to include transport services between the EC and the Far East.

5.5.4 1980 Recommendation on the Torremolinos International Convention for the Safety of Fishing Vessels

On 23 September 1980 the Council of Ministers adopted a Recommendation calling on EC Member States to ratify or accede to the 1977 Torremolinos International Convention for the Safety of Fishing Vessels by 31 July 1982.

5.5.5 1980 Proposal on Port Control of Pollution

On 2 July 1980, the Commission transmitted to the Council of Ministers a proposal for a Directive on the enforcement, in respect of vessels using EC ports, of international standards governing the safety of shipping and the prevention of pollution.[75]

Discussions on the proposals were suspended during 1981 pending completion of the work of the second European conference which was scheduled for 1982. Meanwhile, however, on 15 December 1981, the Council of Ministers adopted a Resolution asserting the need for Member States to take effective action as port-States to ensure that international standards for shipping safety and pollution prevention are correctly observed by all vessels.[76]

5.5.6 1980 Parliamentary resolutions on oil pollution

The Parliament adopted resolutions on aid for areas polluted by oil slicks and on a code of conduct for oil tankers and other vessels carrying noxious substances.[77]

5.5.7 1981 Accession to the EC of Greece

The accession to the EC of Greece in 1981 was a significant event in the development of EC shipping law. Greece is undoubtedly one of the major states in the shipping world.

5.5.8 1981 Council Resolution on its Priorities in the Transport Sector up to 1983

On 26 March 1981, the Council of Ministers adopted a Resolution on its priorities in the transport sector up to 1983. It did not take the opportunity to add further areas.

5.5.9 1981 Decision extending the Collection of Information Regime in respect of the Far East

On 26 March 1981, the Council of Ministers adopted a Decision establishing detailed rules for the collection of information concerning the activities of carriers participating

73. OJ L5, 9 January 1979.
74. OJ L5, 9 January 1979.
75. OJ C192, 30 July 1980; Bull. EC 6-1980, point 2.1.136.
76. See Bull. EC 12-1981.
77. OJ C85, 14 March 1980; OJ C117, 18 April 1980; OJ C147, 20 May 1980.

in cargo liner traffic between the EC Member States and the Far East. This Decision[78] extended the system already in existence in two other areas.

5.5.10 1981 Proposal on Competition Rules and Shipping

On 16 October 1981, the Commission transmitted to the Council a proposal for a Regulation laying down detailed rules on competition (i.e. Articles 85 and 86) in sea transport.[79]

5.5.11 1981 Proposals on Concerted Research on Shore-Based Maritime Navigation Aid Systems

On 24 September 1981, the Commission sent to the Council of Ministers a proposal for a Decision on a three-year concerted research project in the field of shore-based maritime navigation aid systems.

Again on 24 September 1981, the Commission sent to the Council of Ministers a proposal for a Decision authorising the Commission to negotiate an agreement on the proposed three-year concerted research project in the field of shore-based maritime navigation aid systems between the EC and other States participating in European co-operation in the field of scientific and technical research (COST).[80]

The Parliament delivered its opinion on the proposals.[81] In the light of this opinion, the Commission amended its proposals for the Decision adopting a concerted Community research project in the field of shore-based maritime navigation aid systems.

On 13 December 1982, the Council of Ministers finally adopted the Decision.[82]

5.5.12 1982 Extension of the Collection of Information systems

In 1982, the Council of Ministers extended the system for the collection of information concerning the activities of carriers participating in cargo liner traffic between the EC Member States and East Africa, Central America as well as the Far East for a further two years.[83]

5.5.13 1982 Memorandum of Understanding on Port-State Control

A Memorandum of Understanding on Port-State Control was signed at the Ministerial Conference on Maritime Safety in Paris on 26 January 1982.[84]

5.5.14 1983 Economic and Social Committee Opinion on the Commission's proposal on the application of Articles 85 and 86 to shipping

The Economic and Social Committee delivered its Opinion on the Commission's proposal on the Application of Articles 85 and 86 to shipping on 27 January 1983[85]

78. OJ L5, 9 January 1982; Bull. EC 12-1981.
79. See OJ C282, 5 November 1981; Bull. EC 9-1981. point 2.1.27. See also the Fifteenth General Report on the Activities of the European Communities, points 206 and 487.
80. Bull. EC 9-1981, point 2.1.117.
81. OJ C238, 13 September 1982.
82. OJ L378, 31 December 1982.
83. See OJ L368, 28 December 1982; Bull. EC 12-1982.
84. Bull. EC 1-1982, point 2.1.74.
85. CES 73/83.

having adopted it on 10 November 1982. This followed a request from the Council of Ministers on 3 November 1981.[86] On 12 November 1981, the bureau of the ECOSOC had instructed the Section for Transport and Communications to draw up an Opinion on the proposal.[87]

5.5.15 1983 Recommendation on SAR

On 25 July 1983, the Council of Ministers recommended that EC Member States ratify or accede to the 1979 International Convention on Maritime Search and Rescue (SAR).[88]

5.5.16 1983 Countermeasures Decision

On 26 October 1983, the Council of Ministers adopted a Decision whereby Member States which had taken or intended to take countermeasures against non-EC Member States in connection with shipping matters were to consult with the other EC States and the Commission.[89]

5.5.17 1983 Parliament's case against the Commission for failure to elaborate proposals in the area of transport

In 1983, the Parliament instituted proceedings against the Commission alleging inaction in respect of the transport sector. The ECJ declared that in breach of the EEC Treaty, the Council of Ministers had failed to ensure freedom to provide services in the sphere of international transport and to lay down the conditions under which non-resident carriers may operate transport services in a Member State. The court was of the view that the Commission was obliged to elaborate proposals in the transport area.

The Parliament's action provoked Commission reaction: the Commission published policy papers on inland transport in February 1983, civil aviation in March 1984 and maritime transport in March 1985.[90]

5.5.18 1984 Commission Memorandum on Maritime Transport

In December 1984, the Commission sent a communication to the Council of Ministers laying down the main lines of action for a Community shipping policy.[91] Up to then, neither the Commission nor the Council of Ministers had clearly defined the general framework and now a "coherent approach".[92]

86. OJ C282/4, 5 November 1981.
87. CES 211/82.
88. OJ L237, 26 August 1983; Bull. EC 7/8-1983, point 2.1.1980.
89. Bull. EC 6-1983, point 2.1.227.
90. COM(85)90 final, 14 March 1985; reprinted in Bulletin of the EC, Supp.5/85 and OJ C212 of 23 August 1985, pp. 2–21 (proposals only). The case, Case 13/83 has been reported at [1985] ECR 1513 and [1986] CMLR 138.
91. COM(84)668 final.
92. See Commission's Information Memo P-95 of December 1984, p. 1.

5.5.19 1985 Progress Towards a Common Maritime Policy: Commission Communication

5.5.19.1 Introduction

In many ways, EC shipping law really begun in 1985.[93] In March 1985, the Commission published its *Progress Towards a Common Maritime Policy: Maritime Transport* document[94] which was a Communication and a set of Proposals which the Commission forwarded to the Council of Ministers. This was the first "systematic"[95] attempt by the Commission at defining a Community shipping policy. It was the real beginning of EC shipping law because some of the Commission's important proposals were adopted as law by the Council of Ministers at the end of 1986 which was the first serious series of shipping measures.

The background to the Communication was, according to Bredima-Savopoulou and Tzoannos that it

> "was officially approved by the Commission in collegium in December 1984 under the Greek Transport Commissioner, Mr G. Contogeorgis. Thereafter, in January '85 the Transport portfolio was entrusted to the British Commissioner, Mr S. Clinton Davis. From the outset, Mr Clinton Davis made it publicly known that he had certain misgivings about the Memorandum and that he would wish it to be more pronounced over labour issues, flags of convenience and, thus, in its overall approach less liberal. Taking advantage of the fact that in the 'interregnum' between the two Commissioners—over Christmas 1985—the versions in all languages were not ready, the new Commissioner proceeded with some amendments in the texts of the Memorandum, not in the legislative proposals."[96]

It was felt by the Commission, that the Community had then reached a stage in the development of its shipping policy which required a more coherent approach. The objective was said by the Commission to be to provide an overall concept for a Community shipping policy, to review, in the light of these principles, policy developments so far and to propose the new measures which the Commission felt were required for the furtherance of the Community's trading and shipping interests.[97] This

93. Bredima-Savopoulou and Tzoannos comment in *op. cit.* at footnote 15 above: "[t]he year 1985 must be considered a turning point for policy making in the European Community (EC) with respect to its maritime sector, since it was then that the Commission submitted to the Council for the first time a comprehensive memorandum and set of proposals for interlinked measures in support of that sector."

94. COM(85)90 final, 14 March 1985; reprinted in Bulletin of the EC, Supp. 5/85 and OJ C212/2, 23 August 1985 (proposals only). Referred to herein as "*Progress*".

95. Petropolous, "The European Community Transport Policy – An Overview" at *The Future of Shipping in Europe — Key Legal and Commercial Issues*, London, 28–29 June 1990, p. 4.

96. *Op. cit.* at footnote 15 above, pp. 113–114. The authors record these amendments thus: the "wording of the Memorandum concerning open registries has been toned down without it being coupled, however, with a change in the overall policy on open registries. Thus, there are changes to the effect that open registry shipping is considered as having 'undesirable effects' and in some respects may 'not be in conformity with international conventions' and that measures should be taken to eliminate 'unacceptable practices'. In the paragraphs concerning manpower and social aspects there is a series of presentational changes designed to adjust the tone of the section and to stress that social and employment issues are closely linked to international policy. More particularly, attention is drawn to the adverse consequences for the EEC of a reduction in the number of available seafarers. Moreover, an official dialogue between the social partners should be established to promote a greater consensus on general problems in shipping. The new text also calls for a detailed study on the problems of non-domiciled seafarers to be undertaken in this area, whilst the previous text gave a degree of acceptance to EEC owners employing non-EEC nationals. There are also some other changes, such as adding to the list of major long-term factors affecting the structure of Community shipping the following factors: major takeovers, diversification by shipping companies into non-maritime activities and increased influence of financial institutions as beneficial owners of ships. Finally, reference is made to the need for concerted action on hydrography."

97. *Progress*, p. 9.

was the first incisive analysis of the sector and the first comprehensive package of measures to be proposed in the area. Most importantly, this Communication led to the first package of measures to be adopted in the sphere—in December 1986.[98]

The Commission believed that after a number of policy proposals on specific shipping policy matters, the time had come to develop a "more coherent framework" for a Community shipping policy and this document was designed to set out that framework. The Commission believed that this Paper, together with the February 1983 policy paper on inland transport[99] and the March 1984 policy paper on civil aviation[100] met the Parliament's request for a comprehensive approach to the common transport policy.[101]

5.5.19.2 Analysis of the Market

The Maritime Transport Paper recognised the decline of the Community's fleet relative to world tonnage and attributed this decline to the prolonged recession in world trade, a loss of comparative advantage on the part of EC shipping interests, the competition from State trading companies and cargo reservation by developing countries in the case of liner trades, changing patterns of trade and the growth of protectionist practices adopted by other countries. There was not just a decline in numbers and tonnage but there was also an increase in the age of the EC fleet. This decline was in spite of the fact that the EC was the leading trading area in the world: its trade in 1982 with third countries represented 21% by value of world imports and 20% by value of world exports with some 95% of the total trade (in terms of quantity) between the EC and third countries being carried by sea and some 30% (again in terms of quantity) of intra-EC traffic being carried by sea.

The Commission's solution was not to adopt an insular or parochial view but rather to take a broader perspective—it wrote at page 7:

> "in view of the Community's dependence on world trade and the dependence of its shipping interests on international shipping markets, the Commission is of the opinion that the maintenance of a multilateral and commercially orientated Community shipping policy is still in the best interests of the Community's shipping industry, as well as of its user industries and is still the best way of achieving the objectives of the Treaty."

In terms of bulk shipping operations, the Commission concluded that the pursuance of a market-orientated policy was in line with the economic interests of the EC and that open registry shipping are important economic facts for the EC fleet. While recognising these facts, the Commission also believed that they had undesirable effects as well and that in some respects they were not in conformity with international Conventions. It thus argued that measures should be taken to eliminate unacceptable practices and conduct (such as substandard ships).

5.5.19.3 Proposals

The Paper made a number of specific proposals.

The Commission proposed in respect of all forms of shipping a Regulation permitting EC action against cargo reservation practices which damage, or threaten to

98. On the December 1986 package of measures, see para. 5.5.20, below.
99. OJ C154, 13 June 1983; Bull. EC 2-1983, point 2.1.128.
100. OJ C182, 9 July 1984; Bull. EC 2-1984, point 2.1.149.
101. *Progress*, Summary.

damage, EC interests.[102] The Commission believed that this was "one of the areas where Community action is likely to be more effective because of the greater trading weight of the Community and because only Community action can ensure that such countermeasures do not merely result in the diversion of cargo from one Community port to another".[103]

The Commission also proposed a Council Regulation on freedom to provide maritime services.[104] Such a Regulation would apply the principle of freedom to provide services as regards offshore supply services, Member States' trades with third states, the carriage of cargo wholly or partly reserved for the national flag and, with certain specific exceptions, the carriage of passengers or goods by sea between ports in a Member State (including overseas departments of that Member State) (i.e. cabotage).

On 15 May 1979, the Member States and the EC adopted a Regulation (Regulation 954/79) on the ratification of the UN Code of Conduct for Liner Conferences.[105] The UN Code was adopted subject to a number of reservations designed to preserve a market-orientated system as between the industrialised countries and as between OECD liner shipping companies. This left a gap. The gap which had to be filled was a joint definition or interpretation of the "concept of national shipping line" which confers, in Code-based trades, important rights on liner shipping companies. In *Progress*, the Commission put forward a number of criteria for such a definition.[106] The Commission hoped that its criteria would avoid "any discrimination between shipping lines of the Member States and, subject to reciprocity, shipping lines of other OECD countries, without taking away from each Member State the flexibility to take into account its particular national circumstances".[107]

The Commission dealt at some length in *Progress* on the issue of liner conferences and competition. It summarised its position thus:

"[w]hile Regulation 954/79[108] also acknowledges the stabilising role of liner conferences, guaranteeing regular and reliable services to transport users, the Commission undertook at the same time to submit a draft Regulation on the basis of Article 85(3) applying the competition rules of the Treaty to maritime transport. The Commission submitted a draft in 1981,[109] and in the light of the ensuing discussions in the Council and elsewhere has somewhat modified its original ideas. . . . The Commission is concerned about the increasing trend to exclude outside competition from trades in which closed conferences operate. These cases are most serious where a State at one end of the trade route precludes non-conference competition. The Commission's proposal is designed in particular to deal with this problem."[110]

The Commission proposed complementing that proposal with another which attempted to ensure that EC liner shipping could compete with third countries' liner shipping companies on the basis of fair and commercial principles and thus proposed that the Commission should be able to act against unfair practices where they cause or threaten material injury to EC liner conferences.[111]

In 1977 the Council adopted a Decision on EC consultation in regard to Member States' relations with third countries and relating to shipping matters in international

102. *Progress*, p. 47.
103. *Progress*, p. 7.
104. *Progress*, pp. 7 and 49.
105. OJ L121, 17 May 1979.
106. *Progress*, pp. 7 and 53.
107. *Progress*, p. 7.
108. *Ibid.*, at footnote 106 above.
109. OJ C282, 5 November 1981.
110. Set out in *Progress*, at p. 54.
111. *Progress*, p. 58.

organisations.[112] In *Progress*, the Commission proposed a Council Decision amending that Decision so as to allow *ex-ante* consultation on Member States' shipping relations with third States.[113]

The Commission reiterated its enthusiasm for remaining active in the area of maritime safety. To this end, the Commission said that it would pay particular attention to: (a) the development and co-ordination of the system of port State control within the European region and in particular the control of substandard ships and crew conditions; (b) the study of the need for and, if established, the implementation of a coastal navigational system to improve the safety of navigation around the coasts of the EC, including concerted action on hydrography; and (c) the use of the EC's relationship with developing countries to help in the training of their masters, crew and maritime adminstrations.

Similarly, the Commission reiterated its enthusiasm for remaining active in the area of pollution prevention.

The Commission also dealt with the issue of ports. It stated that it was essential that matters relating to ports be taken into account in the context of the development of both the common inland and maritime transport policies.[114] Building on its 1984 proposal designed to eliminate distortions of competition between ports arising from the variations in the national regulation of hinterland traffic,[115] the Commission stated that it would, first, re-examine the State aids applied to ports and would deal with specific aids on the basis of Articles 92 and 93 of the EEC Treaty and, secondly, increase its co-operation with the ports concerning the development of common standards for the exchange of information between ports.[116]

The Commission expressed its willingness to intensify and develop its co-operation in shipping matters with the ACP (African, Caribbean and Pacific) States.

5.5.19.4 Economic and Social Committee's Opinion

On 1 April 1985, the Council of Ministers decided to consult the ECOSOC under Article 198(1) of the EEC Treaty on the Communication and, on 26 July 1985, the Council of Ministers asked the Committee to deliver its Opinion on four of the six Annexes, namely the Draft Council Regulation concerning co-ordinated action to safeguard Free Access to Cargoes in Ocean Trades (Annex II.1), the Draft Council Regulation applying to the Principle of Freedom to Provide Services to Maritime Transport,[117] amendments to the Proposal for a Council Regulation laying down detailed rules for the application of Articles 85 and 86 of the Treaty to Maritime Transport[118] and the Draft Council Regulation on Unfair Pricing Practices in Maritime Transport.[119] The ECOSOC delivered its Opinion on the Communication and some of the proposals on 21 May 1986.[120]

The Committee welcomed:

112. OJ L239, 17 September 1977.
113. *Progress*, pp. 7 and 52.
114. *Progress*, p. 8.
115. OJ C14, 16 January 1985; Bull. EC 12-1984, point 2.1.203.
116. *Progress*, p. 8.
117. *Progress*, Annex II.2.
118. *Progress*, Annex II.5.
119. *Progress*, Annex II.6.
120. TRA/116.

"the publication of this long-awaited document on maritime transport policy because it indicates that at last the Commission has begun to regard maritime transport as an industry in its own right. Until now the Community has lacked a coherent and comprehensive policy for the transport sector and it is now crucial that such a policy should address the means of the Member States' fleets decline, if not reversing it."[121]

None the less, the Committee was scathing in its view of the Commission's proposals:

"[a]lthough the Commission has made a useful attempt to translate the principles of the EEC Treaty into shipping terms, the analysis and policy have a number of deficiencies and the Commission's proposals will not halt the fleet's decline unless these proposals are amended and improved. The situation in the shipping industry is clearly deteriorating yet the Commission does not appear to appreciate fully the seriousness of the situation. The Commission's analysis is confined to a static review of the situation, failing to assess the most recent trends and the outlook for various sectors or to consider the effects of the fundamental change taking place in the level and pattern of world trade."[122]

Instead, it called for a pragmatic and realistic maritime policy which would recognise the international dimension of the industry and its relationship with other maritime industries as well as serve the social, economic and political interests of the EC enabling a prompt and effective response to any threat to these interests.

5.5.20 The 1986 Package[123]

As compared to the first three decades of the EC, there has been a frenzy of activity in the area of shipping during the last decade or so. The corner-stone of this recent activity has been the package of Regulations adopted during the UK Presidency of the Council of Ministers in December 1986 on freedom to provide services,[124] competition,[125] unfair pricing practices[126] and free access to cargoes and ocean trades.[127] These Regulations "completed the foundations for a European shipping policy, following the steps taken since 1977 (consultation procedure,[128] monitoring system,[129] safety at sea[130] and 'Brussels Package'[131])."[132] The Regulations had been proposed in the Commission's Communication to the Council of Ministers entitled *Progress Towards a Common Transport Policy—Maritime Transport*.[133] The adoption of these measures owed a great deal to the work of the British Presidency of the Council of Ministers.

The Package of Measures consisted of four Regulations. It is worth considering the extent to which these measures are protectionist[134] and therefore out of step with the EC's avowed open shipping policy.

121. TRA, para. 2.1.
122. TRA, para. 2.2.
123. See Bredima-Savopoulou and Tzoannos, *op. cit.* at footnote 15, Chapter 8.
124. Regulation 4055/86.
125. Regulation 4056/86.
126. Regulation 4057/86.
127. Regulation 4058/86.
128. Council Decision 77/587/EEC, OJ L239, 17 September 1977.
129. Council Decision 78/774/EEC, OJ L258, 21 September 1978.
130. Council Directives 79/115/EEC and 79/116/EEC, OJ L33, 8 February 1979.
131. Council Regulation (EEC) No. 954/79, OJ L121, 17 May 1979.
132. Report from the Commission to the Council of Ministers on the Implementation of the four Regulations in the field of maritime transport adopted by the Council of Ministers on 22 December 1986, *ibid.*, para. 1.
133. COM(85)90 final.
134. See the comments of UNICE in Agence Europe, *Business Brief*, No. 1135 at p. 4.

5.5.20.1 Regulation 4055/86

Regulation 4055/86[135] applied the principle of freedom to provide services to maritime transport between Member States and between Member States and third countries. The measure was not as broad as the Commission or the British Presidency of the Council of Ministers desired: it did not extend to cabotage. The Council of Ministers asked COREPER to work towards the adoption of a measure to deal with this thorny issue.[136]

5.5.20.2 Regulation 4056/86

Regulation 4056/86[137] laid down detailed rules for the application of Articles 85 and 86 of the EEC Treaty to maritime transport.

Regulation 4056/86 does not boldly and baldly apply Articles 85 and 86 of the EEC Treaty to maritime transport. The Regulation recognises the distinctive characteristics of the maritime transport sector, including its international character and thus allows for negotiations with third states on matters arising. Regulation 4057/86[138] dealt with unfair pricing practices in maritime transport.

Regulation 4058/86[139] concerned co-ordinated action to safeguard free access to cargoes in ocean trades.

5.5.20.3 Statements

The Council of Ministers, the Commission and some national delegations made a number of Statements on shipping which were entered into the minutes of the Council of Ministers.

The first statement concerned Community shipping policy generally and was made by the Council of Ministers. The Council declared that:

> "its adoption of the present Regulations marks only a first stage in the elaboration of a Community shipping policy whose aims are to maintain and develop an efficient competitive shipping industry to ensure the provision of competitive shipping services for the benefit of Community trade."

The Council of Ministers recognised that for these aims to be achieved, an effort was needed to reduce the disparities in operating conditions and costs between the Community fleets as a whole and their foreign competitors. It went on to welcome the Commission's programme of proposals[140] relating to fiscal, social and technical aspects of shipping. The Council then went on to invite the Commission to submit "appropriate proposals as rapidly as possible, with a view to contributing to the completion of the internal market by 1992". Bredima-Savopoulou and Tzoannos comment that this statement "delineates the framework and purposes for future measures to be taken by the EC in the second phase of its common shipping policy".[141]

The second statement, which was made by the Commission, related to the Consultation Procedure in relation to Articles 4(2), 4(6) and 6(5) of Regulation 4058/

135. On Regulation 4055/86, see Chapter 7 below.
136. On cabotage, see paras 7.6 *et seq.*, below.
137. On Regulation 4055/86, see Chapter 12 below.
138. On Regulation 4057/86, see Chapter 13, below.
139. On Regulation 4058/86, see Chapter 14, below.
140. Contained in Annex I to Doc. 8107/86 MAR 48.
141. *Op. cit.* at footnote 15 above, p. 174.

86. The statement "requests the Council [of Ministers] to take up as a matter of priority its proposals to amend the consultation procedure established by Council Decision 77/587/EEC".

The third statement was one by the Council of Ministers on Tramp Shipping and Consortia. It related to Articles 1 and 3 of Regulation 4056/86. In it the Council of Ministers invited the Commission "to study the situation regarding competition in the sectors of passenger shipping, tramp shipping, joint ventures, consortia and agreements between transport users to consider whether it is necessary to submit new proposals". The Council of Ministers said that it regarded joint ventures and consortia which had as their object or effect the achievement of technical improvement or co-operation (within the meaning of Article 2 of Regulation 4056/86) or where the consortia only covered a minor market as falling outside Article 85(1) of the EEC Treaty. The Statement then went on, in the words of Bredima-Savopoulou and Tzoannos:

> "The Commission undertakes to submit within one year from the date of adoption of the Regulation a report to the Council on whether to provide for block exemptions for passenger transport services, joint ventures and consortia,[142] and to submit proposals to that effect if necessary. The Commission will meanwhile examine carefully any request for individual exemption relating to passenger transport services. In doing so, it will examine, *inter alia*, 'the extent to which such agreements are conducive to facilitating services in this area and favour their continuity and their optimum operation'."[143]

5.5.20.4 Assessment of the 1986 Package

The 1986 Package is important but it is only a beginning. Its importance is not to be underestimated—as Dimitri Petropolous, the Head of Division: Maritime Transport in the EC Commission, has said: "[w]ith the adoption of a shipping package of four Council Regulations in December 1986, the Community has now at its disposal the legal instruments that it can use to preserve free and fair competition in world shipping".[144]

To what extent were the four Regulations successful in stemming the tide of flagging out, ageing as well as scrapping or selling but not replacing? Georgios Anastassopoulos, the then Chairman of the Transport Committee of the European Parliament, speaking to the Antwerp Shipping Symposium, "A Future for the Community Fleet", on 6 May 1987, said that the four Regulations "won't suffice to halt the decline. We have welcomed them as a first step towards a Community maritime policy. But the Regulations have not prevented the continuance of flagging out and I am not the only one to fear that they won't prevent it in the future."[145]

The Select Committee of the House of Lords on the European Communities has said that the December 1986 package has "worked well. But they have not stopped the

142. "With regard to the future treatment of consortia, it has been proposed by some shipowner quarters to make the following distinction: the activities of consortia operating within conferences lie within the intent of Regulation 4056. The few consortia operated as single commercial activities should be treated in the same manner as individual shipping companies and should therefore require no special treatment under the competition rules. In the rare cases where a consortium operates outside a conference and is under single company operation it will be obliged to have a rate fixing role and should be subject to a similar group exemption as that provided under Regulation 4056."Alan Bott in "The EEC and Shipping", Institute of Maritime Law, Conference 11/2/88, London.

143. *Op. cit.* at footnote 15 above, p. 175. On the eventual report, see para. 5.5.29 below.

144. "The European Community Transport Policy–An Overview", at The Future of Shipping in Europe–Key Legal and Commercial Issues, London, 28–29 June 1990, p. 2 (personal views).

145. Reprinted in (1987) XXII *European Transport Law* at 200.

decline in the Community merchant fleet. The haemorrhage of economic and potential military resources continues."[146]

5.5.21 The Single European Act

The Single European Act (SEA)[147] has by abolishing the need for unanimity in the Council of Ministers in (*inter alia*) shipping matters facilitated future development. Rabe has commented:

"[a] major step towards the definition of a common Community policy in the sphere of maritime transport was the adoption of the Single European Act. It has had and will have a significant impact on the EEC legislative procedure. Article 84(2) EEC Treaty now clearly spells out that also for sea transport the respective instruments will generally be adopted by a majority vote. This will certainly speed up the process of establishing a common maritime transport policy of the Community."[148]

5.5.22 1987 Antwerp Meeting

In May 1987, a gathering of representatives of the EC Parliament and Commission as well as national shipowners, seafarers and administrations took place in Antwerp.[149] The meeting heard about the decline in the fortunes of EC shipping. But interestingly, for present purposes, the meeting also heard about ways of solving it—while many of these ways have not yet been adopted, some may provide a path for the future. The then Transport Commissioner, Stanley Clinton Davis, said that positive measures were needed to counter the competitive pressures on shipowners to flag out.[150] Many speakers favoured EC governments granting a special tax and social security status for the shipping industry so as to combat the shipping crisis by allowing EC-based shipping companies to compete.[151] There were many calls for an EC-led approach.

5.5.23 1988 Shipbuilding Talks with Japan

In July 1988, the EC and Japan discussed their differences over shipbuilding. They agreed that both sides would work together to raise prices so as to avoid a further decline in the fortunes of EC shipbuilding due to cheap prices in Japanese yards.[152]

5.5.24 1988 Commission Proposal on the Minimum Health and Safety Requirements for Improved Medical Treatment on Board Vessels

The Commision proposed a measure on minimum health and safety requirements for improved medical treatment on board vessels. This will be examined below.

5.5.25 1988 Commission Programme

The Commission in its Programme for 1988 promised that after the first year of application of the 1986 Package,[153] positive measures would be taken to strengthen the

146. See *Community Shipping Measures*, Session 1989–1990, 28th Report, para. 2.
147. On the SEA see para. 3.5.24, above and paras 26.2, 26.4.2, 26.5.3.13, 26.5.4.1.
148. "Recent Developments in EEC Legislation Pertaining to Maritime Transport", at the IBA Conference in Strasbourg, October 1989, Paper No. SG328/A, at p. 2.
149. For the press coverage, see *Lloyd's List*, 7 May 1987, p .1; 8 May 1987, p. 3.
150. *Lloyd's List*, 7 July 1987, p. 1.
151. See *Lloyd's List*, 8 May 1987, p. 3.
152. See *Lloyd's List*, 14 July 1988.
153. On which see para. 5.5.20, above.

position of EC fleets and national shipowners and to allow the use of an EC flag. The Commission had hoped to make progress on cabotage, safety and the carriage of dangerous goods.

5.5.26 August 1989: Positive Measures

In an effort to improve the operating conditions of Community shipping, the Commission published on 3 August 1989 a Communication by it to the Council of Ministers. This document, entitled "A Future for the Community Shipping Industry: Measures to Improve the Operating Conditions of Community Shipping"[154] proposes some measures which might well be adopted. These proposals, which were long awaited,[155] relate to the establishment of an EC shipping register, the effectiveness of port state control, the common definition of an EC shipowner and the application of the freedom to provide services to maritime transport within the EC States. It was the second stage of EC shipping policy.

5.5.26.1 Proposal for a Council Regulation establishing a Community Ship Register and Providing for the Flying of the Community Flag by Sea-Going Vessels

The Commission proposed a Council Regulation to establish a European Community Shipping Register (the EUROS Register). This has not yet been adopted but is examined in Chapter 6 below.

5.5.26.2 Proposal for a Commission Recommendation on Improving the Effectiveness of Port State Control in the Community

The Commission was anxious to promote and strengthen the effectiveness of port state control and this matter is examined below.

5.5.26.3 Proposal for a Council of Ministers Regulation providing for a Common Definition of a Community Shipowner

It is necessary to define a Community Shipowner for a variety of purposes (including the EUROS Register) and thus the Commission proposed a defining Regulation. This matter is discussed in Chapter 6 below.

5.5.26.4 Proposal for a Council of Ministers Regulation applying the Principle of Freedom to Provide Services to Maritime Transport within Member States

The remaining loophole after the adoption of Regulation 4055/86 was cabotage. The Commission proposed a Regulation to deal with this loophole. The Commission's proposal was examined in Chapter 7 below.

154. COM(89)266 final; 3 August 1989. See the Economic and Social Committee Opinion (OJ C56/70, 7 March 1990).

155. See the comments of Rabe in "Recent Developments in EEC Legislation Pertaining to Maritime Transport", at the IBA Conference in Strasbourg, October 1989, Paper No. SG328/A, at p. 2. The proposals of the Commission resulted from an invitation by the Council of Ministers.

5.5.26.5 1990: Proposal for a Council Regulation regarding the Transfer of Ships from one Register to another within the Community

The Commission proposed a Regulation to facilitate the transfer of ships between EC registers. This Regulation has been adopted and is discussed in Chapter 6 below.

5.5.27 Financial and fiscal measures

On 3 August 1989, the Commission published a second document another Communication, this one being entitled "Financial and Fiscal Measures Concerning Shipping Operations with Ships Registered in the Community".[156] The Communication included a series of "Guidelines for the examination of State aids to Community Shipping Companies". This was a document produced for the information of the Council.

5.5.28 June 1990 Resolution on Passenger Ferry Safety

On 19 June 1990, the Council of Ministers and the Representatives of the Governments of the Member States, meeting within the Council of Ministers adopted a Resolution[157] on Improving Passenger Ferry Safety.[158] There had been a number of ferry disasters in Europe over the previous few years, including the *Herald of Free Enterprise* in 1987.

The Resolution called on the Member States and the EC Commission, in their capacity as members or as observer of the International Maritime Organisation of the United Nations (IMO)[159] and the Memorandum of Understanding on Port State Control[160] to press for the urgent identification, elaboration, adoption and implementation of measures which will improve safety of passenger ferries on an international basis in the framework of the IMO and Port State Control Memorandum.

The Council of Ministers and the Representatives of the Governments of the Member States adopted the Resolution aware of: (a) the large number of passengers who travel by passenger ferries in European waters, (b) the essentially international nature of such operations; (c) the necessity of crews being able to function in a satisfactory manner in the event of an emergency; (d) the dangers which can arise from management and communication failures; (e) the potentially large-scale intervention which could be required in the event of an accident involving a passenger ferry; and (f) the fact that the transport of passengers in European waters is carried out by vessels registered both inside and outside the Community, thus requiring any necessary improvement of passenger ferry safety, including the question of crewing, to take place in a broad international context.

5.5.29 1990 Proposal for a Council of Ministers Regulation to grant a Block Exemption for Consortia

The Council of Ministers adopted a Regulation on 25 February 1992 a Regulation to enable the Commission to issue a block exemption to consortia.

156. SEC(89)921 final.
157. On the legal effect of a Resolution, see para. 3.5.2.2.5, above.
158. OJ C206/02, 18 August 1990.
159. On the IMO, see paras 1.3.3, above.
160. On the Memorandum, see paras 23.2.3, below.

5.5.29.1 1991: Permanent Dialogue on the Maritime Industry

On 18 September 1991, the Commission announced the creation of a permanent forum for discussion on the shape of the EC's maritime policy.[161] Having recognised the huge importance of the maritime sector for the EC—the fishing, shipbuilding, offshore and shipping industries provide about two and a half million jobs in the EC—the Commission decided to establish a permanent dialogue between all the parties concerned. This forum will report to the Commission by Summer 1992. The Commission has recognised the need for a coherent response in areas: safety (the Commission is preparing a White Paper on such issues as ferry safety and oil tanker design); research and development; transport; international competition; and the environment. The report is anxiously awaited.

5.6 THE FUTURE

The area of EC shipping law has developed dramatically over the past ten years. It is anticipated that there will be more developments over the next five years. The developments will probably be in competition (including state aids), registration, safety, the environment and external relations.

161. Commission Information Memo P(91)64 of 18 September 1991.

CHAPTER 6

Establishment and Registration

6.1 RIGHT OF ESTABLISHMENT

This chapter examines the right of establishment under the EEC Treaty[1] in the context of shipping.[2] Articles 52–58 of the EEC Treaty deal with the right of establishment. It is to be presumed, in the light of the judgment of the ECJ in Case 167/73 *Commission v. France*,[3] that the rules contained on freedom of establishment contained in Articles 52 to 58 of the EEC Treaty are applicable in the context of sea transport. Thus, national rules restricting the right of establishment of shipping companies in a Member State to nationals or companies in that Member State are inapplicable *vis-à-vis* nationals or companies from other Member States and such infringements may be brought before national courts.[4]

In the context of shipping, the right of establishment mainly revolves around registration.[5] It has been said:

"[Most] Member States favour the view that there is no relation between establishment and registration, since the latter is an act of national sovereignty escaping from the demands of Community Law. On the contrary, the Commission's view is that registration is a corollary of establishment and that, in any event, all financial advantages deriving from the flag should be granted to EC nationals without discrimination. The problem has wider implications because the flag is linked in certain Member States with a series of economic advantages. This is the case of the coastal shipping, the so-called 'cabotage'. The Commission in a report on the economic implications of coastal shipping in the Community concludes that the economic consequences from the lifting of the privilege are minimal. It is noteworthy that a case is pending on this matter before the Court concerning an action of the Commission versus France, the outcome of which will be of paramount importance for the right of registration of vessels in the Community."[6]

1. On the right of establishment generally, see Everling, *The Right of Establishment in the Common Market* (1964). See also Rawlinson and Cornwell-Kelly, *European Community Law*, Chapter 10; Kapteyn and Van Themaat, *Introduction to the Law of the European Communities* (4th edn, 1988), p. 427 *et seq.*; Vaughan (ed.), *Law of the European Communities*, vol. 2, Chapter 16.

For the case law, see, *inter alia*, *Dona v. Mantero* [1976] ECR 1333, [1976] 2 CMLR 578; Case 197/84 *Steinhausser v. City of Biarritz* [1985] ECR 1819, [1986] 1 CMLR 53; Case 270/83 *Commission v. France* [1986] ECR 273; Case 71/76 *Thieffry v. Conseil de l'Ordre des Avocats à la Cour de Paris* [1977] ECR 765, [1977] 2 CMLR 373; Case 11/77 *Patrick v. Ministre des Affairs Culturelles* [1977] ECR 1199, [1977] 2 CMLR 523; Case 16/78 *Choquet* [1978] ECR 2293, [1979] 1 CMLR 535; Case 110–111/78 *Ministère Public et al. v. Van Wesemael and Follachio* [1979] ECR 35, [1979] 3 CMLR 87; Case 107/83 *Ordre des Avocats au Barreau de Paris v. Klopp* [1984] ECR 2971, [1985] 1 CMLR 99; Case 292/86 *Gullung v. Conseil de l'Ordre des Avocats au Barreau de Colmar et al.* [1988] 2 CMLR 57.

2. See Dubois, "Le Principe de la Liberté d'Etablissement et de Prestations de Services en Matière de Transports Maritime", Colloque 10-12/10-79, Institut Méditerranéen des Transports Maritimes, Marseilles.

3. [1973] ECR 359, [1974] 2 CMLR 216. On this case, see para 5.4.8, above.

4. Bredima-Savopoulou and Tzoannos, "In Search of a Common Shipping Policy for the EEC" (1981) 20 *Journal of Common Market Studies* 95 at p. 103.

5. See Dubois, *op. cit* at footnote 2.

6. Bredima-Savopoulou and Tzoannos, *op. cit* at footnote 4.

6.1.1 Concept of right of establishment

The right of establishment involves the entitlement of a person to enter another EC Member State and "establish" there for the purpose of carrying on an economic activity other than under a contract of employment.

The right of establishment as understood in EC law includes the right to take up and pursue activities as a self-employed person as well as to set up and manage undertakings[7] in a Member State.

Freedom of establishment is closely linked to the freedom to provide services.[8] However, it involves a more permanent presence in the host State than merely providing services to undertakings in that second State[9] on a non-permanent basis.[10] For most purposes, it does not matter whether an activity involves the right of establishment or the right to provide services. On the other hand, the matter may be material for present purposes because there is a divergence between the provisions in Article 61 of the EEC Treaty on freedom to provide services and those provisions relating to establishment in the context of transport.

6.1.2 General rule on freedom of establishment

Article 52 of the EEC Treaty provides:

"Within the framework of the provisions set out below,[11] restrictions on the freedom of establishment of nationals of a Member State in the territory of another Member State shall be abolished by progressive stages in the course of the transitional period. Such progressive abolition shall also apply to restrictions on the setting up of agencies, branches or subsidiaries by nationals of any Member State established in the territory of any Member State.

Freedom of establishment shall include the right to take up and pursue activities as self-employed persons and to set up and manage undertakings, in particular companies or firms within the meaning of the second paragraph of Article 58, under the conditions laid down for its own nationals by the law of the country where such establishment is effected, subject to the provisions of the Chapter relating to capital."

The purpose of Article 52 is to ensure that self-employed nationals of one Member State are treated in the same way in another Member State as are nationals of that second State.[12] Or, put another way, a national of Member State X may pursue his freedom of establishment in Member State Y on the same basis as a national of Member State Y.

Article 52 has direct effect.[13,14] In the case of the original six Member States, it had direct effect from the end of the transitional period.[15] In the case of newer Member States, the Article had direct effect from their dates of accession.[16]

The freedom of establishment under the EEC Treaty may be enjoyed by nationals of EC Member States and their families, notwithstanding that some or all of the family

7. On the meaning of "undertakings", see para. 10.1.3.1, below but in essence, an undertaking is any entity carrying on an economic activity

8. Kapteyn and Van Themaat, *op. cit.* at footnote 1, p. 429.

9. See Case 118/75 *Watson and Belmann* [1976] ECR 1185; [1976] 2 CMLR 552.

10. See Case 196/87 *Steymann v. Staatssecretaris van Justitie.*

11. I.e. Arts 52–58 of the EEC Treaty.

12. See Case 221/85 *Commission v. Belgium* [1987] ECR 719; [1988] 1 CMLR 620.

13. On the concept of direct effect, see para. 3.3.5, above.

14. See Case 2/74 *Reyner v. Kingdom of Belgium* [1974] ECR 631; [1974] 2 CMLR 305.

15. I.e. 1 January 1970. See Case 2/74 *Reyner v. Kingdom of Belgium* [1974] ECR 631; [1974] 2 CMLR 305.

16. Case 11/77 *Patrick v. Ministre des Affaires Culturelles* [1977] ECR 1199; [1977] 2 CMLR 523.

members are not nationals of an EC Member State.[17] In the case of companies, freedom of establishment means that a company has a right to transfer its registered office to another Member State after the first Member State has given its consent.[18]

Article 52 allows for freedom of establishment in relation to incidental matters as well such as the establishment of agencies, branches or subsidiaries.[19] It deals not "merely with the establishment of the self-employed or companies but also with the exercise of a profession or management of undertakings".[20] It is clear from the decision of the ECJ in Case 159/78 *Commission v. Italy*[21] that Article 52 does not restrict the duty of a Member State to abolish any national rules which are discriminatory.

Discrimination even by professional bodies is prohibited under the EEC Treaty[22] provided there is the EC dimension: Article 52 may not be invoked to deal with purely domestic matters which have no EC dimension.[23]

Article 52 is implemented by means of a General Programme as well as by directives in particular areas.

6.1.3 Prohibition of new restrictions

Article 53 of the EEC Treaty prohibits Member States from introducing any new restrictions on the right of establishment after they join the EC. It provides: "Member States shall not introduce any new restrictions on the right of establishment in their territories of nationals of other Member States, save as otherwise provided in this Treaty." It is clear from Case 6/64 *Costa v. ENEL*[24] that Article 53 has direct effect.

6.1.4 Implementation of the Treaty provisions on establishment

Article 54 provides for the implementation of the provisions of the EEC Treaty on freedom of establishment by means of a General Programme and the enactment of directives.[25] Article 54 provides:

"1. Before the end of the first stage, the Council[26] shall, acting unanimously on a proposal from the Commission and after consulting the Economic and Social Committee and the European Parliament, draw up a general programme for the abolition of existing restrictions on freedom of establishment within the Community. The Commission shall submit its proposal to the Council during the first two years of the first stage.

The programme shall set out the general conditions under which freedom of establishment is to be attained in the case of each type of activity and in particular the stages by which it is to be attained.

2. In order to implement this general programme or, in the absence of such a programme, in order to achieve a stage in attaining freedom of establishment as regards a particular activity, the

17. Case 48/75 *Royer* [1976] ECR 497; [1976] 2 CMLR 619.
18. Case 81/87 *R v. HM Treasury et al., ex p. Daily Mail and General Trust PLC* [1988] 3 CMLR 713.
19. Case 270/83 *Commission v. France* [1986] ECR 273.
20. Kapteyn and Van Themaat, *op. cit.* at footnote 1, p. 428.
21. [1979] ECR 3247; [1980] 3 CMLR 446.
22. Case 36/74 *Walrave and Koch v. Association Union Cycliste Internationale et al.* [1974] ECR 1405; [1975] 1 CMLR 320.
23. Case 198/86 *Conradi et al. v. Direction de la Concurrence et des Prix des Hauts de la Seine et al.*; Case 20/87 *Ministère Public v. Gauchard*; Case 204/87 *Bekaert v. Procureur de la République de Rennes*; Case 63/86 *Coman v. Italy*; and Case 147/86 *Commission v. Greece*.
24. [1964] ECR 585; [1964] CMLR 426.
25. On the legal status of a directive, see para. 3.5.2.2.2, above.
26. I.e. the Council of Ministers. On the Council of Ministers, see para. 3.4.3, above.

Council shall, acting on a proposal from the Commission, in co-operation with the European Parliament and after consulting the Economic and Social Committee, issue directives, acting unanimously until the end of the first stage and by a qualified majority thereafter.[27]

3. The Council and the Commission shall carry out the duties devolving upon them under the preceding provisions, in particular:

(a) by according, as a general rule, priority treatment to activities where freedom of establishment makes a particularly valuable contribution to the development of production and trade;

(b) by ensuring close co-operation between the competent authorities in the Member States in order to ascertain the particular situation within the Community of the various activities concerned;

(c) by abolishing those administrative procedures and practices, whether resulting from national legislation or from agreements previously concluded between Member States, the maintenance of which would form an obstacle to freedom of establishment;

(d) by ensuring that workers of one Member State employed in the territory of another Member State may remain in that territory for the purpose of taking up activities therein as self-employed persons, where they satisfy the conditions which they would be required to satisfy if they were entering that State at the time when they intended to take up such activities;

(e) by enabling a national of one Member State to acquire and use land and buildings situated in the territory of another Member State, in so far as this does not conflict with the principles laid down in Article 39(2);

(f) by effecting the progressive abolition of restrictions on freedom of establishment in every branch of activity under consideration, both as regards the conditions for setting up agencies, branches or subsidiaries in the territory of a Member State and as regards the subsidiaries in the territory of a Member State and as regards the conditions governing the entry of personnel belonging to the main establishment into managerial or supervisory posts in such agencies, branches or subsidiaries;

(g) by co-ordinating to the necessary extent the safeguards which, for the protection of the interests of members and others, are required by Member States of companies or firms within the meaning of the second paragraph of Article 58 with a view to making such safeguards equivalent throughout the Community.

(h) by satisfying themselves that the conditions of establishment are not distorted by aids granted by Member States."

The General Programme was adopted in 1962.[28] Directive 73/148[29] provides that nationals[30] and specified relatives[31] of the EC Member States must be admitted to any EC Member State on presentation of a passport or national identity card. A large number of directives[32] has been adopted so as to deal with the freedom of establishment in a number of professions and occupations, including architects,[33] carriers of goods by waterway[34] and passenger transport.[35]

6.1.5 Mutual recognition of diplomas, certificates and qualifications

Article 57 provides:

"1. In order to make it easier for persons to take up and pursue activities as self-employed persons, the Council shall, on a proposal from the Commission and in cooperation with the

27. Ed. Paragraph 2 was amended by Art. 6(4) of the SEA.
28. OJ 1962 2/36.
29. OJ 1973 L172/14. This replaced Directive 64/220, OJ 1964 O 56/845.
30. This right does not extend to companies: see Case 81/87 *R v. HM Treasury and Commissioners of Inland Revenue, ex p. Daily Mail and General Trust PLC* [1988] 3 CMLR 713.
31. The relatives do not have to be nationals of a Member State.
32. On the legal nature of directives, see para. 3.5.2.2.2, above.
33. Directive 85/384, OJ 1985 L223/15.
34. Directive 87/540, OJ 1987 L322/20.
35. Directive 74/562, OJ 1970 L308/23.

European Parliament, acting unanimously during the first stage and by a qualified majority thereafter, issue directives for the mutual recognition of diplomas, certificates and other evidence of formal qualifications.

2. For the same purpose, the Council shall, before the end of the transitional period, acting on a proposal from the Commission and after consulting the European Parliament, issue directives for the coordination of the provisions laid down by law, regulation or administrative action in Member States concerning the taking up and pursuit of activities as self-employed persons. Unanimity shall be required for directives the implementation of which involves at least one Member State amendment of the existing principles laid down by law governing the professions with respect to training and conditions of access for natural persons. In other cases the Council shall act by a qualified majority, in cooperation with the European Parliament.

3. In the case of the medical and allied and pharmaceutical professions, the progressive abolition of restrictions shall be dependent upon coordination of the conditions for their exercise in the various Member States."

It had been held that in the absence of directives on mutual recognition of qualifications, where a person who is a national of one EC Member State wishes to practise his or her profession in another Member State and passes the professional examination in that second Member State then that person must be admitted to practice.[36] Directive 89/48[37] alters the situation somewhat by providing for a general system for the recognition of higher education diplomas where there has been at least three years' professional education and training towards a profession.

6.1.6 Exceptions to the freedom of establishment

6.1.6.1 Exception 1: Exercise of official authority

Article 56 of the EEC Treaty is an exception to the freedom of establishment. It provides:

"The provisions of this Chapter shall not apply, so far as any given Member State is concerned, to activities which in that State are connected, even occasionally with the exercise of official authority.

The Council may, acting by a qualified majority on a proposal from the Commission, rule that the provisions of this Chapter shall not apply to certain activities."

This provision must be construed narrowly.[38] It relates to *activities* and not entire professions unless the public activities constitute so much of the profession that the two are inseparable.

6.1.6.2 Exception 2: Public policy

Article 56 of the EEC Treaty provides:

"1. The provisions of this Chapter and measures taken in pursuance thereof shall not prejudice the applicability of provisions laid down by law, regulation or administrative action providing for special treatment for foreign nationals on grounds of public policy, public security or public health.

2. Before the end of the transitional period, the Council shall, acting unanimously on a proposal from the Commission and after consulting the European Parliament, issue directives for the coordination of the aforementioned provisions laid down by law, regulation or administrative action. After the end of the second stage, however, the Council shall, acting by a

36. Case 71/76 *Thieffry v. Conseil de l'Ordre des Avocats* [1977] ECR 765; [1977] 2 CMLR 373.

37. OJ 1989 L19/16.

38. Case 7/68 *Commission v. Italy* [1986] ECR 423; [1969] CMLR 1.

qualified majority on a proposal from the Commission and in co-operation with the European Parliament, issue directives for the coordination of such provisions as, in each Member State, are a matter for regulation or administrative action."

6.1.6.3 Exception 3: Public security

Article 56 of the EEC Treaty provides:

"1. The provisions of this Chapter and measures taken in pursuance thereof shall not prejudice the applicability of provisions laid down by law, regulation or administrative action providing for special treatment for foreign nationals on grounds of public policy, public security or public health.

2. Before the end of the transitional period, the Council shall, acting unanimously on a proposal from the Commission and after consulting the European Parliament, issue directives for the coordination of the aforementioned provisions laid down by law, regulation or administrative action. After the end of the second stage, however, the Council shall, acting by a qualified majority on a proposal from the Commission and in co-operation with the European Parliament, issue directives for the coordination of such provisions as, in each Member State, are a matter for regulation or administrative action."

6.1.6.4 Exception 4: Public health

Article 56 of the EEC Treaty provides:

"1. The provisions of this Chapter and measures taken in pursuance thereof shall not prejudice the applicability of provisions laid down by law, regulation or administrative action providing for special treatment for foreign nationals on grounds of public policy, public security or public health.

2. Before the end of the transitional period, the Council shall, acting unanimously on a proposal from the Commission and after consulting the European Parliament, issue directives for the coordination of the aforementioned provisions laid down by law, regulation or administrative action. After the end of the second stage, however, the Council shall, acting by a qualified majority on a proposal from the Commission and in co-operation with the European Parliament, issue directives for the coordination of such provisions as, in each Member State, are a matter for regulation or administrative action."

The Commission has made a proposal for a Council of Ministers Regulation on a Common Definition of a Community Shipowner.[39]

6.2 REGISTRATION

6.2.1 Introduction

The choice of the State in which to register a ship is an important strategic decision.[40] Flagging out to "flags of convenience"[41] is an everyday phenomenon in world shipping. It is done for a variety of reasons,[42] including, the possibility of lower taxes or no taxes as well as reduced crewing costs.[43]

39. COM(89)266 final. Reprinted in OJ C263, 16 October 1989, p. 17.

40. Burns, "Registration of EC Vessels—Offshore, International or Euroregistry", at *The Future of Shipping in Europe–Key Legal and Commercial Issues*, London, 28–29 June 1990.

41. The Select Committee of the House of Lords on the European Communities defined "flags of convenience" as "States operating ship registries open to all shipowners regardless of nationality" (see *Community Shipping Measures*, 28th Report, para. 1).

42. See UNCTAD Secretariat report *Economic Consequences of the Existence or Lack of a Genuine Link between Vessel and Flag Registry*, TD/B/C.4/168.

43. See Rabe, "Recent Developments in EEC Legislation Pertaining to Maritime Transport", IBA Conference, Strasbourg 1990, pp. 3–4.

There are now four types of registry:

(a) traditional home registries;
(b) traditional open registries;
(c) offshore registries; and
(d) international registries.

6.2.1.1 Traditional home registries

The traditional home registries require the ships which are registered on them to be owned and/or managed and/or manned by persons resident in the State of registry.

6.2.1.2 Traditional open registries

Traditional open registries include such registries as the Bahamas, Bermuda, Cayman Islands, Costa Rica, Cyprus, Honduras, Hong Kong, Lebanon, Liberia, Maldive Islands, Malta, Netherlands Antilles, Panama, Seychelles, Singapore and Somalia.[44] The qualifications for registration on such registries are quite lax. Almost any shipowner can register on these registries by creating a link (even a loose one) with such a registry, as, for example, by buying a shelf company incorporated in that jurisdiction. There are very few restrictions in such matters as safety, the environment or employment imposed on the shipowner by such registries. There may also be tax advantages to registration under such flags. The Committee of Inquiry into Shipping (the so-called "Rochdale Report"[45]) describes the attributes of a registry of convenience in the following terms:

(a) the country of registry allows ownership and/or control of its merchant vessels by non-citizens;
(b) access to the register is easy; a ship may usually be registered at a Consul's office abroad. Equally important, transfer from the registry at the owner's option is not restricted;
(c) taxes on the income from the ships are not levied locally or are low. A registry fee and an annual fee, based on tonnage, are normally the only charges made. A guarantee or acceptable understanding regarding future freedom from taxation may also be given;
(d) the country of registration is a small power with no national requirement under any foreseeable circumstances for all the shipping registered, but receipts from very small charges on a large tonnage may produce a substantial effect on its national income and balance of payments;
(e) manning of ships by non-nationals is freely permitted;
(f) the country of registry has neither the power nor the administrative machinery effectively to impose any government or international regulations; nor has the country the wish to control the companies themselves.[46]

Boczek has defined a flag of convenience as: "a flag of any country allowing the registration of foreign owned and foreign controlled vessels under conditions which,

44. On flags of convenience and their connection (if any) with international maritime fraud, see Ellen and Campbell, *International Maritime Fraud* (1981), Chapter 6.
45. Cmnd. 4337.
46. Cited in Ellen and Campbell, *op. cit.*, at pp 63–64.

for whatever reasons, are convenient and opportune for the persons who are registering the vessels".[47]

The Maritime Transport Committee of the OECD has in its *Study of the Expansion of the Flags of Convenience and of Various Aspects Thereof*, defined a flag of convenience as: "the flag of such countries whose law allows—and indeed makes it easy—for ships owned by foreign nationals or companies to fly those flags in contrast to the practice in the maritime countries where the right to fly the national flag is subject to stringent conditions and involves far-reaching obligations."

6.2.1.3 Offshore registries

The offshore registries are registries based in dependencies or colonies and are designed to attract the fleets of a particular State.[48] Shipowners are attracted to such registries by a package of advantages, including choice of crew[49] and tax privileges, as well as maintaining the right to fly the flag of the State. Examples include Bermuda (UK), the Cayman Islands (UK), the Isle of Man (UK),[50] Kerguelen (France)[51] and the Netherlands Antilles (The Netherlands). For example, a ship registered in the Cayman Islands or the Isle of Man has fewer restrictions placed on it than a ship registered in the UK itself, but the ship may still fly the Red Ensign of the UK. Thus, a ship registered in the Cayman Islands may have a master, officers and crew of any nationality and still fly the Red Ensign, provided that it never visits a UK port. Other offshore registries can be more restrictive but they still remain quite flexible, for example, the Isle of Man allows a shipowner to register there and choose crew (as opposed to officers) from anywhere in the world and still fly the Red Ensign. British shipowners are particularly attracted to such offshore registries—about one-third of the total gross tonnage in British ownership is registered on one of the British offshore registries. There are disadvantages to flagging out one's vessels to such an offshore registry and the most significant is the possibility of having one's ship boycotted unless the agreements relating to the crew's pay and conditions meet the International Transport Federation's standards. The legal status of such registries in the light of EC law is an open question. Another important issue is whether or not ships registered in such locations can benefit from the freedoms embodied in the Treaties? Can they benefit from Regulation 4055/86? Protocol No. 2 to the Act of Accession of the UK states that persons on the Isle of Man or the Channel Islands "shall not benefit from Community provisions relating to the free movement of persons and services".

6.2.1.4 International registries

An international register allows ships registered on it to fly the domestic flag (e.g. ships registered on the Danish International Register may still fly the Danish flag) but are still subject to detailed rules on such matters as ownership, management,[52] manning[53] and

47. *Flags of Convenience* (1962), p. 2.

48. On new registries generally, see Bredima-Savopoulou and Tzoannos, *The Common Shipping Policy of the EEC* (1990), pp. 52–54. On the dangers of offshore registries, see the comments of Commissioner Clinton Davies, *Lloyd's List*, 1 April 1987, p. 1.

49. Sometimes this includes the right to choose officers as well.

50. On the Isle of Man, see *Fairplay*, 25 January 1990, p. 24.

51. Kerguelen is used for dry bulk carriers.

52. E.g. the Norwegian International Ships Register requires a representative office in Norway.

53. E.g. the Norwegian International Ships Register allows a ship on the register to have officers or crew from any State. The master may be from a foreign State provided that he or she has a dispensation from the Norwegian Maritime Directorate.

operation.[54] The Norwegian International Ships Register (NIS) has been the most successful to date.[55] Denmark and Germany both have international registers.

6.2.2 International law on registration

International law is largely concerned with the concept of a "genuine link" between the ship and the State whose flag the ships flies. This is an imprecise term which defies precise definition. None the less, it involves a number of factors, which have been summarised by Marston (in the light of responses to an UNCTAD report[56]) in the following terms:

"(a) the fact of registration; (b) a substantial share of beneficial ownership in the vessel by nationals (individuals or legal entities) of the flag-State; (c) the principal place of business and effective management of the legal entity which has the beneficial ownership of the vessel should be in the flag-State; (d) the principal officers of the legal entity beneficially owning the vessel should be nationals of the flag-State; together with the further factors of national legislation to control effectively the administrative, social, technical, safety and environmental matters as well as adequate national arrangements for the implementation and supervision of such legislation."[57]

It is clear that some registries around the world do not impose such obligations.

6.2.2.1 Geneva Convention on the High Seas 1958

Article 5(1) of the Geneva Convention on the High Seas 1958 dealt with the issue of "the genuine link" in the following terms:

"Each State shall fix the conditions for the granting of its nationality to ships, for the registration of ships in its territory, and for the right to fly its flag. Ships have the nationality of the State whose flag they are entitled to fly. There must exist a genuine link between the State and the ship; in particular, the State must effectively exercise its jurisdiction and control in administrative, technical and social matters over ships flying its flag."

A report, entitled "Economic Consequences of the Existence or Lack of a Genuine Link between Vessel and Flag Registry"[58] and prepared by the UNCTAD Secretariat observed that Article 5 of the Geneva Convention on the High Seas 1958 did not provide "an effective remedy to deal with the practice of registering merchant vessels in countries which may not be in a position to exercise effective jurisdiction and control over such vessels".

6.2.2.2 United Nations Convention on the Law of the Sea 1982

The United Nations Convention on the Law of the Sea (UNCLOS III), which was opened for signature on 10 December 1982, deals with, among other things, the issue of registration.

Article 90 recognises the right of every State, whether coastal or land-locked,[59] to sail ships flying its own flag on the high seas.

54. On new registries generally, see Bredima-Savopoulou and Tzoannos, *op. cit.* at footnote 48, pp. 52–54.
55. In part the success of the NIS is attributable to the K/S system of limited partnership.
56. On the particular UNCTAD report, see para. 6.2.2.1, below.
57. (1986) JWTL 575 at p. 576.
58. TD/B/C.4/168.
59. E.g. Luxembourg.

Article 91 goes on to deal with the nationality of ships. It provides:

"1. Every State shall fix the conditions for the grant of its nationality to ships, for the registration of ships in its territory, and for the right to fly its flag. Ships have the nationality of the State whose flag they are entitled to fly. There must exist a genuine link between the State and the ship.

2. Every State shall issue to ships to which it has granted the right to fly its flag documents to that effect."

This is really no more than Article 5 of the Geneva Convention on the High Seas 1958.

Article 94 deals with the duties of the flag State. It reads:

"1. Every State shall effectively exercise its jurisdiction and control in administrative, technical and social matters over ships flying its flag.

2. In particular every State shall:

(a) maintain a register of ships containing the names and particulars of ships flying its flag, except those which are excluded from generally accepted international regulations on account of their small size; and

(b) assume jurisdiction under its internal law over each ship flying its flag and its master, officers and crew in respect of the administrative, technical and social matters concerning the ship.

3. Every State shall take such measures for ships flying its flag as are necessary to ensure safety at sea with regard, *inter alia*, to:

(a) the construction, equipment and seaworthiness of ships;

(b) the manning of ships, labour conditions, and the training of crews, taking into account the applicable international instruments;

(c) the use of signals, the maintenance of communications and the prevention of collisions.

4. Such measures shall include those necessary to ensure:

(a) that each ship, before registration and thereafter at appropriate intervals, is surveyed by a qualified surveyor of ships, and has on board such charts, nautical publications and navigational equipment and instruments as are appropriate for the safe navigation of the ship;

(b) that each ship is in the charge of a master and officers who possess appropriate qualifications, in particular in seamanship, navigation, communications and marine engineering, and that the crew is appropriate in qualification and numbers for the type, size, machinery and equipment of the ship;

(c) that the master, officers and, to the extent appropriate, the crew are fully conversant with and required to observe the applicable international regulations concerning the safety of life at sea, the prevention of collisions, the prevention, reduction and control of marine pollution, and the maintenance of communications by radio.

5. In taking measures called for in paragraphs 3 and 4 each State is required to conform to generally accepted international regulations, procedures and practices and to take any steps which may be necessary to secure their observance.

6. A State which has clear grounds to believe that proper jurisdiction and control with respect to a ship have not been exercised may report the facts to the flag State. Upon receiving such a report, the flag State shall investigate the matter and, if appropriate, take any action necessary to remedy the situation.

7. Each State shall cause an inquiry to be held by or before a suitably qualified person or persons into every marine casualty or incident of navigation on the high seas involving a ship flying its flag and causing loss of life or serious injury to nationals of another State or serious damage to ships or installations of another State or to the marine environment. The flag State and the other State shall co-operate in the conduct of any inquiry held by that other State into any such marine casualty or incident of navigation."

What does the concept of "genuine link" mean? It is a concept which has defied definition. The United Nations Convention on the Law of the Sea unfortunately does not define it. However, the United Nations adopted in 1986 a Convention on Conditions for the Registration of Ships and this Convention tries to give some meaning to the concept. A "genuine link" means, according to the Convention, that nationals of the flag State participate in the ownership, crewing or management of the ship. In the words of one commentator:

"[a]re these just empty words? The answer so far appears to be yes. One of the fastest growing registries in the world is that of the Bahamas. The Bahamas are a signatory to the 1982 Convention,[60] and indeed are one of the few nations which has ratified it. Yet, under Bahamas law, anyone, of whatever nationality, can register a ship under Bahamas flag; he can manage his ship from wherever he likes, and he can employ officers and crew of whatever nationality he likes."[61]

6.2.2.3 United Nations Convention on the Registration of Ships 1986

The UNCTAD[62] Committee on Shipping adopted Resolution 22(VI) on Economic Co-operation in Merchant Shipping on 9 August 1974. Paragraph 3 of the Resolution read:

"The Committee of Shipping . . . [c]onsiders . . . that the following matters of shipping policy may also be suitable and ripe for harmonisation: the economic consequences for international shipping of the existence or lack of a genuine link between vessel and flag of registry as explicitly defined in international conventions in force, and requests the UNCTAD secretariat to undertake an examination of this matter as soon as possible."

The UNCTAD Secretariat responded by preparing a report which was entitled "Economic Consequences of the Existence or Lack of a Genuine Link between Vessel and Flag Registry"[63] which was published in 1977. This Report pointed out that Article 5 of the Geneva Convention on the High Seas 1958 did not provide "an effective remedy to deal with the practice of registering merchant vessels in countries which may not be in a position to exercise effective jurisdiction and control over such vessels".

After the publication of the report, an *ad hoc* intergovernmental working group was established. It adopted a unanimous resolution to the effect that "the expansion of open-registry fleets has adversely affected the development and competitiveness of fleets of countries which do not offer open-registry facilities, including those of developing countries".

In 1981, the Committee on Shipping resolved to recommend the holding of a conference on the adoption of an international agreement on the conditions for registration of ships. The General Assembly of the UN took up the Committee's call for a conference and on 20 December 1982 resolved that a plenipotentiary conference be held in 1984.[64] The purpose of the conference was to consider the adoption of an international agreement concerning the conditions under which vessels should be accepted on national shipping registers. The Conference opened in July 1984 and was attended by 93 States and a large number of international organisations. A total of 109 States were involved in the drafting of the Convention. The position of States such as Liberia was obvious: they opposed any substantial change in the *status quo*. The United Nations Convention on the Registration of Ships[65] was eventually signed on 7 February 1986. There were States parties to the Convention as of 1 April 1991.

60. I.e. UNCLOS III.

61. Burns, "Registration of EC Vessels—Offshore, International or Euroregistry", at *The Future of Shipping in Europe—Key Legal and Commercial Issues*, London, 28–29 June 1990, p. 5.

62. On UNCTAD, see Chapter 1, above.

63. TD/B/C.4/168.

64. UN GA Res. 37/209.

65. TD/RS/CONF/23. On the Convention, see Marston (1986) 29 JWTL 575.

The purpose of the Convention was to deal with the enormous numbers of ships which are being registered under various flags of convenience, such as Liberia and Panama. The European Parliament later summarised the aims of the Convention (by reference to Article 1 of the Convention) as relating to:

"— definition of the powers and responsibilities of national shipping authorities with respect to a number of problems concerning exercise of their jurisdiction and supervision over ships registered in the State whose flag they fly;
— mandatory updating of national shipping registers and documents specifying the identity of the owner, operator, or other persons in charge;
— specifying the proportions of owning interests and/or crew complements to be accounted for by nationals;
— definition of the role of the flag State, especially as regards involvement of nationals in the management of shipowning companies;
— detailed guidelines on conditions of charter of ships, joint ventures between shipowning companies from different countries, and protection of the interests of countries that supply labour."[66]

6.3 EC PERSPECTIVE ON REGISTRATION

6.3.1 Introduction

Many EC-based shipowners are flagging out their ships on various registries. Indeed, about half (56.4%) of the vessels owned by EC-based owners are registered on "home" registries.[67] In terms of gross registered tonnage, only 51.3% of EC-owned tonnage is registered on one of the EC-home registries.[68]

There are no specific EEC rules on registration, but the general rules would apply *mutatis mutandis*.

There can be no restrictions based on discrimination between nationals of the EC.[69] This applies, in particular, to the freedom of establishment. Yet the registries of most of the Member States discriminate against foreigners (including EC nationals) in some way or other, for example more than one-half of a ship must be British-owned before it may be registered on the British registry.[70] A similar rules appears to exist in France and Belgium. Other Member States require offices, shareholders, directors or principal places of business. These restrictions, in so far as they discriminate between an EC Member State's own nationals and the nationals of another EC Member State, are illegal under EC law.[71] The Commission, the institution charged with the task of enforcing EC law,[72] has not been particularly vigilant in bringing to task the Member States which impose such illegal restrictions.

In 1986, Sir James Scott-Hopkins, a Member of the European Parliament for the UK, asked the Commission the following question: ". . .[D]oes the Commission not

66. The European Parliament's Committee on Transport published a report on the Commission's proposal for a Council decision on the common position to be adopted by Member States when signing and ratifying the United Nations Convention on Conditions for the Registration of Ships (COM(86)523 final); Doc. A2-53/88; Rapporteur: Mr D. Romera I. Alcazar.

67. Mikelis and Dean, "The Fleet Controlled by the European Community—Present Status and Some Historic Trends" (referred to in footnote 2 of para. 2.2.1, above).

68. Mikelis and Dean, *op. cit.* at footnote 67. In the case of the UK, this ratio was as low as 32.7% per Mikelis and Dean, *op. cit.* It was reckoned that two ships a day were changing from an EC flag to another flag to enjoy lower costs: *Lloyd's List*, 6 July 1988, p. 2.

69. EEC, Art.7.

70. Merchant Shipping Act, 1988.

71. See, in particular, Article 7 of the EEC Treaty.

72. See para. 3.4.2, above.

agree that legislation is needed, as a matter of urgency, to enable Member States to co-ordinate the policing of abuses such as the use of flags of convenience to employ sub-standard ships and inadequately trained and underpaid crews?"[73]

Commissioner Stanley Clinton Davies responded:

"... As far as the use of open registry shipping is concerned the Member States coordinate, on the basis of Commission proposals and using the consultation procedure set up in 1977[74], their position together with other states of Group B in the UNCTAD Conference on registration of ships, which has just held its final session in Geneva. The aim is to strengthen the link between ship and flag in order to eliminate abuses of using open registries. The Commission, which shares the Honourable Member's concerns in this field, has given its full support to all the international measures designed to eliminate the abuses associated with some of the open registry fleets.

In addition Member States have coordinated their efforts to eliminate sub-standard shipping and to check on the adequacy of crews through the Memorandum on Port State Control signed in Paris in January 1982. The Memorandum was based on the Commission's proposed directive of June 1980.[75] The Memorandum will be revised at a Ministerial meeting in The Hague in April 1986. In the Commission's view Port State Control has proved an increasingly effective means of dealing with the problems mentioned by the Honourable Member, particularly in view of the controls undertaken with respect to the IMO Convention on Standards of Seafarers' Training. As the Memorandum is applied also by non-Member States further legislation and in particular Community legislation does not at present seem necessary or appropriate."

6.3.2 EC reaction to the UN Convention on the Registration of Ships 1986

6.3.2.1 Commission's Communication

On 25 September 1986, the Commission sent to the Council of Ministers: (a) a Communication on the United Nations Convention on Conditions for the Registration of Ships; and (b) a Proposal for a Council of Ministers Decision on the Common Position to be adopted by Member States when signing and ratifying the United Nations Convention on Conditions for the Registration of Ships.[76]

During the negotiations in Geneva on the Convention, the EC Commission alerted the Member States of the EC that there was a discrepancy between the UN Convention and the EEC Treaty. Articles 8, 9 and 10 of the Convention conflicted with certain provisions of the EEC Treaty. These incompatibilities are discussed in the next three paragraphs. The Commission's objections were not taken into account by the negotiating parties and the Commission then informed the Member States that, in the absence of a textual guarantee of compatibility between the Convention and the provisions of the EEC Treaty, they were debarred under EC law from signing or ratifying the Convention. The Dutch delegation, representing the EC Member States present at the Conference, informed the States gathered at the Conference that the EC States could not sign the Convention. The Commission followed this statement by informing the EC Member States by way of a letter on 4 March 1986 to the effect that no EC Member State should sign the Convention until an agreed form of reservation for EC Member States had been agreed. The Commission was thus of the view that the Member States could enforce the Convention in a manner consistent with their obligations under EC law if, and only if, they make an appropriately worded reservation when signing and ratifying the Convention.

Article 8 of the Convention relates to ownership of ships. It provides:

73. Written Question No. 1955/85.
74. OJ L239 of 17 September 1977.
75. OJ C192 of 30 July 1980, p. 8.
76. COM(86)523 final.

"*Ownership of Ships*

1. Subject to the provisions of Article 7, the flag State shall provide in its laws and regulations for the ownership of ships flying its flag.

2. Subject to the provisions of Article 7, in such laws and regulations the flag State shall include appropriate provisions for participation by that State or its nationals as owners of ships flying its flag or in the ownership of such ships and for the level of such participation. These laws and regulations should be sufficient to permit the flag State to exercise effectively its jurisdiction and control over ships flying its flag."

It is believed that this provision is contrary to Article 7 (no discrimination on grounds of nationality), Articles 52–58 (freedom of establishment) and 67–73 (free movement of capital) of the EEC Treaty.

Article 9 of the Convention relates to hiring of crews. It provides:

"*Manning of Ships*

1. Subject to the provisions of Article 7, a State of registration, when implementing this Convention, shall observe the principle that a satisfactory part of the complement consisting of officers and crew of ships flying its flag be nationals or persons domiciled or lawfully in permanent residence in that State.

2. Subject to the provisions of Article 7 and in pursuance of the goal set out in paragraph 1 of this Article, and in taking necessary steps to this end, the State of registration shall have regard to the following:

a. the availability of qualified seafarers within the State of registration;
b. multilateral or bilateral agreements or other types of arrangements valid and enforceable pursuant to the legislation of the State of registration;
c. the sound and economically viable operation of its ships.

3. The State of registration should implement the provision of paragraph 1 of this Article on a ship, company or fleet basis.

4. The State of registration, in accordance with its laws and regulations, may allow persons of other nationalities to serve on board ships flying its flag in accordance with the relevant provisions of this Convention.

5. In pursuance of the goal set out in paragraph 1 of this Article, the State of registration should, in accordance with shipowners, promote the education and training of its nationals or persons domiciled or lawfully in permanent residence within its territory.

6. The State of registration shall ensure:

a. that the manning of ships flying its flag is of such a level and competence as to ensure compliance with applicable international rules and standards, in particular those regarding safety at sea;
b. that the terms and conditions of employment on board ships flying its flag are in conformity with applicable international rules and standards;
c. that adequate legal procedures exist for the settlement of civil disputes between seafarers employed on ships flying its flag and their employers;
d. that nationals and foreign seafarers have equal access to appropriate legal processes to secure their contractual rights in their relations with their employers."

It is believed that this provision is contrary to Articles 48–51 (free movement of workers) of the EEC Treaty.

Article 10 of the Convention relates to the role of flag States in the management of shipowning companies. It provides:

"*Role of Flag States in respect of the Management of Shipowning Companies and Ships*

1. The State of registration, before entering a ship in its register of ships, shall ensure that the shipowning company or a subsidiary shipowning company is established and/ or has its principal place of business within its territory in accordance with its laws and regulations.

2. Where the shipowning company or a subsidiary shipowning company or the principal place of business of the shipowning company is not established in the flag State, the latter shall ensure, before entering a ship in its register of ships, that there is a representative or management

person who shall be a national of the flag State, or be domiciled therein. Such a representative or management person may be a natural or juridical person who is duly established or incorporated in the flag State, as the case may be, in accordance with its laws and regulations, and duly empowered to act on the shipowner's behalf and account. In particular, this representative or management person should be available for any legal process and to meet the shipowner's responsibilities in accordance with the laws and regulations of the State of registration.

3. The State of registration should ensure that the person or persons accountable for the management and operation of a ship flying its flag are in a position to meet the financial obligations that may arise from the operation of such a ship to cover risks which are normally insured in international maritime transportation in respect of damage to third parties. To this end the State of registration should ensure that ships flying its flag are in a position to provide at all times documents evidencing that an adequate guarantee, such as appropriate insurance or any other equivalent means, has been arranged. Furthermore, the State of registration should ensure that an appropriate mechanism, such as a maritime lien, mutual fund, wage insurance, social security scheme, or any governmental guarantee provided by an appropriate agency of the State of the accountable person, whether that person is an owner or operator, exists to cover wages and related moneys owed to seafarers employed on ships flying its flag in the event of default of payment by their employers. The State of registration may also provide for any other appropriate mechanism to that effect in its laws and regulations."

It is believed that this provision is contrary to Articles 52–58 (freedom of establishment) of the EEC Treaty.

The Commission proposed the following reservation:

"[The Member State concerned] will apply Articles 8, 9 and 10 in conformity with its obligations under the Treaty establishing the European Economic Community, and in particular with those requiring equal treatment of the nationals of the Member States of the Community."

As of 1 April 1991, the Council of Ministers had still not acted on the proposal. However, in case the Council of Ministers does act then a review of the Communication and the proposed Decision would be useful at this juncture.

6.3.2.2 Commission's proposal

The Commission said in its Communication:

"1. In order to eliminate abuses of ship regulations that may become possible through the failure of flag States to meet their international obligations, the Commission fully supports the adoption of measures which aim at strengthening the link between ship and flag State. However, during the conference which led to the [Registration] Convention, the Commission made it clear to the Member States of the Community that they would not be free under Community law to sign or ratify the Convention unless they obtained a clause which rendered the Convention compatible with the EEC Treaty or found another equivalent solution.

2. COREPER[77] decided unanimously on 7 February 1986 that the text of the clause for this purpose which was being negotiated at Geneva was not acceptable as it did not meet the requirements of Community law. It made certain suggestions for the improvement of the clause, but added that if a satisfactory clause could not be negotiated, the delegation holding the Presidency [of the Council of Ministers] should make a declaration on behalf of the Member States to the effect that they would only be able to sign the Convention in conformity with the EEC Treaty. In Geneva the delegations of the Member States decided that they would not be able to renegotiate a satisfactory Community clause. The clause was, accordingly, withdrawn and the Dutch delegation made a declaration on the lines laid down by COREPER.

3. Following the conclusion of the conference at Geneva and the adoption of the text of the Convention the Commission sent a letter of 4 March 1986 to the Member States. The letter pointed out that the conference had ended without it having been determined whether, and if so

77. On the Committee of Permanent Representatives, see para. 3.4.3.5, above.

how, the Convention could be reconciled with the obligations of Member States under Community law. The letter confirmed that the Commission considered that it would be contrary to the obligations of the Member States under the EEC Treaty for them to sign or ratify the Convention without an appropriate reservation. The letter asked the Member States, therefore, to do nothing that could prejudice a final approach to be adopted by the Council [of Ministers] and in particular that the Member States should not sign the Convention until the Council had decided on a common form of reservation to be used by all Member States when signing and ratifying the Convention.

4. The problem of incompatibility between the Convention and the EEC Treaty arises essentially because the Convention requires that:

— the State where a ship is registered must ensure *either* that there is a sufficient participation by its nationals as owners of ships flying its flag or in the ownership of such ships (Article 8) *or* that a satisfactory part of the complement of ships flying its flag consists of officers and crew who are nationals or persons domiciled or lawfully in permanent residence (Article 9);

— the State of registration must ensure that the shipowning company or a subsidiary is established and/or has its principal place of business within its territory and makes further provision for a representative presence (Article 10).

5. Article 8 (ownership) and Article 9 (manning) are alternatives. For those Member States which wish to comply with Article 8, however, the problem arises of reconciling its provisions with the principle of non-discrimination on the ground of nationality (Article 7 of the EEC Treaty),[78] the right of establishment (Articles 52 to 58)[79] and the principle of the free movement of capital (Articles 67 to 73 of the EEC Treaty).[80] For those Member States which wish to comply with the manning provisions of Article 9, the problem arises of reconciling those provisions with the principle of the free movement of workers (Articles 48 to 51 of the EEC Treaty). Finally, Article 10(1) raises questions with respect to the right of establishment (Articles 52 to 58 of the EEC Treaty).[81]

6. As the Commission has pointed out on several occasions these problems necessitated common action by the Member States in order to find a solution. The preferred solution from a Community point of view, given that it was impossible to improve the wording of the Articles in question, would have been a satisfactorily worded clause, which preserved the rights of the Member States to observe their obligations under the EEC Treaty. Another way of achieving the same degree of legal security would have been the negotiation of a protocol of signature to the same effect. Unfortunately neither of these results was achieved.

7. In order to find a solution to the problem which the Community and the Member States now face it becomes necessary to look in some detail at the Articles of the Convention in question. As regards Article 8 (ownership) the Commission notes that the Convention contains no rules on how the concept of nationality shall be defined for the purposes of the application of its provisions. It also notes that the purpose of the ownership provision is to permit the flag State to exercise effectively its jurisdiction and control over ships flying its flag. In the circumstances the Commission considers that Member States, which wish to apply the provisions of Article 8, should do so in applying the extended definition of nationality provided by the EEC Treaty for economic activities coming within its scope. Given the institutional and legal framework of the Community this will not weaken the jurisdiction and control exercised over the ship. A similar approach may be applied in respect of the manning provisions in Article 9. In addition to the arguments mentioned above, it is to be noted that Article 9(2)(b) [of the Convention] allows the State of registration to have regard to multilateral agreements and also that Article 9(4) provides that it may allow persons of other nationalities to serve on board ships flying its flag. Article 10(1) requires the State of registration, before entering a ship on its register, to ensure that the shipowning company or a subsidiary shipowning company is established and/or has its principal place of business within its territory in accordance with its laws and regulations. The Commission considers that it is legitimate to interpret this provision as meaning that the concept of establishment may be interpreted, as far as the Member States are concerned, in accordance

78. See Chapter 3, above.
79. See Chapter 3, above.
80. See Chapter 3, above.
81. See Chapter 3, above.

with the relevant law, that is to say Articles 52 to 58 of the EEC Treaty. On the basis of this approach the application of Article 10 [of the Convention] and the relevant Treaty provisions may be reconciled.

8. In accordance with the above analysis, the Commission considers that Member States can apply the Convention in such a way as to comply with their obligations under Community law, if, but only if, they make a common reservation in appropriate terms, when they sign and ratify this Convention.

9. Under Article 19 of the Vienna Convention [on the Law of Treaties], a State may, when signing or ratifying a treaty, formulate a reservation, in a case other than where reservations are prohibited or only specified reservations are allowed, if the reservation is compatible with the object and purpose of the Treaty. For the reasons explained in paragraph 7 the Commission considers that, to the extent that the common act should be regarded as a reservation, it may be strongly argued that it is compatible with the object and purpose of the Convention on conditions for the registration of ships.

10. It is to be noted, moreover, that reservations may be accepted by other contracting States. Acceptance may be either made expressly or implicitly. In the latter case silence for a period of 12 months suffices. However, a contracting party may object to a reservation and may prevent the Convention from entering into force as between it and the State making the reservation. On the other hand, where the objecting State has not opposed the entry into force of the Treaty between itself and the reserving State, the provisions to which the reservation relates do not apply as between the two States to the extent of the reservation (Articles 20 and 21 of the Vienna Convention).

11. It is inherent in the nature of the common action which must now be adopted, in the absence of a more legally secure solution, that there will be a risk of objection. The Commission would not expect this risk to be serious given:

— the interests which third countries have in the participation of Member States in the Convention, taking into account the importance of the Member States' fleets in world shipping;
— the preparatory work to alert the contracting parties to the Member State's obligations under the EEC Treaty, including the declarations made at the Conference at the time of the adoption of the Convention (ref. para.2 above),
— the arguments which justify the statement on the basis of the particular obligations of the Member States arising from the Treaty, and
— the rather unattractive results to an objecting State of an objection.

Whatever the assessment of the risk, however, it is a risk that cannot be avoided.

12. To give effect to the approach described above, the Commission proposes the annexed Council Decision. This proposal is, in effect, that the Council should adopt a decision whereby on signing and ratifying the Convention, the Member States will be obliged to make a reservation in the following terms:

'[The Member State concerned] will apply Articles 8, 9 and 10 in conformity with its obligations under the Treaty establishing the European Economic Community, and in particular with those requiring equal treatment of the nationals of the Member States of the Community.'

The Commission wishes to make it clear, moreover, that for a Member State to sign or become a party to the Convention without making an appropriate common reservation would be a violation of Community law, and the Commission would use the possibilities provided by Articles 169 and 186 of the EEC Treaty to prevent this, if necessary.

If the Convention does not receive enough ratification to bring it into force, or if, contrary to expectations, there are substantial objections to Member States signing and ratifying it on the basis of the reservation proposed, the Commission would in due course consider whether it would be useful for it to make additional proposals."

6.3.2.3 European Parliament's Report

On 18 May 1988, the European Parliament's Committee on Transport published a report on the Commission's proposal for a Council decision on the common position to be adopted by Member States when signing and ratifying the United Nations Convention on Conditions for the Registration of Ships (COM(86)523 final).[82]

6.3.4 An EC register : EUROS

6.3.4.1 Proposal

The Commission proposed in its August 1989 document "A Future for the Community Shipping Industry: Measures to Improve the Operating Conditions of Community Shipping"[83] the establishment of a Community ship register and for the flying of the Community flag by some sea-going vessels.[84] This is embodied in a proposal for a Council Regulation entitled Draft Council Regulation concerning the Establishment of a Community Ship Register and providing for the flying of the Community Flag by Sea-going Vessels. It would operate in parallel with the national registries in each Member State.

Rabe, addressing the International Bar Association's Section on Business Law in Strasbourg, in 1989, said:

"[t]he proposal to establish a Community Ship Register (EUROS) is intended to reverse both these trends. Its objectives are to present an incentive to Community shipowners to register their ships within the Community and simultaneously to secure the employment of European seafarers in highly-skilled functions and as far as possible of those in other functions. To achieve this the Commission—correctly may I say—does regard as insufficient steps taken by individual Member States, where in some instances already second ship registers have been introduced. In view of the target of establishing a single internal market, the idea is to set up a harmonized system of operating conditions providing for high quality, reliability and safety of the transport services rendered evidenced by the Community flag. This would in the Commission's opinion also lead to a higher degree of convenience of the conditions of competition among Member States."

The Select Committee of the House of Lords on the European Communities has said that the EUROS proposal is "an imaginative idea. But given the long centuries in which law on the high seas has been that of the 'separate flags of nations' it is also fraught with dangers and complexities."[85]

The Register is to be an additional one to the Member States' registries and is not in substitution of them. There would be no obligation to register on it. Vessels registered on EUROS would also remain registered on the national registry.

The Preamble to the proposed Regulation is instructive:

"Whereas the availability of a high quality competitive fleet depends on the availability of a maritime infrastructure within the Community allowing for the preservation of a sufficient number of nationals of Member States to serve as seafarers and a cost level which is competitive;

Whereas the comparative advantage of Community shipping has been eroded over the years, and the fleet flying Member States' flags has suffered a considerable decline, and to the extent that ships have been transferred to third country registers, there has been a severe loss of employment

82. See Doc. A2-53/88. Rapporteur: Mr D. Romera I. Alcazar.

83. COM(89)266 final, 3 August 1989. On 5 July 1988, Manfred Ebel MEP proposed a European flag.

84. See *ibid.* For the amended proposal, see OJC 73/11, 19 March 1991. See "EC attacked over new Euros register", *Lloyd's List*, 13 December 1991, p. 1; "Improved leadership urged for EC shipping", *Lloyd's List*, 10 February 1992, p. 1. Note the moves in South America to adopt a Latin American register (noting the differences): "Latin American register planned", *Lloyd's List*, 25 November 1991, p. 1. The Commission issued a revised proposal on 13 December 1991 (COM (91)483 final) but the comments in this chapter relate to the amendment submitted on 27 February 1991.

85. See Community Shipping Measures, Session 1989-90, 28th Report, para. 2 (footnote omitted).

for Community nationals; and as a result the invisible earnings of the Member States' of the Community have declined;

Whereas the efforts to meet the problem through national measures, either by the establishment of second national registers, to which more favourable conditions are attached, or by granting operating subsidies or aid to related sectors, tend to disperse the effects of the actions undertaken and risk a distortion of competition;

Whereas it is in the Community interest to aim at a structural development of a fleet of vessels, registered in Member States' registers but also identifiable as Community vessels which meet the standards laid down by international maritime conventions and to man these vessels, to the highest possible proportion, with Community seafarers;

Whereas this aim cannot be attained without a reduction of the cost level;

Whereas the establishment of a Community ship register should serve the purpose of creating a channel through which national efforts can be converged, a focus for the employment of Community seafarers, and a trade mark guaranteeing shippers a high quality service;

Whereas the Community ship register will be additional to the national register and should be introduced without delay in order to discourage the trend towards setting up secondary registers;

Whereas the right to register vessels in the Community register should be reserved for natural and legal persons having a genuine link with the Community; whereas, however, this right should also be given under certain conditions and terms to persons who have a genuine link with third countries;

Whereas the vessel to be registered in the Community register should comply with certain conditions; whereas, in particular, the vessel should be and remain registered in a national register; whereas the decisions on the admission to the national register must be taken in compliance with the provisions of the Treaty;

Whereas registration in, and continued membership of, the Community register should depend on compliance with the safety measures required by the international conventions in this respect and any rules in respect of vessels, personnel and seamen established at Community level;

Whereas the number of qualified seafarers from Member States on board vessels registered in this register should be sufficient to meet present and future requirements of the Community fleet, bearing in mind that in order to ensure passengers' safety and to safeguard employment among seafarers of the Member States, the crews of passenger vessels and ferries operating in European waters must consist entirely of Community seafarers;

Whereas seafarers from non-Community countries on vessels registered in this register should be employed on conditions which have been agreed on by their representative organizations and, in the absence of such an agreement, on conditions which comply with internationally agreed standards;

Whereas in order to ensure uniform crew composition for each category of vessel and degree of automation, in view of the substantial divergences that exist between national legislations on this matter, guidelines for the composition of the crews of vessels registered in Euros must be laid down by the Commission on the basis of the principles set out in Resolution A 481 (XII) of the International Maritime Organization and ILO Convention 147 concerning minimum standards in merchant shipping which are internationally recognized and accepted;

Whereas all seafarers on vessels registered in this register should at least benefit from the social security schemes to which they are entitled in the country where they are resident;

Whereas vessels, while remaining on this register, should be able to transfer between the national registers of Member States without technical hindrance, when they comply with the essential technical requirements to be laid down by the Council;

Whereas the right of free movement under Article 48 of the Treaty as implemented by Council Regulation 1612/68[86] applies to employment of nationals of Member States on board vessels registered in the Member States; whereas therefore this right applies to vessels registered in Euros; whereas, however, the effective exercise of that right may be hindered by differences between qualifications and licences issued in the Member States; whereas it is appropriate to provide for recognition of such qualifications and licences for seafarers for the purposes of employment on board vessels in the Community register subject to minimum requirements laid down by the Council;

86. OJ No. L257, 19 October 1968, p. 2.

Whereas registration in this register should be reflected in the right and obligation to fly the European flag which should be afforded a similar degree of protection to that enjoyed by the flags of Member States and third countries;

Whereas the Commission should, in application of the provisions of this regulation, be enabled to adopt implementing provisions concerning the establishment of the register and concerning procedures of registration and deregistration;

Whereas there should be cooperation between the Community register and the national ship registers, including an exchange of information;

Whereas the Member States should take the necessary measures to control and enforce compliance with the provisions of this Regulation;

Whereas the Commission will report annually to the European Parliament and Council on the number of vessels registered in the Community register and the number of Community seafarers employed in those vessels, thus enabling the effectiveness of this regulation to be assessed, and whereas the Commission will if necessary propose any modifications and improvements required."

6.3.4.2 Objective of the proposal

The objective of the proposed Regulation is set out in Article 1 of the proposed Regulation. This provision states that the Regulation provides for: (a) the establishment of a Community ship register for sea-going merchant vessels; (b) the conditions for registration; (c) the provision of certain facilities accruing from such registration; (d) the right to fly the European Community flag on these vessels in addition to the national flag[87]; and (e) associated measures aimed at ensuring the maintenance of social standards and at improving environmental and safety standards.

An advantage of the EUROS system is that such a scheme would facilitate the Commission's review of State aids because the ships registered on it would already have met the conditions set down by the Commission.

6.3.4.3 Legal bases

The legal bases of the proposed Regulation is, according to the preamble to the proposal put forward by the Commission, the EEC Treaty generally and, in particular, Articles 84(2) and 92(3)(d) thereof. It is noteworthy that Article 92(3)(d) was added in on the amended proposal

6.3.4.4 Market reaction

NUMAST (the UK seafaring officers' union) stated in its submission to the UK Department of Transport that the union was "not yet convinced that a Community register which, as proposed, would in essence be a dual register is the only, or even the most effective, means of achieving the objective". It also expressed concern about the criterion suggested for entry to the EUROS and expressed total opposition to the inclusion on the register of bareboat chartered tonnage.

The proposals are regarded by many in the industry as falling short of their aims and geared more towards internal harmonisation than improving the general welfare of shipping within the EC.[88]

The European Parliament called for tax concessions. The Commission's revised draft provides that the income of seafarers on EUROS-registered ships would be

87. Ships registered on EUROS would also have a distinctive marking on their sterns as well.
88. General Council of British Shipping, *Shipping, 1992 and Beyond* (1990), p. 15.

exempt of tax normally levied in EC Member States and this tax would be paid over to the shipowners.

The European Community Shipowners Association (ECSA) rejected the concession on seafarers' taxation. ECSA argued that the proposal is not attractive enough to encourage ships away from flags of convenience because, among other reasons, the tax exemption relates only to EC seafarers on the EUROS register and travelling outside the EC and when they are not involved in cabotage as well as the fact that the exemption only relates to tax and not social welfare. ECSA wanted more: in particular, they wanted a package of positive measures to attract ships.

The Member States do not appear enthusiastic about the Commission's proposals.

6.3.4.5 Establishment of the register

EUROS would be an additional register, i.e. a register which would operate in addition to the registers in each of the Member States. Article 2 of the proposed Regulation provides for the establishment of a Community ship register (to be called "EUROS") on which sea-going merchant vessels may be registered in addition to their national registration in a Member State of the EC.

6.3.4.6 Eligibility to be registered

Registration is not automatic and a number of requirements must be met. According to the Regulation, the Commission shall register a sea-going merchant vessel when the conditions laid down in Article 3, 4 and 5 of the proposed Regulation are met.[89]
Article 3 of the proposed Regulation describes a community vessel owner in the following terms:

> "1. The following who are owners of a vessel registered in the national register of a Member State may apply for registration of the vessel in Euros:
> (a) nationals of the Member States;
> (b) companies formed in accordance with the law of a Member State and having their principal place of business in, and effective control exercised within, the Community, provided that a majority of the members of the board or of the directors of these companies are nationals of the Member States having their domicile or usual residence in the Community.
> (c) Companies formed in accordance with the law of a Member State or of a third country in which nationals of Member States participate by more than 50% or are company shareholders controlling more than 50% of the overall company capital.
> For the purpose of this regulation, a natural or legal person mentioned above will hereafter be referred to as a 'Community vessel owner';
> 2. Where it has been agreed between a third country and the Community that registration of vessels in the register of that third country and in Euros shall be permitted, the term 'nationals of the Member States' shall, for the purposes of paragraph 1(a) and (b), include nationals of the third country concerned."

Article 4 sets out the criteria for vessels eligible for registration:

> "Eligible for registration in Euros is any sea-going merchant vessel with a tonnage of at least 500 grt, built or under construction, which is already registered in a Member State and is used or to be used for the transport of cargo or passengers or any other commercial purpose, if it fulfils the following conditions:

89. Proposed Regulation, Article 2, para. 2.

(a) the vessel must be and remain registered in the national ship register for the duration of its registration in Euros;
(b) the vessel must be owned, and for the duration of its registration in Euros remain owned, by a Community vessel owner;
(c) the vessel shall not be more than 20 years old at the time of its registration in Euros unless it has been completely refurbished and certified by a Member State as complying with the regulations for new ships defined in the 1974 Solas Convention."

Article 5 describes registration:

"1. The Community vessel owner shall apply to the Commission for the registration of a vessel in Euros. He shall submit this application either directly to the Commission or through the competent national authorities which shall forward the application to the Commission.

This application shall be accompanied by:
(a) A certificate of ownership of the vessel issued by the national registration authority;
(b) The measurement certificate of the vessel;
(c) A certified copy of the vessel's certificate of nationality;
(d) If the vessel is mortgaged, a written statement by the mortgage creditors that they consent to the registration of the vessel in Euros.

The Commission may stipulate other documents or certificates that must be submitted in order for a vessel to be registered in Euros.

2. Registration in Euros shall be completed when the following data is recorded in the relevant entry of the vessel:
(a) the name or title of the Community vessel owner and his or its other particulars;
(b) the name, the international call letters, the dimensions, the gross and net registered tonnage, the type and power of the engine and the age of the vessel;
(c) the type of the vessel, its number and port of national registration.

The Commission may also lay down other data concerning the vessel which must be recorded in Euros.

3. The following data shall also be recorded in the register:
(a) changes of ownership or national flag of the vessel;
(b) the deregistration of the vessel.

4. Third parties shall be entitled to receive information of the data concerning a vessel registered in Euros on payment of a reasonable fee."

Article 6 deals with notification:

"1. Where a vessel is registered in or deregistered from Euros the Commission shall notify its national registration authority.

2. Where, for any reason, a vessel is deregistered from the national register, the national register authority shall immediately notify the Commission."

Article 7 on certificates and documents of vessels:

"The following certificates or documents must be kept on board the vessel for the entire duration of its registration in Euros:
(a) The certificates or documents which the vessel is required to have on board under the legislation of the Member State in whose national register the vessel is registered;
(b) The certificate granting the right to fly the European flag;
(c) The certificate of minimum crew composition;
(d) The 'sea-worthiness' certificate issued by a Member State in whose register the vessel is registered."

Article 8 deals with deregistration:

"1. A vessel registered in Euros shall be deleted:
(a) by the Commission, acting *ex officio*, where the vessel ceases to comply with the provisions of this regulation or,
(b) by an application from the Community vessel owner.

2. The deletion of a vessel from the national register of a Member State and its registration in the national register of another Member State at the same time, shall not affect its registration in Euros."

Bare-Boat Charters. Vessels operated by EC vessel owners on the basis of bare-boat charters[90] for a period of at least 12 months may be registered in EUROS during the period of that charter where four conditions are fulfilled: first, the vessel is registered as a bare-boat chartered vessel in a national ship register of a Member State[91]; secondly, the laws of the vessel's initial flag in EUROS allow the registration of a bare-boat chartered vessel in the national register of a Member State[92]; thirdly, the consent of the owner of the vessel and of all mortgage creditors for the registration of the bare-boat in EUROS is obtained[93]; and fourthly, the bare-boat charter has been duly recorded in the register of the vessel's initial flag State.[94]

6.3.4.7 Safety on EUROS-registered ships

Article 10 of the proposed Regulation provides that throughout the period of registration the vessel must be provided with all certificates required by the Member State in whose national register it is registered.

Article 11 deals with the manning of EUROS-registered ships:

"1. Guidelines concerning the manning of vessels registered in Euros shall be laid down by the Commission on the basis of the principles set out in Resolution No A 481 (XII) of 19 November 1981 of the Assembly of the International Maritime Organization (IMO), after consultation with the Joint Committee on Maritime Transport and Member States. The Commission shall adopt the guidelines within the time limit mentioned in Article 24.

2. The Commission shall include in the guidelines provisions ensuring that insofar as requirements concerning safe manning are met and the necessary automation exists, seafarers with multiple qualifications certificates may be employed, provided that specific reference is made to this fact in the minimum manning certificate.

3. Member States shall issue minimum manning certificates in conformity with paragraphs 1 and 2 and shall deliver them to the persons requesting the registration of a vessel in Euros. The Member State shall specify in the minimum manning certificate a language or languages of the crew.

4. At the request of the Community vessel owner concerned or seafarers employed on the vessel who consider that the minimum manning certificate issued by a Member State is not in conformity with the guidelines laid down by the Commission, the Commission will carry out an investigation and will take a decision after consultation with the Member State concerned. The Commission will take the decision within two months of the date of request.

5. The decision of the Commission shall lay down the minimum manning scale of the vessel. The Member State concerned shall issue immediately a new certificate in conformity with the Commission decision.

6. The national authorities shall monitor compliance with the provisions of the minimum manning certificate and impose sanctions where appropriate."

Article 12 deals with the nationality of the crew:

"1. On vessels registered in Euros all officers and at least half of the rest of the crew referred to in their minimum manning certificates shall be nationals of a Member State.

Trainees do not count towards meeting the requirements above.

2. In particular, on passenger vessels or ferries registered in Euros which operate regular lines for passengers or vehicles between the ports of the same Member State or between (1)

90. A bare-boat charter (also termed a charter-party by demise or a demise charter-party) is one whereby the owner simply provides the ship and the charterer supplies its own crew, stores and fuel. The possession and control of the vessel are normally vested in the charterer and are not retained by the owner.

91. *Ibid.*, Article 9(1).

92. *Ibid.*, Article 9(1).

93. *Ibid.*, Article 9(1).

94. *Ibid.*, Article 9(1).

Mediterranean ports or (2) North Sea and Baltic ports or (3) European Atlantic ports or operate cruises with embarkation and disembarkation at any of the above ports, all the officers and the remaining crew referred to in the minimum manning certificate of vessels shall be nationals of the Member States."

Article 13 relates to availability of seafarers:

"1. The Member States shall provide for monitoring on a permanent basis of the availability of seafarers who are nationals of Member States in their ports, and make the information so obtained available to interested parties.

2. Where seafarers who are nationals of the Member States are not available for employment in a vessel registered in Euros that lies in the port of a Member State, under the terms and conditions of the collective wage agreements concluded with their representative organizations, the Member State may grant permission to the master of the vessel to sail on the forthcoming voyage with fewer seafarers who are nationals of the Member States than those provided in Article 12."

Interestingly, there is a provision (Article 14) dealing with wages, working hours and further labour conditions:

"1. Labour conditions and working hours of seafarers, who are not nationals of a Member State, on board vessels registered in Euros, shall be in accordance with the laws and regulations of the Member State in whose national register the vessel is registered and the Community regulations if any.

2. Wages and any other remuneration of seafarers who are not nationals of a Member State on board vessels registered in Euros shall be at least in accordance with the ILO Wages, Hours of Work and Manning (Sea) Recommendation (No 109), 1958, subject to any arrangement on collective wages agreed upon with organizations as referred to in Article 15."

Article 15 relates to collective wage agreements:

"1. Seafarers who are not nationals of a Member State may be employed only on the basis of collective wage agreements concluded with trade unions representing the above seafarers.

2. No collective wage agreement may be concluded with a trade union on behalf of nationals of a third country if such union does not satisfy the conditons of ILO Convention No 87 concerning the freedom of association and protection of the right to organize.

3. The law of the Member State of registration of the vessel or, if explicitly referred to in the agreement, any other Member State, shall apply to such collective wage agreements. The courts of the Member States shall be competent to hear and determine disputes arising out of such agreements and from individual labour contracts drawn up in accordance with and in implementation of such a collective wage agreement.

4. Collective agreements must not contain discriminatory rules based on sex."

Article 16 relates to social security:

"Without prejudice to Article 13(2)(c) of Council Regulation (EEC) No 1408/71[95] and in the absence of a contrary agreement at the level of governments or social partners, social security for seafarers on board vessels registered in Euros shall be the responsibility of the country in which the seafarer has his usual residence unless the legislation of that country expressly provides otherwise, in which case the Member State in whose national register the vessel is registered shall be responsible but in accordance with the legislation generally applicable to seafarers of the country of usual residence.

For the purpose of this provision residence means residence on shore and employment on board a vessel registered in a Member State shall not, of itself, be considered as being residence in that State."

Article 17 states that Articles 14, 15 and 16 shall apply subject to any right conferred or obligations imposed by any other Community legislative act except where such act expressly provides otherwise.

95. OJ No. L149, 5 July 1971, p. 2.

Section 4 of the proposed Regulation entitled "Facilities attached to registration in Euros" provides in Article 18 for the transfer of vessels. Article 18 provides:

"Any vessel registered in Euros and having valid certificates and classification and meeting the essential technical requirements to be laid down by the Council according to the provisions of the Treaty before 31 December 1991, may be transferred to the register of another Member State without the imposition of additional technical requirements."

Article 19 deals with the recognition of seafarers' qualifications:

"The qualifications and licences of seafarers who are nationals of a Member State shall be recognized by the competent authorities of each Member State for the purposes of employment on any vessel registered in Euros, subject to minimum requirements for professional training and experience in the function concerned as required in Directives adopted or to be adopted by the Council, according to the provisions of the Treaty, before 31 December 1991."

Section 5 of the proposed Regulation entitled "European flag, port of registration" deals with the flag. Article 20 ("European Flag") provides:

"1. Vessels registered in Euros are entitled and obliged to fly the European flag in addition to their national flag.

2. Upon registration a certificate conveying the right to fly the European flag will be delivered by the Commission to the applicant for registration."

Article 21 relates to the port of registration of the ship and a vessel registered in EUROS shall bear a relevant identification on its stern under the name of the port of registry in its national registration.

Article 22 relates to rights *in rem* and provides that where a vessel flies the European flag this shall not affect the rights *in rem* and maritime liens on this vessel and/or matters of public, administrative or criminal law which shall continue to be governed by the laws of the national flag Member State.

Article 23 is important (and novel). It relates to the calculation of the age of a vessel. For the purpose of the Regulation the age of a vessel shall be calculated from 1 January of the year following the year in which the vessel was delivered by the shipyards ready for commercial use.

Section 6 relates to some final matters. Article 24 deals with implementing measures:

"The Commission shall, within six months after the adoption of this Regulation, adopt the necessary implementing measures concerning the establishment and functioning of Euros, the procedures for registration and deregistration, the system for monitoring compliance with the provisions of this Regulation and the sanctions in case of failure to observe them and lay down the form and content of the documents concerned, including the certificate concerning the right to fly the European flag, the form of, and rules governing the flying of the flag, and the minimum manning certificate."

Article 25 deals with cooperation:

"1. National authorities and the Commission shall assist each other in applying this Regulation and in checking compliance therewith.

2. Within the framework of this mutual assistance they shall communicate to each other the necessary information."

Article 26 deals with the transitional period. It provides:

"1. Member States shall, within 12 months of the adoption of this Regulation and after consultation with the Commission:

(a) adopt measures to protect the European flag and take the necessary measures to enable those vessels registered in Euros to exercise their right to fly it;

(b) take the necessary measures effectively to control compliance with the relevant provisions of Sections 2, 3 and 5 of this Regulation and of the decisions implementing these provisions which shall be issued by the Commission and to introduce the procedure for imposing sanctions.

2. Such measures shall make express reference to this regulation.
3. Member States shall forthwith communicate to the Commission the measures adopted."

Article 27 discusses reports and review. It states:

"The Commission shall make an annual report to the European Parliament and Council, beginning on 1 July 1993, on the number of vessels registered in Euros and the composition of their crews. It shall also propose to the Council any amendments to this Regulation which may be required."

While Article 28 provides:

"By 31 December 1995 at the latest the Council shall decide on a review of this Regulation on the basis of a proposal from the Commission which shall be submitted by 1 July 1995."

6.3.4.12 Advantages of being registered on EUROS

A vessel which would be registered on EUROS could be registered to the register of another Member State without having additional technical requirements imposed.

There would be a mutual recognition of qualifications and licences of EC national seafarers employed on EUROS-registered vessels. Such qualifications and licences would however have to conform with certain minimum requirements laid down by existing legislation as well as those adopted before 1 July 1991.

6.3.4.13 Assessment of the proposal

As might have been expected, the Commission has been bullish about the prospects of such a Register. The Commission has written that the "proposal . . . will make a major contribution to the objective of furthering the common interest by reinforcing the image and the commercial attractiveness of a high quality service Community fleet".[96]

6.3.5 Council regulation on the transfer of ships from one register to another within the Community

6.3.5.1 Introduction

On 1 June 1990, the Commission published its proposal for a Council Regulation on the Transfer of Ships from one Register to another within the Community.[97] It was adopted as Regulation 613/91 on 4 March 1991.[98] Such a measure is very much needed. It is presently problematical as well as expensive to transfer ships from a register in one State to another because of the different national rules relating to such matters as safety, pollution and so on. States do not generally recognise certificates

96. "Examination of State Aids to Community Shipping Companies", p. 3 (contained in Annex I to *Financial and Fiscal Measures Concerning Shipping Operations with Ships Registered in the Community*, *ibid.*).

97. COM(90)219 final, C3 0186/90, 1 June 1990. Referred to hereafter as "the Proposal".

98. OJ L68/1, 15.3.91.

relating to local requirements issued by each other. These different national rules exist despite the existence of international conventions for two reasons: first, such conventions often allow considerable unharmonised discretion to the State parties; and secondly, some States impose rules over and above the rules laid down in the conventions. The net effects of such rules are: first, the need for tests and surveys to be conducted when a ship is transferring registry so as to ensure that the ship can be re-registered; secondly, new equipment which may not be any better but does meet the transferee State's requirements may have to be purchased; thirdly, equipment may have to be modified to meet the transferee State's requirements. The Commission has commented that the "delays and additional costs to the shipowner arising from these formalities are reflected in the ship's operating costs. It is obvious that such practices are not in accordance with the aims of the Single Market. Moreover, the shipping industry has long since sought the abolition of these obstacles to trade in ships."[99]

In its Competitiveness and Employment Impact Statement, the Commission is of the opinion that the proposed measures would not impose any additional obligations on businesses directly and there would be no indirect obligations on businesses imposed by national, regional or local authorities.[100] In fact, the Commission believes that the competitiveness of Community shipping would be enhanced through the elimination of unnecessary costs involved in the transfer of ships.[101]

6.3.5.2 Background to the proposal

The Commission, in its Communication "A Future for the Community Shipping Industry",[102] identified the need to facilitate the transfer of ships from one register to another. The Commission was of the opinion that the facilitation of such transfer would improve the operating conditions for EC shipping.[103]
The Commission said:

"[a]s a parallel measure to setting up a Community Register, the Commission advocated the mutual recognition of ships' technical equipment on the basis of the 'new approach' to technical harmonisation and standardisation adopted by the Council[104] having regard to IMO Conventions.

The Commission considers that, without prejudice to the safety standards laid down at international level or to the general level of maritime safety, no technical requirements should be imposed which would impede the transfer of a Community-registered vessel from one Community shipowner or flag to another. Consequently, the Commission has suggested that, during the period of time required to set up the Community Register, steps should be taken to abolish nationally imposed technical standards.

Accordingly, in its proposal for the establishment of a Community Register, the Commission proposed that any vessel for which classification documents and certificates have been issued and which complies with the basic technical standards to be adopted by the Council before 1 July

99. *Proposal*, Explanatory Memorandum, p. 1. The Preamble to the proposed Regulation thus provides: ". . . measures to facilitate the transfer of ships within the Community are required to free European shipowners from unnecessary costs and administrative procedures involved in a change of register within the Community and also to improve the operating conditions and the competitive position of Community shipping . . . "

100. Explanatory Memorandum to the proposed Regulation, p. 14.

101. Explanatory Memorandum to the proposed Regulation, p. 14.

102. COM(89) 266final, 3 August 1989.

103. According to the August 1989 document: "A Future for the Community Shipping Industry: Measures to Improve the Operating Conditions of Community Shipping".

104. Council Regulation of 7 May 1985 (OJ C138, 4 June 1985).

1991, as provided for in the Treaty, may be transferred to the register of another Member State without having to comply with additional technical requirements."[105]

The Commission had earlier written:

"At present, if a ship is transferred from one Community register to another, it tends to be re-examined by the regulatory authorities responsible for ship safety and it is by no means uncommon for the new owner to be required to replace equipment already certified by the authorities of the original flag state. This happens because the regulatory authorities tend to have their own lists of approved equipment which owe as much to a wish to erect non-tariff barriers in favour of their own equipment industry as they do to the needs of safety. In the Commission's view this places an unnecessary burden on shipowners. It will, therefore, following up on an idea developed by Germany, establish a Community-wide list of approved equipment as meeting IMO standards, and it will propose a Directive to the effect that ships registered under Community flags may be equipped with any of the items contained on that list. It will not itself seek to approve or disapprove such equipment; this function should remain with the regulatory authorities of the Member States who have the responsibiity for implementing the relevant international conventions in pursuance of which the equipment is certified."[106]

The Council of Ministers at its meeting on 4–5 December 1989 called on the Commission to present a proposal to facilitate transfer of ships between registers, as soon as possible, based on the principles of mutual recognition of existing international standards.[107] The Commission now believes that the best way of meeting the Council of Minister's request is through the means of a short and general Regulation.[108]

In its Explanatory Memorandum to the Proposal, the Commission declared that it:

"is aware that the full free movement of goods will only be reached through the principle of technical harmonisation of ship equipment and certification as defined in the . . . 'new approach'. The Commission is of the opinion that in the meantime a first and positive step in this direction could be reached through the proposed procedure allowing for the free transfer of ships within the Community.

Starting from the principle of compliance with the international Conventions on safety and the prevention of marine pollution, the Commission proposes mutual recognition of the safety level attested to by international certificates when a vessel flying the flag of a Member State of the Community is re-registered in another Member State. Where the vessel concerned complies with international standards, the Member States should undertake not to impose their national technical regulations which sometimes differ from those laid down in international conventions."

It is interesting to note that the Commission, in the Preamble to the proposed Regulation, draws a connection between the facilitation of the transfer of ships and the completion of the internal market. It wrote: "[w]hereas the establishment and functioning of the internal market involves the elimination of technical barriers to the transfer of ships between the national registers while safeguarding a high level of safety of ships and environmental protection in conformity with international regulations."

6.3.5.3 Legislative history

The European Parliament's Committee on Transport and Tourism in its report[109] on the Commission proposal states:

105. *Proposal*, Explanatory Memorandum, p. 2. Footnote omitted.
106. *Progress Towards a Common Transport Policy: Maritime Transport*, *ibid.*, para. 97.
107. Conclusions of the Council Meeting of 4–5 December 1989.
108. Explanatory Memorandum to the Proposed Regulation, p. 4.
109. Doc. A3-0345/90 (rapporteur: Mrs Ursula Braun-Moser).

"1. The transfer of a ship from the register of one Member State to the register of another currently entails a number of difficulties. Member States do not normally recognize certificates issued by other Member States.

2. The technical standards required by the Member States for safety and environmental reasons are based on the current conventions (the IMO standards) but often differ on questions of detail, partly because the scope for interpreting and assessing international standards is exercised differently by the Member States, partly because for various reasons a number of Member States lay down additional technical requirements. In its proposal for a regulation setting up a Community ship register,[110] the Commission proposed that the Council shall take a decision on the harmonisation of technical standards by 1 July 1991.

3. In these circumstances the straightforward and practical solution would seem to be to facilitate the transfer of a ship from one register to another by mutual recognition of certificates issued by the Member States. This is in keeping with the Council's new approach to technical harmonisation and standardisation[111] and does not entail any safety problems, as it complies with IMO standards on all points.

4. Article 1(c) of the Commission proposal takes into account the fact that the job of issuing the required government certificates has largely been handed over to non-governmental classification societies. For historical reasons, these societies have taken over both the classification proper, that is, guaranteeing the strength of the hull and the reliability of the engines, and the issuing of maritime safety certificates on behalf of the government.

5. There must, however, be some means of ensuring that the classification companies to which government duties have been transferred meet the same requirements throughout the Community in order to guarantee that work vital to maritime safety continues to be of high quality. In particular, classification companies should have sufficient experience of and experience in carrying out technical inspections and a worldwide net of surveyors and should be capable of devising and administering recognized technical rules."

The Economic and Social Committee issued its unanimous Opinion on 18 December 1990.[112] The body of its Opinion was:

"4. *General Comments*

4.1 The Committee endorses the Commission proposal, since it clearly facilitates the extension of the single market to the shipping industry. It also addresses questions relating to compatibility with safety and environment-orientated action.

4.2 The process of liberalization is not, however, entirely without problems.

4.2.1. The Commission proposal would, in the medium-term, appear to run counter to the ESC approach. The proposal envisages mutual recognition of certificates until such times as Community requirements are laid down. The ESC has however stated its preference for Community recognition of international standards.

4.2.2. The Committee of course endorses the position expressed in earlier Opinions, adding that international standards should be adopted in such a way that no Community Member State applying particularly high standards of work-place safety should be compelled to lower them.

The Committee also considers that in cutting costs, care must be taken not to compromise safety considerations or generate environmental hazards, at either the national or Community level.

To this end, the Community should, within the international organizations, lobby for the fulfilment of such requirements. If this objective is to be secured, regulations and national responsibilities must be clarified, so as to avoid differences of interpretation.

In any case, and in line with the Committee's stated views, steps should be taken to enhance safety conditions at national level.

4.2.3. The Committee notes the exclusion of passenger vessels and urges the Commission to propose, as soon as possible, a regulation permitting the free transfer of such vessels while ensuring a high level of safety.

110. COM(89)266 final—the Sarlis Report.

111 Resolution of 7 May 1985, OJ C136, 4 June 1985.

112. TRA/202.

4.2.4. The Committee also agrees with the establishment of a committee of experts, but would wish to see consultative machinery similar to that set up by the IMO, involving employers, trade unions, conservationists and consumers, for the resolution of safety issues."

The European Parliament also delivered an opinion.[113]

6.3.5.4 Relationship between the Regulation and other rules

The Commission has stressed in its Explanatory Memorandum to the proposed Regulation that this proposal for the Regulation is without prejudice to: (a) the application by the Member States of the International Maritime Organisation[114] or other international conventions; (b) the application of Community rules pursuant to existing or subsequent legislation; and (c) the role of the International Maritime Organisation[115] in drafting and interpreting international conventions on safety and the prevention of marine pollution.

6.3.5.5 Legal bases

The legal bases of the Regulation are the EEC Treaty generally but also, in particular, Article 84(2)[116] thereof. This means that in the light of the amendment made to Article 84(2)[117] of the EEC Treaty by Article 16(5) of the Single European Act that the Council of Ministers need only to adopt the Regulation by means of a qualified majority.

6.3.5.6 Interpretation

Article 1 of the Regulation is merely an interpretative provision. It defines, for the purposes of the Regulation, three terms, namely, "conventions", "requirements" and "certificates".

The Regulation defines "conventions" as meaning three Conventions (as well as their related Resolutions[118] adopted by the International Maritime Organisation[119]), namely: (a) the 1974 International Convention for the Safety of Life at Sea (1974 SOLAS); (b) the International Convention on Load Lines 1966 (LL66); (c) the International Convention for the Prevention of Pollution from Ships 1973 (as modified by its 1978 Protocol (MARPOL 73/78). These conventions are read (as amended) on 4th March 1991 together with related resolutions of mandatory status adopted by the IMO. Article 1(a) of the Regulation provides that without prejudice to the procedures for amending the conventions, the application, for the purposes of this Regulation, of subsequent amendments thereto which have entered into force shall be decided upon in accordance with the provisions laid down in Article 7 of the Regulation.

The term "requirements" when used in the Regulation means "the safety and pollution prevention requirements as laid down in the Conventions".[120]

113. OJ C19, 28 January 1991.
114. On the IMO, see Chapter 1, above.
115. On the IMO, see Chapter 1, above.
116. On Art. 84(2), see Chapter 4, above.
117. On Art. 84(2), see Chapter 4, above.
118. Resolutions, in this context, do not have the same meaning as the term in EC law. On the meaning of the term "resolution" in EC law, see Chapter 3, above.
119. On the International Maritime Organisation, see Chapter 1, above.
120. Regulation, Article 1.

In the context of the Regulation, the term "certificates" means "certificates issued by or on behalf of a Member State in accordance with the Conventions as well as certificates issued for chemical tankers and gas carriers built before 1 July 1986, in accordance with the Bulk Chemical Code [IMO Resolution A.212 (VIII)] or the Bulk Gas Code [IMO Resolution A.328 (IX)]".[121]

6.3.5.7 Application of the Regulation

Article 2 of the Regulation provides:

"This Regulation shall apply to cargo ships of 500 tons[122] gross tonnage and upwards which:

(a) were built on or after 25 May 1980, or were built before that date, but:
 —compliance of which the requirements for new ships defined in the 1974 Solas Convention and
 —in the case of chemical tankers and gas carriers, compliance with the standards codes referred to in Article 1(c) for ships built on or after 25 May 1980,
 is certified by or on behalf of a Member State and
(b) have been flying the flag of, and registered in, a Member State, and in active service under that flag for at least six months; and
(c) carrying valid certificates."

In its Explanatory Memorandum to the proposed Regulation, the Commission commented:

"The Commission, supported by government experts, considers that passenger ships should not, at this stage, be covered by this Regulation, in view of their distinctive features and their uses: they are often constructed to meet additional requirements other than those laid down in the international conventions since they have to sail in waters affected by particular weather conditions. Furthermore, where these vessels (especially the older ones) are concerned, there are differences in the way in which the conventions are interpreted, particularly as regards the structural rules on fire protection and accident prevention, health and hygiene. Nevertheless the Commission undertakes to examine as soon as possible with the experts the possibility of including passenger vessels in the scope of the regulation, offering all the necessary guarantees on the safety level."[123]

The Explanatory Memorandum to the proposed Regulation provides that Article 2 defines the scope of the Regulation.[124] The Explanatory Memorandum goes on:

"Since application of the SOLAS (1974), LL66 and MARPOL 73/78 Conventions ensures a high level of maritime safety and prevention of pollution by ships which is acceptable within the Community and without prejudice to the application of other international conventions and Community rules, the recognition of certificates is limited to the abovementioned Conventions.

The tonnage limit is that laid down in the Conventions in respect of cargo vessels providing international transport services.

The introduction of an age limit and a requirement that vessels be covered by valid certificates will help to increase the level of safety at sea and the prevention of marine pollution within the Community. Passenger liners are excluded on the grounds of their distinctive characteristics. The conditions governing registration mean that only vessels flying the flag of a Member State of the Community can reap the benefit of this Regulation and ensure that standards of safety and pollution prevention are complied with before transfer."

---

121. Regulation, Article 1.
122. Note: not metric tonnes.
123. Proposed Regulation, Explanatory Memorandum, p. 3.
124. *Ibid.*, p. 5.

6.3.5.8 Obligation on Member State to register

Article 3 of the Regulation embodies the general obligation on the other Member State to register a ship (within the meaning of Article 1 of the Regulation) which is being transferred from another registry.

Under Article 3(1) of the Regulation, Member States would not be entitled to withhold from registration a cargo ship[125] registered in another EC Member State complying with the requirements and carrying valid certificates. However, Member States parties to the Convention on the Protection of the Marine Environment in the Baltic Sea area may impose such additional requirements as provided for in that Convention. Any new certificates issued would be on the same basis.[126]

It would however be wrong to imagine that the transfer of a ship from a registry in an EC Member State to another registry would be entirely straightforward. Article 3(3) provides a minor sting in the tail to Article 3(1). Article 3(3) provides that, on transfer, a ship may be subjected to inspection by the receiving Member State to confirm that the actual condition of the ship and its equipment corresponds with its certificates.

The Commission in its Explanatory Memorandum to the proposed Regulation wrote:

"The non-application of national technical rules, combined with an acceptable level of safety and pollution prevention, makes it easier for vessels which comply with international standards to be transferred from one register to another within the Community without barriers to trade. The issue of new certificates include the acceptance of the interpretations and methods of implementation of the conventions of other Member States made for the purposes of the ships' design and equipment, in so far as they are in compliance with the provisions of the conventions, and of the approvals of particular fittings, materials, appliances or apparatuses, or type thereof, fitted on board the ship. The national governments are responsible for issuing the international certificates relating to the safety of, and the prevention of pollution by vessels and their equipment. The Member State to whose register the vessel is being transferred should retain a limited right of inspection in order to ensure that vessels flying the flag of a Member State of the Community meet with the standard of safety and prevention of marine pollution set by the abovementioned conventions."

Article 3 provides:

"1. Member States shall not withhold from registration, for technical reasons arising from the Conventions, a cargo ship registered in another Member State complying with the requirements and carrying valid certificates and fittings and equipment approved or type-approved in the ship's country of origin.

In so far as on the date of entry into force of this Regulation they are bound by regional agreements for the protection of the marine environment, Member States may impose additional rules which conform with the requirements of the optional annexes to the Conventions.

2. Upon the transfer of the ship, the receiving flag Member State shall issue certificates under the same conditions as under the flag previously flown.

3. Where the certificates are issued by an organization on behalf of a Member State, the latter must ensure that the qualifications, technical experience and staffing of the said organization are such as will enable it, in applying the Conventions, to issue certificates guaranteeing a high level of safety.

The organization must be in a position to develop and update rules and regulations having the quality of accepted technical standards, and must operate with qualified and experienced surveyors so as adequately to assess a ship's condition.

125. Such a cargo ship would be a ship of 500 tons gross tonnage and upwards which will be: (a) built on or after 25 May 1980 or built before that date but certified by a Member State as complying with the regulations for new ships as defined in the 1974 SOLAS Convention; (b) flying the flag of, and registered in, a Member State and in active service under that flag; and (c) carrying valid certificates.

126. Proposed Regulation, Article 3(2).

4. Nevertheless, on transfer, a ship may be subjected to inspection by the receiving flag Member State to confirm that the actual condition of the ship and its equipment corresponds with its certificates and with the statements of compliance referred to in Article 2(a)."

6.3.5.9 No additional requirements for certificates

The Regulation incorporates a prohibition on additional requirements being embodied in certificates and thus attempts to ensure compliance with the principles underlying the Regulation when the certificates issued pursuant to Article 3 are renewed, extended or revised. Article 4 provides:

"In so far as requirements remain unchanged for existing receiving flag ships, at the times of renewal, extension or revision of the certificates issued under Article 3, Member States shall not impose requirements other than those initially prescribed for the full term certificates."

6.3.5.10 Divergences of interpretation

Articles 5 and 7 set up an appeal procedure to safeguard the objectives of the transfer of ships which comply with the international safety and pollution prevention requirements, without barriers to trade and unnecessary costs. Article 5 provides:

"1. Member States shall immediately notify to the Commission any refusal to issue new certificates for reasons based on divergences of interpretation of the requirements or of the provisions which the Conventions leave to the discretion of the Parties.

Unless the Commission is informed of an agreement between the Member States concerned within one month, it shall initiate proceedings in order to take a decision in accordance with the procedure laid down in Article 7.

2. Where a Member State considers that a ship cannot be registered under Article 3 for reasons of serious danger to safety or the environment outside the scope of certificates, registration may be suspended for a period not exceeding three months, and the Member State shall without delay bring the matter before the Commission, giving the reasons therefor. The suspension shall be confirmed or revoked in accordance with the procedure laid down in Article 7."

Article 7 provides:

"Where the procedure laid down in this article is to be followed, the representative of the Commission shall submit to the committee a draft of the measures to be taken. The committee shall deliver its opinion on the draft within a time limit which the chairman may lay down according to the urgency of the matter. The opinion shall be delivered by the majority laid down in Article 148(2) of the EEC Treaty in the case of decisions which the Council is required to adopt on a proposal from the Commission. The votes of the representatives of the Member States within the committee shall be set out in that Article. The chairman shall not vote.

The Commission shall adopt the measures envisaged if they are in accordance with the opinion of the committee.

If the measures envisaged are not in accordance with the opinion of the committee, or if no opinion is delivered, the Commission shall, without delay, submit to the Council a proposal relating to the measures to be taken. The Council shall act by a qualified majority.

If, on the expiry of eight weeks from the date of referral to the Council, the Council has not acted, the proposed measures shall be adopted by the Commission."

6.3.5.12 Committee of maritime experts

The Commission proposed the establishment of a Committee of experts. Article 6 of the Regulation provides that the Commission shall be assisted by a committee composed of representatives of the Member States and chaired by a representative of the Commission. Its function will be to resolve any conflicts of integration which might arise from divergences of interpretation of the requirements of the international safety and pollution prevention conventions or recognition of certificates issued by classification societies.

6.3.5.12.1 The Committee's procedure

Article 7 lays down a procedure. It is wiser to cite Article 7 in its entirety so as to demonstrate the full impact of the procedure:

> "Where the procedure defined in this Article is to be followed the representative of the Commission shall submit to the committee a draft of the measures to be taken. The committee shall deliver its opinion on the draft within a time limit which the chairman may lay down according to the urgency of the matter. The opinion shall be delivered by the majority laid down in Article 148(2) of the EEC Treaty in the case of decisions which the Council is required to adopt on a proposal from the Commission. The votes of the representatives of the Member States within the committee shall be weighted in the manner set out in that Article. The Chairman shall not vote.
>
> The Commission shall adopt the measures envisaged if they are in accordance with the opinion of the committee.
>
> If the measures envisaged are not in accordance with the opinion of the committee, or if no opinion is delivered, the Commission shall, without delay, submit to the Council a proposal relating to the measures to be taken. The Council shall act by a qualified majority.[127]
>
> If, on the expiry of eight weeks from the date of referral to the Council, the Council has not acted, the proposed measures shall be adopted by the Commission."

This procedure is, according to the Commission, in accordance with the Council Decision 87/373 of 13 July 1987 on the exercise by the Commission of implementing powers conferred by the Council of Ministers.[128]

6.3.5.12.2 Entry into force

Article 9 of the Regulation stated that the Regulation would enter into force on 1 January 1992.

6.3.5.13 "National Shipping Line"

In 1986, the Commission in its Communication to the Council on Progress Toward a Common Transport Policy: Maritime Transport proposed a Draft Council Directive concerning a Common Interpretation of the Concept of "National Shipping Line".[129]

The Economic and Social Committee in its Opinion on the Proposal questioned whether the proposal came too late to be useful as a number of States had already adopted a definition while others were well on their way to doing so.[130] And, in any event, the committee believed that the proposal from the Commission was unclear and required re-examination on the part of the Commission.[131]

127. Ed. On the Council of Ministers acting by a qualified majority, see Chapter 3, above.
128. Explanatory Memorandum to the proposed Regulation, p. 6.
129. Annex II.4.
130. Opinion, para. 4.3.1.
131. Opinion, para. 4.3.1.

6.4 DEFINITION OF A COMMUNITY SHIPOWNER

The Commission has proposed a Council Regulation providing for a common definition of a Community shipowner.

6.4.1 Introduction

The Commission has proposed the adoption of a Council Regulation on a common definition of a Community shipowner.[132]

6.4.2 Rationale for the Proposal

The second Recital to the proposal provides that "to an increasing degree Community legislation refers to Community shipowners and there should be a common view on the identity of such a shipowner."

6.4.3 Legal bases

The legal bases for the Regulation would be the EEC Treaty generally and, in particular, Article 84(2) thereof.

6.4.4 Purpose of the proposed Regulation

The purpose of the proposed Regulation, according to Article 1 of the proposal, is to lay down criteria establishing a common definition of a Community shipowner.

6.4.5 The concept of a Community shipowner

Article 4 of the amended proposal provides:

"The following shipowners are regarded as Community shipowners:

1. (a) a national of a Member State, who has his domicile or usual residence in a Member State;
   (b) a company or firm which is formed in accordance with the law of a Member State and which complies with the following conditions:
      (i) the principal place of business is situated and the effective control exercised in a Member State; and
      (ii) a majority of the members of the board or of the directors are nationals of Member States having their domicile or usual residence in the Community or in which nationals of Member States participate by more than 50% or are company shareholders controlling more than 50% of the overall company capital;
2. (a) a national of a Member State who has his domicile or usual residence outside the Community if he is the owner of a vessel registered in a Member State in accordance with its legislation;
   (b) a company or firm formed in accordance with the law of a third country in which nationals of Member States participate by more than 50% or are shareholders controlling more than 50% of the overall company capital provided that it is the owner of a vessel registered in a Member State in accordance with its legislation."

132. COM(91) 54. For the amended version, see OJ C73/25, 19 March 1991.

6.5 PARALLEL REGISTRIES

A number of EC States operate parallel registries. Bredima-Savopolou and Tzoannos comment:

"[t]hese registries enable a shipowner to register his vessels under the national flag but operate it with a high degree of flexibility concerning choice and conditions of employment of factors of production, including labour. Thus, whilst the government of the particular state retains administrative control over the ships in the parallel register, the shipowner can operate under conditions similar to those found in the traditional open registries . . . many European countries are turning in increasing numbers to the invention of a parallel register for the operation of vessels under 'off-shore' conditions as an answer to the loss of competitive advantage *vis-à-vis* third country fleets. This practice is creating a two-tier regime for the operation of ships under the flag of the countries concerned; one with strict control of ship management including employment conditions, and a second with a high degree of flexibility in ship management."[133]

Denmark has an off-shore registry. France has established an "off-shore" or parallel registry in the Kerguelen Islands. Luxembourg has a parallel registry. The Netherlands has an off-shore registry in the Dutch Antilles. The UK has an off-shore registry in the Isle of Man.

A matter of critical concern is the status of each of these "dependent territories" and so on. Article 2 of Protocol No. 3 of the Act of Accession of the UK to the EC provides that the residents of the Isle of Man shall not benefit from EC provisions relating to the free movement of persons and services.

Speaking to the Antwerp Shipping Symposium, 'A Future for the Community Fleet', on 6 May 1987, Georgios Anastassopoulos, the then Chairman of the Transport Committee of the European Parliament, stated that the European Parliament:

"has taken a very strong position against flagging out. And naturally it has never favoured open registries with all their negative for the Community implications [*sic*]. But the question is not a theoretical one. It cannot be resolved by exorcisms. The shipowners have reiterated to us that their conversion to the open registries is the lesser of evils and that it represents for them the only way of survival in a very competitive world environment. They have argued that whilst all other costs don't make a very substantial difference, the difference in manning costs for a bulk carrier or a tanker between a normal European and an open registry amount to half a million dollars a year. . . . There could be no question . . . [t]he European Parliament would welcome the incentives to prevent flagging out. We have to stop it before it is too late. . . . The development of a European flag has aroused much enthusiasm . . . Its time may later come, but it seems . . . that we have still a long way to go. A Community emblem would be a different question, but with more psychological than substantial repercussions."[134]

It is worth noting that a reference has been made to the Court of Justice of the European Communities by judgments of the *Arbeitsgericht* [Labour Court] Bremen, Second Chamber, of 9 October 1990, which were received at the Court Registry on 22 February 1991, for a preliminary ruling in the actions between Sloman Neptun Schiffahrts AG and Bodo Ziesemer, *Seebetriebsrat* [Seamen's representative], on the following question:

"The Court of Justice is requested to give a preliminary ruling on the question whether it is compatible with Articles 92 and 117 of the EEC Treaty that Article 1(2) of the Gesetz zur Einführung eines zusätzlichen Schiffregisters für Seeschiffe unter der Bundesflagge im internationalen Verkehr (Internationales Seeschiffahrtsregister—ISR) [Law on the introduction

133. *Op. cit.*, p. 53.
134. (1987) XXII *European Transport Law*, at p. 199.

of an additional shipping register for ships flying the Federal German flag in international trade (International Shipping Register—ISR)] of 23 March 1989, BGBl. 1, p. 550, makes it possible for foreign seamen with no permanent abode or residence in the Federal Republic of Germany not to be covered by German collective agreements and thus to be employed at lower 'home country' rates and on less favourable employment conditions than comparable German seamen."

The matter is still before the ECJ.

CHAPTER 7

Freedom to Supply Maritime Services

7.1–7.2 INTRODUCTION

One of the cardinal principles of the EC is that nationals of one EC Member State should be legally entitled to provide services to persons residing in another EC Member State. It is a right which is of tremendous significance in all areas of the economy, in particular, banking, insurance, broadcasting and, of course, transport.[1] It is also a freedom which has proved controversial and has generated enormous jurisprudential as well as political argument.

The existence of the freedom to provide services in shipping must not be underestimated. Even if a national of, for example, the UK decides not to provide services to nationals of other Member States, that is not the end of the matter—a national from one of the other Member States might well decide to offer services to UK nationals and thereby steal the UK national's own customers.

7.3 UN LINER CODE

On the United Nations Convention on a Code of Conduct for Liner Conferences, see Chapter 11, below.

7.4 FREEDOM TO PROVIDE SERVICES IN EC LAW[2]

Freedom to provide services is an extremely important principle of EC law. While Articles 59 and 60(3) relate to the provision of services, the position is different in the context of transport. Article 61(1) of the EEC Treaty provides:

> "Freedom to provide services in the field of transport shall be governed by the provisions of the Title relating to transport."

Thus, a special regime has to be established for shipping services.

1. See, for example, Lowe, *The Transport and Distribution Manager's Guide to 1992* (1989), p. 14.
2. See also Aussant, "Freedom to Provide Services in the EC" (1988) 23 Journal of Law and Economics 556.

7.5 REGULATION 4055/86

7.5.1 Introduction

Regulation 4055/86[3] (referred to in this Section as the "Regulation") applies the principle of freedom to provide services to maritime transport between Member States as well as between Member States and third countries. It does not deal with services between ports within one EC Member State (i.e. cabotage).

7.5.2 Purpose

The Regulation was adopted so as to enable shipowners to compete against the restrictions imposed by other countries. It prohibits, in three stages, the sharing of the transport of certain goods between ships of a member State and a Third State. The first stage, which ended on 31 December 1989 saw the phasing out of such restrictions on the carriage between Member States by ships flying a Member State flag. The second stage, which ended on 31 December 1991, involves services between Member States and third countries provided by ships flying a Member State flag. The third stage, which ends on 1 January 1993, involves any ship providing transport between Member States and between Member States and third countries.

According to Dimitri Petropolous, the Head of Division: Maritime Transport at the Commission, in the light of, *inter alia*:

"the direction provided by the Treaty of Rome towards a policy based on market economy principles . . . , the first objective for Community maritime transport policy must be to *safeguard free access to a free world shipping market*. Indeed there is nothing to be gained by a protectionist Community shipping policy. Although the Community is a big cargo generating area you can normally not reserve more than half of the cargo to your own ships — your trading partners can make their claims. As the Community fleet is already carrying around 40% of the Community's foreign trade on vessels registered in the Community, the possible gain, if any, would be small and could place in jeopardy the revenue from which the Community shipping industry gets from cross trading between third countries. Moreover the Community's shipping policy cannot simply look at the position of shipowners. An essential consideration of shipping policy must be that the Community's foreign trade should have the advantages of freight rates arrived at in fair and free competition. Therefore the Community has to defend itself against protectionist measures of other countries whilst at the same time bringing its own house in order in this respect. This is the purpose of the two Community Regulations adopted in December 1986 on *freedom to provide international shipping serveices* (EEC No. 4055/86) and on *free access to ocean trades* (EEC No. 4058/86).[4]

The Preamble reiterates the anti-protectionist approach of the EC towards cargo sharing between some EC Member States and non-Member States

The Preamble contains a recital:

"Whereas the structure of the Community shipping industry is such as to make it appropriate that the provisions of the Regulation should also apply to nationals of the Member States established outside the Community and to shipping companies established outside the Community and controlled by nationals of a Member State, if their vessels are registered in that Member State in accordance with its legislation."

3. Le Bihan & Lebullenger, "Common Maritime Transport Policy: Bilateral Agreements and the Freedom to Provide Services" (1988) 9 YBk EL 209.

4. "The European Community Transport Policy An Overview", at The Future of Shipping in Europe—Key Legal and Commercial Issues, London, 28–29 June 1990, pp. 4–5. (Personal Comments).

Commenting on this Recital, Bredima-Savopoulou and Tzoannos say that this:

"statement implies that accommodation of the Greek registration system has necessitated the provision of an alternative category of beneficiaries of the freedom to provide services in maritime transport. It implies acceptance by the Community of the notion of nationality of ships strengthened with the additional caveat that the shipowning company established outside the EEC will be majority owned by EEC nationals."[5]

The Regulation provides that the freedom to provide maritime transport services between EC Member States and between third States applies in respect of:

(a) Nationals of EC Member States who are established in a Member State other than that of the person for whom the services are provided; and
(b) Nationals of the EC Member States established outside the EC and shipping companies established outside the EC and controlled by nationals of an EC Member State provided their vessels are registered in that EC Member State."

7.5.3 Commercial background

The introduction or maintenance of cargo sharing in bulk trade would seriously affect the trading interests of all countries by increasing transport costs.

7.5.4 Effect

The Regulation is applicable in its entirety and is directly applicable in all EC Member States.[6] It applies to nationals of Member States, whether natural or legal persons, who are established in a Member State other than that of the person, for whom the services are intended. Nationals of EC Member States established outside the EC and shipping companies established outside the EC and controlled by nationals of a Member State are also covered, if their vessels are registered in that EC Member State.

7.5.5 Entry into force

The Regulation entered into force, in accordance with Article 12 of the Regulation, on the day following its publication in the *Official Journal*, namely, on 1 January 1987.

7.5.6 Implementation

Member States are obliged, under Article 10 of the Regulation, to consult with the Commission before adopting laws, regulations or administrative provisions implementing the Regulation. The Member States are also obliged under the provision to communicate any such measures adopted to the Commission.

7.5.7 Basic provision relating to freedom to provide services: Article 1

The essence of the Regulation is embodied in Article 1 of the Regulation:

"1. Freedom to provide maritime transport sevices between Member States and between Member States and third countries shall apply in respect of nationals of Member States who are established in a Member State other than that of the person for whom the services are intended.

5. The Common Shipping Policy of the EEC (1990), p. 176.
6. Reg. 4055/86, Art. 12.

2. The provisions of this Regulation shall also apply to nationals[7] of the Member States established outside the Community and controlled by nationals of a Member State, if their vessels are registered in that Member State in accordance with its legislation.

3. The provisions of Articles 55 to 58 and 62 of this Treaty[8] shall apply to the matters covered by this Regulation.

4. For the purpose of this Regulation, the following shall be considered 'maritime transport services between Member States and between Member States and third countries' where they are normally provided for remuneration:

(a) *intra-Community shipping services*:
the carriage of passengers or goods by sea between any port of a Member State and any port or off-shore installation of another Member State;

(b) *third-country traffic*:
the carriage of passengers or goods by sea between the ports of a Member State and ports or off-shore installations of a third country."

It is thus clear that the Regulation does not apply to services within a Member State, i.e. cabotage despite the Commission's proposal having included such services within the scope of the proposed Regulation but this matter will be dealt with below.[9]

The Council of Ministers is empowered, under Article 7, to extend the provisions of the Regulation to nationals of a third country (i.e. a non-EC Member State) which provide maritime transport services and are established in the EC. It has been commented:

"[t]his provision is basically intended to be used in order to extend the benefit of the liberalization process to other OECD countries which are not Member States of the EEC. It is remarkable, however, that this provision is unduly vague: it does not specify when, how, under what criteria such a Council decision may be taken. This provision may open the door to misinterpretation and claims by nationals of other countries apart from the above group."[10]

7.5.7.1 Timetable: Article 2

Article 2 of the Regulation provides that, by way of derogation from Article 1, unilateral national restrictions in existence before 1 July 1986, on the carriage of certain goods wholly or partly reserved for vessels flying the national flag, shall be phased out (at the latest) in accordance with the timetable set out in Article 2. That timetable provides that carriage between Member States by vessels flying the flag of a Member State was to have been phased out by 31 December 1989; carriage between Member States and third countries by vessels flying the flag of a Member State is to be phased out by 31 December 1991; and, carriage between Member States and between Member States and third countries in other vessels by 1 January 1993. It is only then that there will be a complete freedom for EC nationals to provide services to and from their own EC Member States to other EC States.

Dimitri Petropolous, the Head of Division: Maritime Transport in the Commission has summarised the French position by saying that France:

"has taken the position that its major apparent restriction is not cargo reservation at all. Admittedly, there is a law of 1928 which refers to a reservation of oil in French flag ships or ships chartered by French oil importers. However, it is argued that in practice there is no restriction for other flags since the whole scheme is based on the requirement for oil importers to have sufficient

7. This includes both natural and legal persons.
8. I.e. the EEC Treaty.
9. See para. 7.5, below.
10. Bredima Savopoulou and Tzoannos, *op. cit.*, pp. 116–117.

tonnage available in times of crisis. But there is no obligation on these importers to use that capacity in French trades. The Commission is still studying the legal and practical implications of this regime, as well as some less important apparent restrictions."[11]

Spain has now adopted measures to liberalise their reserved trades for the benefit of shipping companies from other EC States insofar as such companies use ships registered in EC States. Bredima-Savopoulou and Tzoannos record[12] that:

"Spanish Regulation No. 1382 of 18/1/1985 provides for liberalization of maritime transport from the reservation for Spanish flag vessels of the transportation of certain commodities save for an extremely long list of commodities including, *inter alia*: tobacco, coal, lignite, crude oil and other types of oil, petroleum gas, cotton, meat, coffee, wheat, rye, barley, corn, rice, cereal, flour, olivc oil, soya oil, sunflower oil, sugar."

7.5.8 Cargo-sharing arrangements in bilateral agreements: Articles 3 and 4

The phasing out or adjustment of cargo-sharing arrangements contained in existing bilateral agreements concluded by Member States with third countries is provided for in Articles 3 and 4 of the Regulation.

Article 3 simply provides that cargo-sharing arrangements contained in existing bilateral agreements concluded by Member States with third countries shall be phased out or adjusted in accordance with the provisions of Article 4 of the Regulation.

Article 4 of the Regulation provides that:

"1. Existing cargo-sharing arrangements not phased out in accordance with Article 3 shall be adjusted in accordance with Community legislation and in particular:

(a) where trades governed by the United Nations Code of Conduct for Liner Conferences[13] are concerned, they shall comply with this Code and with the obligations of Member States under Regulation (EEC) No.954/79[14];

(b) where trades not governed by the United Nations Code of Conduct for Liner Conferences are concerned, agreement shall be adjusted as soon as possible and in any event before January 1, 1993, so as to provide for fair, free and non discriminatory access by all Community nationals, as defined in Article 1,[15] to the cargo-shares due to the Member State concerned.

2. National action in pursuance of paragraph 1 shall be notified immediately to the Member States and the Commission. The consultation procedure established by Council Decision 77/587/EEC shall apply.

3. Member States shall report to the Commission on progress made on the adjustments referred to in paragraph 1(b), initially every six months and subsequently every year.

4. When difficulties arise in the process of adjusting agreements to bring them into conformity with paragraph 1(b), the Member State concerned shall inform the Council and the Commission. In cases where agreements are incompatible with paragraph 1(b), and where the Member State concerned so asks, the Council shall, acting on a proposal from the Commission, take appropriate action."

The effective date for determining whether an agreement is an "existing one" for the purposes of the Regulation was 1 January 1987.

7.5.9 Cargo-sharing arrangements in future agreements: Article 5

Article 5 of the Regulation explicitly prohibits new cargo sharing arrangements in future agreements except in the most exceptional of circumstances. It provides that:

11. *Op. cit.* at footnote 4, p. 16.
12. *Op. cit.* at footnote 5, p. 206.
13. See Chapter 11, below.
14. See para. 11, above.
15. Ed.

"1. Cargo-sharing arrangements in any future agreements with third countries are prohibited other than in those exceptional circumstances where Community liner shipping companies would not otherwise have an effective opportunity to ply for trade to and from the third country concerned. In those circumstances such arrangements may be permitted in accordance with the provisions of Article 6.

2. In cases where a third country seeks to impose cargo sharing arrangements on Member States in liquid or dry bulk trades, the Council shall take the appropriate action in accordance with Regulation (EEC) No. 4056/86[16] concerning co-ordinated action to safeguard free access to cargoes in ocean trades."

(In respect of the exceptional circumstances outlined in Article 5(1), see Bredima-Savopoulou and Tzoannos at pp. 178–179.)

Article 6 of the Regulation goes on to provide that where a Member State's nationals or shipping companies, as defined in Article 1, paras 1 and 2, are experiencing, or are threatened by, a situation where they do not have an effective opportunity to ply for trade to and from a particular third country, the Member State concerned shall inform the other Member States and the Commission as soon as possible.

The Council of Ministers, acting by qualified majority[17] on a proposal of the Commission, shall decide on the necessary action. Such action may include, in the circumstances envisaged in Article 5(1), the negotiation and conclusion of cargo-sharing arrangements.[18]

If the Council has not decided on the necessary action within six months of a Member State providing information under para. 1, the Member State concerned may take such action as may be for the time being be necessary to preserve an effective opportunity to ply for trade in accordance with Article 5(1).[19]

"4. Any action taken under paragraph 3 shall be in accordance with Community law and provide for fair, free and non- discriminatory access to the relevant cargo-shares by nationals or Community shipping companies as defined in Article 1(1) and (2).

5. National action in pursuance of paragraph 3 shall be notified immediately to the Member States and the Commission. The consultation procedure established by Council Decision 77/587/EEC shall apply."[20]

7.5.10 Non-discrimination between EC nationals on the basis of nationality

As long as restrictions on freedom to supply services have not been abolished, each Member State shall apply such restrictions without discrimination on grounds of nationality or residence to all persons providing services within the meaning of Article 1(1) and (2) of the Regulation.[21] This amplifies the principle of non-discrimination on the basis of nationality enshrined in Article 7 of the EEC Treaty and embodied in EC law generally.[22]

7.5.11 Non-EC nationals

The Council of Ministers is empowered to extend the provisions of the Regulation to nationals of a third country which provide maritime transport services and are

16. See Chapter 12, below.
17. On Council of Ministers' voting procedures, see Chapter 3, above.
18. Art. 6(2).
19. Art. 6(3).
20. See Chapter 19, below.
21. Reg. 4055/86, Art. 9.
22. On the principle of non-discrimination on the basis of nationality, see Chapter 3, above.

established in the EC.[23] This is an open-ended provision which confers on the Council of Ministers a great deal of discretion.

7.5.12 Temporary establishment

Article 8 of the Regulation provides:

"Without prejudice to the provisions of the [EEC] Treaty relating to right of establishment,[24] a person providing a maritime transport service may, in order to do so, temporarily pursue his activity in the Member State where the service is provided, under the same conditions as are imposed by that State on its own nationals."

7.5.13 Review

The EC Council is charged under Article 11 of the Regulation to review, acting in accordance with the provisions of the EEC Treaty, the Regulation before 1 January 1995.[25]

7.5.14 Assessment

The Regulation is vague in many instances. What is meant by the phrase "fair, free and non-discriminatory access"? What is indeed meant by the term "cargo sharing arrangement"?

The Commission in its Seventh Annual Report to the European Parliament on Commission Monitoring of the Application of Community Law[26] state in para. 190:

"As expected in the previous report, it has been possible to withdraw the infringement proceedings against Portugal on preference accorded the carriage of goods by vessels flying the national flag. As a result of cooperation between the Commission and the Portugese authorities, in February 1989, the latter adopted a decree-law to bring the legislation into line with Regulation (EEC) No. 4055/86 applying the principle of freedom to provide services to maritime transport."

7.5.15 French-Corsican Case

Case 48/89 *Corsica Ferries France* v. *Direction Générale des Douanes Françaises* is an interesting judgment on Regulation 4055/86. The ECJ in a succinct and lucid judgment said:[27]

"[1] By judgment of 17 January 1989, which was received at the Court on 23 February 1989, the Cour de Cassation of the French Republic referred to the Court for a preliminary ruling under Article 177 EEC a question on the interpretation of the EEC Treaty, in particular Articles 59, 62 and 84.

[2] Those questions arose in proceedings between Corsica Ferries France (hereinafter referred to as 'Corsica Ferries') and the Direction Générale des Douanes in regard to charges levied on the shipowner in 1981 and 1982 in respect of passengers embarked, disembarked or transferred in Corsican ports.

[3] In regard to those ports, section R.212-20 of the French Code des Ports Maritimes, as amended by the Decree of 12 May 1981, levies a charge on all passengers travelling to Corsica

23. Reg. 4055/86, Art. 7.
24. See Arts 52 *et seq.* of the EEC Treaty.
25. Reg. 4055/86, Art. 11.
26. COM(90) 288 final, 22 May 1990.
27. [1991] 2 CMLR 227.

from mainland France or Sardinia and a charge at an identical rate on all passengers travelling to or from a port situated in Europe or North Africa.

[4] According to Corsica Ferries, that provision is contrary to Article 59 *et seq.* EEC inasmuch as it discriminates between ships plying between Corsica and ports in mainland France, who are not required to pay tax in respect of passengers who embark at a Corsican port, and ships, such as those of Corsica Ferries, plying between Corsica and ports in another State, which are subject to tax both on arrival in and departure from the Corsican port.

[5] Since it considered that an interpretation of certain provisions of the EEC Treaty was necessary, the Cour de Cassatio stayed the proceedings until the Court of Justice had given a preliminary ruling on the following question:

> Must the EEC Treaty, in particular Articles 59, 62 and 84, be interpreted as meaning that a member-State is authorised, in connection with the use by a ship of harbour installations situated in its island territory, to levy charges on the embarkation and disembarkation of passengers when travelling to or arriving from a port situated in another member-State, whilst in the case of travel between two ports situated within national territory those charges are levied only on embarkation at the island port?

[6] Reference is made to the Report for the Hearing for a fuller account of the facts of the case, the course of the procedure and the written observations submitted to the Court, which are mentioned or discussed hereinafter only in so far as is necessary for the reasoning of the Court.

[7] In order to answer the question referred to the Court by the Cour de Cassation, it must first be pointed out that the French legislation at issue in the main proceedings may constitute a restriction on freedom to provide services within the Community within the meaning of Article 59(1) EEC in so far as it discriminates between persons providing transport services between a port situated in national territory and a port situated in another member-State of the Community and persons providing transport services between two ports situated in national territory.

[8] As the Court has decided on various occasions, the Articles of the EEC Treaty concerning the free movement of goods, persons, services and capital are fundamental Community provisions and any restriction, even minor, of that freedom is prohibited.

[9] In the area of freedom to provide services such a restriction may, as the Court pointed out in Case 127/86, *Ministère Public* v. *Ledoux*,[28] result from national tax measures which affect the trader's exercise of that right.

[10] Although Article 59, guaranteeing freedom to provide services within the Community, has been directly and unconditionally applicable since the expiry of the transitional period provided for in Article 8 of the Treaty, under Article 61(1) of the Treaty freedom to provide services in the field of transport is to be governed by the provisions of the title relating to transport (see Joined Cases 209–213/84, *Ministère Public* v. *Asjes*[29] and Case 4/88, *Lambregts Transportbedrijf* v. *Belgian State*.[30]

[11] It follows, as the Court pointed out in *Asjes*,[31] that in the transport sector the objective laid down in Article 59 of the Treaty of abolishing during the transitional period restrictions on freedom to provide services should have been attained in the framework of the common policy provided for in Articles 74 and 75.

[12] With regard in particular to maritime transport, Article 84(2) of the Treaty provides that the Council may decide whether, to what extent and by what procedure appropriate provisions may be laid down for that kind of transport.

[13] It was only in Regulation 4055/86 applying the principle of freedom to provide services to maritime transport between member-States and between member-States and non-member countries, which entered into force on 1 January 1987, that the Council adopted, on the basis of Article 84(2) of the Treaty, the measures necessary to achieve freedom to provide services in maritime transport between member-States.

[14] It must therefore be concluded that in 1981 and 1982, the period at issue in the main proceedings, freedom to provide services in maritime transport had not yet been implemented

28. [1988] ECR 3741.
29. [1986] ECR 1425, [1986] 3 CMLR 173.
30. [1989] ECR 2583, [1991] 1 CMLR 351, at paras [8] & [9].
31. At para. [37].

and that consequently the member-States were entitled to apply provisions such as those at issue in the main proceedings.

[15] That conclusion is not weakened by the fact that those rules were reintroduced into the French Code des Ports Maritimes in 1981 after having been repealed in 1969. In the light of the existence of Article 61(1) of the Treaty, Article 62, which prohibits the member-States from introducing any new restrictions on the freedom to provide services which had in fact been attained at the date of the entry into force of the Treaty, does not apply.

[16] The answer to the question referred to the Court by the Cour de Cassation of the French Republic should therefore be that the EEC Treaty, in particular Articles 59, 61, 62 and 84, did not before the entry into force of Council Regulation 4055/86 of 22 December 1986 applying the principle of freedom to provide services to maritime transport between member-States and between member-States and non-member countries, prevent a member-State from levying, in connection with the usc by a ship of harbour installations situated within its island territory, charges on the embarkation and disembarkation of passengers arriving from or going to a port situated in another member-State, whilst in the case of travel between two ports situated within national territory those charges were levied only on embarkation at the island port.

Costs

[17] The costs incurred by the Government of the French Republic and the Commission of the European Communities, which have submitted observations to the Court, are not recoverable. Since these proceedings are, in so far as the parties to the main proceedings are concerned, in the nature of a step in the action pending before the national court, the decision on costs is a matter for that court.

On those grounds, THE COURT (Second Chamber), in answer to the question submitted to it by the Cour de Cassation of the French Republic by judgment of 17 January 1989,

HEREBY RULES:

> The EEC Treaty, in particular Articles 59, 61, 62 and 84, did not, before the entry into force of Council Regulation 4055/86 of 22 December 1986 applying the principle of freedom to provide services to maritime transport between member-States and between member-States and non-member countries, prevent a member-State from levying, in connection with the use by a ship of harbour installations situated in its island territory, charges on the embarkation and disembarkation of passengers arriving from or going to a port situated in another member-State, whilst in the case of travel between two ports situated within national territory those charges were levied only on embarkation at the island port."

7.5.16 Italy-Algeria Case

In July 1985, Italy informed the other EC Member States and the Commission that it was experiencing difficulties in its trade relations with Algeria because Algeria was demanding that about 80% of goods shipped on liner services between Italy and Algeria be carried on the Algerian state shipping line. The EC and the Member States made representations to Algeria but to little avail.

Italy, acting on its own behalf, then negotiated with Algeria an "Agreement on Maritime Transport and Navigation between the Italian Republic and the People's Democratic Republic of Algeria". This draft Agreement was initialled and signed but not ratified. Article 4 of the draft Italy–Algeria Agreement provided:

> "Shipowners will be responsible for taking the measures necessary for the organisation and sharing of trade in the framework of a conference or other organisation of shipowners for the most effective operation of lines, in accordance with the trade-sharing principle laid down in the Code of Conduct for Liner Conferences and subject to compliance with the international obligations of each party."

On 17 March 1987, Italy notified the draft Agreement to the Commission in accordance with Article 6(5) of Regulation 4055/86. The Commission believed that

Article 4 of the draft Agreement had to be considered in the light of Articles 5(1) and 6(2) of Regulation 4055/86. Article 5(1) of the Regulation provides:

"Cargo-sharing arrangements in any future agreements with any third countries are prohibited other than in those exceptional circumstances where Community liner shipping companies would not otherwise have an effective opportunity to ply for trade to and from the third country concerned. In these circumstances such arrangements may be permitted in accordance with the provisions of Article 6."

Article 6(2) of the Regulation provides:

"The Council, acting by qualified majority on a proposal of the Commission, shall decide on the necessary action. Such action may include, in the circumstances envisaged in Article 5(1), the negotiation and conclusion of cargo-sharing arrangements."

The Commission was of the view that the restrictive condition in Article 5(1) of the Regulation was not met because "Italy would have had an effective opportunity to ply for trade to and from Algeria if it had acceded to the Convention on a Code of Conduct for Liner Conferences adopted at Geneva on 6 April 1974 . . . which would, pursuant to Article 2(4) of the Code, have given its shipping companies access to the traffic in question".[32] Article 2(4) of the Code provides:

"When determining a share of trade within a pool of individual member lines and/or groups of national shipping lines in accordance with Article 2, paragraph 2, the following principles regarding their right to participation in the trade carried by the conference shall be observed, unless otherwise mutually agreed:

(a) The group of national shipping lines of each of two countries the foreign trade between which is carried by the conference shall have equal rights to participate in the freight and volume of traffic generated by their mutual foreign trade and carried by the conference,

(b) Third-country shipping lines, if any, shall have the right to acquire a significant part, such as 20 per cent. in the freight and volume of traffic generated by that trade."

The Commission believed that the proposed Agreement could be operated for so long as Italy was not a party to the Liner Conferences Code. The Commission therefore submitted to the Council of Ministers a draft Decision pursuant to Article 6(2) of the Regulation. The Decision would authorise the Agreement subject to the condition that Italy would accede to the Code as quickly as possible. The Agreement would cease to have effect as soon as the Code of Conduct became applicable to trade between Italy and Algeria or, at the very latest, three years after the adoption of the Council Decision. The draft Agreement would have to be amended in some respects however in advance so as to ensure freedom to provide services and the maintenance of effective competition.

On 17 September 1987, the Council of Ministers adopted Decision 87/475[33] relating to maritime transport between Italy and Algeria. The Preamble to the Decision stated:

"the provisions of the aforementioned Agreement need to be applied in such a way as to avoid a conflict with the obligations of the Member States under Community law, in particular with respect to fair, free and non-discriminatory access to cargoes by Community nationals or shipping companies, including independent lines."

Article 1 of the Decision granted unconditional authorisation to ratify the Agreement "on the understanding" that Italy will accede to the Liner Code as soon as possible.

32. Judgment, para. 8.
33. OJ 1987 L272/37.

On 25 November 1987, the EC Commission instituted proceedings under Article 173(1) of the EEC Treaty to annul Council Decision 87/475.

The Commission raised a number of arguments. First, the Commission maintained that the Decision is contrary to Articles 5 and 6 of the Regulation because (a) it authorised the conclusion of a cargo-sharing arrangement although the requisite conditions were not met and (b) the agreement was contrary to Community law in several respects.

Did Article 4 of the draft Agreement contain a cargo-sharing arrangement? This was the Commission's argument but the Council of Ministers asserted that it simply provided for the establishment of a liner conference (i.e. a group of vessel-operating carriers which provide international liner services for the carriage of cargo and has arrangements on freight rates and other conditions of transport). The ECJ held that it constituted a cargo-sharing arrangement. That said, was there a breach of Articles 5 and 6? The ECJ said:

> "[17] With regard to the breach of Article 5(1) of the regulation on freedom to provide services, the first branch of its submission, the Commission argues that there were no 'exceptional circumstances' within the meaning of that provision such as to justify the conclusion of a cargo-sharing arrangement unlimited in its duration. Such circumstances exist only where there is no means less restrictive of freedom to provide services by which the member-State concerned can obtain access to the trade in question. In this case, Italy could have acceded to the Code of Conduct.
>
> [18] According to the Commission, such accession would at the same time have brought Italy under Council Regulation 954/79 of 15 May 1979, concerning the ratification by member-States of, or their accession to, the United Nations Convention on a Code of Conduct for Liner Conferences (hereinafter referred to as "the regulation on ratification of the Code of Conduct").[34] Under Article 3 of that regulation, cargoes allocated to Italian members of the liner conference would have had to be redistributed fairly among all the Community lines which were members of that conference. The simple reference in Article 4 of the draft agreement between Italy and Algeria to the trade-sharing principle in the Code of Conduct did not make the redistribution rule in Article 3 of the regulation applicable. The draft agreement, says the Commission, thus does not guarantee freedom to provide services to the same degree as the accession of Italy to the Code of Conduct would have done.
>
> [19] The regulation on ratification of the Code of Conduct simply lays down certain obligations which Member States that accede to the Code must observe in order to ensure that the Code is applied in a manner consistent with Community law. Contrary to what the Commission proposed, the regulation does not set a time limit within which accession must take place. The regulation thus does not oblige the Member States to accede to the Code of Conduct.
>
> [20] Nor can Italy's accession to the Code of Conduct be required on the ground that it would guarantee freedom to provide services to a greater extent than the application of the agreement between Italy and Algeria. The agreement may provide the same guarantees in that respect as accession to the Code if it contains appropriate clauses guaranteeing freedom to provide services. The question whether that is the case must be considered in connection with the second branch of this submission.
>
> [21] Consequently, the Council was entitled to refrain from making authorisation to ratify the draft agreement between Italy and Algeria subject to the condition that Italy should accede to the Code of Conduct."

The first branch of the submission was therefore rejected.

In the second branch of the submission, the EC Commission argued that the contested decision is contrary to Article 6(2) of Regulation 4055/86 because under that provision, the Council of Ministers could authorise only measures consistent with Community law; the contested decision is contrary to Community law in two respects:

34. [1979] OJ L121/1.

"[24] The Commission argues first of all that the Council could authorise ratification of the agreement only if it ensured fair, free and non-discriminatory access for companies from other member-States to shares in the traffic between Italy and Algeria. It relies in that regard on Article 6(4) of the regulation on freedom to provide services, according to which member-States which themselves negotiate a cargo-sharing arrangement, after the Council has failed to act for a prolonged period, must ensure such freedom of access. The same requirement necessarily applies to Council decisions authorising a cargo-sharing arrangement.

[25] The Commission goes on to argue that the Council can authorise a cargo-sharing arrangement only if it gives Community companies which are not members of the conference effective access to cargoes transported by the conference. That obligation follows from Article 7(2)(b)(i) of Council Regulation 4056/86 of 22 December 1986, laying down detailed rules for the application of Articles 85 and 86 of the Treaty to maritime transport,[35] which requires that effective competition be maintained.

[26] A comparison of the two claims set out above indicates that the first concerns the redistribution of the Italian share of the trade in question between Community companies which are members of the conference other than Italian companies and the second concerns access to that share of trade on the part of Community companies, from whatever member-State, which are not members of the conference.

[27] With regard to the first claim, it should be observed that Italy is bound to ensure that all Community companies which are members of the conference have access to the trade share allocated to Italian shipowners by the agreement. That obligation follows from Article 1 of the regulation on freedom to provide services, which makes the freedom to provide services applicable to maritime transport. It is confirmed in Article 6(4) of that regulation, which is relied on by the Commission. With regard to the second claim, it should be observed that Article 7(2)(b)(i) of Council Regulation 4056/86 does require that the agreement should preserve the possibility of access by Community companies which are not members of the conference to the trade share allocated to Italian shipowners by the agreement.

[28] According to the Commission, the draft agreement between Italy and Algeria does not meet those two requirements because it contains no specific provisions in that respect.

[29] The Commission argues first of all that the reference to Italy's international obligations contained in Article 4 of the draft agreement is too vague to ensure observance of freedom to provide services and freedom of competition.

[30] Article 4 of the draft agreement is made more specific by Article 1(b) of the contested decision, under which Italy 'will reiterate to Algeria that the provisions of the agreement will be implemented in accordance with Community law'. The second to last recital in the preamble to the contested decision states that the obligations imposed by Community law include the obligation to ensure 'fair, free and non-discriminatory access to cargoes by Community nationals or shipping companies, including independent lines'. Italy's obligation to ensure observance of freedom to provide services and freedom of competition is thus stated in a sufficiently precise manner.

[31] The Commission also objects that the international obligations referred to in Article 4 of the draft agreement cannot be relied on against private parties, that is to say the shipowners that are responsible for applying the agreement.

[32] The fact that the application of the agreement is delegated to private parties cannot prejudice observance of Community law. Italy must adopt the necessary internal measures to ensure that its shipowners grant other Community companies rights of access in accordance with Italy's Community obligations.

[33] Since the Commission has not shown that the agreement, as supplemented by the requirements set out in the contested decision, is contrary to Community law, the second branch of the submission must also be rejected.

[34] Consequently, the first submission must be dismissed."

Turning to the breach of the prohibition of discrimination, the ECJ said:

"[35] This submission is made in the alternative to the first submission, in the event that Articles 5(1) and 6(2) of the Regulation on freedom to provide services did not in themselves

35. [1986] OJ L378/4.

prevent the Council from authorising the contested agreement. The Commission submits that in that case these provisions should be implemented in such a manner as to ensure observance of the prohibition of discrimination laid down in Article 7 of the [EEC] Treaty. According to the Commission, that was not done in this case. However, it does not put forward arguments in that respect separate from those which it made in arguing that the contested decision is contrary to the regulation on freedom to provide services.

[36] Consideration of the first submission has shown that the agreement between Italy and Algeria, as supplemented by the requirements set out in the contested decision, ensures non-discriminatory access on the part of shipping lines from other member-States to cargoes allocated to Italy under the agreement.

[37] Consequently, this submission must also be dismissed."

Then turning to the alleged breach of the obligation to state reasons, the ECJ said:

"[38] The Commission submits that by failing, in the contested decision, to state that Article 4 of the draft agreement contained a cargo-sharing arrangement and to state what were the 'exceptional circumstances' within the meaning of Article 5(1) of the regulation on freedom to provide services which justified the conclusion of such an arrangement the Council failed to comply with its obligation to state reasons pursuant to Article 190 of the Treaty.

[39] It is apparent from the first recital in the preamble to the contested decision that Algerian practices of cargo reservation were at the root of the problem. The second recital shows that the purpose of the draft agreement between Italy and Algeria was to counteract the effects of those practices The contested decision thus gave a sufficient indication of the type of problem with which the agreement whose ratification it authorises was intended to deal. A separate, express statement that this was a cargo-sharing arrangement was therefore nugatory.

[40] With regard to the existence of 'exceptional circumstances' justifying authorisation to ratify the agreement it should be emphasised that the fourth recital in the preamble to the contested decision states that its legal basis is Article 6(2) of the regulation on freedom to provide services and points out that that provision authorises the adoption of measures 'where a member-State's nationals or shipping companies do not have an effective opportunity to ply for trade to and from a particular third country'. It is apparent from that recital that the Council considered that the Algerian practices of cargo reservation had created a situation in which Italy no longer had effective access to trade with that non-member country. The contested decision therefore contains a sufficient explanation of the exceptional circumstances justifying its adoption.

[41] It follows from the foregoing that the submission based on breach of the obligation to state reasons must also be rejected."

Finally, turning to the alleged breach of Article 149 of the Treaty, the ECJ said:

"[42] In its final submission the Commission argues that in adopting the contested decision the Council went beyond the limits of its right of amendment under Article 149(1) of the [EEC] Treaty. Under that provision, it says, the Council can adopt a measure only if it has the same subject-matter and objective as the Commission's proposal. Otherwise the Council's measure must be considered to have been adopted without any proposal. In this case the Commission proposed that the Council should refuse authorisation to ratify the agreement if specific amendments were not made. The Council, on the other hand, granted unconditional authorisation to ratify the agreement. By so doing it completely altered the objective of the Commission's proposal and thus disregarded the limits to its right of amendment.

[43] Article 1 of the proposal submitted by the Commission to the Council with a view to the adoption of the contested decision provided that 'Italy may ratify its Agreement on Maritime Transport and Navigation with Algeria, signed on 28 February 1987, on condition that . . .' The conditions set out in the proposal were intended to make the agreement consistent with Community law. The contested decision also authorises Italy to ratify the agreement, but makes that authorisation subject to certain requirements which, as has been established above, ensure observance of Community law.

[44] It is not therefore necessary for the Court to rule generally on the limits of the right of amendment provided for in Article 149(1) of the Treaty; it is sufficient to hold that in this case, and contrary to what the Commission maintains, the Council did not in any event depart from

the subject-matter of the Commission's proposal and did not alter its objective, that is to say, to ensure that the agreement was applied in compliance with Community law.

[45] Consequently, the submission based on breach of Article 149 of the Treaty cannot be upheld.

[46] It follows from all the foregoing that the action is unfounded and must be dismissed."

7.6 CABOTAGE

7.6.1 Introduction

Europe without walls is a land of opportunity. Cabotage is the provision of a shipping service between ports in any one Member State, including the overseas territories of that State.

Cabotage is an impediment to trade within the EC.[36] The Single Market so ardently desired by the Commission in its June 1985 White Paper will be incomplete without the abolition of cabotage. It is an exception to the free open and competition policy espoused by the Member States and championed by the Commission. Cabotage is an obstacle to the free movement of services within the EC: it is one of the cardinal principles of EC law that nationals of one EC Member State should be legally entitled to provide services to persons in other EC Member States. It is a right which is of tremendous significance in all areas of the economy, in particular, in banking,[37] insurance[38] and of course, transport.[39] It is also a freedom which has proved controversial and has generated considerable jurisprudential and political argument.

The abolition of cabotage is a divisive issue among the Member States of the EC. These States can be categorised (in simple terms) into two groups: the "Northern States" which favour its abolition (because they have little to lose by its abolition and may instead gain from the new services which have opened up) and the "Southern States" which favour the retention of cabotage either in whole or in part because they have so much to lose from its abolition (and perhaps very little to gain).

The implications of the abolition of cabotage must not be underestimated. The Greek Island traffic, the Spanish and Italian coastal traffic as well as a multitude of small routes in France, Greece, Italy, Portugal and Spain would finally be opened up. More generally, the freedom to provide services in shipping must not be underestimated. Even if a national of, for example, Greece decides not to provide services to nationals of other Member States (in Italy or wherever), that is not the end of the matter—a national from one of the other Member States might well decide to offer services to Greek nationals and thereby steal the Greek national's own customers.

Cabotage is a modern but limited form of flag discrimination—a concept which is nothing new. Tudor England pioneered flag discrimination. Cromwell then enacted the Navigation Acts in 1651. The effect of these laws is summarised by Farthing in the following terms:

"trade to and from British colonies, which at a much later stage began to expand significantly, had to be carried in British ships. No foreign-built ships were to be used. Commodities of all sorts, particularly strategic commodities had to be enumerated and their carriage regulated and

36. See "Reforms of Cabotage Urged", *Lloyd's List*, 1 April 1987, p. 3.
37. Directive No. 89/646, OJ 1989 L386/1.
38. Directive No. 88/357, OJ 1988 L172/1.
39. See, for example, Reg. 4055/86, OJ 1986 L378/1.

controlled so that no one else got a look in. There was also general encouragement in the form of grants to British shipowners for the carriage of specified exports such as corn and other agricultural products."[40]

It is clear that in life little changes!

7.6.2 Concept of cabotage

7.6.2.1 Definition

Cabotage is the carriage of passengers or goods by sea between ports in any one Member State, including the overseas territories of that State.

7.6.2.2 State cabotage

Cabotage restrictions are imposed by individual Member States, namely, France, Greece, Italy, Portugal and Spain.

7.6.2.3 EC cabotage

A concept which is not widely known is the concept of EC cabotage, that is to say, that the EC as a whole would become a cabotage region, within which national restrictions would be abolished and a single internal EC market would be established. Cabotage on an EC-level does not really exist because there is no cargo reservation at EC-level except for the UNCTAD Code of Conduct on Liner Conferences. This idea was proposed by France in a Working Paper submitted after the 11 November 1985 Council Meeting. While the idea is attractive in its simplicity, the danger is that if the EC were to adopt such a patently interventionist apporach within its own borders then it would lose its moral right to preach to others about free trade in shipping services.

7.6.3 Commercial overview of cabotage

The volume of cabotage trade within the EC is quite significant. This trade is, for obvious reasons, clustered in the Mediterranean with Greece having about 20 million tonnes of cabotage cargo, Spain with about 40 million tonnes, Italy with about 55 million tonnes. Nonetheless the UK has the largest cabotage trade in the EC having over 65 million tonnes.

In general, cabotage activities involve almost all shipping activities, including the transport of cargo (both wet and dry), passengers (including cruising) and off-shore supplies.

Among the five southern Member States, dry bulk cargo is the most important as far as Greece is concerned but liquid cargoes are more important for France, Italy, Spain and Portugal. Apart from France, the amount of cargo and passengers carried on cabotage services is rising, albeit slowly.

The bulk of cabotage trade is between the mainland and the island as well as between two ports on the mainland. Only a small proportion is between islands and then when it is between islands, it is mainly passengers rather than cargo.

40. *International Shipping: An Introduction to the Policies, Politics and Institutions of the Maritime World* (Lloyd's of London Press Ltd, 1987), pp. 9–10.

The number of passengers transported on cabotage services in the Cabotage States in the EC is reckoned to be around fifty million. Some of these services are short ferry crossings. Greece has a significant cruise liner business which is not equalled by any of the other cabotage states. Some passengers and workers are carried out to offshore installations but this is negligible in the whole picture.

7.6.4 Merits of cabotage

7.6.4.1 Arguments for cabotage

The arguments offered by the five southern EC States for cabotage are mainly strategic ones, involving national security, the need for "public service" routes to islands and remote regions, as well as the need to preserve national fleets and seafarers' jobs.

On occasion, Greece has supported cabotage restrictions on the grounds of national security because of its long-standing dispute with Turkey. Greece believes that some of its islands are in dangerous proximity to Turkey and for security reasons only Greek ships should be servicing such islands. The European Parliament has said that national security is a reason why Member States should be able to restrict national services to national vessels.

Spain and Italy have supported the continuance of cabotage restrictions on the grounds that their removal would have adverse consequences for the jobs and welfare of its seafarers.

At present, goods and passengers are being carried to islands and remote regions where it is not economically viable to do so but there are government subsidies in place which make such operations feasible.

The European Parliament's Committee on Economic and Monetary Affairs in its Interim Report on the Community Shipping Industry in 1976 wrote:

> "16. In cabotage, or coastal trading, within the EEC, there is also some flag discrimination to be found. For example, some Community States' vessels have been excluded from certain Cross-Channel passenger services. The effects of such a practice, may, however, prove to be beneficial, especially where such trade is heavily seasonal. Established shipping companies may use a high revenue during the summer to help finance under-utilised shipping in the winter months, thus providing a service of considerable social and economic benefit."[41]

In essence, the abolition of cabotage would however reduce profits for the shipping companies (which benefit from the restriction) in those Southern States, result in a loss of jobs as well as ships for those national fleets and could result in some services currently being offered having to be withdrawn.

7.6.4.2 Arguments against cabotage

On the other hand, cabotage has few friends north of the Mediterranean. Studies indicate that cabotage results in higher costs in terms of freight and passenger rates. Protected and anti-competitive markets almost invariably lead to higher prices.

It is true to say that even if the rates charged for the shipment of cargo and passengers on particular cabotage routes are not higher than open routes, they may in fact be kept artificially low because of subsidies from the States involved.

41. Doc. 479/76, Rapporteur: Mr J. L. Prescott, para. 14, citing *Finanstidende*, Copenhagen, 31 December 1975. On the report generally, see Chapter 5, above.

A protected environment almost always leads to inefficiencies. The protected environment of cabotage has meant that some protected routes are serviced by inefficient and old ships and as it is, the EC's fleet is older than the fleets of other blocs.

Most particularly, cabotage breaches the concept of equality embodied in such provisions of the EEC Treaty as Article 7. Why should Greek ships be entitled to offer cabotage services along the UK coast but not the other way around?

7.6.5 Cabotage in each of the Member States

In broad terms, France, Greece, Italy, Portugal and Spain favour the retention of cabotage (of these, only Greece has been a hardliner in recent negotiations at the Council meetings) and Belgium, Denmark, Germany, Ireland, The Netherlands and the UK favour its abolition. The matter is not of much direct interest to Luxembourg!

In more specific terms, EC Member States may be classified into four groups of States for the purposes of cabotage: (a) States which have cabotage restrictions; (b) States which do not have cabotage restrictions; (c) States which have limited cabotage restrictions; and (d) States for which the issue does not arise.

7.6.5.1 States which have cabotage restrictions

These States share some general characteristics, namely, they have many islands (e.g. Greece (Aegean), Spain (the Balearics), France (Corsica), Italy (Sicily and Sardinia)) and long coastlines (e.g. Italy and Greece) or remote regions which are difficult to get to otherwise than by sea or air (e.g. Greece). These are the States which are now resisting changes.

7.6.5.1.1 France

France maintains some cabotage restrictions. It has *petit cabotage* which involves trade between French ports as well as *grand cabotage* which involves trade between the ports of Mediterranean France and ports in France's overseas territories such as Guadeloupe and Martinique.

7.6.5.1.2 Greece

Greece maintains cabotage restrictions. The archipelago with its multitude of islands means that Greek opposition to the abolition of cabotage is not too surprising. National trade in goods loaded and unloaded is some 38.5% of the total international trade in goods loaded and unloaded.[42]

7.6.5.1.3 Italy

National trade in goods loaded and unloaded is some 23% of the total international trade in goods loaded and unloaded thus it is a matter of little concern.[43] The long Italian coastline means that cabotage trade can be quite attractive. Italy maintains cabotage restrictions.

42. Eurostat, 1984 figures.
43. Eurostat, 1984 figures.

7.6.5.1.4 Portugal

While Portugal has traditionally maintained some cabotage restrictions, there have been a number of significant moves towards liberalisation since 1988.

7.6.5.1.5 Spain

National trade in goods loaded and unloaded is some 56.6% of the total international trade in goods loaded and unloaded.[44] Spain has an extensive range of cabotage restrictions.

7.6.5.2 States which do not have cabotage restrictions

7.6.5.2.1 Belgium

Belgium does not have any cabotage restrictions because cabotage there is almost unheard of in the light of its short coastline.[45]

7.6.5.2.2 Germany

National trade in goods loaded and unloaded is a mere 2.9% of the total international trade in goods loaded and unloaded thus it is a matter of little concern.[46]

7.6.5.2.3 Ireland

Ireland does not have any cabotage restrictions. Indeed, national trade in goods loaded and unloaded is a mere 2.8% of the total international trade in goods loaded and unloaded thus it is a matter of little concern.[47]

7.6.5.2.4 United Kingdom

National trade in goods loaded and unloaded is some 33.1% of the total international trade in goods loaded and unloaded.[48] The UK has the largest cabotage traffic in the EC. The British have pressed hard for the abolition of cabotage. The British Shipping Minister has spoken out on many occasions on the issue. Mrs Thatcher (then Prime Minister) mentioned the issue in her famous Bruges Speech. They have championed the adoption of EC legislation on the abolition of cabotage for many years.

In 1988, the UK enacted the Merchant Shipping Act. The Act allows the UK to retaliate against other EC States which preserve cabotage restrictions in favour of their own national shipowners and refuse to allow UK shipowners access to domestic routes. The restrictions imposed by the UK could include restrictions on the carriage of goods and passengers between ports in the UK, between British ports and off-shore installations on the UK Continental Shelf and between off-shore installation on the UK Continental Shelf. The restrictions could also extend to cruises originating or

44. Eurostat, 1984 figures.
45. Eurostat, 1984 figures.
46. Eurostat, 1984 figures.
47. Eurostat, 1984 figures.
48. Eurostat, 1984 figures.

terminating in UK ports. These powers, which are quite draconian, have not (yet?) been implemented. If they were implemented then they would almost inevitably face challenge in the UK national courts and in the ECJ as well. In the absence of any agreement on cabotage and were these powers to be implemented, then there would almost certainly be a challenge from Greece.

7.6.5.3 States which have limited cabotage restrictions

7.6.5.3.1 Denmark

National trade in goods loaded and unloaded is some 14.5% of the total international trade in goods loaded and unloaded.[49]

Denmark has cabotage restrictions in relation to trade with the Faroe Islands. Denmark also restricts trade involving vessels up to 500 grt to national flag carriers. Nonetheless it appears to be quite anxious to see the abolition of cabotage in the EC.

7.6.5.4 States for which the issue does not arise

7.6.5.4.1 Luxembourg

Luxembourg is the obvious and only example. It has no coastline and is thus not capable of imposing cabotage restrictions.

7.6.6 Development of the concept of cabotage in EC Law

7.6.6.1 Commission v. France

The decision of the ECJ in *Commission v. France* is important in that it emphasised that the general rules of the EEC Treaty applied to the maritime transport sector.

7.6.6.2 1985 Communication from the Commission to the Council

In its Communication to the Council in 1985 on "Progress Towards a Common Transport Policy: Maritime Transport",[50] the Commission proposed the application of the principle of freedom to provide services to the maritime transport sector.

It included in Annex II-2, a Draft Council Regulation applying the principle of freedom to provide services in sea transport. The Council of European and Japanese National Shipowners' Associations (CENSA) described this proposal as the corner-stone of the 1985 Package. The legislative basis for the Draft Regulation was Article 84, para. 2, of the EEC Treaty.

Article 1(1) of the Draft Regulation provided that restrictions on freedom to provide sea transport services[51] within the Community were to be abolished by 1 July 1986 in

49. Eurostat, 1984 figures.

50. COM(85)90, Annex II-2.

51. The term "freedom to provide sea transport services" included the provision of sea transport services between a Member States and a third country (Art. 2 of the Draft Regulation). Services were considered to be "sea transport services" where they are normally provided for remuneration and shall in particular include: (a) the carriage of passengers or goods by sea between ports in any one Member State, including overseas territories of that State (cabotage); (b) the carriage of passengers or goods by sea between any port in a Member State and installations or structures on the continental shelf of that Member State (offshore supply services); (c) the carriage of passengers or goods by sea between any port in a Member State and any

respect of nationals of Member States who are established in a State of the Community other than that of the person for whom the services are intended. Article 1(2) immediately qualified this general principle by establishing a timetable which provided that in the case of certain sea transport services specified in Article 3(1), restrictions which existed before 1 July 1986 might be retained, but should be progressively abolished during a period of five years after the adoption of the Regulation—however, in the case of cabotage, a period of ten years was allowed. In the case of cabotage between specific regions, however, the ten-year period would not apply where its application would cause "particular difficulties". In such cases, the Member States concerned were to inform the Commission, which would before the end of the tenth year after the adoption of the Regulation present specific proposals which would take account of those difficulties, for the progressive abolition of the relevant restrictions.

Article 4 of the Draft Regulation provided that notwithstanding the application of the principle of freedom to provide services to sea transport services, a Member State may, where necessary in order to maintain sufficient sea transport services in the case of cabotage between the mainland and its islands and between its islands, impose public service obligations as a condition for the right to provide the service.

It is important to remember that Article 5 of the Draft Regulation provided that the Council might, acting unanimously on a proposal from the Commission, extend the provisions of the Draft Regulation (were it enacted) to nationals of a third country which provides sea transport services and are established in the Community.

7.6.6.3 1986 December Package

In December 1986, the Council adopted four Regulations: Regulation 4055/86 applying the principle of freedom to provide services to maritime transport between Member States and between Member States and Third Countries; Regulation 4056/86 laying down detailed rules for the application of Arts 85 and 86 of the EEC Treaty to Maritime Transport; Regulation 4057/86 on unfair pricing practices in maritime transport; and Regulation 4058/86 concerning co-ordinated action to safeguard free access to cargoes in ocean trades. Collectively, these are known as the "December 1986 Package" or the "Brussels Package".

Cabotage proved to be the major impediment to agreement on the Council Regulation applying the Principle of Freedom to Provide Services in Sea Transport. Member States were divided along the North-South Line. Most States were prepared to accept the maintenance of cabotage restrictions in respect of the ordinary services to islands and remote geographical regions (especially, where such services were unprofitable and offered only for public services reasons). There was however a gulf between Member States on the issue of whether or not cabotage restrictions should be lifted in the case of cruising operations. The gap was too wide to be bridged and agreement on cabotage was postponed and a Regulation on freedom to provide serices between Member States and between Member States and third countries (Regulation 4055/86) was adopted[52] instead, leaving cabotage for another day. If the opponents of

port in another Member States (intra-Community shipping services); and (d) the carriage of passengers or goods by sea by a shipping company established in a Member State between the ports of another Member State and ports in a third country (cross-trading).

52. Article 1(4) of which provides that: "For the purposes of this Regulation, the following shall be considered 'maritime transport services between Member States and between Member States and third countries' where they are normally provided for remuneration:

cabotage had stuck to their case, Regulation 4055/86 might not have been adopted at all. As the Commission later wrote:

"[i]n agreeing to the package of four Regulations in the field of transport in December 1986, the Council did not find it possible to decide at that stage on the application of the principle of freedom to provide services in respect of shipping services within the Member States; it therefore agreed that further consideration of this part of the Commission proposal was necessary."[53]

7.6.6.4 1988 Commission Programme

The Commission in its Programme for 1988[54] hoped for progress on cabotage.

7.6.6.5 1989 Positive Measures Programme

In its August 1989 Package of Positive Measures for EC Shipping, the Commission wrote:

"[i]n the context of measures being proposed with the aim of maintaining a more competitive Community fleet, with converging conditions of operation, through the instrument of a parallel Community register, the Commission considers it necessary to make progress with the application to Member States' internal maritime transport of the principle of the freedom to provide services, in view of the completion ofthe internal market by 1993."[55]

It went on to say that:

"[i]n this context, the Commission considers appropriate that the removal of restrictions on the freedom to provide services in Member States' internal maritime transport in respect of nationals and maritime companies of the Member States should be accompanied by conditions in respect of the vessels used to provide the service, so as to ensure a degree of approximation of operating conditions, always taking also due account of the special requirements of certain public services of cabotage which the Member States make in the general interest. The Commission therefore proposes that removal of restrictions is subject to the use of vessels registered in the Community ship register andwhich operate in short-sea trades."[56]

The Commission then appended a proposal for a Council Regulation concerning the application to Member States' internal maritime transport of the freedom to provide services, which incorporated the considerations outlined above by the Commission.[57] This new proposal superseded the earlier one in 1985.

The Commission's proposal has been amended and submitted to the Council of Ministers.[58]

7.6.6.5.1 A brief analysis of the Commission proposal as amended

PREAMBLE

Apart from the usual formal statements, the Preamble to the proposed Regulation states:

(a) *intra-Community shipping services*: the carriage of passengers or goods by sea between any port of a Member State and any port or off-shore installation of another Member State;

(b) *third-country traffic*: the carriage of passengers or goods by sea between the ports of a Member State and ports or off-shore installations of a third country."

53. Positive Measures, para. 113.
54. Bull. EC Supp.1/88, p. 50.
55. Positive Measures, ibid., para. 114.
56. Positive Measures, ibid., para. 115.
57. Positive Measures, ibid., Annex 4.
58. OJ C73/27, 19 March 1991.

"Whereas the principle of freedom to provide services does not yet apply to maritime transport within the Member States;

Whereas it is important to adopt measures with the aim of progressively establishing the internal market over a period expiring on 31 December 1992; whereas the internal market shall comprise an area without internal frontiers in which the free movement of goods, persons, services and capital is ensured;

Whereas the creation of an internal market which covers an area without internal frontiers will have to take into account the priciples of the Treaty with regard to the raising of the standard of living including the improvement of the employment opportunities for workers.

Whereas in accordance with Article 61 of the [EEC] Treaty freedom to provide services in the field of maritime transport is to be governed by the provisions of the Title relating to transport;

Whereas the abolition of restrictions on the provision of maritime transport services within Member States is necessary for the establishment of the single market;

Whereas therefore the principle of freedom to provide services should be applied to maritime transport within Member States;

Whereas this freedom should be subject to conditions in respect of the vessels used to provide the services, so as to ensure a degree of approximation of operating conditions among the persons and companies providing such services;

Whereas the introduction of public services entailing certain rights and obligations for the shipowners concerned may be justified in order to ensure regular transport services on certain links, provided that there is no distinction on the grounds of nationality or residence;

Whereas such conditions are fulfilled by ships registered in the Community ship register established by Council Regulation (EEC) No. . . . and used in short-sea trades . . ."

ENTRY INTO FORCE

Member States would be obliged under Article 6, under the proposed Regulation, to consult the Commission before adopting laws, regulations or administrative provisions implementing the restrictions on cabotage set out in Article 2 of the draft Regulation. Member States would also be obliged to send to the Commission any measures so adopted.

EFFECT

The proposed Council Regulation would, if it enters into force, be binding in its entirety and directly applicable in all Member States.

ARTICLE 1

The essence of the proposed Regulation is embodied in Article 1:

"1. Restrictions on freedom to provide maritime transport service[59] within Member States shall be abolished in respect of the Community shipowners referred to in Article 4 of Regulation No . . on a common definition of a Community shipowner where, in providing these services, they exclusively use vessels registered in the Community ship register not exceeding 6,000 grt, providing that these vessels are allowed to operate in services, if any, within the State which they are registered.

2. The provisions of this Regulation shall also apply to nationals of the Member States established outside the Community and to shipping companies established outside the Community and controlled by nationals of a Member State, if their vessels are registered in that Member State in accordance with its legislation and in the Community ship register and not exceeding 6,000 grt.

3. For the purposes of this Regulation, services shall be considered as "maritime transport services" where they are normally provided for remuneration and shall in particular include:

(a) the carriage of passengers or goods by sea between ports in any one Member State, including overseas departments of that State (cabotage);

59. Ed. On the definition of "maritime transport services", see below.

(b) the carriage of passengers or goods by sea between any port in a Member State and installations or structures on the continental shelf of that Member State (off-shore supply services).

4. The Member State between whose ports the maritime transport services are provided may require that vessels used for these services are manned with nationals of the Member States to the same degree as is required in respect of the vessels flying its own flag which are used for these services and that they shall have similar training to that required of its nationals employed therein."

"Maritime services" are defined quite broadly for the purposes of the proposed Regulation. Article 1(3) of the proposed Council Regulation states that for the purposes of the Regulation, services shall be considered as "maritime transport services" where they are normally provided for remuneration and shall in particular include: (a) the carriage of passengers or goods by sea between ports in any one Member State, including overseas departments of that State (cabotage); (b) the carriage of passengers or goods by sea between any port in a Member State and installations or structures on the continental shelf of that Member State (off-shore supply services).

ARTICLE 2: DEROGATION

Article 2 of the proposed Regulation provides:

"1. Notwithstanding Article 1(1) and (2), a Member State may, where necessary in order to maintain sufficient maritime transport services in the case of cabotage between the mainland and its islands and between its islands, impose public service obligations as acondition for the right to provide the service.

2. For the purpose of this Regulation the law, regulations or administrative conditions imposed by Member States aiming to guarantee the continuity, regularity and efficiency of the services, and the provision of goods of fundamental importance for the economic well-being of such territories shall be considered as public service obligations."

Article 3 of the proposed Regulation provides:

"1. In the event of severe market disruption or serious imbalances between supply and demand in a given geographical area, the Commission shall, either on its own initiative or at the request of a Member State, adopt safeguard measures with a view to appropriately redressing the situation.

2. Where a Member State puts a request to the Commission, the decision shall be adopted within 30 days of receipt of the request duly accompanied by the information considered relevant."

ARTICLE 4

Article 4 of the proposed Regulation provides that Articles 55 to 62 of the EEC Treaty shall apply to the matters covered by the proposed Regulation.

ARTICLE 5

Article 5 of the proposed Regulation provides that without prejudice to the provisions of the EEC Treaty relating to the right of establishment, a person providing a maritime transport service may, in order to do so, temporarily pursue his activity in the Member State where the service is provided, under the same conditions as are imposed by the State on its own nationals.

7.6.7 Outlook

The Commission's Proposals in August 1990 have been given a mixed reception. The Greeks have not accepted them in their entirety. Indeed, most States do not see why the abolition of cabotage has to be linked to the EUROS Register. It is now likely that if cabotage is abolished, it may be done so other than within the confines of EUROS.

If cabotage were completely abolished throughout the EC then there will be opportunities. Greece is one example. The trade between south-east and northern Spain is another. There are also some openings in Italy and Portugal.

The Council of Transport Ministers met in Luxembourg in June. They discussed an Irish proposal to solve the issue. It is understood that this proposal was generally accepted yet no solution was reached.

It seems likely, at the time of writing, that a solution worked out under the Dutch Presidency of the Council of Ministers during the last six months of 1991 will solve the problem even though any solution will not be adopted until at least mid-1992.

CHAPTER 8

Employment and Social Security Law

8.1 INTRODUCTION

One of the saddest trends over the past few years has been the dramatic decline in the number of people employed in the EC shipping industry. A decline was almost inevitable given increasing technology—a 12,000-tonne refrigerated cargo liner would have had a crew of 70 to 80 in the early 1950s, but now the crew would be 18 or less.[1] However, the decline in employment is not due solely to increasing technology.

The tonnage owned by companies in EC Member States has fallen dramatically[2] and this has partly been due to the flagging-out of many ships formerly registered in EC Member States to "registries of convenience" so as to benefit from low-cost crews. This continuing decline not only leads to unemployment and its consequential problems but also a dying off in the skills of seafarers in the EC.[3] In all probability, the best way to secure the employment of EC seafarers is to secure the future of Member State fleets and their registration in EC Member States as well as facilitating the easy exchange of EC seafarers.[4] Nonetheless, the wide differentials in the pay and conditions expected by EC seafarers and those tolerated by some non-EC seafarers means that it will not be enough for there to be a resurgence in the fortunes of a true EC fleet.

EC shipping policy has a social dimension. The policy so far adopted by the Member States has an employment protection dimension. A bipartite committee was established in 1987 to advise the Commission on how best to promote social measures for seafarers in the EC. The *Positive Measures Communication* of 3 August 1989 contained a number of specific measures designed to improve the social conditions of seafarers.

Employment controls may be used as a form of protectionism on the part of a State.[5] For example, a State may protect the jobs of its own seafarers by prohibiting the employment of non-nationals to perform certain tasks (e.g. masters) or indeed, all tasks. Such restrictions formed the basis of an ECJ decision, Case 167/73, *Commission v. France*, which was discussed above[6] and which is briefly described below. A State

1. See Farthing, *International Shipping: An Introduction to the Policies, Politics and Institutions of the Maritime World*, p. 19.
2. See Chapter 2, above.
3. See the Commission in *Progress towards a Common Transport Policy . . .*, and the Economic and Social Committee in Opinion of the Economic and Social Committee on the Communication and Proposals (II.3, II.4) by the Commission to the Council on Progress towards a Common Transport Policy—Maritime Transport, COM(85)90 final, para. 3.2.4.
4. See Opinion of the Economic and Social Committee on the Communication and Proposals (II.3, II.4) by the Commission to the Council on Progress towards a Common Transport Policy—Maritime Transport, COM(85)90 final, para. 3.2.
5. See Bredima-Savopoulou and Tzoannos, *The Common Shipping Policy of the EEC* (1990), p. 36.
6. See Chapter 4, above.

may also establish special tax and social security rules for seafarers and thereby protect the national shipping fleet. Many Member States operate restrictive practices in relation to the employment of seafarers.

Belgium, Denmark, Germany, Greece, the Netherlands and the UK all employ significant numbers of non-EC seafarers.[7] On the other hand, few non-EC national seafarers are employed on ships registered in France, Ireland, Portugal and Spain.

8.2 EC LAW AND EMPLOYMENT GENERALLY

8.2.1 Introduction

Article 3(c) of the EEC Treaty requires "the abolition, as between Member States, of obstacles to freedom of movement of persons". Articles 48–51 deal with free movement of workers, Articles 52–58 deal with freedom of establishment and Articles 59–66 relate to freedom to provide services. All of the relevant EEC Treaty provisions along with most of the secondary legislation has been held to be directly effective.

8.2.2 Free Movement of Workers[8]

Chapter 1 of Title III of the EEC treaty deals with the Free Movement of Workers. This Chapter, which consists of Articles 48–51, is the basic law on the subject. There is more movement of workers in the US than in the EC due to a common language, uniform recognition of qualifications and a largely common culture.

8.2.2.1 Concept of "worker"

The concept of "worker" is not defined in the EEC Treaty.[9] It is understood to include all persons working under a contract of employment, such as salaried employees, executives, manual workers and persons who have performed paid work for a substantial period of time (see Case 53/81 *Levin v. Staatssecretaris van Justitie*[10]). The term "worker" when used in Article 48 of the EEC Treaty has a Community meaning[11] and not a national one. It must be interpreted broadly.[12] The concept "must be defined in accordance with objective criteria which distinguish the employment relationship by reference to the rights and duties of the persons concerned, and the essential feature of an employment relationship is that for a certain period of time a person performs

7. Bredima-Savopoulou and Tzoannos, *op. cit.*, pp. 50–52.

8. On free movement of workers, see O'Keeffe, "Practical Difficulties in the Application of Article 48 of the EEC Treaty" (1982) 19 CML Rev. 35; Pickup, "Reverse Discrimination and Free Movement of Workers" (1989) 23 CML Rev. 135; Steiner, *op. cit.*, Ch.18; Watson, "Free Movement of Workers" (1989) 14 EL Rev. 415. See also Regulation 1612/68. See Case 36/75 *Rutili v. Minister for the Interior*.

9. See Hartley, "Free Movement of Students in European Community Law" (1989) *Cahiers de Droit Europeen*. Article 48 was directly effective since the end of the transition period (Case 167/73 *Commission v. France* [1971] ECR 359 at 372 and Case 41/74 *Van Duyn v. Home Office* [1974] ECR 1337 at 1347. If there is no EC aspect then EC law is not relevant: Case 175/87 *R. v. Saunders* [1977] ECR 1129 at 1135. On the scope of the Article, see Case 15/69 *Uglioga* [1969] ECR 363 and Case 9/74 *Casagrande* [1974] ECR 773.

10. [1982] ECR 1035, [1982] 2 CMLR 454.

11. See Case 66/85 *Lawrie-Blum v. Land Baden-Wurttemberg* [1986] ECR 2121, [1987] 3 CMLR 389 and Case 344/87 *Bettray v. Staatssecretaris van Justitie* [1991] 1 CMLR 459, para.11.

12. See Case 75/63 *Hoekstra (nee Unger) v. BBDA*; Case 66/85 *Lawrie-Blum v. Land Baden-Wurttemberg* [1986] ECR 2121, [1987] 3 CMLR 389 and Case 344/87 *Bettray v. Staatssecretaris van Justitie* [1991] 1 CMLR 459, para.11.

services for and under the direction of another person in return for which he receives remuneration".[13] The person must be pursuing an effective and genuine economic activity.[14] To qualify as a "worker", it is not necessary that the work be of a full-time nature.[15] It need not be particularly productive,[16] but must be "real".[17] The source of the salaries does not matter, for example, it could be state-funded.[18] On the other hand, work which is merely rehabilitatory in nature would not allow free movement under the Treaty.[19]

Regulation 1408/71[20] is applicable in the context of a person insured by a social security scheme.

The concept of nationality is determined, as a general rule, by the national law of the Member State.

The family of a "worker" is not expressly dealt with by the EEC Treaty. Secondary legislation has, however, given members of the worker's family many of the rights conferred on the worker. These rights even extend to members of the EC worker's family who are not themselves nationals of an EC Member State.

No restriction may be imposed on the right of a national of another Member State to enter the territory of a Member State to stay there and to move within it unless his or her presence or conduct would constitute a genuine and sufficiently serious threat to public policy (Case 36/75 *Rutili v. Ministre de l'Interieur*[21]).

A Member State is entitled to limit the freedom of movement of one of its own nationals in respect of it own territory.[22]

A "worker" means, for present purposes, not only those who are currently working but also those who have lost their jobs and are capable of taking up another job.[23]

The provisions relating to free movement of workers also apply to merchant seafarers[24] as well as airline workers.[25]

The provisions would not, however, apply to naval or air force personnel because the navy and air force are not economic activities and, even if they were, such persons are engaged in the "public service".

8.2.2.2 Article 48 of the EEC Treaty

Article 48 of the EEC treaty provides:-

"1. Freedom of movement for workers shall be secured within the Community by the end of the transitional period at the latest.

2. Such freedom of movement shall entail the abolition of any discrimination based on nationality between workers of the Member States as regards employment, remuneration, and other conditions of work and employment.

13. Case 344/87 *Bettray v. Staatssecretaris van Justitie* [1991] 1 CMLR 459, para.12.
14. Case 344/87 *Bettray v. Staatssecretaris van Justitie* [1991] 1 CMLR 459, para.13.
15. Case 139/85 *Kempf v. Staatssecretaris van Justitie* and Case 53/81 *Levin*.
16. Case 344/87 *Bettray v. Staatssecretaris van Justitie* [1991] 1 CMLR 459, para.15.
17. Case 53/81 *Levin*.
18. Case 344/87 *Bettray v. Staatssecretaris van Justitie* [1991] 1 CMLR 459, para.15. See also Case 196/87 *Steymann v. Staatssecretaris van Justitie*.
19. Case 344/87 *Bettray v. Staatssecretaris van Justitie* [1991] 1 CMLR 459, para. 20.
20. OJ 1971 L149/2.
21. [1975] ECR 1219, [1976] 1 CMLR 140.
22. Case 175/78 *R v. Saunders* [1979] ECR 1129, [1979] 2 CMLR 216; Cases 35 and 36/82 *Marson v. Netherlands*; Case 20/87 *Ministère Public v. Gauchard*; Case 180/83 *Moser v. Land Baden-Wurttemberg*.
23. Case 75/63 *Hoekstra (née Unger) v. BBDA*.
24. Case 167/73 *Commission v. France* [1974] ECR 359, [1974] 2 CMLR 216.
25. Case 80/70 *Defrenne v. Sabena*.

3. It shall entail the right, subject to limitations justified on grounds of public policy, public security or public health:
   (a) to accept offers of employment actually made;
   (b) to move freely within the territory of Member States for this purpose;
   (c) to stay in a Member State for the purpose of employment in accordance with the provisions governing the employment of nationals of that State laid down by law, regulation or administrative action:
   (d) to remain in the territory of a Member State after having being employed in that State, subject to conditions which shall be embodied in implementing regulations to be drawn up by the Commission.

4. The provision of this Article shall not apply to employment in the public service."

8.2.2.3 Discrimination on the basis of nationality

Article 48 (2) which provides that the freedom of movement of workers shall entail the abolition of any discrimination based on nationality between workers of the Member States as regards employment, remuneration and other conditions of work and employment is, in essence, a more specific statement of the general provision contained in Article 7 of the EEC Treaty.

8.2.2.3.1 Exceptions to the right

The right to free movement of workers is subject to express derogations on the grounds of public policy, public security, public health and public service.[26]

8.2.2.3.2 Public service[27]

It is clear from Case 225/85 *Commission v. Italian Republic*[28] that before Article 48(4) becomes operable it must be shown that the employment relates to persons who are charged with the exercise of powers conferred by public law or are responsible for safeguarding the general interests of the State[29]: it is not simply every State employee which falls within the scope of the provision.[30] Article 48(4) only relates to *access* to employment.[31]

The concept of "public service" is a Community one[32] and must be interpreted in accordance with EC law rather than in a simple nationalistic manner.

It is widely assumed that the free movement of workers provisions of the EEC Treaty do not apply to ship's captains because of the "public" nature of some of their functions.

26. EEC Treaty, Article 48(4). In relation to public health, see Dir. 64/221. The exceptions must be construed strictly: Case 41/74 *Van Duyn* v. *Home Office* [1974] ECR 1337 at 1350.

27. Wooldridge, "Free Movement of EEC Nationals: The Limitation Based on Public Policy and Public Security " (1977) 2 EL Rev. 190. See Case 149/79 *Commission v. Belgium* [1980] ECR 3881; Case 307/84 *Commission v. France* [1986] ECR 1225; and Case 66/85 *Lawrie-Blum v. Land Baden-Wurttemberg* [1986] ECR 2121.

28. [1987] ECR 2625, [1988] CMLR 635.

29. See Case 33/88 *Allue Coonan v. Universita degli studi di Venezia.*

30. See also Case 149/79 *Commission v. Belgium: Re Public Employees* and Case 66/85 *Lawrie-Blum v. Land Baden Wurttemberg.*

31. See Case 152/73 *Sotgiu v. Deutsche Bundespost.*

32. Case 149/79 *Commission v. Belgium: Re Public Employees.*

8.2.2.4 Article 49 of the EEC Treaty

Article 49 of the EEC Treaty states as follows:

"As soon as this Treaty enters into force, the Council shall, acting by a qualified majority on a proposal from the Commission, in co-operation with the European Parliament and after consulting the Economic Social Committee, issue directives or make regulations setting out the measures required to bring about, by progressive stages, freedom of movement for workers, as defined in Article 48, in particular:

(a) by ensuring close co-operation between national employment services;

(b) by systematically and progressively abolishing those administrative procedures and practices and those qualifying periods in respect of eligibility for available employment, whether resulting from national legislation or from agreements previously concluded between Member States, the maintenance of which would form an obstacle to liberalisation of the movement of workers;

(c) by systematically and progressively abolishing all such qualifying periods and other restrictions provided for either under national legislation or under agreements previously concluded between Member States as imposed on workers of other Member States conditions regarding the free choice of employment other than those imposed on workers of the State concerned;

(d) by setting up appropriate machinery to bring offers of employment into touch with applications for employment and to facilitate the achievement of a balance between supply and demand in the employment market in such away as to avoid serious threats to the standard of living and level of employment in the various regions and industries."

According to the ECJ in Case 167/73 *Commission v. French Republic* (the so-called *French Seafarers Case*)[33] and Case 41/74 *Van Duyn v. Home Office*,[34] Article 49 has direct effect.

8.2.2.5 Assessment

There are many rights existing under EC law which people do not exercise. There is little to indicate that many seafarers have exercised their rights to move to another Member State, except where it is a neighbouring State or one with which they have particular links (such as marital or family ties). The reasons for such a lack of mobility are manifold, but primarily revolve around the difficulty of finding a job, lack of mutual recognition of qualifications and certificates, resistance from unions in the host State and language barriers. Levi Sandri, the then Vice-Chairman of the EC Commission said in 1968 that it is for capital to go where there is labour and not *vice versa*.

8.2.3 Working conditions

Article 117 of the EEC Treaty provides:

"Member States agree upon the need to promote improved working conditions and an improved standard of living for workers, so as to make possible their harmonisation while the improvement is being maintained.

They believe that such a development will ensue not only from the functioning of the common market, which will favour the harmonisation of social systems, but also from the procedures provided for in this Treaty and from the approximation of provisions laid down by law, regulation or administrative action."

33. [1974] ECR 359, [1974] 2 CMLR 216.
34. [1974] ECR 1337, [1975] 1 CMLR 1.

8.2.4 Equal pay

Article 119 of the EEC Treaty provides for equal pay for men and women. The provision reads:

"Each Member State shall during the first stage[35] ensure and subsequently maintain the application of the principle that men and women should receive equal pay for equal work.

For the purpose of this Article, 'pay' means the ordinary basic or minimum wage or salary and any other consideration, whether in cash or in kind, which the worker receives, directly or indirectly, in respect of his employment from his employer.

Equal pay without discrimination based on sex means:

(a) that pay for the same work at piece rates shall be calculated on the basis of the same unit of measurement;

(b) that pay for work at time rates shall be the same for the same job."

8.2.5 Non-discrimination on the basis of nationality between EC nationals

Article 7 of the EEC Treaty provides:

"Within the scope of the application of this Treaty, and without prejudice to any special provisions contained therein, any discrimination on grounds of nationality shall be prohibited."

The provision only applies within the scope of the application of the EEC Treaty. Thus, there must be (as a minimum) an economic activity.[36]

Therefore workers, the self-employed and persons engaged in vocational training[37] could invoke, in appropriate cases, Article 7 of the EEC Treaty where they allege discrimination on the basis of nationality.

Discrimination could take the form of a discriminatory requirement as to residence.[38]

So what is the legality of restrictions imposed by an EC Member State in respect of the employment of non-nationals on board ships flying the flag of that Member State? It is not illegal, on the basis of EC law alone, for an EC Member State to prohibit the employment on board ships flying its flag of persons who are not nationals of an EC Member State.[39]

However, as a general rule, insofar as an EC Member State discriminates between its own nationals and nationals of other EC Member States, then it is in violation of its duties under EC law and the discriminatory law is void. This rule is said to be a general rule for three reasons. First, Portugal and Spain are excluded from this under a transitional arrangement in respect of free movement of labour. The freedom has existed in respect of Greece since 1 January 1988. Secondly, no institutional framework has been established by the Member States so as to facilitate this free movement of seafarers and thus, the free movement is more imaginary than real in the case of ticketed or certified ranks. Thirdly, there are great difficulties existing in respect of the mutual recognition of certificates as well as tickets, and this has not allowed the free movement of seafarers which is allowed under strict law.

35. I.e. the first stage of the formation of the Common Market.
36. Case 36/74 *Walrave and Koch v. Association Union Cycliste Internationale.*
37. See Case 293/84 *Gravier v. City of Liège.*
38. Case 152/73 *Sotgiu v. Deutsche Bundespost.*
39. Article 7 EEC only relates to discrimination between EC nationals.

8.2.6 Employment in shipping in the EC

8.2.6.1 Introduction

As a general rule, each Member State has special rules relating to the employment of seafarers which do not apply to other employees—such special rules exist because of the peculiar nature of the seafaring job.[40]

8.2.6.1.1 Merchant Marine

A table of persons employed in the merchant marine in nine of the Member States for the year 1986 shows that Greece had the largest number of persons employed in this sector, with the UK and the Federal Republic of Germany not too far behind. The full table is:

Member State	*Number and % of State's Total Workers*
Belgium	2,928
Denmark	9,779
France	6,807
FRG	20,470
Greece	31,934
Netherlands	14,218
Portugal	2,913[41]
Spain	19,873
UK	29,781

8.2.6.1.2 Shipbuilding

A table of persons employed in the shipbuilding sector in nine of the Member States for the year 1986 shows that the Federal Republic of Germany had the largest number of persons employed in this sector, with Spain and the Netherlands not too far behind. The full table is:

Member State	*Number and % of State's Total Work Force*	*% of EC Total Work Force*
Belgium	3,871	0.1%
Denmark	12,260	0.5%
France	13,498	0.06%
FRG	38,118	0.02%
Greece	6,328	0.2%
Italy	13,809	0.07%
Netherlands	15,300	0.3%
Portugal	14,150	0.4%
Spain	22,996	0.2%
UK	11,694	0.5%

40. See *ISF Guide to International Maritime Labour Supply* (Lloyd's of London Press Ltd, 1990).
41. 1985 figure.

8.2.6.2 Hollesen Study

A study, known as the Hollesen Study, on the provisions of national collective agreements on seafarers' pay, working hours, off-duty periods and labour costs on board EC vessels, was published by the Commission in June 1980. This study is more formally described as the Survey on Working Hours and Wages in Sea Transport in 1979 in the Member States of the European Communities. The study followed on from a French declaration at the Council of Transport Ministers meeting of 20 February 1979 and showed that there were significant differences between seafarers in different Member States in terms of pay and conditions.

8.3 EC LAW AND THE EMPLOYMENT OF SEAFARERS

The employment of seafarers is a matter of legal regulation and concern, not only on the part of Member States themselves, but also on the part of such organisations as the International Labour Organisation (ILO), the International Maritime Organisation (IMO) and the EC itself.

The Economic and Social Committee commented in 1986 that further improvements in the instruments adopted by organisations such as the IMO and the ILO should continue to be supported and promoted by the EC.

Transport workers sometimes need special protection. The Economic and Social Committee in its Opinion on the Transport Policy of the European Communities in the 1980s stated that a "common transport policy must be socially beneficial by catering for transport needs from an overall economic point of view and by helping to improve the living and working conditions of the people employed in transport".[42]

8.3.1 Training

The Commission has written:

> "98. Good levels of training of crew and shipmasters backed by a system able to enforce and monitor the minimum internationally agreed safety standards are essential elements of any consistent safety policy. In this respect the Commission would like to see a greater use of simulators in training shipmasters. The Convention on Standards of Training and Watchkeeping (STCW), which entered into force in 1984, set the framework for a Community role in helping developing countries to raise the present standards of training of their crews, thus benefiting those countries directly and also the safety of navigation in European waters. In addition developing countries require assistance in building up their national maritime administrations. This requires training of a special nature where Community administrations can play a valuable role.
>
> 99. The agreements of co-operation concluded by the EEC with the countries of the Lomé Convention (ACP) and with several ASEAN and Latin American countries permit financial assistance for training in general and maritime training in particular. The Commission has already helped to develop a programme of seminars for training of trainers in maritime academies of ASEAN, the first of which took place in Malacca in March [19]84. The Commission proposes a larger contribution of and funds for training in the maritime sector.
>
> 100. In addition to this action each European country has already problems to find highly qualified operators in their existing VTSs[43] and, possibly, in future in the European integrated

42. CES 741/82, OJ 326 of 13 December 1982, point 4.4.1.
43. I.e. Vessel traffic management services. On VTS, see below.

network of VTS. The special operational requirements demand a new specialised staff the qualifications and standards of whom are not set. In the light of the positive EUROCONTROL experience in the field of training air traffic control operators the Commission will consider with the Member States whether it is sensible to develop common standards of training for VTS operators in Europe."

The Commission has proposed an improvement in regard to access on the part of seafarers to training, particularly in regard to the new technologies.

8.3.1.1 Hours of working

Excessive working time poses dangers to the health and safety of the seafarers, passengers (where appropriate), ships and the environment.[44]

8.3.1.2 Mutual recognition of qualifications

The EC has, over many years, promoted a programme to facilitate the mutual recognition between Member States of the professional and educational qualifications issued by the authorities of the Member States. Such a recognition is vital to the implementation of the freedom of establishment provisions of the Treaties and can have the effect of raising the standards of proficiency across the Community. Progress has been made in such areas as medicine and architecture.

Commenting on the Commission's Progress towards a Common Transport Policy, the Economic and Social Committee said that it:

"notes the intention of the Commission to develop proposals for the mutual recognition of certificates and points out that mutual recognition must assume an agreed equivalence of entry standards, training and examinations and that such agreement does not currently exist. Moreover the Commission should take into consideration that certain Member States have legislation specifying the nationality of all or part of their crews and that such legislation is often for defence reasons. While defence is not an area for which the Commission is responsible, it cannot be ignored by Member States."[45]

In 1988, the Commission proposed at the Joint Committee on Maritime Transport mutual recognition of junior officers on ships registered in the EC.[46] This was supported by CAACE and GCBS. In the interim, the UK agreed to unilaterally recognise qualifications from certain jurisdictions.

8.3.1.2.1 Directive 87/540

Council Directive 87/540/EEC is officially entitled a Directive "on access to the occupation of carrier of goods by waterway in national and international transport and on mutual recognition of diplomas, certificates and other evidence of formal qualifications for this occupation".

The Commission said, as part of its EUROS proposal, that there would be mutual recognition of qualifications and licences of EC seafarers employed on vessels registered on EUROS.

44. Opinion of the Economic and Social Committee on the Communication and Proposals (II.3, II.4) by the Commission to the Council on Progress towards a Common Transport Policy—Maritime Transport, COM(85)90 final, point 3.2.5.

45. Opinion of the Economic and Social Committee on the Communication and Proposals (II.3, II.4) by the Commission to the Council on Progress towards a Common Transport Policy—Maritime Transport, COM(85)90 final, point 3.2.8.

46. See *Lloyd's List*, 9 December 1988, p. 3.

Denmark and Italy are willing to recognise a certificate issued by a competent authority in another EC Member State as being equivalent to their own certificates. The Federal Republic of Germany recognises a certificate issued by a competent authority in another Member State, provided that the certificate holder has a good knowledge of the German language.

The UK recognises not only its own certificates, but also certificates issued by certain competent authorities in the British Commonwealth and of the Republic of Ireland.

8.3.1.2.2 Belgium, Greece and Ireland

The UK unilaterally announced in December 1988 that it would recognise the certificates issued by the competent authorities of the EC Member States and Norway in respect of all on-board officers below the ranks of master, chief officer and chief engineer.

The Commission is expected to bring forward proposals in this area. Mutual recognition would allow northern operators of ships to utilise cheaper southern crews.

The EC's measures in regard to health on board ships should be compatible with the International Labour Organisation and World Health Organisation standards.

8.3.2 Taxation

Commenting on the Commission's Progress towards a Common Transport Policy, the Economic and Social Committee said that it "welcomes the Commission's support for favourable direct tax regimes for the Community seafarers and believes that the Commission should actively promote this and also explore such means of helping to maintain the employment of EC nationals on vessels of Member States, such as assistance with training and repatriation costs".[47]

8.4 EC SOCIAL SECURITY LAW

8.4.1 Introduction

There is a process in train to develop an EC Social Policy.[48] Seafarers always require special protection from the law. The Phoenicians had a system of compensation for lost or injured seafarers. The Greeks had similar rules.

The need to safeguard the living and working conditions of crews, as well as their level of competence, has been expressed many times in EC legislation[49] and pronouncements.

8.4.2 Joint Committee on Maritime Transport

Directive 87/467/EEC set up a Joint Committee on Maritime Transport.[50]

47. Opinion of the Economic and Social Committee on the Communication and Proposals (II.3, II.4) by the Commission to the Council on Progress towards a Common Transport Policy—Maritime Transport, COM (85)90, final, point 3.2.7.

48. See Merritt, "Social Policy Rethink" (1988/1) *European Affairs* 88; Steiner, "The Right to Welfare, Equality and Equity under Community Law" (1989) 10 ELRev. 21.

49. See for example, Rec. 78/584/EEC, Preamble, Recital 3; OJ L194 July 1978, p. 17

50. OJ 1987 L253.

The Commission believes that the Joint Committee on Maritime Transport (which assists the Commission) would be the most appropriate way of ensuring participation at EC level on the social and economic issues involved in shipping.

On 23 December 1976, the European Parliament's Committee on Economic and Monetary Affairs published its Interim Report on the Community Shipping Industry.[51]

The Report stated:

> "35. Ships flying flags of convenience may well pay their crews lower wages than EEC-registered ships, but within the Community itself there are wide differentials, with a comparative wage ratio sometimes as great as 2:1. Clearly a competitive advantage is available to the shipowners (the majority of whom are British) with lower wage costs, in competing for freight on a world market. And as conference lines have agreed freight rates, here the lower-cost shipowners are enabled to make higher profits than their competitors.
>
> 36. There is a strong argument, therefore, for a harmonisation upwards of wage rates throughout the Community, which would at least remove an element of unfair competition here, and probably enable all Community shipowners to compete more effectively in the world market.
>
> Harmonisation of conditions of competition requires action to be taken not only over wages, but also over conditions of work. There has already been some attempt within the framework of the ILO[52] to formulate international legislation concerning social security and working and health conditions on board ships . . . of the 22 currently valid ILO conventions, most EEC Member States have ratified fewer than half. Moreover, in many instances, the conventions have been accepted but there has been virtually no effort to ensure their implementation. This indicates that there is still a wide field open for harmonisation of working conditions within the Community, and some initiative by the Commission in this field is certainly called for . . ."

In 1987 the Commission published a report entitled "A Social Survey in Maritime Transport". This was subtitled a "Preparatory Study on the Employment and Social Impact of International and National Provisions Regarding Working Conditions in Maritime Transport; and Distortions Affecting both Employment and Competitivity of Community Nationals" and was written by van Poelgeest of the Maritime Economic Research Centre in Rotterdam. It had been requested by the Director-General for Employment and Social Affairs of the Commission and was aimed at trying to identify "to what extent employment related benefits and burdens affect the competitiveness on board EEC vessels, in so far as the responsibility rests with governments".[53]

While it was published in 1987, its conclusions still make interesting reading.

In respect of income tax, it concluded that only four States[54] had some specific regulations allowing seafarers to pay less tax compared with employees ashore. It was interesting to note that Greece had the lowest rate of tax for one of the four ranks or ratings chosen for the survey[55] for A/Bs, but Belgium had the highest at 36.1 per cent for the captain.

In respect of "net annual income", that is to say, after all compulsory deductions (such as income tax, social security contributions, pension premiums and welfare contributions) have been made from gross annual income, there are wide variations: for example, a Belgian captain would be left with 56 per cent of gross salary but a Spanish captain would be left with 71 per cent.

51. Doc.479/76, Rapporteur: Mr J. L. Prescott.
52. I.e. the International Labour Organisation.
53. Page i of the Final Report.
54. Denmark, Finland, Greece and the UK.
55. Namely, captains, chief officers, second engineers and A/Bs (sailors) at zero per cent.

All EC Member States were found to have well protected seafarers in regard to social security issues such as sickness, unemployment, occupational hazards and so on.

In regard to the continuity of employment, there is a wide divergence of practice in relation to ratings, but very little divergence in the case of officers. In regard to ratings, almost all ratings on ships registered in what was then the Federal Republic of Germany were employed on a continuous basis, but only half were so employed in the UK, and only 20 per cent were employed on a continuous basis on Spanish ships. It was reckoned that between 80 per cent and 90 per cent of officers on board vessels registered in EC Member States were employed on a continuous basis with only the remaining 10 per cent to 20 per cent employed on a voyage-only basis.

There was a great divergence between EC Member States on the training of deck officers. In general, the State pays for the education but some States, most notably the UK, operate a cadetship system.

The travelling costs of seafarers were found not to be subsidised by States, except in the cases of Denmark and Finland. Apart from those States, all seafarers were able to benefit from the standard IATA discounts available to repatriating seafarers.

The Report found that there were relatively few low cost non-EC nationals on board EC ships. There were a number of practical restrictions on their employment, including certification requirements and rules in certain cases which actually prohibit their employment.

CHAPTER 9

Introduction to EC Competition Law and Shipping

9.1 INTRODUCTION

There are many practices in the shipping world which are *prima facie* anti-competitive. For example, shipbuilders sometimes combine to exchange forecasts, technical information and designs as well as fix prices; governments offer anti-competitive depreciation allowances, investment grants, training aids, cargo reservation schemes, tax-free reserves and soft loans as well as subsidies[1]; and shipping companies sometimes combine together in anti-competitive cartels or abuse their dominant position in various ways.

Competition in shipping matters is a highly charged political and emotive issue.[2] Many shipping industry spokesmen have denied that EC competition law should have a role to play in the sector. Nonetheless, EC competition law, like the poor, is (almost) always with us. To ignore EC competition law is perilous: for example, a fine imposed in 1991 on one company in the packaging industry for breaches of EC competition law amounted to ECU75,000,000 (i.e. £57,000,000 or US$70,000,000 approximately); a business may be fined up to 10% of its previous year's worldwide turnover. Nonetheless, a delicate balance must be struck when the EC becomes involved in shipping. Kreis has commented that the EC "must protect its interests in the shipping industry without impeding international shipping or imposing barriers on free, worldwide trade".[3]

1. Frankel has commented ("Strategic Planning Applied to Shipping" [1988] 16 *Maritime Policy Management*, No. 2, p. 123) that shipping is often considered as a national asset and as such, induces various governmental interventions which are not necessarily based on commercial sense.
2. See Bredima-Savopoulou and Tzoannos, *The Common Shipping Policy of the EEC* (1990), pp. 62–68 as well as Clough and Randolph, *Shipping and EC Competition Law* (1991), *passim*. See also Kreis, "European Community Competition Policy and International Shipping" (1989–90) 13 *Fordham International Law Journal* 411 and the comments of Hickey in his paper "The Application of the Competition Rules of the European Community to Shipping", at *The Future of Shipping in Europe*, London, 28 June 1990, at p. 1.
3. *Op. cit.*, at footnote 2, at p. 413.

9.2 EEC COMPETITION LAW GENERALLY

EC competition[4,5] is a means of achieving, among other aims, a fair, free[6] and efficient internal market in the EC where businesses[7] may thrive in a competitive environment which is beneficial to the consumer. It is a highly charged political area of law which has huge economic significance. Francis Jacobs has written:

"Competition law is a subject of the highest practical significance to all those doing business in, or with, the Community. A sophisticated and principled body of law has developed over the past thirty years. It affects a vast range of commercial activity. It is implemented by the Commission of the European Communities, endowed for this purpose with a panoply of powers unparalleled in other areas of Community law, or for the most part in national law. It has to be applied by the courts of the Member States. And it has to be observed by all those subject to it. It has the greatest impact on business life in the obvious form that it renders anti-competitive agreements and practices void, exposes firms to intensive investigations and enquiries, and may give rise to very substantial fines. Seen more constructively, it gives firms the opportunity to compete fairly and the opportunity to compete for the advantages of the European market; it protects the consumer; and it compels a more efficient use of economic resources."[8]

Bellamy and Child have written:

"Although not clearly articulated, the Community rules on competition seem to fulfil three broad functions: (i) to prevent barriers to trade being erected by private agreements between undertakings, abuse of monopoly power, or state subsidies; (ii) to preserve effective competition as the spur to the creation of the single market; and (iii) to encourage efficiency, innovation, and lower prices."[9]

9.3 EC COMPETITION LAW AND SHIPPING: THE HISTORY OF THE APPLICATION OF ARTICLES 85 AND 86 OF THE EEC TREATY

9.3.1 1962: Regulation 17/62 implementing EC competition law

It is possible to enforce EC competition law in a number of ways:

4. "Competition" is, in this context, similar to the term "anti-trust" as used in US law or "restrictive practices" in English law. On the relationship between the two systems of law, see Hawk, "The American (anti-trust) revolution: lessons for the EEC?" [1988] ECLR 53. On Article 3(f) EEC Treaty, see Cases 6&7/73 *Instituto Chemioteropico Italiano SpA and Commercial Solvents v. EC Commission* [1974] ECR 223, [1974] 1 CMLR 309.

5. On EC competition law, see, among other books, Bellamy and Child, *Common Market Law of Competition* (3rd edn.); Freeman and Whish, *Butterworths Competition Law* (1991); Goyder, *EEC Competition Law* (1988); Green, *Commercial Agreements and Competition Law: Practice and Procedure in the UK and EEC* (1986); Merkin & Williams, *Competition Law: Antitrust Policy in the UK and the EEC* (1984); Ritter et al., *EEC Competition Law: A Practitioner's Guide* (1991). Van Der Woude, Jones and Lewis, *EEC Competition Law Handbook* (1990); and Whish, *Competition Law* (2nd edn. 1989). See also Riesenfeld, "Antitrust Laws in the EEC" (1966) 50 *California Law Review* 459. On EC competition law and shipping, see Clough and Randolph, *Shipping and EC Competition Law* (1991).

6. The Commission has stated in the Introduction to its *Sixteenth Report on Competition Policy* (1986): "Competition policy has a key role to play in ensuring that the opening of the market yields all the benefits expected of it. It must ensure that these barriers are not replaced by divisions of markets resulting from restrictive business practices or protectionist measures taken by Member States." This reiterates the approach taken in the Introduction to the *Ninth Report on Competition Policy* (1979). See also Cases 56 & 58/84 *Consten and Grundig v. Commission* [1966] ECR 299, at 340.

7. This includes small as well as large businesses: see the comments of the Commission in its Sixteenth Report on Competition Policy (1987), points 22 to 23; Fourteenth Report on Competition Policy (1984), points 22 to 26; and the Twelfth Report on Competition Policy (1982), points 25 to 28.

8. In the Introduction to Goyder, *op. cit.*, p.vii.

9. *Op. cit.* at footnote 5, para.1-025 (footnote omitted)

(a) individuals may enforce it through the courts of the Member States[10];
(b) pending the adoption by the Council of Ministers of regulations conferring (under Article 87 of the EEC Treaty) enforcement powers on the Commission, the competent authorities of the Member States[11] and the Commission may enforce EC competition law by recording infringements by means of reasoned decisions[12]; and
(c) the Commission may enforce EC competition law by the Council of Ministers conferring on the Commission the necessary enforcement powers by virtue of Article 87 of the EEC Treaty.

The last method is the most satisfactory. Regulation 17/62[13] of 6 February 1962 was the means adopted by the Council of Ministers to confer on the Commission the power to enforce Articles 85 and 86 of the EEC Treaty. This does not apply however to maritime transport—it was only in 1986 that the necessary measure was adopted (i.e. Regulation 4056/86).

9.3.2 1962: Regulation 141/62 disapplying EC competition law in the case of transport

While Regulation 17/62 applied to (among other sectors) transport, Regulation 141 of 26 November 1962[14] quickly disapplied Regulation 17/62 in the case of transport. Regulation 141 set back the application of competition law to shipping by almost a quarter of a century.[15] The Regulation disapplied Regulation 17/62 in the cases of "agreements,[16] decisions[17] or concerted practices[18] in the transport sector which have as their object or effect the fixing of transport rates and conditions, the limitation or control of the supply of transport or the sharing of transport markets"[19] and Regulation 17/62 would not apply either to "the abuse of a dominant position, within the meaning of Article 86 of the Treaty, within the transport market".[20] In effect, transport was excluded from the application of Regulation 17/62 by means of Regulation 141/62. This deliberate exclusion has however always been narrowly interpreted.[21]

9.3.3 1968: Regulation 1017/68 applying EC competition law to certain transport modes

Regulation 1017/68[22] of 19 July 1968 applied the competition rules to rail, road and inland waterway transport albeit more leniently than Regulation 17/62. This Regulation was accompanied by a number of other Regulations which dealt with procedure, namely Regulation 1629/69[23] and Regulation 1630/69.[24] It was, however,

10. See Bellamy and Child, *op. cit.* at footnote 5, Chapter 10.
11. Acting under Article 88 of the EEC Treaty.
12. Acting under Article 89 of the EEC Treaty.
13. OJ No. 13, 21 February 1962, p. 204/62.
14. OJ No. 124, 28 November 1962, p. 2751/62. See also OJ Special Edition, 1959–62, at p.291.
15. Aviation also had to wait almost a quarter of a century.
16. *Ed.* on the concept of "agreements", see para. 10.1.3.2.2 below.
17. *Ed.* on the concept of "decisions", see para. 10.1.3.2.3 below.
18. *Ed.* on the concept of "concerted practices", see para. 10.1.3.2.4 below.
19. Regulation 141/62, Article 1.
20. Regulation 141/62, Article 1.
21. See, for example, *Olympic Airways*, OJ 1985 L46/51 and *London-European and Sabena*, OJ 1988 L317/47, where services which were ancillary to transport (e.g. ground handling and computer reservation systems) were held to fall within the scope of Regulation 17/62.
22. OJ L175, 23 July 1968, p. 1. See OJ Special Edition, 1968 (I), at p. 302.
23. OJ Special Edition, 1969 (II), at p. 371.
24. OJ Special Edition, 1969 (II), at p. 381.

more accommodating to the needs of the transport industry than Regulation 17/62 would have been in respect of industry generally.

9.3.4 1973: Accession of Denmark, Ireland and the UK to the EC

As has been mentioned elsewhere in this book,[25] the accession of three coastal States in 1973 stimulated further discussion in the EC on shipping matters. It has often been said that the accession of these three States proved to be the stimulus for the Commission's initiative in taking the *French Seamen's Case*.[26]

9.3.5 1974: Commission v. France

For some years, some commentators believed that the competition rules set out in Articles 85 to 94 of the EEC Treaty did not apply to shipping due to the curious wording of Article 84(2) of the EEC Treaty. This view was rejected by the European Court of Justice in two cases: first in Case 167/73 *Commission v. France*[27] and then in Cases 209 to 213/84 *Nouvelles Frontieres*.[28] The European Court of Justice held in Case 167/73 *Commission v. France*[29] (also known as the *French Seamen's Case*) that despite, Article 84(2) which provided that sea and air transport were not covered by the provisions of Title IV relating to the Common Transport Policy until such time as the Council of Ministers decided to include them, nevertheless sea and air transport were, on the same basis as other modes of transport, subject to the general provisions of the EEC Treaty. Thus, the transport sector is subject to Articles 85 and 86 of the EEC Treaty but implementing Regulations would facilitate the application of competition law.

9.3.6 1978: Commission v. Belgium

The European Court of Justice in Case 156/77 *Commission v. Belgium*[30] confirmed its approach in Case 167/73 *Commission v. France*, namely, that "the rules on competition form part of the general system of the Treaty". Ruttley has commented that "the result" of this case against Belgium and the *French Seamen's Case* was that "it was beyond doubt that the competition rules of the EEC Treaty apply generally to all economic sectors, including transport".[31]

9.3.7 1979: UNCTAD Code

It has been written that the "UNCTAD code has been the cornerstone of the Community's approach to the enforcement of EEC competition rules in the shipping sector. This Code was recognised by the Brussels package which regulates the Community's common position on the UNCTAD Code and its potential conflicts with the EEC Treaty".[32]

25. See Chapter 5, above.
26. [1974] ECR 359; [1974] 2 CMLR 216.
27. *Ibid.*
28. [1986] ECR 1425.
29. [1974] ECR 359; [1974] 2 CMLR 216.
30. [1978] ECR 1881.
31. [1991] 1 ECLR 5, at p. 6.
32. Clough and Randolph, *op. cit.* at footnote 2 above, para.1.1.

9.3.8 Pre-regulation 4056/86 position

The Commission in its Explanatory Memorandum to its 1981 Proposal for a Council Regulation laying down detailed rules for the application of Articles 85 and 86 of the EEC Treaty to maritime transport described the legal position pending the adoption of an implementing provision:

"In this field, pending the entry into force of such rules, Articles 88 and 89 provide the legal basis for action by the Member States or the Community:

- under Article 88, the authorities in Member States shall rule on the admissibility of agreements and on abuse of a dominant position in accordance with the law of their country and with Article 85, in particular para.3, and Article 86;
- Article 89 requires the Commission, in cooperation with the competent authorities in the Member States, who shall give it their assistance, to investigate cases of suspected infringement of the principles of the rules of competition. If it finds that there has been an infringement it shall propose appropriate measures to bring it to an end. If the infringement is not brought to an end, the Commission shall record it in a reasoned decision. It may authorize Member States to take the measures needed to remedy the situation.

This has two consequences. The Commission currently has not the power to enforce the rules of competition efficiently and consistently in the sea transport sector. In order to conduct investigations and secure the termination of infringements, it is dependent on the cooperation of the appropriate national authorities.

On the other hand, in the absence of an implementing regulation, Articles 85 and 86 are directly and fully applicable in each Member State. The national courts have jurisdiction to hear complaints relating to business conduct contrary to those Articles and either to forbid such conduct or not.

Concerning particularly the sea transport sector, there is a risk therefore that there will be delivered within the Community legal decisions which on the one hand are not coherent between one Member State and another, and which will also not take sufficient account of the specified character of the business concerned, which could react to the disadvantage of both shipowners and users. The fact that the Commission has already received three formal complaints about liner conferences shows that this risk is real.

The need therefore to apply Articles 85 and 86 in a consistent fashion throughout the Community and to assure shipowners as well as users of transport a sufficient degree of legal security, requires in itself the adoption of a regulation applying the rules of competition in the sea transport sector.

In these circumstances the Commission has already made clear when it submitted to the Council [of Ministers] a proposal for a regulation, that on the ratification by Member States of the UN Convention relating to a Code of Conduct for Liner Conferences[33] it was not, in principle, opposed to Liner Conferences subject to a detailed examination of the way they function.

When it adopted its regulation[34] the Council [of Ministers] considered that it is recognised that the stabilising role of conferences, by its nature, guarantees regular services to shippers, but that it is necessary to avoid possible breaches of the rules of competition of the [EEC] Treaty by the conferences. It therefore invited the Commission to present to it a proposal for a regulation concerning the application of these rules to sea transport."[35]

Regulation 4055/86 helps competition in the shipping sector by opening up (at least in part) the EC shipping market by applying the principle of freedom to provide maritime transport services between Member States as well as between Member States and third countries.

33. COM(77)686 final, 15 September 1977.
34. OJ L151, 17 May 1979.
35. Commission of the European Communities, *Proposal for a Council Regulation (EEC) laying down detailed rules for the application of Articles 85 and 86 of the Treaty to Maritime Transport*, COM(81)423 final, pp. 1–3.

9.3.9 Regulation 4056/86

The Council of Ministers adopted Regulation 4056/86 to apply competition rules to maritime transport. Chapter 12 below examines the Regulation.

Regulation 4056/86 is a more "mainstream" competition measure. It provides a special regime for shipping in terms of competition law.

9.4 OVERLAP BETWEEN COMPETITION MEASURES RELATING TO TRANSPORT AND GENERAL MEASURES

For present purposes, it may be said that Regulation 17/62 of 6 February 1962 applies Articles 85 and 86 to all economic sectors other than transport; Regulation 1017/68 applies Articles 85 and 86 to road, rail and inland waterway transport; Regulation 4056/86 applies Articles 85 and 86 to maritime transport; and Regulation 3975/87 applies Articles 85 and 86 to air transport.

What if a particular activity straddles a number of the particular sectors? What if an activity involves some elements of a particular sector but is also a matter within the framework of the general economy? It is submitted that there can be no general rule and the classification would turn on the facts of each case; an assessment would have to be made of the material incidents of the activity. For instance, in Case IV/32.328 *London European Airways v. Sabena*[36] the provision of computerised airline reservation systems was seen as falling within the scope of Regulation 17/62 and not Regulation 3975/87. Similarly, ground handling services in airports were considered as falling within the scope of Regulation 17/62 and not Regulation 3975/87 in the *Re Olympic Airways* case.[37] In Case IV/30.373 *Re Agreements on the Protection and Indemnity Clubs,*[38] the case turned on Regulation 17/62. It is submitted that the sale of containers would really fall within the scope of Regulation 17/62 but their transport by sea would normally fall within the scope of Regulation 4056/86.[39]

9.5 CONCLUSION

Competition law applies to shipping[40] and its application is facilitated, in relation to Articles 85 and 86 of the EEC Treaty, by means of Regulation 4056/86. The next chapter examines Articles 85 and 86 generally. Chapter 12 examines in depth Regulation 4056/86 and its accompanying regulation, Regulation 4260/86. The final three chapters in this part on competition deal with State aids,[41] dumping[42] and consortia.

36. OJ 1988 L317/47.
37. [1985] 1 CMLR 730.
38. [1989] CMLR 178.
39. See, in any case, Recital 6 of the proposed block exemption on consortia (OJ 1990 C167/90).
40. On the application of Articles 85 and 86 to transport generally, see Case 167/73 *Commission v. France* (*French Seamen's Case*) [1974] ECR 359, [1974] 2 CMLR 216; Cases 209–213/84, *Ministère Public v. Asjes* (*Nouvelles Frontières*) [1986] ECR 1425, [1986] 3 CMLR 173; and Case 66/86 *Ahmed Saeed* [1990] 4 CMLR 102.
41. This involves the granting of financial assistance by States to companies dumping.
42. This arises where goods or a service from one country is introduced onto another country's market at less than the normal value of that product or service.

It is certain that, as shipping companies around the world are becoming aware of the fact that they may face huge fines by the EC Commission for breaches of competition law, the subject of marine competition law will become hugely important.[43]

43. See "Senior Managers Sacked by SDV", *Lloyd's List*, 17 February 1992, p. 1, for a possible instance of a shipping company being fined.

CHAPTER 10

Articles 85 and 86 of the EEC Treaty

This chapter examines Articles 85 and 86 which are the principal provisions relating to competition in the EEC Treaty. It is an essential chapter because it facilitates an understanding of Regulation 4056/86 and shows how the competition rules of the EEC may be applied to the shipping industry generally.

10.1 ARTICLE 85[1]

10.1.1 Introduction

Certain types of anti-competitive agreements,[2] decisions[3] and concerted practices[4] between independent undertakings[5] which may affect trade between EC Member States and which have as their object or effect[6] the prevention, restriction or distortion of competition within the Common Market are, in the light of Article 85(1) of the EEC Treaty, incompatible with the Common Market and are thus void under Article 85(2) unless they are exempted[7] under Article 85(3). In essence, Article 85 prohibits particular types of restrictive agreements, decisions and concerted practices. It is designed to prevent uncompetitive "co-ordinated market behaviour".[8]

10.1.2 Text of Article 85

Article 85 of the EEC Treaty provides:

"1. The following shall be prohibited as incompatible with the common market: all agreements between undertakings, decisions by associations of undertakings and concerted practices which may affect trade between Member States and which have as their object or effect the prevention, restriction or distortion of competition within the common market, and in particular those which:

1. On Article 85 EEC, see Bellamy and Child, *Common Market Law of Competition* (3rd edn., 1987), Chapter 2; Clough and Randolph, *Shipping and EC Competition Law* (1991); Freeman and Whish, *Butterworths Competition Law* (1991), *passim*; Green, *Commercial Agreements and Competition Law: Practice and Procedure in the UK and EEC* (1986); and Whish, *Competition Law* (2nd edn., 1989), Chapter 1. See also Green, "Article 85 in perspective: stretching jurisdiction, narrowing the concept of a restriction and plugging a few gaps" [1988] ECLR 190. There are many publications dealing with EC competition law generally, see Chapter 9, footnote 5 above.

2. On the concept of "agreement", see para. 10.1.3.2.2, below,

3. On the concept of "decision", see para. 10.1.3.2.3, below.

4. On the concept of "concerted practice", see para. 10.1.3.2.4, below.

5. On the concept of "undertaking", see para. 10.1.3.1, below. On Article 85 of the EEC Treaty and unilateral action, see Freeman and Whish, *op. cit.*, paras. 162–164.

6. On the concepts of "object" and "effect", see para. 10.1.4, below.

7. On the concept of "exemption", see para. 10.1.9, below.

8. Whish, *op. cit.* at footnote 1, p. 212.

(a) directly or indirectly fix purchase or selling prices or any other trading conditions;
(b) limit or control production, markets, technical development, or investment;
(c) share markets or sources of supply;
(d) apply dissimilar conditions to equivalent transactions with other trading parties, thereby placing them at a competitive disadvantage;
(e) make the conclusion of contracts subject to the acceptance by other parties of supplementary obligations which, by their nature or according to commercial usage, have no connection with the subject of such contracts.

2. Any agreements or decisions prohibited pursuant to this Article shall be automatically void.
3. The provision of paragraph 1 may, however, be declared inapplicable in the case of:
— any agreement or category of agreements between undertakings;
— any decision or category of decisions by associations of undertakings;
— any concerted practice or category of concerted practices;

which contributes to improving the production or distribution of goods or to promoting technical or economic progress, while allowing consumers a fair share of the resulting benefit, and which does not:

(a) impose on the undertakings concerned restrictions which are not indispensable to the attainment of these objectives;
(b) afford such undertakings the possibility of eliminating competition in respect of a substantial part of the products in question."

In essence, Article 85 EEC prevents, as a general rule, anti-competitive arrangements between undertakings.

10.1.3 Basic concepts in Article 85

10.1.3.1 Undertaking[9]

10.1.3.1.1 Introduction

Article 85 EEC relates to agreements, decisions or concerted practices entered into by "undertakings". It is thus essential to be able to define what is meant in this context by the term "undertaking". It is important to stress that the definition of undertaking for the purposes of Article 85 EEC is the same, *mutatis mutandis*, for Article 86 EEC.

10.1.3.1.2 Definition

The EEC Treaty does not define what is meant by the term "undertaking". This has not, however, given rise to many problems in the practical application of EEC competition law. The EC institutions take a broad view of the concept. It is submitted that any entity, be it a natural or legal person, engaged in commercial activities (whether or not for profit[10]) may constitute an undertaking for the purposes of EEC

9. See Bellamy and Child, *op. cit.* at footnote 1, paras 2-003–2-015; Clough and Randolph, *op. cit.* at footnote 1, para. 3.2.2.2; Freeman and Whish, *op. cit.*, paras. 107–124; and Whish, *op. cit.* at footnote 1, pp. 213–17. See Cases 209/78 *Von Landewyck v. Commission* [1980] ECR 3125 at 3250; Case 173/83 *Hydrotherm v. Anderoil* [1984] ECR 2999, [1985] 3 CMLR 224, CCH 14,112. See the following Commission decisions: *AOIP/Beyrard* OJ L6/8, 13 January 1976, [1976] 1 CMLR D14, CCH 9801; *ARG/Unipart* OJ L45/34, 18 February 1988, [1988] 4 CMLR 513, CCH 10.968; *LdPE* OJ L 74/21, 17 March 1989, CCH [1989] 1 CEC 2,193; *Polypropylene* OJ L 230/1, 18 August 1986, [1988] 4 CMLR 347, CCH 10,782; *PVC* OJ L74/1, 17 March 1989, CCH [1989] 1 CEC 2,167; *RAI/UNITEL* OJ L157/39, 15 June 1978, [1978] 3 CMLR 306; CCH, 10,009; *Reuter/BASF* OJ L254/40, 17 September 1976, [1976] 2 CMLR D44, CCH 9862; *Welded Steel Mesh* OJ L260/1, 6 September 1989, [1989] 2 CEC 2051; *Zinc Producer Group* OJ L220/27, 17 August 1984, [1985] 2 CMLR 108, CCH 10,617; *P&I Clubs* OJ L376/2, 31 December 1985

10. Commission Decision 85/615/EEC *P&I Clubs* OJ 1985 L376/2, [1989] 4 CMLR 178.

competition law irrespective of whether it supplies goods or services.[11,12] In the *Film Purchases by German Television Stations* case,[13] the Commission said that the "fundamental concept of undertaking in Article 85(1) covers any activity directed at trade in goods or services irrespective of the legal form of the undertaking and regardless of whether or not it is intended to earn profits". In *Polypropylene*[14] the Commission said that the concept of an undertaking was not identical to the concept of legal personality for the purposes of fiscal or company law. Indeed, the term is widely and generously interpreted by the Commission and the ECJ.

10.1.3.1.3 Particular entities

It may be helpful to enumerate some of the entities which have been seen by the Commission and the ECJ as constituting "undertakings" for the purposes of EEC competition law.

Companies It is now almost trite to state that a company is an undertaking for the purposes of EEC competition law.[15]

Partnerships A partnership is an undertaking for the purposes of EEC competition law: in *Re Italian Cast Glass*,[16] a firm which was established by four independent companies to supervise a quota-fixing agreement was held to constitute an undertaking for the purposes of EEC competition law.

State-owned corporations[17] State-owned corporations may be undertakings for the purposes of EEC competition law.[18]

Statutory bodies A body or authority created by statute may constitute an undertaking for the purposes of Articles 85 and 86 EEC[19] provided they are engaged in economic or commercial activities. A rule-making body *per se* would not constitute an undertaking.[20] Equally, quasi-governmental bodies carrying on economic activities may fall within the framework of Articles 85 and 86.[21]

Co-operatives A co-operative is an undertaking for the purposes of EEC competition law.[22]

11. See, for example, Case 90/76 *Van Ameyde v. UCI* [1977] ECR 1091. The rules apply to such services as banking and transport.
12. *Polypropylene* OJ 1986 L230/1; [1988] 4 CMLR 347, on appeal Cases 179/86 etc. *Rhones-Poulenc SA v. Commission.*
13. Commission Decision 89/536/EEC OJ 1989 L284/36, [1990] 4 CMLR 841.
14. Commission Decision 86/398/EEC OJ 1986 L230/1, [1988] 4 CMLR 347, on appeal Cases 179/86 etc. *Rhones-Poulenc SA v. Commission.*
15. This includes trust companies: *Fides* OJ 1979 L57/33, [1979] 1 CMLR 650 and limited partnerships: Case 258/78 *Nungesser v. Commission* [1982] ECR 2015, [1983] 1 CMLR 278. A group of companies may constitute a single economic unit: Cases 48, 49, 51–57 *ICI v. Commission* [1972] ECR 619, [1972] CMLR 557. See Case 170/83 *Hydrotherm v. Compact* [1984] ECR 2999, [1985] 3 CMLR 224.
16. Commission Decision 80/1334/EEC OJ 1980 L383/19, [1982] 4 CMLR 61. See also *Breeders' Rights: Roses* OJ 1985 L369/9.
17. See Bellamy and Child, *op. cit.* at footnote 1 above, para. 2-010.
18. See Case 155/73 *Italian State v. Sacchi* [1974] ECR 409, [1974] 2 CMLR 177 and Case 41/83 *Italy v. Commission* [1985] ECR 873, [1985] 2 CMLR 368.
19. A State authority may still be subject to EC competition law on State aids even though it does not carry on economic activities.
20. See Case 123/83 *BNIC v. Clair* [1985] ECR 391, at p. 395, [1985] 2 CMLR 430, (Opinion of Advocate-General Slynn) and Case 30/87 *Corrine Bodson v. Pompes Funèbres* [1988] ECR 2479, [1989] 4 CMLR 984.
21. Case 258/78 *Nungesesser KG v. Commission* [1982] ECR 2015, [1983] 1 CMLR 278.
22. Case 61/80 *Co-operative Stremsel-en Kleurselfabriek v. Commission* [1981] ECR 851, [1982] 1 CMLR 240; Commission Decision 86/596/EEC *MELDOC* OJ 1986 L348/50, [1989] 4 CMLR 853.

Trade associations A trade association is an undertaking for these purposes. Consequently, agreements between trade associations may fall within the scope of EEC competition law.[23]

Mutual societies and P&I clubs A mutual insurance club, more specifically a Protection and Indemnity Club (i.e. a P&I Club), has been regarded as an undertaking for the purposes of EEC competition law.[24]

Individuals[25] Individuals may constitute undertakings for the purposes of EEC competition law.[26] Sole traders are obvious examples.[27] Consultants are also undertakings.[28] There are many decisions to this effect.[29] In *RAI/UNITEL*,[30] opera singers were held to be undertakings. In *AOIP v. Beyrard*,[31] an individual was held to be an undertaking where a patent licence agreement had been concluded between himself and a company. A *controlling*[32] shareholder was an undertaking in *Vaessen v. Morris*.[33]

Employees[34] An employee acting as an employee would not be an undertaking for the purposes of EEC competition law.[35] A former employee who carries on an independent business in his or her own right would constitute an undertaking for the purposes of EEC competition law.[36]

Trade unions[37] It has been suggested that a trade union "is probably not an undertaking, as it does not carry on commercial activity".[38] This appears to be a correct view but it is submitted that in so far as a trade union represents self-employed persons[39] or engages in commercial activities then it is an undertaking. Whether or not a trade union constitutes an undertaking, it may well have the capacity to lodge a complaint under EEC competition law,[40] thus a seafarer's union may not necessarily be an undertaking under EEC competition law but could still have the *locus standi* under EEC competition law to make a complaint to the Commission alleging breach of that body of law.

23. See e.g. Case 71/74 *FRUBO v. Commission* [1975] ECR 563, [1975] 2 CMLR 123; Case 96/82 *IAZ International Belgium NV v. Commission* [1983] ECR 3369, [1984] 3 CMLR 276; *EATE Levy* OJ 1985 L219/35, [1988] 4 CMLR 698; *Uniform Eurocheques* OJ 1989 L36/16.

24. Commission Decision 85/615/EEC *P and I Clubs* OJ 1985 L376/2, [1989] 4 CMLR 178. See [1985] ECLR 7, and p. 301.

25. See Bellamy and Child, *op. cit.* at footnote 1, para. 2-009.

26. See Case 173/83 *Hydrotherm v. Anderoil* [1984] ECR 2999, [1985] 3 CMLR 224, CCH 14,112; *AOIP/Beyrard* OJ L6/8, 13 January 1976, [1976] 1 CMLR D14, CCH 9801; *RAI/UNITEL* OJ L157/39, 15 June 1978, [1978] 3 CMLR 306, CCH, 10,009; *Reuter/BASF* OJ L254/40, 17 September 1976, [1976] 2 CMLR D44, CCH 9862.

27. See, for example, Case 258/78 *Nungesser v. Commission* [1982] ECR 2015; [1983] 1 CMLR 278.

28. See *Reuter/BASF* OJ 1976 L254/50, [1976] 2 CMLR D44.

29. See, for example, Commission Decision 76/743/EEC *Reuter/BASF* OJ 1976 L254/40, [1976] 2 CMLR D44; Commission Decision 79/86/EEC *Vaessen BV v. Morris* OJ 1979 L19/32, [1979] 1 CMLR 511; Case 35/83 *BAT v. Commission* [1985] ECR 363, [1985] 2 CMLR 470; Case 42/84 *Remia BV and Verenigde Bedrijven Nutricia NV v. Commission* [1985] ECR 2545, [1987] 1 CMLR 1; Commission Decision 85/561/EEC *Breeders' Rights: Roses* OJ 1985 L369/9, [1988] 4 CMLR 193.

30. OJ 1978 L157/39, [1978] 3 CMLR 306.

31. Commission Decision 76/29/EEC OJ 1976 L6/8, [1976] 1 CMLR D14.

32. A shareholder merely holding some shares would probably not constitute an undertaking.

33. OJ 1979 L19/32, [1979] 1 CMLR D14.

34. See Bellamy and Child, *op. cit.* at footnote 1 above, para. 2-007; Freeman and Whish, *op. cit.*, para. 121.

35. Cases 40/73 etc. *Suiker Unie v. Commission* [1975] ECR 1663, at 2007, [1976] 1 CMLR 295 (para.539).

36. Commission Decision 76/743/EEC *Reuter/BASF* OJ 1976 L254/40, [1976] 2 CMLR D44.

37. See Bellamy and Child, *op. cit.*, para. 2-008 as well as Freeman and Whish, *op. cit.*, para. 121.

38. Whish, *op. cit.*, p. 215.

39. See Bellamy and Child, *op. cit.*, para. 2 008.

40. See *BP/Texaco, Sixteenth Report on Competition Policy* (1987), point 43.

Charities In so far as a charity does not carry on a commercial activity then it should not be regarded as an undertaking for present purposes. It is important to stress that the entity must carry on commercial activities but need not have a profit motive[41] or economic purpose.[42]

Foreign trade organisations Many socialist States have or had foreign trade organisations. These have been held to constitute undertakings for the purposes of EEC competition law notwithstanding that they have no separate existence from their States.[43]

Public and local authorities[44] It has long been debated and disputed as to whether local authorities could constitute undertakings for the purposes of EC competition law. In Case 30/87 *Corrine Bodson v. Pompes Funebres des Regions Liberees SA,*[45] the ECJ held that Article 85 EEC did not apply to licensing agreements between French municipalities acting in their capacity as public authorities and entities entrusted with the provision of a public service. It is submitted that where the authority is acting as a public authority exercising *public* functions then it would not have the capacity to be an undertaking for present purposes.

Member States[46] Whether a Member State constitutes an undertaking is an undecided issue. It is submitted that, on the (somewhat weak) basis of Case 30/87 *Corrine Bodson v. Pompes Funebres des Regions Liberees*[47] and the general principles of public international law (developed in recent years) on State immunity, a Member State could be an undertaking in so far as it was engaged in commercial activities which could be conducted by other non-State entities but not where it was engaged in non-commercial activities or State-only commercial activities.

Connected entities generally In some circumstances, the Commission and the courts will treat two or more entities as constituting one single undertaking for the purposes of EC competition law. If the entities constitute one undertaking for present purposes due to identical control or ownership then Article 85 EEC does not (because it cannot) apply in relation to any agreement between them.

Parent and subsidiary[48] An agreement may fall outside the scope of Article 85 EEC where there is so close an economic relationship between the parties that they constitute one economic entity. This has been the approach used by the Commission in dealing with such agreements between parent companies and their subsidiaries.[49] A parent company may be made liable for the wrongdoings of its subsidiaries. A parent company is liable for the activities of its subsidiaries and thus, in the case of a

41. *EEC v. ANSEAU-NAVEWA* OJ 1982 L167/39, [1982] 2 CMLR 193; *Interpar v. GVL mbH* OJ 1982 L370/49, [1982] 1 CMLR 221; *P and I Clubs* OJ 1985 L376/2, [1985] 4 CMLR 178.

42. Case 155/73 *Italian State v. Sacchi* [1974] ECR 409, [1974] 2 CMLR 177.

43. See Commission Decision 85/206/EEC *Aluminium Products* OJ 1985 L92/1, [1987] 3 CMLR 813; and Commission Decision 82/860/EEC OJ 1982 L360/31, [1983] 1 CMLR 703 *Colombian Coffee* OJ 1982 L360/31, [1983] 1 CMLR 703. See also *Fourteenth Report on Competition Policy*, point 57.

44. See Bellamy and Child, *op. cit.*, para.2-012.

45. [1988] ECR 2479, [1989] 4 CMLR 984.

46. See Bellamy and Child, *op. cit.* at footnote 1 above, para.2-011.

47. [1988] ECR 2479, [1989] 4 CMLR 984. See *Irish Aerospace (Belgium) NV v. European Organisation for the Safety of Air Navigation, Financial Times*, 18 July 1991.

48. Bellamy and Child, *op. cit.* at footnote 1 above, para.2-005. See also *Johnson and Johnson* OJ [1980] L 377/16, [1981] 2 CMLR 287.

49. See *Re Zinc Producers' Group* OJ 1984 L220/27, [1985] 2 CMLR 108; *Johnson and Johnson* OJ 1980 L377/16, [1981] 2 CMLR 287; Case 15/74 *Centrafarm v. Sterling Drug* [1974] ECR 1147, at p. 1167 (para. 41); Cases 228 and 229/82 *Ford v Commission (No. 1)* [1984] ECR 1129, [1980] CMLR, *Central Wine Buyers (South Leicester Ltd) v. Moet et Chandon (London) Ltd* OJ 1982 L94/7, [1982] 2 CMLR 166; and Case 107/82 *AEG v. Commission* [1983] ECR 3151, at p. 3199.

distribution agreement, a parent must ensure that competition further down the distribution chain is not anti-competitive.[50] A parent company outside the EC can be made subject to EC competition law where its subsidiary is within the EC.

Principal and agent[51] If the relationship between a principal and agent is such that the agent does not have economic independence (at least in this regard) from the principal then (notwithstanding that they may be legally independent of one another), any agreements (etc.) made between the principal and agent may fall outside the scope of EEC competition law.[52] It is instructive to examine the Commission Notice on Principal-Agent Agreements in such situations.

Branch offices[53] It has been held that a branch office does not in itself constitute an undertaking for the purposes of EEC competition law.[54]

Successive entities If one entity succeeds another so that the liabilities of the former entity are now attributed to the latter entity then the two entities may be treated as a single undertaking for the purposes of EEC competition law and thus Article 85 EEC does not apply. If a member of a cartel has been replaced by another then can the successor organisation be held liable for the "sins" of the earlier organisation? In *PVC*[55] the Commission held that the determining factor is "whether there is a functional and economic continuity between the original infringer and the undertaking into which it was merged". The Commission went on to indicate that it is a matter for EEC law to determine whether or not the new entity is responsible for the conduct of the old one—national law is not conclusive on the issue. It is of interest to note that the ECJ has held (in Cases 29, 30/83 *Compagnie Royale Asturienne des Mines SA and Rheinzink GmbH v. Commission*[56]) that "a change in the legal form and name of an undertaking does not create a new undertaking free of liability for the anti-competitive behaviour of its predecessor when, from an economic point of view, the two are identical".

Foreign entities[57] The mere fact that the entity is incorporated or situate outside the EC does not mean that it cannot be an undertaking for the purposes of EC competition law.

10.1.3.2 Agreements, decisions and concerted practices[58]

10.1.3.2.1 Introduction

Article 85(1) of the EEC Treaty prohibits certain "agreements between undertakings, decisions by associations of undertakings and concerted practices". It is important to determine what is meant in EEC competition law, by the terms "agreement", "decision" and "concerted practice". The definition is a critical one because the Commission has interpreted the terms widely in the past and too wide an interpretation

50. *Johnson and Johnson* OJ 1980 L377/16, [1981] 2 CMLR 287; Cases 100-103/80 *Musique Diffusion Francaise v. Commission* [1983] ECR 1825, [1983] 3 CMLR 221.

51. See Bellamy and Child, *op. cit.* at footnote 1 above, para. 2-007.

52. See *Aluminium Imports from Eastern Europe* OJ 1985 L92/1, at p. 37.

53. See Bellamy and Child, *op. cit.* at footnote 1 above, para. 2-006.

54. *Fire Insurance (D)* OJ 1982 L80/36, [1982] 2 CMLR 159.

55. OJ 1989 L74/1, para. 42.

56. [1984] ECR 1679, [1985] 1 CMLR 688.

57. See Bellamy and Child, *op. cit.* at footnote 1 above, para. 2-014.

58. See Bellamy and Child, *op. cit.* at footnote 1 above, paras 2-016-2-045; Clough and Randolph, *op. cit.* at footnote 1, para. 3.2.2.3; Freeman and Whish, *op. cit.* at footnote 1 above, paras. 125–164; and Whish, *op cit.* at footnote 1, pp. 217–228.

can prove (albeit in limited circumstances) to be the basis of a challenge to the Commission's finding. It is vital to remember that the three concepts overlap[59] and it is rare that a particular course of conduct constitutes only an agreement, a decision or a concerted practice.[60] It is also vital to remember that the list of examples of agreement (and so on) contained in Article 85(1) of the EEC Treaty is not exhaustive. The agreement, decision or concerted practice does not have to be legally enforceable.[61] If it had to be so then all anti-competitive undertakings would have to do is conclude "gentlemen's agreements" (i.e. non-legally binding agreements) and thereby circumvent EEC competition law. The agreement, decision or concerted practice does not have to be in any particular form: for example, it may be an oral agreement.[62] It may even have to be inferred from the circumstances of the case.[63] The economic effect is more important than the legal form.

10.1.3.2.2 Agreements between undertakings[64]

An agreement is a distinct concept from a concerted practice.[65] None the less the two are closely related. If a situation does not amount to an agreement then it may well amount to a concerted practice.[66] Indeed, the Commission, in reaching its findings, has often said that the co-operation between the parties amounts to an agreement or in any event if not an agreement, then a concerted practice.[67] It is thus submitted that for the purposes of EEC law, there is no importance in the distinction.

The agreement may be made in writing, by conduct or orally.[68] There does not have to be any sanction for the enforcement of the "agreement".[69] The mental state of the participants (even where they are unwilling[70]) has been generally ignored by the Commission in their determination as to whether an agreement existed[71] but the participants' unwillingness may be taken into account in assessing fines.[72]

It is useful, but only of limited use, to survey examples of situations which have been held to amount to "agreements" for present purposes.

Legally binding contracts A legally enforceable contract is an agreement for present purposes.[73]

59. See, for example, *Fedetab* OJ 1978 L224/29, at p. 40, [1978] 3 CMLR 524 at 539.
60. See the comments of Advocate-General Reischl in Cases 209/78 etc. *Van Landewyck v. Commission* [1980] ECR 3125, at p. 3310, [1981] 3 CMLR 134 at 185.
61. See Cases 209/78 etc. *Van Landewyck v. Commission* [1980] ECR 3125 at pp. 3250–1, [1981] 3 CMLR 193. Acceptance is not necessary: *BVB/ABB* OJ L7/27, 9 January 1987.
62. *National Panasonic* OJ 1982 L354/28, [1983] 1 CMLR 497, at 504. The rules of a market may be an agreement between participants in the market: *GAFTA Soya Bean Meal Futures Association Ltd* OJ L19/18, 21 January 1987.
63. See Case 28/77 *Tepea v. Commission* [1978] ECR 1391, at pp. 1412–7.
64. See Bellamy and Child, *op. cit.*, paras 2-016–2-030; Freeman and Whish, *op. cit.*, paras. 126–129; and Whish, *op. cit.*, pp. 217–220. The Commission is broadening the concept of "agreement".
65. See Commission Decision 86/398/EEC *Polypropylene* OJ 1986 L230/1, [1988] 4 CMLR 347, para. 86.
66. See Reischl AG in Case 209/78 *Van Landewyck v. Commission* [1980] ECR 3125, at p. 3310, [1981] 3 CMLR 134 at p. 185.
67. E.g. *Re Floral* OJ 1980 L39/51, [1980] 2 CMLR 285.
68. Case 28/77 *Tepea v. Commission* [1978] ECR 1391, [1978] 3 CMLR 392.
69. *Polypropylene* OJ 1986 L230/1, [1988] 4 CMLR 347.
70. See *Hasselblad* OJ 1982 L16/9, [1979] 1 CMLR 448.
71. *Belgian Roofing Felt* OJ 1986 L232/15, on appeal Case 246/86 *Belasco v. Commission*; *Polypropylene* OJ 1986 L230/1, [1988] 4 CMLR 347, on appeal Cases 179/86 etc. *Rhones-Poulenc SA v. Commission*; *PVC* OJ 1989 L74/1; and *LdPE* OJ 1989 L74/21.
72. *Camera Care Ltd v Victor Hasselblad AB* OJ 1982 L161/18, [1982] 2 CMLR 233; *Wood Pulp* OJ [1985] L85/1, [1985] 3 CMLR 474 at para.131, on appeal Cases 89/85 etc. *A Ahlstrom OY v. Commission.*
73. Commission Decision 78/193/EEC *Penney's Trade Mark* OJ 1978 L60/19, [1978] 2 CMLR 100.

Compromise of litigation A compromise of litigation may constitute an agreement for present purposes.[74]

Unenforceable agreement "Gentlemen's agreements" have been held to be agreements for the present purposes.[75]

A series of collective agreements A number of collective agreements may constitute one agreement for present purposes.[76]

Constitution of a trade association The constitution of a trade association has been held to be an agreement for present purposes.[77]

Standard conditions of sale Standard conditions of sale would be agreements for present purposes.[78]

Standard form contracts An agreement set out in a standard form contract has also been held to constitute an agreement for present purposes.[79]

Guidelines An agreement may be merely a set of guidelines issued by various organisations.[80]

Spent agreements It has been held in a number of cases[81] that an agreement which has expired but its effects continue to be felt might be an agreement for the purposes of Article 85.

Conclusion The breadth of meaning attached to the expression "agreement" is clear from the fact that "simple understandings" have been held to constitute agreements for present purposes.[82] It appears that mere "contact" may be sufficient to arouse the suspicions of the Commission. It is also clear that what appears to be a unilateral action may still amount to an agreement because of some tacit understanding on the part of a number of other undertakings.[83] Thus charterparties, cargo sharing agreements and even tacit understandings not to poach each other's customers would fall within the scope of "agreements". The breadth of the term "concerted practice" means that "agreements" may easily be subsumed under the term "concerted practice".

10.1.3.2.3 Decisions by associations of undertakings[84]

Article 85 of the EEC Treaty also applies to certain decisions by associations of undertakings.[85] These associations are normally trade associations, but may well take any form of structure and include various members.[86] They need not be profit-making;

74. *Re Penney's Trade Mark* OJ 1978 L60/19; [1978] 2 CMLR 100.
75. Case 41/69 *ACF Chemiefarma NV v. Commission* [1970] ECR 661.
76. *ENI/Montedison* OJ 1987 L354/28, [1988] 4 CMLR 444.
77. Commission Decision 84/191 *Nuovo CEGAM* OJ [1984] L99/29, [1984] 2 CMLR 484.
78. Case 30/78 *Distillers Company v. Commission* [1980] ECR 2229, [1980] 3 CMLR 121 and Commission Decision 79/68/EEC *Kawasaki Motors* OJ 1979 L16/9, [1979] 1 CMLR 448.
79. *Putz v. Kawasaki Motors (UK) Ltd* OJ 1979 L16/9, [1979] 1 CMLR 448.
80. See *Uniform Eurocheques* OJ 1989 L36/16.
81. For example, Cases 51/75 *EMI Records Ltd v. CBS UK Ltd* [1976] ECR 811, at pp. 848–9, [1976] 2 CMLR 235, at p. 267.
82. *Re Stichting Sigarettenindustrie Agreements* OJ 1982 L232/1, [1982] 3 CMLR 702; *National Panasonic* OJ 1982 L 354/28, [1983] 1 CMLR 497.
83. Case 107/82 *AEG v. Commission* [1983] ECR 3151, at pp. 3194–95. See also Commission Decision 82/506/EEC *Stichting Sigarettenindustrie Agreements* OJ 1982 L 232/1, [1982] 3 CMLR 702.
84. See Bellamy and Child, *op. cit.* at footnote 1 above, paras 2-031–2-032, as well as Freeman and Whish, *op. cit.*, paras. 130–141.
85. See *Publishers Association—Net Book Agreement*, OJ 1989 L22/12. The association need not have legal personality of its own. *Emo* (OJ L11/16, 17 January 1979).
86. See Bellamy and Child, *op. cit.*, para. 2-032.

they may take virtually any form and may be associations of associations. The decisions of associations of undertakings may well be agreements in themselves. It is useful, but only of limited use, to survey examples of situations which have been held to amount to "decisions" for present purposes.

A constitution of a trade association is a decision of an association of undertakings.[87] A recommendation made by the association is a decision.[88] Even a non-binding recommendation can constitute a decision for these purposes.[89] If a trade association recommends to its members to engage in anti-competitive behaviour then not only will the members be liable but, because of this head of liability, the trade association itself will be liable.[90] It may be easier for the EC authorities to prove a decision of an association of undertakings than to prove individual agreements or a concerted practice.[91]

10.1.3.2.4 Concerted practices[92]

Of the three types of measures caught by Article 85, the final one mentioned in Article 85(1) is a "concerted practice".[93] This is the most controversial and complex measure of the three. Undertakings may operate in a parallel manner without there being a concerted practice—the undertakings may simply "read" or react to the market in an identical manner[94]—which is to be expected in an oligopolistic market with a homogeneous product.

In *ICI v. Commission (Dyestuffs)*[95] the ECJ described a "concerted practice" as "a form of co-ordination between undertakings which, without having reached the stage where an agreement properly so-called has been concluded, knowingly substitutes practical co-operation between them for the risks of competition". The ECJ developed this point in *Suiker Unie v. Commission* (*Sugar Cartel*)[96] by saying that Article 85 strictly prohibited:

"any direct or indirect contact between such operators, the object or effect whereof is either to influence the conduct on the market of an actual or potential competitor or to disclose to such a competitor the course of conduct which they themselves have decided to adopt or contemplate adopting on the market."

These two cases are now the pivotal cases on the point.[97] The thrust of the two cases has been summarised by Whish in the following terms: "there must be a mental consensus whereby practical co-operation is *knowingly* substituted for competition, but the

87. *National Sulphuric Acid Association* (OJ L260/24, 3 October 1980), *Publishers' Association* (OJ L22/12, 26 January 1989); *BPICA* OJ 1977 L299/18, [1977] 2 CMLR D43; *Re ASPA* OJ 1970 L 148/9, [1970] CMLR D25.

88. Case 8/72 *Vereeniging van Cementhandelaren v. Commission* [1972] ECR 977, [1973] CMLR 7.

89. Case 96/82 etc. *IAZ International Belgium NV v. Commission* [1983] ECR 3369, [1984] 3 CMLR 276.

90. Commission Decision 82/896/EEC *AROW v. BNIC* OJ 1982 L379/1, [1983] 2 CMLR 240.

91. Whish, *op. cit.* at footnote 1 above, p. 220.

92. See Bellamy and Child, *op. cit.* at footnote 1 above, paras. 2-033–2-045; Clough and Randolph, *op. cit.*, para. 3.2.2.5; Freeman and Whish, *op. cit.*, paras 142–161; and Whish, *op cit.*, at footnote 1, pp. 221–226. See also Case 172/80 *Zuchner v. Bayerische Vereinsbank AG* [1981] ECR 2021, [1982] 1 CMLR 313.

93. See Korah, "Concerted Practices" (1973) 36 MLR 220.

94. See Cases 29, 30/83 *Compagnie Royale Asturienne des Mines SA and Rheinzink GmbH v. Commission* [1984] ECR 1679, [1985] 1 CMLR 688; *Italian Flat Glass* OJ 1989 L33/44.

95. Case 48/69, [1972] ECR 619, [1972] CMLR 557.

96. Cases 40/73 etc. [1975] ECR 1663, [1976] 1 CMLR 295.

97. See Case 172/80 *Zuchner v. Bayerische Vereinsbank AG* [1981] ECR 2021, [1982] 1 CMLR 313.

consensus need not be achieved verbally and can come about by any direct or indirect contact between the parties."[98]

It is of interest that the Commission has held in some cases that a concerted practice did not require proof of a plan.[99] Proof is vital in bringing proceedings. The undertakings may have destroyed faxes, letters, telexes, records and all other documentary evidence. The burden of proof rests on the EC authorities to prove a concerted practice. If there is insufficient evidence for the Commission to say that there was a concerted practice then the Court will be willing to set aside the Commission's decision.[100]

10.1.3.2.5 Agreements, decisions and concerted practices entered into outside the EC

Agreements, decisions and concerted practices entered into outside the EC may still fall within the scope of Article 85 of the EEC Treaty where they have an effect within the EC.[101]

10.1.4 Object or effect of preventing, restricting or distorting competition

10.1.4.1 Introduction

Article 85 of the EEC Treaty prohibits particular agreements, decisions or practices which have as their object or effect the prevention, restriction or distortion of competition. What is meant by "object " or "effect"? Moreover, what is meant by prevention, restriction or distortion of competition? In assessing this issue, regard should be had to the economic effect rather than the legal form.[102]

In Case 56/65 *Société Technique Minière v. Maschinenbau Ulm*[103] the ECJ held that the terms "object" or "effect" are to be read disjunctively. Thus, it is essential first to prove that the object of the agreement was to prevent, restrict or distort competition and then, only if it was not clear that the *object* of an agreement (etc.) was to harm competition would it be necessary to consider whether it had the effect of doing so. Thus, where the *object* of the agreement is to prevent, restrict or distort competition, there is no need to establish the *effect* on competition. Thus, an agreement to fix prices, share markets or impose an export ban will be seen as being anti-competitive.

10.1.4.2 Object

In studying, the "object" of the agreement (etc.) the authorities are not concerned with the subjective intention of the parties but must instead look at the "objective" intention of the agreement (etc.)—i.e. the purpose of the agreement considered in the economic context in which it is to be applied.[104]

98. *Op. cit.*, p. 223.

99. *Polypropylene* OJ 1986 L230/1, [1988] 4 CMLR 347, on appeal Cases 179/86 etc. *Rhones-Poulenc SA v. Commission.*

100. E.g. Cases 40/73 etc. *Suiker Unie v. Commission* [1975] ECR 1663, [1976] 1 CMLR 295; Cases 29,30/83 *Compagnie Royale Asturienne des Mines SA and Rheinzink GmbH v. Commission* [1984] ECR 1679, [1985] 1 CMLR 688.

101. Case 22/71 *Beguelin Import v. GL Import Export* [1971] ECR p. 949, at 959, [1972] CMLR 81.

102. See Freeman and Whish, *op. cit.* at footnote 1 above, paras. 165–205.

103. [1966] ECR 235, at p. 249, [1966] CMLR 357, at p. 375. The whole legal and economic context must be examined.

104. Cases 29, 30/83 *Compagnie Royale Asturienne des Mines SA and Rheinzink GmbH v. Commission* [1984] ECR 1679, [1985] 1 CMLR 688 and Cases 96/82 etc. *IAZ v. Commission* [1983] ECR 3369.

10.1.4.3 Effect

If it is not clear that the "object" of the agreement (etc.) is anti-competitive then regard must be had to the effect of the agreement (etc.). To do so, one must examine the agreement (etc.) in the context of its market:

> "it would be pointless to consider an agreement, decision or practice by reason of its effect if those effects were to be taken distinct from the market in which they are seen to operate, and could only be examined apart from the body of effects, whether convergent or not, surrounding their implementation. Thus in order to examine whether it is caught by Article 85(1) an agreement cannot be examined in isolation from the above context, that is, from the factual or legal circumstances causing it to prevent, restrict or distort competition."[105]

It is necessary to determine the product market, the geographical market, the level of competition in the market and the legal infrastructure (intellectual property laws and so on). The effect must be appreciable.

10.1.4.4 Preventing, restricting and distorting competition

It is legally irrelevant whether the agreement (etc.) prevents, restricts and distorts competition: it is sufficient that it does any one of the three. Distortion is in many ways the "catch-all" term.[106]

10.1.5 Effect on inter-State trade

10.1.5.1 Introduction

Only agreements, decisions or concerted practices which (*inter alia*) affect trade between Member States fall within the scope of Article 85 of the EEC Treaty. The significance of this requirement (i.e. an effect on inter-State trade) is critical. It constitutes the "boundary between the areas respectively covered by Community law and the law of the Member States".[107] If a particular agreement (etc.) is seen as having an effect on inter-State trade then the national competition authorities are thereby excluded and the matter is one for the EC authorities. Thus, this criterion is of critical importance in each case.

A substantial part of the Common Market must be affected. This does not have to be a State and could even be a region in a State.[108]

10.1.5.2 Examples

Examples of agreements (etc.) which have an effect on inter-State trade abound. A contract which prohibits a distributor from selling goods other than on its own

105. Case 23/67 *Brasserie de Haecht v. Wilkin* [1967] ECR 407, [1968] CMLR 26. Certain arrangements have a *per se* effect on competition (e.g. export bans). It is possible to look at the effects on third parties: Case 272/85 *Association nationale des travailleurs independants de la batellerie (Antib) v. Commission* [1987] ECR 2201.

106. *X/Open Group* OJ 1987 L35/36, [1988] 4 CMLR 542.

107. Case 22/82 *Hugin Kassaregister AB v. Commission* [1979] ECR 1869, at p. 1899, [1979] 3 CMLR 345 at p. 373.

108. See *Sugar Cartel* OJ 1973 L140/17. For a contrary (but, it is submitted, wrong) view, see the decision of the Commission in the Douwe Egbert and Van Nelle Merger under Regulation 4064/89 (see Editorial by Julian Maitland-Walker at [1991] 1 ECLR 3).

national market would fall within this category. Whish has commented that: "so wide is the meaning given to this expression in the cases . . . that it would be reasonable to start with a presumption that agreements that restrict competition will fall within Article 85 unless a clear case can be made to the contrary."[109]

It would be useful if there were a test by which one could determine whether or not a particular agreement (etc.) has an effect on inter-State trade. Sadly, there is no single universally acceptable and applicable test. There are, however, two which have developed: the STM test and the Structural test.

Test 1: STM test In Case 56/65 *Société Technique Minière v. Maschinenbau Ulm*[110] the ECJ stated that before Article 85 could apply "it must be possible to foresee with a sufficient degree of probability on the basis of a set of objective factors of law or of facts that the agreement in question may have an influence, direct or indirect, actual or potential, on the pattern of trade between Member States".

Test 2: Structural test This test examines the structure of the market. The ECJ has occasionally utilised this test (in such cases as Cases 6, 7/73 *Commercial Solvents v. Commission,*[111] Case 22/79 *Greenwich Film Production v. SACEM*[112] and Case 7/82 *GVL v. Commission*[113]) and the Commission (in such cases as *Re Vacuum Interrupters Ltd*[114] and *Polypropylene*).[115]

An agreement relating to trading outside the EC may still be subject to Article 85 where it has an effect on trade between the Member States of the EC.[116] In Cases 29, 30/83 *Compagnie Royale Asturienne des Mines SA and Rheinzink GmbH v. Commission*[117] an agreement between two undertakings in respect of exports to the Middle East was held to be subject to EC competition law because the agreement was ultimately a way of protecting the German market.

10.1.6 De minimis doctrine

10.1.6.1 Introduction

Occasionally, an agreement (etc.) falls outside the scope of Article 85 because "it has only an insignificant effect on the market, taking into account the weak position which the persons concerned have on the market of the product in question".[118]

10.1.7 Agreements falling outside Article 85(1)

Some agreements (etc.) fall outside Article 85(1). This section examines a selection of such agreements.

109. *Op. cit.*, p. 243.
110. [1966] ECR 235, [1966] CMLR 357.
111. [1974] ECR 223, [1974] 1 CMLR 309.
112. [1979] ECR 3275, [1980] 1 CMLR 629.
113. [1983] ECR 483, [1983] 3 CMLR 645.
114. [1977] L48/32, [1977] 1 CMLR D67.
115. OJ 1986 L230/1, [1988] 4 CMLR 347.
116. See *Re Franco-Japanese Ballbearings Agreement* OJ 1974 L343/19, [1975] 1 CMLR D8; *Re French and Taiwanese Mushroom Packers* OJ 1975 L29/26, [1975] 1 CMLR D83; *Aluminium Products* OJ 1985 L92/1, [1987] 3 CMLR 813; *Siemens/Fanuc* OJ 1985 L376/29, [1988] 4 CMLR 948.
117. [1984] ECR 1679, [1985] 1 CMLR 688.
118. Case 5/69 *Volk v. Vervaecke* [1969] ECR 295, [1969] CMLR 273.

10.1.7.1 Commission notice agreements

The Commission occasionally publishes "notices" which specify certain types of agreements which are deemed not to infringe Article 85(1). These are often described as "group negative clearances" or "block negative clearances". They are not, however, to be seen as group exemptions or block exemptions. Group or block exemptions are authorised by Regulation (i.e. they constitute EC law), while "group negative clearances" or "block negative clearances" are merely expressions of the Commission's thinking and do not constitute law. Nonetheless, where an undertaking relies in good faith on a Notice, the Commission will not fine such an undertaking.[119] That said, it is wise for an undertaking not to interpret too strictly any Notice from the Commission. There is a Commission *Notice on Agreements of Minor Importance*[120] adopted in 1986 on the subject of minor agreements. The Co-operation Agreements Notice outlines the types of co-operation agreements between independent firms which do not, according to the Commission, violate EC competition law. For the most part, these are joint market research, preparation of statistics and information exchange agreements. The Commission has published a *Notice on Agreements between a Principal and an Agent.*[121] The Commission has also published a *Notice on Agreements between an Undertaking and a Sub-contractor.*[122]

10.1.7.2 Agreements within a single economic unit

Article 85(1) EEC does not relate to agreements (etc.) within a single economic unit. Thus, a parent and subsidiary may enter into an agreement (etc.) which would otherwise be void provided the subsidiary has no "economic independence" from the parent company notwithstanding that it may have a separate legal personality.[123] In such circumstances, a full rigorous examination is made of the facts—for example, shareholdings, directors and actual influence—so as to determine economic independence or dependence.[124] In the case of a company having a majority shareholding in a company then it is presumed that the "parent" controls the subsidiary's business affairs.[125]

An agreement (etc.) between a principal and an agent may fall outside Article 85 EEC where the agent does not have economic independence from the principal (at least in this regard) notwithstanding that the parties may have separate legal personality.

An agreement (etc.) between a contractor and a sub-contractor falls outside Article 85 EEC because of the close economic connection between the parties. It is instructive to see the Commission Notice on this relationship.[126]

10.1.7.3 Objective necessity

Some agreements have been held to be outside the scope of Article 85 EEC because of the "objective necessity" principle. This means that some restrictions in contracts

119. Indeed the Commission may be estopped from doing so.
120. Maitland-Walker, "Notice on Agreements of Minor Importance" [1986] ECLR 337.
121. JO 1962 139/2921.
122. JO [1979] C1/2, [1979] 1 CMLR 264.
123. Case 22/71 *Beguelin Import v. GL Import Export* [1971] ECR 949, [1972] CMLR 81; Case 15/74 *Centrafarm BV v. Sterling Drug Inc* [1974] ECR 1147, [1974] 2 CMLR 480.
124. See Case 107/82 *AEG Telefunken v. Commission* [1983] ECR 3151, [1984] 3 CMLR 325.
125. Warner AG in Cases 6,7/73 *Commercial Solvents v. Commission* [1974] ECR 223, [1974] 1 CMLR 309.
126. JO 1979 C1/2, [1979] 1 CMLR 264.

which have been held to be "objectively necessary" for the performance of those contracts are not within the scope of Article 85 EEC. Thus, restrictive covenants taken on the sale of a business have been held to be "objectively necessary" and thus outside the scope of the provision.[127] Restrictions in a licence on plant breeders' rights have been held to be essential so as to allow the breeder to make full use of the seeds in question.[128] Provisions in a franchise agreement which protect the franchisor's intellectual property rights would also be "objectively necessary".[129]

10.1.7.4 Commercial risk

Occasionally, where a particular agreement (etc.) contains provisions on exclusivity, those provisions will be seen as falling outside Article 85 EEC because of the risk accepted by the distributor, licensee or franchisee.[130]

10.1.7.5 Selective distribution system

Some selective distribution systems fall outside the scope of Article 85 EEC.[131]

10.1.7.6 Mergers

In certain cases, mergers fall outside the scope of Article 85 but this is not such a serious issue since the adoption of Regulation 4064/89 on the control of concentrations.[132]

10.1.7.7 Transfer of assets

In *ENI/Montedison*[133] the Commission held that a swap of assets between two major undertakings in the thermoplastics industry which resulted in BPCL specialising in the production of polyethylene and ICI specialising in PVC was an agreement which distorted competition and was not simply a mere transfer of assets. In the end, an individual exemption was granted.

In *Mecaniver-PPG*[134] the Commission held that a sale of shares amounted to a mere transfer of assets and was thus outside Article 85. Of course, the transfer of assets could have wider implications for competition and could thereby be caught by Article 85.

10.1.7.8 Exemption

An agreement (etc.) which has been exempted by the Commission under Article 85(3) will not be struck down under Article 85(1).

127. Case 42/84 *Remia and Nutricia v. Commission* [1987] 1 CMLR 1. See also *Reuter/BASF* OJ 1976 L254/40, [1976] 2 CMLR D44.
128. Case 27/87 *Erauw-Jacquery v. La Hesbignonne* [1988] 4 CMLR 576.
129. See Case 161/84 *Pronuptia v. Schillgalis* [1986] 1 CMLR 414.
130. Case 56/65 *STM v. Maschinenbau* [1966] ECR 235, [1966] CMLR 357; Case 258/78 *Nungesser v. Commission* [1982] ECR 2015; [1983] 1 CMLR 278.
131. Leigh, "EEC Law and Selective Distribution: Recent Developments" [1986] ECLR 419.
132. OJ 1990 L257/14, 21 September 1990.
133. OJ 1987 L5/13, [1988] 4 CMLR 444.
134. OJ 1985 L35/54, [1985] 3 CMLR 359.

10.1.8 Article 85(2): Voidness [135]

10.1.8.1 Introduction

As a general principle, an agreement etc. which violates Article 85(1) is void by virtue of Article 85(2). Thus, it will be unenforceable in proceedings in national courts because Articles 85 and 86 have direct effect.

10.1.8.2 Text of Article 85(2) EEC

Article 85(2) EEC provides: "Any agreements or decisions prohibited pursuant to this Article shall be automatically void."

10.1.8.3 Penal aspect

An agreement, decision or concerted practice which violates Article 85(1) and is not exempted under Article 85(3) is void under Article 85(2). This means that the parties may be open to fines and may not rely on that agreement, decision or concerted practice in any litigation. Only those provisions of the agreement (etc.) which violate Article 85(1) are void—provided the rest can be severed.[136]

10.1.8.4 Is this really a penalty at all?

If a number of undertakings conspire to distort competition then they may not want their "agreement" to be legally enforceable in court—they are rarely going to petition a court so as to get the court's assistance in enforcing such an agreement.

10.1.9 Article 85(3): Exemptions

10.1.9.1 Introduction

An agreement (etc.) which falls within the scope of Article 85(1) might be exempted by virtue of the provisions of Article 85(3) provided the conditions specified therein are satisfied. Such an exemption will not, however, be forthcoming unless it has been specifically requested. An application for an exemption normally immunises the undertakings involved from fines unless and until the Commission takes a decision on the case.

10.1.9.2 Text of Article 85(3) EEC

Article 85(3) of the EEC Treaty provides as follows:

"The provisions of paragraph 1 may, however, be declared inapplicable in the case of:
- any agreement or category of agreements between undertakings;
- any decision or category of decisions by associations of undertakings;
- any concerted practice or category of concerted practices;

which contributes to improving the production or distribution of goods or to promoting technical or economic progress, while allowing consumers a fair share of the resulting benefit, and which does not:

---

135. See Clough and Randolph, *op. cit.* at footnote 1, para.3.2.3. See also Case 22/71 *Beguelin Import v. G.L. Import-Export* [1971] ECR 949, [1972] CMLR 81.

136. Case 56/65 *Société Technique Minière v. Maschinenbau Ulm* [1966] ECR 235 The question of severability is one of national law (Case 319/82 *Société de Vente de Ciments v. Kerpen* [1985] 1 CMLR 511).

(a) impose on the undertakings concerned restrictions which are not indispensable to the attainment of these objectives;
(b) afford such undertakings the possibility of eliminating competition in respect of a substantial part of the products in question."

10.1.9.3 Conditions for granting exemptions

10.1.9.3.1 Introduction

Exemptions may be granted either (a) individually to an individual agreement, decision or concerted practice or (b) collectively to a species of agreements, decisions or concerted practices. This distinction between individual and group exemptions is discussed below. Meanwhile, the general law relating to exemptions is examined below.

Article 85(3) sets out grounds or conditions for the granting of exemptions by the Commission. These grounds are not, in actual practice, seen as being sacrosanct and absolute. In fact, the Commission operates a very flexible regime and where it wants to exempt a particular agreement then it may do so without specifying the particular ground in Article 85(3).

10.1.9.3.2 Benefit

There must a benefit which is objectively valuable to the EC as a whole. Any advantages in the agreement (etc.) must outweigh the disadvantages.[138]

10.1.9.3.3 Fair share to the consumers

There must be a fair share of the benefit resulting from the agreement (etc.) reaching the consumer. In this situation, the "consumer" does not necessarily mean the private/personal consumer but instead means the user of the product or service.

10.1.9.3.4 No indispensable restrictions

There must be no indispensable restrictions. This does not mean however that there cannot be any restriction, for example, in research and development agreements, it may be indispensable for parent undertakings to agree to refrain from research in an area entrusted to a jointly owned subsidiary.

10.1.9.3.5 No substantial elimination of competition

An agreement (etc.) which *substantially* eliminates competition will not be given an exemption. In *Re WANO Schwarzpulver GmbH*,[139] the Commission refused an exemption in respect of an agreement which would have sealed off the UK market to further infiltration.

138. Cases 56, 58/64 *Consten and Grundig v. Commission* [1966] ECR 299, at p. 348; [1966] CMLR 418, at p. 478.
139. OJ 1978 L322/26, [1979] 1 CMLR 403.

10.1.9.4 Individual exemptions

Under Article 9(1) of Regulation 17/62, the Commission has the power to grant individual exemptions from the sanction of voidness in Article 85(2).

The Commission's decision on the issue of granting an individual exemption is subject to review by the ECJ.

The Commission does not have enough staff to deal with all the possible applications for individual exemption. The granting of individual exemptions is extremely rare. The granting of *block* exemptions and the informal settlement of cases has eased the backlog.

10.1.9.5 Block exemptions

10.1.9.5.1 Introduction

The Commission may, under the powers conferred on it by the Council of Ministers, issue block exemptions. Any agreement falling within the scope of a block exemption is valid without specific authorisation from the Commission and does not need to be specifically notified to the Commission.

Individual agreements should (where possible) be drafted in such a way as to benefit from a block exemption.

A block exemption normally contains three types of clauses: white, black and grey. White clauses are those which are valid *vis-à-vis* the block exemption. Black clauses are those which, if included in the particular agreement, will remove the agreement from the benefit of the block exemption. Grey clauses are those which do not usually fall within Article 85 EEC but are included in the block exemption for the purposes of certainty.

So as to benefit from a block exemption, an agreement (etc.) must come within the generic type envisaged by the Commission when it issued thc block exemption. This is the so-called issue of "characterisation".[140]

10.1.9.5.2 Examples

Regulation 67/67, which was the first block exemption, dealt with exclusive distribution agreements. This was replaced by Regulation 1983/83.[141] Regulation 4056/86[142] is a block exemption for liner conferences.

10.1.9.5.3 Opposition procedure

Some block exemption regulations (e.g. patent licensing, specialisation, research and development, franchising and know-how) provide for an opposition procedure.

The parties must notify the agreement on a Form A/B. They must indicate that they wish to invoke the procedure. If the Commission does not object to the agreement within a specified period then the agreement qualifies for exemption.

140. See, for example, *Italian Cast Glass* OJ 1980 L383/19, [1982] 2 CMLR 61.
141. OJ 1983 L 173/1 (see the corrigendum in OJ 1983 L281/24).
142. OJ L378/3, 31 December 1986.

10.1.9.5.4 Comfort letters

In certain circumstances, the Commission will informally settle a matter by issuing a comfort letter which is not legally binding and does not constitute a final decision at all but is extremely useful and acceptable in many situations.

10.2 ARTICLE 86

10.2.1 Introduction

Article 86 of the EEC Treaty prohibits certain types of abuse of a dominant position.[143] In essence, Article 86 provides that any abuse by one or more undertakings[144] of a dominant position[145] within the Common Market or in a substantial part[146] thereof is prohibited as being incompatible with the Common Market in so far as it may affect trade between Member States of the EC.[147] The Article is designed to control the abusive exercise of monopoly as well as oligopolistic power[148] and is complementary to Article 85 of the EEC Treaty.[149] Article 86 does not prevent the existence of dominant undertakings but it does prohibit the abuse of dominance by an undertaking of any size.[150]

It is important to highlight that, unlike Article 85 of the EEC Treaty, Article 86 of the EEC Treaty does not have an exemption procedure,[151] thus a breach of Article 86 is incurable by way of exemption.

It is interesting to recall that the first formal decision by the Commission in relation to Article 86 was not taken until 1971—fourteen years after the signing of the Treaty. This was the *GEMA* decision.[152] Since 1971, Article 86 EEC has been applied quite frequently and sometimes controversially. Article 86 is as relevant to small undertakings as large ones: size is not the determinant but market share is the key.

10.2.2 Text of Article 86 EEC

Article 86 of the EEC Treaty provides:

"Any abuse by one or more undertakings of a dominant position within the common market or in a substantial part of it shall be prohibited as incompatible with the common market in so far as it may affect trade between Member States. Such abuse may, in particular, consist in:

143. On Article 86 EEC, see Bellamy and Child, *op. cit.* at footnote 1, Chapter 8; Clough and Randolph, *op. cit.* at footnote 1, para.3.2.6; Myles, *EEC Brief* (looseleaf work), vol. 2; Vaughan, *Law of the European Communities* (1986), para.19.51 *et seq.*; Whish, *op. cit.* at footnote 1, Chapter 8. See also Korah, "Interpretation and Application of Article 86 of the Treaty of Rome: Abuse of Dominant Position within the Common Market" [1978] 53 *Notre Dame Lawyer* 768; Temple Lang, "Monopolisation and the Definition of Abuse of a Dominant Position under Article 86 EEC Treaty" (1979) 16 CML Rev. 345.

144. On the concept of "undertakings", see para.10.1.3.1, above.

145. On the concept of "dominant position", see para.10.2.8, below.

146. On the concept of "the common market or in a substantial part" see para.10.1.5, above.

147. On the concept of "affecting trade between Member States" see para.10.1.5, above.

148. Bellamy and Child, *op. cit.* at footnote 1 above, para.8-002.

149. On Article 85 of the EEC Treaty, see para.10.1 *et seq.* above.

150. It is important to recall that an undertaking may be abusing its dominant position without necessarily having a monopoly.

151. On the exemption procedure contained in Article 85 EEC, see para.10.1.9, above. Although a "negative clearance" decision or letter of comfort may be issued (Regulation 17/62, Article 2) generally but not so in the case of Regulation 4056/86.

152. JO 1971 L134/15; [1971] CMLR D35.

(a) directly or indirectly imposing unfair purchase or selling prices or unfair trading conditions;
(b) limiting production, markets or technical development to the prejudice of consumers;
(c) applying dissimilar conditions to equivalent transactions with other trading parties, thereby placing them at a competitive disadvantage;
(d) making the conclusion of contracts subject to acceptance by the other parties of supplementary obligations which, by their nature or according to commercial usage, have no connection with the subject of such contracts."

10.2.3 Importance of economic evidence

Economic evidence is critical in almost all the decisions and cases on competition generally but this is particularly so in Article 86 cases and therefore lawyers contemplating bringing proceedings under that provision are well advised to seek the opinions of economists at an early stage in the proceedings. Whish has written:

"[i]n Article 86 cases, perhaps more than in any other part of UK and EEC competition law, economic analysis is critical. An understanding of the basic economic concepts is vital, since transgressions of Article 86 can have serious consequences. Legal advisers involved in Article 86 cases will often need expert advice from economists in order properly to prepare an offence or defence under Article 86."[153]

This is very true but it is a pity that the ECJ does not always adhere to the principle.[154]

10.2.4 Interpretation of Article 86 EEC

The ECJ has made clear in a number of cases that Article 86 must be interpreted having regard to the spirit, general scheme and wording of the provision as well as to the general objectives of the EEC Treaty itself.[155] Thus, such provisions of the EEC Treaty as Articles 2[156] and 3(f)[157] are of critical concern.[158]

10.2.5 Economic rationale for Article 86 EEC

Korah has set out the economic rationale for Article 86 EEC in the following terms:

"[t]he objection to market power[159] expressed by economists is that a firm,[160] not sufficiently constrained by competitive pressures, may be able to operate inefficiently for long periods, or earn high profits, through charging higher prices than would be possible in more competitive conditions. The higher prices would reduce demand, so that some buyers, who would have been willing to pay the cost (including a normal profit on the funds employed) of an efficient operator, will be disappointed. The resources, that in terms of consumer demand might have been more usefully employed in making the monopolised product, would be devoted to less strongly desired uses. Classical economists objected to the discretion enjoyed by a monopolist. The emphasis of modern economics is even more general, and is focused upon the wide discretion enjoyed by

153. *Op. cit.* at footnote 1, at p. 278 (footnote omitted).

154. See, for example, the *Commercial Solvents v. Commission* case.

155. Case 6/72 *Europemballage Corpn and Continental Can Co Inc v. Commission* [1973] ECR 215, [1973] CMLR 199; Joined Cases 6, 7/73 *Instituto Chemioterapico Italiano SpA and Commercial Solvents Corpn v. Commission* [1974] ECR 223, [1974] 1 CMLR 309; Case 27/76 *United Brands Co v. Commission* [1978] ECR 207, [1978] 1 CMLR 429, ECJ; Case 85/76 *Hoffmann-La Roche and Co AG v. Commission* [1979] ECR 461, [1979] 3 CMLR 211; Case 322/81 *Nederlandsche Banden-Industrie Michelin NV v. Commission* [1983] ECR 3461, [1985] 1 CMLR 282.

156. On Article 2, see Appendix 1, below.

157. On Article 3(f), see Appendix 1 below.

158. On the interpretation generally of Article 86 EEC, see Korah, "Interpretation and Application of Article 86 of the Treaty of Rome: Abuse of Dominant Position within the Common Market" [1978] 53 *Notre Dame Lawyer* 768.

159. *Ed.*, *i.e.* dominance.

160. *Ed.*, *i.e.* undertaking.

firms[161] with market power to pursue a variety of goals and to choose a range of productive means, unconstrained within wide limits by market pressures. In a more competitive market, each firm is limited by the value for money provided by other firms. In most markets many firms may enjoy some discretion over their production and marketing strategies, but this is not the general independence that enables high prices to be maintained over long periods."[162]

10.2.6 Check-list for the successful application of Article 86 EEC

Article 86 EEC is somewhat curiously drafted and thus it may be useful to construct a check-list of the conditions which must be satisfied before Article 86 EEC can be successfully applied:

(1) Is the entity involved an "undertaking"?
(2) Does a dominant position exist?
(3) Does the dominant position exist in the common market or a substantial part of it?
(4) Is there an abuse of that dominant position?
(5) Is it possible that the abuse may have an effect on trade between Member States?

10.2.7 Undertakings

Most of what was written in paragraph 10.1.3.1, above, in relation to Article 85 is also relevant in the context of Article 86. Some points must, however, be made on the concept of an "undertaking" when used in the context of Article 86.[163] First, an undertaking which has a "dominant position" conferred on it by law is still an undertaking and falls within the scope of Article 86.[164] Secondly, as a general rule, no Member State may confer an immunity from Article 86 of the EEC Treaty on an undertaking by conferring on it certain legal privileges. This is based on the duties imposed on a Member State by virtue of Articles 3(f) and 5 of the EEC Treaty.[165] The sole exception to this rule is in regard to the limited privileges which a Member State may confer on an undertaking by virtue of Article 90(2) of the EEC Treaty. This sole exception is also a very limited one in that the Commission and the courts interpret the exception quite narrowly. Thirdly, the dominant position may be held by one undertaking (a monopoly) or it may be held by two or more undertakings (a duopoly or an oligopoly). It appears (though it is far from settled in the case-law of the courts) that not all of the undertakings need engage in the abuse.[166]

10.2.8 Concept of a dominant position or dominance

10.2.8.1 Introduction

Article 86 applies to situations where there has been an abuse of a dominant position. Thus, it is critical to determine, *inter alia*, what constitutes a dominant position.

161. *Ibid.*
162. *Op. cit.*, p.109.
163. See also the comments on undertakings in the context of Article 85 in para. 10.1.3.1 above.
164. Case 311/84 *Centre Belge d'Etudes de Marche Tele-Marketing v. CLT* [1986] 2 CMLR 558, at para.16; Case 26/75 *General Motors v. Commission* [1975] ECR 1367, [1976] 1 CMLR 95; Case 41/83 *Italy v. Commission* [1985] ECR 873, [1985] 2 CMLR 368; and Case 226/84 *BL v. Commission* [1987] 1 CMLR 185.
165. See Whish, *op. cit.* at footnote 1, pp. 276–277.
166. Smit and Herzog, *The Law of the European Economic Community—A Commentary on the EEC Treaty* (looseleaf), p. 3–282.

Dominance can only be determined in respect of a particular market—it is not an abstract concept. There is a wealth of judicial as well as academic[167] discussion on the concept and thus what is presented here is merely a précis of that discussion.

10.2.8.2 There is no definition in the EEC Treaty

The EEC Treaty does not define the concept of "dominant position". Interestingly, Article 66(7) of the ECSC Treaty, which is the comparable provision for the European Coal and Steel Community, makes an attempt at definition.[168]

10.2.8.3 The definition used by the EEC institutions

10.2.8.3.1 Introduction

The ECJ has in a number of cases[169] attempted to determine what constitutes a dominant position and its view may be summarised by the words it used in Case 322/81 *Michelin v. Commission* to define dominance as: ". . . a position of economic strength enjoyed by an undertaking which enables it to hinder the maintenance of effective competition on the relevant market by allowing it to behave to an appreciable extent independently of its competitors and customers and ultimately of consumers."[170] In essence, this means the power to act independently of competitors or to be able to effectively eliminate competition. In Case 6/72 *Continental Can*[171] the ECJ said:

"[u]ndertakings are in a dominant position when they have the power to behave independently, which puts them in a position to act without taking into account their competitors, purchasers or suppliers. That is a position when, because of their share of the market, or of their share of the market combined with the availability of technical knowledge, raw materials or capital, they have the power to determine prices or to control production or distribution for a significant part of the products in question. This power does not necessarily have to derive from an absolute domination permitting the undertakings which hold it to eliminate all will on the part of their economic partners, but it is enough that they be strong enough as a whole to ensure to those undertakings an overall independence of behaviour, even if there are differences in intensity in their influence on the different partial markets."

Temple Lang has written that:

167. See, *inter alia*, Baden Fuller, "Article 86 EEC: Economic Analysis of the Existence of a Dominant Position" (1979) 4 EL Rev 423; Gyselen and Kyriakis, "Article 86 EEC: the Monopoly Power Measurement Issue Revisited" (1986) 11 EL Rev 134; and Korah, "Concept of a Dominant Position within the meaning of Article 86" (1980) 17 CML Rev 395.

168. Article 66(7) ECSC provides: "If the High Authority finds that public or private undertakings which, in law or in fact, hold or acquire in the market for one of the products within its jurisdiction a dominant position shielding them against effective competition in a substantial part of the common market are using that position for purposes contrary to the objectives of this Treaty, it shall make to them such recommendations as may be appropriate to prevent the position from being so used. If these recommendations are not implemented satisfactorily within a reasonable time, the High Authority shall, by decisions taken in consultation with the Government concerned, determine the prices and conditions of sale to be applied by the undertaking in question to draw up production or delivery programmes with which it must comply, subject to liability to the penalties provided for in Articles 58, 59 and 64."

169. E.g. Case 27/76 *United Brands v. Commission* [1978] ECR 207, [1978] 1 CMLR 429; Case 85/76 *Hoffmann-La Roche v. Commission* [1979] ECR 461, [1979] 3 CMLR 211; Case 31/80 *L'Oreal NV v. De Nieuwe AMCK PVBA* [1980] ECR 3775, [1981] 2 CMLR 235; Case 322/81 *Nederlandsche Banden-Industrie Michelin NV v. Commission* [1983] ECR 3461, [1985] 1 CMLR 282.

170. [1983] ECR 3461, [1985] 1 CMLR 282 at para.30. See also Case 27/76 *United Brands v. Commission* [1978] ECR 207, [1978] 1 CMLR 429, paras.65–66.

171. [1973] ECR 215, [1973] CMLR 199.

"a dominant position is economic power, due to lack of competition, of which the holder can take advantage to impede effective competition. An enterprise may have a dominant position, even if effective competition has not been eliminated. To determine whether a dominant position exists, all facts tending to prove or disprove the market power of the enterprise must be taken into account. The effect of a series of findings may be cumulative, especially if only one enterprise on the market enjoys all the competitive advantages considered. No single fact is necessarily decisive."[172]

Dominance is to be decided in each case. It is a question of fact. Market share is not in itself the sole determinant of the issue. Korah has written that undertakings which have over 40% of the market and are considerably larger than other undertakings in that market should be regarded as being dominant.[173]

What are the factors which the courts will take into account in determining the existence or non-existence of dominance? A non-exhaustive list would, it is submitted, include a high degree of vertical integration, technological lead, a highly developed sales network and the absence of potential competition.[174] Regard must be had to the relevant product, geographical and temporal markets.

10.2.8.3.2 The product or services market

It is necessary to determine the relevant product or services[175] market. The ECJ quashed the Commission's decision in the *Continental Can*[176] case because the Commission did not properly define the relevant product market. The Commission has now become more careful[177] and, while a number of challenges have been brought on the basis of the Commission's determinations on "relevant product markets", the ECJ does not readily quash the Commission's determinations on this point alone.[178]

The institutions have shied away from defining what constitutes the "relevant product market". However, it is clear from the judgments that "interchangeability" is the essential element in the definition: if goods or services can be interchanged then they are within the same product market. Thus, the ECJ said in Case 6/72 *Continental Can v. Commission* that it was necessary to look at those "characteristics of the products in question by virtue of which they are particularly apt to satisfy an inelastic need and are only to a limited extent interchangeable with other products".[179] The ECJ said in Case 27/76 *United Brands v. Commission*[180] that the issue of whether a product market existed turned on whether the product can be "singled out by such special features distinguishing it from other fruits that it is only to a limited extent interchangeable with

172. "Some Aspects of Abuse of Dominant Position in European Community Antitrust Law" (1979–1980) 3 *Fordham International Law Forum* 1, at p. 4.

173. *An Introductory Guide to EEC Competition Law and Practice* (Oxford, 1978), p. 115.

174. Myles, *op. cit.*, para. 37.

175. See *Decca Navigator Systems* OJ 1989 L43/27.

176. [1973] ECR 215, [1973] 1 CMLR 199, para.32.

177. Note, however, *Hoffmann v. La Roche* OJ 1976 L223/27, [1977] 2 CMLR D25.

178. Cases 6,7/73 *ICI and Commercial Solvents v. Commission* [1974] ECR 223, [1974] 1 CMLR 309; Case 27/76 *United Brands v. Commission* [1978] ECR 207, [1978] 1 CMLR 429; Case 322/81 *Nederlandsche Banden-Industrie Michelin v. Commission* [1983] ECR 3461, [1985] 1 CMLR 282.

179. [1973] ECR 215, [1973] CMLR 199, at para. 32. In Case 66/86 *Ahmed Saeed* [1990] 4 CMLR 102 or paras. 39 and 40, the ECJ said in relation to a scheduled flight and the issue of dominance): "the test to be employed is whether the scheduled flight on a particular route can be distinguished from the possible alternatives by virtue of specific characteristics as a result of which it is not interchangeable with those alternatives and is affected only to an insignificant degree by competition from them."

180. [1978] ECR 207, [1978] 1 CMLR 429.

them and is only exposed to their competition in a way that is hardly perceptible". In determining interchangeability, regard must be had to, among other things, both demand-side and supply-side interchangeability where relevant and accurate evidence is available.[181] The emphasis is, however, on the demand-side interchangeability.

Cross-elasticity of demand is high where an increase in the price of one product causes a significant switch by consumers to another product. Cross-elasticity is low where an increase in the price of one product will not cause a significant switch by consumers to another product. Thus, for example, an increase in the price of one brand of washing powder ("Brand X") will probably cause an increase in the demand for other brands of cheaper washing powder ("Brand Y" and "Brand Z"). Thus, Brands X, Y and Z are cross-elastic (i.e. cross-elasticity is high). On the other hand, an increase in the price of a brand of washing powder ("Brand X") will probably not cause consumers to switch from buying a more expensive newspaper ("Title A") to a cheaper one ("Title B"). Thus, Brand X and Titles A and B are not cross-elastic to any significant extent.

Products are not interchangeable simply because of their prices. An expensive luxury car may have the same essential physical characteristics as a cheap basic car, but the two would not necessarily be interchangeable at all.

The physical characteristics of the goods involved in the market should be taken into account so as to test interchangeability. Thus, for example, in Case 27/76 *United Brands v. Commission*,[182] the court took into account such physical characteristics of bananas (the goods in question) as their taste, softness, consumption by the old and sick, seedlessness and handling quality.

It is useful in determining the relevant product market, to establish what is the intended use to which the product may be put by the user. Thus, if a consumer requires a product for a particular purpose then that product will be within the same market only as products which satisfy the same purpose.[183] Thus, spare parts may form a separate market from the products for which they are needed or even some spare parts may be distinguishable from the machine itself.[184,185]

In determining the relevant product market, it is often useful to examine the structure of supply and demand on a market. Thus, in Case 322/81 *Nederlandsche Banden-Industrie Michelin v. Commission*,[186] the ECJ found that the replacement tyre market was a distinct market from the new tyre market because replacement tyres were fitted in different circumstances from new tyres. Indeed raw material may constitute a separate product market from the finished product.[187]

The relevant product market may be neatly defined by means of legislation.[188] Thus, in Case 226/84 *BL v. Commission*[189] the market (approval certificates) was held in law by BL in respect of BL vehicles and no one else could interfere.

181. Case 6/72 *Continental Can v. Commission* [1973] ECR 215, [1973] 1 CMLR 199; *Eurofix-Bauco v. Hilti* OJ 1988 L65/19, [1989] 4 CMLR 677.

182. [1978] ECR 207, [1978] 1 CMLR 429.

183. See Cases 6,7/73 *ICI and Commercial Solvents Corpn v. Commission* [1974] ECR 223, [1974] 1 CMLR 309; Case 6/72 *Europemballage Corpn and Continental Can v. Commission* [1973] ECR 215, [1973] CMLR 199; Case 22/78 *Hugin v. Commission* [1979] ECR 1869, [1979] 3 CMLR 345.

184. Case 22/78 *Hugin v. Commission* [1979] ECR 1869, [1979] 3 CMLR 345.

185. Case 238/87 *AB Volvo v. Erik Veng* [1989] 4 CMLR 122.

186. [1983] ECR 3461, [1985] 1 CMLR 282.

187. Cases 6, 7/73 *Commercial Solvents v. Commission* [1974] ECR 223, [1974] 1 CMLR 309.

188 *E.g.* a national or EC law may limit the use to which a product may be put by the user.

189. [1987] 1 CMLR 185.

Occasionally, the Commission and the courts may have recourse to extrinsic evidence. This evidence may take the form of marketing plans or documents. Thus, for example, in *BBI/Boosey and Hawkes (Interim Measures)*,[190] the Commission took into account internal documents in which Boosey and Hawkes identified a discrete or distinct market for British brass band musical instruments as opposed to brass musical instruments generally.

10.2.8.3.3 Supply-side substitutability

Supply-side substitutability should also be taken into account in some cases. This means that the market should be examined from the buyer's perspective.[191] This is, however, of very limited relevance as far as most cases are concerned.

10.2.8.4 Relevant geographical market

The relevant geographical market must also be determined. There must be an area in which the objective conditions of competition are the same for all competitors.[192] The market may be the whole of the EEC,[193] but the market does not have to be geographically enormous: it could be Britain and Ireland[194] or even just Ireland (Northern or Southern).[195] Suffice it to say that if an undertaking operates on a localised basis then it may still possess power over that market.[196] The geographical market may be easily drawn. In *British Telecommunications*[197] the market was easily defined where they related to where particular telecommunications services were available. A particular ferry route is unlikely to be a substantial part of the common market but may be the relevant geographical market.[198]

10.2.8.5 Relevant temporal market

In determining the existence (or non-existence) of dominance, regard must be had to the temporal dimension of the market. An undertaking may, for example, be exposed

190. OJ 1987 L286/36, [1988] 4 CMLR 67.

191. Case 6/72 *Continental Can v Commission* [1973] ECR 215, [1973] CMLR 199.

192. See *Decca Navigator Systems* OJ 1989 L43/27.

193. As in *Hilti* OJ 1988 L65/19, [1989] 4 CMLR 677; on appeal Case 98/88 *Hilti AG v. Commission.*

194. As in *BPB Industries plc* OJ 1989 L10/50, on appeal *British Plasterboard Industries plc and British Gypsum v. Commission.* See also Case 27/76 *United Brands v. Commission* [1978] ECR 207, [1978] CMLR 429, para.44.

195. As in *Magill TV Guide/ITP, BBC and RTE* OJ 1989 L78/43, on appeal Cases 76/89 etc. *RTE v. Commission.*

196. *Cf.* Tenth Report on Competition Policy, point 57.

197. OJ 1982 L360/36, [1983] 1 CMLR 457; upheld on appeal Case 41/83 *Italy v. Commission* [1985] ECR 873, [1985] 2 CMLR 368.

198. In answer to a written question in the European Parliament (Written Question 1377/83 at OJ C38/37, 13.2.84), the EC Commission stated that the Harwich/Hook of Holland route was not a substantial part of the common market. It is interesting to note that the EC Commission may be prepared to treat as a "substantial part" the market for the whole of a member state's liner trade with certain non-EC states, which constitutes a substantial part of the trade between those states and the EC as a whole, because that state is the largest EC trading partner with the states concerned (*e.g.* the investigations into West and Central African trades referred to in the Nineteenth Competition report, para.28)—for further details, see Clough and Randolph, *op. cit.* at footnote 1 above, para.3.2.6.2, footnote 2. Note, however, the 1992 *Aer Lingus/British Midland* decision where the London/Dublin air route must have been a substantial part of the common market.

to competition for parts of the year but entirely immune from it at other times of the year. This may be the case in such markets as fruit[199] or oil.[200]

10.2.11 Market power

10.2.11.1 Introduction

It is also necessary to determine whether or not the undertaking(s) has sufficient market power as to be dominant. In Case 27/76 *United Brands v. Commission*,[201] the ECJ stated that dominance "relates to a position of economic strength enjoyed by an undertaking which enables it to prevent effective competition being maintained on the relevant market by affording it the power to behave to an appreciable extent independently of its competitors, customers and ultimately of its consumers".

10.2.11.2 Measuring market power

If a legal monopoly exists then the undertaking has, *ex hypothesi*, sufficient market power as to be regarded as dominant.

It was argued unsuccessfully in Case 41/83 *Italy v. Commission*[202] and Case 311/84 *Centre Belge d'Etudes de Marche Tele-Marketing v. CLT*[203] that notwithstanding that the undertaking has been granted a legal monopoly, it is still subject to Article 86 EEC, except insofar as it is in any way protected by Article 90(2) EEC.

10.2.11.3 Market shares

Market share is an important (but not the sole) determinant of market power. As a simple rule, the larger the market share, the greater chance of dominance existing. A market share of 100% would constitute dominance![204] A large market share is not in itself the sole determinant of dominance. An undertaking may have a large market share but may be selling its products at a highly marginal rate.

The ECJ said in Case 85/76 *Hoffmann-La Roche v. Commission*:

> "[f]urthermore although the importance of the market shares may vary from one market to another the view may legitimately be taken that very large shares are in themselves, and save in exceptional circumstances, evidence of the existence of a dominant position. An undertaking which has a very large market share and holds it for some time . . . is by virtue of that share in a position of strength."[205]

The Commission might well, however, place great reliance on market share in a case where interim measures are sought and the Commission has to move quickly.[206] In such cases and in cases where the Commission and the courts are placing great emphasis on the market share, it is highly possible that a share of 40% to 45% or more would

199. Case 27/76 *United Brands v. Commission* [1978] ECR 207, [1978] 1 CMLR 429.
200. *ABG* OJ 1977 L117/1, [1977] 2 CMLR D1.
201. [1978] ECR 207, [1978] 1 CMLR 429.
202. [1985] ECR 873, [1985] 2 CMLR 368.
203. [1986] 2 CMLR 558.
204. See *GVL* OJ 1981 L370/49, [1982] 1 CMLR 221.
205. [1979] ECR 461, [1979] 3 CMLR 211. See Case 27/76 *United Brands v. Commission* [1978] ECR 207, [1978] 1 CMLR 429, paras. 65 and 66.
206. *ECS/AKZO* OJ 1983 L252/13, [1983] 3 CMLR 694.

constitute dominance. It has been said that a share of 20% to 40% may, in certain circumstances, amount to dominance.[207]

10.2.11.4 Barriers to entry

As was written above, market share is not the only determinant: it is necessary to look at other "barriers to entry". The Commission and the courts have interpreted the concept of a "barrier to entry" quite widely and what is presented here is a basic list.

10.2.11.4.1 Economies of scale

The ECJ was willing, in Case 27/76 *United Brands v. Commission*,[208] to take into account "economies of scale" as barriers to entry and thus as a factor in determining dominance. It is not just the courts who use the test. The Commission is also willing to take the economies of scale into account in determing the existence of dominance.[209]

10.2.11.4.2 Evidence of the undertakings

The undertakings themselves may (externally and/or internally) express dominance. In *BBI/Boosey and Hawkes: Interim Measures*[210] the managers of Boosey and Hawkes wrote that its instruments were "automatically [the] first choice" of all the brass bands in Britain.

10.2.11.4.3 Price movements

The fact that an undertaking was able unilaterally to raise its prices, with the market following suit, indicated dominance in one case.[211]

10.2.11.4.4 Conduct

The conduct of the undertaking(s) is relevant and admissible in determining whether or not it is in a dominant position in the market place.[212]

10.2.11.4.5 Overall strength and size of the undertaking(s)

Just because an undertaking is large does not mean that it is dominant. However, in Case 85/76 *Hoffmann-La Roche v. Commission*,[213] the Commission did take into account the size of the undertaking in question.

207. Whish, *op. cit.* at footnote 1 above, p. 294. It is worth noting that a loss-making undertaking may be dominant: Case 322/81 *Michelin v. Commission* [1983] ECR 3461, [1985] 1 CMLR 282, para. 59.
208. [1978] ECR 207, [1978] 1 CMLR 429.
209. *BPB Industries plc* OJ 1989 L10/50, at para.116.
210. OJ 1987 L286/36, [1988] 4 CMLR 67, at para.18.
211. *Napier Brown-British Sugar* OJ 1988 L284/41, para. 55.
212. See Case 27/76 *United Brands v. Commission* [1978] ECR 207, [1978] 1 CMLR 429, at para.122; Case 322/81 *Michelin v. Commission* [1983] ECR 3461, [1985] 1 CMLR 282; Decision 88/138 *Eurofix-Bauco v. Hilti* OJ 1988 L65/19, [1989] 4 CMLR 677.
213. [1979] ECR 461, [1979] 3 CMLR 211.

10.2.11.4.6 Legal provisions

National legal rules, such as intellectual property rights, can operate as barriers to entry.[214]

10.2.11.4.7 Deep pocket

The existence of a "deep pocket" on the part of an undertaking may, in practice, be regarded as evidence of dominance.[215]

10.2.12 Within the Common Market or a substantial part of it

If the dominant position is not in the whole or in a substantial part of the common market then Article 86 EEC cannot, by its own terms, apply. This is a form of *de minimis* principle. If an undertaking (or undertakings) operates throughout the EC then there is little difficulty. If an undertaking (or undertakings) operates (or operate) in one Member State or in a part of a Member State then a number of points are worth remembering about the issue of "a substantial part of the Common Market"—which has, incidentally, been defined (rather unhelpfully) by Smit and Herzog as "any non-negligible part of a Member State".[216] First, each Member State is almost certainly "a substantial part of the Common Market" for present purposes.[217] Secondly, a part of a Member State may well constitute "a substantial part of the Common Market" for present purposes.[218] In *Re European Sugar Cartel*, "Southern Germany" was held to constitute a "substantial part" of the Common Market.[219] Thirdly, there are no "fixed percentages". Indeed, in Case 77/77 *BP v. Commission*, the Advocate-General in the case (AG Warner) was of the opinion that the Dutch market for petrol—then 4.6% of the EC total—constituted a substantial part of the common market.[220]

10.2.13 Concept of "Abuse of a Dominant Position"

10.2.13.1 Introduction

Article 86 of the EEC Treaty does not prohibit *per se* an undertaking from having or acquiring a dominant position; but it does prevent an undertaking *abusing* such a position. As the ECJ said in Case 322/81 *Michelin v. Commission*:

> "A finding that an undertaking has a dominant position is not in itself a recrimination (*reproche*) but simply means that, irrespective of the reasons for which it has such a dominant position, the undertaking concerned has a special responsibility not to allow its conduct to impair genuine undistorted competition on the common market."[221]

---

214. Case 22/78 *Hugin v. Commission* [1979] ECR 1869, [1979] 3 CMLR 345.
215. Case 27/76 *United Brands v. Commission* [1979] ECR 461, [1979] 3 CMLR 211, at para.48.
216. Para. 3-257. In Case 40/73 etc. *Suiker Unie v. Commission* [1975] ECR 1663, [1976] 1 CMLR 295, the ECJ stated: "for the purpose of determining whether a specific territory is large enough to amount to a 'substantial part of the common market', the pattern and volume of the production and consumption of the said product as well as the habits and economic opportunities of vendors and purchasers must be considered."
217. Whish, *op. cit.*, p. 301.
218. Case 40/73 *Suiker Unie v. Commission* [1975] ECR 1663, [1976] 1 CMLR 295.
219. [1973] CMLR D65.
220. [1978] ECR 1513, [1978] 3 CMLR 174.
221. *Ibid.*

10.2.13.2 Definition of abuse

Article 86 does not contain an exhaustive list of the "abuses" in which an undertaking could engage when it has a dominant position—the provision has in fact been applied to situations which are not expressly set out in the text—as Whish has commented, Article 86 amounts to a "formidable weapon".[222] Nor does it define the concept of abuse. Juristically, the concept of abuse has been classified into three branches: (a) anti-competitive abuses; (b) explotative abuses; and (c) reprisal abuses.

Temple Lang has offered the following view of the concept of abuse:

> "a dominant enterprise may act contrary to Article 86 for any of the following reasons: (1) if its behaviour takes advantage of economic power to obtain benefits or to impose burdens not obtainable or imposable in conditions of normal and reasonably effective competition, at the expense of the interests of customers or consumers (or, in the case or a dominant buyer, of suppliers). These are "exploitative" abuses; (2) if its behaviour significantly restricts intra-brand or inter-brand competition, or alters the market in such a way that competition is likely to be significantly reduced, or increases or reinforces the dominant firm's economic power. However, normal and legitimate competition is lawful, even if it increases the market share or economic power of the dominant enterprise. These are "anti-competitive" abuses; (3) if its behaviour is calculated to damage or seriously interfere with the business of another enterprise. If these abuses are to be regarded as a separate category, they can be called "reprisal" abuses."[223]

10.2.13.3 Exploitation

Exploitation by an undertaking of its dominant position would normally constitute an abuse of its dominant position.[224]

10.2.13.4 Anti-competitive abuses

Article 86 also applies to anti-competitive behaviour. Such behaviour may be directed against new entrants or existing competitors. Thus, practices such as mergers which would be anti-competitive,[225] price discrimination,[226] requirements contracts and tie-ins,[227] export and import bans,[228] and refusals to supply[229] could be subject to the sanction of Article 86. Article 8 of Regulation 1017/68 gives examples of abuse in the inland transport sector for example, directly or indirectly imposing unfair transport terms.

10.2.14 Effect on inter-State trade

It is submitted that the discussion above, relating to "effect on inter-State trade" is again applicable, *mutatis mutandis* to the provision presently under review and only one further point needs to be made in the present context.

The ECJ stated in the course of its judgment in Cases 6, 7/73 *Commercial Solvents v. Commission*[230] that the requirement of having an effect on inter-State trade was satisfied

222. *Op. cit.* at footnote 1, p. 302. It will be recalled that Article 86 EEC contains four examples.
223. *Ibid.*, pp. 363–364.
224. *British Telecommunications* OJ 1982 L360/36, [1983] 1 CMLR 457.
225. *Cf.* Case 6/72 *Europemballage Corpn and Continental Can Co. Inc. v. Commission* [1973] ECR 215, [1973] CMLR 199.
226. See, for example, *British Telecommunications* OJ [1982] L360/36, [1983] 1 CMLR 457.
227. Case 85/76 *Hoffmann-La Roche v. Commission* [1979] ECR 461, [1979] 3 CMLR 211.
228. *Cf.* Case 40/73 etc. *Suiker Unie v. Commission* [1975] ECR 1663, [1976] 1 CMLR 295.
229. Case 6/73 etc. *Commercial Solvents v. Commission* [1974] ECR 223, [1974] 1 CMLR 309.
230. [1974] ECR 223, [1974] 1 CMLR 309.

where the conduct engaged in by the undertaking(s) resulted in an alteration of the structure of competition in the common market. This is the so-called structural test. It has been applied by the Commission and the courts on a number of occasions—most notably, Cases 27/76 *United Brands v. Commission*[231]; 327/88 *Tetra Pak Rausing SDA v. Commission*; *Napier Brown-British Sugar*[232] and *London European-Sabena.*[233] It is submitted that it is the most suitable test for oligopolistic markets.

10.3 COMPETITION PROCEDURE

This book is about the substantive law of the EC as it relates to shipping. It touches on EC competition law and must, by sheer limitation of size, touch only marginally on competition procedure. Thus, recourse should be had to the established works on this subject for greater depth and detail.[234] What follows here is merely an overview of EC competition procedure generally.[235]

10.3.1 Role of the Commission

The Commission should administer the system of competition in a way which is above politics[236] or reproach. Council Regulation 17/62[237] is the legislative basis for Commission's actions in this area. It relates to the application and enforcement of Articles 85 and 86 of the EEC Treaty.

10.3.2 Role of the national authorities and courts

The various national authorities have a role to play in the enforcement of EEC competition law.[238] The national authorities are competent to apply EEC competition law so long as the EC has not initiated any procedure to enforce the competition rules. They also play a part in the investigation of suspected breaches of EEC competition law. National courts may also grant damages for breaches of EEC competition law.

10.3.3 Initiation of proceedings

Competition cases may be initiated in any one of four ways: notification by the parties to the Commission of their arrangements or activities; a complaint by a third party to the Commission of the arrangements or activities of others; by the initiative of the

231. [1978] ECR 207, [1978] 1 CMLR 429.
232. OJ 1988 L284/41, paras 77-80.
233. OJ 1988 L317/47, [1989] 4 CMLR 662, para. 33.
234. See Kerse, *Antitrust Procedure* (1988) as well as the books mentioned in footnote 1 above. See also Kreis, "Commission Procedures in Competition Proceedings—Recent Reforms in Practice and Law" in 1983 Fordham Corp. L. Inst. 145 (B. Hawk ed., 1984); Kreis, "EEC Commission Investigation Procedures in Competition Cases" (1983) 17 Int'l Law 19.
235. For the details relating to Regulation 4056/86, see Chapter 12, below.
236. See the Editorial by Julian Maitland-Walker entitled "The Unacceptable Face of Politics in Competition Cases" [1991] 1 ECLR 3.
237. OJ Sp.Edn. (Eng.) 1959-1962, p. 57.
238. See Basedow, "National Authorities in European Airline Competition Law" [1988] ECLR 342; Bentil, "Common Market Anti-Trust Law and Restrictive Business Agreements or Practices prompted by National Regulatory Measures" [1988] ECLR 354.

Commission itself to investigate a particular case; or by reason of an investigation by the Commission of a particular industrial sector.

10.3.4 Notification

Notification by the parties to the Commission of their arrangements or activities is a voluntary act. The arrangements may be notified so as to obtain a negative clearance or an individual[239] exemption. A negative clearance indicates that the Commission does not believe that the arrangements violate EC competition law. An exemption admits that there is a violation of Article 85(1) but provides that in the overall context of competition (seen in the light of Article 85(3) of the EEC Treaty), an exemption would be appropriate.

While it is a voluntary decision to notify, there may be a tactical advantage because the Commission may not, as a general rule,[240] fine undertakings in respect of activities carried out after notification and only the Commission may grant an exemption.

10.3.5 Complaints[241]

A complaint may be made by a third party to the Commission of the arrangements or activities of others. The complaint may be made by a Member State, a legal person or a human being. Any complainant other than a Member State must show that it has a legitimate interest. The complaint may be made in writing[242] or orally.

10.3.6 Own-initiative investigations[243]

The Commission has investigated particular undertakings on occasion. It may have learned of developments by, for example, an investigation into another undertaking or by monitoring developments generally.

10.3.7 Sector investigations[244]

The Commission has power to investigate particular industrial sectors. It has used this power on a number of occasions, most notably in the context of the brewing industry.

10.3.8 Conduct of proceedings

10.3.8.1 Fact-finding

The Commission may establish the facts of a particular case either by requesting information from various quarters or conducting investigations.

10.3.8.2 Requests for information[245]

The Commission has power to request information under Article 11 of Regulation 17/62. The Commission may ask the addressee of the request to voluntarily comply with

239. If the arrangements already qualify for a block exemption then no notification is needed.
240. See Regulation 17/62, Article 15(6).
241. See Ritter *et al., op. cit.* at footnote 1 above, pp. 617–622.
242. Form C has been provided by the Commission so as to facilitate complaints.
243. See Ritter *et al., op. cit.* at footnote 1 above, p. 622.
244. This is an important power which may well be used in the shipping sector.
245. See Ritter *et al., op. cit.*, at footnote 1 above, pp. 626–632.

the request or may formally decide to compel the addressee to respond and fine the addressee for not responding.

10.3.8.3 Investigations[246]

The Commission has the power to conduct investigations of premises (including ships) so as to gather information. Some of these investigations are unannounced and are often gloriously described as "dawn-raids". While conducting such an investigation, the Commission may ask questions and take copies or extracts from books or business records.

10.3.8.4 Legal professional privilege

Legal professional privilege may be claimed in certain circumstances but it is not absolute.[247]

10.3.9 Conclusion of proceedings

10.3.9.1 Introduction

A competition case may end in a variety of ways, including, the granting of a negative clearance, the granting of an exemption or the so-called termination of proceedings.

10.3.9.2 Negative clearance

The Commission may decide that the notified arrangements do not violate Article 85(1) or 86 of the EEC Treaty and may decide to grant a "Negative Clearance" which formally states that the arrangements do not violate these Treaty provisions.

10.3.9.3 Exemption

The Commission may decide[248] that the notified arrangements do violate Article 85(1) of the EEC Treaty but may decide to grant an "Exemption" because the arrangements justify the application of Article 85(3).

10.3.9.4 Termination of proceedings

The Commission may also decide to terminate the proceedings. It may decide to impose a fine on the undertakings. Fines may be upto 10% of the undertaking's previous year's worldwide turnover. Decisions of the Commission may be appealed to the ECJ (or, initially, to the Court of First Instance and then to the ECJ on points of law).

10.3.10 Internal compliance[249]

All shipping companies (however small) which operate[250] within the EC should seriously contemplate setting up an Anti-Trust/Compliance Programme. Such a

246. *Ibid.* at footnote 1 above, pp. 632–641.
247. See Ritter *et al.*, *op. cit.* at footnote 1 above, pages 603 and 640.
248. Reg/17/62, Art.6.
249. See Marks, "Setting up-an Anti-Trust Compliance Programme" [1988] ECLR 88 and Stanbrook and Ratliff, "EEC Anti-Trust Audit" [1988] ECLR 334.
250. Whether based within the EC or not.

programme would minimise the exposure to fines and breaches of competition law generally.

CHAPTER 11

Liner Conferences Generally

11.1 INTRODUCTION

The purpose of this chapter is to describe liner conferences generally. Liner conferences are bodies or associations which consist of shipowners who operate regular shipping services for the carriage of general cargo according to fixed schedules and rates on particular routes.[1] The United Nations Conference on Trade and Development defines a liner conference as a

"group of two or more vessel-operating carriers which provides international liner services for the carriage of cargo on a particular route or routes within specified geographical limits and which has an agreement or arrangement, whatever its nature, within the framework of which they operate under uniform or common freight rates and any other agreed conditions with regard to the provision of liner services."

They normally involve price-fixing and market sharing arrangements. It has been written that the sea transport conference is the

"most important regulating instrument created by the shipping companies to govern world line transport. Such conferences lay down for their members, in respect of certain transport regions and lines, binding provisions on freight rates, conditions of carriage and other details of sea transport. Since these conferences cannot be completely controlled by any single state, they are in a position to exercise considerable power."[2]

Liner conferences are normally classified as being either open or closed in terms of their membership.

The debate on liner conferences is a long-standing one which has occasionally raged rather savagely. The proponents of liner conferences argue that they help to co-ordinate shipping services and allow a proper utilisation of resources. The opponents of liner conferences regard them as nothing more than cartels which manipulate markets. Most EC States (with the exception of Greece) have been somewhat non-committal, but they have favoured the closed conference system on occasion.

Unlike the US with its Shipping Acts of 1916 and 1984, European governments have been reluctant to legislate in this area. Such is their reluctance to legislate that they have positively encouraged shipowners and shippers to establish their own self-regulatory

1. On liner conferences, see Herman, *Shipping Conferences* (1983); Marx, *International Shipping Cartels: A Study of Industrial Self-Regulation by Shipping Companies* (1953); Oeter in Bernhardt (ed.), *Encyclopedia of Public International Law*, vol. 11, 1989, p. 197; and Sturmey, *The Code of Conduct and the Review Conference*. On liner conferences and EC law, see Clough and Randolph, *Shipping and EEC Competition Law* (1991), *passim*. See also Krels, "European Community Competition Policy and International Shipping" (1989–90) 13 *Fordham International Law Journal* 411; and Sturmey, "Pragmatic Competition and Liner Shipping" (1990) 14 *Marine Policy* 36.

2. Doc. 5/77; 23 March 1977; Rapporteur: Mr H. Seefeld, para. 58.

regimes. This self-regulatory approach was embodied in the 1964 Note of Understanding concluded between a number of European shippers and shipping companies. This Note was transformed in 1971 into the CENSA–ESC Code of Practice, which was ultimately unacceptable to the developing States.

Until recent years, the regulation of liner conferences was essentially a matter of national law. The English courts held that such conferences were not unlawful. The US legislated by way of the Shipping Act of 1916 to apply the rules of anti-trust law to conferences involving trade between the US and other States.

The European Parliament's Committee on Economic and Monetary Affairs, in its Interim Report on the Community Shipping Industry in 1976, discussed the background to the Code in the following terms:

> "15. Especially since the 1960s and in respect of liners in particular, the South American countries, as well as certain Asian ones, have introduced flag discrimination measures discriminating in favour of ships flying their national flag, measures which usually reserve up to or beyond 50 per cent of incoming or outgoing cargo for these ships. Such measures have enabled the developing countries to achieve a high rate of growth in their world cargo fleet. Their share of total world shipping, however, fell from 7 to just over 6 per cent between 1970 and 1975, despite the declared aim of the United Nations Development Decade that it should rise to 10 per cent. by 1980. Certain EEC States, notably Germany and Italy, have taken some measures to counter this practice. The German Federal Government can restrict conditions of freight contracts and charters between residents of the Federal Republic of Germany and carriers which are residents of the countries which exclude German ships from free competition. Italy restricts the use of ships which discriminate against Italian flag ships; shipments on such vessels are subject to government authorisation."[3]

Liner conferences are generally (but not universally) seen as stabilising and rationalising the lines on which the ships operate.

11.2 UNITED NATIONS CODE OF CONDUCT FOR LINER CONFERENCES

11.2.1 Introduction

In more recent times, liner conferences have not just been of interest to national legal systems. The United Nations Conference on Trade and Development (UNCTAD) turned its attention to conferences in the 1970s[4] and on 6 April 1974, the United Convention on a Code of Conduct for Liner Conferences,[5] which is reprinted in Appendix 2, below, was finally adopted after two years of negotiations. The Code consists of a Convention (containing seven chapters) with an Annex (containing model rules of procedure for international mandatory conciliation) and three attached Resolutions. The Convention on a Code of Conduct for Liner Conferences was the most critical development of the law relating to liner conferences. It establishes agreed norms relating to the conduct of liner conferences. It is a framework Convention.

3. 76, Rapporteur: Mr J. L. Prescott, para.14, citing *Finanstidende*, Copenhagen, 31 December 1975. On the report generally, see para. 11.2.5, below.

4. See UNCTAD Secretariat, *The Regulation of Liner Conferences*, UN Doc.TD/104/ Rev.1 (1972). Juda, "The UNCTAD Liner Code: A Preliminary Examination of the Implementation of the Code of Conduct for Liner Conferences" (1988) JMLC 181. Clough and Randolph (*op. cit.* at footnote 1) state (at p. 2) that the UNCTAD Code "has been the cornerstone of the Community's approach to the enforcement of the EEC competition rules in the shipping sector".

5. (1974) 13 ILM 910. See Shah, "The UN Liner Code of Conduct: Some Key Issues Regarding its Implementation" (1981) 16 ETL 491.

11.2.2 UNCTAD negotiations

The Convention resulted from several years of discussions on the issue.

The discussions stretched back to the first meeting of UNCTAD (the so-called UNCTAD I meeting) in 1964 when it was decided that the "appropriate inter-governmental procedures, including any committee that might be deemed necessary, be established . . . to study and report on economic aspects of shipping that might be referred to it".[6]

At UNCTAD II in 1968, it was resolved that the "governments of Member States of UNCTAD should urge liner conferences and equivalent organisations, directly or through the shipowner members of them, to make provisions in their constitution or working arrangements to the effect that they would discuss with shippers' councils or equivalent bodies questions pertaining to freight rates, conference practices, adequacy of shipping services and other matters of common interest within the consultation machinery of the country or group of countries concerned".[7]

The Consultative Shipping Group[8] drafted (after the 1968 UNCTAD II meeting[9]) guidelines for the behaviour of liner conferences and these guidelines became known as the CENSA Code when adopted by the shipowners' association, CENSA.

The UNCTAD III meeting in Santiago, Chile in 1972 called on the United Nations General Assembly to convene a conference on the subject. Resolution 66 of the Conference, which contained a draft code, called for the adoption of a Code as soon as possible; this Resolution was supported by 74 votes[10] to 19[11] with two abstentions.[12]

The negotiations commenced when the UN Conference of Plenipotentiaries met between 12 November 1973 and 15 December 1973, as well as between 11 March 1974 and 6 April 1974.

11.2.3 Objectives and principles of the Code

The Preamble to the Convention provides that the parties thereto agree to reflect in the Code the following three fundamental objectives and three basic principles:

> "(a) the objective to facilitate the orderly expansion of world sea-borne trade;
> (b) the objective to stimulate the development of regular and efficient liner services adequate to the requirement of the trade concerned;
> (c) the objective to ensure a balance of interests between suppliers and users of liner shipping services;
> (d) the principle that conference practices should not involve any discrimination against the shipowners, shippers or the foreign trade of any country;

6. UNCTAD I: Final Act and Report—Annexes at IV.21, p. 54.

7. UNCTAD II: Report of Shipping Committee, April–May 1970, Annex 1.

8. On the CSG, see Chapter 1, above.

9. At UNCTAD II in 1968, it was resolved that the "governments of Member States of UNCTAD should urge liner conferences and equivalent organisations, directly or through the shipowner members of them, to make provisions in their constitution or working arrangements to the effect that they would discuss with shippers' councils equivalent bodies questions pertaining to freight rates, conference practices, adequacy of shipping services and other matters of common interest within the consultation machinery of the country or group of countries concerned". For further details, see below.

10. The supporters were mainly the developing States. Kreis has commented that they wanted "a larger role in the operation and the profits of the shipping services that affected them" (1989–90) 13 *Fordham International Law Journal* 411.

11. The opponents were mainly the developed States.

12. I.e. Austria and Israel.

(e) the principle that conferences hold meaningful consultations with shippers' organisations, shippers' representatives and shippers on matters of common interest, with, upon request, the participation of appropriate authorities;

(f) the principle that conferences should make available to interested parties pertinent information about their activities which are relevant to those parties and should publish meaningful information on their activities."

11.2.4 Signature and entry into force

The Convention was signed in Geneva on 6 April 1974. Some eighty-three States have signed the Convention.[13]

It entered into force on 6 October 1983 (in accordance with Article 49 of the Code) when the necessary number of ratifications (i.e. twenty-four States with a combined tonnage representing at least 25 per cent of world tonnage) had been lodged for six months.

11.2.5 Perspectives on the Code of Conduct

The Code is a flexible (if not loose) instrument. Despite this flexibility, the essence of the Convention is the 40:40:20 formula, whereby the exporting and importing State's national lines have 40 per cent each of the trade with third State's having the balance of 20 per cent.[14]

The Code has not achieved universal appeal. The United States, Greece, Japan and Brazil have all opposed it. However, for present purposes, the reaction of the EC is the most significant.

It has been said that:

"The UNCTAD Code of Conduct for liner conferences appeared to be one of the most promising legal efforts to change traditional structures of global economy in order to form a New International Economic Order. A steadily growing number of developing countries has used the provisions of the Code as a basis for preferential, i.e. protectionist, legislation aimed at controlling all the shipping business affecting their countries and reserving foreign transports to their own national lines.

These protectionist policies . . . illustrate the dangers conjured by the Code's critics. Flag protectionism tends to eliminate the possibilities of cross-trade, which is likely to cause under-utilisation of shipping capacities, artificially puffed up national fleets and, in the long term, considerably increased freight rates.

Protectionist regulation of liner conferences also leads to an important increase in non-conference shipping, a tendency which could clearly be seen in recent years. A consequence of this tendency is a growing pressure to regulate also non-conference liner shipping after the same protectionist model, which would destroy competition in liner shipping markets completely."[15]

---

13. I.e. Algeria, Argentina, Australia, Bangladesh, Bhutan, Bolivia, Brazil, Bulgaria, Burundi, Canada, Chile, China, Colombia, Cuba, Czechoslovakia, Democratic Yemen, Denmark, Ecuador, Egypt, Finland, France, Gabon, German Democratic Republic, Federal Republic of Germany, Ghana, Greece, Guatemala, Guinea, Honduras, Hungary, India, Indonesia, Iran, Iraq, Italy, Ivory Coast, Jamaica, Japan, Kenya, Kymer Republic, Kuwait, Liberia, Libyan Arab Republic, Madagascar, Malaysia, Mexico, Morocco, Netherlands, New Zealand, Nicaragua, Nigeria, Norway, Pakistan, Panama, Peru, Philippines, Poland, Republic of Korea, Republic of Vietnam, Romania, Senegal, Singapore, Spain, Sri Lanka, Sudan, Sweden, Switzerland, Thailand, Trinidad and Tobago, Tunisia, Turkey, Ukrainian Soviet Socialist Republic, Union of Soviet Socialist Republics, United Arab Emirates, United Kingdom of Great Britain and Northern Ireland, United Republic of Cameroon, United Republic of Tanzania, United States of America, Uruguay, Venezuela, Yugoslavia and Zaire.

14. See the Code, Article 2. This is in contrast to the Norwegian proposal (which was made too late to be negotiated) of 40:60 where 40 per cent would be reserved for any importer or exporter which was a developing country and the remainder would be for ships of any State.

15. See Oeter, *op. cit.* at footnote 1, above, at p. 199.

The European Parliament's Committee on Economic and Monetary Affairs, in its Interim Report on the Community Shipping Industry, said in 1976 that:

"17. The trend towards flag discrimination was reinforced recently by the drafting of the United Nations Convention on a Code of Conduct for Liner Conferences. This Convention upholds as a basic principle that conference practices should not involve any discrimination against shipowners, shippers, or the foreign trade of any country. However, it also introduces the principle of cargo-sharing, on the basis of a 40–40–20 formula (i.e. 40 per cent each by the importing and exporting countries' ships, and 20 per cent by the ships of third countries).

Although the liner conferences (of which there are some 350 in the world, many with headquarters in Europe) involve only some 8 to 10 per cent of the total seaborne trade by volume, the principle involved is an important one, and one whose acceptance could seriously weaken the position of EEC shipping. Moreover, while accepting the desire of the developing countries to play a large part in world shipping as a legitimate one, one might well question whether the method proposed by the United Nations Convention was the best way of achieving this.

According to a study published[16] on shipping in the Third World, developing countries could experience serious difficulties as a result of wide-scale cargo reservation schemes as they are applied to national flag fleets. Such policies, it is suggested, would not only result in a reduction of free competition but would often lead to a reduction in the frequency of services. The report stated that this would produce over-tonnaging which in turn would reduce the efficiency of vessel utilisation and result in increased shipping costs."[17]

It has been written that the "important points" of the Code of Conduct are:

"— The shipping companies of a country which is served by a conference have an inalienable right to membership in that conference.
— Of the transport operations between two countries the shipping companies of those two countries are to have shares of about 40 per cent each, third countries receiving the remaining 20 per cent.
— Provision is made for negotiations and conciliation proceedings between shipping companies and shippers, in which government representatives are to participate.
— The fixing of freight rates is to be based on certain criteria. Set periods are to be observed in the case of increases in freight rates and the introduction of surcharges and currency conversion compensation factors.
— An international mandatory conciliation procedure will help enforce the provisions of the code in the event of disputes."[18]

The Code consists of a statement of objectives and principles, seven chapters and an annex setting out the model rules of procedure for international mandatory conciliation.

11.2.6 Application of the Code

The Code applies (if only, by implication of its Title) at least[19] to liner conferences. The Code defines a liner conference as "a group of two or more vessel-operating carriers which provides international liner services for the carriage of cargo on a particular route or routes within specified geographical limits and which has an agreement or arrangement, whatever its nature, within the framework of which they operate under uniform or common freight rates and any other agreed conditions with respect to the provision of liner services".[20]

16. *Shipping in the Third World*, H. P. Drewry (Shipping Consultants) as quoted in *The Times*, London, 12 January 1976.

17. Doc. 479/76, Rapporteur: Mr J. L. Prescott, para.14, citing *Finanstidende*, Copenhagen, 31 December 1975.

18. Doc. 5/77, 23 March 1977; Rapporteur: Mr H. Seefeld, para.58.

19. See Article 18 of the Code.

20. See Part One, Chapter I of the Code.

11.2.7 Provisions of the Code relating to relations between conference members

11.2.7.1 Introduction

Part One, Chapter II of the Convention deals with relations among member lines. Article 1 relates to membership.

11.2.7.2 Membership

Article 1 relates to membership and provides:

"1. Any national shipping line[21] shall have the right to be a full member of a conference which serves the foreign trade of its country, subject to the criteria set out in Article 1, paragraph 2. Shipping lines which are not national lines in any trade of a conference shall have the right to become full members of that conference, subject to the criteria set out in Article 1, paragraphs 2 and 3, and to the provisions regarding the share of trade as set out in Article 2 as regards third-country shipping lines.

2. A shipping line applying for membership of a conference shall furnish evidence of its ability and intention, ..."

Thus, there is a clear distinction between "national lines", and "non-national lines" with the former finding it easier to apply for membership of conferences.

11.2.7.3 Participation

Article 2 is the basis of the so-called "40:40:20" formula for cargo-sharing. It provides:

"1. Any shipping line admitted to membership of a conference shall have sailing and loading rights in the trades covered by that conference.

2. When a conference operates a pool, all shipping lines members of the conference serving the trade covered by the pool shall have the right to participate in the pool for that trade.

3. For the purpose of determining the share of trade which member lines shall have the right to acquire, the national shipping lines of each country, irrespective of the number of lines, shall be regarded as a single group of shipping lines for that country.

4. When determining a share of trade within a pool of individual member lines and/or groups of national shipping lines in accordance with Article 2, paragraph 2,[22] the following principles regarding their right to participation in the trade carried by the conference shall be observed, unless otherwise mutually agreed:

(a) The group of national shipping lines of each of the two countries the foreign trade between which is carried by the conference shall have equal rights to participate in the freight and volume of traffic generated by their mutual foreign trade and carried by the conference:

(b) Third-country shipping lines, if any, shall have the right to acquire a significant part, such as 20 per cent, in the freight and volume of traffic by that trade.[23]

21. Chapter I provides: "A national line of any given country is a vessel-operating carrier which has its head office of management and its effective control in that country and is recognised as such by an appropriate authority of that country or under the law of that country.

"Lines belonging to and operated by a joint venture involving two or more countries and in whose equity the national interests, public and/or private, of those countries have a substantial share and whose head office of management and whose effective control is in one of those countries can be recognised as a national line by the appropriate authorities of those countries."

22. See above.

23. Clough and Randolph (*op. cit.* footnote 1, at para. 11.1, above) observe at para.1.4.10 of their book: "the following difference in language should be noted. Article 2(4)(a) talks of the 'right to participate' in the trade by the national shipping lines, but Article 2(4)(b) only talks of the 'right to acquire' a significant part of the trade for the third country lines. This implies that although third country shipping lines might come to acquire a significant part of the relevant trade, they might not come to participate in it. This distinction is

5. If, for any one of the countries whose trade is carried by a conference, there are no national shipping lines participating in the carriage of that trade, the share of the trade to which national shipping lines[24] of that country would be entitled under Article 2, paragraph 4 shall be distributed among the individual member lines participating in the trade in proportion to their respective share."

A third country shipping line is defined by Chapter I as being "a vessel-operating carrier in its operations between two countries of which it is not a national shipping line".

11.2.7.4 Decision-making

Article 3 deals with decision-making. Decisions relating to trade between two countries cannot be made without the consent of the national shipping lines of those two states. Article 3 provides:

"The decision-making procedures embodied in a conference agreement shall be based on the equality of all the full member lines; these procedures shall ensure that the voting rules do not hinder the proper work of the conference and the service of the trade and shall define the matters on which decisions will be made by unanimity. However, a decision cannot be taken in respect of matters defined in a conference agreement relating to the trade between two countries without the consent of the national shipping lines of those two countries."

11.2.7.5 Sanctions

Article 4 deals with sanctions in the cases of withdrawals and expulsions of lines. It provides:

"1. A shipping line member of a conference shall be entitled, subject to the provisions regarding withdrawal which are embodied in pool schemes and/or cargo-sharing arrangements, to secure its release, without penalty, from the terms of the conference agreement after giving three months' notice, unless the conference agreement provides for a different time period, although it shall be required to fulfil its obligations as a member of the conference up to the date of its release.

2. A conference may, upon notice to be specified in the conference agreement, suspend or expel a member for significant failure to abide by the terms and conditions of the conference agreement.

3. No expulsion or suspension shall become effective until a statement in writing of the reasons therefor has been given and until any dispute has been settled as provided in chapter VI.

4. Upon withdrawal or expulsion, the line concerned shall be required to pay its share of the outstanding financial obligations of the the conference, up to the date of its withdrawal or expulsion. In cases of withdrawal, suspension or expulsion, the line shall not be relieved of its own financial obligations under the conference agreement or of any of its obligations towards shippers."

11.2.7.6. Self-policing

Article 5 deals with self-policing by conferences. It provides:

"1. A conference shall adopt and keep up to date an illustrative list, which shall be as comprehensive as possible, of practices which are regarded as malpractices and/or breaches of

---

made even more clear in the UK secondary legislation implementing the Code, via the Brussels package. The words 'right to acquire' are deemed to mean 'right to acquire by commercial means'; see the list of mandatory measures in the Merchant Shipping (Liner Conferences) (Mandatory Provisions) Regulations 1985 (SI 1985/406)."

24. On "national shipping lines", see above.

the conference agreement and shall provide effective self-policing machinery to deal with them, with specific provisions requiring:

(a) The fixing of penalties or a range of penalties for malpractices or breaches, to be commensurate with their seriousness;
(b) The examination and impartial review of an adjudication of complaints, and/or decisions taken on complaints, against malpractices or breaches by a person or body unconnected with any of the shipping lines members of the conference or their affiliates, on request by the conference or any other party concerned;
(c) The reporting, on request, on the action taken in connection with complaints against malpractices and/or breaches, and on a basis of anonymity for the parties concerned, to the appropriate authorities of the countries whose trade is served by the conference and of the countries whose shipping lines are members of the conference.

2. Shipping lines and conferences are entitled to the full co-operation of shippers and shippers' organisations in the endeavour to combat malpractices and breaches."

11.2.7.7 Conference agreements

Article 6 deals with the inspection conference agreements by the appropriate authorities. It provides:

"All conference agreements, pooling, berthing and sailing rights agreements and amendments or other documents directly related to, and which affect, such agreements, shall be made available on request to the appropriate authorities of the countries whose trade is served by the conference and of the countries whose shipping lines are members of the conference."

11.2.8 Provisions of the Code relating to relations with shippers

11.2.8.1 Introduction

Chapter III deals with "Relations with Shippers".

11.2.8.2 Loyalty arrangements

Article 7 provides:

"1. The shipping lines members of a conference are entitled to institute and maintain loyalty arrangements with shippers, the form and terms of which are matters for consultation between conference and shippers' organisations or representatives of shippers. These loyalty arrangements shall provide safeguards making explicit the rights of shippers and conference members. These arrangements shall be based on the contract system or any system which is also lawful.

2. Whatever loyalty arrangements are made, the freight rate applicable to loyal shippers shall be determined within a fixed range of percentages of the freight rate applicable to other shippers. Where a change in the differential causes an increase in the rates charged to shippers, the change can be implemented only after 150 days' notice to those shippers or according to regional practice and/or agreement. Disputes in connection with a change of the differential shall be settled as provided in the loyalty agreement.

3. The terms of loyalty arrangements shall provide safeguards making explicit the rights and obligations of shippers and of shipping lines members of the conference in accordance with the following provisions, *inter alia*:

(a) The shipper shall be bound in respect of cargo whose shipment is controlled by him or his affiliated or subsidiary company or his forwarding agent in accordance with the contract of sale of the goods concerned, provided that the shipper shall not, by evasion, subterfuge, or intermediary, attempt to divert cargo in violation of his loyalty commitment;

(b) Where there is a loyalty contract, the extent of actual or liquidated damages and/or penalty shall be specified in the contract. The member lines of the conference may, however, decide to assess lower liquidated damages or to waive the claim to liquidated damages. In any event, the liquidated damages under the contract to be paid to the shipper shall not exceed the freight charges on the particular shipment, computed at the rate provided under the contract;

(c) The shipper shall be entitled to resume full loyalty status, subject to the fulfilment of conditions established by the conference which shall be specified in the loyalty arrangement;

(d) The loyalty arrangement shall set out:

(i) A list of cargo, which may include bulk cargo shipped without mark or count, which is specifically excluded from the scope of the loyalty arrangement;

(ii) A definition of the circumstances in which cargo other than cargo covered by (i) above is considered to be excluded from the scope of the loyalty arrangement;

(iii) The method of settlement of disputes arising under the loyalty arrangement;

(iv) Provision for termination of the loyalty arrangement on request by either a shipper or a conference without penalty, after expiry of a stipulated period of notice, such notice to be given in writing; and

(v) The terms for granting dispensation."

Thus, loyalty arrangements such as dual rate contracts and deferred rebates may exist.

11.2.8.3 Dispensation

Article 8 provides:

"1. Conferences shall provide, within the terms of the loyalty arrangements, that requests by shippers for dispensation shall be examined and a decision given quickly and, if requested, the reasons given in writing where dispensation is withheld. Should a conference fail to confirm, within a period specified in the loyalty arrangement, sufficient space to accommodate a shipper's cargo within a period also specified in the loyalty arrangement, the shipper shall have the right, without being penalised, to utilise any vessel for the cargo in question.

2. In ports where conference services are arranged subject to the availability of a specified minimum of cargo (i.e. on inducement), but either the shipping line does not call, despite due notice by shippers, or the shipping line does not reply within an agreed time to the notice given by shippers, shippers shall automatically have the right, without prejudicing their loyalty status, to use any available vessel for the carriage of their cargo."

11.2.8.4 Availability of tariffs

Article 9 provides for the availability of tariffs and related conditions. In specific terms, the Article provides:

"Tariffs, related conditions, regulations, and any amendments thereto shall be made available on request to shippers, shippers' organisations and other parties concerned at reasonable cost, and they shall be available for examination at offices of shipping lines and their agents. They shall spell out all conditions concerning the application of freight rates and the carriage of any cargo covered by them."

This is mirrored in Regulation 4056/86.

11.2.8.5 Annual reports

Article 10 relates to annual reports and provides:

"Conferences shall provide annually to shippers' organisations, or to representaives of shippers, reports on their activities designed to provide general information of interest to them, including relevant information about consultations held with shippers and shippers' organisations, action taken regarding complaints, changes in membership, and significant changes in service, tariffs and conditions of carriage. Such annual reports shall be submitted, on request, to the appropriate authorities of the countries whose trade is served by the conference concerned."

11.2.8.6 Consultation machinery

Article 11 establishes a consultation machinery. It provides:

"1. There shall be consultations on matters of common interest between a conference, shippers' organisations, representatives of shippers and, where practicable, shippers, which may be designated for that purpose by the appropriate authority if it so desires. These consultations shall take place whenever requested by any of the above-mentioned parties. Appropriate authorities shall have the right, upon request, to participate fully in the consultations, but this does not mean that they play a decision-making role.

2. The following matters, *inter alia*, may be the subject of consultation:
  (a) Changes in general tariff conditions and related regulations;
  (b) Changes in the general level of tariff rates and rates for major commodities;
  (c) Promotional and/or special freight rates;
  (d) Imposition of, and related changes in, surcharges;
  (e) Loyalty arrangements, their establishment or changes in their form and general conditions;
  (f) Changes in the tariff classification of ports;
  (g) Procedure for the supply of necessary information by shippers concerning the expected volume and nature of their cargoes; and
  (h) Presentation of cargo for shipment and the requirement regarding notice of cargo availability.

3. To the extent that they fall within the scope of activity of a conference, the following matters may also be the subject of consultation:
  (a) Operation of cargo inspection services;
  (b) Changes in the pattern of services;
  (c) Effects of the introduction of new technology in the carriage of cargo, in particular unitisation, with consequent reduction of conventional service or loss of direct services; and
  (d) Adequacy and quality of shipping services, including the impact of pooling, berthing or sailing arrangements on the availability of shipping services and freight rates at which shipping services are provided; changes in the areas served and in the regularity of calls by conference vessels.

4. Consultations shall be held before final decisions are taken, unless otherwise provided in this Code. Advance notice shall be given of the intention to take decisions on matters referred to in Article 11, paragraphs 2 and 3. Where this is impossible, urgent decisions may be taken pending the holding of consultations.

5. Consultations shall begin without undue delay and in any event within a maximum period specified in the conference agreement, or in the absence of such a provision in the agreement, not later than 30 days after receipt of the proposal for consultations, unless different periods of time are provided in this Code.

6. When holding consultations, the parties shall use their best efforts to provide relevant information, to hold timely discussions and to clarify matters for the purpose of seeking solutions of the issues concerned. The parties involved shall take account of each other's views and problems and strive to reach agreement consistent with their commercial viability."

It has been commented that the rules in the UNCTAD are very precise but that the rules in Regulation 4056/86 are, by contrast, "vague and general".[25]

25. Clough and Randolph, *op. cit.*, footnote 1, at para. 11.1, para. 1.4.12.3.

11.2.9 Provisions of the Code relating to freight rates

11.2.9.1 Introduction

Chapter IV deals with "Freight Rates".

11.2.9.2 Criteria for freight rate determination

Article 12 of the Code provides:

"In arriving at a decision on questions of tariff policy in all cases mentioned in this Code, the following points shall, unless otherwise provided, be taken into account:

(a) Freight rates shall be fixed at as low a level as is feasible from the commercial point of view and shall permit a reasonable profit for shipowners;

(b) The cost of operations of conferences shall, as a rule, be evaluated for the round voyage of ships, with the outward and inward directions considered as a single whole. Where applicable, the outward and inward voyage should be considered separately. The freight rates should take into account among other factors, the nature of cargoes, the interrelation between weight and cargo measurement, as well as the value of cargoes;

(c) In fixing promotional freight and/or special freight rates for specific goods, the conditions of trade for these goods of the countries served by the conference particularly of developing and land-locked countries, shall be taken into account."

11.2.9.3 Conference tariffs and classification of tariff rates

Article 13 of the Code provides:

"1. Conference tariffs shall not unfairly differentiate between shippers similarly situated. Shipping lines members of a conference shall adhere strictly to the rates, rules and terms shown in the tariffs and other currently valid published documents of the conference and to any special arrangements permitted under this Code.

2. Conference tariffs should be drawn up simply and clearly, containing as few classes/categories as possible, depending on the commodity and, where appropriate, for each class/category; they should also indicate, wherever practicable, in order to facilitate statistical compilation and analysis, the corresponding appropriate code number of the item in accordance with the Standard International Trade Classification, the Brussels Tariff Nomenclature or any other nomenclature that may be internationally adopted; the classification of commodities in the tariffs should, as far as practicable, be prepared in co-operation with shippers' organisations and other national and international organisations concerned."

11.2.9.4 General freight-rate increases

Article 14 of the Code provides:

"1. A conference shall give notice of not less than 150 days, or according to regional practice and/or agreement, to shippers' organisations or representatives of shippers and/or shippers and, where so required, to appropriate authorities of the countries whose trade is served by the conference, of its intention to effect a general increase in freight rates, an indication of its extent, the date of effect and the reasons supporting the proposed increase.

2. At the request of any of the parties prescribed for this purpose in this Code, to be made within an agreed period of time after the receipt of the notice, consultations shall commence, in accordance with the relevant provisions of this Code, within a stipulated period not exceeding 30 days or as previously agreed between the parties concerned; the consultations shall be held in respect of the basis and amounts of the proposed increase and the date from which it is to be given effect.

3. A conference, in an effort to expedite consultations, may or upon the request of any of the parties prescribed in this Code as entitled to participate in consultations on general freight-rate increases shall, where practicable, reasonably before the consultations, submit to the participating parties a report from independent accountants of repute, including, where the requesting parties accept it as one of the bases of consultations, an aggregated analysis of data regarding relevant costs and revenues which in the opinion of the conference necessitate an increase in freight rates.

4. If agreement is reached as a result of the consultations, the freight-rate increase shall take effect from the date indicated in the notice served in accordance with Article 14, paragraph 1, unless a later date is agreed upon between the parties concerned.

5. If no agreement is reached within 30 days of the giving of notice in accordance with Article 14, paragraph 1, and subject to procedures prescribed in this Code, the matter shall be submitted immediately to international mandatory conciliation, in accordance with Chapter VI. The recommendation of the conciliators, if accepted by the parties concerned, shall be binding upon them and shall be implemented, subject to the provisions of Article 14, paragraph 9, with effect from the date mentioned in the conciliators' recommendation.

6. Subject to the provisions of Article 14, paragraph 9, a general freight-rate increase may be implemented by a conference pending the conciliators' recommendation. When making their recommendation, the conciliators should take into account the extent of the above-mentioned increase made by the conference and the period for which it has been in force. In the event that the conference rejects the recommendation of the conciliators, shippers and/or shippers' organisations shall have the right to consider themselves not bound, after appropriate notice, by any arrangement or other contract with that conference which may prevent them from using non-conference shipping lines. Where a loyalty arrangement exists shippers and/or shippers' organisations shall give notice within a period of 30 days to the effect that they no longer consider themselves bound by that arrangement, which notice shall apply from the date mentioned therein, and a period of not less than 30 days and not more than 90 days shall be provided in the loyalty arrangement for this purpose.

7. A deferred rebate which is due to the shipper and which has already been accumulated by the conference shall not be withheld by, or forfeited to, the conference as a result of action by the shipper under Article 14, paragraph 6.

8. If the trade of a country carried by shipping lines members of a conference on a particular route consists largely of one or few basic commodities, any increase in the freight rate on one or more of those commodities shall be treated as a general freight-rate increase, and the appropriate provisions of this Code shall apply.

9. Confernces should institute any general freight-rate increase effective in accordance with this Code for a period of a stated minimum duration, subject always to the rules regarding surcharges and regarding adjustment in freight rates consequent upon fluctuations in foreign exchange rates. The period over which a general freight-rate increase is to apply is an appropriate matter to be considered during consultations conducted in accordance with Article 14, paragraph 2, but unless otherwise agreed between the parties concerned during the consultations, the minimum period of time between the date when one general freight-rate increase becomes effective and the date of notice for the next general freight-rate increase given in accordance with Article 14, paragraph 1 shall not be less than 10 months."

This is a "fundamentally commercial approach".[26]

11.2.9.5 Promotional freight rates

Promotional freight rates are dealt with by Article 15 of the Code. It provides:

"1. Promotional freight rates for non-traditional exports should be instituted by conferences.

2. All necessary and reasonable information justifying the need for a promotional freight rate shall be submitted to a conference by the shippers, shippers' organisations or representatives of shippers concerned.

26. Clough and Randolph, *op. cit.*, para. 1.4.13.1.

3. Special procedures shall be instituted providing for a decision within 30 days from the date of receipt of that information, unless mutually agreed otherwise, on application for promotional freight rates. A clear distinction shall be made between these and general procedures for considering the possibility of reducing freight rates for other commodities or of exempting them from increases.

4. Information regarding the procedures for considering applications for promotional freight rates shall be made available by the conference to shippers and/or shippers' organisations and, on request, to the Governments and/or other appropriate authorities of the countries whose trade is served by the conference.

5. A promotional freight rate shall be established normally for a period of 12 months, unless otherwise mutually agreed between the parties concerned. Prior to the expiry of the period, the promotional freight rate shall be reviewed, on request by the shipper and/or shippers' organisation concerned, when it shall be a matter for the shipper and/or shippers' organisation, at the request of the conference, to show that the continuation of the rate is justified beyond the initial period.

6. When examining a request for a promotional freight rate, the conference may take into account that, while the rate should promote the export of the non-traditional product for which it is sought, it is not likely to create substantial competitive distortions in the export of a similar product from another country served by the conference.

7. Promotional freight rates are not excluded from the imposition of a surcharge or a currency adjustment factor in accordance with Articles 16 and 17.

8. Each shipping line member of a conference serving the relevant ports of a conference trade shall accept, and not unreasonably refuse, a fair share of cargo for which a promotional freight rate has been established by the conference."

11.2.9.6 Surcharges

Article 16 of the Code provides:

"1. Surcharges imposed by a conference to cover sudden or extraordinary increases in costs or losses of revenue shall be regarded as temporary. They shall be reduced in accordance with improvements in the situation or circumstances which they were imposed to meet and shall be cancelled, subject to Article 16, paragraph 6, as soon as the situation or circumstances which prompted their imposition cease to prevail. This shall be indicated at the moment of their imposition, together, as far as possible, with a description of the change in the situation or circumstances which will bring about their increase, reduction or cancellation.

2. Surcharges imposed on cargo moving to or from a particular port shall likewise be regarded as temporary and likewise shall be increased, reduced or cancelled, subject to Article 16, paragraph 6, when the situation in that port changes.

3. Before any surcharge is imposed, whether general or covering only a specific port, notice should be given and there shall be consultation, upon request, in accordance with the procedures of this Code, between the conference concerned and other parties directly affected by the surcharge and prescribed in this Code as entitled to participate in such consultations, save in those exceptional circumstances which warrant immediate imposition of the surcharge. In cases where a surcharge has been imposed without prior consultation, consultations, upon request, shall be held as soon as possible thereafter. Prior to such consultations, conferences shall furnish data which in their opinion justify the imposition of the surcharge.

4. Unless the parties agree otherwise, within a period of 15 days after the receipt of a notice given in accordance with Article 16, paragraph 3, if there is no agreement on the question of the surcharge between the parties concerned referred to in that Article, the relevant provisions for settlement of disputes provided in this Code shall prevail. Unless the parties concerned agree otherwise, the surcharge may, however, be imposed pending resolution of the dispute, if the dispute still remains unresolved at the end of a period of 30 days after the receipt of the above-mentioned notice.

5. In the event of a surcharge being imposed, in exceptional circumstances, without prior consultation as provided in Article 16, paragraph 3, if no agreement is reached through subsequent consultations, the relevant provisions for settlement of disputes provided in this Code shall prevail.

6. Financial loss incurred by the shipping lines members of a conference as a result of any delay on account of consultions and/or other proceedings for resolving disputes regarding imposition of surcharges in accordance with the provisions of this Code, as compared to the date from which the surcharge was to be imposed in terms of the notice given in accordance with Article 16, paragraph 3, may be compensated by an equivalent prolongation of the surcharge before its removal. Conversely, for any surcharge imposed by the conference and subsequently determined and agreed to be unjustified or excessive as a result of consultations or other procedures prescribed in this Code, the amounts so collected or the excess thereof as determined hereinabove, unless otherwise agreed, shall be refunded to the parties concerned, if claimed by them, within a period of 30 days of such claim."

11.2.9.7 Currency changes

Currency changes are dealt with in Article 17 of the Code.

11.2.10 Other substantive aspects of the Code

Part One, Chapter V, deals with other provisions of the Code. The Code is contained in Appendix 2 below.

11.3 THE UN LINER CODE AND EC LAW

11.3.1 Introduction

The importance of the UN Liner Code for EC law is seen in the following statement:

"[g]iven the fact that the EC's only competition block exemption at the moment in the field of sea relates almost exclusively to liner conferences, it is clearly necessary to examine the background and the provisions of those acts which bear on the subject. This stance is supported by the third recital in Council Regulation (EEC) 4056/86 which provides that '. . . the Regulation applying the rules of competition to maritime transport foreseen in the last recital of Council Regulation (EEC) 954/79 should take account of the adoption of the Code'."[27]

The relevant regulation, Regulation 954/79, provides that "the questions covered by the Code are of importance not only to the Member States but also to the Community, in particular from the shipping and trading point of view . . .".[28]

The Member States of EC were not united in its views on the UN Liner Code. This was unfortunate.[29] The vote in April 1974 was a matrix of views.

The following States voted in favour of the Code:

Belgium
France
Germany

The following States voted against the Code:

Denmark
United Kingdom

The following States abstained:

Italy
The Netherlands.

27. Clough and Randolph, *op. cit.*, footnote 1, at para. 11.1.
28. Regulation 954/79, Preamble, Second Recital.
29. Doc.5/77; 23 March 1977; Rapporteur: Mr H. Seefeld, para. 59.

Two States, namely Ireland and Luxembourg, did not attend the Conference. Meanwhile, the EC Commission acted as an observer at the Conference. The lack of unity may well have been fatal "[i]t is extremely regrettable that the Member States of the Community were not able to adopt a joint position in due time, especially since if they had done so it might have been possible to influence the negotiations so that the end result would have been acceptable to all Member States".[30] Regulation 954/79 was the embodiment of the common position of the EC Member States.

11.3.2 Compatibility of the Code with EC law

Some elements of the Code are incompatible with EC law. In particular, the Code would violate against the EC law principles of non-discrimination on the basis of nationality,[31] freedom of establishment in another EC Member State,[32] freedom to provide services to persons in other EC Member States[33] and EC competition law.[34]

11.3.3 Regulation 954/79

Regulation 954/79 is the so-called Brussels Package which enables the Member States of the EC to accede to or ratify the UNCTAD Code.

11.3.4 Legislative history of Regulation 954/79

11.3.4.1 1974: Commission Proposal

On 15 July 1974, the Commission published a Communication entitled "Proposal for a decision of the Council concerning common action by the Member States in respect of the United Nations Convention on a Code of Conduct for Liner Conferences".[35]

This Communication recalled that the general rules of the EEC Treaty applied to sea transport (in the light of Case 167/73 *Commission* v. *France*[36]) and thus the Member States should take a common position on the Convention. In essence, the Commission believed that the Code could damage "certain fundamental interests of the Community".[37] It was later recorded that the proposal involved the Commission proposing that "the Member States should abstain from any measures connected with the signing and ratification of and the accession to [the] Convention (Article 2 of the proposal) and that the Council [of Ministers] should decide by 30 June 1975, on a proposal from the Commission, on a common procedure (Article 1 of the proposal)".[38]

11.3.4.2 1975: Commission Proposal

The Commission followed up its 1974 Communication with another entitled "Proposal concerning the opening of negotiations in respect of the United Nations

30. Doc.5/77; 23 March 1977; Rapporteur: Mr H. Seefeld, para. 59.
31. See Article 7 EEC. See also Chapter 3, above.
32. See Articles 52–58 EEC.
33. See Article 61 EEC.
34. See Articles 85 to 92 EEC.
35. COM(74)1112 final.
36. [1974] ECR 359 and [1974] 2 CMLR 216.
37. See COM(74)1112 final.
38. Doc.5/77; 23 March 1977; Rapporteur: Mr H. Seefeld, para. 61.

Convention on a Code of Conduct for Liner Conferences".[39] This document stated that there were specific incompatibilities between certain provisions of the Code and the EEC Treaty. Specifically, the following incompatibilites arose:

11.3.4.2.1 Code of Conduct: EEC Treaty

Articles 1 and 2 of Chapter II of the Code reduced the effect of the competition rules and resulted in discrimination between Community nationals by reason of their national base as well as shipping companies established in the EC.

Chapter III of the Code does not entirely conform to the provisions of the EC competition law.

Belgium, France and Germany signed the Convention subject to ratification. The Commission protested and instituted proceedings against the States under Article 169 of the EEC Treaty.[40] Scarascia Mugnozza, the Vice-President of the Commission said, while answering a question in the European Parliament, on 13 October 1976:

"The three Member States who have signed the Convention, subject to ratification, declare themselves bound to respect the obligations incumbent on them under the Treaty of Accession to the European Communities and are now ready to suspend ratification unless the Council of Ministers of the Community expressly authorises them to ratify. The Commission will not begin infringement proceedings before the Court of Justice. The Commission has had firm assurances that the three Member States will take active steps at Community level to formulate a common approach to the Code of Conduct. In the meantime, the Member States and the Commission reserve their position on the legal aspects of the problem."

Despite the incompatibility of some aspects of the Code with EC law, the EC decided in 1979 to allow EC Member States and the EC itself to become Contracting Parties to the Code. The EC's decision was embodied in Regulation 954/79. This is the so-called Brussels Package. The reason for this Regulation is that the EC did not want to deprive those developing countries with which it has a special relationship, of the cargo-sharing arrangements involved in the Code.

11.3.4.3 Council of Ministers Decision

On 15 May 1979, the Council of Ministers adopted Regulation 954/79/EEC.[41] Petropolous has commented:

"[t]he political reasons for this lie in the fact that the Community has a special relationship with a great number of developing countries and wanted to give them the benefit of the preferential treatment contained in the Code. The legal means to make the adhesion possible are contained in the "Brussels Package" of 1979 (EEC Regulation No. 954/79)."[42]

Clough and Randolph have commented[43]:

"The Regulation serves two useful purposes, insofar as the Community is concerned. It harmonises the position of the Member States with regard to the UNCTAD Code and it establishes certain common reservations to some of the Code's more 'difficult' provisions.

39. Doc.COM(75)1112 final of 14 March 1975 and Doc.COM(75)302 final of 17 June 1975.
40. On Article 169 of the EEC Treaty, see Chapter 3, above.
41. OJ L121/1, 17 April 1979.
42. Speech, "The European Community Maritime Transport Policy", pp.7–8 at a Conference, "The Future of Shipping in Europe", London, 28–29 June 1990. See also the Preamble to the Regulation.
43. *Op. cit.*, para.1.5.1.

Historically, it also fulfilled a very important role. One effect of the regulation was to allow individual Member States to ratify or accede to the Code. Up until the regulation came into force, too few countries had ratified or acceded to the Code to make it effective. Article 49 of the Code provides that the Code would only come into force six months after the date when no less than 24 States, the combined tonnage of which amounted to at least 25 per cent of world tonnage, had become Contracting Parties to the Code. The effect of the regulation was to allow Member States with important tonnage capacities to become Contracting States and thus trigger the entry of the UNCTAD Code."

In essence, the EC decided that the 40:40:20 formula on cargo sharing was inapplicable as far as the relations between EC Member States were concerned in respect of relations between themselves or between EC members and States which were members of the Organisation for Economic Co-operation and Development (OECD).

11.3.5 Contents of Regulation 954/79

Article 1 provides:

"1. When ratifying the United Nations Convention on a Code of Conduct for Liner Conferences, or when acceding thereto, Member States shall inform the Secretary-General of the United Nations in writing that such ratification or accession has taken place in accordance with this Regulation.

2. The instrument of ratification or accession shall be accompanied by the reservations set out in Annex I."

11.3.5.1 Existing conference

Article 2 of the Regulation deals with existing conferences. It provides:

"1. In the case of an existing conference, each group of shipping lines of the same nationality which are members thereof shall determine by commercial negotiations with another shipping line of that nationality whether the latter may participate as a national shipping line in the said conference.

If a new conference is created, the shipping lines of the same nationality shall determine by commercial negotiations which of them may participate as a national shipping line in the future conference.

2. Where the negotiations referred to in paragraph 1 fail to result in agreement, each Member State may, at the request of one of the lines concerned and after hearing all of them, take the necessary steps to settle the dispute.

3. Each Member State shall ensure that all vessel-operating shipping lines established on its territories under the Treaty establishing the European Economic Community are treated in the same way as lines which have their management head office on its territory and the effective control of which is exercised there."

11.3.5.2 Cargo allocation

Article 3 of the Regulation deals with cargo allocation. It provides:

"1. Where a liner conference operates a pool or a berthing, sailing and/or any other form of cargo allocation agreement in accordance with Article 2 of the Code of Conduct, the volume of cargo to which the group of national shipping lines of each Member State participating in that trade or the shipping lines of the Member States participating in that trade as third country shipping lines are entitled under the Code shall be redistributed, unless a decision is taken to the contrary by all the lines which are members of the Conference and parties to the present redistribution rules. This redistribution of cargo shares shall be carried out on the basis of a unanimous decision by those shipping lines which are members of the conference and participate in the redistribution, with a view to all these lines carrying a fair share of the conference trade

2. The share finally allocated to each participant shall be determined by the application of commercial principles, taking account in particular of:

(a) the volume of cargo carried by the conference and generated by the Member States whose trade is served by it;

(b) past performance of the shipping lines in the trade covered by the pool;

(c) the volume of cargo carried by the conference and shipped through the ports of the Member States;

(d) the needs of the shippers whose cargoes are carried by the conference

3. If no agreement is reached on the redistribution of cargoes referred to in paragraph 1, the matter shall, at the request of one of the parties, be referred to conciliation in accordance with the procedure set out in Annex II. Any dispute not settled by the conciliation procedure may, with the agreement of the parties, be referred to arbitration. In that event, the award of the arbitrator shall be binding.

4. At intervals to be laid down in advance, shares allocated in accordance with paragraphs 1, 2, and 3 shall be regularly reviewed, taking into account the criteria set out in paragraph 2 and in particular from the viewpoint of providing adequate and efficient services to shippers."

11.3.5.3 OECD Member States

The relations with other Member States of the OECD are dealt with by Article 4 of the Regulation. It provides:

"1. In a conference trade between a Member State of the Community and a State which is a party to the Code of Conduct and not an OECD country, a shipping line of another Member State of the OECD wishing to participate in the redistribution provided for in Article 3 of this Regulation may do so subject to reciprocity defined at governmental or ship-owners' level.

2. Without prejudice to paragraph 3 of this Article, Article 2 of the Code of Conduct shall not be applied in conference trades between Member States or, on a reciprocal basis, between such States and the other OECD countries which are parties to the Code.

3. Paragraph 2 of this Article shall not affect the opportunities for participation as third country shipping lines in such trades, in accordance with the principles reflected in Article 2 of the Code of Conduct, of the shipping lines of a developing country which are recognised as national shipping lines under the Code and which are:

(a) already members of a conference serving these trades; or

(b) admitted to such a conference under Article 1(3) of the Code.

4. Articles 3 and 14(9) of the Code of Conduct shall not be applied in conference trades between Member States or, on a reciprocal basis, between such States and other OECD countries which are parties to the code.

5. In conference trades between Member States and between these States and other OECD countries which are parties to the Code of Conduct, the shippers and shipowners of Member States shall not insist on applying the procedures for settling disputes provided for in Chapter VI of the Code in their mutual relationships or, on a reciprocal basis, in relation to shippers and ship-owners of other OECD countries where other procedures for settling disputes have been agreed between them. They shall in particular take full advantage of the possibilities provided by Article 25(1) and (2) of the Code for resolving disputes by means of procedures other than those laid down in Chapter VI of the Code."

6. For the adoption of decisions relating to matters defined in the conference agreement concerning the trade of a Member State, other than those referred to in Article 3 of this Regulation, the national shipping lines of such State shall consult all the other Community lines which are members of the conference before giving or withholding their assent."

11.3.5.4 Decision-making procedures

Article 5 of the Code provides for decision-making procedures.

11.3.5.5 Reservations and interpretative reservations

Annex I to the Regulation sets out the reservations and interpretative reservations which must be entered by the EC Member States when ratifying or acceding to the Convention. These are:

"1. For the purposes of the Code of Conduct, the term 'national shipping line' may, in the case of a Member State of the Community, include any vessel-operating shipping line established on the territory of such Member State in accordance with the EEC Treaty.

2. (a) Without prejudice to paragraph (b) of this reservation, Article 2 of the Code of Conduct shall not be applied in conference trades between the Member States of the Community or, on a reciprocal basis, between such States and the other OECD countries which are parties to the Code."

(b) Point (a) shall not affect the opportunities for participation as third country shipping lines in such trades, in accordance with the principles reflected in Article 2 of the Code, of the shipping lines of a developing country which are recognised as national shipping lines under the Code and which are:

- (i) already members of a conference serving these trades; or
- (ii) admitted to such a conference under Article 1(3) of the Code. Articles 3 and 14(9) of the Code of Conduct shall not be applied in conference trades between the Member States of the Community or, on a reciprocal basis, between such States and the other OECD countries which are parties to the Code

4. In trades to which Article 3 of the Code of Conduct applies, the last sentence of that Article is interpreted as meaning that:

- (a) the two groups of national shipping lines will co-ordinate their positions before voting on matters concerning the trade between their two countries;
- (b) this sentence applies solely to matters which the conference agreement identifies as requiring the assent of both groups of national shipping lines concerned, and not to all matters covered by the conference agreement."

The reservations were necessary because of the otherwise incompatible nature of the Code *vis-à-vis* the EEC Treaty.

11.3.6 Implementation of the UN Code in EC Member States

It is not the purpose of this book to review the implementation of the UN Code in each of the Member States and recourse should be had to the laws of each of those States for details on this point. Suffice it to say, the UK implemented the Liner Code by means of the Merchant Shipping (Liner Conferences) Act 1982 (which entered into force on 23 July 1982) and Denmark, France, Germany as well as the Netherlands have implemented the Code.

CHAPTER 12

Competition: Regulation 4056/86

12.1 INTRODUCTION

Council Regulation 4056/86 of 22 December 1986 (referred to in this chapter as "the Regulation") lays down detailed rules for the application of Articles 85[1] and 86[2] of the EEC Treaty to certain limited forms of maritime transport.[3,4] The rules set out in the Regulation are both substantive and procedural.[5] The Regulation is quite unique: it "presents many peculiar features for which one will look in vain in other Regulations which give effect to the principles of Articles 85 and 86".[6] The Regulation recognises the unique nature of maritime transport.

It has "furthered the self-regulatory mechanism of shipping conferences and their agreements with users".[7] The Regulation applies to the international liner service sector. It grants an open-ended block exemption for cargo liner conferences.

The position of shippers has been improved because of the existence of the Regulation and they have submitted complaints accordingly.

12.2 LEGISLATIVE HISTORY

12.2.1 Introduction

It will be recalled[8] that while Regulation 17/62 implemented Articles 85 and 86 of the EEC Treaty, Regulation 141/62 disapplied Regulation 17/62 in relation to transport.

1. On Article 85 of the EEC Treaty, see Chapter 10, above.
2. On Article 86 of the EEC Treaty, see Chapter 10, above.
3. On the definition of "maritime transport" for present purposes, see para.1.2.6.5, below.
4. OJ 1986 L378/4. For the literature on the Regulation, see, *inter alia*, Clough and Randolph, *Shipping and EC Competition Law* (1991), *passim*; Greaves, *op. cit.*, Chapter 11; Green [1988] ETL 612; Kreis [1988] ETL 562; Kreis [1990] *Fordham International Law Journal* 411; Rycken [1987] ETL 483; Rabe and Schuette [1988] LMCLQ 182; Ruttley, "International Shipping and EEC Competition Law" [1991] 1 ECLR 5; as well as Slot, in Slot and de Woude (eds), *Exploiting the Internal Market: Co-operation and Competition Towards 1992.*

For the background discussion on Regulation 4056/86, see the Report of ECOSOC's Section for Transport and Communications on the Proposal for a Council Regulation (EEC) laying down Detailed Rules for the Application of Articles 85 and 86 of the Treaty to Maritime Transport (CES) 211/82; Interim Report drawn up on behalf of the Committee on Economic and Monetary Affairs on the proposal from the Commission of the European Communities to the Council for a Regulation laying down detailed rules for the application of Articles 85 and 86 of the Treaty to Maritime Transport (Rapporteur: Nyborg) (EP Doc.1–249/84/9).

5. The substantive rules are set out in particular, in Articles 1–9 of the Regulation.
6. Slot, *op. cit.*, at p. 31.
7. Rabe, "Recent Developments in EEC Legislation Pertaining to Maritime Transport", *IBA Strasbourg Conference*, 1989, at p. 12.
8. See Chapters 5 and 9, above.

The absence of a Regulation implementing Articles 85 and 86 of the EEC Treaty could have led to confusion—as the Commission said in an Information Memorandum (prior to the adoption of the Regulation):

"Although the rules on competition, like all the general provisions of the Treaty apply to sea transport, maritime and air transport are[9] the only branches of the economy for which detailed provisions applying those rules have not yet been laid down.

Without provisions of this kind, the Commission does not possess the means to ensure effectively that shipping companies comply with Articles 85 and 86 of the EEC Treaty. What is more, as these Articles are applicable directly by the authorities and courts of the Member States, there is a real risk that bodies of case law may evolve within the Community which will be inconsistent, if not contradictory."[10]

The Regulation came very late in the development of EC competition law. As late as 1982, the ECOSOC's Section on Transport and Competition Law were able to write that air and sea transport were the "only branches of the economy where there are currently no detailed provisions for implementing the competition rules". None the less, the Regulation was heralded for many years. In the Preamble to Regulation 954/79 concerning ratification or accession by EC Member States to the UN Code of Conduct, it was proclaimed that:

"Whereas the stabilizing role of conferences in ensuring reliable services to shippers is recognized, but it is nevertheless necessary to avoid possible breaches by conferences of the rules of competition laid down in the Treaty; whereas the Commission will accordingly forward to the Council [of Ministers] a proposal for a Regulation concerning the application of those rules to sea transport."

The Regulation took a great deal of time to emerge: while the first proposal was submitted by the Commission to the Council of Ministers in 1981, the idea of such a proposal was raised as early as 1975.[11,12] The delay was due to the intensive negotiations and detailed studies which had to be made before EC competition law could be applied to this most unique of areas. During its passage from initiation to adoption, the proposal was formally amended at least four times. The eventual adoption of the Regulation was an important achievement and cleared even further the path for Regulations 3975 and 3976/87 on air transport.

12.2.2 1981 Commission Proposal

On 16 October 1981, a proposal for a Regulation laying down detailed rules for the application of Articles 85 and 86 of the EEC Treaty to maritime transport was finally submitted by the Commission to the Council of Ministers.[13] This was at the instigation of Commissioner Andriessen. The 1981 proposed Regulation did not exempt bulk transport because of a lack of adequate experience in the field.

9. This position has now been altered due to the adoption of the Regulation.

10. At the time of its adoption the "Commission [had] no means of investigating directly cases of suspected infringements of Articles 85 and 86 in maritime transport" (Regulation 4056/86, Preamble, Recital 2).

11. See Fifth Competition Report (1975), at para.15.

12. See the European Parliament's comments in EP. Doc 1-249 (see footnote 4, above), para. 2.

13. COM(81)423; OJ C282, 5 November 1981. See Commission Information Memo P-58, October 1981.

12.2.3 1983 ECOSOC Opinion

On 3 November 1981 the Council of Ministers requested[14] the Economic and Social Committee to furnish an Opinion on the Commission's proposal. On 27 January 1983 the Economic and Social Committee published its Opinion.[15]

This resulted from the Council of Minister's request and the ECOSOC's Bureau deciding on 12 November 1981 to instruct the Section for Transport and Communications to draw up an Opinion on the matter. The Opinion, which was adopted by eighty-nine votes to four with seven abstentions, approved the Commission's proposal subject to some comments.

The ECOSOC contended that there should have been a dual basis of the Regulation, namely, Articles 84(2) and 87.[16] It approved the exclusion of bulk transport but noted the absence of a clear definition of bulk transport.[17] It also stated that the conditions attaching to the exemption were "vague and questionable".[18] The influence of the ECOSOC in the formulation of this Regulation must not be underestimated.

12.2.4 1984 European Parliament's Report

On 12 November 1981, the Council of Ministers requested, pursuant to Article 87 of the EEC Treaty, the European Parliament to deliver an Opinion on the proposal. The President of the European Parliament referred the request to the Committee on Economic and Monetary Affairs, the Legal Affairs Committee as well as the Committee on Transport. On 11 May 1984, the European Parliament's Committee on Economic and Monetary Affairs published an Interim Report[19] on the proposal. The body of the report stated that the Committee:

"2. Welcomes the proposed Regulation on the application of the competition policy provisions laid down in the Treaty to maritime transport and stresses that the main aims of the regulation are compatible with the objectives of the UN Convention of 6 April 1979 on a Code of Conduct for Liner Conferences, which the Member States also accepted in the form of EEC Regulation 954/79 of 15 May 1979[20];

3. Agrees in principle that there should be the greatest possible concordance between the UN Code and the Regulation with respect to the rules of competition laid down in the Treaty and stresses the need for the Regulation to take account of practical experience gained in the implementation of the Code;

4. The Committee on Economic and Monetary Affairs takes the view that, where compatible with the content of the proposed Regulation, the detailed provisions of Articles 4 and 5 should be formulated to correspond closely to the following provisions in the Code:

- non-differentiation between shippers;
- formal consultation between shippers and conferences on matters of common interest;
- loyalty agreements, of which the form and content are the object of negotiation between the conference and shippers;
- access to clearly specified tariffs and similar conditions of transport etc. upon the request of any party concerned;
- services not covered by freight charged;

14. OJ C282/4, 5 November 1981, p. 4.

15. Opinion on the Proposal for a Council Regulation laying down detailed rules for the application of Articles 85 and 86 of the Treaty to Maritime Transport, OJ C77/13, 23.3.83; CES 73/83.

16. *Ibid.*, para.1.1.3. The Regulation, as finally adopted, included this provision.

17. *Ibid.*, para. 1.2.1.

18. *Ibid.*, para. 1.3.6.

19. Doc. 1-249/84/A, Rapporteur: Mr K. Nyborg.

20. OJ L121, 17 May 1979, p. 1.

5. Therefore calls on the Commission to show the necessary flexibility when applying the Regulation and, where such is compatible with the principles of competition policy, to accept that the sector should regulate its own conduct;

6. Considers the Commission's proposed definition of bulk transports to be unclear and recommends that only cargo without mark or count or cargo for which the tariffs have been negotiated should be excluded from the scope of the Regulation;

7. Agrees with the Commission that the question of access by outside shipping companies to conferences and the question of the internal organisation of conferences are covered by the general provisions of the Treaty and that there is therefore no need for an implementing Regulation in this connection; such matters can only be settled case by case;

8. Is aware of the international aspects of liner conferences and the fact that any regulation of these will necessarily come into conflict with the legal positions of those conference parties that are not Member States of the Community; therefore realizes that there is a risk of jurisdictional problems arising in this respect with third countries and wishes to avoid conflicts in this area . . ."

The European Parliament ultimately passed two resolutions on the proposal: the Resolution on the proposal from the EC Commission to the EC Council for a Regulation laying down detailed rules for the application of Articles 85 and 86 of the Treaty to maritime transport[21] and the Resolution embodying the opinion of the European Parliament on Memorandum No.3 from the EC Commission to the EC Council and on the proposals *inter alia* for amendments to the Proposal for a Regulation laying down detailed rules for the application of Articles 85 and 86 of the Treaty to Maritime Transport.[22]

12.2.5 1985 Amended Commission Proposal

A proposal for the Regulation was contained in the Commission's Communication of 14 March 1985 entitled "Progress Towards the Common Transport Policy—Maritime Transport".[23] This was an amended version of the 1981 proposal in the light of, among other things, the opinions of the European Parliament and the Economic and Social Committee. In its Annual Report on Competition for 1985, the Commission identified the major issues deserving amendment:

"(i) redrafting certain definitions (conference, transport user, tramp vessel services) so as to be closer to the wording used by the UN Code of Conduct for Liner Conferences;

(ii) the requirement for application of the block exemption Regulation have been brought down to only one condition (*sine qua non*), namely the principle of non-discrimination. Requirements contained in the earlier version as conditions for application have now been converted into obligations, which while not barring coverage by the block exemption may nevertheless give rise to withdrawal of the benefit thereof;

(iii) adding an obligation of conferences to consult shippers and providing for loyalty agreements covering less than 100% of a shippers cargo;

(iv) a clear and exhaustive definition of the special circumstances having effects incompatible with the conditions laid down in Article 85(3) and justifying the withdrawal of the benefit of the block exemption; these are: acts of third states, acts of conferences and change of market conditions;

(v) the establishment of a differentiated regime for the efficient monitoring of the exempted conference agreements depending on the presence or elimination of outsider competition;

(vi) redrafting Article 8 which provides for the possibility of concluding agreements with third countries."

21. OJ C172/178, 2.7.84.
22. OJ C255/12, 13.10.86.
23. Document COM(85)90 Final.

An examination of part of the Recitals to the Regulation is instructive:

"Whereas the rules of competition form part of the Treaty's general provisions which also apply to maritime transport[24]; whereas detailed rules for applying those provisions are set out in the Chapter of the Treaty dealing with the rules on competition or are to be determined by the procedures laid down therein;

Whereas according to Council Regulation No. 141, Council Regulation No. 17 does not apply to transport; whereas Council Regulation (EEC) No. 1017/68 applies to inland transport only; whereas, consequently, the Commission has no means at present of investigating directly cases of suspected infringement of Articles 85 and 86 in maritime transport; whereas, moreover, the Commission lacks such powers of its own to take decisions or impose penalties as are necessary for it to bring to an end infringements established by it;

Whereas this situation necessitates the adoption of a Regulation applying the rules of competition to maritime transport; whereas Council Regulation (EEC) No. 954/79 of May 15, 1979, concerning the ratification by Member States of, or their accession to, the United Nations Convention on a Code of Conduct for Liner Conferences will then result in the application of the Code of Conduct to a considerable number of conferences serving the Community; whereas the Regulation applying the rules of competition to maritime transport foreseen in the last recital of Regulation (EEC) No. 954/79 should take account of the adoption of the Code; whereas, as far as conferences subject to the Code of Conduct are concerned, the Regulation should supplement the code or make it more precise;

Whereas it appears preferable to exclude tramp vessel services from the scope of this Regulation, rates for these services being freely negotiated on a case-by-case basis in accordance with supply and demand conditions;

Whereas this Regulation should take account of the necessity, on the one hand to provide for implementing rules that enable the Commission to ensure that competition is not unduly distorted within the Common Market, and on the other hand to avoid excessive regulation of the sector."

12.2.6 1986: Commission Amendment

The Commission published an amended proposal on 24 November 1986.[25] The amendment suggested changes to Articles 14 and 15 of the Proposal.

Article 14 related to liaison with the authorities of the Member States. Paragraphs 5 and 6 of the proposal had read:

"5. Consultation shall take place at a joint meeting convened by the Commission; such meeting shall be held not later than fourteen days after dispatch of the notice convening it. This notice shall, in respect of each case to be examined, be accompanied by a summary of the case together with an indication of the most important documents, and a preliminary draft decision.

6. The Advisory Committee may deliver an opinion notwithstanding that some of its members or their alternates are not present. A report of the outcome of the consultative proceedings shall be annexed to the draft decision. It shall not be made public."

12.3 ENTRY INTO FORCE OF THE REGULATION

Regulation 4056/86 entered into force on 1 July 1987.[26]

24. See the judgment of the ECJ in *Commission v. France* (*French Seafarers'* Case) [1974] ECR 359, [1974] 2 CMLR 216; analysed in Chapter 5, above.

25. OJ C324/6, 17.12.86; COM(86) 676 final.

26. Regulation 4056/86, Article 27.

12.4 LEGAL BASES OF THE REGULATION

The Regulation was adopted on the bases of Articles 84(2) and 87 of the EEC Treaty. It will be recalled[27] that Article 84(2) provides that the Council of Ministers may, acting by a qualified majority, decide whether, to what extent and by what procedure appropriate provisions may be laid down for sea and air transport. It will also be recalled[28] that prior to the SEA Article 87 provides for the adoption of Regulations and Directives to give effect to the principles set out in Articles 85 and 86.

The original proposal in 1981 was to be adopted solely on the basis of Article 87.[29] The Economic and Social Committee[30] as well as the European Parliament[31] both objected to this approach. Clough and Randolph comment:

"The importance of the legal basis for the substantive content of Community legislation has been established in numerous cases by the European Court. This includes the difference in voting procedure between majority voting, required under Article 87, and unanimity as required then under Article 84(2). However, in the present context of sea transport, set against the background of uncertainty as to whether the competition rules applied at all without EC Council action under Article 84(2), the dual legal basis has more than procedural significance.

The debate between the EC Council and the EC Commission over legal basis reflects an underlying difference over policy. Article 9 of the Regulation deals predominantly with what must be classified as transport policy, rather than competition policy. It therefore requires an appropriate legal basis which only could have been Article 84(2), in the absence of further progress with a common sea transport policy. However, it is not clear from the Regulation, or its legislative history, whether the EC Council intended the liberal approach applied to closed liner conferences, with the emphasis on self-regulation under the UNCTAD Code, to reflect the triumph of transport policy over competition policy. The result, albeit short-lived, does.

In fact, despite its acceptance of the Brussels package and its endorsement of the UNCTAD Code, the EC Commission throughout the five years of its legislative history tried to introduce in the proposal provisions for preventing conferences from breaching the competition rules. In the end, the provisions falling into that category were brought much closer into line with the UNCTAD Code, as requested, for example, by the European Parliament.

It is understood that the EC Commission eventually adopted the addition of Article 84(2) to the legal basis on the ground that Article 9 of the Regulation is concerned with transport, as opposed to competition policy since it is concerned with international law conflicts. Council Regulation (EEC) 4056/86 was adopted by the EC Council on the dual legal basis.

However, the inclusion of the transport policy legal basis, relating to sea and air transport in Article 84(2), is unusual. This is clear from the fact that the EC Council regulations laying down the procedure for applying the competition rules and enabling the EC Commission to adopt block exemption regulations for certain categories of agreements in the air transport sector were both adopted on the basis of Article 87 alone. The weight given to transport policy signified by the dual legal basis is unlikely to be repeated.

The EC Commission has reinforced recently its opposition to repeating the liberal regime adopted in respect of liner conferences in Council Regulation (EEC) 4056/86, largely because of transport policy considerations, in the case of other sea transport operations such as consortia and multi-modal arrangements."[32]

27. On Article 84(2) of the EEC Treaty, see Chapter 10, above.

28. On Article 87 of the EEC Treaty, see Chapter 10, above.

29. See OJ C282/4, 5.11.81. See also *Ninth Report on Competition Policy*, 1979, para. 15.

30. See Opinion on the Proposal for a Council Regulation laying down detailed rules for the Application of Articles 85 and 86 of the [EEC] Treaty to Maritime Transport, para.1.1, OJ C77/13, 23.3.83

31. Resolution of the European Parliament embodying the Opinion of the European Parliament on Memorandum No.3 from the EC Commission to the EC Council etc., para.40, OJ C255/182, 13.10.86

32. *Op. cit.*, 4.3.

12.5 LEGAL EFFECT

As Article 27 of the Regulation provides, it is binding in its entirety and directly applicable to all Member States.[33] There was no need to have national legislation implementing the measure.[34] The Regulation gave the Commission the means of implementing Articles 85 and 86 in the sphere of maritime transport.

12.6 APPLICATION OF THE REGULATION

12.6.1 Text of Article 1

The Regulation is limited in scope. Article 1 of the Regulation provides:

"1. This Regulation lays down detailed rules for the application of Articles 85 and 86 of the Treaty to maritime transport services.

2. It shall apply only to international maritime transport services from or to one or more Community ports, other than tramp vessel services.

3. For the purposes of this Regulation:

(a) 'tramp vessel services' means the transport of goods in bulk or in break-bulk in a vessel chartered wholly or partly to one or more shippers on the basis of a voyage or time charter or any other form of contract for non-regularly scheduled or non-advertised sailings where the freight rates are freely negotiated case by case in accordance with the conditions of supply and demand;

(b) 'liner conference' means a group of two or more vessel-operating carriers which provides international liner services for the carriage of cargo on a particular route or routes within specified geographical limits and which has an agreement or arrangement, whatever its nature, within the framework of which they operate under uniform or common freight rates and any other agreed conditions with respect to the provision of liner services;

(c) 'transport user' means an undertaking (e.g. shippers, consignees, forwarders, etc.) provided it has entered into, or demonstrates an intention to enter into, a contractual or other arrangement with a conference or shipping line for the shipment of goods, or any association of shippers."

Article 1 of the Regulation differs from Article 1 of the original proposal in 1981 which read:

"1. This regulation lays down detailed rules for the application of Articles 85 and 86 of the Treaty to maritime transport.

2. It shall apply only to international maritime transport operations other than bulk transports from or to one or more Community ports."

The Commission, in its Explanatory Memorandum[35] to that proposed Regulation, wrote:

"In view of the jurisprudence of the Court[36] the regulation affects all sea transport services other than bulk which may affect trade between Member States. In principle it applies to all sea

33. On direct applicability, see Chapter 3, above.

34. See para. 3.5.2.2.1, above, on the legal effect of Regulations.

35. See COM(81)423 final.

36. *Cf.* considerations put forward by the Court in the following judgments: (1) Case 22/71 *Beguelin Import v. SAGL Import-Export* [1971] ECR 949, at p. 959, paras 10 and 11; (2) Case 48/69 *Imperial Chemical Industries Ltd v. Commission* [1972] ECR 619 at pp. 665–6; (3) Cases 6 and 7/73 *Commercial Solvents v. Commission* [1974] ECR 223 at pp. 254–6; and (4) Case 36/74 *Walrave and Koch v. Union Cycliste Internationale* [1974] ECR 1405, at p. 1421.

transport to or from a Community port, even if it concerns transport between the Community and a third country. Restrictive or abusive practices or lines between the Community and third countries may in fact affect trade between Member States by influencing the competitive position of the ports and the undertakings in their area of influence, even if potential, and by disturbing the usual flows of transport at Community level of both exports and imports."

12.6.2 Effect of Article 1

Article 1 provides international liner conferences with an automatic open-ended group exemption subject to certain exceptions. In essence, it applies to liner services only and provides an exemption to certain liner cargo conferences within the meaning of the UNCTAD Code.

12.6.3 Transport services

The Regulation applies only to certain types of maritime transport services.[37] Thus, it does not apply to any activity which is not a "transport" service, thus services which are ancillary or related to transport do not fall within the scope of the Regulation.[38] Travel agency, shipping agency, ships' brokerage or similar "ancillary" activities would not fall within the scope of the Regulation.

12.6.4 International transport services

The Regulation applies only to certain types of international maritime transport services from or to one or more Community ports, other than tramp vessel services.[39] Thus, the Regulation does not apply to maritime transport within an EC Member State or, put another way, it does not apply to cabotage trade in an EC Member State. Nor does it apply to trade between ports in two different States where neither State is a Member State of the EC. There is, of course, nothing stopping Articles 85 and 86 (in themselves) from being applied to such trade where there was an effect on trade between EC Member States but this would prove difficult in the absence of the implementing rules to be found in Regulation 4056/86.[40] The Regulation will apply whenever the international journey begins or ends in an EC port.

12.6.5 Maritime services

The Regulation applies to maritime services. Unfortunately, this term is left undefined by the Regulation. The Commission has interpreted this term narrowly and sees it purely in the context of the sea-leg of a journey.[41] Thus, any other part of a multimodal journey would fall outside Regulation 4056/86.

37. Regulation 4056/86, Article 1(2).

38. For a comparable situation in relation to ground-handling and reservation activities in the airline industry, see *Olympic Airways* OJ 1985 L46/51 and *London-European Airways–Sabena* OJ 1988 L317/47, respectively.

39. Regulation 4056/86, Article 1(2).

40. See Cases 89/85, 104/85, 114/85, 116/85 and 125-9/85 *A. Ahlstrom Osakeyhtio v. EC Commission* [1988] ECR 5193; (known as the *Wood Pulp* case). *Quaere* the use of Articles 88 and 89 in such circumstances

41. See, for example, OJ 1990 C59/2, para. 1; OJ 1990 C130/3, para. 1; OJ 1990 C162/16, para. 20; and the draft Consortia block exemption in OJ 1990 C167/9, Recital 6 (acknowledgement to Ruttley (*op. cit.*) for these citations)

12.6.6 Services other than tramp services

The Regulation applies only to international maritime transport services from or to one or more Community ports, other than tramp vessel services (as defined in the Regulation).[42] The non-application of the Regulation to tramp services was at the insistence of Greece. For the purposes of the Regulation, "tramp vessel services" is generously defined as meaning:

> "the transport of goods in bulk or in break-bulk in a vessel chartered wholly or partly to one or more shippers on the basis of a voyage or time charter or any other form of contract for non-regularly scheduled or non-advertised sailings where the freight rates are freely negotiated case by case in accordance with the conditions of supply and demand."[43]

It is assumed by many commentators (but not all) that this sector operates in a competitive environment in any case. The mere fact that the Regulation does not apply to such services does not prejudice the fact that Articles 85 and 86 do apply. Nor does it prejudice the possibility that the Commission may make a proposal in this area in the future. Nor again, does it prejudice the application of the Regulation (i.e. Regulation 4056/86) where the trade is a tramp one but the freight rate has not been freely negotiated.

Ruttley has enumerated five common types of maritime agreement which fall within the scope of Regulation 4056/86 but they require notification to the Commission and exemption under Article 85(3) as they do not fall within the scope of the block exemptions provided by the Regulation. The five are:

> "(1) joint venture agreements and other consortia agreements (for example, vessel pools),
> (2) exclusive port utilisation agreements,
> (3) management and shared route agreements,
> (4) container 'slot charter' or slot exchange arrangements on vessels,
> (5) agreements between Liner Conferences and independent shipping operators (the so-called 'outsider agreements')."[44]

12.6.7 Transport users

The Regulation only applies to certain agreements between transport users. In the context of the Regulation, a "transport user" is an "undertaking[45] (e.g. shippers, consignees, forwarders etc.) provided it has entered into, or demonstrates an intention to enter into, a contractual or other arrangement with a conference or shipping line for the shipment of goods, or any association of shippers".[46] This is a mirror-image of the term used in the Liner Code Exemption. Who else is included? Bredima-Savopoulou and Tzoannos comment:

> "[i]t is uncertain whether providers of ancillary services (insurers, classification societies, stevedores, shipping agents) are covered by the Regulation or whether they are subject to the ordinary rules of competition. Basically, the Regulation is of direct relevance only to shipowners and operators."[47]

42. Regulation 4056/86, Article 1(2).
43. Regulation 4056/86, Article 1(3)(a). This was a controversial definition and one which resulted after considerable discussion.
44. Ruttley, *op. cit.*, footnote 4 above, at p. 9.
45. On the meaning of the concept of "undertaking", see Chapter 10, above.
46. Regulation 4056/86, Article 1(3)(c).
47. *Op. cit.*, pp. 207–208, footnote 9.

Views differ on this point. It is submitted that such undertakings are engaged in activities which are ancilliary to maritime transport and thus such agreements fall outside the scope of the block exemptions contained in the Regulation. Thus, just as a ground handling agreement is outside the scope of the comparable Regulation on air transport, thus a stevedoring agreement is outside the Regulation.

12.6.8 Agreements between providers of ancillary services

As a general rule, the Regulation provides no exemption for agreements between the providers of ancillary services such as shipping agents or for agreements between maritime transport service operators and the providers of ancillary services. The sole exception is contained in Article 2 of the Regulation.

12.6.9 Passenger traffic

The transport of passengers falls within the scope of the Regulation.[48] Passenger liner conferences are however not included in the definition of "liner conferences" for the purposes of Article 1(3)(b).

12.6.10 Scope

The ambiguous drafting of Article 1 means that there is sufficient doubt that no view can be expressed here as to who are the "beneficiaries" of the Regulation: does it cover ships' agents; classification societies; insurers etc.? The answer will have to be determined by the authorities and will probably turn on the facts of each case.

12.7 TECHNICAL AGREEMENTS

12.7.1 Introduction

Article 2 of the Regulation provides an exemption under Article 85(3) of the EEC Treaty[49] for certain types of agreements, decisions and concerted practices[50] whose *sole* object and effect is to achieve technical improvements or cooperation by means of:

(a) the introduction of uniform application of standards or types in respect of vessels and other means of transport, equipment, supplies or fixed installations;
(b) the exchange or pooling for the purpose of operating transport services, of vessels, space on vessels or slots or other means of transport, staff, equipment or fixed installations;
(c) the organisation and execution of successive or supplementary maritime transport operations and the establishment or application of inclusive rates and conditions for such operations;
(d) the co-ordination of transport timetables for connecting routes;
(e) the consolidation of individual assignments; or
(f) the establishment or application of uniform rules concerning the structure and the conditions governing the application of transport tariffs.

48. See the Nineteenth Report on Competition Policy (1989), para.29.
49. On the concept of an exemption under Article 85(3) of the EEC Treaty, see Chapter 10, above.
50. On the concepts of agreements, decisions and concerted practices, see Chapter 10, above.

An agreement with any ulterior motive will not benefit from the exemption: the *sole* object and effect of the agreement must fall within the scope of Article 2 of the Regulation.

12.7.2 Text of Article 2

Article 2(1) of the Regulation provides:

"1. The prohibition laid down in Article 85(1) of the EEC Treaty shall not apply to agreements[51], decisions[52] and concerted practices[53] whose sole object and effect is to achieve technical improvements or co-operation by means of:

(a) the introduction of uniform application of standards or types in respect of vessels and other means of transport, equipment, supplies or fixed installations;
(b) the exchange or pooling for the purpose of operating transport services, of vessels, space on vessels or slots or other means of transport, staff, equipment or fixed installations;
(c) the organization and execution of successive or supplementary maritime transport operation and the establishment or application of inclusive rates and conditions for such operations;
(d) the co-ordination of transport timetables for connecting routes;
(e) the consolidation of individual assignments;
(f) the establishment or application of uniform rules concerning the structure and the conditions governing the application of transport tariffs.

2. The Commission shall, if necessary, submit to the Council proposals for the amendment of the list contained in paragaph 1."

This is, in effect, a white list.

The original proposal in 1981 was very similar to the provision which was finally adopted. The original provision read as follows (with the changed paragraphs italicised):

"1. The prohibition laid down in Article 85(1) of the Treaty shall not apply to agreements, decisions or concerted practices whose sole object and effect is to achieve technical improvements or co-operation by means of:

(a) the introduction or uniform application of standards or types of vessels and other means of transport, equipment, supplies or fixed installation;
(b) the exchange or pooling, for the purpose of operating transport services, of vessels and other modes of transport, staff, equipment or fixed installations;
(c) the organisation and execution of successive or supplementary maritime transport operations and the establishment and application of inclusive rates and conditions for such operations;
(d) the coordination of transport timetables for connecting routes;
(e) the bulking of individual consignments;
(f) the establishment or application of uniform rules concerning the structure and the conditions governing the application of transport on condition that such rules do not directly or indirectly fix rates and conditions of carriage;

2. The Commission shall, if necessary, submit to the Council proposals for the amendment of the list contained in paragraph 1 of this article."

The Commission commenting on this 1981 Proposal said: "The list of exceptions hardly differs from that of Article 3 of Regulation (EEC) No.1017/68. Account has been taken in particular of the fact this regulation only applies to one mode of

51. On the concept of "agreements" for the purposes of EC competition law, Chapter 10, above.
52. On the concept of "decisions" for the purposes of EC competition law, Chapter 10, above.
53. On the concept of "concerted practices" for the purposes of EC competition law, Chapter 10, above.

transport."[54] This list (which may well be termed a "White List") is also quite similar to that contained in the comparable air transport measure. This list is not closed for ever. Article 2(2) of the Regulation provides that the Commission shall, if necessary, submit to the Council of Ministers proposals for the amendment of the list.

It is worth stressing that the *sole* object and effect must be to conclude a technical agreement. If there is any other motive then the automatic exemption no longer applies.

12.7.2.1 The introduction of uniform application of standards or types in respect of vessels and other means of transport, equipment, supplies or fixed installations

The introduction of uniform application of standards or types in respect of vessels and other means of transport, equipment, supplies or fixed installations is an inherently technical-type agreement.

12.7.2.2 The exchange or pooling for the purpose of operating transport services, of vessels, space on vessels or slots or other means of transport, staff, equipment or fixed installations

The *sole object and effect* of the agreement must be the exchange or pooling for the purpose of operating transport services, of vessels, space on vessels or slots or other means of transport, staff, equipment or fixed installations. It has been commented that the paragraph:

> "makes it clear that the exemption will only apply where the '*sole object and effect*' of the agreement or practice is to achieve technical improvements or co-operation. Accordingly this paragraph does not of itself provide exemption for joint ventures or consortia except of a very restricted kind. It is partly for this reason that the Commission has recently put forward proposals for a new Regulation clarifying the position of joint ventures and consortia."[55]

12.7.2.3 The organisation and execution of successive or supplementary maritime transport operations and the establishment or application of inclusive rates and conditions for such operations

Sub-paragraph (c) of Article 2(1) of the Regulation deals with the organisation and execution of successive or supplementary maritime transport operations and the establishment or application of inclusive rates and conditions for such operations. It has been commented that:

> "Sub-paragraph (c) relates to supplementary transport operations and the establishment of inclusive rates and conditions. In view of the rapid growth of inter-modal transport this is clearly another area where clarification is required since the exemption provided by Article 2(1)(c) will again only apply where the *sole object and effect* of the Agreement or practice is to achieve technical improvements or co-operation. It is therefore hoped that the Regulation which is currently under consideration will clarify the extent to which agreements relating to Inter-modal transport are covered by the Regulation or will lay down further rules."[56]

54. See COM(81)423 final, p. 5.
55. Hickey, *op. cit.*, p. 10.
56. Hickey, *op. cit.*, p. 10.

12.7.2.4 The co-ordination of transport timetables for connecting routes

The co-ordination of transport timetables for connecting routes is a purely technical matter and an agreement which aims or effects solely at the co-ordination of transport timetables for connecting routes will benefit from the automatic exemption contained in Article 2 of the Regulation.

12.7.2.5 The consolidation of individual assignments

The consolidation of individual assignments is again a purely technical matter and any agreement which aims or effects solely the consolidation of individual assignments will benefit from the automatic exemption contained in Article 2 of the Regulation.

12.7.2.6 The establishment or application of uniform rules concerning the structure and the conditions governing the application of transport tariffs

An agreement which aims or effects only the establishment or application of uniform rules concerning the structure and the conditions governing the application of transport tariffs automatically benefits from the exemption contained in Article 2 of the Regulation.

12.7.3 Amendment

It is to be noted that the Council add to, delete from or amend the list of technical agreements upon a proposal from the Commission.

12.8 BLOCK EXEMPTION FOR LINER CONFERENCES

12.8.1 Introduction

The block exemption contained in Article 3 of the Regulation has "provided the long aspired legal security as regards the application of the [EEC] Treaty's competition rules to maritime transport".[57] It is the "main feature" of the Regulation.[58] Articles 3 to 6 represent a far-reaching conditional block exemption for an unlimited time period for conferences and their agreements with users.[59] The exemption may be withdrawn in certain circumstances.

It is not a complete exemption in that conditions and obligations are attached to it.

A block exemption[60] is granted in Article 3 to certain types of liner conferences. However, Article 4 imposes a condition on this exemption and Article 5 imposes an obligation on the exemption.

12.8.2 Liner conferences

A "liner conference" is defined, for the purpose of the Regulation, as being:

57. Rabe, "Recent Developments in EEC Legislation Pertaining to Maritime Transport", IBA Strasbourg Conference 1989, at p. 12.

58. Ruttley, *op. cit.*, at p. 10.

59. Kreis, *op. cit.*, at p. 418.

60. On the meaning of a block exemption, see Chapter 10, above.

"a group of two or more vessel-operating carriers which provides international liner services for the carriage of cargo on a particular route or routes within specified geographical limits and which has an agreement or arrangement, whatever its nature, within the framework of which they operate under uniform or common freight rates and any other agreed conditions with respect to the provision of liner services."[61]

Thus, consortia and joint ventures are not included. Liner conferences are bodies or associations which co-ordinate the operation of regular shipping services for the carriage of general cargo on set routes with fixed schedules and tariffs. Such conferences standardise or harmonise the uniform freight rates, sailings and so on of the members of the conference.

Liner conferences safeguard their centralised system by means of a monopolistic structure operating on four levels:

(a) restricted membership;
(b) cargo sharing and pooling;
(c) loyalty arrangements; and
(d) agreements on a "common tariff" and "general conditions".[62]

12.8.3 Block exemption

Article 3 of the Regulation exempts from Article 85(1) of the EEC Treaty liner conferences (as defined in Article 1(3)(b) of the Regulation[63]) when they have as their objective the fixing of rates and conditions of carriage,[64] and, as the case may be, one or more of the following objectives: (a) the co-ordination of shipping timetables, sailing dates or dates of calls; (b) the determination of the frequency of sailings or calls; (c) the co-ordination or allocation of sailings or calls among members of the conference; (d) the regulation of the carrying capacity offered by each member; or (e) the allocation of cargo or revenue among members. This exemption is, however, subject to the condition imposed by Article 4 of the Regulation.[65]

Kreis has written:

"Substantively, Council Regulation No. 4056/86 on Maritime Transport includes a block exemption for liner conferences and for their agreements with transport users. The exemption is not limited in time. In addition, the Regulation does not obligate parties to notify the Commission of agreements, but companies may do so when they believe their agreements may violate the prohibition against cartels laid down by Article 85(1) of the [EEC] Treaty. An "opposition procedure" has been introduced for granting individual exemptions under Article 85(3), which simplifies and accelerates the process of granting exemptions where appropriate."[66]

12.8.4 Text of Article 3 of the Regulation

"Agreements, decisions and concerted practices of all or part of the members of one or more liner conferences are hereby exempted from the prohibition in Article 85(1) of the Treaty[67],

61. Regulation 4056/86, Article 1(3)(b).
62. See Report of the ECOSOC's Section on Transport and Communications, *ibid.*
63. See Chapter 11, above.
64. This objective is necessary so as to benefit from the block exemption. If it is absent then it would be necessary to seek an individual exemption if the agreement were to otherwise fall within the scope of Article 85(1) of the EEC Treaty.
65. On Article 4 of the Regulation, see Chapter 11, above.
66. *Op. cit.*, at p. 417, footnote omitted.
67. I.e. the EEC Treaty.

subject to the condition imposed by Article 4 of this Regulation, when they have as their objective the fixing of rates and conditions of carriage, and, as the case may be, one or more of the following objectives:

(a) the co-ordination of shipping timetables, sailing dates or dates of calls;
(b) the determination of the frequency of sailings or calls;
(c) the co-ordination or allocation of sailings or calls among members of the conference;
(d) the regulation of the carrying capacity offered by each member;
(e) the allocation of cargo or revenue among members."

The original proposal read:

"1. A liner conference means a group of vessel-operating carriers which provides liner services for the carriage of cargo or passengers on a particular route or routes within specified geographical limits and which jointly fixes freight rates and any other conditions for those services.

2. Agreements, decisions and concerted practices of all or part of the members of a conference or of several conferences are hereby exempted from the prohibition in Article 85(1) of the Treaty[68], subject to the conditions imposed by Article 4 of this regulation, when they have one or more of the following objects:

(a) the fixing of the above-mentioned rates and conditions of carriage and, as the case may be;
(b) the co-ordination of shipping timetables, sailing dates or dates of calls;
(c) the determination of the frequency of sailings or calls;
(d) the co-ordination or allocation of sailings or calls among members of the conference;
(e) the regulation of the carrying capacity offered by each member;
(f) the allocation of cargo or revenue among members."

The Commission in its Explanatory Memorandum to the original proposal[69] said:

"Article 85(2) of the [EEC] Treaty permits the exemption of a category of agreements from the prohibition set out in Article 85(1). It seems advisable to grant such an exemption by category to all conference agreements between shipowners. The conferences represent a considerable part of the transport committed to regular sea services throughout the world, and the fact that UNCTAD has devised a Code of Conduct for Liner Conferences implies in principle the recognition on a world-wide level of their beneficial role.

The exemption concerns the fixing of prices and so-called rationalisation agreements.

As far as prices are concerned, account must be taken of the fact that sea transport, more than any other mode of transport, is characterised by considerable fluctuations, both business and seasonal, in demand for cargo capacity. To this first cause of instability in the level of freight is added, as far as capacity is concerned, a cause which all modes of transportation have in common, that is the very considerable price variations resulting from marginal offers by shipowners wishing to avoid return voyages in ballast or to complete their cargoes.

The instability of freight which would result from the total absence of market regulation would be unfavourable to carriers and users:

— to the carriers who could not base themselves on any forecasts of profitability in order to run, maintain and renew their fleets and who could not give the users a reliable service at fixed prices;
— to the users who could only count on transport under certain conditions, who would be submitted to excessive and unforeseeable variations in freight rates and who, in the longer term, would suffer from a gradual deterioration of the service offered because the fleet had not been modernised.

Both the shipowners and the users try, through price agreements, to introduce some stability in ocean freights.

Rationalization agreements are the logical consequence of price agreements. In order to avoid competition extending to offers of capacity available but also to ensure a proper service for difficult ports, the shipowners have concluded agreements concerning calls and capacity. The

68. I.e. the EEC Treaty.
69. See COM(81)423 final, pp. 6–7.

most elaborate agreements foresee a sharing of tonnage and even revenues, which assures a regular transport of the merchandise alongside even that which is the least remunerative."

The ECOSOC has said that it looks favourably on the conferences, but thinks that the main priority is for any national shipping company which applies to able to join the conference on the same conditions as existing members.[70]

12.8.5 Condition attaching to the block exemption for liner conferences

Article 4 of the Regulation provides a condition to be attached to the exemptions contained in Articles 3 and 6 of the Regulation. Article 4 supplements the UN Code on Liner Conferences. The effect of Article 4 is that differential rates and conditions are only permissible where they are economically justified.

12.8.5.1–12.8.5.3 Text of Article 4

Article 4 of the Regulation provides:

"The exemption provided for in Articles 3 and 6 shall be granted subject to the condition that the agreement, decision or concerted practice shall not, within the common market, cause detriment to certain ports, transport users or carriers by applying for the carriage of the same goods and in the area covered by the agreement, decision or concerted practice, rates and conditions of carriage which differ according to the country of origin or destination or port of loading or discharge, unless such rates or conditions can be economically justified.

Any agreement or decision or, if it is severable, any part of such an agreement or decision not complying with this condition shall be void automatically under Article 85(2) of the Treaty."

12.8.5.4 Commission's Commentary on Article 4

In its Commentary to the provision as adopted, the Commission stated:

"A certain number of conditions are imposed on members of conferences. The general disposition of Article 79(1) of the Treaty which prohibits discrimination on the sole ground of country of origin or destination of the goods transported has been retained. Furthermore, the conditions imposed concerned fidelity agreements, by which the conferences try to secure for a certain period the custom of the shippers or forwarding agents, have as their object that the last mentioned:

(1) retain their freedom to choose their carriers and their ports;
(2) may release themselves from their commitment within a reasonable time period, and
(3) may not have imposed upon them clauses or types of agreements which would restrict their freedom too much.

Finally in order to avoid encroaching on an area regulated by Council Regulation (EEC) No.1017/68 one condition protects the freedom of choice of the users so far as land legs are concerned."[71]

12.8.5.5 Importance of Article 4: Commentary

It has been commented that the importance of Article 4 is:

"apparent from the sanction which is that all or part of an agreement under which a liner conference operated could be automatically void. The condition is however unsatisfactory in that the criteria to be applied are not set out. The level of detriment which may call the condition

70. *Ibid.*, para.2.3.2.
71. *Ibid.*, p. 7.

into play is not defined and the provision that rates or conditions of carriage which differ will have to be economically justified obviously could give rise to considerable debate. In addition there could be considerable scope for argument and debate on the question whether or not the goods in question should be considered as being 'the same goods' for the purposes of Article 4 in circumstances where the classification of goods can vary from country to country."[72]

The concept of "detriment" is an important one and deserves comment.

12.8.6 Obligations attaching to the exemption

12.8.6.1 Introduction

Article 5 of the Regulation states that in order to benefit from the exemption contained in Article 3 of the Regulation, the particular liner conference must comply with obligations in five areas, namely, (a) *consultations;* (b) *loyalty arrangements*; (c) *services not covered by the freight charges*; (d) *availability of tariffs*; and (e) *notification to the Commission of awards at arbitration and recommendations.*

Some of the obligations are taken from the UN Code of Conduct. Indeed, Article 5 is very similar to Article 11 of the Code of Conduct on Liner Conferences.

12.8.6.2 Text of Article 5

"The following obligations shall be attached to the exemption provided for in Article 3:

1. *Consultations*

There shall be consultations for the purpose of seeking solutions on general issues of principle between transport users on the one hand and conferences on the other concerning the rates, conditions and quality of scheduled maritime transport services.
These consultations shall take place whenever requested by any of the abovementioned parties.

2. *Loyalty arrangements*

The shipping lines' members of a conference shall be entitled to institute and maintain loyalty arrangements with transport users, the form and terms of which shall be matters for consultation between the conference and transport users' organizations. These loyalty arrangements shall provide safeguards making explicit the rights of transport users and conference members. These arrangements shall be based on the contract system or any other system which is also lawful.

Loyalty arrangements must comply with the following conditions:

(a) Each conference shall offer transport users a system of immediate rebates or the choice between such a system and a system of deferred rebates:
- under the system of immediate rebates each of the parties shall be entitled to terminate the loyalty arrangement at any time without penalty and subject to a period of notice of not more than six months; this period shall be reduced to three months when the conference rate is the subject of a dispute;
- under the system of deferred rebates neither the loyalty period on the basis of which the rebate is calculated nor the subsequent loyalty period required before payment of the rebate may exceed six months; this period shall be reduced to three months where the conference rate is the subject of a dispute.

(b) The conference shall, after consulting the transport users concerned, set out:
  (i) a list of cargo and any portion of cargo agreed with transport users which is specifically excluded from the scope of the loyalty arrangement; 100% loyalty arrangements may be offered but may not be unilaterally imposed;
  (ii) a list of circumstances in which transport users are released from their obligation of loyalty; these shall include:

72. Hickey, *op. cit.*, p. 11.

— circumstances in which consignments are dispatched from or to a port in the area covered by the conference but not advertised and where the request for a waiver can be justified, and
— those in which waiting time at a port exceeds a period to be determined for each port and for each commodity or class of commodities following consultation of the transport users directly concerned with the proper servicing of the port.

The conference must, however, be informed in advance by the transport user, within a specified period, of his intention to dispatch the consignment from a port not advertised by the conference or to make use of a non-conference vessel at a port served by the conference as soon as he has been able to establish from the published schedule of sailings that the maximum waiting period will be exceeded.

3. *Services not covered by the freight charges*
Transport users shall be entitled to approach the undertakings of their choice in respect of inland transport operations and quayside services not covered by the freight charge or charges on which the shipping line and the transport user have agreed.

4. *Availability of tariffs*
Tariffs, related conditions, regulations and any amendments thereto shall be made available on request to transport users at reasonable cost, or they shall be available for examination at offices of shipping lines and their agents. They shall set out all the conditions concerning loading and discharge, the exact extent of the services covered by the freight charge in proportion to the sea transport and the land transport or by any other charge levied by the shipping line and customary practice in such matters.

5. *Notification to the Commission of awards at arbitration and recommendations*
Awards given at arbitration and recommendations made by conciliators that are accepted by the parties shall be notified forthwith to the Commission when they resolve disputes relating to the practices of conferences referred to in Article 4 and in points 2 and 3 above."

12.8.6.3 Details of the obligations

There are five obligations attaching to the block exemption granted under Article 3 of the Regulation. The obligations are, according to Article 5 of the Regulation, absolute in terms of their application.

12.8.6.4 Consultations

There may be consultations for the purpose of seeking solutions on general issues of principle between transport users on the one hand and conferences on the other concerning the rates, conditions and quality of scheduled maritime transport services.[73] These consultations are to take place whenever requested by the transport users or the conferences.[74]

12.8.6.5 Loyalty arrangements

There is also an obligation in relation to loyalty arrangements. Article 5 of the Regulation provides that the shipping lines' members of a conference are entitled to institute and maintain loyalty arrangements with transport users, the form and terms of which shall be matters for consultation between the conference and transport users' organisations. These loyalty arrangements must provide safeguards making explicit

73. Regulation 4056/86, Article 5(1).
74. *Ibid.*

the rights of transport users and conference members. These arrangements are to be based on the contract system or on any other lawful system.

Article 5 of the Regulation imposes a number of conditions on loyalty arrangements. First, each conference must offer transport users a system of immediate rebates or the choice between such a system and a system of deferred rebates. Under the system of immediate rebates, each of the parties shall be entitled to terminate the loyalty arrangement at any time without penalty and subject to a period of notice of not more than six months; this period shall be reduced to three months when the conference rate is the subject of a dispute.[75] Under the system of deferred rebates, neither the loyalty period on the basis of which the rebate is calculated nor the subsequent loyalty period required before payment of the rebate may exceed six months; this period shall again be reduced to three months where the conference rate is the subject of a dispute.[76] Secondly, the conference shall, after consulting the transport users concerned, set out (i) a list of cargo and any portion of cargo agreed with transport users which is specifically excluded from the scope of the loyalty arrangement, 100% loyalty arrangements may be offered but may not be unilaterally imposed; and (ii) a list of circumstances in which transport users are released from their obligation of loyalty. These shall include: (a) circumstances in which consignments are dispatched from or to a port in the area covered by the conference but not advertised and where the request for a waiver can be justified, and those in which waiting time at a port exceeds a period to be determined for each port and for each commodity or class of commodities following consultation of the transport users directly concerned with the proper servicing of the port.[77]

In regard to these lists, the conference must, however, be informed in advance by the transport user, within a specified period, of his intention to dispatch the consignment from a port not advertised by the conference or to make use of a non-conference vessel at a port served by the conference as soon as he has been able to establish from the published schedule of sailings that the maximum waiting period will be exceeded.[78]

12.8.6.6 Services not covered by the freight charges

Transport users are to be entitled to approach the undertakings of their choice in respect of inland transport operations and quayside services not covered by the freight charge, and charges on which the shipping line and the transport user have agreed.[79]

12.8.6.7 Availability of tariffs

Article 5 of the Regulation provides that tariffs, related conditions, regulations and any amendments thereto shall be made available on request to transport users at reasonable cost, or they shall be available for examination at offices of shipping lines and their agents. They shall set out all the conditions concerning loading and discharge, and exact extent of the services covered by the freight charge in proportion to the sea transport and the land transport or by any other charge levied by the shipping line and customary practice in such matters.

75. Regulation 4056/86, Article 5(2).
76. Regulation 4056/86, Article 5(2).
77. Regulation 4056/86, Article 5(2).
78. Regulation 4056/86, Article 5(2).
79. Regulation 4056/86, Article 5(3).

12.8.6.8 Notification to the Commission of awards at arbitration and recommendations

Article 5 of the Regulation provides that it is an obligation attaching to an exemption under Article 3 of that Regulation that awards given at arbitration and recommendations made by conciliators that are accepted by the parties are to be notified forthwith to the Commission when they resolve disputes relating to the practices of conferences such as discriminations, loyalty arrangements and services not covered by freight rates.

12.9 BLOCK EXEMPTION FOR AGREEMENTS BETWEEN TRANSPORT USERS AND CONFERENCES CONCERNING THE USE OF SCHEDULED MARITIME TRANSPORT SERVICES

12.9.1 Introduction

Article 6 of the Regulation provides that agreements,[80] decisions[81] and concerted practices[82] between transport users,[83] on the one hand, and conferences, on the other, as well as agreements between transport users which may be necessary to that end, concerning the rates, conditions and quality of liner services are exempted under Article 6 of the Regulation from the prohibition laid down in Article 85(1) of the EEC Treaty as long as they are provided for in Article 5(1) and (2) of the Regulation.[84]

It is clear that Article 6 is drafted in a way which is both vague and elusive. It is also clear that given its content, it is "of comparatively narrow scope".[85]

12.9.2 Text of Article 6 of the Regulation

"Agreements, decisions and concerted practices between transport users, on the one hand, and conferences, on the other hand, and agreements between transport users which may be necessary to that end, concerning the rates, conditions and quality of liner services, as long as they are provided for in Articles 5(1) and (2) are hereby exempted from the prohibition laid down in Article 85(1) of the Treaty."

12.9.3 Definition of liner conferences

A liner conference is defined, for the purposes of the Regulation, as being:

"a group of two or more vessel-operating carriers which provides international liner services for the carriage of cargo on a particular route or routes within specified geographical limits and which has an agreement or arrangement, whatever its nature, within the framework of which they operate under uniform or common freight rates and any other agreed conditions with respect to the provision of liner services."[86]

12.9.4 Definition of transport user

A transport user is defined, for the purposes of the Regulation, as being:

80. On the concept of "agreements", see Chapter 10, above.
81. On the concept of "decisions", see Chapter 10, above.
82. On the concept of "concerted practices", see Chapter 10, above.
83. On the concept of "transport users", see Chapter 10, above.
84. On Article 85(1) EEC, see Chapter 10, above.
85. Ruttley, *op. cit.*, p. 13.
86. Regulation 4056/86, Article 1(3)(b).

"an undertaking (e.g. shippers, consignees, forwarders, etc.) provided it has entered into, or demonstrates an intention to enter into, a contractual or other arrangement with a conference or shipping line for the shipment of goods, or any association of shippers."

12.10 MONITORING OF EXEMPTED AGREEMENTS

12.10.1 Introduction

Agreements which benefit from an exemption under the Regulation (i.e. exempted agreements) require monitoring. Article 7 of the Regulation provides for such monitoring. It provides for the monitoring of breaches of an obligation imposed under Article 5 of the Regulation[87] and for effects which are incompatible with Article 85(3) of the EEC Treaty.[88,89]

12.10.2 Text of Article 7 of the Regulation

"1. *Breach of an obligation*

Where the persons concerned are in breach of an obligation which, pursuant to Article 5, attaches to the exemption provided for in Article 3, the Commission may, in order to put an end to such breach and under the conditions laid down in Section II[90]:

— address recommendations to the persons concerned;

— in the event of failure by such persons to observe those recommendations and depending upon the gravity of the breach concerned, adopt a decision that either prohibits them from carrying out or requires them to perform specific acts or, while withdrawing the benefit of the block exemption which they enjoyed, grants them an individual exemption according to Article 11(4) or withdraws the benefit of the block exemption which they enjoyed.

2. *Effects incompatible with Article 85(3)*

(a) Where, owing to special circumstances as described below, agreements, decisions and concerted practices which qualify for the exemption provided for in Articles 3 and 6 have nevertheless effects which are incompatible with the conditions laid down in Article 85(3) of the Treaty, the Commission, on receipt of a complaint or on its own initiative, under the conditions laid down in Section II,[91] shall take the measures described in (c) below. The severity of these measures must be in proportion to the gravity of the situation.

(b) Special circumstances are, *inter alia*, created by:

(i) acts of conferences or a change of market conditions in a given trade resulting in the absence or elimination of actual or potential competition such as restrictive practices whereby the trade is not available to competition; or

(ii) acts of conference which may prevent technical or economic progress or user participation in the benefits;

(iii) acts of third countries which:

— prevent the operation of outsiders in a trade,

— impose unfair tariffs on conference members,

— impose arrangements which otherwise impede technical or economic progress (cargo-sharing, limitations on types of vessels).

(c) (i) If actual or potential competition is absent or may be eliminated as a result of action by a third country, the Commission shall enter into consultations with the competent authorities of the third country concerned, followed if necessary by negotiations under directives to be given by the Council, in order to remedy the situation.

87. Regulation 4056/86, Article 7(1).
88. Regulation 4056/86, Article 7(2).
89. For the text of Article 7, see para.12.10.2, below.
90. I.e. Section II of the Regulation.
91. I.e. Section II of the Regulation.

If the special circumstances result in the absence or elimination of actual or potential competition contrary to Article 85(3)(b) of the Treaty the Commission shall withdraw the benefit of the block exemption. At the same time it shall rule on whether and, if so, under what additional conditions and obligations an individual exemption should be granted to the relevant conference agreement with a view, *inter alia*, to obtaining access to the market for non-conference lines;

(ii) If, as a result of special circumstances as set out in (b), there are effects other than those referred to in (i) hereof, the Commission shall take one or more of the measures described in paragraph 1."

12.10.3 Commentary

Article 7 is critical to the whole Regulation. If there is a breach of an obligation under Article 5 of the Regulation then Article 7(1) of the Regulation comes into focus.

It provides that where the persons concerned are in breach of an obligation which, pursuant to Article 5 of the Regulation, attaches to the exemption provided for in Article 3 of the Regulation, then the Commission may, in order to put an end to such breach and under the conditions laid down in Section II of the Regulation, first, address recommendations to the persons concerned and, secondly, if there is a failure by those persons to observe those recommendations and depending on the gravity of the breach concerned, adopt a decision that either prohibits them from carrying out or requires them to perform specific acts or, while withdrawing the benefit of the block exemption which they enjoyed, grant them an individual exemption according to Article 11(4) of the Regulation or withdraw the benefit of the block exemption altogether.[92] Article 7 means that the Commission has the sole power to monitor exempted agreement.

If the effects of the agreements, decisions or practices involved are incompatible with Article 85(3) EEC then Article 7(2) of the Regulation comes into focus. It provides that where, owing to special circumstances,[93] agreements, decisions and concerted practices which qualify for the exemption provided for in Articles 3 and 6 have nevertheless effects which are incompatible with Article 85(3) EEC, the Commission, on receipt of a complaint or on its own initiative, under the conditions laid down in Section II of the Regulation, take certain measures. Where actual or potential competition is absent or may be eliminated as a result of action by a third country, the Commission shall enter into consultations with the competent authorities of the third country concerned, followed, if necessary, by negotiations under directives to be given by the Council, in order to remedy the situation. The gravity of the measures must be in proportion to the gravity of the situation.[94] If the special circumstances result in the absence or elimination of actual or potential competition contrary to Article 85(3)(b)[95] of the EEC Treaty, the Commission shall withdraw the benefif of the block exemption. At the same time it shall rule on whether and, if so, under what additional conditions

92. Regulation 4056/86, Article 7(1).

93. "Special circumstances" are defined, in this context, as being created by (*inter alia*): (i) acts of conferences or a change of market conditions in a given trade resulting in the absence or elimination of actual or potential competition such as restrictive practices whereby the trade is not available to competition; or (ii) acts of conference which may prevent technical or economic progress or user participation in the benefits; or (iii) acts of third countries which prevent the operation of outsiders in a trade; impose unfair tariffs on conference members or impose arrangements which otherwise impede technical or economic progress (cargo-sharing, limitations on types of vessels).

94. Regulation 4056/86, Article 7(2).

95. On Article 85(3)(6), see Chapter 10, above.

and obligations an individual exemption would be granted to the relevant conference agreement with a view, *inter alia*, to obtaining access to the market for non-conference lines.[96] If, as a result of one of the "special circumstances", there are effects other than these then the Commission shall take one or more of the measures mentioned in Article 7(1) of the Regulation, namely, address recommendations to the persons concerned and, secondly, if there is a failure by those persons to observe those recommendations and depending on the gravity of the breach concerned, adopt a decision that either prohibits them from carrying out or requires them to perform specific acts or, while withdrawing the benefit of the block exemption which they enjoyed, grant them an individual exemption according to Article 11(4) of the Regulation or withdraw the benefit of the block exemption altogether.

12.11 ABUSE OF A DOMINANT POSITION

12.11.1 Introduction

Article 86 of the EEC Treaty prohibits the abuse of a dominant position.[97] Article 8(i) of the Regulation provides that any abuse of a dominant position within the meaning of Article 86 of the EEC Treaty where maritime services (as defined by the Regulation) are concerned shall be automatically prohibited, that is to say, there is no need for a prior decision to that effect. Nor will there be any exemption. Where the Commission, either on its own initiative or at the request of a Member State, or of natural or legal persons claiming a legitimate interest, finds that in any particular case the conduct of conferences benefiting from the exemption laid down in Article 3 of the Regulation, nevertheless has effects which are incompatible with Article 86 of the EEC Treaty, it may withdraw the benefit of the block exemption and take, pursuant to Article 10 of the Regulation, all appropriate measures for the purpose of bringing to an end infringements of Article 86 of the Treaty.[98] Thus, Article 86 applies to otherwise exempt conference agreements.

It has been written that:

"The acts of a conference may not only offend Article 85 and the conditions laid down by Regulation 4056/86, but also Article 86, as the Commission takes the view that the parties in a trade, which are members of a conference, may thereby be in a position of joint dominance. The relevant market in this context will be routes served by the conference and any interchangeable services on these routes, in accordance with Case 66/84 *Ahmed Saeed*. This approach enables the Commission to impose fines directly, and not to bother about the escalating procedure, where they consider that the conference has committed an abuse. It is possible that the application of this approach by the Commission will be contested before the [European] Court of Justice."[99]

12.11.2 Text of Article 8

"*Effects incompatible with Article 86 EEC*

1. The abuse of a dominant position within the meaning of Article 86 of the Treaty shall be prohibited, no prior decision to that effect being required.

96. Regulation 4056/86, Article 7(2)(c).
97. On Article 86 of the EEC Treaty, see Chapter 10, above.
98. Regulation 4056/86, Article 8(2).
99. George Close in a paper entitled "Special Provision for Shipping in EEC Competition Law", addressed to the Norwegian Shipowners, Oslo, p. 13.

2. Where the Commission, either on its own initiative or at the request of a Member State or of natural or legal persons claiming a legitimate interest, finds that in any particular case the conduct of conferences benefiting from the exemption laid down in Article 3 nevertheless has effects which are incompatible with Article 86 of the Treaty, it may withdraw the benefit of the block exemption and take, pursuant to Article 10, all appropriate measures for the purpose of bringing to an end infringements of Article 86 of the Treaty.

3. Before taking a decision under paragraph 2, the Commission may address to the conference concerned recommendations for termination of the infringement."

12.11.3 Commentary

Article 86 EEC prohibits the abuse of a dominant position. Article 8(1) of the Regulation provides that the abuse of a dominant position within the meaning of Article 86 EEC shall be prohibited and no prior decision to that effect is required. Thus, Article 86 EEC applies to otherwise exempt conference agreements.

Article 8(2) of the Regulation goes on to provide that where the Commission finds that in any particular case the conduct of conference benefiting from the exemption laid down in Article 3 of the Regulation nevertheless has effects which are incompatible with Article 86 EEC, it may withdraw the benefit of the block exemption and take, pursuant to Article 10, all appropriate measures for the purpose of bringing to an end infringements of Article 86 EEC. Before taking such a decision, the Commission must however address to the conference recommendations for the termination of the infringement.[100]

12.11.4 Example

Hickey has recorded:

"An illustration of the application of Article 86 [of the EEC Treaty] is provided by the complaint made to the [EC] Commission by Comex [in 1989] following the acquisition by Stena of Houlder Offshore. Comex complained to the Commission that Stena had thus acquired an unfair position in the market for the supply of Diver Support Vessels and that they would be prejudiced as a result. Following negotiations this dispute was resolved by Stena agreeing to time charter one of the DSV's concerned to Comex."[101]

12.12 CONFLICTS OF NATIONAL LAWS

12.12.1 Text of Article 9 of the Regulation

"1. Where the application of this Regulation to certain restrictive practices or clauses is liable to enter into conflict with the provisions laid down by law, regulation or administrative action of certain third countries which would comprise important Community trading and shipping interests, the Commission shall, at the earliest opportunity, undertake with the competent authorities of the third countries concerned, consultations aimed at reconciling as far as possible

100. Regulation 4056/86, Article 8(3).

101. *Op. cit.*, p. 12. Clough and Randolph, *op. cit.* at footnote 1, state at page 116, footnote 2, that while no exemption may be granted from Article 86 EEC "this does not prevent the EC Commission issuing 'negative clearance' decisions or comfort letters, pursuant to Article 2 of Regulation 17/62, declaring that Article 86 (and/or Article 85(1)) does not apply to the conduct in question. However, there is no such provision in Council Regulation (EEC) 4056/86 in the case of conduct directly relating to sea transport. This means that any abuse of a dominant position in the market for international sea transport services from or to one or more Community ports, other than in respect of tramp vessel services, covered by Regulation 4056/86 (i.e. Article 1(2)), will be prohibited without any prior decision to that effect being required (Article 8(1)), without any possibility of 'negative clearance' in appropriate circumstances."

the abovementioned interest with the respect of Community law. The Commission shall inform the Advisory Committee referred to in Article 15 of the outcome of these consultations.

2. Where agreements with third countries need to be negotiated, the Commission shall make recommendations to the Council, which shall authorize the Commission to open the necessary negotiations.

The Commission shall conduct these negotiations in consultation with an Advisory Committee as referred to in Article 15 and within the framework of such directives as the Council may issue to it.

3. In exercising the powers conferred on it by this Article, the Council shall act in accordance with the decision-making procedure laid down in Article 84(2) of the Treaty."

12.12.2 Commentary

Article 9 of the Regulation deals with conflicts of "international" law that is, conflicts with the laws of third states. It provides, in paragraph 1, that where the application of the Regulation to certain restrictive practices or clauses is liable to create a conflict with the provisions laid down by law, regulation or administrative action of certain third countries which would compromise important Community trading and shipping interests, the Commission shall, at the earliest opportunity, undertake with the competent authorities of the third countries concerned, consultations aimed at reconciling as far as possible the abovementioned interest with the respect of Community law. The Commission is obliged under Article 9, para. 1 of the Regulation to inform the Advisory Committee of the outcome of these consultations.

If there is need to conclude agreements with third countries,[102] then the Commission shall make recommendations[103] to the Council which in turn shall[104] authorise the Commission to open the necessary negotiations.[105] The Commission is obliged to conduct these negotiations in consultation with the Advisory Committee referred to in Article 15 of the Regulation and within the framework of any directives which the Council may make.[106,107] Regulation 4056/86, Article 9(2).

The Commission has had contact with such foreign agencies as the US Federal Maritime Commission.[108]

12.13 RULES OF PROCEDURE

Section II of the Regulation sets out rules of procedure.[109] The rules of procedure are similar to the procedural provisions in Regulation 17/62[110] implementing Articles 85 and 86 of the EEC Treaty generally; Regulation 1017/68 relating to the rail, road and inland waterway transport; and Regulation 3975/87[111] in respect of air transport. All in all, however, what has emerged has been described as a "complicated and time-consuming procedure".[112]

102. I.e., non-EC States.

103. On the legal status of Recommendations, see para.3.5.2.2.4, above.

104. In exercising this power, the Council shall act in accordance with the decision-making procedure laid down in Article 84(2) EEC : see Regulation 4056/86, Article 9(3).

105. Regulation 4056/86, Article 9(2).

106 In exercising this power, the Council shall act in accordance with the decision-making procedure laid down in Article 84(2) EEC : see Regulation 4056/86, Article 9(3).

107. Regulation 4056/86, Article 9(2).

108. See *American Shipper*, January 1990, at p. 14 onwards (cited in Ruttley, *op. cit.*, at p. 17).

109. Remember that Article 7 of Section I of Regulation 4056/86 also has procedural implications.

110. OJ 1962, 204; OJ 1959–62, 87. See Kerse, Antitrust Procedure (1987), *passim*.

111. OJ L374/1.

112. ECOSOC (1983), *ibid.*, para.2.9.1.

Three points deserve special mention. First, the parties to an agreement are not obliged to notify their agreements, decisions or concerted practices to the Commission. Secondly, the rules of procedure do not provide for applications for negative clearances.[113] Thirdly, the rules cast the Commission in the roles of investigator, prosecutor and judge.[114]

12.13.1 Complaints

12.13.1.1 Text of Article 10

"Acting on receipt of a complaint or on its own initiative, the Commission shall initiate procedures to terminate any infringement of the provisions of Articles 85(1) or 86 of the Treaty or to enforce Article 7 of this Regulation.

Complaints may be submitted by:

(a) Member States;

(b) Natural or legal persons who claim a legitimate interest."

12.13.1.2 Procedures on complaint or on the Commission's own initiative

Article 10 of the Regulation provides that acting on receipt of a complaint or on its own initiative, the Commission shall initiate procedures to terminate any infringement of the provisions of Articles 85(1)[115] or 86[116] of the EEC Treaty or to enforce Article 7 of the Regulation.[117] The complaint must be made in one of the official languages of the EC. There are no restrictions on the content or form of the complaint.

12.13.1.3 Locus standi to submit a complaint

Article 10 of the Regulation provides that complaints may be submitted by: (a) Member States and (b) natural or legal persons who claim a legitimate interest. Thus, the formal right of complaint accorded to Member State governments under Article 89 of the EEC Treaty now applies to other persons who have a "legitimate interest". The Regulation does not define "legitimate interest"; thus it must be decided on a case-by-case basis.

12.13.2 Result of procedures on complaint or on the Commission's own initiative

12.13.2.1 Introduction

If the Commission finds that there has been an infringement of Articles 85 and/or 86 of the EEC Treaty then recourse must be had to Article 11 of the Regulation.

12.13.2.2 Text of Article 11

"Result of Procedures on Complaint or on the Commission's own Initiative

1. Where the Commission finds that there has been an infringement of Articles 85(1) or 86 of the Treaty, it may by decision require the undertakings or associations of undertakings concerned to bring such infringement to an end.

113. On negative clearances, see para. 10.1.7.1, above.
114. See the comments of thc ECOSOC (1983), ibid. at footnote 4, para.2.11.3.
115. On Article 85(1) EEC, see Chapter 10, above.
116. On Article 86 EEC, see Chapter 10, above.
117. On Article 7 of the Regulation, see Chapter 10, above.

Without prejudice to the other provisions of this Regulation, the Commission may, before taking a decision under the preceding paragraph, address to the undertakings or associations of undertakings concerned, recommendations for termination of the infringement.

2. Paragraph 1 shall apply also to cases falling within Article 7 of this Regulation.

3. If the Commission, acting on a complaint received, concludes that on the evidence before it there are no grounds for intervention under Articles 85(1) or 86 of the Treaty or Article 7 of this Regulation, in respect of any agreement, decision or practice, it shall issue a decision rejecting the complaint as unfounded.

4. If the Commission, whether acting on a complaint received or on its own initiative, concludes that an agreement, decision or concerted practice satisfies the provisions both of Article 85(1) and of Article 85(3) of the Treaty, it shall issue a decision applying Article 85(3). Such decision shall indicate the date from which it is to take effect. This date may be prior to that of the decision."

12.13.2.3 Commentary on Article 11

The result of the procedures on complaint or on the Commission's own initiative is dealt with by Article 11 of the Regulation.

If the Commission finds that there has been an infringement of Articles 85(1) or 86 of the EEC Treaty or Article 7 of the Regulation,[118] it may by way of a decision[119] requiring the undertakings[120] or associations of undertakings[121] concerned to bring such infringement to an end.[122] Without prejudice to the other provisions of the Regulation, the Commission may, before taking a decision under the foregoing procedure, address to the undertakings[123] or associations of undertakings[124] concerned, recommendations[125] for termination of the infringement.[126]

If the Commission, acting on a complaint received, concludes that on the evidence before it there are no grounds for intervention under Articles 85(1) or 86 of the EEC Treaty or Article 7 of Regulation 4056/86, in respect of any agreement, decision or practice, it shall issue a decision rejecting the complaint as unfounded.[127]

If the Commission, whether acting on a complaint received or on its own initiative, concludes that an agreement,[128] decision[129] or concerted practice[130] satisfies the provisions both of Article 85(1)[131] and of Article 85(3)[132] of the EEC Treaty, it shall issue a decision[133] applying Article 85(3).[134] Such decision shall indicate the date from which it is to take effect. This date may be prior to that of the decision.[135]

The Commission is obliged to publish the decisions which it takes pursuant to Article 11.[136] Such publication shall state the names of the parties and the main content

118. Regulation 4056/86, Article 11(2). On Article 7 of Regulation 4056/86, see para.12.10.3, above.
119. On decisions, see above.
120. On undertakings, see above.
121. On associations of undertakings, see above.
122. Regulation 4056/86, Article 11(1), sub-paragraph 1.
123. On undertakings, see above.
124. On associations of undertakings, see above.
125. On recommendations, see above.
126. Regulation 4056/86, Article 11(1), sub-para.2.
127. Regulation 4056/86, Article 11(3).
128. On agreement, see above.
129. On the concept of decision, see above.
130. On concerted practice, see above.
131. On Article 85(1) EEC, see above.
132. On Article 85(1) EEC, see above.
133. On decisions, see above.
134. On Article 85(3) EEC, see paras 4.3.3.2.11 *et seq.*, above.
135. Regulation 4056/86, Article 11(4).
136. Regulation 4056/86, Article 25(1).

of the decision; it shall also have regard to the legitimate interests of the undertakings in the protection of their business secrets.[137]

12.13.3 Opposition procedure

12.13.3.1 Introduction

Article 12 of the Regulation provides for an opposition procedure for any agreement, decision or concerted practice which does not qualify for the block exemption under Article 3 of the Regulation. This opposition procedure facilitates (to some extent) the granting of an individual exemption. Parties to an agreement (etc.) may by formally applying under Article 12 seek an exemption under Article 85(3) for the agreement. Interestingly, Article 12 of the Regulation does not contemplate an application for a negative clearance.

12.13.3.2 Text of Article 12

"*Application of Article 85(3)—Objections*

1. Undertakings and associations of undertakings which seek application of Article 85(3) of the Treaty in respect of agreements, decisions and concerted practices falling within the scope of Article 85(1) to which they are parties shall submit applications to the Commission.

2. If the Commission judges such an application admissible and is in possession of all the available evidence, and no action under Article 10 has been taken against the agreement, decision or concerted practice in question, then it shall publish as soon as possible in the *Official Journal of the European Communities* a summary of the application and invite all interested third parties and the Member States to submit their comments to the Commission within 30 days. Such publications shall have regard to the legitimate interest of undertakings in the protection of their business secrets.

3. Unless the Commission notifies applicants, within 90 days from the date of such publication in the *Official Journal of the European Communities*, that there are serious doubts as to the applicability of Article 85(3), the agreement, decision or concerted practice concerned shall be deemed to be exempt, insofar as it conforms with the description given in the application, from the prohibition for the time already elapsed and for a maximum of six years from the date of publication in the *Official Journal of the European Communities*.

If the Commission finds, after expiry of the 90-day time limit, but before expiry of the 6 year period, that the conditions for applying Article 85(3) are not satisfied, it shall issue a decision declaring that the prohibition in Article 85(1) EEC is applicable. Such decision may be retroactive where the parties concerned have given inaccurate information or where they abuse the exemption from the provisions of Article 85(1).

4. The Commission may notify applicants as referred to in the first subparagraph of paragraph 3 and shall do so if requested by a Member State within 45 days of the forwarding to the Member State of the application in accordance with Article 15(2). This request must be justified on the basis of considerations relating to the competition rules of the Treaty.

If it finds that the conditions of Article 85(1) and of Article 85(3) are satisfied, the Commission shall issue a decision applying Article 85(3). The decision shall indicate the date from which it is to take effect. This date may be prior to the date of the application."

12.13.3.3 Commentary

If undertakings or associations of undertakings seek application of Article 85(3) of the EEC Treaty[138] in respect of agreements, decisions and concerted practices falling within the scope of Article 85(1) EEC to which they are parties then such undertakings or

137. Regulation 4056/86, Article 25(2).

138. I.e. seek an individual exemption.

associations of undertakings shall submit applications to the Commission.[139] Notification is made using the so-called "MAR form".

If the Commission judges such an application to be admissible and it is in possession of all the available evidence, and no action under Article 10 of the Regulation[140] has been taken against the agreement, decision or concerted practice in question, then it shall publish as soon as possible in the *Official Journal of the European Communities* a summary of the application and invite all interested parties and the Member States to submit their comments to the Commission within thirty days.[141]

The Regulation provides for commercial confidentiality because it states that such publications shall have regard to the legitimate interest of undertakings in the protection of their business secrets.[142]

There is then a default-type mechanism. Unless the Commission notifies applicants, within ninety days from the date of the publication in the *Official Journal*, that there are serious doubts as to the applicability of Article 85(3) EEC,[143] then the agreements, decisions or concerted practices concerned shall be deemed to be exempt, insofar as it conforms with the description given in the application, from the prohibition for the time already elapsed and for a maximum of six years from the date of publication in the *Official Journal*.[144] That is not however the end of the matter. If the Commission finds, after the expiry of the ninety-day time limit but before the expiry of the six-year one, that the conditions for applying Article 85(3) are not satisfied, it shall issue a decision declaring that the prohibition in Article 85(1) EEC is applicable. Such decision may be retroactive where the parties concerned have given inaccurate information or where they abuse the exemption from the provisions of Article 85(1) EEC.[145]

The Commission may notify applicants and shall do so, if requested by a Member State within forty-five days of the forwarding to the Member State of the application in accordance with Article 15(2) of the Regulation.[146]

This request must be justified on the basis of considerations relating to the competition rules of the EEC Treaty.[147]

If the Commission finds that the conditions of Articles 85(1) EEC and 85(3) EEC are satisfied, the Commission shall issue a decision[148] applying Article 85(3). Such a decision must indicate the date from which it is to take effect[149] which may be prior to the date of the application.[150] If the Commission issues a decision applying Article 85(3) EEC (i.e. an exemption) and such a decision is taken on the basis of either Article 11(4) or the second paragraph of Article 12(4), then the decision must indicate the period for which it is to be valid.[151] Such a period would normally be not less than six years.[152] The exemption may not be absolute and thus conditions and obligations may be attached to it.[153]

139. Regulation 4056/86, Article 12(1).
140. On which see above.
141. Regulation 4056/86, Article 12(2).
142. Regulation 4056/86, Article 12(2).
143. I.e. the exemption provision in Article 85 EEC.
144. Regulation 4056/86, Article 12(3).
145. Regulation 4056/86, Article 12(3).
146. Regulation 4056/86, Article 12(4).
147. Regulation 4056/86, Article 12(4).
148. On the legal status of decisions, see para.3.5.2.2.3, above.
149. Regulation 4056/86, Article 12(4).
150. Regulation 4056/86, Article 12(4).
151. Regulation 4056/86, Article 13(1).
152. See Regulation 4056/86, Article 13(1).
153. Regulation 4056/86, Article 13(1).

The exemption may be renewed if the conditions for applying Article 85(3) EEC continue to be satisfied.[154]

Conversely, the Commission may revoke or amend the exemption or prohibit some specified act on the part of the parties.[155] The Commission may exercise such powers in four specified circumstances: (a) where there has been a change in any of the facts which were basic to the making of the decision; (b) where the parties commit a breach of any obligation attached to the decision[156]; (c) where the decision is based on incorrect information or was induced by deceit[157]; or (d) where the parties abuse the exemption from the provisions of Article 85(1) EEC granted to them by the decision.[158]

The Commission is obliged to publish the decisions which it takes pursuant to Article 12(3), second paragraph and 12(4).[159]

Such publication shall state the names of the parties and the main content of the decision; it shall also have regard to the legitimate interests of the undertakings in the protection of their business secrets.[160]

Rabe has commented:

"A recurrent topic that has been given a lot of public attention is the possibility under Article 12 of the Regulation of granting exemptions with regard to agreements between conferences and non-conference shipping lines, so-called outsiders. Here an individual decision is necessary since the liner conference block exemption—Article 3 of the Regulation—does not apply. An example are the agreements between the liner conferences serving the US-Europe North Atlantic routes and several major non-conference competitors. These 'tolerated outsider agreements', generally referred to under the common denotation EUROCORDE, were the object of formal complaints by Shippers' Councils. The Commission under Article 10 of the Regulation opened formal proceedings and this triggered applications by the conferences and one outsider for individual exemptions under Article 12 of the Regulation.

A matter of growing concern in the recent past have become the cases where conferences acquired a dominating market position. It has been argued that such a situation has notably developed with regard to the North Atlantic conference. Under such circumstances it is obvious that special attention has to be paid to the question whether the present arrangement adequately secures and implements the Treaty's regime of competition law. The increasing exclusion on non-conference trade definitely affects not just the competitiveness of the Community merchant fleet but has also serious repercussions as regards the competiveness of the Community's exports and imports and thus its foreign trade generally.

The Commission has also directed its attention towards the closed-trade practices of some countries. In these cases national legislative or adminstrative instruments regulate the access to cargo. An example are the central freight offices used in the West Africa trade. The Commission regards these practices as incompatible with the competition rules."[161]

The Commission has received notifications of joint operating agreements between the following ferry companies: (a) SNCF/Sealink (on the France/UK route); (b) SMZ/Sealink (on the Netherlands/UK route); and (c) Sealink/B&I (Ireland/UK route). These notifications are discussed below.

154. Regulation 4056/86, Article 13(2).

155. See Regulation 4056/86, Article 13(3).

156. In this case, the Exemption may be revoked with retrospective effect: Regulation 4056/86, Article 13(2).

157. In this case, the Exemption may be revoked with retrospective effect: Regulation 4056/86, Article 13(2).

158. In this case, the Exemption may be revoked with retrospective effect: Regulation 4056/86, Article 13(2).

159. Regulation 4056/86, Article 25(1).

160. Regulation 4056/86, Article 25(2).

161. Rabe, "Recent Developments in EEC Legislation Pertaining to Maritime Transport", IBA Strasbourg Conference 1989, at pp. 2, 12–13.

12.13.4 Duration and revocation of individual exemptions

12.13.4.1 Introduction

Article 13 of the Regulation deals with the duration and revocation of individual exemptions granted under Articles 11(4) or 12(4) of the Regulation.

12.13.4.2 Text of Article 13

"*Duration and Revocation of Decisions Applying Article 85(3)*

1. Any decision applying Article 85(3) taken under Article 11(4) or under the second subparagraph of Article 12(4) shall indicate the period for which it is to be valid; normally such period shall not be less than six years. Conditions and obligations may be attached to the decision.
2. The decision may be renewed if the conditions for applying Article 85(3) continues to be satisfied.
3. The Commission may revoke or amend its decision or prohibit specified acts by the parties:
   - (a) where there has been a change in any of the facts which were basic to the making of the decision;
   - (b) where the parties commit a breach of any obligation attached to the decision;
   - (c) where the decision is based on incorrect information or was induced by deceit; or
   - (d) where the parties abuse the exemption from the provisions of Article 85(2) granted to them by the decision.

In cases falling within (b), (c) or (d), the decision may be revoked with retroactive effect."

12.13.4.3 Renewal of the exemption

Article 13(2) of the Regulation makes clear that the decision may be renewed if the conditions for applying Article 85(3) continues to be satisfied.

12.13.4.4 Revocation of the exemption

The Commission may revoke its decision in any one of five situations: (a) where there has been a change in any of the facts which were basic to the making of the decision; (b) where the parties commit a breach of any obligation attached to the decision; (c) where the decision is based on incorrect information or was induced by deceit; or (d) where the parties abuse the exemption from the provisions of Article 85(2) granted to them by the decision. In the case of the last three situations, the decision to revoke the decision may be retrospective.

12.13.4.5 Amendment of the exemption

The Commission may amend its decision in any one of four situations: (a) where there has been a change in any of the facts which were basic to the making of the decision; (b) where the parties commit a breach of any obligation attached to the decision; (c) where the decision is based on incorrect information or was induced by deceit; or (d) where the parties abuse the exemption from the provisions of Article 85(2) granted to them by the decision. It would appear from the drafting of Article 13(3) that the decision may not be amended with retrospective effect.

12.13.4.6 Prohibition of specified acts by the parties

The Commission may prohibit specified acts by the parties in any one of four situations: (a) where there has been a change in any of the facts which were basic to the making of the decision; (b) where the parties commit a breach of any obligation attached to the decision; (c) where the decision is based on incorrect information or was induced by deceit; or (d) where the parties abuse the exemption from the provisions of Article 85(2) granted to them by the decision. It would appear from the drafting of Article 13(3) that a prohibition of specified acts by the parties may not be imposed with retrospective effect.

12.13.4.7 Publication of the decision

The Commission is obliged to publish the decisions which it takes pursuant to Article 13(3) of the Regulation.[162] Such publication shall state the names of the parties and the main content of the decision; it shall also have regard to the legitimate interests of the undertakings in the protection of their business secrets.[163]

12.13.5 Powers of the commission

12.13.5.1 Text of Article 14

"Powers
Subject to review of its decision by the Court of Justice, the Commission shall have sole power:
— to impose obligations pursuant to Article 7
— to issue decisions pursuant to Article 85(3).
The authorities of the Member States shall retain the power to decide whether any case falls within the provisions of Article 85(1) or Article 86, until such time as the Commission has initiated a procedure with a view to formulating a decision in the case in question or has sent notification as provided for in the first subparagraph of Article 12(3)."

12.13.5.2 Commentary

The Commission has, by virtue of Article 14 of the Regulation, the sole power (a) to impose obligations pursuant to Article 7 of the Regulation and (b) to issue decisions pursuant to Article 85(3) of the EEC Treaty. The authorities of the Member States retain the power to decide whether any case falls within the provisions of Articles 85(1) or 86 of the EEC Treaty, until such time as the Commission has initiated a procedure with a view to formulating a decision in the case in question or has sent notification as provided for in the first sub-paragraph of Article 12(3) of the Regulation[164,165] The Commission's powers are however subject to review by the Court of Justice.[166]

Articles 85 and 86 are directly applicable in the legal systems of the Member States and thus proceedings may be instituted in the national courts on the bases of Articles 85 and 86. It is worth remembering that the national courts do not have the power to grant exemptions under Article 85(3).

12.13.6 Liaison with the authorities of the member states: Article 15

12.13.6.1 Introduction

Article 15 of the Regulation deals with the possibility of the Commission liaising with the authorities of the Member States of the EC.

162. Regulation 4056/86, Article 25(1).
163. Regulation 4056/86, Article 25(2).
164. On Article 12(3) of the Regulation, see above.
165. Regulation 4056/86, Article 14
166. Regulation 4056/86, Article 14.

12.13.6.2 Text of Article 15

"*Liaison with the Authorities of the Member States*

1. The Commission shall carry out the procedures provided for in this Regulation in close and constant liaison with the competent authorities of the Member States; these authorities shall have the right to express their views on such procedures.

2. The Commission shall immediately forward to the competent authorities of the Member States copies of the complaints and applications, and of the most important documents sent to it or which it sends out in the course of such procedures.

3. An Advisory Committee on agreements and dominant positions in maritime transport shall be consulted prior to the taking of any decision following upon a procedure under Article 10 or of any decision issued under Article 10 or of any decision issued under the second subparagraph of Article 12(3), or under the second subparagraph of paragraph 4 of the same Article. The Advisory Committee shall also be consulted prior to the adoption of the implementing provisions provided for in Article 26.

4. The Advisory Committee shall be composed of officials competent in the sphere of maritime transport and agreements and dominant positions. Each Member State shall nominate two officials to represent it, each of whom may be replaced, in the event of his being prevented from attending, by another official.

5. Consultation shall take place at a joint meeting convened by the Commission; such meeting shall be held not earlier than fourteen days after dispatch of the notice convening it. This notice shall, in respect of each case to be examined, be accompanied by a summary of the case together with an indication of the most important documents, and a preliminary draft decision.

6. The Advisory Committee may deliver an opinion notwithstanding that some of its members or their alternates are not present. A report of the outcome of the consultative proceedings shall be annexed to the draft decision. It shall not be made public."

12.13.6.3 Commentary

Article 15(1) of the Regulation provides that the Commission shall carry out the procedures provided for in the Regulation in close and constant liaison with the competent authorities of the Member States; such authorities having the right to express their views on such procedures.

The Commission is obliged immediately to forward to the competent authorities of the Member States copies of the complaints and applications, and of the most important documents sent to it or which it sends out in the course of such procedures.[167]

Article 15 provides for an Advisory Committee on Agreements and Dominant Positions in Maritime Transport. The Committee is the equivalent for the maritime transport sector of the Advisory Committee on Restrictive Practices which deals with most other industrial sectors. The Maritime Transport Committee is composed of officials competent in the sphere of maritime transport and agreements and dominant positions.[168] Each Member State shall nominate two officials to represent it, each of whom may be replaced, in the event of his being prevented from attending, by another official.[169] The Committee is to be consulted prior to the taking of any decision following upon a procedure under Article 10 of the Regulation, or of any decision issued under the second sub-para. of Article 12(3) of the Regulation, or under the second sub-para. of Article 12(4).[170] The Committee is also to be consulted prior to the adoption of the implementing provisions provided for in Article 26 of the Regulation.[171,172]

167. Regulation 4056/86, Article 15(2).
168. Regulation 4056/86, Article 15(4).
169. Regulation 4056/86, Article 15(4). A similar committee was established for the air transport sector by Article 8 of Regulation 3975/87 (OJ L374/1).
170. Regulation 4056/86, Article 15(3).
171. On the Article 26 implementation provisions, see para.12.13.13, below.
172. Regulation 4056/86, Article 15(3).

Consultation must take place at a joint meeting convened by the Commission with such meeting being held not earlier than fourteen days after the dispatch of the notice convening it.[173] The Committee may deliver an opinion notwithstanding that some of its members or their alternates are not there.[174] Interestingly, the report of the outcome of the consultative proceedings is annexed to the draft decision but it is not made public.[175]

The national authorities are given exceptionally wide powers under the Regulation and it is submitted that the role of the national authorities is minimised in coming years because of the danger of confidential information being circulated to national authorities which may have alternative (commercial) agendas.

12.13.7 Commission requests for information

12.13.7.1 Introduction

So as to carry out its functions under the Regulation, the Commission needs to be able to obtain all necessary information. Article 16 of the Regulation provides for this eventuality.

12.13.7.2 Text of Article 16

"*Requests for Information*

1. In carrying out the duties assigned to it by this Regulation, the Commission may obtain all the necessary information from the Governments and competent authorities of the Member States and from undertakings and associations of undertakings.

2. When asking a request for information to an undertaking or association of undertakings, the Commission shall at the same time forward a copy of the request to the competent authority of the Member State in whose territory the seat of the undertaking or association of undertakings is situated.

3. In its request, the Commission shall state the legal basis and the purpose of the request, and also the penalties provided for in Article 19(1)(b) for supplying incorrect information.

4. The owners of the undertakings or their representatives and, in the case of legal persons, companies or firms, or of associations having no legal personality, the person authorized to represent them by law or by their constitution, shall be bound to supply the information requested.

5. Where an undertaking or association of undertakings does not supply the information requested within the time limit fixed by the Commission, or supplies incomplete information, the Commission shall by decision require the information to be supplied. The decision shall specify what information is required, fix an appropriate time limit within which it is to be supplied and indicate the penalties provided for in Article 19(1)(b) and Article 20(1)(c) and the right to have the decision reviewed by the Court of Justice.

6. The Commission shall at the same time forward a copy of its decision to the competent authority of the Member State in whose territory the seat of the undertaking or association of undertakings is situated.

173. Regulation 4056/86, Article 15(5). Such notice must, in respect of each case to be examined, be accompanied by a summary of the case together with an indication of the most important documents and a preliminary draft decision: Regulation 4056/86, Article 15(5).

174. Regulation 4056/86, Article 15(6).

175. Regulation 4056/86, Article 15(6).

12.13.7.3 Commentary

The Commission has various powers to obtain all the necessary information which it requires for the purpose of carrying out the duties assigned to it under the Regulation.[176]

In its request, the Commission is obliged to state the legal basis and the purpose of the request as well as the penalties provided for in Article 19(1)(b) for supplying incorrect information.[177]

The owners of the undertakings or their representatives and, in the case of legal persons, companies or firms, or of associations having no legal personality, the person authorised to represent them by law or by their constitution, shall be bound to supply the information requested.[178]

If an undertaking or association of undertakings does not supply the information requested within the time limit fixed by the Commission, or supplies incomplete information, the Commission shall by decision require the information to be supplied.[179]

Such a decision shall specify what information is required, fix an appropriate time limit within which it is to be supplied and indicate the penalties provided for in Article 19(1)(b) and Article 20(1)(c) of the Regulation as well as the right to have the decision reviewed by the ECJ.[180] The Commission is obliged under Article 16(6) of the Regulation to forward a copy of the decision to the competent authority of the Member State in whose territory the seat of the undertaking or association of undertakings is situated.[181]

When sending a request for information to an undertaking or association of undertakings, the Commission is obliged to simultaneously forward a copy of the request to the competent authority of the Member State in whose territory the seat of the undertaking is situated.[182]

12.13.8 Investigations

12.13.8.1 Introduction

To request information under Article 16 of the Regulation may prove insufficient or even injudicious because it may "tip-off" a guilty party of Commission action.

12.13.8.2.1 Text of Article 18

"*Investigating Powers of the Commission*

1. In carrying out the duties assigned to it by this Regulation, the Commission may undertake all necessary investigations into undertakings and associations of undertakings.

To this end the officials authorized by the Commission are empowered:

(a) to examine the books and other business records;

(b) to take copies of or extracts from the books and business records;

(c) to ask for oral explanations on the spot;

176. See Regulation 4056/86, Article 16.
177. Regulation 4056/86, Article 16(3).
178. Regulation 4056/86, Article 16(4).
179. Regulation 4056/86, Article 16(5).
180. Regulation 4056/86, Article 16(5).
181. Regulation 4056/86, Article 16(6).
182. Regulation 4056/86, Article 16(2).

(d) to enter any premises, land and vehicles of undertakings.

2. The officials of the Commission authorized for the purpose of these investigations shall exercise their powers upon production of an authorization in writing specifying the subject matter and purpose of the investigation and the penalties provided for in Article 19(1)(c) in cases where production of the required books or other business records is incomplete. In good time before the investigation, the Commission shall inform the competent authority of the Member State in whose territory the same is to be made of the investigation and of the identity of the authorized officials.

3. Undertakings and associations of undertakings are obliged to submit to investigations ordered by a decision of the Commission. The decision shall specify the subject matter and purpose of the investigation, appoint the date on which it is to begin and indicate the penalties provided for in Article 19(1)(c) and Article 20(1)(d) and the right to have the decision reviewed by the Court of Justice.

4. The Commission shall take decisions referred to in paragraph 3 after consultation with the competent authority of the Member State in whose territory the investigation is to be made.

5. Officials of the competent authority of the Member State in whose territory the investigation is to be made, may at the request of such authority or of the Commission, assist the officials of the Commission in carrying out their duties.

6. Where an undertaking opposes an investigation ordered pursuant to this Article, the Member State concerned shall afford the necessary assistance to the officials authorized by the Commission to enable them to make their investigation. To this end, Member States shall take the necessary measures, after consulting the Commission, before 1 January 1989."

12.13.8.2.2 Commentary

The powers of investigation of the Commission are extensive: Article 18(1) of the Regulation provides that in carrying out the duties assigned to it by this Regulation, the Commission may undertake all necessary investigations into undertakings and associations of undertakings.[183] To this end, the officials authorised by the Commission are empowered: (a) to examine the books and other business records; (b) to take copies of or extracts from the books and business records; (c) to ask for oral explanations on the spot; and (d) to enter any premises, land and vehicles of undertakings.[184]

The officials of the Commission authorised for the purpose of these investigations exercise their powers upon production of an authorisation in writing specifying the subject matter and purpose of the investigation and the penalties provided for in Article 19(1)(c) of the Regulation in cases where production of the required books or other business records is incomplete.[185] Article 18(2) of the Regulation provides that, in good time before the investigation, the Commission shall inform the competent authority of the Member State in whose territory the same is to be made of the investigation and of the identity of the authorised officials.[186]

Undertakings and associations of undertakings are obliged to submit to investigations ordered by a decision of the Commission.[187]

The Commission may not take such a decision until it has consulted with the competent authority of the Member State in whose territory the investigation is to be made.[188]

The decision, when it is made, must specify the subject matter and purpose of the investigation, appoint the date on which it is to begin and indicate the penalties

183. Regulation 4056/86, Article 18(1).

184. Regulation 4056/86, Article 18(1). For details of a raid, see "EEC sends Lawyers into UKWAL Offices", *Lloyd's List*, 24 July 1989, p. 1.

185. Regulation 4056/86, Article 18(2).

186. Regulation 4056/86, Article 18(2).

187. Regulation 4056/86, Article 18(3).

188. Regulation 4056/86, Article 18(4).

(provided for in Article 19(1)(c) and Article 20(1)(d) of the Regulation) and the right to have the decision reviewed by the Court of Justice.[189]

If an undertaking opposes an investigation ordered under Article 18 of the Regulation then the Member State concerned is obliged to afford the necessary assistance to the officials authorised by the Commission to enable them to make their investigation.[190]

12.13.8.3 Investigations by authorities of the Member States

12.13.8.3.1 Introduction

The Commission has the power to request the competent authorities of Member States to undertake the investigations which the Commission considers to be necessary under Article 18(1) of the Regulation or which the Commission has ordered by a decision pursuant to Article 18(3) of the Regulation.[191]

The officials of the competent authorities of the Member States responsible for conducting the investigations are entitled to exercise their powers upon production of an authorisation in writing issued by the competent authority of the Member State in whose territory the investigation is to be made.[192] Such an authorisation must specify the subject matter and the purpose of the investigation.[193]

The officials of the competent authority in the Member States may be assisted by Commission officials, at the request of either the Commission or the competent authorities of the Member State involved.[194]

12.13.8.3.2 Text of Article 17

"*Investigations by the authorities of the Member States*

1. At the request of the Commission, the competent authorities of the Member States shall undertake the investigations which the Commission considers to be necessary under Article 18(1), or which it has ordered by decision pursuant to Article 18(3). The officials of the competent authorities of the Member States responsible for conducting these investigations shall exercise their power upon production of an authorisation in writing issued by the competent authority of the Member State in whose territory the investigation is to be made. Such authorisation shall specify the subject matter and purpose of the investigation.

2. If so requested by the Commission or by the competent authority of the Member State in whose territory the investigation is to be made, the Commission officials may assist the officials of such authority in carrying out their duties."

12.13.8.4 Secrecy of information gathered

Information acquired as a result of the application of Articles 17 and 18 of the Regulation may only be used for the purpose of the relevant request or investigation: it may not be used for any other purpose.[195] Without prejudice to the provisions of

189. Regulation 4056/86, Article 18(3).

190. Regulation 4056/86, Article 18(6). To this end, the Member States were obliged to take the necessary measures, after consulting with the Commission, before 1 January 1989.

191. Regulation 4056/86, Article 17(1).

192. Regulation 4056/86, Article 17(1).

193. Regulation 4056/86, Article 17(1).

194. Regulation 4056/86, Article 17(2).

195. Regulation 4056/86, Article 24(1).

Articles 23 and 25 of the Regulation, the Commission and the competent authorities of the Member States, their officials and other servants are prohibited from disclosing information acquired by them as a result of the application of the Regulation and of the kind covered by the obligation of professional secrecy.[196]

It is however possible that general information or surveys which do not contain information relating to particular undertakings or associations of undertakings may be published.[197]

12.13.9 Fines and periodic penalty payments

12.13.9.1 Fines

12.13.9.1.1 Text of Article 19

"*Fines*

1. The Commission may by decision impose on undertakings or associations of undertakings fines of from 100 to 5000 ECU where, intentionally or negligently:
   (a) they supply incorrect or misleading information, either in a communication pursuant to Article 5(5) or in an application pursuant to Article 12; or
   (b) they supply incorrect information in response to a request made pursuant to Article 16(3) or (5), or do not supply information within the time limit fixed by a decision taken under Article 16(5); or
   (c) they produce the required books or other business records in incomplete form during investigations under Article 17 or Article 18, or refuse to submit to an investigation ordered by decision issued in implementation of Article 18(3).
2. The Commission may by decision impose on undertakings or associations of undertakings fines of from 1000 to one million ECU, or a sum in excess thereof but not exceeding 10% of the turnover in the preceding business year of each of the undertakings participating in the infringement, where either intentionally or negligently:
   (a) they infringe Article 85(1) of the Treaty, or do not comply with an obligation imposed under Article 7 of this Regulation;
   (b) they commit a breach of any obligation imposed pursuant to Article 5 or to Article 13(1).

In fixing the amount of the fine, regard shall be had both to the gravity and to the duration of the infringement.

3. Article 15(3) and (4) shall apply.
4. Decisions taken pursuant to paragraphs 1 and 2 shall not be of criminal law nature.

The fines provided for in paragraph 2(a) shall not be imposed in respect of acts taking place after notification to the Commission and before its Decision in application of Article 85(3) of the Treaty, provided they fall within the limits of the activity described in the notification.

However, this provision shall not have effect where the Commission has informed the undertakings concerned that after preliminary examination it is of the opinion that Article 85(1) of the Treaty applies and that application of Article 85(3) is not justified."

12.13.9.1.2 Commentary

It is worth recalling that the fine which can be imposed is up to 10% of the worldwide (i.e. not just the EC) turnover during the previous year.

The ECJ[198] has a jurisdiction under Article 172 of the EEC Treaty to review fines and penalties which have been imposed.

196. Regulation 4056/86, Article 24(2).
197. Regulation 4056/86, Article 24(3)
198. On the ECJ, see para.3.4.6, above.

Procedural wrongdoings The Commission has power under Article 19 of the Regulation to impose fines on undertakings or associations of undertakings. The fines range from 100 to 5,000 ECU.[199] The Commission may impose a fine where, intentionally or negligently, the undertaking or association of undertakings: (a) supply incorrect or misleading information, either in a communication pursuant to Article 5(5) of the Regulation or in an application pursuant to Article 12 of the Regulation[200]; or (b) supply incorrect information in response to a request made pursuant to Article 16(3) or (5) of the Regulation, or do not supply information within the time limit fixed by a decision taken under Article 16(5) of the Regulation; or (c) produce the required books or other business records in incomplete form during investigations under Articles 17 or 18 of the Regulation, or refuse to submit to an investigation ordered by decision issued in implementation of Article 18(3) of the Regulation. It is important to stress that a decision taken pursuant to Article 19(1) is not of a criminal nature.[201]

Substantive wrongdoings The Commission has power to impose, by way of a decision, on undertakings or associations of undertakings fines of from 1,000 to one million ECU, or a sum in excess thereof, but not exceeding 10% of the turnover of the preceding business year of each of the undertakings participating in the infringement, where either intentionally or negligently: (a) they infringe Article 85(1) EEC, or do not comply with an obligation imposed under Article 7 of the Regulation[202]; or (b) they commit a breach of any obligation imposed pursuant to Article 5 or to Article 13(1) of the Regulation.[203]

In fixing the amount of the fine, the Commission must have regard to both the gravity and to the duration of the infringement.[204] It is important to stress that a decision taken pursuant to Article 19(2) is not of a criminal nature.[205]

In regard to fines generally, Article 15(3) and (4) of the Regulation applies.[206]

12.13.9.2 Periodic penalty payments

12.13.9.2.1 Text of Article 20

"*Periodic Penalty Payments*

1. The Commission may by decision impose on undertakings or associations of undertakings periodic penalty payments of from 50 to 1000 ECU per day, calculated from the date appointed by the decision, in order to compel them:
   (a) to put an end to an infringement of Article 85(1) or Article 86 of the Treaty the termination of which it has ordered pursuant to Article 11, or to comply with an obligation imposed pursuant to Article 7;
   (b) to refrain from any act prohibited under Article 13(3);
   (c) to supply complete and correct information which it has requested by decision taken pursuant to Article 16(5);
   (d) to submit to an investigation which it has ordered by decision taken pursuant to Article 18(3).

199. The ECU in this context is the ECU adopted in drawing up the budget of the Community in accordance with Articles 207 and 209 of the EEC Treaty (Regulation 4056/86, Article 22).

200. Regulation 4056/86, Article 19(1)(a).

201. Regulation 4056/86, Article 19(4).

202. In the case of these fines, they shall not be imposed in respect of acts taking place after notification to the Commission and before its Decision in application of Article 85(3) EEC, provided they fall within the limits of the activity described in the notification: Regulation 4056/86, Article 19(4)

203. Regulation 4056/86, Article 19(2).

204. Regulation 4056/86, Article 19(2).

205. Regulation 4056/86, Article 19(4).

206. Regulation 4056/86, Article 19(3).

2. Where the undertakings or associations if undertakings have satisfied the obligation which it was the purpose of the periodic penalty payment to enforce, the Commission may fix the total amount of the periodic penalty payment at a lower figure than that which would arise under the original decision.

3. Article 15(3) and (4) shall apply."

12.13.9.2.2 Commentary

The Commission has the power to impose periodic penalty payments in addition to fines.[207] Article 20(1) of the Regulation provides that the Commission may by decision impose on undertakings or associations of undertakings periodic penalty payments of from 50 to 1,000 ECU[208] per day. The amount is calculated from the date appointed by the decision.[209] The purposes for the periodic penalty payments are as follows: (a) to put an end to an infringement of Article 85(1) EEC or Article 86 EEC, the termination of which the Commission has ordered pursuant to Article 11 of the Regulation, or to comply with an obligation imposed pursuant to Article 7 of the Regulation[210]; (b) to refrain from any act prohibited under Article 13(3) of the Regulation[211]; (c) to supply complete and correct information which it has requested by decision taken pursuant to Article 16(5) of the Regulation[212]; or (d) to submit to an investigation which it has ordered by decision taken pursuant to Article 18(3) of the Regulation.[213] If the undertakings or association of undertakings has satisfied the obligations which it was the purpose of the periodic penalty payment to enforce then the Commission may fix the total amount of the periodic penalty payment at a lower figure than that which would arise under the original decision.[214] Again like fines, Article 15(3) and (4) of the Regulation apply to periodic penalty payments.[215]

12.13.10 Hearings of the parties and others

12.13.10.1 Introduction

In a number of specified situations, the Commission is obliged under the terms of the Regulation to give a hearing to the parties involved.

12.13.10.2 Text of Article 23

"*Hearing of the Parties and of Third Persons*

1. Before taking decisions as provided for in Articles 11, 12(3) second sub-paragraph, and 12(4), 13(3), 19 and 20 the Commission shall give the undertakings concerned the opportunity of being heard on the matters to which the Commission has taken objection.

2. If the Commission or the competent authorities of the Member States consider it necessary, they may also hear other natural or legal persons. Applications to be heard on the part of such persons where they show a sufficient interest shall be granted.

207. Regulation 4056/86, Article 20.

208. ECU in this context is the ECU adopted in drawing up the budgets of the Community in accordance with Articles 207 and 209 EEC: Regulation 4056/86, Article 22.

209. Regulation 4056/86, Article 20(1).

210. Regulation 4056/86, Article 20(1)(a).

211. Regulation 4056/86, Article 20(1)(a).

212. Regulation 4056/86, Article 20(1)(c).

213. Regulation 4056/86, Article 20(1)(d).

214. Regulation 4056/86, Art/20(2).

215. Regulation 4056/86, Art/20(3).

3. Where the Commission intends to give negative clearance pursuant to Article 85(3) of the Treaty, it shall publish a summary of the relevant agreement, decision or concerted practice and invite all interested third parties to submit their observations within a time limit which it shall fix being not less than one month. Publication shall have regard to the legitimate interest of the undertakings in the protection of their business secrets."

12.13.10.3 Commentary

Article 23(1) of the Regulation provides that before taking decisions as provided for in Articles 11, 12(3) second paragraph, and 12(4), 13(3), 19 and 20 of the Regulation, the Commission shall give the undertaking or association of undertakings concerned the opportunity of being heard on the matters to which the Commission has taken objection.

If the Commission or the competent authorities of the Member States consider it necessary then they may also hear other natural or legal persons.[216] The Commission may also entertain other persons and applications where such persons apply to be heard and they demonstrate a sufficient interest in the case.[217]

If the Commission intends to give a negative clearance pursuant to Article 85(3) EEC, it shall publish a summary of the relevant agreement, decision or concerted practice and invite all interested third parties to submit their observations within a time limit which it shall fix, but such time limit shall not be less than one month.[218]

Such publication must have regard to the legitimate interests of the undertakings in the protection of their business interests.[219]

12.13.11 Review by the Court of Justice of the fines and periodical penalty payments

12.13.11.1 Introduction

Article 21 of the Regulation provides that the Court of Justice may review fines and periodical penalty payments.

12.13.11.2 Text of Article 21

"*Review by the Court of Justice*
The Court of Justice shall have unlimited jurisdiction within the meaning of Article 172 of the Treaty to review decisions whereby the Commission has fixed a fine or periodical penalty payment; it may cancel, reduce or increase the fine or periodic penalty payment imposed."

12.13.11.3 Commentary

Article 21 of the Regulation explicitly states that the Court of Justice has unlimited jurisdiction within the meaning of Article 172 EEC[220] to review decisions whereby the Commission has fixed a fine or periodical penalty payment and may cancel, reduce or increase the fine or penalty payment imposed.

216. Regulation 4056/86, Article 23(2).
217. Regulation 4056/86, Article 23(2).
218. Regulation 4056/86, Article 23(3).
219 Regulation 4056/86, Article 23(3).
220. On Article 172 EEC, see paras 3.4.6.6.4, 12.13.9.1.2, above.

12.13.12 *Publication of decisions*

The Commission is obliged to publish the decisions which it takes pursuant to Articles 11, 12(3) second paragraph, 12(4) and 13(3) of the Regulation.[221]

Such publication shall state the names of the parties and the main content of the decision; it shall also have regard to the legitimate interests of the udnertakings in the protection of their business secrets.[222]

12.13.13 *Implementing provisions*

Article 26 of the Regulation provides that the Commission shall have power to adopt implementing provisions concerning the scope of the obligations of communication pursuant to Article 5(5); the form, content and other details of complaints pursuant to Article 10; applications pursuant to Article 12; and the hearings provided for in Article 23(1) and (2) of the Regulation.[223] Regulation 4260/86 is the resultant measure.[224]

This latter Regulation entered into force on 1 January 1989.

12.14 PROCEDURE: COMMISSION REGULATION 4260/88

12.14.1 *Introduction*

Commission Regulation 4260/88 of 16 December 1988 deals with the communications, complaints, applications and hearings provided for in Council Regulation 4056/86.[225] It shall be referred to in this section as "Regulation 4260/86". It also provides for the use of Form MAR which is the equivalent of Form A/B.

Section I of Regulation 4260/88 deals with Notifications, Complaints and Applications.

12.14.2 *Legal basis and background*

Regulation 4260/86 was adopted by the Commission and not the Council of Ministers. Article 26 of Regulation 4056/86 provides that the Commission "shall have power to adopt implementing provisions concerning the scope of the obligation of communication pursuant to Article 5(5), the form, content and other details of complaints pursuant to Article 10, applications pursuant to Article 12 and the hearings provided for in Article 23(1) and (2)".

12.14.3 *Notification*

12.14.3.1 Text of Article 1 of Regulation 4260/86

"*Notifications*

1. Awards at arbitration and recommendations by conciliators accepted by the parties shall be notified to the Commission when they concern the settlement of disputes relating to the practices of conferences referred to in Articles 4 and 5(2) and (3) of Regulation No. 4056/86.

221. Regulation 4056/86, Article 25(1).
222. Regulation 4056/86, Article 25(2).
223. Regulation 4056/86, Article 26.
224. On Regulation 4260/86, see paras 12.14.1, 12.14.4.1 *et seq.*, below.
225. OJ 1988 L376/1. On procedure generally in this area, see Clough and Randolph, *op. cit.*, Chapter 5.

2. The obligation of notification applies to any party to the dispute resolved by the award or recommendation.

3. Notifications shall be submitted forthwith by registered letter with an acknowledgment of receipt or shall be delivered by hand against receipt. They shall be written in one of the official languages of the Community.

Supporting documents shall be either originals or copies. Copies must be certified as true copies of the original. They shall be submitted in their original language. Where the original language is not one of the official languages of the Community, a translation in one of the official languages shall be attached.

4. When representatives of undertakings, of associations of undertakings, or of natural or legal persons sign such notifications, they shall produce written proof that they are authorized to act."

12.14.4 Complaints

12.14.4.1 Introduction

Regulation 4260/88 lays down a procedure for submitting complaints under Regulation 4056/86. This procedure is set out in Article 2 of Regulation 4260/86.

12.14.4.2 Text of Article 2 of Regulation 4260/86

"*Complaints*

1. Complaints pursuant to Article 10 of Regulation No. 4056/86 shall be submitted in writing in one of the official languages of the Community, their form, content and other details being left to the discretion of complainants.

2. Complaints may be submitted by:

(a) Member States

(b) natural or legal persons who claim a legitimate interest.

3. When representatives of undertakings, of associations of undertakings, or of natural or legal persons sign such complaints, they shall produce written proof that they are authorized to act."

12.14.5 Applications for exemptions

12.14.5.1 Introduction

Regulation 4260/88 lays down a procedure for submitting applications for exemptions of the competition rules. This procedure is laid down in Article 4 of Regulation 4260/86.

12.14.5.2 Text of Article 4 of Regulation 4260/86

"*Submission of Applications*

1. Applications pursuant to Article 12 of Regulation 4056/86 shall be submitted on Form MAR shown in Annex I.[226]

2. Several participating undertakings may submit an application on a single form.

3. Applications shall contain the information requested in the form.

4. Fourteen copies of each application and of the supporting documents shall be submitted to the Commission.

5. The supporting documents shall be either originals or copies. Copies must be certified as true copies of the original.

6. Applications shall be in one of the official languages of the Community. Supporting documents shall be submitted in their original language. Where the original language is not one of the official languages, a translation in one of the official languages shall be attached.

226. I.e. Annex I of Regulation 4260/86.

7. The date of submission of an application shall be the date on which it is received by the Commission. Where, however, the application is sent by registered post, it shall be deemed to have been received on the date shown on the postmark of the place of posting.

8. Where an application submitted pursuant to Article 12 of Regulation No.4056/86 falls outside the scope of that Regulation, the Commission shall without delay inform the applicant that it intends to examine the application under the provisions of such other Regulation as is applicable to the case; however, the date of submission of the application shall be the date resulting from paragraph 7. The Commission shall inform the applicant of its reasons and fix a period for him to submit any comments in writing before it conducts its appraisal pursuant to the provisions of that other Regulation."

12.14.6 Hearings

Section II of Regulation 4260/88 lays down the procedure to be followed for hearings when companies have the opportunity to express their views regarding the objections raised against them.

12.14.6.1 Preliminary hearing

12.14.6.1.1 Text of Article 5

Article 5 of Regulation 4260/88 provides:

"Before consulting the Advisory Committee on Agreements and Dominant Positions in the field of Maritime Transport the Commission shall hold a hearing pursuant to Article 23(1) of Regulation 4056/86."

12.14.6.1.2 Text of Article 6

Article 6 of Regulation 4260/88 provides:

"1. The Commission shall inform undertakings and associations of undertakings in writing of the objections raised against them. The communication shall be addressed to each of them or to a joint agent appointed by them.

2. The Commission may inform the parties by giving notice in the Official Journal of the European Communities, if from the circumstances of the case this appears appropriate, in particular where notice is to be given to a number of undertakings but no joint agent has been appointed. The notice shall have regard to the legitimate interest of the undertakings in the protection of their business secrets.

3. A fine or a periodic penalty payment may be imposed on an undertaking or association of undertakings only if the objections were notified in the manner provided for in paragraph 1.

4. The Commission shall, when giving notice of objections, fix a period within which the undertakings and associations of undertakings may inform the Commission of their views."

12.14.7 Communicating awards and recommendations

The Regulation sets out an obligation to communicate to the Commission arbitration awards and recommendations by conciliators.

12.15 PRACTICE TO DATE

12.15.1 Brazilian and Colombian coffee trades

There has been a series of cases.[227] In 1990, the Commission has itself summarised one case in the following terms:

227. Cases No. IV/32.808 and No. IV/33.509.

"71. In July 1988 the Commission received a complaint under Article 10 of Regulation No. 4056/86 made by two West German Coffee importers against the existing liner conferences in the North Europe-Colombia and North Europe-Brazil trades. Articles 4, 7 and 8 of the Regulation are allegedly infringed by the Conferences. The Commission undertook an investigation and, shortly after, the complainants withdrew from their complaint against the Brazilian Conference. The Commission, however, continued its investigation on its own initiative in the Brazilian case.

72. Some new developments have been detected in the trades recently. The Commission is assessing the situation in both trades. In particular, in the Brazilian context, a new complaint under Article 10 has been filed by an independent line in the trade against the conference (*Grimaldi-Cobelfret vs. BEBFC*, Case No. IV/33.509, filed on 2 April 1990). The Commission is at present examining this trade in light also of the information provided by the independent complainants."[228]

12.15.2 Eurocorde

In July 1987, the Commission received formal complaints from two shippers' associations involving the North–Europe–US Atlantic Conference (the "NEAC") and the US Atlantic–North Europe Conference (the "ANEC").[229]

Both associations were complaining about the so-called tolerated outsider agreements ("TOAs") between the conferences serving the North Atlantic trades between Europe and the US and their major competitors. These competitors included the Evergreen Marine Corporation and Polish Ocean Lines. The agreements were known as the Eurocorde Agreements.[230] The Commission commenced formal proceedings.[231]

The Commission then received an application for an individual exemption of the Eurocorde agreement pursuant to Articles 11(4) and 12 of the Regulation.

In 1990, the Commission has itself summarised this case in the following terms:

"Following two complaints lodged by the European Shippers' Councils (ESC) and the British Shippers Council (BSC) the Commission undertook in July 1987 an investigation concerning two agreements passed by the existing liner conferences in the Atlantic US-North Europe trades, with its major independent competitors. Two applications for individual exemption under Article 85(3) of the Treaty were filed simultaneously, first by the conferences and then by one of the outsiders involved.

The Commission has concluded that the agreements might fulfil the conditions for an exemption provided that some modifications are made, and conditions and obligations are imposed. The Commission's services are in consultation so that a decision could be issued before the end of this year."[232]

The Commission ruled in February 1992 that the Agreement did not meet the requirements of Article 85(3) and thus decided against exempting it. The Commission did not however ban the Agreement outright because of the potential damage to market stabilisation. The European Shippers' Council may appeal the Commission decision to the ECJ.

228. Report from the Commission to the Council of Ministers on the Implementation of the Four Regulations in the Field of Maritime Transport adopted by the Council on 22 December 1986, SEC(90) 1594 final, 1 August 1990, paras 71 and 72.

229. See *Seventeenth Report on Competition Policy*, para. 47 (1987).

230. See Vail, "Eurocorde Becomes More Cordial", *American Shipper*, Oct.1987, at p. 38.

231. See Usworth, "EC Body Challenges Eurocorde Agreements", *The Journal of Commerce*, 20 January 1988, Sect.B at 1, col. 4.

232. Report from the Commission to the Council of Ministers on the Implementation of the Four Regulations in the Field of Maritime Transport adopted by the Council on 22 December 1986, SEC(90)1594 final, 1 August 1990, para. 64.

12.15.3 Gulfway

The Commission has received an application for an individual exemption of the Gulfway agreement pursuant to Articles 11(4) and 12 of the Regulation.

12.15.4 Israeli trades

Case No. IV/33.056 deals with trades between Israel and the EC.

In 1990, the Commission has itself summarised this case in the following terms:

"At the beginning of 1989 the Commission received a complaint based on Article 10 of Regulation 4056/86, concerning restrictive practices being applied by the two liner conferences operating between Israel and the United Kingdom and Northern Europe.

These practices were also affecting the liner trades between Israel and the Western Mediterranean and Adriatic.

The Commission is proceeding in the examination of the alleged facts on the basis of the arguments put forward by both sides and the answers provided in reply to requests for information under Article 16(3) of Regulation 4056/86."[233]

12.15.5 RTM/P&O

The Commission was notified of an agreement between P&O and RTM in respect of the UK/Belgium route in response to a request on the part of the Commission for information.[234,235]

12.15.6 Sealink/B&I (operating agreement)

The Commission has received an application for an individual exemption pursuant to Article 12 of the Regulation in respect of Ireland/UK ferry services operated by Sealink and B&I.[236]

The notification was sent to the Member States and the Commission informed the parties concerned that there were serious doubts about Article 85(3) of the EEC Treaty being applicable to the agreement.[237]

The Commission was later informed[238] that the agreement ceased to apply on 1 January 1988 and thus the Commission closed its investigation of the matter.

12.15.7 Sealink/B&I (port dispute)

In 1990, the Commission has itself summarised this case in the following terms:

233. Report from the Commission to the Council of Ministers on the Implementation of the Four Regulations in the Field of Maritime Transport adopted by the Council on 22 December 1986, SEC(90)1594 final, 1 August 1990, para. 75.

234. Report from the Commission to the Council of Ministers on the Implementation of the Four Regulations in the Field of Maritime Transport adopted by the Council on 22 December 1986, SEC(90)1594 final, 1 August 1990, para.67.

235. Case 33.045.

236. Case No. IV/32.385.

237. Report from the Commission to the Council of Ministers on the Implementation of the Four Regulations in the Field of Maritime Transport adopted by the Council on 22 December 1986, SEC(90)1594 final, 1 August 1990, para.65.

238. According to Report from the Commission to the Council of Ministers on the Implementation of the Four Regulations in the Field of Maritime Transport adopted by the Council on 22 December 1986, SEC(90)1594 final, 1 August 1990, para.66.

"73. The Irish authorities approached the Commission in 1988 regarding the conditions of use of the port of Holyhead (United Kingdom). This followed the concern expressed by the Irish B&I company following the refusal of the port authority (Sealink Harbours Ltd. ['SHL']) to grant B&I commercially profitable peak slots.

SHL's position was that it was technically impossible to dovetail slots requested by the Irish company for B&I with those already occupied by its competitor (Sealink).

74. Following a detailed examination of the arguments put forward, the Commission services intervened to advocate a compromise between the two parties. As a result, agreement was reached in principle in July 1989 and entered into force at the beginning of 1990."[239]

12.15.8 Sealink/SMZ

The Commission has received an application for an individual exemption pursuant to Article 12 of the Regulation in respect of cross-channel ferry services operated by Sealink and SMZ.[240] The notification was sent to the Member States and the Commission informed the parties concerned that there were serious doubts about Article 85(3) of the EEC Treaty being applicable to the agreement.[241]

12.15.9 Sealink/SNCF

The Commission received an application for an individual exemption pursuant to Article 12 of the Regulation in respect of cross-channel ferry services operated by Sealink and SNCF.[242] The notification was sent to the Member States and the Commission informed the parties concerned that there were serious doubts about Article 85(3) of the EEC Treaty being applicable to the agreement.[243]

12.15.10 West and Central Africa cases

In 1990, the Commission has itself summarised these cases[244] in the following terms:

"68. In 1987 the Commission was notified under Article 10 of Regulation 4056/86 of various complaints concerning restrictive practices in liner trades between the Community and the west coast of Africa

69. Following a detailed enquiry into the facts submitted, the Commission decided to initiate a formal procedure by sending a statement of objections to four Europe/Africa Liner conferences and 11 Franco-African shipowners' committees (see action under Regulation No.4058/86, paras.86 to 90)

70. The Commission also sent out three statements of objections, respectively to two liner conferences that refused to submit to an investigation required under Article 18(3) of Regulation 4056/86 and to the Secretariat of the shipowners' committees for transmitting incorrect information in response to a request under Article 16(3) of the same Regulation."[245]

239. Report from the Commission to the Council of Ministers on the Implementation of the Four Regulations in the Field of Maritime Transport adopted by the Council on 22 December 1986, SEC(90)1594 final, 1 August 1990, para. 64. See "B&I anger over Sealink 'abuses'", *Irish Independent*, 3 January 1992.

240. Case No. IV/32.383, OJ No.C 17/12, 89.

241. Report from the Commission to the Council of Ministers on the Implementation of the Four Regulations in the Field of Maritime Transport adopted by the Council on 22 December 1986, SEC(90)1594 final, 1 August 1990, para.65.

242. Case No. IV/32.385, OJ No.C 17/8, 21.8.89.

243. Report from the Commission to the Council of Ministers on the Implementation of the Four Regulations in the Field of Maritime Transport adopted by the Council on 22 December 1986, SEC(90)1594 final, 1 August 1990, para.65.

244. Cases No. IV/32.447, 32.448 and 32.450.

245. Report from the Commission to the Council of Ministers on the Implementation of the Four Regulations in the Field of Maritime Transport adopted by the Council on 22 December 1986, SEC(90)1594 final, 1 August 1990, paras. 68–69.

12.15.11 The 1237 Agreement

The Commission has received an application for an individual exemption of the 1237 Agreement pursuant to Articles 11(4) and 12 of the Regulation.[246]

12.15.12 Irish Club rules

Case IV/33.677 relates to the Irish Club rules. The Commission has published a Notice concerning this case.[247]

The Commission has not yet formed a view on the applicability of Article 85(3) of the EEC Treaty to the agreement.

12.16 ASSESSMENT

It has been written that the "purpose of this Regulation as set forth in the preambular paragraphs is to steer a middle course between two evils: undue distortion of competition within the common market by a complete laissez-faire attitude and excessive regulation of the sector. Adoption of the competition rules originates in the misgivings expressed by developing countries in the 1970s about the functioning of the conference system."[248] The same authors have commented that "the Regulation attempts to steer a middle course between conflicting interests of liner conferences and shippers. The result of this Regulation is group exemption to liner conferences couched in the widest possible terms, i.e., a very generous treatment of liner conferences unprecedented in other fields of competition law of the Community."[249]

Helmut Kreis, the former Deputy Head of the Administrative Unit for Transport and Tourism in DGIV, writing personally in 1989 stated that Regulation is a way by which the EC accepted the self-regulatory system enshrined in the United Nations Convention on a Code for Liner Conferences.[250] He has also written that the Regulation is "important because it provides for a fairly liberal regime, increases legal security, and clarifies the relationship between liner conferences and transport users".[251]

Regulation 4056/86 does not provide a complete competition regime in relation to shipping. Towage probably falls outside its scope. The same may be said of salvage and offshore supply services. Many tramp services fall outside its scope. Similarly, many non-scheduled services do as well.

What of successive transport operations, i.e. situations where both maritime and inland transport operations are interconnected in the one operation?

246. See OJ C59/2, 1990.
247. OJ C166, 26.6.91.
248. Bredima-Savopoulou and Tzoannos, *op. cit.*, p. 180, footnote omitted.
249. *Op. cit.*, p.181.
250. (1989–90) 13 Regulation Fordham Int'l LJ 411, at p. 418.
251. *Op. cit.*, p. 418. Clough and Randolph have commented that the Regulation seeks to reconcile the EC's transport policy commitment to the UNCTAD Code and to the scheduled liner cartel, enshrined in the 1979 Brussels package, with the EEC competition rules (p. 151).

CHAPTER 13

Dumping: Regulation 4057/86

13.1 INTRODUCTION

Dumping occurs when a product or service from one country is introduced on to another country's market at less than the normal value of that product or service.[1] This practice has serious consequences for the economy in which the goods or services are dumped because it undermines industry in the economy where goods or services are dumped.

The EC has fallen victim to dumping in a number of areas such as photocopiers, footwear and, most importantly for present purposes, shipping services.[2] There is no doubt that the dumping by some non-EC shipowners of their freight rates on the EC markets has had a detrimental effect on EC shipowners.[3] The EC has responded by adopting Regulation 4057/86,[4] which was the first EC anti-dumping measure to deal with services.[5] The purpose of Regulation 4057/86 is to provide a remedy against:

> "unfair pricing practices by certain third country shipowners engaged in international cargo liner shipping, which causes serious disruption of the freight pattern on a particular route to, from or within the Community and cause or threaten to cause major injury to Community shipowners operating on that route and to Community interests."[6]

13.2 COUNCIL REGULATION 4057/86

13.2.1 Introduction

Many non-EC shipping companies (especially Eastern European and South-East Asian ones) were engaging in unfair practices to the detriment of their EC counterparts. Non-EC shipping companies engaged in various unfair practices consisting of, among other things, cheap freight rates brought about by subsidies from their governments. EC shipping companies suffered as a consequence. There was need for some EC-driven legislation to deal with the issue because there was need for a co-ordinated response to the problem.

1. On dumping in the GATT, see the GATT, Article VI and the Agreement on the Implementation of Article VI of the GATT (the so-called Anti-Dumping Code).
2. On EC dumping law, generally, see Bessler and Williams, *Anti-Dumping and Subsidy Law: The European Communities* as well as Van Bael and Bellis, *Anti-Dumping and other Trade Protection Laws of the EEC* (2nd edn., 1990).
3. On Soviet merchant shipping services being dumped in the EC, see Berstrand, "Soviet Merchant Shipping", *Marine Policy*, March 1990, p. 112.
4. OJ L378/14, 31 December 1986.
5. Anti-dumping measures in the EC and GATT have traditionally dealt only with goods.
6. Regulation 4057/86, Article 1.

On 23 December 1976, the European Parliament's Committee on Economic and Monetary Affairs published its Interim Report on the Community Shipping Industry.[7] The Report stated:

"26. Most countries with a merchant fleet accord it certain subsidies, either direct or through favourable fiscal provisions. The Third World, especially the Arab countries, is rapidly developing its own State fleets. The policies followed by the State-trading countries are of particular concern here, as certain elements making up a significant part of EEC shipping costs, such as insurance, are not included as a shipping cost by lines in State-trading countries, with the results that these latter can naturally charge lower rates. Between 1963 and 1974, the USSR and other Eastern European countries increased their share of world tonnage from 5.2% to 7.6%, while the share of the OECD countries fell from 75.7% to 60%.[8] The gross tonnage of the fleets of State-trading countries has increased by about 400% in 15 years.[9]

27. Because of their different system of calculating costs, and the fact that their personnel receive a different system of remuneration which results in lower wages costs than those for Community fleets, the fleets of State-trading countries have been able to offer freight rates between 10 and 50% lower than those offered by Community shipping; this is, in effect, a practice of dumping.

28. Concern has been expressed in several quarters over the expansion of Soviet and Eastern European shipping fleets. The 'World Trade Review and Outlook' (published by the shipbrokers, Lambert Brothers Shipping) suggests that undercutting of freight rates by the Russians, aided by the East Europeans and some sympathetic developing countries, is making Western liner services insolvent and ripe for State subsidies or public ownership. With nearly 10 million tons already afloat, Russia has the world's largest general cargo liner fleet, nearly a third of which is competing for scarce cargoes at cut rates against western shipping in western ports.[10]

As an example of problems faced, the percentage of the United Kingdom's seaborne exports to the Soviet Union by value, carried in Russian ships in 1975, was 78% and in British ships 18%. The corresponding figures for the United Kingdom's imports from the Soviet Union were 74% and 10% respectively.[11]

The Soviet merchant fleet, according to the General Council of British Shipping, now ranks sixth in the world, and the Soviet Union has the largest conventional cargo liner fleet in the world—6.9 million gross registered tons in 1974 (the UK has 6.4 million). Moreover, the Eastern bloc could account for up to 20 per cent of all liner tonnage on order.[12]

29. The most obvious practices used by Eastern bloc countries, in particular the Soviet Union, to divert cargoes to their own shipping, fell under four main headings:

(a) a strict enforcement of f.o.b. purchase/c.i.f. sale contract terms in their direct trades with no flexibility, resulting in a near total monopoly of cargo movements;

(b) a systematic policy of undercutting in their cross-trading activities by charging freight rates which were uneconomic, certainly in Western terms;

(c) inter-governmental (either bilateral or multilateral) agreements reserving part or all of the cargo moving in the trade;

(d) the establishment of so-called joint shipping agencies in foreign countries without reciprocity; Western shipping companies were not afforded the same possibility to run their business in Eastern bloc countries with the same freedom.[13]

30. Shipping interests have called for Western governments to consider concerted action against uncommercial Eastern bloc practices, and for shippers to bear in mind that the immediate attractions of using Soviet cut rates will only be short-term and there would be a big longer-term price to be paid. Estimates of the significance of the threat from Comecon shipping vary considerably, however; the arguments are complex, and the facts are in some dispute. A

7. Doc. 479/76, Rapporteur: Mr J. L. Prescott.
8. Information from *Lloyd's Register of Shipping*.
9. COM(76)341 final.
10. *The Times*, London, 25 March 1976.
11. *The Times*, London, 27 April 1976.
12. General Council of British Shipping, "Red Ensign versus Red Flag—a Critical Choice".
13. Press release on a speech by Mr W. R. Russell, retiring Chairman of the Council of European and Japanese National Shipowners' Associations (CENSA) in London on 11 December 1975.

study published in February 1976 by Seatrade Publications entitled 'Soviet Shipping' suggests, however, that the expansion of the Russian fleet in the next five years may not be as dramatic as supposed by certain European and American shipping sources. This study makes the following important points:

1. 'A Confidential study from the Committee on European and Japanese National Shipowners' Associations (CENSA) has offered to accept government involvement in their affairs in return for curbs on the "uncommercial practices" of socialist shipping lines'.
2. Soviet shipping minister Timofei Guzhenko stated that the socialist share of world shipping was not expanding since over 80% of world orders for dry cargo ships were being placed by capitalist countries, with socialist countries accounting for only 3% and this was declining.
3. CENSA also accuses Comecon fleets of slashing freight rates on cross trades, and of costing practices which relieve shipping lines of the capital costs of building ships, as well as the cost of insurance. The Russians deny that their companies receive any such government subsidies.
4. 'The US and other western lines can easily outgun the Soviets and other East bloc carriers in both ship capacity and service, but when trade slumps the inoffensive Soviet tonnage becomes a bigger threat.'
5. 'The USSR's modest $200m. trade surplus with the West in 1974, has plummeted to a staggering $5.5 billion deficit in 1975 . . . the Comecon bloc as a whole is in hock to the West to the tune of $12bn.'
6. Soviet shipping has had to cross trade to stay viable, because the USSR's annual tonnage of maritime exports greatly exceeds imports, and cross-trading therefore helps to utilise capacity. In addition, the seasonality of many Soviet sea routes, which are blocked by ice in winter, releases ships elsewhere."

The EC responded with Council Regulation 4057/86 on unfair pricing practices in maritime transport.[14] This is in part a procedural measure and is a hybrid of anti-dumping as well as countervailing duty legislation.[15] It attempts to deal with some of the unfair practices by non-EEC undertakings[16] (especially the State-owned undertakings) in the shipping sector by establishing procedures for those acting on behalf of EC shipping companies who consider themselves injured or threatened by unfair pricing practices to lodge a complaint to the Commission. It only applies to the cargo liner shipping sector, that is to say, services operating on regular routes at regular intervals and operating according to published schedules. Thus, it does not apply to tramp or bulk operations.[17] In essence, the Regulation attempts to protect EC shipping lines from certain unfair pricing practices operated by non-EC shipping lines. The Regulation allows for duties to be imposed on freight rates charged by non-EC shipping operators where the rate charged on a route either to, from or within the EC is unfair. The Regulation also allows for undertakings (*i.e.* commitments) to be accepted

14. OJ 1986/L378/14. On Reg.4057/86, see Bellis, Vermulst and Musquar, "The New EEC Regulation on Unfair Pricing Practices in Maritime Transport: a Forerunner of the Extension of Unfair Trade Competition to Services" (1988) 22 JWTL 47; Elsner, "Unfair Pricing Practices in Maritime Transport" (1988) *European Transport Law* 591; Hutchings, "Unfair Pricing Practices — Procedure," at "The EEC and Shipping", Institute of Maritime Law, Conference, London, 11 November 1988; Randolph, "Dumping: Unfair Pricing Practices of Non-EEC Lines" at "The EEC and Shipping", Institute of Maritime Law, Conference, London, 11 November 1988; Smith, "The EEC's Unfair Pricing Practices Regulation: New Wave of Competition or Protectionism in Community Shipping?" (1988) 11 *Fordham International Law Journal* 883; Steenbergen, "Unfair Pricing Practices in Maritime Transport" at EEC Shipping Law Conference, 4-5/2/88; and Van Bael and Bellis, *op. cit.* at footnote 2 above Part VI.

15. Bellis, Vermulst and Musquar, *op. cit.* at footnote 14 above, at p. 60.

16. In this context, the term "shipowner" includes shipping companies which charter-in tonnage for the purposes of providing a liner service.

17. It would have been difficult to apply the Regulation to such services because they are based on freely negotiated rates which differ from case to case.

from non-EC shipping lines where rates are revised upwards. In summary the Regulation comes into play when the pricing practice (a) is "unfair"; (b) causes serious disruption of the freight pattern on a particular route to, from or within the EC; (c) is in the international cargo liner shipping sector; (d) perpetrated by a non-EC ship operator engaged in international liner services; (e) constitutes a "major injury" to EC ship operators; and (f) it is in the interests of the EC to act to counteract the practice.

Regulation 4057/86 is closely modelled on the EC's anti-dumping legislation, thus in many instances reference to the general EC law relating to dumping will be of assistance in interpreting the Regulation.[18] It is important for shipping companies to ensure that their practices do not fall foul of Regulation 4057/86, or else their services may be subject to redressive duties.

13.2.2 Legal basis

Article 84(2) of the EEC Treaty provides the legal basis for Regulation 4057/86.[19] It is similar, in many ways, to Regulation 2176/84 which is the basic Regulation in EC law laying down the anti-dumping and subsidy law.

13.2.3 Commercial background

The Preamble to the Regulation states that there was reason "to believe, *inter alia*, on the basis of the information system set up by Council Decision 78/774/EEC,[20] that the competitive participation of Community shipowners in international liner shipping is adversely affected by certain unfair practices of shipping lines of third countries"[21] with those unfair practices consisting of "continuous charging of freight rates for the transport of selected commodities which are lower than the lowest freight rates charged for the same commodities by established and representative shipowners"[22] with those pricing practices being made possible "by non-commercial advantages granted by a State which is not a member of the Community".[23] This evidence was the result of the monitoring system established under Decision 77/774/EEC.[24]

13.2.4 Legal history

As is normal, the Regulation started life as a draft submitted by the Commission to the Council of Ministers in the 1985 *Communication on Progress Towards a Common Transport Policy*.[25] The Economic and Social Committee[26] and the European Parliament[27] then delivered their opinions. The Regulation is similar in many ways to Regulation 2423/88,[28] the Anti-Dumping and Anti Subsidy Regulation.

18. See Elsner, *op. cit.* at footnote 14.
19. Regulation 4057/86, Preamble.
20. OJ L258/35, 21 September 1978. See Chapter 19, below.
21. Regulation 4057/86, Preamble, Recital 1.
22. Regulation 4057/86, Preamble, Recital 3.
23. Regulation 4057/86, Preamble, Recital 4.
24. On this system, see Chapter 19, below.
25. COM(85)90 final. On the Communication, see para. 5.5.19, above.
26. OJ C344/31, 31 December 1985.
27. OJ C255/169, 15 October 1986.
28. OJ 1988/L209/1.

13.2.5 Entry into force

Regulation 4057/86 entered into force on 1 July 1987. Being a Regulation, it did not need implementing legislation in each Member State.[29]

13.2.6 Purpose

Article 1 of Regulation 4057/86 provides:

"This Regulation lays down the procedure to be followed in order to respond to unfair pricing practices by certain third country shipowners engaged in international cargo liner shipping, which causes serious disruption of the freight pattern on a particular route to, from or within the Community and cause or threaten to cause major injury to Community shipowners operating on that route or to Community interests."

The Regulation allows the EC to respond to such unfair practices by being able to take redressive action against the unfair pricing practices.[30] It is important to study each of the elements in Article 1 to ensure the correct application of the Regulation.

13.2.7 Application

It is clear from the Regulation itself that it applies only to international cargo liner shipping. The Regulation applies to nationals of the EC who are based outside the EC as well as those EC nationals based within the EC. As Recital 3 of the Preamble to the Regulation provides:

"the structure of the Community shipping industry is such as to make it appropriate that the provisions of this Regulation should also apply to nationals of Member States established outside the Community or cargo shipping companies established outside the Community and controlled by nationals of Member States, if their ships are registered in a Member State in accordance with its legislation."

The twelfth Recital to the Regulation makes plain that this Regulation may not be abused so as to obviate or avoid the application of Regulation 4056/86.[31]

In the light of the definition given in the Regulation for "Community Shipowners" and the general thrust of the Regulation, only shipowners can be beneficiaries under the Regulation.

There is a minimum of four issues to be determined before the Regulation may be applied: (a) the third country shipowner (engaged in international cargo liner shipping) has enjoyed "non-commercial advantages" (which constitute unfair pricing practices); (b) the "normal freight rate" must be determined; (c) the rates actually charged by the third country shipowner must be established; and (d) a comparison must be drawn between the "normal freight rate" and the freight rate actually charged by the third country shipowner with the "dumped" rate causing serious disruption of the freight pattern on a particular route to, from or within the EC.

13.2.8 Concepts

13.2.8.1 Concept of dumping

Dumping occurs where a product or service of one country is introduced into the commerce of another country at less than the normal value of the product or service. In

29. See para. 3.5.2.2.1, above.
30. Regulation 4057/86, Preamble, Recital 5.
31. On Regulation 4056/86, see Chapter 12, above.

the context of this Regulation, it occurs where there are, *inter alia*, charges which are lower than normal freight rates.

13.2.8.2 Concept of an unfair pricing practice

There are no internationally agreed rules as to what constitutes an unfair price in the maritime transport field.[32] However, Article 3(b) of Regulation 4057/86 defines "unfair pricing practices", for the purposes of the Regulation, as the:

> "continuous charging on a particular shipping route to, from or within the Community of freight rates for selected or all commodities which are lower than the normal freight rates charged during a period of at least six months, when such lower freight rates are made possible by the fact that the shipowner concerned enjoys non-commercial advantages which are granted by a State which is not a member of the Community."

Thus, lower freight rates may only be challenged where they result from "non-commercial advantages".

The definition of an unfair pricing practice has a number of elements which must be carefully analysed. Third Country shipowners excludes nationals of Member States established outside the EC or cargo shipping companies established outside the EC but controlled by nationals when their ships are registered in an EC Member State.

13.2.8.3 Concept of non-commercial advantage

The Regulation, as adopted,[33] does not define or give examples of "non-commercial advantages". This is unhelpful for anyone concerned with the Regulation but is understandable given the difficulties associated with defining such a nebulous and capricious concept. As a consequence of this lack of a definition, the EC institutions have reserved to themselves considerable flexibility[34] in their approach to the application of this Regulation—the institutions must however be careful in exercising this discretion lest in their attempts to ensure an open shipping policy, they themselves do not prove to be too protectionist.[35]

The Commission had in its draft proposal to the Council of Ministers provided that the EC could adopt defensive measures against shipowners which enjoyed the advantages of being (a) owned or controlled directly or indirectly by any non-EC Member State; (b) more favourably placed than EC shipowners as to the access to cargo in ocean trades through national legislation; and/or (c) the operators of ships flying the flag of countries which have not ratified and do not implement the international conventions of the IMO and ILO.[36] The Council of Ministers did not, however, adopt the Commission's approach because:

> "this approach would appear to have been both too narrow and too wide: too narrow, because it would have only allowed three distinct situations to fall under the terms of non-commercial advantage, and too wide, because it would have introduced an unnecessary automatism in that, e.g. any State-owned third country shipowner would have fulfilled this condition."[37]

32. Regulation 4057/86, Preamble, Recital 6.
33. The original proposal included some examples of non-commercial advantages.
34. Bellis, Vermulst and Musquar, *op. cit.* at footnote 14, describe this as "a deliberate oversight" which enables "the Community authorities to use the Regulation as a 'catch-all' weapon against any form of government subsidies".
35. See the comments of UNICE in 1135 Agence Europe, *Business Brief*, p. 4.
36. One presumes that the Commission was specifically referring to those Conventions dealing with seafarers' wages and conditions.
37. Elsner, *op. cit.* at footnote 14, at p. 594.

Despite the absence of a definition, it is none the less necessary to give some examples of the concept. In broad terms, subsidies, grants, aids, soft loans, moratoria on debts,[38] and unfair tax breaks[39] as well as cargo reservation schemes[40] could potentially constitute non-commercial advantages. Similarly, the non-adherence to or non-enforcement by a non-EC State of basic international standards on such matters as safety, crewing and so on may constitute an unfair advantage for that State's shipping companies. It might well be deduced that a "non-commercial advantage" is a benefit which does not arise from the normal activity of the market place but is instead a result of the interference by governmental or other forces so as to distort the workings of the normal shipping market.

13.2.8.4 Concept of normal freight rates

There are two tests for establishing the normal freight rate. The first is the so-called third party test. The second analyses the actual costs of the service. Regrettably, the choice of tests, which will always prove critical,[41] will lead to confusion and perhaps conflicting results. It is an important strategic decision in each case as to which test will be used.

The "normal freight rate" is determined (for the purposes of Regulation 4057/86) by taking into account:

(i) the comparable rate actually charged in the ordinary course of shipping business for the like service on the same or a comparable route by established and representative companies not enjoying non-commercial advantages which are granted by a State which is not a member of the EC; or

(ii) otherwise the constructed rate which is determined by taking the costs of comparable companies not enjoying the non-commercial advantages which are granted by a State which is not a member of the EC, plus a reasonable margin of profit. This cost shall be computed on the basis of all costs incurred in the ordinary course of shipping business, both fixed and variable, plus a reasonable amount for overhead expenses.

This first test is the comparable rate actually[42] charged in the ordinary course of the shipping business for a similar service on the same or a similar route by established and representative shipping companies which do not enjoy the non-commercial advantages outlined in the Regulation. There will be a great deal of dispute over whether or not the shipping companies chosen are established at all or comparable to the company being investigated. Similarly, disputes will arise over the comparability of the service or routes involved. Parties who have their rates challenged under this Regulation would be advised to establish differences between their own company, service as well as route and those offered by the Commission as being comparable.

The second test is based on the costs of service. If there is no comparable service offered in the ordinary course of the shipping business (for the purposes of the first test),

38. See *Hyundai* below, at para. 13.2.15.

39. See *Hyundai*, *ibid.*

40. *Ibid.*

41. In *Hyundai*, *ibid.* the company sought to be compared to Jebsen but the final figures were determined by comparison with Eagle Container Line plus a profit margin of 3%.

42. I.e. not constructively.

then the Commission will have to construct the normal freight rate. The Commission will construct the normal freight rate by taking into account the costs of comparable companies[43] not enjoying the non-commercial advantages covered by the Regulation and a reasonable profit margin.[44] These costs are to be computed on the basis of all costs incurred in the ordinary course of the shipping business—both fixed and variable plus a reasonable amount for overhead business.

It has been commented that these tests focus on the prices or costs of what could be termed the "surrogate company" which may even be the complainant company itself.[45]

The Preamble to the Regulation provides that:

> "in order to determine the existence of unfair pricing practices, provision should . . . be made for an appropriate method of calculation [and] when calculating the 'normal freight rate' account should be taken of the comparable rate actually charged by established and representative companies operating within or outside conferences or otherwise of a constructed rate based on the costs of comparable companies plus a reasonable margin of profit."[46]

It is interesting to note that much (but not all) of the Regulation is similar to Regulation 2176/84 on dumping generally.

13.2.8.5 Concept of "serious disruption of a freight pattern"

Once again, the Regulation does not define a key concept. The notion of a "serious disruption of a freight pattern" is a nebulous one. It is probable that some of the causes of injury to EC shipowners would also amount to a serious disruption of a freight pattern. The disruption may arise in regard to services from, to or within the EC.

13.2.8.6 Concept of "injury to Community ship operators"

The existence of injury is necessary for the imposition of redressive duties. In determining the existence of injury, the examination by the EC institutions shall cover two principal factors, namely the freight rates offered by Community ship operators' competitors on the route in question, in particular in order to determine whether they have been significantly lower than the normal freight rate offered by Community ship operators,[47] and the level of service offered by all the companies concerned.

The EC institutions must examine whether the rates offered by the non-EC ship operators are "significantly lower than the normal freight rate" offered by EC shipowners. Comparisons would be made with the freight rates of EC shipowners and, for example, in the *Hyundai* case,[48] the Commission alleged that Hyundai were undercutting the prices charged by EC companies by between 17% and 43%.

The effect of the price cutting and the level of service on EC ship operators may be gauged by taking into account trends in a number of economic indicators such as:

43. Parties who have their rates challenged by the Commission should seriously consider challenging the companies proposed by the Commission and contend that they are not, in fact, comparable at all.
44. The Commission is likely to have considerable discretion as to what constitutes a reasonable profit margin in this context.
45. Bellis, Vermulst and Musquar, *op. cit.* at footnote 14, at p. 50.
46. Regulation 4057/86, Preamble, Recital 5.
47. On the definition of Community shipowner, see para. 13.2.8.8, below.
48. See para. 13.2.15, below.

— sailings,
— utilisation of capacity,
— cargo bookings,
— market share,
— freight rates (that is depression of freight rates or prevention of freight rate increases which would normally have occurred),[49]
— profits,[50]
— return of capital,
— investment,[51] and
— employment.

If a threat of injury is alleged, the Commission may also examine whether it is clearly foreseeable that a particular situation is likely to develop into actual injury. In this regard, account may also be taken of factors such as:

(a) the increase in tonnage deployed on the shipping route where the competition with Community shipowners is taking place;
(b) the capacity which is already available or is to become available in the foreseeable future in the country of the foreign shipowners and the extent to which the tonnage resulting from that capacity is likely to be used on the shipping route referred to above in (a).[52]

The application of the Regulation is difficult to predict because of the absence of any specific indicators as to what is a "major" injury and what is not. This undefined line could prove to be the basis of many challenges by companies alleged to be engaged in unfair practices.

13.2.8.7 Concept of "Community interests"

The fundamental concept "Community interest" is, like many other fundamental concepts in Regulation 4057/86, left undefined. However, Article 12 gives some guidance. It provides that "[i]n deciding on the redressive duties, the Council [of Ministers] shall also take due account of the external trade policy considerations as well as port interests and the shipping policy considerations of the Member States concerned".

13.2.8.8 Concept of third country shipowner

A third country shipowner[53] is a cargo liner shipping company other than a Community shipowner.[54]

According to Regulation 4057/86, an EC shipowner is:

"(a) a cargo shipping company established under the EEC Treaty in a Member State of the EEC; or

49. See para. 13.2.15, below.
50. *Ibid.*
51. *Ibid.*
52. Regulation 4057/86, Article 4(2).
53. This term includes those companies which charter in tonnage so as to provide a cargo liner shipping service.
54. Regulation 4057/86, Article 3(a).

(b) a national of a Member State established outside the EEC provided the company's ships are registered in an EEC Member State in accordance with that State's legislation; or
(c) a cargo shipping company established outside the EEC and controlled by nationals of Member States provided the company's ships are registered in an EEC Member State in accordance with that State's legislation."[55]

The breadth of drafting used in this provision means that there will be considerable flexibility. What of ships registered in Kerugulen?[56] Are they registered in France? It is submitted that the ambiguity of the provision will only be resolved on a case-by-case basis and the EC institutions will decide on the basis of the type of EC interest being undermined by the practice.

13.2.9 Role of EC institutions under the Regulation

13.2.9.1 The Commission

The Seventh Directorate-General of the Commission[57] (DGVII *i.e.* the Transport Directorate General) has responsibility for administering the Regulation. It receives the complaints,[58] conducts the investigations,[59] calculates the duties,[60] accepts any undertakings[61] or terminates proceedings.[62] DGIV (the Competition Directorate-General) normally deals with competition matters, but because of the special problems associated with dumping in shipping, it is DGVII which deals with Regulation 4057/86. It is well to remember that the Commission does not have the power to impose duties.

13.2.9.2 The Council of Ministers

It is only the Council of Ministers[63] which has the legal power to impose a duty. The Commission does not have the power to impose duties.

13.2.9.3 The European Court of Justice

A party affected by a decision of the Council of Ministers to impose duties may appeal to the European Court of Justice. Hyundai appealed to the Court.

13.2.10 Complaints

13.2.10.1 Complaint procedure

It was necessary to establish under the Regulation procedures "for those acting on behalf of the Community shipping industry who consider themselves injured or threatened by unfair pricing practices to lodge a complaint".[64]

55. Regulation 4057/86, Article 3(d).
56. I.e. part of the French Antarctic.
57. On the Commission, see para. 3.4.2. DGVII has responsibility for transport.
58. On complaints, see para. 13.2.10, below.
59. On investigations, see para. 13.2.12, below.
60. On the duties, see para. 13.2.13.4, below.
61. On acceptance of undertakings, see para. 13.2.13.3, below.
62. On the termination of proceedings, see para. 13.2.13.7, below.
63. On the Council of Ministers, see para. 3.4.3, above.
64. Regulation 4057/86, Preamble, Recital.

13.2.10.2 Who may lodge a complaint?

Any natural or legal person, or any association not having legal personality, acting on behalf of the Community shipping industry who considers themselves injured or threatened by unfair pricing practices may lodge a written complaint.[65] This includes seafarers.

If, in the absence of any complaint, a Member State is in possession of sufficient evidence both of unfair pricing practices[66] and of injury resulting therefrom for Community shipowners[67] then that Member State is obliged immediately to communicate such evidence to the Commission.[68]

This complaint mechanism affords EC shipping companies to complain to the Commission and therefore initiate action on particular unfair pricing practices by some non-EC shipping companies. Conversely, non-EC shipping companies need to monitor their activities carefully so that they do not violate the rules contained in Regulation 4057/86 and thereby fall victim of a complaint under that Regulation.

Seafarers' unions are not given an express right under the Regulation to lodge a complaint despite the support for such a right from the Parliament and the Transport Commissioner.

13.2.10.3 Form of complaint

The Regulation provides that the complaint must be made in writing.[69] The Regulation does not however lay down any other formalities for the complaint. There is no particular form to be used, as the case is with many other areas of competition law.

13.2.10.4 Contents of the complaint

The complaint should contain sufficient evidence of the existence of the unfair pricing practice and injury resulting therefrom.[70] This sufficient evidence must demonstrate the existence of the unfair pricing practice and the resulting injury. Such evidence would include details of the routes, cargoes, rates charged or likely to be charged by the EC and non-EC companies, operators, the non-commercial advantages, effects on EC shipping, and the resulting injuries.

While it would be better to approach the Commission with "sufficient evidence" at the beginning, it may well be the case that *prima facie* evidence will suffice so as to encourage the Commission to begin investigations.

If it becomes apparent after consultation that the complaint does not provide sufficient evidence to justify initiating an investigation then the complainant is so informed by the Commission.[71]

In most situations, it would be wiser to have preliminary discussions/consultations with the Commission before lodging the complaint.

65. Regulation 4057/86, Article 5(1). In the light of the *BP/TGWU* (16th Report on Competition Policy and *Scottish Steel Campaign/British Steel* (1991), trade unions may have *locus standi* to complain but they have not been given the express right to do so.
66. As defined in para. 13.2.8.2, above.
67. See para. 13.2.8.6, above.
68. Regulation 4057/86, Article 5(6).
69. Regulation 4057/86, Article 5(1).
70. Regulation 4057/86, Article 5(2).
71. Regulation 4057/86, Article 5(5).

13.2.10.5 To whom is the complaint made?

The complaint may be made to the Commission[72] and the Commission then sends each Member State a copy of the complaint received.[73] Equally, the complaint may be made to a Member State of the EC and that State shall then forward it to the Commission.[74]

13.2.10.6 Confidentiality of the complaint

The complainant may request the Commission to keep certain parts of its complaint confidential. If the Commission is satisfied that parts of its complaint should be kept confidential then it will ask the complainant to prepare a "confidential complaint" (copies of which will only be circulated to the Commission and the Member States) and a "non-confidential complaint" which will be circulated generally.

13.2.10.7 Withdrawal of the complaint

A complaint may be withdrawn.[75] If it is withdrawn then proceedings may be terminated *unless* such termination would not be in the interest of the Community.[76]

13.2.11 Consultation

Provision is made in Article 6 of the Regulation for consultations. Such consultations are a preliminary step before the initiation of proceedings.[77] Article 6(4) provides that consultation shall in particular cover: (a) the existence of unfair pricing practices and the amount thereof; (b) the existence and extent of injury; (c) the causal link between the unfair pricing practices and injury; and (d) the measures which, in the circumstances, are appropriate to prevent or remedy the injury caused by unfair pricing practices and the ways and means for putting such measures into effect. Such consultations shall be held immediately on request by a Member State or on the initiative of the Commission.[78]

Any consultations provided for in the Regulation must take place within an Advisory Committee.[79] The Advisory Committee consists of representatives of each Member State with a representative of the Commission acting as Chairman.[80]

The Committee may either meet or conduct its business in writing. If it meets then it meets when convened by its chairman[81] who shall provide the Member States, as promptly as possible, with all relevant information.[82] Where necessary, consultation may be in writing only and in such case the Commission shall notify the Member States and shall specify a period within which they shall be entitled to express their opinions or to request an oral consultation.[83]

72. Regulation 4057/86, Article 5(3).
73. *Ibid.*
74. Regulation 4057/86, Article 5(3).
75. Regulation 4057/86, Article 5(4).
76. *Ibid.*
77. See Regulation 4057/86, Article 7(1).
78. Regulation 4057/86, Article 6(1).
79. Regulation 4057/86, Article 6(1).
80. Regulation 4057/86, Article 6(1).
81. Regulation 4057/86, Article 5(2).
82. Regulation 4057/86, Article 6(2).
83. Regulation 4057/86, Article 6(3).

The Commission is not bound to accept the views of the Advisory Committee, but it is unlikely that a unanimous view of the Committee will be ignored by the Commission because the views of the Committee may be tantamount to the views of the Member States and those views will probably surface again at the Council of Ministers.

13.2.12 Initiation and investigation

13.2.12.1 Initiation

Consultation[84] is a prerequisite before initiation and investigation. It is only where, after consultation, it is apparent that there is sufficient evidence to justify initiating a proceeding that the Commission may do so.[85]

If it is apparent that there is sufficient evidence to justify initiating a proceeding then the Commission must immediately do three things, namely:

(a) announce the initiation of a proceeding in the *Official Journal of the European Communities*. This notice will invite interested third parties to comment on the investigation;[86,87]
(b) advise the shipowners, shippers and freight forwarders known to the Commission to be concerned and the complainants; and
(c) commence the investigation at Community level, acting in co-operation with the Member States.[88]

In practical terms, the Commission may decide to postpone the initiation of an investigation until it has sufficient staff to deal with the case. The length of an investigation depends on the circumstances of the case, but it would normally take months, rather than weeks, and could take several months or even years.

13.2.12.2 Contents of the investigation

The investigation must cover both unfair pricing practices and injury resulting therefrom and shall be carried out in accordance with Article 5 of the Regulation which lays down some basic rules.

The first of these rules is that an investigation of unfair pricing practices should normally cover a period of not less than six months immediately prior to the initiation of the proceedings.[89] In the *Hyundai* case, it was 10 months.[90]

Where appropriate, the Commission shall seek all the information it deems necessary and attempt to check this information with the shipowners, agents, shippers, freight forwarders, conferences, associations and other organisations, provided that the undertakings or organisations concerned give their consent.[91]

84. On consultation, see para. 13.2.11, above.
85. Regulation 4057/86, Article 7(1).
86. On the confidentiality of information supplied, see para. 13.2.10.6, above.
87. Regulation 4057/86, Article 7(1)(a).
88. Regulation 4057/86, Article 7(1)(a) provides that the announcement in the *Official Journal of the European Communities* must, first, indicate the foreign shipowner concerned and its country of origin, secondly, give a summary of the information received, thirdly, provide that all relevant information should be communicated to the Commission, and, finally, state the period within which interested parties may make known their views in writing and may apply to be heard orally by the Commission.
89. Regulation 4057/86, Article 5(1)(c).
90. See para. 13.2.15, below, on the case.
91. Regulation 4057/86, Article 5(2)(a).

Where necessary the Commission shall, after consultation, carry out investigations in third countries (i.e. non-EC States), provided that the firms concerned give their consent and the government of the country in question has been officially notified and raises no objection and the Commission shall be assisted by officials of those Member States which so request.[92]

The Commission may enlist the help of EC Member States by requesting them to supply information, to carry out all necessary checks and inspections (particularly among shippers, freight forwarders, Community shipowners and their agents) and to carry out investigations in third countries, provided the firms concerned give their consent and the government of the country in question has been officially notified and raises no objection.[93] Member States are obliged to take whatever steps are necessary in order to give effect to requests from the Commission, including sending to the Commission the information requested, together with the results of all inspections, checks or investigations carried out.

13.2.12.3 Invitation to the allegedly guilty party to make their case

The Commission will send *pro forma* questionnaires to the ship operators who are allegedly violating Regulation 4057/86. The time period within which the recipients will have to reply is five weeks from the date of the notification of the investigation in the *Official Journal*, but this may be extended or waived.

13.2.12.4 Co-operation

The Commission does not have the legal power to compel the parties to co-operate with the investigation or supply any information requested by the Commission. It requests co-operation. The Commission would normally carry out on-the-spot verifications at the premises of the informants on the accuracy of the information supplied.

A party whose co-operation is sought by the Commission should carefully consider whether or not it should co-operate. It is almost invariably wiser to co-operate because the Commission might well decide the matter "on the basis of the information available to it" and thereby not take into account the views of parties who did not co-operate.

13.2.12.5 Confidentiality of information supplied

An informant may request the Commission to keep certain parts of its information confidential. If the Commission is satisfied that all or part of the information should be kept confidential then it will do so.

13.2.12.6 Conclusion of the first stages of investigation

After concluding the first stages of investigation, the Commission would be expected to discuss in broad terms its findings with the parties involved. This preliminary-type discussion is often useful (in other areas of EC dumping law) to clarify any misconceptions and allow the parties to make representations to the Commission on any matter of interest.

92. Regulation 4057/86, Article 5(2)(b).
93. Regulation 4057/86, Article 5(3)(a).

13.2.12.7 Formal rights of the parties

The parties have three particular rights. They have a right to:

(a) inspect non-confidential information made available by other parties to the Commission;
(b) a hearing with the Commission;
(c) request a "confrontation meeting" attended by the complainants and the allegedly guilty.

A "confrontation meeting" is a meeting attended by the complainants and the allegedly guilty shipping companies. The meeting would be presided over by a Commission official. There is no obligation on the "other side" (i.e. the party who did not request the meeting) to attend such a meeting.

13.2.13 Outcome of the Commission's investigations

13.2.13.1 Introduction

There are three possible outcomes from the Commission's investigations, namely:

(a) the investigation is terminated without any action being taken; or
(b) the investigation is terminated after the acceptance of an undertaking; or
(c) "redressive duties" are imposed.

13.2.13.2 No action

The proceedings are terminated if the Commission, after consultation, determines that protective measures are unnecessary and no Member State objects within the Advisory Committee.[94] If a Member State does object then the Commission must submit to the Council of Ministers a report on the results of the consultation along with a proposal that the proceedings be terminated.[95] The proceedings will be terminated unless the Council, acting by way of a qualified majority, decides otherwise.[96]

13.2.13.3 Undertakings

13.2.13.3.1 Introduction

The complaint may be "settled" by the non-EC shipowner giving an acceptable written undertaking to the EC Commission.[97] It may be an undertaking to raise the freight rate or withdraw from the service altogether. In this context "undertaking" means a commitment or promise and not its more usual meaning in EC competition law. Undertakings given in dumping cases are not normally published. The acceptance or rejection of the undertaking is a matter of discretion for the Commission.

The acceptance of an undertaking means that a redressive duty would not normally be imposed *per se*. The breach or withdrawal of the undertaking would, however, mean that such a duty could be imposed and imposed with retrospective effect.

94. Regulation 4057/86, Article 9(1).
95. Regulation 4057/86, Article 9(1).
96. Regulation 4057/86, Article 9(1).
97. Regulation 4057/86, Article 10(1).

If the Commission accepts an undertaking but none the less continues with its investigation and finds that there was no breach then the undertaking would lapse.

13.2.13.3.2 Duration of undertakings

An undertaking lapses five years after it was confirmed by the Commission or last amended. It may however continue: where an interested party shows that the expiration would lead to injury or threat of injury then the Commission must conduct a review and the undertakings will remain in force pending the outcome of this review.

13.2.13.3.3 Review of undertakings

The Commission may carry out a review at any time either on its own initiative or at the request of an EC Member State. Any interested party may ask the Commission to review the undertaking provided that at least one year has elapsed since its confirmation.

13.2.13.4 Redressive duties

Article 2 of the Regulation provides that in response to the unfair pricing practices prohibited by the Regulation which cause major injury, redressive duties may be applied by the Community.[98] For example, in the *Hyundai* case, a duty of ECU450 was imposed for each 20ft container. These duties may be imposed where it has been shown on investigation by the Commission that: (a) there is an unfair pricing practice; (b) such practice has caused injury to the Community shipowner; and (c) it is in the interest of the Community to impose duties. The Council of Ministers must also take into account, when deciding whether to impose redressive duties, "the external trade policy considerations as well as the port interests and the shipping policy considerations of the Member States concerned".[99] A threat of major injury may only give rise to an examination.[100]

13.2.13.5 Power to impose redressive duties

Redressive duties may only be imposed by the Council of Ministers following on from a recommendation of the Commission.

13.2.13.6 Calculation of the redressive duties

The redressive duty to be imposed must not exceed the difference between the freight rate charged by the non-EC ship operator and the "normal freight rate"[101] established by the Commission's investigation.

The duty imposed may be related to units of cargo, value of the products or whatever. For example, in *Hyundai* the duty was a fixed amount for each type of

98. Regulation 4057/86 does not confer the power to impose provisional duties.

99. Regulation 4057/86, Article 12. This provision is somewhat unclear. Guidance might be had from the amendment proposed by the Parliament on this issue: ". . . the Council shall take into account that important national interests connected with a Member State's foreign policy are placed in jeopardy when it imposes a duty".

100. Regulation 4057/86, Article 2(2).

101. On the "normal freight rate", see para. 13.2.8.4, above.

container. There is undoubtedly considerable flexibility in the way in which it may be calculated.

13.2.13.7 Imposition of redressive duties

The redressive duties are imposed by way of a Council of Ministers' Regulation. The Regulation must state the reasons for the Regulation, the amount and type of duty, the commodities concerned and the country of origin of the non-EC ship operators. The duties may be imposed on non-EC shipowners only. The duties are applicable to the transport of the particular commodities when they are loaded[102] or unloaded at any EC port.

13.2.13.7.1 Collection of redressive duties

The collection of redressive duties imposed under a Regulation of the Council of Ministers is the task of the customs authorities in the Member States.

13.2.13.7.2 Duration of the redressive duties

An undertaking lapses five years after it was confirmed by the Commission or last amended.[103] It may however continue. Where an interested party shows that the expiration would lead to injury or threat of injury then the Commission must conduct a review and the duties will remain in force pending the outcome of this review.

13.2.13.7.3 Retroactivity of redressive duties

As a general rule, a redressive duty may not be imposed retrospectively. However, such a duty may be imposed when the Council of Ministers determines that an undertaking[104] has been violated or withdrawn.

13.2.13.7.4 Review of redressive duties

The Commission may carry out a review at any time, either on its own initiative or at the request of an EC Member State. Any interested party may ask the Commission to review the duty, provided that at least one year has elapsed since its imposition.

13.2.13.7.5 Refunds of redressive duties

The Regulation lays down procedures for examining applications for refunds of redressive duties.[105] The non-EC shipowner can obtain a refund when the duty collected exceeds the difference between the freight rate actually charged by it and the "normal freight rate" imposed by the Commission.[106] In practice, such a refund might be paid after a considerable delay, if at all.

102. In the *Hyundai* case the duties only related to goods loaded because Hyundai did not discharge relevant cargo in the EC.

103. Regulation 4057/86, Article 15(2).

104. On undertakings, see para. 13.2.13.3, below.

105. Regulation 4057/86, Article 16.

106. Regulation 4057/86, Article 16.

13.2.14 Appeals

In dumping cases generally, it has been recognised that complainants, exporters and importers have the right to bring a regulation imposing anti-dumping duties before the European Court so as to test its validity under EC law. The same right would apply in this context.[107]

13.2.15 Practice to date

Action was taken against Hyundai Marine Company Limited on 20 October 1988 on the basis of Regulation 4057/86[108] when the Commission proposed the imposition of redressive duties on container cargoes shipped from the EC to Australia by Hyundai Merchant Marine Company of Seoul in the Republic of Korea.

This followed a complaint made in August 1987 by the Committee of European Community Shipowners (CAACE[109]) regarding the alleged dumping of freight rates by Hyundai Merchant Marine on the EC–Australian route. The CAACE was acting on behalf of liner shipping companies from Denmark, France, Germany, Italy, The Netherlands, Spain and the UK operating in the liner shipping trade between the EC and Australia and organised in Europe/UK to Australia Conferences.[110] These companies were all the EC shipowners engaged in that particular trade.[111] The CAACE alleged that Hyundai were benefiting from non-commercial advantages offered by the South Korean Government and could thus charge rates 25% to 30% lower than the normal rates charged by CAACE companies.

The Commission opened the proceedings.[112] It was the first proceedings to be opened under Regulation 4057/86. The Commission investigated the matter over a period of 16 months and made visits to Antwerp, Crawley, Hamburg, Ipswich, London, Paris, Rotterdam, Seoul and Trieste. The service operated by Hyundai was compared by the Commission to a service operated by the Eagle Container Line, a Swiss company operating out of Ipswich in the UK,[113] but the basis of this comparison has been challenged by Hyundai which wanted to be compared to a Norwegian company.[114] The Commission rejected the comparison to the Norwegian company because "*inter alia*, [the Norwegian company] entered the trade only in 1985/86 and does not operate a fixed fleet and often calls only at one major Australian port" and was not thus an "appropriate choice".[115]

The Commission held that the complaint was justified: Hyundai had, according to the Commission, been engaged in unfair pricing practices on the Europe to Australia route, thereby causing serious disruption of the freight pattern to the detriment of EC shipowners.

The Commission concluded that Hyundai were benefiting from a number of non-commercial advantages. The first of these related to the cargo reservation scheme under Article 16 of the Korean Maritime Transportation Fostering Act and the second

107. See *Hyundai*, below, in para. 13.2.15.
108. OJ 1989 L4/1.
109. I.e. the Comité des Associations d'Armateurs des Communautes Europeénnes.
110. A Belgian shipowner later joined the proceedings.
111. See Regulation 15/89.
112. OJ 1987 C308/3.
113. See Regulation 15/89, para. 10.
114. Regulation 15/89, para. 12.
115. Regulation 15/89, para. 12.

related to the Shipping Industry Rationalisation Plan (SIRP) operated by the Korean Government since 1984.

According to the Commission, Hyundai were undercutting the normal freight rate by an average of 26% or ECU450 per 20ft container during the ten-month period investigated by the Commission. Hyundai were, according to the Commission, benefiting from a cargo reservation scheme and a rationalisation plan for the shipping industry both operated by the Korean Government.

The Council of Ministers then imposed on 4 January 1989, by way of Regulation (EEC) 15/89,[116] a redressive duty on containerised cargo loaded on to any vessel operated directly or indirectly by Hyundai at any EC port for Australia. The duty was 450ECU for a 20ft container and 900ECU for a 40ft container with no regard for the contents of the container—*pro rata* rates would apply for containers of other sizes. Hyundai then suspended its service. No duty was imposed on bulk cargo.

Hyundai has appealed to the ECJ and a judgment was not to hand when completing this edition.[117]

The Commission, in its Report to the Council of Ministers on 1 August 1990 on the Implementation of the Four Regulations in the Field of Maritime Transport,[118] stated:

> "82. The following conclusions can be drawn from the first case under the Regulation on unfair pricing practices:
>
> — the legal instrument is adequate for its intended purpose;
> — a proceeding can be carried out sufficiently quickly to offer relief where this is justified;
> — national customs authorities can efficiently implement a specific regulation;
> — maritime transport appears to lend itself to attempts to circumvent a redressive duty. Although the current legislation seems to be sufficient for the institutions to cope with this problem where anticipated, it would appear preferable to discourage such attempts from the outset. A clarification of the current legislation therefore appears desirable;
> — a small number of points with regard in particular to customs rules and the procedural rights should be updated to keep up with post-1986 developments in EC customs and anti-dumping legislation on which latter a substantial part of Regulation No. 4057/86 has been modelled."

The Commission continued:

> "84. Market reports seem to indicate that certain third country shipowners against whom complaints were being prepared have changed their rate policies subsequent to the imposition of the duty against HMM. Such reaction can only be welcomed: the value of Regulation 4057/86 is to be seen as much as a deterrent as a tool to take redressive action."

There is little doubt that the Commission will have to utilise the Regulation sparingly: its mere existence and its potency[119] to date has meant that it may well prove to be a deterrent rather than a weapon used in battle.

116. OJ 1989 L4/1.
117. Case 136/89.
118. SEC(90)1594 final, p. 19.
119. This presumes no overturning of the Commission's decision by the ECJ.

CHAPTER 14

Regulation 4058/86

14.1 INTRODUCTION

EEC Council of Ministers Regulation 4058/86[1] concerns co-ordinated action to safeguard free access to cargoes in ocean trade. It provides a procedure to be used where certain trade practices by a third country[2] or its agents threaten to restrict free market access by Member States' shipping companies. The Regulation establishes a procedure for EC States to join together so as to resist cargo-reservation by non-EC States. It comes into operation whenever there is an effect on the merchant fleet or trading interests of a Member State.

The Regulation was adopted because the Member States believed that there was a need to ensure a free competitive environment, particularly for the purposes of the dry and liquid bulk trades.

14.2 APPLICATION

The Regulation applies to all types of shipping services and all types of cargo in international trades. The markets concerned are: (a) liner cargoes in codist trades (except in the case of restrictions from the Code of Conduct on Liner Conferences); (b) liner cargoes in non-codist trades; (c) bulk cargoes and any other cargo on tramp services; (d) passengers; as well as (e) persons and goods to or between offshore installations.

14.3 LEGAL BASES

The legal bases of the Regulation are the EEC Treaty generally and, in particular, Article 84(2) thereof.

14.4 LEGAL HISTORY

The Regulation commenced with a draft submitted by the Commission and was opined on by the European Parliament in 1986[3] as well as the Economic and Social Committee in 1985.[4]

1. OJ L378/21, 31 December 1986. The Regulation is referred to in this chapter as the "Regulation".
2. I.e., a non-EC State.
3. OJ C 255/169, 15 October 1986.
4. OJ C 344/31, 31 December 1985.

14.5 ENTRY INTO FORCE

The Regulation entered into force on 1 July 1987.[5]

14.6 BACKGROUND

The Recitals to the Regulation provide:

"Whereas an increasing number of countries resort to protecting their merchant fleets either unilaterally, through legislation or administrative measures, or through bilateral agreement with other countries;

Whereas certain countries, by virtue of measures they have adopted or practices they have imposed, have distorted the application of the principle of fair and free competition in shipping trade with one or more Community Member States;

Whereas in respect of liner trades the United Nations Convention on a Code of Conduct for Liner Conferences, which entered into force on 6 October 1983, grants certain rights to shipping companies which are members of a conference operating a pool;

Whereas, increasingly, third countries which are contracting parties or signatories to that Convention interpret its provisions in such a way as effectively to expand the rights given under the Convention to their companies both in liner and tramp trades, to the disadvantage of Community companies or companies of other OECD countries, whether conference members or not;

Whereas in respect of bulk trades there is an increasing tendency on the part of third countries to restrict access to bulk cargoes, which poses a serious threat to the freely competitive environment broadly prevailing in the bulk trades; whereas the Member States affirm their commitment to a freely competitive environment as being an essential feature of the dry and liquid bulk trades and are convinced that the introduction of cargo-sharing in these trades will have a serious effect on the trading interests of all countries by substantially increasing transportation costs;

Whereas the restriction of access to bulk cargoes would adversely affect the merchant fleets of the Member States, as well as substantially increasing the transportation costs of such cargoes, and would thereby have a serious effect on the trading interests of the Community;

Whereas the Community should be enabled to provide for coordinated action by Member States if the competitive position of Member States' merchant fleets or Member States' trading interests are adversely affected by cargo reservation to shipping companies of third countries or if required by an international agreement;

Whereas Council Decision 77/587/EEC[6] provides, *inter alia*, for consultation on the various aspects of developments which have taken place in relations between Member States and third countries in shipping matters;

Whereas Council Decision 83/573/EEC[7] provides, *inter alia*, for concertation by Member States of any countermeasures they may take in relation to third countries and for the possibility of a decision on the joint application by Member States of appropriate countermeasures forming part of their national legislation;

Whereas it is necessary to elaborate and refine the machinery provided for in these Decisions with a view to providing for coordinated action by Member States in certain circumstances at the request of a Member State or Member States or on the basis of an international agreement. . . ."

14.7 CONCEPTS

Article 2 of the Regulation sets down the definition of two key concepts: (a) "home-trader" and (b) "cross-trader". A "home-trader" is a "shipping company of a third

5. Regulation 4058/86, Article 9.
6. OJ No. L239, 17 September 1977, p. 23
7. OJ No. L332, 28 November 1983, p. 37.

country which operates a service between its own country and one or more Member States". A "cross-trader" is a "shipping company of a third country which operates a service between another third country and one or more Member States".

14.8 TRIGGERING EVENT

Article 1 of the regulation provides:

"The procedure provided for by this Regulation shall be applicable when action by a third country or by its agents restricts or threatens to restrict free access by shipping companies of Member States or by ships registered in a Member State in accordance with its legislation to the transport of:

— liner cargoes in Code trades, except where such action is taken in accordance with the United Nations Convention on a Code of Conduct for Liner Conferences;
— liner cargoes in non-Code trades;
— bulk cargoes and any other cargo on tramp services;
— passengers;
— persons or goods to or between offshore installations.

This procedure shall be without prejudice to the obligations of the Community and its Member States under international law."

14.9 REQUESTS BY A MEMBER STATE FOR CO-ORDINATED ACTION

14.9.1 Introduction

Article 3 of the Regulation provides that co-ordinated action may be requested by a Member State. The request is to be made to the Commission which will then make the appropriate recommendation or proposal of recommendation to the Council of Ministers. In considering the response, the Council of Ministers must consider the external trade policy considerations as well as the port interests and the shipping policy considerations of the Member States concerned.

14.9.2 Text of Article 3

Article 3 of the Regulation provides:

"Coordinated action may be requested by a Member State.

The request shall be made to the Commission; the latter shall make the appropriate recommendations or proposals to the Council within four weeks.

The Council, acting in accordance with the voting procedure laid down in Article 84(2) of the Treaty, may decide on the coordinated action provided for in Article 4.

In deciding on coordinated action, the Council shall also take due account of the external trade policy considerations as well as the port interests and the shipping policy considerations of the Member States concerned."

It is worth bearing in mind that only a Member State may request co-ordinated action.

14.10 CO-ORDINATED ACTION

14.10.1 Introduction

Co-ordinated action may consist of counter-measures such as the imposition of quotas or taxes or duties. They must only be used however after diplomatic representations have been made.

14.10.2 Text of Article 4

"1.Coordinated action may consist of:

(a) diplomatic representation to the third countries concerned, in particular where their actions threaten to restrict access to trade;

(b) countermeasures directed at the shipping company or companies of the third countries concerned or at the shipping company or companies of other countries which benefit from the action taken by the countries concerned, whether operating as a hometrader or as a cross-trader in Community trades.

Those countermeasures may consist, separately or in combination, of:

(i) the imposition of an obligation to obtain a permit to load, carry or discharge cargoes; such a permit may be subject to conditions or obligations;

(ii) the imposition of a quota;

(iii) the imposition of taxes or duties.

2. Diplomatic representations shall be made before countermeasures are taken.

Such countermeasures shall be without prejudice to the obligations of the European Community and its Member States under international law, shall take into consideration all the interests concerned and shall neither directly nor indirectly lead to deflection of trade within the Community."

14.10.3 Diplomatic representations

In advance of any counter-measures being taken, diplomatic representations must however be made to the non-EC state concerned. This is in accordance with the normal rules of international relations.

14.11 PROCEDURE

Article 5 of the Regulation provides that:

"1. When deciding upon one or more of the countermeasures referred to in Article 4 (1) (b) the Council shall specify, as appropriate, the following:

(a) the developments, which have caused countermeasures to be taken;

(b) the trade or range of ports to which the countermeasures are to apply;

(c) the flag or shipping company of the third country whose cargo reservation measures restrict free access to cargoes in the shipping area concerned;

(d) maximum volume (percentage weight in tonnes, containers) or value of cargo which may be loaded or discharged in ports of Member States;

(e) maximum number of sailings from and to ports of Member States;

(f) amount or percentage and basis of the taxes and duties to be levied and the manner in which they will be collected;

(g) the duration of the countermeasures.

2. Where the countermeasures envisaged by paragraph 1 are not provided for by the national legislation of a Member State they may be taken in accordance with the Council Decision referred to in the third paragraph of Article 3 by the Member State concerned on the basis of this Regulation."

14.12 ACTION BY MEMBER STATES IN DEFAULT OF COUNCIL ACTION

14.12.1 Individual or group action

Article 6 (1) of the Regulation provides that if the Council has not adopted the proposal on co-ordinated action within two months then Member States may apply national measures unilaterally or as a group, if the situation so requires. It is to be presumed that the situation must *objectively* require the action: any other interpretation would be a nonsense.

14.12.2 Urgent action

Article 6 (2) of the Regulation contemplates national urgent action. It provides that Member States may, in cases of urgency, take the necessary national measures on a provisional basis, unilaterally or as a group, even within the two-month period referred to in Article 6 (1) of the Regulation.

14.12.3 Report to the Commission

All national measures must be notified immediately to the Commission.[8]

14.13 CONSULTATION

Article 7 of the Regulation provides that during the period in which the counter-measures are to apply, the Member States and the Commission shall consult each other in accordance with the consultation procedure established in Decision 77/587/EEC[9] every three months or earlier if the need arises, in order to discuss the effects of the counter-measures in force.

14.14 OECD MEMBER STATES

14.14.1 Introduction

Interestingly, co-ordinated action may be taken where other OECD States are restricted and, on the basis of reciprocity, that State and the EC agree to resort to co-ordinated resistance.

14.14.2 Article 8 of the Regulation

Article 8 provides that the procedure provided for by the Regulation may be applied when action by a third country or its agents restricts or threatens to restrict the access of shipping companies of another OECD country where, on a basis of reciprocity, it has been agreed between that country and the Community to resort to co-ordinated

8. Regulation 4058/86, Article 6 (3).
9. See Chapter 19, below.

resistance in the case of restriction of access to cargoes. Such a country may make a request for co-ordinated action and join in such co-ordinated action in accordance with the Regulation.

14.15 HISTORY

Regulation 4058/86 has been used in relation to West and Central Africa. Denmark brought a complaint against a number of activities in the Europe/West Africa trade. It alleged that some of the West African states were engaging in practices which excluded the Danish lines. The complaint was supported by the Greek and Italian governments as well as the European Shippers' Council. Belgium, France and Germany have been somewhat sympathetic to the cause of the West African states. The Council decided that diplomatic representations would be made within the framework of the Lomé Convention. The matter then escalated into a three-pronged attack on the bases of Regulation 4055/86, 4056/86 and 4058/86. The matter was not resolved at the time of writing. There is no doubt that similar problems are and will be experienced around the world.[10]

10. See the Report from the Commission to the Council of Ministers on the Implementation of the Four Regulations in the Field of Maritime Transport adopted by the Council on 22 December 1986, SEC (90) 1594 final.

CHAPTER 15

State Aids

15.1 INTRODUCTION

Many States throughout the world offer financial assistance and fiscal advantages to shipping companies, ports and seafarers to help promote shipping activities. The EC Commission has written:

> "4.10 Most countries with merchant fleets grant them subsidies—some small, some large—either by direct grants or by tax relief measures. It should also be noted that distortions in operating conditions are created by the existence of flags of convenience which grant almost total tax exemption and do not necessarily require the observance of certain safety standards or rules governing working conditions.
>
> 4.11 It does seem, however, that it is the conditions of operation of the merchant fleets of certain state-trading countries which cause most of the problems in this area, since the economic system of these countries allows their shipping companies to operate on international routes without taking account of the 'real' costs (particularly capital costs). The effects of these activities of these countries in the maritime trade sector can, however, be more easily reviewed in the [context of] 'under-cutting'."[1]

Such aid or subsidisation is not new—the British Navigation Acts in 1651 provided for (among other things) the giving of grants to British shipowners. Nor is it unusual among States around the world—such aid is given by many States including most OECD States. Moreover, these aids and subsidies are becoming more common over time.[2]

15.2 PURPOSES OF STATE AIDS

State aids or subsidies may be described as acts

> "by a governmental unit involving either a payment, a remission of charges or supplying commodities or services at less than cost or market price with the intent of achieving a particular objective".[3]

This assistance offered by States (often termed "State aids") generally falls into two general categories: aid to acquire ships (i.e. acquisition aids) and aid to operate ships

1. Communication from the Commission to the Council on the Community's Relations with Non-Member Countries in Shipping Matters, COM(76)341 final.

2. See Ademuni-Odeke, *Shipping in International Trade Relations* (1988), Chapter 8; Farthing, *International Shipping: An Introduction to the Policies, Politics and Institutions of the Maritime World* (1987), pp. 9–10; Hawkins, *Shipping Subsidies and the Balance of Payments* (1989), Chapter 1; and Sturmey, *British Shipping and World Competition* (1961), pp. 28–29.

3. Economic Committee of the United States Congress, *Subsidy and Subsidy-Like Programs of the United States Government*, 1960, p. 8 (cited in Schina, *State Aids under the EEC Treaty: Articles 92 to 94* (1987), at p. 1).

(i.e. operational aids). More particularly, the aid is found in such forms as building subsidies,[4] ship-purchase aids,[5] loan guarantees, scrap and build aids,[6] port aids, operating aids, reduced social security contributions,[7] as well as tax breaks for both the shipping company[8] and the seafarer.[9] Aids can also take the form of cargo preference rules or postal subvention.[10] Some aids are only directed to certain shipping activities such as the coastal trades. It has been written[11] that State aids take a variety of forms in the shipping industry, but include operating subsidies, construction subsidies, credit and loan subsidies, scrap and build subsidies, investment grants, taxation allowances, cargo/flag preference and reservation, cabotage, customs reductions, moratoria and guarantees on loans as well as deductions in social security contributions.

State aids are usually employed for any one or more of the following purposes:

(a) establishment of a shipping industry;
(b) maintenance of a shipping industry;
(c) development of a shipping industry;
(d) the facilitation of public service obligations;
(e) reduction of operation or acquisition costs;
(f) facilitation of other industrial sectors, e.g. by providing transport facilities for manufacturing exporters; as well as
(g) the encouragement and/or maintenance of employment.

15.3 ECONOMICS OF STATE AIDS[12]

In its First Report on Competition Policy in 1971, the Commission was of the view that State aid: "generally means a conflict of interests between the recipient economic agents and their competitors in other Member States".[13]

It has been written:

"[b]y its implementation of EEC Treaty provisions regarding state aid, the Commission reveals a belief that markets work well in the long run but can benefit from selective prodding in the short and medium run. The benefits of economic union are seen as flowing from the unrestricted play of market forces, but the Commission will accept distortions of competition to speed the rate at which markets move towards long-run, competitive, equilibrium.

From this position it follows that state aid, even operating aid, may be permitted in severely depressed areas, to promote employment and development. State aid may be permitted to speed

4. E.g. Japan and Switzerland.
5. E.g. Australia, Ireland and Switzerland.
6. E.g. Japan has had such scrap-and-build grants.
7. E.g. Finland and Sweden.
8. E.g. Norway and the Republic of Ireland. The fiscal advantages offered to shipping often involve depreciation. Shipping companies often benefit from aids which are available to other companies as well.
9. E.g. Greece and Sweden. Aids may well be used for other purposes, *e.g.* to modernise the Manchester Ship Canal: *Lloyd's List*, 15th May 1989, p. 3.
10. See Sturmey, *op. cit.* at footnote 2 above p. 28.
11. According to the list in Hawkins, *op. cit.* at footnote 2 above, at p. 3.
12. See Schina, *op. cit.* at footnote 3 above, para. 1.1; Corden and Fels, *Public Assistance to Industry, Protection and Subsidies in Britain and Germany* (1976); Whiting (ed.), *The Economics of Industrial Statistics* (1976); and the Economic Committee of the United States Congress, *Subsidy and Subsidy-Like Programs of the United States Government*, 1960. See also Sharpe, "Unfair Competition by Public Support of Private Enterprises" (1979) 95 *Law Quarterly Review* 205.
13. At para. 133.

the reorganisation of industries with structural excess capacity. State aid may be permitted to promote genuinely innovative projects of common interest. However, aid which simply keeps unhealthy concerns alive or postpones their inevitable day of reckoning slows the market adjustment process, and is not permitted."[14]

State aids undoubtedly stimulate shipping activity in various jurisdictions. In "most cases" in the EC "they are intended specifically to compensate for the cost handicap national fleets meet on the world market".[15] They can be effective in achieving public goals which cannot be achieved by private means[16] and alleviate distortions in the marketplace. Conversely, such State interference distorts the free market equilibrium which would otherwise exist in the market. As the Commission said in its *Financial and Fiscal Measures Concerning Shipping Operations with Ships Registered in the Community*: "[i]f taken in an uncoordinated way, they present the risk that competition between . . . States is being distorted. This may worsen the conditions under which competitivity has to be restored". State aids have, in the shipping world, the same effect as practices such as flag discrimination.

15.4 STATE AIDS AND EC LAW GENERALLY

15.4.1 Introduction

Many EC Member States provide aid to shipping companies and shipping operations.[17] Some examples will prove instructive. For example, Ireland has a fund to assist shipping companies acquire new or relatively new ships,[18] various fiscal advantages for companies engaged in shipping activities (including a 10% tax rate) and had a Business Expansion Scheme which facilitated investment in shipping activities.

The EC is, in general, opposed to State aids.[19] The Commission has opined:

"[State aids may be] used as form of protectionism, to benefit national producers to give them competitive advantages, to transfer difficulties on to competitors in other States . . . such aids, however beneficial they may appear from a short-term national point of view, could endanger and threaten the unity of the common market."[20]

14. Evans and Martin, "Socially Acceptable Distortion of Competition: Community Policy on State Aid" (1991) 16 ELRev. 79.
15. Commission of the European Communities, *Financial and Fiscal Measures Concerning Shipping Operations with Ships Registered in the Community*, SEC(89)921 final, 3 August 1989, p. 1.
16. See Prest, "The Economic Rationale of Subsidies to Industry" in Whiting (ed.), *The Economics of Industrial Subsidies* (1976), p. 70.
17. See Commission of the European Communities, *Financial and Fiscal Measures Concerning Shipping Operations with Ships Registered in the Community*, SEC(89)921 final, 3 August 1989, *passim*. See "EEC Approves UK Merchant Fleet Aid", *Lloyd's List*, 26 November 1987, p. 3.
18. See the Shipping Investments Grants Act 1987 (annotated by Power, *Irish Current Law Statutes Annotated*).
19. See Dir. 80/273; and the Community Framework for State Aids for Research and Development (published in OJ 1986 C83/2). On EC law and State Aids see Schina, *op. cit.* at footnote 3 (1987). See also Bellamy and Child, *Common Market Law of Competition* (3rd edn., 1987), Chapter 14; Cowrie, "State Aids in the Eighties" (1986) 11 ELRev. 247; Evans and Martin, "Socially Acceptable Distortion of Competition: Community Policy on State Aid" (1991) 16 ELRev. 79; Freeman and Whish (eds.), *Butterworths Competition Law*, Division VIII; Lasok, "State Aids under the EEC Treaty" [1986] ECLR 53; *op. cit.*, "The Commission's Power over Illegal State Aids" [1990] 3 ECLR 125; Quigley, "The Notion of a State Aid in the EEC" (1988) 13 ELRev. 242; and Ross, "A Review of Developments in State Aids 1987–1988" (1989) 26 CML. Rev. 167. See also Harden, "The Approach of English Law to State Aids to Enterprises" [1990] ECLR 100. It would be wrong to see State Aids as being an issue solely of concern to the EC. The OECD has also been concerned with the issue. The issue is also relevant in the context of GATT. It should be noted that the ECSC also has rules on state aids.
20. Twelfth Report on Competition Policy, 1982, point 167.

As Bellamy and Child have written: "The establishment of a true single market and a system of undistorted competition requires that Member States are prohibited from granting to undertakings aids that distort, or threaten to distort, competition and trade between Member States".[21] On the other hand, such aids may stimulate or maintain industry which would not otherwise survive but can provide a valuable social service, economic infrastructure or trading facility.

15.4.2 Introduction to the EEC Treaty rules

Articles 92 to 94 of the EEC Treaty deal with State aids. As a general principle, State aid as defined in Article 92(1) of the EEC Treaty is incompatible with the common market. This is however only a general principle.[22] Derogations are permitted under Article 92(2) and (3). Article 93 provides for a procedural regime conferring on the Commission control over aids. Article 94 then enables the Commission to adopt regulations so as to apply Articles 92 and 93. Schina has succinctly summarised the rules on this area in the following terms: "The provisions of the EEC Treaty on state aids (Article 92 to 94), while not prohibiting state aids outright, invest the Commission with wide discretionary powers to control state aids and take binding decisions against the defaulting states".[23] In exercising these powers, the Commission may take into account economic, social and political factors.[24]

15.4.3 State aids in shipping and EC law

The Commission has in the recent past focused its attention on State aids in the area of shipping. Such attention is long overdue. In August 1989, the Commission published a set of guidelines which it will use in determining whether or not particular State aids contravene Articles 92 and/or 93 of the EEC Treaty.[25] These guidelines are embodied in a document entitled "Financial and Fiscal Measures Concerning Shipping Operations with Ships Registered in the Community".[26] The Commission wrote in this document that if State aids are provided:

"in an uncoordinated way, they present the risk that competition between Member States is . . . distorted. This may worsen the conditions under which competitivity has to be restored. By applying the rules of the [EEC] Treaty to State aids, the Commission intends to diminish such negative effects. Therefore, the Commission has defined the conditions under which State aids to shipping companies may be considered compatible with the common market. The Commission's aim is to increase the efficiency of action already undertaken on a national level by providing a general framework. It also wants to take account of the introduction of a European Community register.[27] Indeed, fiscal and financial measures should be used in a way which would make them appropriate to reach the objectives of the common shipping policy, i.e. the maintenance of ships

21. *Op. cit.* at footnote 2, para. 14-001.

22. There is a rebuttable presumption *per* Advocate-General Darmon in Case 248/84 *Federal Republic of Germany v. EC Commission* [1987] ECR 4013, at p. 4028, [1988] 1 CMLR 591, at p. 596 that aid which falls within the scope of Art. 92(1) of the EEC Treaty is incompatible with the Common Market.

23. *Op. cit.*, para. 32.

24. See Advocate General Warner in Case 78/76 *Firma Steinike und Weinlig v. Bundesamt für Ernährung und Forstwirtschaft* [1977] ECR 595, at p. 582, [1977] 2 CMLR 688, at p. 699.

25. On the two provisions, see paras. 15.4.4–15.4.7 below.

26. SEC(89)921 final, 3 August 1989.

27. On the European Community Register, see Chapter 6, above.

under Community flags and the employment, to the highest possible proportion, of Community seafarers on board such ships."[28]

The guidelines are, according to the Commission: "*general* principles of the Commission on the compatibility of state aids with the common market and are . . . based on the conclusions of the communication on measures to improve the operating conditions of Community shipping, including those in support of a European register."[29]

The rules on State aids are not designed to abolish State aids totally—they are instead designed to prohibit subsidies which distort competition and are contrary to the common good.

Most aspects of State aids are dealt with by Directorate-General IV of the EC Commission. However, State aids as they relate to transport are dealt with by Directorate-General VII.

The Commission in its "Guidelines for the Examination of State Aids to Community Shipping Companies" reviewed a number of operating aids and wrote that these: "in principle are to be considered incompatible with the common market under Article 92(1) of the EEC Treaty. However, without excluding Article 92(2) and 92(3)(a) and (b), state aids in the maritime sector must carefully be assessed in the light of Article 92(2)(c)."[30]

Article 92(2)(c) provides that aid to facilitate the development of certain economic activities or of certain economic areas, where such aid does not adversely affect trading conditions to an extent contrary to the common market, may be considered to be compatible with the common market.

The critical concept is "common interest". The Commission in its "Guidelines for the Examination of State Aids to Community Shipping Companies" wrote that it:

"considers that a strong Community fleet is essential to the Community both for economic and strategic reasons. As the leading world trading entity the Community should not be excessively dependent on third country fleets for its imports and exports, so losing control and influence on the price and quality of transport to and from its territory.

Therefore, the common interest would be met by measures aiming first at the maintenance of ships under Community flags, that is to say countering the flagging out trend, notably by improving their technological equipment, and second by the employment, to the highest possible proportion, of Community seafarers on board such ships.

However, measures taken by individual Member States in order to improve the situation of their fleet are not adequate to strengthen the position of the Community fleet as a whole, in the way described.

Indeed, the compatibility of State aids with the common market must be assessed in a Community context, taking account of the effects it produces on competition between Member State fleets.

Therefore, in spite of the shipping industry's undeniable need for aid, the Commission has to give proposed aids very strict consideration."[31]

15.4.3.1 Compatibility of shipping State aids with EC law: the general principles

The Commission has written in its "Guidelines for the Examination of State Aids to Community Shipping Companies", that State aids not exceeding a ceiling to be defined

28. Commission of the European Communities, *Financial and Fiscal Measures Concerning Shipping Operations with Ships Registered in the Community*, SEC(89)921 final, 3 August 1989. p. 1.

29. "Guidelines for the Examination of State Aids to Community Shipping Companies", p. 1 (Annex I to *Financial and Fiscal Measures Concerning Shipping Operations with Ships Registered in the Community, ibid.*) (emphasis added)

30. "Guidelines for the Examination of State Aids to Community Shipping Companies", *ibid.*, p. 2.

31. "Guidelines for the Examination of State Aids to Community Shipping Companies", *ibid.*, p. 3.

on the basis of the lowest relevant cost difference, could be considered compatible with the common market under Article 92(3)(c) provided they comply with the following constraints:

"(a) *Aid must not be out of proportion to its aim*

On several occasions the Commission has stated that the intensity of the aid granted must be in proportion to the intensity of the problems which it intends to solve.[32] This intensity is represented by the . . . ceiling. This ceiling will be regularly reviewed.

The Commission will take care when confronted with a specified aid scheme, that the total amount of aid granted by itself or in addition to other possible existing schemes does not exceed this ceiling. The compatibility with the common market of investment or operating aids carried out within the framework of a restructuring plan will be examined by the Commission with particular reference to the need for new or modernised ships to meet the requirements set out in the directive establishing a European register.[33]

(b) *Aid must be transparent, temporary and preferably on a declining scale*

The Commission will periodically examine the necessity for each scheme to be maintained in view of the situation of the Community fleet.

(c) *Aid must not specifically contribute to increasing or maintaining capacity in sectors with manifest overcapacity*

The scale of aid schemes to maritime transport in most Member States means that the Commission must be ever more vigilant in exercising its powers in this area. It will ensure that such schemes comply with the general doctrine concerning state aid and do not flout the principles established when the first measures were taken under Community policy for the maritime sector."[34]

15.4.4 Article 92(1) of the EEC Treaty: the prohibition of certain types of aid[35]

15.4.4.1 Article 92(1)

Article 92(1) of the EEC Treaty provides:

"Save as otherwise provided in this Treaty, any aid granted by a Member State or through State resources in any form whatsoever which distorts or threatens to distort competition by favouring certain undertakings or the production of certain goods shall, in so far as it affects trade between Member States, be incompatible with the common market."

15.4.4.2 Purpose of Article 92

The aim of Article 92 is:

"to prevent trade between Member States from being affected by benefits granted by public authorities which, in various forms, distort or threaten to distort competition by favouring certain undertakings or the production of certain goods. Accordingly, Article 92 does not distinguish between the measure of State intervention concerned by reference to their causes or aims but defines them in relation to their effects."[36]

Article 92 is not however "a clear and unqualified prohibition of State aids".[37]

32. See for example "Communication to the Council concerning the Commission's policy on sectoral aids" (COM(78)221).
33. E.g. see Chapter 6, above.
34. *Ibid.*, pp. 4–5.
35. See Schina, *op. cit.* at footnote 3 above, Chapter 2.
36. Case 173/73 *Commission v. Italy* [1974] ECR 709, at p. 718.
37. Schina, *op. cit.* at footnote 3 above, para. 40.

15.4.4.3 Concept of aid[38]

The EEC Treaty does not define an "Aid" for the purposes of Articles 92–94. The absence[39] of a definition facilitates the Commission and the European Court of Justice by allowing them considerable flexibility.[40]

Commentators have defined the concept of aid in different ways. Colliard believed that aid is any measure which favours the competitive position of an undertaking and therefore tends to compensate for an aspect of economic inferiority in a discriminatory way.[41]

The aid may take the form of a capital injection[42] or a reduction in the charges normally incurred by the recipient undertaking.[43] It may take the form of a shareholding or stake in a company so as artificially to assist that company.[44] It may even be paid for "through levies that are obligatory as a result of government action"[45] but not actually paid for by the State. In essence, there is no particular form that aid must take. A large number of arrangements may constitute aids. This list includes[46]:

subsidies;
provision of capital[47];
export aids[48];
a subsidy to cover an operating loss;
an investment grant[49];
payment of bonuses to attract staff to a particular industry[50];
reduced social security payments for particular groups[51];
loans at reduced rates[52];
tax exemptions[53];
carrying on of infrastructural works which would facilitate the production of certain types of goods or services or the production by certain undertakings of such goods or services[54];
exchange rate guarantees[55];

38. See Quigley, "The Notion of a State Aid in the EEC" (1988) 13 EL Rev. 242.
39. The absence of a definition may have been intentional: see Schina, *op. cit.* at footnote 2, para. 43.
40. Case 310/85 *Deufil v. Commission* [1987] ECR 501.
41. In Ganshof van der Meersch, *Le Droit de la Communauté Européenne*, vol. 4, Concurrence, Brussels, 1972, p. 380 (cited in Schina, *op. cit.* at footnote 2 above, at para. 44). In this context it is worth recalling that one must pay particular attention to the effect of the aid: see Case 167/73 *Italy v. Commission* [1974] ECR 709, [1974] 2 CMLR 593.
42. See, for example, Case 84/82 *Germany v. Commission* [1984] ECR 1451 and Cases 296 and 318/82 *Netherlands and Leeuwarder Papierwarenfabriek v. Commission* [1985] ECR 809.
43. Case 30/59 *De Gezamenlijke Steenkolenmijnen in Limburg v. ECSC High Authority* [1961] ECR 1, at p. 19.
44. See the *Commission's Second Report on Competition Policy* (1972), point 124.
45. See Commission Decision 89/296 of 30 March 1989.
46. For a longer list of examples see the Commission's Written Reply to Parliamentary Question No. 48 by Mr Burgbacher of 30 July 1963 published in [1963] JO 2235.
47. Case 234/84 *Belgium v. Commission* [1986] ECR 2263; Case 40/85 *Belgium v. Commission* [1986] ECR 2321, and Case 301/87 *France v. Commission* [1990] ECR 351.
48. Case 30/59 *Steenkolenmijnen v. High Authority* [1961] ECR 1.
49. Case 730/79 *Philip Morris v. Commission* [1980] ECR 2671.
50. Case 30/59 *Steenkolenmijnen v. High Authority* [1961] ECR 1.
51. Cases 6 and 11/69 *Commission v. France* [1969] ECR 523 at 520.
52. Case 323/82 *Intermills v. Commission* [1984] ECR 3809, and Case 57/86 *Greece v. Commission* [1988] ECR 2875, at p. 2871.
53. See Tenth Report on Competition Policy, 1980, point 220; and Schina, *op. cit.*, paras. 52–53.
54. Commission's answer to Parliamentary Question 28/67 by M. Dehousse [1967] JO 2311.
55. See Second Report on Competition Policy, 1972, point 103. Guarantees generally constitute aids

preferential guarantees;
preferential access to State contracts (e.g. postal contracts for ships)[56];
a grant without any consideration[57];
transfer of property at preferential rates; and
State indemnities against losses or assumption of costs.[58]

These examples could easily operate in the shipping industry.

How does one distinguish State Aid from State Investment or State Social Security? In relation to State investment,[59] the Commission has said: "provisions of new capital to firms by governments are in the nature of aid . . . where a private investor in a market economy would not have provided the financing in similar circumstances."[60] In terms of social security, infrastructural improvements or normal fiscal policy, the European Court of Justice has stated that: "Article 92 does not distinguish between the measures of State intervention concerned by reference to their causes or aims but defines them in relation to their effects."[61]

Schina, as well as, Bellamy and Child, has dissected the concept of "State aid" and concluded that it involves five elements: (i) an advantage; (ii) granted by a Member State or through State resources; (iii) favouring certain undertakings or the production of certain goods; (iv) distorting competition; and (v) affecting inter-State trade.[62]

15.4.4.3.1 Advantage

Whatever its form,[63] it is clear that the aid granted must constitute an advantage. For example, in Cases 67/85 etc. *Van Der Koon v. Commission*,[64] the aid given favoured horticulturists which used natural gas over other natural gas users. In Case 61/79 *Amministrazione delle Finanze delle Stato v. Denkavit Italiano*[65] the ECJ stated:

"[Article 92(1)] refers to the decisions of Member States by which the latter, in pursuit of their own economic and social objectives give by unilateral and autonomous decisions, undertakings or other persons resources or procure for them advantages intended to encourage the attainment of the economic and social objectives sought."[66]

A facility granted may well constitute an aid within the meaning of Article 92, notwithstanding that the recipient has provided some benefit to the donor[67] or has

because they remove the element of risk: see Freeman and Whish, *op. cit.*, at footnote 19, paras 42–43. See also the letter of the Commission to Member States on 5 April 1989 on State Guarantees (SG(189) D/G 328.

56. *Second Report on Competition Policy*, 1972, para. 106.

57. See Opinion of Advocate-General Reischl in Case 61/79 *Amministrazione delle Finanze Dello Stato v. Denkavit Italiano Srl* [1980] ECR 1205, at p. 1235, [1981] 3 CMLR 694, at p. 702.

58. Advocate-General Darmon in Case 248/84 *Germany v. EC Commission* [1987] ECR 4013, at p. 4027, [1987] 1 CMLR 591, at p. 596.

59. On this issue, see Case 323/84 *Intermills SA v. Commission* [1984] ECR 3809, [1986] 1 CMLR 614; Case 40/85 *Re Boch: Belgium v. Commission* [1986] ECR 2321, [1988] 2 CMLR 301; and Case 234/84 *Re Meura: Belgium v. Commission* [1986] ECR 2263, [1988] 2 CMLR 331.

60. Commission Decision 87/418 of 4 February 1987, concerning aid to a Belgian steel pipe and tube manufacturer, OJ 1987 L227/45, at p. 47.

61. Case 173/73 *Italy v. Commission* [1974] ECR 709, at p. 718; [1974] 2 CMLR 593, at p. 606.

62. Schina, *op. cit.* at footnote 3 above, para. 40; as well as Bellamy and Child, *Common Market Law of Competition* (3rd ed., 1987), para. 14-003.

63. The form of "aid" is largely irrelevant.

64. [1988] ECR 219.

65. [1980] ECR 1205, at p. 1228, para. 31

66. [1980] ECR 1205, at p. 1228, para. 31.

67. See Case 78/76 *Steinike und Weinlig v. Germany* [1977] ECR 595, at p. 611; Case 290/83 *Commission v.*

assisted the Member State generally in some way[68] provided that the granting of that aid would not have been made in the "normal course"[69] of events. The advantage conferred on the recipient must not contemplate the State getting any "valuable" goods or services in return.[70]

The ECJ said in one case that an aid is wider than a subsidy:

"A subsidy is normally defined as a payment in cash or in kind made in support of an undertaking other than the payment by the purchaser or consumer for the goods or services which it produces. An aid is a very similar concept, which, however, places emphasis on its purpose and seems especially devised for a particular objective which cannot normally be achieved without outside help. The concept of an aid is nevertheless wider than that of a subsidy because it embraces not only positive benefits, such as subsidies themselves, but also interventions which, in various forms, mitigate the charges which are normally included in the budget of an undertaking and which, without, therefore, being subsidies in the strict meaning of the word, are similar in character and have the same effect."[71]

15.4.4.3.2 Aid is provided by a Member State or an emanation of such a State

Article 92 of the EEC Treaty speaks of "any aid granted by a Member State or through State resources". Thus, the aid must come (directly or indirectly) from a Member State.[72] The aid must constitute a "burden on the public finances [of the Member State] in the form either of expenditure or of reduced revenue".[73] That said, it is not important whether it is paid directly by the State or indirectly through other agencies[74]: as the ECJ has stated in Case 78/76 *Steinike und Weinlig v. Germany*:

"The prohibition contained in Article 92(1) covers all aid granted by a Member State or through State resources without its being necessary to make a distinction whether the aid is granted directly by the State or by public or private bodies established or appointed by it to administer the aid. In applying Article 92 regard must primarily be had to the effects of the aid on the undertakings or producers favoured and not the status of the institutions entrusted with the distribution and administration of the aid."[75]

Thus, the aid might be provided by such entities as private bodies administering State aid[76] or local authorities (such as Lander, municipalities or provinces).[77] Thus, in *Swansea Cork Ferries*[78] the aid from State resources (Ireland for the most part) to subsidise a ferry service between Ireland and the UK was being given by the States (the

France [1985] ECR 439, at p. 449, para. 14; and Case 173/73 *Italian Government v. Commission* [1974] ECR 709, [1974] 2 CMLR 593.

68. See Case 323/84 *Intermills v. Commission* [1984] ECR 3809.
69. See Advocate-General Slynn in Case 84/82 *Germany v. Commission* [1984] ECR 1451.
70. See Schina, *op. cit.* at footnote 3 above, para. 50.
71. Case 30/59 *Steenkolenmijnen v. High Authority* [1961] ECR 1, at p. 19.
72. Cases 213/81 etc. *Norddeutsches Vieh- und Fleischkontor v. BALM* [1982] ECR 3583, para. 22; Case 67/85 *Van Der Koon v. Commission* [1988] ECR 21. See Freeman and Whish, *op. cit.* at footnote 19 above paras. 44–46.
73. See the comments of Advocate-General Capotorti in Case 82/77 *Openbaar Ministerie v. van Tiggele* [1978] ECR 25, [1978] CMLR 528.
74. See Case 222/82 *Apple and Pear Development Council v. Lewis* [1983] ECR 4083 at p. 4108 and Case 78/86 *Steinike und Weinlig v. Germany* [1977] ECR 595.
75. [1977] ECR 595, at p. 611.
76. See Case 78/76 *Steinike und Weinlig v. Germany* [1977] ECR 595.
77. Case 323/84 *Intermills v. Commission* [1984] ECR 3809 and Cases 296 and 318/82 *Netherlands and Leeuwarder Papierwarenfabriek v. Commission* [1985] ECR 809. See also the First Report on Competition Policy 1971, paras. 158–159.
78. This case involved a complaint by Irish Ferries against the granting of aid by the UK and Irish Governments to a company jointly owned by local councils in Wales and Ireland.

UK and Ireland) via local councils. Aid which is being granted by the EC but which is channelled through a Member State must be outside the scope of Article 92 by definition.

15.4.4.3.3 Aid favours certain undertakings or the production of certain goods or services

Article 92 of the EEC Treaty provides that an aid is incompatible where it distorts or threatens to distort competition by, among other things, favouring certain undertakings or the production of certain goods.[79] Schina has commented[80]:

"Aid is selective in nature if it applies to any kind of economic activity (including the provision of services), to a sector of the economy, to a branch of industrial activity, to all undertakings in a geographical area or to a group of undertakings sharing certain characteristics (for example, small and medium-sized undertakings and those employing predominantly female labour).[81]

The beneficiary undertakings may be either private or public,[82] but they need not be exclusively national, even though this is usually the case. An aid to the import of scientific instruments and goods of advanced technology to Italy was considered by the Commission to distort competition both in favour of the imported products and of those manufacturers who used them,[83] but if the beneficiary is an institute of scientific research, assistance to it by the state is not covered by Article 92."[84]

15.4.4.3.4 Aid distorts competition

The aid must distort competition.[85] Moreover, competition between Member States of the EC must be distorted. There must be some distortion of competition: a theoretical distortion is not enough.[86]

It is easy to see how State aid may distort competition. In fact, it is difficult to see how such aid would not distort competition. The Commission stated in its Eleventh Report on Competition:

"the effect of the use of aids within the Member States should not be overlooked. While the recipient of aid receives a positive advantage, there are automatic disadvantages for those who do not receive aid. Not only do they have to compete, but the very fact of the granting of subsidies may have wider economic effects in terms of higher rates of interest which further heighten the disadvantage of the non-recipient of aid. It is possible to envisage a situation where efforts to ameliorate the social consequences of the adaptation of crisis sectors can and do lead to the result that potential growth in newer industries, which provide the real future, is retarded if not made impossible."[87]

79. See Schina, *op. cit.* at footnote 3 above, section 2.5.
80. *Op. cit.* at footnote 3 above, paras 106–107.
81. See, for instance, Sixth Report on Competition Policy, 1976, points 253 to 256; and Eleventh Report on Competition Policy, 1981, point 244.
82. I.e. State-owned or privately-owned.
83. Commission Decision 72/261/EEC of 28 June 1972 (1972) OJ L166/12.
84. *Ibid.*
85. See Case 730/79 *Philip Morris v. Commission* [1980] ECR 2671, [1981] 2 CMLR 321. See Freeman and Whish, *op. cit.* at footnote 19 above, paras. 47–49.
86. See Case 248/84 *Federal Republic of Germany v. Commission* [1987] ECR 4013, at p. 4041, [1988] 1 CMLR 591, at p. 608.
87. 1981, point 176.

Nonetheless, the Commission cannot simply assume that there has been an anti-competitive effect on the market: it must set out the circumstances which are the bases for their view.[88] It must assess the distortion. This assessment need only be a somewhat elementary[89] or qualitative one.[90]

15.4.4.3.5 Effect on inter-state trade

The aid must have an effect[91] on trade between Member States of the EC[92]—irrespective of whether the effect decreases or even increases the volume of such trade.[93] Schina has commented[94] that there are two main conditions in which State aid affects trade:

(1) there are channels of trade and competition within the Community in the sector concerned;
(2) aid is not localised or of such small dimension as to have an insignificant effect on competition in the common market.

15.4.4.3.6 Purpose of the aid

The purpose of the aid can be material. If the State is granting an aid which private industry is unlikely to provide by way of a loan then it is quite likely that the payment constitutes an aid falling within the scope of Article 92.[95] If the State takes a shareholding or stake in a company so as to artificially assist the company then that may well constitute an aid.[96] The aid must distort or threaten to distort competition. Thus, it must favour one undertaking in a sector, market or region over another[97] or favour the production of some item (whether a product or a service) of another.

15.4.4.3.7 Juridical nature of Article 92

Article 92 is not directly effective. The European Court of Justice has refused to regard Article 92(1) as having direct application.[98] Article 92(1) may, however, be of direct application where it is given effect by means of a Commission Decision or a Regulation adopted under Article 94 of the EEC Treaty.[99]

88. See Joined Cases 296 and 318/82 *Netherlands and Leeuwarder Papierwarenfabriek BV v. Commission* [1985] ECR 809, [1985] 3 CMLR 380 in which the European Court of Justice stated (at pp. 823 and 396 respectively): "the statement of reasons for a decision [of the Commission] adversely affecting an undertaking must be such as to allow the Court to review its legality and to provide the undertaking concerned with the information necessary to enable it to ascertain whether or not the decision is well-founded". See also Case 248/84 *Germany v. Commission* [1987] ECR 4013, [1989] 1 CMLR 591.

89. See Case 730/79 *Philip Morris Holland BV v. Commission* [1980] ECR 2671, [1981] 2 CMLR 321.

90. Case 47/69 *France v. Commission* [1970] ECR 487, [1970] CMLR 351.

91. This may be a potential effect: see Case 102/87 *France v. Commission* [1988] ECR 4067.

92. EEC Treaty, Art. 92. See Case 47/69 *France v. Commission* [1970] ECR 487, [1970] CMLR 351; Case 40/75 *Produits Bertrand v. Commission* [1976] ECR 1, [1976] 1 CMLR 220; Case 730/79 *Philip Morris v. Commission* [1980] ECR 2671; [1981] 2 CMLR 321.

93. See Opinion of Advocate-General Capotorti in Case 730/79 *Philip Morris v. Commission* [1980] ECR 2671, at p. 2697, [1981] 2 CMLR 321, at p. 329.

94. *Op. cit.* at footnote 3 above, para. 117.

95. See Cases 296 and 318/82 *Netherlands and Leeuwarder Papierwarenfabriek v. Commission* [1985] ECR 809.

96. See the Commission's Second Report on Competition Policy (1972), point 124.

97. See Cases 6 and 11/69 *Commission v. France* [1969] ECR 523, at p. 540; Case 203/82 *Commission v. Italy* [1983] ECR 2525; and Case 52/83 *Commission v. France* [1983] ECR 3707.

98. On the concept of direct application, see para. 3.5.3, above.

99. Case 77/72 *Capolongo v. Maya* [1973] ECR 611, at p. 621, [1974] 1 CMLR 230, at p. 245.

15.4.5 Article 92(2) of the EEC Treaty: the automatic authorisation of certain types of aid

15.4.5.1 Introduction

Article 92(2) of the EEC Treaty authorises certain types of aid.[100] It provides that aid having any of three specified aims is compatible with the common market and thus not illegal *vis-à-vis* the EEC Treaty. It is worth recalling that the Commission has considerable discretion in deciding whether or not a particular aid is compatible with the Common Market by virtue of Article 92(2) of the EEC Treaty.[101]

15.4.5.2 Text of Article 92(2)

Article 92(2) of the EEC Treaty provides:

"The following shall be compatible with the Common Market:
- (a) aid having a social character, granted to individual consumers, provided that such aid is granted without discrimination related to the origin of the products concerned;
- (b) aid to make good the damage caused by natural disasters or exceptional occurrences;
- (c) aid granted to the economy of certain areas of the Federal Republic of Germany affected by the division of Germany, in so far as such aid is required in order to compensate for the economic disadvantages caused by that division."

15.4.5.3 Effect of compatibility

The net effect of Article 92(2) is that three types of aid are declared compatible with the common market *de jure*. The effect of their compatibility with the common market would mean that notification to the Commission would seem somewhat otiose[102] but would still have to be done.[103]

Article 92(2) is an exception to the general prohibition on State aids and is interpreted narrowly.

If the Commission were to refuse authorisation for an aid which fell within the scope of Article 92(2) of the EEC Treaty then the Member State involved could bring proceedings against the Commission under Article 173 of the EEC Treaty.

15.4.5.4 Aid having a social character

Article 92(2)(a) of the EEC Treaty provides that aid having a social character, granted to individual consumers, is compatible with the Treaty provided that such aid is granted without discrimination related to the origin of the products concerned.[104] This exception will be of limited direct application to shipping companies because the aid has to be given to individual consumers.

15.4.5.5 Natural disasters

Article 92(2)(b) of the EEC Treaty provides that aid to make good the damage caused by natural disasters or exceptional occurrences is compatible with the Treaty. This aid

100. See Schina, *op. cit.* at footnote 3 above, Chapter 3.
101. Advocate-General Roemer in Case 77/72 *Capolongo v. Azienda Agricola Maya* [1973] ECR 611, at p. 627, [1972] 1 CMLR 230, at p. 236.
102. As the Commission has no discretion in the matter.
103. Case 730/79 *Philip Morris* [1980] ECR 2671, [1981] 2 CMLR 321
104. See Schina, *op. cit.* at footnote 3 above, para. 3.1. Case 52/71 *Benedetti v. Munari* [1977] ECR 163.

must only repair damage caused by natural disasters or exceptional occurrences. State aid to repair a ship which had been damaged by a natural disaster might therefore be compatible with EC law. *Quaere* whether funding provided by a State to a (State) shipping company to acquire an already-built vessel so as to replace one which was sunk would constitute aid within the meaning of Article 92(2)(b)? If the sunken ship was lost by reason of a natural disaster then it ought to be compatible.

15.4.5.6 Germany

Article 92(2)(c) of the EEC Treaty provides that aid granted to the economy of certain areas of the Federal Republic of Germany affected by the division of Germany, is compatible with the Treaty, in so far as such aid is required in order to compensate for the economic disadvantages caused by that division.

15.4.6 Article 92(3) of the EEC Treaty: the authorisation of certain types of aid in certain circumstances

15.4.6.1 Introduction

Article 92(3) of the EEC Treaty lays down certain aims of aid which *may* be considered as being compatible with the common market. These exemptions are narrowly interpreted—as the Commission stated in its Tenth Report on Competition Policy[105]:

"Exemptions to incompatibility included in Article 92(3) must be strictly interpreted, notably, aid may only be granted when the Commission can establish that it will contribute to the attainment of the objectives specified in the exemption which, under normal market conditions, the recipient firms would not attain by their own actions."

15.4.6.2 Text of Article 92(3)

Article 92(3) of the EEC Treaty provides:

"The following may be considered to be compatible with the Common Market:

(a) aid to promote the economic development of areas where the standard of living is abnormally low or where there is serious underemployment;

(b) aid to promote the execution of an important project of common European interest or to remedy a serious disturbance in the economy of a Member State;

(c) aid to facilitate the development of certain economic activities or of certain economic areas, where such aid does not adversely affect trading conditions to an extent contrary to the common interest. However, the aids granted to shipbuilding as of 1 January 1957 shall, in so far as they serve only to compensate for the absence of customs protection, be progressively reduced under the same conditions as apply to the elimination of customs duties, subject to the provisions of this Treaty concerning common commercial policy towards third countries;

(d) such other categories of aid as may be specified by decision of the Council acting by a qualified majority on a proposal from the Commission."

15.4.6.3 Criteria used by the Commission in deciding to authorise an aid

The Commission has set out the criteria which it uses in deciding whether or not to authorise aid under Article 92(3) of the EEC Treaty.[106]

105. 1980, p. 149.
106. Twelfth Report on Competition Policy (1982), point 160.

The assessment of whether or not the aid should be authorised must be made in the overall European context and not in a national or regional framework.[107]

The aid must be necessary to achieve an aim set out in Article 92(3) which would not otherwise be obtained by normal means.[108]

The Commission has written:

"State aids are in principle incompatible with the common market. The discretionary power of the Commission should only be exercised when the aids proposed by Member States contribute to the achievement of the Community objectives and interests set out in Article 92(3) EEC. The national interest of a Member State or the benefits obtained by the recipient of aid in contributing to the national interest do not by themselves justify the positive exercise of the Commission's discretionary powers."[109]

15.4.6.4 Economic development aids

Aid to promote the economic development of areas where the standard of living is abnormally low or where there is serious underemployment may be authorised.[110] The assessment must be made in a EC-wide context and not simply on a national or regional basis.[111] It is clear that as a general rule the regions must suffer "abnormally low living standards or serious underemployment where the per capita gross domestic product does not exceed 75% of the Community average".[112]

15.4.6.5 Important European project

Aid to promote the execution of an important project of common European interest may be authorised.[113] A maritime equivalent of the Airbus would fall within this rubric.

15.4.6.6 Serious disturbance in the economy

Aid to remedy a serious disturbance in the economy of a Member State may be authorised.[114] Thus, the Commission has stated its willingness to authorise aid to the European aircraft industry so as to overcome its modest position in the world and EC markets.[115]

15.4.6.7 Development of certain economic activities

As a general rule, aid to facilitate the development of certain economic activities or of certain economic areas, where such aid does not adversely affect trading conditions to an extent contrary to the common interest may be authorised.[116]

107. Case 730/79 *Philip Morris v. Commission* [1980] ECR 2671, [1981] 2 CMLR 321, para. 24.
108. Case 730/79 *Philip Morris v. Commission* [1980] ECR 2671, [1981] 2 CMLR 321, para. 16.
109. Tenth Report on Competition Policy, 1980, p. 151.
110. EEC Treaty, Art. 92(3)(a).
111. Case 730/79 *Philip Morris v. Commission* [1980] ECR 2671, [1981] 2 CMLR 321, Case 248/84 *Germany v. Commission* [1987] ECR 4013.
112. See Commission, Eighteenth Report on Competition Policy, 1988, p. 147. For a practical example, see Commission Decision 88/318 of 2 March 1988 on Law No. 64 of 1 March 1986 on aid to the Mezzogiorno, OJ 1988 L143/37.
113. EEC Treaty, Art. 92(3)(b); see Case 730/79 *Philip Morris Holland BV v. Commission* [1980] ECR 2671, [1981] 2 CMLR 321.
114. EEC Treaty, Art. 92(3)(b).
115. See Second Report on Competition Policy (1972), paras 100–103. See also the Greek economy: Seventeenth Report on Competition Policy (1987), points 185–6.
116. EEC Treaty, Art. 92(3)(c). See also Case 248/84 *Germany v. Commission* [1987] ECR 4013.

However, the aids granted to shipbuilding as of 1 January 1957 shall, in so far as they serve only to compensate for the absence of customs protection, be progressively reduced under the same conditions as apply to the elimination of customs duties, subject to the provisions of the EEC Treaty concerning common commercial policy towards third countries.[117]

A decision under Article 92(3)(c) must be taken in an EC-wide context and not simply on a national or regional basis.

Aids which have been authorised under this heading have been both sectoral and regional. In terms of sectoral aids, aids granted to shipbuilding, steel and textiles are three examples. In terms of regional aids, there have been, for example, aids granted to areas such as Ireland, Southern Italy and Portugal.

15.4.6.8 Sectoral aids

Aid granted by a State to a particular sector (such as shipping) is acceptable provided that individual large grants are notified to the Commission.[118] The Commission has stated:

> "It is now the well-established policy of the Commission to accept such general aid schemes subject to one of two conditions, namely, that the Member States concerned informs the Commission of either a regional or sectoral plan of application, or where this is felt not to be possible, that it notifies significant individual cases of application."[119]

In a Communication to the Council of Ministers of 25 May 1978, the Commission has stated its policy on sectoral aids to industries with persistent excess capacity:

> "(i) aids should not be given where their sole effect would be to maintain the *status quo*;
> (ii) . . . while rescue measures may be needed in order to provide a breathing space during which longer-term solutions to a company's difficulties can be worked out, they should not frustrate any necessary reductions in capacity . . . ;
> (iii) since it is a common feature of the industries concerned that capacity is excessive, aids should not be given to investment projects which would result in capacity being increased . . ."

The Commission is concerned to ensure that, in the case of sectoral aid, State aid does not exacerbate existing problems or simply transfer them to another Member State.[120] It is worth bearing in mind that sectoral aid which is approved at one time may be regarded at a later stage in the development of the particular market sector as being incompatible with the Common Market.[121]

15.4.6.9 Aid to build a ship

The issue of shipbuilding aids is dealt with in the chapter relating to shipbuilding.[122]

15.4.6.10 Aid to reduce manning costs

In its Guidelines for the Examination of State Aids to Community Shipping Companies (published in August 1989) the Commission wrote that "[a]id in the field of

117. EEC Treaty, Art. 92(3)(c).
118. Commission Decision 81/626 of 10 July 1981, OJ 1981 L229/12.
119. Commission Decision 81/626 of 10 July 1981, OJ 1981 L229/12.
120. Evans and Martin, *op. cit.* at footnote 19, at p. 92.
121. See the UK's Offshore Supplies Interest Relief Grant (OSIRG) case: Commission Decision 79/496 of 2 May 1979 published in OJ 1979 L127/50.
122. I.e. Chapter 18.

social security and seafarers' income taxation, tending to reduce the costs borne by shipping companies without reducing the level of social security for the seafarers and resulting from the operation of ships registered in the Community may be considered compatible with the common market".[123]

15.4.6.11 Aid for crew relief/employment grants

In its Guidelines for the Examination of State Aids to Community Shipping Companies the Commission wrote that:

"[a]id granted in order to reduce the costs of employing Community crews on ships registered in the Community and operating in distant waters, in the form of payment or reimbursement of the cost of repatriation of seafarers may be considered compatible with the common market provided they do no exceed 50% of the total costs incurred for such reason."[124]

As a general rule, the Commission will approve aid which genuinely assists employment.[125]

15.4.6.12 Aid to training

In its Guidelines for the Examination of State Aids to Community Shipping Companies the Commission wrote that "[a]id granted in order to assist the training costs of seafarers on board ships registered in the Community may be considered compatible with the common market provided that the trainees are employed on a supernumerary basis[126] not having any input into the working of the ships in which they are trained".[127]

15.4.6.13 Aid in the form of special taxation of certain shipping activities

The Commission recognises that: "[a]n important element in encouraging ship modernisation would be fiscal advantage."[128] The Commission also recognises that the tax regimes in each of the Member States differs greatly.[129] Much will turn on the purpose and the discriminatory nature of the tax concession.

In its Guidelines for the Examination of State Aids to Community Shipping Companies the Commission wrote that "[a]id consisting in differential tax treatment on earnings arising from maritime activities of Community shipowners insofar as they operate ships registered in the Community may be considered compatible with the common market".[130]

15.4.6.14 Operating aid

Operating aid is any assistance which "has a direct effect on production costs and on the selling price".[131] The Commission and the European Court of Justice have traditionally

123. *Ibid.*, p. 5.
124. *Ibid.*, p. 5.
125. See Commission, Sixteenth Report on Competition Policy, 1986, p. 138.
126. I.e. signed on the ship but not as a working seafarer.
127. *Ibid.*, p. 6.
128. Commission of the European Communities, "Financial and Fiscal Measures Concerning Shipping Operations with Ships Registered in the Community", SEC(89)921 final, 3 August 1989, p. 2.
129. Commission of the European Communities, "Financial and Fiscal Measures Concerning Shipping Operations with Ships Registered in the Community", SEC(89)921 final, 3 August 1989, p. 3.
130. *Ibid.*, p. 6.
131. Commission Decision 82/744 of 11 October 1982 concerning Italian National Law No. 423/81 of 1

been opposed to such aid[132] because of its tendency to perpetuate operational inefficiencies. The Commission has however been more flexible in its views on operating aid where there is a regional aid dimension to it.[133]

In its Guidelines for the Examination of State Aids to Community Shipping Companies the Commission wrote that any kind of operating aid, other than those mentioned above:

"the aim or effect of which is basically to improve the liquidity situation of the recipients is in principle incompatible with the common market. The Commission will examine such aids on a case-by-case basis, if they are directly linked to a restructuring plan considered compatible with the common market. Rescue aid given to shipping companies experiencing difficulties should comply with the guidelines set out by the Commission in its 8th report on competition policy."[134]

15.4.6.15 Aid to investment

In its Guidelines for the Examination of State Aids to Community Shipping Companies the Commission wrote that:

"[t]o the extent that aids granted to shipping companies are available as aid for building or conversion of ships, particular regard should be had to the provisions of the sixth Council Directive of 26 January 1987 on aid to shipbuilding,[135] whereby such aids are to be counted as indirect contract-related production aid to national yards."[136]

The Sixth Directive has now been superseded by the Seventh Shipbuilding Directive.

15.4.6.16 Restructuring aid

Aid which is granted to restructure a company or industry may well be exempted under Article 92(3)(c) of the EEC Treaty[137] provided the aid is proportional to the problem involved.[138] Such aid must however be aimed at solving structural problems rather than aid aimed at dealing with cyclical or temporary problems.

15.4.6.17 Environmental aid[139]

Aid may sometimes be given by a State so as to protect or repair the environment. There has to be a balance between the so-called "polluter pays" principle and the fact that the polluter may be unable or unwilling to pay.[140] The European Court of Justice has said:

August 1981, on measures for agriculture: OJ 1982 L315/23, at p. 24.

132. See Case 310/85 *Deufil GmbH and Co KG v. Commission* [1987] ECR 901, at p. 926, [1988] 1 CMLR 553, at p. 566.

133. OJ 1988 C212/2

134. Eighth Report on Competition Policy, 1978, para. 228.

135. OJ L69/55, 12 July 1987.

136. *Ibid.*, p. 6.

137. See Commission Decision 87/423 of 11 March 1987 concerning aid which the Belgian Government had granted to a ceramic sanitary ware manufacturer at La Louviere, OJ 1987 L228/39, at p. 40.

138. See Commission Decision No. 81/2320 of 7 August 1981 establishing Community rules for aids to the steel industry, OJ 1981 L228/14, at p. 16.

139. See Commission, Fourth Report on Competition Policy, 1974, pp. 101–106; *op. cit.*, Sixth Report on Competition Policy, 1976, pp. 127–131. See Grabitz, Eberhard and Zacker, "Scope for Action by the EC Member States for the Improvement of Environmental Protection under EEC Law: The Example of Environmental Taxes and Subsidies" (1989) 26 CMLRev. 423.

140. See Commission Decision 77/260 of 22 March 1977 on OJ 1977 L80/23.

"[t]he Commission has based its policy with regard to aid on the view that a project may not be described as being of common European interest for the purposes of Article 92(3)(b) unless it forms part of a transnational European programme supported jointly by a number of governments of Member States, or arises from concerted action by a number of Member States to combat a common threat such as environmental pollution."[141]

The Commission has since said in its *Sixteenth Report on Competition Policy*[142] that environmental aid qualifies from an exemption under Article 92(3)(b) where it satisfies four criteria:

(i) the aid is intended to facilitate the implementation of new environmental standards;
(ii) the net grant equivalent of the aid does not exceed 15% of the value of the aided investment;
(iii) firms receiving aid have had installations in operation for at least two years before the entry into force of the environmental standards in question;
(iv) the eligible firm bears the entire cost of normal replacement investment and operating costs.

It is clear however that the Commission has not been very strenuous in its objections to the granting of State aids for environmental purposes.[143]

15.4.6.18 Aid in the form of public authority holdings in company capital

What if an EC Member State decides to step in and prop up an ailing shipping company which is about to be wound up? Would it make much difference if the company were not in difficulties? What is the relevance of Article 222 of the EEC Treaty? Schina has dealt with the point of State involvement generally:

"54. Article 222 of the EEC Treaty provides that this Treaty shall in no way prejudice the rules in Member States governing the system of property ownership. As a result minority interests (for example, shareholdings, subscription of capital stakes, debentures etc.) acquired by the state in firms agreeing to implement a restructuring plan are not automatically to be regarded as state aids. This is particularly so when such interests are acquired to encourage the development of industries of new advanced technology and the projects are being selected in accordance with commercial and banking criteria. But the position is different with regard to ailing firms. The acquisition of an interest is liable to constitute assistance equivalent to state aid when the state intends to behave not as a normal shareholder or entrepreneur but as a public authority providing support for a firm or product, because of its particular problems. Thus, holdings in firms in difficulties are given advance vetting by the Commission in whatever industry they may be required.[144]

55. In *Kingdom of the Netherlands and Leeuwarder Papierwarenfabriek BV v. Commission*[145] the Court upheld the Commission's treatment of state participation in ailing undertakings. In this case, the holding by a Dutch regional development organisation in the capital of an undertaking in the cardboard carton industry was held to be a state aid by the Court. The reason given was that the undertaking in question could not obtain the finance in the capital markets

141. Joined Cases 62/87 and 72/87 *Executif Regional Wallon and Glaverbel SA v. Commission* [1988] ECR 1573, at p. 1595.

142. 1986, p. 176.

143. See Evans and Martin, *op. cit.* at footnote 19, at p. 104.

144. See Eighth Report on Competition Policy, 1978, point 229; Ninth Report on Competition Policy, 1979, point 185; Commission's answer to Parliamentary Question 1156/81 by Mr Damseaux (1982) OJ C38/10; and Commission Decision 82/73/EEC, (1982) OJ C37/29.

145. Joined Cases 296 and 318/82, Judgment of 13 March 1983; see also Case 323/82 *Intermills v. Commission* [1984] ECR 3809, [1986] 1 CMLR 614.

necessary for its survival, due firstly to its financial structure, secondly to its urgent need of investment for modernisation and thirdly to the overcapacity existing in this sector."[146]

In its *Guidelines for the Examination of State Aids to Community Shipping Companies* the Commission wrote that it had:

"laid down precise criteria in its letter of 17 September 1984 to the Member States [on this issue].[147] The Commission's approach is based on the consideration that aid that is incompatible with the common market is not involved in cases where new capital is contributed to a company in circumstances which would be acceptable to a private investor operating in normal market economy conditions."[148]

15.4.6.19 Rescue aid[149]

What if the State rescues a shipping company which is in financial difficulties? The Commission has made clear in a letter[150] to the Member States that rescue aid is permissible as being compatible with the Common Market where it is given so as to keep the recipient company in business while the underlying causes of the company's difficulties are remedied. The aid must be notified to the Commission in advance. The aid would normally be provided by loans in cash which would bear normal commercial interest rates. The aid would only be provided for the minimum time required to rescue the company and this period would normally be for less than six months. The aid must not have adverse effects on industrial activity in the other Member States. The Commission has also made clear in one of its Decisions[151] that rescue aid "must be in the nature of a remedy for the perceived serious disturbance in the economy of the Member State concerned".

15.4.6.20 Regional policy aid

The Commission has decided that:

"[t]he only circumstances in which the effect on trading conditions caused by regional aid can be regarded as not against the common interest are where it can be shown that the aided region suffers from difficulties that are relatively severe by Community standards, that without the aid market forces would not eliminate these difficulties, that the level of aid is in proportion to the difficulties and that the grant of aid does not unduly distort competition in particular sectors."[152]

Thus, the test of compatibility for regional aid is not a national one but rather a Community-wide one.[153] It is a detailed test which examines a variety of matters but

146. *Op. cit.* at footnote 19 above, paras 54–55. See also Freeman and Whish, *op. cit.* at footnote 19 above, paras. 22–28.

147. Bull. EC 9-1984.

148. *Ibid.*, p. 6. The Commission examines whether the purpose is to obtain income or depreciation—the aim of the ordinary investor. See the Commission memorandum, Bull. EC 9/1984 and Case 234/84 *Belgium v. Commission* [1986] ECR 2263.

149. Case 323/84 *Intermills S.A. v. Commission* [1984] ECR 3809, [1986] 1 CMLR 614; Commission Decision 87/585 of 15 July 1987 on aid granted by the French Government to a producer of textiles, clothing and paper products—*Boussac Saint Frères* OJ 1987 L352/42.

150. 24 January 1979 and discussed in Commission Decision 87/585 of 15 July 1987 on aid granted by the French Government to a producer of textiles, clothing and paper products—*Boussac Saint Frères* OJ 1987 L352/42, at p. 48.

151. Commission Decision 88/167 of 7 October 1987 concerning Law 1386/1983 by which the Greek Government grants aid to Greek industry OJ 1988 L76/18, at p. 21.

152. Commission Decision 87/15 of 19 February 1986 on the compatibility with the Common Market of aid under the German Federal/Land Government Joint Regional Aid Programme (joint programme for the improvement of regional economic structures) in six labour market regions OJ 1987 L12/17, at p. 22.

153. See Communication of the Commission on Regional Aid Systems, OJ 1979 C31/9; the

particularly, the net per capita income of the region *vis-à-vis* the Community as a whole.[154]

15.4.6.21 Research and development aid[155]

The Commission has looked favourably on aids granted for research and development purposes, provided the research and development are substantial and conducted in innovative ways. It has looked particularly favourably on aid granted in a co-ordinated way to an industry in which the EC suffers a disadvantage relative to the rest of the world. This has been especially so in the case of computers. The Commission has also been favourably disposed to such aid where there has been a market failure to allocate sufficient resources to research and development. It is submitted that the current plight of shipping in the EC should encourage the Commission to look equally favourably on aids for research and development in the area of shipping.

15.4.6.22 Small and medium-sized enterprises

The EC has tried to foster small and medium-sized enterprises (SMEs).[156] Aid which is given to a SME so as to overcome its inherent shortcomings[157] will normally[158] be authorised as strengthening and preserving SMEs which are an essential element in a healthy and competitive environment.[159]

15.4.6.23 Other aids which are specified by the Council of Ministers

Other categories of aid as may be specified by decision of the Council of Ministers acting by a qualified majority on a proposal from the Commission may be authorised.[160] This rubric has proved to be the basis for action in the shipbuilding aid programmes.

15.4.7 Article 93 of the EEC Treaty: supervision

15.4.7.1 Text of Article 93

Article 93 of the EEC Treaty provides:

"1. The Commission shall, in co-operation with Member States, keep under constant review all systems of aid existing in those States. It shall propose to the latter any appropriate measures required by the progressive development or by the functioning of the common market.

2. If, after giving notice to the parties concerned to submit their comments, the Commission finds that aid granted by a State or through State resources is not compatible with the common

Communication of the Commission on the Method for the Application of Article 92(3)(a) and (c) to Regional Aids, OJ 1988 C212/2; and the Commission Decision 87/15 of 19 February 1986, OJ 1987 L12/17, at p. 23.

154. For example, see the Commission's discussion of regional aid to Sicily: Commission, Sixth Report on Competition Policy, 1976, p. 108.

155. See Commission, Community Framework for State Aids for Research and Development , OJ 1986 C83/2; *op. cit.*, Eighth Report on Competition Policy, 1978, p. 126.

156. See Action Programme for SMEs, COM(86)445 final, 20 September 1986.

157. See the Commission's Sixth Report on Competition Policy, 1976, p. 132.

158. Provided it is a genuine attempt to overcome the SME's difficulties: see Commission Decision 88/318 of 2 March 1988 on Law No. 64 of 1 March 1986 on aid to the Mezzogiorno, OJ 1988 L143/37, at p. 41.

159. See Commission, Seventeenth Report on Competition Policy, 1987, p. 29.

160. EEC Treaty, Art. 92(3)(d).

market having regard to Article 92, or that such aid is being misused, it shall decide that the State concerned shall abolish or alter such aid within a period of time to be determined by the Commission.

If the State concerned does not comply with this decision within the prescribed time, the Commission or any other interested State may, in derogation from the provisions of Articles 169 and 170, refer the matter to the Court of Justice direct.

On application by a Member State, the Council may, acting unanimously, decide that aid which that State is granting or intends to grant shall be considered to be compatible with the common market, in derogation from the provisions of Article 92 or from the regulations provided for in Article 94, if such a decision is justified by exceptional circumstances. If, as regards the aid in question, the Commission has already initiated the procedure provided for in the first subparagraph of this paragraph, the fact that the State concerned has made its application to the Council shall have the effect of suspending that procedure until the Council has made its attitude known.

If, however, the Council has not made its attitude known within three months of the said application being made, the Commission shall give its decision on the case.

3. The Commission shall be informed, in sufficient time to enable it to submit its comments, of any plans to grant or alter aid. If it considers that any such plan is not compatible with the common market having regard to Article 92, it shall without delay initiate the procedure provided for in paragraph 2. The Member State concerned shall not put its proposed measures into effect until this procedure has resulted in a final decision."

15.4.7.2 Existing aids

Article 93(1) provides that the Commission shall, in co-operation with Member States, keep under constant review all systems of aid existing in those States, and it shall propose to those states any appropriate measures required by the progressive development or by the functioning of the Common Market. These aids were those which existed in a Member State when the EEC Treaty entered into force in relation to that State or those aids which were properly implemented after that time in accordance with the EEC Treaty.[161]

15.4.7.3 Contentious proceedings

If, after giving notice[162] to the parties concerned to submit their comments, the Commission finds that aid granted by a State or through State resources is not compatible with the common market having regard to Article 92, or that such aid is being misused, it shall decide that the State concerned shall abolish or alter such aid within a period of time to be determined by the Commission. If the Commission finds that the aid is not incompatible with the EEC Treaty then it must terminate the proceedings by way of a Decision.[163]

If the State concerned does not comply with this decision within the prescribed time, the Commission or any other interested State may, in derogation from the provisions of Articles 169 and 170, refer the matter to the Court of Justice directly.

On application by a Member State, the Council of Ministers may, acting unanimously, decide that aid which that State is granting or intends to grant shall be considered to be compatible with the common market, in derogation from the provisions of Article 92 or from the regulations provided for in Article 94, if such a

161. See Bellamy and Child, *op. cit.* at footnote 19 above, para. 14–19.
162. See Case 323/84 *Intermills v. Commission* [1984] ECR 3809.
163. Case 120/73 *Lorenz v. Germany* [1973] ECR 1471, at p. 1482.

decision is justified by exceptional circumstances. If, as regards the aid in question, the Commission has already initiated the procedure provided for in the first subparagraph of the paragraph, the fact that the State concerned has made its application to the Council shall have the effect of suspending that procedure until the Council has made its attitude known. It has been commented that the procedure whereby a Member State may appeal to the Council of Ministers for a declaration that aid condemned by the Commission is compatible with the Common Market has fallen into disuse.[164] If, however, the Council of Ministers has not made its attitude known within three months of the said application being made, the Commission shall give its decision on the case.

15.4.7.4 New aids

The Commission must be informed, in sufficient time to enable it to submit its comments, of any plans to grant or alter aid. If it considers that any such plan is not compatible with the common market having regard to Article 92, it shall without delay initiate the procedure provided for in paragraph 2.[165] The Member State concerned shall not put its proposed measures into effect until this procedure has resulted in a final decision.[166] It is clear from Cases 91 and 127/83 *Heineken*[167] that while a Member State is obliged to notify the Commission, it need not notify anyone else.

15.4.7.5 Article 93 and the doctrine of direct effect

Article 93(3) has direct effect.[168] It is submitted that the rest of the Article does not have such effect. Thus, as Bellamy and Child contend, a private party in a Member State can seek a declaration that the implementation of an aid is contrary to Article 93(3).[169]

15.4.8 Article 94 of the EEC Treaty: the legislative powers

15.4.8.1 Introduction

Article 94 has been used, among other provisions, as a Treaty basis for Regulation 1107/70 on the granting of aids for transport by rail, road and inland waterway.

15.4.8.2 Text of Article 94

Article 94 of the EEC Treaty provides:

"The Council may, acting by a qualified majority on a proposal from the Commission, make any appropriate regulations for the application of Articles 92 and 93 and may in particular determine the conditions in which Article 93(3) shall apply and the categories of aid exempted from this procedure."

15.4.9 Challenging State aids

Article 92 does not have direct effect and cannot therefore be invoked in proceedings before the national courts.[170] Article 93(3) has direct effect.[171] It is submitted that the rest

164. Evans and Martin, *op. cit.* at footnote 19, above, at p. 80.
165. EEC Treaty, Article 93(3).
166. EEC Treaty, Article 93(3).
167. [1984] ECR 3424, at p. 3952.
168. Case 6/64 *Costa v. ENEL* [1964] ECR 585 and Case 120/73 *Lorenz v. Germany* [1973] ECR 1471.
169. *Op. cit.* at footnote 19, above, para. 14-24, footnote omitted.
170. See para. 15.4.7.5, above.
171. Case 6/64 *Costa v. ENEL* [1964] ECR 585 and Case 120/73 *Lorenz v. Germany* [1973] ECR 1471.

of the Article does not have such effect. Thus, as Bellamy and Child contend, a private party in a Member State can seek a declaration that the implementation of an aid is contrary to Article 93(3).[172]

It is worth recalling that the Commission has considerable discretion in deciding whether or not a particular aid is compatible with the Common Market by virtue of Article 92(2) of the EEC Treaty.

Where the Commission decides that an aid is unauthorised then it may order a Member State to require the repayment of that aid.[173]

If the Commission addresses a decision to a Member State prohibiting a particular aid then the beneficiary of that aid would have sufficient *locus standi* under Article 173 of the EEC Treaty[174] to challenge the Commission's decision.[175]

It is no defence for a Member State when its aid is being challenged to say that other Member States are carrying out the same programmes—as the European Court of Justice said in Case 78/76 *Firma Steinike und Weinlig v. Bundesamt für Ernährung und Forstwirtschaft*:

> "Any breach by a member-State of an obligation under the Treaty in connection with the prohibition laid down in Article 92 cannot be justified by the fact that other member-States are also failing to fulfil this obligation. The effects of more than one distortion of competition on trade between member-States do not cancel one another out but accumulate and the damaging consequences to the Common Market are increased."[176]

15.4.10 Conclusions

It has been observed that the framework adopted in the EEC Treaty:

> "has left the Commission considerable discretion to fashion for itself a policy on State aid. The early policy of the Commission concentrated on efforts to reduce the amount of aid granted by Member States under the guise of regional policy and in the form of assistance to sectors in crisis. There is increasing recognition of the positive role which state aid can play in the implementation of regional policy and more recent horizontal policies such as environmental policy and [Research and Development] policy. The challenge for the Commission in 1992 and beyond is to reconcile the requirements of such interventionist policies with the maintenance of free competition within the Community."[177]

15.5 STATE AIDS AND SHIPBUILDING

Chapter 18 of this book deals with the issue of state aids and shipbuilding.

172. *Op. cit.* at footnote 19, above, para. 14–24, footnote omitted.
173. Case 70/72 *Commission v. Germany* [1973] ECR 813, at p. 829.
174. On EEC Treaty, Article 173, see para. 3.4.6.6.5, above.
175. Case 730/79 *Philip Morris v. Commission* [1980] ECR 2671.
176. [1977] ECR 595, at p. 598, [1977] 2 CMLR 688, at p. 723.
177. Evans and Martin, *op. cit.* at footnote 19, above, at p. 79.

CHAPTER 16

Consortia

16.1 INTRODUCTION

Consortia may be defined as: "coalitions of several independent shipping lines seeking some form of co-operation in order to maintain profitability through rationalisation in the widest sense and to spread the expense of investment in container operations."[1] They normally involve such conditions as joint fleet operations, joint terminal contracts or operations, joint offices, joint equipment pools, the pooling of cargoes or revenues, joint marketing, joint documentation or joint price fixing.[2] Their purposes vary—examples of the Statement of Purposes in various consortia agreements include:

"the purpose of the Agreement is to establish a joint service/consortium capable of securing the economies and advantages of modern shipping technology through co-ordinated management of roll-on/roll-off, container or similar modern vessels, and all related activities"; or

"to enable the parties to operate a service as defined in the agreement in the most economical and efficient way; to promote and maximize the trade and the movement of cargoes between the points and ports referred to"; or

"the purpose of this Agreement is to authorize the parties to continue their joint service in the trades covered by this Agreement."[3]

It was estimated by the European Commission that there were about fifty-seven consortia operating worldwide as of June 1990.[4] At least forty of these fifty-seven operate in EC liner trades.[5] There is in fact a heavy presence of European shipping companies in consortia. There is also an overlap between membership of consortia and conferences.

The Commission in the Communication on consortia[6] identified the background to the development of consortia and wrote:

"2.1 The Commission is aware of present and prospective developments and organisational changes in world shipping and the implications which these may have for the Community's shipping and competition policies. Competition in the liner shipping industry has created the need for companies to be efficient in order to compete on the world market. The shipping industry

1. Communication by the Commission, Report on the Possibility of a Group Exemption for Consortia Agreements in Liner Shipping, COM(90)260 final (referred to in this chapter as the "Communication"), para. 3.2.

On consortia, see Green, "Consortia and Multi-Modal Transport", Second EEC Shipping Law Conference, Antwerp, 7–8 February 1991; Mylonas-Widdall, "Consortia regulation draft approved", *Lloyd's List*, 20 December 1991, p. 4.

2. Communication, *op. cit.* at footnote 1, above, para. 3.2.
3. Communication, *op. cit.* at footnote 1, above, para. 3.2.
4. Communication, *op. cit.* at footnote 1, above, para. 3.2.
5. Communication, *op. cit.* at footnote 1, above, para. 3.2.
6. See footnote 1, above.

is a capital intensive one, with a high proportion of fixed to variable costs. Ships therefore need to be as fully utilised as possible if the capital costs are to be covered. Individual enterprises acting alone without having strong financial resources are in a vulnerable position if heavy overcapacity shows itself on their particular trade routes.

2.2 The development of container services has increased pressures for co-operation and rationalisation, especially on the longer deep sea trade routes. Because of the large amounts of cargo which can be handled daily from a containership, operators have been able to use bigger ships without increasing, and indeed even reducing, port time. However, since the amount of cargo available remains much the same, fewer of the larger ships are needed to serve a particular trade. Community shipowners have difficulty to operate with container ships of the size needed to obtain the available economies of scale and thus minimise costs, whilst maintaining a satisfactory frequency of service.

2.3 Other related pressures towards closer association between operators on containerised trade routes were that:

— the establishment of a container service necessitated an initial capital investment greater than that required to replace tonnage on conventional services. Individual lines therefore hesitated to make this investment on their own account;

— container ships were less free to transfer from one trade to another because many were designed for a particular trade route; in addition many ports did not have the equipment and infrastructure to handle container ships (a problem which still exists in some developing countries).

2.4 These pressures for co-operation led individual shipping lines to enter into joint fleet operations usually described as consortia."

In essence, consortia are merely another way of reducing costs and enhancing efficiency.[7]

16.2 JURIDICAL NATURE OF CONSORTIA

The juridical nature of consortia is a matter of critical concern. Are they subject to Regulation 4056/86?[8] Are they concentrations and thus subject to the Merger Control Regulation?

The Commission has concluded, based on its review of the consortia agreements submitted to it, that they do not constitute mergers or concentrations because of (a) the provisions relating to termination with different periods of notice and (b) there is no evidence of a transfer of assets or activities to the consortium.[9] It is submitted that such a view is reasonable in the circumstances. Consortia are merely vehicles (of limited duration) used by various shipping companies (who still remain largely independent) so as to exploit particular market opportunities and that various companies may be a member of more than one consortium. The partners do not completely and irreversibly transfer all of their assets to the consortium. If they did and the consortium fell within the scope of Regulation 4064/89 (the so-called "Merger Control Regulation") then they would fall outside the scope of Regulation 4056/86 because of Article 22(2) of Regulation 4064/89.[10]

7. Green, *op. cit.* at footnote 1, p. 2.

8. On Regulation 4056/86, see Chapter 12, above.

9. Communication, *op. cit.* at footnote 1, above, para. 5.1.

10. Statement for entry into the Council minutes entitled "Commission Statement re Article 3(2), first indent of the Merger Control Regulation," Doc. No. 10958/89 RC 51 at p. 4, 19 December 1989. It is possible that a particular consortium may be a concentration within the meaning of Regulation 4064/89 and thus the question must be individually examined.

The Commission has also concluded that consortia are not normally[11] pure technical agreements and thus they fall outside the scope of the exemption in Article 2 of Regulation 4056/86.[12] This is in direct contradiction to the views of CAACE and CENSA. The Commission reasoned thus:

"The information available suggests that there are few if any consortia agreements whose sole object and effect are to achieve technical improvements or co-operation in the sense of Article 2 of Regulation No. 4056/86.[13]

All but two of the 23 agreements[14] examined contain arrangements not only on joint fleet and terminal operations but also on pooling and/or conference rights, pricing, marketing or inland operations. One of the two exceptions concerns a Slot Charter Agreement containing arrangements on joint schedule and space/slot exchange and arrangements on capacity restrictions for one of the parties regarding certain European ports. The other case concerns an agreement containing arrangements on joint fleet and terminal operations. However, it also provides for cost sharing arrangements for ships, administration and equipment. In addition it provides that conference trading rights may only be exercised by agreement of the consortium policy committee and that the parties, without having joint marketing, 'may combine their interests'.

In all these cases the consortium's sole object and effect are not purely technical.[15]

There are, according to CAACE's descriptive list,[16] some other consortia agreements limited to arrangements on joint fleet and terminal operations. However, these agreements cannot be regarded as purely technical since for instance one agreement also contains, *inter alia*, the parties' agreement to avoid unreasonable or unfair sales and marketing competition amongst themselves through a common freight policy. Such agreements restrict competition and cannot be considered as having exclusively technical objects and effects. Finally, the parties to consortia agreements regulate the use of their vessel capacities in given trade routes and are actual or potential competitors.

For all these reasons consortia cannot, other than perhaps in very exceptional cases, be considered as falling within the scope of Article 2 of Council Regulation 4056/86."[17]

It is equally necessary to consider whether consortia fall within the scope of the conferences block exemption. In the words of the Commission:

"conferences are arrangements which exist essentially to ensure that their members charge the same rates of freight. Some conferences also agree members' participation in a particular trade (which is defined either as sailing rights, i.e. the right to berth x number of sailings per annum from one area to another or as percentage shares in the trade) or even 'pool' either earnings or liftings (freight tons) or both: the intention generally being to equate 'share' with earnings and liftings."[18]

The Commission is clear that consortia are not covered by the Conference block exemption in Regulation 4056/86:

"Consortia are pursuing different objectives and are different in organisation [from consortia]. The size of container ships (say 3 to 6 conventional ships = 1 container ship) means that most single shipping companies are no longer capable of providing, on their own, a satisfactory liner service to shippers. To be viable, a shipping service must perform a frequent, say weekly, service to its customers. Rationalisation of schedules is, therefore, a *sine qua non* of liner shipping with

11. It would be possible but unlikely that a consortium agreement would be a technical agreement within the meaning of Article 2 of Regulation 4056/86.
12. See Chapter 12, above, on Regulation 4056/86.
13. *Ibid.*
14. The agreements were examined by the Commission in its study for its Communication.
15. On the significance of technical agreements, see Article 2 of Regulation 4056/86.
16. This was a list of consortia agreements submitted by the CAACE to the Commission.
17. Communication, para. 5.2.
18. Communication, para. 5.3.

each participating line being allocated slots for each sailing. This is not the role of conferences. Shipowners agree that consortia are different from conferences.

Consortia agreements restrict or eliminate competition between the parties in some or all of the following areas:

- the provision and use of capacity and transport facilities;
- timings and sailings;
- marketing;
- inland operations;
- their policies as conference members; and
- price competition (which is eliminated either by conference membership, or by arrangements in the consortium agreements which are to that extent equivalent to a conference agreement, or by some combination of the two).

A considerable number of consortia agreements thus contain restrictive arrangements which go beyond the scope of Article 3 of Council Regulation No. 4056/86 and would therefore not be covered by the block exemption for conferences, even if they could be considered as conference agreements . . .

Consortia are increasingly concerned with combined sea/land door-to-door transport. Multilateral agreements on combined sea/land transport are not covered by the conference block exemption, which applies only to the maritime sector.[19]

5.4 It follows that consortia agreements which restrict competition and affect trade between Member States must, if they are not to be considered null and void in accordance with Article 85(2) of the Treaty, be covered either by an individual or by a block exemption. In view of the number of consortia agreements and the need for shipowners to retain the flexibility necessary to change their agreements in response to changing competitive circumstances, it is desirable for administrative reasons to give a group exemption as far as possible. Accordingly, the Commission has examined the scope for granting such a group exemption."

It is reasonably clear that consortia, even where acting as conference members, are not conferences in themselves.

16.3 COMMERCIAL VIEW ON CONSORTIA

The views of the industry on consortia are mixed.[20] The Commission summarises these views in the following terms:

"4.1 CAACE and CENSA have argued, in various submissions to the Commission,[21] that Community shipping lines need to participate in consortia in order 'not to be put at a disadvantage compared with their competitors, the single entity, multi-trade giants'.[22] In their view consortia are either excepted, as technical agreements, under Article 2 of Regulation No. 4056/86,[23] or are covered by the block exemption in Article 3 of the same regulation.[24] For cases not so covered there should be a group exemption. These views were not shared by the Union of Greek shipowners who argued that the Commission should only grant individual exemptions, where appropriate.

4.2 The British Shippers' Council has informed the Commission that, in its view, consortia are covered neither by Article 2[25] nor by Article 3 of Regulation No. 4056/86[26] and that a new block exemption would be inappropriate. Individual exemptions should be granted only with special conditions and obligations. The European Shippers' Council hold similar views, arguing

19. Communication, para. 5.3.
20. Kemball, *The Business of Shipping*, pp. 219–222.
21. In connection with the Communication mentioned in footnote 1 above.
22. In particular, those large shipping companies from south-east Asia.
23. See Chapter 12, above.
24. See Chapter 12, above.
25. See Chapter 12, above.
26. See Chapter 12, above.

that consortia should apply for individual exemption and that conditions and obligations, including an obligation to meaningful consultations with shippers, should be attached."[27]

It has been commented[28] that it is possible to identify certain common categories of consortia, in particular, consortia which involve:

- joint scheduling;
- slot and space exchanges;
- equipment pools;
- joint offices;
- joint terminal operations;
- cargo sharing;
- revenue sharing arrangements;
- joint sales and joint use of bills of lading;
- price fixing;
- shared inland operations (e.g. joint consolidation and haulage).[29]

16.4 1990 COMMUNICATION ON CONSORTIA

16.4.1 Introduction

On 18 June 1990, the Commission sent a Communication[30] to the Council of Ministers which contained a report on the possibility of a group exemption[31] for consortia agreements[32] in liner shipping[33] as well as a proposal for a Council Regulation on the application of Article 85(3) of the EEC Treaty[34] to certain categories of agreements, decisions and concerted practices between shipping companies.

16.4.2 Background to the communication on consortia

When the Council of Ministers adopted the Regulation 4056/86[35] as part of the December 1986 Package of Measures,[36] the Commission undertook to report to the Council of Ministers within one year on whether it was appropriate to provide for block exemptions[37] for consortia and to make proposals where necessary.[38] This followed the Council of Ministers' statement when it adopted Regulation 4056/86:

"The Council of Ministers invites the Commission to study the situation regarding competition in the sectors of passenger shipping, tramp shipping, joint ventures, consortia and agreements between transport users to consider whether it is necessary to submit new proposals. The Council notes, however, that where the object and effect of joint ventures and consortia is either to

27. Communication, *op. cit.* at footnote 1, above, para. 4.
28. Green, *op. cit.* at footnote 1, above, pp. 5–6.
29. Green, *op. cit.* at footnote 1, above, pp. 5–6.
30. COM(90)260 final, 18 June 1990.
31. A group exemption is a block licence under Article 85(3) for certain types of arrangements under Article 85(1).
32. On consortia agreements, see Chapter 11, above.
33. On liner shipping, see Chapter 11, above.
34. Article 85(3) of the EEC Treaty is the exemption provision for Article 85(1)..
35. On Regulation 4056/86 generally, see Chapter 12, above.
36. COM (89) 266 final.
37. On block exemptions, see para. 31, above.
38. Council Doc. No. 11584/86 MAR 84 of 19 December 1986, Annex III.

achieve technical improvements or co-operation as provided for in Article 2 of the Regulation or where close-knit consortia only cover minor market shares, the prohibition laid down in Article 85(1) of the Treaty does not apply to them."[39]

While the Commission made an interim report in 1988, it was unable to make such a final report[40] to the Council of Ministers in the light of the fact that "despite its repeated efforts to complete its work within one year because the industry did not make available to it a sufficient number of consortia agreements to constitute a satisfactory basis for analysis".[41]

16.5 THE NEED FOR THE BLOCK EXEMPTION

Having discounted the possibility that consortia would be either technical agreements[42] or conferences[43] and thus outside any exempting provisions, the Commission decided that it was necessary to specifically exempt consortia agreements. The Commission decided against a policy of granting individual exemptions as and when agreements were notified because of the "number of consortia agreements and the need for shipowners to retain the flexibility necessary to change their agreements in response to changing economic circumstances, it is desirable for administrative reasons to give a group exemption as far as possible".[44]

The Commission justified the exemption on the basis that the EC's shipping industry:

"needs to attain the necessary economies of scale to compete on the world liner conference market. Consortia can help to provide the necessary means for improving the productivity of liner shipping services and promoting technical and economic progress by facilitating and encouraging the use of containers.

Users of the shipping services offered by consortia obtain several important advantages. First, they are ensured regular sailings at prices which do not depend on which ships are used for their containers. Second, economies of scale in the use of ships and on-shore facilities are achieved. Third, since consortia tend to bring about higher levels of capacity utilisation, costs are reduced for this reason also. Fourth, consortia increase the quality of shipping services by using more modern ships and equipment as well as port facilities. Last, but not least, through provision of joint inland services they are responding to many shippers' requirements for efficient door-to-door transport.

Thus, users can obtain a share of the benefits resulting from the improvement in productivity and service. However, any group exemption must give a sufficient guarantee that consortia are able to realise their advantages to the fullest extent and that users get a fair share of the resulting rationalisation and reduction in costs.

In order, therefore, to ensure that all the requirements of Article 85(3) are met it would be necessary, *inter alia*, to attach to the block exemption certain conditions and/or obligations to ensure that a fair share of the benefits would be passed on to shippers and that competition in respect of a substantial part of the trades in question was not eliminated."[45]

The Commission continued its defence of the need for a separate block exemption and not simply amendments to the various Regulations in issue (i.e. Regulations 17/62,[46]

39. Council Doc. No. 11584/86, MAR 84, of 19 December 1986, Annex III.
40. See Doc. No. 4130/MAR 3, 11 January 1988 and Doc. No. 10048/88 MAR 38 of 13 December 1988.
41. COM(90)260 final, para. 1.2.
42. And thus within Article 2 of Regulation 4056/86.
43. I.e. liner conferences.
44. Communication, para. 5.4.
45. Communication, para. 6.1.
46. I.e. the general implementing Regulation for competition generally.

1017/68[47] and 4056/86[48]) by saying that such an "independent, self-contained regulation" was necessary because of (a) the great variety of different consortia arrangements operating under different circumstances, (b) the impossibility of drafting a block exemption for joint ventures (and consortia are after all, a specialised form of joint venture), and (c) the fact that many consortia deal with multi-modal transport operations which fall partly within the scope of Regulation 4056/86[49] and partly under Regulation 1017/68[50] and, in so far as containers are concerned, partly under Regulation No.17/62[51,52] Some consortia agreements can fall within the scope of Regulation 4056/86 but clearly not all such agreements. It is more realistic to imagine that a separate block exemption is needed because Consortia Agreements often involve transport other than international sea transport and thus would not fall within the scope of Regulations 4056/86. It is submitted that given the ever-changing composition of most consortia, it would be very difficult to avoid a situation where virtually every change in membership might require separate applications for individual exemptions.

16.6 CONTENTS OF THE COUNCIL OF MINISTERS REGULATION[53]

On 25 February 1992, the Council of Ministers adopted Regulation 479/92 to provide a block exemption for consortia. It is an enabling regulation.

16.6.1 Purpose

The Regulation states that:

"Whereas Article 85(1) of the [EEC] Treaty may in accordance with Article 85(3) thereof be declared inapplicable to categories of agreements, decisions and concerted practices which fulfill the conditions contained in Article 85(3);

Whereas, pursuant to Article 87 of the [EEC] Treaty, the provisions for the application of Article 85(3) of the Treaty should be adopted by way of Regulation; whereas, according to Article 87(2)(b), such a Regulation must lay down detailed rules for the application of Article 85(3), taking into account the need to ensure effective supervision, on the one hand, and to simplify administration to the greatest possible extent on the other; whereas, according to Article 87(2)(d), such a Regulation is required to define the respective funtions of the Commission and of the Court of Justice;

Whereas liner shipping is a capital intensive industry; whereas containerization has increased pressures for co-operation and rationalization; whereas the Community shipping industry needs to attain the necessary economies of scale in order to compete successfully on the world liner shipping market;

Whereas joint service agreements between liner shipping companies with the aim of rationalising their operations by means of technical, operational and/or commercial arrangements (described in shipping circles as consortia) can help to provide the necessary means for improving the productivity of liner shipping services and promoting technical and economic progress;

47. I.e. the implementing Regulation for road, rail and inland waterway.
48. I.e. the implementing Regulation for maritime transport.
49. In respect of the maritime transport aspect.
50. In respect of the inland waterway, road or railway aspects.
51. In respect of any aspect not covered by Regulation 1017/68 or 4056/86.
52. Communication, para. 6.2.
53. Regulation 479/92, OJ L55/3, 29 February 1992. For the Commission proposal, see OJC 167/9, 10 July 1990. For the Opinions of the Parliament and the ECOSOC, see OJ C 305/39, 25 November 1991 and OJ C 69/16, 18 March 1991 respectively.

Having regard to the importance of maritime transport for the development of the Community's trade and the role which consortia agreements can fulfil in this respect, taking account of the special features of international liner shipping;

Whereas the legalization of these agreements is a measure which can make a positive contribution to improving the competitiveness of shipping in the Community;

Whereas users of the shipping services offered by consortia can obtain a share of the benefits resulting from the improvements in productivity and service, by means of, *inter alia*, regularity, cost reductions derived from higher levels of capacity utilization, and better service quality stemming from improved vessels and equipment.

Whereas the Commission should be enabled to declare by way of Regulation that the provisions of Article 85(1) of the Treaty do not apply to certain categories of consortia agreements, decisions and concerted practices, in order to make it easier for undertakings to cooperate in ways which are economically desirable and without adverse effect from the point of view of competition policy;

Whereas the Commission, in close and constant liaison with the competent authorities of the Member States, should be able to define precisely the scope of these exemptions and the conditions attached to them;

Whereas consortia in liner shipping are a specialized and complex type of joint venture; whereas there is a great variety of different consortia agreements operating in different circumstances; whereas the scope, parties, activities or terms of consortia are frequently altered; whereas the Commission should therefore be given the responsibility of defining from time to time the consortia to which the group exemption should apply;

Whereas, in order to ensure that all the conditions of Article 85(3) of the Treaty are met, conditions should be attached to group exemptions to ensure in particular that a fair share of the benefits will be passed on to shippers and that competition is not eliminated;

Whereas pursuant to Article 11(4) of Council Regulation (EEC) No. 4056/86 of 22 December 1986 laying down detailed rules for the application of Articles 85 and 86 of the EEC Treaty to maritime transport the Commission may provide that a decision taken in accordance with Article 85(3) of the Treaty shall apply with retrospective effect; whereas it is desirable that the Commission be empowered to adopt, by Regulation, provisions to that effect;

Whereas notification of agreements, decisions and concerted practices falling within the scope of this Regulation must not be made compulsory, it being primarily the responsibility of undertakings to see to it that they conform to the rules on competition, and in particular to the conditions laid down by the subsequent Regulation implementing this Regulation;

Whereas there can be no exemption if the conditions set out in Article 85(3) of the Treaty are not satisfied; whereas the Commission should therefore have power to take the appropriate measures where an agreement proves to have effects incompatible with Article 85(3) of the Treaty; whereas the Commission should consequently be able first to address recommendations to the parties and then to take decisions . . ."

It is worth dwelling for a moment on whether consortia agreements violate Article 85(1) of the EEC Treaty at all. Consortia agreements vary as much as joint venture agreements and each should be examined individually. Thus, it is possible that some consortia agreements do not violate Article 85(1) because the parties are not actual or potential competitors or the agreement is really promoting competition rather than restricting it. None the less, there is no doubt that there are many consortia agreements which do fall foul of Article 85(1) of the EEC Treaty and need to be exempted.[54]

16.6.2 Form of the proposed block exemption

The Commission was anxious, in proposing a block exemption, to have an "independent, self-contained regulation, rather than an amendment or addition to any existing regulation"[55] for three specific reasons, namely:

54. *Quaere* whether consortia agreements can violate Art. 86 of the EEC Treaty. It is submitted that in so far as "joint dominance" may violate Art. 86 then a consortia agreement may violate that provision.

55. Communication, *ibid.* at footnote 1 above, para. 6.2.

"— there is a great variety of different consortia arrangements operating under different circumstances;
— consortia are a specialized form of joint venture. Despite the efforts of the Commission's services and the interested industries, it has proved impossible to draft a block exemption for joint ventures in general;
— many consortia deal with multi-modal transport operations which fall partly within the scope of Regulation No. 4056/86 and partly under Regulation No. 1017/68 and, insofar as containers are concerned, partly under Regulation No. 17/62."[56]

Of the three reasons, the second and third are the strongest.

16.6.3 Scope of the block exemption

The Regulation deals with multimodal as well as purely maritime consortia. Thus, it would have to be adopted on the bases of, *inter alia*, Regulations 17/62, 1017/68 and 4056/86.[57]

16.6.4 Provision for an exemption regulation

Article 1 of the Regulation provides:

"1. Without prejudice to the application of Regulation (EEC) No. 4056/86, the Commission may by regulation and in accordance with Article 85(3) of the Treaty, declare that Article 85(1) of the Treaty shall not apply to certain categories of agreements between undertakings, decisions of associations of undertakings and concerted practices that have as an object to promote or establish cooperation in the joint operation of maritime transport services between liner shipping companies, for the purpose of rationalizing their operations by means of technical, operational and/or commercial arrangements—with the exception of price fixing (consortia).

2. Such regulation adopted pursuant to paragraph 1 shall define the categories of agreements, decisions and concerted practices to which it applies and shall specify the conditions and obligations under which, pursuant to Article 85(3) of the Treaty, they shall be considered exempted from the application of Article 85(1) of the Treaty."

16.6.5 Duration and effect of the exemption

Article 2 of the Regulation provides:

"1. The Regulation adopted pursuant to Article 1 shall apply for a period of five years, calculated as from the date of its entry into force.

2. It may be repealed or amended where circumstances have changed with respect to any of the facts which were basic to its adoption."

Article 3 of the Regulation provides:

"The regulation adopted pursuant to Article 1 may include a provision stating that it applies with retroactive effect to agreements, decisions and concerted practices which were in existence at the date of entry into force of such regulation, provided they comply with the conditions established in that regulation."

16.6.6 Consultation

Article 4 of the Regulation provides:

56. Communication, *ibid.* at footnote 1, above, para. 6.2.
57. Communication, *ibid.* at footnote 1, above, para. 6.3.

"Before adopting its regulation, the Commission shall publish a draft thereof to enable all persons and organizations concerned to submit their comments within such reasonable time limit as the commission shall fix but in no case less than one month."

Thus, before the Block Exemption is adopted, there will have to be consultation. Article 5 of the Regulation goes on to provide:

"1. Before publishing the draft regulation and before adopting the regulation the Commission shall consult: the Advisory Committee on Agreements and Dominant Position in Maritime Transport established by Article 15(3) of Regulation (EEC) No. 4056/86.

2. Paragraphs 5 and 6 of Regulation (EEC) No. 4056/86, relating to consultation with the Advisory Committee, shall apply, it being understood that joint meetings with the Commission shall take place not earlier than one month after dispatch of the notice convening them."

16.6.7 Breaches

Article 6 of the Regulation provides:

"1. Where the persons concerned are in breach of a condition or obligation attaching to an exemption granted by the Regulation adopted pursuant to Article 1, the Commission may, in order to put an end to such a breach:

— address recommendations to the persons concerned, and
— in the event of failure by such persons to observe those recommendations, and depending on the gravity of the breach concerned, adopt a decision that either prohibits them from carrying out, or requires them to perform specific acts or, while withdrawing the benefit of the group exemption which they enjoyed, grants them an individual exemption in accordance with Article 11(4) of Regulation (EEC) No. 4056/86, or withdraws the benefit of the group exemption which they enjoyed.

2. Where the Commission, either on its own initiative or at the request of a Member State or of natural or legal persons claiming a legitimate interest, finds that in any particular case an agreement, decision or concerted practice to which the group exemption granted by the Regulation adopted pursuant to Article 1 applies, nevertheless has effects which are incompatible with Article 85(3) of the Treaty or within the prohibition of Article 86, it may withdraw the benefit of the group exemption from those agreements, decisions or concerted practices and take all appropriate measures for the purpose of bringing these infringements to an end, pursuant to Article 13 of Regulation (EEC) No. 4056/86.

3. Before taking a decision under paragraph 2, the Commission may address recommendations for termination of the infringement to the persons concerned."

16.6.8 Entry into force

Article 7 of the Regulation provides that it entered into force on the day following its publication in the *Official Journal of the European Communities*, that is to say, 1 March 1992.

The UK Shipping Minister, Mr McLoughlin, expressed his hope, prior to the publication of the Commission proposal, that it would create a sound regulatory framework with minimal governmental interference.[58] He also expressed the hope that the resultant regime would not be unwieldy in its bureaucracy and he pointed out that the US version requires 200 staff to operate.[59] The Council of Ministers has given the Commission the power to adopt a block exemption on consortia. It will be fascinating to see what happens next.

58. GCBS Seminar on Shipping and the Single Market, 26 February 1990.
59. *Ibid.*

CHAPTER 17

European Community Marine Environmental Law

17.1 INTRODUCTION

The protection of the marine environment has been a concern of the international community for many decades.[1] The EC is an important forum for such concern[2] and it has adopted (especially in recent times) over 170 legislative measures relating to the environment generally, including many relating to the marine environment. This paper examines the environmental law of the EC and how it relates to shipping.[3] Some elements of the EC law relating to marine pollution are generated within the EC while the rest comes from the participation of the EC in international fora such as the various Commissions relating to international watercourses and rivers such as the Rhine.

In the late 1980s and early 1990s, the environment has become an issue of geopolitical significance and concern. This apparent new-found interest in the environment is however deceptive. There has been a keen international interest in the environment generally (and the marine environment in particular) for much longer. Environmental cases such as *The Trail Smelter Arbitration: US v. Canada*[4] and *The Corfu Channel Case (Merits): UK v. Albania*[5] were decided half a century or so ago. It is hoped that the contemporary interest in this most precious of resources will not be lost as quickly as it was (apparently) gained.

1. On international marine environment law, see Bell and Bell, *Environmental Law* (1991); Bothe, "Oil Pollution Conventions" in Bernhardt (ed.), *Encyclopedia of Public International Law*, vol. 11 (1989), p. 245 and Salmon in Bernhardt (ed.), *Encyclopedia of Public International Law*, vol. 11 (1989), p. 200.

2. See Freestone, *Environmental Protection in EC Law* (NYP); Haigh, *EEC Environmental Policy and Britain* (2nd edn, 1989); Johnson and Corcelle, *The Environmental Policy of the European Communities* (1989); Johnson, *The Pollution Policy of the European Communities*, 2nd edn (1983); Kramer, *EEC Treaty and Environmental Protection* (1990); and Saetevik, *Environmental Co-operation between North Sea States* (1988).

See also Booth and Green, "European Community Environmental Programme and UK Law" (1975–76) 1 EL Rev 444 and 535; Haagsma, "The EC's Environmental Policy: A Case Study in Federalism" (1988) 12 *Fordham Int'l L.J.* 311; Hayward, "The Role and Activities of the European Communities in the Protection and the Preservation of the Marine Environment of the North Sea" (1990) *International Journal of Estuarine and Coastal Law* 101, Jans, "Article 7 EEC and a Non-Discriminatory Transfrontier Environmental Policy" (1988/1) LIEI 21; Nollkaemper, "The European Community and International Environmental Co-operation: Legal Aspects of External Community Powers" (1987/2) LIEI 55.

See also the papers of the First Annual Summer School in Environmental Law: Module II-EC Law, July 1990. Newspaper coverage of this issue includes "EEC Forms Pollution Task Force", *Lloyd's List*, 17 September 1987, p. 1.

3. See Abecassis and Jarashow, *Oil Pollution from Ships* (2nd edn., 1985) and Johnson, *The Pollution Control Policy of the European Communities* (1983), pp. 84–92 and Myles, *op. cit.*, pp. 3–332 to 3–336.

4. (1941) 3 RIAA 1905, 1965–1966.

5. [1949] ICJ Rep. 4.

17.2 THE 1950s

17.2.1 1957: The EEC Treaty

The original EEC Treaty, drafted in 1957, did not expressly provide for environmental matters. This is not too surprising given the fact that the link between economics and the environment was not as well appreciated then as it is now. However, the absence of express terms in the EEC Treaty was not fatal: Articles 100 and 235 allow for the adoption of rules in circumstances where the Treaty contains no express provisions and these two provisions formed the bases for action in this area.

Article 100 provides:

"The Council[6] shall, acting unanimously on a proposal from the Commission, issue directives for the approximation of such provisions laid down by law, regulation or administrative action in Member States as directly affect the establishment or functioning of the common market.

The European Parliament and the Economic and Social Committee shall be consulted in the case of directives whose implementation would, in one or more Member States, involve the amendment of legislation."

Article 235 provides:

"If action by the Community should prove necessary to attain, in the course of the operation of the common market, one of the objectives of the Community and this Treaty has not provided the necessary powers, the Council shall, acting unanimously on a proposal from the Commission and after consulting the European Parliament, take the appropriate measures."

These two Articles have proved useful as the bases for action by the EC in regard to the environment.[7] Moreover, Article 2 stated that the Community's task is to provide throughout the Community a harmonious development of economic activities. It is submitted that this task may well have an environmental dimension.

17.3 THE 1960s

17.3.1. Introduction

The 1960s saw the slow build-up of the interest in the environment which has now reached a crescendo. Concerns during the 1960s about "the Bomb", marine pollution, space exploration and the pharmaceutical industry were the foundations for modern environmental law.

17.3.2 1967: Torrey Canyon

The *Torrey Canyon* incident was extremely significant in the development of EC environment law.[8] The *Torrey Canyon* was a US-owned and chartered but Liberian

6. *Ed.* i.e. the Council of Ministers.

7. E.g. Dir. 76/464 on pollution caused by certain dangerous substances discharged into the aquatic environment of the Community.

8. On the *Torrey Canyon* incident generally, see Brown, "The Lessons of the Torrey Canyon: International Law Aspects" (1968) 21 CLP 113; Healy, "The CMI and IMCO Draft Conventions on Civil Liability for Oil Pollution" (1969–1970) 1 JMLC 93; Keeton, "The Lessons of the Torrey Canyon: English Law Aspects" (1968) 21 CLP 94; Nanda, "The Torrey Canyon Disaster: Some Legal Aspects" (1967) 44 Denver LJ 400; "Report of the Board of Investigation in the Matter of the Stranding of the SS Torrey Canyon on March 18, 1967" (1967) 6 ILM 480; UK Secretary of State, "The Torrey Canyon" (Cmnd. 3246 (1967)); Stansfield, "The Torrey Canyon" in Bernhardt (ed.), *Encyclopedia of Public International Law*, vol. 11 (1989), p. 333; Sweeney, "Oil Pollution of the Oceans" (1968–69) 37 *Fordham Law Rev.* 155; Utton, "Protective Measures and the Torrey Canyon" (1967–1968) 9 *Boston College Int'l and Comp. Law Rev.* 613.

registered supertanker which ran aground on 18 March 1967 on the Seven Stones' Reef between the Scilly Isles and Lands End while on its way from Mina Al Ahamadi in the Persian Gulf to Milford Haven in Wales. At the time, it was carrying some 119,328 tons of crude oil. While it ran aground in international waters, its cargo posed a threat to both the French and UK coastlines. All attempts to refloat the vessel or to transfer her cargo to another ship were impeded by bad weather. On 27 March 1967, the UK Government decided to burn the oil slicks as well as bomb the ship so as to open her cargo tanks and burn the oil contained in them. While all the oil in the ship's vicinity was destroyed by this action, some 80,000 tons escaped and still threatened the UK and French coastlines.

The *Torrey Canyon* incident raised a number of issues of international law. It is a general rule of international law that the flag State of the ship has jurisdiction over the ship while she is on the high seas so then how come the UK had the jurisdiction to bomb the ship? Of course, one argument raised at the time was that the UK was not bombing the ship but rather preventing pollution of its coastline. Interestingly, much later (in 1980) the International Law Commission was of the view that the UK's action was an act of necessity and was thus permissible under international law.[9] More importantly for present purposes, the UK referred the incident and its implications to the International Maritime Consultative Organisation (now the International Maritime Organisation)[10] at an extraordinary meeting on 4 May 1967. As a result, two Conventions were adopted. The first Convention, namely, the Convention relating to Intervention on the High Seas in Cases of Oil Pollution Casualties of 29 November 1969[11] authorises States parties to the Convention to take "such measures on the high seas as may be necessary to prevent, mitigate or eliminate grave and imminent danger to their coastline"[12] from oil pollution. The second Convention, namely, the Convention on Civil Liability for Oil Pollution Damage of 29 November 1969[13] provides that a shipowner which causes oil pollution damage may limit its liability by establishing a fund for compensation.

The significance of the *Torrey Canyon* also lies in the facts that the incident first, "caused the community of nations to address the legal problems of massive accidental oil pollution at sea, thereby providing legal grounds for coastal State intervention and a cogent regime for limited liability"[14]; while secondly, it concentrated the minds of European States (in particular, the UK and France) to oil pollution from ships.

17.4 THE 1970s

17.4.1 1972: UN Conference in Stockholm

The global concerns of the 1960s began to mature in the form of a United Nations (UN) Conference on the Environment which was held in Stockholm in 1972. The Conference called for concerted action on the environment. It highlighted the need for

9. See Stansfield, *op. cit.*, at p. 334. See (1980) 2 YILC.
10. On this organisation, see para. 1.3.3, above.
11. UNTS, vol. 970, p. 212.
12. Convention, Art. 1.
13. UNTS, vol. 973, p. 3. On the Convention, see Healy, "The International Convention on Civil Liability for Oil Pollution Damage" (1970) 1 JMLC 317.
14. Stansfield, *op. cit.*, p. 334.

action in many areas of the environment, including the marine environment. In its Declaration[15] which was made by 113 States, a set of principles was laid down, including the following:

"*Principle 1*
Man has the fundamental right to freedom, equality and adequate conditions of life, in an environment of a quality that permits a life of dignity and well-being, and he bears a solemn responsibility to protect and improve the environment for present and future generations. In this respect, policies promoting or perpetuating apartheid, racial segregation, discrimination, colonial and other forms of oppression and foreign domination stand condemned and must be eliminated.

Principle 2
The natural resources of the earth including the air, water, land, flora and fauna and especially representative samples of natural ecosystems must be safeguarded for the benefit of present and future generations through careful planning or management, as appropriate. . . .

Principle 7
States shall take all possible steps to prevent pollution of the seas by substances that are liable to create hazards to human health, to harm living resources and marine life, to damage amenities or to interfere with other legitimate users of the sea. . . ."

17.4.2 1972 and 1973: EC responses to the UN Conference

The EC responded to the UN Conference: in October 1972 the Paris Summit Conference of Community Heads of State or Government (the beginnings of the modern European Council) stressed the need for an environmental policy and called for the establishment of an action programme before 31 July 1973. The EC also responded in 1973, by developing the principles of an EC environmental policy: these principles were that:

— pollution should be prevented at source rather than seeking to remedy the effects;
— environmental policy should be compatible with economic and social development;
— environmental policy considerations should be taken into account in the planning processes; and
— the polluter should pay for damage caused.[16]

These principles were embodied in the First Action Programme.

17.4.3 1973: the First Action Programme[17]

17.4.3.1 The Action Programmes

The EC has so far adopted four consecutive Action Programmes for the Environment. The first related to the 1973–1976 period.[18] The second related to the 1977–1981 period.[19] The third programme related to the years 1982–1986.[20] At the time of writing, the current one is the 1987–1992 programme.[21]

15. (1972) 11 ILM 1416.
16. See OJ C112, 20 December 1973.
17. OJ 1973 C112/1.
18. OJ 1973 C112/1.
19. OJ 1977 C39/1.
20. OJ 1983 C46/1.
21. OJ 1987 C328/1.

17.4.3.2 1973: The 1973 Action Programme

The 1973–1977 Action Programme converted the four Principles into three specific "actions": first, to reduce and prevent pollution and nuisances; secondly, to improve the environment and quality of life; and thirdly, EC or Member States must take action in international environmental organisations.

The First Action Programme classified marine pollution as coming from four principal sources:

(a) discharge from land;
(b) deliberate dumping of waste at sea;
(c) exploitation of marine and sub-marine resources, especially exploitation of the seabed; and
(d) sea transport and navigation.

The same Programme recognised that marine pollution is one of the most dangerous of all forms of pollution because it affects the fundamental biological and ecological balances of the planet as well as the nutritional, recreational and social needs of humanity. The Programme recognised that marine pollution affected the whole of the EC because pollution affects the transport of goods by sea.

17.4.4 1973: establishment of an Environmental and Consumer Protection Service

In 1973, an Environmental and Consumer Protection Service was established within the EC Commission. This Service is now embodied within Directorates A and B of Directorate-General XI of the Commission which handles Environment, Nuclear Safety and Civil Protection.[22] Directorate B of DG XI has responsibility for water pollution.

17.4.5 1975: Paris Convention for the Prevention of Marine Pollution from Land-Based Sources

The EC has become a party to, or has signed, a number of international treaties governing a number of environmental issues. In 1975, Decision 75/437 was adopted on the conclusion of the Paris Convention for the Prevention of Marine Pollution from Land-Based Sources.[23]

17.4.6 1975: Council Recommendation on the "Polluter Pays" principle

The Council of Ministers adopted a Recommendation on the "Polluter Pays" principle.[24]

17.4.7 1976: discharge of effluent from land: Directive 76/464

On 4 May 1976, the Council of Ministers adopted Directive 76/464 on pollution caused by certain dangerous substances discharged into the aquatic environment of the

22. DG XI's official address is rue de la Loi 200, B–1049 Brussels (tel: 235 11 11).
23. OJ 1975 L194/5.
24. OJ 1975 L194.

Community.[25] Article 2 of this Directive required Member States to "take the appropriate steps to eliminate pollution of the waters referred to in Article 1[26] by the dangerous substances in the families and groups of substances in List I of the Annex and to reduce pollution of the said waters by the dangerous substances in the families and groups of substances in List II of the Annex, in accordance with this Directive".[27]

17.4.8 1976: deliberate dumping of waste at sea

The deliberate dumping of waste at sea is the subject of a number of international Conventions, most notably, the Oslo[28] and London[29] Conventions.

The First Action Programme accepted that the application of the international Conventions in this area meant that the EC Member States would have to adopt national legislation so as to implement such international measures and that such national implementing legislation would have to be coordinated by the EC.

On 12 January 1976, the Commission put forward a proposal for a Directive on dumping wastes at sea. The proposed Directive absolutely prohibited "particularly harmful substances" but permitted (by way of licences) the discharge of certain other harmful waste and matters.

17.4.9 Bravo drilling rig in the Ekofisk field

On 22 April 1977, a blow-out of oil and gas occurred on the Bravo drilling rig in the Ekofisk field in the North Sea (a sector under the supervision of Norway—not a member of the EC). By the time the blow-out was plugged eight days later, some 20,000 tonnes of oil had been discharged into the sea. While the incident need not detain discussion too much at this point, it did none the less have some significance for the development of EC environmental law in that it was very much in the mind of the Commission when it brought forward its Communication to the Council of Ministers on measures for the prevention, control and reduction of pollution caused by accidental discharges of hydrocarbons into the sea.[30]

17.4.10 1977: exploitation of marine and sub-marine resources, especially exploitation of the seabed

The Commission sent a Communication to the Council of Ministers on 9 June 1977 on the measures necessary for the prevention, control and reduction of pollution caused by accidental discharges of hydrocarbons into the sea. This was accompanied by a draft resolution on the issue.

25. OJ L129/23, 18 May 1976. As at 1 June 1990, this has not been altered.

26. *Ed.* Dir. 76/464, Article 1 provides that the Directive applies to inland surface water, territorial waters, internal coastal waters and ground water.

27. Dir. 76/464, Article 2.

28. This Convention is more properly described as the Convention for the Prevention of Marine Pollution by Dumping from Ships and Aircraft, concerning the areas of the north-east Atlantic, the North Sea and their Dependent Seas. It was signed at Oslo on 15 February 1972 and entered into force on 7 April 1974.

29. This Convention is more properly described as the Convention on the Dumping of Wastes at Sea, concerning all the seas in the world. It was signed at London on 13 November 1972 and entered into force on 31 August 1975.

30. This is discussed below ("Exploitation of marine and sub-marine resources, especially exploitation of the seabed").

Johnson records:

"The Commission was of the opinion that the Community should have powers and means allowing it to take action in such situations [as the Ekofisk incident], so expressing the solidarity of the Member States among themselves and towards non-member countries hit by a disaster of this type, since the protection of the seas was a duty for all the countries of the international community in the interest of future generations.

[According to the Commission] the following measures should [have been] implemented as soon as possible[31]:

- the establishment of a "data bank" at Community level recording the means available for taking action in the event of accidental discharges of hydrocarbons
- the development of a research programme into the technologies for collecting and dispersing hydrocarbons, into what happens to hydrocarbons in the sea and into their effects on marine fauna and flora.

The Commission also intended to appoint a group of high-level experts to examine the causes, circumstances and effects of recent accidents involving considerable spills of hydrocarbons in the sea, the remedies and preventive measures. The group would also be responsible for studying preparations for an environmental impact report on installations for prospecting and drilling for hydrocarbons at sea. It could also prepare the formulation of Community positions aiming at the efficient implementation of international agreements on:

1. the prevention of marine pollution in the prospecting and drilling for hydrocarbons;
2. the civil liability for damage caused by pollution with hydrocarbons and the establishment of a compensation fund."[32]

17.4.11 The Second Action Programme[33]

The Second Action Programme on the Environment, adopted on 13 June 1977 (following a Resolution of 17 May 1977), repeated many of the key features of the First Programme and expanded the thinking on the subject a little by saying that "a number of important provisions already adopted or contemplated constituted the basis for a coherent policy designed to prevent and reduce this type of pollution at Community level".

17.4.12 1977 Commission Communication to the Council of Ministers on the Reorganisation of the Community Shipbuilding Industry

On 9 December 1977, the Commission sent a Communication to the Council of Ministers on the Reorganisation of the Community Shipbuilding Industry.[34] It suggested an interesting use of environmental protection! The Communication discussed the decline in the fortunes of the EC shipbuilding industry. It mentioned that there was the transfer of a significant portion of the world fleet to flags of convenience and this "has brought into the shipping market vessels which present both operating hazards (substandard ships) and a threat to the marine environment. . . ."[35] The Commission then recorded that international bodies were then "trying to devise means of combating this form of unfair competition. The Community should step up the action it is already taking in this direction by taking steps towards the adoption of practical measures in the near future".[36] It went on to suggest that "[c]ertain

31. *Op. cit.*, pp. 87–88.
32. Op. cit., *The Pollution Control Policy of the European Communities*, pp. 87–88.
33. OJ 1977 C39/1.
34. Bull. EC, Supp. 7/77.
35. *Ibid.*, para. 15.
36. *Ibid.*, para. 16.

environmental measures could lead to a partial reduction of the excess capacity in tanker fleets and also appreciably stimulate the conversion of existing tankers".[37]

17.4.13 Amoco Cadiz

The *Amoco Cadiz* polluted the French coast in March 1978.[38] The French Foreign Minister, M. Guiringaud, asked the EC Council of Ministers at its 4 April 1978 meeting to adopt and implement a number of practical measures relating to oil pollution.

17.4.14 1978: Copenhagen Summit

The Copenhagen summit of the European Council on 7 and 8 April 1978 established pollution prevention and maritime safety as priority areas for Community action. In a later Council Resolution, it was stated that "the European Council took the view that the Community should make the prevention and control of marine pollution, in particular by hydrocarbons, an important objective of its action".[39]

In 1978, the Commission submitted an outline plan for action in the area of pollution to the Council. The thrust of the Commission's view was that the EC should lend its weight to the action already being taken by various international organisations rather than hope to draw up new regulations of its own. None the less, the Commission proposed that the EC should take action of its own accord in specified areas.

17.4.15 Council Resolution of 26 June 1978

17.4.15.1 Introduction

On 26 June 1978 the EEC Council resolved to set up an action programme of the European Communities on the control and reduction of pollution caused by hydrocarbons discharged at sea.[40]

17.4.15.2 Background

The European Parliament as well as the Economic and Social Committee both gave their Opinions on 13 June 1978.

17.4.15.3 Resolution in the context of the Action Programmes

The Council in its Resolution drew inspiration from the Action Programmes. It states in the Preamble to the Resolution:

> "Whereas the European Communities' Action Programmes on the Environment stressed the paramount importance to Western Europe that effective action be taken against the dangers inherent in the carriage of hydrocarbons, including the threat of serious pollution of coastal areas from accidents on the high seas and specified that the protection of marine waters to ensure that ecological balances are preserved is a priority task."[41]

37. *Ibid.*, para. 16 (footnote omitted).

38. On the *Amoco Cadiz* incident, see Gundling in Bernhardt (ed.), *Encyclopedia of Public International Law*, vol. 11 (1989), p. 31.

39. Council Resolution of 26 June 1978 setting up an action programme of the European Communities on the control and reduction of pollution caused by hydrocarbons discharged at sea.

40. OJ C162, 8 July 1978, p. 1.

41. Resolution, Preamble, Recital 2.

17.4.15.4 Rationale of the Resolution

The Council states in the Preamble to the Resolution:

"Whereas the authorities of the Member States the responsibility of which it is to take action in the event of pollution of the sea by hydrocarbons must have very prompt access to information on the human and material resources which can be deployed for the control of such pollution;

Whereas, in order quickly to counteract or even to prevent accidental pollution by hydrocarbons, these authorities must be able to ascertain particulars of the features of the vessels and offshore structures liable to cause such pollution and must be informed of any violations which may have been committed by vessels in the territorial waters of the Member States;

Whereas these authorities must be able to call on the assistance, at very short notice, of specialists who are fully and suitably trained in the control of marine pollution by hydrocarbons; whereas the equipment used for this purpose must be immediately available for use;

Whereas it is necessary to study the details of a possible Community contribution to work relating to the design and development of clean-up vessels, in view of its high cost;

Whereas the legal provisions on insurance against risks of accidental pollution by hydrocarbons must guarantee adequate compensation for the victims of such pollution;

Whereas research should be carried out to improve mechanical and chemical methods of treating hydrocarbons discharged at sea and to further knowledge regarding the subsequent history of such hydrocarbons and their effects on marine flora and fauna;

Whereas the action to be taken pursuant to this resolution may in no event exempt operators from their liability under civil or criminal law;

Whereas the Commission must have at its disposal the resources to prepare the detailed proposals provided for in the programme annexed hereto;

Whereas there are already international agreements dealing with measures for control of pollution from hydrocarbons to which Member States are party and there is a need to complement such agreements while avoiding duplication. . . ."

17.4.15.5 Essence of the Resolution

The essence of the Resolution is that the Council approved the "broad lines of approach" laid down in the Action Programme annexed to the Resolution.

The Annex contains the Action Programme of the European Communities on the control and reduction of pollution caused by hydrocarbons discharged at sea. It provides:

"The Commission will undertake the preliminary studies to identify what gaps need to be filled in the current framework of measures to control and reduce pollution caused by hydrocarbons discharged at sea and to propose appropriate action, at Community level and, if necessary, within the framework of international organizations or agreements. In the light of these studies, the Commission will place appropriate proposals before the Council as soon as possible. These studies will cover the following fields:

1. Computer processing of the existing data, or data still to be collected, on ways of dealing with marine pollution by hydrocarbons with a view to the immediate use of such data in the event of accidental pollution.

The study undertaken by the Commission will relate to any steps which might need to be taken so as to ensure that Member States, and if necessary interested third countries, have complete, rapid and reliable information on ways of dealing with marine pollution by hydrocarbons. The information studied will include in particular:

— the team of qualified personnel to combat marine pollution by hydrocarbons, the specific qualifications of such teams and practical particulars of how such teams can be called in; the availability of products and equipment for the chemical treatment of hydrocarbons (dispersants, precipitating agents, aerator-agitators and dispersant spreading equipment);
— availability of equipment for the mechanical treatment of hydrocarbons and

the specifications of the ships and equipment from which these operations can be carried out (speed and stability of vessels, equipment fitted) and their location;

— availability of the required coastline-protection resources (oil slick containment equipment, oil absorbants or precipitating agents, gels enabling dispersants to be used on rocks or structures, aerator-agitator and recovery equipment for use in shallow-waters and beach-cleaning equipment).

This study will consider in particular the conditions under which the collection and computer processing of this information, which should be constantly updated, can be achieved at minimum cost and avoiding any duplication. Possibilities exist already both at national level and within the framework of existing international agreements [and] will need to be fully explored.

2. Study of the availability for the Member States of relevant data on tankers liable to pollute the waters around the Community and the coasts of the Member States and on off-shore structures under the jurisdiction of the Member States.

The study undertaken by the Commission would be aimed at:

(a) investigating to what extent Member States may as of now have rapidly available complete and reliable information relating to:
   — the structural features of the tankers and offshore structures in question and emergency plans for prompt intervention,
   — any infringements committed in the territorial waters.

(b) investigating, if necessary, the means of making this information more readily available."

The Council also noted that the Commission would undertake the studies before submitting appropriate proposals as soon as possible for the implementation of this programme.

The Council also undertook to take a decision on the proposals within nine months from the date of their submission by the Commission or, as the case may be, of the date of forwarding of the opinions of the European Parliament as well as the Economic and Social Committee.

Finally, the Council called on the Member States to provide the Commission, at its request and on a case by case basis, with all the information needed to apply the Resolution.

17.4.16 1978 Council Recommendation on Ratification of Safety Conventions

17.4.16.1 Introduction

On 26 June 1978, the Council of Ministers meeting at Luxembourg recommended (by way of Council Recommendation 78/584/EEC[42]) to the Member States of the EC that, where they had not already done so, they should, where appropriate, sign, ratify or accede to a number of international Conventions on safety in shipping. The Conventions in question were: the 1974 International Convention for the Safety of Life at Sea (SOLAS); the 1978 Protocol relating to the 1974 International Convention for the Safety of Life at Sea; the 1973 international Convention for the Prevention of Pollution by Ships (MARPOL), as amended by the 1978 Protocol; and Convention No. 147 concerning minimum standards in merchant ships, adopted by the International Labour Conference in 1976.

One of the interesting features of the Recommendation is that EC Member States were recommended that they should inform in writing the Secretary-General of the Inter-Government Maritime Consultative Organisation or the International Maritime

42. OJ L194, 19 July 1978, p. 17.

Organisation (as appropriate) that their signing, ratification or accession had regard to the Recommendation.

17.4.16.2 Background to the Recommendation

The Commission proposed the Recommendation. The Economic and Social Committee delivered its opinion on 21 June 1978 and the European Parliament also delivered its opinion.[43]

Earlier, the European Council on 7 and 8 April 1978 declared that the prevention of and the fight against marine pollution, particularly from hydrocarbons, must be a major objective for Community action. The Council had also asked the Council of Ministers (acting on the basis of a proposal from the Commission) and the Member States to take appropriate measures without delay within the Community and to adopt common attitudes in the appropriate international bodies on the swift implementation of existing international rules in this area, in particular, those regarding the minimum standards for the operation of ships.

17.4.16.3 Conventions referred to in the Recommendation

The Conventions referred to in the Recommendation were (a) the 1973 international Convention for the Prevention of Pollution by Ships (MARPOL); (b) the 1974 international Convention for the Safety of Life at Sea (SOLAS)[44]; (c) the 1976 ILO Convention No. 147 Concerning Minimum Standards in Merchant Ships[45]; (d) the 1978 Protocol relating to the 1974 international Convention for the Safety of Life at Sea; and, (e) the 1978 MARPOL Protocol.

17.4.17 1978: measures relating to titanium dioxide

Titanium dioxide is a highly pollutant agent which is used in a variety of industries such as the plastics and paints industries. If titanium dioxide has contact with sea water than it becomes a highly destructive red mud.

On 20 February 1978, the Council of Ministers adopted Directive 78/176 on waste from the titanium dioxide industry.[46] The Directive has since been amended. The aim of the Directive is "the prevention and progressive reduction, with a view to its elimination, of pollution caused by waste from the titanium dioxide industry".[47]

Member States are obliged to

> "take the necessary measures to ensure that waste is disposed of without endangering human health and without harming the environment, and in particular:
> — without risk to water, air, soil and plants and animals;
> — without deleteriously affecting beauty-spots or the countryside."[48]

43. OJ C163, 10 July 1978, p. 17.
44. Member States which had not already done so were recommended by Recommendation 78/584/EEC to sign, ratify or accede to (as the case may be) the SOLAS Convention as soon as possible and, in any event, by 1 January 1979.
45. Member States which had not already done so were recommended by Recommendation 78/584/EEC to ratify or accede to the ILO Convention by 1 April 1979.
46. OJ L54/19.
47. Dir. 78/176, Article 1(1).
48. Dir. 78/176, Article 2.

The "discharge, dumping, storage, tipping and injection of waste are prohibited unless prior authorisation is issued by the competent authority of the Member State in whose territory the waste is produced. Prior authorisation must also be issued by the competent authority of the Member State".[49] This authorisation may only be for a limited period but it may be renewed.[50]

The surveillance and monitoring of disposal is covered by Annex II of the Directive.

17.4.18 Recommendation 79/114 on the ratification of the 1978 international Convention on Standards of Training, Certification and Watchkeeping for Seafarers

This Recommendation recommended Member States to sign the 1978 international Convention on Standards of Training, Certification and Watchkeeping for Seafarers by 1 April 1979 and to ratify it as soon as possible and not later than 31 December 1980. The Member States were also recommended to inform the Secretary-General of the Inter-Governmental Maritime Consultative Organisation that they have signed and ratified the Convention in accordance with the Recommendation.

17.5 THE 1980s

17.5.1 1980–1982: port state control

In June 1980 the Commission proposed a Directive on Port State Control. Discussions began in the Council's group of experts. The French Government short-circuited the work of this group by convening in Paris, in December 1980, a regional conference of the ministers of the nine maritime EC States as well as Norway, Spain, Sweden and Portugal.[51] This Paris Conference set up a Working Group. On 26 January 1982, the maritime authorities of the relevant States approved the Group's work and a Memorandum of Understanding on Port State Control in Implementing Agreements on Maritime Safety and Protection of the Maritime Environment was adopted and entered into force on 1 July 1982.[52] This Memorandum embodied much of the proposals of the Commission.

The Memorandum recognises that the "principal responsibility for the effective application of standards laid down in international instruments rests upon the authorities of the State whose flag a ship is entitled to fly"[53] but recognises nonetheless "that effective action by port States is required to prevent the operation of substandard ships".[54]

Under the Memorandum, the maritime authority of each of the parties to the Memorandum agreed to maintain an effective system of port state control with a view to ensuring that, without discrimination as to flag, foreign merchant ships visiting its State comply with the standards laid down in the relevant instruments as defined in

49. Dir. 78/176, Article 4(1).
50. Dir. 78/176, Article 4(2).
51. The Final Declaration of the Conference underlined the need to increase maritime safety and the protection of the marine environment as well as the importance of improving living and working conditions on board ships.
52. [1982] 21 ILM 1.
53. Memorandum, Preamble.
54. *Ibid.*

Section 2[55] of the Memorandum. These relevant instruments were the 1966 international Convention on Load Lines; the 1974 international Convention for the Safety of Life at Sea; the 1978 Protocol relating to the international Convention for the Safety of Life at Sea; the 1973 international Convention for the Prevention of Pollution from Ships as modified by the 1978 Protocol; the 1978 international Convention on Standards of Training, Certification and Watchkeeping for Seafarers; the 1972 Convention on the International Regulations for Preventing Collisions at Sea; and the 1976 ILO Merchant Shipping (Minimum Standards) Convention.

17.5.2 Commission Decision 80/686 setting up an advisory committee on the control and reduction of pollution caused by hydrocarbons discharged at sea

Commission Decision 80/686 set up an advisory committee on the control and reduction of pollution caused by hydrocarbons discharged at sea.

17.5.3 1982: United Nations Convention on the Law of the Sea (UNCLOS III)

While the United Nations Convention on the Law of the Sea (UNCLOS III)[56] has received a mixed reaction, there can be little doubt of the laudatory nature of its provisions relating to the marine environment. Its relevance at this juncture is the participation by the EC in the UNCLOS III Conference.

Article 192 (entitled "General Obligation") provides: "States have the obligation to protect and preserve the marine environment."

Article 193 (entitled "Sovereign right of States to exploit their natural resources") balances the environmental duty with the right to exploit natural resources. It provides:

> "States have the sovereign right to exploit their natural resources pursuant to their environmental policies and in accordance with their duty to protect and preserve the marine environment."

17.5.4 1983: Communication

In 1983, a Commission Communication was published and it concerned the granting of financial support for pilot projects for the control and reduction of pollution caused by hydrocarbons discharged at sea.[57]

17.5.5 1983: Council Recommendation on SAR

On 25 July 1983, the EEC Council recommended in Recommendation 83/419/EEC that inasmuch as they have not already done so, the Member States ratify or accede to the 1979 International Convention on Maritime Search and Rescue as soon as they can.

17.5.6 1985: Single European Act amended the EEC Treaty

The adoption of the Single European Act (SEA) was a critical step in the development of EC environmental law because it amended the EEC Treaty so as to expressly provide

55. Memorandum, Section 1.2.
56. [1982] 21 ILM 1261.
57. OJ L194/17, 19 July 1978.

for environmental protection. In specific terms, Article 25 of the SEA inserted a new Title to the Treaty, namely, Title VII to Part Three.

Article 130r of the EEC Treaty (as amended) reads:

"1. Action by the Community relating to the environment shall have the following objectives:
— to preserve, protect and improve the quality of the environment
— to contribute towards protecting human health;
— to ensure a prudent and rational utilization of natural resources.

2. Action by the Community relating to the environment shall be based on the principles that preventive action should be taken, that environmental damage should as a priority be rectified at source, and that the polluter should pay. Environmental protection requirements shall be a component of the Community's other policies.

3. In preparing its action relating to the environment, the Community shall take account of:
— available scientific and technical data;
— environmental conditions in the various regions of the Community;
— the potential benefits and costs of action or lack of action;
— the economic and social development of the Community as a whole and the balanced development of its regions.

4. The Community shall take action relating to the environment to the extent to which the objectives referred to in paragraph 1 can be attained better at Community level than at the level of the individual Member States. Without prejudice to certain measures of a Community nature, the Member States shall finance and implement the other measures.

5. Within their respective spheres of competence, the Community and the Member States shall cooperate with third countries and with the relevant international organizations. The arrangements for Community co-operation may be the subject of agreements between the Community and the third parties concerned, which shall be negotiated and concluded in accordance with Article 228.

The previous paragraph shall be without prejudice to Member States' competence to negotiate in international bodies and to conclude international agreements."

Article 130r of the EEC Treaty (as amended) reads:

"The Council, acting unanimously on a proposal from the Commission and after consulting the European Parliament and the Economic and Social Committee, shall decide what action is to be taken by the Community.

The Council shall, under the conditions laid down in the preceding subparagraph, define those matters on which decisions are to be taken by a qualified majority."

Article 130t of the EEC Treaty (as amended) reads:

"The protective measures adopted in common pursuant to Article 130s shall not prevent any Member State from maintaining or introducing more stringent protective measures compatible with this Treaty."

17.5.7 1986: Community information system

Council Decision 86/85 established a Community information system for the control and reduction of pollution caused by the spillage of hydrocarbons and other harmful resources at sea.[58] Decision 88/346/EEC extended Decision 86/85 to inland waterways.[59]

This system was used in a number of instance. Most notably, the *Kowloon Bridge* and the *Capo Emma* off the south-western coasts of Ireland in 1986.

58. OJ No. L77/33, 22 March 1986.
59. OJ No. L158/32, 25 June 1988.

17.5.8 1987–1988: European Environmental Year

In March 1986, the European Council adopted a Resolution approving an action programme for the European Year of the Environment (March 1987 to March 1988).[60] This Resolution followed on from proposals forwarded by the Commission to the Council in February 1986.[61]

17.5.9 1987: The Fourth Action Programme[62]

The 1987–1992 Programme was adopted by way of a Resolution on 18 October 1987. It has been commented that the "fourth environmental action programme envisages the combating of marine pollution from specific or diffused sources, *inter alia*, by the implementation of Council Directive 76/464/EEC on dangerous substances . . . and by the general improvement of the Community's aquatic environment and, in particular, the North Sea and the Mediterranean."[63]

17.5.10 1987: European parliamentary question on the seaworthiness of vessels operating in Community waters

In 1987, Mr Thomas Raftery, then a Member of the European Parliament, asked the Commission the following question:

"Following the recent disaster involving the iron ore carrier 'Kowloon Bridge' off the south-west coast of Ireland and the near-disaster of the oil tanker 'Capo Emma' in the same area, what action will the Commission take to ensure higher standards of seaworthiness of vessels operating in Community waters?"

Stanley Clinton Davies, the Commissioner with responsibility for transport, responded:

"The honourable Member raises a very important question. May I begin by saying that I remain convinced that flag state control must remain the primary way of applying standards. Nonetheless, the development of port state enforcement is proving to be an effective way of combating the operation of substandard shipping.

The application of port state control in European waters under the Paris Memorandum of Understanding extends beyond the eleven European Community Maritime States to Norway, Sweden and Finland. No less than 10,000 ships are being inspected each year by these maritime authorities in order to ensure respect for the relevant international conventions.

The Commission is encouraged to note that the Canadian and United States coastguards are now making their inspection reports available to European authorities. Since Japan is also instituting a system of port state control, we should soon be in a position where it will be virtually impossible for a substandard ship to contemplate a visit to any Community port with any degree of equanimity.

I would not wish to give the impression that I am complacent about the progress of port state control. Indeed, two members of the Community are still a long way behind with their inspection timetable and I shall be keeping a close check on the progress that they make this year to meet their obligations.

Moreover, I am not convinced that enough is being done about the port state enforcement of ILO standards. It has been argued that it is more difficult for an inspector to check for compliance with International Labour Organization standards than with, for example, the Solas

60. OJ No. C46/1, 17 February 1983.
61. COM (86) 76 final. See Bull. EC No. 2 of 1986.
62. OJ 1987 C328/1.
63. Myles, *op. cit.*, p. 3–332.

Convention. There may be some truth in that, but it is not a justification for neglecting those standards altogether. Accordingly, the Commission intends to set up a small working party with the ILO, the port state control secretariat, ship owners and seafaring unions, to examine these practical problems in an attempt to draw up more positive guidelines to surveyors on these human aspects of the port state enforcement of international standards. So in this way we would hope to contribute to the eradication from Community ports and Community waters of shipping which is substandard in the widest sense of the word."

Mr Raftery continued:

"Thank you, Commissioner, for your very comprehensive answer. Could I ask, what proportion of the ships are being checked for seaworthiness, and whether a higher proportion of ships flying flags of convenience are being checked than ships flying normal national flags? Is the Commission going to be more active in this whole area in future in the light of the two serious disasters which occurred off the south coast of Ireland [and] one almost equally serious disaster which miraculously was just avoided?"

The Commissioner responded:

"I think I am right in saying that about 60% of ships visiting ports are in general terms now being checked. I stand to be corrected as to the exact proportion, but I think that is roughly the situation.

Yes, more flag of convenience ships are being inspected than has been the case hitherto. I have given an average figure for the number of inspections being carried out. Last year the figure in fact rose to something like 12,000 inspections. Just over 300 ships were detained or delayed until deficiencies were put right.

The number of flag of convenience vessels is higher than the number of Community ships but, nonetheless, it is a matter of grave concern to me that Community ships should be defying these essential safety standards. Community shipping of course has no right to derogate from those standards at all. So we are extremely vigilant about these matters. We shall continue to be and I hope that the number of inspections over the forthcoming years will be substantially increased."

17.5.11 Mediterranean

In November 1988, the Commission adopted a Communication on action to protect the Mediterranean marine environment. This was the so-called MEDSPA strategy.

17.5.12 Marine Science and Technology Programme (MAST) 1989–1992 [64]

The MAST programme from 1989 to 1992 is indicative of the level of research which is being carried either by or for the EC in the area of marine pollution.

17.6 THE 1990s

17.6.1 Introduction

The 1990s are the Green Years. Both the EC and its Member States have enacted laws and developed policies in this area at a pace never seen before. Sadly, few of them have any direct relevance for shipping.

64. OJ No. L200, 13 July 1989.

17.6.2 1990: European Environment Agency Regulation

Council of Ministers Regulation 1210/90 on the establishment of the European Environment Agency and the European Environment Information and Observation Network[65] was an important milestone. Yet it has not been able to achieve much in the marine environmental sphere.

17.6.3 1990 Resolution on the Prevention of Accidents causing Marine Pollution

17.6.3.1 Introduction

On 19 June 1990, the Council of Ministers adopted a Resolution[66] on the Prevention of Accidents Causing Marine Pollution.[67]

17.6.3.2 Background

The Council of Ministers sets out in its Preamble the thinking that went into adopting the Resolution.

The Council regretted the:

"great damage to the marine ecosystem of the Community caused by the discharge of more than 100,000 tonnes of mineral oil as a result of the accidents which occurred in the last fortnight of 1989 involving the tankers 'Aragon', flying the Spanish flag, and 'Khark-V', flying the Iranian flag, in the Atlantic waters near the archipelagoes of two Member States, as well as the accident involving the tanker 'Seawind Dos', of a similar nature."

The Council was conscious that such damage could give rise to calamitous consequences for fauna and flora and other natural resources of the area. It was also aware that such maritime accidents have aroused considerable public concern, threatening to undermine the legitimate use of the coasts for recreational purposes, with the resulting negative repercussions on the touristic resources of the Member States. The Council recalled the enormous material and environmental damage caused in various regions of the Community by other accidents of this nature, including the *Torrey Canyon* and the *Amoco Cadiz*.

The Council went on to say in the Preamble that it was:

"considering that the world fleet of VLCC[68] ships has aged and there is no prospect of its being renewed in the short term as well as the deterioration and lack of appropriate maintenance of a large number of VLCC tankers, and the additional factor of risky navigation in maritime zones in bad, and sometimes extreme meteorological conditions, and on highly congested traffic routes;

Conscious of the fact that the most appropriate method of combating maritime disasters is to insist on prevention as far as possibilities allow, bearing in mind that the most effective way of combating marine pollution is its prevention;

Conscious that the Community must be duly prepared to cope with this type of incident in Community waters and taking into account that the extent of the damage caused by pollution is directly related to the speed of response and the degree of coordination between the national and international services available . . ."

The Council went on to recognise that the IMO represents the focal point for preventing and combating marine pollution at the international level.

65. OJ 1990 L120/1.
66. Resolutions are not binding in EC law.
67. Res. 90/C 206/1.
68. *Ed.* i.e. very large crude carriers.

17.6.3.3 Ensuring that EC ships are safe

The first article of the Resolution provides that Member States will endeavour to provide themselves with an adequate and efficient maritime administration which is capable of ensuring strict compliance with the technical rules on safety at sea and the prevention of marine pollution by ships flying their flags, in accordance with the provisions of the relevant international Conventions, in particular the SOLAS and MARPOL Conventions.

17.6.3.4 Inspections on foreign ships docking in EC ports

The Resolution provides that the maritime administration of the Member States will intensify its inspections on foreign ships docking in Community ports in order to make sure, as far as possible, that they do not present an unacceptable risk to the safety of human life at sea or to the integrity of the marine ecosystem. In particular, they will in any case attain the objectives for a minimum number of inspections provided for in the Paris memorandum of Understanding on port State control.[69]

The Resolution calls on Member States to ensure that their maritime inspectors carry out, in the course of ensuring that EC ships are safe and the carrying out of inspections on foreign ships docking in EC ports, checks (particularly through the safe manning document) on the qualification of the people making up the crew of the ships (especially tankers).[70] In so doing, the Resolution calls on the Member States' maritime inspectors to have particular regard to the observance of rule 13 of Chapter V of the SOLAS Convention and the provisions of the STCW Convention of 1978.[71]

Member States are called upon by Article 4 of the Resolution to always give reciprocal support in identifying the origin of, monitoring and combating pollution by crude oil and other substances prejudicial to the Community's marine environment. In particular, the Member States will take the steps which might be considered necessary in order to guarantee that in the event of any maritime accident which threatens the ecosystem of the Community waters, a rapid, efficient and co-ordinated response is given by all Member States' administrations, bringing to bear the most appropriate and accessible means in accordance with the circumstances.[72]

17.6.3.5 Requests for the Commission to act

The Resolution calls on the Commission to start promoting and improving the instrument of Community action organised in the form of the "task force", providing it with the necessary resources and the precise functions required for co-ordination and rapidity of response.[73]

The Resolution also called on the Commission to continue as a matter of urgency with its research task with regard to the project for the establishment of a system of safety at sea, based on control posts and shore-based navigation aid systems, in accordance with the general framework of COST projects 301 and 311, with the aim of providing proper protection for waters which are essential routes for the Community's maritime traffic.[74]

69. Article 2.
70. Resolution, Article 3.
71. Resolution, Article 3.
72. Resolution, Article 4.
73. Resolution, Article 5.
74. Resolution, Article 6

17.6.4 Environmental Information Directive

The Council has adopted a Directive on the freedom of access to information on the environment[75] but is of relatively marginal significance in the context of the marine environment.

17.6.5 Shipment of radioactive wastes

The Commission has proposed new rules in relation to the transport of radioactive wastes.[76]

17.6.6 North Sea

In February 1991, the EC Commission published a proposal on specific action (NORSPA) for the coastal waters and the coastal areas of the Irish Sea, North Sea, Baltic Sea and the North-East Atlantic Ocean.[77] The programme would specifically protect these coastal waters and areas. The Commission anticipated the expenditure of about 10m ECU during its first two years.

17.7 CONCLUSION

Where does all this lead to? The EC constitutes a single internal environment. The environment never recognises the political boundaries of the Member States, thus it is only inevitable that the EC should have a key role to play in regard to the protection of the environment.

The role of the EC is strengthened by the willingness of many individuals and common-interest groupings to notify violations, propose new rules and generally develop the law.[78] None the less, there is an interesting balance to be struck between the willingness of the EC to be involved in environmental matters and its aims in the fields of economics and society.[79]

Sadly, the EC has not proved to be effective enough in the area of the marine environment. Certainly, projects such as the Blue Flag have proved useful but in terms of the "big picture" one must say that the EC has not been as effective as it could be. But perhaps it has been as effective as its Member States have let it be. While the Commission and the Council have significant legislative roles, both the Parliament and the Court of Justice will have to contribute substantially to the development of the law in this area, if there is to be any progress at all.[80]

75. COM (90) 91 final; OJ 1990 No. C102/6.
76. COM (89) 559, OJ C5, 10 January 1990.
77. COM (90) 498.
78. See Case 187/87 *Saarland and Others v. Ministry of Commerce and Others* [1989] 1 CMLR 529.
79. The EC Commission has stated (*Commission Work Programme for 1990*, para. 142) that it is "no longer possible to maintain the quality of life and sustain economic growth without taking account of the environment".
80. In regard to the ECJ, see, for example, Case 302/86 *Commission v. Denmark* [1989] 1 CMLR 619.

CHAPTER 18

Shipbuilding

18.1 INTRODUCTION

The purpose of this chapter is to review the EC law relating to shipbuilding,[1] including the State aids granted to shipbuilding and the Reneval Programme for shipyards.

A State's policy on shipbuilding can normally be directly related to its policy on shipping generally[2]—thus, for example, a State wishing to foster and maintain its shipping fleet may also support its shipbuilding industry and, conversely, a State wishing to bolster its shipbuilding industry may oblige its shipping companies to build a portion of their ships in home yards and may provide aid to facilitate this protectionism.

The plight of shipbuilding in the EC is in large measure dependent on the plight of EC shipping: shipbuilding in the EC is very dependent on the fortunes of EC shipping.

A vital and competitive shipbuilding industry is strategically important for the EC. The Preamble to the Seventh Shipbuilding Directive[3] states:

> "a competitive shipbuilding industry is of vital interest to the Community and contributes to its economic and social development by providing a substantial market for a range of industries, including those using advanced technology; whereas it contributes also to the maintenance of employment in a number of regions, including some which are already suffering a high rate of unemployment; whereas this is also true of ship conversion and ship repair."

This chapter should be read in conjunction with Chapter 15 on State Aids.

18.2 COMMERCIAL OVERVIEW

On 23 December 1976, the European Parliament's Committee on Economic and Monetary Affairs published its Interim Report on the Community Shipping Industry.[4] The Report stated:

1. The term "shipbuilding" is used to include ship conversion and ship repair (unless the context requires otherwise).

2. Bredima-Savopoulou and Tzoannos, *The Common Shipping Policy of the EEC* (1990), p. 54 *et seq.*; Bredima and Tzoannos, "In Search of a Common Shipping Policy for the EEC" (1981) 20 JCMS 95, at 111–112; EC, *Panorama of EC Industry 1989*, Chapter 15. See also "Plans to Help Former Shipyard Areas", *Lloyd's List*, 17 July 1987, p. 1; "European Call for Sanctions in Shipbuilding", *Lloyd's List*, 23 October 1987, p. 1; "Japan set to abolish shipyard subsidies", *Lloyd's List*, 10 December 1991, p. 1. See also the EC Commission's Press Release, "Commission to Investigate Aid to Greek Shipbuilding" (IP(89)235).

3. Dir.90/684/EEC, OJ L380/27, 31 December 1990. See para. 19.9.7, below. The Preamble to the Third Shipbuilding Directive (Dir.75/432/EEC) had read: "Whereas a sound and competitive shipbuilding industry is necessary to the Community; whereas it contributes to its economic and social development, by providing a substantial market for a range of sectors, including those using advanced technology, and as an employer in a number of Community regions; whereas this is also the case with ship conversion and ship repair . . .".

4. Doc. 479/76, Rapporteur: Mr J. L. Prescott.

"37. The shipbuilding industry is extremely important to the Community, directly employing more than 400,000 people, and also providing work for a further one million or so in various supply industries, whose deliveries of goods or services represent about 60% of shipyard turnover.

The industry is also extremely important for regional policy, as it is often located in regions where the structure of industry is scarcely diversified.[5] In 1975 almost 8 million grt was completed in Community shipyards, the largest producers being Germany (some 2m grt) followed by the UK, Denmark, France, Italy and the Netherlands (in order of importance, each producing around 1m grt). In comparison, Japan produced almost 17m grt, and the rest of the world 9m."

Shipbuilding enjoyed a boom during the 1960s and early 1970s. Such a boom was caused by the success experienced and the growth expected in the world's economies during that time. During 1974–6, production was about 33 million grt.[6] However, a depression began in the mid 1970s. Between 1976 and 1979, vessel completions around the world fell by some 37 per cent. However, in the EC, this decline was some 42 per cent.[7] By the late 1980s, the crisis was serious and almost irreversible.[8]

So why did this depression occur around the world? Such was the increase in orders that the crisis of the mid 1970s and 1980s might well have occurred due to over-capacity, even without the oil crises of 1973 and 1978.

There has been a huge decline in the fortunes of shipbuilding in the EC. In 1976, the volume of output totalled 5,927 million cgrt[9,10] but, by 1987, this had fallen to 1,719 million cgt.[11,12] This was more than a three-fold drop and when translated into the EC's position in the world of shipbuilding, it meant a decline from 26.8 per cent of world production to 18.6 per cent.[13]

In employment terms, 273,000 people were employed in EC shipyards in 1980, but this had fallen to 139,000 working in 71 yards by 1987.[14] The crisis in shipbuilding meant that there were large-scale redundancies during the 1970s and early 1980s. In the EC, employment declined by some 36 per cent between 1975 and 1979.[15] The numbers employed in new shipbuilding in 1987[16] were as follows:

Belgium	2,548
Denmark	7,000
Germany	12,875
Greece	1,621
France	8,940
Ireland	n/a

5. See "Communication from the Commission to the Council on Shipbuilding", 26 May 1976 (COM(76)224 final).
6. *Ibid.*, para. 2.
7. Lloyd's figure: Bredima and Tzoannos (1981) 20 JCMS 95, at p. 111.
8. Newspaper coverage of this issue includes "Yard Crisis to Cost 45,000 EEC Jobs", *Lloyd's List*, 24 August 1987, p. 1.
9. CGRT means compensated gross registered tonnes—coefficient 1978.
10. See *Panorama of EC Industry 1989*, p. 15–1.
11. CGT means compensated gross tons—coefficient 1984.
12. See *Panorama of EC Industry 1989*, p. 15–1.
13. In terms of the vessels actually built in the EC, it is worth noting that they are mainly in the categories of passenger vessels (in particular, ferries) and other non-cargo carrying vessels such as fishing vessels. See *Panorama of EC Industry 1989*, p. 15–2.
14. See *Panorama of EC Industry 1989*, p. 15–1.
15. Commission of the European Communities, *Report on the State of the Shipbuilding Industry in the Community*, COM(80)443 final.
16. See *Panorama of EC Industry 1989*, p. 15–4.

Italy	9,500
Luxembourg	n/a
Netherlands	3,600
Portugal	5,020
Spain	17,300
UK	8,000

In part, the EC yards were not to blame for this decline. There has been an over-capacity in recent years: between 1973 and 1987, worldwide fleet volume has increased by 30 per cent, but transport volume has decreased by 10 per cent.[17] On the other hand, much of the decline in the fortunes of EC yards was due to the competitive pressure from South-East Asian and Japanese yards who benefited from (at the very least) economies of scale and links with other industries. South Korean yards benefited from government subsidies and low labour costs—for example, hourly labour costs in 1987 amounted to ECU17 per hour in South Korea, but some ECU62 in the Netherlands, ECU69 in Germany and ECU34 in the UK. The Commission in its Communication to the Council of Ministers, Reorganisation of the Community Shipbuilding Industry,[18] stated that the "difficulties in new shipbuilding result from a world-wide structural imbalance between production capacity and demand; they are relatively worse for the Community industry on account of the competitive weakness of Community shipyards in comparison with non-European competitors". More thoroughly, the decline may be attributed to seven major reasons. First, and foremost, while production facilities in some Member States had been modernised, EC shipbuilding was structurally inefficient. Secondly, there were a large number of yards in the EC. Thirdly, the competitors in Japan were integrated into large industrial groups which could economically shelter the yards during bad times. Fourthly, wages and social security costs were very high in the EC.[19] Fifthly, the decline in the EC fleet meant that as many owners placed their orders close to home, there was a consequential decline in the orders placed at EC shipyards. Sixthly, currency depreciation played its part. Seventhly, smaller scale production in the EC was not as efficient as the South-East Asian competitors.

On 12 May 1976, the EC Member States, and Norway, Sweden, Finland, Spain, Portugal and Japan, signed, under the auspices of the OECD,[20] the so-called "General Guidelines for Government Policies in the Shipbuilding Industry". This agreement was designed to restore, in the medium term, the balance between supply and demand.

The EC sought to intervene and solve the problem as well. Bredima-Savopoulou and Tzoannos commented in 1981:

> "The Commission's intervention with respect to the problems of shipbuilding has three dimensions: (a) it attempts to harmonise government subsidies to the shipbuilding sector within the Community, (b) it has proposed a number of measures at Community level which would encourage the shipbuilding industry to undertake the necessary structural changes in order to become competitive in the world market, whilst at the same time boosting demand in order to alleviate the social consequences of the crisis and (c) it has taken action at international level to induce other countries, especially Japan, to try and reduce shipbuilding overcapacity."

---

17. See *Panorama of EC Industry 1989*, p. 15–1.
18. 9 December 1977, Bull. EC, Supp. 7/77, para. 1, footnote omitted.
19. See Communication, para. 3.
20. On the OECD and shipping, see Chapter 1, above.

18.2.1 Protectionist practices

Individual EC Member States responded in a number of ways to the crisis in shipbuilding. First, some directed their navies and State shipping companies to place orders at home as opposed to foreign shipyards. Secondly, some Member States gave aid either to their shipyards (to subsidise prices), or shipping companies (to subsidise costs) or both. The aid given was huge,[21] but perhaps not very effective. Thirdly, individual yards made staff redundant and restricted recruitment. Such nationalist approaches could only go so far in attempting to solve an international crisis. There was need for action by the world shipbuilding community generally.

Individual shipyards responded by banning overtime, introducing short-time working, reducing working hours and curbing new recruitment.

In Italy, the State-owned shipping group, Finmare, has to place its orders for new ships with the state-owned shipbuilding group, Fincantieri.

In Portugal, new ships to be built by Portuguese companies have to be built in Portuguese yards.

As a general rule, shipyards in EC Member States rely quite heavily on orders from shipping companies in their own Member State.[22]

18.3 1977 COMMUNICATION ON SHIPBUILDING

On 9 December 1977, the Commission sent a Communication to the Council of Ministers on the Reorganisation of the Community Shipbuilding Industry.[23] Such an initiative was necessary because the EC's shipbuilding industry was in serious difficulties: there were serious fears for the jobs of many of the 165,000 employed in EC shipyards.[24] This Communication dealt with three main issues: the problems of EC shipbuilding; the objectives of EC intervention; and EC action.

18.3.1 Problems of EC shipbuilding

The problems of EC shipbuilding may be expressed in these terms: in 1960, the first nine Member States of the EC represented 50.9 per cent of the world's shipbuilding output; by 1970, this had fallen to 27.8 per cent and, by 1975, it had fallen to 22.3 per cent.[25] The Communication recognised that the EC had a shipbuilding crisis[26] and that this crisis was particularly bad for the EC in the light of the competitive weakness of EC shipyards in comparison with non-EC competitors,[27] particularly, the South-East Asian yards.

In the Communication, the Commission stated that its interest in the problem of shipbuilding has "two aspects", namely:

"— competition: so far Community action on the industry has been almost entirely limited to successive directives coordinating aids to shipbuilding. Their main objective was to

21. See Communication, para. 7.
22. Bredima-Savopoulou and Tzoannos, *op. cit.*, p. 58.
23. Bull.EC, Supp. 7/77.
24. See Communication, para. 12.
25. The European Parliament's Committee on Economic and Monetary Affairs published its Interim Report on the Community Shipping Industry, para. 38.
26. *Ibid.*, para. 1.
27. *Ibid.*, para. 1.

harmonise public intervention in the sector and reduce the level of those aids most damaging to intra-Community competition;
— financial: since its inception, the European Regional Development Fund (ERDF) has paid out an estimated 78.65 million u.a. in regions where there is a high concentration of shipbuilding. The sum covers 225 projects involving a total investment of 1,470 million u.a. and the creation or preservation of 34,112 jobs in France, Germany, Italy and in the United Kingdom where, in addition, 111 industrial-infrastructure projects have been aided in the said regions."

"Intervention by the Social Fund to benefit workers in the industry has been modest and the Council did not take up the Commission's proposal for applying Art. 4 of the decision on the use of the Social Fund,[28] submitted in January 1974."[29,30]

18.3.2 Objectives of EC intervention

The Communication identified that the first objective of EC policy on shipbuilding must be to make EC yards competitive in the world market.[31] Thus it wrote in 1977, the EC's "attention should be directed chiefly to the new building of seagoing non-naval ships,[32] since this is the segment of the industry in which the structural problem of overcapacity and competitiveness is acute. The other sub-sectors, while less affected by the structural problem, are more sensitive to the short-term economic situation". Thus, the Communication continued, there was a need to reorganise the yards in the EC so that they are competitive in the world market.

In the debate on the balance between the interests of the shipping industry and the shipbuilding industry, the Commission declared "[a]s the cost of transport is a very important factor in the Community's economy, the Commission does not consider that the interests of the shipping industry should in any way be subordinated to those of shipbuilders".[33]

The Commission was of the opinion that there was a need for a quantitative and qualitative adjustment of structures to foreseeable demand. It said that "[q]uantitatively, it will be necessary, in the industry's own interests as well as in the interests of the workers whose jobs in the shipyards will otherwise disappear entirely, to adjust production capacities to market prospects in an orderly fashion" and "[q]uantitatively, moves to adapt production capacities quantitatively must be accompanied by efforts to improve production facilities so that they may survive without aid and become competitive in the world market."[34]

It is interesting to note the views of the Commission in relation to employment:

"13. Once the objective of reorganisation has been defined for the industry, the consequences for employment must be drawn; these will be of two kinds:
— retraining of workers within yards where the latter undertake internal conversion as part of the qualitative adaptation of production facilities;
— redeployment outside the industry: here the Community should bring into play all its resources for creating jobs outside shipbuilding, both within the yards themselves and,

28. OJ L28 of 4 February 1971.
29. OJ C13 of 12 February 1974.
30. Communication, para. 9.
31. *Ibid.*, para. 10.
32. At this stage it does not seem appropriate to include warships because the building of these highly sophisticated vessels is not affected by the crisis.
33. Communication, para. 10.
34. Communication, para. 11.

more particularly, for those made redundant, every effort being made to site the activities in the same district or region as the affected yards, so that these new activities may benefit from the skills of the workers concerned; this process of creating new jobs must be accompanied by suitable social measures.

In view of an expected level of demand of about 2.4 million cgrt[35] in the early 1980s, the Commission estimates that an effective restructuring operation in this sector could affect approximately 75,000 jobs. 15,000 of which it is estimated will be vacated by natural wastage. If the operation is extended to directly related industries, these would be affected in the same proportion which would make approximately 30,000 persons redundant.

14. As such results can only be achieved gradually, it will be necessary to continue to resort to holding actions which are essential for the direct or indirect support of employment.

The Commission considers that, if the objective is to be achieved, Community action would be acceptable to the general public and to the workers only if it takes full account of the different situations in the industry in each Member State, and the position the industry occupies in the economy of the Member State or region. Whether this operation will be used to demonstrate the Community's solidarity will depend on the political will of the Council."[36]

The Communication mentioned that there was the transfer of a significant proportion of the world fleet to flags of convenience and this "has brought into the shipping market vessels which present both operating hazards (substandard ships) and a threat to the marine environment".[37] The Commission then recorded that international bodies were then "trying to devise means of combating this form of unfair competition. The Community should step up the action it is already taking in this direction by taking steps towards the adoption of practical measures in the near future".[38] It went on to suggest that "[c]ertain environmental measures could lead to a partial reduction of the excess capacity in tanker fleets and also appreciably stimulate the conversion of existing tankers"[39] and more "stringent safety regulations would remove unfair advantages enjoyed by ships of non-member countries, particularly those registered under flags of convenience, and thus act to the advantage of the shipbuilding industry, either directly (conversions and repairs), or indirectly (ships would be scrapped more quickly, and this would speed up the improvement of the transport market). Such regulations could also limit the trend for our shipowners to register their vessels under flags of convenience".[40]

18.3.4 EC action

The Commission identified certain key courses of action which were indispensable for the successful reorganisation of the EC shipbuilding industry. These indispensable courses of action were:

"— since (private or public) initiatives in the Member States do not cancel one another out the Commission continues with, and steps up, its measures to make these initiatives less opaque and to co-ordinate them;
— the intervention concentrates less and less on maintaining hopeless situations and turns increasingly to re-establishing maximum efficiency in the undertakings and, above all, to creating new jobs in other activities;
— contacts with all the parties concerned are maintained and strengthened; the Commission is already in regular contact with employer, managerial and trade union

35. Compensated gross registered tonnes—coefficient 1978.
36. Communication, p. 10 (footnote omitted).
37. *Ibid.*, para. 15.
38. *Ibid.*, para. 16.
39. *Ibid.*, para. 16 (footnote omitted).
40. *Ibid.*, para. 16.

bodies and these contacts should be intensified; also, to obtain a clearer appreciation of the possibilities of meeting the type likely to face Community shipyards, these contacts should be extended to the industrial and trade union organisations concerned with Community shipping;

— there is greater, permanent concentration between the Community's public authorities under Community auspices and with due regard for the spheres of competence deriving from the EEC Treaty;

— Community action continues, with appropriate procedures, throughout the crisis situation in the industry."[41]

In terms of reorganising the shipbuilding sector, the Commission believed that reorganisation was contingent upon the determination of a quantitative "indicator" of the level of demand to which the shipbuilding industry's production should be geared—with such an indicator being geared to demand.[42]

The topic of shipbuilding aids is a controversial one[43] and the comments of the Commission in the Communication deserve repetition in full:

"In order to avoid the situation whereby national aids granted to undertakings—in the vain hope of a recovery in the near future—divert the recipients' attention from the need to modernise their production facilities—a necessary condition of stability in Community shipbuilding—the Commission, in its proposal for a fourth directive, sought to co-ordinate these aids with a view to reorganising the sector in a manner consistent with the quantitative indicator.

With previous directives the Community tried to remove those barriers to competition in shipbuilding which were not in the common interest. The directives therefore covered a very wide range of aids affecting the shipbuilding market.

Against the current background of imminent crisis in the industry the Commission has now made proposals specifically geared to enabling the Member States to deal with the situation.[44]

Such measures are, however, acceptable only within limits and only in so far as they do not worsen conditions of competition to an extent prejudicial to the common interest.

Measures of this type must also be in line with the reorganisation objectives, the aim of which is to make the industry competitive and capable of functioning without aid.

The Commission's proposal for a fourth directive, sent to the Council on 4 November 1977, takes abundant account of the industry's structural problems and should therefore not be regarded simply as a legal framework for limiting the granting of aids but as an essential element of an industrial approach.

The proposal also covers Member States' aids to shipowners and provides that such aids may not discriminate against shipyards of other Member States."[45]

18.3.4.1 Committee

The Commission concluded by calling on the Council of Ministers to set up, in order to permit a better understanding of the shipbuilding sector and its problems at an EC level, a standing body in the form of a committee of senior officials briefed to contribute to the progressive adjustment of production capacities to demand, as far as possible on the basis of national programmes, but taking account of changes in forecast worldwide supply and demand.[46] This Committee would be known as the Shipbuilding Committee and would advise the Council and the Commission as well as contribute towards the co-ordination of national and EC policies.[47] The purpose of the

41. *Ibid.*, para. 19.
42. *Ibid.*, para. 20.
43. See Chapter 15, above.
44. Bull.EC, 10–1977, point 2.1.19.
45. Communication, para. 21.
46. Communication, para. 31. See Proposal for a Council decision setting up a Shipbuilding Committee, annexed to the Communication.
47. See Article 1 of the Proposal for a Council Decision setting up a Shipbuilding Committee, appended to the Reorganisation of the Community Shipbuilding Industry, ibid., at p. 21.

Committee would be, according to the Proposal, to monitor trends in the level of demand and contribute towards organising the adjustment of production capacities to that level and improving production structures.[48]

18.4 1978 COUNCIL OF MINISTERS RESOLUTION

In 1978, the Council of Ministers adopted a resolution stressing the need to maintain within the EC a competitive and healthy shipbuilding industry.[49] The Resolution also stressed the need to make qualitative and quantitative adjustments to the shipbuilding sector. Directive 81/363 later summarised the Resolution as stressing "the need to maintain within the Community a healthy and competitive shipbuilding industry whose scale of activity should be consistent with the size of the Community's seaborne trade and respect its economic, social and strategic importance".[50]

18.5 COMMISSION PROPOSAL

The 1978 Council Resolution[51] led to the Commission proposing a scheme to promote the scrapping and building of new ships of new vessels in EC yards. This proposal was embodied in a Communication from the Commission to the Council on a Scheme to Promote the Scrapping and Building of Ocean-Going Ships.[52] By 1981, not accepted.

18.6 FIRST REPORT ON SHIPBUILDING

In 1979 the Commission published its first half-yearly report on shipbuilding.[53]

18.7 1986 PARLIAMENTARY RESOLUTION

On 11 September 1986, the European Parliament resolved that (a) an integrated approach of financing a ship-and-build policy should be adopted and (b) there was need to identify the nature of the demand for shipbuilding and shipyard services. More specifically, the Parliament proposed:

> "(i) a *scrap and build policy* based on Articles 92, 93 and 94 of the [EEC] Treaty which provides for aids granted by States compatible with the Common Market, such as aids to shipbuilding with a view of eliminating surplus capacity, of modernising the shipyards and of promoting economic development;
>
> (ii) a system of Community *investment incentives* that would replace direct and indirect subsidies of national governments to shipowners with a view of creating a climate which would encourage Community shipowners to place orders with Community shipyards;

48. See Article 2 of the Proposal for a Council Decision setting up a Shipbuilding Committee, appended to the Reorganisation of the Community Shipbuilding Industry, *ibid.*, at p. 21.
49. OJ C229/1, 27 September 1978.
50. Dir. 81/363/EEC, Recital 3.
51. See above.
52. *Bulletin of the European Communities*, Supp. 7/79.
53. Supp. 7/79, Bull.EC.

(iii) an *integrated system of financing* the scrap-and-build policy from Community sources such as the European Regional Development Fund, the Social Fund, the scheme offered by the European Investment Bank and the New Community Instrument with a view of encouraging Community shipowners to flag-in Community registries by reducing their fixed costs and by offering incentives through a coordinated package of financing aimed at reducing flagging-out."[54]

18.8 1987 COMMISSION COMMUNICATION ON SHIPBUILDING

The Commission forwarded a Second Communication on shipbuilding to the Council of Ministers on 31 July 1987.[55] The Communication took the Sixth Council Directive on Shipbuilding as its base.

18.8.1 Key proposals

The Commission proposed two measures:

(a) a Community programme under the European Regional Development Fund designed to benefit reconversion in shipbuilding areas and involving ECU200m during the period 1988 to 1990;
(b) a specific Community programme of accompanying social measures intended to benefit workers in shipbuilding, made redundant or threatened with redundancy, and involving ECU71.5m during the period 1988 to 1990.

18.8.2 Reaction to the communication

The European Parliament's Committee on Budgets in its Opinion on Shipbuilding[56] that the Second Communication was "the first to contain a realistic analysis of the future marketing potential of the Community shipbuilding industry". The Committee, while welcoming the Reneval Programme, thought that the timetable for the Programme was vague and needed a longer time-frame (in specific terms, five years).

18.9 RENEVAL PROGRAMME

18.9.1 Introduction

Regulation 2506/88 (the Reneval Regulation) instituted a Community programme (the "Reneval Programme") to assist the conversion of shipbuilding areas.[57] It was not, however, the first programme: the Council adopted Regulation 2617/80 on 7 October 1980[58] so as to institute a specific Community regional development measure contributing to overcoming constraints on the development of new economic activities in certain zones adversely affected by restructuring of the shipbuilding programme.

54. As summarised by the Committee on Transport in its Opinion on Shipbuilding (Ser.A, Doc.A2–66/68).
55. COM(87)275 final.
56. Ser.A, Doc.A2–26/88.
57. OJ L225/24, 15 August 1988. It resulted from a Commission proposal (OJ C291/8, 31 October 1987) which was opined on by the European Parliament (OJ C187, 18 July 1988), as well as the Economic and Social Committee (OJ C356/49, 31 December 1987).
58. OJ L271/16, 15 January 1980.

The Reneval Programme resulted from a Commission proposal in 1987.[59,60] It is best seen in the light of the Council's Regulation on the European Regional Development Fund.[61] Article 7(4) of that Regulation provides "for participation by the [European Regional Development] Fund in Community programmes the purpose of which is to help in solving serious problems affecting the socio-economic situation in one or more regions and which are designed to provide a better link between the Community's objectives for the structural development or conversion of regions and the objectives of other Community policies".[62] There has been a reduction in shipbuilding, ship conversion and ship repair capacity in the EC, and an even greater reduction in employment in those activities.[63] The Regulation recites:

> "a number of areas in the Community which are highly dependent on shipbuilding and which have already suffered major job losses as a result of the decline in shipbuilding are likely to see a worsening of these adverse consequences;
> the Community should support the effort which must be made to replace jobs lost as a result of restructuring through the development of new sources of appropriate employment in other sectors in the regions affected."[64]

18.9.2 Establishment of the Reneval Programme

Article 1 of the Reneval Regulation provides:

> "A Community programme within the meaning of Article 7 of the Fund Regulation that makes a major contribution to the conversion of certain declining industrial regions in the Community adversely affected by the restructuring of the shipbuilding industry is hereby established."

In this context, the "Fund Regulation" means Regulation 1787/84.[65]

The Reneval Regulation entered into force on 16 August 1988.[66]

18.9.3 Purpose of the Reneval Programme

Article 2 of the Reneval Regulation succinctly states the purpose of the Programme:

> "The purpose of the Community programme shall be to contribute, in the areas concerned, to the removal of obstacles to the development of new, job-creating economic activities. To this end, the programme shall provide for the implementation of a series of consistent, multiannual measures aimed at improving the infrastructure and the physical and social environment in the areas concerned, as well as the establishment of new activities, the growth of small and medium-sized undertakings and the development of innovation. The Community programme shall thereby seek to provide a better link between the Community's objectives for the conversion of regions and the objectives of the Community's policy on shipbuilding."

18.9.4 Criteria and areas of application: Article 3(1)

Article 3(1)(a) provides that the Reneval Programme is concerned with those "areas which have experienced substantial job losses in shipbuilding in the past three years

59. See OJ C291/8, 31 October 1987 and the amendments forwarded on 19 May 1988 and 28 June 1988.
60. For the Parliament's Opinion, see OJ C187, 18 July 1988 and for the ECOSOC's Opinion, see OJ C356/49, 31 December 1987.
61. Regulation 1787/84 of 19 June 1984 (OJ L169/1, 28 June 1984).
62. In the words of the Second Recital to Regulation 2506/88.
63. Regulation 2506/88, Recital 3.
64. Regulation 2506/88, Recitals 4 and 5.
65. OJ L169/1, 28 June 1984.
66. Regulation 2506/88, Article 9.

and not earlier than 1 January 1984, or which are currently experiencing or threatened with such losses, whenever this sector determines their economic development, such losses resulting in a serious aggravation of unemployment in these areas".

The Reneval Programme also concerns:

"areas which correspond or belong to a NUTS level III territorial unit satisfying all the following criteria:

— the average rate of unemployment must have been above the recorded Community average in the last three years;
— the percentage share of industrial employment in total employment must have equalled or exceeded the Community average in any reference year since 1975 (included);
— there must have been an observable fall in industrial employment compared with the reference year chosen in accordance with the preceding incident".

but this is provided they also satisfy the sectoral criteria stated in Article 3(1)(a).

It is worth noting that the programme may be extended to adjoining areas satisfying the criteria set out in Article 3.[67] The Reneval Programme shall apply to those areas provided that the Commission reaches a decision to that effect.[68]

By way of an exception, in accordance with Article 3(3) of the Reneval Regulation, the Reneval Programme automatically applied to the Murcia region in Spain and the Setubal region in Portugal when the Reneval Regulation entered into force[69] because of the major job losses in shipbuilding which had occurred in those regions.

18.9.5 Decision-making process: Article 3(2)

The procedure for the application of the Reneval Programme was set out in Article 3(2) of the Reneval Regulation. A Member State had to submit an application to the Commission in respect of an area which may qualify under the Reneval Programme. Applications had to be submitted by 30 April 1990. They had to be supported by the requisite information, notably concerning job losses in shipbuilding. The Commission had to take its decision within three months of the date on which the Member State made its application.

Article 3(3) provided for an exceptional procedure. It stated that as soon as the Regulation entered into force, the Reneval Programme automatically applied to the areas in Spain and Portugal in which major job losses in shipbuilding have occurred in the years preceding the period used in Article 3(1), namely, the Murcia region in Spain and the Setubal area in Portugal.

18.9.6 Permitted activities for the Reneval Programme

Article 4 provides that the Fund may participate, under the Reneval Programme in operations such as those set out in Article 4 of Regulation 2617/80 with the exception of point 2 thereof.

18.9.7 Financing of the Reneval Programme

Article 5 of the Reneval Regulation provides that the programme is to be financed jointly by the Member State concerned and the EC.[70] Assistance from the Fund, which

67. Regulation 2506/88, Article 3(1).
68. Regulation 2506/88, Article 3(2).
69. I.e. 16 August 1988.
70. Regulation 2506/88, Article 5(1).

may not exceed 55 per cent of the total public expenditure taken into account in the programme, shall be provided from the appropriations entered for this purpose in the general budget of the EC.[71] The Community contribution for each type of operation may not, under Article 5(1) of the Reneval Regulation, exceed the rate fixed in Article 5(1) of Regulation 2617/80/EEC with the exception of point (b). With regard to the infrastructure referred to in the second paragraph of Article 4 of the Reneval Regulation, Community participation may be up to 50 per cent of public expenditure.[72]

Portugal is an exception to these general rules on financing. Article 5(2) of the Reneval Regulation provides that where the Community programme concerns areas in Portugal, the level of the Fund participation was to be increased until 31 December 1990 by twenty percentage points, subject to a ceiling of 70 per cent.

Article 8 of the Reneval Regulation provides that the amount of Fund assistance may not exceed the amount laid down by the Commission when adopting the programme agreement referred to in Article 13(1) of the Fund Regulation.

18.9.8 Form of the aid

All or part of the aid may be in the form of a capital grant or an interest subsidy.[73]

Aid granted under the Reneval Programme shall not be combined with aid granted for the same project under specific Community measures introduced pursuant to the former Fund Regulation 724/75/EEC or Regulation 3634/85/EEC.[74] Article 6(3) of the Reneval Regulation goes on to say that "the aid referred to in Article 5(1)(c) and (e) of Regulation 2617/80 and, where it benefits businesses directly, the aid referred to in Article 5(1)(g) of the said Regulation, may not have the effect of reducing the share of expenditure met by recipient businesses to less than 20 per cent of total expenditure".

18.9.9 Entities eligible for funding

Article 6(2) provides that the following shall be eligible for Fund assistance in respect of the operations referred to in Article 4 of the Reneval Regulation:

- (a) public authorities;
- (b) local and regional authorities;
- (c) local and regional development corporations;
- (d) other businesses, co-operatives or self-employed persons carrying on a productive activity.

18.9.10 Procedure

Article 7(1) of the Reneval Regulation provides that the programme of assistance drawn up by the competent authorities in the Member States concerned shall be sent to the Commission:

"(a) in respect of the areas referred to in Article 3(3),[75] within six months of the date of entry into force of this Regulation;

71. Regulation 2506/88, Article 5(1).
72. Regulation 2506/88, Article 5(1).
73. Regulation 2506/88, Article 6(1).
74. Regulation 2506/88, Article 6(1).
75. See Regulation 2506/88.

(b) in respect of the areas referred to in Article 3(2),[76] from the date on which the Member State submits an application relating to the areas which may qualify under the Community programme and at the latest within six months of the date of the Commission decision to be adopted pursuant to the said paragraph 2.

Where the Commission's decision relates to an area already referred to in Article 3(3) or covered by a Commission decision within the meaning of Article 3(2), the programme of assistance shall be adopted accordingly."

18.9.11 Duration of the programme

The duration of the programme of assistance may not extend beyond 31 December 1993.[77]

18.9.12 The Reneval Areas: the practice to date

It is useful to examine some examples.

18.9.12.1 France

18.9.12.1.1 Decision 90/205: Certain Coastal Zones of Le Havre, Dieppe and Fecamp

The coastal zone of the Le Havre, Dieppe and Fecamp employment areas as defined by the following canton:

"the 10 cantons of Le Havre, the cantons of Criquetot-L'Esneval."

18.9.12.2 Germany

18.9.12.2.1 Decision 89/539/EEC: Kreisfreie Stadt in Lubeck

Article 1 of Decision 89/539 of 21 September 1989[78] provides that the Kreisfreie Stadt of Lubeck in Germany satisfied the criteria in the Reneval Programme and that programme applied to that area.

18.9.12.2.2 Decision 89/448/EEC: City Region of Hamburg–Zentrum

Article 1 of Decision 89/448 of 13 July 1989 provides that the city region of Hamburg–Zentrum in the then Federal Republic of Germany[79] satisfied the criteria in the Reneval Programme and that programme applied to that area.

18.9.12.3 Netherlands

18.9.12.3.1 Decision 89/484: Rijn Delta and certain other areas

Article 1 of Commission Decision 89/484/EEC[80] provides that:

"The Rijn-Delta, comprising the communes of Alblasserdam, Capelle aan den Ijssel, Dordrecht, Gorinchem, Hardixveld-Giessendam, Hendrik-Ido-Ambacht, Krimpen aan den Ijssel,

76. See Regulation 2506/88.
77. Regulation 2506/88, Article 7(2).
78. I.e. prior to German unification.
79. OJ L214/16, 1989.
80. OJ L235/37, 12 August 1989.

Maasluis, Nieuw-Lekkerland, Papendrecht, Ridderkerk, Rotterdam, Rozenburg, Schiedam, Sleidrecht, Vlaardingen and Zwijndrecht in the Corop areas of Groot-Rijnmond and Zuidoost Zuid-Holland, and Amsterdam-Noord in the Corop area of Groot-Amsterdam in the Netherlands are hereby found to satisfy the criteria in Article 3(1) of Regulation (EEC) No. 2506/88. The Community programme instituted by that Regulation shall therefore apply to those areas."

18.9.12.4 Spain

18.9.12.4.1 Decision 91/91: La Coruna, Pontevedra and Vizcaya

The provinces of La Coruna and Pontevedra in the Autonomous Community of Galacia and the province of Vizcaya in the Autonomous Community of the Basque Country were deemed under Article 1 of Commission Decision 91/91/EEC[81] to satisfy the criteria in Article 3(1) of Regulation 2506/88 and thus the Reneval Programme applied to that area.

18.9.12.5 United Kingdom

18.9.12.5.1 Decision 89/541: Plymouth travel-to-work area

The Plymouth travel-to-work area in the counties of Devon and Cornwall was deemed under Article 1 of Commission Decision 89/541/EEC[82] to satisfy the criteria in Article 3(1) of Regulation 2506/88 and thus the Reneval Programme applied to that area.

18.9.12.5.2 Decision 90/602: Wirral and Sefton

The districts of Wirral and Sefton in the county of Merseyside in the UK were deemed under Article 1 of Commission Decision 90/602/EEC[83] to satisfy the criteria in Article 3(1) of Regulation 2506/88 and thus the Reneval Programme applied to that area.

18.10 SHIPBUILDING AIDS

The plight of some shipyards has led various governments to provide aids, subsidies and tax breaks so as to stimulate activity at such yards.[84] On 23 December 1976, the European Parliament's Committee on Economic and Monetary Affairs published its Interim Report on the Community Shipping Industry.[85] The Report recorded some examples which would prove instructive:

"A recent report[86] states that 'yards in virtually every major shipbuilding country are now quoting for new orders on terms which contravene the intent, if not the letter, of the Organisation for Economic Cooperation and Development's Understanding on Export Credits'. A case is cited of a West German shipyard indicating to Egyptian officials seeking to

81. OJ L50/24, 23 February 1991.
82. OJ L288/29, 6 October 1989.
83. OJ L315/33, 15 November 1990.
84. See the European Parliament's Committee on Economic and Monetary Affairs published its Interim Report on the Community Shipping Industry, para. 42 *et seq.*
85. Doc. 479/76, Rapporteur: Mr J. L. Prescott.
86. *The Times*, London, 26 January 1976.

order ships that the 30% down payment (which the understanding requires to be paid in the pre-delivery period) could be provided in the form of capital aid made available by the German government for development projects.

The Budgets Comittee of the Bundestag voted at the begining of April,[87] 'to lift a restriction which had barred German shipowners placing orders with German yards from claiming both interest rate subsidies under the country's shipyard aid scheme and direct subvention under the shipping line aid fund. It also decided to reduce the subventions that German shipping lines could claim when placing orders abroad'.

The British Government has decided to extend to home shipowners the insurance inflation scheme which has been available to foreign customers on capital goods. This measure[88] had been delayed by difficulties over gaining approval from the EEC authorities in Brussels. In response to pressure from the European Commission, this cost escalation scheme will cover goods imported from other Member States for incorporation into ships being built in the United Kingdom. The Commission's requirement of degressivity having also been complied with, the Commission has proposed that the Council should amend its directive 75/432/EEC on aid to shipbuilding to permit this British scheme.[89]

As a final example of increasing aids to shipbuilding, one notes that the West German Transport Ministry announced in April 1976 that the shipbuilding aid programme for the current year would be stepped up (from the DM 110m originally planned) to DM 170m."

State aids do not necessarily help to resolve the difficulties of European shipyards—the Commission has stated that it is "to be feared that uncoordinated measures by individual countries would be ineffective and, because of their protectionist effect, lead only to disruption of competition and a partitioning of the market".[90] It is submitted that the Commission's view is correct. None the less, it would be impossible to outlaw aid completely[91]—as the Preamble to the Seventh Shipbuilding Directive[92] states:

"a complete abolition of aid to the sector is still not possible in view of the present market situation and in view of the need to encourage restructuring in many yards."

None the less:

"a tight and selective aid policy should be continued in order to support the present trend in production towards more technologically-advanced ships and in order to ensure fair and uniform conditions for intra-Community competition . . . [and] such a policy constitutes the most appropriate approach in terms of ensuring the maintenance of a sufficient level of activity in European shipyards and, thereby, the survival of an efficient and competitive European shipbuilding industry."

The Commission in its First Report on Competition Policy[93] stated at para. 168:

"Shipbuilding is one of the few industries to benefit from production aid throughout the world.

This has led to a genuine 'aid rush' during the period 1969–1970 for which there are several reasons.

As against other industries, shipbuilding cannot be protected by conventional commercial policy measures (customs duties and quantitative restrictions) without prejudicing shipbuilders who carry out their business on markets where competition is extremely active. The export of ships, therefore, also involves the export of certain manufactured products which are incorporated in the ships and which could, as such, not easily be exported without encountering

87. *The Times*, London, 12 April 1976.

88. *The Times*, London, 9 April 1976.

89. COM(76)321 final, 30 July 1976.

90. COM(76)224 final, p. 9.

91. The Council of Ministers stated in the Preamble to the Third Shipbuilding Directive (Dir. 75/432/EEC): "aid to shipbuilding should not . . . adversely affect trading conditions to an extent contrary to the common interest".

92. Dir. 90/684/EEC, OJ L380/27, 31 December 1990.

93. 1972.

certain obstacles, especially customs duties. Fostering an increase in tonnage by lowering prices of ships and maintaining freight prices at a low level could also be to the advantage of economies which are largely dependent upon seagoing trade.

Thus, thanks to aid, some non-member countries have been able to build up an important, and in one particular case, a dominating position on the world market. This situation could not be ignored by the traditional shipbuilding countries of Western Europe, because of the regional and social considerations arising from the location of a number of shipyards. Their reactions were also motivated by shipping and industrial policy considerations, since shipbuilding, being essentially an assembly industry, considerably influences the economy as a whole.

It would have been better to normalise the competition conditions on a world-wide basis rather than to adopt national protection measures which are bound to foster outbidding in the matter of aid. This was done within the OECD, which groups the world's main shipbuilding countries, but the effective results of this work have only started to show themselves in 1971. In the meantime, measures had to be taken in Europe, and in the Community in particular, both at national and at Community levels. Since 1972, to aid traditionally granted in France and Italy was added aid granted in Germany, followed by aid granted in the Netherlands and in Belgium from 1967 onwards.

For its part, the Commission submitted to the Council [of Ministers], in 1965, a draft directive concerning the granting of aid to shipbuilding with a view to correcting distortions of competition on the international shipbuilding market. The directive was only adopted by the Council in July 1969."[94]

18.10.1 First shipbuilding directive

The First Shipbuilding Directive, Directive 69/262/EEC[95] provided that aid should be no more than ten per cent of the price contractually fixed before the beginning of the works, for the purchase of new vessels or for "works of transformation". Ten per cent was chosen because this was estimated to be the level of harm suffered by EC shipyards as a result of the distortion of competition in the world market.[96]

The Commission later discussed the First Shipbuilding Directive in the following terms:

"The directive of 1969 achieved its aims, which were to protect the Community shipbuilding industry and harmonise aid granted within the Community.

Although the Community shipbuilding industry had suffered a recession until 1967, the position, in quantitative terms, had improved slightly by 1969 and stabilised after that. The improvement is more marked in qualititative terms, as the European industry has specialised, in recent years, in the construction of ships of greater value added adapted to the requirements of modern maritime transport.

Action taken to compensate distortions of competition was accompanied by structural measures intended to speed up the adaptation of the sector to the new market conditions and to technical progress. Because of the results obtained and as a positive result of the 1969 directive, there has been a relative improvement in the Community's position.

The balance-sheet with regard to the harmonisation of specific aid within the Community is equally satisfactory.

In the early stages the situation was quite erratic, with aid exceeding 30% of the selling price in France and Italy, while elsewhere no aid was granted at all. Since 1967, the situation has tended to become more balanced, the figure for national aid dropping, within a few years, to around 10%, with the exception of Italy where the figure was still higher. Since the beginning of 1971, a downward alignment has been recorded, and now the average fluctuates around 5%, here again with the exception of Italy, where the figure for aid still hovers around the maximum rate of the 10% fixed by the directive. In some Member States, however, there are general aid systems which

94. OJ L206 of 15 August 1969, p. 25.
95. OJ L206/25, 15 August 1969.
96. First Report on Competition Policy, *op. cit.*, para. 168.

are to a large extent granted for shipbuilding and which, added to the specific aid, appreciably affect price for ships.

Efforts within the OECD for normalising competition conditions on the international market have resulted in two OECD Council resolutions being successively adopted on 30 May 1969 and 16 December 1970 respectively, which laid down the optimum credit conditions for the export of ships, a ceiling which was not to be exceeded. The last arrangement had an important effect in reducing export credit aid, since the rates of interest for this particular export credit had to remain below the figure of 7.5%. In addition, the OECD took action in order to arrive rapidly at an overall agreement which would result in the progressive abolition of all forms of aid to the industry. The need for protection on the part of the Community shipping industry is therefore no longer so great."

18.10.2 Second shipbuilding directive

The Second Shipbuilding Directive, Directive 72/273/EEC[97] reduced the maximum permissible aid. The ceiling was lowered to 5 per cent of the contract price in 1972 and 4 per cent in 1973. In specific terms, Article 1 provided:

"Aids and interventions to assist shipbuilding may be considered compatible with the common market in so far as they satisfy the conditions set out in Articles 2 and 3."

Article 2 provided:

"Grants of aid and interventions may be made for the following purposes:

(a) the building, in a shipyard of the Community, of metal-hulled sea-going vessels being any of the following:

- merchant vessels for the carriage of cargo and/or passengers of not less than 150 gross registered tons;
- fishing vessels of not less than 150 gross registered tons;
- dredgers of not less than 150 gross registered tons;
- tugs of not less than 500hp;

(b) the conversion, in a shipyard of the Community, of metal-hulled sea-going vessels of not less than 5000 gross registered tons, on condition that conversion operations entail radical alterations to the cargo plan, the hull or the main propulsion system of such vessels.

Article 3 then provided:

"1. Aid or intervention for the building or conversion of ships falling within Article 2 may consist of:

(a) export credit facilities in respect of ships, provided that such facilities satisfy the conditions laid down in the understanding on Export Credit for Ships contained in the Resolution of the Council of the OECD of 16 September 1970;

(b) other credit facilties for sales and conversions of ships provided that the conditions referred to in (a) are satisfied;

(c) any form of aid or intervention coming within Article 1, other than those specified under (a) and (b), the amount of which, subject to exemption, does not exceed 5% of the relevant contract price in 1972 and 4% of the contract price in 1973.

2. Grants exceeding the aforementioned ceilings shall in the following cases be treated as exemptions for the purposes of paragraph 1(c)

- where the excess is due to the operation of a scheme of insurance against exceptional rises in costs;
- where the grant is to the Italian shipbuilding industry, provided that such grants are progressively reduced at a rate at least equal to that indicated under (c), and there is at the same time put into operation a programme for the rationalisation of Italian shipbuilding industry designed to make the industry properly competitive at the European level not later than the end of 1976;

97. OJ L169/28, 27 July 1972.

— where the excess is the result of indirect aid or intervention for the building or conversion of ships.

3. The contract price means the sale price fixed by contract, taking account of any price revision clause.

4. The Council, acting by a qualified majority on a proposal from the Commission, shall modify this Article as and when appropriate."

Thus the OECD conditions were adopted by this Directive in respect of export credits to ships.

There was also an anti-discriminatory mechanism built into the Directive. Article 5 provided:

"The Member States shall refrain from any discriminatory practices calculated to favour within their national territories the building or conversion of ships or the manufacture of products intended to form part of such ships."

It was anticipated that four new States would join the EC on 1 January 1973 (i.e. during the life of the Directive). One of the four, Norway, did not do so following a referendum of its people. None the less, Article 6 made provision for the accession of the four States:

"On the entry into force of the Treaty concerning the Accession of the Kingdom of Denmark, Ireland, the Kingdom of Norway and the United Kingdom of Great Britain and Northern Ireland to the European Economic Community and the European Atomic Energy Community:

(a) the following temporary exceptions to subparagraph (a) of Article 2 shall apply:
- — the minimum tonnage level for aid and intervention in the United Kingdom of Great Britain and Northern Ireland in respect of the aforementioned shipbuilding operations shall be 100 gross registered tons;
- — the minimum tonnage level for aid and intervention in the Kingdom of Norway in respect of the construction of fishing vessels shall be 50 gross registered tons;

(b) the following indent shall be added to Article 3(2):
'where the grant is to the Irish shipbuilding industry'."

The Second Directive was due to apply until 31 December 1973.[98] It was extended by means of Directive 74/643 until June 1975. Schina records: "[t]his extension was caused by the long debate within the Council on the Third Directive, by which the Commission wanted to increase its control of State aids to shipbuilding."[99] The Commission in its Third Report on Competition Policy (published in May 1974) wrote that when the draft third Directive and its proposals:

"were examined by the Council, it was . . . found that the problems dealt with in the Commission's proposals were too important and too wide in scope to be dealt with by the Council before the end of the year. Adopting a proposal from the Commission to this effect, the Council therefore decided to extend the duration of the Second Directive until 30 June 1974; this will enable the Council to carry out a thorough examination of the new proposed aids Directive and of the guidelines for an industrial policy for shipbuilding submitted at the same time."

18.10.2.1 Study

Article 7(2) of the Second Shipbuilding Directive provided:

"The Commission shall as soon as possible undertake a study of trends in supply and demand on the world shipbuilding market and of the overall effect of aids and interventions significantly affecting, whether directly or indirectly, the conditions of competition and trade on that market

98. Dir. 72/273, Article 7(1)

99. *Op. cit.*, para. 274.

within the Community. It shall submit to the Council proposals based on the results of this study. The Council shall act on these proposals, immediately if possible, but in any event not later than the end of 1973."

The Commission in its Third Report on Competition Policy (published in May 1974) wrote:

"90. The second Council Directive[100] on shipbuilding aids provided that the Commission would examine the various aspects of the imbalance between supply and demand on the shipbuilding market and all State aid and intervention directly or indirectly affecting the conditions of competition and trade in this field. Using the results of the study, the Commission was to endeavour to provide solutions to the overcapacity problem which might arise and to the aids problem, by submitting to the Council proposals for action to prevent supply developing in such a way as to jeopardise the desired balance, and a new draft directive coordinating in the common interest all aid and intervention to shipbuilding and ship conversions[.] The Council was in theory to act upon these proposals by 31 December 1973 at the latest, the date on which the second Directive was to lapse.

91. The study made by the Commission, in collaboration with the national experts of the nine Member States and in liaison with the OECD, showed that world shipbuilding capacity could well exceed, in the middle of the present decade, the expected growth of requirements, and points to a risk of excess capacity for the end of this period. It is unlikely that the currently full order books of the shipyards will be maintained, given that foreseeable requirements for sea transport are developing at a slower pace and are likely to be met without delay. The difficulties which would arise from such a situation would particularly affect Community shipbuilding, since the Community's restructuring drive is not yet completed and its competitive capacity remains generally below that of some of its competitors.

92. An industrial policy for European shipbuilding must therefore aim to close this gap in order to make the industry competitive on a world-wide basis within a maximum period of four years so that it can, in the best conditions, face the situation of surplus capacity that can be foreseen. The Commission's shipbuilding proposals sent to the Council at the end of October 1973 are directed towards attaining this objective through a policy of restructuring and of investment coordinated at Community level.

This policy would be based essentially upon support for investments in the Community shipyards with a view to boosting investment during the 1974–1977 period, given that after this period, with the risk of excess capacity, action taken could come too late. The policy advocated would comprise both reconversion measures and social measures, including the intervention of the Social Fund, since it is by no means certain that some shipyards will, in future years, not have changed their activities because the cost of maintaining operations has already or is likely to become prohibitive. In addition, the policy will be supported by a research and development programme, necessitated, *inter alia*, by the deficiencies of the small- and medium-scale shipyards in this respect. Equally, these shipyards should be urged to collaborate in market research, so as to enable them to adjust their production better to demand and to increase their outlets.

93. In general, this approach to substitute for the aids given so far to shipyard production incentives that will eventually render their structures competitive without any State support. This approach, underlying the two previous Council Directives concerning aid to shipbuilding, constitutes the main feature of the draft third Directive, which has been submitted by the Commission to the Council . . ."

18.10.2.1.1 Direct aids and intervention

"94. The reduction in direct aids to production, i.e. those bearing a direct relation to the price of ships, would be pursued in accordance, moreover, with the guidelines of the OECD General Arrangements, which provide for the complete termination, by 1 November 1975, of aids liable to distort competition in the industry.

The second Directive fixed the ceiling of direct aid at 5% of the contractual price in 1972 and 4% in 1973. Since this Directive allowed for a number of exemptions to these ceilings and since,

100. OJ L169 27 July 1972, p. 28.

in several new Member States, the level of aids was relatively high, it was proposed that the new ceilings will now include some aids which had not been included in the ceiling fixed by the previous directives. Furthermore, a more detailed method for assessing the aids has been formulated, and this will enable compliance with the ceilings to be verified more accurately. The Directive, whose duration would be fixed at four years, does not lay down a specific ceiling for 1976 and 1977; it is, nevertheless, agreed that the rate of decline must be at least one point per year; the OECD general arrangement provides for the complete abolition of direct aids by the end of 1975, when the results obtained under this arrangement should be examined."

18.10.2.1.2 Aids for the sale of ships

"95. As regards credits granted for the sale of ships, the second Directive made reference to the OECD agreement (most favourable rate 7.5%, payment on account 20%, maximum duration 8 years) and in fact it thus confined itself to harmonising the conditions for obtaining one of the factors of production, in this case, credit, but not the aids themselves; the latter consist of the difference between the normal cost of borrowing capital, which can vary from State to State, and the rate of preferential credit granted. The 7.5% rate would thus give a varying degree of assistance depending on the Member State. A ceiling should therefore be fixed for these aids. The maximum subsidy which the shipbuilder may receive when a ship is sold will be restricted to five percentage points in relation to the normal cost of borrowing. The Commission and the Member States will endeavour to have this limitation adopted within the OECD."

18.10.2.1.3 Investment aids

"96. While it considers that for the reasons given above, investment in the shipyards of the Community should be facilitated, the Commission is of the opinion that the efficiency of aids conferred for this purpose must be increased, by granting them only after examination of the objectives relating to areas and industries concerned that are to be attained and of the results which may be expected in terms of increased competitiveness of the shipyards qualifying. To this end, the draft directive provides that prior notification of plans for investment aid and intervention exceeding four million u.a.[101] will have to be given to the Commission for multilateral examination."

18.10.2.1.4 Emergency measures

"97. Any emergency measures taken by Member States in the form of aids or interventions aimed at safeguarding the continued operations of an undertaking or the employment it provides will be taken only when they are justified by the need for avoiding acute social difficulties and in so far as they enable the competitive position of the undertaking receiving assistance to be restored within a reasonable period of time.

The draft third Directive thus covers all direct and indirect aids which Community shipyards may receive.

When these proposals were examined by the Council, it was, however, found that the problems dealt with in the Commission's proposals were too important and too wide in scope to be dealt with by the Council before the end of the year. Adopting a proposal from the Commission to this effect, the Council therefore decided to extend the duration of the Second Directive until 30 June 1974; this will enable the Council to carry out a thorough examination of the new proposed aids Directive and of the guidelines for an industrial policy for shipbuilding submitted at the same time."

18.10.3 Third shipbuilding directive

The Third Shipbuilding Directive, Directive 75/432[102] was adopted on 10 July 1975. It was due to apply until 31 December 1977.[103]

101. I.e. ECU.
102. OJ L192/27, 1975.
103. Dir. 75/432, Article 9.

18.10.3.1 Background to the Directive

The background to the Directive is clear from its Preamble:

"... Whereas Council Directive No. 72/273/EEC[104] of 20 July 1972 on aid to shipbuilding, which was designed to offset distortions in competition on the world market, has helped to reduce and harmonise direct aids to shipbuilding in the Community; whereas this Directive, last extended by Directive No. 74/59/EEC,[105] expired on 30 June 1975;

Whereas the position of shipbuilding in the Community has improved since the adoption of Directive 72/273/EEC, due to favourable market developments and to the rationalisation and restructuring efforts of shipyards; whereas, however, if undertakings are to be made competitive and a balance achieved in this sector, these efforts must be intensified; whereas this is particularly urgent in view of the serious difficulties threatening the sector; ...

Whereas the objectives of a competitive and balanced shipbuilding industry require an appropriate adjustment of production structures so that the undertakings in the sector may eventually be able to follow general economic developments and meet competition on the world market without the support of intervention by the public authorities and so that the investment efforts of the sector are compatible with the world balance between supply and demand;

Whereas distortions in competition on the world market have been reduced through a series of understandings concluded by the main shipbuilding countries within the framework of the OECD with the object of harmonising export credit conditions for ships; whereas, within this same organisation, the principal shipbuilding countries have concluded a general arrangement on the progressive reduction of specific aid measures distorting competition in the shipbuilding industry, with a view to their abolition by 1 November 1975;

Whereas, furthermore, the objective of making the shipbuilding industry competitive in a relatively short time requires consideration of the overall effects of aids and interventions directly or indirectly affecting competition and trade conditions on the market for the building, conversion or repair of ships;

Whereas the continued application of aids to shipbuilding has a protective effect which was justifiable in the past but is not likely in the long term significantly to improve the world competitiveness of the Community shipbuilding industry; whereas, however, elimination of such aids must take place gradually to enable shipyards to adjust to the new conditions;

Whereas aid to shipbuilding should not, however, adversely affect trading conditions to an extent contrary to the common interest. ..."

18.10.3.2 Essence of the Directive

Article 1 of the Directive provided:

"Aid and intervention to assist shipbuilding may be considered compatible with the common market, under this Directive, in so far as they satisfy the conditions set out in Article 2(1) and (2) and Article 3."

Article 2 then provides:

"1. Article 1 shall apply to aid and intervention for the building, in the Community, of the following metal-hulled sea-going vessels:

- merchant vessels for the carriage of cargo and/or passengers of not less than 150 gross registered tons,
- fishing vessels of not less than 150 gross registered tons,
- dredgers of not less than 150 gross registered tons,
- tugs of not less than 500hp.

2. (a) Article 1 shall apply to the aid and intervention referred to in paragraph 1 until 31 December 1975 only, on condition that their present level is not increased.

(b) Nevertheless, Article 1 shall apply beyond 31 December 1975 when these aids and interventions are granted:

104. OJ L169, 27 July 1972, p. 28. The Second Shipbuilding Directive.

105. OJ L38, 11 February 1974, p. 1.

— in Ireland, provided that such aids and interventions are progressively reduced and that there is at the same time a rationalisation plan,
— in Italy, provided that such aids and interventions are progressively reduced and that there is at the same time put into operation a plan for the rationalisation of the shipbuilding industry the effect of which would be to make the industry properly competitive and able to continue without such measures,
— in France, in the form of a price guarantee introduced–under the specific intervention scheme to assist shipbuilding—by the law of 24 May 1951, provided that the terms of this scheme are made progressively more restrictive.

3. The Member States shall provide a table, for the exclusive use of the Commission, based on the specimen given in Annex I,[106] setting out the decisions on the aid and intervention referred to in paragraph 1 and an estimate of their effects. This information will be provided on 1 March of each year in respect of the decisions taken during the second half of the previous calendar year and on 1 September for those taken in the first half of the current calendar year.

The Commission shall regularly draw up an overall report to serve as the basis for discussion with national experts."

While Article 3 provides:

"Article 1 shall apply to aid and intervention in the form of credit facilities for export and for all other sales of ships, provided that such facilities satisfy the conditions laid down in the understanding on export credit for ships contained in the resolution of the Council of the OECD of 18 July 1974, or in any agreements replacing it.

These aids and interventions may apply under the same conditions to the conversion of metal-hulled sea-going vessels of not less than 5,000 gross registered tons, on condition that conversion operations entail radical alterations to the cargo plan, the hull or the propulsion system."

Article 6 of the Directive provides:

"The Member States shall refrain from any intervention measures to promote within their national territories the building, conversion and repair of ships to be used for navigation or for use at sea and the manufacture of products intended to form part of such ships, other than those provided for in Articles 2 and 3 or those considered compatible with the common market under Articles 92 and 93 of the Treaty."[107]

18.10.3.3 Reporting mechanism

Article 4 of the Directive provided:

"The Member States shall inform the Commission of their decisions to grant aid to investments in shipbuilding, conversion or repair yards where the amount of such investment is in excess of five million units of account. This information shall be provided every year in the form of a table based on the specimen in Annex II[108]: on 1 March, in respect of the decisions taken in the second half of the previous calendar year and on 1 September for those taken in the first half of the current calendar year."

Article 5 goes on to provide:

"The Member States shall inform the Commission of their rules and procedures for implementing the aid and intervention systems to assist the building, conversion and repair of ships before such rules and procedures enter into force."

18.10.3.4 Emergency aid

Article 5 of the Directive provides:

106. See Annex I to the Directive.
107. On Articles 92 and 93 of the EEC Treaty, see Chapter 13, above, generally.
108. See Annex II to the Directive.

"Aid and intervention of a conservatory nature intended as a temporary solution for the rescue of a shipbuilding, ship conversion or ship repair undertaking pending a solution to the problems confronting the undertaking concerned shall be notified individually to the Commission, pursuant to Article 93 of the Treaty."

The Council of Ministers expressed the forlorn hope that as a general rule, aids could be abolished by November 1975.[109]

18.10.4 Fourth shipbuilding directive

18.10.4.1 Introduction

The Fourth Shipbuilding Directive, Directive 78/338/EEC,[110] was adopted on 4 April 1978.

18.10.4.2 Legal bases

The legal bases for the Directive were Article 92(3)(d) and 113 of the EEC Treaty.

18.10.4.3 Commercial background

The plight of the EC's shipbuilding industry is obvious from one of the recitals which read:

"the position of shipbuilding has considerably worsened during the last few years; whereas Community shipyards face a general fall in demand and acute price competition on a contracted world market; whereas the result of this has been a serious reduction in orders, aggravating the structural problems of the industry and indeed threatening its existence."

The extent of the problem legitimated the granting of aid in certain cases. Again, one of the recitals to the Directive is instructive:

"if the situation in the industry were normal, the continuation of aid to its operation would not be justified since it would serve only as a protective measure"

18.10.4.4 Duration

Due to the delay in adopting the Fifth Shipbuilding Directive[111] the Fourth Shipbuilding Directive was extended until 31 March 1981.

18.10.4.5 Concept of shipbuilding

Article 1 of the Fourth Directive defines shipbuilding in the following terms:

"the building, in the Community, of the following metal-hulled, sea-going vessels:
- merchant vessels for the carriage of passengers and/or cargo, of not less than 150 gross registered tons;
- fishing vessels of not less than 150 gross registered tons;
- dredgers or ships for other work at sea, excluding self-propelled drilling platforms, of not less than 150 gross registered tons;
- tugs of not less than 500 hp."

109. Article 2.
110. OJ L98/19, 1978.
111. See para. 18.10.5, below.

18.10.4.6 Concept of ship-conversion

Article 1 of the Fourth Directive defines ship-conversion in the following terms:

"the conversion of metal-hulled sea-going vessels of not less than 5,000 gross registered tons, apart from the exception mentioned in Article 2, on condition that conversion operations entail radical alterations to the cargo plan, the hull or the propulsion system."

18.10.4.7 Concept of ship-repair

Article 1 of the Fourth Directive defines ship-repair in the following terms:

"the repair of the following metal-hulled, sea-going vessels:
- — merchant vessels for the carriage of passengers and/or cargo, of not less than 150 gross registered tons;
- — fishing vessels of not less than 150 gross registered tons;
- — dredgers or ships for other work at sea, excluding self-propelled drilling platforms, of not less than 150 gross registered tons;
- — tugs of not less than 500 hp."

18.10.4.8 Concept of sale

Article 1 of the Fourth Directive states that sale means all sales of the following metal-hulled, sea-going vessels:

- "— merchant vessels for the carriage of passengers and/or cargo, of not less than 150 gross registered tons;
- — fishing vessels of not less than 150 gross registered tons;
- — dredgers or ships for other work at sea, excluding self-propelled drilling platforms, of not less than 150 gross registered tons;
- — tugs of not less than 500 hp."

18.10.4.9 Concept of state aid

Article 1 of the Fourth Directive defines State Aid as meaning the aid referred to in Articles 92 and 93 of the EEC Treaty and "this concept shall cover not only aid granted by the State itself but also that granted by regional or local authorities.

"the building, in the Community, of the following metal-hulled, sea-going vessels:
- — merchant vessels for the carriage of passengers and/or cargo, of not less than 150 gross registered tons;
- — fishing vessels of not less than 150 gross registered tons;
- — dredgers or ships for other work at sea, excluding self-propelled drilling platforms, of not less than 150 gross registered tons;
- — tugs of not less than 500 hp."

18.10.4.10 Credit facilities

Article 2 states that aid and intervention in the form of credit facilities was to be considered compatible with the common market whether (a) for all sales or conversions of vessels or (b) for the conversion of vessels of not less than 1,000 gross registered tons where it is a case of matching terms offered by a shipbuilder from a non-member country. Such aid and intervention had however to comply with the OECD Council resolution of 18 July 1974 or with any agreements which may supersede that resolution.[112]

112. Dir. 78/338/EEC, Article 2.

18.10.4.11 Relationship between the Directive and the EEC Treaty rules relating to state aids

Article 3 of the Directive made clear that notwithstanding the specific provisions of the Directive, the general provisions of Articles 92 and 93 of the EEC Treaty were to be fully applicable to the shipbuilding, ship-conversion and ship-repair industry.

Article 10 of the Directive provides that the Member States "shall refrain from any aid and intervention, other than that provided for in Articles 2 to 7 [of the Directive] or that considered compatible with the common market under Articles 92 and 93 of the [EEC] Treaty,[113] to promote within their national territories the building, conversion or repair of ships or the manufacture of products intended to form part thereof".

18.10.4.12 Investment aid

Article 4(1) of the Directive categorically stated:

"Member States shall not grant sectoral aid for the creation of new shipyards or for investment in existing yards if such aid would be liable to increase the Member State's building capacity.

In applying general or regional investment aid schemes to the shipbuilding sector, Member States shall take all practicable steps to ensure that aided investment does not lead either to increases in the capacity of the sector in a Member State, or to the creation of employment which is not of a stable nature. To this end, plans for such application of general or regional aid schemes leading to increases in shipbuilding capacity in a Member State must be communicated to the Commission not less than three weeks before they are put into effect."

Paragraph 2 of the same Article contains a procedure for such notification:

"The Member States shall inform the Commission of their decisions to grant aid to investments in shipbuilding, ship-conversion or ship-repair yards where the amount of such investment is in excess of five million European units of account. This information shall be provided in the form of a table based on the specimen in Annex I, on 1 March in respect of decisions taken in the second half of the previous calendar year and on 1 September in respect of those taken in the first half of the current calendar year."

18.10.4.13 Rescue aids

Article 5 of the Directive dealt with rescue aids to cope with the serious social problems arising out of the decline in shipbuilding. There was need for prior notification to the Commission of any proposed aid. The Article provided:

"Aid and intervention intended as a temporary solution for the rescue of a shipbuilding, ship-conversion or ship-repair undertaking pending a definitive solution to the problems confronting the undertaking concerned, in order to deal with acute social problems, may be considered compatible with the common market under this Directive. Plans for such aid and intervention shall, pursuant to Article 93(3) of the Treaty, be notified to the Commission individually and in advance. They may not be put into effect before the Commission has given its agreement. The Commission shall adopt a position on the plans as soon as possible, taking account of the urgency of each individual case."

18.10.4.14 Crisis aid

Article 6 of the Directive dealt with production aid to remedy a serious crisis which caused a substantial reduction in orders. Such aid had to be authorised by the

113. On Articles 92 and 93 of the EEC Treaty, see Chapter 15, above, *passim*.

Commission. The maximum level of such aid was 30 per cent. This level could only be exceeded in the most exceptional circumstances where the proposed aid had been notified in advance and authorised. This production aid had to be linked to some industrial restructuring objective. It could not be used to affect trading conditions to an extent contrary to the common interest when the assisted plan was in competition with a tender from a yard in another Member State.

In specific terms, the Article provided:

"1. Production aid and intervention may be considered compatible with the common market under this Directive if they are granted in order to remedy the serious crisis which is causing a substantial reduction in orders on hand in a Member State and consequently a decrease in production.

Such aid and intervention shall be progressively reduced; it shall be granted only if linked to the attainment of industrial restructuring objectives with a view to making the industry competitive and able to operate with aid or intervention.

The rate at which such aid is reduced shall in particular take account of the acuteness of the crisis in the Member State concerned.

When assessing the compatibility of such measures with the common market and in particular the level of aid and intervention, the Commission shall pay particular attention to the situation on the market, the gravity of the crisis on the basis of the balance of the work-load for the shipyards and the need for appropriate adaptation of production capacity to the conditions prevailing on the market.

The Commission shall assess the maximum level of aid and intervention which may be granted for the application of the various aid schemes. Authorisation to exceed this level may be given only as an exceptional measure, after the Commission has been notified. Such exceptions may not be put into effect unless the Commission has given its agreement. The Commission shall adopt a position as possible, taking account of the urgency of each individual case.

2. The Commission shall be given prior notification of any proposed individual aid or intervention under the measures referred to in paragraph 1 where the proposal is in competition with a tender from a yard in another Member State. Such proposals may not be implemented before the Commission has given its agreement. The Commission shall verify that such aid does not affect trading conditions to an extent contrary to the common interest.

3. The Member States shall supply the Commission with a table, for the exclusive use of the Commission, based on the specimen in Annex II,[114] setting out the decisions on the aid and intervention referred to in paragraph 1 and an estimate of their effects. They shall also provide a report on the attainment of industrial restructuring objectives.

This information shall be provided on 1 March in respect of decisions taken during the second half of the previous calendar year, and on 1 September in respect of those taken in the first half of the current calendar year.

The Commission shall verify, on the basis of the information referred to in the first and second subparagraphs and of the state of the order books in the Member State concerned, whether efforts to attain the industrial restructuring objectives mentioned in paragraph 1 and the crisis measures which have been applied are contributing genuinely and in an equitable manner to the adaptation of the industry to the new conditions on the world shipbuilding market.

On the basis of the information communicated to it, the Commission shall regularly draw up an overall report to serve as a basis for discussion with national experts. This report shall state *inter alia* the maximum level of aid and intervention obtaining in each Member State during the period in question.

4. Annex III lists the types of aid and intervention which are considered compatible with the common market under paragraph 1 and those considered compatible under Article 7.

The Commission shall modify the list in Annex III[115] on the basis of the decisions it takes regarding proposed aid and intervention, or existing schemes."

114. See Annex II to the Directive.

115. See Annex III to the Directive.

18.10.4.15 Cost-escalation insurance

Article 7 of the Directive provides:

"Intervention in the form of cost-escalation insurance may be considered compatible with the common market under this Directive, subject to the conditions listed in Article 6(1), first and second subparagraphs, and in paragraphs 3 and 4."

18.10.4.16 Non-discrimination

Article 8 of the Directive provided that aids granted to shipowners for the purchase of ships should not discriminate against the shipyards of other Member States. To bolster this prohibition on non-discrimination, Member States are obliged to draw up reports when such aid is granted to their own shipowners on a selective basis.[116]

18.10.5 Fifth shipbuilding directive

18.10.5.1 Introduction

On 28 April 1981 the Fifth Shipbuilding Directive, Directive 81/363/EEC,[117] was adopted.[118]

18.10.5.2 Duration

Due to the delay in adopting the Sixth Shipbuilding Directive[119] the Fifth Shipbuilding Directive was extended until 31 December 1984[120] and re-extended until 31st December 1986.[121]

18.10.5.3 Legal basis

The legal basis of the Fifth Shipbuilding Directive is the EEC Treaty generally but, in particular, Articles 92(3)(d) and 113 thereof. Article 92(3)(d) of the EEC Treaty provides that the Council of Ministers may decide to declare specified categories of aid as being compatible with the Common Market even though those categories were not specified in the EEC Treaty itself.[122] Article 113 of the EEC Treaty relates to the Common Commercial Policy.[123]

116. Article 8 provides:
"[t]his information shall be provided in the form of a table for the exclusive use of the Commission, based on the specimen in Annex IX. The Member States shall communicate the information required under points 1 and 2 of that Annex half-yearly on 1 March in respect of decisions to grant aid taken in the second half of the previous calendar year and on 1 September in respect of those taken in the first half of the current calendar year. They shall communicate the information required under points 3 and 4 of that Annex annually on 1 March in respect of decisions to grant aid taken during the preceding calendar year. The Commission shall draw up overall reports at regular intervals summarising the information thus supplied.

These reports shall be discussed with the Member States in order to ensure that there is no discrimination in the shipbuilding industry as a result of such aid. These provisions are entirely without prejudice to any future Community rules on aid to shipowners."

117. OJ L137/39, 23 May 1981.
118. On the Directive, see Schina, *op. cit.*, pp. 88–93.
119. See para. 18.10.6, below.
120. Dir. 82/880/EEC of 21 December 1982; OJ L371/46, December 1982.
121. Dir. 85/2/EEC of 18 December 1984; OJ L2/13, January 1985.
122. For the text of Article 92(3)(d) of the EEC Treaty, see Appendix 1, below.
123. For the text of Article 113 of the EEC Treaty, see Appendix 1, below.

18.10.5.4 Entry into force

The Fifth Directive took effect on 28 April 1981.

18.10.5.5 Commercial Background

The plight of the EC's shipbuilding industry is obvious from one of the recitals which read:

"the situation of the shipbuilding industry has continued to be unfavourable during the period of operation of Council Directive 78/338/EEC of 4 April 1978[124]; whereas this situation has in particular taken the form of an imbalance between the production capacity of the industry and demand, leading to low price levels;

Whereas shipbuilding undertakings in the Community have therefore been obliged to draw frequently on their financial reserves to take orders, thus reducing their chance of implementing the structural adaptations needed to face the prevailing market conditions in the longer term."

The extent of the problem legitimated the granting of aid in certain cases. Again, one of the recitals to the Directive is instructive:

"if the situation in the industry were normal, the continuation of aid to its operation would not be justified since, its effect being mainly that of conservation, it is not likely to bring any lasting improvement in the Community shipbuilding industry's competitiveness.

. . . the continuation of the crisis has serious consequences for the shipbuilding industry which may make the immediate abolition of such aid impossible."

18.10.5.6 Duration

Due to the delay in adopting the Sixth Shipbuilding Directive[125] the Fifth Shipbuilding Directive was extended.

18.10.5.7 Concept of shipbuilding

Article 1 of the Fifth Directive defines shipbuilding in the following terms:

"the building in the Community of the following metal-hulled, sea-going vessels:
- merchant vessels for the carriage of passengers and/or cargo, of not less than 150 gross registered tons;
- fishing vessels of not less than 150 gross registered tons;
- dredgers or ships for other work at sea, of not less than 150 gross registered tons;
- tugs of not less than 365 kW."

It is to be noted that in respect of dredgers or ships for other work at sea, the Fourth Directive excluded "self-propelled drilling platforms", but this is not the case with the Fifth Shipbuilding Directive.

18.10.5.8 Concept of ship-conversion

Article 1 of the Fifth Directive defines ship-conversion in the following terms:

"the conversion of metal-hulled sea-going vessels of not less than 1,000 gross registered tons, on condition that conversion operations entail radical alterations to the cargo plan, the hull or the propulsion system."

124. I.e. the Fourth Shipbuilding Directive.
125. See para. 18.10.6, below.

18.10.5.9 Concept of ship-repair

Article 1 of the Fifth Directive defines ship-repair in the following terms:

"the repair of the following metal-hulled, sea-going vessels:
- merchant vessels for the carriage of passengers and/or cargo, of not less than 150 gross registered tons;
- fishing vessels of not less than 150 gross registered tons;
- dredgers or ships for other work at sea, of not less than 150 gross registered tons;
- tugs of not less than 365 kW."

18.10.5.10 Concept of sale

Article 1 of the Fourth Directive states that sale means all sales of the following metal-hulled, sea-going vessels:

"the repair of the following metal-hulled, sea-going vessels:
- merchant vessels for the carriage of passengers and/or cargo, of not less than 150 gross registered tons;
- fishing vessels of not less than 150 gross registered tons;
- dredgers or ships for other work at sea, of not less than 150 gross registered tons;
- tugs of not less than 365 kW."

18.10.5.11 Concept of aid

Article 1 of the Fifth Directive defines Aid as meaning:

"State aid within the meaning of Articles 92 and 93 of the [EEC] Treaty, including not only aid granted by the State itself but also that granted by regional or local authorities and any aid elements contained in the financing measures taken by Member States in respect of the shipbuilding or ship-repair undertakings which they directly or indirectly control and which do not count as the provision of risk capital according to standard company practice in a market economy.

Such aid may be considered compatible with the common market provided that it complies with the criteria for derogation contained in this Directive."

18.10.5.12 Credit facilities

Article 2 states that aid in the form of credit facilities for all sales and conversions could be considered compatible with the common market provided it complies with the OECD Council resolution of 30 January 1980 or with any agreements replacing the resolution.[126]

18.10.5.13 Relationship between the Directive and the EEC Treaty rules relating to state aids

Article 3 of the Directive made clear that notwithstanding the specific provisions of the Directive, the general provisions of Articles 92 and 93 of the EEC Treaty were to be fully applicable to the shipbuilding, ship-conversion and ship-repair industry.

Article 10 of the Directive provides that the Member States:

"shall refrain from any aid and intervention, other than that provided for in Articles 2 to 7 [of the Directive] or that considered compatible with the common market under Articles 92 and 93 of

126. See the OECD Council resolution of 30 January 1980 generally for credit facilities.

the [EEC] Treaty,[127] to promote within their national territories the building, conversion or repair of ships or the manufacture of products intended to form part thereof."

18.10.5.14 Investment aid

Article 4(1) of the Directive categorically stated:

"Member States shall not grant sectoral aid for the creation of new shipyards or for investment in existing yards if such aid would be liable to increase the Member State's building capacity.

In applying general or regional investment aid schemes to the shipbuilding sector, Member States shall take all practicable steps to ensure that aided investment does not lead either to increases in the capacity of the sector in a Member State, or to the creation of employment which is not of a stable nature. To this end, plans for such application of general or regional aid schemes leading to increases in shipbuilding capacity in a Member State must be communicated to the Commission not less than three weeks before they are put into effect."

Paragraph 2 of the same Article contains a procedure for such notification:

"The Member States shall inform the Commission of their decisions to grant aid to investments in shipbuilding, ship-conversion or ship-repair yards where the amount of such investment is in excess of five million European units of account. This information shall be provided in the form of a table based on the specimen in Annex I, on 1 March in respect of decisions taken in the second half of the previous calendar year and on 1 September in respect of those taken in the first half of the current calendar year."

18.10.5.15 Rescue aids

Article 5 of the Directive dealt with rescue aids to cope with the serious social problems arising out of the decline in shipbuilding. There was need for prior notification to the Commission of any proposed aid. The Article provided:

"Aid and intervention intended as a temporary solution for the rescue of a shipbuilding, ship-conversion or ship-repair undertaking pending a definitive solution to the problems confronting thee undertaking concerned, in order to deal with acute social problems, may be considered compatible with the common market under this Directive. Plans for such aid and intervention shall, pursuant to Article 93(3) of the Treaty, be notified to the Commission individually and in advance. They may not be put into effect before the Commission has given its agreement. The Commission shall adopt a position on the plans as soon as possible, taking account of the urgency of each individual case."

18.10.5.16 Crisis aid

Article 6 of the Directive dealt with production aid to remedy a serious crisis which caused a substantial reduction in orders. Such aid had to be authorised by the Commission. The maximum level of such aid was 30 per cent. This level could only be exceeded in the most exceptional circumstances where the proposed aid had been notified in advance and authorised. This production aid had to be linked to some industrial restructuring objective. It could not be used to affect trading conditions to an extent contrary to the common interest when the assisted plan was in competition with a tender from a yard in another Member State.

In specific terms, the Article provided:

"1. Production aid and intervention may be considered compatible with the common market under this Directive if they are granted in order to remedy the serious crisis which is causing a

127. On Articles 92 and 93 of the EEC Treaty, see Chapter 15, above.

substantial reduction in orders on hand in a Member State and consequently a decrease in production.

Such aid and intervention shall be progressively reduced; it shall be granted only if linked to the attainment of industrial restructuring objectives with a view to making the industry competitive and able to operate with aid or intervention.

The rate at which such aid is reduced shall in particular take account of the acuteness of the crisis in the Member State concerned.

When assessing the compatibility of such measures with the common market and in particular the level of aid and intervention, the Commission shall pay particular attention to the situation on the market, the gravity of the crisis on the basis of the balance of the work-load for the shipyards and the need for appropriate adaptation of production capacity to the conditions prevailing on the market.

The Commission shall assess the maximum level of aid and intervention which may be granted for the application of the various aid schemes. Authorisation to exceed this level may be given only as an exceptional measure, after the Commission has been notified. Such exceptions may not be put into effect unless the Commission has given its agreement. The Commission shall adopt a position as possible, taking account of the urgency of each individual case.

2. The Commission shall be given prior notification of any proposed individual aid or intervention under the measures referred to in paragraph 1 where the proposal is in competition with a tender from a yard in another Member State. Such proposals may not be implemented before the Commission has given its agreement. The Commission shall verify that such aid does not affect trading conditions to an extent contrary to the common interest.

3. The Member States shall supply the Commission with a table, for the exclusive use of the Commission, based on the specimen in Annex II,[128] setting out the decisions on the aid and intervention referred to in paragraph 1 and an estimate of their effects. They shall also provide a report on the attainment of industrial restructuring objectives.

This information shall be provided on 1 March in respect of decisions taken during the second half of the previous calendar year, and on 1 September in respect of those taken in the first half of the current calendar year.

The Commission shall verify, on the basis of the information referred to in the first and second subparagraphs and of the state of the order books in the Member State concerned, whether efforts to attain the industrial restructuring objectives mentioned in paragraph 1 and the crisis measures which have been applied are contributing genuinely and in an equitable manner to the adaptation of the industry to the new conditions on the world shipbuilding market.

On the basis of the information communicated to it, the Commission shall regularly draw up an overall report to serve as a basis for discussion with national experts. This report shall state *inter alia* the maximum level of aid and intervention obtaining in each Member State during the period in question.

4. Annex III lists the types of aid and intervention which are considered compatible with the common market under paragraph 1 and those considered compatible under Article 7.

The Commission shall modify the list in Annex III[129] on the basis of the decisions it takes regarding proposed aid and intervention, or existing schemes."

18.10.5.17 Cost-escalation insurance

Article 7 of the Directive provides:

"Intervention in the form of cost-escalation insurance may be considered compatible with the common market under this Directive, subject to the conditions listed in Article 6(1), first and second subparagraphs, and in paragraphs 3 and 4."

18.10.5.18 Non-discrimination

Article 8 of the Directive provided that aids granted to shipowners for the purchase of ships should not discriminate against the shipyards of other Member States. To bolster

128. See below.
129. See Annex III of the Directive.

this prohibition on non-discrimination, Member States are obliged to draw up reports when such aid is granted to their own shipowners on a selective basis.[130]

18.10.6 Sixth shipbuilding directive

On 26 January 1987, the Council of Ministers adopted the Sixth Shipbuilding Directive, Directive 87/167/EEC.

18.10.6.1 Duration

The Sixth Shipbuilding Directive expired on 31 December 1990.

18.10.6.1.1 Article 4(5)

The Commission in a press release[131] of 20 April 1989 stated:

"The Commission has decided to adopt a negative decision in respect of German aid for a contract concerning the construction of a 1700cgt winetanker for the German shipowner Paul Hase. The Sixth Shipbuilding Directive (Article 4(5)) provides that where there is competition between yards in different Member States for the same order, the Commission will only permit the lowest aid level unless a higher aid level within the maximum production aid ceiling is necessary to ensure that the contract remains with the Community.

In June 1987 the Dutch authorities asked the Commission to intervene in a case of intra-Community competition for the building of the above vessel. Yards in Germany and the Netherlands were involved in the bidding for the contract. As both Member States concerned eventually advised the Commission that they would not grant aid to the contract, the Commission decided to close the case. Subsequently, the German Government notified its intention to grant production aid after all, and referred to competition from a third country. The aid would amount to 1,734,000DM (871m ECU) equivalent to 16.6% of contract value. The Dutch Government did not alter its plan not to grant aid.

In July 1988 the Commission opened a procedure against the German Government in order to limit the aid level to that of the Dutch Government (i.e. zero), at the same time establishing the higher level was not necessary to retain the contract in the Community.

The German authorities have refused to align their aid package to the Dutch level arguing that the offers made by the competing yards are not comparable under the terms of Article 4(5) of the Sixth Directive and claiming that the Dutch yard was not involved in the competition throughout the tendering procedure. The Commission has concluded that in fact there was competition between the two yards and that the aid level proposed may have influenced the shipowner's choice of yard and thereby distorted competition. For this reason the Commission has decided to adopt a negative decision against Germany.

Under the terms of the decision, Germany has two months in which to abolish the proposed aid."

---

130. Article 8 provides: "[t]his information shall be provided in the form of a table for the exclusive use of the Commission, based on the specimen in Annex IX. The Member States shall communicate the information required under points 1 and 2 of that Annex half-yearly on 1 March in respect of decisions to grant aid taken in the second half of the previous calendar year and on 1 September in respect of those taken in the first half of the current calendar year. They shall communicate the information required under points 3 and 4 of that Annex annually on 1 March in respect of decisions to grant aid taken during the preceding calendar year. The Commission shall draw up overall reports at regular intervals summarising the information thus supplied.

These reports shall be discussed with the Member States in order to ensure that there is no discrimination in the shipbuilding industry as a result of such aid. These provisions are entirely without prejudice to any future Community rules on aid to shipowners."

131. IP(89)253.

18.10.6.2 Implementation

Article 12(2) of the Directive obliged the Commission to report to the European Parliament and the Council of Ministers on the first two years' application and implementation of the Directive.

The Commission's report was issued at the end of February 1989 and was published on 18 April 1989.[132]

18.10.6.3 Spain and Portugal

Directive 87/167/EEC gave an interim period of adjustment to Portugal and Spain.

It has been written:

"Prior to the Sixth Directive, permitted state aid levels were negotiated bilaterally between Member States and the Commission. The Sixth Directive approach was based on market developments. Thus aid ceilings were based on the *cost* of building certain types of ships in the most efficient European yards and the *price* at which the world market leaders were offering such ships for sale. The ceilings were intended to include all aid which has a bearing on an owner's decision to purchase a ship in a Community yard. On the introduction of the Sixth Directive, the aid ceiling was 28% of build cost for large ships and 20% for ships costing less than ECU 6m (L4.2mn). For calendar year 1990 the levels will be 20% and 14%, reflecting the improved efficiency of European yards and higher prices in the Far East.

Member States can choose at what level within the ceiling they wish to give production aid, if at all. Aid for restructuring, closure, research and development are not limited by the ceiling. All these aids must first be approved by the Commission and are assessed on an individual basis."

One of the most celebrated of all building aid cases involved Brittany Ferries.[133]

18.10.6.4 Assessment

On 22 December 1988, the Commission reduced the EEC limit on shipbuilding subsidies by 2% to 26% from 1989. Subsidies on small ships worth up to 6m ECU ($7m) were reduced by 4% to an upper limit of 16%. The Sixth Shipbuilding Directive was replaced by the Seventh Shipbuilding Directive, namely, Directive 90/684.[134]

The Council of Ministers in adopting the Seventh Shipbuilding Directive[135] stated in the Second Recital to that Directive:

"Whereas the aid policy laid down in that[136] Directive has in general met the objectives set out at its introduction . . ."

The Council of Ministers also said in the Preamble to the Seventh Shipbuilding Directive that:

"the basic aid policy laid down in Directive 87/167/EEC, differentiating between, on the one hand, production aid based on a common ceiling and, on the other, restructuring aid supporting desirable structural changes, remains the most appropriate way of ensuring that the industry is competitive in the long term . . . ."

---

132. SEC(89)518 final.

133. See "UK Seeks EEC Probe into Brittany Ferries Order", *Lloyd's List*, 9 May 1987, p. 1; "Threat to Freeze French Ship Subsidy", *Lloyd's List*, 18 June 1990, p. 3; "EEC Awaits Brittany Ferries Subsidy Information", *Lloyd's List*, 12 May 1987, p. 3. Another case involving the Sixth Directive was NESL in the UK in the context of reopening a shipbuilding yard after aid had been granted on its closure: see "NESL plans hit trouble with EEC", *Lloyd's List*, 1 July 1989, p. 1.

134. OJ L380/27, 31 December 1990. See para. 19.9.7, below.

135. Dir. 90/684/EEC, OJ L380/27, 31 December 1990. On this Directive, see para. 18.9.7, below.

136. I.e. The Sixth Directive.

thus endorsing the approach taken in the Sixth Shipbuilding Directive.

18.10.7 Seventh shipbuilding directive

18.10.7.1 Background

The Seventh Shipbuilding Directive, Directive 90/684/EEC,[137] was adopted by the Council of Ministers on 21 December 1990. It was rendered necessary by the fact that the Sixth Shipbuilding Directive, Directive 87/167/EEC of 26 January 1987 was due to expire on 31 December 1990.[138]

One of its purposes is to "ensure fair competition at an international level among shipyards through a balanced and equitable elimination of all existing impediments to normal competition conditions and must provide a suitable instrument for counteracting all illegal practices and forms of assistance inconsistent with the agreement".[139]

18.10.7.1.1 Commission proposal

The Commission proposed the Seventh Shipbuilding Directive in 1990.[140] The Commission in an Information Memorandum published in May 1990[141] had stated:

"The European Commission has decided to propose a Seventh Directive on aid to shipbuilding to the Council of Ministers, prolonging for two years the basic policy of the current Sixth Directive which expires at the end of 1990.

The two-year extension ties in with the Commission's present efforts inside the OECD to support the US initiative to reach an international agreement, within that period, between the world's major shipbuilding nations on a balanced phasing out of aid and other obstacles to normal competition in shipbuilding and ship repair.

The Commission's proposal to the Council differs from the present aid directive in that Spain and Portugal which, as new Member States, had been accorded a four-year transitional arrangement until the end of 1990, will be fully subject to the same shipbuilding aid rules as the other Member States of the Community.

Furthermore, the proposal tightens up the existing provisions, mainly as regards the definition of small ships, for which only limited aid is allowed, the use of development aid tied to ships, for which only limited aid is allowed, the irreversibility of aided shipyard closures and of the monitoring rules. . . ."

18.10.7.1.2 Opinion of the European Parliament

The European Parliament delivered its Opinion on 23 November 1990.

18.10.7.1.3 Opinion of the Economic and Social Committee

The Economic and Social Committee[142] delivered an Opinion.[143]

137. OJ L380/27, 31 December 1990.
138. See Directive 90/684, Recital 1.
139. Dir. 90/684, Recital 6.
140. OJ C223/4, 7 September 1990.
141. Reprinted in the [1990] *International Business Lawyer* 293.
142. On the ECOSOC, see Chapter 3, above.
143. OJ C332, 31 December 1990.

18.10.7.1.4 Commercial Background

The Council of Ministers in its Recitals to the Seventh Shipbuilding Directive states:

"Whereas although since 1989 there have been significant improvements in the world market for shipbuilding, a satisfactory equilibrium between supply and demand has still not been established and the price improvements which have taken place are still insufficient in the overall context to restore a normal market situation within the sector, allowing prices to reflect full production costs and a reasonable return on invested capital;

Whereas the positive international trend is likely to lead to a normalisation of the market, provided the consequences of the Gulf crisis are faced properly and the reasons behind the symptoms of crisis in the world economy are understood;

Whereas, parallel to this market amelioration, international efforts are being deployed within the Organization for Economic Cooperation and Development (OECD) framework to reach a multilateral agreement between the world's most important shipbuilding nations on a rapid phasing-out of all direct and indirect public support measures to shipbuilding, ship conversion and ship repair and of other obstacles to re-establishing normal and fair competition conditions in the sector;

Whereas this agreement must ensure fair competition at an international level among shipyards through a balanced and equitable elimination of all existing impediments to normal competition conditions and must provide a suitable instrument for counteracting all illegal practices and forms of assistance inconsistent with the agreement."

18.10.7.2 International context

The Directive is expressed to be without prejudice to the amendments necessary to comply with international obligations entered into by the Community.[144]

18.10.7.3 Legal basis

The legal basis of the Seventh Shipbuilding Directive is the EEC Treaty generally but, in particular, Articles 92(3)(d) and 113 thereof. Article 92(3)(d) of the EEC Treaty provides that the Council of Ministers may decide to declare specified categories of aid as being compatible with the Common Market even though those categories were not specified in the EEC Treaty itself. Article 113 of the EEC Treaty provides:

18.10.7.4 Entry into force

The Seventh Directive took effect on 1 January 1991.

18.10.7.5 Approach

The Recitals to the Seventh Shipbuilding Directive[145] state that "increased efficiency is a principal objective pursued by this Directive".

The Recitals to the Seventh Shipbuilding Directive[146] states:

"a competitive shipbuilding industry is of vital interest to the Community and contributes to its economic and social development by providing a substantial market for a range of industries, including those using advanced technology; whereas it contributes also to the maintenance of employment in a number of regions, including some which are already suffering a high rate of unemployment; whereas this is also true of ship conversion and ship repair."

144. Dir. 90/684, Recital 7.
145. Dir. 90/684/EEC, OJ L 380/27, 31 December 1990. On this Directive, see para. 18.9.7, below.
146. Dir. 90/684/EEC, OJ L380/27, 31 December 1990. See para. 18.9.7, below.

none the less the "yearly review of the production aid ceiling should always aim at its progressive reduction".[147]

The Council of Ministers in adopting the Seventh Shipbuilding Directive[148] stated in the Recitals:

"the basic aid policy laid down in Directive 87/167/EEC,[149] differentiating between, on the one hand, production aid based on a common ceiling and, on the other, restructuring aid supporting desirable structural changes, remains the most appropriate way of ensuring that the industry is competitive in the long term."

The Recitals to the Seventh Shipbuilding Directive[150] also state:

"there is every reason, for the sake of transparency and equity, to continue to include in the present aid policy indirect aid granted to shipbuilding through investment aid to shipowners for the building and conversion of ships."

It is interesting to notice that the Council of Ministers is anxious to develop the building of "high-tech" vessels at EC shipyards. The Recitals to the Seventh Shipbuilding Directive[151] state:

"every effort should be made to encourage the introduction of high-technological vessels in Community yards."

Should not the fruits of this introduction be given only to EC shipowners? Or is it enough that EC shipyards benefit?

18.10.7.6 Concept of aid

Article 1 of the Seventh Shipbuilding Directive provides that "aid" means:

"State aid within the meaning of Articles 92 and 93 of the [EEC] Treaty, including not only aid granted by the State itself but also that granted by regional or local authorities and any aid elements contained in the financing measures taken by Member States in respect of the shipbuilding or ship repair undertakings which they directly or indirectly control and which do not count as the provision of risk capital according to standard company practice in a market economy.

Such aid may be considered compatible with the common market provided that it complies with the criteria for derogation contained in this Directive."

18.10.7.7 Concept of shipbuilding

Shipbuilding is defined in Article 1 of the Seventh Shipbuilding Directive as meaning the building in the Community of the following metal-hulled sea-going vessels:

"(a) merchant ships for the carriage of passengers and/or cargo, of not less than 100GRT;
(b) fishing vessels of not less than 100GRT;
(c) dredgers or ships for other work at sea of not less than 100GRT excluding drilling platforms; or
(d) tugs of not less than 365kW."

147. Recital to the Seventh Shipbuilding Directive.
148. Dir. 90/684/EEC, OJ L380/27, 31 Decemeber 1990. On this Directive, see para. 18.9.7, below.
149. I.e. the Sixth Shipbuilding Directive.
150. Dir. 90/684/EEC, OJ L380/27, 31 December 1990. On this Directive, see para. 18.9.7, below.
151. Dir. 90/684/EEC, OJ L380/27, 31 December 1990. On this Directive, see para. 18.9.7, below.

18.10.7.8 Concept of ship-conversion

Ship-conversion is defined in Article 1 of the Seventh Shipbuilding Directive as meaning the conversion in the Community of metal-hulled sea-going vessels, as defined in Article 1(a)[152] of the Directive, of not less than 1,000 GRT, on condition that conversion operations entail radical alterations to the cargo plan, the hull or the propulsion system or the passenger accommodation.

One of the Recitals to the Seventh Shipbuilding Directive states:

"the reduced level of aid acceptable for ship conversion and for small specialised vessels, for which the competition is mainly intra-European, should be applied, based on experience, to the largest possible section of this market."

18.10.7.9 Concept of ship-repair

Ship-repair is defined in Article 1 of the Seventh Shipbuilding Directive as meaning the repair of metal-hulled sea-going vessels which are any one of the following four categories:

"(a) merchant ships for the carriage of passengers and/or cargo, of not less than 100GRT;
(b) fishing vessels of not less than 100GRT;
(c) dredgers or ships for other work at sea of not less than 100GRT excluding drilling platforms; or
(d) tugs of not less than 365kW."

The Council of Ministers in adopting the Seventh Shipbuilding Directive[153] stated in the Recitals:

"although it is proposed to treat ship conversion in the same way as shipbuilding to a certain extent, aid to the ship-repair sector should not be permitted, in view of the continuing overcapacity in this sector, except for investments, closure and research and development aid."

18.10.7.10 Concept of contract value before aid

Article 1 of the Seventh Shipbuilding Directive provides that "contract value before aid" means "the price laid down in the contract plus any aid granted directly to the shipyard".

18.10.7.11 Specific areas of the EC

18.10.7.11.1 Spain and Portugal

The transitional arrangements which had been accorded to Spain and Portugal ended on 31 December 1990. However, "as the stage of restructuring of the Spanish shipbuilding industry has still not reached a level where it is competitive with the other Member States of the Community, a specific further two-year restructuring programme should be carried out while exemption from the production aid ceiling should be allowed for 1991".[154]

152. I.e. (a) merchant ships for the carriage of passengers and/or cargo; (b) fishing vessels; (c) dredgers or ships for other work at sea excluding drilling platforms; or (d) tugs of not less than 365kW.

153. Dir. 90/684/EEC, OJ L380/27, 31 December 1990. On this Directive, see para. 18.9.7, below.

154. Recital to the Seventh Shipbuilding Directive.

18.10.7.11.2 Greece

The Recitals to the Seventh Shipbuilding Directive[155] state:

"a short-term financial restructuring of the shipbuilding industry in Greece is necessary in order to enable its public owners to restore its competitiveness by selling off to new owners."

18.10.7.11.3 "German Democratic Republic"

The transitional arrangements which had been accorded to the territory of the former German Democratic Republic ended on 31 December 1990.

18.10.7.12 Discriminatory practices

Article 2 of the Seventh Shipbuilding Directive provides:

"No aid granted pursuant to this Directive may be conditional upon discriminatory practices as to products originating in other Member States."

18.10.7.13 Aid to shipowners

Article 3 of the Seventh Shipbuilding Directive deals with aid granted to shipowners.

Article 3(1) of the Seventh Shipbuilding Directive provides that all forms of aid to shipowners or to third parties which are available as aid for the building or conversion of ships shall be subject to the notification rules in Article 11 of that Directive. This aid shall include credit facilities, guarantees and tax concessions granted to shipowners or third parties for those purposes.[156] Article 11 is discussed below.[157] This is however "without prejudice to changes in the Community rules on aid to shipowners provided that observance of the principle of transparency of aid for shipbuilding and ship conversion is ensured".[158]

Article 3(2) of the Seventh Shipbuilding Directive provides that grant equivalent of the aid will be subject in full to the rules set out in Article 4 of the Directive where the aid is actually used for the building or conversion of ships in Community shipyards. Article 4 of the Directive deals with contract-related production aid. This is however "without prejudice to changes in the Community rules on aid to shipowners provided that observance of the principle of transparency of aid for shipbuilding and ship conversion is ensured."[159]

Article 3(2) of the Seventh Shipbuilding Directive goes on to provide that grants equivalent of the aid will be subject in full to the rules set out in Article 12 of the Directive where the aid is actually used for the building or conversion of ships in Community shipyards. Article 12 of the Directive deals with monitoring. This is however "without prejudice to changes in the Community rules on aid to shipowners provided that observance of the principle of transparency of aid for shipbuilding and ship conversion is ensured".[160]

155. Dir. 90/684/EEC, OJ L380/27, 31 December 1990.
156. Dir. 90/684/EEC, Article 3(1).
157. See Appendix 2, below.
158. Dir. 90/684/EEC, Article 3(4).
159. Dir. 90/684/EEC, Article 3(4).
160. Dir. 90/684/EEC, Article 3(4).

A general rule that aid "granted by a Member State to its shipowners or to third parties in that State for the building or conversion of ships may not lead to distortions of competition between national shipyards and shipyards in other Member States in the placing of orders" is laid down in Article 3(3) of the Seventh Shipbuilding Directive. This is however "without prejudice to changes in the Community rules on aid to shipowners provided that observance of the principle of transparency of aid for shipbuilding and ship conversion is ensured".[161]

18.10.7.14 Operating aid

Chapter II of the Directive (comprising of Articles 4 and 5) deals with operating aid.

18.10.7.14.1 Ceilings

Article 4(1) of the Seventh Shipbuilding Directive provides that production aid in favour of shipbuilding[162] and ship conversion[163] may be considered compatible with the common market[164] provided that the total amount of aid granted in support of any individual contract does not exceed, in grant equivalent, a common maximum ceiling expressed as a percentage of the contract value before aid[165]—that is to say, the so-called "ceiling".

The ceiling is fixed, according to Article 4(2) of the Seventh Shipbuilding Directive, by the Commission with reference to the prevailing difference between the cost structures of the most competitive Community yards and the prices charged by their main international competitors with particular regard to the market segments in which the Community yards remain relatively most competitive. However, the Commission must pay particular attention to ensuring that the aid for the building of small specialised vessels, a market segment normally served by small yards, in particular small ships of a contract value of less than ECU10 million and for which the competition is mainly inter-European, is kept at the lowest possible level, nevertheless allowing for the particular situation in Greece. These rules apply to all types of ship conversion, irrespective of the value of the contract.

The ceiling is to be reviewed every twelve months.[166] It may be reviewed more frequently than every twelve months where exceptional circumstances warrant it.[167] However, every review must be made with the aim of progressively reviewing the ceiling.[168] In every review, "the Commission shall also ensure that there are no undue concentrations of shipbuilding activities in specific market segments to an extent contrary to Community interests".[169]

The aid ceiling for 1991 is 13% but 9% for ships with a contract value of less than ECU10m and for ship conversion. This is a reduction from the 1990 levels of 20% and 14% respectively. The aid ceiling for 1992 is 9% for production aid in EC shipyards and 4.5% for contracts less than ECU10m.

161. Dir. 90/684/EEC, Article 3(4).
162. For the definition of "shipbuilding", for present purposes, see above.
163. For the definition of "ship conversion", for present purposes, see above.
164. I.e. not illegal under EC law.
165. Article 1 of the Seventh Shipbuilding Directive provides that "contract value before aid" means "the price laid down in the contract plus any aid granted directly to the shipyard".
166. Dir. 90/684/EEC, Article 4(3).
167. Dir. 90/684/EEC, Article 4(3).
168. Dir. 90/684/EEC, Article 4(3).
169. Dir. 90/684/EEC, Article 4(3).

As a general rule, the aid ceiling applicable to a contract is that in force at the date of the signature of the final contract.[170] Thus, care should be taken to ensure the appropriate time of signing. As a general rule, the contract should signed as soon as possible because the aid ceiling levels will be progressively reduced rather than increased. However, this general rule "shall not apply in respect of any ship delivered more than three years from the date of signing of the final contract. In such cases, the ceiling applicable to that contract shall be that in force three years before the date of delivery of the ship".[171] The Commission may grant an extension of this three-year delivery limit when "this is justified by the technical complexity of the individual shipbuilding project concerned or by delays resulting from unexpected disruptions of a substantial and defensible nature in the working programme of a yard".[172]

The ceiling will apply to all forms of production aid granted directly to the yards as well as aid covered by Article 3(2) of the Seventh Shipbuilding Directive.[173,174] This is irrespective of whether the aid is granted under the sectoral, general or regional aid schemes.[175]

18.10.7.15 Restructuring aid

Chapter III of the Directive (comprising of Articles 6 to 9) deals with restructuring aid.

18.10.7.15.1 Investment aid

Article 6(1) of the Seventh Shipbuilding Directive provides that:

> "Investment aid, whether specific or non-specific, may not be granted for the creation of new shipyards or for investment in existing yards unless it is linked to a restructuring plan which does not involve any increase in the shipbuilding capacity of the yard or unless it is directly linked to a corresponding irreversible reduction in the capacity of other yards in the same Member State over the same period.
>
> Such aid may not be granted to ship repair yards unless linked to a restructuring plan which results in a reduction in the overall ship repair capacity of the Member State concerned. In this context the Commission may take into account capacity reductions carried out in the immediately preceding years."

Investment may be deemed compatible with the common market provided that (a) the amount and intensity of the aid are justified by the extent of the restructuring involved and (b) the aid is limited to supporting expenditure directly related to the investment.[176]

Article 6(2) goes on to provide that:

> "[Article 6(1)] shall not apply to the opening of a new shipyard in a Member State which otherwise would have no shipbuilding facilities or to investments in a Member State's only existing yard, provided that the effect of the yard in question on the Community is minimal."

170. Dir. 90/684/EEC, Article 4(3).
171. Dir. 90/684/EEC, Article 4(3).
172. Dir. 90/684/EEC, Article 4(3).
173. Article 3(2) of the Seventh Shipbuilding Directive provides that the grants equivalent of the aid will be subject in full to the rules set out in Article 4 of the Directive where the aid is actually used for the building or conversion of ships in Community shipyards. Article 4 of the Directive deals with contract-related production aid. This is, however, "without prejudice to changes in the Community rules on aid to shipowners provided that observance of the principle of transparency of aid for shipbuilding and ship conversion is ensured".
174. Dir. 90/684/EEC, Article 4(4).
175. Dir. 90/684/EEC, Article 4(4).
176. Dir. 90/684/EEC, Article 6(3).

In examining investment aid under Article 6, the Commission must take account of "the extent of the contribution of the investment programme concerned to such Community objectives for the sector as innovation, specialisation, working conditions, health, safety and the environment".[177]

18.10.7.15.2 Aid for closures

Article 7 of the Seventh Shipbuilding Directive deals with aid for closures of shipyards.

Article 7(1) provides that aid to defray the normal costs resulting from the partial or total closure of shipbuilding or ship repair yards may be considered compatible with the common market provided that the capacity reduction resulting from such aid is of a genuine and irreversible nature.[178]

The closure must be "irreversible".[179] In order to establish this irreversible nature of aided closures, the Member State concerned must ensure that the closed shipbuilding and ship repair facilities remain closed for a period of not less than five years.[180] During this five-year period, the closed site may not be used for activities in anticipation of a return to shipbuilding after the expiry of the five-year period, thus it may not be developed or rebuilt or in any way prepared for a reopening.[181] The concept of "irreversibility" is not absolute however: Article 7(1) of the Seventh Directive provides:

> "In order to establish the irreversible nature of aided closures, the Member State concerned shall ensure that the closed shipbuilding and ship repair facilities remain closed for a period of not less than five years.
>
> Within this five-year period, the closed site may not be used for activities in anticipation of a return to shipbuilding after the expiry of the five-year period.
>
> *If, after a period of five years but before the tenth anniversary of the closure, a Member State wishes to reopen a closed shipbuilding or ship repair facility, it must obtain the Commission's prior approval.*
>
> The Commission's decision will be taken with reference both to the currently existing worldwide balance between supply and demand and to whether it is envisaged that aid is to be granted for reopening the facilities."[182]

By implication, a yard may be reopened after ten years without the Commission's approval and without having to repay any aid granted.

The types of aid which are allowable are, in particular,[183]

- payments to workers made redundant or retired before legal retirement age[184];
- counselling services to workers made or to be made redundant or retired before legal retirement age including payments made by yards to facilitate the creation of small undertakings[185];
- payments to workers for vocational training;[186];

177. Dir. 90/684/EEC, Article 6(4).
178. Dir. 90/684/EEC, Article 7(1).
179. Dir. 90/684/EEC, Article 7(1).
180. Dir. 90/684/EEC, Article 7(1).
181. Dir. 90/684/EEC, Article 7(1).
182. Dir. 90/684/EEC, Article 7(1), emphasis added.
183. Dir. 90/684/EEC, Article 7(2) uses the term "in particular" thus, by implication, other costs could, in appropriate circumstances, be included.
184. Dir. 90/684/EEC, Article 7(2).
185. Dir. 90/684/EEC, Article 7(2).
186. Dir. 90/684/EEC, Article 7(2).

— expenditure incurred for the development of the yard, its buildings, installations and infrastructure for use other than that specified in Article 1(a), (b) and (c) of the Seventh Directive[187]; and
— in the event of total closure of a yard, the residual book value of its installations (ignoring that portion of any revaluation since 1 January 1982 which exceeds the national inflation rate).[188]

The amount and intensity of the aid must be justified by the extent of the restructuring involved.[189] Account may be taken of the structural problems of the region concerned and, in the case of conversion to other industrial activities, of the Community legislation and rules applicable to the new sector concerned.[190]

18.10.7.15.3 Aid for research and development

Article 8 of the Seventh Directive deals with aid for research and development. Given the age of EC shipping and its relatively poor state of technological development,[191] it is essential that the EC rules on State Aids allow for the authorisation of Research and Development aid.

Article 8 states:

> "1. Aid to defray expenditure by shipbuilding and ship repair undertakings for research and development projects may be considered compatible with the common market.
> 2. For the purposes of this Directive, the eligible costs shall be only those relating to fundamental research, basic industrial research and applied research and development, all as defined by the Commission in Annex I to the Community framework for State aids for research and development,[192] excluding those related to industrial application and commercial exploitation of the results."

18.10.7.16 Monitoring

Part V of the Seventh Shipbuilding Directive deals with the monitoring procedure.

The Recitals to the Seventh Shipbuilding Directive[193] state:

> "the efficiency of the present aid policy and confidence in it can only be obtained by close and timely monitoring by the Commission of Member States' implementation of the aid rules; whereas, therefore, compliance by Member States with their reporting obligations, on which such a monitoring system is based, should be secured by providing for the suspension of all outstanding payments of aid already approved until all due reports have been received by the Commission; whereas this provision must also apply to the non-transmission of reports relating to aid schemes which have already been authorised."

18.10.7.17 Spain

Spain joined the EC late relative to the all the other Member States (apart from Portugal).[194] It is thus perhaps not surprising to find exceptions relating to the application of the Seventh Shipbuilding Directive to Spain.

187. Dir. 90/684/EEC, Article 7(2).
188. Dir. 90/684/EEC, Article 7(2).
189. Dir. 90/684/EEC, Article 7(3).
190. Dir. 90/684/EEC, Article 7(3).
191. See Chapter 2, above.
192. OJ C83, 11 April 1986, p. 2.
193. Dir. 90/684/EEC, OJ L380/27, 31 December 1990. See "German Subsidies under Review", *Lloyd's List*, 20 December 1991, p. 3.
194. See Chapter 3, above.

Article 9(1) of the Seventh Shipbuilding Directive provides:

"With the exception of the second sub paragraph of Article 4(5), Chapter II of this Directive shall not be applicable to Spain until 1 January 1992."

Thus, in essence, the rules relating to operating aid have no application to Spain before 1 January 1992.

Article 9(2) provides that in respect of 1991 (i.e. before Chapter II applies), operating aid for shipbuilding and ship conversion in Spain may be considered compatible with the common market provided that:

— Spain's shipbuilding industry carries out, in addition to the 1987 to 1990 restructuring programme and according to the timetable set, all the restructuring measures laid down in the supplementary restructuring plan for 1991 and 1992 submitted to the Commission by the Spanish Government,
— the Spanish Government, jointly with the Commission, mandates an independent consultancy to monitor the implementation, according to the timetable, of the aforementioned restructuring programme; this consultancy shall supply six-monthly reports to the Commission and the Spanish authorities containing details of the progress that the sector has made, in compliance with the restructuring plan, in order to be capable of operating with the same aid level as the other Member States,
— where the six-monthly reports give reason to doubt that the shipbuilding industry will attain the planned level of competitiveness, the Spanish Government will take measures to reinforce the restructuring of the sector which are accepted by the Commission as capable of rectifying the situation,
— operating aid is reduced from the 1990 level."

18.10.7.18 Balance

The next few years will prove interesting. It is believed by some commentators that shipbuilding aids will be eliminated by the end of 1994. If aids are not eliminated then some States, such as Denmark[195] may decide to institute proceedings in the ECJ. It is interesting that since OECD negotiations began in September 1989, the EC has reduced its aid level from 26% to 9% in 1992.

195. See "Denmark may act against EC on subsidies", *Lloyd's List*, 14 December 1991, p. 1.

CHAPTER 19

The EC's Relations in Shipping Matters with the Rest of the World

19.1 INTRODUCTION

Shipping is by its very nature an international activity.[1] This chapter provides an overview of the EC's external relations with the rest of the world in regard to shipping matters.[2]

In a 1984 Press Release, the Commission stated:

"[a]ny Community shipping policy must, inevitably, grant pride of place to international aspects, i.e. to the relations between Member States and non-member countries. Even the intra-Community aspects of such a policy must take the international context into account. In the Commission's view, there are a number of problems in this area which could be tackled more effectively by the Community rather than the Member States individually."[3]

There is need for a single EC external policy in relation to shipping matters. In 1977, the European Parliament's Committee on Regional Policy, Regional Planning and Transport published an Interim Report on the Sea Transport Problems in the Community and stated:

"There have been many changes since 1957: the Community has been enlarged by countries that are particularly important in world shipping. The Community has established the beginnings of a common external economic policy, but this cannot work if it overlooks one of the most important instruments of Europe's external trade, namely sea transport. Sooner than it would like, the Community is being forced by world economic developments and by its overseas partners to speak with one voice and to adopt a common position. In all major questions of world economic policy sea transport has again and again played an important role for the Community."[4]

The need for such a policy is evident from the fact that the EC has had on-going discussions (and occasionally battles) with, among others, the US,[5] the former USSR

1. See Farthing, *International Shipping: An Introduction to the Policies, Politics and Institutions of the Maritime World* (Lloyd's of London Press Ltd, 1987). See Sberro, *The EC's External Relations in the Transport Sector* (1991).

2. There are instances where the EC has external relations with non-Member States on shipping matters which are not covered in this chapter (e.g. Reg. 4055/86), but which are discussed elsewhere in this book. So, too, the relations between the EC and the State Trading countries are not reviewed in this chapter because the matter is now of historical interest: see the Economic and Social Committee in its Opinion on the EEC's Transport Problems with East European Countries (1977), for some background.

3. P-95, December 1984. This is in contradiction to the now much-favoured notion of subsidiarity.

4. Working Documents; Doc.5/77; 23 March 1977; Rapporteur: Mr H. Seefeld, para. 4.

5. See, for example, "EEC Lashes US Oil Policy", *Lloyd's List*, 29 May 1987, p. 2.

and other State-trading countries, Japan[6] as well as West Africa in shipping and related matters. There is little doubt but that these discussions and battles will rage well into the future.

19.2 THE LAW RELATING TO THE EXTERNAL RELATIONS OF THE EC

19.2.1 Introduction

The law and practice concerning the external relations of the EC are fascinating subjects but go beyond the scope of this book.[7]

These subjects embrace such matters as the EC's commercial policy, development policy and relations with States around the world. A mere summary will have to suffice for present purposes.

The Member States of the EC are each sovereign and independent States. None the less they have each transferred some of their sovereignty and independence to the EC.[8,9]

It is inevitable that the EC will have contact with non-Member States and international organisations around the world. Such contact takes the form of international trade,[10] competition and development arrangements. Much of this co-operation takes place within the confines of European Political Co-operation (EPC): Article 30(5) of the SEA requires that the external policies of the EC and the policies agreed within the EPC are to be consistent.

19.2.2 Provisions of the EC Treaties

19.2.2.1 ECSC Treaty

In relation to the ECSC, Article 6 of its Treaty provides:

"The Community shall have legal personality.

In international relations, the Community shall enjoy the legal capacity it requires to perform its functions and attain its objectives.

In each of the Member States, the Community shall enjoy the most extensive legal capacity afforded to legal persons constituted in that State; it may, in particular, acquire or dispose of movable and immovable property and may be a party to legal proceedings.

The Community shall be represented by its institutions, each within the limits of its powers.

Thus, in international relations, the Community shall enjoy the legal capacity it requires to perform its functions and attain its objectives. This means that it has limited functional international personality: limited to its own functions."

19.2.2.2 Euratom or EAEC Treaty

In relation to Euratom, Article 101 of its Treaty provides:

6. See, "EEC Warns Japan", *Lloyd's List*, 27 April 1990, p. 3.

7. See Kapteyn and Van Themaat, *op. cit.*, Chapter XI; Mathijsen, *op. cit.*, p. 231–56; and Vaughan (ed.), *op. cit.*, Part 4.

8. This transfer has been problematical.

9. Note the reactions of Denmark and Ireland to the SEA.

10. See Arts 113, 114 and 224 EEC. Note also the sanctions imposed on Argentina, Iran, Iraq, Rhodesia, South Africa and the former USSR. See Kuyper, *The Implementation of International Sanctions* (1978) as well as Kuyper again in O'Keeffe and Schermers (eds.), *Essays in European Law and Integration* (1982) at p. 141.

"The Community may, within the limits of its powers and jurisdiction, enter into obligations by concluding agreements or contracts with a third State, an international organisation or a national of a third State.

Such agreements or contracts shall be negotiated by the Commission in accordance with the directives of the Council: they shall be concluded by the Commission with the approval of the Council, which shall act by a qualified majority.

Agreements or contracts whose implementation does not require action by the Council and can be effected within the limits of the relevant budget shall, however, be negotiated and concluded solely by the Commission; the Commission shall keep the Council informed."

19.2.2.3 EEC Treaty

Article 101 and Article 113 of the EEC Treaty are directly relevant. Article 110 provides that by establishing a customs union between themselves Member States aim to contribute, in the common interest, to the harmonious development of world trade, the progressive abolition of restrictions on international trade and the lowering of customs barriers. The common commercial policy must take into account the favourable effect which the abolition of customs duties between Member States may have on the increase in the competitive strength of undertakings in those States. Some of the international "trade and shipping" agreements were negotiated jointly on the basis of Article 113.[11] In this regard, the Council of Minister's Decision of 16 December 1969 on the progressive standardisation of agreements concerning commercial relations between Member States and third countries and on the negotiation of Community agreements[12] is relevant. The absence of a common shipping policy has been the cause of weakness in terms of negotiating such agreements.[13]

19.2.2.3.1 Treaty-making powers

Article 228 of the EEC Treaty provides:

"1. Where this Treaty provides for the conclusion of agreements between the Community and one or more States or an international organisation, such agreements shall be negotiated by the Commission. Subject to the powers vested in the Commission in this field, such agreements shall be concluded by the Council, after consulting the European Parliament where required by this Treaty.

The Council, the Commission or a Member State may obtain beforehand the opinion of the Court of Justice as to whether an agreement envisaged is compatible with the provisions of this Treaty. Where the opinion of the Court of Justice is adverse, the agreement may enter into force only in accordance with Article 236.

2. Agreements concluded under these conditions shall be binding on the institutions of the Community and on Member States."

19.2.2.3.2 Relations with the United Nations and GATT

Article 229 provides:

"It shall be for the Commission to ensure the maintenance of all appropriate relations with the organs of the United Nations, of its specialised agencies and of the General Agreement on Tariffs and Trade.

11. Doc. 5/77; 23 March 1977; Rapporteur: Mr H. Seefeld, para. 30.
12. OJ L326, 29 December 1969.
13. Doc. 5/77; 23 March 1977; Rapporteur: Mr H. Seefeld, para. 32. For the text of Article 113, see Appendix 1, below.

The Commission shall also maintain such relations as are appropriate with all international organisations. None the less the absence of an express provision has not hampered the recognition of the international personality of the EEC."

19.2.2.3.3 Relations with the Council of Europe

Article 230 provides:

"The Community shall establish all appropriate forms of co-operation with the Council of Europe."

The Council has very limited relevance for shipping matters.

19.2.2.3.4 Relations with the Organisation for Economic Co-operation and Development

Article 231 provides:

"The Community shall establish close co-operation with the Organisation for European Economic Co-operation, the details to be determined by common accord."

The Organisation for European Economic Co-operation (OEEC) later became known as the Organisation for Economic Co-operation and Development (OECD).[14]

19.3 CONSULTATION PROCEDURE IN SHIPPING MATTERS

19.3.1 Introduction

On 13 September 1977, the EEC Council adopted Decision[15] 77/587/EEC to set up a consultation procedure on relations between Member States and third countries in shipping matters and on action relating to such matters in international organisations.[16] It was one of the first ever measures in EC shipping law

19.3.2 Purpose

The purpose of the Decision may be gleaned from the Preamble to the Decision which provides:

"Whereas, to make allowance for developments affecting world shipping and for their consequences for the Member States, it is desirable that problems of common interest with regard to relations between Member States and third countries in shipping matters and to action relating to such matters in international organisations should be identified in good time;

Whereas it is desirable to facilitate exchanges of information and consultations on such matters and to promote co-ordination, where appropriate, of the action taken by the Member States in international organisations;

Whereas each Member State should give the benefit of its experience in relations to third countries in shipping matters to the other Member States and to the Commission;

Whereas information in this field is regularly exchanged in certain international organisations; whereas these procedures should be supplemented at Community level by exchanges of information between the Member States and the Commission . . ."

14. On the work of the OECD in shipping, see Chapter 1, above.
15. On the nature of decisions in EC law, see Chapter 3, above.
16. OJ L239/23, 17 September 1977.

19.3.3 Background

Some non-EC shipping companies were engaged in practices which distorted competition by resorting to flag discrimination, dumping, subsidies, tax concessions as well as non-adherence and non-enforcement of international safety standards.

The Decision owes its origin to a proposal from the Commission to the Council of Ministers in June 1976 which was embodied in a Communication entitled "Communication from the Commission to the Council on the Community's Relations with Non-Member Countries in Shipping Matters".[17] This Memorandum was written because the EC was "facing increasing problems in its relations with non-member countries in shipping matters".[18] The three-fold purpose of the Communication was to:

"(i) underline the importance of shipping to the Community;
(ii) outline the main problems affecting shipping in the Community's relations with non-member countries; [and]
(iii) suggest Community measures to meet these problems."[19]

In this Communication, the Commission (in its own words):

"advocated that the Community should take steps to counter the growing discrimination, increasingly frequent market-disrupting practices and the dumping methods to which Community shipping is being exposed by the policies of other countries. To halt the spreading distortions of competition in sea transport, the Community should not only resort to bilateral and multilateral agreements to deal with the problem, but should also, where necessary, envisage limiting shares of traffic and imposing compensatory levies."[20]

This Communication was the first time that the Commission had adopted an overall position on the difficulties facing the merchant fleets of the Member States.[21]

The Commission elsewhere surveyed the factual background to the Decision in the following terms:

"The sea transport sector is going through an increasingly serious crisis. The measures adopted by certain foreign governments (especially those of the State trading countries, of certain developing countries and of some developed countries), increasingly restrain the freedom to provide services in this field, especially on regular routes, and have now reached a level which is very harmful to Community interests.

The unfavourable effect of these measures (which most often reserve an increasingly substantial part of cargoes for the national flag) arise in three ways:

(a) a loss of revenue (present and future) for the Community's shipping companies (which represent a turnover of about 13,000 million u.a., employ more than 300,000 people and make a very considerable contribution to the balance of payments);
(b) a relative decline in the carrying capacity controlled by the Member States, the effect of which is a lower degree of security of supply in the event of crisis or conflict (the share of the Community's shipping companies for world fleet dropped from 40 per cent in 1958 to 24 per cent in 1975);
(c) a loss of efficiency for the Community's foreign trade, 90 per cent of which depends on maritime transport and which suffers from the artificial restraints because of the inefficiency which they create, especially as regards the regular routes."[22]

17. COM(76)341 final, 30 June 1976. On the Communication and the background thereto, see Commission's Information Memo P 51 of July 1976.

18. Communication, *ibid.*, para. 1.1.

19. *Ibid.*, para. 1.

20. EC Commission, *Information: Transport*, No. 132/76 entitled "The European Community and Sea Traffic with Non-Member States".

21. *Ibid.*

22. Commission's Information Memo, P-51, July 1976, p. 1. The abbreviation "u.a." stands for "units of account".

The Commission also wrote elsewhere that:

"[t]he greatest problems are . . . caused by the rise of the merchant fleets of the State-trading countries. The economic system of the East Bloc countries, in which costs play a different role from in free market economies, enables their shipping lines easily to underquote freight rates even though no real competitive advantage exists.

Capital costs, the most important cost factor in this capital-intensive industry, thus play a subordinate role in the fleets of the State-trading countries. Insurance premiums, sometimes quite considerable, are paid by the state. Bunker fuel is supplied in Soviet ports at much lower prices than in the West. These three factors together make it possible for the shipping lines of the State-trading countries to apply freight rates which are on average 30 per cent below the market level. The system of selling cif and purchasing fob[23] offers further scope for influencing the choice of vessels.

Although the Member States of the Council for Mutual Economic Assistance account for only 5 per cent of world trade, as a result of these dumping practices their share of the world fleet of cargo liners is 16 per cent. In trade between the USA and the Federal Republic of Germany, Eastern European freighters are already carrying 13 per cent of total freight. In ports in the Netherlands, they take on nearly as much cargo as Dutch vessels, while in German ports their share is already half of that of the German shipping lines. The attempt of the Soviet merchant marine to gain a footing on the route between Western Europe and East Africa is also significant.

Soviet vessels now carry 70 per cent of sea-borne trade between the Community and the USSR. It should also be noted that vessels from the State-trading countries may load and unload freely in Community ports, but Community countries' fleets may not do likewise in ports in State-trading countries.

As a result of dumping by the State-trading coutries, Western European shipping lines are suffering a growing loss of revenue, which reduces the returns on investments in shipping and will eventually lead to a further relative decline of the Western European merchant fleet. Dumping also entails a political danger. If the fleets of the State-trading countries should ever get into a dominant position, they could one day be in a position to impose their conditions on Community countries' trade.

All these practices raise political problems. The Commission therefore takes the view that the Community must act. Up until now, some Member States, basing themselves on the Treaty of Rome,[24] have been unwilling to recognise that the Community has any competence in shipping matters. Nevertheless, such matters have recently been mentioned in the exchanges of letters relating to trade agreements. In GATT, flag discrimination has at the insistence of the Commission been included in the list of non-tariff barriers to trade. The Commission feels that Community action would clearly be more effective than moves by individual member countries. Shipping problems should therefore be discussed at future bilateral negotiations with non-member countries and should also be brought up at multilateral level. Where necessary, countermeasures should also be taken to maintain the efficiency of Community shipping lines."[25]

The fleets of the developing countries had grown almost three-fold and the world fleet generally had actually tripled during the 1959–76 period. The flags of convenience had grown more than three times and the fleets of State-trading countries had quadrupled in tonnage during the same period. On the other hand, the EC's share of the world market had fallen from 40% to 24%. This was a depressing picture for the EC but was compounded by the fact that while the EC's fleet was declining, world trade was increasing[26] which meant that the EC's fleet could not benefit from the upturn.

The discriminatory practices engaged in by some other States had begun to affect freight prices and this would have a consequential effect on the EC's Commercial Policy generally.

23. By selling cif and purchasing fob, one reserves to oneself the choice of carrier.

24. I.e. the EEC Treaty.

25. Commission, "The European Community and Sea Traffic With Non-Member States", Information: Transport, 132/76, pp. 2–3.

26. During 1958–76, trade between the EC and the rest of the world grew by about 400%.

Why had the EC not reacted earlier? In a significant passage in an Information Memorandum published by it in July 1976, the Commission said:

"[i]n the past, Community action to deal with this adverse development has had an extremely limited scope, *especially owing to the reluctance of certain Member States to recognise that the Community has had the necessary powers in this field or to grant them.* However, it has become vital to reach an agreement on the substance of the action to be taken to protect the fundamental interests of the Community and its Member States, while deferring laying down the legal procedures until the appropriate time."[27]

In its 1976 Communication to the Council of Ministers on the Community's Relations with Non-Member Countries in Shipping Matters,[28] the Commission stated:

"4.1 The Community shipping companies are experiencing serious problems at two levels: at the cyclical level because of the effects of the economic crisis on these companies, especially in the oil transport sector, and on the political level because of the increasingly restrictive practices adopted by the governments of certain non-member countries in the field of international shipping relations . . .

4.2 The political difficulties are due to the determination of some foreign governments to gain a larger share of international maritime trade, by recourse to measures which create distortions in respect of the free supply of services on the market. They consist, in particular, of measures of flag discrimination, state financing of deficits of national shipping companies, and dumping practices. Other difficulties are created by tax exemptions and the disregard of safety measures."

It then went on to identify the specific difficulties encountered by EC shipping companies in external maritime trade, namely flag discrimination,[29] subsidies[30] and under-quoting by the East Bloc countries.[31] This was the first time that the Commission adopted an overall position on the difficulties facing the merchant fleets of the Member States.

In respect of flag discrimination, the Commission stated:

"4.3 The trend towards increased government intervention has often taken the form of flag discrimination, especially since the mid-sixties, and particularly in the liner trades. This usually means that countries reserve sometimes more than 50 per cent of cargoes for vessels flying the national flag. The Latin American and certain Asian countries are particularly prone to this practice.[32]

Such measures have helped to enable developing countries to obtain a very high growth rate for their merchant fleets and to increase their share of the world cargo liner fleet to 15 per cent.

4.4 The desire of some developing—and of some developed—countries to secure for their own vessels a large share of their sea-borne transport found institutional expression in April 1974 in the adoption of a Convention on a Code of Conduct for Liner Conferences. The text represents the result of negotiations initiated in 1973 at the request of the General Assembly of the United Nations and under the auspices of UNCTAD, and in which virtually all the countries with a merchant fleet participated. These negotiations, the objective of which was to improve the system of liner conferences, were explicitly approached with the aim of taking particular account of the special needs and problems of developing countries in this field.

4.5 This spirit was not respected, since the final text provides for the general application of national cargo reservation to all countries, irrespective of their level of development or their economic system.

---

27. *Ibid.*, p. 1 (emphasis added).
28. COM(76) 341 final. See Press Release P–51, July 1976.
29. COM(76) 314 final, paras 4.3–4.9.
30. COM(76) 314 final, paras 4.10–4.11.
31. COM(76) 314 final, paras 4.12–4.18.
32. The same objectives can be achieved indirectly, e.g. by the application of a system of sales cif and purchases fob, leaving the choice of vessel to the exporter and importer respectively.

4.6 Consequently, in practice the application of the Convention in its present form results in the generalised institutionalisation of discrimination in favour of national flags by allowing 'cargo-generating countries' at each end of a shipping route to reserve up to some 40 per cent of their cargoes for vessels flying their own flags, leaving 20 per cent for shippers from third countries . . .

4.8 Finally, it should be recalled that discriminatory measures applied on a unilateral basis are not resorted to exclusively by developing countries, but that the practices of certain developed market economy countries create, or threaten to create, serious damage. This is especially the case with certain discriminatory measures applied, or possibly to be applied in the future, by the United States. For example, the US Administration interprets the 'Jones Act', reserving national US coastal waters to vessels flying the Amercian flag, in such a way as to refuse foreign shipping companies the right to trans-ship containers arriving from abroad in an American port and consigned to another port in that country. European container vessel operators are thus put in a very unfavourable competitive position on the world's most important shipping route, the North Atlantic. Furthermore, a draft bill has just been laid before Congress to reserve to US flag vessels 30 per cent of oil imported into the United States. The direct impact of the adoption of such legislation on European shipowners would probably be more important than most of the industrial measures applied by other foreign governments (not to speak of the risk of an even more serious snowball effect) . . .

4.9 As for state-trading countries, their system of state commerce allows them to pursue a determined trading policy under which their purchases are systematically made on a fob basis and their sales on a cif basis. This allows the state agencies of these countries to choose the means of transport which suits them (normally their own ships) and thus to apply indirectly flag discrimination, which has had the effect of permitting them to reserve to their own ships 70 per cent or more of their bilateral trade with the Community."[33]

In respect of subsidies, the Commission stated:

"4.10 Most countries with merchant fleets grant them subsidies—some small, some large—either by direct grants or by tax relief measures. It should also be noted that distortions in operating conditions are created by the existence of flags of convenience which grant almost total tax exemption and do not necessarily require that the observance of certain safety standards or rules governing working conditions.

4.11 It does seem, however, that it is the conditions of operation of the merchant fleets of certain state-trading countries which cause most of the problems in this area, since the economic system of these countries allows their shipping companies to operate on international routes without taking account of the 'real' costs (particularly capital costs). The effects of these activities of these countries in the maritime trade sector can, however, be more easily reviewed in the [context of] 'under-cutting'."[34]

In respect of under-quoting by East Bloc countries, the Commission stated:

"4.12 The merchant fleets of the state-trading countries have grown more rapidly than those of any other category of country since the fifties and have become particularly important in the cargo liner sector. This extremely rapid expansion—400 per cent in fifteen years—was made possible by the economic system of these countries which allowed their shipping companies to compete on the international market without paying the same attention as the market economy countries to capital costs, which form a large part of the total costs of this highly capital-intensive industry. Furthermore, insurance premiums, which are very important in this sector, are covered by the state and bunker fuel is delivered (at least in the USSR ports) at prices much lower than the Western level. All these factors taken together enable the state-trading countries to apply freight rates which on average are about 30 per cent below the market level. The system of selling cif and buying fob used by these countries . . . permits them to exercise a further control over the cargoes involved in their own foreign trade.

4.13 Although the international trade of CMEA (COMECON) member countries only represents about 5 per cent of international trade in general cargo, their share of the world fleet of

33. COM(76) 341 final.
34. COM(76) 341 final.

general cargo vessels is already 16 per cent, and 20 per cent of the vessels on order. Of the total trade between the USA and the Federal Republic of Germany, the fleets of state-trading countries already transport about 13 per cent. In the Dutch ports, they already lift nearly as much cargo as Dutch shipowners, and their share of trade in the German ports amounts to half of that of German shipowners. Another specific example concerns the route W. Europe–E. Africa which currently employs between thirty and forty vessels (most of which are European). In September 1975, the USSR announced its intention of putting twelve Russian vessels on this route, which in itself does not represent a commercial interest for that country. More than 70 per cent of the bilateral sea-borne trade between the EEC and the USSR is carried by vessels belonging to the USSR.

4.14 This expansion was of course motivated by political and military reasons, but also by a desire to secure convertible currrency revenue in a sector which, despite the large number of flag discrimination practices, is still almost completely open as far as traffic between developed countries is concerned."

The Commission then proposed a number of measures which it later summarised in the following terms:

"(a) the common interests should be protected with the aim of arriving at a common policy which would include, if necessary, the negotiation of purely maritime agreements between the Community and non-member countries. In the meantime there is a need for concentration at Community level regarding the measures to be taken in connection with the bilateral agreements concluded between Member States and certain non-member countries;

(b) the Member States and the Commission should closely co-ordinate their positions within the international organisations responsible for sea transport or in the context of other multilateral discussions so that Community or joint action can be taken as the case may be;

(c) whenever it is appropriate, clauses on sea transport should be included in the guidelines for negotiating agreements between the Community and non-member countries;

(d) whenever appropriate, questions concerning sea transport should be raised where there is contact between the Community and non-member countries, even outside the framework of commercial or other agreements with the country in question;

(e) the Commission should examine, in conjunction with the Member States, the case for adopting other measures in the sea transport sector, including countermeasures."[35]

19.3.4 Legal bases

The legal bases for the Decision were, in general, the EEC Treaty and, in particular, Article 84, paragraph 2 of the EEC Treaty, as originally drafted.

19.3.5 Scope of the consultation

Article 1 of the Decision provides that:

"The Member States and the Commission shall consult each other, in accordance with the procedures laid down in this Decision:

(a) on questions concerning shipping matters and dealt with in international organisations, and

(b) on the various aspects of development which have taken place in relations between Member States and third countries in shipping matters, and on the functioning of bilateral and multilateral agreements concluded in this sphere. . ."

The consultations shall be held at the request of a Member State or of the Commission, within one month of the request or at the earliest opportunity in urgent cases.

35. EC Commission, Information Memo P-51, July 1976, p. 2.

19.3.6 Purposes of consultation

The purposes of consultation depend on the nature of the consultation.

In regard to consultations on questions concerning shipping matters and dealt with in international organisations, the main aims of such consultation shall be (a) to determine jointly whether the questions raise problems of common interest and (b) depending on the nature of such problems, to either (i) consider jointly whether Member States' action within the international organizations concerned should be co-ordinated and (ii) consider jointly any other approach which might be appropriate.[36] The Member States and the Commission are obliged to exchange any relevant information as soon as possible.[37]

For the purposes of the consultations on the various aspects of development which have taken place in relations between Member States and third countries in shipping matters, and on the functioning of bilateral or multilateral agreements concluded in this sphere, each Member State shall inform the other Member States and the Commission of the various aspects of developments which have taken place in its relations with third countries in shipping matters, and of the operation of bilateral or multilateral agreements concluded in this field, if it considers this likely to contribute to the identification of problems of common interest.[38]

The main aims of such consultations shall be to examine the implications of the information provided and to consider any approach which might be appropriate.[39]

19.3.7 Channels and confidentiality of consultation

The channel for the exchanges of information is the General Secretariat of the Council.[40] The consultations provided for in the Decision take place within the framework of the Council of Ministers.[41]

All information and consultation provided for in the Decision is covered by what the Decision describes as "professional secrecy".[42]

One presumes that an action for damages would lie in the ECJ against the institution which divulged any secret information.[43]

19.3.8 Review

Article 5 of the Decision provides that at the end of a period of three years following the date of notification of the Decision, the Council was obliged to re-examine the consultation procedure with a view to amending or supplementing it, if experience shows that to be necessary. The Decision had not been amended up until the time of writing. Regard must be had to paragraph 19.6, below, relating to counter-measures.

36. Decision 77/587/EEC, Art.2(1).
37. Decision 77/587/EEC, Art.2(2).
38. Decision 77/587/EEC, Art.3(1).
39. Decision 77/587/EEC, Art.3(2).
40. Decision 77/587/EEC, Art.4. Decision 77/587/EEC is reprinted as Appendix 2, below. On the General Secretariat of the Council of Ministers, see para. 19.4.3.6, above.
41. Decision 77/587/EEC, Art.4(2). Decision 77/587/EEC is reprinted as Appendix 2, below. On the Council of Ministers, see para. 19.4.3, above.
42. Decision 77/587/EEC, Art.4(3). Decision 77/587/EEC is reprinted as Appendix 2, below.
43. See Case 145/83, 53/84 *Adams v. Commission* [1985] ECR 3539.

19.4 MARKET MONITORING

19.4.1 Decision 78/774/EEC

19.4.1.1 Introduction

On 19 September 1978, the Council of Ministers adopted Decision 78/774/EEC concerning the activities of certain third countries in the field of cargo sharing.[44] This Decision provided that information systems would be established so as to enable the EC institutions to be kept informed of the activities of the fleets of third States (i.e. non-Member States of the EC) whose practices are harmful to the shipping interests of the EC and its Member States. This information system was to monitor, in particular, any activities which adversely affect the competitive participation of the fleets of the EC States in international maritime trade. Such an information system would have to facilitate consultation at EC level.[45]

19.4.1.2 Legal bases

The principal legal bases of the Decision were the EEC Treaty generally and, in particular, Article 84(2) of the EEC Treaty.[46]

19.4.1.3 Legislative history

The Decision was the culmination of a draft Decision submitted to the Council by the Commission and which was commented on by the Parliament[47] in 1978 as well as the Economic and Social Committee on 1 June 1978.

19.4.1.4 Article 1: The essence of the Decision

Article 1 of the Decision[48] (as originally adopted) provides:

> "1. Each Member State shall take all the necessary measures to institute a system allowing it to collect information on the activities of the fleets of third countries whose practices are harmful to the shipping interests of the Member States and in particular in so far as these activities adversely affect the competitive participation of the fleets of Member States in international maritime trade.
>
> 2. This system must enable each Member State, to the extent necessary to attain the objectives referred to in para. 1, to collect information on:
> - the level of cargo shipping services offered;
> - the nature, volume, value, origin and destination of goods loaded or unloaded in the Member States concerned by the ships engaged in these services; and
> - the level of tariffs charged for such services."

19.4.1.5 Article 2: Application

Article 2 of the Decision (as originally adopted) provided:

44. See OJ L258/35, 21 September 1978.
45. See Dec.78/774/EEC, Preamble, Recital 1.
46. See Dec.78/774/EEC, Preamble.
47. See OJ C131, 5 June 1978, p. 4.
48. I.e. Dec.78/774/EEC.

"1. The Council, acting unanimously, shall decide to which third countries' fleets the information system shall be jointly applied.

2. The Decision referred to in paragraph 1 shall specify the type of cargo shipping to which the information system is to apply, the date of its introduction, the intervals at which the information is to be provided and which of the types of information listed in Article 1 are to be collected.

3. Each Member State shall forward to the Commission, periodically or at the request of the latter, the information produced by its information system.

4. The Commission shall collate the information for the Community as a whole. Article 4 of the Council Decision 77/587/EEC of 13 September 1977 setting up a consultation procedure on relations between Member States and third countries in shipping matters and on action relating to such matters in international organisations[49] shall apply to that information."

19.4.1.5.1 Amendment to Article 2(1)

Article 1 of Council Decision 89/242/EEC[50] provides that the first paragraph of Article 2 of Decision 78/774/EEC be replaced by the following:

"(1) The Council, acting by a qualified majority, shall decide to which third countries' fleets the information system shall be jointly applied."

This amendment took effect on 5 April 1989. The background to the amendment is apparent from the Preamble to the Decision:

"Whereas Decision 78/774/EEC provides the basis for an information system concerning the activities of certain third countries in the field of cargo shipping,

Whereas Article 2 of that Decision provides for decisions on the application of the information system to third countries' fleets to be taken unanimously,

Whereas it is necessary to amend this procedure in the light of the revised Article 84(2) of the [EEC] Treaty, which provides for voting by qualified majority, . . .

The change had been proposed by the Commission on 21 December 1988.[51] The European Parliament approved of the change by way of its normal legislative resolution."[52]

19.4.1.6 Legislative resolution

"Embodying the opinion of the European Parliament on the proposal from the Commission to the Council for a decision amending Decision 78/774/EEC concerning the activities of certain third countries in the field of cargo shipping

The European Parliament,

- having regard to the proposal from the Commission to the Council[53]
- having been consulted by the Council pursuant to Article 84(2) of the EEC Treaty (Doc. C2–305/88),
- considering the proposed legal basis to be appropriate,
- having regard to the report of the Committee on Transport (Doc. A2–388/88),

1. Approves the Commission's proposal in accordance with the vote thereon;

2. Calls on the Council to notify Parliament should it intend to depart from the text approved by Parliament;

3. Asks to be consulted again should the Council intend to make substantial modifications to the Commission's proposal;

49. OJ L239, 17 September 1977, p. 23. On Dec.77/587/EEC, see para.19.3, above.
50. OJ L97/47, 11 April 1989. See Appendix 2, below.
51. COM(88)748 final/2. Reprinted in OJ C28/10, 3 February 1989.
52. Doc. A2–388/88, reprinted in OJ C69/230, 20 March 1989.
53. COM(88)748 final.

4. Instructs its President to forward this opinion to the Council and Commission."

19.4.1.7 Observations of the Committee

The Economic and Social Committee commented:[54]

"2.4 The . . . proposal for a Council Directive to amend Decision 78/774/EEC, to provide for voting by qualified majority rather than by unanimity, is a necessary consequence of the revision to Article 84(2) of the [EEC] Treaty under the Single European Act and is . . . approved."

19.4.1.8 Article 3: Evaluation

Article 3 of the 1978 Decision provides that:

"The Member States and the Commission shall examine regularly, within the framework of the consultation procedure established by Decision 77/587/EEC and on the basis *inter alia* of the information produced by the information system referred to in Article 1, the activities of the fleets of the third countries specified in the Decisions referred to in Article 2."

19.4.1.9 Article 4: National legislation

Article 4 of the 1978 Decision provides that:

"The Council, acting unanimously, may decide on the joint application by Member States, in their relations with a third country or group of third countries regarding which a Decision referred to in Article 2 has been adopted, of appropriate counter-measures forming part of their national legislation."

19.4.1.10 Article 5: National systems

Article 5 of the 1978 Decision provides that:

"The Member States shall retain the right to apply unilaterally their national information systems and counter-measures."

In this regard, note should be made of Article 4 of Dec. 83/573,[55] which provides that the Member States are free to apply national counter-measures unilaterally despite the adoption of Decision 83/573/EEC concerning counter-measures in the field of international merchant shipping.

19.4.1.11 Article 6: Implementation

Article 6 of the Decision provides that:

"The Member States shall, as soon as possible and at the latest by 31 December 1978, after consulting the Commission, adopt the laws, regulations and administrative provisions necessary to implement this Decision."

19.4.2 Decision 79/4/EEC

19.4.2.1 Introduction

On 19 December 1978, the Council of Ministers adopted Decision 79/4/EEC[56] on the collection of information concerning the activities of carriers participating in cargo liner traffic in certain areas of operation.

54. OJ C71/25 at 26, 20 March 1989.
55. See para. 19.6.1, below.
56. OJ L5/31, 9 January 1979.

19.4.2.2 Legal bases

The EEC Treaty was the general legal basis for Decision 79/4/EEC with Article 84(2) EEC being the specific legal basis.

19.4.2.3 Legislative history

The Commission submitted a draft Decision.[57] The European Parliament then approved it,[58] as did the Economic and Social Committee.[59]

19.4.2.4 Factual background

The Preamble to the Decision provides:

"there is need for surveillance of the activities of all shipping companies participating in certain cargo liner traffic operations from and to the Community, if there is reason to think that certain carriers are not following the rules of competition in accordance with the principles of market economy and are adversely affecting the competitive position of Member State fleets in international maritime trade . . ."

19.4.2.5 Extension of the information collected

Article 1 of the Decision provides:

"From 1 January 1979 to 31 December 1980, each Member State shall collect the information specified in Annex I for all carriers participating in cargo liner traffic in the areas of operation specified in Annex II, in so far as these carriers serve its ports. The information for each half-year shall be forwarded to the Commission as soon as possible and in any case not later than three months after the end of the period concerned."

Annex I provided:

"Information to be collected

1. *Liner services operated*[60]
   (a) Name of company and service.
   (b) Area of operation (see Annex II).
   (c) Date of establishment, modification or termination of liner service.
   (d) Vessels employed (name, flag, vessel type (e.g. general cargo, container, roll-on-roll-off, lighter carrier), dwt, grt and TEU).
   (e) Arrivals and departures per vessel.
   (f) Conference membership; if yes, which conference or section thereof?
2. *Liner cargo carried*
   (a) Flag.
   (b) Area of operation.
   (c) Total liner cargo loaded from country of loading, origin or dispatch in incoming traffic, total liner cargo carried to country of unloading and/or destination in outgoing traffic, in weight and/or freight tonnes
   (d) Specification of types of commodities.
3. *Information concerning transport rates*

Member States shall use their best endeavours to provide information on transport rates. This information should be based on current average rates by carrier, paid for selected commodities."

57. The Commission is the institution which proposes drafts to the Council of Ministers.
58. OJ C296/50, 11 December 1978.
59. Opinion delivered on 29/30 November 1978.
60. The first six monthly return should describe the situation at the start of the six months concerned, changes which occurred during the period and the situation at the end of the period. Subsequent returns should describe changes occurring during the period and the situation at the end of it.

Annex II provided:

"List of areas of operation

1. Between the Member States and East Africa (Somalia, Kenya, Uganda, Zambia, Tanzania, Mozambique).

2. Between the Member States and Central America (East and West Coasts—from Mexico's southern frontier to Panama inclusive, with the exclusion of the West Indies)."

By virtue of Article 1 of Decision 90/545, the date is now "31 December 1991" while "in the areas of operation specified in Annex II" is replaced by "in the areas of operation specified in Part 1 of Annex II".

19.4.2.6 Assessment

The Council of Ministers later said that the information gathered under this Decision (as well as others) "gives ground for concern about the competitive position of Member State liner companies because of the nature of the competition which they face from certain carriers in the areas of operation referred to in Annex II to Decision 79/4/EEC".[61]

19.4.3 Decision 80/1181/EEC[62]

19.4.3.1 Introduction

The Council of Ministers later said that the information gathered under this Decision (as well as others) "gives ground for concern about the competitive position of Member State liner companies because of the nature of the competition which they face from certain carriers in the areas of operation referred to in Annex II to Decision 79/4/EEC".[63]

19.4.4 Decision 81/189/EEC[64]

19.4.4.1 Introduction

This Decision provided that between 1 July 1981 and 31 December 1982, each Member State had to collect certain information outlined in Annex 1 of the Decision concerning cargo liner traffic between that State and each of the countries listed in Annex II of the Decision.

19.4.4.2 Annex I

Annex I relates to the information to be collected. It fell within four categories: (1) liner services operated; (2) liner cargo carried; (3) information concerning freight rates; and (4) sources of information and methodology.

19.4.4.3 Annex II

Annex II listed the States under scrutiny as Japan, Taiwan, Hong Kong, Malaysia, Singapore, Republic of Korea, the Philippines and Thailand.

61. Decision 89/243/EEC, Preamble, Recital 1.
62. OJ L350/44, 23 December 1980.
63. Decision 89/243/EEC, Preamble, Recital 1.
64. OJ L88/32, 2 April 1981.

19.4.5 *Decision 82/870/EEC*[65]

The Council of Ministers later said that the information gathered under this Decision (as well as others) "gives ground for concern about the competitive position of Member State liner companies because of the nature of the competition which they face from certain carriers in the areas of operation referred to in Annex II to Decision 79/4/EEC".[66]

19.4.7 *Decision 84/656/EEC*[67]

The Council of Ministers later said that the information gathered under this Decision (as well as others) "gives ground for concern about the competitive position of Member State liner companies because of the nature of the competition which they face from certain carriers in the areas of operation referred to in Annex II to Decision 79/4/EEC".[68]

19.4.8 *Decision 86/646/EEC*

Decision 89/242/EEC,[69] amended Decision 86/646/EEC by extending the duration of that Decision by another year until 31 December 1989.

The Council of Ministers later said that the information gathered under this Decision (as well as others) "gives ground for concern about the competitive position of Member State liner companies because of the nature of the competition which they face from certain carriers in the areas of operation referred to in Annex II to Decision 79/4/EEC".[70]

19.4.9 *Decision 89/242/EEC*

Decision 89/242/EEC,[71] amended Decision 78/774/EEC by amending the voting procedure. The amendment is discussed above.

19.4.10 *Decision 89/243/EEC*

Decision 89/242/EEC,[72] amended Decision 86/646/EEC by extending the duration of that Decision by another year until 31 December 1989. A draft of Decision 89/242 had been submitted by the Commission earlier that year.[73]

19.4.11 *Decision 90/545/EEC*[74]

19.4.11.1 Introduction

Council Decision 90/545/EEC extended the collection of information on the activities of carriers participating in cargo liner traffic in a certain area of operation. The

65. OJ L368/42, 28 December 1982.
66. Decision 89/243/EEC, Preamble, Recital 1.
67. OJ L341/91, 29 December 1984.
68. Decision 89/243/EEC, Preamble, Recital 1.
69. OJ L97/48, 11 April 1989.
70. Decision 89/243/EEC, Preamble, Recital 1.
71. OJ L97/47, 11 April 1989.
72. OJ L97/48, 11 April 1989.
73. OJ C28/9, 3 February 1989.
74. OJ L311/32, 10 November 1990.

Economic and Social Committee delivered an Opinion on 25 January 1989 on the proposed Council Directive extending the collection of information concerning the activities of carriers participating in cargo liner traffic.

19.4.11.2 Background

The Preamble to Decision 90/545/EEC provides:

"Having regard to the Treaty establishing the European Economic Community, and in particular Article 84(2) thereof,

Having regard to Council Decision 78/774/EEC of 19 September 1989 concerning the activities of certain third countries in the field of cargo shipping,[75] as amended by Decision 89/242/EEC,[76]

Having regard to the proposal from the Commission,

Whereas the collection of information on the competitive position of Member State liner companies in the trades referred to in Annex II to Decision 79/4/EEC,[77] and Article 2 of Decision 80/1181/EEC[78] was last extended by one year until 31 December 1989 by Decision 89/243/EEC[79];

Whereas recent developments in the trade under consideration lead to the conclusion that the collection of information on the activities of carriers participating in cargo liner traffic between the Community and East Africa should be extended by two years, namely, until the end of 1991 . . ."

19.4.11.3 Essence of the Decision

By virtue of Article 1 of Decision 90/545, the date for operation is now "31 December 1991" while "in the areas of operation specified in Annex II" is replaced by "in the areas of operation specified in Part 1 of Annex II".

19.5 INTERNATIONAL SAFETY CONVENTIONS

19.5.1 Introduction

The Council of Ministers has adopted a number of measures relating to the ratification by EC Member States of various international Conventions relating to safety.

On 26 June 1978, the Council of Ministers meeting at Luxembourg recommended,[80] by way of Council Recommendation 78/584/EEC,[81] to the Member States of the EC that, where they had not already done so, they should, where appropriate, sign, ratify or accede to a number of international Conventions on safety in shipping.[82]

On 21 December 1978, the EEC Council of Ministers recommended[83] in Recommendation 79/114/EEC the ratification of the 1978 international Convention on Standards of Training, Certification and Watchkeeping for Seafarers.[84]

75. OJ L258, 21 September 1978, p. 35.
76. OJ L97, 11 April 1989, p. 47.
77. OJ L5, 9 January 1931.
78. OJ L350, 23 December 1980, p. 44.
79. OJ L350, 23 December 1980, p. 44.
80. On the juridical nature of a Recommendation in EC law see Chapter 3, above.
81. OJ L194, 19 July 1978, p. 17.
82. See para. 19.6.2, below.
83. On the legal effect of a Recommendation, see Chapter 3, above.
84. OJ L33/31, 8 February 1979. See para. 19.6.2, below.

On 25 July 1983, the EEC Council of Ministers recommended in Recommendation 83/419/EEC that inasmuch as they have not already done so, the States ratify or accede to the 1979 international Convention on Search and Rescue as soon as they can.[85]

19.5.2 1978 Council of Ministers Recommendation on the ratification of safety conventions

19.5.2.1 Introduction

On 26 June 1978, the Council of Ministers meeting at Luxembourg recommended,[86] by way of Council Recommendation 78/584/EEC,[87] to the Member States of the EC that, where they had not already done so, they should, where appropriate, sign, ratify or accede to a number of international conventions on safety in shipping.

19.5.2.2 Background to the Recommendation

The Commission[88] proposed the Recommendation on ratification of safety conventions.[89] The Economic and Social Committee[90] delivered its opinion on 21 June 1978[91] and the European Parliament[92] also delivered its Opinion.[93] Earlier, the European Council[94] of 7 and 8 April 1978 declared that the prevention of and the fight against marine pollution, particularly from hydrocarbons, must be a major objective for Community action. The European Council[95] had also asked the Council of Ministers (acting on the basis of a proposal from the Commission) and the Member States to take appropriate measures without delay within the Community and to adopt common attitudes in the appropriate international bodies on the swift implementation of existing international rules in this area, in particular, those regarding the minimum standards for the operation of ships.

19.5.2.3 Conventions referred to in the Recommendation

The Conventions in question were: the 1974 international Convention for the safety of life at sea (SOLAS)[96]; the 1978 Protocol relating to the 1974 international Convention for the safety of life at sea; the 1973 international Convention for the prevention of pollution by ships (MARPOL), as amended by the 1978 Protocol; and Convention No. 147 concerning minimum standards in merchants ships, adopted by the International Labour Conference in 1976.[97]

85. See para. 19.6.4, below.
86. On the juridical nature of a Recommendation in EC law see Chapter 3, above.
87. OJ L194, 19 July 1978, p. 17.
88. On the Commission, see Chapter 3, above.
89. OJ L194/17, 19 July 1978.
90. On the Economic and Social Committee, see Chapter 3, above.
91. Delivered on 21 June 1978.
92. On the European Parliament, see Chapter 3, above.
93. OJ C163, 10 July 1978, p. 17.
94. On the European Council, see Chapter 3, above.
95. On the European Council, see Chapter 3, above.
96. Member States which had not already done so were recommended by Recommendation 78/584/EEC to sign, ratify or accede to (as the case may be) the SOLAS Convention as soon as possible and, in any event, by 1 January 1979.
97. Member States which had not already done so were recommended by Recommendation 78/584/EEC

19.5.2.4 Procedure for ratification or accession

One of the interesting features of the Recommendation is that EC Member States were recommended that they should inform in writing the Secretary-General of the Inter-Government Maritime Consultative Organisation or the International Labour Organisation (as appropriate) that their signing, ratification or accession has had regard to the Recommendation.

19.5.3 1978 Council of Ministers Recommendation on the ratification of the 1978 International Convention on Standards of Training, Certification and Watchkeeping for Seafarers

On 21 December 1978, the EEC Council of Ministers recommended[98] in Recommendation 79/114/EEC the ratification of the 1978 international Convention on Standards of Training, Certification and Watchkeeping for Seafarers.[99]

19.5.4 1983 Council of Ministers Recommendation on SAR

On 25 July 1983, the EEC Council of Ministers recommended[100] in Recommendation 83/419/EEC that in as much as they have not already done so, the Member States ratify or accede to the 1979 international Convention on Maritime Search and Rescue as soon as they can. This Convention, popularly referred to as SAR, was approved in Hamburg on 27 April 1979 in Hamburg under the auspices of the International Maritime Consultative Organisation (IMCO). The Council, in its Preamble to Recommendation 83/419/EEC, said that "in view of the great importance of the . . . Convention with regard to the search for and possible rescue of persons in distress at sea, the Convention should enter into force as soon as possible" and that "ratification or accession by all the Member States [of the EC] will not only help to bring the Convention into force in accordance with the principles of international law but will also ensure a unified search and rescue service in the coastal waters of the Community and thereby increase the effectiveness of the Convention".

19.6 COUNTER-MEASURES

19.6.1 1983 Council Decision concerning counter-measures in the field of international merchant shipping

19.6.1.1 Introduction

On 26 October 1983 the Council of Ministers adopted Decision 83/573/EEC concerning counter-measures in the field of international merchant shipping.[101]

to ratify or accede to the ILO Convention by 1 April 1979.

98. On the legal effect of a Recommendation, see Chapter 3, above.

99. OJ L33/31, 8 February 1979.

100. On the Council's power of recommendation, see Chapter 3, above.

101. OJ L332/37, 28 November 1983.

19.6.1.2 Legal bases

The legal bases of the Decision were the EEC Treaty generally and, in particular, Article 84(2)[102] thereof.

19.6.1.3 Factual background

The factual background to the Decision is apparent from the Preamble which reads:

"Whereas the results of the maritime information system set up under the provisions of Decisions 78/774/EEC,[103] 79/4/EEC,[104] 80/1181/EEC,[105] 81/189/EEC,[106] and 82/870/EEC,[107] together with the the experience of certain Member States, show that it would be advisable to define an appropriate Community procedure concerning counter-measures in the field of international merchant shipping in relation to third countries to be taken by the Member States concerned . . ."

19.6.1.4 Obligation to consult

Article 1 of the Decision provides for an obligation to consult. In specific terms, it provides:

"A Member State which has adopted or intends to adopt counter-measures in the field of international merchant shipping in relation to third countries shall consult the other Member States and the Commission in accordance with the consultation procedure established by Decision 77/587/EEC."[108]

In relation to this consultation, the provisions of Article 3 of the Decision should be borne in mind.[109]

19.6.1.5 Desirability of co-ordination of measures

Article 2 of the Decision provides:

"1. The Member States shall endeavour, within the framework of the consultation referred to in Article 1, to concert any counter-measures they may take.

2. The Council may, acting unanimously, decide on the joint application by Member States of appropriate counter-measures forming part of their national legislation."

19.6.1.6 Procedural matters

Article 3 of the Decision provides:

"When engaging in the consultation referred to in Article 1, Member States should, if appropriate, specify as far as possible the following:

(a) the developments which have caused counter-measures to be taken;
(b) the shipping area to which the counter-measure is to apply;
(c) the nature of the shipping service affected (for example liner traffic);

102. I.e. the pre-SEA Article 84(2) EEC.
103. OJ L258/35, 21 September 1978. See Appendix 2, below.
104. OJ L5/31, 9 January 1979. See Appendix 2, below.
105. OJ L350/44, 23 December 1980. See Appendix 2, below.
106. OJ L88/32, 2 April 1981. See Appendix 2, below.
107. OJ L368/42, 28 December 1982. See Appendix 2, below.
108. OJ L239/23, 17 September 1977. See Appendix 2, below.
109. See para. 19.6.1.6, above.

(d) the nature of the counter-measures taken or to be taken;
(e) the duration of the counter-measure;
(f) the proportionality of the counter-measure to be damage suffered."

19.6.1.7 Counter-measures

Article 4 of the Decision provides:

"The Member States shall remain free to apply national counter-measures unilaterally."

19.7 BILATERAL RELATIONS

19.7.1 Council Decision 87/475 relating to maritime transport between Italy and Algeria

On 17 September 1987, the Council of Ministers adopted Council Decision 87/475 relating to Maritime Transport between Italy and Algeria.[110]

19.8 INTERNATIONAL ORGANISATIONS

There is a large number of international organisations (both inter-governmental and non-governmental in nature) which are involved in shipping. Many of them have been surveyed at para. 19.3, above. Suffice it to say presently that the EC must take an active part in such international organisations and use its strong collective advice to the full. It has been stated by a Committee of the European Parliament that the "Community should . . . adopt a common position and speak with one voice in all these organisations".[111]

19.8.1 United Nations

19.8.1.1 Introduction

The United Nations (UN) is the premier universal international organisation.[112] It has some involvement with shipping affairs and this involvement has been reviewed in Chapter 1, above.

Article 229 of the EEC Treaty provides:

"It shall be for the Commission to ensure the maintenance of all appropriate relations with the organs of the United Nations, of its specialised agencies and of the General Agreement on Tariffs and Trade.

The Commission shall also maintain such relations as are appropriate with all international organisations. None the less the absence of an express provision has not hampered the recognition of the international personality of the EEC."

19.8.1.2 Liner Conferences

The EEC Council of Ministers adopted Regulation 954/79 of 15 May 1979 concerning the ratification by Member States of, or their accession to, the United Nations Convention on a Code of Conduct for Liner Conferences.[113]

110. OJ L272/37, 25 September 87.
111. The European Parliament's Committee on Regional Policy, Regional Planning and Transport its Interim report on the Sea Transport Problems in the Community, *op. cit.*, para. 28.
112. See Chapter 1, above.
113. OJ L121/1, 17 May 79.

19.8.2 UNCLOS III

The Third United Nations Conference on the Law of the Sea (UNCLOS III) ended, after almost nine years of negotiation, on 30 April 1982, with the adoption of the United Nations Convention on the Law of the Sea (known as UNCLOS III).[114]

The Convention was adopted by 130 votes in favour, 4 against and 17 abstentions. There were no EC States among the opponents but there were seven EC Member States among the abstainers: Belgium; the Federal Republic of Germany[115]; Italy; Luxembourg; the Netherlands; Spain; and the UK.[116]

It was opened for signature on 10 December 1982.

19.8.2.1 United Nations Economic Commission for Europe

The United Nations Economic Commission for Europe in Geneva has discussed such shipping matters as the simplification of customs clearance.

19.8.3 International Maritime Organisation and International Maritime Consultative Organisation

The International Maritime Organisation (IMO) and International Maritime Consultative Organisation (IMCO) are the premier universal international shipping organisations.[117] They have considerable involvement with shipping affairs and this involvement has been reviewed in Chapter 1, above.

19.8.4 International Labour Organisation

The International Labour Organisation (ILO) is the principal international organisation dealing with employment matters.[118]

It has conducted a number of projects (many leading to International Conventions) in the area of the employment of seafarers. The Member States of the EC have ratified some (but not all) of these Conventions and it has been suggested that the EC could assume a co-ordinating function in regard to the ratification by these Member States of those Conventions.[119]

19.8.5 General Agreement on Tariffs and Trade as well as General Agreement on Trade in Services

The General Agreement on Tariffs and Trade (GATT), as well as General Agreement on Trade in Services (GATS) are two important fora where the EC must maintain a united front on all trade matters (including shipping). Flag discrimination has been

114. On the Conference, see, *inter alia*, UN General Assembly Resolution 3067(XXVIII).
On the EC and the Conference, see, Simmonds, "The Commuity's Participation in the UN Law of the Sea Convention", in O'Keefe and Schermers, *Essays in European Law and Integration*, 1982, p. 179.

115. Incidentally, the German Democratic Republic also abstained.

116. The reasons for their opposition falls outside the scope of this work, but suffice it to say that the larger EC States objected to the Deep-Sea Bed provisions of the Convention.

117. See Chapter 1, above.

118. See Chapter 1, above.

119. Interim Report on Sea Transport Problems in the Community, EP Doc.5/77, para. 22 (Rapporteur: Seefeld).

included as one of "Non-Tariff Barriers" within GATT's List of Non-Tariff Barriers. The EC will have to become more vigilant and careful in its preparation of a united voice at GATT and GATS negotiations. In the current round of GATS negotiations, the EC may back down from its stance on shipping policy liberalisation so as to achieve overall success at the GATS talks.

19.8.6 European Free Trade Association

The EC has had close links for many years with EFTA. These links appear to be intensifying due to the negotiation of an accord to extend EC trade, competition and industrial rules to EFTA on 1 January 1993.

CHAPTER 20

The EC and Safety at Sea

20.1 INTRODUCTION

This chapter examines the law of the EC relating to the safety of shipping.

There have been many major shipping disasters in or near the EC during the last 30 years and these have focused the mind of the EC on matters relating to ships' safety. The *Torrey Canyon*, *Amoco Cadiz*, *Herald of Free Enterprise* and *Scandinavian Star* are all notable examples. Safety continues to be an issue of the highest priority: for example, more than one bulk carrier a month now sinks and more than 300 seafarers have lost their lives on bulk carriers during the period 1989–1991.

The year 1987 was the worst for lives lost at sea during peacetime: 3,841 lives were lost (with 3,132 on one ship, the *Dona Paz*, alone).

The EC is committed to a policy of safety. The Council of Ministers stated in 1978 in its Recommendation on the ratification of Conventions on Safety in Shipping, "safety in shipping must be improved".[1]

The Commission has written that the "Community has a major interest in the maintenance and improvement of standards of ship safety, both from the point of view of its seafarers and from that of the protection of the maritime environment".[2]

The EC has occasionally linked safety with "the living and working conditions of crews and their level of competence".[3]

The transportation of hydrocarbons has raised particular problems. As the EEC Council of Ministers recognised in 1978 in its Recommendation on the ratification of Conventions on safety in shipping:

> "there is a fundamental interest in seeing effective action undertaken to reduce the risks inherent in the transport of hydrocarbons, in particular the danger of severe coastal pollution as the result of accidents on the high seas [and] this fundamental interest is underlined by the European Communities' environment action programmes."[4]

Tragedies such as the loss of the *Herald of Free Enterprise* in March 1987 which led to the deaths of 188 people highlight the enormous attention which must be paid to safety at sea. Loss at sea of life, ships and cargo can never be totally eliminated, but such loss may be minimised.

The EC has a better safety record than many regions around the world. None the less, it has been reckoned (but disputed) that nearly half of the Mediterranean passenger and car ferries have such grave safety problems that their use is not recommended by a German consumers' organisation.[5]

1. Recommendation 78/584/EEC, Recital 3.
2. *Progress Towards a Common Transport Policy: Maritime Transport*, COM(85)90 final, para. 87.
3. Recommendation 78/584/EEC, Recital 3.
4. Recommendation 78/584/EEC, Recital 2.
5. See "Ferry Safety Fears in Mediterranean", *Lloyd's List*, 1 November 1989.

20.1.1 International legislation

There is an extensive range of international conventions and recommendations on maritime safety.[6] These result mainly from the work of the International Maritime Organisation and other UN organisations.[7] This chapter only examines the rules and role of the EC in the areas of safety at sea.

20.2 EC MEASURES AND DEVELOPMENTS

20.2.1 1978 Council Recommendation on ratification of safety conventions

20.2.1.1 Introduction

On 26 June 1978, the Council meeting at Luxembourg recommended[8] (by way of Council Recommendation 78/584/EEC[9]) to the Member States of the EC that, where they had not already done so, they should, where appropriate, sign, ratify or accede to a number of international conventions on safety in shipping. The Conventions in question were: the 1974 International Convention for the Safety of Life at Sea (SOLAS); the 1978 Protocol Relating to the 1974 International Convention for the Safety of Life at Sea; the 1973 International Convention for the Prevention of Pollution by Ships (MARPOL), as amended by the 1978 Protocol; and Convention No. 147 concerning minimum standards in merchants ships, adopted by the International Labour Conference in 1976.

One of the interesting features of the Recommendation is that EC Member States were recommended that they should inform in writing the Secretary-General of the Intergovernment Maritime Consultative Organisation or the International Labour Organisation (as appropriate) that their signing, ratification or accession had regard to the Recommendation.

20.2.1.2 Background to the Recommendation

The Commission proposed the Recommendation. The Economic and Social Committee delivered its opinion on 21 June 1978 and the European Parliament also delivered its opinion.[10]

Earlier, the European Council on 7 and 8 April 1978 declared that the prevention of and the fight against marine pollution, particularly from hydrocarbons, must be a major objective for Community action. The Council had also asked the Council of Ministers (acting on the basis of a proposal from the Commission) and the Member States to take appropriate measures without delay within the Community and to adopt common attitudes in the appropriate international bodies on the swift implementation of existing international rules in this area, in particular, those regarding the minimum standards for the operation of ships.

6. See Bruer in Bernhardt (ed.), *Encyclopedia of Public International Law* 7, vol. 11, 1989, p. 224.
7. See Chapter 16, above.
8. On the juridical nature of a Recommendation in EC law see Chapter 3, above.
9. OJ L194/17, 19 July 1978, p. 17.
10. OJ C163/17, 10 July 1978, p. 17.

20.2.1.3 Conventions referred to in the Recommendation

The Conventions referred to in the Recommendation were the 1973 International Convention for the Prevention of Pollution by Ships (MARPOL); the 1974 International Convention on the Safety of Life at Sea (SOLAS); the 1976 ILO Convention No. 147 Concerning Minimum Standards in Merchant Ships; the 1978 Protocol relating to the 1974 International Convention on the Safety of Life at Sea; and the 1978 MARPOL Protocol.

20.2.2 1978 Council Recommendation on the ratification of the 1978 international Convention on Standards of Training, Certification and Watchkeeping for Seafarers

On 21 December 1978, the Council of Ministers adopted Recommendation 79/114 on the ratification of the 1978 Watchkeepers Convention.[11] The Recommendation recommended that the Member States sign the 1978 international Convention on Standards of Training, Certification and Watchkeeping for seafarers by 1 April 1979 and ratify it as soon as possible and not later than 31 December 1980. Again, Member States were recommended to inform the Secretary-General of the Inter-Government Maritime Consultative Organisation that they have signed and ratified the Convention in accordance with the Recommendation.

20.2.3. Deep-sea pilots directives

On 21 December 1978 the Council of Ministers adopted Directive 79/115 concerning pilotage of vessels by deep-sea pilots in the North Sea and English Channel.[12] This Directive is examined in Chapter 22, below.

20.2.4. Tankers

Again on 21 December 1978, the Council of Ministers adopted Directive 79/116 concerning the minimum requirements for certain tankers entering or leaving Community ports.[13] This is examined in Chapter 23, below.

20.2.5 Fishing vessels

On 23 September 1980, the Council of Ministers adopted a Recommendation on the ratification of the Torremolinos International Convention for the Safety of Fishing Vessels.[14] As this book does not deal with fishing vessels, the Recommendation need not be discussed here.

20.20.6 Greek Government

On 10 July 1982 the Commission adopted an Opinion addressed to the Greek Government regarding the implementation of the Council Directive of 21 December

11. OJ L194/17, 19 April 1978.
12. OJ L33/32, 8 February 1979.
13. OJ L33/33, 8 February 1979. See the amendment published at OJ L315/16, 11 December 1979.
14. OJ L259/29, 2 October 1980.

1978, concerning minimum requirements for certain tankers entering or leaving Community ports, and Council Directive of 6 December 1979 amending the abovementioned Directive.[15] This Opinion is considered in Chapter 23, below.

20.2.7 1983 Council Recommendation on SAR

On 25 July 1983, the EEC Council recommended[16] in Recommendation 83/419/EEC that in as much as they have not already done so, the Member States ratify or accede to the 1979 International Convention on Maritime Search and Rescue as soon as they can. This Convention, popularly referred to as SAR, was approved in Hamburg on 27 April 1979 under the auspices of the Intergovernmental Maritime Consultative Organisation (IMCO). The Council, in its Preamble to Recommendation 83/419/EEC, said that "in view of the great importance of the . . . Convention with regard to the search for and possible rescue of persons in distress at sea, the Convention should enter into force as soon as possible" and that "ratification or accession by all the Member States [of the EC] will not only help to bring the Convention into force in accordance with the principles of international law but will also ensure a unified search and rescue service in the coastal waters of the Community and thereby increase the effectiveness of the Convention".

20.2.8 1987 European Parliamentary Question on the Seaworthiness of Vessels Operating in Community Waters

Mr Thomas Raftery, a Member of the European Parliament, asked the Commission the following question:

"Following the recent disaster involving the iron ore carrier 'Kowloon Bridge' off the south-west coast of Ireland and the near-disaster of the oil tanker Capo Emma in the same area, what action will the Commission take to ensure higher standards of seaworthiness of vessels operating in Community waters?"

Mr Stanley Clinton Davies, the Commissioner with responsibility for transport, responded:

"The honourable Member raises a very important question. May I begin by saying that I remain convinced that flag state control must remain the primary way of applying standards. None the less, the development of port state enforcement is proving to be an effective way of combating the operation of substandard shipping.

The application of port state control in European waters under the Paris memorandum of understanding extends beyond the eleven European Community Maritime States to Norway, Sweden and Finland. No less than 10,000 ships are being inspected each year by these maritime authorities in order to ensure respect for the relevant international conventions.

The Commission is encouraged to note that the Canadian and United States coastguards are now making their inspection reports available to European authorities. Since Japan is also instituting a system of port state control, we should soon be in a position where it will be virtually impossible for a substandard ship to contemplate a visit to any Community port with any degree of equanimity.

I would not wish to give the impression that I am complacent about the progress of port state control. Indeed, two members of the Community are still a long way behind with their inspection

15. The Directive of 6 December 1979 amends Dir. 79/116 by replacing the text of item A.(i)(g) of Art. 1(1) and adding new entries to section C of the Annex to Directive 79/116.

16. On the Council's power of recommendation, see Chapter 3. The Recommendation is published at OJ L237/34, 26 August 1983.

timetable and I shall be keeping a close check on the progress that they make this year to meet their obligations.

Moreover, I am not convinced that enough is being done about the port state enforcement of ILO standards. It has been argued that it is more difficult for an inspector to check for compliance with International Labour Organisation standards than with, for example, the SOLAS Convention. There may be some truth in that, but it is not a justification for neglecting those standards altogether. Accordingly, the Commission intends to set up a small working party with the ILO, the port state control secretariat, ship owners and seafaring unions, to examine these practical problems in an attempt to draw up more positive guidelines to surveyors on these human aspects of the port state enforcement of international standards. So in this way we would hope to contribute to the eradication from Community ports and Community waters of shipping which is substandard in the widest sense of the word."

Mr Raftery continued

"Thank you, Commissioner, for your very comprehensive answer. Could I ask what proportion of the ships are being checked for seaworthiness, and whether a higher proportion of ships flying flags of convenience are being checked than ships flying normal national flags? Is the Commission going to be more active in this whole area in future in the light of the two serious disasters which occurred off the south coast of Ireland one almost equally serious disaster which miraculously was just avoided?"

The Commissioner responded:

"I think I am right in saying that about 60 per cent of ships visiting ports are in general terms now being checked. I stand to be corrected as to the exact proportion, but I think that is roughly the situation.

Yes, more flags of convenience ships are being inspected than has been the case hitherto. I have given an average figure for the number of inspections being carried out. Last year the figure in fact rose to something like 12,000 inspections. Just over 300 ships were detained or delayed until deficiencies were put right.

The number of flag of convenience vessels is higher than the number of Community ships but, nonetheless, it is a matter of grave concern to me that Community ships should be defying these essential safety standards. Community shipping of course has no right to derogate from those standards at all. So we are extremely vigilant about these matters. We shall continue to be and I hope that the number of inspections over the forthcoming years will be substantially increased."

20.2.9 1989: Parliament's Resolution on Safety at Sea

On 17 March 1989, the European Parliament[17] adopted a Resolution[18] on safety at sea.

20.2.10 1990: Council of Ministers Resolution on Passenger Ferry Safety

On 19 June 1990, the Council of Ministers[19] and the Representatives of the Governments of the Member States, meeting within the Council, adopted a Resolution[20] on Improving Passenger Ferry Safety.[21] There had been a number of ferry disasters in Europe over the previous few years, including the *Herald of Free Enterprise* in March 1987 and the *Scandinavian Star* in 1990.

The Resolution called on the Member States and the EC Commission, in their capacity as members or as observer of the International Maritime Organisation of the

17. On the European Parliament, see Chapter 3, above.
18. On the legal status of a Resolution, see Chapter 3, above.
19. On the Council of Ministers, see Chapter 3, above.
20. On the legal effect of a Resolution, see Chapter 3, above.
21. OJ C206/02, 18 August 1990.

United Nations (IMO)[22] and the Memorandum of Understanding on Port State Control[23] to press for the urgent identification, elaboration, adoption and implementation of measures which will improve safety of passenger ferries on an international basis in the framework of the IMO and Port State Control Memorandum.

The Council of Ministers and the representatives of the governments of the Member States adopted the Resolution aware of:

(a) the large number of passengers who travel by passenger ferries in European waters;
(b) the essentially international nature of such operations;
(c) the necessity of crews being able to function in a satisfactory manner in the event of an emergency;
(d) the dangers which can arise from management and communication failures;
(e) the potentially large-scale intervention which could be required in the event of an accident involving a passenger ferry; and
(f) the fact that the transport of passengers in European waters is carried out by vessels registered both inside and outside the Community, thus requiring any necessary improvement of passenger ferry safety, including the question of crewing, to take place in a broad international context.

20.2.11 Council Directive on the Minimum Safety and Health Requirements for Improved Medical Treatment on Board Vessels

20.2.11.1 Introduction

The Council of Ministers has adopted a Directive on the Minimum Safety and Health Requirements for Improved Medical Treatment on Board Vessels (Directive 92/29 of 31 March 1992).[24] The Commission had consultations with the Advisory Committee on Safety, Hygiene and Health Protection at Work.

20.2.11.2 Background

The Commission has, in the past, envisaged the adoption of measures to ensure medical treatment at sea.[25] In its proposal the Commission made clear that a vessel is "a workplace which requires special attention on account of its mobility, its geographical isolation, and the potentially high risks to safety and health of the workers on board",[26] thus, the Commission contended, "there is a need for vessels to have on board adequate medical equipment and medicines, properly maintained and checked at regular intervals, to permit the effective treatment of the crew and, in certain cases, avoid disembarkations at sea or diversions of vessels, which are not only costly but can also delay treatment".[27] The improvement of medical treatment at sea would

22. On the IMO, see Chapter 1, above.
23. On the Memorandum, see Appendix 2, below.
24. OJ L113/19, 30 April 1992. On the Commission proposal see COM(90)272 final–SYN 278; see OJ C183/6, 24 July 1990 and OJ C74/11, 20 March 1991. On the Commission's policy in this area, see its Communication in its Programme.
25. See the Commission's *Communication on its Programme concerning Safety, Hygiene and Health at Sea* reprinted in OJ C28/2, 3 February 1988.
26. Preamble to the Proposed Directive.
27. Proposed Directive, Recital 3.

then make it "desirable to promote training in and information on the use of medical supplies and of the various remote medical consultation facilities".[28]

The proposal had been drawn up after consultation with the Advisory Committee on Safety, Hygiene and Health Protection at Work.

The Directive provided in its Preamble:

> "Whereas vessels should have adequate medical supplies, kept in good order and checked at regular intervals, so that workers can obtain the necessary medical treatment at sea;
> Whereas in order to ensure appropriate medical treatment at sea, training and information of seafarers should be encouraged as regards the use of medical supplies;
> Whereas the use of long-distance medical consultation methods constitutes an efficient way of contributing to the protection of the safety and health of workers . . .".

20.2.11.3 Legal basis

The legal basis of the Directive is the EEC Treaty generally and Article 118A[29] in particular.[30]

The Directive recognises that a vessel constitutes "a workplace involving a wide range of risks, bearing in mind, *inter alia*, its geographical isolation, where appropriate, requires special attention".

20.2.11.4 Basic concepts

20.2.11.4.1 Antidote

An antidote is defined, for the purposes of the Directive, by Article 1 of the Directive as being:

> "a substance used to prevent or treat a harmful effect or effects, direct or indirect, of one or more substances included in the list of dangerous substances in Annex III [of the Directive.]"

20.2.11.4.2 Medical supplies

Medical supplies are defined, for the purposes of the Directive, by Article 1 of the Directive as being:

> "medicines, medical equipment and antidotes, including any antidotes that may be required under the terms of Article 3(1) a non-exhaustive list of which is given in Annex II [of the Directive.]"

20.2.11.4.3 Owner

Article 1 of the Directive provides that the term "owner" means, for the purposes of that Directive, "the registered owner of a vessel unless that vessel has been chartered by demise or is managed, either wholly or in part, by a natural or legal person other than the registered owner under the terms of a management agreement; in that case the owner shall be construed as the demise charterer or natural or legal person managing the vessel as appropriate".

28. Proposed Directive, Recital 4.
29. For the text of Article 118A, see Appendix 1, below.
30. Recital 1.

20.2.11.4.4 Vessel

A vessel is defined, for the purposes of the Directive, by Article 1 of the Directive as being:

"any vessel flying the flag of a Member State, or registered under the plenary jurisdiction of a Member State, seagoing or estuary-fishing, publicly or privately owned, excluding:
— inland navigation vessels.
— warships,
— pleasure boats used for non-commercial purposes and not manned by professional crews,
— tugs operating in harbour areas.
Vessels shall be classed in three categories in accordance with Annex I."

20.2.11.4.5 Worker

A worker is defined, for the purposes of the Directive, by Article 1 of the Directive as being:

"any person who is employed or retained in whatever capacity on board a vessel, including trainees and apprentices, but excluding pilots."

20.2.11.5 Obligation to have medical supplies on board

Member States would be obliged under Article 2 of the Directive to take measures necessary to ensure that the vessels under their jurisdiction always have adequate medicines and medical equipment on board.[31]

The quantities to be carried would have to take account of the nature and destination of the trip and the number of crew members.[32]

The contents of the medical supplies are to be detailed on a checklist.[33]

Article 2 provides:

"*Medicines and medical equipment—Sick-bay—doctor*
Each Member State shall take the measures necessary to ensure that:

1. (a) every vessel flying its flag or registered under its plenary jurisdiction always carries on board medical supplies which meet at least, in terms of quality, the specifications of Annex II sections I and II for the category of vessel to which it belongs;
   (b) the quantities of medicinal products and medical equipment to be carried depend on the nature of the voyage—in particular ports of call, destination, duration—the type or types of work to be carried out during the voyage, the nature of the cargo and the number of workers;
   (c) the content of the medicines and medical equipment included in the medical supplies shall be detailed on a checklist corresponding at least to the general framework laid down in Annex IV, sections A, B and C II 1 and II 2;
2. (a) for each of its life-rafts and life-boats, every vessel flying its flag or registered under its plenary jurisdiction carries a watertight medicine chest at least containing the medical supplies specified in Annex II, sections I and II, for category C vessels;
   (b) the content of these chests is also detailed on the checklist referred to in paragraph 1(c);
3. every vessel flying its flag or registered under its plenary jurisdiction, of more than 500 gross registered tonnes, with a crew of 15 or more workers and engaged on a voyage of more than three days, has a sick-bay in which medical treatment can be administered under satisfactory material and hygienic conditions;

31. Directive, Article 2.
32. Directive, Article 2.
33. Directive, Article 2.

4. every vessel flying its flag or registered under its plenary jurisdiction, with a crew of 100 or more workers and engaged on an international voyage of more than three days, has a doctor responsible for the medical care of the workers on board."

20.2.11.6 Obligation on ships to carry antidotes

Article 3 of the Directive deals with dangerous substances. Member States would have two separate obligations depending on the type of vessel involved.

First, Member States are obliged to ensure that any vessel under their jurisdiction carrying any of the dangerous substances set out in Section III of Annex III to the Directive has medical supplies, including the appropriate antidotes set out in Annex II of the Directive.[34]

Secondly, Member States would be obliged in the case of ferry-type vessels, whose conditions of operation do not always allow them to know well enough in advance the nature of the dangerous substances being transported, all the antidotes listed in Section III of Annex II are carried on board.[35] However, on a regular route where the crossing is due to last less than two hours, the antidotes may be limited to those which have to be administered within a period not exceeding the duration of the crossing.[36]

20.2.11.7 Allocation of responsibilities

Member States will be obliged to ensure that:

"Each Member State shall take the measures necessary to ensure that:

1. (a) the provision and replenishment of the medical supplies of any vessel flying its flag or registered under its plenary jurisdiction are undertaken on the exclusive responsibility of the owner, without any expense to the workers;

(b) the management of the medical supplies is placed under the responsibility of the captain of the vessel; he may, without prejudice to this responsibility, delegate the use and maintenance of the medical supplies to one or more workers specially designated by reason of their competence;

2. the medical supplies are maintained in good condition and replenished and/or replaced as soon as possible, and in every case as a priority part of normal revictualling procedures;

3. in an emergency established by the captain as far as possible after having obtained a medical opinion, the required medicines, medical equipment and antidotes which are not available on board are made available as soon as possible."[37]

20.2.11.8 Information and training

Article 5 of the Directive provides:

"Each Member State shall take the measures necessary to ensure that:

1. medical supplies are accompanied by one or more guides to their use, including instructions for use of at least the antidotes required in Annex II section III;

2. all persons receiving professional maritime training and intending to work on board ship have been given basic training in the medical and emergency measures to be taken immediately in the event of an accident or serious medical emergency;

3. the captain and any worker or workers to whom he delegates the use of the medical supplies pursuant to Article 4(1)(b) have received special training updated periodically, at least every five

34. Directive, Article 3(1).
35. Directive, Article 3(2).
36. Directive, Article 3(2).
37. Directive, Article 4.

years, taking into account the specific risks and needs connected with the different categories of vessel and in accordance with the general guidelines set out in Annex V."

The Member States would be obliged to take appropriate measures to ensure that the medical supplies[38] are accompanied by a guide to their use, including instructions for the use of the antidotes.[39,40]

20.2.11.9 Training

The Directive envisages general training for the crew, as well as special training for the captain and those members of the crew who have been specially delegated to use the ship's medical supplies.[41]

In terms of general training, the proposed Directive provides that Member States would be obliged to take all appropriate measures to ensure that during their professional maritime training all persons intending to work on board are given instruction in the medical and emergency measures to be taken immediately in the event of an accident or serious emergency.[42]

In terms of special training, the Directive provides that Member States would be obliged to take all appropriate measures to ensure that the captain and the worker or workers to whom he or she delegates the use of the ship's medical supplies[43] have received special training, taking into account the specific risks and needs connected with the different categories of vessels and in accordance with the general guidelines set out in Annex V of the Directive.[44]

20.2.11.10 Data centres

The EC Member States will be obliged under this Directive to designate one or more centres to provide any data which may be required to improve emergency treatment for crew members.[45] The transmission system used would have to be, in accordance with Article 6 of the Directive, ensure that the data remain confidential.

20.2.11.11 Inspection

Member States will be obliged to take "appropriate measures" to ensure that a competent authority carries out annual checks on all vessels flying their flags only to determine whether the medical supplies carried correspond to the checklist provided for pursuant to the Directive.[46]

20.2.11.12 Adaptation of the annexes

Provision is made in Article 8 of the Directive for the adaptation of the annexes. These adaptations would be made in the light of technical progress, changes in international regulations or specifications and new findings in this field.[47]

38. On medical supplies, see Article 4 of the Directive.
39. On antidotes, see Article 3 of the Directive.
40. Directive, Article 5(1).
41. Directive, Article 5.
42. Directive, Article 5.
43. See Article 4 of the Directive on medical supplies.
44. Directive, Article 5(3).
45. Directive, Article 6.
46. Directive, Article 7
47. Directive, Article 8.

So as to assist in the making of such changes, the Commission will be assisted by a committee composed of the representatives of the EC Member States.[48] The committee would be chaired by a representative of the Commission[49] who would submit to the committee a draft of the measures to be taken.[50] It would be the function of the committee to deliver its opinion on the draft within a time limit which the chairman may lay down according to the urgency of the matter.[51] This opinion would be delivered by the majority laid down in Article 148(2) of the EEC Treaty[52] in the case of decisions which the Council of Ministers is required to adopt on a proposal from the Commission.[53]

The votes of the representatives of the Member States within the committee shall be weighted in the manner set out in Article 148 of the EEC Treaty but the chairman will not have a vote. The Commission would be obliged to adopt the measures envisaged if they are in accordance with the opinion of the committee.[54]

If the measures envisaged are not in accordance with committee's opinion, or if no opinion is delivered, the Commission shall, without delay, submit to the Council of Ministers, a proposal relating to the measures to be taken and the Council of Ministers shall act by a qualified majority.[55]

If, after three months from referring them to the Council of Ministers, the Council of Ministers has not acted then the proposed measures shall be adopted by the Commission.[56]

20.2.11.13 Entry into force

The Directive provides that Member States are obliged to bring into force the laws, regulations and administrative provisions necessary for compliance with the Directive by 31 December 1994.[57]

20.2.11.14 Conclusion

There is little doubt that the adoption of the Directive is welcome because "there is a need to provide for additional measures for medical assistance at sea in order to take account of technological and medical progress and thus ensure better protection of the health and safety"[58] of seafarers.

48. Directive, Article 8.
49. Directive, Article 8.
50. Directive, Article 8.
51. Directive, Article 8.
52. For the text of Article 148(2) EEC, see Appendix 4, below.
53. Directive, Article 8.
54. Directive, Article 8.
55. Directive, Article 8.
56. Directive, Article 8.
57. Directive, Article 9(1).
58. Directive, Recital 5.

CHAPTER 21

Navigation

21.1 INTRODUCTION

The EC has been marginally concerned with navigation issues. This concern is growing.

21.2 DECISION 82/887

On 13 December 1982, the Council of Ministers adopted Decision 82/887/EEC adopting a concerted action project for the European Economic Community in the field of shore-based marine navigation aid systems. This was the so-called "COST 301" Research Programme. The Commission later wrote:

"The main objective of COST 301 is to consider the need for and if appropriate to propose means to improve the safety of navigation in European waters through an integrated network of shore-based centres. The purpose of these centres, (known as Vessel Traffic Management Services/ VTMS or VTS) would be, through better organisation and management of traffic flow, to reduce risks of collisions, strandings and rammings, and therefore enhance safety at sea and prevent pollution of seas and coastal areas...

An additional objective of the programme is to consider how to make the best possible use of such an integrated network to provide a service to the maritime community concerned (mariners, shipowners, governments, administrations, port authorities, search and rescue services, etc.): this service should be able to make available to these users the information they need, in a form and timescale that meets their requirements."[1]

Finland, Norway, Sweden and Spain joined the project by signing in 1983 an Agreement of Co-operation.

21.3 DECISION 92/143: RADIONAVIGATION SYSTEMS

21.3.1 Introduction

On 25 February 1992, the Council of Ministers adopted Decision 92/143 on Radionavigation Systems for Europe.[2]

21.3.2 Legal bases

The legal bases of the Decision were the EEC Treaty generally as well as Article 84(2) thereof in particular.

1. Progress Towards a Common Transport Policy: Maritime Transport, COM(85)90 final, paras 93–4.
2. OJ L59/17, 4 March 1992.

21.3.3 Legislative history

The Decision had a short gestation. The Commission's proposals were formally published in 1991,[3] the European Parliament[4] as well as the Economic and Social Committee[5] delivered their Opinions that same year, and the Council adopted the Decision in February 1992.[6]

21.3.4 Technical background

The technical background to Decision 92/143 is clear from the Preamble which recites:

"... Whereas the 1974 International Convention for the Safety of Life at Sea (SOLAS 1974) drafted under the auspices of the International Maritime Organization (IMO), requires contracting parties to arrange for the establishment and maintenance of such aids to navigation as the volume of traffic and the degree of risk warrant;

Whereas, in its Resolution A.666 (16), the IMO refers both to the need for a worldwide radionavigation system and to the possibility of regional applications of terrestrial systems such as Chayka, Decca Navigator, Loran-C, Omega and Differential Omega;

Whereas the International Association of Lighthouse Authorities confirms that, in order to meet the needs of maritime navigation, a terrestrial radionavigation system is necessary until general-purpose satellite systems are widely available, and also thereafter in parallel to such systems for the foreseeable future;

Whereas it is a concern of the Community to ensure the highest degree of safety of navigation and protection of the marine environment;

Whereas the United States Coastguard has decided to terminate its Loran-C commitments outside the United States of America as from 1994 and intends to offer the Loran-C facilities to the relevant host nations;

Whereas certain Member States intend to participate in one or more regional agreements on the establishment of Loran-C chains covering North-West Europe and the North Atlantic, the Mediterranean, the Iberian Peninsula and the Baltic, while a number of these areas are already covered by terrestrial systems, such as Decca and Omega;

Whereas Member States are not required to abandon existing radionavigation systems, such as Decca and Omega, provided they fulfil their Loran-C obligations in accordance with regional agreements;

Whereas the Loran-C system in particular satisfies international requirements and its more general application does not prejudice the development of satellite aids to navigation, especially as combined coverage by satellite and Loran-C will offer an excellent degree of system verification and continuity of radionavigation coverage for the benefit of maritime safety and environmental protection;

Whereas the establishment of regional Loran-C systems must ensure coherent and complete coverage of the European maritime area, avoiding as much as possible the imposition of additional costs upon the users of existing terrestrial radionavigation systems. . . ."

21.3.5 Role of the Member States

Article 1 of the Decision provides:

"1. Without prejudice to existing radionavigation systems, Member States which participate in or join regional agreements on Loran-C shall do so in a way which fulfils international objectives.

2. With regard to their participation in the regional agreements referred to in paragraph 1, Member States shall seek to achieve the radionavigation configurations which cover the widest possible geographical area in Europe and in neighbouring waters."

3. OJ C53/71, 28 February 1991 and OJ C317/16, 7 December 1991.
4. OJ C280/32, 28 October 1991.
5. OJ C159/22, 17 June 1991.
6. OJ L59/17, 4 March 1992.

This does not require Member States to abandon existing radionavigation systems but instead provides that those States which participate in or join regional agreements on Loran-C shall do so in a way which fulfils international objectives.

21.3.6 Role of the Commission

Article 2 of the Decision relates to the role of the Commission. It provides:

> "The Commission shall:
> — ensure coordination between the Member States participating in the regional agreements referred to in paragraph 1 with a view to ensuring compatibility between the Loran-C chains introduced at regional level,
> — encourage the development of receivers, which take account of the ongoing development of satellite systems and the enhancement of the present Loran-C system,
> — pursue its work with a view to setting up a radionavigation plan which takes into account the development of satellite navigation systems, of existing terrestrial systems and of the radionavigation plans of the Member States, and
> — propose the necessary measures to the Council should the need arise."

21.3.7 Role of the Commission and Member States jointly

Article 3 provides for the Commission and the Member States to act jointly to support efforts to set up a world-wide radionavigation system. It provides:

> "As members or observers within the International Association of Lighthouse Authorities, Member States and the Commission shall support efforts to set up a worldwide radionavigation system including European regional Loran-C chains with the purpose of enlarging worldwide Loran-C coverage in order to improve the safety of navigation and protection of the marine environment."

CHAPTER 22

Pilotage

22.1 INTRODUCTION

This short chapter concentrates on the 1978 North Sea Pilotage Directive.[1]

22.2 THE 1978 NORTH SEA PILOTAGE DIRECTIVE

22.2.1 Introduction

On 21 December 1978, the EEC Council of Ministers adopted a Directive concerning pilotage of vessels by deep-sea pilots in the North Sea and English Channel. This was Directive 79/115/EEC.

22.2.2 Legal bases

The legal bases of this Directive were the EEC Treaty generally and Article 84(2) in particular.

22.2.3 Purpose

The purpose of the Directive is set out in the Preamble to it which reads:

"[w]hereas for the sake of safety at sea and of preventing marine pollution, it is necessary to ensure that vessels wishing to use the services of pilots in the North Sea and English Channel can call on adequately qualified deep-sea pilots, and to promote the employment of such pilots in vessels flying the flags of Member States."

22.2.4 Obligation on certain states to provide qualified pilots

Article 1(1) of the Directive provides that the Member States which have coasts bordering on the North Sea or English Channel are obliged to take all necessary and appropriate measures to ensure that vessels availing themselves of the services of a deep-sea pilot for pilotage in the North Sea or the English Channel be provided with adequately qualified deep-sea pilots in possession of a certificate delivered by a competent authority of one of these Member States certifying that such pilots are qualified to pilot vessels in the North Sea and the English Channel.

1. Dir.79/115/EEC.

22.2.5 Member States are obliged to encourage ships which fly their flags to use qualified pilots

Article 1(2) of the Directive is apparently addressed to all Member States of the EC in that it provides that "[e]ach Member State" is obliged to take all necessary and appropriate measures to encourage vessels flying its national flag to avail themselves, in the North Sea and the English Channel, of the services of only those deep-sea pilots who are in possession of a certificate as referred to in Article 1(1) or of an equivalent certificate delivered by another North Sea coastal State, when seeking the assistance of deep-sea pilots.

22.2.6 Implementation

Article 2 provides that after consulting the Commission, Member States were obliged to bring into force the laws, regulations and administrative provisions necessary to comply with the Directive not later than 1 January 1980 and were obliged to inform the Commission thereof.

22.3 1985 COMMISSION MEMORANDUM ON SHIPPING

The former EC Commissioner for Transport, Lord Stanley Clinton Davis, was reported, at the time of the Commission's 1985 Memorandum being published, as emphasising the need for concerted action in the field of pilotage.

CHAPTER 23

Ports and Port State Control

23.1 PORTS

Ports are as much an integral part of EC shipping policy as ships. The EC has examined the topic of ports on a number of occasions, but there has not been a great deal of legislative action.

Attention has been focused on ports since 1961 when the topic was discussed in a report made to the European Parliament.[1] Attention was again focused on the issue in 1967[2] and 1972[3] when further reports were made to the European Parliament. In 1970, the Commission published its *Note on Port Options on a Community Basis*.[4]

The Commission followed up this note by holding plenary meetings of major European ports: the first two of which led to the drawing up of terms of reference for a working group.[5] The Commission reviewed its work between 1972 and 1980 in the following terms:

"102. . . . the Commission's services worked closely with representatives of the major port authorities of the Community in the production of two reports. The first of these[6] set out the major differences in practice as regards the financing of infrastructure, superstructure and operations both between the ports of the various Member States and often between the ports of a single country. The second[7] attempted to determine whether these differences led to serious distortions to competition.

The majority of port experts did not think that the existing differences warranted a specific port policy on the part of the Community. There are, however, aspects of port policy where in the view of the Commission Community action would be useful. The Community's ports are a critical link in the transport chain between sea and inland transport. It is therefore essential that port aspects are taken into account in the context of the development of both the inland and the maritime aspects of the common transport policy. It is in this sense that the Commission will consider Parliament's recommendations on matters affecting ports.

103. In order to identify possible areas of work at Community level it seems relevant in today's transport policy context to review and update the Commission's conclusions on some of the main issues which were examined in . . . earlier reports . . . :

— the influence of national and Community transport policies on conditions of competition between the ports of the Member States;

1. Document EP 106 of 11 December 1961 (Rapporteur: Kaptcyn).
2. Document EP 140 of 24 November 1967 (Rapporteur: Seifriz).
3. *Report on Port Policy within the Framework of the European Community* (Doc.EP 10/72) of 12 April 1972.
4. Document 16/VII/71 of 24 March 1970.
5. See Report of an Enquiry into the Current Situation in the Major Community Seaports drawn up by the Port Working Group (CB-22-77-863).
6. Report on an Enquiry into the current situation in the Major Community Seaports drawn up by the Port Working Group (CB-22-77-863).
7. Report of the Port Working Group (VII/440/80) (Internal Working Paper).

— the influence of charging policies and of state aids to ports on competition between the ports of the Member States."[8]

In respect of the first item, namely, the influence of national and Community transport policies on conditions of competition between the ports of the Member States, the Commission wrote:

"*Hinterland Traffic*

104. The organisation of the market in hinterland transport has an important bearing on competition between the Community's seaports. While it is not the only factor determining the competitive positions of a seaport and a customer's decision to use its services rather than those of rival ports, a port's intrinsic appeal is unquestionably enhanced the more versatile the services it can provide in the way of transport links with the hinterland and the more flexible the rates charged.

105. For years now a debate has been going on between the German seaports and various modes of transport by land. This, coupled with public utterances on the debate by experts in this field and the views expressed by the competent German authorities, attests to the topicality—although not the novelty—of this aspect of transport policy both in Germany and elsewhere. Furthermore, [the European] Parliament has, in various reports, emphasised the importance of finding adequate solutions in this matter.

106. But the problem is not confined to competition between the German seaports and the ARA (Amsterdam, Rotterdam, Anterp) range of ports: it affects competition between all Community ports, i.e. between the North Sea, the Atlantic and the Mediterranean, and between individual ports in each of these groups.

107. The markets where one port enjoys an unassailable position are few and far between and in any case on the small side. Most of the Community's continental heartland can be regarded—increasingly so as a result of the constant improvement in the technical and organisational efficiency of inland modes of transport—as a collection of geographical areas each of which could be served by several ports.

108. Competition between the seaports to serve these areas can, where transport is concerned, only function under optimum conditions if each of these markets is regulated along much the same lines, i.e. if the ports and their customers are offered comparable terms from the point of view of quantity and quality in comparable circumstances.

109. This is not the case at present. The nub of the problem facing Germany, for instance, is that hinterland transport is subject for the most part to a regulated system of competition involving, in particular, a relatively rigid set of compulsory tariffs for road haulage and inland waterway transport, a rigid capacity limitation on commercial road hauliers and all the intervention by public authorities that this entails. By contrast, hinterland transport to and from the rival ARA ports is predominantly international in nature and enjoys complete freedom of commercial activity in Rhine shipping and a freer regime, in respect of access and tariffs, in the road haulage market.

110. There is evidence of similar discrepancies in other transport markets making up the hinterland of several seaports with overlapping catchment areas, for instance competition between North Sea and Adriatic ports. The rivalry between these ports has led to a situation in Italy where goods being carried to and from Trieste are no longer subject to quotas and road hauliers are not obliged to obtain authorisation.

111. It is difficult, if not impossible, to say what the effects of such distortions of competition have been. Statistics produced in the debate going on within Germany show that figures cannot be advanced to prove what the actual effects are in view of the multitude of factors that influence the volume of traffic at a particular port over long periods of time.

112. It is obvious, however, that a port with access to a variety of freely competing inland modes of transport charging market rates may, all other things being equal, have a competitive edge over rivals whose hinterland communications are regulated by state or quasi-public cartels governing market access and prices.

113. In the Commission's view, there is no satisfactory regulatory method to harmonise the conditions of competition on such different routes facing such a widespread set of conditions.

8. *Progress towards a Common Transport Policy: Maritime Transport*, COM(85)90 final, paras 102–3.

The only genuine harmonisation possible is that brought about by the free operation of the market. It would be conceivable and practicable and meet the objective of equating competition between ports to abolish all restrictions on access, notably in the area of quota-fixing, and abolish fixed tariffs in respect of the carriage of exports and imports to and from all Community ports, whether on international or on national routes.

114. This so-called corridor approach does not pose any insurmountable technical problems, and the system can also be monitored. It would serve its purpose in view of its limited objectives and could also serve to promote the Community's external trade.

115. It should be stressed—to avoid any misunderstanding—that such an approach is not designed to iron out any natural advantages or disadvantages in the competitive positions of the various seaports. In view of the objectives of the EEC Treaty, the aim is and must be solely to do away with artificial distortions stemming from discrepancies in market regulations and out-of-date measures.

116. A solution of this nature will stand the test of achieving fair competition between the seaports. With this end in view the Commission has already initiated consultations on such a proposal and has recently presented a proposal to the Council.

Maritime Aspects

117. As regards shipping all measures aimed at favouring, directly or indirectly, the national fleet of a Member State and/or of its trading partners tend to have an effect on the distribution of the tonnage handled by ports. Thus, for instance, unilateral or bilateral cargo reservation measures by Member States or third countries can distort competition between ports. The Commission's proposals on the application of the competition rules of the [EEC] Treaty to sea transport, and on the application of the principle of freedom to provide services to shipping will serve to remove the dangers of a distortion of competition between ports.

118. It is alleged that Community legislation concerning the environment and shipping safety have, because of national differences in the implementation and policing of these measures, caused distortions of competition between Community ports. The same allegation is sometimes made in respect of the Community's monitoring exercise in respect of seaborne trade between the Community, Central America, East Africa and the Far East. The Commission has so far not received any substantive evidence to corroborate these allegations. But it keeps developments in this respect under review."

In respect of the second item, namely, the influence of charging policies and of state aids to ports on competition between the ports of the Member States, the Commission went on to write:

"119. Charging policies in the ports vary from one Member State to another and from one port to another. It is generally considered that some three-quarters of the costs involved when a ship calling to load or discharge a full cargo in port are made up of cargo handling charges (mainly stevedoring charges) and only one quarter of port charges imposed by the port authority or other public body. This relationship tends to vary, however, for some other ships such as specialised offshore vessels, passenger cruise ships or ships calling to load or discharge part cargoes to take on bunkers or for repair. Work undertaken by the Port Working Group between 1977 and 1980 revealed that, for example, most port authorities made no specific charge for use of the deepwater access channel or for the use of buoys and lights and it was not possible to find out whether the port dues charged covered such items. The Commission estimates that about 5 per cent of the total transport costs are port charges; and the 1980 report had already concluded that port charges did not seem to constitute the major determining factor in the choice of a port. In fact, no single factor can be identified to regularly determine this choice. There is always a whole array of qualitative and quantitative aspects involved. Their weight varies over time and as a function of the commodity to be shipped, the terms of shipment and the origin and destination of the commodity. Therefore, the Commission does not deem it useful nor necessary at present to embark on the complex task of harmonising the charging policies of the Community's ports.

120. As regards port aids, the effect of direct national port aids on competition between ports was also examined in 1980 by the Port Working Group of the Commission . . . and at that time it concluded that national aids to ports did not lead to serious distortions to competition. At this

stage, therefore the Commission will not attempt to draw up guidelines for the application of the Treaty to state aids to ports; but it will deal with specific aids, if required, directly on the basis of Articles 92 and 93 of the [EEC] Treaty and it will review the general situation from time to time and study further the different port aid systems existing in the Member States. Other aids. such as regional aids and aids to facilitate the development of certain economic activities which may also have a bearing on competition between ports will be taken into account as well in the Commission's considerations regarding their compatibility with the common market."

This work of the Commission in the area of ports culminated in 1981 in the submission of a report to Parliament on its work towards a Community Port Policy.[9] The European Parliament approved the Carossino Report on the Role of Ports in the Common Transport Policy on 11 March 1983.[10]

23.2 PORT STATE CONTROL

23.2.1 Introduction

The control exercised by States in their own ports over ships visiting those ports (i.e. Port State control) is an important way of dealing with safety and pollution. It is embodied in Chapter I, Part B, Regulation 19 of the SOLAS Convention (as amended). This regulation provides that:

- first, every ship is subject to the port State control of another party to SOLAS;
- secondly, control is directed towards verifying the validity of the ship's certificates; and
- thirdly, where there are clear grounds for believing that the condition of the ship or of its equipment does not correspond substantially with the contents of the certificates or with the provisions of the Convention, the ship shall not sail until the defects are remedied.

23.2.2 Commission proposal for a directive on Port State Control

In June 1980, the Commission proposed a Directive concerning the enforcement in respect of shipping using Community ports of international standards for shipping safety and pollution prevention, known as "Port State Control".[11] As the Commission itself later recorded: "[d]iscussions in the Council [of Ministers] were overtaken by events as the French government convened a meeting of the maritime authorities of thirteen (the nine Member States plus Norway, Sweden, Spain, Portugal and later Finland) European countries to discuss the issue."[12]

23.2.3 The Memorandum of Understanding on Port State Control

All the maritime States of the EC have signed the Memorandum of Understanding on Port State control.[13]

9. Report on Community Port Policy (Doc.EP 73.762).
10. European Parliament, Report on the Role of Ports in the Common Transport Policy, 15 November 1982, P E 80/050/final; Report on the Problems of Maritime Transport in the Community, 23 March 1977, P E 47.110/final. See also the *Report of an Enquiry into the Current Situation in the Major Commodity Sea-Ports drawn up by the Port Working Group* (1992).
11. COM(80)360 final.
12. *Progress Towards a Common Transport Policy: Maritime Transport*, COM(85)90 final, para. 88.
13. 26 January 1982. Published in (1982) 21 ILM 1.

Port State control was organised on a regional basis between the States which bordered the North Sea.

The Memorandum was negotiated at the Regional European Conference on Maritime Safety. It was signed in Paris on 26 January 1982 and entered into force on 1 July 1982. It obliges its signatories to sign and ratify a number of international conventions regarding safety of life at sea; standards of employment and accommodation on board ships; and the protection of the marine environment. More specifically, the Conventions in question are: International Convention on Load Lines, 1966; Convention on the International Regulations for Preventing Collisions at Sea, 1972; International Convention for the Prevention of Pollution from Ships, 1973 (as modified by the Protocol of 1978); International Convention for the Safety of Life at Sea, 1974 (as amended by the Protocol of 1978); Merchant Shipping (Minimum Standards) Convention, 1976 (ILO Convention No.147); International Convention on Standards of Training, Certification and Watchkeeping for Seafarers, 1978.

Its aim is to "ensure that the standards set by various international Conventions in the maritime safety area were being implemented in an effective and harmonised manner. To this end the signatories undertook to inspect within three years 25 per cent of the individual foreign flag merchant ships entering their ports, to detain or delay ships with deficiencies until such deficiencies were put right, to set up an information system to assist each other in the choice of ships for inspection and to ratify all the relevant international conventions."[14]

By 30 June 1984, some 18,000 inspections had been made resulting in the detention or delay of over 700 ships which had serious deficiencies. The system was bolstered by the creation of a real-time computerised information system in St Malo so as to provide a databank of information for inspectors.

The Memorandum has proved useful but deserves further strengthening. The Commission has proposed improving the effectiveness of the system (see below).

23.2.4 Commission Recommendation on improving the effectiveness of Port State Control in the Community[15]

The Commission included in its Positive Measures[16] communication a Recommendation[17] that the EC Member States should perform their obligations under the Memorandum where they have not already done so.

23.2.4.1 Rationale

The Preamble to the proposed Recommendation read:

"Whereas the safety of life at sea, acceptable standards of living and working conditions on board ships and the protection of the marine environment must be maintained and promoted;

Whereas the principal responsibility for the effective application of these standards as laid down in international instruments rests upon the relevant authorities of the State whose flag a ship is entitled to fly;

Whereas effective action in the form of Port State Control is, nevertheless, necessary to ensure proper application of these standards in order to rescue and prevent substandard shipping;

14. *Progress Towards a Common Transport Policy: Maritime Transport*, COM(85)90 final, para. 88.
15. COM(89)266 final, OJ C263, 16 October 1989, p. 15.
16. COM(89)266 final, 3 August 1989.
17. On the legal effect of a Recommendation, see Chapter 3, above.

Whereas all the maritime nations of the European Economic Community are signatories of the Memorandum of Understanding on Port State Control;

Whereas it is essential that all international conventions under the Memorandum of Understanding are duly signed and ratified by all Member States;

Whereas correct application of the international conventions referred to in the Memorandum of Understanding on Port State Control requires uniform and effective checking by Member States who are signatories to the aforesaid Memorandum;

Whereas it is necessary to ensure that the target number of inspections on individual foreign merchant ships visiting the ports of signatories to the Memorandum is achieved in order to reduce and prevent substandard shipping and in order to avoid distortions of conditions of competition between ports within the Community;

Whereas for these purposes a full and uniform system of Port State Control should be in force throughout the Community."

In essence the Recommendation had three objectives: first, to reduce and prevent substandard shipping; secondly, to avoid distortions of conditions of competition; and, thirdly, to ensure that a full and uniform system of port state control operates throughout the EC.

23.2.4.2 Ratification of the International Conventions covered by the Memorandum of Understanding

The Recommendation recommends that Member States ratify certain Conventions in pursuance of their obligations under the Memorandum of Understanding. These Conventions are: International Convention on Load Lines, 1966; Convention on the International Regulations for Preventing Collisions at Sea, 1972; International Convention for the Prevention of Pollution from Ships, 1973 (as modified by the Protocol of 1978); International Convention for the Safety of Life at Sea, 1974 (as amended by the Protocol of 1978); Merchant Shipping (Minimum Standards) Convention, 1976 (ILO Convention No. 147); International Convention on Standards of Training, Certification and Watchkeeping for Seafarers, 1978.

The Recommendation also recommends that those Member States, which have not yet ratified the optional Annexes to the International Convention for the Prevention of Pollution from Ships 1973 (as amended by the Protocol of 1978 (MARPOL 73/78)) do so forthwith.

23.2.4.3 Implementation of the International Conventions covered by the Memorandum of Understanding

The Recommendation recommends that those Member States, which are signatories to the Memorandum of Understanding, ensure that:

"1. a minimum annual total of 25 per cent of the number of individual foreign merchant ships visiting their ports are inspected in accordance with the provisions of the Memorandum of Understanding;

2. the inspection procedures laid down in the Manual for Surveyors adopted by the Port State Control Committee are strictly applied;

3. adequate resources, both financial and manpower, are provided to ensure a full implementation of their obligations under the Memorandum of Understanding on Port State Control."

23.2.4.4 Follow-up

The Recommendation provides that the Commission request Member States to inform it within twelve months of the adoption of the Recommendation of the measures they have taken in the field.

23.2.5 1982 Commission Opinion

On 1 July 1982, the Commission adopted an Opinion addressed to the Greek Government regarding the implementation of the 1978 Council Directive,[18] concerning minimum requirements for certain tankers entering or leaving Community ports, and of the Council Directive of 6 December 1979 amending the 1978 Council Directive. This Opinion, Opinion 82/452/EEC read:

> "1. In a letter dated 13 August 1981 the Office of the Permanent Representative of Greece to the European Communities sent the Commission, under Article 3 of each of the two Directives in question,[19,20] Presidential Decree No.618/81 of 8 June 1981 concerning minimum requirements for certain tankers entering or leaving Greek ports.
>
> 2. Examination of that Decree has satisfied the Commission that the Greek Government has fully complied with the provisions of both the Directives in question."

In 1986, Sir James Scott-Hopkins, a Member of the European Parliament for the UK, asked the Commission the following question:

> "[D]oes the Commission not agree that legislation is needed, as a matter of urgency, to enable Member States to coordinate the policing of abuses such as the use of flags of convenience to employ sub-standard ships and inadequately trained and underpaid crews?"[21]

Commissioner Stanley Clinton Davies responded:

> "As far as the use of open registry shipping is concerned the Member States co-ordinate, on the basis of Commission proposals and using the consultation procedure set up in 1977,[22] their position together with other states of Group B in the UNCTAD Conference on registration of ships, which has just held its final session in Geneva. The aim is to strengthen the link between ship and flag in order to eliminate abuses of using open registries. The Commission, which shares the Honourable Member's concerns in this field, has given its full support to all the international measures designed to eliminate the abuses associated with some of the open registry fleets.
>
> In addition Member States have coordinated their efforts to eliminate sub-standard shipping and to check on the adequacy of crews through the Memorandum on Port State Control signed in Paris in January 1982. The Memorandum was based on the Commission's proposed Directive of June 1980.[23]
>
> The Memorandum will be revised at a Ministerial meeting in The Hague in April 1986. In the Commission's view Port State Control has proved an increasingly effective means of dealing with the problems mentioned by the Honourable Member, particularly in view of the controls undertaken with respect to the IMO Convention on Standards of Seafarers' Training. As the Memorandum is applied also by non-Member States further legislation and in particular Community legislation does not at present seem necessary or appropriate."

23.2.5.1 1986 progress towards a Common Transport Policy: Maritime Transport

In giving its Opinion on the Communication, the Economic and Social Committee commented:

18. 21 December 1978.
19. OJ L33, 8 February 1979, p. 11.
20. OJ L315, 11 December 1979, p. 16.
21. Written Question No. 1955/85.
22. OJ L239 of 17 September 1977.
23. OJ C192 of 30 July 1980, p. 8.

"3.5.1 The Committee feels that greater weight should be attached by the Commission to the adverse affects of disparities in port charges and light dues since these are important factors to ship operators in their choice of ports. Furthermore, the Committee notes that certain liner Conference Services operating between Member States and third countries practise price discrimination on cargo shipped as between ports of one Member State and another to destinations in third countries. Such practice is inconsistent with the principle of fair and equal competition for all and should be discontinued.

3.5.2 The Committee welcomes the Commission's proposal that a Community wide dimension should be given to the provision of port waste facilities, as required under MARPOL. It feels that the Commission should initiate a proposal for the provision of such facilities on a much wider basis than at present with either Community or national funding for the establishment of reception facilities. Further the Commission should investigate the feasibility of using laid up tankers for the reception of oily wastes and possibly other wastes. The provision of port reception facilities should be considered within the context of EC infrastructure policy and priority areas should include the Mediterranean and also the North Sea."

The Economic and Social Committee also commented:

"3.4.1 The Committee fully supports the concept of port state control as the necessary complement of the exercise of flag jurisdiction. In particular it supports the 1982 Paris Memorandum which stressed the importance of vessels of all flags adhering to the generally accepted IMO and ILO Conventions and coordinated the approach of the EC and Nordic countries to inspections of vessels visiting their ports.

3.4.2 However there should be full disclosure of deficiencies classified by flag type and degree of seriousness gathered from port state inspections and an investigation into whether the inspections are uniformly carried out through the Community's ports. Unless there is such a disclosure and unless it can be demonstrated that these inspections are being conducted on a uniform basis, then a statement as in the Commission's memorandum, that there is little evidence that competitive pressures among the various ports of the Community are undermining the application of port state control is far from convincing.

3.4.3 The Committee further considers that the Commission should explore the possibility of introducing a system of coastal state control so that vessels passing through EC waters are subject to the same standards as vessels entering ports, since the safety of seafarers, vessels, the public and the environment is no less at risk from vessels which are sailing through the waters of port state control signatories without visiting a port in a signatory state than those from which do visit a signatory state's port. The Committee recognises that there are a number of practical and legal difficulties in establishing a system of coastal state control but considers that the subject merits investigation."

CHAPTER 24

Carriage of Goods and Passengers by Sea

24.1 PASSENGER BAGGAGE

24.1.1 The proposed elimination of controls on passenger baggage on intra-community sea crossings

On 3 August 1990, the Commission submitted a proposal for a Council Regulation (EEC) concerning the elimination of controls and formalities applicable to the cabin and checked baggage of passengers taking an intra-Community flight and the baggage of passengers making an intra-Community sea crossing.[1]

24.1.2 Background

The Preamble to the proposed Regulation provides:

"Whereas Article 8a of the [EEC] Treaty provides that the internal market shall comprise an area without internal frontiers in which the free movement, in particular, of goods is ensured; whereas in this context ports and airports stand apart as either may constitute, at the same time, an external frontier and an internal border; whereas the application of the principle of freedom of movement should result, *inter alia*, in the elimination of controls on the cabin and checked baggage of passengers taking an intra-Community flight and the baggage of passengers making an intra-Community sea crossing; . . .

Whereas maritime transport may involve different types of voyage and whereas the concept of an intra-Community sea crossing must be defined;

Whereas the elimination of the controls and formalities applicable to baggage on intra-Community flights and sea crossings does not rule out the possibility of maintaining safety checks . . ."

24.1.3 Legal basis

The legal basis for the proposed Regulation is the EEC Treaty generally and Article 100 thereof in particular.

24.1.4 Basic regime

Article 1 of the proposed Regulation provides (in relation to maritime transport):

1. See COM(90)370 final–SYN 289. The proposed Regulation is reprinted in OJ C 212/8, 25 August 1990.

"Without prejudice to the safety checks applicable in . . . sea transport, no controls or formalities shall be carried out in respect of . . . the baggage of passengers making an intra-Community sea crossing."[2]

24.1.5 Basic concepts relating to sea transport

In the context of the proposed Regulation, an "intra-Community sea crossing" means "a sea crossing"[3] where the port of departure and port of arrival are situated in Community customs territory and the journey is made by a vessel crossing regularly between two or more specified Community ports.[4,5]

24.1.6 Limitations

The proposed Regulation would not, as presently drafted, apply to either:

- the baggage of passengers using a maritime service effected in one vessel and comprising successive legs departing from, terminating in or calling at a non-Community port[6]: or
- the baggage of passengers on board pleasure craft, i.e. private boats intended for recreational use whose itinerary depends on the wishes of the user.[7]

24.1.7 Committee on Community Transit

Article 5 of the proposed Regulation provides that the Committee on Community Transit (which is to be established) would be responsible for the implementation of Articles 6 and 7 of the proposed Regulation. Article 6 provides that the Committee "may examine any question relating to the application of this Regulation submitted to its chairman either on his own initiative or at the request of the representative of a Member State". Article 7, which is more detailed, provides:

"The Commission shall, after consulting the Committee, adopt the provisions necessary for the application of this Regulation.

The representative of the Commission shall submit to the Committee a draft of the measures to be taken. The Committee shall deliver its opinion on the draft, within a time limit which the chairman may lay down according to the urgency of the matter, if necessary by taking a vote.

The opinion shall be recorded in the minutes; in addition, each Member State shall have the right to ask to have its position recorded in the minutes.

The Commission shall take the utmost account of the opinion delivered by the Committee. It shall inform the Committee of the manner in which its opinion has been taken into account."

24.1.8 Application

The Commission has proposed that the Regulation would apply from 1 January 1993.

2. In the context of the proposed Regulation, a "Community port" means "any port situated in Community customs territory" (proposed Regulation, Article 2(4)).
3. In the context of the proposed Regulation, a "sea crossing" means "the movement of a vessel between two ports without any intermediate stop" (proposed Regulation, Article 2(5)).
4. In the context of the proposed Regulation, a "Community port" means "any port situated in Community customs territory" (proposed Regulation, Article 2(4)).
5. Proposed Regulation, Article 2(6).
6. In the context of the proposed Regulation, a "Community port" means "any port situated in Community customs territory" (proposed Regulation, Article 2(4)).
7. Proposed Regulation, Article 3.

24.2 FARES

On 22 June 1987, the Commission adopted Decision 87/359/EEC concerning reductions in air and sea transport fares available only to Spanish nationals resident in the Canary Islands and the Balearic Islands.[8]

The Commission acted on the basis of Article 90(1) and (3) of the EEC Treaty.

Spain had introduced, by way of Decree-Laws 22/62 of 14 June 1962[9] and Law No. 46/81 of 29 December 1981[10] special arrangements relating to transport under which certain persons travelling between continental Spain and the Canary as well as Balearic Islands were granted reductions in fares for air and sea transport.

In specific terms, Article 2 of the Decree-Law 22/62 concerning air links with the Canary Islands provided from a State subsidy amounting to 33 per cent of the price for tickets on scheduled passenger services on that route and Article 3 required transport undertakings receiving the subsidy to reduce the price of their tickets by the same amount. Article 1 of the Decree-Law expressly provided that the State subsidies for air transport services to and from the Canary Islands were applicable only to tickets used by Spanish nationals resident on the Islands. Law 46/81 concerned air and sea links with the Balearic Islands and provided in a similar way for a State subsidy allowing reduced fares to be charged on scheduled transport services between the archipelago and the rest of Spain. Article 2 of the Law provided for a reduction in fares amounting to 25 per cent of the fare for sailings between the archipelago and the rest of Spain and to 10 per cent of the fare for sailings between islands within the archipelago. Articles 3 and 4 of the Law provided that the relevant undertakings, which are required to grant the reductions in fares, would be reimbursed by the State for the resulting loss of revenue. Article 1 of the Law provided that only Spanish nationals resident in the Balearic Islands are eligible for the reduction in fares.

The special arrangements provided for by Decree-Law No. 22/62 and Law No. 46/81 were reinforced by Article 1 of Royal Decree No. 3269/82 of 12 November 1982.[11]

This provided that the reductions in fares for scheduled passenger transport services provided for in Decree-Law No. 22/62 and Law No. 46/81 and granted through the intermediary of the publicly owned transport companies are to be available only to Spanish nationals who, at the time of purchasing their tickets, can provide evidence that they are resident in the provinces of the Balearic Islands, Las Palmas and Santa Cruz de Tenerife.

A number of private individuals as well as Members of the European Parliament objected to these arrangements and objected to the Commission. A formal complaint was ultimately lodged with the Commission.[12] The Commission later said, in the course of its Decision, that:

> "By restricting eligibility for the reduced-fare air and sea transport arrangements to Spanish nationals resident in the Canary and Balearic Islands, Spain is clearly placing them at an advantage over nationals of other Member States similarly resident in the islands.
>
> The transport arrangements applied by Spain are of obvious economic importance in view of the number of nationals of other Member States in the islands, the cost of transport between the islands and continental Spain, and the scale of the reduction granted only to Spanish residents."

8. OJ L194, 15 July 1987, p. 28.
9. See Decree-Law No. 22/62 of 14 June 1962, *Boletin Oficial del Estado* No.143, 15 June 1962.
10. *Boletin Oficial del Estado*, No. 312, 30 December 1981.
11. *Boletin Oficial del Estado*, No. 287, 30 November 1982.
12. See Recital 6 of Dec.87/359/EEC, OJ L194/28, 15 July 1987.

The Commission made representations to the Spanish Government on 23 December 1986 expressing its view that the arrangements were incompatible with the Treaty. It reiterated its position on 5 February 1987. The Commission then reaffirmed its position on 4 March 1987 after the Commission had received the Spanish authorities' comments and statement that the arrangements would continue.

The Commission, in its Decision of 22 June 1987 reasoned thus:

"10. Article 90(1) of the EEC Treaty provides that, in the case of public undertakings, Member States shall neither enact nor maintain in force any measure contrary to the rules contained in the Treaty, in particular to the rules provided for in Article 7 and Articles 85 to 94. The same requirement applies to undertakings to which Member States grant special or exclusive rights.

11. By continuing to apply after 1 January 1986[13] the preferential transport fare arrangements introduced by Decree-Law No. 22/62 of 14 June 1962 and Law No. 46/81 of 29 December 1981, Spain had maintained in force in the case of public undertakings, namely the national transport companies Iberia and Transmediterranea,[14] measures within the meaning of Article 90(1) of the EEC Treaty.

12. Article 90(3) of the EEC Treaty provides that the Commission shall secure the application of the provisions of Article 90 and shall, where necessary, address appropriate Directives or Decisions to Member States.

13. Pursuant to Article 90(1), the provisions of Article 7 of the EEC Treaty must in particular be observed. These prohibit any discrimination on grounds of nationality.

14. Since, even though no exception clause is provided for in the transitional measures laid down in the Act of Accession,"[15]

The Commission thus decided, in Article 1 of its Decision that:

"The following provisions are hereby declared incompatible with the provisions of Article 90(1), in conjunction with those of Article 7, of the EEC Treaty:

— Article 1 of Spanish Decree-Law No. 22/62 on the subsidisation of air transport links with the Canary Islands,
— Article 1 of Spanish Law No. 46/81 on the subsidisation of fares for Spanish nationals resident in the Balearic Islands,
— Article 1 of Spanish Royal Decree No. 3269/82 on the certification of residence for the purposes of the subsidisation of fares and the payment of the subsidy towards scheduled transport services between the peninsula, the Canary Islands and the Balearic Islands, to the extent that they restrict the application of the reductions in transport fares for which they provide to Spanish nationals resident in the provinces of the Balearic Islands, Las Palmas and Santa Cruz de Tenerife to the exclusion of nationals of other Member States resident in the islands."

The Commission gave Spain two months from the date of notification of the Decision of the measures to inform the Commission of the measures which Spain proposed taking to comply with the Decision.[16]

24.3 TRAVEL ALLOWANCES

At its meeting of 18 March 1991, the EC finance ministers agreed to increase the EC traveller's allowance by 50 per cent as and from 1 July 1991.

13. *Ed.* the date of accession of Spain to the EC.

14. The Spanish State held 99 per cent and 95 per cent, respectively, of their share capital (Source: Dec.87/359/EEC, Recital 9).

15. Spain has continued to apply its preferential transport arrangements. The discrimination on grounds of nationality must be brought to an end.

16. Decision 87/359/EEC, Article 2.

CHAPTER 25

Litigious Aspects of EC Shipping Law: the Convention on Jurisdiction and the Enforcement of Judgments in Civil and Commercial Matters

25.1 INTRODUCTION

The Convention on Jurisdiction and the Enforcement of Judgments in Civil and Commercial Matters[1] (referred to in this chapter as the "Convention"[2]) is of critical concern to those involved in EC shipping law. This chapter constitutes an elementary introduction to the Convention and pays special attention to those aspects relating to shipping.

The Convention was signed by the original six Member States of the EC[3] on 23 September 1968 and entered into force on 1 February 1973. The six new Member States of the EC have all acceded to the Convention as a condition of their membership of the EC.[4,5]

The Convention is largely founded on Article 220 of the EEC Treaty[6] which obliged the Member States which are parties to that Treaty to enter into negotiations to

1. On the Convention, see Dashwood, Halcon and White, *A Guide to the Civil Jurisdiction and Judgments Convention* (1987); Kaye, *Civil Jurisdiction and Enforcement of Foreign Judgments* (1987); O'Malley and Layton (eds), *European Civil Practice* (1989), Part 2. See also Bogaert, "Ius Vigilantibus: Tactics of Forum Shopping under the EEC Judgments Convention?" [1988] 9 ECLR 1; Collier, *Conflict of Laws* (1987), Chapter 9; Kohler, "Practical Experience of the Brussels Jurisdiction and Judgments Convention in the Six Original Contracting States" (1985) 34 ICLQ 563; Lone, "Free Movement of Judgments in the EEC" (1986) 35 ICLQ 629; Kohler, "The Case Law of the ECJ on the Judgments Convention" (1982) 7 ELR 3, at p. 103; Lipstein, "Enforcement of Judgments under the Jurisdiction and Judgments Convention: Safeguards" (1987) 36 ICLQ 873.

See also Bercow, "Security for Costs—Europe and Beyond", *Lloyd's List*, 13 December 1991, p. 5; Keates, "When is an English Court 'seised' of proceedings?" *Lloyd's List*, 22 November 1991, p. 10; Moore, "Judges still have to interpret the provisions of 1982 Act", *Lloyd's List*, 17 January 1992, p. 4.

2. It is also known as the "Brussels Convention", but this terminology is not used here because of any confusion which may be caused to the reader by virtue of the Arrest Convention of 1952 also being called the "Brussels Convention".

3. Namely, Belgium, France, Germany, Italy, Luxembourg and The Netherlands.

4. On the conditional aspect, see Article 63 of the Convention.

5. Denmark, Ireland and the UK acceded in 1978 (the so-called "1978 Accession Convention": OJ L304, 30 October 1978). The Convention and the Protocol became operable between the original Six and Denmark on 1 November 1986. The Convention and the Protocol became operable between those seven States and the UK on 1 January 1987. The Convention and the Protocol became operable between those eight States and Ireland on 1 June 1988. Greece acceded by way of an Accession Agreement signed on 25 October 1982 by the so-called "1982 Accession Convention". Spain and Portugal acceded by the San Sebastian Convention by the so-called "San Sebastian Convention".

6. For Article 220 of the EEC Treaty, see Appendix 1 below.

simplify the procedures associated with the recognition and enforcement of judgments by the courts of those States.[7] It has largely replaced an incomplete series of bilateral conventions between some of the Member States of the EC.[8] The Convention has grown to include a Protocol on Interpretation which was adopted in 1971 and is now one of the most important elements of EC shipping litigation law.

O'Malley and Layton have succinctly summarised the scheme of the Convention in the following terms:

"The general scheme of the . . . Convention is to provide uniform and directly applicable rules of jurisdiction which form part of the law of each of the Contracting States. The courts of those states are bound to consider their jurisdiction in the light of those rules in any case to which the Convention applies. The Convention then provides that judgments given by the courts of the Contracting States are to be accorded virtually automatic recognition and enforcement in the other Contracting States, and lays down a uniform procedure to be followed for that purpose. It provides that the jurisdiction of the court of origin may only be reviewed in a few exceptional cases and permits recognition and enforcement to be refused only in limited and tightly defined circumstances."[9]

The Preamble to the Convention is instructive as to the Convention's purpose and effect. It provides:

"The High Contracting Parties to the Treaty establishing the European Economic Community,[10]

Desiring to implement the provisions of Article 220 of that Treaty by virtue of which they undertook to secure the simplification of formalities governing the reciprocal recognition and enforcement of judgments of courts or tribunals;

Anxious to strengthen in the Community the legal protection of persons therein established;

Considering that it is necessary for this purpose to determine the international jurisdiction of their courts, to facilitate recognition and to introduce an expeditious procedure for securing the enforcement of judgments, authentic instruments and court settlements;

Have decided to conclude this Convention . . ."

The European Court of Justice almost[11] invariably interprets the Convention in accordance with principles of Community law rather than in accordance with the law of the Member State where the case is being tried.[12]

The Convention does not affect the domestic law of the Member States *per se*[13] but each of the Member States have had to enact domestic legislation so as to implement the Convention.[14] The Convention was given domestic effect in the UK by means of the Civil Jurisdiction and Judgments Act 1982 (referred to in this chapter as the "UK Act").[15] This UK Act: "signified a radical departure from the common law and statutory rules as regards the jurisdiction of the English courts over persons who are domiciled in other member states of the European Community and with respect to the

7. See *Industrie Tessili v. Dunlop* [1976] ECR 1473, at p. 1484.
8. See Convention, Article 55.
9. *Op. cit.*, at footnote 1, para. 13.08.
10. *Ed.* referred to in this book as the "EEC Treaty".
11. The European Court of Justice sometimes leaves procedural matters for interpretation according to national law.
12. For an exceptional example, see *Tessili v. Dunlop* [1976] ECR 1473.
13. See *Sanicentral GmbH v. Collin* [1979] ECR 3423, at p. 3492, para. 5.
14. E.g. in the Republic of Ireland, the legislation is principally embodied in the Jurisdiction of Courts and Enforcement of Judgments (European Communities) Act 1988.
15. See Collins, *The Civil Jurisdiction and Judgments Act 1982* (1983). See also Collier, *Conflict of Laws* (1987), Chapter 9; Kerr (1978) 75 LS Gaz 1190; Newman, "Background and Scheme of the Civil Jurisdiction and Judgments Act 1982" in *Jurisdiction and Enforcement of Judgments in Europe* (1985).

recognition and enforcement of judgments of the courts of other Member States".[16] It entered into force on 1 January 1987

Collier goes on succinctly to summarise the "radical departure" in the following terms:

"[t]he . . . Convention lays down uniform rules governing jurisdiction of the domestic courts of member states and then provides that recognition and enforcement of judgments of such courts are, with very limited exception, to be automatic. It departs in five main ways, from the [pre-] existing principles of English law governing jurisdiction and recognition and enforcement of judgments. First, jurisdiction exercised on the basis of the defendant's presence in England alone is prohibited. Secondly, if the defendant is outside England but the action falls within the jurisdiction of the English courts, service upon him is a matter of right and not merely within the courts' discretion. Thirdly, if the English court has jurisdiction it probably has no discretion to stay the action on the ground that another court is a more convenient forum, unless that court has already been seised of the case. Fourthly, the grounds for refusal of recognition or enforcement of judgments are very limited indeed, especially as regards investigation of the jurisdiction of the court which pronounced the judgment. Fifthly, judgments other than money judgments can be enforced."[17]

The UK Act provides that the Convention is given the force of law in the UK[18] with due regard to the reports of the rapporteurs—these rapporteurs drew up special reports on the Convention. The UK Act also provides that any question as to the meaning of the Convention must, where it has not been referred to the European Court of Justice for a preliminary ruling under Article 177 of the EEC Treaty,[19] be decided according to the principles laid down by the European Court of Justice. It is worth recalling that the Convention takes precedence over the laws of each of the Member States.[20]

25.2 SCOPE OF THE CONVENTION

25.2.1 Subject-matter of the Convention

Article 1 of the Convention[21] provides that the Convention shall "apply in civil and commercial matters whatever the nature of the court or tribunal". Civil and commercial matters (a term which is not defined in the Convention but which must be given a Community rather than a national meaning[22]) would include employment[23] and insurance. However, the Convention "shall not extend, in particular, to revenue, customs or administrative matters",[24] or apply to:

(a) "the status or legal capacity of natural persons, rights in property arising out of a matrimonial relationship, wills and succession";[25]

16. Collier, *op. cit.*, at footnote 15, p. 113.
17. *Op. cit.*, at p. 115, footnote omitted.
18. Section 2.
19. On Article 177 of the EEC Treaty, see Chapter 3, above.
20. *Sanicentral GmbH v. Collin* [1979] ECR 3423, at p. 3492 para. 5.
21. On Article 1, see Jenard, *op. cit.*, paras 32–54; Schlosser, *op. cit.*, paras 20–68; Collins, *op. cit.*, pp. 17–31; Dashwood, Halcon and White, *op. cit.*, pp. 9–15 and 69–79; Hartley, *op. cit.*, pp. 10–22 and 96–97; Kaye, *op. cit.*, pp. 62–156; and O'Malley and Layton, *op. cit.*, paras 14.03–14.35.
22. See *LTU v. Eurocontrol* [1976] ECR 1541; and *Netherlands State v. Ruffer* [1980] ECR 3807.
23. *Sanicentral v. Collin* [1979] ECR 3423.
24. This latter disqualification was added by Article 3 of the 1978 Accession Convention.
25. Convention, Article 1. See *de Cavel v. de Cavel (No. 1)* [1979] ECR 1055, [1979] 2 CMLR 547; *de Cavel v. de Cavel (No. 2)* [1980] ECR 731, and Case 25/81 *W v. H* [1982] ECR 731, [1983] 2 CMLR 125.

(b) "bankruptcy, proceedings relating to the winding-up of insolvent companies or other legal persons, judicial arrangements, compositions and analogous proceedings"[26];
(c) "social security"[27]; or
(d) "arbitration."[28]

The European Court of Justice decided in Case 29/76 *LTU v. Eurocontrol*[29] that the Convention did not apply to the exercise by a public authority of its functions. Similarly, in Case 814/79 *Netherlands v. Ruffer*[30] the European Court of Justice classified the claim by the Dutch Public Waterways Authority for reimbursement of the expenses incurred in removing the wreck of a German vessel as falling outside the ambit of "civil and commercial matters", because it fell within the scope of a public authority exercising its functions (i.e. an administrative act).[31]

If a case falls partly within the Convention and partly outside it then a court may have jurisdiction over the case where the court would have jurisdiction over it under the Convention (in so far as it is relevant) and its own internal law (in so far as it is relevant). If a court only has jurisdiction under the Convention over part of the case then where the case is severable then the court must exercise jurisdiction over that part.[32] If the case is not severable then, unfortunately, each case must be decided on its own merits[33] —which is an unsatisfactory situation because it hampers predictability.

The exception relating to arbitration is a matter of some dispute.[34] O'Malley and Layton comment on those aspects of the exception which are clear:

"It is clear that the Convention does not extend to the recognition and enforcement of arbitral awards as such, nor to judgments which incorporate such awards, notwithstanding that arbitration is one of the matters referred to in Article 220 of the EEC Treaty which forms the basis for the 1968 Convention. It is generally accepted, too, that the Convention does not apply to court proceedings which are really part of the arbitration process, whether that process is yet to be started, is in progress or has been concluded. So, for example, proceedings are excluded from the scope of the Convention if they are for the principal purpose of appointing an arbitrator, fixing the place for the arbitration, setting aside an arbitral award, or ruling on points of law arising during the course of the arbitration."[35]

If there is doubt over whether the Convention applies to a particular matter then the European Court of Justice has power to give a preliminary ruling under the 1971 Protocol on Interpretation.

In *Mare Rich & Co. AG v. Società Italiana Impianti S.p.A.*,[36] the ECJ was asked to consider whether the exception in Article 1(4) of the Convention extended (a) to any

26. Convention, Article 1. See Case 133/78 *Gourdain v. Nadler* [1979] ECR 733, [1979] 3 CMLR 180.
27. Convention, Article 1.
28. Convention, Article 1.
29. [1976] ECR 1541, [1979] 1 CMLR 88.
30. [1980] ECR 3807, [1981] 3 CMLR 293.
31. The European Court of Justice stated at para. 15 of its judgment: "[t]he fact that in recovering those costs the administering agent acts pursuant to a debt which arises from an act of public authority is sufficient for its action, whatever the nature of the proceedings afforded by national law for that purpose, to be treated as being outside the ambit of the Brussels Convention".
32. See *Bianco v. Andreas Kufferath*, Giust. Civ. 1980, I, p. 103 (the Italian Court of Cassation).
33. See O'Malley and Layton, *op. cit.*, at footnote 1, para. 14.06.
34. See O'Malley and Layton, *op. cit.*, at footnote 1, para. 14.31.
35. *Op. cit.*, para. 14.31 (footnotes omitted).
36. [1992] 1 Lloyd's Rep. 342.

litigation or judgments and, if so, (b) to litigation or judgments where the initial existence of an arbitration agreement is in issue. The court said that "by excluding arbitration from the scope of the Convention on the ground that it was already covered by international conventions, the Contracting Parties intended to exclude arbitration in its entirety, including proceedings before national courts." It continued: "it must be pointed out that the appointment of an arbitrator by a national court is a measure adopted by the State as part of the process of setting arbitration proceedings in motion. Such a measure therefore comes within the sphere of arbitration and is thus covered by the exclusion contained in Article 1(4) of the Convention."

25.2.2 Geographical scope [37]

The Convention applies to the twelve Member States of the EC. In respect of the UK, the Convention did not automatically extend to the Isle of Man and the Channel Islands, and left the UK to decide whether or not to apply the Convention to those areas.

There must be an international[38] element to a case before the Convention becomes applicable.

Many (but not all) of the principles of the Convention have been reflected in the Lugano Convention which was opened for signature on 16 September 1988 between the Member States of the EC and the Member States of the European Free Trade Association (EFTA). This allows for some degree of uniformity in terms of jurisdiction and enforcement of judgments throughout 18 European States.

25.3 JURISDICTION

25.3.1 Introduction

Title II of the Convention contains direct rules on jurisdiction.

25.3.1.1 General rule

The general rule under the Convention is that persons domiciled in a contracting State are to be sued only in that State (i.e. the domicile of the defendant is the key to the court's jurisdiction). Thus, the domicile or nationality of the plaintiff is irrelevant, as is the nationality of the defendant.

25.3.1.2 Exceptions to the general rule on jurisdiction

The general rule is subject to a number of exceptions. First, some other court may have exclusive jurisdiction.[39] Secondly, a defendant who is a party to a contractual arrangement (such as a charterparty) may submit to another jurisdiction (such as England).[40]

37. See Article 60.
38. More accurately, there must be a choice of two or more legal systems.
39. See Article 16 of the Convention and para. 25.3.6, below.
40. See Article 17 of the Convention and para. 25.3.6, below.

25.3.1.3 Domicile

25.3.1.3.1 Convention provisions relating to domicile

The Convention does not define domicile. None the less the concept has an equivalent (but not identical) meaning in each of the Member States. Article 52[41] of the Convention provides uniform rules for the choice of law:

"In order to determine whether a party is domiciled in the Contracting State whose courts are seised of the matter, the court shall apply its internal law.

If a party is not domiciled in the State whose courts are seised of the matter, then, in order to determine whether the party is domiciled in another Contracting State, the court can apply the law of that State."

Article 53[42] provides:

"For the purposes of this Convention, the seat of a company or other legal person or association of natural or legal persons shall be treated as its domicile. However, in order to determine that seat, the court shall apply its rules of private international law.

In order to determine whether a trust is domiciled in the Contracting State whose courts are seised of the matter, the court shall apply its rules of private international law."

25.3.1.3.2 UK statutory rules relating to domicile

A statutory definition of domicile is provided, for the purposes of the UK Act, by sections 41 and 42 of that Act. Section 41 of the UK Act (which deals with the domicile of individuals) provides:

"(1) Subject to Article 52 (which contains provisions for determining whether a party is domiciled in a Contracting State), the following provisions of this section determine, for the purposes of the 1968 Convention and this Act, whether an individual is domiciled in the United Kingdom or in a particular part of, or place in, the United Kingdom or in a state other than a Contracting State.

(2) An individual is domiciled in the United Kingdom if and only if

(a) he is resident in the United Kingdom; and

(b) the nature and circumstances of his residence indicate that he has a substantial connection with the United Kingdom.

(3) Subject to subsection (5), an individual is domiciled in a particular part of the United Kingdom if and only if—

(a) he is resident in that part; and

(b) the nature and circumstances of his residence indicate that he has a substantial connection with that part.

(4) An individual is domiciled in a particular place in the United Kingdom if and only if he

(a) is domiciled in the part of the United Kingdom in which that place is situated; and

(b) is resident in that place.

(5) An individual who is domiciled in the United Kingdom but in whose case the requirements of subsection (3)(b) are not satisfied to any particular part of the United Kingdom shall be treated as domiciled in the part of the United Kingdom in which he is resident.

41. Article 52 of the Convention had a third paragraph which was deleted by Article 15 of the 1989 Accession Convention and which read: "the domicile of a party shall, however, be determined in accordance with his national law if, by that law, his domicile depends on that of another person or on the seat of an authority".

On Article 52, see Jenard, *op. cit.*, paras 66–77; Schlosser, *op. cit.*, paras 71–74; Collins, *op. cit.*, pp. 37–40; Dashwood, Halcon and White, *op. cit.*, pp. 19–21 and 183–184; Hartley, *op. cit.* at footnote 1, pp. 24–30; Kaye, *op. cit.* at footnote 1, pp. 278–319; and O'Malley and Layton, *op. cit.* at footnote 1, paras 31.01–31.23.

42. On Article 53, see Jenard, *op. cit.*, paras 245–246; Schlosser, *op. cit.*, paras 75, 114–120 and 227; Collins, *op. cit.*, pp. 37 and 40–44; Dashwood, Halcon and White, *op. cit.*, pp. 20–21 and 184–186; Hartley, *op. cit.*, pp. 30–31; Kaye, *op. cit.*, pp. 319–339; and O'Malley and Layton, *op. cit.*, paras. 31.23–31.32.

(6) In the case of an individual who
(a) is resident in the United Kingdom, or in a particular part of the United Kingdom; and
(b) has been so resident for the last three months or more,
the requirements of subsection (2)(b) or, as the case may be, subsection (3)(b) shall be presumed to be fulfilled unless the contrary is proved.
(7) An individual is domiciled in a state other than a Contracting State if and only if—
(a) he is resident in that state; and
(b) the nature and circumstances of his residence indicate that he has a substantial connection with that state."

Section 42 of the UK Act (which deals with the domicile and seat of a corporation or association) provides:

"(1) For the purposes of this Act the seat of a corporation or association (as determined by this section) shall be treated as its domicile.
(2) The following provisions of this section determine where a corporation or association has its seat
(a) for the purpose of Article 53 (which for the purposes of the 1968 Convention equates the domicile of such a body with its seat); and
(b) for the purposes of this Act other than the provisions mentioned in section 43(1)(b) and (c).
(3) A corporation or association has its seat in the United Kingdom if and only if—
(a) it was incorporated or formed under law of a part of the United Kingdom and has its registered office or some other official address in the United Kingdom; or
(b) its central management and control is exercised in the United Kingdom.
(4) A corporation or association has its seat in a particular part of the United Kingdom if and only if it has its seat in the United Kingdom and
(a) it has its registered office or some other official address in that part; or
(b) its central management and control is exercised in that part; or
(c) it has a place of business in that part.
(5) A corporation or association has its seat in a particular place in the United Kingdom if and only if it has its seat in the part of the United Kingdom in which that place is situated and
(a) it has its registered office or some other official address in that place; or
(b) its central management and control is exercised in that place; or
(c) it has a place of business in that place.
(6) Subject to subsection (7), a corporation or association has its seat in a state other than the United Kingdom if and only if
(a) it was incorporated or formed under the law of that state and has its registered office or some other official address there; or
(b) its central management and control is exercised in that state.
(7) A corporation or association shall not be regarded as having its seat in a Contracting State other than the United Kingdom if it is shown that the courts of that state would not regard it as having its seat there.
(8) In this section
'business' includes any activity carried on by a corporation or association, and 'place of business' shall be construed accordingly;
'official address', in relation to a corporation or association, means an address which it is required by law to register, notify or maintain for the purpose of receiving notices or other communications."

Section 43 of the UK Act deals with the seat of a corporation or association for the purposes of Article 16(2) of the Convention[43] and related provisions. It reads:

"(1) The following provisions of this section determine where a corporation or association has its seat for the purposes of
(a) Article 16(2) (which confers exclusive jurisdicition over proceedings relating to the formation or dissolution of such bodies, or to the decisions of their organs);

43. On Article 16(2) of the Convention, see para. 25.3.6, below.

(b) Articles 5A and 16(2) in Schedule 4; and
(c) Rules 2(12) and 4(1)(b) in Schedule 8.

(2) A corporation or association has its seat in the United Kingdom if and only if—
(a) it was incorporated or formed under the law of a part of the United Kingdom; or
(b) its central management and control is exercised in the United Kingdom.

(3) A corporation or association has its seat in a particular part of the United Kingdom if and only if it has its seat in the United Kingdom and
(a) subject to subsection (5), it was incorporated or formed under the law of that part; or
(b) being incorporated or formed under the law of a state other than the United Kingdom, its central management and control is exercised in that part.

(4) A corporation or association has its seat in a particular place in Scotland and only if it has its seat in Scotland and
(a) it has its registered office or some other official address in Scotland in that place; or
(b) it has no registered office or other official address in Scotland, but its central management and control is exercised in that place.

(5) A corporation or association incorporated or formed under
(a) an enactment forming part of the law of more than one part of the United Kingdom; or
(b) an instrument having effect in the domestic law of more than one part of the United Kingdom shall, if it has a registered office, be taken to have its seat in the part of the United Kingdom in which that office is situated, and not in any other part of the United Kingdom.

(6) Subject to subsection (7), a corporation or association has its seat in a Contracting State other than the United Kingdom if and only if—
(a) it was incorporated or formed under the law of that state; or
(b) its central management and control is exercised in that state.

(7) A corporation or association shall not be regarded as having its seat in a Contracting State other than the United Kingdom if
(a) it has its seat in the United Kingdom by virtue of subsection (2)(a); or
(b) it is shown that the courts of that other state would not regard it for the purposes of Article 16(2) as having its seat there.

(8) In this section 'official address' has the same meaning as in section 42."

Section 44 of the UK Act deals with persons who are deemed to be domiciled in the UK for certain purposes. It provides:

"(1) This section applies to
(a) proceedings within Section 3 of Title II of the 1968 Convention (insurance contracts), and
(b) proceedings within Section 4 of that Title (consumer contracts).

(2) A person who, for the purposes of proceedings to which this section applies arising out of the operations of a branch, agency or other establishment in the United Kingdom, is deemed for the purposes of the 1968 Convention to be domiciled in the United Kingdom by virtue of
(a) Article 8, second paragraph (insurers); or
(b) Article 13, second paragraph (suppliers of goods, services or credit to consumers), shall, for the purposes of those proceedings, be treated for the purposes of this Act as so domiciled and as domiciled in the part of the United Kingdom in which the branch, agency or stablishment in question is situated."

Section 45 deals with the domcile of trusts and section 46 deals with the domicile of the Crown. Neither section need detain this discussion as neither are particularly relevant for present purposes.

25.3.2 General provisions

25.3.2.1 Persons domiciled in a contracting State

Article 2[44] sets down the general rule that subject to the provisions of the Convention,

44. On Article 2 of the Convention, see Jenard, *op. cit.*, paras 62–65; Schlosser, *op. cit.*; paras 82–86; Collins, *op. cit.*, pp. 45–47; Dashwood, Halcon and White, *op. cit.* pp. 21–22 and 84–86; Hartley, *op. cit.*, pp. 23–31 and 42–43; Kaye, *op. cit.*, pp. 253–265; and O'Malley and Layton, *op. cit.*, paras 16.01–16.08.

persons domiciled in a contracting State shall, whatever their nationality, be sued in the courts of that State and persons who are not nationals of the State in which they are domiciled shall be governed by the rules of jurisdiction applicable to nationals of that State.

Persons who are domiciled in a contracting State may be sued in the courts of another contracting State only by virtue of the rules set out in sections 2 to 6 of Title II of the Convention (i.e. Articles 5–18) and certain provisions specified in Article 3 of the Convention may not be applied against them.[45] Article 3[46] provides as follows:

"Persons domiciled in a Contracting State may be sued in the courts of another Contracting State only by virtue of the rules set out in Sections 2 to 6 of this Title.

In particular the following provisions shall not be applicable against them:

- in Belgium: Article 15 of the civil code (Code civil—Burgerlijk Wetboek) and Article 638 of the judicial code (Code judiciare—Gerechtelijk Wetboek),
- in Denmark: Article 246(2) and (3) of the law on civil procedure (Lov om rettens pleje),
- in the Federal Republic of Germany: Article 23 of the code of civil procedure (Zivilprozessordnung),
- in Greece: Article 40 of the code of civil procedure *Κώδικας Πολιτικῆς Δικονομίας*,
- in France: Articles 14 and 15 of the civil code (Code civil),
- in Ireland: the rules which enable jurisdiction to be founded on the document instituting the proceedings having been served on the defendant during his temporary presence in Ireland,
- in Italy: Articles 2 and 4, Nos.1 and 2 of the code of civil procedure (Codice di procedura civile),
- in Luxembourg: Articles 14 and 15 of the civil code (Code civil),
- in the Netherlands: Articles 126(3) and 127 of the code of civil procedure (Wetboek van Burgerlijke Rechtsvordering),
- in Portugal: Article 65(1)(c), Article 65(2) and Article 65A(c) of the code of civil procedure (Codigo de Processo Civil) and Article 11 of the code of labour procedure (Codigo de Processo de Trabalho),
- in the United Kingdom: the rules which enable jurisdiction to be founded on:

(a) the document instituting the proceedings having been served on the defendant during his temporary presence in the United Kingdom; or
(b) the presence within the United Kingdom of property belonging to the defendant; or
(c) the seizure by the plaintiff of property situated in the United Kingdom."

25.3.2.2 Defendants not domiciled in a contracting State

If the defendant is not domiciled in a contracting State then the jurisdiction of the courts of each contracting State must, subject to the provisions of Article 16 of the Convention,[47] be determined by the law of that State.[48] As against such a defendant, any person domiciled in a contracting State may, whatever his nationality, avail himself in that State of the rules of jurisdiction there in force, and in particular those specified in Article 3, second paragraph, in the same way as the nationals of that State.[49]

45. NB Articles 21 23 and 57 of the Convention.

46. On Article 3 of the Convention, see Jenard, *op. cit.*, paras 82–88; Schlosser, *op. cit.*, paras 83–88; Collins, *op. cit.*, pp. 47–59; Dashwood, Halcon and White, *op. cit.*, pp. 86–87; Hartley, *op. cit.*, pp. 8; Kaye, *op. cit.*, pp. 265–269; and O'Malley and Layton, *op. cit.*, paras 16.09–16.14.

47. Article 16 deals with the exclusive jurisdiction of the courts. On Article 16, see para. 25.3.6, below and see Jenard, *op. cit.*, paras 131 and 153; Schlosser, *op. cit.*, paras 162–165; Collins, *op. cit.*, pp. 77–78; Dashwood, Halcon and White, *op. cit.*, pp. 29–30 and 115–121; Hartley, *op. cit.*, pp. 63–64; Kaye, *op. cit.*, pp. 871–883; and O'Malley and Layton, *op. cit.*, paras 20.01–20.46.

48. See Convention, Article 4.

49. See Convention, Article 4.

25.3.3 Special jurisdiction

Section 2 of Title II of the Convention[50] deals with Special Jurisdiction. In addition to being liable to suit in the jurisdiction in which the person is domiciled, the person domiciled in a contracting State may also be sued in another contracting State in certain specified cases of so-called special jurisdiction. The effect of suing a person in the special jurisdiction is that the jurisdiction of the courts of that person's domicile is ousted.

25.3.3.1 Article 5: Introduction

A person who is domiciled in a contracting State may be sued, in another contracting State, under Article 5 of the Convention, in seven specific instances. There are other cases specified in Article 6.

25.3.3.2 Article 5(1): Contract[51]

Article 5(1) of the Convention provides that a person who is domiciled in a contracting State may, in another contracting State, be sued:

"in matters relating to a contract, in the courts for the place of performance of the obligation in question; in matters relating to individual contracts of employment, this place is that where the employee habitually carries out his work, or if the employee does not habitually carry out his work in any one country, the employer may also be sued in the courts for the place where the business which engaged the employee was or is now situated."

The term "contract" has a Community law definition rather than a mere national one.

The term "contract" includes membership of an association.[52]

The jurisdiction exists even where the defendant denies that there is or was a contract.[53]

O'Malley and Layton have commented[54]:

"For a national court to decide whether there is jurisdiction under [Article 5(1)] it must answer a particularly complex series of questions. In summary, and subject to . . . qualifications . . . , the questions are as follows. First, the court must decide whether the dispute concerns a matter relating to a contract, according to an independent interpretation of that concept.[55] Secondly, it must decide what the obligation in question is, again according to an independent interpretation. Thirdly, it must apply its own conflicts of law rules to find the law applicable to that obligation. Fourthly, it must apply that law to decide whether the place of performance is within its territorial jurisdiction. If it is, the court must decide, fifthly, whether any of a number of other, relatively unimportant, provisions . . . affect its applicability. If not, and only then, it must accept jurisdiction."

The qualifications are also summarised by O'Malley and Layton:[56]

50. I.e. Articles 5–6A.

51. On Article 5 of the Convention, see Jenard, *op. cit.*, paras 97–106; Schlosser, *op. cit.*, paras 133; Collins, *op. cit.*, pp. 51–56; Dashwood, Halcon and White, *op. cit.*, pp. 22–23 and 90–95; Hartley, *op. cit.*, pp. 43–48; Kaye, *op. cit.*, pp. 489–527; as well as O'Malley and Layton, *op. cit.*, paras 17.02–17.30. See *Union Transport v. Continental Lines* [1992] 1 Lloyd's Rep. 229.

52. *Martin Peters Baunnternehmung GmbH v. Zuid Nederlandse Aannemers Vereniging* [1983] ECR 987.

53. *Effer v. Kantner* [1982] ECR 987.

54. *Op. cit.*, para. 17.03 (footnotes omitted)

55. See *Martin Peters v. ZNAV* [1983] ECR 987, at p. 1002 (para. 13)

56. *Op. cit.*, para. 17.03 (footnotes omitted).

"First, a choice of jurisdiction clause may be effective under Article 17. Secondly, as a transitional measure, if the parties expressly agreed in writing, before the 1978 Convention came into force,[57] that a contract was to be governed by English law, the English courts retain the right to exercise jurisdiction in the dispute. Thirdly, Luxembourg domicilaries sued under this paragraph need not submit to the jurisdiction and if they do not, the court must declare of its own motion that it has no jurisdiction. Fourthly, there are special provisions relating to employment disputes between the master and a crew member of a ship registered in Denmark or Ireland."[58]

It is important to stress that the special provisions relating to employment disputes have been altered since O'Malley and Layton published their book. Article Vb of the 1968 Annexed Protocol now provides:

"In proceedings involving a dispute between the master and a member of the crew of a sea-going ship registered in Denmark, in Greece, in Ireland or in Portugal, concerning remuneration or other conditions of service, a court in a Contracting State shall establish whether the diplomatic or consular officer responsible for the ship has been notified of the dispute. It shall stay the proceedings so long as as he has not been notified. It shall of its own motion decline jurisdiction if the officer, having been duly notified, has exercised the powers accorded to him in the matter by a consular convention, or in the absence of such a convention has, within the time allowed, raised any objection to the exercise of such jurisdiction."

Schlosser in his report on Article Vb states[59]:

"The new Article Vb of the Protocol annexed to the 1968 Convention is based on a request by Denmark founded on Danish tradition. This has become part of the Danish Seamen's Law No. 420 of 18 June 1973 which states that disputes between a crew member and a shipmaster of a Danish vessel may not be brought before foreign courts. The same principle is also embodied in some consular conventions between Denmark and other States. Following a specific request from the Irish delegation, the scope of this provision has also been extended to Irish ships."

Where a court accepts jurisdiction and breaches Article Vb then the courts of the other contracting States must recognise and enforce the judgment granted because this is not one of the cases open to review under Article 28 of the Convention.

Article 5(1) only relates to contract and not quasi-contract.

It is interesting to determine what is the "place of performance". In Case 12/76 *Industrie Tessili Italiana Como v. Dunlop AG* [60] the European Court of Justice held:

"It is for the court before which the matter is brought to establish under the Convention whether the place of performance is situated within its territorial jurisdiction. For this purpose it must determine in accordance with its own rules of conflict of laws what is the law applicable to the legal relationship in question and define in accordance with that law the place of performance of the contractual obligation in question."[61]

25.3.3.3 Article 5(2): Maintenance[62]

Article 5(2) provides that a person who is domiciled in a contracting State may, in another contracting State, be sued:

57. 1 January 1987 in the United Kingdom.
58. 1968 Protocol, Article Vb.
59. *Op. cit.*, para. 132.
60. [1976] ECR 1473.
61. [1976] ECR 1473, at p. 1485 (paras 13–14).
62. On Article 5(2) of the Convention, see Jenard, *op. cit.*, paras 107–110; Schlosser, *op. cit.*, paras 36–42 and 90–108; Collins, *op. cit.*, pp. 57–58; Dashwood, Halcon and White, *op. cit.*, pp. 24–26 and 95–96; Hartley, *op. cit.*, pp. 18–19 and 48–50; Kaye, *op. cit.*, pp. 527–561; and O'Malley and Layton, *op. cit.*, paras 17.31–17.43.

"in matters relating to maintenance, in the courts for the place where the maintenance creditor is domiciled or habitually resident or, if the matter is ancillary to proceedings concerning the status of a person, in the court which, according to its own law, has jurisdiction to entertain those proceedings, unless that jurisdiction is based solely on the nationality of one of the parties."

25.3.3.4 Article 5(3): Tort, delict and quasi-delict[63]

Article 5(3) provides that a person who is domiciled in a contracting State may, in another contracting State, be sued "in matters relating to tort, delict or quasi-delict, in the courts for the place where the harmful event occurred".

Advocate-General Warner stated in Case 814/79 *Netherlands v. Ruffer*[64] that the classification of a cause of action as being tortious is a matter to be determined in accordance with Community (as opposed to national) concepts.

The concepts of "tort, delict or quasi-delict" must be given an independent EC meaning.[65]

The "place where the harmful event occurred" means where the wrong conduct occurred or where the plaintiff suffered the harm or damage.[66] In the words of the European Court of Justice, "the defendant may be sued, at the option of the plaintiff, either in the courts for the place where the damage occurred or in the courts for the place of the event which gives rise to and is at the origin of that damage".[67] O'Malley and Layton comment on the multiple jurisdiction problem:

"Where a multiplicity of jurisdictions is available, the rules on *lis pendens* and related actions[68] will go some way to resolve conflicts of jurisdiction and reduce the likelihood of conflicting decisions. Where a plaintiff has sued to judgment in one jurisdiction, he will not be permitted to start a fresh action on the same cause of action in another juridiction;[69] but it may be that the effect of the *Bier*[70] decision, in cases involving a choice of places where the harmful event can be said to have occurred, is that even by starting an action for tort, delict or quasi-delict in the courts for one such place, a plaintiff will be taken to have elected that forum to the exclusion of others, although, it is submitted, that would probably be too narrow an application of the European Court's decision in the case of continuing wrongs."[71]

25.3.3.5 Article 5(4): Civil claims in criminal proceedings[72]

Article 5(4) of the Convention provides that a person who is domiciled in a contracting State may, in another contracting State, be sued: "as regards a civil claim for damages or restitution which is based on an act giving rise to criminal proceedings, in the court seised of those proceedings, to the extent that the court has jurisdiction under its own law to entertain civil proceedings."

63. On Article 5(3) of the Convention, see Jenard, *op. cit.*, para. 111; Schlosser, *op. cit.*, para. 134; Collins, *op. cit.*, pp. 58–61; Dashwood, Halcon and White, *op. cit.*, pp. 22 and 96–97; Hartley, *op. cit.*, pp. 50–52; Kaye, *op. cit.*, pp. 561–588; and O'Malley and Layton, *op. cit.*, paras. 17.44–17.52

64. [1980] ECR 3807, at p. 3833.

65. See Case 189/87 *Kalfelis v. Schroder, Munchmeyer, Hengst & Co.*; *Martin Peters v. ZNAV* [1983] ECR 987.

66. See *Handelskwerkrij G. J. Bier BV v. Mines de Potasse d'Alsace SA* [1978] ECR 1735.

67. In *Bier v. Mines de Potasse d'Alsace* [1976] ECR 1735, at p. 1748–1749.

68. Articles 21 *et seq.*

69. *De Wolf v. Cox BV* [1976] ECR 1758.

70. [1978] ECR 1735.

71. *Op. cit.*, para. 17.49 (some footnotes omitted).

72. On Article 5(4) of the Convention, see Jenard, *op. cit.*, paras 38 and 114; Collins, *op. cit.*, p. 61; Dashwood, Halcon and White, *op. cit.*, pp. 23 and 97; Hartley, *op. cit.*, pp. 52–53; Kaye, *op. cit.*, pp. 588–589; and O'Malley and Layton, *op. cit.*, paras 17.53–17.54.

25.3.3.6 Article 5(5): Branches, agencies and other establishments[73]

Article 5(5) provides that a person who is domiciled in a contracting State may, in another contracting State, be sued: "as regards a dispute arising out of the operations of a branch, agency or other establishment, in the courts for the place where the branch, agency or other establishment is situated."

Again, these concepts must be given a Community meaning rather than a purely national one.[74] The branch or agency must be a place of business which is equipped to carry on business on its own behalf.[75] The dispute must emanate from the operations of the branch

25.3.3.7 Article 5(6): Trusts[76]

Article 5(6) provides that a person who is domiciled in a contracting State may, in another contracting State, be sued: "as settlor, trustee or beneficiary of a trust created by the operation of a statute, or by a written instrument, or created orally and evidenced in writing, in the courts of the Contracting State in which the trust is domiciled". This point was added to the Convention by Article 5(4) of the 1978 Accession Convention.

25.3.3.8 Article 5(7): Salvage[77]

Article 5(7) provides that a person who is domiciled in a contracting State may, in another contracting State, be sued:

"as regards a dispute concerning the payment of remuneration claimed in respect of the salvage of cargo or freight, in the court under the authority of which the cargo or freight in question:
(a) has been arrested to secure such payment, or
(b) could have been so arrested, but bail or other security has been given;
provided that this provision shall apply only if it is claimed that the defendant has an interest in the cargo or freight or had such an interest at the time of salvage."

This point was added to the Convention by Article 5(4) of the 1978 Accession Convention.

Article 5(7) exists so as to take into account the way in which the English courts exercise their *in rem* jurisdiction in claims for remuneration for salvage of cargo or freight.

O'Malley and Layton comment on Article 5(7) in the following terms:

"The wording of the paragraph makes it clear, though, that it is not every case where the claim is secured by a maritime lien that is envisaged, but only salvage claims and only then it is the defendant has (or had at the time of salvage) an interest in the cargo or freight.[78] The reason why

73. On Article 5(5) of the Convention, see Jenard, *op. cit.*, para. 115; Collins, *op. cit.*, pp. 61–64; Dashwood, Halcon and White, *op. cit.*, pp. 23–24 and 97–100; Hartley, *op. cit.*, pp. 53–54; Kaye, *op. cit.*, pp. 589–610; and O'Malley and Layton, *op. cit.*, paras 17.55–17.64.

74. *Somafer v. Saar-Ferngas* [1978] ECR 2183.

75. Case 14/76 *De Bloos v. Bouyer* [1976] ECR 1497, [1977] 1 CMLR 60.

76. On Article 5(6) of the Convention, see Schlosser, *op. cit.*, paras 109–120; Collins, *op. cit.*, pp. 64–65; Dashwood, Halcon and White, *op. cit.*, pp. 26 and 100; Hartley, *op. cit.*, p. 55; Kaye, *op. cit.*, pp. 610–632; and O'Malley and Layton, *op. cit.*, paras 17.65–17.69.

77. See Schlosser, *op. cit.*, paras 121–123; Collins, *op. cit.*, p. 65; Dashwood *et al.*, *op. cit.*, pp. 26–27, 100; Hartley, *op. cit.*, pp. 55–56; Kaye, *op. cit.*, pp. 632–634; Maxwell, *op. cit.*, para. 5.66; as well as O'Malley and Layton, *op. cit.*, paras 17.70–17.72.

78. In this respect, it seems that the jurisdiction is narrower than that permitted by English law, which permits an action *in rem* against cargo or freight irrespective of its ownership: Supreme Court Act 1981, s. 21(3).

the jurisdiction covers freight as well as cargo is to cater for the case in which the freight is payable conditionally upon the safe arrival of the cargo at its destination. If it had not been salved, no freight would have been payable and it is appropriate that the salvor should have a prior right to be satisfied out of the freight.[79]

Such jurisdiction in the case of ships is covered by Article 7 of the Brussels Convention of May 10, 1952 of the Arrest of Sea-going Ships,[80] which continues to have effect under Article 57 of the 1968 Convention. That Convention does not refer to the arrest of cargo or freight and, but for Article 5(7), the 1968 Convention would have deprived the English courts of that basis of jurisdiction as against defendants domiciled in other Contracting States. The Brussels Convention of 1952 also does not provide for jurisdiction in cases where the ship has been released against bail or other security. This omission is not repaired in respect of ships by the 1968 Convention, but the problem is avoided in respect of cargo and freight by Article 5(7)(b).

The terms of the paragraph ought probably to be given an independent interpretation, but the European Court of Justice is almost certain, it is suggested, to follow the meanings given to its various expressions in international maritime law generally.

If the jurisdiction of a court in England and Wales or Northern Ireland is invoked under this paragraph, and the court then stays or dismisses the proceedings on the ground that the dispute should be submitted to arbitration or to the determination of a court elsewhere, the court has power to preserve the security under section 26 of the 1982 Act, in addition to its general powers under Article 24 to grant interim relief in the absence of substantive jurisdiction. But where the action falls within the 1968 Convention, the court has only limited powers to stay or dismiss the proceedings, notably under the provisions in Articles 21 or 23 relating to *lis pendens* and related actions."[81]

The Schlosser Report states:

"121. The exercise of jurisdiction in maritime matters has traditionally played a far greater role in the United Kingdom than in the Continental States of the Community. The scope of the international competence of the courts, as it has been developed in the United Kingdom, has become of worldwide significance for admiralty jurisdiction. This factor is reflected not least in the Brussels Conventions of 1952 and 1957.[82] It would have been inappropriate to limit the exercise of admiralty jurisdiction to the basis of jurisdiction included in the 1968 Convention in its original form. If a ship is arrested in a State because of an internationally recognized maritime claim, it would be unreasonable to expect the creditor to seek a decision on his claim before the courts of the shipowner's domicile. For this reason, the Working Party gave lengthy consideration to the possible inclusion of a special section on admiralty jurisdiction in Title II. Article 36 of the [1978] Accession Convention is derived from an earlier draft prepared for that purpose.[83] Parallel negotiations on Article 57 of the 1968 Convention did, however, lead to a generally acceptable interpretation which will enable States party to the Convention on maritime law to assume jurisdiction on any particular matter dealt with in that Convention, even in respect of persons domiciled in a Community State which is not a party to that Convention.[84] Furthermore, all delegations are in support of a Joint Declaration urging the Community States to accede to the most important of all the Conventions on maritime law, namely the Brussels Convention of 10 May 1952.[85] The Working Party, confident that this Joint Declaration will be adopted and implemented, finally dropped its plans for a section dealing with admiralty jurisdiction. This would also avoid interfering with the general principles of the 1968 Convention, and maintain a clear dividing line between its scope and that of other Conventions.

Two issues remain outstanding, however, since they are not fully covered by the Brussels Conventions of 1952 and 1957: jurisdiction in the event of the arrest of salvaged cargo or freight

79. Schlosser, para. 122.

80. This Convention is given effect in English law by ss. 20–22 of the Supreme Court Act 1981, and s. 26 of the Civil Jurisdiction and Judgments Act 1982. See also *The Nordglimt* [1987] 2 Lloyd's Rep. 470.

81. *Op. cit.*, paras 17.71–17.72 (some footnotes omitted).

82. See para. 238 *et seq.* of the Schlosser Report.

83. See para. 131 of the Schlosser Report.

84. See para. 236 *et seq.* of the Schlosser Report.

85. See para. 238 of the Schlosser Report.

(the new Article 5(7)) (1) and actions for limitation of liability in maritime matters (the new Article 6A) (2). Moreover, until Denmark and Ireland accede to the Brussels Arrest Convention of 10 May 1952, transitional provisions had also to be introduced (3). Finally, a particularity affecting only Denmark and Ireland (4) still remained to be settled.

1 Jurisdiction in connection with the arrest of salvaged cargo or freight

122. (a) The Brussels Convention of 1952 allows a claimant, *inter alia*, to invoke the jurisdiction of a State in which a ship had been arrested on account of a salvage claim (Article 7(1)(b)). Implicit in this provision is a rule of substantive law. A claim to remuneration for salvage entitles the salvage firm to a maritime lien on the ship. A similar lien in favour of a salvage firm can also exist on the cargo; this can be of some economic importance, if it is the cargo rather than the ship which was salvaged, or if the salvaged ship is so badly damaged that its value is less than the cost of the salvage operation. The value of the cargo of a modern supertanker can amount to a considerable sum. Finally, prior rights can also arise in regard to freight. If freight is payable solely in the event of the safe arrival of the cargo at the place of destination, it is appropriate that the salvage firm should have a prior right to be satisfied out of the claim to freight which was preserved due to the salvage of the cargo.

Accordingly United Kingdom law provides that a salvage firm may apply for the arrest of the salvaged cargo or the freight claim preserved due to its intervention and may also apply to the court concerned for a final decision on its claims to remuneration for salvage. Jurisdiction of this kind is similar in scope to the provisions of Article 7 of the Brussels Convention of 1952. As there i s no other Covention on the arrest of salvaged cargo and freight which would remain applicable under Article 57 [of the 1968 Convention], the United Kingdom would, on acceding to the 1968 Convention, have suffered an unacceptable loss of jurisdiction if a special provision had not been introduced.

123. (b) The proposed solution applies the underlying principle of Article 7 of the Brussels Convention of 1952 to jurisdiction after the arrest of salvaged cargo or freight claims.

Under Article 24 of the 1968 Convention, there is no limitation on national laws with regard to the granting of provisional legal safeguards including arrest. However, they could not provide that arrest, whether authorized or effected, should suffice to found jurisdiction as to the substance of the matter. The exception introduced in Article 5(7)(a) is confined to arrest to safeguard a salvage claim.

Article 5(7)(b) introduces an extension of jurisdiction not expressly modelled on the Brussels Convention of 1952. It is a result of practical experience. After salvage operations—whether involving a ship, cargo or freight—arrest is sometimes ordered, but not actually carried into effect, because bail or other security has been provided. This must be sufficient to confer jurisdiction on the arresting court to decide also on the substance of the matter.

The object of the provision is to confer jurisdiction only with regard to those claims which are secured by a maritime lien. If the owner of a ship in difficulties has concluded a contract for its salvage, as his contract with the cargo owner frequently obliges him to do, any disputes arising from the former contract will not be governed by this provision."

25.3.3.9 Article 6: Special jurisdiction

A person domiciled in a contracting State may also be sued, under Article 6 of the Convention, in instances over and above those set out in Article 5. O'Malley and Layton have succinctly stated the essence of Article 6 in these terms: "Article 6 provides rules of special jurisdiction based on a connection between the dispute and a particular court, where the connection is the litigation of another related dispute before that court."[86]

86. *Op. cit.*, para. 17.74, footnote omitted.

25.3.3.10 Article 6(1): Co-defendants[87]

A person domiciled in a contracting State may also be sued, under Article 6(1) of the Convention: "where he is one of a number of defendants, in the courts for the place where any one of them is domiciled". The claims brought against the co-defendants must be linked.[88] The second co-defendant may be domiciled anywhere in the world.

25.3.3.11 Article 6(2): Third parties[89]

A person domiciled in a contracting State may also be sued, under Article 6(2) of the Convention "as a third party in an action on a warranty or guarantee or in any other third party proceedings, in the court seised of the original proceedings, unless these were instituted solely with the object of removing him from the jurisdiction of the court which would be competent in his case". This may not be relied upon in respect of Germany.[90]

25.3.3.12 Article 6(3): Counterclaims[91]

A person domiciled in a contracting State may also be sued, under Article 6(3) of the Convention "on a counter-claim arising from the same contract or facts on which the original claim was based, in the court in which the original claim is pending". Thus, the counterclaim must be brought in the same court as the one in which the main action is being tried.

25.3.3.13 Article 6(4): Certain combined actions

A person domiciled in a contracting State may also be sued, under Article 6(4) of the Convention "in matters relating to a contract, if the action may be combined with an action against the same defendant in matters relating to rights *in rem* in immovable property, in the court of the Contracting State in which the property is situated". This point was added by Article 5 of the 1989 Accession Convention.

25.3.3.14 Article 6A: Limitation of liability actions in respect of the operation of ships[92]

Article 6a of the Convention, which was inserted by Article 6 of the 1978 Accession Convention, provides that: "Where by virtue of this Convention a court of a

87. On Article 6(1) of the Convention, see Jenard, *op. cit.*, para. 116; Collins, *op. cit.*, pp. 65–66; Dashwood, Halcon and White, *op. cit.*, p. 101; Hartley, *op. cit.*, p. 57; Kaye, *op. cit.*, pp. 634–644; and O'Malley and Layton, *op. cit.*, paras 17.75–17.81.

88. *Kalfelis v. Schroder, Munchmeyer, Hengst & Co.* (para. 9). This link is established where the matter is so interlinked that separate proceedings would prove expensive and unnecessary (*Kalfelis v. Schroder, Munchmeyer, Hengst & Co.*, para. 12).

89. On Article 6(2) of the Convention, see Jenard, *op. cit.*, paras 118–124; Schlosser, *op. cit.*, para. 135; Collins, *op. cit.*, pp. 66–67; Dashwood, Halcon and White, *op. cit.*, pp. 101–102; Hartley, *op. cit.*, p. 57; Kaye, *op. cit.*, pp. 645–651; and O'Malley and Layton, *op. cit.*, paras 17.82–17.89.

90. Article V of the 1968 Protocol.

91. On Article 6(3) of the Convention, see Jenard, *op. cit.*, para. 125; Collins, *op. cit.*, p. 67; Hartley, *op. cit.*, p. 57; Kaye, *op. cit.*, pp. 652–664; and O'Malley and Layton, *op. cit.*, paras 17.90–17.95.

92. On Article 6A of the Convention, see Schlosser, *op. cit.*, paras 124–130; Collins, *op. cit.*, pp. 67–68; Dashwood, Halcon and White, *op. cit.*, p. 102; Hartley, *op. cit.*, pp. 55–56; Kaye, *op. cit.*, pp. 799–803; and O'Malley and Layton, *op. cit.*, paras 17.96–17.98.

contracting State has jurisdiction in actions relating to liability from the use or operation of a ship, that court, or any other court substituted for this purpose by internal law of that State, shall also have jurisdiction over claims for limitation of such liability."

Given the importance of this provision for present purposes, the opportunity has been taken to cite in detail many of the commentaries on the provision.

Schlosser states:

"*2. Jurisdiction to order a limitation of liability*

124. It is not easy to say precisely how the application of Article 57 of the 1968 Convention[93] links up with that of the International Convention of 10 October 1957 relating to the limitation of the liability of owners of seagoing ships[94] (see end of paragraph 128) and with relevant national laws. The latter Convention contains no express provisions directly affecting international jurisdiction or the enforcement of judgments. The Working Party did not consider that it was its task to deal systematically with the issues raised by that Convention and to devise proposals for solving them. It would, however, be particularly unfortunate in certain respects if the jurisidictional lacunae of the 1957 Convention on the limitation of liability were carried over into the 1968 Convention and were supplemented in accordance with the general provisions on jurisdiction of that Convention.

A distinction needs to be drawn between three differing aspects arising in connection with the limitation of liability in matters of maritime law. First, a procedure exists for setting up and allocating the liability fund. Secondly, the entitlement to damages against the shipowner must be judicially determined. Finally, and distinct from both, there is the assessment of limitation of liability regarding a given claim.

The procedural details giving effect to these three aspects vary in the different legal systems of the Community.

125. Under one system, which is followed in particular in the United Kingdom, limitation of liability necessitates an action against one of the claimants—either by way of originating proceedings or, if an action has already been brought against the shipowner, as a counterclaim. The liability fund is set up at the court dealing with the limitation of liability issue, and other claimants must also lodge their claims with the same court.

126. Under the system obtaining in Germany, for example, proceedings for the limitation of liability are started not by means of an action brought against a claimant, but by a simple application which is not directed 'against' any person, and which leads to the setting up of the fund.

If the application is successful, all claimants must lodge their claims with that court. If any disputes arise about the validity of any of the claims lodged, they have to be dealt with by special proceedings taking the form of an action by the claimant against the fund administrator, creditor or shipowner contesting the claim. Under this system an independent action by the shipowner against the claimant in connection with limitation of liability is also possible. Such an action leads not to the setting up of a liability fund or to an immediately effective limitation of liability, but merely establishes whether liability is subject to potential limitation, in case of future proceedings to assess the extent of such liability.

127. The new Article 6a does not apply to an action by a claimant against the shipowner, fund administrator or other competing claimants, nor to the collective proceedings for creating and allocating the liability fund, but only to the independent action brought by a shipowner against a claimant (a). Otherwise the present provisions of the 1968 Convention whch are relevant to limitation of maritime liability apply (b).

128. (a) The actual or potential limitation of the liability of a shipowner can, however, in all legal systems of the Community be used otherwise than as a defence. If a shipowner anticipates a liability claim, it may be in his interest to take the initiative by asking for a declaration that he has only limited or potentially limited liability for the claim. In that case he can choose from one of the jurisdictions which are competent by virtue of Articles 2 to 6. According to these provisions,

93. Article 57 is a non-prejudice clause.

94. The new Convention on the limitation of liability for maritime claims, signed in London on 19 November 1976, was not yet in force at the end of the Working Party's discussions.

he cannot bring an action in the courts of his domicile. Since, however, he could be sued in those courts, it would be desirable to allow him to have recourse to this jurisdiction. It is the purpose of Article 6a to provide for this. Moreover, apart from the Brussels Convention of 1952, this is the only jurisdiction where the shipowner could reasonably concentrate all actions affecting limitation of his liability. The result for English law (see paragraph 125) is that the fund can be set up and allocated by that same court. In addition, Article 6a makes it clear that proceedings for limitation of liability can also be brought by the shipowner in any other court which has jurisdiction over the claim. It also enables national legislation to give jurisdiction to a court within their territory other than the court which would normally have jurisdiction.

129. (b) For proceedings concerning the validity as such of a claim against a shipowner, Articles 2 to 6 are exclusively applicable. In addition, Article 22 is always applicable. If proceedings to limit liability have been brought in one State, a court in another State which has before it an application to establish or to limit liability may stay the proceedings or even decline jurisdiction.

130. (c) A clear distinction must be drawn between the question of jurisdiction and the question which substantive law on limitation of liability is to be applied. This need not be the law of the State whose courts have jurisdiction for assessing the limitation of liability. The law applicable for the limitation of liability also defines more precisely the type of case in which limitation of liability can be claimed at all."

O'Malley and Layton comment:

"The Schlosser Report describes the nature and purpose of claims for limitation of liability in maritime matters and the different types of procedure commonly adopted by the Contracting Parties in respect of such claims.[95] Proceedings for the limitation of liability are those by which a shipowner or other person who is a potential defendant to a maritime claim can take the initiative in seeking to limit his liability. Such proceedings, which take different forms in different Contracting States, do not necessarily involve proceedings against a claimant, but where they take the form of an action by (typically) a shipowner, Article 6A provides an additional jurisdiction.

The rule of jurisdiction provided by this Article is in addition to those which would otherwise be available to a shipowner or other potential defendant under Articles 2 to 6 or, pursuant to Article 57, under a specialised convention.[96] Jurisdiction under Articles 17 and 18, on the other hand, would take priority over this Article. Article 6A enables him as plaintiff to bring the limitation proceedings in any court which would have jurisdiction over him as defendant if the proceedings concerned the use or operation of a ship, or in any other court substituted for this purpose by national law. It is irrelevant whether or not that court would have had jurisdiction over the defendant (i.e. the claimant) apart from this Article.

If the proceedings concern the validity of a claim against a shipowner, rather than the size of the claim, they do not fall within Article 6A, but only within Articles 2 to 6[97] (or, if they are relevant, Articles 16 to 18). Article 6A does not affect the question of what law is applicable to the claim,[98] so if the applicable law does not provide for limitation actions, the jurisdiction under this Article cannot be successfully invoked. Also, Article 6A does not affect Article 22, which may be applied to stay the limitation action if the claimant's action is started first."[99]

95. Schlosser, para. 124 *et seq.* A description of such proceedings is beyond the scope of this work. In English law, they may be brought under the Merchant Shipping Acts 1894 to 1981. See also, R.S.C., Ord. 75, rr37 to 40, 1 *Halsbury's Laws* (4th ed.), paras 353–355, 461–472; *British Shipping Laws*, Vols. 1, 4, 11.

96. International convention of 10 October 1957 relating to the limitation of the liability of owners of sea-going ships (Cmnd. 353), Merchant Shipping (Liability of Shipowners and Others) Act 1958; Athens Convention on the Carriage of Passengers and their Luggage by Sea 1974 (Cmnd. 6326), Sched. 3 of the Merchant Shipping Act 1979; London convention on limitation of liability for maritime claims, of 19 November 1976 (Cmnd. 7035), Sched. 4 of the Merchant Shipping Act 1979; Brussels Convention of 10 May 1952 on the arrest of sea-going ships (Cmnd. 8954). See Gaskell, "The Zeebrugge Disaster: Application of the Athens Convention 1974" (1987) 137 NLJ 285, at pp. 322, 383.

97. Schlosser, para. 129.

98. Schlosser, para. 130.

99. *Op. cit.* at footnote 1, para. 17.97 (some foonotes omitted).

25.3.4 Insurance

Section 3 of Title II of the Convention (i.e. Articles 7–12A) deals with jurisdiction in matters relating to insurance.[100] It seeks to redress the balance of power between the insurer and the insured: as the European Court of Justice has stated:

"It is apparent from a consideration of the provisions of that section in the light of the documents leading to their enactment that in affording the insured a wider range of jurisdiction than that available to the insurer and in excluding any possibility of a clause conferring jurisdiction for the benefit of the insurer their purpose was to protect the insured who is most frequently faced with a predetermined contract the clauses of which are no longer negotiable and who is in a weaker economic position."[101]

In matters relating to insurance, jurisdiction is determined by that section, without prejudice to the provisions of Articles 4 and 5(5).[102] O'Malley and Layton comment:

"[t]he effect of the reference to Article 4 is to limit the scope of Articles 7 to 12A to cases where the defendant is domiciled in a Contracting State, whether the defendant is insurer, the insured, the policy-holder or beneficiary . . . [and the effect of the reference to Article 5(5)] is to provide a basis of jurisdiction under that provision in addition to those provided by Articles 7 to 12A."[103]

Article 8[104] (as amended by Article 7 of the 1978 Accession Convention) provides general rules of jurisdiction:

"An insurer domiciled in a Contracting State may be sued:

1. in the courts of the State where he is domiciled; or
2. in another Contracting State, in the courts for the place where the policy-holder is domiciled; or
3. if he is a co-insurer, in the courts of a Contracting State in which proceedings are brought against the leading insurer.

An insurer who is not domiciled in a Contracting State but has a branch, agency or other establishment in one of the Contracting States shall, in disputes arising out of the operations of the branch, agency or establishment, be deemed to be domiciled in that State."

Article 9 of the Convention[105] provides: "In respect of liability insurance or insurance of immovable property, the insurer may in addition be sued in the courts for the place where the harmful event occurred. The same applies if movable and immovable property are covered by the same insurance policy and both are adversely affected by the same contingency."

Article 10 of the Convention[106] provides:

"In respect of liability insurance, the insurer may also, if the law of the court permits it, be joined in proceedings which the injured party had brought against the insured.

---

100. In this context, the term "insurance" must be given an independent meaning within the context of the Convention and not a nationalistic one. Insurance in this context probably does not include reinsurance: see Schlosser, *op. cit.*, para. 151. See *New Hampshire Insurance Co.* v. *Strabag Bau & Ors.* [1992] 1 Lloyd's Rep. 361, C.A.

101. *Gerling Konzern AG v. Amministrazione del Tesoro dello Stato* [1983] ECR 2503, at p. 2516, para. 17.

102. Convention, Article 7.

103. *Op. cit.*, paras 18.04–18.05 (footnote omitted).

104. On Article 8 of the Convention, see Jenard, *op. cit.*, paras 137–140; Schlosser, *op. cit.*, paras 149–152; Collins, *op. cit.*, pp. 64 and 71; Hartley, *op. cit.*, pp. 60–61; Kaye, *op. cit.*, pp. 809–812; and O'Malley and Layton, *op. cit.*, paras 18.11–18.22.

105. On Article 9 of the Convention, see Jenard, *op. cit.*, para. 141; Schlosser, *op. cit.*, paras 136–139; Collins, *op. cit.*, p. 71; Hartley, *op. cit.*, p. 61; Kaye, *op. cit.*, p. 812; and O'Malley and Layton, *op. cit.*, paras 18.23–18.31.

106. On Article 11, see Jenard, *op. cit.*, para. 147; Collins, *op. cit.*, p. 72; Dashwood, Halcon and White, *op. cit.*, p. 27 as well as O'Malley and Layton, *op. cit.*, para 18.42 *et seq.*

The provisions of Articles 7, 8 and 9 shall apply to actions brought by the injured party directly against the insurer, where such direct actions are permitted.

If the law governing such direct action provides that the policy-holder or the insured may be joined as a party to the action, the same court shall have jurisdiction over them."

Article 11 of the Convention[107] provides:

"Without prejudice to the provisions of the third paragraph of Article 10, an insurer may bring proceedings only in the courts of the Contracting State in which the defendant is domiciled, irrespective of whether he is the policy-holder, the insured or a beneficiary.

The provisions of this Section shall not affect the right to bring a counterclaim in the court in which, in accordance with this Section, the original claim is pending."

Article 12[108] of the Convention provides:

"The provisions of this Section may be departed from only by agreement on jurisdiction:

1. which is entered into after the dispute has arisen, or
2. which allows the policy-holder, the insured or a beneficiary to bring proceedings in courts other than those indicated in this Section, or
3. which is concluded between a policy-holder and an insurer, both of whom are domiciled in the same Contracting State, and which has the effect of conferring jurisdiction on the courts of that State even if the harmful event were to occur abroad, provided that such an agreement is not contrary to the law of that State, or
4. which is concluded with a policy-holder who is not domiciled in a Contracting State, except in so far as the insurance is compulsory or relates to immovable property in a Contracting State, or
5. which relates to a contract of insurance in so far as it covers one or more of the risks set out in Article 12a."

Article 12a[109] provides that the following are the risks referred to in point 5 of Article 12:

"1. Any loss of or damage to:
(a) sea-going ships, installations situated offshore or on the high seas, or aircraft, arising from perils which relate to their use for commercial purposes;
(b) goods in transit other than passengers' baggage where the transit consists of or includes carriage by such ships or aircraft;

2. Any liability, other than for bodily injury to passengers or loss of or damage to their baggage:
(a) arising out of the use or operation of ships, installations or aircraft as referred to in point 1(a) above in so far as the law of the Contracting State in which such aircraft are registered does not prohibit agreements on jurisdiction regarding insurance of such risks;
(b) for loss or damage caused by goods in transit as described in point 1(b) above;

3. Any financial loss connected with the use or operation of ships, installations or aircraft as referred to in point 1(a) above, in particular loss of freight or charter-hire;

4. Any risk or interest connected with any of those referred to in (1) to (3) above."

Thus, the parties to a contract of marine insurance may enter into a jurisdiction agreement under Articles 12(5) and 17. The rationale for departing from the consumer protection approach of section 3 of Title II of the Convention (i.e. Articles 7–12A) is that the parties to such insurance are more than able to take care of themselves economically.

107. On Article 10, see Jenard, *op. cit.*, paras 142–146; Schlosser, *op. cit.*, para 148; Collins, *op. cit.*, pp. 71–72; as well as O'Malley and Layton, *op. cit.*, para. 18.42 *et seq.*

108. As amended by Article 8 of the 1978 Accession Convention.

109. Schlosser, *op. cit.*, paras 140–147.

25.3.5 Consumer contracts

Articles 13–15 of the Convention deals with jurisdiction over consumer contracts. These are designed to offer consumers greater protection.

Article 13 provides:[110]

"In proceedings concerning a contract concluded by a person for a purpose which can be regarded as being outside his trade or profession, hereinafter called 'the consumer', jurisdiction shall be determined by this section, without prejudice to the provisions of Articles 4 and 5(5), if it is:

1. a contract for the sale of goods on instalment credit terms, or
2. a contract for a loan repayable by instalments, or for any other form of credit, made to finance the sale of goods, or
3. any other contract for the supply of goods or a contract for the supply of services, and
   (a) in the State of the consumer's domicile the conclusion of the contract was preceded by a specific invitation addressed to him or by advertising, and
   (b) the consumer took in that State the steps necessary for the conclusion of the contract.

Where a consumer enters into a contract with a party who is not domiciled in a Contracting State but has a branch, agency or other establishment in one of the Contracting States, that party shall, in disputes arising out of the operations of the branch, agency or establishment, be deemed to be domiciled in that State.

This section shall not apply to contracts of transport."

Article 14[111] provides:

"A consumer may bring proceedings against the other party to contract either in the courts of the Contracting State in which that party is domiciled or in the courts of the Contracting State in which he is himself domiciled.

Proceedings may be brought against a consumer by the other party to the contract only in the courts of the Contracting State in which the consumer is domiciled.

These provisions shall not affect the right to bring a counterclaim in the court in which, in accordance with this Section, the original claim is pending."

Article 15[112] provides:

"The provisions of this Section may be departed from only by an agreement:

1. which is entered into after the dispute has arisen, or
2. which allows the consumer to bring proceedings in courts other than those indicated in this Section, or
3. which is entered into by the consumer and the other party to the contract, both of whom are at the time of the conclusion of the contract domiciled or habitually resident in the same Contracting State, and which confers jurisdiction on the courts of that State, provided that such an agreement is not contrary to the law of that State."

25.3.6 Exclusive jurisdiction

In certain circumstances, courts other than those of the defendant's domicile have exclusive jurisdiction. These circumstances are set out in Articles 16 and 17 of the Convention.[113]

Article 16[114] is the first of the two articles of the Convention dealing with exclusive jurisdiction. It provides:

110. See O'Malley and Layton, *op. cit.*, para. 18.43 *et seq.*
111. See O'Malley and Layton, *op. cit.*, para. 19.25 *et seq.*
112. See O'Malley and Layton, *op. cit.*, para. 19.34 *et seq.*
113. On Article 17 of the Convention, see para. 25.3.7.1, below.
114. See O'Malley and Layton, *op. cit.*, Chapter 20.

"The following courts shall have exclusive jurisdiction, regardless of domicile:

1. (a) in proceedings which have as their object rights in rem in immovable property or tenancies of immovable property, the courts of the Contracting State in which the property is situated;
   (b) however, in proceedings which have as their object tenancies of immovable property concluded for temporary private use for a maximum period of six consecutive months, the courts of the Contracting State in which the defendant is domiciled shall also have jurisdiction, provided that the landlord and the tenant are natural persons and are domiciled in the same Contracting State;
2. in proceedings which have as their object the validity of the constitution, the nullity or the dissolution of companies or other legal persons or associations of natural or legal persons, or the decisions of their organs, the courts of the Contracting State in which the company, legal person or association has its seat;
3. in proceedings which have as their object the validity of entries in public registers, the courts of the Contracting State in which the register is kept;
4. in proceedings concerned with the registration or validity of patents, trade marks, designs, or other similar rights required to be deposited or registered, the courts of the Contracting State in which the deposit or registration has been applied for, has taken place or is under the terms of an international convention deemed to have taken place;
5. in proceedings concerned with the enforcement of judgments, the courts of the Contracting State in which the judgment has been or is to be enforced."

25.3.6.1 Proceedings have as their object rights in rem

The courts of the *situs* of the property have exclusive jurisdiction where the proceedings have as their object rights *in rem*. Collier states that in relation to proceedings *in rem* such proceedings "include those involving title to or possession of property, but probably not an action for damage to it."[115,116]

25.3.6.2 Tenancies of immovable property

The courts of the *situs* of the property have exclusive jurisdiction where the proceedings involve tenancies of immovable property. This is a limited exception.[117]

25.3.6.3 Certain proceedings involving a company

The courts of the State where a company has its seat have exclusive jurisdiction in proceedings concerning the validity of the company's constitution or the decisions of the company's organs. More exactly, "in proceedings which have as their object the validity of the constitution, the nullity or the dissolution of companies or other legal persons or associations of natural or legal persons, or the decisions of their organs, the courts of the contracting State in which the company, legal person or association has its seat"[118] have exclusive jurisdiction.

25.3.6.4 Validity of Acts on public registers

In proceedings which have as their object the validity of entries in public registers, the courts of the contracting State in which the register is kept have exclusive jurisdiction.

115. Schlosser Report, paras 169–172.
116. *Op. cit.*, at p. 124.
117. See Case 73/77 *Sanders v. van der Putte* [1977] ECR 2383, [1978] 1 CMLR 331 and Case 241/83 *Rosler v. Rottwinkel* [1986] ECR 99, [1985] 1 CMLR 806.
118. Convention, Article 16(2).

25.3.6.5 Intellectual property proceedings

As a general rule, the place of deposit or registration of an instrument of intellectual property is where proceedings must be taken. More exactly, "in proceedings concerned with the registration or validity of patents, trade marks, designs, or other similar rights required to be deposited or registered, the courts of the contracting State in which the deposit or registration has been applied for, has taken place or is under the terms of an international convention deemed to have taken place"[119] have exclusive jurisdiction.

25.3.6.6. Enforcement of judgments

In the case of the enforcement of judgments, the courts of the State where the judgment is to be or has been enforced are the courts which have exclusive jurisdiction. More specifically, "in proceedings concerned with the enforcement of judgments, the courts of the contracting State in which the judgment has been or is to be enforced"[120] have exclusive jurisdiction.

25.3.7 Prorogation of jurisdiction

Section 6 of Title II (i.e. Articles 17–18) deals with the prorogation of jurisdiction. A contractually binding agreement to submit a dispute to the courts of one of the Member States automatically ousts the jurisdiction of the other contracting States with the exception of those States which possess exclusive jurisdiction by virtue of Article 16.[121]

25.3.7.1. Article 17: Jurisdiction agreements

Article 17[122] provides:

"If the parties, one or more of whom is domiciled in a Contracting State, have agreed that a court or the courts of a Contracting State are to have jurisdiction to settle any disputes which have arisen or which may arise in connection with a particular legal relationship, that court or those courts shall have exclusive jurisdiction. Such an agreement conferring jurisdiction shall be either:

(a) in writing or evidenced in writing; or
(b) in a form which accords with practices which the parties have established between themselves; or
(c) in international trade or commerce, in a form which accords with a usage of which the parties are or ought to have been aware and which in such trade or commerce is widely known to, and regularly observed by, parties to contracts of the type involved in the particular trade or commerce concerned.

Where such an agreement is concluded by parties, none of whom is domiciled in a Contracting State, the courts of other Contracting States shall have no jurisdiction over their disputes unless the court or courts chosen have declined jurisdiction.

The court or courts of a Contracting State on which a trust instrument has conferred jurisdiction shall have exclusive jurisdiction in any proceedings brought against a settlor, trustee or beneficiary, if relations between these persons or their rights or obligations under the trust are involved.

Agreements or provisions of a trust instrument conferring jurisdiction shall have no legal force if they are contrary to the provisions of Articles 12 or 15, or if the courts whose jurisdiction they purport to exclude have exclusive jurisdiction by virtue of Article 16.

119. Convention, Article 16(2).
120. Convention, Article 16(2).
121. A consumer contract containing such a clause must comply with Articles 13–15 of the Convention.
122. As amended by Article 11 of the 1978 Accession Convention and by Article 7 of the 1989 Accession Convention.

If an agreement conferring jurisdiction was concluded for the benefit of only one of the parties, that party shall retain the right to bring proceedings in any other court which has jurisdiction by virtue of this Convention.

In matters relating to individual contracts of employment an agreement conferring jurisdiction shall have legal force only if it entered into force after the dispute has arisen or if the employee invokes it to seise courts other than those for the defendant's domicile or those specified in Article 5(1)."

The municipal law of a contracting State cannot invalidate an agreement which is otherwise valid under Article 17 of the Convention.[123]

In terms of form, an oral agreement which has been confirmed in writing by one party and to which the other party does not object, is valid for present purposes.[124]

In Case 201/82 *Gerling Konzern v Amministrazione del Tesoro*[125] (a case involving a policy of insurance) the European Court of Justice held that third parties "even if they have not expressly signed the . . . clause, may rely upon it, provided that, as between the insurer and the policy-holder, the condition as to writing laid down by Article 17 of the Convention has been satisfied and provided that the consent of the insurer in that respect has been clearly manifested".[126]

The parties to a contract may choose any number of courts in different contracting States.[127]

A contractually agreed jurisdiction is not however completely exclusive due to Article 18.[128]

25.3.7.2. Article 18: Jurisdiction by submission[129]

Article 18 provides:

"Apart from jurisdiction derived from other provisions of this Convention, a court of a Contracting State before whom a defendant enters an appearance shall have jurisdiction. This rule shall not apply where appearance was entered solely to contest the jurisdiction, or where another court has exclusive jurisdiction by virtue of Article 16."

25.3.8 Examination as to jurisdiction and admissibility

Section 7 of Title II (i.e. Articles 19–20) deals with the Examination as to Jurisdiction and Admissibility.

Article 19[130] provides:

"Where a court of a Contracting State is seised of a claim which is principally concerned with a matter over which the courts of another Contracting State have exclusive jurisdiction by virtue of Article 16, it shall declare of its own motion that it has no jurisdiction."

The purpose of this provision is to ensure that the courts of contracting States respect each other's jurisdiction.[131] It complements Article 16.[132]

Article 20[133] states:

123. Case 25/79 *Sanicentral v. Collin* [1979] ECR 3423, [1979] 2 CMLR 164.
124. Case 221/84 *Berghoefer GmbH v. ASA* [1985] ECR 1517, [1980] 1 CMLR 566.
125. [1983] ECR 2503, [1984] 3 CMLR 638.
126. [1983] ECR 2503, at p. 2518.
127. See Case 23/78 *Meeth v. Glacetal* [1978] ECR 2133, [1979] 1 CMLR 520.
128. See O'Malley and Layton, *op. cit.*, para. 21.38.
129. *Op. cit.*
130. See O'Malley and Layton, *op. cit.*, Chapter 22.
131. See O'Malley and Layton, *op. cit.*, para. 22.02.
132. On Article 16, see above.
133. See O'Malley and Layton, *op. cit.*, para. 22.11.

"Where a defendant domiciled in one Contracting State is sued in a court of another Contracting State and does not enter an appearance, the court shall declare of its own motion that it has no jurisdiction unless its jurisdiction is derived from the provisions of this Convention.

The court shall stay the proceedings so long as it is not shown that the defendant has not been able to receive the document instituting the proceedings or an equivalent document in sufficient time to enable him to arrange for his defence, or that all necessary steps have been taken to this end.

The provisions of the foregoing paragraph shall be replaced by those of Article 15 of the Hague Convention of November 15, 1965 on the service abroad of judicial and extrajudicial documents in civil or commercial matters, if the document instituting the proceedings or notice thereof had to be transmitted abroad in accordance with that Convention."

25.3.9 Lis pendens—related actions

Article 21[134] of the Convention, as amended by Article 8 of the 1989 Accession Convention, provides:

"Where proceedings involving the same cause of action and between the same parties are brought in the courts of different Contracting States, any court other than the court first seised shall of its own motion stay its proceedings until such time as the jurisdiction of the court first seised is established.

Where the jurisdiction of the court first seised is established, any court other than the court first seised decline jurisdiction in favour of that court."

Article 22[135] of the Convention states:

"Where related actions are brought in the courts of different Contracting States, any court other than the court first seised may, while the actions are pending at first instance, stay its proceedings.

A court other than the court first seised may also, on the application of one of the parties, decline jurisdiction if the law of that court permits the consolidation of related actions and the court first seised has jurisdiction over both actions.

For the purposes of this Article, actions are deemed to be related where they are so closely connected that it is expedient to hear and determine them together to avoid the risk of irreconcilable judgments resulting from separate proceedings."

Article 23[136] then provides: "Where actions come within the exclusive jurisdiction of several courts, any court other than the court first seised shall decline jurisdiction in favour of that court."

In *Zeiger v. Salinitri*[137] the ECJ held that the court "first seised" was the court for which the requirements for proceedings to become "definitively pending" were first fulfilled. In *Dresser UK Ltd v. Falcongate Freight Management Ltd.*[138] the English Court of Appeal held that, as a general rule, service of proceedings was the appropriate moment for the English court to become seised of proceedings.

25.3.10 Provisional, including protective, measures

Article 24[139] of the Convention deals with interim relief. It is embodied in section 9 of Title II and provides: "Applications may be made to the courts of a Contracting State for such provisional, including protective, measures, as may be available under the law

134. See Keates, "When is an English Court 'seised' of proceedings", *Lloyd's List*, 22 November 1991, p. 10.
135. See O'Malley and Layton, *op. cit.*, Chapter 23.
136. *Op. cit.*
137. [1984] ECR 2397.
138. [1991] 2 Lloyd's Rep. 557. See also *The Freccia del Nord* [1989] 1 Lloyd's Rep. 338 (overrruled).
139. See O'Malley and Layton, *op. cit.*, Chapter 24.

of that State, even if, under this Convention, the courts of another Contracting State have jurisdiction as to the substance of the matter."

25.4 RECOGNITION AND ENFORCEMENT

25.4.1 Introduction

Title III of the Convention deals with the recognition and enforcement of judgments. It is divided into three sections: recogntion[140]; enforcement[141]; and common provisions.[142]

25.4.1.1 Concept of judgment[143]

For the purposes of the Convention, a "judgment" means according to Article 25,[144] "any judgment given by a court or tribunal of a Contracting State, whatever the judgment may be called, including a decree, order, decision or writ of execution, as well as the determination of costs or expenses by an officer of the court".[145] The judgment must be rendered in a case falling within the scope of the Convention (i.e. civil and commercial matters).[146]

Collier succinctly states:

"[a]lthough provisional measures, such as an interim injunction, are within the Convention and are enforceable, provided the defendant was amenable to the jurisdiction,[147] the rights of defence must have been observed and they cannot be enforced if they were ordered in the absene of the defendant and intended to be enforced without advance notice to him."[148]

25.4.2 Recognition

25.4.2.1 Principles of recognition

Article 26[149] provides:

"A judgment given in a Contracting State shall be recognised in the other Contracting States without any special procedures being required.

Any interested party who raises the recognition of a judgment as the principal issue in a dispute may, in accordance with the procedures provided for in Sections 2 and 3 of this Title, apply for a decision that the judgment be recognised.

If the outcome of proceedings in a court of a Contracting State depends on the determination of an incidental question of recognition that court shall have jurisdiction over that question.

The advantage of the Article 26 procedure is that recognition is automatic."

25.4.2.2 Instances of non-recognition of judgments

Article 27[150] deals with the circumstances in which a judgment[151] shall not be recognised. It sets out five circumstances when judgments are not recognised. There is a

140. Title III, s. 1 (i.e. Articles 26–30).
141. Title III, s. 2 (i.e. Articles 31–45).
142. Title III, s. 3 (i.e. Articles 46–49).
143. See O'Malley and Layton, *op. cit.*, Chapter 25.
144. *Op. cit.*
145. Convention, Article 25.
146. On the scope of the Convention, see para. 25.2, above.
147. *de Cavel v. de Cavel (No. 1)* [1979] ECR 1055.
148. *Denilauler v. Couchet Frères* [1980] ECR 1553, at p. 1570.
149. See O'Malley and Layton, *op. cit.*, Chapter 27.
150. *Op. cit.*
151. Within the meaning of Article 25 of the Convention: see para. 25.4.1.1, above.

sixth circumstance outlined in Article 28 of the Convention. However, in no circumstances may a judgment be reviewed as to its substance.[152]

25.4.2.2.1 Article 27(1): Public policy[153]

Article 27(1) provides that a judgment[154] shall not be recognised if "such recognition is contrary to public policy in the State in which recognition is sought". It is hard to imagine this occurring in practice.

25.4.2.2.2 Article 27(2): Judgment in default of appearance[155]

Article 27(2) provides that a judgment[156] shall not be recognised "where it was given in default of appearance, if the defendant was not duly served with the document which instituted the proceedings or with an equivalent document in sufficient time to enable him to arrange for his defence". A case which discusses this point is Case 166/80 *Klomps v. Michel.*[157]

25.4.2.2.3 Article 27(3): Conflicting judgments[158]

Article 27(3) provides that a judgment[159] shall not be recognised if "the judgment is irreconcilable with a judgment given in a dispute between the same parties in the State in which recognition is sought".

25.4.2.2.4 Article 27(4): Preliminary questions and private international law[160]

Article 27(4)[161] provides that a judgment[162] shall not be recognised if:

"the courts of the State of origin, in order to arrive at its judgment, has decided a preliminary question concerning the status or legal capacity of natural persons, rights in property arising out of a matrimonial relationship, wills or succession in a way that conflicts with a rule of the private international law of the State in which the recognition is sought, unless the same result would have been reached by the application of the rules of private international law of that State."

25.4.2.2.5 Article 27(5): Conflicts between judgments from non-contracting States[163]

Article 27(5)[164] provides that a judgment[165] shall not be recognised if "the judgment is irreconcilable with an earlier judgment given in a non-contracting State involving the same cause of action and between the same parties, provided that this latter judgment fulfils the conditions necessary for its recognition in the state addressed."

152. Convention, Article 29. See para. 25.4.2.2.7, below.
153. See O'Malley and Layton, *op. cit.*, Chapter 27.
154. Within the meaning of Article 25 of the Convention: see para. 25.4.1.1, above.
155. See O'Malley and Layton, *op. cit.*, Chapter 25.
156. Within the meaning of Article 25 of the Convention: see para. 25.4.1.1, above.
157. [1981] ECR 1593, [1982] 2 CMLR 773.
158. See O'Malley and Layton, *op. cit.*, para. 27.43.
159. Within the meaning of Article 25 of the Convention: see para. 25.4.1.1, above.
160. See O'Malley and Layton, *op. cit.*, para. 27.52.
161. As amended by Annex 1(a)(2) first sub-paragraph to the 1989 Accession Convention.
162. Within the meaning of Article 25 of the Convention: see para. 25.4.1.1, above.
163. See O'Malley and Layton, *op. cit.*, para. 27.59.
164. As added by Article 13(2) of the 1978 Accession Convention and amended by Annex I(d)(2) second sub-paragraph to the 1989 Accession Convention.
165. Within the meaning of Article 25 of the Convention: see para. 25.4.1.1, above.

25.4.2.2.6. Article 28: Exceptions[166]

Article 28 goes on to provide:

"Moreover, a judgment shall not be recognized if it conflicts with the provisions of Sections 3, 4 or 5 of Title II,[167] or in a case provided for in Article 59.[168]

In its examination of the grounds of jurisdiction referred to in the foregoing paragraph, the court or authority applied to shall be bound by the findings of fact on which the court of the State or origin based its jurisdiction.

Subject to the provisions of the first paragraph, the jurisdiction of the court of the State of origin may not be reviewed; the test of public policy referred to in point 1 of Article 27 may not be applied to the rules relating to jurisdiction."

In essence, "with respect to the jurisdiction of the foreign court, if and only if the jurisdiction assumed by that court conflicts with the provisions regarding insurance and consumer contracts or regarding exclusive jurisdiction"[169] will the judgment not be recognised.

25.4.2.2.7 Article 29: Prohibition on review of the substance of the judgment[170]

Article 29 simply provides that "[u]nder no circumstances may a foreign judgment be reviewed as to its substance."

25.4.2.2.8 Article 30[171]

Article 30[172] provides:

"A court of a Contracting State in which recognition is sought of a judgment given in another contracting State may stay the proceedings if an ordinary appeal against the judgment has been lodged.

A court of a contracting State in which recognition is sought of a judgment given in Ireland or the United Kingdom may stay the proceedings if enforcement is suspended in the State of origin, by reason of an appeal."

25.4.3. Enforcement

Section 2 of Title III of the Convention deals with enforcement in the context of the recognition of judgments.

Article 31[173] of the Convention provides that a judgment given in a contracting State and enforceable in that State shall be enforced in another contracting State when, on the application of any interested party, it has been declared enforceable there.[174] However, in the UK, such a judgment shall be enforced in England and Wales, in Scotland, or in Northern Ireland when, on the application of any interested party, it has been registered for enforcement in that part of the UK.[175]

166. See O'Malley and Layton, *op. cit.*
167. See above.
168. See O'Malley and Layton, *op. cit.*, para. 33.24.
169. Collier, *op. cit.*, p. 130.
170. See O'Malley and Layton, *op. cit.*, para. 27.35.
171. *Op. cit.*, para. 27.78.
172. The second sub-paragraph was added by Article 14 of the 1978 Accession Convention and amended by Annex I(d)(4) to the 1989 Accession Convention.
173. See O'Malley and Layton, *op. cit.*, para. 28.01.
174. Convention, Article 31.
175. Convention, Article 31.

The application for the enforcement of a foreign judgment must be submitted to one of the tribunals set out in Article 32(1). These tribunals are:

"— in Belgium, to the tribunal de première instance or rechtbank van eerste aanleg,
— in Denmark, to the byret,
— in the Federal Republic of Germany, to the presiding judge of a chamber of the Landgericht,
— in Greece, to the *μονομελές πρωτοδικεῖο*,
— in Spain, to the Juzgado de Primera Instancia,
— in France, to the presiding judge of the tribunal de grande instance,
— in Ireland, to the High Court,
— in Italy, to the corte d'appello,
— in Luxembourg, to the presiding judge of the tribunal d'arrondissement,
— in the Netherlands, to the presiding judge of the arrondissementsrechtbank,
— in Portugal, to the Tribunal Judicial de Circulo,
— in the UK:
1. in England and Wales, to the High Court of Justice, or in the case of maintenance judgments to the Magistrates' Court on transmission by the Secretary of State;
2. in Scotland, to the Court of Session, or in the case of a maintenance judgment to the Sheriff Court on transmission by the Secretary of State;
3. in Northern Ireland, to the High Court of Justice, or in the case of a maintenance judgment to the Magistrates' Court on transmission by the Secretary of State"

Article 32(2) provides that the jurisdiction of local courts shall be determined by reference to the place of domicile of the party against whom enforcement is sought. If the person is not domiciled in the State in which enforcement is sought, it shall be determined by reference to the place of enforcement.

The procedure for making the application is to be governed by the law of the State in which enforcement is sought.[176] The applicant must give an address for service of process within the area of jurisdiction of the court applied to.[177] However, if the law of the State in which enforcement is sought does not provide for the furnishing of such an address, the applicant shall appoint a representative *ad litem*.[178] Under Article 33, the application must be accompanied by the documents referred to in Articles 46 and 47 of the Convention.

The court to which application for enforcement is made must give its decision without delay.[179] The party against whom the enforcement is sought is not entitled at this stage of the proceedings to make any submissions on the application.[180] Application is made *ex parte*.[181]

The foreign judgment must not be reviewed as to its substance.[182]

The application may only be refused for one of the reasons specified in Articles 27 and 28 of the Convention.[183]

The appropriate official of the court before which the enforcement is sought is obliged to bring, without delay, the decision given on the application to the notice of the applicant in accordance with the procedure laid down by the law of the State in which enforcement is sought.[184]

176. Convention, Article 33(1).
177. Convention, Article 33, para. 2.
178. Convention, Article 33, para. 2.
179. Convention, Article 34, para. 1.
180. Convention, Article 34, para. 1.
181. Convention, Article 34.
182. Convention, Article 34, para. 3.
183. Convention, Article 34, para. 2.
184. Convention, Article 35.

If enforcement is authorised then the party against whom enforcement is sought may appeal against the decision within one month of service thereof.[185] If that party is domiciled in a State which is a party to the Convention but a State other than the one in which the decision authorising enforcement was given then the time for appealling shall be two months and shall run from the date of service, either on him or her in person or at his or her residence[186] but no extension of time may be granted on account of distance.[187] During the time specified for such an appeal and until any such appeal has been determined, no measures of enforcement may be taken other than protective measures taken against the property of the party against whom enforcement is sought.[188] The decision authorising enforcement shall carry with it the power to proceed to any such protective measures.[189]

An appeal against the decision authorising enforcement is to be lodged in accordance with the rules governing procedure in contentious matters in the following courts:

> "— in Belgium, with the tribunal de première instance or rechtbank van eerste aanleg,
> — in Denmark, with the landsret,
> — in the Federal Republic of Germany, with the Oberlandesgericht,
> — in Greece, with the *ἐφετεῖο*,
> — in Spain, with the Audencia Provincial,
> — in France, with the court d'appel,
> — in Ireland, to the High Court,
> — in Italy, with the corte d'appello,
> — in Luxembourg, with the Cour supérieure de justice sitting as a court of civil appeal,
> — in the Netherlands, with the arrondissementsrechtbank,
> — in Portugal, with the Tribunal de Relaçao
> — in the UK:
> 1. in England and Wales, with the High Court of Justice, or in the case of maintenance judgments to the Magistrates' Court;
> 2. in Scotland, to the Court of Session, or in the case of a maintenance judgment to the Sheriff Court;
> 3. in Northern Ireland, to the High Court of Justice, or in the case of a maintenance judgment to the Magistrates' Court."

The judgment given on appeal may be contested in only a certain number of courts:

> "— in Belgium, Greece, Spain, France, Italy, Luxembourg and in the Netherlands, by an appeal in cassation,
> — in Denmark, by an appeal to the hojesteret, with the leave of the Minister for Justice,
> — in the Federal Republic of Germany, by a Rechtsbeschwerde,
> — in Ireland, by an appeal on a point of law to the Supreme Court,
> — in Portugal, by an appeal on a point of law,
> — in the UK, by a single further appeal on a point of law."[190]

Article 38[191] of the Convention provides that the court with which the appeal under Article 37(1)[192] is lodged may, on the application of the appellant, stay the proceedings

185. Convention, Article 36.
186. Convention, Article 36.
187. Convention, Article 36.
188. Convention, Article 39.
189. Convention, Article 39.
190. Convention, Article 37.
191. See O'Malley and Layton, *op. cit.*, para 28.43 *et seq.*
192. See O'Malley and Layton, *op. cit.*, para 28.38 *et seq.*

if an ordinary appeal has been lodged against the judgment in the State of origin or if the time for such an appeal has not yet expired; in the latter case, the court may specify the time within which such an appeal is to be lodged. Where the judgment was given in Ireland or the United Kingdom, any form of appeal available in the State of origin shall be treated as an ordinary appeal for those purposes.[193] The court may also make enforcement conditional on the provision of such security as it shall determine.[194]

If the application for enforcement is refused then the applicant may appeal:

"— in Belgium, to the cour d'appel or hof van beroep,
— in Denmark, to the landsret,
— in the Federal Republic of Germany, to the Oberlandesgericht,
— in Greece, to the ἐφετεῖο,
— in Spain, to the Audencia Provincial,
— in France, to the court d'appel,
— in Ireland, to the High Court,
— in Italy, to the corte d'appello,
— in Luxembourg, to the Cour supérieure de justice sitting as a court of civil appeal,
— in the Netherlands, to the gerechtshof,
— in Portugal, to the Tribunal de Relaçao,
— in the UK:
  1. in England and Wales, to the High Court of Justice, or in the case of maintenance judgments to the Magistrates' Court;
  2. in Scotland, to the Court of Session, or in the case of a maintenance judgment to the Sheriff Court;
  3. in Northern Ireland, to the High Court of Justice, or in the case of a maintenance judgment to the Magistrates' Court."

The party against whom enforcement is sought must be summoned to appear before the appellate court.[195] If the person fails to appear then the provisions of the second and third paragraphs of Article 20 of the Judgments Convention shall apply even where he is not domiciled in any of the contracting States.[196]

A judgment given on an appeal provided for in Article 40 may be contested only:

"— in Belgium, Greece, Spain, France, Italy, Luxembourg and in the Netherlands, by an appeal in cassation,
— in Denmark, by an appeal to the hojesteret, with the leave of the Minister for Justice,
— in the Federal Republic of Germany, by a Rechtsbeschwerde,
— in Ireland, by an appeal on a point of law to the Supreme Court,
— in Portugal, by an appeal on a point of law;
— in the UK, by a single further appeal on a point of law."[197]

If a foreign judgment has been given in respect of several matters and enforcement cannot be authorised for all of them, the court shall authorise enforcement for one or more of them.[198] An applicant may request partial enforcement of a judgment.[199]

193. Convention, Article 38.
194. Convention, Article 38.
195. Convention, Article 40(2).
196. Convention, Article 40(2).
197. Convention, Article 41.
198. Convention, Article 42.
199. Convention, Article 42.

25.4.3.1 A foreign judgment ordering a periodic payment

A foreign judgment which orders a periodic payment by way of a penalty shall be enforceable in the State in which enforcement is sought only if the amount of the payment has been finally determined by the courts of the State of origin.[200]

25.4.3.2 Legal aid

An applicant who, in the State of origin has benefited from complete or partial legal aid or exemption from costs or expenses, shall be entitled, in the procedures provided for in Articles 32 to 35 of the Convention, to benefit from the most favourable legal aid or the most extensive exemption from costs or expenses provided for by the law of the State addressed.[201] However, an applicant who requests the enforcement of a decision given by an administrative authority in Denmark in respect of a maintenance order may, in the State addressed, claim the benefits referred to in the first paragraph if he presents a statement from the Danish Ministry of Justice to the effect that he fulfils the economic requirements to qualify for the grant of complete or partial legal aid or exemption from costs or expenses.[202]

25.4.3.3. No security, bond or deposit

Article 45 of the Convention states that no security, bond or deposit, however described, shall be required of a party who in one contracting State applies for enforcement of a judgment given in another contracting State on the ground that he is a foreign national or that he is not domiciled or resident in the State in which enforcement is sought.

25.4.4. Common rules for recognition and enforcement

Section 3 of Title III of the Convention[203] consists of four articles which relate to both recognition and enforcement of judgments.

A party seeking recognition or applying for enforcement of a judgment must produce: (a) a copy of the judgment which satisfies the conditions necessary to establish its authenticity[204]; and (b) in the case of a judgment given in default, the original or a certified true copy of the document which establishes that the party in default was served with the document instituting the proceedings or with an equivalent document.[205] If the documents referred to under heading (b) are not produced then the court may specify a time for their production, accept equivalent documents or, if it considers that it has sufficient information before it, dispense with their production.[206] If the court so requires, a translation of the documents shall be produced; the translation shall be produced; the translation shall be certified by a person qualified to do so in one of the contracting States.[207] No legalisation or other similar formality is required in respect of any of these documents.[208]

200. Convention, Article 43.
201. Convention, Article 44.
202. Convention, Article 44.
203. I.e. Articles 46–9 of the Convention.
204. Convention, Article 46.
205. Convention, Article 46.
206. Convention, Article 48.
207. Convention, Article 48.
208. Convention, Article 49.

A party applying for enforcement shall also produce: (a) documents which establish that, according to the law of the State of origin the judgment is enforceable and has been served; and (b) where appropriate, a document showing that the applicant is in receipt of legal aid in the State of origin.[209] If the documents referred to under heading (b) are not produced then the court may specify a time for their production, accept equivalent documents or, if it considers that it has sufficient information before it, dispense with their production.[210] If the court so requires, a translation of the documents shall be produced; the translation shall be certified by a person qualified to do so in one of the contracting States.[211] No legalisation or other similar formality is required in respect of any of these documents.[212]

25.4.5 Authentic instruments and court settlements

Article 50 of the Convention provides:

"A document which has been formally drawn up or registered as an authentic instrument and is enforceable in one Contracting State shall, in another Contracting State, be declared enforceable there, on application made in accordance with the procedures provided for in Article 31 *et seq.* The application may be refused only if enforcement of the instrument is contrary to public policy in the State addressed.

The instrument produced must satisfy the conditions necessary to establish its authenticity in the State of origin.

The provisions of Section 3 of Title III[213] shall apply as appropriate."

25.4.5.1 Approved settlements

Article 51 of the Convention deals with the situation where a settlement has been approved by a court. The Article provides: "A settlement which has been approved by a court in the course of proceedings and is enforceable in the State in which it was concluded shall be enforceable in the State addressed under the same conditions as authentic instruments."

25.5 MISCELLANEOUS MATTERS

Article 54a of the Convention[214] provides:

"For a period of three years from 1 November 1986 for Denmark and from 1 June 1988 for Ireland, jurisdiction in maritime matters shall be determined in these States not only in accordance with the provisions of Title II, but also in accordance with the provisions of paragraphs 1 to 6 following. However, upon the entry into force of the International Convention relating to the arrest of sea-going ships, signed at Brussels on 10 May 1952, for one of these States, these provisions shall cease to have effect for that State.

"1. A person who is domiciled in a Contracting State may be sued in the courts of one of the States mentioned above in respect of a maritime claim if the ship to which the claim relates or any other ship owned by him has been arrested by judicial process within the territory of the latter

209. Convention, Article 47.
210. Convention, Article 48.
211. Convention, Article 48.
212. Convention, Article 49.
213. On s. 3 of Title III of the Convention, see para. 25.3.4, above.
214. As added by Article 17 of the 1989 Accession Convention.

State to secure the claim, or could have been so arrested there but bail or other security has been given, and either:

(a) the claimant is domiciled in the latter State; or
(b) the claim arose in the latter State; or
(c) the claim concerns the voyage during which the arrest was made or could have been made; or
(d) the claim arises out of a collision or out of damage caused by a ship to another ship or to goods or persons on board either ship, either by the execution or non-execution of a manoeuvre or by the non-observance of regulations; or
(e) the claim is for salvage; or
(f) the claim is in respect of a mortgage or hypothecation of the ship arrested.

2. A claimant may arrest either the particular ship to which the maritime claim relates, or any other ship which is owned by the person who was, at the time when the maritime claim arose, the owner of the particular ship. However, only the particular ship to which the maritime claim relates may be arrested in respect of the maritime claims set out in (5)(o), (p) or (q) of this Article.

3. Ships shall be deemed to be in the same ownership when all the shares therein are owned by the same person or persons.

4. When in the case of a charter by demise of a ship the charterer alone is liable in respect of a maritime claim relating to that ship, the claimant may arrest that ship or any other ship owned by the charterer, but no other ship owned by the owner may be arrested in respect of such claim. The same shall aply to any case in which a person other than the owner of a ship is liable in respect of a maritime claim relating to that ship.

5. The expression "maritime claim" means a claim arising out of one or more of the following:

(a) damage caused by any ship either in collision or otherwise;
(b) loss of life or personal injury caused by any ship or occurring in connection with the operation on any ship;
(c) salvage;
(d) agreement relating to the use or hire of any ship whether by charterparty or otherwise;
(e) agreement relating to the carriage of goods in any ship whether by charterparty or otherwise;
(f) loss of or damage to goods including baggage carried in any ship;
(g) general average;
(h) bottomry;
(i) towage;
(j) pilotage;
(k) goods or materials wherever supplied to a ship for her operation or maintenance;
(l) construction, repair or equipment of any ship or dock charges and dues;
(m) wages of masters, officers or crew;
(n) master's disbursements, including disbursements made by shippers, charterers or agents on behalf of a ship or her owner;
(o) dispute as to the title to or ownership of any ship;
(p) disputes between co-owners of any ship as to the ownership, possession, employment or earnings of that ship;
(q) the mortgage or hypothecation of any ship.

6. In Denmark, the expression 'arrest' shall be deemed as regards the maritime claims referred to in 5(o) and (p) of this Article, to include a 'forbud', where that is the only procedure allowed in respect of such a claim under Articles 656 to 653 of the law on civil procedure (lov om rettens pleje)."

An interesting miscellaneous aspect of the Convention is the critically important fact that it is now more difficult to obtain security for costs in the English courts against a foreign plaintiff where that person is domiciled in a contracting State.[215]

215. See Bercow, "Security for Costs Europe and Beyond", *Lloyd's List*, 13 December 1991, p. 5, as well as *Berkeley Administration Inc. v. McClelland* [1990] 1 All ER 958.

CHAPTER 26

The Challenges of the Internal Market for Shipping: the 1992 Programme

26.1 INTRODUCTION

26.1.1 Need to be aware of the 1992 programme and "Maastricht"

It is imperative for all shipping companies (whether based in the EC or not) to examine the concept, contents and consequences of the EC's Internal Market Programme (the so-called "1992 Programme" or "Single Market Programme") both generally in terms of the economy as a whole and particularly in relation to shipping.[1] It is equally imperative to appreciate the trend towards economic and monetary union in the EC. The dramatic increase in trade due to the 1992 Programme, and the consequential creation of the largest single market in the world, will mean a consequential increase in the goods and passengers carried on European shipping.

26.1.2 Great changes

The world generally and Europe particularly are undergoing metamorphic changes at present. The easing of the USA–USSR Cold War, the opening up of Eastern Europe, the breaking-up of the USSR and the Internalisation[2] of the EC's market are individually staggering events but to have the three occurring simultaneously is nothing short of spectacular.

1. See the Commission's White Paper to the Council of Ministers, "Completing the Internal Market" of June 1985.

There is no shortage of literature on the 1992 Programme. Among the most useful publications are Butt, "Implementing the European Internal Market: Problem and Prospects," (1988); Calingaert, *The 1992 Challenge from Europe: Development of the European Community's Internal Market* (1988); *Cecchini, 1992: The Benefits of a Single Market* (1988); Clifford Chance, *Guide to 1993* (2nd edn., 1990); Cutler *et al.*, *1992—The Struggle for Europe* (1989); Dewhurst, *Your Business in 1992* (1989); Dudley, *1992: Strategies for the Single Market* (Rev.edn., 1990); EC, *Europe Without Frontiers* (1987); Emerson *et al.*, *The Economics of 1992: The EC Commission's Assessment of the Economic Effects of Completing the Internal Market* (1988); Featherstone, *The Successful Manager's Guide to 1992* (1990); Heseltine, *The Challenge of Europe: Can Britain Win?* (1989); Lodge, *The European Community and the Challenge of the Future* (1989); Owen and Dynes, *The Times Guide to 1992* (1989); Broderick and Calmann, "Introduction to a New Europe: A Primer for 1992", *International Business Lawyer*, January 1992, p. 9; Mayer, "The Single European Market now part of the UK business culture", *Lloyd's List*, 17 April 1989, p. 10; O'Connor, "Oil majors confident about Single Market", *Lloyd's List*, 12 April 1989, p. 5. See also the GCBS' paper "1992—The EC Internal Market: Impact on Shipping".

2. As well as possible federalisation.

26.1.3 Prospect of "1992"

Businesses throughout the world are making detailed plans for the advent of the EC's single market. Cross-border mergers and acquisitions grew to an all-time high in the late 1980s. International joint ventures are becoming ever more popular. Many companies are engaging in language training, asset acquisition and product development on scales never before witnessed in Europe.

26.1.4 Objectives of the EC

The 1992 Programme is best understood when one reviews the objectives of the EC and one bears in mind that by the early or mid-1980s it looked as if many of these objectives would never be met. Article 2 of the EEC Treaty provides:

"The Community shall have as its task, by establishing a common market and progressively approximating the economic policies of Member States, to promote throughout the Community a harmonious development of economic activities, a continuous and balanced expansion, an increase in stability, an accelerated raising of the standard of living and closer relations between the States belonging to it."

The EC had achieved a great deal in its first thirty years: tariffs and quantitative restrictions affecting trade between EC States were abolished, that is to say, a Customs Union was established. Moreover, a Common Customs Tariff[3] was created so that the EC was not just a Customs Union but also a single economic zone of sorts. None the less, many Non-Tariff Barriers (NTBs) remained. By the mid-1980s, the internal or common market seemed illusory. Something had to be done. The remedy chosen by the EC Member States was the so-called "1992 Programme" or "Internal Market Programme".

26.2 THE CONCEPT OF THE INTERNAL MARKET

The Internal Market comprises of "an area without internal frontiers in which the free movement of goods, persons, services and capital is ensured in accordance with the provisions" of the EEC Treaty.[4]

It is anticipated that the EC will be a self-contained unit. Article 8A of the EEC Treaty (as inserted by the Single European Act[5] (the "SEA")) envisages that the internal market will be achieved by 31 December 1992. This market would consist of over 350 million people and be the largest trade bloc in the world.

26.3 THE RATIONALE FOR THE INTERNAL MARKET

What is the rationale behind the drive to complete the Internal Market by 31 December 1992?[6]

3. I.e. the same tariff would be applied to the same type of product wherever it is being imported into the EC.

4. EEC Treaty, Article 8A. On Article 8A, see Editorial in (1989) 26 CML Rev. 1

5. On the SEA, see Chapter 3, above.

6. See Clifford Chance, *op. cit.*, Chapter 3 and Giersch, "Eurosclerosis—What is the Cure?" [1987] 4 *European Affairs* 33.

26.3.1 Revitalisation of EC industry

26.3.1.1 Problems

EC industry was in the slow lane by the mid-1970s/early 1980s.[7] The EC's share of world trade had fallen significantly over the years. Meanwhile, the Americans and the Japanese were expanding their world trade shares while the EC was suffering. The indicators were obvious. In the 1979-1985 period, the US increased its share of world trade by 0.7% and the Japanese by as much as 5.4% but the EC's share fell by 1.4%. This was most noticeable in the technology sector where, during the same period, the EC's share fell by 2.2% while the US share rose by 3.3% and Japan's share increased by a staggering 5.5%. During that same time, investment in the EC was poorer than in either the US or Japan: investment in the US and Japan rose by 30% and 31% respectively while the EC achieved a growth of investment of only 4%—over seven times worse. Productivity in the EC was much less than in the US and shamefully less than comparable productivity in Japan. One statistic brings this point home. For every one unit produced in the EC's electrical goods sector, two were produced in the US and five in Japan. Commentators spoke of "Eurosclerosis". The world was looking elsewhere than the EC for development (particularly, the Pacific Basin).

26.3.1.2 Cure

The United States of America is a single and reasonably well integrated market. On the contrary, the EC was essentially twelve separate and small markets. Its divisions led to inefficiencies. An obvious solution was to integrate or internalise the twelve markets into one and thereby reduce costs[8] (i.e. benefiting from economies of scale by pooling expenses such as research, development, production and distribution) and harnessing the competitive pressures from a more efficient market. It was thought that the EC needed liberal "supply-side" economics in conjunction with some attendant reflationary demand-side stimulants. The economies of scale of a giant[9] single market were too good to be ignored according to the proposers of the 1992 programme.

26.3.2 Revitalisation of the EC organisation

26.3.2.1 Problem

International organisations often involve more promise than performance. The United Nations has not achieved the hopes and aspirations declared at the San Francisco Conference and set out in the Charter of the United Nations. The Council of Europe has proved successful in only a few areas. Similarly, the political momentum of the EC appeared to have gone by the early 1980s, (if not the late 1970s). The speed of progress in the late 1950s and 1960s was not maintained. The EC appeared lethargic by the late 1970s and early 1980s. The two oil crises in the 1970s, the recessions and the political instability within the EC caused their problems. It was even beginning to look like a failure or, at least, not the success hoped for by many. Changes were needed.

7. See Albert and Ball, "Towards European Recovery in the 1980s", Working Documents 1983–1984, European Parliament, Luxembourg.
8. *Cf.* Cecchini, *op. cit.*, *passim.*
9. The EC represents approximately 20% of world trade.

26.3.2.2 Cure

The Member States decided (consciously or unconsciously), by agreeing to the 1992 Programme, to revitalise the EC. The organisation now had a common task—the completion of the Internal Market. The Member States decided to support a process of revitalisation and rejuvenation because the economic and hence political benefits were almost certain.[10]

26.4 BACKGROUND TO THE INTERNAL MARKET PROGRAMME

26.4.1 Introduction

The journey to "1992" has been long and unpredictable. The signatories to the Treaty of Rome which established the EEC in 1957 intended that a Community Customs Union be established which meant that all customs duties and quantitative restrictions as well as all charges and other measures having an equivalent effect on imports and exports between Member States were to be abolished. The framers of the Treaty of Rome intended that a Common Customs Tariff would be established which would mean that the same level of tariffs would be charged on all goods imported from non-Member States. The customs duties were abolished between the original Six by 1968. The Common Customs Tariff was created but this was not enough.[11]

The six new Member States acceding in 1973, 1981 and 1985 interrupted the progress. The recession and oil crises of the 1970s as well as political in-fighting slowed up progress.

26.4.2 Progress

Progress was needed but was difficult to achieve.[12] The European Council had made a number of declarations relating to the need to establish an Internal Market. The Commission proposed measures in 1982 so as to free trade in the EC. In Copenhagen, at its meeting on 3–4 December 1982, the European Council had declared that it "instructs the Council [of Ministers] . . . to decide, before the end of March 1983, on the priority measures proposed by the Commission to reinforce the internal market." In Fontainebleau, the European Council, at its meeting on 25 and 26 June 1984, asked

10. Cutler *et al.*, *1992—The Struggle for Europe* (1989) comment (at page 45): "it is necessary to emphasise that the 1992 programme for removing [Non-Tariff Barriers] and creating a single market is an economic instrument which serves the political end of European unification.

11. It has been written (in Cutler *et al.*, *1992—The Struggle for Europe* (1989), at page 44): "[t]he abolition of tariffs twenty years ago did not create a single, integrated market. A variety of non-tariff barriers continued to impede the free movement of goods, capital and labour within the EC. These non-tariff barriers, or NTBs, include a variety of border controls and checks, differences in national technical regulations and standards, government preferences for domestic procedures in public procurement, exchange controls, fluctuating exchange controls, fluctuating exchange rates and differences in national tax regimes. Under the 1992 programme, the EC proposes to remove many of these barriers and promises to create a single integrated market."

12. It is worth noting that the progress was achieved only after much consideration (note the Tindemans Report (1975), the Spierenburg Report (1979), the Solemn Declaration on European Union (1983), the Draft Treaty on European Union (the so-called Spinelli Treaty) (1984), the Adonnino Report (1985) and, the Dooge Report (1985)) and controversy (note the resistance by Denmark, Greece and the UK to an inter-governmental conference being held in Luxembourg in 1985 to discuss European Union as well as the referenda on the Single European Act in Denmark and Ireland).

the Council of Ministers and the Member States "to put in hand without delay a study of the measures which could be taken to bring about in the near future . . . the abolition of all police and customs formalities for people crossing intra-Community frontiers". Six months later, at its Dublin Summit, the European Council agreed that the Council of Ministers "should take steps to complete the Internal Market, including implementation of European standards". The Commission in its Programme for 1985 then asked the European Council "to pledge itself to completion of a fully unified internal market by 1992 and to approve the necessary programme together with a realistic and binding timetable". Finally, at the Brussels Summit on 29 and 30 March 1985, the European Council "laid particular emphasis on [the need] to achieve a single large market by 1992 thereby creating a more favourable environment for stimulating enterprise, competition and trade [and] called upon the Commission to draw up a detailed programme with a specific timetable before its next meeting".

The Commission's White Paper presented to the Europe Council, "Completing the Internal Market"[13] in June 1985 was the detailed programme containing a specific timetable. It was designed to "spell out the programme and timetable"[14] for the completion of the Internal Market. The Paper contained some 43 proposals relating to agriculture, 33 relating to taxation, 25 relating to food, 23 relating to trade, 18 relating to medicine, 17 relating to transport, 16 relating to machinery, 13 relating to the chemical industry, 9 relating to company law, 9 relating to customs barriers, 9 relating to technology, 9 relating to banking, 9 relating to insurance, 8 relating to education, 8 relating to social policy, 6 dealing with consumer protection, 6 relating to public procurement, 6 relating to securities, 5 relating to the environment, 4 relating to capital movements, 3 dealing with telecommunications, 2 relating to copyright, 2 relating to biotechnology as well as 1 each relating to competition and tourism. If the Programme is followed to the letter then economists (appointed by the Commission) estimate that the reduction in costs will be in the order of 89 to 110 billion ECU and the benefits of more effective competition in the EC marketplace could be in the order of 84 billion to 147 billion ECU.[15]

Thus, the benefits of the 1992 Programme would amount to somewhere between 173 billion to 257 billion ECU. The estimates are that the collective Gross Domestic Product of the EC Member States will increase by some 4.5% to 7%; consumer prices will fall by between 4.5% and 6%; as well as between 1.75 million and 5 million jobs would be created. One of the EC's most important missions appears likely to be achieved on 31 December 1992—a quarter of a century late! It has been written that the

> "internal market programme was based on the belief that by dismantling [the] non-tariff barriers a supply-side shock, in conjunction with some reflationary demand-side measures, would give a major boost to trade within the EC, creating new jobs, and would allow Community-based firms to compete more effectively in the wider world market".[16]

The Internal Market Programme would have been difficult to achieve given the traditional requirement of unanimous voting in the Council of Ministers. The legislative regime needed to be changed. The SEA[17] was to be the instrument of

13. COM(85) 310.
14. Commission White Paper, *Completing the Internal Market*, para. 3.
15. The range of these figures typifies the inexactitude associated with the predictions of the gains and effects of the Internal Market generally.
16. Featherstone, *op. cit.*, p. 5.
17. On the SEA, see Chapter 3, above.

change. It was signed in 1986 and entered into force on 1 July 1987. It changed the EC's law-making process allowing for speedier decisions, allowed for majority voting in certain circumstances and laid the foundation for development of particular EC policies. The completion of the internal market is one of the most important of these policies.[18]

It might never have been possible to adopt the 1992 Programme if the Council of Ministers still operated a unanimous voting rule.

The Internal White Paper of June 1985 contained some 300 proposals. These 300 were later reduced to 279 because a few were withdrawn and others were combined with others. The Commission tabled 175 of the 279 by May 1987. The Commission had submitted 208 proposals to the Council of Ministers and the Council had completely adopted 69 of them by March 1988. By the end of 1988, the 1992 Programme was declared by the Commission in its Half-Way Report to be "irreversible". The proposals are designed to overcome "The Three Barriers". Three main barriers to market efficiency and internalisation have been diagnosed: physical barriers (such as customs, excise and immigration posts); technical barriers (such as varying standards and regulations); and fiscal barriers. Surveys of industrialists indicate that the physical and technical barriers are the most irksome and costly to EC businesses. These three barriers form the rubric of the discussion below of the Internal Market Programme.

The completion of the internal market is not an event—it is a process. The process is in train but there is no guarantee that the market will be fully internalised by 31 December 1992. The dates which have been set down are targets and not deadlines. None the less, even if the EC adopts all the appropriate measures (the Regulations, Directives and so on) by 31 December 1992, is that the end? Is that it? Clearly not. It is important to remember that Directives require incorporation into the domestic law of the Member States. This incorporation may be made later than 31 December 1992.[19]

It may be done inadequately or it may be done incompletely and there will be cases brought against Member States for failure to properly implement the Directives. It would not surprise me if the internal market is the cause of disputes in the Council, arguments in the Commission and cases in the ECJ right up until the end of the millenium.

26.5 THE CONTENTS OF THE INTERNAL MARKET PROGRAMME

26.5.1 Physical barriers[20]

26.5.1.2 Introduction

There are physical impediments and barriers to free trade in the EC. Customs posts and immigration barriers are obvious examples. These barriers are there for such purposes as the enforcement of national trade quotas and revenue laws, the operation of agricultural compensation schemes, the examination of animals and foodstuffs as well as the collection of duties and statistics. They all cost time and money: perhaps as much as 8.3 billion ECU. Such barriers can also sap Community spirit—EC citizens who are

18. EEC Treaty, Article 8A as inserted by the SEA.
19. Delays are notorious—e.g. the Product Liability Directive.
20. See the Commission's White Paper to the Council of Ministers, "Completing the Internal Market" of June 1985, Part One and Clifford Chance, *The CCH Guide to 1993: Changes in EEC Law* (1989), 202–204.

stopped, searched and questioned at various borders do not feel part of one Community. These physical barriers are of greatest significance in five countries (namely, Belgium, Greece, Italy, Portugal and Spain) and such industries as agriculture, textiles, fibres, mineral oil refining, tourism and leather.

It is estimated that the existence of these barriers costs 8.3 billion ECU which amount to 1.7% of total intra-EC trade. Physical barriers affect all businesses but especially the smaller ones who cannot cope with the red-tape involved in a small volume of transactions. Progress is needed, especially in the Mediterranean States and Belgium where the problems associated with physical barriers appear to be at their worst. None the less there are opponents to the notion of removing physical barriers because of the possible spread of terrorism, drugs and other criminal activities. There is also a fiscal dimension to removing the physical borders in that "fiscal shopping" will be easier. The elimination of the physical barriers will be of greatest relevance to Belgium, Greece, Italy, Portugal and Spain.

26.5.1.3 Movement of goods

26.5.1.3.1 Introduction

The existence of border posts slows down the transport of goods and services[21] around the EC. These border posts will remain for so long as there are fiscal differences between the Member States.

26.5.1.3.2 Single administrative document

The introduction of the Single Administrative Document (SAD)[22] on 1 January 1988 has accelerated the speed at which goods move around the EC. Before the SAD there was a plethora of differing forms (up to 100) which had to be completed at border posts. Since the introduction of the SAD there has been only one form (the SAD) which is a standard form which is readily comprehensible to everyone involved in transporting goods around the EC.

26.5.1.3.3 Quota system

The Council of Ministers adopted Regulation 1841/88[23] to abolish all national bilateral quotas on the carriage of goods between Member States from 1 January 1991. This new system replaces the pre-existing regime which involved a complex series of bilateral agreements between Member States. This series of bilateral agreements often led to inefficiency: for example, a lorry might deliver goods to Germany from France but might have to travel back empty because of a lack of a quota.

26.5.1.3.4 Cabotage of goods

The abolition of the quota system did not liberalise the road transport market completely. The abolition of the quota system allowed hauliers to travel around the EC

21. I.e. where persons providing services have to clear their equipment at sea, air and land border posts.
22. OJ L79, 21 March 1985. See *New Law Journal*, 14 August 1987, p. 763.
23. OJ 1988 L163/1. This Regulation was strongly opposed by Germany.

but did not allow them to offer their services within another Member State (cabotage).[24] The Commission proposed the abolition of cabotage.[25]

In December 1989, the Council of Ministers adopted a diluted form of cabotage. Regulation No. 4059/89[26] provided that from 1 July 1990 Member States will be supplied with 15,000 cabotage permits which would be valid for two months or up to 30,000 such permits for one month. The number increases by ten per cent. each year until the end of 1992. The mater will then be reviewed.

26.5.1.3.5 Customs presentation charges

The Council of Ministers has adopted a measure to provide for the abolition of customs presentation charges.[27]

26.5.1.3.6 Transit advice note

A transit advice note which would be produced each time an external EC border is crossed on the same trip has been introduced.[28]

26.5.1.3.7 Veterinary checks

The Council of Ministers has adopted a number of Directives so as to abolish veterinary and phytosanitary border controls.[29]

26.5.1.3.8 Size of trucks on EC roads

The UK and Ireland imposed a limit of 38 tonnes on trucks using their roads. At the June 1989 Transport Ministers Council, both countries agreed to abide by the EC-wide standard of 40 tonnes but have until 1999 to comply with the change.

26.5.1.3.9 Banalisation

In December 1988, the Council of Ministers adopted Reg. No. 4283/88[30] providing for the introduction of common border posts whereby all formalities are confined to one border post instead of the present two posts. This is a process known as banalisation.

26.5.1.4 Movement of persons

Prior to the 1992 Programme, the EC had made considerable progress in facilitating the free movement of persons between the EC Member States. In 1981, the Council of Ministers approved the introduction of a European Passport.[31]

24. On cabotage generally, see Chapter 7, above.
25. COM(85)611.
26. OJ 1989 L390/3.
27. OJ L157, 12 June 1986.
28. OJ L51, 27 February 1990.
29. See COM(90) 90 fin, Annex I, pp. 4–13.
30. OJ 1988 L 382/1.
31. This is a standard, EC-wide passport issued by each Member State but in a common format and style.

26.5.1.4.1 Schengen Agreement

A number of Member States (namely, Belgium, France, Germany, the Netherlands and Luxembourg) concluded an Agreement known as the Schengen Agreement[32] on 14 June 1985 which abolished border controls between themselves in 1990 instead of the proposed 1993. The entry into force of this Agreement was delayed by events in Eastern Europe (most notably, the Unification of Germany[33]) but after the signing of some Complementary Agreements, the Agreement entered into force on 19 June 1990. The Schengen Agreement was similar to the earlier Benelux Union Treaty of 1958 which transferred all controls on the movement of peoples between Belgium, Luxembourg and the Netherlands to the external border. As an aside, one must question the compatibility of such agreements which afford special treatment to some EC nationals but not to all with Article 7 of the EEC Treaty which prohibits discrimination between EC nationals in respect of matters covered by that Treaty.

26.5.1.4.2 Asylum

Following discussions at the June 1990 Dublin Summit, the EC is working on a common external policy in the area of asylum.[34]

26.5.1.4.3 Non-active persons

The Council of Ministers has long discussed the rights of so-called "non-active persons" (i.e. students, retired persons and those persons who would not otherwise hold the right to reside in an EC Member State) to reside in the EC. The right of such people to reside is a troublesome issue for some States because these people are net beneficiaries from the economy of the State rather than contributors (in an economic sense). The debate has raged for many years.[35]

The Council of Ministers reached political agreement on them in December 1989. The Directive has been finally adopted.[36]

The material significance of them is that, for example, a British retired seafarer would have the right to retire to Spain.

26.5.2 Technical barriers[37]

26.5.2.1 Introduction[38]

The Commission stated in its June 1985 White Paper on the Internal Market:

". . . barriers created by different national product regulations and standards have a double-edged effect: they not only add extra costs, but they also distort production patterns; increase

32. Named after the town where the Agreement was signed.

33. I.e. the unification of the Federal Republic of Germany and the former German Democratic Republic.

34. The right of a national from one State (or no State) to remain in another State. This is a highly political issue which is now to be seen in the context of the Maastricht Treaty.

35. The debate has raged since the 1970s.

36. OJ L180, 13 July 1990.

37. See the Commission's White Paper to the Council of Ministers, "Completing the Internal Market" of June 1985, Part Two; Clifford Chance, *The CCH Guide to 1993: Changes in EEC Law* (1989), 204–205; and EC Commission, *The Removal of Technical Barriers to Trade*, European File 18/88 (1988).

38. The cost of technical barriers has not yet been fully established but from a survey of a basket of industries which constitute 43% of the EC's total industrial output, technical barriers cost the EC some three to four billion ECUs.

unit costs; increase stock holding costs; discourage business co-operation, and fundamentally frustrate the creation of a common market for industrial products. Until such barriers are removed, Community manufacturers are forced to focus on national rather than Continental markets and are unable to benefit from the economics of scale which a truly unified internal market offers."[39]

Divergent technical standards caused serious problems in such areas as financial services, construction, safety, taxation and, most importantly (for present purposes), transport.

26.5.2.2 The Commission's White Paper

The EC has traditionally used two approaches to overcome technical standards: the first involves mutual recognition of standards while the second involves the harmonisation of differing standards.

The mutual recognition approach is embodied in the so-called *Cassis de Dijon* case.[40]

In this case, the ECJ held that where a product is lawfully produced and marketed in one Member State then it should be capable of being sold without restriction[41] in any of the other Member States. That is to say, the standards of one Member State (i.e. the State of Production) would be mutually recognised by the other Member State (i.e. the State of Sale). This approach is useful but limited: it depends on a case being brought to the ECJ and does not deal with cases where differing national standards address similar public interest issues in different ways.[42]

Thus the Commission has also sought to *harmonise* the technical standards relating to each product. While the Commission has used this approach for over a quarter of a century, the results were not good because the Council of Ministers normally had to decide on each new standard on the basis of a unanimous vote. Such an approach was slow and sometimes led to comical results[43]

The Commission proposed in its June 1985 White Paper on the Internal Market[44] a "new approach" to technical barriers. The White Paper proposed that in some sectors there should be a distinction between essential safety requirements (which are to be established by the Council of Ministers[45] in harmonisation Directives) and technical specifications (which are to be established by European or national standards). The European standards would be set by such organisations as the European Committee for Standardisation (CEN), the European Committee for Electrotechnical Standardisation (CENLEC) and the European Telecommunications Standardisation Institute (ETSI). If a product is tested, approved and certified (according to national and European standards) in an exporting EC Member State then it may benefit from free movement throughout the EC on the basis of the principle of mutual recognition.[46]

39. COM 85 (310).
40. Case 120/78 *Rewe-Zentral AG v Bundesmonopolverwaltung für Branntwein* [1979] ECR 649, (known as the *Cassis de Dijon* case).
41. Subject to such exceptions as public health, consumer protection etc.
42. Clifford Chance, *op. cit.*, para. 205.
43. E.g. the apocryphal standardisation of the sausage, ice cream and the "pint" of beer are examples of the type of process involved.
44. See also COM(85)19 final: *Technical Harmonisation and Standards: A New Approach.*
45. Since the SEA, unanimous votes may not be essential in all cases.
46. See Case 120/78 *Rewe-Zentral AG v Bundesmonopolverwaltung für Branntwein* [1979] ECR 649, (known as the *Cassis de Dijon* case).

And in other sectors, standards would be set by national authorities but there would be a system of mutual recognition of each other's standards. Harmonisation would be at a minimum whereas maximum use would be made of mutual recognition: harmonise the essentials[47] and mutually recognise the rest.

The new system has worked well for pressure vessels,[48] toys,[49] construction products,[50] electrical interference/electro-magnetic compatibility and machine safety.[51]

26.5.2.3 New standards

In order to prevent new technical standards becoming barriers to trade, Directive 83/189[52] obliges Member States to notify the Commission in advance of proposed regulations setting down technical standards.

26.5.2.4 Mutual recognition of qualifications

A significant technical barrier to the free movement of persons around the EC is the frequent non-recognition by some Member States of qualifications issued by other Member States.

Some progress has been made to have mutual recognition of diplomas and vocational training. Other progress has related to doctors,[53] nurses,[54] dentists,[55] architects, pharmacists and midwives.[56] Such progress has been slow and long-drawn out. For example, it took fifteen years to agree measures relating to architects.

The Commission[57] decided[58] that the best approach is to harmonise in a number of sectors the minimum requirements for qualification, experience and supervised training but leave the rest to "mutual recognition". The Council of Ministers has thus adopted a Directive on a general system for the recognition of higher education diplomas awarded on completion of professional education and training of at least three years' duration.[59]

26.5.2.5 Capital movements

The barriers to free movement of capital between EC Member States are significant impediments to the creation of an integrated market.

26.5.2.6 Free movement of capital

The Council of Ministers adopted Directive 88/361[60] requiring Member States to abolish restrictions on capital movements between persons resident in different EC

47. E.g. health, safety and consumer concerns.
48. OJ L220/87, 8 August 1987.
49. OJ L187/88, 16 July 1988.
50. OJ L40/89 of 11 February 1989.
51. OJ L183/89, 29 June 1989.
52. OJ 1983 L109/8 (as amended by Dir.88/182, OJ L81/75).
53. 1976.
54. 1979.
55. 1980.
56. 1983.
57. 1983.
58. In the 1992 White Paper.
59. Dir. 89/48, OJ 1989 L19/16.
60. OJ 1988 L178/5, 8 July 1988.

Member States. The Directive entered into force on 1 July 1990. Some Member States obtained derogations until 1992 to comply with the Directive. The Directive has huge significance. It will allow anyone the possibility of depositing or borrowing money anywhere in the EC.

26.5.2.7 Balance of payments

The Council of Ministers adopted Regulation 1969/88[61] designed to provide medium-term financial support to Member States' balances of payments.

26.5.3 Public procurement[62]

26.5.3.1 Introduction

One area where technical standards raise their ugly head is that of public procurement.[63]

Public procurement means the purchase by governmental organisations and agencies of goods and services for public consumption. There is no doubt that this is a very large market but its exact size has proved difficult to estimate. Estimates vary from 240 billion to 340 billion ECU or, put another way, 6.8% to 9.8% of the EC's GDP. Public procurement problems are very serious in Italy and Spain.[64]

It would be naive to imagine that these contracts are placed at home because the home suppliers are cheaper—they are placed at home for simple nationalistic and political reasons whatever the economic cost.[65]

If the public procurement process was opened up then how much would be saved? Cecchini estimates that the saving (based on 1984 figures) would be in the order of 4.4 billion ECU.[66]

Partial progress has been achieved—particularly by the adoption of Public Supply Directive 88/295[67] which has strengthened the pre-existing situation very much[68]—but this progress has only been partial in that it applies only to large (200,000+ ECU) contracts and not in the water, energy or transport sectors or indeed, telecommunications. Transport is one of those industries which has benefited most from such nationalism.

26.5.3.2 Supplies

Directive 88/295 on public supplies entered into force on 1 January 1989.[69]

61. OJ 1988 L178/1.
62. Clifford Chance, *op. cit.*, para. 512 *et seq.*
63. See Clifford Chance, *The CCH Guide to 1993: Changes in EEC Law* (1989), 205 and 509. See also Dir. No.88/295, OJ 1988 L 127/1; Dir. No.89/440, OJ 1989 L210/1; and Dir. No.89/665, OJ 1989 L 395/33.
64. See Clifford Chance, *The CCH Guide to 1993: Changes in EEC Law* (1989), 304.
65. Interestingly, EC governments award more public procurement in some industries to non-EC undertakings than to undertakings from other EC States; for example, in the construction industry, US contractors won six billion ECUs of public procurement contracts in 1986 in the EC but EC undertakings won only 0.6 billion ECUs in the same market in the same year.
66. This figure has been disputed by some economists.
67. OJ 1988 L 127/1.
68. *Cf.* Directives 71/304, 71/305, 71/306, 77/62 and 80/767.
69. OJ 1988 L127/1.

26.5.3.3 Public works

Directive 89/440 on public works entered into force on 19 July 1990 (except for Greece, Portugal and Spain where it enters into force on 1 March 1992).[70]

The Directive covered regional and local authorities in the Member States as well as bodies governed by public law. The financial threshold was raised from ECU 1 million to ECU 5 million. Transparency of tendering was improved. It excluded the water, energy, transport and communication industries.

26.5.3.4 Water, energy, transport and communication

The original EC public procurement rules did not extend to the water, energy, transport and communication industries (the "WETT industries"). A measure has now been adopted so as to include the WETT industries within the public procurement rules.

26.5.3.5 Procedural rules for the award of public procurement contracts

Directive 89/665[71] established a harmonisation mechanism on the application of procedural rules for the award of public supply and public works contracts. It is a monitoring mechanism. The Directive allows the Commission to intervene and examine on an urgent basis an alleged infringement of the public procurement rules even before the contract is awarded.

26.5.3.6 Company law[72]

26.5.3.6.1 Introduction

The diverse technical rules relating to companies cause difficulties for businesses in Europe. If a business wishes to sell its services in the twelve Member States then it may have to establish twelve separate companies—each having their own separate rules. For example, a ferry business operating between Britain and the Netherlands may well establish a number of English and Dutch companies to perform various functions (for example, marketing, port services, freight forwarding and so on). Sometimes this plethora of companies is desirable for tax planning but very often it is more of an encumbrance than a bonus.

EC company law is concerned with such matters as corporate structures, control of mergers and acquisitions, accounting, protection of the public and development of Small and Medium-Sized Enterprises (SMEs).

26.5.3.6.2 Merger control regulation[73]

The Council of Ministers adopted Regulation 4064/89[74] on 21 December 1989. This Regulation, known popularly as the Merger Control Regulation, provides an EEC-

70. OJ 1989 L210/1.
71. OJ 1989 L395/33.
72. See Prentice, *EEC Directives on Company Law and Financial Markets* (1991).
73. There is an extensive literature available on the Regulation: see Cook and Kerse, *EEC Merger Regulation* (1991) and the literature cited therein.
74. OJ L257/13, 21 September 1990.

based mechanism for the control of large-scale concentrations. It entered into force on 21 September 1990. The Regulation demarcates the competence of the Commission and the Member State to deal with large mergers and acquisitions (collectively referred to in the Regulation as "Concentrations"): the Commission will normally deal with the concentrations which have a "Community Dimension" while the Member States will deal with the others. A concentration has a "Community Dimension" where:

"— the aggregrate worldwide turnover of all the undertakings concerned is more than ECU 5 billion; and
— the aggregate Community-wide turnover of at least two of the undertakings concerned is more than ECU 250 million;
— unless more than two-thirds of the EC-wide turnover is in a single EC Member State."

Thus, if a very large shipping company is considering acquiring or merging with another (even though they may both be incorporated outside the EC[75]) then its advisors must advert to the possible application of the Merger Control Regulation. There is a detailed procedure associated with the Regulation[76] and care should be taken that it is closely followed. Non-conformity with the Regulation would expose undertakings to fines and periodic penalties.

26.5.3.6.3 European company statute[77]

If a shipping company wishes to operate in each of the EC Member States then it would have to establish a separate company in each State. It would make sense if one company could operate throughout the EC. Thus, the Commission has proposed the *Societas Europaea* (SE) or European Company based on EC law.[78] It could be formed by the merger[79] of two companies already based in the EC or by the establishment of a subsidiary or holding company. The SE would have its registered office in one of the Member States. The structure of the SE would be similar to that proposed for large companies.

26.5.3.6.4 European economic interest groupings[80]

Council Regulation 2137/85[81] created a new form of corporate structure for EC businesses. The Regulation created the European Economic Interest Grouping (EEIG) which is a non-profit making joint venture-type structure which facilitates co-operation between businesses established in different EC Member States. An EEIG is registered in one of the EC Member States but has a personality which transcends all the Member States. The members of the EEIG retain their independence. It would particularly suit small and medium-sized enterprises. The EEIG is non-profit making in itself: if it makes a profit then such profits are taxable in the hands of the members. The EEIG is tax-transparent. It must have members from two or more EC Member States. An EEIG may not have more than 500 employees. It may not invite subscription for capital from members of the public.

75. Many of the cases under the MCR involve non-EC companies.
76. The procedure contemplates the filing of a form (form CO): see Regulation 4064/89 *passim*.
77. See OJ 1989 C263/41.
78. OJ C176/1, 8 July 1991.
79. See below.
80. See Israel, "The EEIG—A Major Step Forward for Community Law" (1988) 9 *The Company Lawyer* 14; Power, "European Economic Interest Groupings" (1990) ILT 19. See also, "Spanish EEIGs leave the legislative starting blocks," *International Tax Review*, June 1991, p. 29.
81. OJ 1985 L199/1, entered into force on 1 July 1989.

In the context of shipping, companies established in different EC Member States could combine some of their operations through the medium of an EEIG. For example, shipping companies could pool their marketing, accounting, administrative, planning, research or distribution networks through the medium of an EEIG.

26.5.3.6.5 Single-member limited liability companies[82]

The so-called Twelfth Company Law Directive[83] provides for the establishment of a company with one member (i.e. shareholder). This is a legal person unknown to the legal systems of many of the Member States but is quite useful for entrepreneurs acting on their own.

26.5.3.6.6 Disclosure of information by branch offices[84]

The Council of Ministers has decided, by adopting Directive 89/666,[85] that a branch set up in a Member State by a company which is incorporated in another Member State must disclose certain documents and particulars as required by the Member State in which the branch is situate. The purpose of this measure was to equalise the position of branches and subsidiaries.

26.5.3.6.7 Amendments to the directives on accounts[86]

A number of EC Directives[87] require certain corporate bodies to prepare and publish accounts containing certain items of sensitive information (for example, profit levels). These measures do not extend to unlimited companies or partnerships. The Council of Ministers has now remedied this "loophole" and the requirement will soon be extended to them.[88]

Thus, a large shipping limited liability company incorporated in one of the Member States has to publish certain "sensitive" information about itself while unlimited liability ones will have to publish such information in the near future.

26.5.3.6.8 Structure of Public Limited Companies[89]

The Commission proposed the introduction of a two-tier management system for Public Limited Companies (PLCs).[90]

The first tier would consist of a Management Organ which would manage the company. The second tier, the Supervisory Organ, would supervise and control the Management Organ. This system, which is well-established in Germany, is anathema to the British Government and unattractive to some other Governments. The Commission has diluted the proposal somewhat and divided the proposal into two separate proposals.

82. See OJ L395, 30 December 1989, Power, (1990) 2 ICCLR.
83. OJ L395, 30 December 1989
84. Branch means a branch in an EC Member State. OJ L395, 30 December 1989.
85. OJ 1989 L395/36, 30 December 1989.
86. OJ 1989 L395/36, 30 December 1989. The fourth and seventh Company Law Directives deal with the format, content and publication of company accounts.
87. Namely, Dir.78/660 (OJ 1978 L222/11) and 83/349 (OJ 1983 L193/1).
88. Unlimited companies and partnerships which have a limited company as a partner will have to file accounts.
89. This is the successor to the Vreedling Proposal.
90. OJ 1983 C240/2.

26.5.3.6.9 Small and medium-sized enterprises[91]

The EC is anxious to stimulate activity in the small and medium-sized enterprise sector. Thus, it has adopted an Action Programme, created various programmes and provided for the financing of certain enterprises to develop this important sector.

26.5.3.7 Banking[92]

26.5.3.7.1 Introduction

The EC Member States have traditionally had differing technical regulations relating to banking. These barriers have impeded the free movement of services and freedom of establishment. The barriers are illustrated by the example of a bank from one EC Member State which wants to establish a branch in each of the other EC Member States but has to comply with the differing laws of each of those eleven other Member States. The solution would be to have the bank complying with one set of regulations. As it would be too difficult to harmonise all the regulations into one set, it would be much better to have that bank conform with its home regulations and continue to be supervised by its home State regulators.

26.5.3.7.2 Second Banking Directive[93]

The Second Banking Directive was adopted in December 1989.[94] Its purpose is to allow banks established in one EC Member State to offer services or establish branches in other Member States without the need for authorisation from the host States while always remaining under the supervision of the home State. Its significance for banking generally is enormous but its relevance in the context of shipping finance is limited because this banking sector is in any case already one of the most international.

26.5.3.7.3 Own funds Directive[95]

Directive 89/299[96] harmonises the capital requirements of banks by setting standards of capital adequacy and defining common standards for the measurement of "own funds" which a bank must hold.

26.5.3.7.4 Solvency ratio Directive[97]

Directive 89/647[98] gives weighting to each of the risks which a bank may incur when lending money. A bank's own funds must be at least 8 per cent of all its risk assets (including off-balance sheet items). Ship's mortgages have a weighting of 100 per cent.

91. Known in EC jargon as "SMEs".
92. See Adkins, "The Single Banking Market of the EEC: the Story So Far" [1990] 6 JIBL 251; Baltensperger and Dermine, "Banking Deregulation", *Economic Policy*, No. 4, pp. 63–109.
93. OJ L386, 30 December 1989. The First Directive was in 1977.
94. Directive 89/646, OJ 1989 L386/1.
95. OJ L124, 4 May 1989.This relates to the funds which a bank must have.
96. OJ 1989 L124/16.
97. OJ L386, 30 December 1989. This relates to the ratio between own funds and loans. See Stokes, "Significance of Directive on ship purchase finance", *Lloyd's List*, 26 March 1990, p. 2.
98. OJ 1989 L386/14.

26.5.3.7.5 Large exposures[99]

The Commission has recommended that no bank should over-expose itself to one client or client group.[100] In specific terms, it should not expose more than 15 per cent of its own funds to one client. This Recommendation is being converted into a binding measure. It has significance for banks which tend heavily to shipping because of the heavy weighting attached to movable assets.

26.5.3.10 Insurance[101]

26.5.3.10.1 Introduction

The EC Member States have traditionally had differing technical regulations relating to insurance. These barriers have impeded the free movement of services and freedom of establishment. There is as much a need for an internal insurance market as there is a need for an internal banking market. The aims are first, to facilitate insurers to establish themselves anywhere in the EC or to offer services anywhere in the EC while secondly, allowing the prospective insured an opportunity of availing himself of policies from any insurance company in the EC.

The EC Commission has proposed measures in both the life and non-life sectors. This section will concentrate on the non-life sector given its relevance for shipping.

26.5.3.10.2 Non-life insurance

More progress has been achieved in the area of non-life insurance than life insurance. Three framework Directives have been proposed and adopted in this area.

26.5.3.10.3 Freedom of establishment

Directive 73/240[102] provides for freedom of establishment of non-life insurance companies. A non-life insurance company established in one EC Member State may establish itself in another Member State subject to authorisation from the host Member State and compliance with the laws of that host State. This right of establishment was extended to Switzerland by means of an international agreement concluded in October 1989.

26.5.3.10.4 Freedom to provide services[103]

Directive 88/357[104] provides for non-life insurance companies with the right to provide their services in any of the other EC Member States. In the case of large risks,[105]

99. This relates to the degree to which credit institutions may extend themselves, i.e., lending "excessive" amounts to a particular entity or industry.

100. Recommendation No.87/62 (OJ 1987 L33/10).

101. See Dassesse, "EEC Insurance Market and 1992: Significance of Fiscal and Tariff Issues" (1990) LMCLQ 176; Eurostudy Special Report, *Insurance 1992*; Jones, *1992—The Changing Face of Financial Services*.

102. OJ 1973 L228/20.

103. On the difference between freedom of establishment and freedom to provide services see Chapter 6, above.

104. OJ 1988 L172/1.

105. Large risks are classified according to the nature of the risk (including a maritime risk) or to the size of the policyholder.

companies may offer their services freely throughout the EC on the basis of home State control. In the case of mass risks, there is an element of control being exerted by the host State.

26.5.3.10.5 Life insurance

This chapter does not deal with life insurance because it is largely irrelevant for present purposes.

26.5.3.10.6 Reinsurance

Freedom of establishment[106] and freedom to provide insurance services[107] was conferred by Directive 64/225.[108]

26.5.3.10.7 Insurance intermediaries

Intermediaries have the right to carry on business in other EC Member States.

26.5.3.11 Securities

There is a set of measures (many of which have been adopted) relating to securities but as they are not directly relevant they need not detain discussion. These measures include a proposed Investment Services Directive,[109] a Directive concerning the conditions for admission of securities to official Stock Exchange Listing,[110] a Directive on the Particulars in a Prospectus for Admission to Listing,[111] a Directive on Undertakings for Collective Investments in Transferable Securities (UCITS),[112] a Directive providing for the publication of periodic information by listed companies,[113] a Directive on Public Offerings of Non-Listed Securities,[114] an Anti-Raider Directive[115] and a Directive on Insider Dealing.[116]

26.5.3.12 Competition[117]

26.5.3.12.1 Introduction

The Commission wrote in its White Paper:

"A strong competition policy will play a fundamental role in maintaining and strengthening the internal market. It will contribute to an improved allocation of resources and to reinforcement of the efficiency and competitiveness of European companies. As the Community moves to

106. On freedom of establishment generally, see Chapter 6, above.
107. On freedom to provide services, see Chapter 7, above.
108. OJ 1963–64, Eng.Spec.Ed., p. 131.
109. OJ 1990 C42/7.
110. Dir.79/279, OJ 1979 L66/21.
111. Dir.80/390, OJ 1980 L100/1.
112. Dir.85/611, OJ 1985 L375/3.
113. Dir.82/121, OJ 1982 L48/26.
114. Dir.89/298, OJ 1989 L124/8.
115. Dir.88/627, OJ 1988 L348/62.
116. Dir.89/592, OJ 1989 L334/30
117. See Chapters 9–16, above.

complete the Internal Market, it will be necessary to ensure that anti-competitive practices do not engender new forms of local protectionism which would only lead to a re-partitioning of the market."

26.5.3.12.2 State aids[118]

The Commission wrote in its White Paper that in the context of maintaining and strengthening the internal market:

"it will be particularly important that the Community discipline on state aids be rigorously enforced. There are tendencies to spend large amounts of public funds on state aids to uncompetitive industries and enterprises. Often, they not only distort competition but also in the long run undermine efforts to increase European competitiveness. They represent a drain on scarce public resources and they threaten to defeat efforts to build the internal market. As the physical and technical barriers inside the Community are removed, the Commission will see to it that a rigorous policy is pursued in regard to state aids so that public resources are not used to confer artificial advantage to some firms over others. An effective Community discipline will make it possible to ensure that available resources are directed away from non-visible activities towards competitive and job creating industries of the future."

26.5.3.12.3 Mergers[119]

There has been a huge growth in the number and value of mergers and acquisitions since the announcement of the White Paper. The Commission is anxious that such concentration of commercial undertakings does not lead to unfair competition. The Commission has acted to control such developments but it lacked any effective power to do so.[120]

The situation is now remedied and the so-called Merger Control Regulation[121] gives the Commission the power to intervene in (albeit large) mergers and acquisitions which threaten the competitive balance of the Community. This Regulation has been discussed above.[122]

26.5.3.13 Environment[123]

The SEA has confirmed that the Environment is one of the fundamental concerns of the EC and this concern has manifested itself in the plethora (around 200) of measures adopted by the EC on the environment. While not strictly part of the White Paper, there is a set of environmental measures which are associated with the 1992 Programme. The first measure sets exhaust emission standards for small cars.[124]

The second proposes the imposition of strict liability on waste producers.[125]

The third relates to the operation of the European Environmental Agency which will assist the Commission in developing the EC's Environmental Policy.

118. See Chapter 15, above.
110. See above.
120. See such cases as 6/72 *Europemballage Cooperation and Continental Can v. EC Commission* [1973] ECR 215 and Joined Cases 142 and 156/87 *British American Tobacco v. EC Commission* [1987] ECR 4487.
121. Regulation 4064/89, OJ 1989 L395/1.
122. See para. 26.5.3.6.2, above.
123. See Chapter 17, above.
124. Dir.89/458, OJ 1989 L226/1.
125. OJ 1989 C251/3.

26.5.3.14 Miscellaneous areas

There are many aspects of the 1992 Programme which are important in other contexts but which do not have any direct relevance for shipping, thus they will be mentioned only briefly.

Telecommunications[126] is a sector which has been subject to considerable governmental regulation. These regulations differ between Member States. Thus the 1992 Programme is designed to "standardise" the rules to some extent. Allied in some ways to the telecommunications area is the Media[127] and the Commission has again proposed certain measures aimed to the "Europeanisation" of the media in Europe.

The Commission has proposed a range of measures relating to information technology[128] including research programmes such as BRITE, ESPRIT, AIM, APOLLO, DELTA, and EUROTRA.

In regard to intellectual property,[129] there is a set of proposals (some of which have been adopted) to remove some of the technical barriers to the creation of the Internal Market caused by differences in the rules relating to intellectual property. As these do not have any direct relevance for shipping, they are not dealt with in this book and recourse should be had to other works where the reader is specifically interested.[130]

26.5.4 Fiscal barriers[131]

26.5.4.1 Introduction

There are different rates of taxation operating in each of the Member States.[132] This leads to disparities in such areas as prices, incomes, excise duties, investments and so on. There is at present a great deal of what might be termed "fiscal shopping"—the searching around for the right fiscal jurisdiction. These fiscal disparities are to the detriment of almost everyone. There is a great deal of "frontier control activity" which is essentially wasteful.

The Commission has now arrived at the view that uniformity in indirect taxation is not a prerequsite to the internal market. Partial harmonisation or approximation would suffice.[133] This system works well in the United States. There is a great deal of political reality in this view.

VAT rates in EC Member States range from 0% to 38%. At first, the Commission envisaged a uniform rate of tax on mineral oils, tobacco and alcohol. This would have been the most attractive approach. By December 1988, it was clear that harmonisation was the most which could be achieved.[134]

These changes mean various things for each of the Member States. Some 30% of consumer spending in the UK which presently falls outside the scope of indirect tax

126. See Clifford Chance, *op. cit.*, para. 613 *et seq.*
127. See Clifford Chance, *op. cit.*, para. 618 *et seq.*
128. See Clifford Chance, *op. cit.*, para. 610 *et seq.*
129. Intellectual property relates to such areas as copyright, patents, trade marks, etc.
130. See Clifford Chance, *op. cit.*, para. 525 *et seq.*
131. See the Commission's White Paper to the Council of Ministers, "Completing the Internal Market" of June 1985, Part Three and Clifford Chance, *The CCH Guide to 1993: Changes in EEC Law* (1989), 206–207.
132. Rates of Valued Added Tax (VAT) vary in the EC from between 0% to 38%. Excise duties vary from zero to 10.5 ECU on bottles of alcohol.
133. The proposal from the Commission is for a band of 2.5 to 3% on either side of each target rate of VAT.
134. Unification would prove impossible.

would be brought within the VAT net. In Ireland and Denmark, there is likely to be a reduction in tobacco and alcohol prices.

Excise duties differ between Member States. Duties on alcohol are at the highest in the UK, Ireland and Denmark and at their lowest in Italy and Greece. These differences mean that the retail prices of such commodities vary significantly throughout the EC. An internal market could not survive with such dramatic disparities—otherwise, to take a stock example, people from the Republic of Ireland might cross the border to buy goods in Northern Ireland. The existence of varying excise duties implies the need for customs posts at the borders.

There are proposals for the interlinking of EC bonded warehouses.[135]

At present, the fiscal regimes in many of the Member States prevent efficient and smooth cross-border investment.[136]

A number of proposals from the Commission would facilitate such activity which will prove vital to the success of an internalised Europe. One proposed Directive would exempt the profits of a subsidiary from tax in the parent company's jurisdiction.[137]

The bases on which taxes (especially in the business sector) are determined vary substantially between fiscal jurisdictions. Double taxation is a related problem. The Council of Ministers has adopted a Directive to provide for an arbitration procedure so as to deal with disputes over double taxation.[138]

Initially it was proposed to abolish duty free concessions between EC Member States.

There is a great need to harmonise the fiscal rules in each of the Member States.[139] If there is no harmonisation then border posts will have to remain intact.

The task of achieving agreement on fiscal changes is not an easy one. The Single European Act[140] retained the rule that the Council of Ministers had to *unanimously* approve changes in taxation.

26.6 EXTERNAL DIMENSION TO THE 1992 PROGRAMME[141]

26.6.1 Introduction

Is the EC preparing itself to take on the world as a single entity or is it getting its own house in order? Is the Internal Market programme designed to allow the EC to compete more effectively with the rest of the world or is it to make the EC more efficient in itself with an overall increase in the standard of living within the EC?

The completion of the Internal Market is one of the major important global events in the decade. It has implications not just for the EC Member States but the entire world. The initial discussions of the internal market gave the impression that the programme was to make Europe internally more efficient and thereby allow, for example, a Greek company to compete in Spain on the same efficient terms as a Spanish company.

135. I.e. warehouses where duty-free goods are stored.

136. *Cf.* European Research Associates, *Obstacles to Transborder Business Activity*, *passim.*

137. See Clifford Chance, *The CCH Guide to 1993: Changes in EEC Law* (1989), 505.

138. OJ L225, 20 August 1990. Double tax relates to the possibility of two or more tax systems applying to one situation.

139. So as to overcome the barriers to trade between EC Member States.

140. On the SEA, see Chapter 3, above.

141. See Henderson, "1992: The External Dimension", Group of Thirty, Occasional Papers 25.

26.6.2 Fortress Europe

The completion of the internal market does have external significance. There is a school of thought that an internalised Europe will be like a fortress taking on the rest of the world. Some believe that the EC will adopt "EC" standards which are materially different from standards elsewhere in the world and thereby handicap non-EC industries—this now seems unlikely, at least in the case of the USA, following the EC's invitation to US officials to participate in the setting of EC standards. Even if this scenario is adopted and the drawbridge is lifted on 31 December 1992 then would the wider world benefit? Yes, it could. Foreign-owned businesses already established within the EC will benefit from the Internal Market. For example, a US-owned company which has a subsidiary in Belgium could compete on the same terms as a Belgian company for a Belgian government public procurement contract.

Yet it is almost impossible to imagine that an internalised Europe would be a fortress against the rest of the world. The European Council, at its June 1988 meeting, said:

"[t]he internal market should not close in on itself. In conformity with the provisions of GATT, the Community should be open to third countries, and must negotiate with those countries, where necessary, to ensure access to their markets for Community exports. It will seek to preserve the balance of advantage accorded, while respecting the unity and the identity of the internal market of the Community."

This view is in accordance with the views of such influential EC officials as the former EC Commissioner for External Trade, Willy De Clercq, who said that Europe "should never forget that our own interests are best served by remaining open to the world". It is now clear that the EC will not be a fortress.

26.6.3 Relations with international organisations

The precise relationship between the EC and non-Member States or international organisations is a fascinating study in the law and politics of external relations.

26.6.3.1 European Free Trade Association

The European Free Trade Association (EFTA) is the EC's largest trading bloc partner. The EC Commission has stated that the EC is committed to closer co-operation with EFTA. The EC has over the years developed an extensive range of contacts and conventions with EFTA. The EC and EFTA have created a free trade zone between them—but it must be remembered that the EC has a kind of inner sanctum (a customs union) within this free trade zone. Austria (a member of EFTA) has applied to join the EC.

The EC and EFTA have concluded an agreement to develop a European Economic Area in which many of the EC rules will apply in the EFTA states. This Agreement is extremely important. Space does not permit a full discussion of the Agreement at this juncture.

26.7 ECONOMIC AND MONETARY UNION

At its Hanover Summit in June 1988 the European Council requested the Commission to make proposals relating to economic and monetary union. The Commission's proposals were well-received at the June 1989 Summit in Madrid. An economic and monetary union would facilitate the internalisation of the market. The Maastricht Arrangements concluded in December 1991 and signed in February 1992 will, if ratified and implemented fully, create an economic and monetary union.

26.8 1992 AND SHIPPING

In many ways, the 1992 Programme is of more direct relevance to short-sea shipping companies, including ferry operators, than long-haul companies.

The completion of the Internal Market will result in an increase in economic activity generally in the EC which will have a consequential effect on the amount of goods and number of passengers carried by sea. Transport companies generally will benefit from reduced warehouse costs, reduced licensing costs, increased trade and greater liberalisation of trade procedures.

CHAPTER 27

Conclusions

27.1 INTRODUCTION

A number of conclusions emerge after reviewing the law of the EC as it relates to shipping. These conclusions are intrinsically interesting but are also important in terms of the future development of EC shipping law.

27.2 THE EC IS ON A TRAJECTORY OF GROWTH

As an international organisation, the EC is on a trajectory of growth. The twelve Member States (some of the richest and most economically advanced in the world) are moving closer together (economically, monetarily, politically as well as in many other ways). They are a force to be reckoned with by the rest of the world. Austria, Finland, Sweden and Turkey have all expressed an interest in joining.

27.3 THE PLACE OF THE EC IN WORLD SHIPPING

The boundaries of the European Community are not the boundaries of shipping. There is no way that the EC will ever control all aspects of shipping as if the industry were in an EC-controlled incubator. Nonetheless, the EC is concerned with shipping and the legal regulation of this international industry.

27.4 EC SHIPPING LAW IS OF RECENT ORIGIN

While EC law has always applied to shipping (albeit in a modified form), the body of EC shipping law is of recent origin. The 1974 case of *Commission v. France*[1] was the first major judicial development in EC shipping law: yet the opportunities afforded by the ECJ in that case were not grasped by the other institutions for many years. The 1979 Brussels Package was the first legislative package. The Treaties left considerable initiative in the hands of the Commission and discretion at the feet of the Council of Ministers: the hesitancy of the latter and the paralysis of the former for many years has hampered the development of the law in this area.

1. Case 167/74 *Commission v. France* [1974] ECR 359; [1974] 2 CMLR 216.

27.5 THERE IS HARDLY ANY LIMIT TO THE POSSIBLE APPLICATION OF EC LAW TO SHIPPING YET THERE IS A LIMIT TO THE POSSIBLE DEVELOPMENT OF EC SHIPPING LAW

EC law applies to virtually every economic activity, including shipping. Thus, the application of EC law to shipping must not be underestimated. The decisions of the ECJ Case C213/89 *R. v. Secretary of State for Transport, ex parte Factortame (No. 2)*[2] and Case 167/74 *Commission v. France* are demonstrative of the application of this body of law to shipping matters.

In 1977, the European Parliament's Committee on Regional Policy, Regional Planning and Transport published an Interim Report on the Sea Transport Problems in the Community and stated:

> "[A] frequently heard argument is that since sea transport is subject to world-wide ramifications and world-wide rules, it should not be forced into the 'narrow confines' of Community regulations, which would only represent a step backwards compared with world-wide arrangements.
>
> There is no logic to this argument, popular though it may be. What European industry is not subject to world-wide ramifications? Is it not simply true to say of the European economy, with its dependence on imports of raw materials and its vital need to export, that everything we do has world-wide ramifications? Even the cereals which grow in our fields are subject to world-wide rules, which in some respects go further than world arrangements for sea transport."[3]

The EC must be vigilant in ensuring that third States and other organisations do not damage EC shipping interests.[4]

Mrs Bredima-Savopoulou was Rapporteur for the Economic and Social Committee in its Opinion on the Proposal for a Council Directive concerning minimum requirements for vessels entering or leaving Community ports carrying packages of dangerous or polluting goods. She wrote in her Opinion:

> "The Community has two alternatives: it could either introduce different standards and requirements of its own, or it could work towards effective implementation of international standards. ... The Committee recommends that the Community follow the second course of action by complying with the international standards laid down by specialized international maritime agencies, by incorporating these into Community legislation and by ensuring that these standards are strictly observed."[5]

There has to be close co-operation between the EC and such bodies as the Internationalen Transportarbeiterfoderation (ITF), the Weltverbandes der Arbeit (WVA) and the Associations of Shipowners in the European Communities (CAACE).

The seafaring skills which were so commonly found in such Member States as the UK must not be left to die. It is difficult to re-establish such skills.

27.6 EC TRANSPORT POLICY HAS BEEN SLOW TO DEVELOP

The EC's transport policy has been slow to develop and, insofar as it has developed, has done so in a piecemeal fashion.

2. [1991] AC 603; [1990] 3 WLR 818; [1991] 1 All ER 70.
3. Working Documents; Doc.5/77; 23 March 1977; Rapporteur: Mr H. Seefeld, para.9.
4. See "EEC sends lawyers into UKWAL offices", *Lloyd's List*, 24 July 1989, p. 1.
5. OJ No. C 329, 30 December 1989.

27.7 EC SHIPPING POLICY HAS NOT BEEN ENTIRELY SUCCESSFUL

The Select Committee of the House of Lords wrote in its Report *Community Shipping Measures*[6]:

"[m]ost—though not all—of the measures . . . proposed [in 1985] were adopted by the Council [of Ministers] in December 1986. . . . So far as they went, they seem to have worked well. But they have not stopped the decline in the Community merchant fleet. The haemorrhage of economic and potential military resources continues."[7]

The Commission did not however stand idly by forever. In August 1990, it proposed the Positive Measures package.

27.8 IS SHIPPING A PUBLIC SERVICE OR MERELY ANOTHER SERVICE IN THE MARKET PLACE?

The public service nature of shipping needs to be given its proper place. Too great an emphasis means that the market will not operate efficiently and too little emphasis and society will not benefit from the shipping industry.

27.9 EC SHIPPING LAW IS ONLY A COMPONENT OF INTERNATIONAL SHIPPING LAW

The advent of such organisations as the United Nations, the United Nations Conference on Trade and Development, the International Labour Organisation, the International Maritime Organisation and specific treaty relationships between States (falling short of international organisations) means that EC law is only one of the constituent elements of international shipping law. The EC must maintain a unified front at these organisations if it is to prove powerful and influential. The international dimension of shipping[8] means that the law of the European Community relating to it will always be only a component part.

27.10 THE FORMULATION OF EC SHIPPING LAW REQUIRES THE INVOLVEMENT OF ALL PARTNERS

The former Commissioner for Transport, Stanley Clinton Davis, said there had to be a strengthening of the dialogue between the social partners: "Each has to comprehend the problems of the other; each has to be mutually supportive."[9]

6. European Communities Committee 28th Report 1989–90 (HL Paper 90).
7. *Ibid.*, para.1.
8. Clough and Randolph, *Shipping and EC Competition Law* (1991) comment (at para.2.1): "EEC Sea Transport Policy must . . . take into account the existence of bilateral agreements, the different systems of regulation in different parts of the world including national cargo reservation systems, total cargo allocation measures such as those in West and Central Africa, the open conference system in the United States and the closed conference system which has prevailed in Europe for over a century."
9. "Maritime Transport", IP(85) 60, 7 March 1985.

27.11 EC SHIPPING LAW AND POLICY MUST SEEK TO PROTECT EC SHIPOWNERS, SEAFARERS AND ALL THOSE INVOLVED IN THE EC SHIPPING INDUSTRY

EC shipping policy might well include a co-ordinated grant, taxation, research, qualifications and services policy so as to improve the lot of EC's shipowners, seafarers and all those involved in the EC shipping industry.

APPENDIX 1

Treaty of Rome

PART ONE. PRINCIPLES

Article 1

By this Treaty, the High Contracting Parties establish among themselves a EUROPEAN ECONOMIC COMMUNITY.

Article 2

The Community shall have as its task, by establishing a common market and progressively approximating the economic policies of Member States, to promote throughout the Community a harmonious development of economic activities, a continuous and balanced expansion, an increase in stability, an accelerated raising of the standard of living and closer relations between the States belonging to it.

Article 3

For the purposes set out in article 2, the activities of the Community shall include, as provided in this Treaty and in accordance with the timetable set out therein:

(a) the elimination, as between Member States, of customs duties and of quantitative restrictions on the import and export of goods, and of all other measures having equivalent effect;

(b) the establishment of a common customs tariff and of a common commercial policy towards third countries;

(c) the abolition, as between Member States, of obstacles to freedom of movement for persons, services and capital;

(d) the adoption of a common policy in the sphere of agriculture;

(e) the adoption of a common policy in the sphere of transport;

(f) the institution of a system ensuring that competition in the common market is not distorted;

(g) the application of procedures by which the economic policies of Member States can be co-ordinated and disequilibria in their balances of payments remedied;

(h) the approximation of the laws of Member States to the extent required for the proper functioning of the common market;

(i) the creation of a European Social Fund in order to improve employment opportunities for workers and to contribute to the raising of their standard of living;

(j) the establishment of a European Investment Bank to facilitate the economic expansion of the Community by opening up fresh resources;

(k) the association of the overseas countries and territories in order to increase trade and to promote jointly economic and social development.

Article 4

1. The tasks entrusted to the Community shall be carried out by the following institutions:

a European Parliament,
a Council,
a Commission,
a Court of Justice.

Each institution shall act within the limits of the powers conferred upon it by this Treaty.

2. The Council and the Commission shall be assisted by an Economic and Social Committee acting in an advisory capacity.

3. The audit shall be carried out by a Court of Auditors acting within the limits of the powers conferred upon it by this Treaty.

Article 5

Member States shall take all appropriate measures, whether general or particular, to ensure fulfilment of the obligations arising out of this Treaty or resulting from action taken by the institutions of the Community. They shall facilitate the achievement of the Community's tasks.

They shall abstain from any measure which could jeopardise the attainment of the objectives of this Treaty.

Article 6

1. Member States shall, in close co-operation with the institutions of the Community, co-ordinate their respective economic policies to the extent necessary to attain the objectives of this Treaty.

2. The institutions of the Community shall take care not to prejudice the internal and external financial stability of the Member States.

Article 7

Within the scope of application of this Treaty, and without prejudice to any special provisions contained therein, any discrimination on grounds of nationality shall be prohibited.

The Council may, on a proposal from the Commission and in co-operation with the European Parliament, adopt, by a qualified majority, rules designed to prohibit such discrimination.

Article 8

1. The common market shall be progressively established during a transitional period of twelve years.

This transitional period shall be divided into three stages of four years each; the length of each stage may be altered in accordance with the provisions set out below.

2. To each stage there shall be assigned a set of actions to be initiated and carried through concurrently.

3. Transition from the first to the second stage shall be conditional upon a finding that the objectives specifically laid down in this Treaty for the first stage have in fact been attained in substance and that, subject to the exceptions and procedures provided for in this Treaty, the obligations have been fulfilled.

This finding shall be made at the end of the fourth year by the Council, acting unanimously on a report from the Commission. A Member State may not, however, prevent unanimity by relying upon the non-fulfilment of its own obligations. Failing unanimity, the first stage shall automatically be extended for one year.

At the end of the fifth year, the Council shall make its finding under the same conditions. Failing unanimity, the first stage shall automatically be extended for a further year.

At the end of the sixth year, the Council shall make its finding, acting by a qualified majority on a report from the Commission.

4. Within one month of the last-mentioned vote any Member State which voted with the minority or, if the required majority was not obtained, any Member State shall be entitled to call upon the Council to appoint an arbitration board whose decision shall be binding upon all

Member States and upon the institutions of the Community. The arbitration board shall consist of three members appointed by the Council acting unanimously on a proposal from the Commission.

If the Council has not appointed the members of the arbitration board within one month of being called upon to do so, they shall be appointed by the Court of Justice within a further period of one month.

The arbitration board shall elect its own Chairman.

The board shall make its award within six months of the date of the Council vote referred to in the last sub-paragraph of paragraph 3.

5. The second and third stages may not be extended or curtailed except by a decision of the Council, acting unanimously on a proposal from the Commission.

6. Nothing in the preceding paragraphs shall cause the transitional period to last more than fifteen years after the entry into force of this Treaty.

7. Save for the exceptions or derogations provided for in this Treaty, the expiry of the transitional period shall constitute the latest date by which all the rules laid down must enter into force and all the measures required for establishing the common market must be implemented.

Article 8a

The Community shall adopt measures with the aim of progressively establishing the internal market over a period expiring on 31 December 1992, in accordance with the provisions of this Article and of Articles 8b, 8c, 28, 57 (2), 59, 70 (1), 84, 99, 100a and 100b and without prejudice to the other provisions of this Treaty.

The internal market shall comprise an area without internal frontiers in which the free movement of goods, persons, services and capital is ensured in accordance with the provisions of this Treaty.

Article 8b

The Commission shall report to the Council before 31 December 1988 and again before 31 December 1990 on the progress made towards achieving the internal market within the time limit fixed in Article 8a.

The Council, acting by a qualified majority on a proposal from the Commission, shall determine the guidelines and conditions necessary to ensure balanced progress in all the sectors concerned.

Article 8c

When drawing up its proposals with a view to achieving the objectives set out in Article 8a, the Commission shall take into account the extent of the effort that certain economies showing differences in development will have to sustain during the period of establishment of the internal market and it may propose appropriate provisions.

If these provisions take the form of derogations, they must be of a temporary nature and must cause the least possible disturbance to the functioning of the common market.

PART TWO. FOUNDATIONS OF THE COMMUNITY

TITLE I. FREE MOVEMENT OF GOODS

Article 9

1. The Community shall be based upon a customs union which shall cover all trade in goods and which shall involve the prohibition between Member States of customs duties on imports and exports and of all charges having equivalent effect, and the adoption of a common customs tariff in their relations with third countries.

2. The provisions of Chapter 1, Section 1, and of Chapter 2, of this Title shall apply to products originating in Member States and to products coming from third countries which are in free circulation in Member States.

Article 10

1. Products coming from a third country shall be considered to be in free circulation in a Member State if the import formalities have been complied with and any customs duties or charges having equivalent effect which are payable have been levied in that Member State, and if they have not benefited from a total or partial drawback of such duties or charges.

2. The Commission shall, before the end of the first year after the entry into force of this Treaty, determine the methods of administrative co-operation to be adopted for the purpose of applying Article 9 (2), taking into account the need to reduce as much as possible formalities imposed on trade.

Before the end of the first year after the entry into force of this Treaty, the Commission shall lay down the provisions applicable, as regards trade between Member States, to goods originating in another Member State in whose manufacture products have been used on which the exporting. Member State has not levied the appropriate customs duties or charges having equivalent effect, or which have benefited from a total or partial drawback of such duties or charges.

In adopting these provisions, the Commission shall take into account the rules for the elimination of customs duties within the Community and for the progressive application of the common customs tariff.

Article 11

Member States shall take all appropriate measures to enable Governments to carry out, within the periods of time laid down, the obligations with regard to customs duties which devolve upon them pursuant to this Treaty.

CHAPTER 1—THE CUSTOMS UNION

Section 1—Elimination of customs duties between Member States

Article 12

Member States shall refrain from introducing between themselves any new customs duties on imports or exports or any charges having equivalent effect, and from increasing those which they already apply in their trade with each other.

Article 13

1. Customs duties on imports in force between Member States shall be progressively abolished by them during the transitional period in accordance with Articles 14 and 15.

2. Charges having an effect equivalent to customs duties on imports, in force between Member States, shall be progressively abolished by them during the transitional period. The Commission shall determine by means of directives the timetable for such abolition. It shall be guided by the rules contained in Article 14 (2) and (3) and by the directives issued by the Council pursuant to Article 14 (2).

Article 14

1. For each product, the basic duty to which the successive reductions shall be applied shall be the duty applied on 1 January 1957.

2. The timetable for the reductions shall be determined as follows:

(a) during the first stage, the first reduction shall be made one year after the date when this Treaty enters into force; the second reduction, eighteen months later; the third reduction, at the end of the fourth year after the date when this Treaty enters into force;

(b) during the second stage, a reduction shall be made eighteen months after that stage begins; a second reduction, eighteen months after the preceding one; a third reduction, one year later;

(c) any remaining reductions shall be made during the third stage; the Council shall, acting by a qualified majority on a proposal from the Commission, determine the timetable therefor by means of directives.

3. At the time of the first reduction, Member States shall introduce between themselves a duty on each product equal to the basic duty minus 10%.

At the time of each subsequent reduction, each Member State shall reduce its customs duties as a whole in such manner as to lower by 10% its total customs receipts as defined in paragraph 4 and to reduce the duty on each product by at least 5% of the basic duty.

In the case, however, of products on which the duty is still in excess of 30%, each reduction must be at least 10% of the basic duty.

4. The total customs receipts of each Member State, as referred to in paragraph 3, shall be calculated by multiplying the value of its imports from other Member States during 1956 by the basic duties.

5. Any special problems raised in applying paragraphs 1 to 4 shall be settled by directives issued by the Council acting by a qualified majority on a proposal from the Commission.

6. Member States shall report to the Commission on the manner in which effect has been given to the preceding rules for the reduction of duties. They shall endeavour to ensure that the reduction made in the duties on each product shall amount:

— at the end of the first stage, to at least 25% of the basic duty;

— at the end of the second stage, to at least 50% of the basic duty.

If the Commission finds that there is a risk that the objective laid down in Article 13, and the percentages laid down in this paragraph, cannot be attained, it shall make all appropriate recommendations to Member States.

7. The provisions of this Article may be amended by the Council, acting unanimously on a proposal from the Commission and after consulting the European Parliament.

Article 15

1. Irrespective of the provisions of Article 14, any Member State may, in the course of the transitional period, suspend in whole or in part the collection of duties applied by it to products imported from other Member States. It shall inform the other Member States and the Commission thereof.

2. The Member States declare their readiness to reduce customs duties against the other Member States more rapidly than is provided for in Article 14 if their general economic situation and the situation of the economic sector concerned so permit.

To this end, the Commission shall make recommendations to the Member States concerned.

Article 16

Member States shall abolish between themselves customs duties on exports and charges having equivalent effect by the end of the first stage at the latest.

Article 17

1. The provisions of Articles 9 to 15 (1) shall also apply to customs duties of a fiscal nature. Such duties shall not, however, be taken into consideration for the purpose of calculating either total customs receipts or the reduction of customs duties as a whole as referred to in Article 14 (3) and (4).

Such duties shall, at each reduction, be lowered by not less than 10% of the basic duty. Member States may reduce such duties more rapidly than is provided for in Article 14.

2. Member States shall, before the end of the first year after the entry into force of this Treaty, inform the Commission of their customs duties of a fiscal nature.

3. Member States shall retain the right to substitute for these duties an internal tax which complies with the provisions of Article 95.

4. If the Commission finds that substitution for any customs duty of a fiscal nature meets with serious difficulties in a Member State, it shall authorise that State to retain the duty on condition that it shall abolish it not later than six years after the entry into force of this Treaty. Such authorisation must be applied for before the end of the first year after the entry into force of this Treaty.

Section 2—Setting up of the common customs tariff

Article 18

The Member States declare their readiness to contribute to the development of international trade and the lowering of barriers to trade by entering into agreements designed, on a basis of reciprocity and mutual advantage, to reduce customs duties below the general level of which they could avail themselves as a result of the establishment of a customs union between them.

Article 19

1. Subject to the conditions and within the limits provided for hereinafter, duties in the common customs tariff shall be at the level of the arithmetical average of the duties applied in the four customs territories comprised in the Community.

2. The duties taken as the basis for calculating this average shall be those applied by Member States on 1 January 1957.

In the case of the Italian tariff, however, the duty applied shall be that without the temporary 10% reduction. Furthermore, with respect to items on which the Italian tariff contains a conventional duty, this duty shall be substituted for the duty applied as defined above, provided that it does not exceed the latter by more than 10%. Where the conventional duty exceeds the duty applies as defined above by more than 10%, the latter duty plus 10% shall be taken as the basis for calculating the arithmetical average.

With regard to the tariff headings in List A, the duties shown in that List shall, for the purpose of calculating the arithmetical average, be substituted for the duties applied.

3. The duties in the common customs tariff shall not exceed:
   (a) 3% for products within the tariff headings in List B;
   (b) 10% for products within the tariff headings in List C;
   (c) 15% for products within the tariff headings in List D;
   (d) 25% for products within the tariff headings in List E; where, in respect of such products, the tariff of the Benelux countries contains a duty not exceeding 3%, such duty shall, for the purpose of calculating the arithmetical average, be raised to 12%.

4. List F prescribes the duties applicable to the products listed therein.

5. The Lists of tariff headings referred to in this Article and in Article 20 are set out in Annex I to this Treaty.

Article 20

The duties applicable to the products in List G shall be determined by negotiation between the Member States. Each Member State may add further products to this List to a value not exceeding 2% of the total value of its imports from third countries in the course of the year 1956.

The Commission shall take all appropriate steps to ensure that such negotiations shall be undertaken before the end of the second year after the entry into force of this Treaty and be concluded before the end of the first stage.

If, for certain products, no agreement can be reached within these periods, the Council shall, on a proposal from the Commission, acting unanimously until the end of the second stage and by a qualified majority thereafter, determine the duties in the common customs tariff.

Article 21

1. Technical difficulties which may arise in applying Articles 19 and 20 shall be resolved, within two years of the entry into force of this Treaty, by directives issued by the Council acting by a qualified majority on a proposal from the Commission.

2. Before the end of the first stage, or at latest when the duties are determined, the Council shall, acting by a qualified majority on a proposal from the Commission, decide on any adjustments required in the interests of the internal consistency of the common customs tariff as a result of applying the rules set out in Articles 19 and 20, taking account in particular of the degree of processing undergone by the various goods to which the common tariff applies.

Article 22

The Commission shall, within two years of the entry into force of this Treaty, determine the extent to which the customs duties of a fiscal nature referred to in Article 17 (2) shall be taken into account in calculating the arithmetical average provided for in Article 19 (1). The Commission shall take account of any protective character which such duties may have.

Within six months of such determination, any Member State may request that the procedure provided for in Article 20 should be applied to the product in question, but in this event the percentage limit provided in that Article shall not be applicable to that State.

Article 23

1. For the purpose of the progressive introduction of the common customs tariff, Member States shall amend their tariffs applicable to third countries as follows:

(a) in the case of tariff headings on which the duties applied in practice on 1 January 1957 do not differ by more than 15% in either direction from the duties in the common customs tariff, the latter duties shall be applied at the end of the fourth year after the entry into force of this Treaty;

(b) in any other case, each Member State shall, as from the same date, apply a duty reducing by 30% the difference between the duty applied in practice on 1 January 1957 and the duty in the common customs tariff;

(c) at the end of the second stage this difference shall again be reduced by 30%;

(d) in the case of tariff headings for which the duties in the common customs tariff are not yet available at the end of the first stage, each Member State shall, within six months of the Council's action in accordance with Article 20, apply such duties as would result from application of the rules contained in this paragraph.

2. Where a Member State has been granted an authorisation under Article 17(4), it need not, for as long as that authorisation remains valid, apply the preceding provisions to the tariff headings to which the authorisation applies. When such authorisation expires, the Member State concerned shall apply such duty as would have resulted from application of the rules contained in paragraph 1.

3. The common customs tariff shall be applied in its entirety by the end of the transitional period at the latest.

Article 24

Member States shall remain free to change their duties more rapidly than is provided for in Article 23 in order to bring them into line with the common customs tariff.

Article 25

1. If the Commission finds that the production in Member States of particular products contained in Lists B, C and D is insufficient to supply the demands of one of the Member States, and that such supply traditionally depends to a considerable extent on imports from third countries, the Council shall, acting by a qualified majority on a proposal from the Commission, grant the Member State concerned tariff quotas at a reduced rate of duty or duty free.

Such quotas may not exceed the limits beyond which the risk might arise of activities being transferred to the detriment of other Member States.

2. In the case of the products in List E, and of those in List G for which the rates of duty have been determined in accordance with the procedure provided for in the third paragraph of Article 20, the Commission shall, where a change in sources of supply or shortage of supplies within the Community is such as to entail harmful consequences for the processing industries of a Member State, at the request of that Member State, grant it tariff quotas at a reduced rate of duty or duty free.

Such quotas may not exceed the limits beyond which the risk might arise of activities being transferred to the detriment of other Member States.

3. In the case of the products listed in Annex II to this Treaty, the Commission may authorise any Member State to suspend, in whole or in part, collection of the duties applicable or may grant such Member State tariff quotas at a reduced rate of duty or duty free, provided that no serious disturbance of the market of the products concerned results therefrom.

4. The Commission shall periodically examine tariff quotas granted pursuant to this Article.

Article 26

The Commission may authorise any Member State encountering special difficulties to postpone the lowering or raising of duties provided for in Article 23 in respect of particular headings in its tariff.

Such authorisation may only be granted for a limited period and in respect of tariff headings which, taken together, represent for such State not more than 5% of the value of its imports from third countries in the course of the latest year for which statistical data are available.

Article 27

Before the end of the first stage, Member States shall, in so far as may be necessary, take steps to approximate their provisions laid down by law, regulation or administrative action in respect of customs matters. To this end, the Commission shall make all appropriate recommendations to Member States.

Article 28

Any autonomous alteration or suspension of duties in the common customs tariff shall be decided by the Council acting by a qualified majority on a proposal from the Commission.

Article 29

In carrying out the tasks entrusted to it under this Section the Commission shall be guided by:

(a) the need to promote trade between Member States and third countries;

(b) developments in conditions of competition within the Community in so far as they lead to an improvement in the competitive capacity of undertakings;

(c) the requirements of the Community as regards the supply of raw materials and semi-finished goods; in this connection the Commission shall take care to avoid distorting conditions of competition between Member States in respect of finished goods;

(d) the need to avoid serious disturbances in the economies of Member States and to ensure rational development of production and an expansion of consumption within the Community.

CHAPTER 2—ELIMINATION OF QUANTITATIVE RESTRICTIONS BETWEEN MEMBER STATES

Article 30

Quantitative restrictions on imports and all measures having equivalent effect shall, without prejudice to the following provisions, be prohibited between Member States.

Article 31

Member States shall refrain from introducing between themselves any new quantitative restrictions or measures having equivalent effect.

This obligation shall, however, relate only to the degree of liberalisation attained in pursuance of the decisions of the Council of the organisation for European Economic Co-operation of 14 January 1955. Member States shall supply the Commission, not later than six months after the entry into force of this Treaty, with lists of the products liberalised by them in pursuance of these decisions. These lists shall be consolidated between Member States.

Article 32

In their trade with one another Member States shall refrain from making more restrictive the quotas and measures having equivalent effect existing at the date of the entry into force of this Treaty.

These quotas shall be abolished by the end of the transitional period at the latest. During that period, they shall be progressively abolished in accordance with the following provisions.

Article 33

1. One year after the entry into force of this Treaty, each Member State shall convert any bilateral quotas open to any other Member States into global quotas open without discrimination to all other Member States.

On the same date, Member States shall increase the aggregate of the global quotas so established in such a manner as to bring about an increase of not less than 20% in their total value as compared with the preceding year. The global quota for each product, however, shall be increased by not less than 10%.

The quotas shall be increased annually in accordance with the same rules and in the same proportions in relation to the preceding year.

The fourth increase shall take place at the end of the fourth year after the entry into force of this Treaty; the fifth, one year after the beginning of the second stage.

2. Where, in the case of a product which has not been liberalised, the global quota does not amount to 3% of the national production of the State concerned, a quota equal to not less than 3% of such national production shall be introduced not later than one year after the entry into force of this Treaty. This quota shall be raised to 4% at the end of the second year, and to 5% at the end of the third. Thereafter, the Member State concerned shall increase the quota by not less than 15% annually.

Where there is no such national production, the Commission shall take a decision establishing an appropriate quota.

3. At the end of the tenth year, each quota shall be equal to not less than 20% of the national production.

4. If the Commission finds by means of a decision that during two successive years the imports of any product have been below the level of the quota opened, this global quota shall not be taken into account in calculating the total value of the global quotas. In such case, the Member State shall abolish quota restrictions on the product concerned.

5. In the case of quotas representing more than 20% of the national production of the product concerned, the Council may, acting by a qualified majority on a proposal from the Commission, reduce the minimum percentage of 10% laid down in paragraph 1. This alteration shall not, however, affect the obligation to increase the total value of global quotas by 20% annually.

6. Member States which have exceeded their obligations as regards the degree of liberalisation attained in pursuance of the decisions of the Council of the organisation for European Economic Co-operation of 14 January 1955 shall be entitled, when calculating the annual total increase of 20% provided for in paragraph 1, to take into account the amount of imports liberalised by autonomous action. Such calculation shall be submitted to the Commission for its prior approval.

7. The Commission shall issue directives establishing the procedure and timetable in accordance with which Member States shall abolish, as between themselves, any measures in existence when this Treaty enters into force which have an effect equivalent to quotas.

8. If the Commission finds that the application of the provisions of this Article, and in particular of the provisions concerning percentages, makes it impossible to ensure that the abolition of quotas provided for in the second paragraph of Article 32 is carried out progressively, the Council may, on a proposal from the Commission, acting unanimously during the first stage and by a qualified majority thereafter, amend the procedure laid down in this Article and may, in particular, increase the percentages fixed.

Article 34

1. Quantitative restrictions on exports, and all measures having equivalent effect, shall be prohibited between Member States.

2. Member States shall, by the end of the first stage at the latest, abolish all quantitative restrictions on exports and any measures having equivalent effect which are in existence when this Treaty enters into force.

Article 35

The Member States declare their readiness to abolish quantitative restrictions on imports from and exports to other Member States more rapidly than is provided for in the preceding Articles, if their general economic situation and the situation of the economic sector concerned so permit.

To this end, the Commission shall make recommendations to the Member States concerned.

Article 36

The provisions of Articles 30 to 34 shall not preclude prohibitions or restrictions on imports, exports or goods in transit justified on grounds of public morality, public policy or public security; the protection of health and life of humans, animals or plants; the protection of national treasures possessing artistic, historic or archaeological value; or the protection of industrial and commercial property. Such prohibitions or restrictions shall not, however, constitute a means of arbitrary discrimination or a disguised restriction on trade between Member States.

1. Member States shall progressively adjust any State monopolies of a commercial character so as to ensure that when the transitional period has ended no discrimination regarding the conditions under which goods are procured and marketed exists between nationals of Member States.

The provisions of this Article shall apply to any body through which a Member State, in law or in fact, either directly or indirectly supervises, determines or appreciably influences imports or exports between Member States. These provisions shall likewise apply to monopolies delegated by the State to others.

2. Member States shall refrain from introducing any new measure which is contrary to the principles laid down in paragraph 1 or which restricts the scope of the Articles dealing with the abolition of customs duties and quantitative restrictions between Member States.

3. The timetable for the measures referred to in paragraph 1 shall be harmonised with the abolition of quantitative restrictions on the same products provided for in Articles 30 to 34.

If a product is subject to a State monopoly of a commercial character in only one or some Member States, the Commission may authorise the other Member States to apply protective measures until the adjustment provided for in paragraph 1 has been effected; the Commission shall determine the conditions and details of such measures.

4. If a State monopoly of a commercial character has rules which are designed to make it easier to dispose of agricultural products or obtain for them the best return, steps should be taken in applying the rules contained in this Article to ensure equivalent safeguards for the employment and standard of living of the producers concerned, account being taken of the adjustments that will be possible and the specialisation that will be needed with the passage of time.

5. The obligations on Member States shall be binding only in so far as they are compatible with existing international agreements.

6. With effect from the first stage the Commission shall make recommendations as to the manner in which and the timetable according to which the adjustment provided for in this Article shall be carried out.

TITLE II. AGRICULTURE

Article 38

1. The common market shall extend to agriculture and trade in agricultural products. "Agricultural products" means the products of the soil, of stock-farming and of fisheries and products of first-stage processing directly related to these products.

2. Save as otherwise provided in Articles 39 to 46, the rules laid down for the establishment of the common market shall apply to agricultural products.

3. The products subject to the provisions of Articles 39 to 46 are listed in Annex II to this Treaty. Within two years of the entry into force of this Treaty, however, the Council shall, acting by a qualified majority on a proposal from the Commission, decide what products are to be added to this list.

4. The operation and development of the common market for agricultural products must be accompanied by the establishment of a common agricultural policy among the Member States.

Article 39

1. The objectives of the common agricultural policy shall be:
   - (a) to increase agricultural productivity by promoting technical progress and by ensuring the rational development of agricultural production and the optimum utilisation of the factors of production, in particular labour;
   - (b) thus to ensure a fair standard of living for the agricultural community, in particular by increasing the individual earnings of persons engaged in agriculture;
   - (c) to stabilise markets;
   - (d) to assure the availability of supplies;
   - (e) to ensure that supplies reach consumers at reasonable prices.

2. In working out the common agricultural policy and the special methods for its application, account shall be taken of:
   - (a) the particular nature of agricultural activity, which results from the social structure of agriculture and from structural and natural disparities between the various agricultural regions;
   - (b) the need to effect the appropriate adjustments by degrees;
   - (c) the fact that in the Member States agriculture constitutes a sector closely linked with the economy as a whole.

Article 40

1. Member States shall develop the common agricultural policy by degrees during the transitional period and shall bring it into force by the end of that period at the latest.

2. In order to attain the objectives set out in Article 39 a common organisation of agricultural markets shall be established.

This organisation shall take one of the following forms, depending on the product concerned:
   - (a) common rules on competition;
   - (b) compulsory co-ordination of the various national market organisations;
   - (c) a European market organisation.

3. The common organisation established in accordance with paragraph 2 may include all measures required to attain the objectives set out in Article 39, in particular regulation of prices, aids for the production and marketing of the various products, storage and carry-over arrangements and common machinery for stabilising imports or exports.

The common organisation shall be limited to pursuit of the objectives set out in Article 39 and shall exclude any discrimination between producers or consumers within the Community.

Any common price policy shall be based on common criteria and uniform methods of calculation.

4. In order to enable the common organisation referred to in paragraph 2 to attain its objectives, one or more agricultural guidance and guarantee funds may be set up.

Article 41

To enable the objectives set out in Article 39 to be attained, provision may be made within the framework of the common agricultural policy for measures such as:

(a) an effective co-ordination of efforts in the spheres of vocational training, of research and of the dissemination of agricultural knowledge; this may include joint financing of projects or institutions;

(b) joint measures to promote consumption of certain products.

Article 42

The provisions of the Chapter relating to rules on competition shall apply to production of and trade in agricultural products only to the extent determined by the Council within the framework of Article 43 (2) and (3) and in accordance with the procedure laid down therein, account being taken of the objectives set out in Article 39.

The Council may, in particular, authorise the granting of aid:

(a) for the protection of enterprises handicapped by structural or natural conditions;

(b) within the framework of economic development programmes.

Article 43

1. In order to evolve the broad lines of a common agricultural policy, the Commission shall, immediately this Treaty enters into force, convene a conference of the Member States with a view to making a comparison of their agricultural policies, in particular by producing a statement of their resources and needs.

2. Having taken into account the work of the conference provided for in paragraph 1, after consulting the Economic and Social Committee and within two years of the entry into force of this Treaty, the Commission shall submit proposals for working out and implementing the common agricultural policy, including the replacement of the national organisations by one of the forms of common organisation provided for in Article 40 (2), and for implementing the measures specified in this Title.

These proposals shall take account of the interdependence of the agricultural matters mentioned in this Title.

The Council shall, on a proposal from the Commission and after consulting the European Parliament, acting unanimously during the first two stages and by a qualified majority thereafter, make regulations, issue directives, or take decisions, without prejudice to any recommendations it may also make.

3. The Council may, acting by a qualified majority and in accordance with paragraph 2, replace the national market organisations by the common organisation provided for in Article 40 (2) if:

(a) the common organisation offers Member States which are opposed to this measure and which have an organisation of their own for the production in question equivalent safeguards for the employment and standard of living of the producers concerned, account being taken of the adjustments that will be possible and the specialisation that will be needed with the passage of time;

(b) such an organisation ensures conditions for trade within the Community similar to those existing in a national market.

4. If a common organisation for certain raw materials is established before a common organisation exists for the corresponding processed products, such raw materials as are used for processed products intended for export to third countries may be imported from outside the Community.

Article 44

1. In so far as progressive abolition of customs duties and quantitative restrictions between Member States may result in prices likely to jeopardise the attainment of the objectives set out in Article 39, each Member State shall, during the transitional period, be entitled to apply to particular products, in a non-discriminatory manner and in substitution for quotas and to such an extent as shall not impede the expansion of the volume of trade provided for in Article 45 (2), a system of minimum prices below which imports may be either:

— temporarily suspended or reduced; or
— allowed, but subjected to the condition that they are made at a price higher than the minimum price for the product concerned.

In the latter case the minimum prices shall not include customs duties.

2. Minimum prices shall neither cause a reduction of the trade existing between Member States when this Treaty enters into force nor form an obstacle to progressive expansion of this trade. Minimum prices shall not be applied so as to form an obstacle to the development of a natural preference between Member States.

3. As soon as this Treaty enters into force the Council shall, on a proposal from the Commission, determine objective criteria for the establishment of minimum price systems and for the fixing of such prices.

These criteria shall in particular take account of the average national production costs in the Member State applying the minimum price, of the position of the various undertakings concerned in relation to such average production costs, and of the need to promote both the progressive improvement of agricultural practice and the adjustments and specialisation needed within the common market.

The Commission shall further propose a procedure for revising these criteria in order to allow for and speed up technical progress and to approximate prices progressively within the common market.

These criteria and the procedure for revising them shall be determined by the Council acting unanimously within three years of the entry into force of this Treaty.

4. Until the decision of the Council takes effect, Member States may fix minimum prices on condition that these are communicated beforehand to the Commission and to the other Member States so that they may submit their comments.

Once the Council has taken its decision, Member States shall fix minimum prices on the basis of the criteria determined as above.

The Council may, acting by a qualified majority on a proposal from the Commission, rectify any decisions taken by Member States which do not conform to the criteria defined above.

5. If it does not prove possible to determine the said objective criteria for certain products by the beginning of the third stage, the Council may, acting by a qualified majority on a proposal from the Commission, vary the minimum prices applied to these products.

6. At the end of the transitional period, a table of minimum prices still in force shall be drawn up. The Council shall, acting on a proposal from the Commission and by a majority of nine votes in accordance with the weighting laid down in the first subparagraph of Article 148(2), determine the system to be applied within the framework of the common agricultural policy.

Article 45

1. Until national market organisations have been replaced by one of the forms of common organisation referred to in Article 40 (2), trade in products in respect of which certain Member States:

— have arrangements designed to guarantee national producers a market for their products; and
— are in need of imports,

shall be developed by the conclusion of long-term agreements or contracts between importing and exporting Member States.

These agreements or contracts shall be directed towards the progressive abolition of any discrimination in the application of these arrangements to the various producers within the Community.

Such agreements or contracts shall be concluded during the first stage; account shall be taken of the principle of reciprocity.

2. As regards quantities, these agreements or contracts shall be based on the average volume of trade between Member States in the products concerned during the three years before the entry into force of this Treaty and shall provide for an increase in the volume of trade within the limits of existing requirements, account being taken of traditional patterns of trade.

As regards prices, these agreements or contracts shall enable producers to dispose of the agreed quantities at prices which shall be progressively approximated to those paid to national producers on the domestic market of the purchasing country.

This approximation shall proceed as steadily as possible and shall be completed by the end of the transitional period at the latest.

Prices shall be negotiated between the parties concerned within the framework of directives issued by the Commission for the purpose of implementing the two preceding sub-paragraphs.

If the first stage is extended, these agreements or contracts shall continue to be carried out in accordance with the conditions applicable at the end of the fourth year after the entry into force of this Treaty, the obligation to increase quantities and to approximate prices being suspended until the transition to the second stage.

Member States shall avail themselves of any opportunity open to them under their legislation, particularly in respect of import policy, to ensure the conclusion and carrying out of these agreements or contracts.

3. To the extent that Member States require raw materials for the manufacture of products to be exported outside the Community in competition with products of third countries, the above agreements or contracts shall not form an obstacle to the importation of raw materials for this purpose from third countries. This provision shall not, however, apply if the Council unanimously decides to make provision for payments required to compensate for the higher price paid on goods imported for this purpose on the basis of these agreements or contracts in relation to the delivered price of the same goods purchased on the world market.

Article 46

Where in a Member State a product is subject to a national market organisation or to internal rules having equivalent effect which affect the competitive position of similar production in another Member State, a countervailing charge shall be applied by Member States to imports of this product coming from the Member State where such organisation or rules exist, unless that State applies a countervailing charge on export.

The Commission shall fix the amount of these charges at the level required to redress the balance; it may also authorise other measures, the conditions and details of which it shall determine.

Article 47

As for the functions to be performed by the Economic and Social Committee in pursuance of this Title, its agricultural section shall hold itself at the disposal of the Commission to prepare, in accordance with the provisions of Articles 197 and 198, the deliberations of the Committee.

TITLE III. FREE MOVEMENT OF PERSONS, SERVICES AND CAPITAL

CHAPTER 1—WORKERS

Article 48

1. Freedom of movement for workers shall be secured within the Community by the end of the transitional period at the latest.

2. Such freedom of movement shall entail the abolition of any discrimination based on nationality between workers of the Member States as regards employment, remuneration and other conditions of work and employment.

3. It shall entail the right, subject to limitations justified on grounds of public policy, public security or public health:

(a) to accept offers of employment actually made;
(b) to move freely within the territory of Member States for this purpose;
(c) to stay in a Member State for the purpose of employment in accordance with the provisions governing the employment of nationals of that State laid down by law, regulation or administrative action;
(d) to remain in the territory of a Member State after having been employed in that State, subject to conditions which shall be embodied in implementing regulations to be drawn up by the Commission.

4. The provisions of this Article shall not apply to employment in the public service.

Article 49

As soon as this Treaty enters into force, the Council shall, acting by a qualified majority on a proposal from the Commission, in co-operation with the European Parliament and after consulting the Economic and Social Committee, issue directives or make regulations setting out the measures required to bring about, by progressive stages, freedom of movement for workers, as defined in Article 48, in particular:

(a) by ensuring close co-operation between national employment services;
(b) by systematically and progressively abolishing those administrative procedures and practices and those qualifying periods in respect of eligibility for available employment, whether resulting from national legislation or from agreements previously concluded between Member States, the maintenance of which would form an obstacle to liberalisation of the movement of workers;
(c) by systematically and progressively abolishing all such qualifying periods and other restrictions provided for either under national legislation or under agreements previously concluded between Member States as imposed on workers of other Member States conditions regarding the free choice of employment other than those imposed on workers of the State concerned;
(d) by setting up appropriate machinery to bring offers of employment into touch with applications for employment and to facilitate the achievement of a balance between supply and demand in the employment market in such a way as to avoid serious threats to the standard of living and level of employment in the various regions and industries.

Article 50

Member States shall, within the framework of a joint programme, encourage the exchange of young workers.

Article 51

The Council shall, acting unanimously on a proposal from the Commission, adopt such measures in the field of social security as are necessary to provide freedom of movement for workers; to this end, it shall make arrangements to secure for migrant workers and their dependants:

(a) aggregation, for the purpose of acquiring and retaining the right to benefit and of calculating the amount of benefit, of all periods taken into account under the laws of the several countries;
(b) payment of benefits to persons resident in the territories of Member States.

CHAPTER 2—RIGHT OF ESTABLISHMENT

Article 52

Within the framework of the provisions set out below, restrictions on the freedom of establishment of nationals of a Member State in the territory of another Member State shall be abolished by progressive stages in the course of the transitional period. Such progressive abolition shall also apply to restrictions on the setting up of agencies, branches or subsidiaries by nationals of any Member State established in the territory of any Member State.

Freedom of establishment shall include the right to take up and pursue activities as self-employed persons and to set up and manage undertakings, in particular companies or firms within the meaning of the second paragraph of Article 58, under the conditions laid down for its own nationals by the law of the country where such establishment is effected, subject to the provisions of the Chapter relating to capital.

Article 53

Member States shall not introduce any new restrictions on the right of establishment in their territories of nationals of other Member States, save as otherwise provided in this Treaty.

Article 54

1. Before the end of the first stage, the Council shall, acting unanimously on a proposal from the Commission and after consulting the Economic and Social Committee and the European Parliament, draw up a general programme for the abolition of existing restrictions on freedom of establishment within the Community. The Commission shall submit its proposal to the Council during the first two years of the first stage.

The programme shall set out the general conditions under which freedom of establishment is to be attained in the case of each type of activity and in particular the stages by which it is to be attained.

2. In order to implement this general programme or, in the absence of such programme, in order to achieve a stage in attaining freedom of establishment as regards a particular activity, the Council shall, acting on a proposal from the Commission, in co-operation with the European Parliament and after consulting the Economic and Social Committee, issue directives, acting unanimously until the end of the first stage and by a qualified majority thereafter.

3. The Council and the Commission shall carry out the duties devolving upon them under the preceding provisions, in particular:

(a) by according, as a general rule, priority treatment to activities where freedom of establishment makes a particularly valuable contribution to the development of production and trade;

(b) by ensuring close co-operation between the competent authorities in the Member States in order to ascertain the particular situation within the Community of the various activities concerned;

(c) by abolishing those administrative procedures and practices, whether resulting from national legislation or from agreements previously concluded between Member States, the maintenance of which would form an obstacle to freedom of establishment;

(d) by ensuring that workers of one Member State employed in the territory of another Member State may remain in that territory for the purpose of taking up activities therein as self-employed persons, where they satisfy the conditions which they would be required to satisfy if they were entering that State at the time when they intended to take up such activities;

(e) by enabling a national of one Member State to acquire and use land and buildings situated in the territory of another Member State, in so far as this does not conflict with the principles laid down in Article 39 (2);

(f) by effecting the progressive abolition of restrictions on freedom of establishment in every branch of activity under consideration, both as regards the conditions for setting up agencies, branches and subsidiaries in the territory of a Member State and as regards the conditions governing the entry of personnel belonging to the main establishment into managerial or supervisory posts in such agencies, branches or subsidiaries;

(g) by co-ordinating to the necessary extent the safeguards which, for the protection of the interests of members and others, are required by Member States of companies or firms within the meaning of the second paragraph of Article 58 with a view to making such safeguards equivalent throughout the Community;

(h) by satisfying themselves that the conditions of establishment are not distorted by aids granted by Member States.

Article 55

The provisions of this Chapter shall not apply, so far as any given Member State is concerned, to activities which in that State are connected, even occasionally, with the exercise of official authority.

The Council may, acting by a qualified majority on a proposal from the Commission, rule that the provisions of this Chapter shall not apply to certain activities.

Article 56

1. The provisions of this Chapter and measures taken in pursuance thereof shall not prejudice the applicability of provisions laid down by law, regulation or administrative action providing for special treatment for foreign nationals on grounds of public policy, public security or public health.

2. Before the end of the transitional period, the Council shall, acting unanimously on a proposal from the Commission and after consulting the European Parliament, issue directives for the co-ordination of the aforementioned provisions laid down by law, regulation or administrative action. After the end of the second stage, however, the Council shall, acting by a qualified majority on a proposal from the Commission and in co-operation with the European Parliament, issue directives for the co-ordination of such provisions as, in each Member State, are a matter for regulation or administrative action.

Article 57

1. In order to make it easier for persons to take up and pursue activities as self-employed persons, the Council shall, on a proposal from the Commission and in co-operation with the European Parliament, acting unanimously during the first stage and by a qualified majority thereafter, issue directives for the mutual recognition of diplomas, certificates and other evidence of formal qualifications.

2. For the same purpose, the Council shall, before the end of the transitional period, acting on a proposal from the Commission and after consulting the European Parliament, issue directives for the co-ordination of the provisions laid down by law, regulation or administrative action in Member States concerning the taking up and pursuit of activities as self-employed persons. Unanimity shall be required for directives the implementation of which involves in at least one Member State amendment of the existing principles laid down by law governing the professions with respect to training and conditions of access for natural persons. In other cases the Council shall act by a qualified majority, in co-operation with the European Parliament.

3. In the case of the medical and allied and pharmaceutical professions, the progressive abolition of restrictions shall be dependent upon co-ordination of the conditions for their exercise in the various Member States.

Article 58

Companies or firms formed in accordance with the law of a Member State and having their registered office, central administration or principal place of business within the Community shall, for the purposes of this Chapter, be treated in the same way as natural persons who are nationals of Member States.

"Companies or firms" means companies or firms constituted under civil or commercial law, including cooperative societies, and other legal persons governed by public or private law, save for those which are non-profit-making.

CHAPTER 3—SERVICES

Article 59

Within the framework of the provisions set out below, restrictions on freedom to provide services within the Community shall be progressively abolished during the transitional period in respect of nationals of Member States who are established in a State of the Community other than that of the person for whom the services are intended.

The Council may, acting by a qualified majority on a proposal from the Commission, extend the provisions of this Chapter to nationals of a third country who provide services and who are established within the Community.

Article 60

Services shall be considered to be "services" within the meaning of this Treaty where they are normally provided for remuneration, in so far as they are not governed by the provisions relating to freedom of movement for goods, capital and persons.

"Services" shall in particular include:

(a) activities of an industrial character;
(b) activities of a commercial character;
(c) activities of craftsmen;
(d) activities of the professions.

Without prejudice to the provisions of the Chapter relating to the right of establishment, the person providing a service may, in order to do so, temporarily pursue his activity in the State where the service is provided, under the same conditions as are imposed by that State on its own nationals.

Article 61

1. Freedom to provide services in the field of transport shall be governed by the provisions of the Title relating to transport.

2. The liberalisation of banking and insurance services connected with movements of capital shall be effected in step with the progressive liberalisation of movement of capital.

Article 62

Save as otherwise provided in this Treaty, Member States shall not introduce any new restrictions on the freedom to provide services which have in fact been attained at the date of the entry into force of this Treaty.

Article 63

1. Before the end of the first stage, the Council shall, acting unanimously on a proposal from the Commission and after consulting the Economic and Social Committee and the European Parliament, draw up a general programme for the abolition of existing restrictions on freedom to provide services within the Community. The Commission shall submit its proposal to the Council during the first two years of the first stage.

The programme shall set out the general conditions under which and the stages by which each type of service is to be liberalised.

2. In order to implement this general programme or, in the absence of such programme, in order to achieve a stage in the liberalisation of a specific service, the Council shall, on a proposal from the Commission and after consulting the Economic and Social Committee and the European Parliament, issue directives, acting unanimously until the end of the first stage and by a qualified majority thereafter.

3. As regards the proposals and decisions referred to in paragraphs 1 and 2, priority shall as a general rule be given to those services which directly affect production costs or the liberalisation of which helps to promote trade in goods.

Article 64

The Member States declare their readiness to undertake the liberalisation of services beyond the extent required by the directives issued pursuant to Article 63(2), if their general economic situation and the situation of the economic sector concerned so permit.

To this end, the Commission shall make recommendations to the Member States concerned.

Article 65

As long as restrictions on freedom to provide services have not been abolished, each Member State shall apply such restrictions without distinction on grounds of nationality or residence to all persons providing services within the meaning of the first paragraph of Article 59.

Article 66

The provisions of Articles 55 to 58 shall apply to the matters covered by this Chapter.

CHAPTER 4—CAPITAL

Article 67

1. During the transitional period and to the extent necessary to ensure the proper functioning of the common market, Member States shall progressively abolish between themselves all restrictions on the movement of capital belonging to persons resident in Member States and any discrimination based on the nationality or on the place of residence of the parties or on the place where such capital is invested.

2. Current payments connected with the movement of capital between Member States shall be freed from all restrictions by the end of the first stage at the latest.

Article 68

1. Member States shall, as regards the matters dealt with in this Chapter, be as liberal as possible in granting such exchange authorisations as are still necessary after the entry into force of this Treaty.

2. Where a Member State applies to the movements of capital liberalised in accordance with the provisions of this Chapter the domestic rules governing the capital market and the credit system, it shall do so in a non-discriminatory manner.

3. Loans for the direct or indirect financing of a Member State or its regional or local authorities shall not be issued or placed in other Member States unless the States concerned have reached agreement thereon. This provision shall not preclude the application of Article 22 of the Protocol on the Statute of the European Investment Bank.

Article 69

The Council shall, on a proposal from the Commission, which for this purpose shall consult the Monetary Committee provided for in Article 105, issue the necessary directives for the progressive implementation of the provisions of Article 67, acting unanimously during the first two stages and by a qualified majority thereafter.

Article 70

1. The Commission shall propose to the Council measures for the progressive co-ordination of the exchange policies of Member States in respect of the movement of capital between those States and third countries. For this purpose the Council shall issue directives, acting by a qualified majority. It shall endeavour to attain the highest possible degree of liberalisation. Unanimity shall be required for measures which constitute a step back as regards the liberalisation of capital movements.

2. Where the measures taken in accordance with paragraph 1 do not permit the elimination of differences between the exchange rules of Member States and where such differences could lead persons resident in one of the Member States to use the freer transfer facilities within the Community which are provided for in Article 67 in order to evade the rules of one of the Member

States concerning the movement of capital to or from third countries, that State may, after consulting the other Member States and the Commission, take appropriate measures to overcome these difficulties.

Should the Council find that these measures are restricting the free movement of capital within the Community to a greater extent than is required for the purpose of overcoming the difficulties, it may, acting by a qualified majority on a proposal from the Commission, decide that the State concerned shall amend or abolish these measures.

Article 71

Member States shall endeavour to avoid introducing within the Community any new exchange restrictions on the movement of capital and current payments connected with such movements, and shall endeavour not to make existing rules more restrictive.

They declare their readiness to go beyond the degree of liberalisation of capital movements provided for in the preceding Articles in so far as their economic situation, in particular the situation of their balance of payments, so permits.

The Commission may, after consulting the Monetary Committee, make recommendations to Member States on this subject.

Article 72

Member States shall keep the Commission informed of any movements of capital to and from third countries which come to their knowledge. The Commission may deliver to Member States any opinions which it considers appropriate on this subject.

Article 73

1. If movements of capital lead to disturbances in the functioning of the capital market in any Member State, the Commission shall, after consulting the Monetary Committee, authorise that State to take protective measures in the field of capital movements, the conditions and details of which the Commission shall determine.

The Council may, acting by a qualified majority, revoke this authorisation or amend the conditions or details thereof.

2. A Member State which is in difficulties may, however, on grounds of secrecy or urgency, take the measures mentioned above, where this proves necessary, on its own initiative. The Commission and the other Member States shall be informed of such measures by the date of their entry into force at the latest. In this event the Commission may, after consulting the Monetary Committee, decide that the State concerned shall amend or abolish the measures.

TITLE IV. TRANSPORT

Article 74

The objectives of this Treaty shall, in matters governed by this Title, be pursued by Member States within the framework of a common transport policy.

Article 75

1. For the purpose of implementing Article 74, and taking into account the distinctive features of transport, the Council shall, acting unanimously until the end of the second stage and by a qualified majority thereafter, lay down, on a proposal from the Commission and after consulting the Economic and Social Committee and the European Parliament:

(a) common rules applicable to international transport to or from the territory of a Member State or passing across the territory of one or more Member States;

(b) the conditions under which non-resident carriers may operate transport services within a Member State;

(c) any other appropriate provisions.

2. The provisions referred to in (a) and (b) of paragraph 1 shall be laid down during the transitional period.

3. By way of derogation from the procedure provided for in paragraph 1, where the application of provisions concerning the principles of the regulatory system for transport would be liable to have a serious effect on the standard of living and on employment in certain areas and on the operation of transport facilities, they shall be laid down by the Council acting unanimously. In so doing, the Council shall take into account the need for adaptation to the economic development which will result from establishing the common market.

Article 76

Until the provisions referred to in Article 75 (1) have been laid down, no Member State may, without the unanimous approval of the Council, make the various provisions governing the subject when this Treaty enters into force less favourable in their direct or indirect effect on carriers of other Member States as compared with carriers who are nationals of that State.

Article 77

Aids shall be compatible with this Treaty if they meet the needs of co-ordination of transport or if they represent re-imbursement for the discharge of certain obligations inherent in the concept of a public service.

Article 78

Any measures taken within the framework of this Treaty in respect of transport rates and conditions shall take account of the economic circumstances of carriers.

Article 79

1. In the case of transport within the Community, discrimination which takes the form of carriers charging different rates and imposing different conditions for the carriage of the same goods over the same transport links on grounds of the country of origin or of destination of the goods in question, shall be abolished, at the latest, before the end of the second stage.

2. Paragraph 1 shall not prevent the Council from adopting other measures in pursuance of Article 75 (1).

3. Within two years of the entry into force of this Treaty, the Council shall, acting by a qualified majority on a proposal from the Commission and after consulting the Economic and Social Committee, lay down rules for implementing the provisions of paragraph 1.

The Council may in particular lay down the provisions needed to enable the institutions of the Community to secure compliance with the rule laid down in paragraph 1 and to ensure that users benefit from it to the full.

4. The Commission shall, acting on its own initiative or on application by a Member State, investigate any cases of discrimination falling within paragraph 1 and, after consulting any Member State concerned, shall take the necessary decisions within the framework of the rules laid down in accordance with the provisions of paragraph 3.

Article 80

1. The imposition by a Member State, in respect of transport operations carried out within the Community, of rates and conditions involving any element of support or protection in the interest of one or more particular undertakings or industries shall be prohibited as from the beginning of the second stage, unless authorised by the Commission.

2. The Commission shall, acting on its own initiative or on application by a Member State, examine the rates and conditions referred to in paragraph 1 taking account in particular of the requirements of an appropriate regional economic policy, the needs of underdeveloped areas

and the problems of areas seriously affected by political circumstances on the one hand, and of the effects of such rates and conditions on competition between the different modes of transport on the other.

After consulting each Member State concerned, the Commission shall take the necessary decisions.

3. The prohibition provided for in paragraph 1 shall not apply to tariffs fixed to meet competition.

Article 81

Charges or dues in respect of the crossing of frontiers which are charged by a carrier in addition to the transport rates shall not exceed a reasonable level after taking the costs actually incurred thereby into account.

Member States shall endeavour to reduce these costs progressively.

The Commission may make recommendations to Member States for the application of this Article.

Article 82

The provisions of this Title shall not form an obstacle to the application of measures taken in the Federal Republic of Germany to the extent that such measures are required in order to compensate for the economic disadvantages caused by the division of Germany to the economy of certain areas of the Federal Republic affected by that division.

Article 83

An Advisory Committee, consisting of experts designated by the Governments of Member States, shall be attached to the Commission. The Commission, whenever it considers it desirable, shall consult the Committee on transport matters without prejudice to the powers of the transport section of the Economic and Social Committee.

Article 84

1. The provisions of this Title shall apply to transport by rail, road and inland waterway.

2. The Council may, acting by a qualified majority, decide whether, to what extent and by what procedure appropriate provisions may be laid down for sea and air transport.

The procedural provisions of Article 75 (1) and (3) shall apply.

PART THREE. POLICY OF THE COMMUNITY

TITLE I. COMMON RULES

CHAPTER 1—RULES ON COMPETITION

Section 1—Rules applying to undertakings

Article 85

1. The following shall be prohibited as incompatible with the common market: all agreements between undertakings, decisions by associations of undertakings and concerted practices which may affect trade between Member States and which have as their object or effect the prevention, restriction or distortion of competition within the common market, and in particular those which:

(a) directly or indirectly fix purchase or selling prices or any other trading conditions;

(b) limit or control production, markets, technical development, or investment;

(c) share markets or sources of supply;
(d) apply dissimilar conditions to equivalent transactions with other trading parties, thereby placing them at a competitive disadvantage;
(e) make the conclusion of contracts subject to acceptance by the other parties of supplementary obligations which, by their nature or according to commercial usage, have no connection with the subject of such contracts.

2. Any agreements or decisions prohibited pursuant to this Article shall be automatically void.

3. The provisions of paragraph 1 may, however, be declared inapplicable in the case of:
— any agreement or category of agreements between undertakings;
— any decision or category of decisions by associations of undertakings;
— any concerted practice or category of concerted practices;

which contributes to improving the production or distribution of goods or to promoting technical or economic progress while allowing consumers a fair share of the resulting benefit, and which does not:
(a) impose on the undertakings concerned restrictions which are not indispensable to the attainment of these objectives;
(b) afford such undertakings the possibility of eliminating competition in respect of a substantial part of the products in question.

Article 86

Any abuse by one or more undertakings of a dominant position within the common market or in a substantial part of it shall be prohibited as incompatible with the common market in so far as it may affect trade between Member States.

Such abuse may, in particular, consist in:
(a) directly or indirectly imposing unfair purchase or selling prices or other unfair trading conditions;
(b) limiting production, markets or technical development to the prejudice of consumers;
(c) applying dissimilar conditions to equivalent transactions with other trading parties, thereby placing them at a competitive disadvantage;
(d) making the conclusion of contracts subject to acceptance by the other parties of supplementary obligations which, by their nature or according to commercial usage, have no connection with the subject of such contracts.

Article 87

1. Within three years of the entry into force of this Treaty the Council shall, acting unanimously on a proposal from the Commission and after consulting the European Parliament, adopt any appropriate regulations or directives to give effect to the principles set out in Articles 85 and 86.

If such provisions have not been adopted within the period mentioned, they shall be laid down by the Council, acting by a qualified majority on a proposal from the Commission and after consulting the European Parliament.

2. The regulations or directives referred to in paragraph 1 shall be designed in particular:
(a) to ensure compliance with the prohibitions laid down in Article 85 (1) and in Article 86 by making provision for fines and periodic penalty payments;
(b) to lay down detailed rules for the application of Article 85 (3), taking into account the need to ensure effective supervision on the one hand, and to simplify administration to the greatest possible extent on the other;
(c) to define, if need be, in the various branches of the economy, the scope of the provisions of Articles 85 and 86;
(d) to define the respective functions of the Commission and of the Court of Justice in applying the provisions laid down in this paragraph;
(e) to determine the relationship between national laws and the provisions contained in this Section or adopted pursuant to this Article.

Article 88

Until the entry into force of the provisions adopted in pursuance of Article 87, the authorities in Member States shall rule on the admissibility of agreements, decisions and concerted practices and on abuse of a dominant position in the common market in accordance with the law of their country and with the provisions of Article 85, in particular paragraph 3, and of Article 86.

Article 89

1. Without prejudice to Article 88, the Commission shall, as soon as it takes up its duties, ensure the application of the principles laid down in Articles 85 and 86. On application by a Member State or on its own initiative, and in co-operation with the competent authorities in the Member States, who shall give it their assistance, the Commission shall investigate cases of suspected infringement of these principles. If it finds that there has been an infringement, it shall propose appropriate measures to bring it to an end.

2. If the infringement is not brought to an end, the Commission shall record such infringement of the principles in a reasoned decision. The Commission may publish its decision and authorise Member States to take the measures, the conditions and details of which it shall determine, needed to remedy the situation.

Article 90

1. In the case of public undertakings and undertakings to which Member States grant special or exclusive rights, Member States shall neither enact nor maintain in force any measure contrary to the rules contained in this Treaty, in particular those rules provided for in Article 7 and Articles 85 to 94.

2. Undertakings entrusted with the operation of services of general economic interest or having the character of a revenue-producing monopoly shall be subject to the rules contained in this Treaty, in particular to the rules on competiton, in so far as the application of such rules does not obstruct the performance, in law or in fact, of the particular tasks assigned to them. The development of trade must not be affected to such an extent as would be contrary to the interests of the Community.

3. The Commission shall ensure the application of the provisions of this Article and shall, where necessary, address appropriate directives or decisions to Member States.

Section 2—Dumping

Article 91

1. If during the transitional period, the Commission, on application by a Member State or by any other interested party, finds that dumping is being practised within the common market, it shall address recommendations to the person or persons with whom such practices originate for the purpose of putting an end to them.

Should the practices continue, the Commission shall authorise the injured Member State to take protective measures, the conditions and details of which the Commission shall determine.

2. As soon as this Treaty enters into force, products which originate in or are in free circulation in one Member State and which have been exported to another Member State shall, on reimportation, be admitted into the territory of the first-mentioned State free of all customs duties, quantitative restrictions or measures having equivalent effect. The Commission shall lay down appropriate rules for the application of this paragraph.

Section 3—Aids granted by States

Article 92

1. Save as otherwise provided in this Treaty, any aid granted by a Member State or through State resources in any form whatsoever which distorts or threatens to distort competition by favouring certain undertakings or the production of certain goods shall, in so far as it affects trade between Member States, be incompatible with the common market.

2. The following shall be compatible with the common market:
   (a) aid having a social character, granted to individual consumers, provided that such aid is granted without discrimination related to the origin of the products concerned;
   (b) aid to make good the damage caused by natural disasters or exceptional occurrences;
   (c) aid granted to the economy of certain areas of the Federal Republic of Germany affected by the division of Germany in so far as such aid is required in order to compensate for the economic disadvantages caused by that division.
3. The following may be considered to be compatible with the common market:
   (a) aid to promote the economic development of areas where the standard of living is abnormally low or where there is serious under-employment;
   (b) aid to promote the execution of an important project of common European interest or to remedy a serious disturbance in the economy of a Member State;
   (c) aid to facilitate the development of certain economic activities or of certain economic areas, where such aid does not adversely affect trading conditions to an extent contrary to the common interest. However, the aids granted to ship building as of 1 January 1957 shall, in so far as they serve only to compensate for the absence of customs protection, be progressively reduced under the same conditions as apply to the elimination of customs duties, subject to the provisions of this Treaty concerning common commercial policy towards third countries;
   (d) such other categories of aid as may be specified by decision of the Council acting by a qualified majority on a proposal from the Commission.

Article 93

1. The Commission shall, in co-operation with Member States, keep under constant review all systems of aid existing in those States. It shall propose to the latter any appropriate measures required by the progressive development or by the functioning of the common market.

2. If, after giving notice to the parties concerned to submit their comments, the Commission finds that aid granted by a State or through State resources is not compatible with the common market having regard to Article 92, or that such aid is being misused, it shall decide that the State concerned shall abolish or alter such aid within a period of time to be determined by the Commission.

If the State concerned does not comply with the decision within the prescribed time, the Commission or any other interested State may, in derogation from the provisions of Articles 169 and 170, refer the matter to the Court of Justice direct.

On application by a Member State, the Council, may, acting unanimously, decide that aid which that State is granting or intends to grant shall be considered to be compatible with the common market, in derogation from the provisions of Article 92 or from the regulations provided for in Article 94, if such a decision is justified by exceptional circumstances. If, as regards the aid in question, the Commission has already initiated the procedure provided for in the first sub-paragraph of this paragraph, the fact that the State concerned has made its application to the Council shall have the effect of suspending that procedure until the Council has made its attitude known.

If, however, the Council has not made its attitude known within three months of the said application being made, the Commission shall give its decision on the case.

3. The Commission shall be informed, in sufficient time to enable it to submit its comments, of any plans to grant or alter aid. If it considers that any such plan is not compatible with the common market having regard to Article 92, it shall without delay initiate the procedure provided for in paragraph 2. The Member State concerned shall not put its proposed measures into effect until this procedure has resulted in a final decision.

Article 94

The Council may, acting by a qualified majority on a proposal from the Commission, make any appropriate regulations for the application of Articles 92 and 93 and may in particular determine the conditions in which Article 93 (3) shall apply and the categories of aid exempted from this procedure.

CHAPTER 2—TAX PROVISIONS

Article 95

No Member State shall impose, directly or indirectly, on the products of other Member States any internal taxation of any kind in excess of that imposed directly or indirectly on similar domestic products.

Furthermore, no Member State shall impose on the products of other Member States any internal taxation of such a nature as to afford indirect protection to other products.

Member States shall, not later than at the beginning of the second stage, repeal or amend any provisions existing when this Treaty enters into force which conflict with the preceding rules.

Article 96

Where products are exported to the territory of any Member State, any repayment of internal taxation shall not exceed the internal taxation imposed on them, whether directly or indirectly.

Article 97

Member States which levy a turnover tax calculated on a cumulative multistage tax system may, in the case of internal taxation imposed by them on imported products or of repayments allowed by them on exported products, establish average rates for products or groups of products, provided that there is no infringement of the principles laid down in Articles 95 and 96.

Where the average rates established by a Member State do not conform to these principles, the Commission shall address appropriate directives or decisions to the State concerned.

Article 98

In the case of charges other than turnover taxes, excise duties and other forms of indirect taxation, remissions and repayments in respect of exports to other Member States may not be granted and countervailing charges in respect of imports from Member States may not be imposed unless the measures contemplated have been previously approved for a limited period by the Council acting by a qualified majority on a proposal from the Commission.

Article 99

The Council shall, acting unanimously on a proposal from the Commission and after consulting the European Parliament, adopt provisions for the harmonisation of legislation concerning turnover taxes, excise duties and other forms of indirect taxation to the extent that such harmonisation is necessary to ensure the establishment and the functioning of the internal market within the time-limit laid down in Article 8a.

CHAPTER 3—APPROXIMATION OF LAWS

Article 100

The Council shall, acting unanimously on a proposal from the Commission, issue directives for the approximation of such provisions laid down by law, regulation or administrative action in Member States as directly affect the establishment or functioning of the common market.

The European Parliament and the Economic and Social Committee shall be consulted in the case of directives whose implementation would, in one or more Member States, involve the amendment of legislation.

Article 100a

1. By way of derogation from Article 100 and save where otherwise provided in this Treaty, the following provisions shall apply for the achievement of the objectives set out in Article 8a.

The Council shall, acting by a qualified majority on a proposal from the Commission in co-operation with the European Parliament and after consulting the Economic and Social Committee, adopt the measures for the approximation of the provisions laid down by law, regulation or adminstrative action in Member States which have as their object the establishment and functioning of the internal market.

2. Paragraph 1 shall not apply to fiscal provisions, to those relating to the free movement of persons nor to those relating to the rights and interests of employed persons.

3. The Commission, in its proposals envisaged in paragraph 1 concerning health, safety, environmental protection and consumer protection, will take as a base a high level of protection.

4. If, after the adoption of a harmonisation measure by the Council acting by a qualified majority, a Member State deems it necessary to apply national provisions on grounds of major needs referred to in Article 36, or relating to protection of the environment or the working environment, it shall notify the Commission of these provisions.

The Commission shall confirm the provisions involved after having verified that they are not a means of arbitrary discrimination or a disguised restriction on trade between Member States.

By way of derogation from the procedure laid down in Articles 169 and 170, the Commission or any Member State may bring the matter directly before the Court of Justice if it considers that another Member State is making improper use of the powers provided for in this Article.

5. The harmonisation measures referred to above shall, in appropriate cases, include a safeguard clause authorising the Member States to take, for one or more of the non-economic reasons referred to in Article 36, provisional measures subject to a Community control procedure.

Article 100b

1. During 1992, the Commission shall, together with each Member State, draw up an inventory of national laws, regulations and administrative provisions which fall under Article 100a and which have not been harmonised pursuant to that Article.

The Council, acting in accordance with the provisions of Article 100a, may decide that the provisions in force in a Member State must be recognised as being equivalent to those applied by another Member State.

2. The provisions of Article 100a (4) shall apply by analogy.

3. The Commission shall draw up the inventory referred to in the first sub-paragraph of paragraph 1 and shall submit appropriate proposals in good time to allow the Council to act before the end of 1992.

Article 101

Where the Commission finds that a difference between the provisions laid down by law, regulation or administrative action in Member States is distorting the conditions of competition in the common market and that the resultant distortion needs to be eliminated, it shall consult the Member States concerned.

If such consultation does not result in an agreement eliminating the distortion in question, the Council shall, on a proposal from the Commission, acting unanimously during the first stage and by a qualified majority thereafter, issue the necessary directives. The Commission and the Council may take any other appropriate measures provided for in this Treaty.

Article 102

1. Where there is reason to fear that the adoption or amendment of a provision laid down by law, regulation or administrative action may cause distortion within the meaning of Article 101, a Member State desiring to proceed therewith shall consult the Commission. After consulting the Member States, the Commission shall recommend to the States concerned such measures as may be appropriate to avoid the distortion in question.

2. If a State desiring to introduce or amend its own provisions does not comply with the recommendation addressed to it by the Commission, other Member States shall not be required,

in pursuance of Article 101, to amend their own provisions in order to eliminate such distortion. If the Member State which has ignored the recommendation of the Commission causes distortion detrimental only to itself, the provisions of Article 101 shall not apply.

TITLE II. ECONOMIC POLICY

CHAPTER 1—CO-OPERATION IN ECONOMIC AND MONETARY POLICY (ECONOMIC AND MONETARY UNION)

Article 102a

1. In order to ensure the convergence of economic and monetary policies which is necessary for the further development of the Community, Member States shall co-operate in accordance with the objectives of Article 104. In so doing, they shall take account of the experience acquired in co-operation within the framework of the European Monetary System (EMS) and in developing the ECU, and shall respect existing powers in this field.

2. In so far as further development in the field of economic and monetary policy necessitates institutional changes, the provisions of Article 236 shall be applicable. The Monetary Committee and the Committee of Governors of the Central Banks shall also be consulted regarding institutional changes in the monetary area.

CHAPTER 2—CONJUNCTURAL POLICY

Article 103

1. Member States shall regard their conjunctural policies as a matter of common concern. They shall consult each other and the Commission on the measures to be taken in the light of the prevailing circumstances.

2. Without prejudice to any other procedures provided for in this Treaty, the Council may, acting unanimously on a proposal from the Commission, decide upon the measures appropriate to the situation.

3. Acting by a qualified majority on a proposal from the Commission, the Council shall, where required, issue any directives needed to give effect to the measures decided upon under paragraph 2.

4. The procedures provided for in this Article shall also apply if any difficulty should arise in the supply of certain products.

CHAPTER 3—BALANCE OF PAYMENTS

Article 104

Each Member State shall pursue the economic policy needed to ensure the equilibrium of its overall balance of payments and to maintain confidence in its currency, while taking care to ensure a high level of employment and a stable level of prices.

Article 105

1. In order to facilitate attainment of the objectives set out in Article 104, Member States shall co-ordinate their economic policies. They shall for this purpose provide for co-operation between their appropriate administrative departments and between their central banks.

The Commission shall submit to the Council recommendations on how to achieve such co-operation.

2. In order to promote co-ordination of the policies of Member States in the monetary field to the full extent needed for the functioning of the common market, a Monetary Committee with advisory status is hereby set up. It shall have the following tasks:

— to keep under review the monetary and financial situation of the Member States and of the Community and the general payments system of the Member States and to

report regularly thereon to the Council and to the Commission;
— to deliver opinions at the request of the Council or of the Commission or on its own initiative, for submission to these institutions.

The Member States and the Commission shall each appoint two members of the Monetary Committee.

Article 106

1. Each Member State undertakes to authorise, in the currency of the Member State in which the creditor or the beneficiary resides, any payments connected with the movement of goods, services or capital, and any transfers of capital and earnings, to the extent that the movement of goods, services, capital and persons between Member States has been liberalised pursuant to this Treaty.

The Member States declare their readiness to undertake the liberalisation of payments beyond the extent provided in the preceding sub-paragraph, in so far as their economic situation in general and the state of their balance of payments in particular so permit.

2. In so far as movements of goods, services, and capital are limited only by restrictions on payments connected therewith, these restrictions shall be progressively abolished by applying, *mutatis mutandis*, the provisions of the Chapters relating to the abolition of quantitative restrictions, to the liberalisation of services and to the free movement of capital.

3. Member States undertake not to introduce between themselves any new restrictions on transfers connected with the invisible transactions listed in Annex III to this Treaty.

The progressive abolition of existing restrictions shall be effected in accordance with the provisions of Articles 63 to 65, in so far as such abolition is not governed by the provisions contained in paragraphs 1 and 2 or by the Chapter relating to the free movement of capital.

4. If need be, Member States shall consult each other on the measures to be taken to enable the payments and transfers mentioned in this Article to be effected; such measures shall not prejudice the attainment of the objectives set out in this Chapter.

Article 107

1. Each Member State shall treat its policy with regard to rates of exchange as a matter of common concern.

2. If a Member State makes an alteration in its rate of exchange which is inconsistent with the objectives set out in Article 104 and which seriously distorts conditions of competition, the Commission may, after consulting the Monetary Committee, authorise other Member States to take for a strictly limited period the necessary measures, the conditions and details of which it shall determine, in order to counter the consequences of such alteration.

Article 108

1. Where a Member State is in difficulties or is seriously threatened with difficulties as regards its balance of payments either as a result of an overall disequilibrium in its balance of payments, or as a result of the type of currency at its disposal, and where such difficulties are liable in particular to jeopardise the functioning of the common market or the progressive implementation of the common commercial policy, the Commission shall immediately investigate the position of the State in question and the action which, making use of all the means at its disposal, that State has taken or may take in accordance with the provisions of Article 104. The Commission shall state what measures it recommends the State concerned to take.

If the action taken by a Member State and the measures suggested by the Commission do not prove sufficient to overcome the difficulties which have arisen or which threaten, the Commission shall, after consulting the Monetary Committee, recommend to the Council the granting of mutual assistance and appropriate methods therefor.

The Commission shall keep the Council regularly informed of the situation and of how it is developing.

2. The Council, acting by a qualified majority, shall grant such mutual assistance; it shall adopt directives or decisions laying down the condition and details of such assistance, which may take such forms as:

(a) a concerted approach to or within any other international organisations to which Member States may have recourse;

(b) measures needed to avoid deflection of trade where the State which is in difficulties maintains or reintroduces quantitative restrictions against third countries;

(c) the granting of limited credits by other Member States, subject to their agreement.

During the transitional period, mutual assistance may also take the form of special reductions in customs duties or enlargements of quotas in order to facilitate an increase in imports from the State which is in difficulties, subject to the agreement of the States by which such measures would have to be taken.

3. If the mutual assistance recommended by the Commission is not granted by the Council or if the mutual assistance granted and the measures taken are insufficient, the Commission shall authorise the State which is in difficulties to take protective measures, the conditions and details of which the Commission shall determine.

Such authorisation may be revoked and such conditions and details may be changed by the Council acting by a qualified majority.

Article 109

1. Where a sudden crisis in the balance of payments occurs and a decision within the meaning of Article 108 (2) is not immediately taken, the Member State concerned may, as a precaution, take the necessary protective measures. Such measures must cause the least possible disturbance in the functioning of the common market and must not be wider in scope than is strictly necessary to remedy the sudden difficulties which have arisen.

2. The Commission and the other Member States shall be informed of such protective measures not later than when they enter into force. The Commission may recommend to the Council the granting of mutual assistance under Article 108.

3. After the Commission has delivered an opinion and the Monetary Committee has been consulted, the Council may, acting by a qualified majority, decide that the State concerned shall amend, suspend or abolish the protective measures referred to above.

CHAPTER 4—COMMERCIAL POLICY

Article 110

By establishing a customs union between themselves Member States aim to contribute, in the common interest, to the harmonious development of world trade, the progressive abolition of restrictions on international trade and the lowering of customs barriers.

The common commercial policy shall take into account the favourable effect which the abolition of customs duties between Member States may have on the increase in the competitive strength of undertakings in those States.

Article 111

The following provisions shall, without prejudice to Articles 115 and 116, apply during the transitional period:

1. Member States shall co-ordinate their trade relations with third countries so as to bring about, by the end of the transitional period, the conditions needed for implementing a common policy in the field of external trade.

The Commission shall submit to the Council proposals regarding the procedure for common action to be followed during the transitional period and regarding the achievement of uniformity in their commercial policies.

2. The Commission shall submit to the Council recommendations for tariff negotiations with third countries in respect of the common customs tariff.

The Council shall authorise the Commission to open such negotiations.

The Commission shall conduct these negotiations in consultation with a special committee appointed by the Council to assist the Commission in this task and within the framework of such directives as the Council may issue to it.

3. In exercising the powers conferred upon it by this Article, the Council shall act unanimously during the first two stages and by a qualified majority thereafter.

4. Member States shall, in consultation with the Commission, take all necessary measures, particularly those designed to bring about an adjustment of tariff agreements in force with third countries, in order that the entry into force of the common customs tariff shall not be delayed.

5. Member States shall aim at securing as high a level of uniformity as possible between themselves as regards their liberalisation lists in relation to third countries or groups of third countries. To this end, the Commission shall make all appropriate recommendations to Member States.

If Member States abolish or reduce quantitative restrictions in relation to third countries, they shall inform the Commission beforehand and shall accord the same treatment to other Member States.

Article 112

1. Without prejudice to obligations undertaken by them within the framework of other international organisations, Member States shall, before the end of the transitional period, progressively harmonise the systems whereby they grant aid for exports to third countries, to the extent necessary to ensure that competition between undertakings of the Community is not distorted.

On a proposal from the Commission, the Council, shall, acting unanimously until the end of the second state and by a qualified majority thereafter, issue any directives needed for this purpose.

2. The preceding provisions shall not apply to such drawback of customs duties or charges having equivalent effect nor to such repayment of indirect taxation including turnover taxes, excise duties and other indirect taxes as is allowed when goods are exported from a Member State to a third country, in so far as such drawback or repayment does not exceed the amount imposed, directly or indirectly, on the products exported.

Article 113

1. After the transitional period has ended, the common commercial policy shall be based on uniform principles, particularly in regard to changes in tariff rates, the conclusion of tariff and trade agreements, the achievement of uniformity in measures of liberalisation, export policy and measures to protect trade such as those to be taken in case of dumping or subsidies.

2. The Commission shall submit proposals to the Council for implementing the common commercial policy.

3. Where agreements with third countries need to be negotiated, the Commission shall make recommendations to the Council, which shall authorise the Commission to open the necessary negotiations.

The Commission shall conduct these negotiations in consultation with a special committee appointed by the Council to assist the Commission in this task and within the framework of such directives as the Council may issue to it.

4. In exercising the powers conferred upon it by this Article, the Council shall act by a qualified majority.

Article 114

The agreements referred to in Article 111 (2) and in Article 113 shall be concluded by the Council on behalf of the Community, acting unanimously during the first two stages and by a qualified majority thereafter.

Article 115

In order to ensure that the execution of measures of commercial policy taken in accordance with this Treaty by any Member State is not obstructed by deflection of trade, or where differences between such measures lead to economic difficulties in one or more of the Member States, the Commission shall recommend the methods for the requisite co-operation between Member States. Failing this, the Commission shall authorise Member States to take the necessary protective measures, the conditions and details of which it shall determine.

In case of urgency during the transitional period, Member States may themselves take the necessary measures and shall notify them to the other Member States and to the Commission, which may decide that the States concerned shall amend or abolish such measures.

In the selection of such measures, priority shall be given to those which cause the least disturbance to the functioning of the common market and which take into account the need to expedite, as far as possible, the introduction of the common customs tariff.

Article 116

From the end of the transitional period onwards, Member States shall, in respect of all matters of particular interest to the common market, proceed within the framework of international organisations of an economic character only by common action. To this end, the Commission shall submit to the Council, which shall act by a qualified majority, proposals concerning the scope and implementation of such common action.

During the transitional period, Member States shall consult each other for the purpose of concerting the action they take and adopting as far as possible a uniform attitude.

TITLE III. SOCIAL POLICY

CHAPTER 1—SOCIAL PROVISIONS

Article 117

Member States agree upon the need to promote improved working conditions and an improved standard of living for workers, so as to make possible their harmonisation while the improvement is being maintained.

They believe that such a development will ensue not only from the functioning of the common market, which will favour the harmonisation of social systems, but also from the procedures provided for in this Treaty and from the approximation of provisions laid down by law, regulation or administrative action.

Article 118

Without prejudice to the other provisions of this Treaty and in conformity with its general objectives, the Commission shall have the task of promoting close co-operation between Member States in the social field, particularly in matters relating to:

- employment;
- labour law and working conditions;
- basic and advanced vocational training;
- social security;
- prevention of occupational accidents and diseases;
- occupational hygiene;
- the right of association, and collective bargaining between employers and workers.

To this end, the Commission shall act in close contact with Member States by making studies, delivering opinions and arranging consultations both on problems arising at national level and on those of concern to international organisations.

Before delivering the opinions provided for in this Article, the Commission shall consult the Economic and Social Committee.

Article 118a

1. Member States shall pay particular attention to encouraging improvements, especially in the working environment, as regards the health and safety of workers, and shall set as their

objective the harmonisation of conditions in this area, while maintaining the improvements made.

2. In order to help achieve the objective laid down in the first paragraph, the Council, acting by a qualified majority on a proposal from the Commission, in co-operation with the European Parliament and after consulting the Economic and Social Committee, shall adopt, by means of directives, minimum requirements for gradual implementation, having regard to the conditions and technical rules obtaining in each of the Member States.

Such directives shall avoid imposing administrative, financial and legal constraints in a way which would hold back the creation and development of small and medium-sized undertakings.

3. The provisions adopted pursuant to this Article shall not prevent any Member State from maintaining or introducing more stringent measures for the protection of working conditions compatible with this Treaty.

Article 118b[1]

The Commission shall endeavour to develop the dialogue between management and labour at European level which could, if the two sides consider it desirable, lead to relations based on agreement.

Article 119

Each Member State shall during the first stage ensure and subsequently maintain the application of the principle that men and women should receive equal pay for equal work.

For the purpose of this Article, "pay" means the ordinary basic or minimum wage or salary and any other consideration, whether in cash or in kind, which the worker receives, directly or indirectly, in respect of his employment from his employer.

Equal pay without discrimination based on sex means:

(a) that pay for the same work at piece rates shall be calculated on the basis of the same unit of measurement;

(b) that pay for work at time rates shall be the same for the same job.

Article 120

Member States shall endeavour to maintain the existing equivalence between paid holiday schemes.

Article 121

The Council may, acting unanimously and after consulting the Economic and Social Committee, assign to the Commission tasks in connection with the implementation of common measures, particularly as regards social security for the migrant workers referred to in Articles 48 to 51.

Article 122

The Commission shall include a separate chapter on social developments within the Community in its annual report to the European Parliament.

The European Parliament may invite the Commission to draw up reports on any particular problems concerning social conditions.

CHAPTER 2—THE EUROPEAN SOCIAL FUND

Article 123

In order to improve employment opportunities for workers in the common market and to contribute thereby to raising the standard of living, a European Social Fund is hereby

1. As added by the Single European Act, Article 22.

established in accordance with the provisions set out below; it shall have the task of rendering the employment of workers easier and of increasing their geographical and occupational mobility within the Community.

Article 124

The Fund shall be administered by the Commission.

The Commission shall be assisted in this task by a Committee presided over by a member of the Commission and composed of representatives of Governments, trade unions and employers' organisations.

Article 125

1. On application by a Member State the Fund shall, within the framework of the rules provided for in Article 127, meet 50% of the expenditure incurred after the entry into force of this Treaty by that State or by a body governed by public law for the purposes of:

(a) ensuring productive re-employment of workers by means of:
vocational retraining;
resettlement allowances;

(b) granting aid for the benefit of workers whose employment is reduced or temporarily suspended, in whole or in part, as a result of the conversion of an undertaking to other production, in order that they may retain the same wage level pending their full re-employment.

2. Assistance granted by the Fund towards the cost of vocational retraining shall be granted only if the unemployed workers could not be found employment except in a new occupation and only if they have been in productive employment for at least six months in the occupation for which they have been retrained.

Assistance towards resettlement allowances shall be granted only if the unemployed workers have been caused to change their home within the Community and have been in productive employment for at least six months in their new place of residence.

Assistance for workers in the case of the conversion of an undertaking shall be granted only if:

(a) the workers concerned have again been fully employed in that undertaking for at least six months;

(b) the Government concerned has submitted a plan beforehand, drawn up by the undertaking in question, for that particular conversion and for financing it;

(c) the Commission has given its prior approval to the conversion plan.

Article 126

When the transitional period has ended, the Council, after receiving the opinion of the Commission and after consulting the Economic and Social Committee and the European Parliament, may:

(a) rule, by a qualified majority, that all or part of the assistance referred to in Article 125 shall no longer be granted; or

(b) unanimously determine what new tasks may be entrusted to the Fund within the framework of its terms of reference as laid down in Article 123.

Article 127

The Council shall, acting by a qualified majority on a proposal from the Commission and after consulting the Economic and Social Committee and the European Parliament, lay down the provisions required to implement Articles 124 to 126; in particular it shall determine in detail the conditions under which assistance shall be granted by the Fund in accordance with Article 125 and the classes of undertakings whose workers shall benefit from the assistance provided for in Article 125 (1)(b).

Article 128

The Council shall, acting on a proposal from the Commission and after consulting the Economic and Social Committee, lay down general principles for implementing a common vocational training policy capable of contributing to the harmonious development both of the national economies and of the common market.

TITLE IV. THE EUROPEAN INVESTMENT BANK

Article 129

A European Investment Bank is hereby established; it shall have legal personality.

The members of the European Investment Bank shall be the Member States.

The Statute of the European Investment Bank is laid down in a Protocol annexed to this Treaty.

Article 130

The task of the European Investment Bank shall be to contribute, by having recourse to the capital market and utilising its own resources, to the balanced and steady development of the common market in the interest of the Community. For this purpose the Bank shall, operating on a non-profit-making basis, grant loans and give guarantees which facilitate the financing of the following projects in all sectors of the economy:

(a) projects for developing less-developed regions;

(b) projects for modernising or converting undertakings or for developing fresh activities called for by the progressive establishment of the common market, where these projects are of such a size or nature that they cannot be entirely financed by the various means available in the individual Member States;

(c) projects of common interest to several Member States which are of such a size or nature that they cannot be entirely financed by the various means available in the individual Member States.

TITLE V. ECONOMIC AND SOCIAL COHESION[2]

Article 130a

In order to promote its overall harmonious development, the Community shall develop and pursue its actions leading to the strengthening of its economic and social cohesion.

In particular the Community shall aim at reducing disparities between the various regions and the backwardness of the least-favoured regions.

Article 130b

Member States shall conduct their economic policies, and shall co-ordinate them, in such a way as, in addition, to attain the objectives set out in Article 130a. The implementation of the common policies and of the internal market shall take into account the objectives set out in Article 130a and in Article 130c and shall contribute to their achievement. The Community shall support the achievement of these objectives by the action it takes through the structural Funds (European Agricultural Guidance and Guarantee Fund, Guidance Section, European Social Fund, European Regional Development Fund), the European Investment Bank and the other existing financial instruments.

2. Title V and Articles therein added by the Single European Act, Article 23.

Article 130c

The European Regional Development Fund is intended to help redress the principal regional imbalances in the Community through participating in the development and structural adjustment of regions whose development is lagging behind and in the conversion of declining industrial regions.

Article 130d

Once the Single European Act enters into force the Commission shall submit a comprehensive proposal to the Council, the purpose of which will be to make such amendments to the structure and operational rules of the existing structural Funds (European Agricultural Guidance and Guarantee Fund, Guidance Section, European Social Fund, European Regional Development Fund) as are necessary to clarify and rationalise their tasks in order to contribute to the achievement of the objectives set out in Article 130a and Article 130c, to increase their efficiency and to co-ordinate their activities between themselves and with the operations of the existing financial instruments. The Council shall act unanimously on this proposal within a period of one year, after consulting the European Parliament and the Economic and Social Committee.

Article 130e

After adoption of the decision referred to in Article 130d, implementing decisions relating to the European Regional Development Fund shall be taken by the Council, acting by a qualified majority on a proposal from the Commission and in co-operation with the European Parliament.

With regard to the European Agricultural Guidance and Guarantee Fund, Guidance Section and the European Social Fund, Articles 43, 126 and 127 remain applicable respectively.

TITLE VI. RESEARCH AND TECHNOLOGICAL DEVELOPMENT[3]

Article 130f

1. The Community's aim shall be to strengthen the scientific and technological basis of European industry and to encourage it to become more competitive at international level.

2. In order to achieve this, it shall encourage undertakings including small and medium-sized undertakings, research centres and universities in their research and technological development activities; it shall support their efforts to co-operate with one another, aiming, notably, at enabling undertakings to exploit the Community's internal market potential to the full, in particular through the opening up of national public contracts, the definition of common standards and the removal of legal and fiscal barriers to that co-operation.

3. In the achievement of these aims, special account shall be taken of the connection between the common research and technological development effort, the establishment of the internal market and the implementation of common policies, particularly as regards competition and trade.

Article 130g

In pursuing these objectives the Community shall carry out the following activities, complementing the activities carried out in the Member States:

(a) implementation of research, technological development and demonstration programmes, by promoting co-operation with undertakings, research centres and universities;

(b) promotion of co-operation in the field of Community research, technological development and demonstration with third countries and international organisations;

3. Title VI and Articles therein added by the Single European Act, Article 24.

(c) dissemination and optimisation of the results of activities in Community research, technological development and demonstration;
(d) stimulation of the training and mobility of researchers in the Community.

Article 130h

Member States shall, in liaison with the Commission, co-ordinate among themselves the policies and programmes carried out at national level. In close contact with the Member States, the Commission may take any useful initiative to promote such co-ordination.

Article 130i

1. The Community shall adopt a multi-annual framework programme setting out all its activities. The framework programme shall lay down the scientific and technical objectives, define their respective priorities, set out the main lines of the activities envisaged and fix the amount deemed necessary, the detailed rules for financial participation by the Community in the programme as a whole and the breakdown of this amount between the various activities envisaged.

2. The framework programme may be adapted or supplemented, as the situation changes.

Article 130k

The framework programme shall be implemented through specific programmes developed within each activity. Each specific programme shall define the detailed rules for implementing it, fix its duration and provide for the means deemed necessary.

The Council shall define the detailed arrangements for the dissemination of knowledge resulting from the specific programmes.

Article 130l

In implementing the multi-annual framework programme, supplementary programmes may be decided on involving the participation of certain Member States only, which shall finance them subject to possible Community participation.

The Council shall adopt the rules applicable to supplementary programmes, particularly as regards the dissemination of knowledge and the access of other Member States.

Article 130m

In implementing the multi-annual framework programme, the Community may make provision, with the agreement of the Member States concerned, for participation in research and development programmes undertaken by several Member States, including participation in the structures created for the execution of those programmes.

Article 130n

In implementing the multi-annual framework programme, the Community may make provision for co-operation in Community research, technological development and demonstration with third countries or international organisations.

The detailed arrangements for such co-operation may be the subject of international agreements between the Community and the third parties concerned which shall be negotiated and concluded in accordance with Article 228.

Article 130o

The Community may set up joint undertakings or any other structure necessary for the efficient execution of programmes of Community research, technological development and demonstration.

Article 130p

1. The detailed arrangements for financing each programme, including any Community contribution, shall be established at the time of the adoption of the programme.

2. The amount of the Community's annual contribution shall be laid down under the budgetary procedure, without prejudice to other possible methods of Community financing. The estimated cost of the specific programmes must not in aggregate exceed the financial provision in the framework programme.

Article 130q

1. The Council shall, acting unanimously on a proposal from the Commission and after consulting the European Parliament and the Economic and Social Committee, adopt the provisions referred to in Articles 130i and 130o.

2. The Council shall, acting by a qualified majority on a proposal from the Commission, after consulting the Economic and Social Committee, and in co-operation with the European Parliament, adopt the provisions referred to in Articles 130k, 130l, 130m, 130n and 130p. The adoption of these supplementary programmes shall also require the agreement of the Member States concerned.

TITLE VII. ENVIRONMENT[4]

Article 130r

1. Action by the Community relating to the environment shall have the following objectives:
   (i) to preserve, protect and improve the quality of the environment;
   (ii) to contribute towards protecting human health;
   (iii) to ensure a prudent and rational utilisation of natural resources.

2. Action by the Community relating to the environment shall be based on the principles that preventive action should be taken, that environmental damage should as a priority be rectified at source, and that the polluter should pay. Environmental protection requirements shall be a component of the Community's other policies.

3. In preparing its action relating to the environment, the Community shall take account of:
   (i) available scientific and technical data;
   (ii) environmental conditions in the various regions of the Community;
   (iii) the potential benefits and costs of action or of lack of action;
   (iv) the economic and social development of the Community as a whole and the balanced development of its regions.

4. The Community shall take action relating to the environment to the extent to which the objectives referred to in paragraph 1 can be attained better at Community level than at the level of the individual Member States. Without prejudice to certain measures of a Community nature, the Member States shall finance and implement the other measures.

5. Within their respective spheres of competence, the Community and the Member States shall co-operate with third countries and with the relevant international organisations. The arrangements for Community co-operation may be the subject of agreements between the Community and the third parties concerned, which shall be negotiated and concluded in accordance with Article 228.

The previous paragraph shall be without prejudice to Member States' competence to negotiate in international bodies and to conclude international agreements.

Article 130s

The Council, acting unanimously on a proposal from the Commission and after consulting the European Parliament and the Economic and Social Committee, shall decide what action is to be taken by the Community.

4. Title VII and Articles therein added by the Single European Act, Article 25.

The Council shall, under the conditions laid down in the preceding sub-paragraph, define those matters on which decisions are to be taken by a qualified majority.

Article 130t

The protective measures adopted in common pursuant to Article 130s shall not prevent any Member State from maintaining or introducing more stringent protective measures compatible with this Treaty.

PART FOUR. ASSOCIATION OF THE OVERSEAS COUNTRIES AND TERRITORIES

Article 131

The Member States agree to associate with the Community the non-European countries and territories which have special relations with Belgium, Denmark, France, Italy, the Netherlands and the United Kingdom. These countries and territories (hereinafter called the "countries and territories") are listed in Annex IV to this Treaty.

The purpose of association shall be to promote the economic and social development of the countries and territories and to establish close economic relations between them and the Community as a whole.

In accordance with the principles set out in the Preamble to this Treaty, association shall serve primarily to further the interests and prosperity of the inhabitants of these countries and territories in order to lead them to the economic, social and cultural development to which they aspire.

Article 132

Association shall have the following objectives:

1. Member States shall apply to their trade with the countries and territories the same treatment as they accord each other pursuant to this Treaty.
2. Each country or territory shall apply to its trade with Member States and with the other countries and territories the same treatment as that which it applies to the European State with which it has special relations.
3. The Member States shall contribute to the investments required for the progressive development of these countries and territories.
4. For investments financed by the Community, participation in tenders and supplies shall be open on equal terms to all natural and legal persons who are nationals of a Member State or of one of the countries and territories.
5. In relations between Member States and the countries and territories the right of establishment of nationals and companies or firms shall be regulated in accordance with the provisions and procedures laid down in the Chapter relating to the right of establishment and on a non-discriminatory basis, subject to any special provisions laid down pursuant to Article 136.

Article 133

1. Customs duties on imports into the Member States of goods originating in the countries and territories shall be completely abolished in conformity with the progressive abolition of customs duties between Member States in accordance with the provisions of this Treaty.
2. Customs duties on imports into each country or territory from Member States or from the other countries or territories shall be progressively abolished in accordance with the provisions of Articles 12, 13, 14, 15 and 17.
3. The countries and territories may, however, levy customs duties which meet the needs of their development and industrialisation or produce revenue for their budgets.

The duties referred to in the preceding sub-paragraph shall nevertheless be progressively reduced to the level of those imposed on imports of products from the Member State with which each country or territory has special relations. The percentages and the timetable of the reductions provided for under this Treaty shall apply to the difference between the duty imposed on a product coming from the Member State which has special relations with the country or territory concerned and the duty imposed on the same product coming from within the Community on entry into the importing country or territory.

4. Paragraph 2 shall not apply to countries and territories which, by reason of the particular international obligations by which they are bound, already apply a non-discriminatory customs tariff when this Treaty enters into force.

5. The introduction of or any change in customs duties imposed on goods imported into the countries and territories shall not, either in law or in fact, give rise to any direct or indirect discrimination between imports from the various Member States.

Article 134

If the level of the duties applicable to goods from a third country on entry into a country or territory is liable, when the provisions of Article 133 (1) have been applied, to cause deflections of trade to the detriment of any Member State, the latter may request the Commission to propose to the other Member States the measures needed to remedy the situation.

Article 135

Subject to the provisions relating to public health, public security or public policy, freedom of movement within Member States for workers from the countries and territories, and within the countries and territories for workers from Member States, shall be governed by agreements to be concluded subsequently with the unanimous approval of Member States.

Article 136

For an initial period of five years after the entry into force of this Treaty, the details of and procedure for the association of the countries and territories with the Community shall be determined by an Implementing Convention annexed to this Treaty.

Before the Convention referred to in the preceding paragraph expires, the Council shall, acting unanimously, lay down provisions for a further period, on the basis of the experience acquired and of the principles set out in this Treaty.

Article 136a

The provisions of Articles 131 to 136 shall apply to Greenland, subject to the specific provisions for Greenland set out in the Protocol on special arrangements for Greenland, annexed to this Treaty.

PART FIVE. INSTITUTIONS OF THE COMMUNITY

TITLE I. PROVISIONS GOVERNING THE INSTITUTIONS

CHAPTER 1—THE INSTITUTIONS

Section 1—The European Parliament

Article 137

The European Parliament, which shall consist of representatives of the peoples of the States brought together in the Community, shall exercise the advisory and supervisory powers which are conferred upon it by this Treaty.

Article 138

[Paragraphs 1 and 2 lapsed on 17 July 1979 in accordance with the Act concerning the election of the representatives of the European Parliament. See Act concerning the election of the representatives of the European Parliament, art 1: "The representatives in the European Parliament of the peoples of the States brought together in the Community shall be elected by direct universal suffrage." See Act concerning the election of the representatives of the European Parliament, art 2:

The number of representatives elected in each Member State is as follows:

Belgium	24
Denmark	16
Germany	81
Greece	24
Spain	60
France	81
Ireland	15
Italy	81
Luxembourg	6
Netherlands	25
Portugal	24
United Kingdom	81]

3. The European Parliament shall draw up proposals for elections by direct universal suffrage in accordance with a uniform procedure in all Member States.

The Council shall, acting unanimously, lay down the appropriate provisions which it shall recommend to Member States for adoption in accordance with their respective constitutional requirements.

Article 139

The European Parliament shall hold an annual session. It shall meet, without requiring to be convened, on the second Tuesday in March.

The European Parliament may meet in extraordinary session at the request of a majority of its members or at the request of the Council or of the Commission.

Article 140

The European Parliament shall elect its President and its officers from among its members.

Members of the Commission may attend all meetings and shall, at their request, be heard on behalf of the Commission.

The Commission shall reply orally or in writing to questions put to it by the European Parliament or by its members.

The Council shall be heard by the European Parliament in accordance with the conditions laid down by the Council in its rules of procedure.

Article 141

Save as otherwise provided in this Treaty, the European Parliament shall act by an absolute majority of the votes cast.

The rules of procedure shall determine the quorum.

Article 142

The European Parliament shall adopt its rules of procedure, acting by a majority of its members.

The proceedings of the European Parliament shall be published in the manner laid down in its rules of procedure.

Article 143

The European Parliament shall discuss in open session the annual general report submitted to it by the Commission.

Article 144

If a motion of censure on the activities of the Commission is tabled before it, the European Parliament shall not vote thereon until at least three days after the motion has been tabled and only by open vote.

If the motion of censure is carried by a two-thirds majority of the votes cast, representing a majority of the members of the European Parliament, the members of the Commission shall resign as a body. They shall continue to deal with current business until they are replaced in accordance with Article 158.

Section 2—The Council

Article 145

To ensure that the objectives set out in this Treaty are attained, the Council shall, in accordance with the provisions of this Treaty:

— ensure co-ordination of the general economic policies of the Member States;

— have power to take decisions;

— confer on the Commission, in the acts which the Council adopts, powers for the implementation of the rules which the Council lays down. The Council may impose certain requirements in respect of the exercise of these powers. The Council may also reserve the right, in specific cases, to exercise directly implementing powers itself. The procedures referred to above must be consonant with principles and rules to be laid down in advance by the Council, acting unanimously on a proposal from the Commission and after obtaining the opinion of the European Parliament.

Article 146

[Repealed by the Merger Treaty, Article 7.]

Article 147

[Repealed by the Merger Treaty, Article 7.]

Article 148

1. Save as otherwise provided in this Treaty, the Council shall act by a majority of its members.

2. Where the Council is required to act by a qualified majority, the votes of its members shall be weighted as follows:

Belgium	5
Denmark	3
Germany	10
Greece	5
Spain	8
France	10
Ireland	3
Italy	10
Luxembourg	2
Netherlands	5
Portugal	5
United Kingdom	10

For their adoption, acts of the Council shall require at least:

— 54 votes in favour where this Treaty requires them to be adopted on a proposal from the Commission,

— 54 votes in favour, cast by at least eight members, in other cases.

3. Abstentions by members present in person or represented shall not prevent the adoption by the Council of acts which require unanimity.

Article 149

1. Where, in pursuance of this Treaty, the Council acts on a proposal from the Commission, unanimity shall be required for an act constituting an amendment to that proposal.

2. Where, in pursuance of this Treaty, the Council acts in co-operation with the European Parliament, the following procedure shall apply:

(a) The Council, acting by a qualified majority under the conditions of paragraph 1, on a proposal from the Commission and after obtaining the opinion of the European Parliament, shall adopt a common position.

(b) The Council's common position shall be communicated to the European Parliament. The Council and the Commission shall inform the European Parliament fully of the reasons which led the Council to adopt its common position and also of the Commission's position. If, within three months of such communication, the European Parliament approves this common position or has not taken a decision within that period, the Council shall definitively adopt the act in question in accordance with the common position.

(c) The European Parliament may within the period of three months referred to in point (b), by an absolute majority of its component members, propose amendments to the Council's common position. The European Parliament may also, by the same majority, reject the Council's common position. The result of the proceedings shall be transmitted to the Council and the Commission. If the European Parliament has rejected the Council's common position, unanimity shall be required for the Council to act on a second reading.

(d) The Commission shall, within a period of one month, re-examine the proposal on the basis of which the Council adopted its common position, by taking into account the amendments proposed by the European Parliament.

The Commission shall forward to the Council, at the same time as its re-examined proposal, the amendments of the European Parliament which it has not accepted, and shall express its opinion on them. The Council may adopt these amendments unanimously.

(e) The Council, acting by a qualified majority, shall adopt the proposal as re-examined by the Commission.

Unanimity shall be required for the Council to amend the proposal as re-examined by the Commission.

(f) In the cases referred to in points (c), (d) and (e), the Council shall be required to act within a period of three months. If no decision is taken within this period, the Commission proposal shall be deemed not have been adopted.

(g) The periods referred to in points (b) and (f) may be extended by a maximum of one month by common accord between the Council and the European Parliament.

3. As long as the Council has not acted, the Commission may alter its proposal at any time during the procedures mentioned in paragraphs 1 and 2.

Article 150

Where a vote is taken, any member of the Council may also act on behalf of not more than one other member.

Article 151

[Repealed by the Merger Treaty, Article 7.]

Article 152

The Council may request the Commission to undertake any studies which the Council considers desirable for the attainment of the common objectives, and to submit to it any appropriate proposals.

Article 153

The Council shall, after receiving an opinion from the Commission, determine the rules governing the committees provided for in this Treaty.

Article 154

[Repealed by the Merger Treaty, Article 7.]

Section 3—The Commission

Article 155

In order to ensure the proper functioning and development of the common market, the Commission shall:

— ensure that the provisions of this Treaty and the measures taken by the institutions pursuant thereto are applied;
— formulate recommendations or deliver opinions on matters dealt with in this Treaty, if it expressly so provides or if the Commission considers it necessary;
— have its own power of decision and participate in the shaping of measures taken by the Council and by the European Parliament in the manner provided for in this Treaty;
— exercise the powers conferred on it by the Council for the implementation of the rules laid down by the latter.

Articles 156 to 163

[Repealed by the Merger Treaty, Article 19.]

Section 4—The Court of Justice

Article 164

The Court of Justice shall ensure that in the interpretation and application of this Treaty the law is observed.

Article 165

The Court of Justice shall consist of 13 Judges.

The Court of Justice shall sit in plenary session. It may, however, form Chambers, each consisting of three or five Judges, either to undertake certain preparatory inquiries or to adjudicate on particular categories of cases in accordance with rules laid down for these purposes.

Whenever the Court of Justice hears cases brought before it by a Member State or by one of the institutions of the Community or, to the extent that the Chambers of the Court do not have the requisite jurisdiction under the Rules of Procedure, has to give preliminary rulings on questions submitted to it pursuant to Article 177, it shall sit in plenary session.

Should the Court of Justice so request, the Council may, acting unanimously, increase the number of Judges and make the necessary adjustments to the second and third paragraphs of this Article and to the second paragraph of Article 167.

Article 166

The Court of Justice shall be assisted by six Advocates-General.

It shall be the duty of the Advocate-General, acting with complete impartiality and independence, to make, in open court, reasoned submissions on cases brought before the Court of Justice, in order to assist the Court in the performance of the task assigned to it in Article 164.

Should the Court of Justice so request, the Council may, acting unanimously, increase the number of Advocates-General and make the necessary adjustments to the third paragraph of Article 167.

Article 167

The Judges and Advocates-General shall be chosen from persons whose independence is beyond doubt and who possess the qualifications required for appointment to the highest judicial offices in their respective countries or who are jurisconsults of recognised competence; they shall be appointed by common accord of the Governments of the Member States for a term of six years.

Every three years there shall be a partial replacement of the Judges. Seven and six Judges shall be replaced alternately.

Every three years there shall be a partial replacement of the Advocates-General. Three Advocates-General shall be replaced on each occasion.

Retiring Judges and Advocates-General shall be eligible for re-appointment.

The Judges shall elect the President of the Court of Justice from among their number for a term of three years. He may be re-elected.

Article 168

The Court of Justice shall appoint its Registrar and lay down the rules governing his service.

Article 168a

1. At the request of the Court of Justice and after consulting the Commission and the European Parliament, the Council may, acting unanimously, attach to the Court of Justice a court with jurisdiction to hear and determine at first instance, subject to a right of appeal to the Court of Justice on points of law only and in accordance with the conditions laid down by the Statute, certain classes of action or proceeding brought by natural or legal persons. That court shall not be competent to hear and determine actions brought by Member States or by Community institutions or questions referred for a preliminary ruling under Article 177.

2. The Council, following the procedure laid down in paragraph 1, shall determine the composition of that court and adopt the necessary adjustments and additional provisions to the Statute of the Court of Justice. Unless the Council decides otherwise, the provisions of this Treaty relating to the Court of Justice, in particular the provisions of the Protocol on the Statute of the Court of Justice, shall apply to that court.

3. The members of that court shall be chosen from persons whose independence is beyond doubt and who possess the ability required for appointment to judicial office; they shall be appointed by common accord of the Governments of the Member States for a term of six years. The membership shall be partially renewed every three years. Retiring members shall be eligible for re-appointment.

4. That court shall establish its rules for procedure in agreement with the Court of Justice. Those rules shall require the unanimous approval of the Council.

Article 169

If the Commission considers that a Member State has failed to fulfil an obligation under this Treaty, it shall deliver a reasoned opinion on the matter after giving the State concerned the opportunity to submit its observations.

If the State concerned does not comply with the opinion within the period laid down by the Commission, the latter may bring the matter before the Court of Justice.

Article 170

A Member State which considers that another Member State has failed to fulfil an obligation under this Treaty may bring the matter before the Court of Justice.

Before a Member State brings an action against another Member State for an alleged infringement of an obligation under this Treaty, it shall bring the matter before the Commission.

The Commission shall deliver a reasoned opinion after each of the States concerned has been given the opportunity to submit its own case and its observations on the other party's case both orally and in writing.

If the Commission has not delivered an opinion within three months of the date on which the matter was brought before it, the absence of such opinion shall not prevent the matter from being brought before the Court of Justice.

Article 171

If the Court of Justice finds that a Member State has failed to fulfil an obligation under this Treaty, the State shall be required to take the necessary measures to comply with the judgment of the Court of Justice.

Article 172

Regulations made by the Council pursuant to the provisions of this Treaty may give the Court of Justice unlimited jurisdiction in regard to the penalties provided for in such regulations.

Article 173

The Court of Justice shall review the legality of acts of the Council and the Commission other than recommendations or opinions. It shall for this purpose have jurisdiction in actions brought by a Member State, the Council or the Commission on grounds of lack of competence, infringement of an essential procedural requirement, infringement of this Treaty or of any rule of law relating to its application, or misuse of powers.

Any natural or legal person may, under the same conditions, institute proceedings against a decision addressed to that person or against a decision which, although in the form of a regulation or a decision addressed to another person, is of direct and individual concern to the former.

The proceedings provided for in this Article shall be instituted within two months of the publication of the measure, or of its notification to the plaintiff, or, in the absence thereof, of the day on which it came to the knowledge of the latter, as the case may be.

Article 174

If the action is well founded, the Court of Justice shall declare the act concerned to be void.

In the case of a regulation, however, the Court of Justice shall, if it considers this necessary, state which of the effects of the regulation which it has declared void shall be considered as definitive.

Article 175

Should the Council or the Commission, in infringement of this Treaty, fail to act, the Member States and the other institutions of the Community may bring an action before the Court of Justice to have the infringement established.

The action shall be admissible only if the institution concerned has first been called upon to act. If, within two months of being so called upon, the institution concerned has not defined its position, the action may be brought within a further period of two months.

Any natural or legal person may, under the conditions laid down in the preceding paragraphs, complain to the Court of Justice that an institution of the Community has failed to address to that person any act other than a recommendation or an opinion.

Article 176

The institution whose act has been declared void or whose failure to act has been declared contrary to this Treaty shall be required to take the necessary measures to comply with the judgment of the Court of Justice.

This obligation shall not affect any obligation which may result from the application of the second paragraph of Article 215.

Article 177

The Court of Justice shall have jurisdiction to give preliminary rulings concerning:

(a) the interpretation of this Treaty;
(b) the validity and interpretation of acts of the institutions of the Community;
(c) the interpretation of the statutes of bodies established by an act of the Council, where those statutes so provide.

Where such a question is raised before any court or tribunal of a Member State, that court or tribunal may, if it considers that a decision on the question is necessary to enable it to give judgment, request the Court of justice to give a ruling thereon.

Where any such question is raised in a case pending before a court or tribunal of a Member State, against whose decisions there is no judicial remedy under national law, that court or tribunal shall bring the matter before the Court of Justice.

Article 178

The Court of Justice shall have jurisdiction in disputes relating to the compensation for damage provided for in the second paragraph of Article 215.

Article 179

The Court of Justice shall have jurisdicton in any dispute between the Community and its servants within the limits and under the conditions laid down in the Staff Regulations or the Conditions of Employment

Article 180

The Court of Justice shall, within the limits hereinafter laid down, have jurisdiction in disputes concerning:

(a) the fulfilment by Member States of obligations under the Statute of the European Investment Bank. In this connection, the Board of Directors of the Bank shall enjoy the powers conferred upon the Commission by Article 169;
(b) measures adopted by the Board of Governors of the Bank. In this connection, any Member State, the Commission or the Board of Directors of the Bank may institute proceedings under the conditions laid down in Article 173;
(c) measures adopted by the Board of Directors of the Bank. Proceedings against such measures may be instituted only by Member States or by the Commission, under the conditions laid down in Article 173, and solely on the grounds of non-compliance with the procedure provided for in Article 21 (2), (5), (6) and (7) of the Statute of the Bank.

Article 181

The Court of Justice shall have jurisdiction to give judgment pursuant to any arbitration clause contained in a contract concluded by or on behalf of the Community, whether that contract be governed by public or private law.

Article 182

The Court of Justice shall have jurisdiction in any dispute between Member States which relates to the subject matter of this Treaty if the dispute is submitted to it under a special agreement between the parties.

Article 183

Save where jurisdiction is conferred on the Court of Justice by this Treaty, disputes to which the Community is a party shall not on that ground be excluded from the jurisdiction of the courts or tribunals of the Member States.

Article 184

Notwithstanding the expiry of the period laid down in the third paragraph of Article 173, any party may, in proceedings in which a regulation of the Council or of the Commission is in issue, plead the grounds specified in the first paragraph of Article 173, in order to invoke before the Court of Justice the inapplicability of that regulation.

Article 185

Actions brought before the Court of Justice shall not have suspensory effect. The Court of Justice may, however, if it considers that circumstances so require, order that application of the contested act be suspended.

Article 186

The Court of Justice may in any cases before it prescribe any necessary interim measures.

Article 187

The judgments of the Court of Justice shall be enforceable under the conditions laid down in Article 192.

Article 188

The Statute of the Court of Justice is laid down in a separate Protocol.

The Council may, acting unanimously at the request of the Court of Justice and after consulting the Commission and the European Parliament, amend the provisions of Title III of the Statute.

The Court of Justice shall adopt its rules of procedure. These shall require the unanimous approval of the Council.

CHAPTER 2—PROVISIONS COMMON TO SEVERAL INSTITUTIONS

Article 189

In order to carry out their task the Council and the Commission shall, in accordance with the provisions of this Treaty, make regulations, issue directives, take decisions, make recommendations or deliver opinions.

A regulation shall have general application. It shall be binding in its entirety and directly applicable in all Member States.

A directive shall be binding, as to the result to be achieved, upon each Member State to which it is addressed, but shall leave to the national authorities the choice of form and methods.

A decision shall be binding in its entirety upon those to whom it is addressed. Recommendations and opinions shall have no binding force.

Article 190

Regulations, directives and decisions of the Council and of the Commission shall state the reasons on which they are based and shall refer to any proposals or opinions which were required to be obtained pursuant to this Treaty.

Article 191

Regulations shall be published in the Official Journal of the Community. They shall enter into force on the date specified in them or, in the absence thereof, on the twentieth day following their publication.

Directives and decisions shall be notified to those to whom they are addressed and shall take effect upon such notification.

Article 192

Decisions of the Council or of the Commission which impose a pecuniary obligation on persons other than States shall be enforceable.

Enforcement shall be governed by the rules of civil procedure in force in the State in the territory of which it is carried out. The order for its enforcement shall be appended to the decision, without other formality than verification of the authenticity of the decision, by the national authority which the Government of each Member State shall designate for this purpose and shall make known to the Commission and to the Court of Justice.

When these formalities have been completed on application by the party concerned, the latter may proceed to enforcement in accordance with the national law, by bringing the matter directly before the competent authority.

Enforcement may be suspended only by a decision of the Court of Justice. However, the courts of the country concerned shall have jurisdiction over complaints that enforcement is being carried out in an irregular manner.

CHAPTER 3—THE ECONOMIC AND SOCIAL COMMITTEE

Article 193

An Economic and Social Committee is hereby established. It shall have advisory status.

The Committee shall consist of representatives of the various categories of economic and social activity, in particular, representatives of producers, farmers, carriers, workers, dealers, craftsmen, professional occupations and representatives of the general public.

Article 194

The number of members of the Committee shall be as follows:

Belgium	12
Denmark	9
Germany	24
Greece	12
Spain	21
France	24
Ireland	9
Italy	24
Luxembourg	6
Netherlands	12
Portugal	12
United Kingdom	24

The members of the Committee shall be appointed by the Council, acting unanimously, for four years. Their appointments shall be renewable.

The members of the Committee shall be appointed in their personal capacity and may not be bound by any mandatory instructions.

Article 195

1. For the appointment of the members of the Committee, each Member State shall provide the Council with a list containing twice as many candidates as there are seats allotted to its nationals.

The composition of the Committee shall take account of the need to ensure adequate representation of the various categories of economic and social activity.

2. The Council shall consult the Commission. It may obtain the opinion of European bodies which are representative of the various economic and social sectors to which the activities of the Community are of concern.

Article 196

The Committee shall elect its chairman and officers from among its members for a term of two years.

It shall adopt its rules of procedure and shall submit them to the Council for its approval, which must be unanimous.

The Committee shall be convened by its chairman at the request of the Council or of the Commission.

Article 197

The Committee shall include specialised sections for the principal fields covered by this Treaty.

In particular, it shall contain an agricultural section and a transport section, which are the subject of special provisions in the Titles relating to agriculture and transport.

These specialised sections shall operate within the general terms of reference of the Committee. They may not be consulted independently of the Committee.

Sub-committees may also be established within the Committee to prepare, on specific questions or in specific fields, draft opinions to be submitted to the Committee for its consideration.

The rules of procedure shall lay down the methods of composition and the terms of reference of the specialised sections and of the sub-committees.

Article 198

The Committee must be consulted by the Council or by the Commission where this Treaty so provides. The Committee may be consulted by these institutions in all cases in which they consider it appropriate.

The Council or the Commission shall, if it considers it necessary, set the Committee, for the submission of its opinion, a time limit which may not be less than ten days from the date on which the chairman receives notification to this effect. Upon expiry of the time limit, the absence of an opinion shall not prevent further action.

The opinion of the Committee and that of the specialised section, together with a record of the proceedings, shall be forwarded to the Council and to the Commission.

TITLE II. FINANCIAL PROVISIONS

Article 199

All items of revenue and expenditure of the Community, including those relating to the European Social Fund, shall be included in estimates to be drawn up for each financial year and shall be shown in the budget.

The revenue and expenditure shown in the budget shall be in balance.

Article 200

1. The budget revenue shall include, irrespective of any other revenue, financial contributions of Member States on the following scale:

Belgium	7.9
Germany	28
France	28

Italy	28
Luxembourg	0.2
Netherlands	7.9

2. The financial contributions of Member States to cover the expenditure of the European Social Fund, however, shall be determined on the following scale:

Belgium	08.8
Germany	32
France	32
Italy	20
Luxembourg	0.2
Netherlands	7

3. The scales may be modified by the Council, acting unanimously.

Article 201

The Commission shall examine the conditions under which the financial contributions Member States provided for in Article 200 could be replaced by the Community's own resources, in particular by revenue accruing from the common customs tariff when it has been finally introduced.

To this end, the Commission shall submit proposals to the Council.

After consulting the European Parliament on these proposals the Council may, acting unanimously, lay down the appropriate provisions, which it shall recommend to the Member States for adoption in accordance with their respective constitutional requirements.

Article 202

The expenditure shown in the budget shall be authorised for one financial year, unless the regulations made pursuant to Article 209 provide otherwise.

In accordance with conditions to be laid down pursuant to Article 209, any appropriations, other than those relating to staff expenditure, that are unexpended at the end of the financial year may be carried forward to the next financial year only.

Appropriations shall be classified under different chapters grouping items of expenditure according to their nature or purpose and subdivided, as far as may be necessary, in accordance with the regulations made pursuant to Article 209.

The expenditure of the European Parliament, the Council, the Commission and the Court of Justice shall be set out in separate parts of the budget, without prejudice to special arrangements for certain common items of expenditure.

Article 203

1. The financial year shall run from 1 January to 31 December.

2. Each institution of the Community shall, before 1 July, draw up estimates of its expenditure. The Commission shall consolidate these estimates in a preliminary draft budget. It shall attach thereto an opinion which may contain different estimates.

The preliminary draft budget shall contain an estimate of revenue and an estimate of expenditure.

3. The Commission shall place the preliminary draft budget before the Council not later than 1 September of the year preceding that in which the budget is to be implemented.

The Council shall consult the Commission and, where appropriate, the other institutions concerned whenever it intends to depart from the preliminary draft budget.

The Council, acting by a qualified majority, shall establish the draft budget and forward it to the European Parliament.

4. The draft budget shall be placed before the European Parliament not later than 5 October of the year preceding that in which the budget is to be implemented.

The European Parliament shall have the right to amend the draft budget, acting by a majority of its members, and to propose to the Council, acting by an absolute majority of the votes cast, modifications to the draft budget relating to expenditure necessarily resulting from this Treaty or from acts adopted in accordance therewith.

If, within 45 days of the draft budget being placed before it, the European Parliament has given its approval, the budget shall stand as finally adopted. If within this period the European Parliament has not amended the draft budget nor proposed any modifications thereto, the budget shall be deemed to be finally adopted.

If within this period the European Parliament has adopted amendments or proposed modifications, the draft budget together with the amendments or proposed modifications shall be forwarded to the Council.

5. After discussing the draft budget with the Commission and, where appropriate, with the other institutions concerned, the Council shall act under the following conditions:

(a) the Council may, acting by a qualified majority, modify any of the amendments adopted by the European Parliament;

(b) with regard to the proposed modifications:

— where a modification proposed by the European Parliament does not have the effect of increasing the total amount of the expenditure of an institution, owing in particular to the fact that the increase in expenditure which it would involve would be expressly compensated by one or more proposed modifications correspondingly reducing expenditure, the Council may, acting by a qualified majority, reject the proposed modification. In the absence of a decision to reject it, the proposed modification shall stand as accepted:

— where a modification proposed by the European Parliament has the effect of increasing the total amount of the expenditure of an institution, the Council may, acting by a qualified majority, accept this proposed modification. In the absence of a decision to accept it, the proposed modification shall stand as rejected;

— where, in pursuance of one of the two preceding sub-paragraphs, the Council has rejected a proposed modification, it may, acting by a qualified majority, either retain the amount shown in the draft budget or fix another amount.

The draft budget shall be modified on the basis of the proposed modifications accepted by the Council.

If, within 15 days of the draft budget being placed before, it, the Council has not modified any of the amendments adopted by the European Parliament and if the modifications proposed by the latter have been accepted, the budget shall be deemed to be finally adopted. The Council shall inform the European Parliament that it has not modified any of the amendments and that the proposed modifications have been accepted.

If within this period the Council has modified one or more of the amendments adopted by the European Parliament or if the modifications proposed by the latter have been rejected or modified, the modified draft budget shall again be forwarded to the European Parliament. The Council shall inform the European Parliament of the results of its deliberations.

6. Within 15 days of the draft budget being placed before it, the European Parliament, which shall have been notified of the action taken on its proposed modifications, may, acting by a majority of its members and three-fifths of the votes cast, amend or reject the modifications to its amendments made by the Council and shall adopt the budget accordingly. If within this period the European Parliament has not acted, the budget shall be deemed to be finally adopted.

7. When the procedure provided for in this Article has been completed, the President of the European Parliament shall declare that the budget has been finally adopted.

8. However, the European Parliament acting by a majority of its members and two-thirds of the votes cast, may if there are important reasons reject the draft budget and ask for a new draft to be submitted to it.

9. A maximum rate of increase in relation to the expenditure of the same type to be incurred during the current year shall be fixed annually for the total expenditure other than that necessarily resulting from this Treaty or from acts adopted in accordance therewith.

The Commission shall, after consulting the Economic Policy Committee, declare what this maximum rate is as it results from:

— the trend, in terms of volume, of the gross national product within the Community;

— the average variation in the budgets of the Member States; and

— the trend of the cost of living during the preceding financial year.

The maximum rate shall be communicated, before 1 May, to all the institutions of the Community. The latter shall be required to conform to this during the budgetary procedure, subject to the provisions of the fourth and fifth sub-paragraphs of this paragraph.

If, in respect of expenditure other than that necessarily resulting from this Treaty or from acts adopted in accordance therewith, the actual rate of increase in the draft budget, established by the Council is over half the maximum rate, the European Parliament may, exercising its right of amendment, further increase the total amount of that expenditure to a limit not exceeding half the maximum rate.

Where the European Parliament, the Council or the Commission consider that the activities of the Communities require that the rate determined according to the procedure laid down in this paragraph should be exceeded, another rate may be fixed by agreement between the Council, acting by a qualified majority, and the European Parliament, acting by a majority of its members and three-fifths of the votes cast.

10. Each institution shall exercise the power conferred upon it by this Article, with due regard for the provisions of the Treaty and for acts adopted in accordance therewith, in particular those relating to the Communities' own resources and to the balance between revenue and expenditure.

Article 204

If, at the beginning of a financial year, the budget has not yet been voted, a sum equivalent to not more than one-twelfth of the budget appropriations for the preceding financial year may be spent each month in respect of any chapter or other subdivision of the budget in accordance with the provisions of the Regulations made pursuant to Article 209; this arrangement shall not, however, have the effect of placing at the disposal of the Commission appropriations in excess of one-twelfth of those provided for in the draft budget in course of preparation.

The Council may, acting by a qualified majority, provided that the other conditions laid down in the first sub-paragraph are observed, authorise expenditure in excess of one-twelfth.

If the decision relates to expenditure which does not necessarily result from this Treaty or from acts adopted in accordance therewith, the Council shall forward it immediately to the European Parliament; within 30 days the European Parliament, acting by a majority of its members and three-fifths of the votes cast, may adopt a different decision on the expenditure in excess of the one-twelfth referred to in the first sub-paragraph. This part of the decision of the Council shall be suspended until the European Parliament has taken its decision. If within the period the European Parliament has not taken a decision which differs from the decision of the Council, the latter shall be deemed to be finally adopted.

The decisions referred to in the second and third sub-paragraphs shall lay down the necessary measures relating to resources to ensure application of this Article.

Article 205

The Commission shall implement the budget, in accordance with the provisions of the regulations made pursuant to Article 209, on its own responsibility and within the limits of the appropriations.

The regulations shall lay down detailed rules for each institution concerning its part in effecting its own expenditure.

Within the budget, the Commission may, subject to the limits and conditions laid down in the regulations made pursuant to Article 209, transfer appropriations from one chapter to another or from one subdivision to another.

Article 205a

The Commission shall submit annually to the Council and to the European Parliament the accounts of the preceding financial year relating to the implementation of the budget. The Commission shall also forward to them a financial statement of the assets and liabilities of the Community.

Article 206

1. A Court of Auditors is hereby established.

2. The Court of Auditors shall consist of 12 members.

3. The members of the Court of Auditors shall be chosen from among persons who belong or have belonged in their respective countries to external audit bodies or who are especially qualified for this office. Their independence must be beyond doubt.

4. The members of the Court of Auditors shall be appointed for a term of six years by the Council, acting unanimously after consulting the European Parliament.

However, when the first appointments are made, four members of the Court of Auditors, chosen by lot, shall be appointed for a term of office of four years only.

The members of the Court of Auditors shall be eligible for re-appointment.

They shall elect the President of the Court of Auditors from among their number for a term of three years. The President may be re-elected.

5. The members of the Court of Auditors shall, in the general interest of the Community, be completely independent in the performance of their duties.

In the performance of these duties, they shall neither seek nor take instructions from any government or from any other body. They shall refrain from any action incompatible with their duties.

6. The members of the Court of Auditors may not, during their term of office, engage in any other occupation, whether gainful or not. When entering upon their duties they shall give a solemn undertaking that, both during and after their term of office, they will respect the obligations arising therefrom and in particular their duty to behave with integrity and discretion as regards the acceptance, after they have ceased to hold office, of certain appointments or benefits.

7. Apart from normal replacement, or death, the duties of a member of the Court of Auditors shall end when he resigns, or is compulsorily retired by a ruling of the Court of Justice pursuant to paragraph 8.

The vacancy thus caused shall be filled for the remainder of the member's term of office.

Save in the case of compulsory retirement, members of the Court of Auditors shall remain in office until they have been replaced.

8. A member of the Court of Auditors may be deprived of his office or of his right to a pension or other benefits in its stead only if the Court of Justice, at the request of the Court of Auditors, finds that he no longer fulfils the requisite conditions or meets the obligations arising from his office.

9. The Council, acting by a qualified majority, shall determine the conditions of employment of the President and the members of the Court of Auditors and in particular their salaries, allowances and pensions. It shall also, by the same majority, determine any payment to be made instead of remuneration.

10. The provisions of the Protocol on the Privileges and Immunities of the European Communities applicable to the Judges of the Court of Justice shall also apply to the members of the Court of Auditors.

Article 206a

1. The Court of Auditors shall examine the accounts of all revenue and expenditure of the Community. It shall also examine the accounts of all revenue and expenditure of all bodies set up by the Community in so far as the relevant constituent instrument does not preclude such examination.

2. The Court of Auditors shall examine whether all revenue has been received and all expenditure incurred in a lawful and regular manner and whether the financial management has been sound.

The audit of revenue shall be carried out on the basis both of the amounts established as due and the amounts actually paid to the Community.

The audit of expenditure shall be carried out on the basis both of commitments undertaken and payments made.

These audits may be carried out before the closure of accounts for the financial year in question.

3. The audit shall be based on records and, if necessary, performed on the spot in the institutions of the Community and in the Member States. In the Member States the audit shall be

carried out in liaison with the national audit bodies or, if these do not have the necessary powers, with the competent national departments. These bodies or departments shall inform the Court of Auditors whether they intend to take part in the audit.

The institutions of the Community and the national audit bodies or, if these do not have the necessary powers, the competent national departments, shall forward to the Court of Auditors, at its request, any document or information necessary to carry out its task.

4. The Court of Auditors shall draw up an annual report after the close of each financial year. It shall be forwarded to the institutions of the Community and shall be published, together with the replies of these institutions to the observations of the Court of Auditors, in the *Official Journal of the European Communities*.

The Court of Auditors may also, at any time, submit observations on specific questions and deliver opinions at the request of one of the institutions of the Community.

It shall adopt its annual reports or opinions by a majority of its members.

It shall assist the European Parliament and the Council in exercising their powers of control over the implementation of the budget.

Article 206b

The European Parliament, acting on a recommendation from the Council which shall act by a qualified majority, shall give a discharge to the Commission in respect of the implementation of the budget. To this end, the Council and the European Parliament in turn shall examine the accounts and the financial statement referred to in Article 205a and the annual report by the Court of Auditors together with the replies of the institutions under audit to the observations of the Court of Auditors.

Article 207

The budget shall be drawn up in the unit of account determined in accordance with the provisions of the regulations made pursuant to Article 209.

The financial contributions provided for in Article 200 (1) shall be placed at the disposal of the Community by the Member States in their national currencies.

The available balances of these contributions shall be deposited with the Treasuries of Member States or with bodies designated by them. While on deposit, such funds shall retain the value corresponding to the parity, at the date of deposit, in relation to the unit of account referred to in the first paragraph.

The balances may be invested on terms to be agreed between the Commission and the Member State concerned.

The regulations made pursuant to Article 209 shall lay down the technical conditions under which financial operations relating to the European Social Fund shall be carried out.

Article 208

The Commission may, provided it notifies the competent authorities of the Member States concerned, transfer into the currency of one of the Member States its holdings in the currency of another Member State, to the extent necessary to enable them to be used for purposes which come within the scope of this Treaty. The Commission shall as far as possible avoid making such transfers if it possesses cash or liquid assets in the currencies which it needs.

The Commission shall deal with each Member State through the authority designated by the State concerned. In carrying out financial operations the Commission shall employ the services of the bank of issue of the Member State concerned or of any other financial institution approved by that State.

Article 209

The Council, acting unanimously on a proposal from the Commission and after consulting the European Parliament and obtaining the opinion of the Court of Auditors, shall:

(a) make Financial Regulations specifying in particular the procedure to be adopted for establishing and implementing the budget and for presenting and auditing accounts;
(b) determine the methods and procedure whereby the budget revenue provided under the arrangements relating to the Communities' own resources shall be made available to the Commission, and determine the measures to be applied, if need be, to meet cash requirements;
(c) lay down rules concerning the responsibility of authorising officers and accounting officers and concerning appropriate arrangements for inspection.

PART SIX. GENERAL AND FINAL PROVISIONS

Article 210

The Community shall have legal personality.

Article 211

In each of the Member States, the Community shall enjoy the most extensive legal capacity accorded to legal persons under their laws; it may, in particular, acquire or dispose of movable and immovable property and may be a party to legal proceedings. To this end, the Community shall be represented by the Commission.

Article 212

[Repealed by the Merger Treaty, Article 24 (2).]

Article 213

The Commission may, within the limits and under the conditions laid down by the Council in accordance with the provisions of this Treaty, collect any information and carry out any checks required for the performance of the tasks entrusted to it.

Article 214

The members of the institutions of the Community, the members of committees, and the officials and other servants of the Community shall be required, even after their duties have ceased, not to disclose information of the kind covered by the obligation of professional secrecy, in particular information about undertakings, their business relations or their cost components.

Article 215

The contractual liability of the Community shall be governed by the law applicable to the contract in question.

In the case of non-contractual liability, the Community shall, in accordance with the general principles common to the laws of the Member States, make good any damage caused by its institutions or by its servants in the performance of their duties.

The personal liability of its servants towards the Community shall be governed by the provisions laid down in their Staff Regulations or in the Conditions of Employment applicable to them.

Article 216

The seat of the institutions of the Community shall be determined by common accord of the Governments of the Member States.

Article 217

The rules governing the languages of the institutions of the Community shall, without prejudice to the provisions contained in the rules of procedure of the Court of Justice, be determined by the Council, acting unanimously.

Article 218

[Repealed by the Merger Treaty, Article 28.]

Article 219

Member States undertake not to submit a dispute concerning the interpretation or application of this Treaty to any method of settlement other than those provided for therein.

Article 220

Member States shall, so far as is necessary, enter into negotiations with each other with a view to securing for the benefit of their nationals:

— the protection of persons and the enjoyment and protection of rights under the same conditions as those accorded by each State to its own nationals;
— the abolition of double taxation within the Community;
— the mutual recognition of companies or firms within the meaning of the second paragraph of Article 58, the retention of legal personality in the event of transfer of their seat from one country to another, and the possibility of mergers between companies or firms governed by the laws of different countries;
— the simplification of formalities governing the reciprocal recognition and enforcement of judgments of courts or tribunals and of arbitration awards.

Article 221

Within three years of the entry into force of this Treaty, Member States shall accord nationals of the other Member States the same treatment as their own nationals as regards participation in the capital of companies or firms within the meaning of Article 58, without prejudice to the application of the other provisions of this Treaty.

Article 222

This Treaty shall in no way prejudice the rules in Member States governing the system of property ownership.

Article 223

1. The provisions of this Treaty shall not preclude the application of the following rules:
   (a) No Member State shall be obliged to supply information the disclosure of which it considers contrary to the essential interests of its security;
   (b) Any Member State may take such measures as it considers necessary for the protection of the essential interests of its security which are connected with the production of or trade in arms, munitions and war material; such measures shall not adversely affect the conditions of competition in the common market regarding products which are not intended for specifically military purposes.

2. During the first year after the entry into force of this Treaty, the Council shall, acting unanimously, draw up a list of products to which the provisions of paragraph 1(b) shall apply.

3. The Council may, acting unanimously on a proposal from the Commission, make changes in this list.

Article 224

Member States shall consult each other with a view to taking together the steps needed to prevent the functioning of the common market being affected by measures which a Member State may be called upon to take in the event of serious internal disturbances affecting the maintenance of law and order, in the event of war, serious international tension constituting a threat of war, or in order to carry out obligations it has accepted for the purpose of maintaining peace and international security.

Article 225

If measures taken in the circumstances referred to in Articles 223 and 224 have the effect of distorting the conditions of competition in the common market, the Commission shall, together with the State concerned, examine how these measures can be adjusted to the rules laid down in this Treaty.

By way of derogation from the procedure laid down in Articles 169 and 170, the Commission or any Member State may bring the matter directly before the Court of Justice if it considers that another Member State is making improper use of the powers provided for in Articles 223 and 224. The Court of Justice shall give its ruling *in camera*.

Article 226

1. If, during the transitional period, difficulties arise which are serious and liable to persist in any sector of the economy or which could bring about serious deterioration in the economic situation of a given area, a Member State may apply for authorisation to take protective measures in order to rectify the situation and adjust the sector concerned to the economy of the common market.

2. On application by the State concerned, the Commission shall, by emergency procedure, determine without delay the protective measures which it considers necessary, specifying the circumstances and the manner in which they are to be put into effect.

3. The measures authorised under paragraph 2 may involve derogations from the rules of this Treaty, to such an extent and for such periods as are strictly necessary in order to attain the objectives referred to in paragraph 1. Priority shall be given to such measures as will least disturb the functioning of the common market.

Article 227

1. This Treaty shall apply to the Kingdom of Belgium, the Kingdom of Denmark, the Federal Republic of Germany, the Hellenic Republic, the Kingdom of Spain, the French Republic, Ireland, the Italian Republic, the Grand Duchy of Luxembourg, the Kingdom of the Netherlands, the Portuguese Republic and the United Kingdom of Great Britain and Northern Ireland.

2. With regard to Algeria and the French overseas departments, the general and particular provisions of this Treaty relating to:

- the free movement of goods;
- agriculture, save for Article 40(4);
- the liberalisation of services;
- the rules on competition;
- the protective measures provided for in Articles 108, 109 and 226;
- the institutions;

shall apply as soon as this Treaty enters into force.

The conditions under which the other provisions of this Treaty are to apply shall be determined, within two years of the entry into force of this Treaty, by decisions of the Council, acting unanimously on a proposal from the Commission.

The institutions of the Community will, within the framework of the procedures provided for in this Treaty, in particular Article 226, take care that the economic and social development of these areas is made possible.

3. The special arrangements for association set out in Part Four of this Treaty shall apply to the overseas countries and territories listed in Annex IV to this Treaty.

This Treaty shall not apply to those overseas countries and territories having special relations with the United Kingdom of Great Britain and Northern Ireland which are not included in the aforementioned list.

4. The provisions of this Treaty shall apply to the European territories for whose external relations a Member State is responsible.

5. Notwithstanding the preceding paragraphs:

(a) This Treaty shall not apply to the Faroe Islands. The Government of the Kingdom of Denmark may, however, give notice, by a declaration deposited by 31 December 1975 at the latest with the Government of the Italian Republic, which shall transmit a certified copy thereof to each of the Governments of the other Member States, that this Treaty shall apply to those Islands. In that event, this Treaty shall apply to those Islands from the first day of the second month following the deposit of the declaration.

(b) This Treaty shall not apply to the Sovereign Base Areas of the United Kingdom of Great Britain and Northern Ireland in Cyprus.

(c) This Treaty shall apply to the Channel Islands and the Isle of Man only to the extent necessary to ensure the implementation of the arrangements for those islands set out in the Treaty concerning the accession of new Member States to the European Economic Community and to the European Atomic Energy Community signed on 22 January 1972.

Article 228

1. Where this Treaty provides for the conclusion of agreements between the Community and one or more States or an international organisation, such agreements shall be negotiated by the Commission. Subject to the powers vested in the Commission in this field, such agreements shall be concluded by the Council, after consulting the European Parliament where required by this Treaty.

The Council, the Commission or a Member State may obtain beforehand the opinion of the Court of Justice as to whether an agreement envisaged is compatible with the provisions of this Treaty. Where the opinion of the Court of Justice is adverse, the agreement may enter into force only in accordance with Article 236.

2. Agreements concluded under these conditions shall be binding on the institutions of the Community and on Member States.

Article 229

It shall be for the Commission to ensure the maintenance of all appropriate relations with the organs of the United Nations, of its specialised agencies and of the General Agreement on Tariffs and Trade.

The Commission shall also maintain such relations as are appropriate with all international organisations.

Article 230

The Community shall establish all appropriate forms of co-operation with the Council of Europe.

Article 231

The Community shall establish close co-operation with the Organisation for European Economic Co-operation, the details to be determined by common accord.

Article 232

1. The provisions of this Treaty shall not affect the provisions of the Treaty establishing the European Coal and Steel Community, in particular as regards the rights and obligations of Member States, the powers of the institutions of that Community and the rules laid down by that Treaty for the functioning of the common market in coal and steel.

2. The provisions of this Treaty shall not derogate from those of the Treaty establishing the European Atomic Energy Community.

Article 233

The provisions of this Treaty shall not preclude the existence or completion of regional unions between Belgium and Luxembourg, or between Belgium, Luxembourg and the Netherlands, to the extent that the objectives of these regional unions are not attained by application of this Treaty.

Article 234

The rights and obligations arising from agreements concluded before the entry into force of this Treaty between one or more Member States on the one hand, and one or more third countries on the other, shall not be affected by the provisions of this Treaty.

To the extent that such agreements are not compatible with this Treaty, the Member State or States concerned shall take all appropriate steps to eliminate the incompatibilities established. Member States shall, where necessary, assist each other to this end and shall, where appropriate, adopt a common attitude.

In applying the agreements referred to in the first paragraph, Member States shall take into account the fact that the advantages accorded under this Treaty by each Member State form an integral part of the establishment of the Community and are thereby inseparably linked with the creation of common institutions, the conferring of powers upon them and the granting of the same advantages by all the other Member States.

Article 235

If action by the Community should prove necessary to attain, in the course of the operation of the common market, one of the objectives of the Community and this Treaty has not provided the necessary powers, the Council shall, acting unanimously on a proposal from the Commission and after consulting the European Parliament, take the appropriate measures.

Article 236

The Government of any Member State or the Commission may submit to the Council proposals for the amendment of this Treaty.

If the Council, after consulting the European Parliament and, where appropriate, the Commission, delivers an opinion in favour of calling a conference of representatives of the Governments of the Member States, the conference shall be convened by the President of the Council for the purpose of determining by common accord the amendments to be made to this Treaty.

The amendments shall enter into force after being ratified by all the Member States in accordance with their respective constitutional requirements.

Article 237

Any European State may apply to become a member of the Community. It shall address its application to the Council, which shall act unanimously after consulting the Commission and after receiving the assent of the European Parliament which shall act by an absolute majority of its component members.

The conditions of admission and the adjustments to this Treaty necessitated thereby shall be the subject of an agreement between the Member States and the applicant State. This agreement shall be submitted for ratification by all the Contracting States in accordance with their respective constitutional requirements.

Article 238

The Community may conclude with a third State, a union of States or an international organisation agreements establishing an association involving reciprocal rights and obligations, common action and special procedures.

These agreements shall be concluded by the Council, acting unanimously and after receiving the assent of the European Parliament which shall act by an absolute majority of its component members.

Where such agreements call for amendments to this Treaty, these amendments shall first be adopted in accordance with the procedure laid down in Article 236.

Article 239

The Protocols annexed to this Treaty by common accord of the Member States shall form an integral part thereof.

Article 240

This Treaty is concluded for an unlimited period.

SETTING UP OF THE INSTITUTIONS

Article 241

The Council shall meet within one month of the entry into force of this Treaty

Article 242

The Council shall, within three months of its first meeting, take all appropriate measures to constitute the Economic and Social Committee.

Article 243

The Assembly shall meet within two months of the first meeting of the Council, having been convened by the President of the Council, in order to elect its officers and draw up its rules of procedure. Pending the election of its officers, the oldest member shall take the chair.

Article 244

The Court of Justice shall take up its duties as soon as its members have been appointed. Its first President shall be appointed for three years in the same manner as its members.

The Court of Justice shall adopt its rules of procedure within three months of taking up its duties.

No matter may be brought before the Court of Justice until its rules of procedure have been published. The time within which an action must be brought shall run only from the date of this publication.

Upon his appointment, the President of the Court of Justice shall exercise the powers conferred upon him by this Treaty.

Article 245

The Commission shall take up its duties and assume the responsibilities conferred upon it by this Treaty as soon as its members have been appointed.

Upon taking up its duties, the Commission shall undertake the studies and arrange the contacts needed for making an overall survey of the economic situation of the Community.

Article 246

1. The first financial year shall run from the date on which this Treaty enters into force until 31 December following. Should this Treaty, however, enter into force during the second half of the year, the first financial year shall run until 31 December of the following year.

2. Until the budget for the first financial year has been established, Member States shall make the Community interest-free advances which shall be deducted from their financial contributions to the implementation of the budget.

3. Until the Staff Regulations of officials and the Conditions of Employment of other servants of the Community provided for in Article 212 have been laid down, each institution shall recruit the staff it needs and to this end conclude contracts of limited duration.

Each institution shall examine together with the Council any question concerning the number, remuneration and distribution of posts.

FINAL PROVISIONS

Article 247

This Treaty shall be ratified by the High Contracting Parties in accordance with their respective constitutional requirements. The instruments of ratification shall be deposited with the Government of the Italian Republic.

The Treaty shall enter into force on the first day of the month following the deposit of the instrument of ratification by the last signatory State to take this step. If, however, such deposit is made less than fifteen days before the beginning of the following month, this Treaty shall not enter into force until the first day of the second month after the date of such deposit.

Article 248

This Treaty, drawn up in a single original in the Dutch, French, German and Italian languages, all four texts being equally authentic, shall be deposited in the archives of the Government of the Italian Republic, which shall transmit a certified copy to each of the Governments of the other signatory States.

Rome, 25 March 1957.

APPENDIX 2

Council Decisions, Recommendations and Resolutions UN Liner Code Convention

1. COUNCIL DECISION OF 13 SEPTEMBER 1977 SETTING UP A CONSULTATION PROCEDURE ON RELATIONS BETWEEN MEMBER STATES AND THIRD COUNTRIES IN SHIPPING MATTERS AND ON ACTION RELATING TO SUCH MATTERS IN INTERNATIONAL ORGANIZATIONS (77/587/EEC)

THE COUNCIL OF THE EUROPEAN COMMUNITIES,

Having regard to the Treaty establishing the European Economic Community, and in particular Article 84(2) thereof,

Whereas, to make allowance for developments affecting world shipping and for their consequences for the Member States, it is desirable that problems of common interest with regard to relations between Member States and third countries in shipping matters and to action relating to such matters in international organizations should be identified in good time;

Whereas it is desirable to facilitate exchanges of information and consultations on such matters and to promote coordination, where appropriate, of the action taken by the Member States in international organizations;

Whereas each Member State should give the benefit of its experience in relations with third countries in shipping matters to the other Member States and to the Commission;

Whereas information in this field is regularly exchanged in certain international organizations; whereas these procedures should be supplemented at Community level by exchanges of information between the Member States and the Commission,

HAS ADOPTED THIS DECISION:

Article 1

The Member States and the Commission shall consult each other, in accordance with the procedures laid down in this Decision:

(a) on questions concerning shipping matters and dealt with in international organizations, and

(b) on the various aspects of development which have taken place in relations between Members States and third countries in shipping matters, and on the functioning of bilateral or multilateral agreements concluded in this sphere.

The consultations shall be held at the request of a Member State or of the Commission, within one month of the request or at the earliest opportunity in urgent cases.

Article 2

1. The main aims of the consultations provided for in Article 1 under (a) shall be:

(a) to determine jointly whether the questions raise problems of common interest;
(b) depending upon the nature of such problems:
— to consider jointly whether Member States' action within the international organizations concerned should be coordinated,
— to consider jointly any other approach which might be appropriate.

2. The Member States and the Commission shall as soon as possible exchange any information of relevance to the aims described in paragraph 1.

Article 3

1. For the purposes of the consultations referred to in Article 1 under (b), each Member State shall inform the other Member States and the Commission of the various aspects of developments which have taken place in its relations with third countries in shipping matters, and of the operation of bilateral or multilateral agreements concluded in this field, if it considers this likely to contribute to the identification of problems of common interest.

2. The main aims of the consultations referred to in paragraph 1 shall be to examine the implications of the information provided and to consider any approach which might be appropriate.

3. The Commission shall provide the Member States with any information which it possesses regarding the matters referred to in paragraph 1.

Article 4

1. The exchanges of information provided for in this Decision shall take place through the General Secretariat of the Council.

2. The consultations provided for in this Decision shall take place within the framework of the Council.

3. The information and consultations provided for in this Decision shall be covered by professional secrecy.

Article 5

At the end of a period of three years following the date of notification of this Decision, the Council shall re-examine the consultation procedure with a view to amending or supplementing it, if experience shows this to be necessary.

Article 6

This Decision is addressed to the Member States.

Done at Brussels, 13 September 1977.

For the Council
The President
A. HUMBLET

2. COUNCIL RECOMMENDATION OF 26 JUNE 1978 ON THE RATIFICATION OF CONVENTIONS ON SAFETY IN SHIPPING (78/584/EEC)

THE COUNCIL OF THE EUROPEAN COMMUNITIES,

Having regard to the Treaty establishing the European Economic Community,

Having regard to the proposal from the Commission,

Having regard to the opinion of the European Parliament,[1]

Having regard to the opinion of the Economic and Social Committee,[2]

Whereas the European Council of 7 and 8 April 1978 declared that the prevention of and the fight against marine pollution, particularly from hydrocarbons, must be a major objective for Community action; whereas it asked the Council, acting on a proposal from the Commission, and the Member States to take appropriate measures without delay within the Community and to adopt common attitudes in the appropriate international bodies on the swift implementation of existing international rules in this field, in particular those regarding minimum standards for the operation of ships;

Whereas there is a fundamental interest in seeing effective action undertaken to reduce the risks inherent in the transport of hydrocarbons, in particular the danger of severe coastal pollution as the fault of accidents on the high seas, and whereas this fundamental interest is underlined by the European Communities' environment action programmes;

Whereas safety in shipping must be improved and the living and working conditions of crews and their level of competence better safeguarded;

Whereas Community action in this field in the framework of specialized international bodies, particularly the IMCO and the ILO and their respective Conventions, may be jeopardized if too long a period were to elapse between the conclusions of those Conventions and their entry into force;

Whereas the 1974 International Convention for the safety of life at sea (SOLAS) and the 1978 Protocol relating thereto and ILO Convention No 147 concerning minimum standards in merchant ships of 1976, which have not yet entered into force, can make a substantial contribution towards improving both technical and welfare standards affecting, respectively, the safety of ships and their equipment and the living and working conditions of their crews;

Whereas the 1973 Convention for the prevention of pollution by ships (MARPOL), as amended by the 1978 Protocol, can make a substantial contribution towards protecting the marine environment against pollution by ships, particularly oil tankers;

Whereas the signing and ratification by or the accession of all the Member States could accelerate the entry into force and increase the effectiveness of these Conventions,

HEREBY RECOMMENDS:

— that, where they have not already done so, the Member States, where appropriate, sign the following international conventions and ratify or accede to them:
— the 1974 International Convention for the safety of life at sea (SOLAS),
— the 1978 Protocol relating to the 1974 International Convention for the safety of life at sea,
— the 1973 International Convention for the prevention of pollution by ships (MARPOL), as amended by the 1978 Protocol,
— Convention No 147 concerning minimum standards in merchants ships, adopted by the International Labour Conference in 1976;
— that signing, ratification or accession by the Member States, as the case may be, take place by the following dates:
— the 1974 SOLAS Convention:
ratification or accession as soon as possible and, in any event, by 1 January 1979,
— the Protocol thereto (1978):
— signing as soon as possible and by 1 March 1979 at the latest,

1. OJ No C 163, 10 July 1978, p. 17.
2. Opinion delivered on 21 June 1978 (not yet published in the Official Journal).

— ratification as soon as possible and, in any event, by 30 June 1979,
— the Protocol (1978) amending and supplementing the MARPOL Convention (1973) and Annex 1 thereto:
— signing by 1 June 1979,
— ratification by 1 June 1980,
— ILO Convention No 147:
ratification or accession by 1 April 1979;
— that the Member States inform in writing the Secretary-General of the Inter-Governmental Maritime Consultative Organization or the International Labour Organization, as appropriate, that their signing, ratification or accession has had regard to this recommendation.

Done at Luxembourg, 26 June 1978.

For the Council
The President
K. B. ANDERSEN

3. COUNCIL RESOLUTION OF 26 JUNE 1978 SETTING UP AN ACTION PROGRAMME OF THE EUROPEAN COMMUNITIES ON THE CONTROL AND REDUCTION OF POLLUTION CAUSED BY HYDROCARBONS DISCHARGED AT SEA

THE COUNCIL OF THE EUROPEAN COMMUNITIES,

Having regard to the Treaty establishing the European Economic Community,

Having regard to the draft from the Commission,

Having regard to the opinion of the European Parliament,[1]

Having regard to the opinion of the Economic and Social Committee,[2]

Whereas at its meeting in Copenhagen on 7 and 8 April 1978, the European Council took the view that the Community should make the prevention and control of marine pollution, in particular by hydrocarbons, an important objective of its action;

Whereas the European Communities' Action Programmes on the Environment[3] stressed the paramount importance to Western Europe that effective action be taken against the dangers inherent in the carriage of hydrocarbons, including the threat of serious pollution of coastal areas from accidents on the high seas and specified that the protection of marine waters to ensure that ecological balances are preserved is a priority task;

Whereas the authorities of the Member States the responsibility of which it is to take action in the event of pollution of the sea by hydrocarbons must have very prompt access to information on the human and material resources which can be deployed for the control of such pollution;

Whereas, in order quickly to counteract or even to prevent accidental pollution by hydrocarbons, these authorities must be able to ascertain particulars of the features of the vessels and offshore structures liable to cause such pollution and must be informed of any violations which may have been committed by vessels in the territorial waters of the Member States;

Whereas these authorities must be able to call on the assistance, at very short notice, of specialists who are fully and suitably trained in the control of marine pollution by hydrocarbons; whereas the equipment used for this purpose must be immediately available for use;

Whereas it is necessary to study the details of a possible Community contribution to work relating to the design and development of clean-up vessels, in view of its high cost;

Whereas the legal provisions on insurance against the risks of accidental pollution by hydrocarbons must guarantee adequate compensation for the victims of such pollution;

Whereas research should be carried out to improve mechanical and chemical methods of treating hydrocarbons discharged at sea and to further knowledge regarding the subsequent history of such hydrocarbons and their effects on marine flora and fauna;

Whereas the action to be taken pursuant to this resolution may in no event exempt operators from their liability under civil or criminal law;

Whereas the Commission must have at its disposal the resources to prepare the detailed proposals provided for in the programme annexed hereto;

Whereas there are already international agreements dealing with measures for control of pollution from hydrocarbons to which Member States are party and there is a need to complement such agreements while avoiding duplication;

Approves the broad lines of approach laid down in the action programme contained in the Annex;

Notes that the Commission will undertake the studies before submitting appropriate proposals as soon as possible for the implementation of this programme;

Undertakes to take a decision on these proposals within nine months from the date of their submission by the Commission or, as the case may be, of the date of forwarding of the opinions of the European Parliament and the Economic and Social Committee;

Calls on the Member States to provide the Commission, at its request and on a case by case basis, with all the information needed to apply this resolution.

1. Opinion delivered on 13 June 1978 (not yet published in the Official Journal).
2. Opinion delivered on 13 June 1978 (not yet published in the Official Journal).
3. OJ No C 112, 20 December 1973, p. 1 and OJ No C 139, 13 June 1977, p. 1.

ANNEX. ACTION PROGRAMME OF THE EUROPEAN COMMUNITIES ON THE CONTROL AND REDUCTION OF POLLUTION CAUSED BY HYDROCARBONS DISCHARGED AT SEA

The Commission will undertake the preliminary studies to identify what gaps need to be filled in the current framework of measures to control and reduce pollution caused by hydrocarbons discharged at sea and to propose appropriate action, at Community level and, if necessary, within the framework of international organizations or agreements. In the light of these studies, the Commission will place appropriate proposals before the Council as soon as possible. These studies will cover the following fields:

1. Computer processing of the existing data, or data still to be collected, on ways of dealing with marine pollution by hydrocarbons with a view to the immediate use of such data in the event of accidental pollution

The study undertaken by the Commission will relate to any steps which might need to be taken so as to ensure that Member States, and if necessary interested third countries, have complete, rapid and reliable information on ways of dealing with marine pollution by hydrocarbons. The information studies will include in particular:

— the team of qualified personnel to combat marine pollution by hydrocarbons, the specific qualifications of such teams and practical particulars of how such teams can be called in;

— the availability of products and equipment for the chemical treatment of hydrocarbons (dispersants, precipitating agents, aerator-agitators and dispersant spreading equipment);

— availability of equipment for the mechanical treatment of hydrocarbons and the specifications of the ships and equipment from which these operations can be carried out (speed and stability of vessels, equipment fitted) and their location;

— availability of the required coastline-protection resources (oil slick containment equipment, oil absorbants or precipitating agents, gels enabling dispersants to be used on rocks or structures, aerator-agitator and recovery equipment for use in shallow waters and beach-cleaning equipment).

This study will consider in particular the conditions under which the collection and computer processing of this information, which should be constantly updated, can be achieved at minimum cost and avoiding any duplication. Possibilities existing already both at national level and within the framework of existing international agreements will need to be fully explored.

2. Study of the availability for the Member States of relevant data on tankers liable to pollute the waters around the Community and the coasts of the Member States and on off-shore structures under the jurisdiction of the Member States

The study undertaken by the Commission would be aimed at:

(a) investigating to what extent Member States may as of now have rapidly available complete and reliable information relating to:
  — the structural features of the tankers and offshore structures in question and emergency plans for prompt intervention,
  — any infringements committed in the territorial waters.

(b) investigating, if necessary, the means of making this information more readily available.

4. COUNCIL DECISION OF 19 SEPTEMBER 1978 CONCERNING THE ACTIVITIES OF CERTAIN THIRD COUNTRIES IN THE FIELD OF CARGO SHIPPING (78/774/EEC)

THE COUNCIL OF THE EUROPEAN COMMUNITIES,

Having regard to the Treaty establishing the European Economic Community, and in particular Article 84 (2) thereof,

Having regard to the draft Decision submitted by the Commission,

Having regard to the opinion of the European Parliament,[1]

Having regard to the opinion of the Economic and Social Committee,[2]

Whereas information systems should be established to enable the Community institutions to be kept informed of the activities of the fleets of third countries whose practices are harmful to the shipping interests of the Member States and in particular in so far as these activities adversely affect the competitive participation of the fleets of Member States in international maritime trade; whereas these information systems must facilitate consultation at Community level;

Whereas the possibility should be provided for the necessary measures to be adopted at Community level for the joint exercise by Member States of their powers to adopt counter-measures in respect of the cargo shipping activities of certain third countries,

HAS ADOPTED THIS DECISION:

Article 1

1. Each Member State shall take all the necessary measures to institute a system allowing it to collect information on the activities of the fleets of third countries whose practices are harmful to the shipping interests of the Member States and in particular in so far as these activities adversely affect the competitive participation of the fleets of Member States in international maritime trade.

2. This system must enable each Member State, to the extent necessary to attain the objectives referred to in paragraph 1, to collect information on:

- the level of cargo shipping services offered,
- the nature, volume, value, origin and destination of goods loaded or unloaded in the Member States concerned by the ships engaged in these services, and
- the level of tariffs charged for such services.

Article 2

1. The Council, acting unanimously, shall decide to which third countries' fleets the information system shall be jointly applied.

2. The Decision referred to in paragraph 1 shall specify the type of cargo shipping to which the information system is to apply, the date of its introduction, the intervals at which the information is to be provided and which of the types of information listed in Article 1 are to be collected.

3. Each Member State shall forward to the Commission, periodically or at the request of the latter, the information produced by its information system.

4. The Commission shall collate the information for the Community as a whole. Article 4 of Council Decision 77/587/EEC of 13 September 1977 setting up a consultation procedure on relations between Member States and third countries in shipping matters and on action relating to such matters in international organizations[3] shall apply to that information.

Article 3

The Member States and the Commission shall examine regularly, within the framework of the consultation procedure established by Decision 77/587/EEC and on the basis *inter alia* of the

1. OJ No C 131, 5 June 1978, p. 40.
2. Opinion delivered on 1 June 1978 (not yet published in the Official Journal).
3. OJ No L 239, 17 September 1977, p. 23.

information produced by the information system referred to in Article 1, the activities of the fleets of the third countries specified in the Decisions referred to in Article 2.

Article 4

The Council, acting unanimously, may decide on the joint application by Member States, in their relations with a third country or group of third countries regarding which a Decision referred to in Article 2 has been adopted, of appropriate counter-measures forming part of their national legislation.

Article 5

The Member States shall retain the right to apply unilaterally their national information systems and counter-measures.

Article 6

The Member States shall, as soon as possible and at the latest by 31 December 1978, after consulting the Commission, adopt the laws, regulations and administrative provisions necessary to implement this Decision.

Article 7

This Decision is addressed to the Member States.

Done at Brussels, 19 September 1978.

For the Council
The President
H. D. GENSCHER

5. COUNCIL DECISION OF 19 DECEMBER 1978 ON THE COLLECTION OF INFORMATION CONCERNING THE ACTIVITIES OF CARRIERS PARTICIPATING IN CARGO LINER TRAFFIC IN CERTAIN AREAS OF OPERATION (79/4/EEC)

THE COUNCIL OF THE EUROPEAN COMMUNITIES,

Having regard to the Treaty establishing the European Economic Community, and in particular Article 84 (2) thereof,

Having regard to Council Decision 78/774/EEC of 19 September 1978 concerning the activities of certain third countries in the field of cargo shipping,[1]

Having regard to the draft Decision submitted by the Commission,

Having regard to the opinion of the European Parliament,[2]

Having regard to the opinion of the Economic and Social Committee,[3]

Whereas there is need for surveillance of the activities of all shipping companies participating in certain cargo liner traffic operations from and to the Community, if there is reason to think that certain carriers are not following the rules of competition in accordance with the principles of market economy and are adversely affecting the competitive position of Member State fleets in international maritime trade,

HAS ADOPTED THIS DECISION:

Article 1

From 1 January 1979 to 31 December 1980, each Member State shall collect the information specified in Annex I for all carriers participating in cargo liner traffic in the areas of operation specified in Annex II, in so far as these carriers serve its ports. The information for each half-year shall be forwarded to the Commission as soon as possible and in any case not later than three months after the end of the period concerned.

Article 2

This Decision is addressed to the Member States.

Done at Brussels, 19 December 1978.

For the Council
The President
G. BAUM

ANNEX I. INFORMATION TO BE COLLECTED

1. Liner services operated[4]

(a) Name of company and service.
(b) Area of operation (see Annex II).
(c) Date of establishment, modification or termination of liner service.
(d) Vessels employed (name, flag, vessel type (e.g. general cargo, container, roll-on roll-off, lighter carrier), dwt, grt and TEU).
(e) Arrivals and departures per vessel.
(f) Conference membership; if yes, which conference or section thereof?

1. OJ No L 258, 21 September 1978, p. 35.
2. OJ No C 296, 11 December 1978, p. 50.
3. Opinion delivered on 29/30 November 1978 (not yet published in the Official Journal).
4. The first six-monthly return should describe the situation at the start of the six months concerned, changes which occurred during the period and the situation at the end of the period. Subsequent returns should describe changes occurring during the period and the situation at the end of it.

2. Liner cargo carried

(a) Flag.
(b) Area of operation.
(c) Total liner cargo loaded from country of loading, origin or dispatch in incoming traffic, total liner cargo carried to country of unloading and/or destination in outgoing traffic, in weight and/or freight tonnes.
(d) Specification of types of commodities.

3. Information concerning transport rates

Member States shall use their best endeavours to provide information on transport rates. This information should be based on current average rates by carrier, paid for selected commodities.

ANNEX II. LIST OF AREAS OF OPERATION

1. Between the Member States and East Africa (Somalia, Kenya, Uganda, Zambia, Tanzania, Mozambique).
2. Between the Member States and Central America (East and West Coasts—from Mexico's southern frontier to Panama inclusive, with the exclusion of the West Indies).

6. COUNCIL RECOMMENDATION OF 21 DECEMBER 1978 ON THE RATIFICATION OF THE 1978 INTERNATIONAL CONVENTION ON STANDARDS OF TRAINING, CERTIFICATION AND WATCHKEEPING FOR SEAFARERS (79/114/EEC)

THE COUNCIL OF THE EUROPEAN COMMUNITIES,

Having regard to the Treaty establishing the European Economic Community, and in particular Article 84 (2) thereof,

Whereas, at its meeting on 7 and 8 April 1978 in Copenhagen, the European Council declared that the Community should make the prevention and combating of marine pollution, particularly from hydrocarbons, a major objective;

Whereas, at its meeting on 6 and 7 July 1978 in Bremen, the European Council deemed it necessary, taking into account the proposals of individual Member States and the Commission, to take further measures to increase the safety of maritime traffic;

Whereas an International Convention on standards of training, certification and watchkeeping for seafarers was adopted in London in July 1978;

Whereas, in the interest of shipping safety and the prevention of pollution, this Convention should enter into force as soon as possible; whereas the early ratification of the Convention by the Member States would constitute a major contribution to the achievement of that objective,

HEREBY RECOMMENDS:

— that the Member States sign the 1978 International Convention on standards of training, certification and watchkeeping for seafarers by 1 April 1979 and ratify it as soon as possible and not later than 31 December 1980;

— that the Member States inform the Secretary-General of the Inter-Governmental Maritime Consultative Organization that they have signed and ratified the Convention in accordance with this recommendation.

Done at Brussels, 21 December 1978.

For the Council
The President
OTTO GRAF LAMBSDORFF

7. COUNCIL DIRECTIVE OF 21 DECEMBER 1978 CONCERNING PILOTAGE OF VESSELS BY DEEP-SEA PILOTS IN THE NORTH SEA AND ENGLISH CHANNEL (79/115/EEC)

THE COUNCIL OF THE EUROPEAN COMMUNITIES,

Having regard to the Treaty establishing the European Economic Community, and in particular Article 84 (2) thereof,

Whereas for the sake of safety at sea and of preventing marine pollution, it is necessary to ensure that vessels wishing to use the services of pilots in the North Sea and English Channel can call on adequately qualified deep-sea pilots, and to promote the employment of such pilots in vessels flying the flags of Member States,

HAS ADOPTED THIS DIRECTIVE:

Article 1

1. The Member States which have coasts bordering on the North Sea or English Channel shall take all necessary and appropriate measures to ensure that vessels availing themselves of the services of a deep-sea pilot for pilotage in the North Sea or the English Channel be provided with adequately qualified deep-sea pilots in possession of a certificate delivered by a competent authority of one of these Member States certifying that such pilots are qualified to pilot vessels in the North Sea and the English Channel.

2. Each Member State shall take all necessary and appropriate measures to encourage vessels flying its national flag to avail themselves, in the North Sea and the English Channel, of the services of only those deep-sea pilots who are in possession of a certificate as referred to in paragraph 1 or of an equivalent certificate delivered by another North Sea coastal State, when seeking the assistance of deep-sea pilots.

Article 2

After consulting the Commission, Member States shall bring into force the laws, regulations and administrative provisions necessary to comply with this Directive not later than 1 January 1980. They shall forthwith inform the Commission thereof.

Article 3

This Directive is addressed to the Member States.

Done at Brussels, 21 December 1978.

For the Council
The President
OTTO GRAF LAMBSDORFF

8. COUNCIL DIRECTIVE OF 21 DECEMBER 1978 CONCERNING MINIMUM REQUIREMENTS FOR CERTAIN TANKERS ENTERING OR LEAVING COMMUNITY PORTS (79/116/EEC)

THE COUNCIL OF THE EUROPEAN COMMUNITIES,

Having regard to the Treaty establishing the European Economic Community, and in particular Article 84 (2) thereof,

Whereas, to reduce the risk of incidents involving tankers entering or leaving Member States' ports, the said tankers should be required to comply in advance with certain minimum requirements before entering and while traversing the territorial waters adjacent to the port of destination or departure;

Whereas the competent authorities should be informed of any deficiency potentially deleterious to the safety of shipping and to the marine environment; whereas a Member State in which the competent authorities are informed of circumstances involving or increasing the risk that another Member State's sea and coastal areas may be endangered should inform that Member State forthwith;

HAS ADOPTED THIS DIRECTIVE:

Article 1

1. Member States shall take all necessary and appropriate measures to ensure that oil, gas and chemical tankers of 1,600 gross registered tons and over—whether fully or partly laden—and including those empty but not yet degassed or purged of hazardous residues, entering or leaving the seaports of their territory shall, as a minimum:

A. in advance of entering,
   (i) notify the competent authority of the Member State in which the port is situated of the following information ("notification"):
      (a) name and call sign of the vessel,
      (b) nationality of the vessel,
      (c) length and draught of the vessel,
      (d) port of destination,
      (e) estimated time of arrival at the port of destination or the pilot station, as required by the competent authority,
      (f) general information on the nature and quantity of cargo,
      (g) where chemicals are being transported, information on whether or not the vessel is in possession of a certificate stating that it is a "new vessel" under the terms of the IMCO code for the construction and equipment of ships carrying dangerous chemicals in bulk,
      (h) whether or not there are any deficiencies or incidents which may decrease the normal safe manoeuvrability of the vessel, affect the safety and easy flow of traffic or constitute a hazard to the marine environment and adjacent areas;
   (ii) complete truly and accurately a tanker check list as reproduced in the Annex to this Directive and make it available to the pilot for his information and to the competent authority, if it so requests.

B. while traversing the territorial waters adjacent to the port of entry or departure,
   (i) inform the competent authorities of any deficiencies and incidents which may decrease the normal safe manoeuvrability of the vessel, affect the safety and easy flow of traffic or constitute a hazard to the marine environment and adjacent areas,
   (ii) as soon as possible establish radiotelephony communication with the coastal radio stations designated for that purpose, preferably on VHF—in particular, with the nearest radar station, if available—and maintain such communication,
   (iii) make use, as far as possible, especially in conditions of restricted visibility, of the services provided by radar stations,
   (iv) make use of pilots, in accordance with practice and with the regulations determined by the competent authorities.

2. If the pilot learns that there are any deficiencies which may prejudice the safe navigation of the vessel, he shall immediately report these to the competent authority.

3. Member States may derogate from paragraphs 1 and 2 where the state of navigational aids, the local situation or the traffic conditions so require or permit.

Article 2

Any Member State the competent authorities of which have been informed, in accordance with Article 1 or in some other way, of facts which involve or increase the risk for another Member State of a hazard being posed to certain maritime and coastal zones, shall take whatever measures are appropriate to inform the Member State concerned thereof as soon as possible.

Article 3

Before 1 January 1980, Member States shall, after consulting the Commission, adopt the laws, regulations and administrative provisions necessary to implement this Directive. They shall inform the Commission and the other Member States of the measures taken, as well as of any provisions providing for derogations under Article 1 (3).

Article 4

This Directive is addressed to the Member States.

Done at Brussels, 21 December 1978.

For the Council
The President
OTTO GRAF LAMSDORFF

ANNEX: TANKER CHECK LIST

A. Vessel identification			
Name of vessel	Owner		
Flag	Call sign	Year built	
Port of registry	Length overall	Gross tonnage	
Classification society			
Class notation	Hull	Machinery	
Propulsion machinery	Output		
Agent			
Draught: forward	amidships	aft	
Kind of cargo loaded (according to tank loading plan)	Volume of Cargo loaded		
B. Safety installations aboard	In good working order		Deficiencies
1. Construction and technical equipment	Yes	No	
Main and auxiliary engines	☐	☐	
Main steering gear	☐	☐	
Auxiliary steering gear	☐	☐	
Anchor gear	☐	☐	
Fixed fire-extinguishing system	☐	☐	
2. Navigational equipment			
Manoeuvring characteristics available	☐	☐	
First radar installation	☐	☐	
Second radar installation	☐	☐	
Gyro compass	☐	☐	
Standard magnetic compass	☐	☐	
Radio direction-finding apparatus	☐	☐	
Echo-sounding device	☐	☐	

	Other electronic position fixing aids	☐	☐
3.	Radio equipment		
	Radiotelegraphy installation	☐	☐
	Radiotelephony installation (VHF)	☐	☐

	Certificates/documents valid on board	
C. Safety certificates and other documents	Yes	No
Cargo ship safety construction certificate	☐	☐
Cargo ship safety equipment certificate	☐	☐
Cargo ship safety radiotelegraphy certificate	☐	☐
Ship safety radiotelephony certificate	☐	☐
Load line certificate	☐	☐
Classification certificate	☐	☐
Oil liability certificate	☐	☐
Oil record book filled in	☐	☐

D. Officers and ratings	Yes	No	Certificate of competency (detailed description and serial number) Name, place country of issuing authority[1]
Master	☐	☐	
Chief mate	☐	☐	
Second mate	☐	☐	
Third mate	☐	☐	
Chief engineer	☐	☐	
First engineer officer	☐	☐	
Second engineer officer	☐	☐	
Third engineer officer	☐	☐	
Radio officer	☐	☐	
Total number of ratings	Deck	Engine room	
Deep-sea pilot taken aboard	☐	☐	
Date	Signature of the master or, if he is indisposed, of the deputy		

1. Member States may decide to exclude from the check list the part of section D relating to certificates of competency.

9. COUNCIL REGULATION OF 15 MAY 1979 CONCERNING THE RATIFICATION BY MEMBER STATES OF, OR THEIR ACCESSION TO, THE UNITED NATIONS CONVENTION ON A CODE OF CONDUCT FOR LINER CONFERENCES (79/954/EEC)

THE COUNCIL OF THE EUROPEAN COMMUNITIES,

Having regard to the Treaty establishing the European Economic Community, and in particular Article 84 (2) thereof,

Having regard to the draft Regulation submitted by the Commission,

Having regard to the opinion of the European Parliament,[1]

Having regard to the opinion of the Economic and Social Committee,[2]

Whereas a Convention on a Code of Conduct for Liner Conferences has been drawn up by a Conference convened under the auspices of the United Nations Conference on Trade and Development and is open for ratification or accession;

Whereas the questions covered by the Code of Conduct are of importance not only to the Member States but also to the Community, in particular from the shipping and trading viewpoints, and it is therefore important that a common position should be adopted in relation to this Code:

Whereas this common position should respect the principles and objectives of the Treaty and make a major contribution to meeting the aspirations of developing countries in the field of shipping while at the same time pursuing the objective of the continuing application in this field of the commercial principles applied by shipping lines of the OECD countries and in trades between these countries;

Whereas to secure observance of these principles and objectives, since the Code of Conduct contains no provision allowing the accession of the Community as such, it is important that Member States ratify or accede to the Code of Conduct subject to certain arrangements provided for in this Regulation,

Whereas the stabilizing role of conferences in ensuring reliable services to shippers is recognized, but it is nevertheless necessary to avoid possible breaches by conferences of the rules of competition laid down in the Treaty; whereas the Commission will accordingly forward to the Council a proposal for a Regulation concerning the application of those rules to sea transport.

HAS ADOPTED THIS REGULATION:

Article 1

1. When ratifying the United Nations Convention on a Code of Conduct for Liner Conferences, or when acceding thereto, Member States shall inform the Secretary-General of the United Nations in writing that such ratification or accession has taken place in accordance with this Regulation.

2. The instrument of ratification or accession shall be accompanied by the reservations set out in Annex 1.

Article 2

1. In the case of an existing conference, each group of shipping lines of the same nationality which are members thereof shall determine by commercial negotiations with another shipping line of that nationality whether the latter may participate as a national shipping line in the said conference.

If a new conference is created, the shipping lines of the same nationality shall determine by commercial negotiations which of them may participate as a national shipping line in the future conference.

1. OJ No C 131, 5 June 1978, p. 34.
2. OJ No C 269, 13 November 1978, p. 46.

2. Where the negotiations referred to in paragraph 1 fail to result in agreement, each Member State may, at the request of one of the lines concerned and after hearing all of them, take the necessary steps to settle the dispute.

3. Each Member State shall ensure that all vessel-operating shipping lines established on its territory under the Treaty establishing the European Economic Community are treated in the same way as lines which have their management head office on its territory and the effective control of which is exercised there.

Article 3

1. Where a liner conference operates a pool or a berthing, sailing and/or any other form of cargo allocation agreement in accordance with Article 2 of the Code of Conduct, the volume of cargo to which the group of national shipping lines of each Member State participating in that trade or the shipping lines of the Member States participating in that trade as third country shipping lines are entitled under the Code shall be redistributed, unless a decision is taken to the contrary by all the lines which are members of the Conference and parties to the present redistribution rules. This redistribution of cargo shares shall be carried out on the basis of a unanimous decision by those shipping lines which are members of the conference and participate in the redistribution, with a view to all these lines carrying a fair share of the conference trade.

2. The share finally allocated to each participant shall be determined by the application of commercial principles, taking account in particular of:

(a) the volume of cargo carried by the conference and generated by the Member States whose trade is served by it;

(b) past performance of the shipping lines in the trade covered by the pool;

(c) the volume of cargo carried by the conference and shipped through the ports of the Member States;

(d) the needs of the shippers whose cargoes are carried by the conference.

3. If no agreement it reached on the redistribution of cargoes referred to in paragraph 1, the matter shall, at the request of one of the parties, be referred to conciliation in accordance with the procedure set out in Annex II. Any dispute not settled by the conciliation procedure may, with the agreement of the parties, be referred to arbitration. In that event, the award of the arbitrator shall be binding.

4. At intervals to be laid down in advance, shares allocated in accordance with paragraph 1, 2 and 3 shall be regularly reviewed, taking into account the criteria set out in paragraph 2 and in particular from the viewpoint of providing adequate and efficient services to shippers.

Article 4

1. In a conference trade between a Member State of the Community and a State which is a party to the Code of Conduct and not an OECD country, a shipping line of another Member State of the OECD wishing to participate in the redistribution provided for in Article 3 of this Regulation may do so subject to reciprocity defined at governmental or ship-owners' level.

2. Without prejudice to paragraph 3 of this Article, Article 2 of the Code of Conduct shall not be applied in conference trades between Member States or, on a reciprocal basis, between such States and the other OECD countries which are parties to the Code.

3. Paragraph 2 of this Article shall not affect the opportunities for participation as third country shipping lines in such trades, in accordance with the principles reflected in Article 2 of the Code of Conduct, of the shipping lines of a developing country which are recognized as national shipping lines under the Code and which are:

(a) already members of a conference serving these trades; or

(b) admitted to such a conference under Article 1 (3) of the Code.

4. Articles 3 and 14 (9) of the Code of Conduct shall not be applied in conference trades between Member States or, on a reciprocal basis, between such States and other OECD countries which are parties to the code.

5. In conference trades between Member States and between these States and other OECD countries which are parties to the Code of Conduct, the shippers and ship-owners of Member States shall not insist on applying the procedures for settling disputes provided for in Chapter VI

of the Code in their mutual relationships or, on a reciprocal basis, in relation to shippers and ship-owners of other OECD countries where other procedures for settling disputes have been agreed between them. They shall in particular take full advantage of the possibilities provided by Article 25 (1) and (2) of the Code for resolving disputes by means of procedures other than those laid down in Chapter VI of the Code.

Article 5

For the adoption of decisions relating to matters defined in the conference agreements concerning the trade of a Member State, other than those referred to in Article 3 of this Regulation, the national shipping lines of such State shall consult all the other Community lines which are members of the conference before giving or withholding their assent.

Article 6

Member States shall, in due course and after consulting the Commission, adopt the laws, regulations or administrative provisions necessary for the implementation of this Regulation.

This Regulation shall be binding in its entirety and directly applicable in all Member States.

Done at Brussels, 15 May 1979.

For the Council
The President
R. BOULIN

ANNEX I. RESERVATIONS

When ratifying the Convention or when acceding thereto, Member States shall enter the following three reservations and interpretative reservation:

1. For the purposes of the Code of Conduct, the term "national shipping line" may, in the case of a Member State of the Community, include any vessel-operating shipping line established on the territory of such Member State in accordance with the EEC Treaty.

2. (a) Without prejudice to paragraph (b) of this reservation, Article 2 of the Code of Conduct shall not be applied in conference trades between the Member States of the Community or, on a reciprocal basis, between such States and the other OECD countries which are parties to the Code.
   (b) Point (a) shall not affect the opportunities for participation as third country shipping lines in such trades, in accordance with the principles reflected in Article 2 of the Code, of the shipping lines of a developing country which are recognized as national shipping lines under the Code and which are:
      (i) already members of a conference serving these trades; or
      (ii) admitted to such a conference under Article 1 (3) of the Code.

3. Articles 3 and 14 (9) of the Code of Conduct shall not be applied in conference trades between the Member States of the Community or, on a reciprocal basis, between such States and the other OECD countries which are parties to the Code.

4. In trades to which Article 3 of the Code of Conduct applies, the last sentence of that Article is interpreted as meaning that:
   (a) the two groups of national shipping lines will coordinate their positions before voting on matters concerning the trade between their two countries;
   (b) this sentence applies solely to matters which the conference agreement identifies as requiring the assent of both groups of national shipping lines concerned, and not to all matters covered by the conference agreement.

ANNEX II. CONCILIATION REFERRED TO IN ARTICLE 3 (3)

The parties to the dispute shall designate one or more conciliators.

Should they fail to agree on the matter, each of the parties to the dispute shall designate a conciliator and the conciliators thus designated shall co-opt another conciliator to act as chairman. Should a party fail to designate a conciliator or the conciliators designated by the parties fail to reach agreement on the chairman, the President of the International Chamber of Commerce shall, at the request of one of the parties, make the necessary designations.

The conciliators shall make every endeavour to settle the dispute. They shall decide on the procedure to be followed. Their fees shall be paid by the parties to the dispute.

10. COUNCIL DIRECTIVE OF 6 DECEMBER 1979 AMENDING DIRECTIVE 79/116/EEC CONCERNING MINIMUM REQUIREMENTS FOR CERTAIN TANKERS ENTERING OR LEAVING COMMUNITY PORTS (79/1034/EEC)

THE COUNCIL OF THE EUROPEAN COMMUNITIES,

Having regard to the Treaty establishing the European Economic Community, and in particular Article 84 (2) thereof,

Whereas it has proved necessary to make certain amendments of a technical nature to Council Directive 79/116/EEC of 21 December 1978 concerning minimum requirements for certain tankers entering or leaving Community ports,[1]

HAS ADOPTED THIS DIRECTIVE:

Article 1

In Article 1 (1) of Directive 79/116/EEC the text of item A. (i) (g) shall be replaced by the following:

"(g) where chemicals are being transported in bulk, information on whether or not the vessel is in possession of a certificate of fitness under the terms of the IMCO code for the construction and equipment of ships carrying dangerous chemicals in bulk, or

where liquefied gases are being transported in bulk, information on whether or not the vessel is in possession of a certificate of fitness under the terms of the IMCO code for the construction and equipment of ships carrying liquefied gases in bulk."

Article 2

In the Annex to Directive 79/116/EEC the following entries shall be added to section C:

Certificate of fitness for the carriage of dangerous chemicals in bulk under ☐ ☐ the terms of the IMCO code.

Certificate of fitness for the carriage of liquefied gases under the terms of the ☐ ☐ IMCO code.

Article 3

Member States shall bring into force, after consulting the Commission, the laws, regulations and administrative provisions necessary to implement this Directive as soon as possible, and in any case by 31 December 1980. They shall inform the Commission and the other Member States thereof.

Article 4

This Directive is addressed to Member States.

Done at Brussels, 6 December 1979.

For the Council
The President
L. PRETI

1. OJ No L 33, 8 February 1979, p. 33.

11. COUNCIL RECOMMENDATION OF 23 SEPTEMBER 1980 ON THE RATIFICATION OF THE TORREMOLINOS INTERNATIONAL CONVENTION FOR THE SAFETY OF FISHING VESSELS (1977) (80/907/EEC)

THE COUNCIL OF THE EUROPEAN COMMUNITIES,

Having regard to the Treaty establishing the European Economic Community, and in particular Article 84 (2) thereof,

Whereas the Torremolinos International Convention for the Safety of Fishing Vessels (1977), can help to promote the safety of ships in general and the safety of fishing vessels in particular;

Whereas ratification or accession by all the Member States can accelerate the entry into force of this Convention,

HEREBY RECOMMENDS:

—that, where they have not already done so, the Member States ratify the Torremolinos International Convention for the Safety of Fishing Vessels (1977), or accede thereto as soon as possible and not later than 31 July 1982;

—that the Member States inform the Secretary-General of the Inter-Governmental Maritime Consultative Organization that they have ratified or acceded to the Convention with regard to this recommendation.

Done at Brussels, 23 September 1980.

For the Council
The President
J. SANTER

12. COUNCIL DECISION OF 4 DECEMBER 1980 AMENDING AND SUPPLEMENTING DECISION 79/4/EEC ON THE COLLECTION OF INFORMATION CONCERNING THE ACTIVITIES OF CARRIERS PARTICIPATING IN CARGO LINER TRAFFIC IN CERTAIN AREAS OF OPERATION (80/1181/EEC)

THE COUNCIL OF THE EUROPEAN COMMUNITIES,

Having regard to the Treaty establishing the European Economic Community and in particular Article 84 (2) thereof,

Having regard to Council Decision 78/774/EEC of 19 September 1978 concerning the activities of certain third countries in the field of cargo shipping,[1]

Having regard to Council Decision 79/4/EEC of 19 December 1978 on the collection of information concerning the activities of carriers participating in cargo liner traffic in certain areas of operation,[2]

Having regard to the draft Decision submitted by the Commission,

Whereas the information collected under Decision 79/4/EEC gives grounds for concern about the competitive position of Member State shipping companies because of the nature of the competition which they face from certain third country carriers in the trades in question; whereas the collection of information about these trades should therefore continue;

Whereas there are indications that the competitive position of the fleets of Member State shipping companies is being adversely affected in the trade between the Community and the Far East by competition from certain carriers which are not following the rules of competition in accordance with the principles of market economy; whereas information should also be collected concerning transport between Member States and the Far East.

HAS ADOPTED THIS DECISION:

Article 1

In Article 1 of Council Decision 79/4/EEC "31 December 1980" shall be replaced by "31 December 1982".

Article 2

Member States shall collect information concerning transport between the Member States and the Far East (Japan, Taiwan, Hong Kong, Malaysia, Singapore, Republic of Korea, the Philippines, Thailand).

Detailed rules for the collection of this information shall be adopted by the Council not later than 31 March 1981.

Article 3

This Decision is addressed to the Member States.

Done at Brussels, 4 December 1980.

For the Council
The President
J. BARTHEL

1. OJ No L 258, 21 September 1978, p. 35 and E.T.L. vol. XXII, 3, p. 227.
2. OJ No. L. 5, 9 January 1979, p. 31 and E.T.L. vol. XXII, 3, p. 229.

13. COUNCIL DECISION OF 26 MARCH 1981 ESTABLISHING DETAILED RULES FOR THE COLLECTION OF INFORMATION CONCERNING THE ACTIVITIES OF CARRIERS PARTICIPATING IN CARGO LINER TRAFFIC BETWEEN THE MEMBER STATES AND THE FAR EAST (81/189/EEC)

THE COUNCIL OF THE EUROPEAN COMMUNITIES,

Having regard to the Treaty establishing the European Economic Community, and in particular Article 84 (2) thereof,

Having regard to the draft Decision submitted by the Commission,

Whereas Article 2 of Council Decision 80/1181/EEC of 4 December 1980 amending and supplementing Decision 79/4/EEC on the collection of information concerning the activities of carriers participating in cargo liner traffic in certain areas of operation provides[1] for the Member States to collect information concerning transport between the Member States and the Far East, and states that detailed rules for the collection of this information shall be adopted by the Council not later than 31 March 1981,

HAS ADOPTED THIS DECISION:

Article 1

From 1 July 1981 to 31 December 1982, each Member State shall collect the information specified in Annex I concerning cargo liner traffic between that State and each of the countries listed in Annex II. The information for each half-year shall be forwarded to the Commission as soon as possible and in any case not later than three months after the end of the period concerned.

Article 2

This Decision is addressed to the Member States.

Done at Brussels, 26 March 1981.

For the Council
The President
D. S. TUIJNMAN

ANNEX I. INFORMATION TO BE COLLECTED

1. Liner services operated

(a) Name of company and service, and flag of the vessels employed;
(b) Far East countries served (see Annex II);
(c) Conference membership.

2. Liner cargo carried

(a) Flag;
(b) Far East country concerned;
(c) total liner cargo carried from country of loading, origin or despatch in incoming traffic and to country of unloading and/or destination in outgoing traffic, in weight tonnes;
(d) total number of containers (in TEUs) and/or total weight of goods carried from country of loading, origin or despatch in incoming traffic, and to country of unloading and/or destination in outgoing traffic.

1. OJ No. L 350, 23 December 1980, p. 44.

3. Information concerning freight rates

Member States shall use their best endeavours to provide information on freight rates.

4. Sources of information and methodology

The returns shall describe the sources of the information collected and the methodology used.

ANNEX II. LIST OF COUNTRIES

Japan
Taiwan
Hong Kong
Malaysia
Singapore
Republic of Korea
The Philippines
Thailand

14. COUNCIL DECISION OF 13 DECEMBER 1982 ADOPTING A CONCERTED ACTION PROJECT FOR THE EUROPEAN ECONOMIC COMMUNITY IN THE FIELD OF SHORE-BASED MARINE NAVIGATION AID SYSTEMS (82/887/EEC)

THE COUNCIL OF THE EUROPEAN COMMUNITIES

Having regard to the Treaty establishing the European Economic Community, and in particular Article 235 thereof,

Having regard to the draft from the Commission,[1]

Having regard to the opinion of the European Parliament,[2]

Having regard to the opinion of the Economic and Social Commitee,[3]

Whereas a concerted action project for Community research in the field of marine navigation aid systems may contribute to the reduction of the risk of accidents in coastal areas and ports, and, consequently, to the protection of human life and the safety of ships and their cargo, and the prevention of pollution on the shore and in coastal waters;

Whereas a research programme in the field of marine navigation aid systems was proposed in 1979 by the Finnish and French delegations within the framework of European cooperation in the field of scientific and technical research (COST); whereas the Scientific and Technical Research Committee (Crest) acknowledged the Community interest of the said programme on 8 April 1981;

Whereas in its resolution of 14 January 1974 on an initial outline programme of the European Communities in the field of science and technology[4] the Council emphasized that an appropriate approach should be adopted towards the whole range of available ways and means, including concerted action projects, and that, wherenver it proved desirable, non-member States, particularly European ones, should be associated in those projects;

Whereas the Member States intend to implement, in accordance with the rules and procedures applicable to their national programmes, the research projects described in Annex I and are prepared to coordinate them at Community level for a period of three years;

Whereas international organizations are carrying out projects in this field; whereas account should be taken of such projects so as to preclude duplication of effort; whereas certain equipment and procedures should, if appropriate, be the subject of agreements within the framework of the competent organizations;

Whereas the implementation of this research requires a financial outlay of the order of 10 million ECU on the part of the Community and the Member States;

Considering the opinion delivered by Crest on the Commission proposal;

HAS DECIDED AS FOLLOWS:

Article 1

The Community shall implement, over a period of three years from 1 January 1983, a concerted action research project in the field of shore-based marine navigation aid systems, hereinafter referred to as "the project".

The project shall consist of the coordination at Community level of the research defined in Annex I forming part of the research programmes of the Member States, taking into account the work being carried out in the field in question by international organizations and ensuring that the international character of marine navigation, and consequently of all the rules governing it, is borne in mind.

Article 2

The Commission shall be responsible for the coordination referred to in Article 1.

1. OJ No. C 256, 8 October 1981, p. 7.
2. OJ No. C 238, 13 September 1982, p. 111.
3. OJ No. C 348, 31 December 1981, p. 24.
4. OJ No. C 7, 29 January 1974, p. 6.

Article 3

The funds estimated as necessary for the Community contribution to the coordination should be 2.1 million ECU including expenditure on a staff of one.

Article 4

To help implement the project, a Concerted Action Committee for shore-based marine navigation aid systems hereinafter referred to as "the committee", shall be set up.

A project leader shall be appointed by the Commission in agreement with the committee.

The terms of reference and composition of the committee are set out in Annex II hereto.

The committee shall adopt its own rules of procedure. The committee secretariat shall be provided by the Commission.

Article 5

1. In accordance with a procedure to be laid down by the Commission after consulting the committee, States participating in the project and the Community shall exchange all useful information concerning the implementation of research relating to the project on a regular basis. Participating Member States shall supply the Commission with all the information needed for coordination purposes. They shall also endeavour to supply the Commission with information on research on the subject which is either planned or has been carried out by bodies for which they are not responsible. Such information shall be treated as confidential if the Member State supplying it so requests.

2. The Commission shall establish annual progress reports on the basis of the information supplied and shall forward them to the Member States and to the European Parliament.

3. At the end of the coordination period, the Commission, after consulting the committee, shall forward to the Member States and to the European Parliament a general report on the implementation and results of the project. It shall publish this report six months after it has been forwarded to the Member States unless one of the Member States objects. In the latter event the report shall be distributed, on request, only to those institutions and undertakings whose research or production activities justify access to the results of the research carried out under this project. The Commission may provide for the report to remain confidential and not to be disclosed to third parties.

Article 6

In accordance with Article 228 of the Treaty the Community may conclude an agreement with third States, and in particular with those participating in COST, with a view to ensuring coordination between the Community's project and the corresponding programmes in those States.

Done at Brussels, 13 December 1982.

For the Council
The President
U. ELLEMANN-JENSEN

ANNEX I. PROJECT CONTENT

1. A study of requirements for precise navigation and ship manoeuvring in confined areas under various hydro-meteorological conditions.

2. A study to develop factors and criteria that can serve as a common determinant for marine traffic problem definition. As a second stage application of these factors and criteria to European waters.

3. An inventory of existing shore-based marine traffic systems in Western Europe, stating:
— geographical coverage,

— type of service provided,
— rules governing operation of the service,
— traffic intensity in the area,
— types of traffic in the area.

4. A study of vessel identification methods, for use both in the control of traffic by the monitoring stations and in ship-to-ship communications.

Indicative breakdown of research

Research topics	Breakdown of research								
	B	D	DK	F	GR	I	IRL	NL	UK
1. Movement of ships in confined ares	×			×		×		×	×
2. (a) Criteria for standard identification of problem areas for marine traffic	×			×		×		×	×
(b) Identification of problem areas for marine navigation	×			×	×	×		×	×
3. Inventory of shore-based marine traffic systems in Western Europe				×	×	×		×	×
4. Identification of ships						×	×	×	×
5. Specifications and standards for pinpointing and precise tracking of ships under way				×		×	×	×	×
6. Shore-to-ship communication methods						×		×	×
7. Harmonization of the procedures of marine traffic services				×		×		×	×

5. A study of methods to enable the monitoring stations to pin-point and track a vessel with accuracy.

6. Methods of shore-to-ship and ship-to-ship communication and data exchange systems between monitoring stations and ships.

7. A study of the harmonization of the procedures of traffic, information and guidance services for shipping in Western Europe.

Among the international organizations with most competence in this area which have been or are working on the above research topics are the following:

— International Maritime Organization (IMO),
— International Association of Lighthouse Authorities (IALA).
— International Association of Ports and Harbours (IAPH).

The list is not exhaustive.

ANNEX II. TERMS OF REFERENCE AND COMPOSITION OF THE CONCERTED ACTION COMMITTEE FOR SHORE-BASED MARINE NAVIGATION AID SYSTEMS

1. The committee shall:
   1.1. contribute to the optimum implementation of the project by giving its opinion on all aspects of its progress;
   1.2. evaluate the results of the project and draw conclusions as to their application;
   1.3. be responsible for the exchange of information referred to in Article 5(1);
   1.4. keep track of national research work carried out in the fields covered by the project, in particular by keeping itself informed about scientific and technical developments which might have an influence on its implementation;
   1.5. take care to avoid duplicating studies and research work being carried out by the competent international organizations, taking account of the international framework in which certain provisions should, where necessary, be adopted;
   1.6. provide guidelines for the project leader;
   1.7. assist the Commission in the selection of contractors and the allocation of the corresponding appropriations.

2. The committee's reports and opinions shall be forwarded to the Commission and the Member States taking part in the project. The Commission shall forward these opinions to Crest.

3. The committee shall be composed of the persons responsible for coordinating the national research activities included in the project, a delegate from the Commission and the project leader. Each member may be accompanied by experts. Wherever it deems it is useful, the committee may invite observers from the relevant international organizations (see Annex I).

15. COUNCIL DECISION OF 16 DECEMBER 1982 EXTENDING THE COLLECTION OF INFORMATION CONCERNING THE ACTIVITIES OF CARRIERS PARTICIPATING IN CARGO LINER TRAFFIC IN CERTAIN AREAS OF OPERATION, CARRIED OUT UNDER DECISIONS 79/4/EEC, 80/1181/EEC AND 81/189/EEC (82/870/EEC)

THE COUNCIL OF THE EUROPEAN COMMUNITIES

Having regard to the Treaty establishing the European Economic Community, and in particular Article 84 (2) thereof,

Having regard to Council Decision 78/774/EEC of 19 September 1978 concerning the activities of certain third countries in the field of cargo shipping,[1]

Having regard to the proposal for a Decision submitted by the Commission,

Whereas the information collected under Decisions 79/4/EEC[2] and 80/1181/EEC[3] give grounds for concern about the competitive position of Member State shipping companies because of the nature of the competition which they face from certain carriers in the areas of operation referred to in Annex II of Decision 79/4/EEC; whereas the collection of information about traffic in these areas should therefore continue;

Whereas it is desirable to obtain a more complete picture of traffic between the EEC and the countries mentioned in Article 2 of Decision 80/1181/EEC, the detailed rules for which are established in Decision 81/189/EEC[4]; whereas the collection of information about this traffic should therefore continue.

HAS ADOPTED THIS DECISION:

Article 1

Article 1 of Decision 79/4/EEC is hereby amended as follows: "31 December 1982" shall be replaced by "31 December 1984".

Article 2

Article 1 of Decision 81/189/EEC is hereby amended as follows: "31 December 1982" shall be replaced by "31 December 1984".

Article 3

This Decision is addressed to the Member States.

Done at Brussels, 16 December 1982.

For the Council
The President
A. MELCHIOR

1. OJ No. L 258, 21 September 1978, p. 35 and E.T.L. vol. XXII, 3, p. 227.
2. OJ No. L 5, 9 January 1979, p. 31 and E.T.L. vol. XXII, 3, p. 229.
3. OJ No. L 350, 23 December 1980, p. 44 and E.T.L. vol. XXII, 3, p. 231.
4. OJ No. L 88, 2 April 1981, p. 32.

16. COUNCIL DECISION OF 28 MARCH 1983 ON THE CONCLUSION OF THE COMMUNITY-COST CONCERTATION AGREEMENT ON A CONCERTED ACTION PROJECT IN THE FIELD OF SHORE-BASED MARINE NAVIGATION AID SYSTEMS (COST PROJECT 301) (83/124/EEC)

THE COUNCIL OF THE EUROPEAN COMMUNITIES,

Having regard to the Treaty establishing the European Economic Community,

Having regard to Council Decision 82/887/EEC of 13 December 1982 adopting a concerted action project for the European Economic Community in the field of shore-based marine navigation aid systems[1], and in particular Article 6 thereof,

Having regard to the Council Decision of 4 May 1982 authorizing the Commission to negotiate an Agreement between the Community and the non-member States participating in the European cooperation in the field of scientific and technical research for the implementation of a concerted action project on shore-based marine navigation aid systems,

Having regard to the draft Decision submitted by the Commission,

Whereas the Commission has completed the negotiations concerning the Agreement in question; whereas the Agreement should therefore be approved,

HAS DECIDED AS FOLLOWS:

Article 1

The Community-COST Concertation Agreement on a concerted action project in the field of shore-based maritime navigation aid systems (COST Project 301) is hereby approved on behalf of the Community.

The text of the Agreement is attached to this Decision.

Article 2

The President of the Council is hereby authorized to designate the persons empowered to sign the Agreement in order to bind the Community.

Done at Brussels, 28 March 1983.

For the Council
The President
J. ERTL

COMMUNITY-COST CONCERTATION AGREEMENT ON A CONCERTED ACTION PROJECT IN THE FIELD OF SHORE-BASED MARINE NAVIGATION AID SYSTEMS (COST PROJECT 301)

THE EUROPEAN ECONOMIC COMMUNITY,

hereinafter referred to as "the Community",
and

THE SIGNATORY STATES TO THIS AGREEMENT,

hereinafter referred to as "the participating non-member States",

Whereas a European concerted action project in the field of maritime navigation aid systems may contribute to the reduction of the risk of accidents in coastal areas and ports and,

1. OJ No. L 378, 31 December 1982, p. 32 and E.T.L. XXII, 3, p. 255.

consequently, to the protection of human life and the safety of ships and their cargo, and the prevention of pollution on the shore and in coastal waters;

Whereas a research programme in the field of maritime navigation aid systems was proposed in 1979 by Finnish and French delegations within the framework of European Cooperation in the field of Scientific and Technical Research (COST);

Whereas, by its Decision of 14 December 1982, the Council of the European Communities adopted a Community concerted action project in the field of shore-based maritime navigation aid systems;

Whereas the Member States of the Community and the participating non-member States, hereinafter referred to as "the States", intend, subject to the rules and procedures applicable to their national programmes, to carry out the research described in Annex A and are prepared to integrate such research into a process of concertation which they consider will be of mutual benefit;

Whereas international organizations are carrying out projects in this field; whereas account should be taken of such projects so as to preclude duplication of effort; whereas certain equipment and procedures should, if appropriate, be the subject of agreements within the framework of the competent organizations;

Whereas the implementation of the research covered by the concerted action project will require a financial contribution of approximately 13 million ECU from the States,

HAVE AGREED AS FOLLOWS:

Article 1

The Community and the participating non-member States, hereinafter referred to as "the Contracting Parties", shall participate for a period extending until 31 December 1985 in a concerted action project in the field of shore-based navigation aid systems.

This project shall consist in concertation between the Community concerted action programme and the corresponding programmes of the participating non-member States. Research areas covered by this agreement are listed in Annex A.

The States shall remain entirely responsible for the research carried out by their national institutions or bodies.

Article 2

A Community-COST Concertation Committee on Action for Shore-Based Marine Navigation Aid Systems, hereinafter referred to as "the Committee", is hereby set up, within which concertation between the Contracting Parties shall be effected.

The Committee shall draw up its rules of procedure. Its Secretariat will be provided by the Commission of the European Communities, hereinafter referred to as "the Commission".

The terms of reference and the composition of this Committee are defined in Annex B.

Article 3

In order to ensure optimum efficiency in the execution of this concerted action project, a project leader shall be appointed by the Commission in agreement with the delegates representing the participating non-member States on the Committee.

Article 4

The maximum financial contribution by the Contracting Parties to the coordination costs for the period referred to in the first paragraph of Article 1 shall be:

— 2,100,000 ECU from the Community,
— 60,000 ECU from each participating non-member State.

In addition, each participating non-member State shall pay an amount calculated by applying to a basic amount of 1,500,000 ECU, representing a part of the Community contribution, the ratio between the gross domestic products of the State concerned for 1980 and the sum of the gross domestic product of the Community and of that State for 1980.

The ECU is defined by the Financial Regulation applicable to the general budget of the European Communities and by the financial arrangements adopted pursuant thereto.

The rules governing the financing of this Agreement are set out in Annex C.

Article 5

1. Through the Committee, the States shall exchange all useful information resulting from the execution of the research covered by the concerted action project. They shall also endeavour to provide information on similar research planned or carried out by other bodies. Any information shall be treated as confidential if the State which provides it so requests.

2. In agreement with the Committee, the Commission shall prepare annual progress reports on the basis of the information supplied and shall forward them to the States.

3. At the end of the concertation period, the Commission shall, in agreement with the Committee, forward to the States a consolidated report on the execution and results of the project. This report shall be published by the Commission not later than six months after it has been forwarded, unless a State objects. In that case the report shall be treated as confidential and shall be forwarded, on request and with the agreement of the Committee, solely to the institutions and undertakings whose research or production activities justify access to knowledge resulting from the performance of the research covered by the concerted action project.

Article 6

1. This Agreement shall be open for signature by the Community and by the non-member States of that Community which took part in the Ministerial Conference held in Brussels on 22 and 23 November 1971.

2. As a condition precedent to its participation in the concerted action project defined in Article 1, each of the Contracting Parties shall, after signing this Agreement, have notified the Secretary-General of the Council of the European Communities not later than 31 December 1983 of the completion of the procedures necessary under its internal provisions for the implementation of this Agreement.

3. For the Contracting Parties which have transmitted the notification provided for in paragraph 2, this Agreement shall come into force on the first day of the month following that in which the Community and at least one of the participating non-member States transmitted these notifications.

For those Contracting Parties which transmit the notification after the entry into force of this Agreement, it shall come into force on the first day of the second month following the month in which the notification was transmitted.

Contracting Parties which have not transmitted this notification when this Agreement comes into force shall be able to take part in the work of the Committee without voting rights until 31 December 1983.

4. The Secretary-General of the Council of the European Communities shall inform each of the Contracting Parties of the notifications provided for in paragraph 2 and of the date of entry into force of this Agreement.

Article 7

This Agreement shall apply, on the one hand, to the territories in which the Treaty establishing the European Economic Community is applied, under the conditions laid down in that Treaty and, on the other hand, to the territories of the participating non-member States.

Article 8

This Agreement, drawn up in a single original in the Danish, Dutch, English, French, German, Greek and Italian languages, each text being equally authentic, shall be deposited in the archives of the General Secretariat of the Council of the European Communities which shall transmit a certified copy to each of the Contracting Parties.

ANNEX A

I. Content of the Concerted Action Project

1. A study of requirements for precise navigation and ship manoeuvring in confined areas under various hydro-meteorological conditions.

2. A study to develop factors and criteria that can serve as a common determinant for marine traffic problem definition. As a second stage application of these factors and criteria to European waters.

3. An inventory of existing shore-based marine traffic systems in Western Europe, stating:
   - geographical coverage,
   - type of service provided,
   - rules governing operation of the service,
   - traffic intensity in the area,
   - types of traffic in the area.

4. A study of vessel identification methods, for use both in the control of traffic by the monitoring stations and in ship-to-ship communications.

5. A study of methods to enable the monitoring stations to pin-point and track a vessel with accuracy.

6. Methods of shore-to-ship and ship-to-ship communication and data exchange systems between monitoring stations and ships.

7. A study of the harmonization of the procedure of traffic, information and guidance services for shipping in Western Europe.

II. Research areas covered by the agreement

1. Movement of ships in confined areas.
2. (a) Criteria for standard identification of problem areas for marine traffic.
   (b) Identification of problem areas for marine navigation.
3. Inventory of shore-based marine traffic systems in Western Europe.
4. Identification of ships.
5. Specifications and standard for pin-pointing and precise tracking of ships under way.
6. Shore-to-ship communication methods.
7. Harmonization of the procedures of traffic services.

Among the international organizations with most competence in this area which have been or are working on the above research topics are the following:
- International Maritime Organization (IMO),
- International Association of Lighthouse Authorities (IALA),
- International Association of Ports and Harbours (IAPH).

This list is not exhaustive.

ANNEX B. TERMS OF REFERENCE AND COMPOSITION OF THE COMMUNITY-COST CONCERTATION COMMITTEE

"Action for shore-based marine navigation aid systems"

1. The Committee shall:
   1.1. contribute to the optimum implementation of the project by giving its opinion on all aspects of its progress;
   1.2. evaluate the results of the project and draw conclusions as to their application;
   1.3. be responsible for the exchange of information referred to in Article 5 (1);
   1.4. keep track of national research work carried out in the fields covered by the project, in particular by keeping itself informed about scientific and technical developments which might have an influence on its implementation;
   1.5. take care to avoid duplicating studies and research work being carried out by the competent international organizations, taking account of the international framework in which certain provisions should, where necessary, be adopted;
   1.6. provide guidelines for the project leader;

1.7. assist the Commission in the selection of contractors and the allocation of the corresponding appropriations.

2. The reports and opinions of the Committee shall be transmitted to the States.

3. The Committee shall be composed of one delegate from the Commission, as coordinator of the Community concerted action project, one delegate from each participating non-member State, one delegate from each Member State representing its national programme and the project leader. Each delegate may be accompanied by experts. Wherever it deems it is useful, the Committee may invite observers from the relevant international organizations (see Annex A).

ANNEX C. FINANCING RULES

Article 1

This Annex lays down the financial rules referred to in Article 4 of the Community-COST Concertation Agreement.

Article 2

At the beginning of each financial year, the Commission shall send to each of the participating non-member States a call for funds corresponding to its share of the annual coordination costs under the Agreement, calculated in proportion to the maximum amounts laid down in Article 4 of the Agreement.

This contribution shall be expressed both in ECU and the currency of the participating non-member State concerned, the value of the ECU being defined in the Financial Regulation applicable to the general budget of the European Communities and its value determined on the date of the call for funds.

The total contributions shall cover the travel and subsistence costs of the delegates to the Committee, in addition to the coordination costs proper.

Each participating non-member State shall pay its annual contribution to the coordination costs under the Agreement at the beginning of each year, and by 31 March at the latest. Any delay in the payment of the annual contribution shall give rise to the payment of interest by the participating non-member State concerned at a rate equal to the highest discount rate obtaining in the States on the due date. The rate shall be increased by 0.25 of a percentage point for each month of delay. The increased rate shall be applied to the entire period of delay. However, such interest shall be chargeable only if payment is effected more than three months after the issue of a call for funds by the Commission.

Article 3

The funds paid by participating non-member States shall be credited to the concerted action project as budget receipts allocated to a heading in the statement of the revenue of the general budget of the European Communities (Commission section).

Article 4

The provisional timetable for the coordination costs referred to in Article 4 of the Agreement is annexed hereto.

Article 5

The Financial Regulation applicable to the general budget of the European Communities shall apply to the management of the appropriations.

Article 6

At the end of each financial year, a statement of appropriations for the concerted action project shall be prepared and transmitted to the participating non-member States for information.

PROVISIONAL TIMETABLE FOR THE COORDINATION COSTS RELATING TO THE CONCERTED ACTION PROJECT ON SHORE-BASED MARITIME NAVIGATION AID SYSTEMS (COST PROJECT 301)

(ECU)

	1983	1984	1985	Total
I. Initial estimate of overall requirements: – Staff – Administrative operating expenditure – Contracts for studies	200 000 (Staff and administrative operating expenditure) 600 000	200 000 800 000	200 000 100 000	600 000 1 500 000
Total	800 000	1 000 000	300 000	2 100 000
II. Revised estimate of expenditure taking into account additional requirements arriving from the accession of participating non-member States: – Staff – Administrative operating expenditure – Contracts for studies	$800\,000 + \Sigma_i a_i$	$1\,000\,000 + \Sigma_i b_i$	$300\,000 + \Sigma_i c_i$	$2\,100\,000 + \Sigma_i a_i + \Sigma_i b_i + \Sigma_i c_i$
III. Difference between I and II to be covered by contribution from participating non-member States:	$\Sigma_i a_i$	$\Sigma_i b_i$	$\Sigma_i c_i$	$\Sigma_i a_i + \Sigma_i b_i + \Sigma_i c_i$

$$a_i = 20\,000 + 600\,000 \frac{GDP_{pns}}{GDP_{EC} + GDP_{pns}}$$

$$b_i = 20\,000 + 800\,000 \frac{GDP_{pns}}{GDP_{EC} + GDP_{i}}$$

$$c_i = 20\,000 + 100\,000 \frac{GDP_{pns}}{GDP_{EC} + GDP_{pns}}$$

GDP = Gross Domestic Product
pns = participating non-member State
EC = European Community

17. COUNCIL RECOMMENDATION OF 25 JULY 1983 ON THE RATIFICATION OF OR ACCESSION TO THE 1979 INTERNATIONAL CONVENTION ON MARITIME SEARCH AND RESCUE (SAR) (83/419/EEC)

THE COUNCIL OF THE EUROPEAN COMMUNITIES,

Having regard to the Treaty establishing the European Economic Community,

Whereas on 27 April 1979 an International Convention on Maritime Search and Rescue was approved in Hamburg under the auspices of the Inter-governmental Maritime Consultative Organization (IMCO);

Whereas, in view of the great importance of the said Convention with regard to the search for and rescue of persons in distress at sea, the Convention should enter into force as soon as possible;

Whereas ratification or accession by all the Member States will not only help to bring the Convention into force in accordance with the principles of international law but will also ensure a unified search and rescue service in the coastal waters of the Community and thereby increase the effectiveness of the Convention,

HEREBY RECOMMENDS:

that inasmuch as they have not already done so, the Member States ratify or accede to the 1979 International Convention on Maritime Search and Rescue as soon as they can.

Done at Brussels, 25 July 1983.

For the Council
The President
C. SIMITIS

18. COUNCIL DECISION OF 26 OCTOBER 1983 CONCERNING COUNTER-MEASURES IN THE FIELD OF INTERNATIONAL MERCHANT SHIPPING (83/573/EEC)

THE COUNCIL OF THE EUROPEAN COMMUNITIES,

Having regard to the Treaty establishing the European Economic Community, and in particular Article 84 (2) thereof,

Whereas the results of the maritime information system set up under the provision of Decisions 78/774/EEC,[1] 79/4/EEC,[2] 80//1181/EEC,[3] 81/189/EEC[4] and 82/870/EEC,[5] together with the experience of certain Member States, show that it would be advisable to define an appropriate Community procedure concerning counter-measures in the field of international merchant shipping in relation to third countries to be taken by the Member States concerned,

HAS ADOPTED THIS DECISION:

Article 1

A Member State which has adopted or intends to adopt counter-measures in the field of international merchant shipping in relation to third countries shall consult the other Member States and the Commission in accordance with the consultation procedure established by Decision 77/587/EEC.[6]

Article 2

1. The Member States shall endeavour, within the framework of the consultation referred to in Article 1, to concert any counter-measures they may take.
2. The Council may, acting unanimously, decide on the joint application by Member States of appropriate counter-measures forming part of their national legislation.

Article 3

When engaging in the consultation referred to in Article 1, Member States should, if appropriate, specify as far as possible the following:

(a) the developments which have caused counter-measures to be taken;
(b) the shipping area to which the counter-measure is to apply;
(c) the nature of the shipping service affected (for example liner traffic);
(d) the nature of the counter-measures taken or to be taken;
(e) the duration of the counter-measure;
(f) the proportionality of the counter-measure to the damage suffered.

Article 4

The Member States shall remain free to apply national counter-measures unilaterally.

Article 5

The Decision is addressed to the Member States.

Done at Luxembourg, 26 October 1983.

For the Council
The President
G. MORAITIS

1. OJ No. L 258, 21 September 1978, p. 35 and E.T.L. vol. XXII, 3, p. 227.
2. OJ No. L 5, 9 January 1979, p. 31 and E.T.L. vol. XXII, 3, p. 229.
3. OJ No. L 350, 23 December 1980, p. 44 and E.T.L. vol. XXII, 3, p. 231.
4. OJ No. L 88, 2 April 1981, p. 32.
5. OJ No. L 368, 28 December 1982, p. 42.
6. OJ No. L 239, 17 September 1977, p. 23 and E.T.L. vol. XXII, 3, p. 220.

19. COUNCIL DECISION OF 18 DECEMBER 1984 EXTENDING THE COLLECTION OF INFORMATION CONCERNING THE ACTIVITIES OF CARRIERS PARTICIPATING IN CARGO LINER TRAFFIC IN CERTAIN AREAS OF OPERATION (84/656/EEC)

THE COUNCIL OF THE EUROPEAN COMMUNITIES,

Having regard to the Treaty establishing the European Economic Community, and in particular Article 84 (2) thereof,

Having regard to Council Decision 78/774/EEC of 19 September 1978 concerning the activities of certain third countries in the field of cargo shipping,[1]

Having regard to the draft Decision submitted by the Commission,

Whereas the information collected under Decisions 79/4/EEC,[2] 80/1181/EEC,[3] 82/870/EEC[4] gives grounds for concern about the competitive position of Member State liner companies because of the nature of the competition which they face from certain carriers in the areas of operation referred to in Annex II to Decision 79/4/EEC; whereas the collection of information about traffic in these areas should therefore continue;

Whereas the information collected about the traffic between the Community and the countries referred to in Article 2 of Decision 80/1181/EEC, in respect of which detailed rules are established in Decision 81/189/EEC,[5] which was extended by Decision 82/870/EEC also gives grounds for concern about the competitive position of Member State liner companies; whereas the collection of information about this traffic should therefore continue.

HAS ADOPTED THIS DECISION:

Article 1

In Articles 1 and 2 of Decision 82/870/EEC, "31 December 1984" is hereby replaced by "31 December 1986".

Article 2

This Decision shall apply from 1 January 1985.

Article 3

This Decision is addressed to the Member States.

Done at Brussels, 18 December 1984.

For the Council
The President
P. BARRY

1. OJ No. L 258, 21 September 1978, p. 35 and E.T.L. vol. XXII, 3, p. 227.
2. OJ No. L 5, 9 January 1979, p. 31 and E.T.L. vol. XXII, 3, p. 229.
3. OJ No. L 350, 23 December 1980, p. 44 and E.T.L. vol. XXII, 3, p. 231.
4. OJ No. L 368, 28 December 1982, p. 42
5. OJ No. L 88, 2 April 1981, p. 32.

20. COUNCIL DECISION OF 16 DECEMBER 1986 EXTENDING THE COLLECTION OF INFORMATION CONCERNING THE ACTIVITIES OF CARRIERS PARTICIPATING IN CARGO LINER TRAFFIC IN CERTAIN AREAS OF OPERATION (86/646/EEC)

THE COUNCIL OF THE EUROPEAN COMMUNITIES,

Having regard to the Treaty establishing the European Economic Community, and in particular Article 84 (2) thereof,

Having regard to Council Decision 78/774/EEC of 19 September 1978 concerning the activities of certain third countries in the field of cargo shipping,[1]

Having regard to the draft Decision submitted by the Commission,

Whereas the information collected under Decisions 79/4/EEC,[2] 80/1181/EEC,[3] 82/870/EEC,[4] 84/656/EEC[5] gives ground for concern about the competitive position of Member State liner companies because of the nature of the competition which they face from certain carriers in the trades referred to in Annex II to Council Decision 79/4/EEC; whereas the collection of information about traffic in these areas should therefore continue;

Whereas the information collected about the traffic between the Community and the countries referred to in Article 2 of Decision 80/1181/EEC, in respect of which detailed rules are established in Decision 81/189/EEC,[6] which was extended by Decisions 82/870/EEC and 84/656/EEC, also gives ground for concern about the competitive position of Member State liner companies; whereas the collection of information about this traffic should therefore continue,

HAS ADOPTED THIS DECISION:

Article 1

In Article 1 of Decision 84/656/EEC, "31 December 1986" is hereby replaced by "31 December 1988".

Article 2

This Decision shall apply from 1 January 1987.

Article 3

This Decision is addressed to the Member States.

Done at Brussels, 16 December 1986.

For the Council
The President
J. MOORE

1. OJ No. L 258, 21 September 1978, p. 35 and E.T.L. vol. XXII, 3, p. 227.
2. OJ No. L 5, 9 January 1979, p. 31 and E.T.L. vol. XXII, 3, p. 229.
3. OJ No. L 350, 23 December 1980, p. 44 and E.T.L. vol. XXII, 3, p. 231.
4. OJ No. L 368, 28 December 1982, p. 42. and E.T.L. vol. XXII, 3, p. 235.
5. OJ No. L 341, 29 December 1984, p. 91 and E.T.L. vol. XXII, 3, p. 237.
6. OJ No. L 88, 2 April 1981, p. 32.

21. COUNCIL REGULATION (EEC) No 4055/86 OF 22 DECEMBER 1986 APPLYING THE PRINCIPLE OF FREEDOM TO PROVIDE SERVICES TO MARITIME TRANSPORT BETWEEN MEMBER STATES AND BETWEEN MEMBER STATES AND THIRD COUNTRIES

THE COUNCIL OF THE EUROPEAN COMMUNITIES,

Having regard to the Treaty establishing the European Economic Community, and in particular Article 84 (2) thereof,

Having regard to the draft Regulation submitted by the Commission,

Having regard to the opinion of the European Parliament,[1]

Having regard to the opinion of the Economic and Social Committee,[2]

Whereas the abolition, as between Member States, of obstacles to freedom of movement for services is laid down by Article 3 of the Treaty as one of the activities of the Community;

Whereas in accordance with Article 61 of the Treaty freedom to provide services in the field of maritime transport is to be governed by the provisions of the Title relating to transport;

Whereas the application of this principle within the Community is also a necessary condition for effectively pursuing, in relation to third countries, a policy aiming at safeguarding the continuing application of commercial principles in shipping;

Whereas Council Regulation (EEC) No 954/79[3] preserves, *inter alia*, within conferences competitive access to that part of cargo liner shipping which is not covered by commitments to national shipping lines of third countries under the United Nations Convention on a Code of Conduct for Liner Conferences, when ratified by Member States;

Whereas, taking into account the fact that the Code of Conduct has not yet been ratified by all Member States and that certain third countries are not likely to ratify it, the Code is not yet applied in all Community trades nor is it likely to apply in the future in some of these trades;

Whereas the Code of Conduct applies only to liner conferences and the cargo carried by their members, and not to independent lines or to shipping companies operating in the field of bulk or tramp shipping, where the Community aims at maintaining a regime of fair and free competition;

Whereas the Community fully endorses Resolution No 2 adopted by the United Nations Conference of Plenipotentiaries on a Code of Conduct for Liner Conferences and which states that in the interests of sound development of liner shipping services, non-conference shipping liners should not be prevented from operating as long as they adhere to the principle of fair competition on a commercial basis;

Whereas the Member States affirm their commitment to a freely competitive environment as being an essential feature of the dry and liquid bulk trades and are convinced that the introduction of cargo-sharing in these trades will have a serious effect on the trading interests of all countries by substantially increasing transportation costs;

Whereas Community shipowners are increasingly faced with new restrictions, imposed by third countries, on the freedom to provide maritime transport services for shippers established in their own country, in other Member States or in the third countries concerned, which may have harmful effects on Community trades as a whole;

Whereas some of the above mentioned restrictions are incorporated in bilateral agreements between third countries and some Member States, while other restrictions are reflected in similar provisions in the legislation or in administrative practices of some Member States;

Whereas therefore the principle of freedom to provide services should now be applied to maritime transport between Member States and between Member States and third countries so as progressively to abolish existing restrictions and prevent the introduction of new restrictions;

Whereas the structure of the Community shipping industry is such as to make it appropriate that the provisions of this Regulation should also apply to nationals of the Member States established outside the Community and to shipping companies established outside the

1. OJ No. C 255, 13 October 1986, p. 169.
2. OJ No. C 172, 2 July 1984, p. 178.
3. OJ No. L 121, 17 May 1979, p. 1.

Community and controlled by nationals of a Member State, if their vessels are registered in that Member State in accordance with its legislation;

Whereas provision should be made for reasonable transitional periods in accordance with the character of the type of transport concerned,

HAS ADOPTED THIS REGULATION:

Article 1

1. Freedom to provide maritime transport services between Member States and between Member States and third countries shall apply in respect of nationals of Member States who are established in a Member State other than that of the person for whom the services are intended.

2. The provisions of this Regulation shall also apply to nationals of the Member States established outside the Community and to shipping companies established outside the Community and controlled by nationals of a Member State, if their vessels are registered in that Member State in accordance with its legislation.

3. The provisions of Articles 55 to 58 and 62 of the Treaty shall apply to the matters covered by this Regulation.

3. For the purpose of this Regulation, the following shall be considered 'maritime transport services between Member States and between Member States and third countries' where they are normally provided for remuneration:

(a) *intra-Community shipping services:*
the carriage of passengers or goods by sea between any port of a Member State and any port or off-shore installation of another Member State;

(b) *third-country traffic:*
the carriage of passengers or goods by sea between the ports of a Member State and ports or off-shore installations of a third country.

Article 2

By way of derogation from Article 1, unilateral national restrictions in existence before 1 July 1986 on the carriage of certain goods wholly or partly reserved for vessels flying the national flag, shall be phased out at the latest in accordance with the following timetable:

— carriage between Member States by vessels flying the flag of a Member State: 31 December 1989

— carriage between Member States and third countries by vessels flying the flag of a Member State: 31 December 1991

— carriage between Member States and between Member States and third countries in other vessels: 1 January 1993

Article 3

Cargo-sharing arrangements contained in existing bilateral agreements concluded by Member States with third countries shall be phased out or adjusted in accordance with the provisions of Article 4.

Article 4

1. Existing cargo-sharing arrangements not phased out in accordance with Article 3 shall be adjusted in accordance with Community legislation and in particular:

(a) where trades governed by the United Nations Code of Conduct for Liner Conferences are concerned, they shall comply with this Code and with the obligations of Member States under Regulation (EEC) No 954/79;

(b) where trades not governed by the United Nations Code of Conduct for Liner Conferences are concerned, agreement shall be adjusted as soon as possible and in any event before 1 January 1993 so as to provide for fair, free and non-discriminatory access by all Community nationals, as defined in Article 1, to the cargo shares due to the Member States concerned.

2. National action in pursuance of paragraph 1 shall be notified immediately to the Member States and the Commission. The consultation procedure established by Council Decision 77/587/EEC shall apply.

3. Member States shall report to the Commission on progress made on the adjustments referred to in paragraph 1 (b), initially every six months and subsequently every year.

4. When difficulties arise in the process of adjusting agreements to bring them into conformity with paragraph 1 (b), the Member State concerned shall inform the Council and the Commission. In cases where agreements are incompatible with paragraph 1 (b) and where the Member State concerned so asks, the Council shall, acting on a proposal from the Commission, take appropriate action.

Article 5

1. Cargo-sharing arrangements in any future agreements with third countries are prohibited other than in those exceptional circumstances where Community liner shipping companies would not otherwise have an effective opportunity to ply for trade to and from the third country concerned. In these circumstances such arrangements may be permitted in accordance with the provisions of Article 6.

2. In cases where a third country seeks to impose cargo-sharing arrangements on Member States in liquid or dry bulk trades, the Council shall take the appropriate action in accordance with Regulation (EEC) No 4058/86 concerning coordinated action to safeguard free access to cargoes in ocean trades.

Article 6

1. If a Member State's nationals or shipping companies, as defined in Article 1, paragraphs 1 and 2, are experiencing, or are threatened by, a situation where they do not have an active opportunity to ply for trade to and from a particular third country, the Member State concerned shall inform the other Member States and the Commission as soon as possible.

2. The Council, acting by qualified majority on a proposal of the Commission, shall decide on the necessary action. Such action may include, in the circumstances envisaged in Article 5 (1), the negotiation and conclusion of cargo-sharing arrangements.

3. If the Council has not decided on the necessary action within six months of a Member State providing information under paragraph 1, the Member State concerned may take such action as may for the time being be necessary to preserve an effective opportunity to ply for trade in accordance with Article 5 (1).

4. Any action taken under paragraph 3 shall be in accordance with Community law and provide for fair, free and non-discriminatory access to the relevant cargo shares by nationals or Community shipping companies, as defined in Article 1 (1) and (2).

5. National action in pursuance of paragraph 3 shall be notified immediately to the Member States and the Commission. The consultation procedure established by Council Decision 77/587/EEC shall apply.

Article 7

The Council, acting in accordance with the conditions laid down in the Treaty, may extend the provisions of this Regulation to nationals of a third country who provide maritime transport services and are established in the Community.

Article 8

Without prejudice to the provisions of the Treaty relating to right of establishment, a person providing a maritime transport service may, in order to do so, temporarily pursue his activity in the Member State where the service is provided, under the same conditions as are imposed by that State on its own nationals.

Article 9

As long as restrictions on freedom to provide services have not been abolished, each Member State shall apply such restrictions without distinction on grounds of nationality or residence to all persons providing services within the meaning of Article 1 (1) and (2).

Article 10

Member States shall, before adopting laws, regulations or administrative provisions in implementation of this Regulation consult the Commission and shall communicate to the latter any such measures so adopted.

Article 11

The Council, acting in accordance with the provisions laid down in the Treaty, shall review this Regulation before 1 January 1995.

Article 12

This Regulation shall enter into force on the day following its publication in the *Official Journal of the European Communities.*

It shall be binding in its entirety and directly applicable in all Member States.

Done at Brussels, 22 December 1986.

For the Council
The President
G. SHAW

22. COUNCIL REGULATION (EEC) No 4056/86 OF 22 DECEMBER 1986 LAYING DOWN DETAILED RULES FOR THE APPLICATION OF ARTICLES 85 AND 86 OF THE TREATY TO MARITIME TRANSPORT

THE COUNCIL OF THE EUROPEAN COMMUNITIES,

Having regard to the Treaty establishing the European Economic Community, and in particular Articles 84 (2) and 87 thereof,

Having regard to the proposal from the Commission,

Having regard to the opinion of the European Parliament,[1]

Having regard to the opinion of the Economic and Social Committee,[2]

Whereas the rules on competition form part of the Treaty's general provisions which also apply to maritime transport; whereas detailed rules for applying those provisions are set out in the Chapter of the Treaty dealing with the rules on competition or are to be determined by the procedures laid down therein;

Whereas according to Council Regulation No 141[3], Council Regulation No 17[4] does not apply to transport; whereas Council Regulation (EEC) No 1017/68[5] applies to inland transport only; whereas, consequently, the Commission has no means at present of investigating directly cases of suspected infringement of Articles 85 and 86 in maritime transport; whereas, moreover, the Commission lacks such powers of its own to take decisions or impose penalties as are necessary for it to bring to an end infringements established by it;

Whereas this situation necessitates the adoption of a Regulation applying the rules of competition to maritime transport; whereas Council Regulation (EEC) No 954/79 of 15 May 1979 concerning the ratification by Member States of, or their accession to, the United Nations Convention on a Code of Conduct for Liner Conferences[6] will result in the application of the Code of Conduct to a considerable number of conferences serving the Community; whereas the Regulation applying the rules of competition to maritime transport foreseen in the last recital of Regulation (EEC) No 954/79 should take account of the adoption of the Code; whereas, as far as conferences subject to the Code of Conduct are concerned, the Regulation should supplement the Code or make it more precise;

Whereas it appears preferable to exclude tramp vessel services from the scope of this Regulation, rates for these services being freely negotiated on a case-by-case basis in accordance with supply and demand conditions;

Whereas this Regulation should take account of the necessity, on the one hand to provide for implementing rules that enable the Commission to ensure that competition is not unduly distorted within the common market, and on the other hand to avoid excessive regulation of the sector;

Whereas this Regulation should define the scope of the provisions of Articles 85 and 86 of the Treaty, taking into account the distinctive characteristics of maritime transport; whereas trade between Member States may be affected where restrictive practices or abuses concern international maritime transport, including intra-Community transport, from or to Community ports; whereas such restrictive practices or abuses may influence competition, firstly, between ports in different Member States by altering their respective catchment areas, and secondly, between activities in those catchment areas, and disturb trade patterns within the common market;

Whereas certain types of technical agreement, decisions and concerted practices may be excluded from the prohibition on restrictive practices on the ground that they do not, as a general rule, restrict competition;

Whereas provision should be made for block exemption of liner conferences; whereas liner conferences have a stabilizing effect, assuring shippers of reliable services; whereas they

1. OJ No. C 172, 2 July 1984, p. 178; OJ No. C 255, 13 October 1986, p. 169.
2. OJ No. C 77, 21 March 1983, p. 13; OJ No. C 344, 31 December 1985, p. 31.
3. OJ No. 124, 28 November 1962, p. 2751/62.
4. OJ No. 13, 21 February 1962, p. 204/62.
5. OJ No. L 175, 23 July 1968, p. 1.
6. OJ No. L 121, 17 May 1979, p. 1.

contribute generally to providing adequate efficient scheduled maritime transport services and give fair consideration to the interests of users; whereas such results cannot be obtained without the cooperation that shipping companies promote within conferences in relation to rates and, where appropriate, availability of capacity or allocation of cargo for shipment, and income; whereas in most cases conferences continue to be subject to effective competition from both non-conference scheduled services and, in certain circumstances, from tramp services and from other modes of transport; whereas the mobility of fleets, which is a characteristic feature of the structure of availability in the shipping field, subjects conferences to constant competition which they are unable as a rule to eliminate as far as a substantial proportion of the shipping services in question is concerned;

Whereas, however, in order to prevent conferences from engaging in practices which are incompatible with Article 85 (3) of the Treaty, certain conditions and obligations should be attached to the exemption;

Whereas the aim of the conditions should be to prevent conferences from imposing restrictions on competition which are not indispensable to the attainment of the objectives on the basis of which exemption is granted; whereas, to this end, conferences should not, in respect of a given route, apply rates and conditions of carriage which are differentiated solely by reference to the country of origin or destination of the goods carried and thus cause within the Community deflections of trade that are harmful to certain ports, shippers, carriers or providers of services ancillary to transport; whereas, furthermore, loyalty arrangements should be permitted only in accordance with rules which do not restrict unilaterally the freedom of users and consequently competition in the shipping industry, without prejudice, however, to the right of a conference to impose penalties on users who seek by improper means to evade the obligation of loyalty required in exchange for the rebates, reduced freight rates or commission granted to them by the conference; whereas users must be free to determine the undertakings to which they have recourse in respect of inland transport or quayside services not covered by the freight charge or by other charges agreed with the shipping line;

Whereas certain obligations should also attach to the exemption; whereas in this respect users must at all times be in a position to acquaint themselves with the rates and conditions of carriage applied by members of the conference, since in the case of inland transports organized by shippers, the latter continue to be subject to Regulation (EEC) No 1017/68; whereas provision should be made that awards given at arbitration and recommendations made by conciliators and accepted by the parties be notified forthwith to the Commission in order to enable it to verify that conferences are not thereby exempted from the conditions provided for in the Regulation and thus do not infringe the provisions of Articles 85 and 86;

Whereas consultations between users or associations of users and conferences are liable to secure a more efficient operation of maritime transport services which takes better account of users' requirements; whereas, consequently, certain restrictive practices which could ensue from such consultations should be exempted;

Whereas there can be no exemption if the conditions set out in Article 85 (3) are not satisfied; whereas the Commission must therefore have power to take the appropriate measures where an agreement or concerted practice owing to special circumstances proves to have certain effects incompatible with Article 85 (3); whereas, in view of the specific role fulfilled by the conferences in the sector of the liner services, the reaction of the Commission should be progressive and proportionate; whereas the Commission should consequently have the power first to address recommendations, then to take decisions;

Whereas the automatic nullity provided for in Article 85 (3) in respect of agreements or decisions which have not been granted exemption pursuant to Article 85 (3) owing to their discriminatory or other features applies only to the elements of the agreement covered by the prohibition of Article 85 (1) and applies to the agreement in its entirety only if those elements do not appear to be severable from the whole of the agreement whereas the Commission should therefore, if it finds an infringement of the block exemption, either specify what elements of the agreement are by the prohibition and consequently automatically void, or indicate the reasons why those elements are not severable from the rest of the agreement and why the agreement is therefore void in its entirety;

Whereas, in view of the characteristics of international maritime transport, account should be taken of the fact that the application of this Regulation to certain restrictive practices or abuses may result in conflicts with the laws and rules of certain third countries and prove harmful to important Community trading and shipping interests; whereas consultation and, where appropriate, negotiations authorized by the Council should be undertaken by the Commission with those countries in pursuance of the maritime transport policy of the Community;

Whereas this Regulation should make provision for the procedures, decision-making powers and penalties that are necessary to ensure compliance with the prohibitions laid down in Article 85 (1) and Article 86, as well as the conditions governing the application of Article 85 (3);

Whereas account should be taken in this respect of the procedural provisions of Regulation (EEC) No 1017/68 applicable to inland transport operations which takes account of certain distinctive features of transport operations viewed as a whole;

Whereas, in particular, in view of the special characteristics of maritime transport, it is primarily the responsibility of undertakings to see to it that their agreements, decisions and concerted practices conform to the rules on competition, and consequently their notification to the Commission need not be made compulsory;

Whereas in certain circumstances undertakings may, however, wish to apply to the Commission for confirmation that their agreements, decisions and concerted practices are in conformity with the provisions in force; whereas a simplified procedure should be laid down for such cases,

HAS ADOPTED THIS REGULATION:

SECTION I

Article 1. Subject-matter and scope of the Regulation

1. This Regulation lays down detailed rules for the application of Articles 85 and 86 of the Treaty to maritime transport services.
2. It shall apply only to international maritime transport services from or to one or more Community ports, other than tramp vessel services.
3. For the purposes of this Regulation:
   (a) 'tramp vessel services' means the transport of goods in bulk or in break-bulk in a vessel chartered wholly or partly to one or more shippers on the basis of a voyage or time charter or any other form of contract for non-regularly scheduled or non-advertised sailings where the freight rates are freely negotiated case by case in accordance with the conditions of supply and demand;
   (b) 'liner conference' means a group of two or more vessel-operating carriers which provides international liner services for the carriage of cargo on a particular route or routes within specified geographical limits and which has an agreement or arrangement, whatever its nature, within the framework of which they operate under uniform or common freight rates and any other agreed conditions with respect to the provision of liner services;
   (c) 'transport user' means an undertaking (e.g. shippers, consignees, forwarders, etc.) provided it has entered into, or demonstrates an intention to enter into, a contractual or other arrangement with a conference or shipping line for the shipment of goods, or any association of shippers.

Article 2. Technical agreements

1. The prohibition laid down in Article 85 (1) of the Treaty shall not apply to agreements, decisions and concerted practices whose sole object and effect is to achieve technical improvements or cooperation by means of:
   (a) the introduction or uniform application of standards or types in respect of vessels and other means of transport, equipment, supplies or fixed installations;
   (b) the exchange or pooling for the purpose of operating transport services, of vessels, space on vessels or slots and other means of transport, staff, equipment or fixed installations;
   (c) the organization and execution of successive or supplementary maritime transport

operations and the establishment or application of inclusive rates and conditions for such operations;

(d) the coordination of transport timetables for connecting routes;

(e) the consolidation of individual consignments;

(f) the establishment or application of uniform rules concerning the structure and the conditions governing the application of transport tariffs.

2. The Commission shall, if necessary, submit to the Council proposals for the amendment of the list contained in paragraph 1.

Article 3. Exemption for agreements between carriers concerning the operation of scheduled maritime transport services

Agreements, decisions and concerted practices of all or part of the members of one or more liner conferences are hereby exempted from the prohibition in Article 85 (1) of the Treaty, subject to the condition imposed by Article 4 of this Regulation, when they have as their objective the fixing of rates and conditions of carriage, and, as the case may be, one or more of the following objectives:

(a) the coordination of shipping timetables, sailing dates or dates of calls;

(b) the determination of the frequency of sailings or calls;

(c) the coordination or allocation of sailings or calls among members of the conference;

(d) the regulation of the carrying capacity offered by each member;

(e) the allocation of cargo or revenue among members.

Article 4. Condition attaching to exemption

The exemption provided for in Articles 3 and 6 shall be granted subject to the condition that the agreement, decision or concerted practice shall not, within the common market, cause detriment to certain ports, transport users or carriers by applying for the carriage of the same goods and in the area covered by the agreement, decision or concerted practice, rates and conditions of carriage which differ according to the country of origin or destination or port of loading or discharge, unless such rates or conditions can be economically justified.

Any agreement or decision or, if it is severable, any part of such an agreement or decision not complying with the preceding paragraph shall automatically be void pursuant to Article 85 (2) of the Treaty.

Article 5. Obligations attaching to exemption

The following obligations shall be attached to the exemption provided for in Article 3:

1. Consultations

There shall be consultations for the purpose of seeking solutions on general issues of principle between transport users on the one hand and conferences on the other concerning the rates, conditions and quality of scheduled maritime transport services.

These consultations shall take place whenever requested by any of the above mentioned parties.

2. Loyalty arrangements

The shipping lines' members of a conference shall be entitled to institute and maintain loyalty arrangements with transport users, the form and terms of which shall be matters for consultation between the conference and transport users' organizations. These loyalty arrangements shall provide safeguards making explicit the rights of transport users and conference members. These arrangements shall be based on the contract system or any other system which is also lawful.

Loyalty arrangements must comply with the following conditions:

(a) Each conference shall offer transport users a system of immediate rebates or the choice between such a system and a system of deferred rebates:

- under the system of immediate rebates each of the parties shall be entitled to terminate the loyalty arrangement at any time without penalty and subject to a period of notice of not more than six months; this period shall be reduced to three months when the conference rate is the subject of a dispute;
- under the system of deferred rebates neither the loyalty period on the basis of which the rebate is calculated nor the subsequent loyalty period required before payment of the rebate may exceed six months; this period shall be reduced to three months where the conference rate is the subject of a dispute.

(b) The conference shall, after consulting the transport users concerned, set out:

(i) a list of cargo and any portion of cargo agreed with transport users which is specifically excluded from the scope of the loaylty arrangement; 100% loyalty arrangements may be offered but may not be unilaterally imposed;

(ii) a list of circumstances in which transport users are released from their obligation of loyalty; these shall include:

- circumstances in which consignments are dispatched from or to a port in the area covered by the conference but not advertised and where the request for a waiver can be justified, and
- those in which waiting time at a port exceeds a period to be determined for each port and for each commodity or class of commodities following consultation of the transport users directly concerned with the proper servicing of the port.

The conference must, however, be informed in advance by the transport user, within a specified period, of his intention to dispatch the consignment from a port not advertised by the conference or to make use of a non-conference vessel at a port served by the conference as soon as he has been able to establish from the published schedule of sailings that the maximum waiting period will be exceeded.

3. Services not covered by the freight charges

Transport users shall be entitled to approach the undertakings of their choice in respect of inland transport operations and quayside services not covered by the freight charge or charges on which the shipping line and the transport user have agreed.

4. Availability of tariffs

Tariffs, related conditions, regulations and any amendments thereto shall be made available on request to transport users at reasonable cost, or they shall be available for examination at offices of shipping lines and their agents. They shall set out all the conditions concerning loading and discharge, the exact extent of the services covered by the freight charge in proportion to the sea transport and the land transport or by any other charge levied by the shipping line and customary practice in such matters.

5. Notification to the Commisison of awards at arbitration and recommendations

Awards given at arbitration and recommendations made by conciliators that are accepted by the parties shall be notified forthwith to the Commission when they resolve disputes relating to the practices of conferences referred to in Article 4 and in points 2 and 3 above.

Article 6. Exemption for agreements between transport users and conferences concerning the use of scheduled maritime transport services

Agreements, decisions and concerned pratices between transport users, on the one hand, and conferences, on the other hand, and agreements between transport users which may be necessary to that end, concerning the rates, conditions and quality of liner services, as long as they are provided for in Article 5 (1) and (2) are hereby exempted from the prohibition laid down in Article 85 (1) of the Treaty.

Article 7. Monitoring of exempted agreements

1. Breach of an obligation

Where the persons concerned are in breach of an obligation which, pursuant to Article 5, attaches to the exemption provided for in Article 3, the Commission may, in order to put an end to such breach and under the conditions laid down in Section II:

— address recommendations to the persons concerned;
— in the event of failure by such persons to observe those recommendations and depending upon the gravity of the breach concerned, adopt a decision that either prohibits them from carrying out or requires them to perform specific acts or, while withdrawing the benefit of the block exemption which they enjoyed, grants them an individual exemption according to Article 11 (4) or withdraws the benefit of the block exemption which they enjoyed.

2. Effects incompatible with Article 85 (3)

(a) Where, owing to special circumstances as described below, agreements, decisions and concerted practices which qualify for the exemption provided for in Articles 3 and 6 have nevertheless effects which are incompatible with the conditions laid down in Article 85 (3) of the Treaty, the Commission, on receipt of a complaint or on its own initiative, under the conditions laid down in Section II, shall take the measures described in (c) below. The severity of these measures must be in proportion to the gravity of the situation.

(b) Special circumstances are, *inter alia*, created by:
   (i) acts of conferences or a change of market conditions in a given trade resulting in the absence or elimination of actual or potential competition such as restrictive practices whereby the trade is not available to competition; or
   (ii) acts of conference which may prevent technical or economic progress or user participation in the benefits;
   (iii) acts of third countries which:
      — prevent the operation of outsiders in a trade,
      — impose unfair tariffs on conference members,
      — impose arrangements which otherwise impede technical or economic progress (cargo-sharing, limitations on types of vessels).

(c) (i) If actual or potential competition is absent or may be eliminated as a result of action by a third country, the Commission shall enter into consultations with the competent authorities of the third country concerned, followed if necessary by negotiations under directives to be given by the Council, in order to remedy the situation.

   If the special circumstances result in the absence or elimination of actual or potential competition contrary to Article 85(3)(b) of the Treaty the Commission shall withdraw the benefit of the block exemption. At the same time it shall rule on whether and, if so, under what additional conditions and obligations an individual exemption should be granted to the relevant conference agreement with a view, *inter alia*, to obtaining access to the market for non-conference lines;

   (ii) If, as a result of special circumstances as set out in (b), there are effects other than those referred to in (i) hereof, the Commission shall take one or more of the measures described in paragraph 1.

Article 8. Effects incompatible with Article 86 of the Treaty

1. The abuse of a dominant position within the meaning of Article 86 of the Treaty shall be prohibited, no prior decision to that effect being required.

2. Where the Commission, either on its own initiative or at the request of a Member State or of natural or legal persons claiming a legitimate interest, finds that in any particular case the conduct of conferences benefiting from the exemption laid down in Article 3 nevertheless has effects which are incompatible with Article 86 of the Treaty, it may withdraw the benefit of the block exemption and take, pursuant to Article 10, all appropriate measures for the purpose of bringing to an end infringements of Article 86 of the Treaty.

3. Before taking a decision under paragraph 2, the Commission may address to the conference concerned recommendations for termination of the infringement.

Article 9. Conflicts of international law

1. Where the application of this Regulation to certain restrictive practices or clauses is liable to enter into conflict with the provisions laid down by law, regulation or administrative action of certain third countries which would compromise important Community trading and shipping interests, the Commission shall, at the earliest opportunity, undertake with the competent authorities of the third countries concerned, consultations aimed at reconciling as far as possible the above mentioned interest with the respect of Community law. The Commission shall inform the Advisory Committee referred to in Article 15 of the outcome of these consultations.

2. Where agreements with third countries need to be negotiated, the Commission shall make recommendations to the Council, which shall authorize the Commission to open the necessary negotiations.

The Commission shall conduct these negotiations in consultation with an Advisory Committee as referred to in Article 15 and within the framework of such directives as the Council may issue to it.

3. In exercising the powers conferred on it by this Article, the Council shall act in accordance with the decision-making procedure laid down in Article 84 (2) of the Treaty.

SECTION II. RULES OF PROCEDURE

Article 10. Procedures on complaint or on the Commission's own initiative

Acting on receipt of a complaint or on its own initiative, the Commission shall initiate procedures to terminate any infringement of the provisions of Articles 85 (1) or 86 of the Treaty or to enforce Article 7 of this Regulation.

Complaints may be submitted by:

(a) Member States;

(b) natural or legal persons who claim a legitimate interest.

Article 11. Result of procedures on complaint or on the Commission's own initiative

1. Where the Commission finds that there has been an infringement of Articles 85 (1) or 86 of the Treaty, it may by decision require the undertakings or associations of undertakings concerned to bring such infringement to an end.

Without prejudice to the other provisions of this Regulation, the Commission may, before taking a decision under the preceding subparagraph, address to the undertakings or associations of undertakings concerned recommendations for termination of the infringement.

2. Paragraph 1 shall apply also to cases falling within Article 7 of this Regulation.

3. If the Commission, acting on a complaint received, concludes that on the evidence before it there are no grounds for intervention under Articles 85 (1) or 86 of the Treaty or Article 7 of this Regulation, in respect of any agreement, decision or practice, it shall issue a decision rejecting the complaint as unfounded.

4. If the Commission, whether acting on a complaint received or on its own initiative, concludes that an agreement, decision or concerted practice satisfies the provisions both of Article 85 (1) and of Article 85 (3) of the Treaty, it shall issue a decision applying Article 85 (3). Such decision shall indicate the date from which it is to take effect. This date may be prior to that of the decision.

Article 12. Application of Article 85 (3)—objections

1. Undertakings and associations of undertakings which seek application of Article 85(3) of the Treaty in respect of agreements, decisions and concerted practices falling within the provisions of Article 85(1) to which they are parties shall submit applications to the Commission.

2. If the Commission judges an application admissible and is in possession of all the available evidence, and no action under Article 10 has been taken against the agreement, decisions or concerted practice in question, then it shall publish as soon as possible in the *Official Journal of the European Communities* a summary of the application and invite all interested third parties and the Member States to submit their comments to the Commission within 30 days. Such publication shall have regard to the legitimate interest of undertakings in the protection of their business secrets.

3. Unless the Commission notifies applicants, within 90 days from the date of such publication in the *Official Journal of the European Communities*, that there are serious doubts as to the applicability of Article 85 (3), the agreement, decision or concerted practice shall be deemed exempt, insofar as it conforms with the description given in the application, from the prohibition for the time already elapsed and for a maximum of six years from the date of publication in the *Official Journal of the European Communities*.

If the Commission finds, after expiry of the 90-day time limit, but before expiry of the six-year period, that the conditions for applying Article 85 (3) are not satisfied, it shall issue a decision declaring that the prohibition in Article 85 (1) is applicable. Such decision may be retroactive where the parties concerned have given inaccurate information or where they abuse the exemption from the provisions of Article 85 (1).

4. The Commission may notify applicants as referred to in the first subparagraph of paragraph 3 and shall do so if requested by a Member State within 45 days of the forwarding to the Member State of the application in accordance with Article 15 (2). This request must be justified on the basis of considerations relating to the competition rules of the Treaty.

If it finds that the conditions of Article 85(1) and of Article 85(3) are satisfied, the Commission shall issue a decision applying Article 85(3). The decision shall indicate the date from which it is to take effect. This date may be prior to that of the application.

Article 13. Duration and revocation of decisions applying Article 85 (3)

1. Any decision applying Article 85(3) taken under Article 11(4) or under the second subparagraph of Article 12(4) shall indicate the period for which it is to be valid; normally such period shall not be less than six years. Conditions and obligations may be attached to the decision.

2. The decision may be renewed if the conditions for applying Article 85(3) continue to be satisfied.

3. The Commission may revoke or amend its decision or prohibit specified acts by the parties:

(a) where there has been a change in any of the facts which were basic to the making of the decision;

(b) where the parties commit a breach of any obligation attached to the decision;

(c) where the decision is based on incorrect information or was induced by deceit, or

(d) where the parties abuse the exemption from the provisions of Article 85 (1) granted to them by the decision.

In cases falling within (b), (c) or (d), the decision may be revoked with retroactive effect.

Article 14. Powers

Subject to review of its decision by the Court of Justice, the Commission shall have sole power:

— to impose obligations pursuant to Article 7;

— to issue decisions pursuant to Article 85 (3).

The authorities of the Member States shall retain the power to decide whether any case falls within the provisions of Article 85 (1) or Article 86, until such time as the Commission has initiated a procedure with a view to formulating a decision in the case in question or has sent notification as provided for in the first subparagraph of Article 12 (3).

Article 15. Liaison with the authorities of the Member States

1. The Commission shall carry out the procedures provided for in this Regulation in close and constant liaison with the competent authorities of the Member States; these authorities shall have the right to express their views on such procedures.

2. The Commission shall immediately forward to the competent authorities of the Member States copies of the complaints and applications, and of the most important documents sent to it or which it sends out in the course of such procedures.

3. An Advisory Committee on agreements and dominant positions in maritime transport shall be consulted prior to the taking of any decision following upon a procedure under Article 10 or of any decision issued under the second subparagraph of Article 12 (3), or under the second subparagraph of paragraph 4 of the same Article. The Advisory Committee shall also be consulted prior to the adoption of the implementing provisions provided for in Article 26.

4. The Advisory Committee shall be composed of officials competent in the sphere of maritime transport and agreements and dominant positions. Each Member State shall nominate two officials to represent it, each of whom may be replaced, in the event of his being prevented from attending, by another official.

5. Consultation shall take place at a joint meeting convened by the Commission; such meeting shall be held not earlier than fourteen days after dispatch of the notice convening it. This notice shall, in respect of each case to be examined, be accompanied by a summary of the case together with an indication of the most important documents, and a preliminary draft decision.

6. The Advisory Committee may deliver an opinion notwithstanding that some of its members or their alternates are not present. A report of the outcome of the consultative proceedings shall be annexed to the draft decision. It shall not be made public.

Article 16. Requests for information

1. In carrying out the duties assigned to it by this Regulation, the Commission may obtain all necessary information from the Governments and competent authorities of the Member States and from undertakings and associations of undertakings.

2. When sending a request for information to an undertaking or association of undertakings, the Commission shall at the same time forward a copy of the request to the competent authority of the Member State in whose territory the seat of the undertaking or association of undertakings is situated.

3. In its request, the Commission shall state the legal basis and the purpose of the request, and also the penalties provided for in Article 19 (1) (b) for supplying incorrect information.

4. The owners of the undertakings or their representatives and, in the case of legal persons, companies or firms, or of associations having no legal personality, the person authorized to represent them by law or by their constitution, shall be bound to supply the information requested.

5. Where an undertaking or association of undertakings does not supply the information requested within the time limit fixed by the Commission, or supplies incomplete information, the Commission shall by decision require the information to be supplied. The decision shall specify what information is required, fix an appropriate time limit within which it is to be supplied and indicate the penalties provided for in Article 19 (1) (b) and Article 20 (1) (c) and the right to have the decision reviewed by the Court of Justice.

6. The Commission shall at the same time forward a copy of its decision to the competent authority of the Member State in whose territory the seat of the undertaking or association of undertakings is situated.

Article 17. Investigations by the authorities of the Member States

1. At the request of the Commission, the competent authorities of the Member States shall undertake the investigations which the Commission considers to be necessary under Article 18 (1), or which it has ordered by decision pursuant to Article 18 (3). The officials of the competent authorities of the Member States responsible for conducting these investigations shall exercise their powers upon production of an authorization in writing issued by the competent authority

of the Member State in whose territory the investigation is to be made. Such authorization shall specify the subject matter and purpose of the investigation.

2. If so requested by the Commission or by the competent authority of the Member State in whose territory the investigation is to be made, Commission officials may assist the officials of such authority in carrying out their duties.

Article 18. Investigating powers of the Commission

1. In carrying out the duties assigned to it by this Regulation, the Commission may undertake all necessary investigations into undertakings and associations of undertakings.

To this end the officials authorized by the Commission are empowered:

(a) to examine the books and other business records;
(b) to take copies of or extracts from the books and business records:
(c) to ask for oral explanations on the spot;
(d) to enter any premises, land and vehicles of undertakings.

2. The officials of the Commission authorized for the purpose of these investigations shall exercise their powers upon production of an authorization in writing specifying the subject matter and purpose of the investigation and the penalties provided for in Article 19 (1) (c) in cases where production of the required books or other business records is incomplete. In good time before the investigation, the Commission shall inform the competent authority of the Member State in whose territory the same is to be made of the investigation and of the identity of the authorized officials.

3. Undertakings and associations of undertakings shall submit to investigations ordered by decision of the Commission. The decision shall specify the subject matter and purpose of the investigation, appoint the date on which it is to begin and indicate the penalties provided for in Article 19 (1) (c) and Article 20 (1) (d) and the right to have the decision reviewed by the Court of Justice.

4. The Commission shall take decisions referred to in paragraph 3 after consultation with the competent authority of the Member State in whose territory the investigation is to be made.

5. Officials of the competent authority of the Member State in whose territory the investigation is to be made, may at the request of such authority or of the Commission, assist the officials of the Commission in carrying out their duties.

6. Where an undertaking opposes an investigation ordered pursuant to this Article, the Member State concerned shall afford the necessary assistance to the officials authorized by the Commission to enable them to make their investigation. To this end, Member States shall take the necessary measures, after consulting the Commission, before 1 January 1989.

Article 19. Fines

1. The Commission may by decision impose on undertakings or associations of undertakings fines of from 100 to 5,000 ECU where, intentionally or negligently:

(a) they supply incorrect or misleading information, either in a communication pursuant to Article 5 (5) or in an application pursuant to Article 12; or
(b) they supply incorrect information in response to a request made pursuant to Article 16 (3) or (5), or do not supply information within the time limit fixed by a decision taken under Article 16 (5); or
(c) they produce the required books or other business records in incomplete form during investigations under Article 17 or Article 18, or refuse to submit to an investigation ordered by decision issued in implementation of Article 18 (3).

2. The Commission may by decision impose on undertakings or associations of undertakings fines of from 1,000 to one million ECU, or a sum in excess thereof but not exceeding 10% of the turnover in the preceding business year of each of the undertakings participating in the infringement, where either intentionally or negligently:

(a) they infringe Article 85 (1) or Article 86 of the Treaty, or do not comply with an obligation imposed under Article 7 of this Regulation;
(b) they commit a breach of any obligation imposed pursuant to Article 5 or to Article 13 (1).

In fixing the amount of the fine, regard shall be had both to the gravity and to the duration of the infringement.

3. Article 15 (3) and (4) shall apply.

4. Decisions taken pursuant to paragraphs 1 and 2 shall not be of criminal law nature.

The fines provided for in paragraph 2 (a) shall not be imposed in respect of acts taking place after notification to the Commission and before its Decision in application of Article 85 (3) of the Treaty, provided they fall within the limits of the activity described in the notification.

However, this provision shall not have effect where the Commission has informed the undertakings concerned that after preliminary examination it is of the opinion that Article 85 (1) of the Treaty applies and that application of Article 85 (3) is not justified.

Article 20. Periodic penalty payments

1. The Commission may by decision impose on undertakings or associations of undertakings periodic penalty payments of from 50 to 1,000 ECU per day, calculated from the date appointed by the decision, in order to compel them:
   (a) to put an end to an infringement of Article 85 (1) or Article 86 of the Treaty the termination of which it has ordered pursuant to Article 11, or to comply with an obligation imposed pursuant to Article 7;
   (b) to refrain from any act prohibited under Article 13 (3);
   (c) to supply complete and correct information which it has requested by decision taken pursuant to Article 16 (5);
   (d) to submit to an investigation which it has ordered by decision taken pursuant to Article 18 (3).

2. Where the undertakings or associations of undertakings have satisfied the obligation which it was the purpose of the periodic penalty payment to enforce, the Commission may fix the total amount of the periodic penalty payment at a lower figure than that which would arise under the original decision.

3. Article 15 (3) and (4) shall apply.

Article 21. Review by the Court of Justice

The Court of Justice shall have unlimited jurisdiction within the meaning of Article 172 of the Treaty to review decisions whereby the Commission has fixed a fine or periodic penalty payment; it may cancel, reduce or increase the fine or periodic penalty payment imposed.

Article 22. Unit of account

For the purpose of applying Articles 19 to 21 the ECU shall be that adopted in drawing up the budget of the Community in accordance with Articles 207 and 209 of the Treaty.

Article 23. Hearing of the parties and of third persons

1. Before taking decisions as provided for in Articles 11, 12 (3) second subparagraph, and 12 (4), 13 (3), 19 and 20, the Commission shall give the undertakings or associations of undertakings concerned the opportunity of being heard on the matters to which the Commission has taken objection.

2. If the Commission or the competent authorities of the Member States consider it necessary, they may also hear other natural or legal persons. Applications to be heard on the part of such persons where they show a sufficient interest shall be granted.

3. Where the Commission intends to give negative clearance pursuant to Article 85 (3) of the Treaty, it shall publish a summary of the relevant agreement, decision or concerted practice and invite all interested third parties to submit their observations within a time limit which it shall fix being not less than one month. Publication shall have regard to the legitimate interest of undertakings in the protection of their business secrets.

Article 24. Professional secrecy

1. Information acquired as a result of the application of Articles 17 and 18 shall be used only for the purpose of the relevant request or investigation.

2. Without prejudice to the provisions of Articles 23 and 25, the Commission and the competent authorities of the Member States, their officials and other servants shall not disclose information acquired by them as a result of the application of this Regulation and of the kind covered by the obligation of professional secrecy.

3. The provisions of paragraphs 1 and 2 shall not prevent publication of general information or surveys which do not contain information relating to particular undertakings or associations of undertakings.

Article 25. Publication of decisions

1. The Commission shall publish the decisions which it takes pursuant to Articles 11, 12 (3), second paragraph, 12 (4) and 13 (3).

2. The publication shall state the names of the parties and the main content of the decision; it shall have regard to the legitimate interest of undertakings in the protection of their business secrets.

Article 26. Implementing provisions

The Commission shall have power to adopt implementing provisions concerning the scope of the obligation of communication pursuant to Article 5 (5), the form, content and other details of complaints pursuant to Article 10, applications pursuant to Article 12 and the hearings provided for in Article 23 (1) and (2).

Article 27. Entry into force

This Regulation shall enter into force on 1 July 1987.

This Regulation shall be binding in its entirety and directly applicable in all Member States.

Done at Brussels, 22 December 1986.

For the Council
The President
G. SHAW

23. COUNCIL REGULATION (EEC) No 4057/86 OF 22 DECEMBER 1986 ON UNFAIR PRICING PRACTICES IN MARITIME TRANSPORT

THE COUNCIL OF THE EUROPEAN COMMUNITIES,

Having regard to the Treaty establishing the European Economic Community, and in particular Article 84 (2) thereof,

Having regard to the draft Regulation submitted by the Commission,

Having regard to the opinion of the European Parliament,[1]

Having regard to the opinion of the Economic and Social Committee,[2]

Whereas there is reason to believe, *inter alia* on the basis of the information system set up by Council Decision 78/774/EEC,[3] that the competitive participation of Community shipowners in international liner shipping is adversely affected by certain unfair practices of shipping lines of third countries;

Whereas the structure of the Community shipping industry is such as to make it appropriate that the provisions of this Regulation should also apply to nationals of Member States established outside the Community or cargo shipping companies established outside the Community and controlled by nationals of Member States, if their ships are registered in a Member State in accordance with its legislation;

Whereas such unfair practices consist of continuous charging in freight rates for the transport of selected commodities which are lower than the lowest freight rates charged for the same commodities by established and representative shipowners;

Whereas such pricing practices are made possible by non-commercial advantages granted by a State which is not a member of the Community;

Whereas the Community should be able to take redressive action against such pricing practices;

Whereas there are no internationally agreed rules as to what constitutes an unfair price in the maritime transport field;

Whereas, in order to determine the existence of unfair pricing practices, provision should therefore be made for an appropriate method of calculation; whereas when calculating the 'normal freight rate' account should be taken of the comparable rate actually charged by established and representative companies operating within or outside conferences or otherwise of a constructed rate based on the costs of comparable companies plus a reasonable margin of profit;

Whereas appropriate factors relevant for the determination of injury should be laid down;

Whereas it is necessary to lay down the procedures for those acting on behalf of the Community shipping industry who consider themselves injured or threatened by unfair pricing practices to lodge a complaint; whereas it seems appropriate to make it clear that in the case of withdrawal of a complaint, proceedings may, but need not necessarily, be terminated;

Whereas there should be cooperation between the Member States and the Commission both as regards information about the existence of unfair pricing practices and injury resulting therefrom, and as regards the subsequent examination of the matter at Community level; whereas, to this end, consultations should take place within an Advisory Committee;

Whereas it is appropriate to lay down clearly the rules of procedure to be followed during the investigation, in particular the rights and obligations of the Community authorities and the parties involved, and the conditions under which interested parties may have access to information and may ask to be informed of the principal facts and considerations on the basis of which it is intended to propose the introduction of a redressive duty;

Whereas, in order to discourage unfair pricing practices, but without preventing, restricting or distorting price competition by non-conference lines, providing that they are working on a fair and commercial basis, it is appropriate to provide, in cases where the facts as finally established show that there is an unfair pricing practice and injury, for the possibility of imposing redressive duties on particular grounds;

1. OJ No. C 255, 15 October 1986, p. 169.
2. OJ No. C 344, 31 December 1985, p. 31.
3. OJ No. L 258, 21 September 1978, p. 35.

Whereas it is essential, in order to ensure that redressive duties are levied in a correct and uniform manner, that common rules for the application of such duties be laid down; whereas, by reason of the nature of the said duties, such rules may differ from the rules for the levying of normal import duties;

Whereas open and fair procedures should be provided for the review of measures taken and for the investigation to be reopened when circumstances so require;

Whereas appropriate procedures should be established for examining applications for refund of redressive duties,

HAS ADOPTED THIS REGULATION:

Article 1. Objective

This Regulation lays down the procedure to be followed in order to respond to unfair pricing practices by certain third country shipowners engaged in international cargo liner shipping, which cause serious disruption of the freight pattern on a particular route to, from or within the Community and cause or threaten to cause major injury to Community shipowners operating on the route and to Community interests.

Article 2

In response to unfair pricing practices as described in Article 1 which cause major injury, a redressive duty may be applied by the Community.

A threat of major injury may only give rise to an examination within the meaning of Article 4.

Article 3

For the purposes of this Regulation:

(a) 'third country shipowner' means cargo liner shipping companies other than those mentioned under (d);

(b) 'unfair pricing practices' means the continuous charging on a particular shipping route to, from or within the Community of freight rates for selected or all commodities which are lower than the normal freight rates charged during a period of at least six months, when such lower freight rates are made possible by the fact that the shipowner concerned enjoys non-commercial advantages which are granted by a State which is not a member of the Community;

(c) the 'normal freight rate' shall be determined taking into account:

(i) the comparable rate actually charged in the ordinary course of shipping business for the like service on the same or comparable route by established and representative companies not enjoying the advantages in (b);

(ii) or otherwise the constructed rate which is determined by taking the costs of comparable companies not enjoying the advantages in (b) plus a reasonable margin of profit. This cost shall be computed on the basis of all costs incurred in the ordinary course of shipping business, both fixed and variable, plus a reasonable amount for overhead expenses.

(d) 'Community shipowners' means:

— all cargo shipping companies established under the Treaty in a Member State of the Community;

— nationals of Member States established outside the Community or cargo shipping companies established outside the Community and controlled by nationals of Member States, if their ships are registered in a Member State in accordance with its legislation.

Article 4. Examination of injury

1. Examination of injury shall cover the following factors:

(a) the freight rates offered by Community shipowners' competitors on the route in question, in particular in order to determine whether they have been significantly lower than the normal freight rate offered by Community shipowners, taking into account the level of service offered by all the companies concerned;

(b) the effect of the above factor on Community shipowners as indicated by trends in a number of economic indicators such as:
— sailings,
— utilization of capacity,
— cargo bookings,
— market share,
— freight rates (that is depression of freight rates or prevention of freight rate increases which would normally have occurred),
— profits,
— return of capital,
— investment,
— employment.

2. Where a threat of injury is alleged, the Commission may also examine whether it is clearly foreseeable that a particular situation is likely to develop into actual injury. In this regard, account may also be taken of factors such as:

(a) the increase in tonnage deployed on the shipping route where the competition with Community shipowners is taking place;

(b) the capacity which is already available or is to become available in the foreseeable future in the country of the foreign shipowners and the extent to which the tonnage resulting from that capacity is likely to be used on the shipping route referred to in (a).

3. Injury caused by other factors which, either individually or in combination, are also adversely affecting Community shipowners must not be attributed to the practices in question.

Article 5. Complaint

1. Any natural or legal person, or any association not having legal personality, acting on behalf of the Community shipping industry who consider themselves injured or threatened by unfair pricing practices may lodge a written complaint.

2. The complaint shall contain sufficient evidence of the existence of the unfair pricing practice and injury resulting therefrom.

3. The complaint may be submitted to the Commission, or a Member State, which shall forward it to the Commission. The Commission shall send Member States a copy of any complaint it receives.

4. The complaint may be withdrawn, in which case proceedings may be terminated unless such termination would not be in the interest of the Community.

5. Where it becomes apparent after consultation that the complaint does not provide sufficient evidence to justify initiating an investigation, then the complainant shall be so informed.

6. Where, in the absence of any complaint, a Member State is in possession of sufficient evidence both of unfair pricing practices and of injury resulting therefrom for Community shipowners, it shall immediately communicate such evidence to the Commission.

Article 6. Consultations

1. Any consultations provided for in this Regulation shall take place within an Advisory Committee, which shall consist of representatives of each Member State, with a representative of the Commission as Chairman. Consultations shall be held immediately on request by a Member State or on the initiative of the Commission.

2. The Committee shall meet when convened by its Chairman. He shall provide the Member States, as promptly as possible, with all relevant information.

3. Where necessary, consultation may be in writing only; in such case the Commission shall notify the Member States and shall specify a period within which they shall be entitled to express their opinions or to request an oral consultation.

4. Consultation shall in particular cover:

(a) the existence of unfair pricing practices and the amount thereof;
(b) the existence and extent of injury;
(c) the causal link between the unfair pricing practices and injury;
(d) the measures which, in the circumstances, are appropriate to prevent or remedy the injury caused by unfair pricing practices and the ways and means for putting such measures into effect.

Article 7. Initiation and subsequent investigation

1. Where, after consultation, it is apparent that there is sufficient evidence to justify initiating a proceeding the Commission shall immediately:

(a) announce the initiation of a proceeding in the *Official Journal of the European Communities*; such announcements shall indicate the foreign shipowner concerned and his country of origin, give a summary of the information received, and provide that all relevant information is to be communicated to the Commission; it shall state the period within which interested parties may make known their views in writing and may apply to be heard orally by the Commission in accordance with paragraph 5;
(b) so advise the shipowners, shippers and freight forwarders known to the Commission to be concerned and the complainants;
(c) commence the investigation at Community level, acting in cooperation with the Member States; such investigation shall cover both unfair pricing practices and injury resulting therefrom and shall be carried out in accordance with paragraphs 2 to 8; the investigation of unfair pricing practices shall normally cover a period of not less than six months immediately prior to the initiation of the proceeding.

2. (a) Where appropriate the Commission shall seek all the information it deems necessary and attempt to check this information with the shipowners, agents, shippers, freight forwarders, conferences, associations and other organizations, provided that the undertakings or organizations concerned give their consent.

(b) Where necessary the Commission shall, after consultation, carry out investigations in third countries, provided that the firms concerned give their consent and the government of the country in question has been officially notified and raises no objection. The Commission shall be assisted by officials of those Member States which so request.

3. (a) The Commission may request Member States:

— to supply information,
— to carry out all necessary checks and inspections, particularly amongst shippers, freight forwarders, Community shipowners and their agents,
— to carry out investigations in third countries, provided the firms concerned give their consent and the government of the country in question has been officially notified and raises no objection.

(b) Member States shall take whatever steps are necessary in order to give effect to requests from the Commission. They shall send to the Commission the information requested together with the results of all inspections, checks or investigations carried out.

(c) Where this information is of general interest or where its transmission has been requested by a Member State, the Commission shall forward it to the Member States provided it is not confidential, in which case a non-confidential summary shall be forwarded.

(d) Officials of the Commission shall be authorized, if the Commission or a Member State so requests, to assist the officials of Member States in carrying out their duties.

4. (a) The complainant and the shippers and shipowners known to be concerned may inspect all information made available to the Commission by any party to an investigation as distinct from internal documents prepared by the authorities of the Community or its Member States provided that it is relevant to the defence of their interests and not confidential within the meaning of Article 8 and that it is used by the Commission in the investigation. To this end, they shall address a written request to the Commission, indicating the information required.

(b) Shipowners subject to investigation and the complainant may request to be informed of the essential facts and considerations on the basis of which it is intended to recommend the imposition of redressive duties.

(c) (i) Requests for information pursuant to (b) shall:

— be addressed to the Commission in writing,
— specify the particular issues on which information is sought.

(ii) The information may be given either orally or in writing, as considered appropriate by the Commission. It shall not prejudice any subsequent decision which may be taken by the Council. Confidential information shall be treated in accordance with Article 8.

(iii) Information shall normally be given no later than 15 days prior to the submission by the Commission of any proposal for action pursuant to Article 11. Representations made after the information is given may be taken into consideration only if received within a period to be set by the Commission in each case, which shall be at least 10 days, due consideration being given to the urgency of the matter.

5. The Commission may hear the interested parties. It shall so hear them if they have, within the periods prescribed in the notice published in the *Official Journal of the European Communities*, made a written request for a hearing showing that they are an interested party likely to be affected by the result of the proceeding and that there are particular reasons why they should be given a hearing.

6. Furthermore, the Commission shall, on request, give the parties directly concerned an opportunity to meet, so that opposing views may be presented and any argument put forward by way of rebuttal. In providing this opportunity the Commission shall take account of the need to preserve confidentiality and of the convenience of the parties. There shall be no obligation on any part to attend a meeting and failure to do so shall not be prejudicial to that party's case.

7. (a) This Article shall not preclude the Council from reaching preliminary determinations or from applying measures expeditiously.

(b) In cases in which any interested party refuses access to, or otherwise does not provide, necessary information within a reasonable period, or significantly impedes the investigation, findings, affirmative or negative, may be made on the basis of the facts available.

8. Proceedings on unfair pricing practices shall not constitute a bar to customs clearance of the goods to which the freight rates concerned apply.

9. (a) An investigation shall be concluded either by its termination or by action pursuant to Article 11. Conclusion should normally take place within one year of the initiation of the proceeding.

(b) A proceeding shall be concluded either by the termination of the investigation without the imposition of duties and without the acceptance of undertakings or by the expiry or repeal of such duties or by the lapse of undertakings in accordance with Articles 14 or 15.

Article 8. Confidentiality

1. Information received in pursuance of this Regulation shall be used only for the purpose for which it was requested.

2. (a) Neither the Council, nor the Commission, nor Member States, nor the officials of any of these, shall reveal any information received in pursuance of this Regulation of which confidential treatment has been requested by its supplier, without specific permission from the supplier.

(b) Each request for confidential treatment shall indicate why the information is confidential and shall be accompanied by a non-confidential summary of the information, or a statement of the reasons why the information is not susceptible of such summary.

3. Information will ordinarily be considered to be confidential if its disclosure is likely to have a significantly adverse effect upon the supplier or the source of such information.

4. However, if it appears that a request for confidentiality is not warranted and if the supplier is either unwilling to make the information public or to authorize its disclosure in generalized or summary form, the information in question may be disregarded.

The information may also be disregarded where such request is warranted and where the supplier is unwilling to submit a non-confidential summary, provided that the information is susceptible of such summary.

5. This Article shall not preclude the disclosure of general information by the Community authorities and in particular of the reasons on which decisions taken in pursuance of this Regulation are based, or disclosure of the evidence relied on by the Community authorities insofar as necessary to explain those reasons in court proceedings. Such disclosure must take into

account the legitimate interest of the parties concerned that their business secrets should not be divulged.

Article 9. Termination of proceedings where protective measures are unnecessary

1. If it becomes apparent after consultation that protective measures are unnecessary, then, where no objection is raised within the Advisory Committee referred to in Article 6 (1), the proceeding shall be terminated. In all other cases the Commission shall submit to the Council forthwith a report on the results of the consultation, together with a proposal that the proceeding be terminated. The proceeding shall stand terminated if, within one month, the Council, acting by a qualified majority, has not decided otherwise.

2. The Commission shall inform the parties known to be concerned and shall announce the termination in the *Official Journal of the European Communities* setting forth its basic conclusions and a summary or the reasons therefor.

Article 10. Undertakings

1. Where, during the course of investigation, undertakings are offered which the Commission, after consultation, considers acceptable, the investigation may be terminated without the imposition of redressive duties.

Save in exceptional circumstances, undertakings may not be offered later than the end of the period during which representations may be made under Article 7 (4) (c) (iii). The termination shall be decided in conformity with the procedure laid down in Article 9 (1) and information shall be given and notice published in accordance with Article 9 (2).

2. The undertakings referred to under paragraph 1 are those under which rates are revised to an extent such that the Commission is satisfied that the unfair pricing practice, or the injurious effects thereof, are eliminated.

3. Undertakings may be suggested by the Commission, but the fact that such undertakings are not offered or an invitation to do so is not accepted, shall not prejudice consideration of the case. However, the continuation of unfair pricing practices may be taken as evidence that a threat of injury is more likely to be realized.

4. If the undertakings are accepted, the investigation of injury shall nevertheless be completed if the Commission, after consultation, so decides or if request is made by the Community shipowners concerned. In such a case, if the Commission, after consultation, makes a determination of no injury, the undertaking shall automatically lapse. However, where a determination of no threat of injury is due mainly to the existence of an undertaking, the Commission may require that the undertaking be maintained.

5. The Commission may require any party from whom an undertaking has been accepted to provide periodically information relevant to the fulfilment of such undertakings, and to permit verification of pertinent data. Non-compliance with such requirements shall be construed as a violation of the undertaking.

Article 11. Redressive duties

Where investigation shows that there is an unfair pricing practice, that injury is caused by it and that the interests of the Community make Community intervention necessary, the Commission shall propose to the Council, after the consultations provided for in Article 6, that it introduce a redressive duty. The Council, acting by a qualified majority, shall take a Decision within two months.

Article 12

In deciding on the redressive duties, the Council shall also take due account of the external trade policy considerations as well as the port interests and the shipping policy considerations of the Member States concerned.

Article 13. General provisions on duties

1. Redressive duties shall be imposed on the foreign shipowners concerned by regulation.

2. Such regulation shall indicate in particular the amount and type of duty imposed, the commodity or commodities transported, the name and the country of origin of the foreign shipowner concerned and the reasons on which the Regulation is based.

3. The amount of the duties shall not exceed the difference between the freight rate charged and the normal freight rate referred to in Article 3 (c). It shall be less if such lesser duty would be adequate to remove the injury.

4. (a) Duties shall be neither imposed nor increased with retroactive effect and shall apply to the transport of commodities which, after entry into force of such duties, are loaded or discharged in a Community port.

(b) However, where the Council determines that an undertaking has been violated or withdrawn, the redressive duties may be imposed, on a proposal from the Commission, on the transport of commodities which were loaded or discharged in a Community port not more than 90 days prior to the date of application of these duties, except that in the case of violation or withdrawal of an undertaking such retroactive assessment shall not apply to the transport of commodities which were loaded or discharged in a Community port before the violation or withdrawal. These duties may be calculated on the basis of the facts established before the acceptance of the undertaking.

5. Duties shall be collected by Member States in the form, at the rate and according to the other criteria laid down when the duties were imposed, and independently of the customs duties, taxes and other charges normally imposed on imports of goods transported.

6. Permission to load or discharge cargo in a Community port may be made conditional upon the provision of security for the amount of the duties.

Article 14. Review

1. Regulations imposing redressive duties and decisions to accept undertakings shall be subject to review, in whole or in part, where warranted. Such review may be held either at the request of a Member State or on the initiative of the Commission. A review shall also be held where an interested party so requests and submits evidence of changed circumstances sufficient to justify the need for such review, provided that at least one year has elapsed since the conclusion of the investigation. Such requests shall be addressed to the Commission, which shall inform the Member States.

2. Where, after consultation, it becomes apparent that review is warranted, the investigation shall be re-opened in accordance with Article 7, where the circumstances so require. Such reopening shall not *per se* affect the measures in operation.

3. Where warranted by the review, carried out either with or without reopening of the investigation, the measures shall be amended, repealed or annulled by the Community institution competent for their adoption.

Article 15

1. Subject to paragraph 2, redressive duties and undertakings shall lapse after five years from the date on which they entered into force or were last amended or confirmed.

2. The Commission shall normally, after consultation and within six months prior to the expiry of the five year period, publish in the *Official Journal of the European Communities* a notice of the impending expiry of the measure in question and inform Community shipowners known to be concerned. This notice shall state the period within which interested parties may make known their views in writing and may apply to be given a hearing by the Commission in accordance with Article 7 (5).

Where an interested party shows that the expiry of the measure would again lead to injury or threat of injury, the Commission shall carry out a review of the measure. The measure shall remain in force pending the outcome of this review.

Where redressive duties and undertakings lapse under this Article the Commission shall publish a notice to that effect in the *Official Journal of the European Communities*.

Article 16. Refund

1. Where the shipowner concerned can show that the duty collected exceeds the difference between the freight rate charged and the normal freight rate referred to in Article 3 (c) the excess amount shall be reimbursed.

2. In order to request the reimbursement referred to in paragraph 1, the foreign shipowner may submit an application to the Commission. The application shall be submitted via the member State within the territory of which the commodities transported were loaded or discharged and within three months of the date on which the amount of the redressive duties to be levied was duly determined by the competent authorities.

The Member State shall forward the application to the Commission as soon as possible, either with or without an opinion as to its merits.

The Commission shall inform the other Member States forthwith and give its opinion on the matter. If the Member States agree with the opinion given by the Commission or do not object to it within one month of being informed, the Commission may decide in accordance with the said opinion. In all other cases, the Commission shall, after consultation, decide whether and to what extent the application should be granted.

Article 17. Final provisions

This Regulation shall not preclude the application of any special rules laid down in agreements concluded between the Community and third countries.

Article 18. Entry into force

This Regulation shall enter into force on 1 July 1987.

This Regulation shall be binding in its entirety and directly applicable in all Member States.

Done at Brussels, 22 December 1986.

For the Council
The President
G. SHAW

24. COUNCIL REGULATION (EEC) No 4058/86 OF 22 DECEMBER 1986 CONCERNING COORDINATED ACTION TO SAFEGUARD FREE ACCESS TO CARGOES IN OCEAN TRADES

THE COUNCIL OF THE EUROPEAN COMMUNITIES,

Having regard to the Treaty establishing the European Economic Community, and in particular Article 84 (2) thereof,

Having regard to the draft Regulation submitted by the Commission,

Having regard to the opinion of the European Parliament,[1]

Having regard to the opinion of the Economic and Social Committee,[2]

Whereas an increasing number of countries resort to protecting their merchant fleets either unilaterally, through legislation or administrative measures, or through bilateral agreements with other countries;

Whereas certain countries, by virtue of measures they have adopted or practices they have imposed, have distorted the application of the principle of fair and free competition in shipping trade with one or more Community Member States;

Whereas in respect of liner trades the United Nations Convention on a Code of Conduct for Liner Conferences, which entered into force on 6 October 1983, grants certain rights to shipping companies which are members of a conference operating a pool;

Whereas, increasingly, third countries which are contracting parties or signatories to that Convention interpret its provisions in such a way as effectively to expand the rights given under the Convention to their companies both in liner and tramp trades, to the disadvantage of Community companies or companies of other OECD countries, whether conference members or not;

Whereas in respect of bulk trades there is an increasing tendency on the part of third countries to restrict access to bulk cargoes, which poses a serious threat to the freely competitive environment broadly prevailing in the bulk trades; whereas the Member States affirm their commitment to a freely competitive environment as being an essential feature of the dry and liquid bulk trades and are convinced that the introduction of cargo-sharing in these trades will have a serious effect on the trading interests of all countries by substantially increasing transportation costs;

Whereas the restriction of access to bulk cargoes would adversely affect the merchant fleets of the Member States, as well as substantially increasing the transportation costs of such cargoes, and would thereby have a serious effect on the trading interests of the Community;

Whereas the Community should be enabled to provide for coordinated action by Member States if the competitive position of Member States' merchant fleets or Member States' trading interests are adversely affected by cargo reservation to shipping companies of third countries or if required by an international agreement;

Whereas Council Decision 77/587/EEC[3] provides, *inter alia*, for consultation on the various aspects of developments which have taken place in relations between Member States and third countries in shipping matters;

Whereas Council Decision 83/573/EEC[4] provides, *inter alia*, for concertation by Member States of any countermeasures they may take in relation to third countries and for the possibility of a decision on the joint application by Member States of appropriate countermeasures forming part of their national legislation;

Whereas it is necessary to elaborate and refine the machinery provided for in these Decisions with a view to providing for coordinated action by Member States in certain circumstances at the request of a Member State or Member States or on the basis of an international agreement,

HAS ADOPTED THIS REGULATION:

1. OJ No. C 255, 15 October 1986, p. 169.
2. OJ No. C 344, 31 December 1985, p. 31.
3. OJ No. L 239, 17 October 1977, p. 23.
4. OJ No. L 332, 28 November 1983, p. 37.

Article 1

The procedure provided for by this Regulation shall be applicable when action by a third country or by its agents restricts or threatens to restrict free access by shipping companies of Member States or by ships registered in a Member State in accordance with its legislation to the transport of:

— liner cargoes in Code trades, except where such action is taken in accordance with the United Nations Convention on a Code of Conduct for Liner Conferences;
— liner cargoes in non-Code trades;
— bulk cargoes and any other cargo on tramp services;
— passengers;
— persons or goods to or between offshore installations.

This procedure shall be without prejudice to the obligations of the Community and its Member States under international law.

Article 2

For the purposes of this Regulation:

— 'home-trader' means a shipping company of a third country which operates a service between its own country and one or more Member States;
— 'cross-trader' means a shipping company of a third country which operates a service between another third country and one or more Member States.

Article 3

Coordinated action may be requested by a Member State.

The request shall be made to the Commission; the latter shall make the appropriate recommendations or proposals to the Council within four weeks.

The Council, acting in accordance with the voting procedure laid down in Article 84 (2) or the Treaty, may decide on the coordinated action provided for in Article 4.

In deciding on coordinated action, the Council shall also take due account of the external trade policy considerations as well as the port interests and the shipping policy considerations of the Member States concerned.

Article 4

1. Coordinated action may consist of:

(a) diplomatic representation to the third countries concerned, in particular where their actions threaten to restrict access to trade;

(b) counter-measures directed at the shipping company or companies of the third countries concerned or at the shipping company or companies of other countries which benefit from the action taken by the countries concerned, whether operating as a hometrader or as a cross-trader in Community trades.

Those countermeasures may consist, separately or in combination, of:

(i) the imposition of an obligation to obtain a permit to load, carry or discharge cargoes; such a permit may be subject to conditions or obligations;

(ii) the imposition of a quota;

(iii) the imposition of taxes or duties.

2. Diplomatic representations shall be made before countermeasures are taken.

Such countermeasures shall be without prejudice to the obligations of the European Community and its Member States under international law, shall take into consideration all the interests concerned and shall neither directly nor indirectly lead to deflection of trade within the Community.

Article 5

1. When deciding upon one or more of the countermeasures referred to in Article 4 (1) (b) the Council shall specify, as appropriate, the following:

(a) the developments which have caused countermeasures to be taken;
(b) the trade or range of ports to which the countermeasures are to apply;
(c) the flag or shipping company of the hird country whose cargo reservation measures restrict free access to cargoes in the shipping area concerned;
(d) maximum volume (percentage, weight in tonnes, containers) or value of cargo which may be loaded or discharged in ports of Member States;
(e) maximum number of sailings from and to ports of Member States;
(f) amount or percentage and basis of the taxes and duties to be levied and the manner in which they will be collected;
(g) the duration of the countermeasures.

2. Where the countermeasures envisaged by paragraph 1 are not provided for by the national legislation of a Member State they may be taken in accordance with the Council Decision referred to in the third paragraph of Article 3 by the Member State concerned on the basis of this Regulation.

Article 6

1. If the Council has not adopted the proposal on coordinated action within a period of two months, Member States may apply national measures unilaterally or as a group, if the situation so requires.

2. However, Member States may, in cases of urgency, take the necessary national measures on a provisional basis, unilaterally or as a group, even within the two-month period referred to in paragraph 1.

3. National measures taken in pursuance of this Article shall be notified immediately to the Commission and to the other Member States.

Article 7

During the period in which the countermeasures are to apply, the Member States and the Commission shall consult each other in accordance with the consultation procedure established by Decision 77/587/EEC every three months or earlier if the need arises, in order to discuss the effects of the countermeasures in force.

Article 8

The procedure provided for by this Regulation may be applied when action by a third country or its agents restricts or threatens to restrict the access of shipping companies of another OECD country where, on a basis of reciprocity, it has been agreed between that country and the Community to resort to coordinated resistance in the case of restriction of access to cargoes.

Such country may make a request for coordinated action and join in such coordinated action in accordance with this Regulation.

Article 9

This Regulation shall enter into force on 1 July 1987.

This Regulation shall be binding in its entirety and directly applicable in all Member States.

Done at Brussels, 22 December 1986.

For the Council
The President
G. SHAW

25. REGULATION No 4260/88 OF 16 DECEMBER 1988[1] ON THE COMMUNICATIONS, COMPLAINTS AND APPLICATIONS AND THE HEARINGS PROVIDED FOR IN COUNCIL REGULATION No 4056/86 LAYING DOWN DETAILED RULES FOR THE APPLICATION OF ARTICLES 85 AND 86 OF THE TREATY TO MARITIME TRANSPORT

THE COMMISSION OF THE EUROPEAN COMMUNITIES,

Having regard to the Treaty establishing the European Economic Community,

Having regard to Council Regulation No. 4056/86 of 22 December 1986 laying down detailed rules for the application of Articles 85 and 86 of the Treaty to maritime transport (O.J. 1986 L378/4), and in particular Articles 26 thereof,

Having regard to the opinion of the Advisory Committee on Agreements and Dominant Positions in the field of Maritime Transport,

Whereas, pursuant to Article 26 of Regulation No. 4056/86, the Commission is empowered to adopt implementing provisions concerning the scope of the obligation of communication pursuant to Article 5 (5), the form, content and other details of complaints pursuant to Article 10 and of applications pursuant to Article 12 and the hearings provided for in Article 23 (1) and (2) of that Regulation;

Whereas the obligation of communication to the Commission of awards at arbitration and recommendations by conciliators provided for in Article 5 (5) of Regulation No. 4056/86 concerns the settlement of disputes relating to the practices of conferences referred to in Articles 4 and 5 (2) and (3) of that Regulation; whereas it seems appropriate to make the procedure for this notification as simple as possible; whereas it is appropriate, therefore, to provide for notifications to be made in writing, attaching the documents containing the text of the awards and recommendations concerned;

Whereas complaints pursuant to Article 10 of Regulation No. 4056/86 may make it easier for the Commission to take action for infringement of Articles 85 and 86 of the EEC Treaty in the field of maritime transport; whereas it could consequently seem appropriate to make the procedure for submitting complaints as simple as possible; whereas it is appropriate, therefore, to provide for complaints to be submitted in one written copy, the form, content and details being left to the discretion of the complainants;

Whereas the submission of the applications pursuant to Article 12 of Regulation No. 4056/86 may have important legal consequences for each undertaking which is a party to an agreement, decision or concerted practice; whereas each undertaking should, therefore, have the right to submit such applications to the Commission; whereas, on the other hand, if an undertaking makes use of that right, it must so inform the other undertakings which are parties to the agreement, decision or concerted practice, in order that they may protect their interests;

Whereas it is for the undertakings and associations of undertakings to inform the Commission of the facts and circumstances in support of the applications submitted in accordance with Article 12 of Regulation No. 4056/86;

Whereas it is desirable to prescribe that forms be used for applications in order, in the interest of all concerned, to simplify and expedite examination thereof by the competent departments;

Whereas in most cases the Commission will in the course of the procedure for the hearings provided for in Article 23 (1) and (2) of Regulation No. 4056/86 already be in close touch with the participating undertakings or associations of undertakings and they will accordingly have the opportunity of making known their views regarding the objections raised against them;

Whereas in accordance with Article 23 (1) and (2) of Regulation No. 4056/86 and with the rights of the defence, the undertakings and associations of undertakings concerned must have the right on conclusion of the procedure to submit their comments on the whole of the objections raised against them which the Commission proposes to deal with in its decisions;

Whereas persons other than the undertakings or associations of undertakings which are involved in the procedure may have an interest in being heard; whereas, pursuant to the second sentence of Article 23 (2) of Regulation No. 4056/86, such persons should have the opportunity of being heard if they apply and show that they have a sufficient interest;

1. OJ No. L 376/1, 1988.

Whereas it is desirable to enable persons who pursuant to Article 10 of Regulation No. 4056/86 have lodged a complaint to submit their comments where the Commission considers that on the basis of the information in its possession there are insufficient grounds for action;

Whereas the various persons entitled to submit comments must do so in writing, both in their own interest and in the interests of good administration, without prejudice to an oral procedure where appropriate to supplement the written procedure;

Whereas it is necessary to define the rights of persons who are to be heard, and in particular the conditions upon which they may be represented or assisted and the setting and calculation of time limits;

Whereas the Advisory Committee on Restrictive Practices and Dominant Positions in Maritime Transport delivers its opinion on the basis of a preliminary draft Decision; whereas it must therefore be consulted concerning a case after the inquiry in that case has been completed; whereas such consultation does not prevent the Commission from re-opening an inquiry if need be,

HAS ADOPTED THIS REGULATION:

SECTION I—NOTIFICATIONS, COMPLAINTS AND APPLICATIONS

Article 1. Notifications

1. Awards at arbitration and recommendations by conciliators accepted by the parties shall be notified to the Commission when they concern the settlement of disputes relating to the practices of conferences referred to in Articles 4 and 5 (2) and (3) of Regulation No. 4056/86.

2. The obligation of notification applies to any party to the dispute resolved by the award or recommendation.

3. Notifications shall be submitted forthwith by registered letter with an acknowledgement of receipt or shall be delivered by hand against receipt. They shall be written in one of the official languages of the Community.

Supporting documents shall be either originals or copies. Copies must be certified as true copies of the original. They shall be submitted in their original language. Where the original language is not one of the official languages of the Community, a translation in one of the official languages shall be attached.

4. When representatives of undertakings, of associations of undertakings, or of natural or legal persons sign such notifications, they shall produce written proof that they are authorised to act.

Article 2. Complaints

1. Complaints pursuant to Article 10 of Regulation No. 4056/86 shall be submitted in writing in one of the official languages of the Community, their form, content and other details being left to the discretion of complainants.

2. Complaints may be submitted by:

(a) Member States

(b) natural or legal persons who claim a legitimate interest.

3. When representatives of undertakings, of associations of undertakings, or of natural or legal persons sign such complaints, they shall produce written proof that they are authorised to act.

Article 3. Persons entitled to submit applications

1. Any undertaking which is party to agreements, decisions or practices of the kind described in Article 85 (1) of the Treaty may submit an application under Article 12 of Regulation No. 4056/86. Where the application is submitted by some but not all of the undertakings concerned, they shall give notice to the others.

2. Where applications under Article 12 of Regulation No. 4056/86 are signed by representatives of undertakings, of associations of undertakings, or of natural or legal persons, such representatives shall produce written proof that they are authorised to act.

3. Where a joint application is submitted, a joint representative shall be appointed.

Article 4. Submission of applications

1. Applications pursuant to Article 12 of Regulation No. 4056/86 shall be submitted on Form MAR shown in Annex I.
2. Several participating undertakings may submit an application on a single form.
3. Applications shall contain the information requested in the form.
4. Fourteen copies of each application and of the supporting documents shall be submitted to the Commission.
5. The supporting documents shall be either originals or copies. Copies must be certified as true copies of the original.
6. Applications shall be in one of the official languages of the Community. Supporting documents shall be submitted in their original language. Where the original language is not one of the official languages, a translation in one of the official languages shall be attached.
7. The date of submission of an application shall be the date on which it is received by the Commission. Where however, the application is sent by registered post, it shall be deemed to have been received on the date shown on the postmark of the place of posting.
8. Where an application submitted pursuant to Article 12 of Regulation No. 4056/86 falls outside the scope of that Regulation, the Commission shall without delay inform the applicant that it intends to examine the application under the provisions of such other Regulation as is applicable to the case; however, the date of submission of the application shall be the date resulting from paragraph 7. The Commission shall inform the applicant of its reasons and fix a period for him to submit any comments in writing before it conducts its appraisal pursuant to the provisions of that other Regulation.

SECTION II—HEARINGS

Article 5. Hearing to be held

Before consulting the Advisory Committee on Agreements and Dominant Positions in the field of Maritime Transport, the Commission shall hold a hearing pursuant to Article 23 (1) of Regulation No. 4056/86.

Article 6. Notice of Commission's objections

1. The Commission shall inform undertakings and associations of undertakings in writing of the objections raised against them. The communication shall be addressed to each of them or to a joint agent appointed by them.
2. The Commission may inform the parties by giving notice in the *Official Journal of the European Communities* if from the circumstances of the case this appears appropriate, in particular where notice is to be given to a number of undertakings but no joint agent has been appointed. The notice shall have regard to the legitimate interest of the undertakings in the protection of their business secrets.
3. A fine or a periodic penalty payment may be imposed on an undertaking or association of undertakings only if the objections were notified in the manner provided for in paragraph 1.
4. The Commission shall, when giving notice of objections, fix a period within which the undertakings and associations of undertakings may inform the Commission of their views.

Article 7. Written comments of parties

1. Undertakings and associations of undertakings shall, within the appointed period, make known in writing their views concerning the objections raised against them.
2. They may in their written comments set out all matters relevant to their defence.
3. They may attach any relevant documents in proof of the facts set out. They may also propose that the Commission hear persons who may corroborate those facts.

Article 8. Decisions limited to matters to which views expressed

The Commission shall in its Decision deal only with those objections raised against undertakings and associations of undertakings in respect of which they have been afforded the opportunity of making known their views.

Article 9. Comments of third parties

If natural or legal persons showing a sufficient interest apply to be heard pursuant to Article 23 (2) of Regulation No. 4056/86 the Commission shall afford them the opportunity of making known their views in writing within such period as it shall fix.

Article 10. No action on complaint

Where the Commission, having received a complaint pursuant to Article 10 of Regulation No. 4056/86, considers that on the basis of the information in its possession there are insufficient grounds for acting on the complaint, it shall inform the persons who submitted the complaint of its reasons and fix a period for them to submit any further comments in writing.

Article 11. Opportunity for oral argument

1. The Commission shall afford to persons who have so requested in their written comments the opportunity to put forward their arguments orally, if those persons show a sufficient interest or if the Commission proposes to impose on them a fine or periodic penalty payment.
2. The Commission may likewise afford to any other person the opportunity of orally expressing his views.

Article 12. Summoning of persons to be heard

1. The Commission shall summon the persons to be heard to attend on such date as it shall appoint.
2. It shall forthwith transmit a copy of the summons to the competent authorities of the Member States, who may appoint an official to take part in the hearing.

Article 13. Conduct of hearings

1. Hearings shall be conducted by the persons appointed by the Commission for that purpose.
2. Persons summoned to attend shall either appear in person or be represented by legal representatives or by representatives authorised by their constitution. Undertakings and associations of undertakings may, moreover, be represented by a duly authorised agent appointed from among their permanent staff.

Persons heard by the Commission may be assisted by lawyers or university teachers who are entitled to plead before the Court of Justice of the European Communities in accordance with Article 17 of the Protocol on the Statute of the Court, or by other qualified persons.

3. Hearings shall not be public. Persons shall be heard separately or in the presence of other persons summoned to attend. In the latter case, regard shall be had to the legitimate interest of the undertakings in the protection of their business secrets.
4. The essential content of the statements made by each person heard shall be recorded in minutes which shall be read and approved by him.

Article 14. Sending of information and summonses

Without prejudice to Article 6 (2), information and summonses from the Commission shall be sent to the addressees by registered letter with acknowledgement of receipt, or shall be delivered by hand against receipt.

Article 15. Time limits

1. In fixing the periods provided for in Articles 4 (8), 6, 9 and 10, the Commission shall have regard both to the time required for preparation of comments and to the urgency of the case. A period shall be not less than two weeks; it may be extended.

2. Periods shall run from the day following receipt of a communication or delivery thereof by hand.

3. Written comments must reach the Commission or be dispatched by registered letter before expiry of the period. Where the period would expire on a Sunday or a public holiday, it shall be extended up to the end of the next following working day. For the purpose of calculating the extension, public holidays shall, in cases where the relevant date is the date of receipt of written comments, be those set out in Annex II to this Regulation, and in cases where the relevant date is the date of dispatch, those appointed by law in the country of dispatch.

Article 16. Effective date

This Regulation shall enter into force on the day following its publication in the *Official Journal of the European Communities*.

This Regulation shall be binding in its entirety and directly applicable in all Member States.

ANNEX I

This form must be accompanied by an annex containing the information specified in the attached Complementary Note.
The form and annex must be supplied in fourteen copies (two for the Commission and one for each Member State). Supply three copies of any relevant agreement and one copy of other supporting documents.

FORM MAR

Please do not forget to complete the Acknowledgement of Receipt annexed.
If space is insufficient, please use extra pages, specifying to which item on the form they relate.

TO THE COMMISSION OF THE EUROPEAN COMMUNITIES

Directorate-General for Competition
200, rue de la Loi
B-1049 Brussels
Application under Article 12 of Council Regulation No 4056/86 of 22 December 1986 with a view to obtaining a decision under Article 85(3) of the Treaty establishing the European Economic Community.

Identity of the parties

1. *Identity of applicant*

Full name and address, telephone, telex and facsimile numbers, and brief description of the undertaking(s) or association(s) of undertakings submitting the application.

For partnerships, sole traders or any other unincorporated body trading under a business name, give, also, the name, forename(s) and address of the proprietor(s) or partner(s).

Where an application is submitted on behalf of some other person (or is submitted by more than one person) the name, address and position of the representative (or joint representative) must be given, together with proof of his authority to act. Where an application or notification is submitted by or on behalf of more than one person they should appoint a joint representative. (Article 3 (2) and (3) of Commission Regulation No 4260).

2. *Identity of any other parties*

Full name and address and brief description of any other parties to the agreement, decision or concerted practice (hereinafter referred to as 'the arrangements').

State what steps have been taken to inform these other parties of this application.

(This information is not necessary in respect of standard contracts which an undertaking submitting the application has concluded or intends to conclude with a number of parties.)

Purpose of this application
(see Complementary Note)

(Please answer yes or no to the question)

Would you be satisfied with a comfort letter? (See the end of Section VII of the Complementary Note.)

The undersigned declare that the information given above and in the . . . pages annexed hereto is correct to the best of their knowledge and belief, that all estimates are identified as such and are their best estimates of the underlying facts and that all the opinions expressed are sincere. They are aware of the provisions of Article 19 (1) (a) of Regulation (EEC) No 4056/86 (see attached Complementary Note).

Place and date . . . .

Signatures: . . . .
. . . .
. . . .

COMMISSION
OF THE
EUROPEAN COMMUNITIES

Directorate-General for Competition

Brussels . . . .

To

ACKNOWLEDGEMENT OF RECEIPT

(This form will be returned to the address inserted above if the top half is completed in a single copy by the person lodging it)

Your application dated: . . . .
. . . .

concerning: . . . .

Your reference: . . . .

Parties:

1. . . . .
2. . . . . and others

(There is no need to name the other undertakings party to the arrangement)

(To be completed by the Commission.)

was received on: . . . .

and registered under No IV/MAR/ . . . .

Please quote the above number in all correspondence

Provisional address:
200, rue de la Loi
B-1049 Brussels

Telephone:
Direct line: 235 . . . .

Telephone exchange: 235 11 11

Telex:
COMEU B 21877

Telegraphic address:
COMEUR Brussels

ANNEX II. LIST OF PUBLIC HOLIDAYS

New Year	1 Jan
Good Friday	
Easter Saturday	
Easter Monday	
Labour Day	1 May
Schuman Plan Day	9 May
Ascension Day	
Whit Monday	
Belgian National Day	21 July
Assumption	15 Aug
All Saints	1 Nov
All Souls	2 Nov
Christmas Eve	24 Dec
Christmas Day	25 Dec
The day following Christmas Day	26 Dec
New Year's Eve	31 Dec

26. PROPOSAL FOR A COUNCIL REGULATION ESTABLISHING A COMMUNITY SHIP REGISTER AND PROVIDING FOR THE FLYING OF THE COMMUNITY FLAG BY SEA-GOING VESSELS (COM(89) 266 FINAL) (SUBMITTED BY THE COMMISSION TO THE COUNCIL ON 2 AUGUST 1989) (89/C 263/02)

THE COUNCIL OF THE EUROPEAN COMMUNITIES,

Having regard to the Treaty establishing the European Economic Community, and in particular Article 84 (2) thereof,

Having regard to the proposal of the Commission,

Having regard to the opinion of the European Parliament,

Having regard to the opinion of the Economic and Social Committee,

Whereas shipping is an indispensable element in trade between the Member States and between Member States and third countries;

Whereas the availability of a high quality and truly competitive fleet depends, on the one hand, on the availability of a maritime infrastructure within the Community including a reserve of nationals of Member States to serve as seafarers and, on the other hand, a cost level which is competitive;

Whereas the fleet flying Member States' flags has suffered a considerable decline over the years and to the extent that ships have been transferred to third country registers, there has been a severe loss of employment for Community nationals;

Whereas the efforts to meet the problem through national measures, inter alia the establishment of second national registers, to which more favourable conditions are attached, tend to disperse the effects of the actions undertaken and risk a distortion of competition;

Whereas it is in the Community interest to aim at a structural development of a fleet of vessels, registered in Member States registers but also identifiable as ships serving Community needs, which comply with the standards of the maritime conventions, and whose crew includes as a minimum a specified number of trained seafarers from Member States;

Whereas this aim cannot be attained without a reduction of the cost level;

Whereas the Commission has developed guidelines for the examination of State aids to be given by the Member States to Community shipping companies;

Whereas the establishment of a Community ship register should serve the purpose of creating a channel through which national efforts can be converged, a pool of Community seafarers and a trade mark guaranteeing shippers a high quality service;

Whereas the Community ship register will be additional to the national register;

Whereas the right to register vessels in the Community register should be reserved for natural and legal persons having a certain link with the Community; whereas, however, this right should also be given under certain conditions to persons having a link with a given third country;

Whereas the vessel to be registered in the Community register should comply with certain conditions; whereas, in particular, the vessel should be and remain registered in a national register; whereas the decisions on the admission to the national register must be taken in compliance with the provisions of the Treaty;

Whereas registration in the Community register should depend on compliance with the safety measures required by the international conventions in this respect;

Whereas the number of trained seafarers from Member States on board of vessels registered in this register should be sufficient to meet future requirements of the Community fleet;

Whereas seafarers from non-Community countries on vessels registered in this register should be employed on conditions in conformity with internationally agreed standards, unless otherwise mutually agreed with their representative organisations;

Whereas all seafarers on vessels registered in this register should at least benefit from the social security schemes to which they are entitled in the country where they are resident;

Whereas vessels, while remaining on this register, should be able to transfer between the national registers of Member States without technical hindrance, when they comply with the essential technical requirements to be laid down by the Council;

Whereas the right of free movement under Article 48 of the Treaty as implemented by Council Regulation (EEC) No 1612/68[1] applies to employment of nationals of Member States on board

1. OJ No. L 257, 19 October 1968, p. 2.

vessels registered in the Member States; whereas therefore this right applies to vessels registered in EUROS; whereas, however, the effective exercise of that right may be hindered by differences between qualifications and licences issued in the Member States; whereas it is appropriate to provide for recognition of such qualifications and licences for seafarers for the purposes of employment on board vessels in the Community register subject to minimum requirements laid down by the Council;

Whereas registration in this register should be reflected in the right and obligation to fly the European flag;

Whereas the Commission should be enabled to adopt implementing provisions concerning the establishment of the register and concerning procedures of registration and deregistration;

Whereas there should be cooperation between the Community register and the national ship registers, including an exchange of information;

Whereas the Member States should take the necessary measures to control and enforce compliance with the provisions of this Regulation;

HAS ADOPTED THIS REGULATION

SECTION 1. SCOPE OF THE REGULATION

Article 1. Objective

This Regulation provides for:

— the establishment of a Community ship register for sea-going merchant vessels,
— the conditions for registration,
— certain facilities accruing from such registration,
— the right to fly the European flag on these vessels in addition to the national flag.

SECTION 2. THE REGISTER, VESSEL OWNERS AND VESSELS

Article 2. Establishment of the register

A Community ship register (hereafter called 'EUROS') is hereby established in which sea-going merchant vessels may be registered in addition to their national registration in a Member State.

The Commission shall register when the conditions laid down in Articles 3, 4 and 5 are met. It shall deregister a vessel when it no longer conforms to the provisions of this Regulation.

Article 3. Persons entitled to have a vessel registered in EUROS

1. The following may apply for registration of a vessel in EUROS:
   (a) nationals of the Member States established in a Member State and pursuing shipping activities;
   (b) a shipping company formed in accordance with the law of a Member State and having its principal place of business in, and effective control exercised within the Community, provided that the majority of the capital of that company is owned by nationals of the Member States or the majority of the board of the company consists of such nationals, who have their domicile or usual residence in the Community;
   (c) nationals of Member States established outside the Community or shipping companies established outside the Community and controlled by nationals of a Member State, if the vessels owned or operated by them are registered in that Member State in accordance with its legislation;

2. For the purpose of this regulation, a natural or legal person meant in paragraph 1 will hereafter be referred to as a 'Community vessel owner';

3. Where it has been agreed between a third country and the Community that registration of vessels in each other's register shall be permitted, the term 'nationals of the Member States' shall, for the purposes only of paragraph 1 (a) and (b), include nationals of the third country concerned.

Article 4. Vessels eligible for registration

Eligible for registration in EUROS is any sea-going merchant vessel of at least 500 grt, built or under construction, which is already registered in a Member State, and entitled to fly the flag of that Member State and used or to be used in national or international trade for the transport of cargo or passengers or any other commercial purpose, if it fulfils the following conditions:

(a) the vessel must be and remain registered in the national ship register for the duration of its registration in EUROS;

(b) the vessel must be owned and for the duration of its registration in EUROS remain owned by a person entitled to register a vessel in EUROS, or operated by a Community vessel owner on the basis of a bare-boat charter in accordance with the provisions of Article 5;

(c) the vessel shall not be more than 20 years old.

Article 5. Bare-boat charters

Vessels operated by Community vessel owners on the basis of a bare-boat charter may be registered in EUROS during the period of that charter if the following conditions are fulfilled:

1. the vessel is registered as a bare-boat chartered vessel in a national ship register of a Member State;
2. the laws of the vessel's initial flag country allow bare-boat registration in another country;
3. the consent of the owner of the vessel and of all mortgage creditors for the registration of the bare-boat is obtained; and
4. the bare-boat charter is duly recorded in the register of the vessel's initial flag country.

SECTION 3. SAFETY, MANNING AND CREW

Article 6. Safety

Throughout the period of registration the vessel must be provided with all certificates required by the Member State concerned.

Article 7. Nationality of crew

On vessels registered in EUROS all officers and at least half of the rest of the crew shall be nationals of a Member State.

Trainees do not count towards meeting the requirements above.

Article 8. Wages, working hours and further labour conditions

Wages, working hours and further labour conditions of seafarers, who are not nationals of a Member State, on board vessels registered in EUROS, shall be in accordance with the Wages of the International Labour Organization (ILO), Hours of Work and Manning (SeA) Recommendation (No 109), 1958, subject to any arrangement on collective wages agreed upon with organizations as referred to in Article 9.

Article 9. Collective wage agreements

1. If Community vessel owners who have registered the vessels which they own or operate in EUROS employ seafarers who are not nationals of a Member State such seafarers may be employed only on the basis of collective wage agreements concluded with trade unions or similar organizations of the country where they are resident.

2. No collective wage agreement may be concluded with a foreign trade union or similar organization on behalf of nationals of a third country if such trade union or organization does

not satisfy the conditions of ILO Convention No 87 concerning the freedom of association and protection of the right to organize.

3. The law of the Member State of registration of the vessel or, if explicitly referred to in the agreement, any other Member State, shall apply to such collective wage agreements. The courts of the Member State concerned shall be competent to hear and determine disputes arising out of such agreements.

Article 10. Social security

Without prejudice to Article 13 (2) (c) of Council Regulation (EEC) No 1408/71[2] and unless otherwise mutually agreed at the level of governments or social partners, social security for seafarers on board vessels registered in EUROS shall be the responsibility of the country in which the seafarer is resident unless the legislation of that country expressly provides otherwise, in which case the Member State of registration shall be responsible but in accordance with the legislation of the country of residence.

For the purpose of this provision residence means residence on shore and employment on board a vessel registered in a Member State shall not of itself, be considered as being residence in that State.

Article 11

Articles 8, 9 and 10 shall apply subject to any right conferred or obligations imposed by any other Community legislative act except where such act expressly provides otherwise.

SECTION 4. FACILITIES ATTACHED TO REGISTRATION IN EUROS

Article 12. Transfer of vessels

Any vessel registered in EUROS and having valid certificates and classification and meeting the essential technical requirements to be laid down by the Council according to the provisions of the Treaty before 1 July 1991, may be transferred to the register of another Member State without the imposition of additional technical requirements.

Article 13. Recognition of seafarers' qualifications

The qualifications and licences of seafarers who are nationals of a Member State shall be recognised by the competent authorities of each Member State for the purposes of employment on any vessel registered in EUROS, subject to minimum requirements for professional training and experience in the function concerned as required in Directives adopted or to be adopted by the Council, according to the provisions of the Treaty, before 1 July 1991.

SECTION 5. EUROPEAN FLAG, PORT OF REGISTRATION

Article 14. European flag

1. Vessels registered in EUROS are entitled and obliged to fly the European flag in addition to their national flag.

2. Upon registration a certificate conveying the right to fly the European flag will be delivered by the Commission to the applicant for registration.

2. OJ No. L 149, 5 July 1971, p. 2.

Article 15. Port of registration

A vessel registered in EUROS shall bear a relevant identification on its stern under the name of the port of registry in its national register.

SECTION 6. FINAL PROVISIONS

Article 16. Implementing measures

The Commission shall, within six months after the adoption of this regulation, adopt the necessary implementing measures concerning the establishment of EUROS, the procedures for registration and deregistration, the form and content of the documents concerned, including the certificate concerning the right to fly the European flag, the form of, and rules governing the flying of, the flag, and the identification of vessels on the register.

Article 17. Cooperation

1. National authorities and the Commission shall assist each other in applying this Regulation and in checking compliance therewith.

2. Within the framework of this mutual assistance they shall communicate to each other the necessary information with respect to registration and deregistration.

Article 18. Transitional period

1. Member States shall, within six months after the adoption of this Regulation and after consultation with the Commission, take the necessary measures to:

- organise effective controls to ensure compliance with the requirements laid down in Sections 2, 3 and 5,
- impose sanctions in case of non-compliance with those requirements,
- enable vessels registered in EUROS to exercise the right to fly the European flag.

2. Such measures shall make express reference to this Regulation.

3. Member States shall forthwith communicate to the Commission the measures adopted.

Article 19. Entry into force

This Regulation shall enter into force on 1 January 1991.

This Regulation shall be binding in its entirety and directly applicable in all Member States.

27. COMMISSION RECOMMENDATION ON IMPROVING THE EFFECTIVENESS OF PORT STATE CONTROL IN THE COMMUNITY (COM (89) 266 FINAL) (SUBMITTED BY THE COMMISSION TO THE COUNCIL ON 2 AUGUST 1989) (89/C 263/03)

THE COMMISSION OF THE EUROPEAN COMMUNITIES,

Having regard to the Treaty establishing the European Economic Community,

Whereas the safety of life at sea, acceptable standards of living and working conditions on board ships and the protection of the marine environment must be maintained and promoted;

Whereas the principal responsibility for the effective application of these standards as laid down in international instruments rests upon the relevant authorities of the State whose flag a ship is entitled to fly;

Whereas effective action in the form of Port State Control is, nevertheless, necessary to ensure proper application of these standards in order to reduce and prevent substandard shipping;

Whereas all the maritime nations of the European Economic Community are signatories of the Memorandum of Understanding on Port State Control;

Whereas it is essential that all international conventions under the Memorandum of Understanding are duly signed and ratified by all Member States;

Whereas correct application of the international conventions referred to in the Memorandum of Understanding on Port State Control requires uniform and effective checking by Member States who are signatories to the aforesaid Memorandum;

Whereas it is necessary to ensure that the target number of inspections on individual foreign merchant ships visiting the ports of signatories to the Memorandum is achieved in order to reduce and prevent substandard shipping and in order to avoid distortions of conditions of competition between ports within the Community;

Whereas for these purposes a full and uniform system of Port State Control should be in force throughout the Community;

HEREBY RECOMMENDS THE MEMBER STATES to take the following measures in pursuance of their obligations under the Memorandum of Understanding on Port State Control (MOU):

I. With regard to ratification of the International Conventions covered by the Memorandum of Understanding

1. those Member States, which have not yet ratified the International Conventions cited below, to do so forthwith:
   - the International Convention on Load Lines, 1966,
   - the International Convention for the Safety of Life at Sea, 1974, as amended by the Protocol of 1978,
   - the International Convention for the Prevention of Pollution from Ships, 1973, as modified by the Protocol of 1978,
   - the International Convention on Standards of Training, Certification and Watchkeeping for Seafarers, 1978,
   - the Convention on the International Regulations for Preventing Collisions at Sea, 1972,
   - the Merchant Shipping (Minimum Standards) Convention, 1976 [Convention of the [International Labour Organization (ILO) No 147];
2. those Member States which have not yet ratified the optional annexes to the International Convention for the Prevention of Pollution from Ships, 1973, as amended by the Protocol of 1978 [International Convention for the Prevention of Pollution from ships (MARPOL 73/78)], to do so forthwith.

II. With regard to the implementation of the International Conventions covered by the Memorandum of Understanding

Member States, which are signatories to the Memorandum of Understanding, to ensure that

1. a minimum annual total of 25% of the number of individual foreign merchant ships visiting their ports are inspected in accordance with the provisions of the Memorandum of Understanding;

2. the inspection procedures laid down in the Manual for Surveyors adopted by the Port State Control Committee are strictly applied;

3. adequate resources, both financial and manpower, are provided to ensure a full implementation of their obligations under the Memorandum of Understanding on Port State Control.

The Commission requests Member States to inform it within twelve months of the adoption of the Recommendation of the measures they have taken in this field.

28. COUNCIL RESOLUTION OF 19 JUNE 1990 ON THE PREVENTION OF ACCIDENTS CAUSING MARINE POLLUTION (90/C 206/01)

THE COUNCIL OF THE EUROPEAN COMMUNITIES,

Regretting the great damage to the marine ecosystem of the Community caused by the discharge of more than 100,000 tonnes of mineral oil as a result of the accidents which occurred in the last fortnight of 1989 involving the tankers 'Aragon', flying the Spanish flag, and 'Khark-V', flying the Iranian flag, in the Atlantic waters near the archipelagos of two Member States, as well as the accident involving the tanker 'Seawind Dos', of a similar nature;

Whereas this damage could give rise to calamitous consequences for fauna and flora and other natural resources of the area;

Whereas the said maritime accidents have aroused considerable public concern, threatening to undermine the legitimate use of the coasts for recreational purposes, with the resulting negative repercussions on the touristic resources of the Member States;

Recalling the enormous material and environmental damage caused in other regions of the Community by other accidents of this nature, some sadly notorious such as those involving the tankers 'Torrey Canyon' and 'Amoco Cadiz';

Concerned about the alarming frequency of this kind of maritime accident;

Considering that the world fleet of VLCC ships has aged and there is no prospect of its being renewed in the short term as well as the deterioration and lack of appropriate maintenance of a large number of VLCC tankers, and the additional factor of risky navigation in maritime zones in bad, and sometimes extreme, meteorological conditions, and on highly congested traffic routes;

Conscious of the fact that the most appropriate method of combating maritime disasters is to insist on prevention as far as possibilities will allow, bearing in mind that the most effective way of combating marine pollution is its prevention;

Conscious that the Community must be duly prepared to cope with this type of incident in Community waters and taking into account that the extent of the damage caused by pollution is directly related to the speed of response and the degree of coordination between the national and international services available;

Recognizing that the International Maritime Organization (IMO) represents the focal point for preventing and combating marine pollution at international level;

Recalling that the IMO has drawn up specific rules and provisions for preventing and combating marine pollution and that various countries, including all the Member States of the Community, agreed in Paris to carry out inspections on ships docking in their ports;

Having regard to the resolution of the European Parliament of 17 March 1989 on safety at sea, and the Commission recommendation on improving the effectiveness of port State control in the Community, which the Commission submitted to the Council on 2 August 1989,

HEREBY ADOPTS THE FOLLOWING RESOLUTION:

1. Member States will endeavour to provide themselves with an adequate and efficient maritime administration which is capable of ensuring strict compliance with the technical rules on safety at sea and the prevention of marine pollution by ships flying their flags, in accordance with the provisions of the relevant international conventions, in particular the Solas and Marpol Conventions.

2. The maritime administration of the Member States will intensify its inspections on foreign ships docking in Community ports in order to make sure, as far as possible, that they do not present an unacceptable risk to the safety of human life at sea or to the integrity of the marine ecosystem. In particular, they will in any case attain the objectives for a minimum number of inspections provided for in the Paris memorandum on port State control.

3. Member States will ensure that their maritime inspectors carry out, in the course of the activities provided for in paragraphs 2 and 3, checks, particularly through the safe manning document, on the qualification of the people making up the crew of ships, especially of tankers, paying particular attention to the observance of rule 13 of Chapter V of the Solas Convention and the provisions of the STCW Convention of 1978.

4. Member States will, as far as possible, always give reciprocal support in identifying the origin of, monitoring and combating pollution by crude oil and other substances prejudicial to the Community's marine environment. In particular, the Member States will take the steps which might be considered necessary in order to guarantee that in the event of any maritime accident which threatens the ecosystem of Community waters, a rapid, efficient and coordinated response is given by all Member States' administrations, bringing to bear the most appropriate and accessible means in accordance with the circumstances.

5. The Commission is requested to start promoting and improving the instrument of Community action organized in the form of the 'task force', providing it with the necessary resources and the precise functions required for coordination and rapidity of response.

6. At the same time, the Commission is earnestly requested to continue as a matter of urgency with its research task with regard to the project for the establishment of a system of safety at sea, based on control posts and shore-based navigation aid systems, in accordance with the general framework of COST projects 301 and 311, with the aim of providing proper protection for waters which are essential routes for the Community's maritime traffic.

29. RESOLUTION OF THE COUNCIL AND OF THE REPRESENTATIVES OF THE GOVERNMENTS OF THE MEMBER STATES, MEETING WITHIN THE COUNCIL, OF 19 JUNE 1990 ON IMPROVING PASSENGER FERRY SAFETY (90/C 206/02)

THE COUNCIL OF THE EUROPEAN COMMUNITIES AND THE REPRESENTATIVES OF THE GOVERNMENTS OF THE MEMBER STATES, MEETING WITHIN THE COUNCIL,

Aware of:

— the large number of passengers who travel by passenger ferries in European waters,
— the essentially international nature of such operations,
— the necessity of crews being able to function in a satisfactory manner in the event of an emergency,
— the dangers which can arise from management and communication failures,
— the potentially large-scale intervention which could be required in the event of an accident involving a passenger ferry,
— the fact that the transport of passengers in European waters is carried out by vessels registered both inside and outside the Community, thus requiring any necessary improvement of passenger ferry safety, including the question of crewing, to take place in a broad international context;

Wishing to improve the safety of passenger ferries;

CALLS UPON the Member States and the Commission, in their capacity as members or as observer of

(a) the International Maritime Organization of the United Nations,
(b) the memorandum of understanding on port State control,

to press for the urgent identification, elaboration, adoption and implementation of measures which will improve safety of passenger ferries on an international basis in the framework of the aforementioned fora.

30. COUNCIL REGULATION (EEC) NO 613/91 OF 4 MARCH 1991 ON THE TRANSFER OF SHIPS FROM ONE REGISTER TO ANOTHER WITHIN THE COMMUNITY

THE COUNCIL OF THE EUROPEAN COMMUNITIES

Having regard to the Treaty establishing the European Economic Community, and in particular Article 84 (2) thereof,

Having regard to the proposal from the Commission,[1]

Having regard to the opinion of the European Parliament,[2]

Having regard to the opinion of the Economic and Social Committee,[3]

Whereas the establishment and functioning of the internal market involve the elimination of technical barriers to the transfer of ships between Member States' national registers; whereas measures to facilitate the transfer of ships within the Community are also required to free European shipowners from the costs and administrative procedures involved in a change of register within the Community and also to improve thereby the operating conditions and competitive position of Community shipping;

Whereas it is necessary, at the same time, to safeguard a high level of ship safety and environmental protection, in compliance with international Conventions;

Whereas the transfer of ships flying the flag of a Member State between the registers of Member States must not, therefore, be impeded by technical barriers, provided that the ships are recognized as complying with the provisions of these international Conventions;

Whereas the issue of international certificates for safety and pollution prevention, provided for under the 1974 International Convention for the Safety of Life at Sea (1974 Solas), the 1966 International Convention on Load Lines (LL 1966), the 1973 International Convention for the Prevention of Pollution from Ships, as amended by the 1978 Protocol (Marpol 73/78) and the related resolutions of mandatory status adopted by the International Maritime Organization (IMO), is the responsibility of States; whereas, where private organizations issue certificates on behalf of a Member State, in accordance with the said Conventions, they also do so on that Member State's responsibility, as defined in those Conventions;

Whereas the international Conventions leave important points of interpretation to the discretion of individual contracting States; whereas, based on their respective interpretation of the Conventions, Governments of Member States issue, to all ships flying their flags that are subject to the provisions of these Conventions, international certificates certifying their compliance with these provisions; whereas the Member States enforce national technical regulations, some provisions of which contain requirements other than those in the international Conventions and associated technical standards; whereas an appropriate procedure should be established in view of solving divergences in the interpretation of existing requirements which may occur upon a request for transfer of ships and in order to take into account the introduction of new provisions in those Conventions;

Whereas this Regulation does not in any way prejudge the preparation and interpretation of conventions by the International Maritime Organization (IMO);

Whereas ships benefiting from the provisions of the Regulation must have been registered and in active service under the flag of a Member State for at least six months so as to give the latter sufficient time to check their condition;

Whereas a committee should be set up to assist the Commission in implementing and interpreting this Regulation with a view to achieving the objective of facilitating the transfer of ships within the Community while ensuring that standards of maritime safety and environmental protection are not reduced,

1. OJ No C 153, 22 June 1990, p. 14.
2. OJ No C 19, 28 January 1991.
3. OJ No C 60, 8 March 1991.

HAS ADOPTED THIS REGULATION:

Article 1

For the purposes of this Regulation:

(a) "Conventions" means the 1974 International Convention for the Safety of Life at Sea (1974 Solas), the 1966 International Convention on Load Lines (LL66) and the International Convention for the Prevention of Pollution from Ships (Marpol 73/78), together with the amendments thereto in force at the date of adoption of this Regulation, and related resolutions of mandatory status adopted by the International Maritime Organization (IMO);

Without prejudice to the procedures for amending the said Conventions, the application, for the purposes of this Regulation, of subsequent amendments thereto which have entered into force shall be decided upon in accordance with the procedure laid down in Article 7;

(b) "requirements" means the safety and pollution prevention requirements laid down in the Conventions;

(c) "certificates" means certificates issued by or on behalf of a Member State in accordance with the Conventions as well as certificates issued for chemical tankers and gas carriers built before 1 July 1986, in accordance with the Bulk Chemical Code [IMO Resolution A.212 (VII)] or the Bulk Gas Carrier Code [IMO Resolution A.328 (IX)].

Article 2

This Regulation shall apply to cargo ships of 500 tons gross tonnage and upwards which:

(a) were built on or after 25 May 1980, or
were built before that date, but:
— compliance of which with the regulations for new ships defined in the 1974 Solas Convention, and
— in the case of chemical tankers and gas carriers, compliance with the standards codes referred to in Article 1 (c) for ships built on or after 25 May 1980,
is certified by or on behalf of a Member State; and

(b) have been flying the flag of, and registered in, a Member State, and in active service under that flag for at least six months; and

(c) carry valid certificates.

Article 3

1. Member States shall not withhold from registration, for technical reasons arising from the Conventions, a cargo ship registered in another Member State complying with the requirements and carrying valid certificates and fittings and equipment approved or type-approved in the ship's country of origin.

In so far as on the date of entry into force of this Regulation they are bound by regional agreements for the protection of the marine environment, Member States may impose additional rules which conform with the requirements of the optional annexes to the Conventions.

2. Upon the transfer of the ship, the receiving flag Member State shall issue certificates under the same conditions as under the flag previously flown.

3. Where the certificates are issued by an organization on behalf of a Member State, the latter must ensure that the qualifications, technical experience and staffing of the said organization are such as will enable it, in applying the Conventions, to issue certificates guaranteeing a high level of safety.

The organization must be in a position to develop and update rules and regulations having the quality of accepted technical standards, and must operate with qualified and experienced surveyors so as adequately to assess a ship's condition.

4. Nevertheless, on transfer, a ship may be subjected to inspection by the receiving flag Member State to confirm that the actual condition of the ship and its equipment corresponds with its certificates and with the statements of compliance referred to in Article 2 (a).

Article 4

In so far as requirements remain unchanged for existing ships, at the time of renewal, extension or revision of the certificates issued under Article 3, receiving flag Member States shall not impose requirements other than those initially prescribed for the full-term certificates.

Article 5

1. Member States shall immediately notify to the Commission any refusal to issue new certificates for reasons based on divergences of interpretation of the requirements or of the provisions which the Conventions leave to the discretion of the Parties.

Unless the Commission is informed of an agreement between the Member States concerned within one month, it shall initiate proceedings in order to take a decision in accordance with the procedure laid down in Article 7.

2. Where a Member State considers that a ship cannot be registered under Article 3 for reasons of serious danger to safety or the environment outside the scope of certificates, registration may be suspended for a period not exceeding three months, and the Member State shall without delay bring the matter before the Commission, giving the reasons therefor. The suspension shall be confirmed or revoked in accordance with the procedure laid down in Article 7.

Article 6

The Commission shall be assisted by a committee composed of representatives of the Member States and chaired by a representative of the Commission.

Article 7

Where the procedure laid down in this Article is to be followed, the representative of the Commission shall submit to the committee a draft of the measures to be taken. The committee shall deliver its opinion on the draft within a time limit which the chairman may lay down according to the urgency of the matter. The opinion shall be delivered by the majority laid down in Article 148 (2) of the EEC Treaty in the case of decisions which the Council is required to adopt on a proposal from the Commission. The votes of the representatives of the Member States within the committee shall be weighted in the manner set out in that Article. The chairman shall not vote.

The Commission shall adopt the measures envisaged if they are in accordance with the opinion of the committee.

If the measures envisaged are not in accordance with the opinion of the committee, or if no opinion is delivered, the Commission shall, without delay, submit to the Council a proposal relating to the measures to be taken. The Council shall act by a qualified majority.

If, on the expiry of eight weeks from the date of referral to the Council, the Council has not acted, the proposed measures shall be adopted by the Commission.

Article 8

The committee may also be consulted by the Commission on any matter relating to the implementation and interpretation of this Regulation and, in particular, in order to ensure that standards of maritime safety and environmental protection are not reduced.

The committee shall draw up its rules of procedure.

Article 9

This Regulation shall enter into force on 1 January 1992.

This Regulation shall be binding in its entirety and directly applicable in all Member States.

Done at Brussels, 4 March 1991.

For the Council
The President
J. F. POOS

31. COUNCIL REGULATION (EEC) No 479/92 OF 25 FEBRUARY 1992 ON THE APPLICATION OF ARTICLE 85(3) OF THE TREATY TO CERTAIN CATEGORIES OF AGREEMENTS, DECISIONS AND CONCERTED PRACTICES BETWEEN LINER SHIPPING COMPANIES (CONSORTIA)

THE COUNCIL OF THE EUROPEAN COMMUNITIES

Having regard to the Treaty establishing the European Economic Community, and in particular Article 87 thereof.

Having regard to the proposal from the Commission.[1]

Having regard to the opinion of the European Parliament.[2]

Having regard to the opinion of the Economic and Social Committee.[3]

Whereas Article 85(1) of the Treaty may in accordance with Article 85(3) thereof be declared inapplicable to categories of agreements, decisions and concerted practices which fulfil the conditions contained in Article 85(3);

Whereas, pursuant to Article 87 of the Treaty, the provisions for the application of Article 85(3) of the Treaty should be adopted by way of Regulation; whereas, according to Article 87(2)(b), such a Regulation must lay down detailed rules for the application of Article 85(3), taking into account the need to ensure effective supervision, on the one hand, and to simplify administration to the greatest possible extent on the other; whereas, according to Article 87(2)(d), such a Regulation is required to define the respective functions of the Commission and the Court of Justice;

Whereas liner shipping is a capital intensive industry; whereas containerization has increased pressures for cooperation and rationalization; whereas the Community shipping industry needs to attain the necessary economies of scale in order to compete successfully on the world liner shipping market;

Whereas joint-service agreements between liner shipping companies with the aim of rationalizing their operations by means of technical, operational and/or commercial arrangements (described in shipping circles as consortia) can help to provide the necessary means for improving the productivity of liner shipping services and promoting technical and economic progress;

Having regard to the importance of maritime transport for the development of the Community's trade and the role which consortia agreements can fulfil in this respect, taking account of the special features of international liner shipping;

Whereas the legalization of these agreements is a measure which can make a positive contribution to improving the competitiveness of shipping in the Community;

Whereas users of the shipping services offered by consortia can obtain a share of the benefits resulting from the improvements in productivity and service, by means of, *inter alia*, regularity, cost reductions derived from higher levels of capacity utilization, and better service quality stemming from improved vessels and equipment;

Whereas the Commission should be enabled to declare by way of Regulation that the provisions of Article 85(1) of the Treaty do not apply to certain categories of consortia agreements, decisions and concerted practices, in order to make it easier for undertakings to cooperate in ways which are economically desirable and without adverse effect from the point of view of competition policy;

Whereas the Commission, in close and constant liaison with the competent authorities of the Member States, should be able to define precisely the scope of these exemptions and the conditions attached to them;

1. OJ No C 167, 10 July 1990, p. 9.
2. OJ No C 305, 25 November 1991, p. 39.
3. OJ No C 69, 18 March 1991, p. 16.

Whereas consortia in liner shipping are a specialized and complex type of joint venture; whereas there is a great variety of different consortia agreements operating in different circumstances; whereas the scope, parties, activities or terms of consortia are frequently altered; whereas the Commission should therefore be given the responsibility of defining from time to time the consortia to which a group exemption should apply;

Whereas in order to ensure that all the conditions of Article 85(3) of the Treaty are met, conditions should be attached to group exemptions to ensure in particular that a fair share of the benefits will be passed on to shippers and that competition is not eliminated;

Whereas pursuant to Article 11(4) of Council Regulation (EEC) No 4056/86 of 22 December 1986 laying down detailed rules for the application of Articles 85 and 86 of the Treaty to maritime transport[4] the Commission may provide that a decision taken in accordance with Article 85(3) of the Treaty shall apply with retroactive effect; whereas it is desirable that the Commission be empowered to adopt, by Regulation, provisions to that effect;

Whereas notification of agreements, decisions and concerted practices falling within the scope of this Regulation must not be made compulsory, it being primarily the responsibility of undertakings to see to it that they conform to the rules on competition, and in particular to the conditions laid down by the subsequent Commission Regulation implementing this Regulation;

Whereas there can be no exemption if the conditions set out in Article 85(3) of the Treaty are not satisfied; whereas the Commission should therefore have power to take the appropriate measures where an agreement proves to have effects incompatible with Article 85(3) of the Treaty; whereas the Commission should be able first to address recommendations to the parties and then to take decisions,

HAS ADOPTED THIS REGULATION:

Article 1

1. Without prejudice to the application of Regulation (EEC) No 4056/86, the Commission may by regulation and in accordance with Article 85(3) of the Treaty, declare that Article 85(1) of the Treaty shall not apply to certain categories of agreements between undertakings, decisions of associations of undertakings and concerted practices that have as an object to promote or establish cooperation in the joint operation of maritime transport services between liner shipping companies, for the purpose of rationalizing their operations by means of technical, operational and/or commercial arrangements—with the exception of price fixing (consortia).
2. Such regulation adopted pursuant to paragraph 1 shall define the categories of agreements, decisions and concerted practices to which it applies and shall specify the conditions and obligations under which, pursuant to Article 85(3) of the Treaty, they shall be considered exempted from the application of Article 85(1) of the Treaty.

Article 2

1. The regulation adopted pursuant to Article 1 shall apply for a period of five years, calculated as from the date of its entry into force.
2. It may be repealed or amended where circumstances have changed with respect to any of the facts which were basic to its adoption.

Article 3

The regulation adopted pursuant to Article 1 may include a provision stating that it applies with retroactive effect to agreements, decisions and concerted practices which were in existence at the date of entry into force of such regulation, provided they comply with the conditions established in that regulaion.

4. OJ No L 378, 31 December 1986, p. 4.

Article 4

Before adopting its regulation, the Commission shall publish a draft thereof to enable all the persons and organizations concerned to submit their comments within such reasonable time limit as the Commission shall fix, but in no case less than one month.

Article 5

1. Before publishing the draft regulation and before adopting the regulation, the Commission shall consult the Advisory Committee on Agreements and Dóminant Positions in Maritime Transport established by Article 15(3) of Regulation (EEC) No 4056/86.

2. Paragraphs 5 and 6 of Article 15 of Regulation (EEC) No 4056/86 relating to consultation with the Advisory Committee, shall apply, it being understood that joint meetings with the Commission shall take place not earlier than one month after dispatch of the notice convening them.

Article 6

1. Where the persons concerned are in breach of a condition or obligation attaching to an exemption granted by the Regulation adopted pursuant to Article 1, the Commission may, in order to put an end to such a breach:

— address recommendations to the persons concerned, and

— in the event of failure by such persons to observe those recommendations, and depending on the gravity of the breach concerned, adopt a decision that either prohibits them from carrying out, or requires them to perform specific acts or, while withdrawing the benefit of the group exemption which they enjoyed, grants them an individual exemption in accordance with Article 11(4) of Regulation (EEC) No 4056/86, or withdraws the benefit of the group exemption which they enjoyed.

2. Where the Commission, either on its own initiative or at the request of a Member State or of natural or legal persons claiming a legitimate interest, finds that in a particular case an agreement, decision or concerted practice to which the group exemption granted by the Regulation adopted pursuant to Article 1 applies, nevertheless has effects which are incompatible with Article 85(3) of the Treaty or with the prohibition laid down in Article 86 of the Treaty, it may withdraw the benefit of the group exemption from those agreements, decisions or concerted practices and take all appropriate measures for the purpose of bringing these infringements to an end, pursuant to Article 13 of Regulation (EEC) No 4056/86.

3. Before taking a decision under paragraph 2, the Commission may address recommendations for termination of the infringement to the persons concerned.

Article 7

This Regulation shall enter into force on the day following its publication in the *Official Journal of the European Communities*.

This Regulation shall be binding in its entirety and directly applicable in all Member States.

Done at Brussels, 25 February 1992

For the Council
The President
VITOR MARTINS

32. COUNCIL DECISION OF 25 FEBRUARY 1992 ON RADIONAVIGATION SYSTEMS FOR EUROPE (92/143/EEC)

THE COUNCIL OF THE EUROPEAN COMMUNITIES,

Having regard to the Treaty establishing the European Economic Community, and in particular Article 84 (2) thereof,

Having regard to the proposal from the Commission,[1]

Having regard to the opinion of the European Parliament,[2]

Having regard to the opinion of the Economic and Social Committee,[3]

Whereas the 1974 International Convention for the Safety of Life at Sea (Solas 1974) drafted under the auspices of the International Maritime Organization (IMO), requires contracting parties to arrange for the establishment and maintenance of such aids to navigation as the volume of traffic and the degree of risk warrant;

Whereas, in its Resolution A.666 (16), the IMO refers both to the need for a worldwide radionavigation system and to the possibility of regional applications of terrestrial systems such as Chayka, Decca Navigator, Loran-C, Omega and Differential Omega;

Whereas the International Association of Lighthouse Authorities confirms that, in order to meet the needs of maritime navigation, a terrestrial radionavigation system is necessary until general-purpose satellite systems are widely available, and also thereafter in parallel to such systems for the foreseeable future;

Whereas it is a concern of the Community to ensure the highest degree of safety of navigation and protection of the marine environment;

Whereas the United States Coastguard has decided to terminate its Loran-C commitments outside the United States of America as from 1994 and intends to offer the Loran-C facilities to the relevant host nations;

Whereas certain Member States intend to participate in one or more regional agreements on the establishment of Loran-C chains covering North-West Europe and the North Atlantic, the Mediterranean, the Iberian Peninsula and the Baltic, while a number of these areas are already covered by terrestrial systems, such as Decca and Omega;

Whereas Member States are not required to abandon existing radionavigation systems, such as Decca and Omega, provided they fulfil their Loran-C obligations in accordance with regional agreements;

Whereas the Loran-C system in particular satisfies international requirements and its more general application does not prejudice the development of satellite aids to navigation, especially as combined coverage by satellite and Loran-C will offer an excellent degree of system verification and continuity of radionavigation coverage for the benefit of maritime safety and environmental protection;

Whereas the establishment of regional Loran-C systems must ensure coherent and complete coverage of the European maritime area, avoiding as much as possible the imposition of additional costs upon the users of existing terrestrial radionavigation systems,

HAS ADOPTED THIS DECISION:

Article 1

1. Without prejudice to existing radionavigation systems, Member States which participate in or join regional agreements on Loran-C shall do so in a way which fulfils international objectives.

1. OJ No C 53, 28 February 1991, p. 71, and OJ No C 317, 7 December 1991, p. 16.
2. OJ No C 280, 28 October 1991, p. 32.
3. OJ No C 159, 17 June 1991, p. 22.

2. With regard to their participation in the regional agreements referred to in paragraph 1, Member States shall seek to achieve the radionavigation configurations which cover the widest possible geographical area in Europe and in neighbouring waters.

Article 2

The Commission shall:

— ensure coordination between the Member States participating in the regional agreements referred to in paragraph 1 with a view to ensuring compatibility between the Loran-C chains introduced at regional level,

— encourage the development of receivers, which take account of the ongoing development of satellite systems and the enhancement of the present Loran-C system,

— pursue its work with a view to setting up a radionavigation plan which takes into account the development of satellite navigation systems, of existing terrestrial systems and of the radionavigation plans of the Member States, and

— propose the necessary measures to the Council should the need arise.

Article 3

As members or observers within the International Association of Lighthouse Authorities, Member States and the Commission shall support efforts to set up a worldwide radionavigation system including European regional Loran-C chains with the purpose of enlarging worldwide Loran-C coverage in order to improve the safety of navigation and protection of the marine environment.

Article 4

This Decision is addressed to the Member States.

Done at Brussels, 25 February 1992.

For the Council
The President
VITOR MARTINS

33. UNITED NATIONS CONVENTION ON A CODE OF CONDUCT FOR LINER CONFERENCES

UN LINER CODE CONVENTION
OBJECTIVES AND PRINCIPLES

The Contracting Parties to the present Convention,

Desiring to improve the liner conference system,

Recognising the need for a universally acceptable code of conduct for liner conferences,

Taking into account the special needs and problems of the developing countries with respect to the activities of liner conferences serving their foreign trade,

Agreeing to reflect in the Code the following fundamental objectives and basic principles:

(a) The objective to facilitate the orderly expansion of world sea-borne trade;
(b) The objective to stimulate the development of regular and efficient liner services adequate to the requirement of the trade concerned;
(c) The objective to ensure a balance of interests between suppliers and users of liner shipping services;
(d) The principle that conference practices should not involve any discrimination against the shipowners, shippers or the foreign trade of any country;
(e) The principle that conferences hold meaningful consultations with shippers' organisations, shippers' representatives and shippers on matters of common interest, with, upon request, the participation of appropriate authorities;
(f) The principle that conferences should make available to interested parties pertinent information about their activities which are relevant to those parties and should publish meaningful information on their activities,

Have agreed as follows:

PART ONE

CHAPTER I. DEFINITIONS

Liner conference or conference

A group of two or more vessel-operating carriers which provides international liner services for the carriage of cargo on a particular route or routes within specified geographical limits and which has an agreement or arrangement, whatever its nature, within the framework of which they operate under uniform or common freight rates and any other agreed conditions with respect to the provision of liner services.

National shipping line

A national shipping line of any given country is a vessel-operating carrier which has its head office of management and its effective control in that country and is recognised as such by an appropriate authority of that country or under the law of that country.

Lines belonging to and operated by a joint venture involving two or more countries and in whose equity the national interests, public and/or private, of those countries have a substantial share and whose head office of management and whose effective control is in one of those countries can be recognised as a national line by the appropriate authorities of those countries.

Third-country shipping line

A vessel-operating carrier in its operations between two countries of which it is not a national shipping line.

Shipper

A person or entity who has entered into, or who demonstrates an intention to enter into, a contractual or other arrangement with a conference or shipping line for the shipment of goods in which he has a beneficial interest.

Shippers' organisation

An association or equivalent body which promotes, represents and protects the interests of shippers and if those authorities so desire, is recognised in that capacity by the appropriate authority or authorities of the country whose shippers it represents.

Goods carried by the conference

Cargo transported by shipping lines members of a conference in accordance with the conference agreement.

Appropriate authority

Either a government or a body designated by a government or by national legislation to perform any of the functions ascribed to such authority by the provisions of this Code.

Promotional freight rate

A rate instituted for promoting the carriage of non-traditional exports of the country concerned.

Special freight rate

A preferential freight rate, other than a promotional freight rate, which may be negotiated between the parties concerned.

CHAPTER II. RELATIONS AMONG MEMBER LINES

Article 1. Membership

1. Any national shipping line shall have the right to be a full member of a conference which serves the foreign trade of its country, subject to the criteria set out in Article 1, paragraph 2. Shipping lines which are not national lines in any trade of a conference shall have the right to become full members of that conference subject to the criteria set out in Article 1, paragraphs 2 and 3, and to the provisions regarding the share of trade as set out in Article 2 as regards third-country shipping lines.

2. A shipping line applying for membership of a conference shall furnish evidence of its ability and intention, which may include the use of chartered tonnage, provided the criteria of this paragraph are met, to operate a regular, adequate and efficient service on a long-term basis as defined in the conference agreement within the framework of the conference, shall undertake to abide by all the terms and conditions of the conference agreement, and shall deposit a financial guarantee to cover any outstanding financial obligation in the event of subsequent withdrawal, suspension or expulsion from membership, if so required under the conference agreement.

3. In considering an application for membership by a shipping line which is not a national line in any trade of the conference concerned, in addition to the provisions of Article 1, paragraph 2, the following criteria, inter alia, should be taken into account:

(a) The existing volume of the trade on the route or routes served by the conference and prospects for its growth;

(b) The adequacy of shipping space for the existing and prospective volume of trade on the route or routes served by the conference;

(c) The probable effect of admission of the shipping line to the conference on the efficiency and quality of the conference service;

(d) The current participation of the shipping line in trade on the same route or routes outside the framework of a conference; and

(e) The current participation of the shipping line on the same route or routes within the framework of another conference.

The above criteria shall not be applied so as to subvert the implementation of the provisions relating to participation in trade set out in Article 2.

4. An application for admission or readmission to membership shall be promptly decided upon and the decision communicated by a conference to an applicant promptly, and in no case later than six months from the date of application. When a shipping line is refused admission or readmission the conference shall, at the same time give in writing the grounds for such refusal.

5. When considering applications for admission, a conference shall take into account the views put forward by shippers and shippers' organisations of the countries whose trade is carried by the conference, as well as the views of appropriate authorities if they so request.

6. In addition to the criteria for admission set out in Article 1, paragraph 2, a shipping line applying for readmission shall also give evidence of having fulfilled its obligations in accordance with Article 4, paragraphs 1 and 4. The conference may give special scrutiny to the circumstances under which the line left the conference.

Article 2. Participation in trade

1. Any shipping line admitted to membership of a conference shall have sailing and loading rights in the trades covered by that conference.

2. When a conference operates a pool, all shipping lines members of the conference serving the trade covered by the pool shall have the right to participate in the pool for that trade.

3. For the purpose of determining the share of trade which member lines shall have the right to acquire, the national shipping lines of each country, irrespective of the number of lines, shall be regarded as a single group of shipping lines for that country.

4. When determining a share of trade within a pool of individual member lines and/or groups of national shipping lines in accordance with Article 2, paragraph 2, the following principles regarding their right to participation in the trade carried by the conference shall be observed, unless otherwise mutually agreed:

(a) The group of national shipping lines of each of two countries the foreign trade between which is carried by the conference shall have equal rights to participate in the freight and volume of traffic generated by their mutual foreign trade and carried by the conference;

(b) Third-country shipping lines, if any, shall have the right to acquire a significant part, such as 20 per cent, in the freight and volume of traffic generated by that trade.

5. If, for any one of the countries whose trade is carried by a conference, there are no national shipping lines participating in the carriage of that trade, the share of the trade to which national shipping lines of that country would be entitled under Article 2, paragraph 4 shall be distributed among the individual member lines participating in the trade in proportion to their respective share.

6. If the national shipping lines of one country decide not to carry their full share of the trade, that portion of their share of the trade which they do not carry shall be distributed among the individual member lines participating in the trade in proportion to their respective shares.

7. If the national shipping lines of the countries concerned do not participate in the trade between those countries covered by a conference, the shares of trade carried by the conference between those countries shall be allocated between the participating member lines of third countries by commercial negotiations, between those lines.

8. The national shipping lines of a region, members of a conference, at one end of the trade covered by the conference, may redistribute amongst themselves by mutual agreement the shares in trades allocated to them, in accordance with Article 2, paragraphs 4 to 7 inclusive.

9. Subject to the provisions of Article 2, paragraphs 4 to 8 inclusive regarding shares of trade among individual shipping lines or groups of shipping lines, pooling or trade-sharing agreements shall be reviewed by the conference periodically, at intervals to be stipulated in those agreements and in accordance with criteria to be specified in the conference agreement.

10. The application of the present Article shall commence as soon as possible after entry into force of the present Convention and shall be completed within a transition period which in no

case shall be longer than two years, taking into account the specific situation in each of the trades concerned.

11. Shipping lines members of a conference shall be entitled to operate chartered ships to fulfil their conference obligations.

12. The criteria for sharing and the revision of shares as set out in Article 2, paragraphs 1 and 11 inclusive shall apply when, in the absence of a pool, there exists berthing, sailing and/or any other form of cargo allocation agreement.

13. Where no pooling, berthing, sailing or other trade participation agreements exist in a conference, either group of national shipping lines, members of the conference, may require that pooling arrangements be introduced, in respect of the trade between their countries carried by the conference, in conformity with the provisions of Article 2, paragraph 4; or alternatively they may require that the sailings be so adjusted as to provide an opportunity to these lines to enjoy substantially the same rights to participate in the trade between those two countries carried by the conference as they would have enjoyed under the provisions of Article 2, paragraph 4. Any such request shall be considered and decided by the conference. If there is no agreement to institute such a pool or adjustment of sailings among the members of the conference, the groups of national shipping lines of the countries at both ends of the trade shall have a majority vote in deciding to establish such a pool or adjustment of sailings. The matter shall be decided upon within a period not exceeding six months from the receipt of the request.

14. In the event of a disagreement between the national shipping lines of the countries at either end whose trade is served by the conference with regard to whether or not pooling shall be introduced, they may require that within the conference sailings be so adjusted as to provide an opportunity to these lines to enjoy substantially the same rights to participate in the trade between those two countries carried by the conference as they would have enjoyed under the provisions of Article 2, paragraph 4. In the event that there are no national shipping lines in one of the countries whose trade is served by the conference, the national shipping line or lines of the other country may make the same request. The conference shall use its best endeavours to meet this request. If, however, this request is not met, the appropriate authorities of the countries at both ends of the trade may take up the matter if they so wish and make their views known to the parties concerned for their consideration. If no agreement is reached, the dispute shall be dealt with in accordance with the procedures established in this Code.

15. Other shipping lines, members of a conference, may also request that pooling or sailing agreements be introduced, and the request shall be considered by the conference in accordance with the relevant provisions of this Code.

16. A conference shall provide for appropriate measures in any conference pooling agreement to cover cases where the cargo has been shut out by a member line for any reason excepting late presentation by the shipper. Such agreement shall provide that a vessel with unbooked space, capable of being used, be allowed to lift the cargo, even in excess of the pool share of the line in the trade, if otherwise the cargo would be shut out and delayed beyond a period set by the conference.

17. The provisions of Article 2, paragraphs 1 to 16 inclusive concern all goods regardless of their origin, their destination or the use for which they are intended, with the exception of military equipment for national defence purposes.

Article 3. Decision-making procedures

The decision-making procedures embodied in a conference agreement shall be based on the equality of all the full member lines; these procedures shall ensure that the voting rules do not hinder the proper work of the conference and the service of the trade and shall define the matters on which decisions will be made by unanimity. However, a decision cannot be taken in respect of matters defined in a conference agreement relating to the trade between two countries without the consent of the national shipping lines of those two countries.

Article 4. Sanctions

1. A shipping line member of a conference shall be entitled, subject to the provisions regarding withdrawal which are embodied in pool schemes and/or cargo-sharing arrangements, to secure

its release, without penalty, from the terms of the conference agreement after giving three months' notice, unless the conference agreement provides for a different time period, although it shall be required to fulfil its obligations as a member of the conference up to the date of its release.

2. A conference may, upon notice to be specified in the conference agreement, suspend or expel a member for significant failure to abide by the terms and conditions of the conference agreement.

3. No expulsion or suspension shall become effective until a statement in writing of the reasons therefor has been given and until any dispute has been settled as provided in chapter VI.

4. Upon withdrawal or expulsion, the line concerned shall be required to pay its share of the outstanding financial obligations of the conference, up to the date of its withdrawal or expulsion. In cases of withdrawal, suspension or expulsion, the line shall not be relieved of its own financial obligations under the conference agreement or of any of its obligations towards shippers.

Article 5. Self-policing

1. A conference shall adopt and keep up to date an illustrative list, which shall be as comprehensive as possible, of practices which are regarded as malpractices and/or breaches of the conference agreement and shall provide effective self-policing machinery to deal with them, with specific provisions requiring:

(a) The fixing of penalties or a range of penalties for malpractices or breaches, to be commensurate with their seriousness;

(b) The examination and impartial review of an adjudication of complaints, and/or decisions taken on complaints, against malpractices or breaches by a person or body unconnected with any of the shipping lines members of the conference or their affiliates, on request by the conference or any other party concerned;

(c) The reporting, on request, on the action taken in connection with complaints against malpractices and/or breaches, and on a basis of anonymity for the parties concerned, to the appropriate authorities of the countries whose trade is served by the conference and of the countries whose shipping lines are members of the conference.

2. Shipping lines and conferences are entitled to the full co-operation of shippers and shippers' organisations in the endeavour to combat malpractices and breaches.

Article 6. Conference agreements

All conference agreements, pooling, berthing and sailing rights agreements and amendments or other documents directly related to, and which affect, such agreements, shall be made available on request to the appropriate authorities of the countries whose trade is served by the conference and of the countries whose shipping lines are members of the conference.

CHAPTER III. RELATIONS WITH SHIPPERS

Article 7. Loyalty arrangements

1. The shipping lines members of a conference are entitled to institute and maintain loyalty arrangements with shippers, the form and terms of which are matters for consultation between conference and shippers' organisations or representatives of shippers. These loyalty arrangements shall provide safeguards making explicit the rights of shippers and conference members. These arrangements shall be based on the contract system or any system which is also lawful.

2. Whatever loyalty arrangements are made, the freight rate applicable to loyal shippers shall be determined within a fixed range of percentages of the freight rate applicable to other shippers. Where a change in the differential causes an increase in the rates charged to shippers, the change can be implemented only after 150 days' notice to those shippers or according to regional practice and and/or agreement. Disputes in connection with a change of the differential shall be settled as provided in the loyalty agreement.

3. The terms of loyalty arrangements shall provide safeguards making explicit the rights and obligations of shippers and of shipping lines members of the conference in accordance with the following provisions, inter alia:

(a) The shipper shall be bound in respect of cargo whose shipment is controlled by him or his affiliated or subsidiary company or his forwarding agent in accordance with the contract of sale of the goods concerned, provided that the shipper shall not, by evasion, subterfuge, or intermediary, attempt to divert cargo in violation of his loyalty commitment;

(b) Where there is a loyalty contract, the extent of actual or liquidated damages and/or penalty shall be specified in the contract. The member lines of the conference may, however, decide to assess lower liquidated damages or to waive the claim to liquidated damages. In any event, the liquidated damages under the contract to be paid to the shipper shall not exceed the freight charges on the particular shipment, computed at the rate provided under the contract;

(c) The shipper shall be entitled to resume full loyalty status, subject to the fulfilment of conditions established by the conference which shall be specified in the loyalty arrangement;

(d) The loyalty arrangement shall set out:
   (i) A list of cargo, which may include bulk cargo shipped without mark or count, which is specifically excluded from the scope of the loyalty arrangement;
   (ii) A definition of the circumstances in which cargo other than cargo covered by (i) above is considered to be excluded from the scope of the loyalty arrangement;
   (iii) The method of settlement of disputes arising under the loyalty arrangement;
   (iv) Provision for termination of the loyalty arrangement on request by either a shipper or a conference without penalty, after expiry of a stipulated period of notice, such notice to be given in writing; and
   (v) The terms for granting dispensation.

4. If there is a dispute between a conference and a shippers' organisation, representatives of shippers and/or shippers about the form or terms of a proposed loyalty arrangement, either party may refer the matter for resolution under appropriate procedure as set out in this Code.

Article 8. Dispensation

1. Conferences shall provide, within the terms of the loyalty arrangements, that requests by shippers for dispensation shall be examined and a decision given quickly and, if requested, the reasons given in writing where dispensation is withheld. Should a conference fail to confirm, within a period specified in the loyalty arrangement, sufficient space to accommodate a shipper's cargo within a period also specified in the loyalty arrangement, the shipper shall have the right, without being penalised, to utilise any vessel for the cargo in question.

2. In ports where conference services are arranged subject to the availability of a specified minimum of cargo (i.e. on inducement), but either the shipping line does not call, despite due notice by shippers, or the shipping line does not reply within an agreed time to the notice given by shippers, shippers shall automatically have the right, without prejudicing their loyalty status, to use any available vessel for the carriage of their cargo.

Article 9. Availability of tariffs and related conditions and/or regulations

Tariffs, related conditions, regulations, and any amendments thereto shall be made available on request to shippers, shippers' organisations and other parties concerned at reasonable cost, and they shall be available for examination at offices of shipping lines and their agents. They shall spell out all conditions concerning the application of freight rates and the carriage of any cargo covered by them.

Article 10. Annual reports

Conferences shall provide annually to shippers' organisations, or to representatives of shippers, reports on their activities designed to provide general information of interest to them, including relevant information about consultations held with shippers and shippers' organisations, action taken regarding complaints, changes in membership, and significant changes in service, tariffs and conditions of carriage. Such annual reports shall be submitted, on request, to the appropriate authorities of the countries whose trade is served by the conference concerned.

Article 11. Consultation machinery

1. There shall be consultations on matters of common interest between a conference, shippers' organisations, representatives of shippers and, where practicable, shippers, which may be designated for that purpose by the appropriate authority if it so desires. These consultations shall take place whenever requested by any of the above-mentioned parties. Appropriate authorities shall have the right, upon request, to participate fully in the consultations, but this does not mean that they play a decision-making role.

2. The following matters, inter alia, may be the subject of consultation:

(a) Changes in general tariff conditions and related regulations;
(b) Changes in the general level of tariff rates and rates for major commodities;
(c) Promotional and/or special freight rates;
(d) Imposition of, and related changes in, surcharges;
(e) Loyalty arrangements, their establishment or changes in their form and general conditions;
(f) Changes in the tariff classification of ports;
(g) Procedure for the supply of necessary information by shippers concerning the expected volume and nature of their cargoes; and
(h) Presentation of cargo for shipment and the requirement regarding notice of cargo availability.

3. To the extent that they fall within the scope of activity of a conference, the following matters may also be the subject of consultation:

(a) Operation of cargo inspection services;
(b) Changes in the pattern of services;
(c) Effects of the introduction of new technology in the carriage of cargo, in particular unitisation, with consequent reduction of conventional service or loss of direct services; and
(d) Adequacy and quality of shipping services, including the impact of pooling, berthing or sailing arrangements on the availability of shipping services and freight rates at which shipping services are provided; changes in the areas served and in the regularity of calls by conference vessels.

4. Consultations shall be held before final decisions are taken, unless otherwise provided in this Code. Advance notice shall be given of the intention to take decisions on matters referred to in Article 11, paragraphs 2 and 3. Where this is impossible, urgent decisions may be taken pending the holding of consultations.

5. Consultations shall begin without undue delay and in any event within a maximum period specified in the conference agreement, or in the absence of such a provision in the agreement, not later than 30 days after receipt of the proposal for consultations, unless different periods of time are provided in this Code.

6. When holding consultations, the parties shall use their best efforts to provide relevant information, to hold timely discussions and to clarify matters for the purpose of seeking solutions of the issues concerned. The parties involved shall take account of each other's views and problems and strive to reach agreement consistent with their commercial viability

CHAPTER IV. FREIGHT RATES

Article 12. Criteria for freight-rate determination

In arriving at a decision on questions of tariff policy in all cases mentioned in this Code, the following points shall, unless otherwise provided, be taken into account:

(a) Freight rates shall be fixed at as low a level as is feasible from the commercial point of view and shall permit a reasonable profit for shipowners;
(b) The cost of operations of conferences shall, as a rule, be evaluated for the round voyage of ships, with the outward and inward directions considered as a single whole.

Where applicable, the outward and inward voyage should be considered separately. The freight rates should take into account among other factors, the nature of cargoes, the interrelation between weight and cargo measurement, as well as the value of cargoes;

(c) In fixing promotional freight rates and/or special freight rates for specific goods, the conditions of trade for these goods of the countries served by the conference particularly of developing and land-locked countries, shall be taken into account.

Article 13. Conference tariffs and classification of tariff rates

1. Conference tariffs shall not unfairly differentiate between shippers similarly situated. Shipping lines members of a conference shall adhere strictly to the rates, rules and terms shown in the tariffs and other currently valid published documents of the conference and to any special arrangements permitted under this Code.

2. Conference tariffs should be drawn up simply and clearly, containing as few classes/categories as possible, depending on the commodity and, where appropriate, for each class/category; they should also indicate, wherever practicable, in order to facilitate statistical compilation and analysis, the corresponding appropriate code number of the item in accordance with the Standard International Trade Classification, the Brussels Tariff Nomenclature or any other nomenclature that may be internationally adopted; the classification of commodities in the tariffs should, as far as practicable, be prepared in co-operation with shippers' organisations and other national and international organisations concerned.

Article 14. General freight-rate increases

1. A conference shall give notice of not less than 150 days, or according to regional practice and/or agreement, to shippers' organisations or representatives of shippers and/or shippers and, where so required, to appropriate authorities of the countries whose trade is served by the conference, of its intention to effect a general increase in freight rates, an indication of its extent, the date of effect and the reasons supporting the proposed increase.

2. At the request of any of the parties prescribed for this purpose in this Code, to be made within an agreed period of time after the receipt of the notice, consultations shall commence, in accordance with the relevant provisions of this Code, within a stipulated period not exceeding 30 days or as previously agreed between the parties concerned; the consultations shall be held in respect of the basis and amounts of the proposed increase and the date from which it is to be given effect.

3. A conference, in an effort to expedite consultations, may or upon the request of any of the parties prescribed in this Code as entitled to participate in consultations on general freight-rate increases shall, where practicable, reasonably before the consultations, submit to the participating parties a report from independent accountants of repute, including, where the requesting parties accept it as one of the bases of consultations, an aggregated analysis of data regarding relevant costs and revenues which in the opinion of the conference necessitate an increase in freight rates.

4. If agreement is reached as a result of the consultations, the freight-rate increase shall take effect from the date indicated in the notice served in accordance with Article 14, paragraph 1, unless a later date is agreed upon between the parties concerned.

5. If no agreement is reached within 30 days of the giving of notice in accordance with Article 14, paragraph 1, and subject to procedures prescribed in this Code, the matter shall be submitted immediately to international mandatory conciliation, in accordance with Chapter VI. The recommendation of the conciliators, if accepted by the parties concerned, shall be binding upon them and shall be implemented, subject to the provisions of Article 14, paragraph 9, with effect from the date mentioned in the conciliators' recommendation.

6. Subject to the provisions of Article 14, paragraph 9, a general freight-rate increase may be implemented by a conference pending the conciliators' recommendation. When making their recommendation, the conciliators should take into account the extent of the above-mentioned increase made by the conference and the period for which it has been in force. In the event that

the conference rejects the recommendation of the conciliators, shippers and/or shippers' organisations shall have the right to consider themselves not bound, after appropriate notice, by any arrangement or other contract with that conference which may prevent them from using non-conference shipping lines. Where a loyalty arrangement exists shippers and/or shippers' organisations shall give notice within a period of 30 days to the effect that they no longer consider themselves bound by that arrangement, which notice shall apply from the date mentioned therein, and a period of not less than 30 days and not more than 90 days shall be provided in the loyalty arrangement for this purpose.

7. A deferred rebate which is due to the shipper and which has already been accumulated by the conference shall not be withheld by, or forfeited to, the conference as a result of action by the shipper under Article 14, paragraph 6.

8. If the trade of a country carried by shipping lines members of a conference on a particular route consists largely of one or few basic commodities, any increase in the freight rate on one or more of those commodities shall be treated as a general freight-rate increase, and the appropriate provisions of this Code shall apply.

9. Conferences should institute any general freight-rate increase effective in accordance with this Code for a period of a stated minimum duration, subject always to the rules regarding surcharges and regarding adjustment in freight rates consequent upon fluctuations in foreign exchange rates. The period over which a general freight-rate increase is to apply is an appropriate matter to be considered during consultations conducted in accordance with Article 14, paragraph 2, but unless otherwise agreed between the parties concerned during the consultations, the minimum period of time between the date when one general freight-rate increase becomes effective and the date of notice for the next general freight-rate increase given in accordance with Article 14, paragraph 1 shall not be less than 10 months.

Article 15. Promotional freight rates

1. Promotional freight rates for non-traditional exports should be instituted by conferences.

2. All necessary and reasonable information justifying the need for a promotional freight rate shall be submitted to a conference by the shippers, shippers' organisations or representatives of shippers concerned.

3. Special procedures shall be instituted providing for a decision within 30 days from the date of receipt of that information, unless mutually agreed otherwise, on application for promotional freight rates. A clear distinction shall be made between these and general procedures for considering the possibility of reducing freight rates for other commodities or of exempting them from increases.

4. Information regarding the procedures for considering applications for promotional freight rates shall be made available by the conference to shippers and/or shippers' organisations and, on request, to the Governments and/or other appropriate authorities of the countries whose trade is served by the conference.

5. A promotional freight rate shall be established normally for a period of 12 months, unless otherwise mutually agreed between the parties concerned. Prior to the expiry of the period, the promotional freight rate shall be reviewed, on request by the shipper and/or shippers' organisation concerned, when it shall be a matter for the shipper and/or shippers' organisation, at the request of the conference, to show that the continuation of the rate is justified beyond the initial period.

6. When examining a request for a promotional freight rate, the conference may take into account that, while the rate should promote the export of the non-traditional product for which it is sought, it is not likely to create substantial competitive distortions in the export of a similar product from another country served by the conference.

7. Promotional freight rates are not excluded from the imposition of a surcharge or a currency adjustment factor in accordance with Articles 16 and 17.

8. Each shipping line member of a conference serving the relevant ports of a conference trade shall accept, and not unreasonably refuse, a fair share of cargo for which a promotional freight rate has been established by the conference.

Article 16. Surcharges

1. Surcharges imposed by a conference to cover sudden or extraordinary increases in costs or losses of revenue shall be regarded as temporary. They shall be reduced in accordance with improvements in the situation or circumstances which they were imposed to meet and shall be cancelled, subject to Article 16, paragraph 6, as soon as the situation or circumstances which prompted their imposition cease to prevail. This shall be indicated at the moment of their imposition, together, as far as possible, with a description of the change in the situation or circumstances which will bring about their increase, reduction or cancellation.

2. Surcharges imposed on cargo moving to or from a particular port shall likewise be regarded as temporary and likewise shall be increased, reduced or cancelled, subject to Article 16, paragraph 6, when the situation in that port changes.

3. Before any surcharge is imposed, whether general or covering only a specific port, notice should be given and there shall be consultation, upon request, in accordance with the procedures of this Code, between the conference concerned and other parties directly affected by the surcharge and prescribed in this Code as entitled to participate in such consultations, save in those exceptional circumstances which warrant immediate imposition of the surcharge. In cases where a surcharge has been imposed without prior consultation, consultations, upon request, shall be held as soon as possible thereafter. Prior to such consultations, conferences shall furnish data which in their opinion justify the imposition of the surcharge.

4. Unless the parties agree otherwise, within a period of 15 days after the receipt of a notice given in accordance with Article 16, paragraph 3, if there is no agreement on the question of the surcharge between the parties concerned referred to in that Article, the relevant provisions for settlement of disputes provided in this Code shall prevail. Unless the parties concerned agree otherwise, the surcharge may, however, be imposed pending resolution of the dispute, if the dispute still remains unresolved at the end of a period of 30 days after the receipt of the above-mentioned notice.

5. In the event of a surcharge being imposed, in exceptional circumstances, without prior consultation as provided in Article 16, paragraph 3, if no agreement is reached through subsequent consultations, the relevant provisions for settlement of disputes provided in this Code shall prevail.

6. Financial loss incurred by the shipping lines members of a conference as a result of any delay on account of consultations and/or other proceedings for resolving disputes regarding imposition of surcharges in accordance with the provisions of this Code, as compared to the date from which the surcharge was to be imposed in terms of the notice given in accordance with Article 16, paragraph 3, may be compensated by an equivalent prolongation of the surcharge before its removal. Conversely, for any surcharge imposed by the conference and subsequently determined and agreed to be unjustified or excessive as a result of consultations or other procedures prescribed in this Code, the amounts so collected or the excess thereof as determined hereinabove, unless otherwise agreed, shall be refunded to the parties concerned, if claimed by them, within a period of 30 days of such claim.

Article 17. Currency changes

1. Exchange rate changes, including formal devaluation or revaluation, which lead to changes in the aggregate operational costs and/or revenues of the shipping lines members of a conference relating to their operations within the conference provide a valid reason for the introduction of a currency adjustment factor or for a change in the freight rates. The adjustment or change shall be such that in the aggregate the member lines concerned neither gain nor lose, as far as possible, as a result of the adjustment or change. The adjustment or change may take the form of currency surcharges or discounts or of increases or decreases in the freight rates.

2. Such adjustments or changes shall be subject to notice, which should be arranged in accordance with regional practice, where such practice exists, and there shall be consultations in accordance with the provisions of this Code between the conference concerned and the other parties directly affected and prescribed in this Code as entitled to participate in consultations, save in those exceptional circumstances which warrant immediate imposition of the currency adjustment factor or freight-rate change. In the event that this has been done without prior

consultations, consultations shall be held as soon as possible thereafter. The consultations should be on the application, size and date of the implementation of the currency adjustment factor or freight-rate change, and the same procedures shall be followed for this purpose as are prescribed in Article 16, paragraphs 4 and 5, in respect of surcharges. Such consultations should take place and be completed within a period not exceeding 15 days from the date when the intention to apply a currency surcharge or to effect a freight-rate change is announced.

3. If no agreement is reached within 15 days through consultations, the relevant provisions for settlement of disputes provided in this Code shall prevail.

4. The provisions of Article 16, paragraph 6 shall apply, adapted as necessary to currency adjustment factors and freight-rate changes dealt with in the present Article.

CHAPTER V. OTHER MATTERS

Article 18. Fighting ships

Members of a conference shall not use fighting ships in the conference trade for the purpose of excluding, preventing or reducing competition by driving a shipping line not a member of the conference out of the said trade.

Article 19. Adequacy of service

1. Conferences should take necessary and appropriate measures to ensure that their member lines provide regular, adequate and efficient service of the required frequency on the routes they serve and shall arrange such services so as to avoid as far as possible bunching and gapping of sailings. Conferences should also take into consideration any special measures necessary in arranging services to handle seasonal variations in cargo volumes.

2. Conferences and other parties prescribed in this Code as entitled to participate in consultations, including appropriate authorities if they so desire, should keep under review, and should maintain close co-operation regarding the demand for shipping space, the adequacy and suitability of service, and in particular the possibilities for rationalisation and for increasing the efficiency of services. Benefits identified as accruing from rationalisation of services shall be fairly reflected in the level of freight rates.

3. In respect of any port for which conference services are supplied only subject to the availability of a specified minimum of cargo, that minimum shall be specified in the tariff. Shippers should give adequate notice of the availability of such cargo.

Article 20. Head office of a conference

A conference shall as a rule establish its head office in a country whose trade is served by that conference, unless agreed otherwise by the shipping lines members of that conference.

Article 21. Representation

Conferences shall establish local representation in all countries served, except that where there are practical reasons to the contrary the representation may be on a regional basis. The name and addresses of representatives shall be readily available, and these representatives shall ensure that the views of shippers and conferences are made rapidly known to each other with a view to expediting prompt decisions. When a conference considers it suitable, it shall provide for adequate delegation of powers of decision to its representatives.

Article 22. Contents of conference agreements, trade participation agreements and loyalty arrangements

Conference agreements, trade participation agreements and loyalty arrangements shall conform to the applicable requirements of this Code and may include such other provisions as may be agreed which are not inconsistent with this Code.

PART TWO

CHAPTER VI. PROVISIONS AND MACHINERY FOR SETTLEMENT OF DISPUTES

A. General Provisions

Article 23

1. The provisions of this Chapter shall apply whenever there is a dispute relating to the application or operation of the provisions of this Code between the following parties:

(a) A conference and a shipping line;
(b) The shipping lines members of a conference;
(c) A conference or a shipping line member thereof and a shippers' organisation or representatives of shippers or shippers; and
(d) Two or more conferences.

For the purposes of this chapter the term "party" means the original parties to the dispute as well as third parties which have joined the proceedings in accordance with (a) of Article 34.

2. Disputes between shipping lines of the same flag, as well as those between organisations belonging to the same country, shall be settled within the framework of the national jurisdiction of that country, unless this creates serious difficulties in the fulfilment of the provisions of this Code.

3. The parties to a dispute shall first attempt to settle it by an exchange of views or direct negotiations with the intention of finding a mutually satisfactory solution.

4. Disputes between the parties referred to in Article 23, paragraph 1 relating to:

(a) Refusal of admission of a national shipping line to a conference serving the foreign trade of the country of that shipping line;
(b) Refusal of admission of a third-country shipping line to a conference;
(c) Expulsion from a conference;
(d) Inconsistency of a conference agreement with this Code;
(e) A general freight-rate increase;
(f) Surcharges;
(g) Changes in freight rates or the imposition of a currency adjustment factor due to exchange rate changes;
(h) Participation in trade; and
(i) The form and terms of proposed loyalty arrangements

which have not been resolved through an exchange of views or direct negotiations shall, at the request of any of the parties to the dispute, be referred to international mandatory conciliation in accordance with the provisions of this Chapter.

Article 24

1. The conciliation procedure is initiated at the request of one of the parties to the dispute.

2. The request shall be made:

(a) In disputes relating to membership of conferences: not later than 60 days from the date of receipt by the applicant of the conference decision, including the reasons therefor, in accordance with Article 1, paragraph 4 and Article 4, paragraph 3;
(b) In disputes relating to general freight-rate increases: not later than the date of expiry of the period of notice specified in Article 14, paragraph 1;
(c) In disputes relating to surcharges: not later than the date of expiry of the 30-day period specified in Article 16, paragraph 1 or, where no notice has been given not later that 15 days from the date when the surcharge was put into effect; and
(d) In disputes relating to changes in freight rates or the imposition of a currency adjustment factor due to exchange rate changes: not later than five days after the date of expiry of the period specified in Article 17, paragraph 3.

3. The provisions of Article 24, paragraph 2 shall not apply to a dispute which is referred to international mandatory conciliation in accordance with Article 25, paragraph 3.

4. Requests for conciliation in disputes other than those referred to in Article 24, paragraph 2, may be made at any time.

5. The time-limits specified in Article 24, paragraph 2 may be extended by agreement between the parties.

6. A request for conciliation shall be considered to have been duly made if it is proved that the request has been sent to the other party by registered letter, telegram or teleprinter or has been served on it within the time-limits specified in Article 24, paragraphs 2 or 5.

7. Where no request has been made within the time-limits specified in Article 24, paragraphs 2 or 5, the decision of the conference shall be final and no proceedings under this chapter may be brought by any party to the dispute to challenge that decision.

Article 25

1. Where the parties have agreed that disputes referred to in Article 23, paragraph 4(a), (b), (c), (d), (h) and (i) shall be resolved through procedures other than those established in that Article, or agree on procedures to resolve a particular dispute that has arisen between them, such disputes shall, at the request of any of the parties to the dispute, be resolved as provided for in their agreement.

2. The provisions of Article 25, paragraph 1 apply also to the disputes referred to in Article 23, paragraph 4(e), (f) and (g), unless national legislation, rules or regulations prevent shippers from having this freedom of choice.

3. Where conciliation proceedings have been initiated, such proceedings shall have precedence over remedies available under national law. If a party seeks remedies under national law in respect of a dispute to which this chapter applies without invoking the procedures provided for in this Chapter, then, upon the request of a respondent to those proceedings, they shall be stayed and the dispute shall be referred to the procedures defined in this chapter by the court or other authority where the national remedies are sought.

Article 26

1. The Contracting Parties shall confer upon conferences and shippers' organisations such capacity as is necessary for the application of the provisions of this chapter. In particular:

(a) A conference or a shippers' organisation may institute proceedings as a party or be named as a party to proceedings in its collective capacity;

(b) Any notification to a conference or shippers' organisation in its collective capacity shall also constitute a notification to each member of such conference or shippers' organisation;

(c) A notification to a conference or shippers' organisation shall be transmitted to the address of the head office of the conference or shippers' organisation. Each conference or shippers' organisation shall register the address of its head office with the Registrar appointed in accordance with Article 46, paragraph 1. In the event that a conference or a shippers' organisation fails to register or has no head office, a notification to any member in the name of the conference or shippers' organisation shall be deemed to be notification to such conference or organisation.

2. Acceptance or rejection by a conference or shippers' organisation of a recommendation by conciliators shall be deemed to be acceptance or rejection of such a recommendation by each member thereof.

Article 27

Unless the parties agree otherwise, the conciliators may decide to make a recommendation on the basis of written submissions without oral proceedings.

B. International Mandatory Conciliation

Article 28

In international mandatory conciliation the appropriate authorities of a Contracting Party shall, if they so request, participate in the conciliation proceedings in support of a party being a national of that Contracting Party, or in support of a party having a dispute arising in the context of the foreign trade of that Contracting Party. The appropriate authority may alternatively act as an observer in such conciliation proceedings.

Article 29

1. In international mandatory conciliation the proceedings shall be held in the place unanimously agreed to by the parties or, failing such agreement, in the place decided upon by the conciliators.

2. In determining the place of conciliation proceedings the parties and the conciliators shall take into account, inter alia, countries which are closely connected with the dispute, bearing in mind the country of the shipping line concerned and, especially when the dispute is related to cargo, the country where the cargo originates.

Article 30

1. For the purposes of this chapter an international panel of conciliators shall be established, consisting of experts of high repute or experience in the fields of law, economics of sea transport, or foreign trade and finance, as determined by the Contracting Parties selecting them, who shall serve in an independent capacity.

2. Each Contracting Party may at any time nominate members of the panel up to a total of 12, and shall communicate their names to the Registrar. The nominations shall be for periods of six years each and may be renewed. In the event of the death, incapacity or resignation of a member of the panel, the Contracting Party which nominated such person shall nominate a replacement for the remainder of his term of office. A nomination takes effect from the date on which the communication of the nomination is received by the Registrar.

3. The Registrar shall maintain the panel list and shall regularly inform the Contracting Parties of the composition of the panel.

Article 31

1. The purpose of conciliation is to reach an amicable settlement of the dispute through recommendations formulated by independent conciliators.

2. The conciliators shall identify and clarify the issues in dispute, seek for this purpose any information from the parties, and on the basis thereof, submit to the parties a recommendation for the settlement of the dispute.

3. The parties shall co-operate in good faith with the conciliators in order to enable them to carry out their functions.

4. Subject to the provisions of Article 25, paragraph 2, the parties to the dispute may at any time during the conciliation proceedings decide in agreement to have recourse to a different procedure for the settlement of their dispute. The parties to a dispute which has been made subject to proceedings other than those provided for in this chapter may decide by mutual agreement to have recourse to international mandatory conciliation.

Article 32

1. The conciliation proceedings shall be conducted either by one conciliator or by an uneven number of conciliators agreed upon or designated by the parties.

2. Where the parties cannot agree on the number or the appointment of the conciliators as provided in Article 32, paragraph 1, the conciliation proceedings shall be conducted by three conciliators, one appointed by each party in the statement(s) of claim and reply respectively, and the third by the two conciliators thus appointed, who shall act as chairman.

3. If the reply does not name a conciliator to be appointed in cases where Article 32, paragraph 2 would apply, the second conciliator shall, within 30 days following the receipt of the statement of claim, be chosen by lot by the conciliator appointed in the statement of claim from among the members of the panel nominated by the Contracting Party or Parties of which the respondent(s) is (are) a national(s).

4. Where the conciliators appointed in accordance with Article 32, paragraphs 2 or 3 cannot agree on the appointment of the third conciliator within 15 days following the date of the appointment of the second conciliator, he shall, within the following 5 days, be chosen by lot by the appointed conciliators. Prior to the drawing by lot:

(a) No member of the panel of conciliators having the same nationality as either of the two appointed conciliators shall be eligible for selection by lot;

(b) Each of the two appointed conciliators may exclude from the list of the panel of conciliators an equal number of them subject to the requirement that at least 30 members of the panel shall remain eligible for selection by lot.

Article 33

1. Where several parties request conciliation with the same respondent in respect of the same issue, or of issues which are closely connected, that respondent may request the consolidation of those cases.

2. The request for conciliation shall be considered and decided upon by majority vote by the chairmen of the conciliators so far chosen. If such request is allowed, the chairmen will designate the conciliators to consider the consolidated cases from among the conciliators so far appointed or chosen, provided that an uneven number of conciliators is chosen and that the conciliator first appointed by each party shall be one of the conciliators considering the consolidated case.

Article 34

Any party, other than an appropriate authority referred to in Article 28, if conciliation has been initiated, may join in the proceedings:

either

(a) As a party, in case of a direct economic interest;

or

(b) As a supporting party to one of the original parties, in case of an indirect economic interest,

unless either of the original parties objects to such joinder.

Article 35

1. The recommendations of the conciliators shall be made in accordance with the provisions of this Code.

2. When the Code is silent upon any point, the conciliators shall apply the law which the parties agree at the time the conciliation proceedings commence or thereafter, but not later than the time of submission of evidence to the conciliators. Failing such agreement, the law which in the opinion of the conciliators is most closely connected with the dispute shall be applicable.

3. The conciliators shall not decide ex aequo et borro upon the dispute unless the parties so agree after the dispute has arisen.

4. The conciliators shall not bring a finding of non liquet on the ground of obscurity of the law.

5. The conciliators may recommend those remedies and reliefs which are provided in the law applicable to the dispute.

Article 36

The recommendations of the conciliators shall include reasons.

Article 37

1. Unless the parties have agreed before, during or after the conciliation procedure that the recommendation of the conciliators shall be binding, the recommendation shall become binding by acceptance by the parties. A recommendation which has been accepted by some parties to a dispute shall be binding between those parties only.

2. Acceptance of the recommendation must be communicated by the parties to the conciliators, at an address specified by them, not later than 30 days after receipt of the notification of the recommendation; otherwise, it shall be considered that the recommendation has not been accepted.

3. Any party which does not accept the recommendation shall notify the conciliators and the other parties, within 30 days following the period specified in Article 37, paragraph 2 of its grounds for rejection of the recommendation, comprehensively and in writing.

4. When the recommendation has been accepted by the parties, the conciliators shall immediately draw up and sign a record of settlement, at which time the recommendation shall become binding upon those parties. If the recommendation has not been accepted by all parties, the conciliators shall draw up a report with respect to those parties rejecting the recommendation, noting the dispute and the failure of those parties to settle the dispute.

5. A recommendation which has become binding upon the parties shall be implemented by them immediately or at such later time as is specified in the recommendation.

6. Any party may make its acceptance conditional upon acceptance by all or any of the other parties to the dispute.

Article 38

1. A recommendation shall constitute a final determination of a dispute as between the parties which accept it, except to the extent that the recommendation is not recognized and enforced in accordance with the provisions of Article 39.

2. "Recommendation" included an interpretation, clarification or revision of the recommendation made by the conciliators before the recommendation has been accepted.

Article 39

1. Each Contracting Party shall recognise a recommendation as binding between the parties which have accepted it and shall, subject to the provisions of article 39, paragraphs 2 and 3, enforce, at the request of any such party, all obligations imposed by the recommendations as if it were a final judgment of a court of that Contracting Party.

2. A recommendation shall not be recognised and enforced at the request of a party referred to in Article 39, paragraph 1 only if the court or other competent authority of the country where recognition and enforcement is sought is satisfied that:

(a) Any party which accepted that recommendation was, under the law applicable to it, under some legal incapacity at the time of acceptance;

(b) Fraud or coercion has been used in the making of the recommendations;

(c) The recommendation is contrary to public policy (ordre public) in the country of enforcement; or

(d) The composition of the conciliators, or the conciliation procedure, was not in accordance with the provisions of this Code.

3. Any part of the recommendation shall not be enforced and recognised if the court or other competent authority is satisfied that such part comes within any of the subparagraphs of Article 39, paragraph 2 and can be separated from other parts of the recommendation. If such part cannot be separated, the entire recommendation shall not be enforced and recognised.

Article 40

1. Where the recommendation has been accepted by all the parties, the recommendation and the reasons therefor may be published with the consent of all the parties.

2. Where the recommendation has been rejected by one or more of the parties but has been accepted by one or more of the parties:

(a) The party or parties rejecting the recommendation shall publish its or their grounds for rejection, given pursuant to Article 37, paragraph 3, and may at the same time publish the recommendation and the reasons therefor;

(b) A party which has accepted the recommendation may publish the recommendation and the reasons therefor; it may also publish the grounds for rejection given by another party unless such other party has already published its rejection and the grounds therefor in accordance with Article 40, paragraph 2(a).

3. Where the recommendation has not been accepted by any of the parties, each party may publish the recommendation and the reasons therefor and also its own rejection and the grounds therefor.

Article 41

1. Documents and statements containing factual information supplied by any party to its conciliators shall be made public unless that party or a majority of the conciliators agrees otherwise.

2. Such documents and statements supplied by a party may be tendered by that party in support of its case in subsequent proceedings arising from the same dispute and between the same parties.

Article 42

Where the recommendation has not become binding upon the parties, no views expressed or reasons given by the conciliators, or concessions or offers made by the parties for the purpose of the conciliation procedure, shall affect the legal rights and obligations of any of the parties.

Article 43

1. (a) The costs of the conciliators and all costs of the administration of the conciliation proceedings shall be borne equally by the parties to the proceedings, unless they agree otherwise.

(b) When the conciliation proceedings have been initiated, the conciliators shall be entitled to require an advance or security for the costs referred to in Article 43, paragraph 1(a).

2. Each party shall bear all expenses it incurs in connection with the proceedings, unless the parties agree otherwise.

3. Notwithstanding the provisions of Article 43, paragraphs 1 and 2, the conciliators may, having decided unanimously that a party has brought a claim vexatiously or frivolously, assess against that party any or all of the costs of other parties to the proceedings. Such decision shall be final and binding on all the parties.

Article 44

1. Failure of a party to appear or to present its case at any stage of the proceedings shall not be deemed an admission of the other party's assertions. In that event, the other party may, at its choice, request the conciliators to close the proceedings or to deal with the questions presented to them and submit a recommendation in accordance with the provisions for making recommendations set out in this Code.

2. Before closing the proceedings, the conciliators shall grant the party failing to appear or to present its case a period of grace, not exceeding 10 days, unless they are satisfied that the party does not intend to appear or to present its case.

3. Failure to observe procedural time-limits laid down in the Code or determined by the conciliators, in particular time-limits relating to the submission of statements or information, shall be considered a failure to appear in the proceedings.

4. Where the proceedings have been closed owing to one party's failure to appear or to present its case, the conciliators shall draw up a report noting that party's failure.

Article 45

1. The conciliators shall follow the procedures stipulated in this Code.

2. The rules of procedure annexed to the present Convention shall be considered as model rules for the guidance of conciliators. The conciliators may, by mutual consent, use, supplement

or amend the rules contained in the annex or formulate their own rules of procedure to the extent that such supplementary, amended or other rules are not inconsistent with the provisions of this Code.

3. If the parties agree that it may be in the interest of achieving an expeditious and inexpensive solution of the conciliation proceedings, they may mutually agree to rules of procedure which are not inconsistent with the provisions of this Code.

4. The conciliators shall formulate their recommendation by consensus or failing that shall decide by majority vote.

5. The conciliation proceedings shall finish and the recommendation of the conciliators shall be delivered not later than six months from the date on which the conciliators are appointed, except in the cases referred to in Article 23, paragraph 4(e), (f), and (g), for which the time limits in Article 14, paragraph 1 and Article 16, paragraph 4 shall be valid. The period of six months may be extended by agreement of the parties.

C. Institutional Machinery

Article 46

1. Six months before the entry into force of the present Convention, the Secretary-General of the United Nations shall, subject to the approval of the General Assembly of the United Nations, and taking into account the views expressed by the Contracting Parties, appoint a Registrar, who may be assisted by such additional staff as may be necessary for the performance of the functions listed in Article 46, paragraph 2. Administrative services for the registrar and his assistants shall be provided by the United Nations Office at Geneva.

2. The Registrar shall perform the following functions in consultation with the Contracting Parties as appropriate:

(a) Maintain the list of conciliators of the international panel of conciliators and regularly inform the Contracting Parties of the composition of the panel;

(b) Provide the names and addresses of the conciliators to the parties concerned on request;

(c) Receive and maintain copies of requests for conciliation, replies, recommendation, acceptances, or rejections, including reasons therefor;

(d) Furnish on request, and at their cost, copies of recommendations and reasons for rejection to the shippers' organisations, conferences and Governments, subject to the provisions of Article 40;

(e) Make available information of a non-confidential nature on completed conciliation cases, and without attribution to the parties concerned, for the purposes of preparation of material for the Review Conference referred to in Article 52; and

(f) The other functions prescribed for the Registrar in Article 26, paragraph 1(c) and Article 30, paragraphs 2 and 3.

CHAPTER VII. FINAL CLAUSES

Article 47. Implementation

1. Each Contracting Party shall take such legislative or other measures as may be necessary to implement the present Convention.

2. Each Contracting Party shall communicate to the Secretary-General of the United Nations, who shall be the depositary, the text of the legislative or other measures which it has taken in order to implement the present Convention.

Article 48. Signature, ratification, acceptance, approval and accession

1. The present Convention shall remain open for signature as from 1 July 1974 until and including 30 June 1975 at United Nations Headquarters and shall thereafter remain open for accession.

2. All States are entitled to become Contracting Parties to the present Convention by:

(a) Signature subject to and followed by ratification, acceptance or approval; or

(b) Signature without reservation as to ratification, acceptance or approval; or
(c) Accession.

3. Ratification, acceptance, approval or accession shall be effected by the deposit of an instrument to this effect with the depositary.

Article 49. Entry into force

1. The present Convention shall enter into force six months after the date on which not less than 24 States, the combined tonnage of which amounts to at least 25 per cent of world tonnage, have become Contracting Parties to it in accordance with Article 48. For the purpose of the present Article the tonnage shall be deemed to be that contained in Lloyd's Register of Shipping—Statistical Tables 1973, table 2 "World Fleets—Analysis by Principal Types", in respect to general cargo (including passenger/cargo) ships and container (fully cellular) ships, exclusive of the United States reserve fleet and the American and Canadian Great Lakes fleets.

2. For each State which thereafter ratifies, accepts, approves or accedes to it, the present Convention shall come into force six months after deposit by such State of the appropriate instrument.

3. Any State which becomes a Contracting Party to the present Convention after the entry into force of an amendment shall, failing an expression of a different intention by that State:
(a) Be considered as a Party to the present Convention amended; and
(b) Be considered as a Party to the unamended Convention in relation to any Party to the present Convention not bound by the amendment.

Article 50. Denunciation

1. The present Convention may be denounced by any Contracting Party at any time after the expiration of a period of two years from the date on which the Convention has entered into force.

2. Denunciation shall be notified to the depositary in writing, and shall take effect one year, or such longer period as may be specified in the instrument of denunciation, after the date of receipt by the depositary.

Article 51. Amendments

1. Any Contracting Party may propose one or more amendments to the present Convention by communicating the amendments to the depositary. The depositary shall circulate such amendments among the Contracting Parties, for their acceptance, and among States entitled to become Contracting Parties to the present Convention which are not Contracting Parties, for their information.

2. Each proposed amendment circulated in accordance with Article 51, paragraph 1 shall be deemed to have been accepted if no Contracting Party communicates an objection thereto to the depositary within 12 months following the date of its circulation by the depositary. If a Contracting Party communicates an objection to the proposed amendment, such amendment shall not be considered as accepted and shall not be put into effect.

3. If no objection has been communicated, the amendment shall enter into force for all Contracting Parties six months after the expiry date of the period of 12 months referred to in Article 51, paragraph 2.

Article 52. Review Conferences

1. A Review Conference shall be convened by the depositary five years from the date on which the present Convention comes into force to review the working of the Convention, with particular reference to its implication, and to consider and adopt appropriate amendments.

2. The depositary shall, four years from the date on which the present Convention comes into force, seek the views of all States entitled to attend the review Conference and shall, on the basis of the views received, prepare and circulate a draft agenda as well as amendments proposed for consideration by the Conference.

3. Further review conferences shall be similarly convened every five years, or at any time after the first Review Conference, at the request of one-third of the Contracting Parties to the present Convention, unless the first Review Conference decides otherwise.

4. Nothwithstanding the provisions of Article 52, paragraph 1, if the present Convention has not entered into force five years from the date of the adoption of the Final Act of the United Nations Conference of Plenipotentiaries on a Code of Conduct for Liner Conferences a Review Conference shall, at the request of one-third of the States entitled to become Contracting Parties to the present Convention, be convened by the Secretary-General of the United Nations, subject to the approval of the General Assembly, in order to review the provisions of the Convention and its annex and to consider and adopt appropriate amendments.

Article 53. Functions of the depositary

1. The depositary shall notify the signatory and acceding States of:
   (a) Signatures, ratifications, acceptances, approvals and accessions in accordance with Article 48;
   (b) The date on which the present Convention enters into force in accordance with Article 49;
   (c) Denunciations of the present Convention in accordance with Article 50;
   (d) Reservations to the present Convention and the withdrawal of reservations;
   (e) The text of the legislative or other measures which each Contracting Party has taken in order to implement the present Convention in accordance with Article 47;
   (f) Proposed amendments and objections to proposed amendments in accordance with Article 51; and
   (g) Entry into force of amendments in accordance with Article 51, paragraph 3.
2. The depositary shall also undertake such actions as are necessary under Article 52.

Article 54. Authentic texts—deposit

The original of the present Convention, of which the Chinese, English, French, Russian and Spanish texts are equally authentic, will be deposited with the Secretary-General of the United Nations.

IN WITNESS WHEREOF the undersigned, having been duly authorised to this effect by their respective Governments, have signed the present Convention, on the dates appearing opposite their signatures.

ANNEX TO THE CONVENTION

MODEL RULES OF PROCEDURE FOR INTERNATIONAL MANDATORY CONCILIATION

Rule 1

1. Any party wishing to institute conciliation proceedings under the Code shall address a request to the effect in writing, accompanied by a statement of claim to the other party, and copied to the Registrar.
2. The statement of claim shall:
   (a) Designate precisely each party to the dispute and state the address of each;
   (b) Contain a summary statement of pertinent facts, the issues in dispute and the claimant's proposal for the settlement of the dispute;
   (c) State whether an oral hearing is desired and, if so, and to the the extent then known, the names and addresses of persons to give evidence, including experts' evidence, for the claimant;
   (d) Be accompanied by such supporting documentation and relevant agreements and arrangements entered into by the parties as the claimant may consider necessary at the time of making the claim;

(e) Indicate the number of conciliators required, any proposal concerning the appointment of conciliators, or the name of the conciliator appointed by the claimant in accordance with Article 32, paragraph 2; and
(f) Contain proposals, if any, regarding rules of procedure.

3. The statement of claim shall be dated and shall be signed by the party.

Rule 2

1. If the respondent decided to reply to the claim, he shall, within 30 days following the date of his receipt of the statement of claim, transmit a reply to the other party and copied to the Registrar.

2. The reply shall:
(a) Contain a summary statement of pertinent facts opposed to the contentions in the statement of claim, the respondent's proposal, if any, for the settlement of the dispute and any remedy claimed by him with a view to the settlement of the dispute;
(b) State whether an oral hearing is desired and, if so, and to the extent then known, the names and addresses of persons to give evidence, including experts' evidence for the respondent;
(c) Be accompanied by such supporting documentation and relevant agreements and arrangements entered into by the parties as the respondent may consider necessary at the time of making the reply;
(d) Indicate the number of conciliators required, any proposal concerning the appointment of conciliators, or the name of the conciliator appointed by the respondent in accordance with Article 32, paragraph 2; and
(e) Contain proposals, if any, regarding rules of procedure.

3. The reply shall be dated and shall be signed by the party.

Rule 3

1. Any person or other interest desiring to participate in conciliation proceedings under Article 34 shall transmit a written request to the parties to the dispute, with a copy to the Registrar.

2. If participation in accordance with (a) of Article 34 is desired, the request shall set forth the grounds therefor, including the information required under rule 1, paragraph 2(a), (b) and (d).

3. If participation in accordance with (b) of Article 34 is desired, the request shall state the grounds therefor and which of the original parties would be supported.

4. Any objection to a request for joinder by such a party shall be sent by the objecting party, with a copy to the other party, within seven days of receipt of the request.

5. In the event that two or more proceedings are consolidated, subsequent requests for third-party participation shall be transmitted to all parties concerned, each of which may object in accordance with the present rule.

Rule 4

By agreement between the parties to the dispute, on motion by either party, and after affording the parties an opportunity of being heard, the conciliators may order the consolidation or separation for all or any claims then pending between the same parties.

Rule 5

1. Any party may challenge a conciliator where circumstances exist that cause justifiable doubts as to his independence.

2. Notice of challenge, stating reasons therefor, should be made prior to the date of the closing of the proceedings, before the conciliators have rendered their recommendation. Any such challenge shall be heard promptly and shall be determined by majority vote of the conciliators in the first instance, as a preliminary point, in cases where more then one conciliator has been appointed. The decision in such cases shall be final.

3. A conciliator who has died, resigned, become incapacitated or disqualified shall be replaced promptly.

4. Proceedings interrupted in this way shall continue from the point where they were interrupted, unless it is agreed by the parties or ordered by the conciliators that a review or rehearing of any oral testimony take place.

Rule 6

The conciliators shall be judges of their own jurisdiction and/or competence within the provisions of the Code.

Rule 7

1. The conciliators shall receive and consider all written statements, documents, affidavits, publications or any other evidence, including oral evidence, which may be submitted to them by or on behalf of any of the parties, and shall give such weight thereto as in the judgement such evidence merits.

2. (a) Each party may submit to the conciliators any material it considers relevant, and at the time of such submission shall deliver certified copies to any other party to the proceedings, which party shall be given a reasonable opportunity to reply thereto;
   (b) The conciliators shall be the sole judges of the relevance and materiality of the evidence submitted to them by the parties;
   (c) The conciliators may ask the parties to produce such additional evidence as they may deem necessary to an understanding and determination of the dispute, provided that, if such additional evidence is produced, the other parties to the proceeding shall have a reasonable opportunity to comment thereon.

Rule 8

1. Whenever a period of days for the doing of any act is provided for in the Code or in these rules, the day from which the period begins to run shall not be counted, and the last day of the period shall be counted except where the last day is a Saturday, Sunday or a public holiday at the place of conciliation, in which case the last day shall be the next business day.

2. When the time provided for is less than seven days, intermediate Saturdays, Sundays and public holidays shall be excluded from the computation.

Rule 9

Subject to the provisions relating to procedural time-limits in the Code, the conciliators may, on a motion by one of the parties or pursuant to agreement between them, extend any such time-limit which has been fixed by the conciliators.

Rule 10

1. The conciliators shall fix the order of business and, unless otherwise agreed, the date and hour of each session.

2. Unless the parties otherwise agree, the proceedings shall take place in private.

3. The conciliators shall specifically inquire of all the parties whether they have any further evidence to submit before declaring the proceedings closed, and a noting thereof shall be recorded.

Rule 11

Conciliator's recommendations shall be in writing and shall include:
   (a) The precise designation and address of each party;
   (b) A description of the method of appointing conciliators, including their names;

(c) A summary of the conciliation proceedings, as the conciliators deem appropriate;
(e) A summary statement of the facts found by the conciliators;
(f) A summary of the submissions of the parties;
(g) Pronouncements on the issues in dispute, together with the reasons therefor;
(h) The signatures of the conciliators and the date of each signature; and
(i) An address for the communication of the acceptance or rejection of the recommendation.

Rule 12

The recommendation shall, so far as possible, contain a pronouncement on costs in accordance with the provisions of the Code. If the recommendation does not contain a full pronouncement on costs, the conciliators shall, as soon as possible after the recommendation, and in any event not later that 60 days thereafter, make a pronouncement in writing regarding costs as provided in the Code.

Rule 13

Conciliators' recommendations shall also take into account previous and similar cases whenever this would facilitate a more uniform implementation of the Code and observance of conciliators' recommendations.

Index

All references are to paragraph number

Abuse of dominant position
  Regulation 4056/86, 12.11, *and see* Article 86
Action Programme for a Common Transport Policy 1962, 5.3.3
Age profile, 2.2.3
Aids. *See* State Aids
Antwerp Meeting 1987, 5.5.22
Article 85, EEC Treaty, 10.1
  agreements, 10.1.3.2
  agreements falling outside, 10.1.7
    agreements of minor importance, 10.1.7.1
    agreements within single economic unit, 10.1.7.2
    commercial risk, 10.1.7.4
    Commission notice agreements, 10.1.7.1
    co-operation agreements, 10.1.7.1
    exemption, 10.1.7.8
    objective necessity, 10.1.7.3
    principal and agent, 10.1.7.1
    selective distribution system, 10.1.7.6
    sub-contractors, 10.1.7.1
    transfer of assets, 10.1.7.7
  basic concepts, 10.1.3
  concerted practices, 10.1.3.2
  de minimis doctrine, 10.1.6
  decisions, 10.1.3.2
  distorting competition, 10.1.4
  effect on inter-state trade, 10.1.5
  exemptions, 10.1.9
    block, 10.1.9.5
    conditions for granting, 10.1.9.3
    individual, 10.1.9.4
  preventing competition, 10.1.4
  restricting competition, 10.1.4
  text, 10.1.2
  undertaking, 10.1.3.1
    definition, 10.1.3.1.2
  voidness, 10.1.8
    penal aspect, 10.1.8.3
Article 86, 10.2
  abuse of dominant position, 10.2.13
    abuse, definition, 10.2.13.2
    anti-competitive abuses, 10.2.13.4
    exploitation, 10.2.13.3
  check-list for successful application, 10.2.6
  concept of dominant position or dominance, 10.2.8
  demand-side interchangeability, 10.2.8.5
    cross-elasticities of demand. 10.2.8.5.1

Article 86—*cont.*
  demand-side interchangeability—*cont.*
    extrinsic evidence, 10.2.8.5.7
    intended use, 10.2.8.5.4
    physical characteristics, 10.2.8.5.3
    price, 10.2.8.5.2
    statutory markets, 10.2.8.5.6
    structure of supply and demand, 10.2.8.5.5
  economic rationale, 10.2.5
  effect on inter-State trade, 10.2.14
  importance of economic evidence, 10.2.3
  interpretation, 10.2.4
  introduction, 10.2.1
  market power, 10.2.11
    barriers to entry, 10.2.11.4
    conduct, 10.2.11.8
    deep pocket, 10.2.11.11
    economies of scale, 10.2.11.5
    evidence of undertakings, 10.2.11.6
    legal provisions, 10.2.11.10
    measuring, 10.2.11.2
    overall strength and size of undertaking, 10.2.11.9
    price movements, 10.2.11.7
  market shares, 10.2.11.3
  product or services market, 10.2.8.3.2
  relevant geographical market, 10.2.8.4
  relevant temporal market, 10.2.8.5
  supply-side substitutability, 10.2.8.8.3.3
  text, 10.2.2
  undertakings, 10.2.7
  "within the Common Market or a substantial part of it", 10.2.12
Article 87, 3.4.3.3, 9.3.1, 12.2.3, 12.2.4, 12.4
Article 90(1), 24.2
Article 90(2), 10.2.7, 10.2.11.2
Article 90(3), 24.2
Article 92(1), 15.4.4
  concept of aid, 15.4.4.3
  judicial nature, 15.4.4.3.7
  purpose, 15.4.4.2
Article 92(2), 15.4.5
  text, 15.4.5.2
Article 92(3), 15.4.6
  aid for crew relief/employment grants, 15.4.6.11
  aid to build ship, 15.4.6.9
  aid to investment, 15.4.6.15
  aid to reduce manning costs, 15.4.6.10

Article 92(3)—*cont.*
aid to training, 15.4.6.12
aids specified by Council of Ministers, 15.4.6.23
criteria used by Commission in deciding to authorise aid, 15.4.6.3
development of economic activities, 15.4.6.7
economic development aids, 15.4.6.4
environmental aid, 15.4.6.17
important European project, 15.4.6.5
operating aid, 15.4.6.14
public authority holdings in company capital, 15.4.6.18
regional policy aid, 15.4.6.20
rescue aid, 15.4.6.19
research and development aid, 15.4.6.21
restructuring aid, 15.4.6.16
sectoral aids, 15.4.6.8
serious disturbance in economy, 15.4.6.6
small and medium-sized enterprises, 15.4.6.22
special taxation of shipping activities, 15.4.6.13
text, 15.4.6.2
Article 93, 15.4.7
text, 15.4.7.1
Article 94, 15.4.8
challenging, 15.4.9
compatibility, 15.4.5.3
compatibility with EC law, 15.4.3.1
distorting competition, 15.4.4.3.4
economies of, 15.3
effect of inter-state trade, 15.4.4.3.5
EC law, and, 15.4
favouring undertakings or production of goods or services, 15.4.4.3.3
Germany, 15.4.5.6
natural disasters, 15.4.5.5
purpose of, 15.4.4.3.6
purposes, 15.2
social character, 15.4.5.4
state, provided by, 15.4.4.3.2

Bahamas, 2.4.10
Belgium, 2.3.2
age profile, 2.3.2.4
employment, 2.3.2.5
general comments, 2.3.2.6
number of ships, 2.3.2.2
tonnage, 2.3.2.3
Benelux Union, 3.3.4
Bodson's proposals, 5.4.2
Bulk carriers, 2.2.4.4

Cabotage, 7.6
commercial overview, 7.6.3
concept, 7.6.2
development of concept in EC law, 7.6.6
Italian solution, 7.6.8
merits, 7.6.4
outlook, 7.6.7
Positive Measures Programme 1989, 7.6.6.5
states for which issue does not arise, 7.6.5.4
states with limited restrictions, 7.6.5.3
Cabotage—*cont.*
states with no restrictions, 7.6.5.2
states with restrictions, 7.6.5.1
Cargo, 2.2.4.1
Cargo reservations, 24.3
bilateral cargo sharing agreements, 24.3.2
Carriage of Goods and Passengers by Sea, 24.1–24.3
fares, 24.2
travel allowances, 24.3
China, 2.4.4
Code of Conduct for Liner Conferences, 5.4.11
Collection of information Decision 1978, 5.4.18
Collection of information systems, extension 1982, 5.5.12
Combined carriers, 2.2.4.7
Comecon, 1.3.21, 2.4.12
Commercial overview of Shipping in EC, 2.1–2.5
Commission's Communication to Council 24 October 1973, 5.4.4
Commission Memorandum on Maritime Transport 1984, 5.5.18
Commission Programme 1988, 5.5.25
Commission Proposal on Minimum Health and Safety Requirements 1988, 5.5.24
Commission Regulation 4260/88, 12.14
applications for exemptions, 12.14.5
background, 12.14.2
communicating awards and recommendations, 12.14.7
complaints, 12.14.4
hearings, 12.14.6
legal basis, 12.14.2
notification, 12.14.3
Community shipowner
meaning, 6.4
Competition
Regulation 4056/86. *See* Regulation 4056/86
Competition procedure, 10.3
Commission, 10.3.1
complaints, 10.3.5
conclusion of proceedings, 10.3.9
conduct of proceedings, 10.3.8
fact-finding, 10.3.8.1
initiation of proceedings, 10.3.3
investigations, 10.3.8.3
judicial review of Commission decisions, 10.3.10
legal professional privilege, 10.3.8.4
national authorities, 10.3.2
notification, 10.3.4
own-initiative investigations, 10.3.6
requests for information, 10.3.8.2
sector investigations, 10.3.7
Conflicts of national laws
Regulation 4056/86, 12.12
Congress of Europe, 3.3.3
Consortia, 16.1–16.6
commercial view on, 16.3
communication on, 16.4
background to, 16.4.2

Consortia—*cont.*
judicial nature, 16.2
meaning, 16.1
proposed block exemption, need for, 16.5
breaches, 16.6.7
consultation, 16.6.6
duration, 16.6.5
effect, 16.6.5
entry into force, 16.6.8
form, 16.6.2
provision for, 16.6.4
scope, 16.6.3
proposed Regulation, 16.6
purpose, 16.6.1
Consultation procedure 1977, 5.4.15
Consultative Shipping Group, 1.3.17
Containers, 2.2.4.5
Council Decisions, App 2
activities of third countries in field of cargo shipping, App 2; 4
collection of information concerning activities of carriers participating in cargo liner traffic, App 2; 5, 12, 13, 15, 19, 20
concerted action project in field of shore-based marine navigation aid systems, App 2; 14, 16
consultation procedure on relations between member states, App 2; 1
counter-measures in field of international merchant shipping, App 2; 18
Council Directives, App 2
minimum requirements for tankers entering or leaving Community ports, App 2; 8, 10
pilotage of vessels by deep-sea pilots in North Sea and English Channel, App 2; 7
Council of Europe, 3.3.5
Council of Ministers Recommendation on ratification of 1978 International Convention, 19.5.3
Council of Ministers Recommendation on ratification of safety conventions 1978, 19.5.2
Council of Ministers Recommendation on SAR, 19.5.4
Council Recommendations App 2
improving effectiveness of port state control App 2; 27
ratification of Conventions on safety in shipping App 2; 2
ratification of 1978 Convention on standards of training certification and watchkeeping for seafarers App 2; 6
ratification of or accession to SAR Convention App 2; 17
ratification of Torremolinos Convention App 2; 11
Council Regulations App 2
application of Article 85(3) of the Treaty to certain categories of agreements, decisions and concerted practices between liner Shipping companies (Consortia) App 2; 30
Council Regulations App 2—*cont.*
application of principle of freedom to provide services to maritime transport App 2; 21
Community Ship Register App 2; 26
coordinated action to safeguard free access to cargoes in ocean trades App 2; 24
detailed rules for application of Articles 85 and 86 to maritime transport App 2; 22
applications App 2; 25
communications App 2; 25
complaints App 2; 25
hearings App 2; 25
flying of Community flag by sea-going vessels App 2; 26
ratification by member states of accession to UN Convention on Code of Conduct for Liner Conferences App 2; 9
unfair pricing practices in maritime transport App 2; 23
Council Resolution on Priorities in Transport Sector 1981, 5.5.8
Council Resolutions App 2
action programme on control and reduction of pollution caused by hydrocarbons discharged at sea App 2; 3
improving passenger ferry safety App 2; 29
prevention of accidents causing marine pollution App 2; 28
Counter-measures, 19.6
Council Decision 1983, 19.6.1
legal basis, 19.6.1.2
Counter-measures Decision 1983, 5.5.16
Convention on Jurisdiction and Enforcement of Judgments in Civil and Commercial Matters, 25.1–25.5
agencies, 25.3.3.6
approved settlements, 25.4.5.1
authentic instruments, 25.4.5
branches, 25.3.3.6
civil claims in criminal proceedings, 25.3.3.5
co-defendants, 25.3.3.10
combined actions, 25.3.3.13
common rules for recognition and enforcement, 25.4.4
consumer contracts, 25.3.5
contract, 25.3.3.2
counterclaims, 25.3.3.12
domicile, 25.3.1.3
defendants not domiciled in contracting state, 25.3.2.2
persons domiciled in contracting state, 25.3.2.1
UK statutory rules, 25.3.1.3.2
enforcement, 25.4.3
foreign judgment ordering periodic payment, 25.4.3.1
legal aid, 25.4.3.2
no security, bond or deposit, 25.4.3.3
examination as to jurisdiction and admissibility, 25.3.8
exclusive jurisdiction, 25.3.6
intellectual property proceedings, 25.3.6.5

Convention on Jurisdiction and Enforcement of Judgments in Civil and Commercial Matters—*cont.*
geographical scope, 25.2.2
insurance, 25.3.4
jurisdiction, 25.3
jurisdiction agreements, 25.3.7.1
jurisdiction by submission, 25.3.7.2
limitation of liability actions in respect of operation of ships, 25.3.3.14
lis pendens-related actions, 25.3.9
maintenance, 25.3.3.3
maritime matters, 25.5
prorogation of jurisdiction, 25.3.7
provisional measures, 25.3.10
recognition, 25.4.2
instances of non-recognition, 25.4.2.2
principles, 25.4.2.1
public policy, and, 25.4.2.2.1
recognition and enforcement, 25.4
salvage, 25.3.3.8
scope, 25.2
special jurisdiction, 25.3.3, 25.3.3.9
subject-matters, 25.2.1
third parties, 25.3.3.11
tort, delict and quasi-delict, 25.3.3.4
trusts, 25.3.3.7
Court of First Instance, 3.4.6
Customs co-operation Council, 1.3.16
Cyprus, 2.4.11

Decision extending Collection of Information Regime in respect of Far East 1981, 5.5.9
Decision in respect of liner trades between EC and East Africa/Central America 1978, 5.4.20
Decision on relations with state trading countries 1978, 5.4.16
Denmark, 2.3.3
age profile, 2.3.3.3
employment, 2.3.3.4
general comments, 2.3.3.5
number of ships, 2.3.3.1
tonnage, 2.3.3.2
Developing Countries, 2.4.7
Draft Council Resolution concerning Priorities and Timetable for Decisions 1980, 5.5.2
Dumping, 13.1–13.2
concept, 13.2.8.1
Council Regulation 4057/86, 13.2
appeals, 13.2.14
application, 13.2.7
commercial background, 13.2.3
"Community interests", 13.2.8.6
complaints, 13.2.10
consultation, 13.2.11
entry into force, 13.2.5
initiation, 13.2.12.1
"injury to Community ship operators", 13.2.8.6
investigation, 13.2.12.2–13.2.12.7
legal basis, 13.2.2

Dumping—*cont.*
Council Regulation 4057/86—*cont.*
legal history, 13.2.4
non-commercial advantage, 13.2.8.3
normal freight rates, 13.2.8.4
outcome of Commission's investigations, 13.2.13
practice to date, 13.2.15
purpose, 13.2.6
redressive duties, 13.2.13.4
calculation, 13.2.13.6
imposition, 13.2.13.7
power to impose, 13.2.13.5
role of EC institutions, 13.2.9
"serious disruption of a freight pattern", 13.2.8.5
third country shipowner, 13.2.8.7
undertakings, 13.2.13.3
unfair pricing practice, 13.2.8.2

EC competition law, 9.1–9.5
Commission *v*. Belgium, 9.3.6
Commission *v*. France, 9.3.5
Denmark, accession to EC, 9.3.4
history of articles 85 and 86, EEC Treaty, 9.3
Ireland, accession to EC, 9.3.4
overlap between transport and general measures, 9.4
pre-regulation 4056/86 position, 9.3.8
Regulation 17/62, 9.3.1
Regulation 141/62, 9.3.2
Regulation 1017/68, 9.3.3
UK accession to EC, 9.3.4
UNCTAD Code, 9.3.7
EC in shipping world, 2.4, 27.3
EC Transport law, 4.1–4.5
administration, 4.1.5
adoption, 4.1.5
air transport, 4.3.3
Commission Regulation 2671/88, 4.3.3.2.13
Commission Regulation 2672/88, 4.3.3.2.14
Commission Regulation 2673/88, 4.3.3.2.15
Commission Regulation 4261/88, 4.3.3.2.16
Council Decision 80/50, 4.3.3.2.1
Council Decision 87/602, 4.3.3.2.8
Council Directive 80/51, 4.3.3.2.2, 4.3.3.2.11
Council Directive 80/1266, 4.3.3.2.3
Council Directive 83/416, 4.3.3.2.5
Council Directive 86/216, 4.3.3.2.6
Council Directive 87/601, 4.3.3.2.7
Council Directive 89/629, 4.3.3.2.18
Council Directive 90/449, 4.3.3.2.19
Council Recommendation 81/560, 4.3.3.2.4
Council Regulation 3975/87/EEC, 4.3.3.2.10
Council Regulation 3976/87/EEC, 4.3.3.2.12
Council Regulation 2299/89/EEC, 4.3.3.2.17
Council Regulation 2342/90/EEC, 4.3.3.2.20
Council Regulation 2343/90/EEC, 4.3.3.2.21
Decision 87/359/EEC, 4.3.3.2.9
Regulation 2343/90/EEC, 4.3.3.2.19
Regulation 82/91, 4.3.3.2.22
Regulation 83/91, 4.3.3.2.23

EC Transport law—*cont.*
air transport—*cont.*
Regulation 84/91, 4.3.3.2.24
Regulation 294/91, 4.3.3.2.25
Regulation 295/91, 4.3.3.2.26
competition, 4.4.2
consultation, 4.4.8
ECSC Treaty. *See* ECSC Treaty
EEC Treaty. *See* EEC Treaty
external relations, 4.4.9
infrastructure costs, 4.4.3
inland waterway, 4.3.4
inspection of goods, 4.4.4
legal bases, 4.1.4
luggage traffic, 4.4.7
passenger traffic, 4.4.7
position of transport in EC treaties, 4.2
prior examination, 4.4.8
public service, 4.4.6
rail transport, 4.3.2
Decision 75/327, 4.3.2.4
Decision 82/529, 4.3.2.9
Decision 83/418, 4.3.2.8
Directive 80/1177, 4.3.27
Package of Measures 1991, 4.3.2.10
Recommendation 1984, 4.3.2.9
Regulation 1192/69, 4.3.2.2
Regulation 2830/77, 4.3.2.5
Regulation 2183/78, 4.3.2.6
Resolution 1970, 4.3.2.3
Resolution 1981, 4.3.2.7
road transport, 4.3.1
ASOR Agreement 1972, 4.3.1.8, 4.3.1.17
Customs Convention 1978, 4.3.1.13
Decision 25 June 1979, 4.3.1.15
Directive 65/269, 4.3.1.3
Directive 74/561, 4.3.1.9
Directive 74/562, 4.3.1.10
Directive 76/914, 4.3.1.11
Directive 78/546, 4.3.1.14
Directive 83/463, 4.3.1.18
Directive 84/647, 4.3.1.19
Directive 87/1544, 4.3.1.20
Regulation 1177/66, 4.3.1.3a
Regulation 1018/68, 4.3.1.4
Regulation 543/69, 4.3.1.5
Regulation 516/72, 45.3.1.6
Regulation 517/72, 4.3.1.7
Regulation 3237/76, 4.3.1.12
Regulation 3690/86, 4.3.1.20
Regulation 1841/88, 4.3.1.21
Regulation 4059/89, 4.3.1.22
TIR Convention 1981, 4.3.1.16
1962 Directive, 4.3.1.2
summertime arrangements, 4.4.5
transport committees, 4.4.1
transport sectors, 4.3
Economic and monetary union, 26.9
Economic and Social Committee Opinion on application of Articles 85 and 86, 1983, 5.5.14
Economic and Social Committee Opinion on Flags of Convenience 1979, 5.4.24
Economic Commission for Europe, 1.3.9
ECSC Rail Tariff, 5.4.5
ECSC Treaty, 4.2.1
article 4, 4.2.1.2
text, 4.2.1.2.1
article 70, 4.2.1.3
commentary, 4.2.1.3.2
text, 4.2.1.3.1
EEC Treaty, and, 4.2.2.15
EEC Treaty, 4.2.2
article 3, 4.2.2.2
commentary, 4.2.2.2.2
text, 4.2.2.2.1
article 4, 4.2.1.2
commentary, 4.2.1.2.2
article 61, 4.2.2.3
commentary, 4.2.2.3.2
text, 4.2.2.3.1
article 74, 4.2.2.4
commentary, 4.2.2.4.2
text, 4.2.2.4.1
article 75, 4.2.2.5
commentary, 4.2.2.5.2
text, 4.2.2.5.1
article 76, 4.2.2.6
commentary, 4.2.2.6.2
text, 4.2.2.6.1
article 77, 4.2.2.7
commentary, 4.2.2.7.2
text, 4.2.2.7.1
article 78, 4.2.2.8
commentary, 4.2.2.8.2
text, 4.2.2.8.1
article 79, 4.2.2.9
commentary, 4.2.2.9.2
text, 4.2.2.9.1
article 80, 4.2.2.10
commentary, 4.2.2.10.2
text, 4.2.2.10.1
article 81, 4.2.2.11
commentary, 4.2.2.11.2
text, 4.2.2.11.1
article 82, 4.2.2.12
commentary, 4.2.2.12.2
text, 4.2.2.12.1
article 83, 4.2.2.13
commentary, 4.2.2.13.2
text, 4.2.2.13.1
article 84, 4.2.2.14
commentary, 4.2.2.14.2
text, 4.2.2.14.1
ECSC Treaty, and, 4.2.2.15
transport provisions, 4.2.2
Employment, 2.2.5, 8.1–8.3
Article 48, EEC Treaty, 8.2.2.2
Article 49, EEC Treaty, 8.2.2.4
discrimination on basis of nationality, 8.2.2.3
EC law, 8.2
equal pay, 8.2.4

Employment—*cont.*
free movement of workers, 8.2.2
Hollesen Study, 8.2.6.2
non-discrimination on basis of nationality between EC nationals, 8.2.5
seafarers, EC law, 8.3
hours of working, 8.3.1.1
mutual recognition of qualifications, 8.3.1.2
taxation, 8.3.2
training, 8.3.1
shipping in EC, in, 8.2.6
merchant marine, 8.2.6.1.1
shipbuilding, 8.2.6.1.2
worker, concept of, 8.2.2.1
working conditions, 8.2.3
Enlargement of EC 1973, 5.4.3
Environmental law, 17.1–17.7
accidental discharges of hydrocarbons into the sea, 17.4.10
Action Programmes, 17.4.3, 17.4.11, 17.4.15.3, 17.5.9
Amoco Cadiz, 17.4.13
Bravo drilling rig, 17.4.9
Commission Communication 1983, 17.5.4
Commission Decision (80/686), advisory committee on pollution, 17.5.2
Copenhagen Summit, 17.4.14
Council Resolution, 26 June 1978, 17.4.15
deliberate dumping of waste at sea, 17.4.8
Directive on Discharge of Effluent from Land (76/464), 17.4.7
EC response to UN Conference, 17.4.2
EEC treaty, 17.2.1
Environmental Information Directive, 17.6.4
Environmental and Consumer Protection Service, 17.4.4
Environmental Year, 17.5.8
European Environment Agency Regulation, 17.6.2
Information system, 17.5.7
Marine Science and Technology Programme, 17.5.12
Mediterranean, 17.5.11
North Sea, 17.6.6
Paris Convention for the Prevention of Marine Pollution from Land-Based Sources, 17.4.5
parliamentary question on seaworthiness, 17.5.10
port state control, 17.5.10
Recommendation on "Polluter Pays" principle, 17.4.6
Recommendation on ratification of STCW Convention, 17.4.18
Recommendation on Safety Conventions, 17.4.16
Recommendation on SAR, 17.5.5
Resolution on Prevention of Accidents causing Pollution, 17.6.3
shipbuilding industry reorganisation, 17.4.12
shipment of radioactive wastes, 17.6.5
Single European Act, 17.5.6
Environmental law—*cont.*
titanium dioxide, measures relating to, 17.4.17
Torrey Canyon, 17.3.2
UN Conference in Stockholm, 17.2.3
UNCLOS III, 17.5.3
Establishment, right of, 6.1
concept, 6.1.1
exceptions, 6.1.6
exercise of official authority, 6.1.6.1
general rule, 6.1.2
implementation of Treaty provisions, 6.1.4
mutual recognition of diplomas, certificates and qualifications, 6.1.5
prohibition of new restrictions, 6.1.3
public health, 6.1.6.4
public policy, 6.1.6.2
public security, 6.1.6.3
Euratom, 3.3.9
European Atomic Energy Community, 3.2.3
European Coal and Steel Community, 3.2.2, 3.3.8
European Community, 1.1, 3.1–3.5. *See also* EC
accession treaties, 3.5.2.1.2
accessions, 3.3.15
agreements, 3.5.2.2.7
Britain's position, 3.3.12
challenging legality of Community measures, 3.5.9
Commission, 3.4.2
composition, 3.4.2.2
DG IV, 3.4.2.5
DG VII, 3.4.2.6
functions, 3.4.2.3
operation, 3.4.2.4
Council of Ministers, 3.4.3
composition, 3.4.3.2
COREPER, 3.4.3.5
functions, 3.4.3.3
General Secretariat, 3.4.3.6
operation, 3.4.3.4
voting, 3.4.3.4
Court of Auditors, 3.4.7.3
Customs Union, 3.3.14
decisions, 3.5.2.2.3
direct applicability, 3.5.3
direct effect, 3.5.3
Directives, 3.5.2.2.2
Eastern Europe, 3.3.21
Economic and Social Committee, 3.4.7.1
enforcement of law in courts of Member States, 3.5.8
European Council, 3.4.4
European integration, 3.3.1
European Investment Bank, 3.4.7.2
evolution of, 11.2
failure to achieve common transport policy, 4.1.3
financial treaties, 3.5.2.1.4
Foundation Treaties, 3.5.2.1.1
fundamental principles of law, 3.5.7
future of, 1.1.7
general principles of law, 3.5.2.2.8

European Community—*cont.*
history, 3.3
importance of transport in, 4.1.1
institutional treaties, 3.5.2.1.3
Internal Market White Paper, 3.3.19
interpretation of community law, 3.5.6
law, 3.5
Maastricht Treaty, 3.5.2.1.6
Merger Treaty, 3.3.13
need to achieve common transport policy, 4.1.2
opinions of Advocates-General, 3.5.2.2.10
organic structure, 3.4
population, 1.1.4
primary law, 3.5.2.1
publication of community law, 3.5.4
recommendations, 3.5.2.2.4
Regulations, 3.5.2.2.1
relations with ILO, 1.3.4.4
relationship between community law and national laws, 3.5.5
resolutions, 3.5.2.2.5
secondary law, 3.5.2.2
shipping in, 1.2 *See also* Shipping in the EC
Single European Act, 3.3.20, 3.5.2.1.5
sources of law, 3.5.2
three European Communities, 1.1.1
Tindemans Report, 3.3.16
transport in, 1.1.6
world's largest trading bloc, 1.1.3
1992 Programme, 1.1.5
European Court of Justice, 3.4.6
actions for inactivity, 3.4.6.6.6
case law, 3.5.2.2.9
functions, 3.4.6.2
jurisdiction, 3.4.6.6
operation, 3.4.6.4
opinions on external relations, 3.4.6.6.10
personnel, 3.4.6.3
preliminary references, 3.4.6.6.9
procedure, 3.4.6.5
staff disputes, 3.4.6.6.8
European Defence Treaty, 3.3.10
European Free Trade Association, 1.3.20, 3.3.11
European Monetary System, 3.3.17
European Parliament, 3.4.5
Bureau, 3.4.5.7
Committees, 3.4.5.9
direct elections to, 3.3.18
election, 3.4.5.5
functions, 3.4.5.10
members, 3.4.5.3
officers, 3.4.5.6
operation, 3.4.5.10
president, 3.4.5.6
seat, 3.4.5.2
Secretariat, 3.4.5.8
tenure, 3.4.5.4
EUROS, 6.3.4
advantages of being registered on, 6.3.4.12
assessment of proposal, 6.3.4.13
eligibility to be registered, 6.3.4.6
EUROS—*cont.*
establishment of register, 6.3.4.5
legal basis, 6.3.4.3
market reaction, 6.3.4.4
objective of proposal, 6.3.4.2
proposal, 6.3.4.1
safety on EUROS-registered ships, 6.3.4.7
Extension of 1978 Collection of Information Decision 1980, 5.5.3
External relations of EC, 19.1–19.8
bilateral relations, 19.7.1
consultation procedure, 19.3
background, 19.3.3
channels, 19.3.7
confidentiality, 19.3.7
legal bases, 19.3.4
purposes, 19.3.2, 19.3.6
review, 19.3.8
scope, 19.3.5
counter-measures. *See* Counter-measures
Euratom Treaty, 19.2.2.2
relations with Council of Europe, 19.2.2.3.3
relations with OECD, 19.2.2.3.4
relations with UN and GATT, 19.2.2.3.2
treaty-making powers, 19.2.2.3.1
ECSC Treaty, 19.2.2.1
EEC Treaty, 19.2.2.3
market monitoring, 19.4. *See also* Market monitoring

Financial and Fiscal Measures 1989, 5.5.27
Flagging-out, 2.2.9
Foundation Treaties, 5.2
France, 2.3.4
age profile, 2.3.4.3
employment, 2.3.4.4
general comments, 2.3.4.5
number of ships, 2.3.4.1
tonnage, 2.3.4.2
Freedom to supply maritime services, 7.1–7.6
EC law, 7.4
Regulation 4055/86, 7.5
assessment, 7.5.14
basic provision, 7.5.7
cargo-sharing arrangements in bilateral agreements, 7.5.8
cargo-sharing arrangements in future agreements, 7.5.9
French–Corsican Case, 7.5.15
Italy–Algeria Case, 7.5.16
purpose, 7.5.2
timetable, 7.5.7.1
Freight rates
UN Liner Code, 11.2.9
French initiative 1975, 5.4.10
French Seaman's Case 1973, 5.4.8

GATS, 19.8.5
General Agreement on Tariffs and Trade (GATT), 1.3.18, 19.8.5
Germany, 2.3.5
age profile, 2.3.5.3

Germany—*cont.*
employment, 2.3.5.4
general comments, 2.3.5.5
number of ships, 2.3.5.1
tonnage, 2.3.5.2
Goods. *See* Carriage of Goods and Passengers by Sea
Greece, 2.3.6
accession to EC 1981, 5.5.7
age profile, 2.3.6.4
employment, 2.3.6.5
general comments, 2.3.6.6
number of ships, 2.3.6.2
tonnage, 2.3.6.3

Historical overview, 5.1–5.6
Hong Kong, 2.4.5

Interim Report of European Parliament's Committee on Economic and Monetary Affairs 1976, 5.4.13
Interim Report of European Parliament's Committee on Sea Transport Problems 1977, 5.4.14
Internal Market, 26.1–26.10
background to programme, 26.4
banalisation, 26.5.1.3.9
banking, 26.5.3.7
benefits of programme, 26.7
company law, 26.5.3.6
competition, 26.5.3.12
concept, 26.2
contents of programme, 26.5
environment, 26.5.3.13
European company statute, 26.5.3.6.3
European economic interest groupings, 26.5.3.6.4
external dimension, 26.6
fortress Europe, 26.6.2
insurance, 26.5.3.10
insurance intermediaries, 26.5.3.10.7
large exposures, 26.5.3.7.5
merger control regulation, 26.5.3.6.2
mergers, 26.5.3.12.3
movement of goods, 26.5.1.3
movement of persons, 26.5.1.4
mutual recognition of qualifications, 26.5.2.4
non-active persons, 26.5.1.4.3
physical barriers, 26.5.1
public procurement, 26.5.3
public works, 26.5.3.3
rationale for, 26.3
relations with international organisations, 26.6.3
removal of fiscal barriers, 26.5.4
revitalisation of EC industry, 26.3.1
revitalisation of EC organisation, 26.3.2
securities, 26.5.3.11
shipping, and, 26.8
single administrative document, 26.5.1.3.2
single-member limited liability companies, 26.5.3.6.5
Internal Market—*cont.*
solvency ratio directive, 26.5.3.7.4
state aids, 26.5.3.12.2
structure of public limited companies, 26.5.3.6.8
technical barriers, 26.5.2
White Paper, 3.3.19
International Atomic Energy Agency, 1.3.14
International Labour Organisation, 1.3.4, 19.8.4
activities, 1.3.4.3
organic structure, 1.3.4.2
organisational structure, 1.3.4.2
relations with EC, 1.3.4.4
Intergovernmental Maritime Consultative Organisation, 1.3.3.2, 19.8.3
International Maritime Organisation, 1.3.3, 1.3.3.4, 19.8.3
committees, 1.3.3.4
International Maritime Satellite Organisation, 1.3.11
assessment, 1.3.11.3
membership, 1.3.11.1
operation, 1.3.11.2
organic structure, 1.3.11.2
International Non-Governmental Organisations, 1.3.22
International organisations, 1.3, 19.8
assessment, 1.3.23
International Safety Conventions, 19.5
Ireland, 2.3.7
age profile, 2.3.7.4
general comments, 2.3.7.5–2.3.7.6
number of ships, 2.3.7.2
tonnage, 2.3.7.3
Italy, 2.3.8
age profile, 2.3.8.4
employment, 2.3.8.5
general comments, 2.3.8.6
number of ships, 2.3.8.2
tonnage, 2.3.8.3

Liner conferences, 11.1–11.3
block exemption for, 12.8
availability of tariffs, 12.8.6.7
condition attaching to, 12.8.5
consultations, 12.8.6.4
loyalty arrangements, 12.8.6.5
notification to Commission of awards at arbitration and recommendations, 12.8.6.8
obligations attaching to, 12.8.6
services not covered by freight charges, 12.8.6.6
text of Article 3, Regulation 4056/86, 12.8.4
text of Article 4, Regulation 4056/86, 12.8.5.1
meaning, 12.8.2, 12.9.3
United Nations Code of Conduct, 11.2. *See also* UN Liner Code
Liquid gas carriers, 2.2.4.6
Luxembourg, 2.3.9

Maastricht Treaty, 3.5.2.1.6
Market monitoring, 19.4
  Decision 78/774/EEC, 19.4.1
  Decision 79/4/EEC, 19.4.2
    extension of information collected, 19.4.2.5
  Decision 80/1181/EEC, 19.4.3
  Decision 81/189/EEC, 19.4.4
  Decision 82/870/EEC, 19.4.5
  Decision 83/573/EEC, 19.4.6
  Decision 84/656/EEC, 19.4.7
  Decision 86/646/EEC, 19.4.8
  Decision 89/242/EEC, 19.4.9
  Decision 89/243/EEC, 19.4.10
  Decision 90/545/EEC, 19.4.11
  legislative resolution, 19.4.1.6
Market sectors, 2.2.4
Marshall Aid, 3.3.2
Member states
  attitudes, 2.3.1.1
  overview of shipping in, 2.3
  policies, 2.3.1.1
Memorandum from Commission to Council 1960, 5.3.1
Memorandum of understanding on Port-State Control 1982, 5.5.13
Memorandum on basic approach to be adopted in Common Transport Policy 1961, 5.3.2
Merchant marine, 2.2.5.1
Merger control regulation, 26.5.3.6.2
Ministerial Conference of West and Central African States, 1.3.19
Multimodalism, 24.4

NATO, 3.3.6
Navigation, 21.1–21.3
  COST 301, 21.2
  radio-navigation systems, 21.3 *et seq.*
  shore-based marine navigation aid systems, 21.2
Netherlands, 2.3.10
  age profile, 2.3.10.4
  employment, 2.3.10.5
  general comments, 2.3.10.6
  number of ships, 2.3.10.2
  tonnage, 2.3.10.3
1992 Programme. *See* Internal Market
North Sea Pilotage Directive, 22.2
  encouragement of ships to use qualified pilots, 22.2.5
  implementation, 22.2.6
  legal basis, 22.2.2
  obligation to provide pilots, 22.2.4
  purpose, 22.2.3
Norway, 2.4.6

Offshore registries, 2.4.9
Oil crisis 1973, 5.4.7
Oil tankers, 2.2.4.3
Open registries, 2.4.8
Ore carriers, 2.2.4.4
Organisation for Economic Co-operation and Development (OECD), 1.3.15
Organisation of European Economic Co-operation, 3.3.2

Package of Regulations 1986, 5.5.20
Parliament proceedings against Commission 1983, 5.5.17
Parliamentary Resolution on Community's Relations with Comecon States 1979, 5.4.23
Parliamentary Resolution on Oil Pollution 1980, 5.5.6
Parliamentary Resolution on Shipping Accidents 1979, 5.4.22
Passenger baggage, 24.5
  Committee on Community Transit, 24.5.7
Passengers, 2.2.4.2. *See also* Carriage of Goods and Passengers by Sea
Pilotage, 22.1–22.3
  Commission Memorandum on Shipping 1985, 22.3
Port state control, 23.2
  Commission Opinion 1982, 23.2.5
  Commission proposal for Directive, 23.2.2
  Commission Recommendation on improving effectiveness, 23.2.4
  Memorandum of Understanding, 23.2.3
  progress towards Common Transport Policy, 23.2.5.1
Ports, 23.1
  hinterland traffic, 23.1
Ports 1974, 5.4.9
Portugal, 2.3.11
  age profile, 2.3.11.4
  employment, 2.3.11.5
  general comments, 2.3.11.6
  number of ships, 2.3.11.2
  tonnage, 2.3.11.3
Positive Measures August 1989, 5.5.26
Progress towards Common Maritime Policy
  Commission communication 1985, 5.5.19
Proposal for Council of Ministers Regulation to grant Block Exemption for Consortia 1990, 5.5.29
Proposal on competition Rules and Shipping 1981, 5.5.10
Proposals on Concerted Research on Shore-Based Maritime Navigation Aid Systems 1981, 5.5.11
Proposals on Port Control of Pollution 1980, 5.5.5
Protectionism, 2.2.8

Ratification of UN Code of Conduct for Liner Conferences 1979, 5.4.21
Recommendation on SAR 1983, 5.5.15
Recommendation on Torremolinos Convention 1980, 5.5.4
Registration, 6.2
  Community shipowner, 6.4
  EC perspective on, 6.3.1
  EC reaction to UN Convention, 6.3.2
  EC register: EUROS, 6.3.4. *See also* EUROS
  Geneva Convention on High Seas 1958, 6.2.2.1

Registration—*cont.*
international law, 6.2.2
international registries, 6.2.1.4
offshore registries, 6.2.1.3
parallel registries, 6.5
proposal for regulation on transfer of ships from one register to another, 6.3.5
application, 6.3.5.7
background to, 6.3.5.2
Committee of experts, 6.3.5.12
legal bases, 6.3.5.5
"National Shipping Line", 6.3.5.13
obligation on Member State, 6.3.5.8
relationship with other rules, 6.3.5.4
traditional home registries, 6.2.1.1
traditional open registries, 6.2.1.2
United Nations Convention on Law of the Sea 1982, 6.2.2.2
United Nations Convention on Registration of Ships 1986, 6.2.2.3
Regulation 4056/86, 12.1–12.6
1237 Agreement, 12.15.11
abuse of dominant position, 12.11
agreements between providers of ancillary services, 12.6.8
amended Commission proposal 1985, 12.2.5
application, 12.6.1
assessment, 12.16
block exemption
agreements between transport users and conferences, 12.9
block exemption for Liner Conferences, 12.8. *See also* Liner Conferences
Brazilian and Colombian coffee trades, 12.15.1
Commission Proposal 1981, 12.2.2
Commission requests for information, 12.13.7
complaint procedures, 12.13.1, 12.13.2
conflicts of national laws, 12.12
consolidation of individual assignments, 12.7.2.5
co-ordination of transport timetables, 12.7.2.4
duration of individual exemptions, 12.13.4
ECOSOC opinion, 12.2.3
effect of article, 12.6.2
entry into force, 12.3
Eurocorde, 12.15.2
European Parliament Report 1984, 12.2.4
exchange or pooling, 12.7.2.2
fines, 12.13.9
review by Court of Justice, 12.13.11
first Commission amendment 1986, 12.2.6
Gulfway, 12.15.3
hearings, 12.13.10
implementary provisions, 12.13.13
international transport services, 12.6.4
investigations, 12.13.8
Irish Club rules, 12.15.12
Israeli trades, 12.15.4
legal bases, 12.4
legal effect, 12.5
legislative history, 12.2.1
Regulation 4056/86—*cont.*
liaison with authorities of member states, 12.13.6
maritime services, 12.6.5
monitoring of exempted agreements, 12.10
opposition procedure, 12.13.3
passenger traffic, 12.6.9
periodic penalty payments, 12.13.9
review by court of justice, 12.13.11
powers of Commission, 12.13.5
practice to date, 12.15
publication of decisions, 12.13.12
revocation of individual exemptions, 12.13.4
RTM/P & O, 12.15.5
rules of procedure, 12.13
scope, 12.6.10
Sealink/B & I (operating agreement), 12.15.6
Sealink/SM2, 12.15.8
Sealink/SNCF, 12.15.9
second Commission amendment 1986, 12.2.7
services other than tramp services, 12.6.6
successive or supplementary maritime operations, 12.7.2.3
technical agreements, 12.7
text of Article 1, 12.6.1
text of Article 2, 12.7.2
transport services, 12.6.3
transport users, 12.6.7
uniform application of standards or types, 12.7.2.1
uniform rules concerning transport tariffs, 12.7.2.6
West and Central Africa cases, 12.15.10
Regulation 4058/86, 14.1 *et seq.*
action by Member States in default of Council action, 14.12
application, 14.2
background, 14.6
concepts, 14.7
co-ordinated action, 14.10
requests by Member State for, 14.9
consultation, 14.13
entry into force, 14.5
history, 14.15
OECD Member States, 14.14
procedure, 14.11
Regulations Competition and Shipping 1962, 5.3.4
Resolution on Passenger Ferry Safety 1990, 5.5.28

Safety, 20.1–20.2
Council Recommendation on ratification of STCW Convention, 20.2.2
Council Recommendation on ratification of safety conventions 1978, 20.2.1
background, 20.2.1.2
Council Recommendation on SAR, 20.2.7
deep sea pilots, 20.2.3
European Parliamentary Question 1987, 20.2.8
European Parliament Resolution on Safety at Sea, 20.2.9

Safety—*cont.*
fishing vessels, 20.2.5
medical treatment on board vessels, 20.2.11
adaption of annexes, 20.2.8.12
antidotes, 20.2.11.4.1, 20.2.11.6
data centres, 20.2.8.10
information, 20.2.11.8
inspection, 20.2.11.11
supplies, 20.2.11.4.2, 20.2.11.5
training, 20.2.8.9
passenger ferries, 20.2.7
tankers, 20.2.4, 20.2.6
Schumann Declaration, 3.3.7
Shipbuilding, 2.2.5.2, 18.1–18.10
aids, 18.10
commercial overview, 18.2
Commission Communication 1987, 18.8
Commission Proposal, 18.5
Committee, 18.3.4.1
Communication 1977, 18.3
Council of Ministers Resolution 1978, 18.4
EC action, 18.3.4
Fifth Directive, 18.10.5
commercial background, 18.10.5.5
concept of aid, 18.10.5.11
concept of sale, 18.10.5.10
concept of shipbuilding, 18.10.5.7
concept of ship-conversion, 18.10.5.8
concept of ship-repair, 18.10.5.9
cost-escalation insurance, 18.10.5.17
credit facilities, 18.10.5.12
crisis aid, 18.10.5.16
duration, 18.10.5.2
investment aid, 18.10.5.14
legal basis, 18.10.5.3
non-discrimination, 18.10.5.18
relationship with EEC Treaty Rules, 18.10.5.13
rescue aids, 18.10.5.15
First Commission Report, 18.6
First Directive, 18.10.1
Fourth directive, 18.10.4
commercial background, 18.10.4.3
concept of shipbuilding, 18.10.4.5
concept of ship-conversion, 18.10.4.6
concept of ship-repair, 18.10.4.7
concept of sale, 18.10.4.8
concept of state aid, 18.10.4.9
cost-escalation insurance, 18.10.4.15
credit facilities, 18.10.4.10
crisis aid, 18.10.4.14
duration, 18.10.4.4
investment aid, 18.10.4.12
legal bases, 18.10.4.2
non-discrimination, 18.10.4.16
relationship between Directive and EEC Treaty Rules, 18.10.4.11
rescue aids, 18.10.4.13
objectives of EC intervention, 18.3.2
Parliamentary Resolution 1986, 18.7
problems in EC, 18.3.1
protectionist practices, 18.2.1
Shipbuilding—*cont.*
Reneval Programme, 18.9
areas of application, 18.9.4
criteria, 18.9.4
decision-making process, 18.9.5
duration, 18.9.11
entities eligible for funding, 18.9.9.
establishment, 18.9.2
financing of, 18.9.7
form of aid, 18.9.8
France, 18.9.12.1
Germany, 18.9.12.1
Netherlands, 18.9.12.3
permitted activities for, 18.9.6
procedure, 18.9.10
purpose, 18.9.3
Spain, 18.9.12.4
United Kingdom, 18.9.12.5
Second Directive, 18.10.2
Seventh Directive, 18.10.7
approach, 18.10.7.5
commercial background, 18.10.7.1.4
international context, 18.10.7.2
monitoring, 18.10.7.16
operating aid, 18.10.7.14
restructuring aid, 18.10.7.15
Spain, 18.10.7.17
specific areas of EC, 18.10.7.11
Sixth Directive, 18.10.6
Study, 18.10.2.1
aids for sale of ships, 18.10.2.1.2
direct aids and intervention, 18.10.2.1.1
emergency measures, 18.10.2.1.4
investment aids, 18.10.2.1.3
Third Directive, 18.10.3
background, 18.10.3.1
emergency aid, 18.10.3.4
essence of, 18.10.3.2
reporting mechanism, 18.10.3.3
Shipbuilding talks with Japan 1988, 5.5.23
Shipping crisis 1970s and 1980s, 5.4.24, 5.5.1
Shipping in the EC, 1.2
competition dimension to policy, 1.2.1.9
earner of foreign currency, 1.2.1.4
employer, 1.2.1.3
environmental dimension to policy, 1.2.1.8
EC policy, 1.2.1
internal balances, 1.2.1.6
lack of comprehensive policy, 1.2.1.12
law, 1.2.2
application, 27.5
limit to development, 27.5
recent origin, 27.4
open/non-protectionist policy, 1.2.1.5
relationship of policy to international obligations of EC Member States, 1.2.1.10
role in internal market, 1.2.1.2
social dimension to policy, 1.2.1.7
staggered or strategic development of policy, whether, 1.2.1.11
strategic significance, 1.2.1.1
Ship's inspection proposals 1978, 5.4.17

Single European Act, 5.5.21
Social security law, 8.4.2
  Joint Committee on Maritime Transport, 8.4.2
Spain, 2.3.12
  age profile, 2.3.12.4
  employment, 2.3.12.5
  general comments, 2.3.12.6
  number of ships, 2.3.12.2
  Seventh Shipbuilding Directive and, 18.10.7.17
  tonnage, 2.3.12.3
State aids, 15.1–15.5
  advantage, 15.4.4.3.1
State of shipping in EC, 2.2
  future developments, 2.2.10

Tanker disasters, 5.4.16
Taxation, 2.2.7
Technology, 2.2.6
Tonnage, 2.2.2
  beneficially owned in EC trust registered outside, 2.2.2.2
  distribution, 2.2.2.3
  owned and registered in EC, 2.2.2.1
Torrey Canyon, 17.2.2
Travel allowances, 24.8
Treaty of Rome, App 1
  agriculture, App 1, 38–47
  approximation of laws, App 1, 100–102
  association of overseas countries and territories, App 1, 131–136a
  balance of payments, App 1, 104–109
  commercial policy, App 1, 110–116
  Commission, App 1, 155
  competition rules, App 1, 85–94
    aids granted by States, App 1, 92–94
    dumping, App 1, 91
    undertakings, App 1, 85–90
  Conjunctural policy, App 1, 103
  Council, App 1, 145–154
  Court of Justice, App 1, 164–188
  Customs Union, App 1, 12–29
  Economic and monetary union, App 1, 102a
  Economic and social cohesion, App 1, 130a–130e
  Economic and Social Committee, App 1, 193–198
  Economic policy, App 1, 102a–116
  Elimination of customs duties between Member States, App 1, 12–17
  Elimination of quantitative restrictions between Member States, App 1, 30–37
  Environment, App 1, 130r–130t
  European Investment Bank, App 1, 129, 130
  European Parliament, App 1, 137–144
  European Social Fund, App 1, 123–128
  final provisions, App 1, 247–248
  financial provisions, App 1, 199–209
  free movement of goods, App 1, 9–37
  free movement of persons, services and capital, App 1, 48–73
    capital, App 1, 67–73
Treaty of Rome—*cont.*
  free movement of persons, services and capital—*cont.*
    right of establishment, App 1, 52–58
    services, App 1, 59–66
    workers, App 1, 48–51
  general provisions, App 1, 210–240
  institutions of Community, App 1, 137–209
  policy of Community, App 1, 85–130t
  principles, App 1, 1–8c
  provisions common to several institutions, App 1, 189–192
  research and technological development, App 1, 130f–130q
  setting up of common customs tariff, App 1, 18–29
  setting up of institutions, App 1, 241–246
  social policy, App 1, 117–128
  social provisions, App 1, 117–122
  tax provisions, App 1, 95–99
  transport, App 1, 74–84

UNCLOS III, 19.8.2
Undertaking
  definition, 10.1.3.1.2
United Kingdom, 2.3.13
  age profile, 2.3.13.4
  employment, 2.3.13.5
  general comments, 2.3.13.6
  number of ships, 2.3.13.2
  tonnage, 2.3.13.3
United Nations, 1.3.2, 19.8.1
United Nations Commission on International Trade Law, 1.3.8
United Nations Conference on Trade and Development, 1.3.7
UN Economic Commission for Europe, 3.3.2
United Nations Educational, Scientific and Cultural Organisation, 1.3.12
United Nations Environment Programme, 1.3.10
  activities, 1.3.10.3
  organisation, 1.3.10.2
UN Liner Code, 7.3, 11.2
  annual reports, 11.2.8.5
  application, 11.2.6
  availability of tariffs, 11.2.8.4
  compatibility with EC law, 11.3.2
  Conference agreements, 11.2.7.7
  consultation machinery, 11.2.8.6
  decision-making, 11.2.7.4
  dispensation, 11.2.8.3
  EC law, and, 11.3
  EEC treaty, and, 11.3.4.2.1
  entry into force, 11.2.4
  freight rates, 11.2.9
  implementation in EC member states, 11.3.6
  loyalty arrangements, 11.2.8.2
  membership, 11.2.7.2
  objectives, 11.2.3
  participation, 11.2.7.3
  perspectives on, 11.2.5
  principles, 11.2.3

UN Liner Code—*cont.*
provisions relating to relations between conference members, 11.2.7
provisions relating to relations with shippers, 11.2.8
Regulation 954/79, 11.3.3–11.3.5
contents, 11.3.5
legislative history, 11.3.4
sanctions, 11.2.7.5
self-policing, 11.2.7.6
signature, 11.2.4

UN Liner Code—*cont.*
UNCTAD negotiations, and, 11.2.2
United States of America, 2.4.2
USSR, former, 2.4.3

World Health Organisation, 1.3.13

1960s, 5.3.1–5.3.4
1970s, 5.4
1980s, 5.5